A C C I   R . ' S

DATE DUE

APR 2 6 2010

MAY 1 7 2010

W I   R D
F R   : Y

"[—

"Coo   ilarly
ple   ."

detail   question:
'How did a patriotic American come to lead the great
struggle to destroy the United States?' "
—*Booklist*

"[Cooper's] success is evident in the subtleties
of his portrayal of Davis."
—*The Times-Picayune*

WILLIAM J. COOPER, JR.

Jefferson Davis, American

William J. Cooper, Jr., is Boyd Professor of History at Louisiana State University. In addition to numerous articles, essays, and reviews, he is the author of *The Conservative Regime: South Carolina, 1877–1890; The South and the Politics of Slavery, 1828–1856;* and *Liberty and Slavery: Southern Politics to 1860,* as well as coauthor of *The American South: A History.* He lives in Baton Rouge.

ALSO BY WILLIAM J. COOPER, JR.

The American South: A History
(with Thomas E. Terrill)

Liberty and Slavery: Southern Politics to 1860

The South and the Politics of Slavery, 1828–1856

The Conservative Regime: South Carolina, 1877–1890

EDITOR

Writing the Civil War: The Quest to Understand
(with James M. McPherson)

A Master's Due: Essays in Honor of David Herbert Donald
(with Michael F. Holt and John M. McCardell, Jr.)

Social Relations in Our Southern States
by Daniel R. Hundley

JEFFERSON DAVIS,
AMERICAN

JEFFERSON DAVIS,
AMERICAN

William J. Cooper, Jr.

VINTAGE CIVIL WAR LIBRARY

Vintage Books

A Division of Random House, Inc.

New York

FIRST VINTAGE CIVIL WAR LIBRARY EDITION,
NOVEMBER 2001

The Library of Congress has cataloged the Knopf edition as follows:
Cooper, William J. (William James), Jr.
Jefferson Davis, American / William J. Cooper, Jr.—1st ed.
p. cm.
Includes bibliographical references (p.) and index.
ISBN 0-394-56916-4
1. Davis, Jefferson, 1808–1889. 2. Presidents—Confederate States of America—Biography. 3. Confederate States of America—Biography. 4. Statesmen—United States—Biography. I. Title.
E467.1.D26 C66 2000
973.7'13'092—dc21
[B]
00-062006

Vintage ISBN: 0-375-72542-3

Author photograph © Jim Zietz

www.vintagebooks.com

Printed in the United States of America
10 9 8 7 6 5 4 3

FRONTISPIECE:
Jefferson Davis, c. 1860 (photograph by Mathew Brady).
Courtesy Library of Congress

IN MEMORIAM

Mamie Mayes Cooper
1916–1998

William James Cooper
1903–1999

CONTENTS

ILLUSTRATIONS

MAPS

This is the story of a man of his time who had a significant impact on his time, and thus on history. Jefferson Davis is a major figure in American history whose principal importance comes from his role in the central event of the country's history, the Civil War.

Because of Davis's significance, he has had many biographers. There have been at least sixteen accounts of his life, the first appearing in 1868, and they range from brief sketches to multivolume treatments. The authors, who have included two major literary figures and serious scholars as well as rabid partisans, have all taken their measure of Davis, a man who understood the importance of biography for historical reputation. "Men live in the estimation of posterity not by their deeds alone," he wrote, "but by their historian also."

Overall, Davis has not fared well in the estimation of historians. He is generally portrayed as an ideologue with poor political skills and as a second-rate leader with a bureaucratic mind-set, who failed spectacularly in his star role, especially when compared to Abraham Lincoln. With a brittle, ill-tempered personality, the portrayal continues, he was unable or unwilling to grow with responsibility. According to this assessment, that shortcoming was particularly apparent and disastrous in his micromanagement of his generals and in his inability to appreciate the political dimensions of the war he was fighting. Of all the words written about Davis, perhaps the most influential appeared in an essay published four decades ago by the eminent historian David M. Potter. Addressing the question of why the Confederacy lost the Civil War, Potter concluded that Davis, because of the faults summarized above, bore the major responsibility. Potter made his condemnation even more explicit and damning when he suggested that if Lincoln and Davis had exchanged positions, the Confederacy might have prevailed.[1]

I did not start my journey with Jefferson Davis to explain Confederate defeat, and that never became my chief interest. I did find a complex man, however. Even though Davis always professed his loyalty to the Constitution, he left the Union with his state, became president of the Confederate States of America, and directed the mighty effort to break up the Union. Although he and his cause failed, the vastness of the war and the profound consequences that issued from it assure its primacy and his prominence. How a patriotic American came to lead the great struggle to destroy the United States is a major issue in my book.

Yet Davis was more than a war chieftain. By 1860, he stood as one of America's most accomplished political leaders. A superb politician, he dominated his state of Mississippi. As a hero in the Mexican War, as a notable cabinet officer, and as a prominent member of the United States Senate, Jefferson Davis commanded respect across the nation. He was spoken of as a man who could legitimately aspire to his country's highest office. And he did become president, but not of the United States.

Although the defeat of the Confederacy ended Davis's active political life, he retained influence in the postwar years. His two-year imprisonment endeared him to former Confederates, who saw him as suffering for their sake. In a fundamental sense he became the embodiment of the Lost Cause, an essential theme in the history of the South after 1865. Even more important, Davis articulated the outlook of the white South that shaped both southern and national history from the 1870s well on into the twentieth century.

At the outset I want to address one matter. Race and the place of African-Americans in American society were central in Davis's life. His stance on an issue that still vexes the nation more than a century after his death would win no kudos in our time. For his entire life he believed in the superiority of the white race. He also owned slaves, defended slavery as moral and as a social good, and fought a great war to maintain it. After 1865, he opposed new rights for blacks. He rejoiced at the collapse of Reconstruction and the reassertion of white authority with its accompanying black subordination. No reader of this book can condone any of these attitudes. But my goal is to understand Jefferson Davis as a man of his time, not condemn him for not being a man of my time. In his age his views were not at all unusual, much less radical. In Davis's lifetime almost every white American and Western European believed that whites were superior to blacks. In addition, millions of Americans, northerners as well as southerners, accepted slavery as a

constitutionally sanctioned and legal institution. I will not keep pointing out that his outlook is different from mine and from that of our own
era. I should not need to.

Davis constantly talked about liberty, its preciousness and his commitment to it. He also interpreted the Confederacy as the legitimate
depository of constitutional liberty. He perceived no contradiction
between his faith in liberty and the existence of slavery. From at least
the time of the American Revolution white southerners defined their
liberty, in part, as their right to own slaves and to decide the fate of the
institution without any outside interference. While such a concept is
utterly foreign to our thinking, it was fundamental to white southerners
until 1865.[2]

The story that follows centers on Jefferson Davis and how he inter-
acted with the people around him, the world he lived in, and the great
events he was caught up in.

JEFFERSON DAVIS,
AMERICAN

"The Saddest Day of My Life"

January 21, 1861, was cold, just above freezing, and partly cloudy in Washington, D.C. Senator Jefferson Davis of Mississippi did not relish his mission. "The saddest day of my life," Davis called it. On this Monday Davis journeyed, as he had so often, from the house on I Street to the Capitol and its Senate chamber.[1]

In that place he had flourished; it was his public home. With its paneled walls and mahogany desks, the new chamber, in use for only two years, bespoke the dignity Davis always associated with the Senate. The iron-and-glass skylights accented the institution's importance by focusing light on the floor where senators sat and spoke while the surrounding galleries remained shadowy. That design feature surely pleased Davis, for he believed no other part of government more consequential.[2]

Being a senator suited the fifty-two-year-old Davis. He prized being a member of that body more than any other public office he had ever held. In it he had risen to a position of authority and prestige. Acknowledged as a leader of the South, he had seen his reputation pass far beyond sectional borders. The *New York Times* designated him "the Cicero of the Senate," while *Harper's Weekly* identified him as "the Bayard of Congress, *sans peur et sans reproche* . . . emphatically 'one of those born to command.' "[3]

But this day offered Jefferson Davis no rewards. Severe facial pain caused by neuralgia, one of the maladies that had plagued him since his desperate struggle with malaria a quarter century earlier, left him greatly distressed and weakened. In fact he had been confined to his room for more than a week, and his physician feared him too unwell to speak in public. Physical discomfort was not the chief of his concerns on this Monday, however. "Unutterable griefs" afflicted him. Today would mark his final appearance in his beloved Senate. Mississippi had not voted him out of office, but neither was he leaving voluntarily.[4]

Ever since Davis's return from the Mexican War in 1847 and his almost immediate entry into the Senate, he had striven to preserve what he always called the Union of "our Fathers." For him that phrase had a double meaning, actual and symbolic. He cherished the knowledge that his own father had been a Revolutionary soldier. The Declaration of Independence and the Constitution he considered his political testaments. His faith in them, as he saw it, made him an ideological as well as a biological son of the generation that had created the United States.

To this Union, Davis had given his full devotion. In 1824, as a youth of sixteen, he took a formal oath of loyalty on the plain at West Point. His four years at the Military Academy and the succeeding seven years on active duty as an officer in the U.S. Army gave form to his visceral feeling of loyalty. That commitment intensified in the Mexican War, where he participated in heavy fighting and sustained a painful wound.

When Davis entered the Senate chamber that wintry January day, he knew that the Union he held dear was gone. The increasingly bitter tension between North and South over slavery, sectional power, and the nature of the Union had finally reached the breaking point following the election of Abraham Lincoln to the presidency in November 1860. States in the Deep South immediately began moving toward secession.

Congress had convened on December 3, 1860, and had at once become the epicenter of the crisis. Strutting southern fire-eaters eager for secession joyfully proclaimed that at last the perfidious Union was dead. Self-assured Republicans, savoring their victory, paid scant attention to the South, which they despised and knew little about. Still, the long history of sectional compromise, which stretched back to the Constitutional Convention in Philadelphia in 1787, provided a tradition of political adjustment and gave hope to those, North and South, who were attempting to devise a plan that would mollify southern fears of a Republican administration and at the same time not deprive the Republicans of their sense of triumph.

Americans crowded into the Capitol, both actually and vicariously. Everywhere newspapers were full of what was and was not happening. Rumors abounded: settlement was at hand; no settlement was possible. In the Federal city, visiting the House of Representatives and the Senate became almost a full-time occupation. So much time was spent in the galleries that many ladies took "their sewing or crocheting." And that was not all. A regular Senate watcher noted that "all of us who are not absolutely spiritual provide ourselves with a lunch." The Senate gallery turned into "the fashionable place of reunion."[5]

One who often sat in the Senate gallery was Varina Howell Davis, the wife of Jefferson Davis for sixteen years. Varina Davis thoroughly enjoyed the bustle and excitement of Washington, where she had spent most of the 1850s. With her husband in either the cabinet or the Senate for all but eighteen months of the decade, she was more at home in the capital than in her native Mississippi. The thirty-four-year-old Varina, known for her sharp wit and rapier retorts, led an active social life revolving around several women friends, though she also enjoyed parties and the company of men. Some found her too prickly, however.

Although they made strenuous efforts in December and on into January, advocates of compromise did not succeed. With Congress ensnared in political and sectional webs, events outside Washington swept to the forefront and deepened the crisis. Talk of secession was quickly transformed into the fact of secession. On December 20, 1860, South Carolina formally left the Union. The remaining Deep South states, west to Texas, seemed to be headed along that same course. Southern senators and congressmen started going home to stand with their states. In Mississippi a convention met to decide its fate and that of the Union; on January 9, 1861, the delegates voted 84 to 15 to take their state out of the Union. The news quickly flashed to Washington via telegraph.

Davis had expected this decision, but even when he learned of it, he remained in Washington, pending his receipt of formal notification of Mississippi's secession. By this time Davis also knew that in early February the seceding states would send delegates to Montgomery, Alabama, to form a southern confederacy. His lingering did not mean that he was unsure about his own path. He knew what he must do. "Now I come to the hard task of announcing to you that the hour is at hand which closes my connection with the United States, for the independence and Union of which my father bled and in the service of which I have sought to emulate the example he set for my guidance," he told former president Franklin Pierce. "The stern conviction of necessity, the demand of honor" governed his action.[6]

On the twenty-first, those who pressed into the Senate chamber saw Davis in his final moment of national power. Though "pale and evidently suffering," he still commanded attention. Just under six feet tall, slender, with the erect military bearing that had marked his posture

Jefferson Davis, c. 1860 (photograph by Mathew Brady).
Library of Congress

since West Point, Davis had presence. His face was more striking than handsome. In many ways the eyes predominated. Icy blue and intense, full, deepset, they drew in listeners, though a film, the legacy of a ravaging ophthalmologic disease in 1858, partially covered the left one. By this time gray tinged his brown hair, wrinkles lined his full forehead, and his features had a sharply chiseled look. High, prominent cheekbones accentuated hollow cheeks. Thin lips curved above a strong chin displaying a fringe beard.[7]

Rising to speak early in the afternoon, with "firm & manly" manner

Jefferson Davis faced his colleagues and a crowded chamber. The gallery was full, with barely standing room available. Ladies were even sitting on the floor against the wall. To ensure herself a seat, Varina Davis had sent a servant at 7 a.m. to hold her a place. Four southern senators, the two Alabamians and the two Floridians, preceded the Mississippian. With what Davis termed "heart wringing words," he announced to his audience that he had received "satisfactory evidence" that Mississippi, "by a solemn ordinance of her people in convention assembled, ha[d] declared her separation from the United States." The independence of Mississippi, he continued, meant that he was no longer a citizen of the United States, and certainly no role remained for him in the United States Senate, for he would never play the obstructionist. Acknowledging that the time for argument had passed, Davis still thought it appropriate "to say something on the part of the State I here represent, on an occasion so solemn as this."[8]

Davis began his brief remarks, which probably lasted about fifteen minutes, by reminding his fellow senators that "for many years" his insistence on "State sovereignty" included "the right of a State to secede from the Union." Thus, whether or not he agreed with the action of Mississippi, his "allegiance" bound him to abide by it. But he hastened to add that he did believe Mississippi had "justifiable cause" to end her connection with the United States. According to Davis, the disconnection meant that all the benefits of the Union, "and they are known to be many," had been surrendered.

In Davis's view the justification for his state's decision was simple yet profound—"a belief that we are to be deprived in the Union of the rights which our Fathers have bequeathed to us." He asserted that the anchors of liberty for the South and southerners, the Declaration of Independence and the Constitution, had been pulled up in the cause of antislavery and racial equality to support "an attack upon [southern] social institutions." The Declaration, Davis proclaimed, had trumpeted the great truth that "no man was born—to use the language of Mr. Jefferson—booted and spurred to ride over the rest of mankind; that men were created equal—meaning the men of the political community." These "great principles," in Davis's interpretation, were now "invoked to maintain the position of the equality of the races." Davis, on the contrary, insisted that the precepts of the Declaration referred solely to "each member of the body politic." In his reading "they ha[d] no reference to the slave." To Davis the meaning of the Constitution had been equally corrupted. He noted that the Constitution provided for "that very class of persons as property." "They were not," he pointed out, "put upon the footing of equality with white men."

As Davis perceived the political world, the subversion of the founding documents, from protection of slave property to assaults upon it, endangered the liberty of white southerners. To his mind the southern recourse was clear: "we recur to the principles upon which our Government was founded." We declare, he went on, "the right to withdraw from a Government which thus perverted threatens to be destructive of our rights." When the South proclaimed its independence, it "but tr[od] in the path of our Fathers." Davis further defined his understanding of secession as defensive by asserting that the South seceded "not in hostility to others, not to injure any section of the country, not even for our own pecuniary benefit; but from the high and solemn motive of defending and protecting the rights we inherited, and which it is our sacred duty to transmit unshorn to our children."

He underscored that secession did not signify enmity, either on his part or on that of his constituents. He addressed those with whom he had sharply disagreed: "I . . . now say in the presence of my God, I wish you well." Both he and those who elected him, Davis avowed, hoped for peaceful relations with their former associates.

At the same time he let all know that he and the other southerners leaving the Union understood the hazard of their undertaking. If the North denied the right of separation, Davis said forthrightly, "We will invoke the God of our fathers who delivered them from the power of the lion, to protect us from the ravages of the bear; and thus, putting our trust in God and in our own firm hearts and strong arms, we will vindicate the right as best we may."

Concluding, Davis became quite personal, even intimate. He noticed several senators with whom he had long served, and he admitted that there had been "points of collision." But now he jettisoned all ill will and acrimony. "I carry with me," he assured his colleagues, "no hostile remembrance. Whatever offense I have given which has not been redressed, or for which satisfaction has not been demanded, I have, Senators, in this hour of our parting, to offer you my apology for any pain which, in heat of discussion, I have inflicted." Then, in the last words Jefferson Davis ever uttered in the United States Capitol, he addressed the vice president and the senators: "it only remains for me to bid you a final adieu."

Davis's conclusion met with an emotional response. Both senators and spectators had given "the utmost attention" to all five southerners.

Now listeners and observers seemed "spellbound." His farewell "left many in tears"; it even "drew tears from the eyes of many Senators." Soon, however, senators, Republicans as well as Democrats, began moving toward Davis and his fellow seceders, where "a general and very cordial shaking of hands took place." At last, a "grief-stricken" Davis departed from the chamber and the building.[9]

His immersion in the day was not yet over. Six weeks later he would speak of his remarks as not merely words, "but rather leaves torn from the book of fate." Even though that book would provide him with twenty-eight more years filled with momentous events and tumultuous emotions, this year remained unique. In the evening a colleague spent several hours with Davis, who was preparing to start for Mississippi the next day. He reported Davis in "great agony" and "tortured" emotionally and physically. Earlier, talking with friends just after his senatorial farewell, Davis held the hand of one; "this is the saddest day of my life." And he meant it; he never forgot 1861, when the Union he treasured disappeared. After the Civil War he would even sign the books he acquired on page 61.[10]

CHAPTER ONE

"There My Memories Begin"

Jefferson Davis was born on June 3, 1808, in Christian County, Kentucky. Located in the west-central section of the state and bordering Tennessee, Christian County at that time was a sparsely settled part of the western frontier. The infant was named for his father's political hero, the sitting president of the United States, Thomas Jefferson. His parents also gave him a middle name, which by early manhood he dropped completely; only the initial F. survived. For Samuel Emory Davis in his early fifties and his forty-eight-year-old wife, Jane Cook Davis, this boy, their tenth child, would be their last.[1]

In searching for a home on the American frontier, Samuel Davis followed literally in the steps of his father. Samuel's grandfather, the first of this Davis family on this side of the Atlantic Ocean, emigrated from Wales to Philadelphia, perhaps as early as 1701, when a number of Welsh Baptists landed in the Pennsylvania port, and surely before 1720. The place and date of Evan Davis's birth are not known. All genealogical authorities agree on his Welshness, and he was undoubtedly born sometime during the final two decades of the seventeenth century. He had a wife, but only her first name has survived. When and where he and Mary Davis were married is also unknown.[2]

Evan Davis found Philadelphia and Pennsylvania hospitable to his efforts to advance his station and to raise a family. He spent the remainder of his life in the city. The colony's tolerant religious policy permitted him to remain loyal to his Baptist faith. Even though Evan Davis spent most of his working years as a carter, he managed to accumulate enough money to buy property. A deed conveying a city lot to him in 1734 carries the colony's first official notice of him. Although he became a property owner, he never learned to read or write. Neither did his wife. All of his legal documents, including his will, he signed with his mark. Late in life he changed occupations to become an innkeeper. When his will was drawn up in 1743, he identified himself as a carter; but the inventory of his estate prepared after his death in 1747 listed him as an innkeeper. Mary survived him for eleven years, dying in 1758.

While Evan Davis was striving to improve his financial status, he and Mary were caring for a large family. They had six children, five sons and one daughter. At the time Evan Davis had his will written, four of them had reached their maturity. He evidently favored the two youngest, who were both still under twenty-one, for he provided that Joseph and Evan Jr. should receive larger shares of his estate than their brothers and sister. In addition to their portions of the property, they were bequeathed cash payments—Joseph £10 and Evan Jr. £20, quite respectable sums, payable when each became twenty-one. The four elder Davis siblings never left Philadelphia, but the two youngest emulated their father in his youth and struck out for new horizons.

Once both reached twenty-one and were in possession of the money from their father's estate, Joseph and Evan Jr. headed southward, probably around 1750. Initially they went to South Carolina. The historical record does not indicate why they chose that destination, nor does it designate how they traveled or where they first located. In all likelihood they stopped either in Charleston or the Welsh Neck, a settlement about 100 miles northeast of the city, populated by Welsh Baptists. Joseph stayed in South Carolina, ultimately settling near Broad River. Evan decided on a different course.

Before departing from his brother, Evan found another partner. In South Carolina he met and married Mary Emory Williams, a widow with two sons. As in the case of his parents, neither the place nor the date of the younger Evan's wedding is known. Additionally, no evidence gives the date when Evan and Mary Davis moved on to Wilkes County, Georgia. But both the marriage and the journey had to have taken place by 1756, for in that year the Davises, living in Georgia, had their first and only child. Named for a paternal uncle and his mother's family, Samuel Emory Davis was also the only grandchild of the senior Evan and Mary Davis.

Evan Davis, Jr., died soon after the birth of his son, though exactly when is unknown. It had to be prior to 1762, for in that year one of his older brothers, William, purchased the property in his father's estate from his living siblings. The deed omitted Evan's name along with that of another brother, both of whom were deceased. After Evan's death his widow evidently lost touch with his brothers, for her name is not mentioned in the 1762 deed. In 1767, when William Davis sold the Davis property to someone outside the family, the deed contained the names of neither Mary Davis nor Samuel Emory Davis. Although Samuel certainly possessed a legitimate claim to his father's part of the property, his uncle William left him out of the transaction. Whether William Davis acted out of ignorance or malice cannot now be ascertained. Clearly, however, young Samuel Davis was deprived of his inheritance from his grandfather Davis's estate.

Samuel grew up with his mother and two stepbrothers on a farm in Wilkes County. No details about his early years have survived. When the American Revolution convulsed the Georgia and South Carolina frontiers, Samuel Davis entered the conflict and the historical record. With his stepbrothers, Samuel joined the patriot militia and fought as a private soldier in both Georgia and South Carolina. In 1779 he formed and led a company that participated in the sieges of Savannah and Augusta.[3]

In mid-1782, when hostilities ended in Georgia, Samuel Davis returned to Wilkes County. Although his mother had died before he returned, Samuel did not long remain without a woman prominent in his life. In South Carolina during the war he met Jane Cook, from a Scots-Irish family, whom he married in 1783. He and his new bride began clearing a farm on 200 acres beside Little River in Wilkes County, land which the state of Georgia had given him for his military service in the Revolution.

For the next several years Samuel and Jane Davis strove to enhance their position. An ambitious young man, Samuel was able to add substantially to his acreage from the abundant, inexpensive land on the Georgia and South Carolina borderlands. By 1785 he owned around 4,000 acres of predominantly uncleared land. A year earlier Samuel and Jane had greeted their first child, Joseph Emory. Holding to the Baptist faith of his forebears, Samuel joined with fellow settlers to organize a local Baptist church and build a log chapel, though Jane did not become a member. By 1787 Samuel had acquired his first slave, a woman named Winnie. All the while his and Jane's family grew. By early in the new decade four more babies, three boys and a girl, had arrived.

Still, Samuel Davis was dissatisfied. Even in the 1780s white fears and Indian depredations disrupted life on the Georgia frontier, undermining the safety and value of many of Samuel's acres. With or without Indians, the prosperity enjoyed by some of his neighbors eluded him. In 1793 he turned away from Georgia toward what he saw as a better opportunity. Disposing of his property and joining South Carolina relatives of Jane, Samuel Davis took his family north and west to the new state of Kentucky. They journeyed along the trail taken by thousands of hopeful and aspiring settlers across the Appalachian Mountains and through the Cumberland Gap.

Once in Kentucky, Samuel Davis did not quickly find a location to his liking. He had to pass through the rich Bluegrass region because much of the land had already been occupied and because the remainder was too expensive. Before the end of the 1790s he had tried two different places, in Mercer and Warren Counties, where he had worked hard to establish a farm in the wilderness. Initially he rented land until he bought a 100-acre plot, but he remained discontented. By 1800 he had moved his family farther west and south to Christian County.

Christian County seemed to be a good choice for the wandering and growing Samuel Davis clan. He cleared and plowed his 200-acre farm with the help of his older children and his two slaves. When he sold his Warren County land in 1801, he used the proceeds to buy another slave and more horses. Raising tobacco, corn, and wheat as well as cattle, hogs, and horses, Samuel Davis became a successful pioneer farmer, and he added to his acres. At the same time his family was expanding. In 1797 Jane Davis gave birth to a daughter, their sixth child and first in Kentucky. During the next decade four more—three girls and one boy—would become part of the large family. Adding to their responsibilities, Samuel and Jane Davis obtained a tavern license and became innkeepers.

As a sign of his increased prosperity Samuel Davis built a new cabin on the site of present-day Fairview, then in Christian County, now partly in Todd County. He put up a double log cabin with two large rooms on either side of a covered passageway, the classic dogtrot design. Each room had its own fireplace and a small shed attached in the rear. The timbers were cut in nearby forests and were hewed into shape by hand. Hand-wrought iron nails and heavy wooden pins kept the logs in place. The cabin contained puncheon floors and heavy wooden doors hung on leather hinges fastened with wooden buttons. The glass panes, undoubtedly the most expensive detail in the house, stood out in the small windows. Sticks and mud, the stack construc-

Birthplace of Jefferson Davis.
Library of Congress

tion, were used for the chimneys at each end of the house. A well in the yard provided the water, known throughout the neighborhood for its quality.[4]

In this cabin on June 3, 1808, Jefferson F. Davis became the tenth and final child born to Samuel and Jane Davis. By then the two oldest boys had moved out, but eight Davis children lived in the cabin with their parents.

Despite his apparent success in Christian County, Samuel Davis decided shortly after the birth of his newest son once again to move west. Precisely why he made that decision is not clear, but the ambition that brought him to Kentucky surely helped take him away from the state. Evidently, he still had not done well enough. He began selling his 1,100-acre farm and buying additional horses and slaves. Around 1810 he yet again turned his face westward and southward. He was not thinking, however, of a nearby county or even an adjoining state. Samuel Davis took aim on a site some 600 miles southwest of Christian County, Bayou Teche, in southern Louisiana. With an entourage of wife, children, slaves, and animals, he made the arduous overland trek in about two months. But the supposedly permanent location in Louisiana turned out to be only a temporary halt. After less than a year in that swampy region, pestilential mosquitoes and recurring illnesses among the younger children prompted still another move.

This time Samuel Davis, now in his mid-fifties, charted a sharply shorter course. The new destination would be only some 100 miles to the north in Wilkinson County in the southwestern corner of Mississippi Territory, which would become in 1817 the state of Mississippi. Samuel Davis located what would be his final stopping place on a small farm two miles east of Woodville, the county seat. The county tax rolls placed him there in 1810.[5]

During the next decade Davis occupied himself with the tasks of an aspiring, energetic farmer. He cleared land; he began planting crops. When he could, he purchased land, more land, and more slaves. He also commenced construction of a new home for his wife and children. At the onset, before any house existed, the Davises camped out, at least for a while. Probably Samuel began as a renter, but by 1813 he had purchased a small piece of property, and by 1820 he owned almost 400 acres, including cleared and uncleared land. His slave force also increased from six in 1810 to twelve in 1816, the maximum he would ever possess. In 1820 he had eleven slaves.[6]

With the help of Davis's sons and his slaves, the land began producing. Samuel Davis was never a wealthy man; he worked in his fields beside his slaves and sons, with cotton as the chief money crop, though he also raised the usual cereals, vegetables, forage, fodder, and animals. Family tradition remarks on the plentiful fruit trees and on Jane Davis's omnipresent flowers, particularly the roses she loved. The place was called Poplar Grove, from the large poplar trees on it. The house, also named Poplar Grove, was completed before 1817.

Samuel Davis's house differed markedly from his cabin in Christian County. Using cypress, he constructed a modest story-and-a-half frame cottage, not a plantation mansion. Built on a center-hall plan, Poplar Grove has two rooms on either side of the first floor and is one room deep on the second. With a small sitting room or library in the gable between the upstairs bedrooms, the house has seven rooms, including a parlor and a dining room, and two chimneys that originally provided outlets for six fireplaces. The kitchen was a separate building in the rear. Large double doors, louvered shutters, and a gallery extending the full length of the front facade embellish the house. A Palladian window in the central gable, two marble mantels, and six-panel doors with painted graining add refined features to the simple but finely executed structure.[7]

"There my memories begin," Jefferson Davis, in the last year of his life, wrote of Woodville and Poplar Grove. Specifically, he remembered seeing the wound inflicted on his brother Samuel's horse at the Battle of New Orleans, which occurred in January 1815. Young Jefferson spent his early boyhood on a farm touching the edge of the American wilderness. There, loving parents, older siblings, especially attentive sisters, and black slaves surrounded him.[8]

In moving more than 1,000 miles and changing residence a half dozen times, Samuel Davis for more than two decades sought unremittingly to improve his station and provide more abundantly for his family. Yet the recollections of those who lived in his house, including Jefferson Davis, did not describe a driven man. They recalled "a silent, undemonstrative man," to his children "rather suggestive than dictatorial," and "strictly a religious governor of his family." In addition, Samuel Davis impressed observers with his "wonderful physical activity." Jefferson recollected one occasion when his then sixty-four-year-old father, trying to mount a difficult horse, vaulted from the ground into the saddle. Like most people of their status in their time and place, neither Samuel nor Jane Davis had any formal education but both were literate. Nothing suggests that any of their first nine children had any more contact with formal schooling than they did. By this time, however, Joseph, the eldest, who had started out in Kentucky as a storekeeper's apprentice, had become an attorney after having read law in both Kentucky and Mississippi. For the youthful Jefferson, his father envisioned a different educational path.[9]

Jefferson did not begin differently. At age five he had started school in "the usual log-cabin schoolhouse" that often provided the only semblance of formal education on the rural frontier, where schools of any kind were scarce. For two years he and his sister Mary, two years older, traveled a mile from their home with their lunch in a bucket to the local log cabin. When composing his "Autobiographical Sketch," an elderly Jefferson Davis had few kind words for the teachers in these backwoods establishments. According to Davis, their attainments rarely exceeded "the three R's" and "their patrons" demanded no more. Moreover, they believed that "the oil of the birch was the proper lubrication for any want of intelligence." Floggings punctuated the school day.

Only the copybook matched the birch as a pedagogical tool. The teacher would write at the top of every page in the copybook "the pothooks, letters, sentences" that their students would then copy on every line of the paper. This format also sufficed for arithmetic. After working through "the examples in the arithmetic," the student would write them out in the copybook. This methodology rested on the assumption that completion of the book meant understanding the process. Not to Jefferson Davis: he maintained that "a bright boy" could repeat all the rules but could give no reason for any of them.[10]

Samuel Davis had no intention of permitting this rudimentary drilling to form even the base of Jefferson's education. To accomplish his purpose he looked back to Kentucky. In his former state a school run by the Dominican order of the Roman Catholic Church offered the kind of educational opportunity that Samuel obviously wanted for his youngest son. How Samuel found out about St. Thomas College is not clear. It opened about the time he left Kentucky; possibly Joseph, who did not migrate to Mississippi until 1811, knew about it; or possibly friends back in Kentucky told Samuel about it. Whatever the case, Samuel Davis acted decisively. His Baptist faith did not deter him from sending his young boy to a Roman Catholic school. He made the arrangements for Jefferson to go, including finding a way for the child to make the overland journey of hundreds of miles. And he kept all these plans from his wife. Jane Davis did not know that her husband intended to send her seven-year-old son, her baby, away to a school so distant as to be practically in another universe. In fact, she was not at home when Jefferson departed.[11]

Sometime in the late spring of 1816, before Jefferson's eighth birthday on June 3, he set out on an almost incredible journey. Without saying good-bye to his mother, the lad joined a party consisting of Major Thomas Hinds and his relatives, including a son of Jefferson's age. Each boy rode a pony. They struck out through what residents called "the Wilderness," the Natchez Trace stretching for about 500 miles between Natchez, Mississippi, thirty-five miles from Woodville and on the great river, and Nashville, Tennessee. Before regular steamboat travel the Trace provided the main route north from the lower Mississippi Valley. Travelers of all types, including the river men who had brought the flatboats down the Ohio and Mississippi Rivers, traversed the Trace. Rough characters and bandits abounded. The Trace also ran through Choctaw Indian territory, but this fact caused little concern because amicable relations predominated between Choctaws and whites. There were a few taverns or "stands" along the way, but mostly the journeyers slept under the stars.

After several weeks on the road and without incident, the Hinds party reached its first important stop, just outside Nashville. There

Major Hinds visited his old commander from the Battle of New Orleans, General Andrew Jackson, at his home, the Hermitage. Jackson received all with such hospitality that they stayed for "several weeks." Youthful Jefferson Davis came face-to-face with an authentic hero. The boy had certainly heard about the general, the victor at New Orleans and the vanquisher of the Indians, who had a larger-than-life image in the Southwest. Besides, his brother Samuel had been in Major Hinds's unit at New Orleans. Toward the end of his life Davis characterized this meeting with a man of Jackson's stature as "a stand-point of no small advantage" for a young boy. He did not find the fearsome, profane warrior he had been told about. Instead, he found Jackson "always very gentle and considerate." The general's "unaffected and well-bred courtesy" deeply impressed him. And the hero always said grace at the table. For Jefferson there was also plenty of time for boys' activities with Major Hinds's son and General Jackson's adopted son. Davis remembered the pony races and that the old soldier would not let the boys wrestle, fearing that they might begin fighting. Everyone left the Hermitage "with great regret." More than seven decades later, Davis wrote, "in me he inspired reverence and affection that has remained with me through my whole life."[12]

After this extended visit, Major Hinds took his charges on northward into Kentucky. By mid-July he delivered young Jefferson Davis to the officials at St. Thomas College. The college records stipulate that Davis arrived and paid fees of $65 on July 16, 1816. Now eight years old, Jefferson Davis stepped into a new world far removed from the familiar faces and precincts of Poplar Grove.[13]

St. Thomas, Davis's home for the next two years, was the first Roman Catholic educational institution west of the Allegheny Mountains. Located in Washington County in central Kentucky, it was part of a religious complex that included St. Rose Convent and Seminary. Father Samuel Wilson's role exemplified the interrelationship among the units. As prior, he directed the entire enterprise; he was also president of the college and on the faculty of both college and seminary. In addition to the educational and religious mission, there was a working farm that produced food for students, staff, and the market.[14]

By modern definitions St. Thomas College was no college at all, but rather a preparatory school, with both boarding and day students. St. Thomas obviously accepted and accommodated quite young students.

The scarcity of records makes it impossible to date its opening precisely, but it had definitely begun operations by 1809. The college building, where Davis lived and went to class, was not completed until 1812. An imposing three-story brick structure, it stood by Cartwright Creek, two miles from the present town of Springfield. Davis attended during a flourishing period for St. Thomas. Later, the financial dislocation caused by the Panic of 1819 hurt the college. The opening of other Roman Catholic schools and the placing of a bishop in Cincinnati led to a reduction in staff. In 1828, the doors of St. Thomas were finally closed.

In the mid-1810s, the school clearly enjoyed a positive reputation that stretched far beyond its immediate environment. Students came from Indiana, Louisiana, Michigan, Mississippi, and Missouri, as well as Kentucky. As many as 200 boys made up the student body. Boarders paid for their education with cash and with their labor. From the beginning, St. Thomas accepted all applicants. The school calendar was quite flexible; students entered whenever they appeared. The calendar evidently did not provide for formal vacations because the boarding students remained in residence throughout the year.

Sectarianism did not characterize St. Thomas. Admissions policy was not tied to religious affiliation. From the outset, both Catholics and non-Catholics were welcome, and a substantial number of non-Catholics were always enrolled. Although all students had to attend religious exercises, proselytism did not form a central part of the program. In fact, when Jefferson Davis told Father Wilson that he wanted to become a Catholic, the old priest kindly put him off. As Davis recollected, Father Wilson "handed me a biscuit and a bit of cheese, and told me that for the present I had better take some Catholic food."[15]

The year Jefferson Davis entered, St. Thomas had five full-time faculty members, four priests and a layman. They taught in a curriculum that concentrated on offerings emphasized by the academic institutions of that day. Latin and Greek were stressed. In his old age Davis recalled that the foundation he received in ancient languages at St. Thomas served him well when he got to college. The faculty also gave instruction in French, Italian, history, literature, science, and music.

Davis thrived, even though he was among the youngest boys and claimed to be the smallest. He had fond memories of some of the priests who taught him. One of them, who was particularly solicitous, put a small bed in his own room for the little boy to use. Even though Davis had been sent far from Wilkinson County, he was not forgotten at home. His parents did write to him, but none of their letters survived.[16]

Study and work did not take up all of young Jefferson's two years at St. Thomas. With more than 100 boys in one place, play and antics were bound to occur. Davis recorded an episode in which he participated. Several boys decided to "revolt" against the old priest in whose room Davis slept. To initiate the prank, Jefferson agreed to blow out the candle that always burned in the room. On the appointed night, after all was quiet, he extinguished the flame. Then the other plotters hurled vegetables and "all kinds of missiles" into the priest's quarters. As soon as light could be restored, a search for the culprits commenced. Davis reported that his confederates "were all sound asleep," but not he. "I was the only wakeful one," he wrote. Although the priests questioned him "severely," he responded that he knew little and would not divulge that. Punishment was directed.

The targeted priest, "who had especial care" of Davis, took him to a small room on the top floor. There, the old man strapped the boy down "to a kind of cot, which was arranged to facilitate the punishment of the boys." This priest, who, according to Davis, "loved me dearly," paused before striking the lad. He pleaded with Davis. "If you tell me what you know, no matter how little, I will let you off." Davis replied, "I know one thing, I know who blew out the light." After the priest reaffirmed the offer of clemency, Davis confessed, "I blew it out." The priest honored his commitment, but he had "a long talk" with the juvenile malefactor, which, Davis remembered, "moved me to tears and prevented me from co-operating with the boys again in their schemes of mischief."[17]

After two years at St. Thomas, Jefferson, now ten, returned to Mississippi. His mother had grown impatient to have him back. In the late spring of 1818 he left with Charles Green, a Mississippian reading law in Kentucky, who had been his guardian during his time at St. Thomas. On this journey the youthful Davis would not repeat the lengthy march over the Natchez Trace. With Green he started for Louisville to catch one of the steamboats by then navigating the Ohio and Mississippi Rivers. Davis's first steamboat trip greatly impressed him. He was struck by the numerous passengers who would get on board the new wonders and ride a few miles just for the experience. Then they would disembark and return by carriage to Louisville. Even seven decades later the names of the boat and its captain were still fresh in his mind: the *Aetna* with Captain Robinson DeHart.[18]

He embarked on the *Aetna* in good spirits. He was going home, and he had just bested a mountebank who tried to take advantage of him with the old stratagem of the learned pig, a phenomenon that had originated in England in the 1780s. The owner of a pig trained the animal to perform any number of a variety of tasks, including spelling names and other words, solving arithmetical problems, telling time, and reading thoughts of members of the audience. Some pigs became quite adept, and the learned pig turned into a popular attraction. From fees and wagers the pig's master could profit handsomely. A commentator, albeit unfriendly, observed that the learned pig "gave great satisfaction to all who saw him, and filled his tormentor's pocket with money." By 1797 this four-footed enticement had crossed the Atlantic. An advertisement in a New York City newspaper touted a porker "who could read, spell, tell the time of day by any person's watch in the audience, and distinguish ladies from gentlemen in the audience."[19]

The trickster encountered by Davis in Louisville claimed that he knew a pig who could outspell Jefferson. To prove it, he offered to bet the young scholar ninepence. Davis accepted the wager, and, as he later told the story, "spelt against the pig." The youngster turned out to be more learned than his porcine opponent, for as he reported, "the pig spelled as well as his master could and no better." "By beating a pig in spelling," Davis began his homeward journey ninepence richer.[20]

After a "slow and uneventful" river voyage brought him back to Mississippi, Jefferson headed for Poplar Grove accompanied by an older brother, Isaac, fifteen years his senior. When the pair reached Woodville, Isaac urged his young sibling to go on home alone—he wanted Jefferson to conceal his identity in order to discover whether his parents would recognize him. In his "Autobiographical Sketch," Jefferson Davis recounted the moment: "I found my dear old mother sitting near the door, and, walking up with an assumed air to hide a throbbing heart, I asked her if there had been any stray horses round there. She said she had seen a stray boy, and clasped me in her arms."

That embrace underscored for the youthful Jefferson his mother's love. He returned her affection. Late in life he remarked that he had never "ceased to cherish a tender memory of the loving care of that mother, in whom there was so much to admire and nothing to remember save good." To him "her beauty and sprightliness of mind" singled her out. It was a "graceful poetic mind, which, with much of her personal beauty," he lovingly remembered, "she retained to extreme old age."[21]

Following his happy reunion with his mother, Jefferson asked about his father. Told that his father was in the field, the impatient boy went immediately to see him. Jefferson recognized that his father, though possessing "deep feeling," tried "to repress the expression of it whenever practicable." But this time the feeling caused by the unexpected appearance of his youngest child moved Samuel Davis. "He took me in his arms with more emotion than I had ever seen him exhibit, and kissed me repeatedly," Jefferson recorded. He added: "I remember wondering why my father should have kissed so big a boy."[22]

Home once more in the bosom of a loving family, Jefferson Davis quickly found himself in another schoolroom. Because the schools in Wilkinson County had not improved, Jefferson was sent off to Jefferson College in Washington, Mississippi, six miles east of Natchez. Founded in 1811, Jefferson College, in Davis's student days, was, like St. Thomas, a preparatory school, not a college. When Davis matriculated in 1818, the school had four teachers. The enrollment did not match the numbers at St. Thomas, but the curriculum, which emphasized the classical languages, was quite similar. Jefferson was enrolled there for only a very short time.[23]

Finally, the possibility of obtaining a decent education had opened in Wilkinson County with the organization of the Wilkinson County Academy, headed by John A. Shaw from Boston. No teacher like Shaw had ever before appeared in Wilkinson County. He had nothing in common with the previous masters of the three R's. Samuel Davis brought Jefferson back to Poplar Grove and placed him in the new academy. For the next five years Jefferson lived at home and regularly attended John Shaw's school.

John Shaw left a marked imprint on his young student. Davis saw him as "the first of a new class of teachers in our neighborhood." Others of similar ability followed Shaw and brought more effective teaching, which greatly improved the performance of their students. Calling Shaw "a scholarly man" and "a quiet, just man," Davis professed, "I am sure he taught me more in the time I was with him than I ever learned from any one else."[24]

Shaw did not succeed in every undertaking. To augment his teaching income, he took on the task of preaching every Sunday. But because Woodville had no church building, he held services in the courthouse. The boys at the academy were required to join the congregation. Before long his students made up his only audience; the adults stopped coming. Asserting that the absence of adult worshippers indicated his ineffectiveness, Shaw gave up his ministerial duties. He then devoted himself totally to the academy. After a time Shaw returned to Massachusetts, but later he ended up in charge of public schools in New Orleans.[25]

Despite his later profession of respect and admiration for John Shaw, the youthful Jefferson Davis on one occasion questioned the value of school. He received an assignment that he believed beyond his ability to memorize. Protests to the instructor brought no reduction in the quantity of material assigned. In class the next day young Jefferson had not mastered the subject matter. Upon the threat of sanctions, he took his books, went home, and told his father.

Samuel Davis offered the rebellious scholar an alternative. "Of course, it is for you to elect whether you will work with head or hands," father informed son. But he did not stop there: "My son could not be an idler. I want more cotton-pickers and will give you work." Next morning the recalcitrant student with bag in hand walked to the cotton field. For two days he participated in the hot, hard physical labor with the other cotton pickers, including slaves. As Davis remembered, the experience persuaded him that school was "the lesser evil." Upon leaving the field on the second day, he told his father of his new view. Samuel Davis listened to the resigning farmhand with "perfect seriousness." Then he spoke about "the disadvantages" of a man "gently bred" working as a laborer. He concluded by telling his son that if he felt the same way tomorrow, he should return to the classroom. That is precisely what Jefferson Davis did. And he suffered no consequences, for the teacher took no notice of his absence—in Jefferson's opinion, because his father had so arranged it.[26]

Jefferson Davis pursued his studies at the Wilkinson County Academy until his early teenage years. By the spring of 1823 it was decided that for his education to progress he would have to enter a real college. Going to college meant, of course, that once again he would have to leave home and Woodville. Without doubt Samuel Davis participated in this decision; he had always desired the best possible education for his youngest son. By this time, however, his eldest, Joseph, twenty-four years older than his brother Jefferson, was also probably involved. Joseph had become a prominent and prosperous attorney in Natchez as well as a substantial landowner. At the same time, Samuel Davis's financial fortunes were in decline. He was even unable to complete payment for the land he had bought; to aid his father, Joseph in 1822 had purchased the family farm. Thus, Joseph's financial support as well as advice was critical. Never hesitating to profess his praise and respect for Joseph, Jefferson later described him as "my beau ideal when I was a boy," who became "my mentor and greatest benefactor." That relationship began even before Samuel Davis's death in 1824. In 1823, the Davises concurred. For the best collegiate opportunity the fourteen-year-old Jefferson would retrace his steps to the state of his birth.[27]

CHAPTER TWO

"Put Away the Grog"

The Davises looked toward Kentucky because no colleges existed in Mississippi. Moreover, Transylvania University in Lexington had acquired a sterling reputation in much of the West. With the decision made about Transylvania, the youthful Jefferson sometime in the late winter or early spring of 1823 began his second trip northward. Unlike his first time seven years earlier, the historical record is silent on this second journey. But at some point, after the spring semester had already begun, the teenager reached Lexington.

In the early 1820s, Lexington, in the center of the rich Bluegrass region, was an impressive place, and the young Mississippi farm boy surely took note. Observers tried to capture the appeal and the distinctiveness of both the setting and the town. "Poetry cannot paint groves more beautiful, or fields more luxuriant," wrote one; "the country neither hilly nor gentle; but gently waving." Some 5,000 people resided in a town where "the streets are broad, straight, paved, clean and have rows of trees on each side." Most of the homes were of brick, with a "rural and charming appearance." In addition to its attractiveness, Lexington was also a cosmopolitan town, notably so for a community of its size. The Athenaeum stocked newspapers and periodicals from East Coast cities. The public library held 6,000 books; in addition, the library at Transylvania contained more than 5,000 volumes, and the two debating societies owned another 1,000.[1]

Transylvania contributed the vitality and resources of a flourishing institution of higher learning. By the time Davis entered, Transylvania had become a "proud university" with some 400 students—an enrollment that matched the numbers at Princeton and Harvard. The university included a preparatory school and programs in law and medicine, as well as an undergraduate curriculum. It had not always been so. As recently as 1818, Transylvania had been little more than a grammar school with fewer than 80 students. In that year Horace Holley came to Lexington as the school's new president. Holley, a New England Unitarian minister, worked with zeal and dedication to transform Transylvania. With his energy and sense of purpose, along with generous financial assistance from the state of Kentucky, he succeeded.[2]

Presidents of colleges and universities have always been important, but in the antebellum period they were absolutely critical to the welfare of their institutions. The president was not only the chief administrative officer but also a key member of the faculty, who invariably taught the required senior course on moral philosophy that was the capstone of the curriculum. Additionally, he served as the main fund-raiser, the chief public-relations official, and the dean of students. Presidents could make powerful imprints, and Horace Holley surely did. But his success was short-lived; by the late 1820s sectarian disputes and political difficulties led to Holley's departure and the decline of Transylvania. Still, for a time, Horace Holley turned Transylvania into a thriving and sophisticated university that offered its students a first-class education. Such it was when Jefferson Davis arrived. In fact, it was as much a university as any other place in the United States. The college building, "a handsome edifice of three stories surmounted by a tall and ornamental cupola, affording not only capacious lecture and recitation rooms, etc., but numerous apartments for students," formed the centerpiece of the campus. On three sides stood the fine brick homes and broad, paved streets so characteristic of Lexington. To the north of the campus extended the cultivated fields and beautiful rolling countryside of the Bluegrass. Leading citizens of the area, including the eminent political figure Henry Clay, sat on the board of trustees.[3]

Holley recognized, of course, that an impressive academic building and notable trustees were not enough, that the kind of university he envisioned required a quality faculty and superb scholarly resources. And he obtained both. As early as 1821 he sent a faculty member to Europe with $17,000 to purchase books. The scientific equipment was "exceptionally complete for the time," including botanical microscopes, an achromatic telescope, magnets, barometers, prisms, a model of a human figure for anatomy, and more than 40,000 botanical and natural history specimens. As professor of philosophy and belles lettres, Holley led a faculty that in 1823 totaled thirteen members covering ancient languages, modern languages, history, mathematics, natural history, botany, chemistry, natural philosophy, anatomy, surgery, medicine, obstetrics and diseases of women, common and statute law, and national and civil law.[4]

To take advantage of the university that Holley had built, students had to meet entrance requirements and pay fees. Tuition was $35, along with a $5 registration fee. Annual expenses for board, lodging, fuel, lights, and laundry were estimated at $105. The requirements for admission, like those at most colleges of the day, emphasized the classical languages. Applicants must have a "good knowledge" of Greek and Latin grammar, the Greek New Testament, *Collectanea Graeca Minora*, Virgil, the orations of Cicero and Sallust. Familiarity with ancient and modern geography was expected. Finally, the prospective student had to understand common arithmetic.

Fourteen-year-old Jefferson Davis officially encountered Transylvania when he faced the entrance tests. Because of his solid background in the classical languages, the Greek and Latin portions posed him no problems. Nothing gave him difficulty but the arithmetic; there his experience was altogether different. The faculty found him inadequately prepared for admission to the sophomore class, Jefferson's wish. Explaining his shortcomings in later years, Davis maintained that mathematics had not been stressed in Wilkinson County Academy. The faculty, not concerned with the cause of the deficiency, decided that he must join the freshman class. Davis recalled that this decision "quite disappointed" him. It meant that he would be placed with mostly younger boys, whereas heretofore he had been grouped with older boys. "I felt my pride offended," he remembered. He obviously made his feelings known in a persuasive way, for the mathematics professor agreed to tutor him privately for the remainder of the session and through the summer. With that proviso the faculty allowed him into the sophomore class, albeit on probation. In the fall he would be examined for full admission to the junior class; during the spring and summer Jefferson did the necessary extra work. At the beginning of the fall semester he passed the requisite examination and became a full-fledged junior.[5]

The undergraduate Jefferson Davis flourished at Transylvania. He received an excellent classical education in ancient languages, history, and science. Though arduous, the prescribed daily schedule certainly did not occupy all of a student's time. At daybreak, collegians had to attend daily prayer in the chapel. Classes dominated the morning, with dinner at 2 p.m. Afternoons were mostly free, and many students participated in athletics. Davis took some of that time for private lessons in French and dance.[6]

As an old man, Davis spoke fondly of certain classes and professors. He always believed the pronunciation of Greek and Latin taught by his classics professor to be "the purest and best of our time." He remembered his history professor, the Reverend Robert H. Bishop, a Scotsman with a broad accent, a devout Presbyterian, as a man of "large attainments and very varied knowledge," whose lectures impressed him for "their wide information [and] for their keen appreciation of the characteristics of mankind." Professor Bishop had a memorable classroom style. Inattentive or unprepared students could spark an explosion. "Ye're like Jacks, and if you can't learn through the ears you shall learn through the back."[7]

At the end of his junior year in June 1824, Jefferson took examinations with his classmates. A public event, the examinations drew many townspeople who gathered to watch and hear the faculty test the students. The testing began at 10 a.m., adjourned at 1 p.m. for dinner, resumed at 3 p.m., and continued until sunset. Acquitting himself with distinction, Davis received honors and was chosen to give an address at the upcoming junior class exhibition scheduled for June 18. He entitled the speech "An Address on Friendship." No record of his remarks survives, but he evidently made a positive impression in his first appearance at a public rostrum. A local newspaper reported: "Davis on friendship made friends of the hearers."[8]

Jefferson succeeded socially as well as academically at Transylvania. He made friends, including people he would later work with in Congress like David Rice Atchison, who became a senator from Missouri. George W. Jones of Indiana, a future senator from Iowa, remained devoted to Davis until Davis's death. Davis joined the Union-Philosophical Society, one of two debating societies at the university. Sponsoring dinners with wine, they provided social along with intellectual activities.[9]

Davis was well liked. Jones, though surely a partisan observer, recalled that Davis "was considered the best looking as he was the most intelligent and best loved student in the University." Perhaps long affection colored Jones's opinion. But at a celebration held by the Union-Philosophical Society just seven months after Davis had departed for West Point, a classmate offered a toast—"To the health and prosperity of Jefferson Davis, late a student of Transylvania University, now a cadet at West Point: may he become the pride of our country and the idol of our army."[10]

At Transylvania, Jefferson Davis witnessed more than the world of students. He lived with the family of Joseph Ficklin in their brick home on the southwestern corner of High and Limestone Streets. A friend of the Davis family, Ficklin provided the teenaged Jefferson a home away from home. Davis never forgot Ficklin, whom he later visited and called his "friend and guardian" while at Transylvania. Several other students boarded at the Ficklin home, which also served as a center of community activity. As postmaster and a newspaper editor, Ficklin was a well-known Lexingtonian, who had numerous callers. His residence was a lively place.[11]

In June 1824 the world seemed right with the sixteen-year-old Jefferson Davis. He had prospered at Transylvania, succeeding both in the classroom and with his fellow students. This agreeable situation lasted but fleetingly, however. In July he learned that his father had died. It was a terrible blow. "You must imagine," he explained to his sister-in-law Susannah, "I cannot describe the shock my feelings sustained, at that sad intelligence." Jefferson respected and loved his father, and Samuel Davis's recent and growing financial problems had troubled his youngest child. Writing to his sister Amanda, the youthful Jefferson gave full expression to these feelings. "He was a parent ever dear to me, but rendered more (if possible) by the disastrous storms that attended the winter of his old age."[12]

Samuel Davis's quest for prosperity, which carried him hundreds of miles and underlay several new starts, ended calamitously. Sometime after 1820 his fortunes began a headlong retreat. He had to sell his land to Joseph. Then he made an arduous journey to Philadelphia, searching vainly to recoup some of his lost inheritance from his grandfather Davis. From Philadelphia in the summer of 1823, a distressed father wrote his college-student son a melancholy letter of what might have been. "If I had applied some thirty year ago," Samuel grieved, "I might now have been immensely rich but I fear all is lost here by the lapse of time." Yet Samuel, his old drive still flickering, pledged, "I shall continue to search every thing to the extent before I leave here which will likely be late in Aug. or early in Septr."[13]

The search yielded nothing. Back in Mississippi, Samuel tried to work his farm, now owned by Joseph, with his third son, also named Samuel, but "some Misunderstanding" between father and son wrecked that effort. Following that debacle, the father headed for his son Joseph's new plantation some 100 miles north in Warren County fronting the river. En route, he became sick with fever and died on July 4 shortly after reaching his destination. Samuel Davis was buried there, not back at Poplar Grove.[14]

Although Samuel did not leave a substantial estate, he still provided Jefferson with a powerful legacy. Samuel Davis's belief in education, his insistence on it, surely helped shape his youngest child. In that generally sad letter from Philadelphia, the father voiced delight that the son was in college, and expounded on that: "Remember the short lessons of instruction offered you before our parting use every possible means to acquire usefull knowledge as knowledge is power the want of which has brought mischiefs and misery on your father in old age. That you may be happy & shine in society when your father is beyond the reach of harm is the most ardent desire of his heart."[15]

Samuel Davis's death had a profound impact on the youthful Jefferson. He not only lost his father at an impressionable age; his oldest brother became entrenched as a surrogate father. Joseph, as noted earlier, had already assumed critical importance in Jefferson's life, for he was surely involved in the decision to send the boy to Transylvania. Now, however, Joseph had a different design. Just as committed to Jefferson's education as their father had been, Joseph was also quite ambitious for his youngest brother. Clearly, Transylvania did not fulfill his hopes. He obtained through Secretary of War John C. Calhoun an appointment for Jefferson to the United States Military Academy at West Point, New York.

Jefferson's reaction to Joseph's plans and the possibility of West Point was not surprising. He had surely known for some time about the exertions to gain him an appointment, though he did not receive his official notification, dated March 11, until the summer of 1824. Once notified, Jefferson formally accepted the appointment, though not without reluctance. As a triumphant rising senior, he really did not want to leave Lexington and Transylvania for West Point, where he would enter a completely new environment and have to begin as a freshman.[16]

"It was no desire of mine to go," he admitted to his sister Amanda, but still he was a dutiful sixteen-year-old who respected the wishes of his oldest brother-become-father. Acknowledging the dynamics, he confessed to this sister, "as Brother Joe evinced some anxiety for me to do so, I was not disposed to object." Making clear that he understood the seriousness of the change impending in his life with the move to West Point, Jefferson recognized that "I will probably remain four years." At the height of his triumph in Lexington, he headed north and east for another, quite different world.[17]

The historical record is silent on Jefferson's journey from Kentucky to New York, except for specifying that he left Lexington in early August and arrived at West Point sometime after September 1. As did most travelers to West Point, he most probably went to New York City, where he took a steamboat for the roughly forty-mile trip up the Hudson River.

The physical setting of the United States Military Academy is impressive indeed. West Point sits atop a bluff that rises 190 feet above the western shore of the wide and majestic Hudson. At the top, the land basically flattens out to form a plain. When Jefferson Davis first saw the place, it had a lush and bucolic appearance, which it retains even today. In his time the grounds seemed almost in a "state of nature." Footpaths crossed the rocky and bare plain. Woods reached down nearly to the Academy grounds. The ruins of Revolutionary forts, huts, and graves scattered among the hills furnished concrete reminders to the cadets that their school occupied a site important in the birth of the nation.[18]

In 1824, the spare physical plant seemed to match the geographic seclusion. The Academy could boast of but four stone buildings, each with a stucco facade. The Academy building, with its two stories, contained classrooms, laboratories, a library, and a chapel. The North and South Barracks, the former with four stories and the latter with three, served as dormitories for the cadets, whose numbers varied but generally ranged between 200 and 250. Finally, there was a two-story mess hall, which contained a small hotel for Academy guests. On the west side of the plain, away from the cadet area, stood the superintendent's quarters and a row of houses for faculty.

Jefferson Davis initially encountered West Point when he took the entrance examination. His appointment did not guarantee his admission, but only the right to be examined for admission. By Davis's day prospective freshmen, or "plebes" in Academy terminology, were supposed to appear in early June for the summer camp held on the plain. Before the beginning of the fall semester in September, the faculty assessed their academic qualifications to become full-fledged cadets. By all accounts the examination was far from rigorous, yet substantial numbers failed because of inferior or nonexistent preparation, especially in mathematics.

Jefferson's late appearance precluded his following the ordained schedule. In his letter to Secretary of War Calhoun accepting his appointment, Jefferson announced his forthcoming tardiness: "am not able to go on before sept. for reasons I will explain to the superintendent on my arrival." The reasons remain unknown, but his delay ensured that he would miss the entire summer encampment. Evidently Davis's reasons for his lateness were persuasive, or this regulation was not yet strictly enforced, for he suffered no penalty. The entrance examination was another matter, however. Upon reaching West Point, Davis learned that the entrance examination had already been given, that successful candidates had been admitted, and that classes had begun.[19]

At this juncture, Davis remembered, "chance favored me." A cadet from the class of 1824 who had been allowed to withdraw for health reasons showed up and requested a special exam that would enable him to graduate. That exception was permitted, and simultaneously, through the intervention of Captain Ethan Allan Hitchcock, who had met the Davis family while on recruiting duty in Natchez, an exception was made as well for Jefferson Davis.

Davis recalled an anxiety replaced by serendipity. Along with the notification that he would be examined came word from Captain Hitchcock that arithmetic would be the chief topic. An apprehensive Davis indicated that he knew little arithmetic, though he did know some algebra and geometry. Alarmed, Captain Hitchcock brought Davis an arithmetic text and told him to study fractions and proportions. Once more Jefferson found himself bedeviled by his old nemesis. Hardly had he begun to study, Davis later wrote, when he was ordered to appear for the examination. From the mathematics professor he received a couple of questions on vulgar fractions and one asking for an explanation of the difference between vulgar and decimal fractions. Davis's algebra enabled him to handle them. Then came one on proportions which he also answered correctly. The "Certainly, certainly" pronounced by his inquisitor relieved the nervous youth, who always believed he had been given credit for more than he knew. The next task, a demonstration that he could read and write legibly, posed no problem. When the French professor took his turn, he did not focus on French. Learning that the young candidate read Greek, this obviously frustrated classicist "launched into a discussion of some questions as to the construction of Greek, with which he was so delighted that he kept on till the superintendent stopped him, and that broke up my examination." "Since that time," Davis maintained in the last year of his life, "I have never believed that an examination formed a very conclusive rule of decision upon the qualifications of a person subjected to its test."[20] Qualified or not, Jefferson Davis commenced his plebe year at West Point.

Davis's West Point was literally the creation of the superintendent who halted his entrance examination, Brevet Lieutenant Colonel Sylvanus Thayer, whose convictions and judgments molded West Point just as Horace Holley's had underlain the shaping of Transylvania. Thayer, however, left a vastly more important legacy, for his impact on West Point lasted well into the twentieth century, and in some ways lives on even now. A New Englander, Thayer graduated from Dartmouth College in 1807, but because things military, especially Napoleon, and the soldier's life had always fascinated him, he went to the Academy at West Point, founded just five years earlier. Thayer's preparation at Dartmouth enabled him to race through the Academy's courses, and after only one year he received his commission. He joined the Corps of Engineers, served in the War of 1812, and in 1815 was sent to Europe for study. Upon his return, President James Monroe in 1817 named him superintendent of West Point. At that moment the Academy was in disarray, wracked by factionalism and abysmal morale. Thayer proved to be a propitious choice.

Sylvanus Thayer had a clear sense of what he wanted to make of West Point. Impressed by what he had seen and heard in France, especially at the École Polytechnique, which was at that time the most famous military school in the world, Thayer wanted to create an American version. His vision had two interrelated dimensions: the academic mission, entailing both curriculum and pedagogy; and the conduct and discipline of the cadet corps.

Thayer's ideas on curriculum differed sharply from those then prevailing among conventional pedagogues as well as from those of the reformers at Harvard. The former remained wedded to their fixed course centered on the classical languages, while the latter advocated electives, modern languages, and liberalism. Thayer envisioned a fixed curriculum, but not one that revolved around Greek and Latin. Thayer's West Point would be an engineering school, the first in the United States. Cadets would take required mathematics and science courses each semester; Greek and Latin would not even be taught.

French, however, was a requirement because Thayer believed that the best books on mathematics, engineering, and the art of war were in French. Physics (then called natural philosophy), chemistry, and engineering, mostly civil, complemented the mathematics courses. Cadets also had to take drawing to enable them to present data and designs graphically, not for the sake of artistic expression. Immersed in mathematics and science, they barely encountered the humanities and social sciences, except for French. The chaplain did teach to first classmen, or seniors, a smorgasbord course that included ethics, geography, history, and law. Courses on specifically military subjects like tactics, strategy, or even military history were not at all central in Thayer's scheme.

Thayer believed in a specific pedagogical system just as firmly as he did in his curriculum. He organized the cadets into four classes: fourth class or plebe, third class or sophomore, second class or junior, and first class or senior. In every subject taught during the four years, the approach did not alter. Every student recited in every class every day; instructors gave daily marks on the recitation; cadets discovered their standing weekly when grades were posted. Examinations were held at the end of each semester, in January and in June. In the June examination the Board of Visitors, a distinguished group that Thayer used to help advance the Academy with Congress and the public, witnessed Thayer and the faculty question the cadets. For the latter, facing simultaneously Superintendent Thayer, the faculty, and the Board of Visitors was doubtless a formidable experience.

For Thayer, conduct and discipline were as important as curriculum and pedagogy. West Point was a regimented place. The daily schedule allowed for practically no free time. Reveille came at dawn. Quickly dressing, the cadets formed for roll call, then returned to clean their rooms. They studied from 6 to 7 a.m., when they marched to breakfast. The cadets marched to all activities in formation. Following breakfast, a half hour of recreation was permitted. Classes ran from 8 a.m. until 1 p.m., the dinner hour. At 2 p.m. classes resumed and lasted for two more hours. Weather permitting, the cadets drilled from 4 until 6; if not, study and recreation filled those two hours. Supper was served at 6 p.m. From 7 to 9:30 more study; then another half hour of recreation, with taps at 10 p.m. Only on Sunday afternoons, the Fourth of July, Christmas Day, and New Year's Day did the cadets have any respite from their mandated regimen.

Rules and regulations pervaded the institution and cadet life. Of course each cadet wore the prescribed uniform—gray pants, vest, and coat; blue fatigue jacket and pants; white duck pants for summer; black leather hat seven inches high and topped with a pompom; high-top black shoes. To help ensure that each cadet was judged on merit alone, Thayer banned all financial distinctions. Cadets were not permitted to receive money, or even to have money. Their government payment, $16 per month plus $12 per month subsistence allowance, went into an account from which they drew for various items, like uniforms. Prohibitions included alcohol, tobacco, playing cards, novels, plays, and leaving the Academy grounds. There was also no hazing; every student from plebe to first classman stood as a full member of the cadet brotherhood. Emphasizing that equality, intermingling among the cadets of all four classes was commonplace.

Thayer devised a structure of demerits to enforce his regulations. For each infraction of any rule a cadet received demerits according to the seriousness of the incident. The possibilities were legion, from a candlestick out of place, to inattention at drill, to missing a class or a formation. For the most serious violations cadets could face trial by court-martial. Demerits became a part of class standing. A confirmed rebel could not do well even if he performed superbly in the classroom. The accumulation of 200 demerits in a single year could result in separation from the Academy. Cadets lived in this world from the summer encampment preceding their plebe year until their graduation. Only once during their four years, in their second summer, were cadets usually permitted to leave the grounds. A tough, demanding place, West Point suffered considerable attrition. In each class those that fell by the wayside reached 50 percent and beyond. But those who made it through the four years forged a powerful common bond.

Thayer's system concluded with class standing. Each year ended with all cadets given their rank in their class based on academic performance combined with the record of demerits. For Thayer this ranking served a larger purpose: the assignment of young officer-graduates to various branches of the army on the basis solely of their records, rather than of favoritism or political influence. Those at the top of each class, around 12 percent, would go into the Corps of Engineers, the elite branch. Cadets next down the line got assignments in the artillery or cavalry, while the lowest portion of each class joined the infantry.

Jefferson Davis spent four years, from age sixteen to age twenty, in this military monastery. His academic performance precluded his ever being at the top of his class. The honors he had won at Transylvania belonged to a different time and place. Never adept at mathematics,

Davis clearly struggled with the many courses he now had to take. Mathematics, science, and engineering accounted for over 70 percent of classroom hours and made up 55 percent of the score for class rank. At the close of his plebe year he finished forty-third out of seventy-one in mathematics; the next year he was thirty-third out of forty-nine; and as a second classman he stood thirtieth out of thirty-seven in physics. Although at times he did much better in other subjects, such as French and drawing, his highest standing came as a plebe, when he finished in the middle of the class. Thereafter his standing declined, and he ultimately graduated twenty-third in a class of thirty-three.[21]

The discipline or conduct portion of the grading undoubtedly contributed heavily to Davis's declining class rank. Starting off as a dutiful cadet obeying regulations, he committed just over two dozen offenses as a plebe. Quickly afterwards, however, a cascade of demerits piled up against him. In his final year he amassed 137, which in the corps as a whole ranked him 163 of 208.[22]

Most of Davis's demerits came from infractions committed by large numbers of cadets. They included making unnecessary noise during study time, allowing noise on his post, failure to police his room, inattention at drill, lingering in bed after reveille, and hair too long. Then there were also more serious ones, such as absences from drill, parade, and laboratory, firing his musket from the window of his room, and disobeying a special order. Still, it was the frequency of Davis's violations that kept him in trouble. He clearly did not commit himself to abide by the rules governing the conduct of the cadet corps. He was certainly no Robert E. Lee, class of 1829, who went through the Academy without receiving even one demerit. Davis willingly and knowingly challenged the system in both small and large matters. His brother Joseph worried that Jefferson might end up in the guardhouse.[23]

On three occasions Jefferson's risk-taking jeopardized his survival at West Point. Any of them could have gotten him shipped home, and one did result in his arraignment before a court-martial. Another led to a serious injury. All of them involved alcohol, either the quest for it or the drinking of it, or both.

The initial incident occurred in Davis's first summer. The preceding year he had reached West Point too late to participate in the encampment, but in the summer of 1825 he lived on the plain in a tent, as did all the cadets. On the night of July 31 the rain fell in torrents and flooded a number of tents, Davis's among them. Washed out of bed, Davis and several comrades decided to visit Benny Havens's tavern.[24]

Located in Buttermilk Falls, two miles from West Point, Benny Havens's tavern was off-limits to cadets. Havens had worked for a sutler serving the Academy, but lost his job when discovered selling alcohol to a cadet. Thereupon, in 1824, he set up his own tavern, which he ran until after the Civil War. "The most famous establishment in all West Point history," it has been called. For cadets willing to chance apprehension and punishment Benny Havens's became a haven indeed. Havens sold cadets food and, more important, alcohol, in the form of hard cider, cider and ale flip, and porter. A staunch friend of the future officers, he welcomed them to his tavern, offered them credit when needed, accepted barter for drinks, and on occasion held barrels of whiskey brought back by cadets returning from furlough. One miserable youth, Edgar Allan Poe, who remained a cadet less than a year, called him "the sole congenial soul in the entire God-forsaken place."[25]

Jefferson and his companions followed a well-worn path to Benny Havens's. Unfortunately for them, however, on that Sunday, Captain Hitchcock also showed up at the tavern. He reported running into the wandering boys. All of them were arrested and scheduled for trial by general court-martial.[26]

Davis's case came before the court on August 3. The seventeen-year-old boy had to confront the reality that he was in a most precarious position. Asked if he had any objection to any member of the court, Davis responded negatively. Davis then argued that the regulations he had been accused of violating did not apply to him. He asserted that "the new regulations were to him in the nature of an *ex post facto* law, having never been published to his corps." The court rejected that claim.

In the formal procedure of the military, Cadet Davis was accused of violating two paragraphs of general army regulations that pertained to cadets. The first charge specified that on July 31 he had ventured "beyond the limits prescribed to Cadets at West Point without permission." The second was divided into two parts: (1) that on July 31 he "did drink spirituous and intoxicating liquor"; and (2) that on the same day he "did go to a public house or place where spirituous liquors are sold, kept by one Benjamin Havens. . . ." Davis admitted guilt to the first, and to the latter part of the second. But he denied that he had been drinking. Immediately after the reading of the charges and Davis's response, Captain Hitchcock testified for the prosecution. Recounting that he saw Davis "at the time specified" at Benny Havens's with several friends, the captain made a crucial point: "all of whom except one appeared to be under the influence of spirituous liquor." Hitchcock admitted, however, that he "did not see Mr. Davis make use of any liquor, and judged that he had used it perhaps more from the circumstances in which I saw him than from either his conduct or appearance generally." When Davis spotted him, Hitchcock continued, "he exhibited extreme embarrassment bordering upon meekness." Hitchcock considered that such behavior "might have proceeded from being found in the circumstances I stated," but he concluded that "the use of spirituous liquors" was involved. That Davis had been drinking, Hitchcock had "not a doubt of it."

Having to cope with this devastating testimony, Davis initially tried to persuade the court that he was not a wayward, undisciplined scamp. He called in his defense both Captain Hitchcock and Commandant of Cadets Major William J. Worth, who was then in fact presiding over the court-martial. Both officers confirmed that Davis's "general deportment" had been "marked by correct and strict attention to his duty. . . ." Heretofore he had not "committed any offense which called for animadversion." Having obtained these positive statements about his character and record, Davis requested that the court give him until the following morning to prepare his defense.

On the morning of August 4, Cadet Davis addressed his judges. His defense comprised the classic ingredients for teenagers accused of serious offenses—ignorance or inapplicability of rules, admitting only what cannot possibly be denied, invoking technicalities, and rationalizing, all tempered by a plea for mercy. "It is with feelings of greatest embarrassment," Davis began. He did not think it fair to be "tried by laws which with respect to my knowledge have just sprung into existence. . . ." But he hurried on, knowing that on the previous day the court had ruled against him on that very point. Next, he contended that though he had certainly left the post, "circumstances may perhaps in some degree justify the deed"—the heavy rain that flooded his tent.

Acknowledging that he had previously pleaded guilty to visiting "a public house and place where liquors are sold," Davis now wanted "to qualify" his admission. He told the court that the critical part of the regulation addressed whether a cadet visited such an establishment to buy liquor. Thus, merely going to a place did not alone constitute violation. "As no evidence has been produced to prove that we did procure or use spirituous liquor," Davis denied that Benny Havens's could be defined as a public house. After all, he noted, cadets could legally patronize other stores that had liquor for sale.

Davis denied unequivocally that he had been drinking. He rightly pointed out that Captain Hitchcock had not observed him imbibing. Neither did any of his comrades testify against him; nor he against any of them. Called as a witness in the case of one of his companions, Davis had tried unsuccessfully to narrow the definition of spirituous liquor so as to exclude hard cider and porter. He stressed that he had seen no one drinking. On this point Davis may have been relying on a traditional cadet stratagem for escaping the incrimination of buddies. When a group gathered for drinking, they turned away from one another and faced the wall at the moment when cup met lips. Each of them could then always swear that he never saw anyone actually take a drink. His "embarrassed" behavior Davis attributed to his having been caught at Benny Havens's, in his words, a situation "certainly enough to have confused any Cadet." A forceful declaration followed: "I cannot believe that the Court would if previously acquainted with the circumstances have shown so little respect to my feelings as to have charged me (on such weak evidence) with conduct so contrary to principles of a soldier & a man of honor."[27]

In concluding his defense, the youthful Davis spoke with a sharply different accent in imploring the court to weigh a quite different matter. "I do trust," Davis closed, "that the Court will bear in mind the maxim that it is better a hundred guilty escape than one righteous person be condemned, and on testimony so circumstantial shall confidentially look forward to an honorable acquittal."

Davis's multifaceted argument did not persuade the court. On that very same day it found Jefferson and his colleagues guilty as charged and sentenced them "to be dismissed from the service of the United States." Simultaneously the court "in consideration of his former good conduct recommend[ed] the remission of said sentence." Superintendent Thayer accepted that verdict. Davis had survived, barely. He had his conduct as a dutiful plebe to thank for his continuing at West Point and becoming a third classman.

The second incident took place a little over a year later, in August 1826. Once again the magnet of Benny Havens's drew Davis into serious trouble, though not the official or judicial kind. Jefferson and a friend headed for their favorite watering hole "on a little frolic—of course without leave." Word reached the tavern that an instructor was approaching. Leaving immediately to return to the Academy, Jefferson and his comrade took "a short cut to get back to barracks." In his pell-mell march up the steep path toward the plain, Jefferson fell. He tumbled some sixty feet down to the riverbank. Luckily for him he grabbed a small tree which tempered "the force of his fall," though it mangled a hand. Davis's companion cried out: "Jeff, are you dead?" A suffering Davis remembered wanting to laugh but hurting too much to do so. Although no record detailing his injuries exists, they were obviously quite severe. He was carried as sick on all monthly returns from August through November. Davis himself later wrote that he spent four months in the hospital, where he "rarely saw any one even when it was thought I was about to die, then some of my friends were allowed to stay with me at night."[28]

Despite his having been away from the post without permission and his lengthy hospital stay, surviving records indicate that this time Jefferson escaped serious disciplinary and academic consequences. The records do not reveal whether or not he had been inebriated. Although Davis did poorly in his classes in the fall semester, no evidence connects that performance to his hospitalization. His grades had been falling since his plebe year. Still, Jefferson did end the year 1826 under arrest for yet another youthful caper, the Christmas eggnog riot of 1826, notorious in the annals of West Point.[29]

Student tradition and Academy authority collided on Christmas Day, 1826. For a number of years cadets had been in the habit of holding drinking parties in the barracks before reveille on Christmas morning. Officers did not interfere with this practice, even though drinking by cadets was forbidden except when officially sanctioned. Authorization was given on rare occasions, especially for the Fourth of July, but on July 4, 1825, events got out of hand. At least Superintendent Thayer thought so. Intoxicated students organized a snake dance, hoisted Commandant Worth on their shoulders, and carried him to the barracks. As a result, Thayer banned all liquor, no exceptions. And the celebration on the Fourth of July, 1826, was dry. At the same time, of course, an unknown number of cadets surreptitiously continued to imbibe spirituous liquors.

As Christmas 1826 drew near, some cadets, including Jefferson Davis, planned to celebrate in the customary way. Word got out that the holiday festivities would once again entail the Christmas morning drinking. Determined to prevent any such activity, Superintendent

Thayer and Commandant Worth placed all tactical officers on duty on Christmas Eve night. They were to patrol the cadet area.

Without question Davis was deeply involved in planning the event. He and two others were designated to obtain the alcohol. None other than Benny Havens supplied the essential liquid, two half-gallon jugs, which the cadets smuggled into North Barracks. Early on Christmas morning the participants planned to mix and drink eggnog in two designated rooms on the upper floors of North Barracks. Revelry began after midnight. To that point the tactical officers had not foiled the celebrants.

But shortly after 4 a.m., authority intruded. In North Barracks, Captain Ethan Hitchcock, hearing "walking" and an "increase of noise," marched toward the source and "observed a collection of cadets at No. 5." When he entered the room, he discovered a group of carousers. At this point Cadet Jefferson Davis rushed in shouting—too late—"Put away the grog, Captain Hitchcock is coming." Captain Hitchcock was already there, and he immediately placed Davis under arrest and ordered him to his room. Without responding, Davis complied.[30]

That prompt compliance undoubtedly saved Davis's West Point career. After his departure, pandemonium broke loose. Drunk cadets ran amuck. They abused officers; they reeled through the barracks shouting, some with swords, some with muskets, some with bayonets; one fired a musket; another threw a log at an officer. Finally reveille was sounded. Cadets poured out of the two barracks. The Christmas eggnog riot was over.

Thayer directed Worth to head a full Court of Inquiry. Twenty-two cadets, including Davis, were under arrest; seventy others, one-third of the corps, were implicated. Thayer realized that he could not charge so many students: the institution probably could not have survived the shock. Finally, after careful scrutiny and deliberation, the superintendent decided that the nineteen cadets most deeply involved would go before a court-martial; fifty-three others would receive lesser punishments. All nineteen tried by court-martial were convicted and sentenced to be dismissed. Seven, however, were saved by the court's recommendation of clemency. Thus, one dozen cadets involuntarily departed.

Jefferson Davis amazingly escaped any punishment. Testimony at the trial established that he had been in on the affair from the beginning. Two cadets testified that he was or appeared to be drunk.

Another swore that Davis offered him a drink. Davis's claim six decades later that he was not drunk must rest on an interpretation of the word. Yet he never had to answer to that charge. In his only appearance before the court-martial, he was asked no questions about his involvement.[31]

The documents do not explain Davis's incredible good fortune. Clearly his instant, unquestioning obedience of Captain Hitchcock's order was critical. Whether or not he was intoxicated, he completely missed the riot. Whether he passed out in his room or just had sense enough not to venture out will never be known. Davis's absence from the scene when the really serious offenses took place made him a prime contender for removal from the court-martial list. After all, Thayer was searching for ways to excuse people. Whatever the particulars, on February 8, 1827, Davis was released from arrest.[32]

Even though nothing else so serious as these three events occurred in Davis's last year and a half, it is not at all surprising that he never achieved much military rank in the cadet corps. For the summer encampment held after Davis's second year, he received an appointment as fourth sergeant of the First Company. In August 1826, he was named sergeant of the color guard. Then as a first classman he joined fifteen other cadets in a Hose Company designed to combat fires. None of these posts represented a significant leadership position.[33]

Although Cadet Davis never achieved academic or military distinction, he obviously made friends. He was never alone in those risky escapades. At West Point and afterwards Davis spoke of "the set" with whom he associated. Composed mostly of southerners, it included Albert Sidney Johnston and Leonidas Polk, both in the class of 1826, and both of whom Jefferson admired as cadets and long afterward. He also would certainly have known two Virginians in the class behind him, Robert E. Lee and Joseph E. Johnston, though he was not close to either. Even in the last decade of his life Davis never forgot his old West Point companions, and he still corresponded with some of them.[34]

Jefferson's "set" may have tried to ameliorate their spartan cadet existence. In the only surviving letter from his four years at West Point, he asked his brother Joseph for money. Although he "fe[lt] a delicacy" in once again requesting money, Jefferson's delicate feelings were insufficient to restrain him. Whether his cadet pay would suffice, Jefferson told Joseph, "depends entirely upon the company I keep." "*The Yankee part of the corps find their pay entirely sufficient some even more,*" he disclosed. Revealing a bit of snobbery as well as sectional chauvinism, the plebe Jefferson remarked, *"but these are not such as I formed an acquaintance with on* my arrival." Nor would he now "select" them as "associates." Concluding, he adopted a haughty tone: "enough of this as you have never been connected with them, you cannot know *how pittiful they generally* are." Whether Joseph sent Jefferson money on this or any other occasion is not known. Jefferson's view of northerners did change by the time of his graduation, and later he praised the nationalizing effect of a West Point education.[35]

Davis apparently never left West Point for any extended period during his four years. Thayer's system provided for a furlough during the summer between the third class and the second class years, but no record mentions Davis taking any such leave. He was, however, granted a one-week leave in mid-July 1825, probably in connection with Joseph's coming to the Academy. Joseph did travel north that summer, and his itinerary included West Point. He had as companions William B. and Margaret K. Howell of Natchez, future father-in-law and mother-in-law of Jefferson. All three appeared at West Point. Delighted to see his surrogate father, Jefferson ran to the landing and embraced Joseph. The young man's "beautiful blue eyes and graceful strong figure" impressed Margaret Howell, who also spoke of "his open bright expression."[36]

Finally, the senior examinations came in June 1828. Cadet Jefferson Davis passed, though without distinction. Thayer's scheme, in which class standing determined army branch, put Davis in the infantry. An order from the War Department dated July 14, 1828, appointed Davis as brevet second lieutenant in the infantry to rank from July 1.[37]

Jefferson Davis never spoke favorably about any of his instructors at West Point. He only mentioned one, and that one quite negatively, though he gave no name. No comments from Davis on Sylvanus Thayer have survived, but it is most unlikely that he would have had much positive to say about the creator of a system he obviously disliked. Thayer, for his part, had no use for Davis. In 1855, when Davis was secretary of war, Thayer vented: "Neither [Davis] nor my opinion of him have changed since I knew him as a cadet. If I am not deceived, he intends to leave his mark in the Army & also at West Point & a *black* mark it will be I fear. He is a recreant and unnatural son, would have pleasure in giving his Alma Mater a kick & would disclaim her, if he could."[38]

In one fundamental sense Thayer was absolutely wrong. Although Jefferson Davis was never a prize cadet, he absolutely prized West

Point. Its imprint never left him. His lifelong military bearing he acquired there. The friendships and the fond memories prompted by them never faded. In his public career as a congressman, a senator, and a cabinet officer, he steadfastly defended and supported his alma mater. In his mind West Point helped undergird the well-being of the nation. As secretary of war he wrote that "those who have received their education at West Point, taken as a body, are perhaps more free from purely sectional prejudices, and more national in their feelings than the same number of persons to be found elsewhere in our country."[39]

With his commission in hand the new second lieutenant received orders to report to the Infantry School of Practice at Jefferson Barracks in Missouri.[40]

CHAPTER THREE

"Ever Ready to Render My Best Services"

Sometime after July 14, 1828, Brevet Second Lieutenant Jefferson Davis left West Point bound for Mississippi. Along with the other new infantry officers, he had been given leave until October 30. Davis had not been home for more than five years, since he began college in the spring of 1823. In all that time he saw a member of his family only once, when his brother Joseph visited West Point in 1825. Yet his journey southward was not a rapid one.

From Lexington, Kentucky, in late August, Davis wrote his superiors for permission to extend his graduation leave. Informing the army that "the commencement of the sickly season" in Mississippi made him anxious about going that far south, he asked for an extension of his furlough until December 31. He buttressed his case with two additional reasons. "Unavoidably detained" in the North, he had not covered the distance he had expected. At the same time he told the army about his almost six-year absence from home. Whatever its particular reason, the army granted his request. The lack of urgency for new officers to report on active duty certainly contributed to the positive response Davis received.[1]

Exactly when he reached Wilkinson County is not known. Undoubtedly he and his family experienced a happy reunion. Although no direct evidence reveals either activities or emotions among the Davises in the fall of 1828, family news and expressions of devotion filled the college letters between Jefferson and other Davises. From Transylvania, Jefferson told his sister to kiss her child for him. In his only remaining letter from West Point he mentioned four siblings and a niece. Moreover, when he wrote the army to have his leave extended, he made clear his desire to remain "some time with my relations."[2]

This homecoming and the year 1828 ended together. With his leave expiring, Lieutenant Davis departed for his first duty station, Jefferson Barracks, ten miles south of St. Louis, Missouri. As the site of the Infantry School of Practice, Jefferson Barracks served as a collection point for young officers. Davis's new orders of December 31, 1828, had assigned him to the First Infantry Regiment, but still at Jefferson Barracks.[3]

Upon his arrival at Jefferson Barracks, Lieutenant Davis confronted the sharp contrast between West Point and the army. As a well-trained graduate of the Military Academy, he reported to headquarters on January 11, 1829, in full uniform, but he found neither the colonel commanding nor the lieutenant colonel. The former was away on special duty; the latter was under arrest. The acting commander, a major, was not there either. To find him Davis was directed to the commissary. There, as Davis remembered, he came upon the major "alone, seated at a table with a pack of cards before him, intently occupied in a game of solitaire." Responding to the lieutenant's formal salute, the major "invited [Davis] to take a seat, and continued his game. After a few minutes the major looked up and inquired: 'Young man, do you play solitaire? Finest game in the world! You can cheat as much as you please and have nobody to detect it.' "[4]

In the next six and a half years Jefferson Davis would learn much about the United States Army. In 1830 the entire force totaled fewer than 6,000 men. Its mission focused on coastal defense and on protecting the advancing settlers from the Indians they were displacing. Most of the troops were scattered across the western frontier, chiefly along the length of the Mississippi River Valley, in isolated posts often populated by fewer than 100 soldiers and a handful of others. Quarrelsomeness, drinking, even violence became almost endemic in an officer corps that could anticipate no continuing military education, few chances for promotion, and limited social outlets. Resignations were common. "The profession of arms is a dull one in a time of peace . . ." wrote one of Davis's commanders. This disenchanted officer continued, "I find More treachery and deception practised in the Army than I ever expected to find with a Body of Men who Call themselves Gentlemen."[5]

The isolation and masculinity of the camps and forts could seem like an extension of West Point, but not always. Usually only senior officers, and not all of them, brought along wives and families. They were indeed rare. Unattached women were even rarer. Sharp differences from the Military Academy stood out; the tight control and esprit de corps dominant among the cadets did not often appear on the frontier. Lieutenant Davis would experience almost every side of this army.

He did not long remain at Jefferson Barracks. On March 24, 1829, he received orders to report to the headquarters of the First Infantry Regiment at Fort Crawford in Michigan Territory, now in the state of Wisconsin. Located at the junction of the Wisconsin and Mississippi Rivers, Fort Crawford was situated right beside Prairie du Chien, a long-established trading center but little more than a village. With a population ranging upward of 500, depending upon the season of the year, Prairie du Chien attracted traders, trappers, and hunters, both Indian and white. Responding to the westward movement of Americans after the War of 1812, the U.S. government founded Fort Crawford in 1816. When Davis arrived thirteen years later, it was largely unfinished. Because the original fort had been located in the lowlands subject to flooding, in 1825 the army chose a new site on higher ground, yet in the very next year ordered its abandonment. The outbreak of Indian troubles in 1827 led to its reopening, but in 1829 much work remained to be done.[6]

Soon after Davis's arrival at Fort Crawford, the regimental commander, Colonel Willoughby Morgan, sent his new lieutenant on to Fort Winnebago, some 180 miles northeast of Fort Crawford at the portage between the Wisconsin River flowing southwest toward the Mississippi and the Fox River heading northeast toward Lake Michigan at Green Bay. The fort stood on the east bank of the Fox about two miles from the Wisconsin. Because of the Indian difficulties, the army in 1828 directed construction of Fort Winnebago at this strategically critical point between Green Bay and Fort Crawford. When Davis reached the still largely unbuilt fort, he stood literally in the midst of a great wilderness.[7]

Davis's first assignment turned him into a construction superintendent. At the time he reported, Fort Winnebago consisted of "only log huts connected by a stockade." The post commander, Major David E. Twiggs, put the young lieutenant in charge of working parties to obtain materials for the construction of blockhouses, barracks, and stores. One group went to the pine forests farther up the Wisconsin; another attacked the hardwood forests on a different stream. When the timber came down the Wisconsin, the water ran so high that it spread in a broad sheet across the portage to the Fox. Taking advantage of the

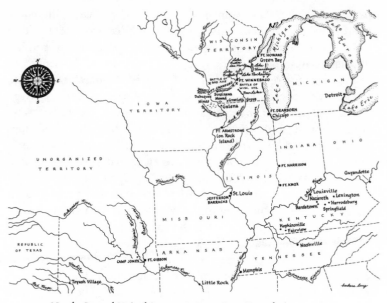

North-Central United States, 1808–40; State Boundaries, ca. 1840.
Papers of Jefferson Davis, *I, with permission of the LSU Press*

temporary water course, Davis and his construction unit built rafts and floated the lumber all the way to Fort Winnebago.[8]

Lieutenant Davis did more than gather building materials. He also had a short-lived career as a furniture-maker when officers' quarters were under his charge. Mrs. John H. Kinzie, the wife of the Indian agent at the fort, remembered the furnishings. The bedstand she described as "of proportions amply sufficient to have accommodated Og, the king of Bashan, with Mrs. Og and the children into the bargain." She also marveled at an "edifice" designed for universal storage from clothes to china upon which Davis and his helpers had "exhausted all of their architectural skill." Mrs. Kinzie detailed this "structure": its "timbers had been grooved and carved"; the front pillars "swelled in and out in a most fanciful manner"; not only paneled, the doors also "radiated out in a way to excite the imagination of all unsophisticated eyes." This showpiece had one problem, however. The numerous shelves were so close together that getting even a gravy boat between them proved almost impossible. The reason for this shelving, according to Davis, derived from the designer's original purpose, for each shelf to hold an officer's coat without folding. Mrs. Kinzie and Major

Twiggs's wife "christened the whole affair, in honor of its projector, a 'Davis.'"[9]

Lieutenant Davis's contributions to the improvement of Fort Winnebago did not end his military construction career. Two years later, when back at Fort Crawford, he took on an important task in the rebuilding and expansion of that post. His new commanding officer, Colonel Zachary Taylor, assigned him to oversee the logging and sawmill operation that provided the lumber for the reconstruction project. This time Davis operated on the Yellow River (in present-day Iowa) about twelve miles northwest of Prairie du Chien. This work lasted for approximately six weeks.[10]

Jefferson Davis certainly did not spend all of his time in building enterprises. Like most young officers, he experienced an enormous variety of duties. Between 1829 and 1835 he served as a company commander, acting assistant quartermaster, assistant commissary of subsistence, and adjutant. He also saw detached service on recruiting duty and searching for deserters.[11]

At times these jobs could be quite tedious. Army bureaucracy and regulations required incredibly detailed record-keeping, especially in the quartermaster and commissary areas. In August 1830, Washington informed Davis that in his quarterly account for commissary activities he had made an error of 7 cents. Later that year he explained to the quartermaster general his actions regarding five oxen, one horse, and six small boats that had all been condemned. Then there was the correspondence over the conversion into bulk of 3,678 rations of extra whiskey. Did that amount come out as 118 gallons 2 gills or 114 gallons 30 gills? In 1831 the Office of the Commissary General corrected Davis's reporting on the 68 pounds of candles he had sold to officers. He had sold them at 14 cents a pound instead of the 14.5 cents he should have charged with the incorporation of transportation costs. Davis responded that he believed his calculations correct: transportation had cost 1.5 cents per pound, actually 1.47 cents.[12]

At other times Davis's assignments could be both exciting and trying, especially when on detached service. Literally one of the first white Americans in northern Illinois, and what would become Wisconsin and Iowa, he traversed much of the northwestern wilderness. In 1829 he made one of the first journeys from the portage to Chicago. He remembered the delays caused by "wandering through bogs" and going three and a half days without food and thirty-six hours without water. Killing a pheasant and its brood enabled the lieutenant and his men to "escape starvation." Davis's arrival underscored the extraordinary nature of his trek. The appearance of a white man on the bank of the Chicago River opposite Fort Dearborn created a stir within the garrison. In later years Davis maintained that he led the first party of white Americans to the site of Madison, Wisconsin, then known as Four Lakes Country.[13]

The wilderness landscape captured his imagination. Writing of the countryside around Fort Winnebago to sister Lucinda, Davis described the prairie as "new beautiful and being studded by islands of woods possess[ing] by a variety in the scene an advantage over west Prairies." Enchanted by the Fox River, he pictured "a sluggish and very crooked river its banks low and the grass grow[ing] to the water's edge which makes it look beautiful at a distance." Water "so clear that you could see the fish swimming all through it" impressed him. In a lengthy 1831 report to the quartermaster general he catalogued the routes and provided a detailed description of the countryside for more than 100 miles in every direction of Fort Winnebago. "A country richly clothed with grass" pervaded his world. Marshes, boggy bayous, deep ravines, rapids, and swift streams all caught the eye of the young lieutenant.[14]

One major assignment took him far beyond the narrow confines of army posts and omnipresent regulations. In October 1831 Colonel Morgan ordered him to lead a detachment to the Dubuques Mines, near present-day Dubuque, Iowa, to prevent the outbreak of hostilities between pioneers and Indians. American settlers were eager for the opportunity to mine lead in that area, but the Fox and Sauk (sometimes Sac) Indians retained the land. By an unratified treaty of July 31, 1831, the Fox and the Sauk agreed to remain on the west side of the Mississippi, and the whites were to stay on the east bank. Zealous settlers determined to press across the river, however, and violence threatened. When Lieutenant Davis showed up, he discovered that the reports of white intrusion on the western bank were accurate. He also reported that he feared more white intruders. Although he wanted to thwart mining activity by obstructing navigation in the streams the miners used for transporting lead from mines to furnaces, he realized that he had an insufficient force. Thus, he maintained his position of guarding the mines and keeping red and white apart, which he did successfully through the winter.[15]

According to a later account, his personality and persuasiveness were also critical in keeping the peace. Refusing to use force against the miners, Davis listened carefully to their interpretation of their rights.

After hearing them out, he responded that "time and patience" would eventually give them access to the mines. For the time being, however, Davis insisted that they would have to stay away. At one point he defused a hostile crowd by saluting them as friends and asking them to drink to the success of his plan. Upon hearing his offer to treat all, the recalcitrant miners cheered him.[16]

Lieutenant Jefferson Davis did more than learn his trade as a junior officer. In a long letter written during his first army summer to his sister Lucinda, he reflected upon himself and his place in the world, as thoughtful young people so often do. Although he did not find the army exciting, he admitted, "I know of nothing else that I could do which I would like better." Compatriots with "genteel" manners made for a general congeniality. Furthermore, "as far as morality is deemed necessary in the intercourse of men in the world it is strictly observed." "Dissipation," Davis noted, was "less common than among the citizens of Mississippi." If drunkards appear, "they are dismissed from the service."

Still reflecting on the rightness of his occupation, he mused that if he had returned directly to Mississippi from Transylvania, "I might have made a tolerable respectable citizen." West Point, however, "made me a different creature from that which nature had designed me to be," and getting along with civilians might prove difficult. Still, Davis insisted that he would "endeavour to improve myself as much as circumstances will admit." Army duties did not require serious thinking and called for "but small inducement to study." And like most other men, most of his fellow officers did not "labour for the love of it." Contrasting his own attitude, Davis informed his sister that he had ordered some books from New York City. He also hoped that he might someday be stationed at a post where he had access to a library.

Jefferson Davis simply did not know what he wanted from the future. Acknowledging Lucinda's anxiety about him, he was straightforward. "If I had any definite plan I would most willingly unfold it to you." But he had none, except for his projected reading program. From that he expected "to acquire general information," though he planned to concentrate on "legal reading." He believed that focus appropriate, for "if at any time I should determine on a civil course of life I think I would prefer the practice of law to any other profession." If, on the other hand, he remained in the army, "a knowledge of law" would qualify him for the responsibilities of a judge advocate, "an honorable and frequently pleasing and profita[ble] duty."

Writing on his twenty-first birthday, Davis admitted the collision between youthful aspirations and harsh reality. "When I was a boy and dreamed with my eyes open as most do I thought of ripening fame at this age of wealth and power." He continued, "As I grew older I saw the folly of this but still thought at the age of [twenty-one] I should be on the high way to all ambition desired." That time had arrived, however, and he was "the same poor being that I was at fifteen with the exception of a petty appointment which may long remain as small as it is at present." That reality he faced as so many other young people have, but the realization did not drag him down. "Yet I am not distressed for I behold myself a member though an humble one of an honorable profession in which sychophancy . . . is not necessary to success. . . ."[17]

The twenty-one-year-old Davis evinced pride in his profession while trying to come to terms with uncertainty about himself and his future. At the same time he obviously struggled with his emotional state. He had largely been on his own from age fourteen when he entered Transylvania. At sixteen he confessed the pain caused him by his father's death. The correspondence with his family underscores its importance. Even so, he now lived far away from those he cherished and who cherished him. The loneliness and harsh conditions of far-flung frontier posts with their seemingly unending winters provided much time for pondering. Self-examination in those circumstances could lead to an enveloping sadness, which he clearly confronted. He also shared his confrontation. In 1833 a loving niece, Joseph's oldest daughter, who was his contemporary, warned him against "that ever preying *viper* melancholy." As an antidote she urged: "cherish ambition, cherish pride, and run from excitement to excitement." "You have cause to look for happiness," she wrote, "and that you may gather it[s] sweet blossoms to your bosom at last, do I fondly pray."[18]

Despite the great distances and lengthy absences, Lieutenant Davis clung to his family. The surviving letters, though few and all written to him, show that his mother, his brother Joseph, sisters, sister-in-law, brother-in-law, nieces, and nephews all cared enormously for him. Warm and chatty, the letters are filled with family news and expressions of love and concern for a loved one far away. As often with young people, Jefferson never wrote frequently enough for the folks at home. His correspondents recurrently talked about how much his letters meant to them, and always wanted him to write more regularly. In late 1833, Joseph's wife, Eliza, told him that his mother "is resolved upon paying you a visit" unless more letters reached her.[19]

In addition to requesting that Jefferson improve as a correspondent, his family also expressed a great desire to see him. In turn, home never strayed too far from Jefferson's mind. Whenever he thought of any other occupations, he placed himself in Mississippi. Though visits home could not be routine, a young niece remembered them as joyful. Between his postgraduation furlough in the fall of 1828 and the end of his military service in the spring of 1835, he returned to Mississippi only twice. He served for more than three years before receiving the first extensive leave that permitted him to return to Mississippi. Departing from Fort Crawford in late March 1832, he headed home. Writing from Woodville in mid-April, Lieutenant Davis requested an extension of his leave. He was granted four additional months, though the Black Hawk War interrupted his stay. Then three years later, in March 1835, he was granted a furlough for a trip home. This time he resigned from the army at the conclusion of his leave.[20]

While maintaining contact with home was vital for Jefferson Davis, one person retained special importance, his brother Joseph. Aware of "the consequences you seem to attach to my opinion," Joseph recognized his centrality for his youngest sibling. Joseph also loved Jefferson dearly, but did not dictate to him. Using his influence cautiously, Joseph informed Jefferson that he would advise, but Jefferson must make his own decisions. "No One can judge for an other, and the worst of all reasons," Joseph reminded the young lieutenant, "is that such a one *said so.*" In charting "a plan of life," Joseph counseled, "we should look to the end and take not the shortest route but the surest that which is beset with the fewest difficulty and the most pleasant to travel." Even though Jefferson Davis had lost his actual father, the young man had a sage and sensible surrogate father.[21]

The advice that Jefferson must make his own decisions about his future came in July 1832, when Jefferson was on leave in Mississippi. At that moment Lieutenant Davis was surely contemplating a change in occupation. He had in mind going to work for a railroad proposed for southwest Mississippi, and he wanted Joseph's opinion. Joseph gave it directly. He had doubts about the future of the "small comy.," but Jefferson had to make his own decision. Lieutenant Davis decided to stay with the army, though no evidence details his decision-making.[22]

Although Jefferson Davis spent most of the time between 1829 and 1835 far from home and family, he had with him a constant human reminder of that special place and those special people. Throughout his army career Lieutenant Davis was accompanied by James Pemberton, his slave. At that time it was not at all unusual for army officers on active duty to have servants with them, including slaves. In fact, army regulations authorized a payment for the maintenance of officers' servants. Each time the army paid Lieutenant Davis, he also received an allowance for one servant. The annual base pay for a second lieutenant was $300, which with allowances for subsistence and a servant went up to $834 for an infantry officer, with additional allowances possible. While on active duty Davis had no income save his army salary.[23]

Originally the property of Samuel Davis, James Pemberton was the first slave Jefferson Davis ever owned. Samuel had specified in 1823 that James Pemberton belonged to his son Jefferson. Although there are no particulars on the legal title passing to Jefferson, family members never questioned his ownership. Pemberton, however, did not leave Wilkinson County to join his master until Jefferson Davis was on active duty in the army. Lieutenant Davis was single, but his slave evidently had a wife. Even though slave marriages were not recognized in Mississippi law, or in any other slave states, probably the great majority of slave owners recognized alliances between slaves, as did the Davises with James Pemberton. Family letters to the lieutenant report on the well-being of Julia Ann and a son, the wife and child of James Pemberton. They also ask for news of the absent husband and father.[24]

The historical record is not revealing on the interaction between Lieutenant Davis and James Pemberton. Serving with Davis in various posts, Pemberton remained loyal to his master. No record of disciplinary problems or attempts to escape survives. But by every appearance a mutual respect and devotion grew over the years. One later account describes Pemberton nursing Davis through a serious winter illness. As for Davis, his actions spoke vividly. When he resigned from the army in 1835 to begin a career as a planter, he placed James Pemberton in charge of the land clearing. Later he made Pemberton his overseer.[25]

Even in isolated posts, Lieutenant Davis's social life extended beyond his family and James Pemberton. In the army he ran into some of his old West Point chums like Albert Sidney Johnston. In addition, he met new people like Captain William S. Harney, a fellow officer at Fort Winnebago. Eight years Davis's senior and a ten-year veteran, Harney became a boon companion whom Davis would admire into old age. At Fort Winnebago, Davis also shared a most pleasant association with Indian agent John H. Kinzie and his wife. The Kinzies felt close enough to Davis for their daughter to request a favor during the Civil War and remark on "Auld lang syne" on the frontier.[26]

His location in the Northwest provided the opportunity to renew his friendship with a Transylvania intimate, George W. Jones. While searching for deserters from Fort Crawford, Davis learned that Jones lived in the general area. When he came upon Jones's cabin one night, the two college mates enjoyed a happy reunion. Thereafter Lieutenant Davis often visited at Sinsinawa Mound, Jones's home located in present-day southwestern Wisconsin. The two men cemented a friendship that remained firm until Davis's death six decades later.[27]

The social and sporting activities popular with young officers occupied much of their time and certainly attracted Davis. Not unexpectedly, hunting, fishing, and animals were central. Expeditions frequently proceeded into the wilderness to take advantage of the unlimited supply of wildlife, from wolves to rabbits. Some pursuits went beyond hunting. There were foxhunts, but with a difference: frontiersmen would bring in wolves, and the officers would chase them with "horse and hound." At times the entertainment turned in a more brutal direction. The officers would stage fights between dogs and wolves. One of Davis's friends took pride in his ability to wrestle wolves successfully.[28]

Not all off-duty exertions revolved around wild animals. Winter sleigh rides offered diversion and excitement. Enjoying horses immensely, Davis had the reputation of being able to ride anything. On one occasion he narrowly escaped serious injury when he jumped from a horse that had tried to throw him and reared until it fell. When the horse rose, the intrepid rider leaped once again into the saddle.[29]

Young Lieutenant Davis proved that he was not only active but also physically strong and courageous. Searching for trespassing settlers west of the Mississippi one winter, Davis found himself caught in a snowstorm. He found refuge in a cave where he stayed the night; that the cave was an Indian sepulchre did not deter him. Once, when crossing the Mississippi, his horse refused to swim. Davis sprang from the horse's back and tried to guide the animal, swimming with bridle in one hand and gun in the other. Refusing to follow his rider's lead, the recalcitrant and frightened horse threatened to drown them both. Davis placed his foot on the horse's shoulder, pushed off, and swam for the opposite shore. As he scrambled upon the bank, his mount almost clambered over him.[30]

Several accounts demonstrate Davis's ability to defend himself. Approaching him as he was sitting on some lumber, a discharged soldier asked if he was an officer. Hearing a positive answer, the soldier told Davis to prepare, for he had sworn to whip the first officer he encountered. Immediately Davis bounded up and knocked the man down. The downed pugilist announced that Davis was a gentleman and not the officer he was seeking. Another time, for an unknown reason, Lieutenant Davis found himself in combat with a lean, muscular carpenter standing six feet four inches and weighing 185 pounds. After some sparring, Davis decided he could flatten his opponent and delivered a mighty blow. Unfazed, the carpenter grabbed Davis in a bear hug. Fearing he would lose, Davis resorted to a trick he had learned as a boy wrestling with slaves. He caught the carpenter by the collar, sprang upward and backward. As the carpenter rushed to pin him down, the prone Davis nailed his adversary in the stomach with both feet and knocked him on his back. A superior officer arrived and stopped the fight, though Davis wanted to continue.[31]

Not only strong and vigorous, Lieutenant Davis in his early twenties was also a handsome and engaging young man. Remaining slim, just as at West Point, made him seem taller than his five feet eleven inches. He probably weighed less than 150 pounds. Davis's smooth face and bright coloring made him look especially youthful. His personality along with a "gay laugh" charmed many of his compatriots. A fellow officer said he always comported himself as "a corteous gentleman," though at times, as even Davis later admitted, he could be arrogant and sarcastic. On horseback he could dazzle. Riding through a parade ground in "white drill Pants, made quite narrow at the boot, and quite wide at the thigh, and undress coat," he attracted attention. In one trooper's opinion, no one else could have made "a more gallant and dashing Dragoon."[32]

The spirited lieutenant certainly evinced an interest in the opposite sex normal for a young man of his age and time. At Jefferson Barracks, even before he headed for the Northwest, he reveled in female attentiveness. Writing to one sister, he noted with pride that the pin she had given him "drew attention in ball rooms" from Missouri girls. But, trying to appear older than twenty-one, he added that if he had been four years younger, their solicitude "might have made me vain. . . ."[33]

Evenings at frontier posts were enlivened when nearby settlers hosted what they called "gumbo balls," named for the chief refreshment. At these affairs the officers mingled with the "respectable" young, single women who always attended. The civilian and military guests danced to music usually provided by a local fiddler.[34]

Sometime in 1832 while stationed at Fort Crawford, Jefferson Davis evidently for the first time seriously courted a young woman. He was attracted to Mary Dodge, daughter of Major Henry Dodge, who would later be Davis's commanding officer in the Dragoons. She and Davis enjoyed special occasions together, including a sleigh ride that ended when the sleigh capsized in a snowdrift and the courting couple were pitched into a snowbank. Of course, her father and uncle teased Mary about her beau. Although Jefferson and Mary were delighted with each other for a while, their romance did not lead toward marriage. No documents record the end of the courtship, but Davis forever cherished his joyous time with Mary Dodge. Writing to her a half century later, he treasured "the pleasant memories of one springtime" when they shared "the flowers of youth's happy garden."[35]

The extent of Davis's participation in the common army diversions of alcohol and gambling is not totally clear. According to the historical record, he never got into trouble on either count. Later in life, both Davis and his wife zealously guarded his self-proclaimed image of never drinking or gambling. Davis did not have a history of gambling, though the outcome of horse races certainly interested him. Yet it is difficult to believe that the bon vivant of the West Point years utterly disappeared. A considerable distance separates some drinking from drinking that would cause official problems.[36]

Anecdotal evidence indicates that Davis's cadet persona did survive. One recollection places him at a wedding reception where after substantial imbibing he became the "leading spirit" of the party and captain of the dancers. The fancy he took to a young Indian girl, niece of his hostess, the Indian wife of a settler with French antecedents, led to his taking "improper liberties." His advances resulted in a confrontation with the girl's inebriated brother. Knives and pistols were drawn; Davis's commanding officer intervened to prevent violence. Whether or not this particular episode ever happened, Davis surely made every effort to enjoy his off-duty time.[37]

In his assignments on the frontier, Lieutenant Davis was part of a military force whose chief mission was to prevent conflict between settlers and Indians, and, if that effort failed, to protect the settlers. Davis made unfriendly contact with Indians only infrequently. Although at the Dubuques Mines he did a superb job of keeping miners and Indians apart, incidents did occur when he confronted the natives. On a reconnaissance patrol out from Fort Winnebago, Lieutenant Davis and his party encountered a group of Indians. One blocked the path, and the others attempted to turn Davis's unit in the wrong direction. Davis acted promptly. Charging the blockader, Davis grasped him by the hair and dragged him for a distance. This quick action so disconcerted the Indians that Davis and his men proceeded without further challenge.[38]

Despite that dramatic episode, Lieutenant Davis spent very little time between 1829 and 1835 facing Indians in combat situations. He also missed the greater part of the major military event that took place during his tour of duty, the Black Hawk War. During the spring and summer of 1832, Ma-Ka-Tai-Me-She-Kia-Kiak, or Black Hawk, a sixty-five-year-old Sauk warrior, led a small band from his tribe in an uneven and ultimately disastrous contest against the Illinois militia and the regular United States Army. While Indians and soldiers marched and fought through northern Illinois and southern Wisconsin, Jefferson Davis spent most of these months on leave.[39]

The war stemmed from Black Hawk's long-standing hostility toward the Americans, which dated back to his service on the British side in the War of 1812. He became increasingly unhappy with a treaty negotiated in 1804 by his tribe and the Fox with the United States, by which the Indians gave up their considerable holdings in western Illinois and southern Wisconsin. In return the United States paid a nominal annuity of $1,000 and permitted the tribes to remain on government-owned land. But after surveys and sale to white settlers, the Indians would have to move west of the Mississippi, where the United States would honor their land claims and protect them. By 1830 the increasing white settlement prompted the government to commence selling the land. Thinking removal west of the Mississippi inevitable, most of the Sauk and Fox began establishing new villages in present-day Iowa. Black Hawk, however, refused to go along.

Rallying dissidents to his cause and believing advisers who predicted that other tribes as well as the British from Canada would aid him, Black Hawk challenged American authority and power. Although conflict was averted in 1831, it broke out the next year. Misunderstandings and failed opportunities to settle matters brought bloodshed in May 1832. For the next three months the army, the militia, and Black Hawk mostly marched and occasionally fought inconclusive skirmishes. Finally, in early August, the Americans caught up with Black Hawk's beleaguered band near the mouth of the Bad Axe River on the east bank of the Mississippi. The resulting Battle of Bad Axe, in which 150 Indians were killed, ended the Black Hawk War.

Jefferson Davis may have been at Bad Axe, but before then he surely did not take part in the war. Several authorities have described him as a full-fledged participant, and in later years Davis claimed for himself a significant presence in the conflict. In this instance Davis's memory failed him just as surely as the other commentators based their conclusions on erroneous or incomplete information.[40]

The record is clear. On March 26, 1832, Lieutenant Davis left Fort Crawford for Mississippi with a sixty-day furlough. By the end of the month he had reached St. Louis. In mid-April he mailed a letter from Natchez, and in May he was at Woodville, where he remained until at least July 9. In the meantime he had requested and been given a four-month extension of his leave. He did not stay in Mississippi through the summer, however. The muster roll from Fort Crawford lists him as having rejoined his unit on August 18, 1832. News of the hostilities evidently brought him back to the army. But even if he had departed from Woodville promptly after July 9, the most efficient mode of transportation, the steamboat, could not have delivered him to Fort Crawford before July 21 or 22. Then Davis would have had to travel to the army in the field. Thus, if he fought at all, it could only have been on August 2, 1832, at the Battle of Bad Axe.[41]

While it is impossible to be absolutely certain whether or not Davis saw combat, there is no doubt about his major contribution to the American effort. Although Black Hawk managed to escape from the debacle at Bad Axe, he did not long retain his freedom. By the end of August he was captured by a party of Winnebago and delivered to the Indian agent at Prairie du Chien, who handed the prisoner over to Colonel Zachary Taylor at Fort Crawford. Taylor assigned an escort to take Black Hawk and some 100 other Sauk captives down to Jefferson Barracks. After cholera struck the detail, Taylor had to make some changes in personnel. This time Lieutenant Jefferson Davis was instructed to head a second detachment and make sure that Black Hawk arrived safely at Jefferson Barracks.[42]

On September 3, the steamboat with Lieutenant Davis and his charges aboard set out from Fort Crawford. During the weeklong journey down the Mississippi to Jefferson Barracks, the young army officer and the venerable Indian warrior developed a mutual respect. Davis admired the campaign Black Hawk had commanded as well as his bearing in captivity. When the boat stopped at Galena, Illinois, Davis did his best to keep Black Hawk from becoming a public spectacle. He did prevent onlookers crowding the boat from entering Black Hawk's quarters.

Black Hawk appreciated Davis's consideration. In his autobiography, the defeated warrior wrote fondly of the "young war chief, who treated us all with much kindness." Calling his captor "a good and brave young chief," Black Hawk reported that he was "much pleased" with Davis's conduct. According to Black Hawk, Davis recognized "what his own feelings would have been if he had been placed in a similar situation, that we did not want to have a gaping crowd around us."[43]

At Jefferson Barracks, however, Davis could not keep away all who wanted to see the great Black Hawk. Now held in shackles, Black Hawk attracted many prospective viewers. On one occasion Davis was directed to permit "several gentlemen" to observe Black Hawk and some of his comrades. Annoyed, Davis commented, "Oh, Sir! Gentlemen, here is the Grand Llama of Tartary, worshipped in foreign parts and here is the real live lion stuffed with straw." Noticing Davis's discomfort, one of the party, Washington Irving, "laughed heartily" and remarked, "I see, Sir, you do not like the part of showman." Thereupon, the famous writer and the obscure lieutenant engaged in "some pleasant conversation."[44]

Following his assignment with Black Hawk, Davis resumed his interrupted furlough. Then in January 1833 he returned to Fort Crawford, where he would remain until spring. For his first four years on active duty Davis served in the Northwest, but in his final two years he moved to the Southwest. The shift occurred because in March 1833 Congress authorized a cavalry regiment to operate on the frontier. This new elite unit, designated simply the Dragoons, was designed to combine the speed of horses with the firepower of muskets to provide a mobile force for the protection of settlers. The secretary of war decided to station the Dragoons at Jefferson Barracks. Davis's commander at Fort Crawford, Colonel Zachary Taylor, gave him an assignment plum by naming him one of the junior officers who would go from the First Infantry to the Dragoons. In April, he left Fort Crawford for duty with the Dragoons. His orders sent him directly to Lexington, Kentucky, where he spent around two months successfully recruiting troopers for the new regiment. Finally on July 11, 1833, he reported to regimental headquarters at Jefferson Barracks.[45]

While Davis responded promptly to his new orders, he grasped the opportunity presented for his promotion. He had entered the army in 1828 as a brevet second lieutenant, as did all new Academy graduates. In March 1831 the brevet was dropped when he received his commission as second lieutenant in the First Infantry, to rank from July 1, 1828, the date of his graduation from West Point. Promotion in the regular army came slowly at best, and at irregular intervals certainly. Only the promotion, resignation, or death of incumbents, or the creation of new units, opened up opportunities for advancement.

When he joined the Dragoons, Davis realized that his previous regimental rank made him senior to the three first lieutenants in his new regiment. He pointed this out to the secretary of war, while emphasizing his loyalty and obedience. "I am as ever ready to render my best services wherever the Government may require them, not doubting but that I shall receive all to which I am entitled." Then he detailed the relative ranking. Two months later Davis's commanding officer, Colonel Henry Dodge, recommended Davis's promotion, telling the War Department that "due to his Merit," Davis deserved the promotion. These entreaties were successful, for in February 1834 Davis was promoted to first lieutenant, Dragoons, to rank from March 4, 1833, the date of his assignment to the regiment. The promotion carried with it an increase in pay and allowances of approximately $250 per year.[46]

Davis's case for promotion was certainly not hurt by Colonel Dodge's naming him on August 29 adjutant of the regiment. Previously the first field-grade officer to arrive at Jefferson Barracks had appointed Davis adjutant of the squadron, composed of the earliest reporting companies. Then when Colonel Dodge appeared, he made Davis's appointment official, and for the entire regiment. In this capacity Lieutenant Davis acted as chief aide to Colonel Dodge, whom he had known back at Fort Crawford. As adjutant, Davis occupied a critical position. All orders went through him, usually bearing his signature for the commander. They covered a wide range, from the appointment of special duties like courts-martial, to normal housekeeping matters like orders designating staff officers. In addition, he coordinated the activities of the companies that made up the regiment.[47]

Adjutant Davis's first major task was to plan for the move of the Dragoons from Jefferson Barracks to its permanent station, Fort Gibson in Arkansas Territory (now in Oklahoma) on the Arkansas River, fifty miles northwest of Fort Smith. On October 26, 1833, a directive from the War Department had reached Jefferson Barracks instructing Colonel Dodge to set up regimental headquarters at Fort Gibson. The orders stipulated that Colonel Dodge should act "as early as practicable," which he interpreted to mean promptly. Within a month all necessary preparations had been made; by November 20 the column pulled out of Jefferson Barracks.[48]

The troopers of the Dragoons long remembered the 450-mile journey to Fort Gibson. The march commenced before the recruits had

South-Central United States, 1808–40; State Boundaries, ca. 1840.
Papers of Jefferson Davis, *I, with permission of the LSU Press*

received their full complement of uniforms and weapons. Traveling in a southwesterly direction over largely uncharted land, the regiment coped with a shortage of supplies as it battled both the elements and the terrain. On the third day out a snowstorm struck soldiers ill prepared for the freezing weather. The final part of the trek proved especially onerous. Struggling through thick canebrakes sapped the energy of tired and hungry troops. Food ran short. During the last two days on the trail many men "had eaten scarce a mouthful." When the regiment finally reached Fort Gibson on December 14, "weariness and extreme fatigue" showed "upon every countenance."[49]

Fort Gibson was no paradise, but rather a primitive frontier post. A regimental officer lamented the absence of "comfortable quarters." Many men spent a severe winter in tents, which provided little protection when the temperature plummeted to zero and even below. The horses fared no better. There were no stables and little corn. The troopers had to turn the animals loose "to sustain a miserable existence on cane in an Arkansas bottom."[50]

Colonel Dodge ordered the establishment of regimental headquarters for the winter at Camp Jackson, one mile west of Fort Gibson. The men assigned there did not fare much better than their comrades still at Fort Gibson. "We are now quartered in large barrack-rooms, built of oak shingles," wrote a cavalryman. They offered little protection from the cold and the roofs leaked, but "buffalo robes kept water from saddles, knapsacks, and clothing, and preserved a dry sleeping place for the night." All in all the barracks, in the words of an occupant, offered "comfort scarcely equal to a country barn."[51]

Jefferson Davis spent an eventful winter at Camp Jackson. For the first time in his twenty-five and a half years he became seriously ill. Bronchial difficulties plagued him. He even talked to a superior officer about getting a surgeon's certificate that would declare him medically unfit for duty. He did not take that step, however. Similar symptoms reappeared the following winter when an army physician diagnosed "an affection of the lungs," which he termed "a chronic complaint." The doctor believed "the vicissitudes of the weather—the changible climate" responsible for Davis's illness. Thereafter bronchial and respiratory problems would remain a constant throughout Davis's life.[52]

In February 1834 Lieutenant Davis resigned as adjutant. Precisely why he decided to relinquish this favored position is not at all clear. Army records only indicate his resignation and his reassignment to one of the new companies that joined the regiment. At least part of the reason was personal difficulties with Colonel Dodge. Although Dodge had selected Davis as his adjutant and had recommended his promotion to first lieutenant, the two had fallen out. Complaining that Davis and Major Richard Mason desired to "Harrass me in Small Matters," Dodge condemned both officers as "Now two of My Most inveterate enemies." There is no evidence concerning what brought about this sharp change in the men's relationship. Despite his feelings Colonel Dodge did not attempt to discipline Davis formally or to have him transferred from the Dragoons.[53]

In the spring of 1834 the War Department decided to send the Dragoons on an expedition to the Pawnee Pict village 250 miles southwest of Fort Gibson (in present-day Oklahoma). The government wanted to make a show of strength in the heartland of the Comanche, the Kiowa, and the Pawnee. No treaties had yet been made with these tribes, and they posed a danger both to the increasing number of traders on the Santa Fe Trail and to the Indians arriving in the territory from east of the Mississippi because of removal. The secretary of war believed that an appearance by the Dragoons in this country would encourage greater respect for the United States from the Indians.[54]

By mid-June Colonel Dodge started westward with around 500 men, including Lieutenant Jefferson Davis. The Dragoons found the going extremely arduous. Rough terrain made great demands on horses and riders. The oppressive heat, as high as 105 degrees in the shade, debilitated all. One trooper exclaimed that "the sun with all his scorching rays came pouring down upon us almost hot enough to have roasted an egg in the sand." Every day men fell by the way. Shooting buffalo and rabbits along with observing roving bands of Indians and herds of wild horses broke the monotony, but gave no relief from the sun and the shortage of provisions. On July 21, the force—reduced to 183—reached its destination. Colonel Dodge and the Indians met in council for several days. Impressed with the colonel and his mounted soldiers, several chiefs agreed to return with the Dragoons for further talks at Fort Gibson.[55]

The Dragoons started east on July 25. Not having fully recovered from the harshness of the outward journey, the men experienced an even tougher return trip. Hunger, thirst, and the omnipresent heat so enervated the troopers that many believed they had reached their limits of endurance. Water was always scarce; the diet consisted chiefly of mule and horse meat bought from the Indians. Men and horses suffered mightily. Ravaged by heat prostration, exhaustion, typhus, and dysentery, the column finally reached Fort Gibson on August 15. The two-month trek had been almost as devastating as a battle. Colonel Dodge judged that "perhaps their never has been a campaign that operated more severely on men and horses."[56]

Lieutenant Davis came through the ordeal reasonably fit. The official journal kept on the mission usually specified sick officers; Jefferson Davis's name was never listed. In later years he remembered sighting buffalo and killing a bear, though mostly the heat and the lack of food and water.[57]

Back at Fort Gibson, Davis found himself assigned to a detachment commanded by his friend Major Mason. These companies were directed to construct a camp on the Arkansas River some twenty miles above Fort Gibson. On August 30 Major Mason appointed Davis acting assistant quartermaster and acting assistant commissary of subsistence, jobs he had previously held at Fort Winnebago. In these capacities Davis procured building supplies for what became Camp Jones and provisions for the troops who constructed and manned it. When Davis relinquished these duties in November, he spent much time supervising the actual construction.[58]

Off-duty activities were quite similar to those he had known earlier in his army career. Attending horse races was a popular pastime. He and Lieutenant Lucius B. Northrop, with whom he had been a cadet, vied with each other in picking the fastest horse. Wolf fights also captured the attention of Davis and his peers.[59]

Up to this time, the late fall of 1834, Jefferson Davis had never been in serious official trouble. Unlike Cadet Davis, Lieutenant Davis was not constantly at war with rules and regulations. Personal squabbles, like the difficulties with Colonel Dodge, surely took place, but they remained on a personal, not official, level. Such an episode had occurred at Fort Crawford, probably in 1832. Four officers were detailed to serve on a court-martial, including Lieutenant Davis, his commanding officer Colonel Zachary Taylor, Major Thomas Smith, and another, unknown lieutenant. According to custom, and Colonel Taylor's preference, each officer sitting on such a court-martial was supposed to wear his full-dress uniform. The lieutenant, who had just been sent up from Jefferson Barracks, did not have that attire with him. He asked his fellow officers to excuse him from the requirement of wearing it. Colonel Taylor said no; Major Smith said yes. The colonel and the major soundly disliked each other. For whatever reason, perhaps not thinking it a significant issue, Davis sided with Major Smith. Thus, the court made the requested exception. It is not clear why Colonel Taylor did not exercise the prerogative of rank, but he evidently did not. He did become furious, however. "Highly incensed," he forbade Davis from coming to his quarters as a guest. Still, there was no official repercussion.[60]

One incident did become at least partially official. While serving as a quartermaster in 1830, Davis had an official altercation, but it led nowhere. Unhappy with the response by the quartermaster's office in St. Louis to his requisition for stationery, Davis wrote, "I Shall avoid making any call on you, which it may be optionary with you to grant or refuse." The quartermaster in St. Louis forwarded Davis's letter to the quartermaster general in Washington, calling the language "insubordinate and highly disrespectful." The quartermaster general agreed. Describing Davis's conduct as "repugnant to every sound principle of service," he asked Davis's commanding general to take appropriate action. But there is no record of any such disciplinary measure being taken. In all probability the infantry general thought his infantry lieutenant had dealt with the quartermaster's office just as it deserved.[61]

In December 1834, however, Lieutenant Davis confronted serious official trouble. Following a run-in with Major Mason, his commanding officer as well as a friend and messmate, Davis found himself under arrest awaiting a general court-martial. On the cold, rainy morning of December 24, Davis, though awake and fully dressed, remained in his tent and missed reveille. Mason appeared, noticed Davis's absence, and sent for his subordinate, who reported promptly. The difficulties arose when the major and the lieutenant faced each other that wet, wintry morning. Each interpreted their interaction dramatically differently. An offended Major Mason charged Lieutenant Davis with "Conduct subversive of good order and Military Discipline." He stated his case in the specification brought before the court-martial, which convened at Fort Gibson on February 12, 1835.[62]

At the court-martial Major Mason testified that when Lieutenant Davis responded to the order to present himself, he asked why Davis had been absent from reveille. Davis replied, "because I was not out of my tent, and Regulations require when it rains that roll shall be call'd in quarters by Chiefs of squads." Mason said he then told Davis, "you know it is my order that all officers of this command attend the Reveille roll call of their respective Companies." According to Mason, Davis listened, then in an "insubordinate and contemptuous manner" walked away uttering "Hum!" Believing that Davis was being disrespectful, Mason called him back and so stated to him. Further, he told Davis to consider himself under arrest and to return to his quarters. As Mason reported, Davis stood in place and "stared me full in the face." In Mason's version, not until the third statement of his order did Davis go to his quarters. And, in Mason's words, Davis obeyed only after asking "in a disrespectful and contemptuous manner" whether his superior was finished with him.

Lieutenant Jefferson Davis took this matter seriously. The accusation not only threatened his army career, it also maligned his public reputation and challenged his sense of himself. Put simply, his honor had been questioned. In his summation before the court-martial, Davis announced his desire to "wipe away the discredit which belongs to my arrest." He asserted that "the humble and narrow reputation which a subaltern can acquire by years of the most rigid performance of his duty, is little worth in the wide world of Fame, but yet is something to himself." This classic combining of the public and private dimensions of reputation formed the fundamental underpinning to the idea of honor in Jefferson Davis's own mind and in the South.

To defend himself before a panel of thirteen officers, with Brigadier General Matthew Arbuckle as president of the court, Davis presented an imaginative and thorough defense. Not surprisingly, he denied his accuser's interpretation of the encounter. He knew, however, that denial alone would not suffice for a successful defense. To help him present his case he called eight witnesses: his company commander, three fellow lieutenants, a surgeon, two sergeants, and a private.

Through the questioning of these witnesses Davis hoped to accomplish several goals. Citing the experiences of Captain David Perkins and Lieutenant James Izard, Davis cast doubt on the efficacy, and even the existence, of Major Mason's order regarding attendance at reveille. Izard testified that because of sickness he had missed reveille and suffered no consequences. Captain Perkins followed with the statement that he had missed reveille because of bad weather with no adverse reaction from Major Mason; furthermore, he declared that he knew of no written order. Davis then produced Surgeon John Porter, who stated that the inclement weather on December 24 could have been detrimental to Davis's bronchial condition, and the surgeon testified further that Mason was aware of Davis's health problems.

Davis also countered Mason's version of their conversation, and his description of Davis's attitude. While passing nearby at the moment the two officers were speaking to each other, Sergeant David Sample noted nothing disrespectful in Davis's conduct. Finally, Lieutenant Northrop, who talked with Davis upon his return to quarters, maintained that Davis was in a good mood. The two discussed the incident, and neither thought anything would come of it.

Captain Perkins and Lieutenant James Bowman helped Davis out on one aspect of this particular matter. When Davis asked Perkins whether calmness before Mason might irritate him, Perkins said it would when Mason was trying to correct someone. Perkins also revealed that Mason had spoken harshly to him, Perkins, on three occasions. Lieutenant Bowman went even further: He informed the court that he had known Mason to berate an officer in a fashion that no proud man could accept.

The court also unknowingly offered its assistance. Intervening, the staff judge advocate asked Mason, "Might not the usual manner of the accused be considered disrespectful or even contemptuous by one not well acquainted with him?" This was surely Mason's chance to buttress his charge and tarnish Davis. He did not do so, however. He answered that Davis's general conduct had always been that of "a corteous gentleman."

Davis also took pains to demonstrate that he had been a good officer who carried out his assignments efficiently. Suggesting otherwise to the court, Major Mason described Davis as formerly conscientious but at Camp Jones lacking in energy. In contrast, Captain Perkins testified that since May, when Davis joined his company, the lieutenant had "habitually attended" to his duties. Both sergeants, Sample and John Budd, swore that Davis performed superbly supervising construction at Camp Jones. Their testimony made clear that Davis's projects had not fallen behind others in completion. Lieutenant Izard affirmed that in his view Major Mason had been unnecessarily strict on small duties in camp. According to Izard, the major cared insufficiently about the progress and completion of a task and too much about whether an officer was continuously present on-site. In his defense Davis presented himself as an able, dedicated officer maltreated by a martinet who for whatever reason wanted to punish and embarrass a particular subordinate. Davis even suggested that Mason acted out of some undefined "irritation."

The trial lasted five days, three taken up with the presentation of the defense. After Davis's summary statement on February 19, 1835, the room was cleared for the court to consider its ruling. As a part of deliberations the staff judge advocate read the entire proceedings to the court. The court decided in Davis's favor. Although it held him guilty of the specification, or the basic facts, it excepted all references to "highly disrespectful, insubordinate and contemptuous conduct." The court ascribed "no criminality to the facts of which he is found Guilty." Thus, deciding he was not guilty of the charge, the court acquitted Lieutenant Davis.

Following the verdict of the court-martial, Davis requested a furlough. As in his previous applications for leave, he specified personal and family matters as the reasons requiring his absence from duty. On March 10, he was granted a forty-day leave. There was a singular difference this time, however. When Davis departed from Fort Gibson, he left with General Arbuckle his resignation from the army, to be sent forward if he did not return to duty.[63]

Davis did not take this step because he had failed as an army officer. His commanding officers at Fort Winnebago and Fort Crawford had been pleased with him. Colonel Taylor had sent him to the Dragoons, a signal recognition. Remembering Davis from Fort Winnebago, Lieutenant Colonel Twiggs in February 1835 asked that Davis be assigned to his command at New Orleans to help with major construction. "I have no hesitation in Saying," Twiggs wrote, "that [Davis] is as well, *if not bettor* qualified for that duty, than any officer of my acquaintance."[64]

In the Southwest he had also performed ably, and his acquittal vindicated his own version of his service. The commanding general at Fort Gibson concurred. Lieutenant Davis had clearly impressed General Arbuckle, who, when sending Davis's resignation forward to the army's Western Department, referred to the lieutenant as "a young officer of much intelligence and great promise." He hoped that departmental headquarters would have information that Davis had changed his mind.[65]

General Arbuckle's hopes were in vain. In fact, Davis had also informed the Western Department of his wish to resign. Finally on June 24 the adjutant general in Washington published orders announcing Davis's resignation, effective June 30, 1835.[66]

Like many of his contemporaries in the 1830s, Jefferson Davis left the army for new opportunities. He had thought about it earlier. In 1832 he had seriously considered signing on with a proposed new railroad in Mississippi. And he had surely talked with his brother Joseph and his brother-in-law William Stamps about joining one of them in a farming venture. After his resignation he would follow that course with Joseph. But something even more important prompted the new direction taken by the twenty-six-year-old former first lieutenant—a young woman named Sarah Knox Taylor.

CHAPTER FOUR

"Located in a Very Retired Place"

In August 1832, eighteen-year-old Sarah Knox Taylor came with her mother, Margaret Smith Taylor, and a younger sister and brother, Elizabeth and Richard, to join her father, Colonel Zachary Taylor, at Fort Crawford. Commanding officer of the First Infantry Regiment, Colonel Taylor was also Lieutenant Davis's superior at Fort Crawford from the spring of 1832 to the spring of 1833. There Sarah Knox met Jefferson Davis, and there a friendship developed that grew into love.

Sarah Knox Taylor, known generally as Knox, was a bright and delightful young woman. Born at Fort Knox in Vincennes, Indiana Territory, on March 6, 1814, she had been given an excellent education for a girl of her time and place. In Louisville, Kentucky, the home base of Colonel Taylor and his family, she had been tutored by Thomas Elliott; she then attended the Pickett School in Cincinnati. The only extant likeness of her is a stylized portrait of a girlish teenager with long flowing hair, a rounded chin, and a prominent forehead framing luminous eyes. Her winsome personality charmed her contemporaries, who commented on her intelligence and wit and also noted her long hair, hazel eyes, and her slender, diminutive stature. They disagreed, however, on other characteristics. One noticed her dark coloring and her "exquisitely beautiful figure," but felt the forehead too pronounced for true beauty, while another described her as "extremely pretty." Her cousin remembered Knox as "very handsome, as graceful as a nymph and the best dancer in the State of Kentucky."[1]

A young man in love, Jefferson Davis followed the convention of his day and asked Knox's father for her hand and his blessing on their marriage. But although Knox surely wanted her father to respond positively, Colonel Taylor refused to sanction the proposed match. Margaret Taylor concurred. At the outset, at least, the senior Taylors had

Sarah Knox Taylor (painting by J. B. Reid).
Louisiana State Museum, New Orleans

nothing against Davis personally. It was just that neither wanted their daughter to be an army wife. Colonel Taylor had an especially strong opinion about the difficulties army life posed for wives and families. "I knew enough of the family life of an officer," he told a colleague; "I scarcely knew my own children or they me." He held to that position even though in 1829 his eldest daughter, Ann, had married an army officer.[2]

Soon, however, personal concerns reinforced Colonel Taylor's opposition to the marriage. For some reason—it may have been the court-martial vote—Taylor turned against Jefferson Davis. He went so far as to forbid his subordinate to visit in his home, and he certainly wanted his daughter's romance with the lieutenant to end. Although the depth of Taylor's animosity is uncertain, the story that Davis wanted to challenge him to a duel is most certainly apocryphal. Equally fanciful are accounts that Taylor never harbored hard feelings. He was clearly miffed, and for a time quite cold to Davis.[3]

Knox Taylor proved to possess as strong and independent a personality as her father. Although she respected his wishes about not marrying Davis, at least for the time being, she informed him that she would never marry any other. She kept on seeing her lieutenant, who also persevered despite his colonel's displeasure and personal animus. Even with parental objections and within the confines of Fort Crawford, the young couple managed to carry on their courtship with the assistance of friends. When Captain and Mrs. Samuel MacRee invited Knox for a visit to their tent, they informed Davis, who would stop by at that time. Knox's friend Mary Street, daughter of the resident Indian agent, arranged similar invitations. Thus, visiting Mary Street's home, Davis would find Knox present.

Of course, in the small world of Fort Crawford it was most unlikely that these meetings could have been kept secret from Colonel Taylor. Margaret Taylor's opposition had already softened somewhat, and after a time even the colonel moderated his stance. Then Knox and Jefferson could meet more openly. When Knox took her younger sister and brother out for walks, Jefferson would join the trio. Thereupon Knox would permit the youngsters to romp and play, leaving the sweethearts alone together.[4]

By early 1833, Jefferson and Knox had pledged their love and their futures to each other. They became engaged, even though Colonel Taylor still would not give his consent to marriage. The historical record is silent on whether or not his unhappiness about his daughter and Davis had anything to do with making the lieutenant available for the Dragoons. Taylor had never acted against Davis professionally; in fact, some officers believed that he had exhibited favoritism toward Davis. There is also no record of the reaction to the engagement within the Davis family, though Jefferson informed relatives about his feelings for Knox.[5]

When Davis departed Fort Crawford in the spring of 1833 for the Dragoons, he took Knox's love with him. In the face of Colonel Taylor's adamant opposition, they decided not to marry then, but they broke off neither their courtship nor their intention ultimately to wed. They evidently decided to wait and see if Colonel Taylor would change his mind.

After leaving Fort Crawford, Davis did not see his fiancée again for more than two years. His passion for her did not fade, however. In December 1834 from Fort Gibson, he wrote the only surviving letter between them. The pangs of their eighteen-month separation leap from the page: "Oh! how I long to lay my head upon that breast which beats in unison with my own, to turn from the sickening nights of worldly duplicity and look in those eyes so eloquent of purity and love." Such "intense feeling" could lead to superstition. Davis admitted that his recent dreams, which he called our "weakest thoughts," frightened him. He saw his Knox, "a sacrifice to your parents," standing on the verge of marrying someone else. The arrival of a letter from her, Jefferson rejoiced, "has driven many mad notions from my brain." "I have kissed it often," he confessed.

Jefferson wanted her to have no doubt about her importance to him. He promised that "whatever I may be hereafter I will ascribe to you." "Neglected by you," he continued, "I should be worse than nothing and if the few good qualities I possess shall under your smiles yield a fruit it will be your's as the grain is the husbandman's." He vowed that he and she were one. "I have no secrets from you, you have a right to ask me any question without an apology." Their future he saw in the flower—"hearts ease"—she had given him: "it is as bright as ever."

The two of them had obviously been discussing their marriage, for Davis regretted that their union would separate Knox from her "earliest and best friends." Recognizing the emotionally unsettling situation, he praised her for the strength that would enable her to take such a large step. "Very few," he wrote, "have that measure of firmness." He confided what she certainly knew: "as you are the first with whom I ever [s]ought to have one fortune so you would be the last from whom I would expect desertion." He expected from his cherished one "all that intellect and dignified pride brings."

Davis then turned to more practical matters. Assuring Knox that her "preference to a meeting elsewhere than Prarie-du-Chien and [her] desire to avoid any embarrassment [that] might widen the breach made already cannot be greater than my own," he agreed their reunion should take place somewhere else. And that wonderful meeting would be "soon." He suggested that if she knew when she would be in St. Louis, he could join her there. At least they would rejoin each other in Kentucky. During the wait, he hoped she found "in the society of the Prarie enough to amuse if not to please."

He assured her that "the griefs over which we weep are not those to be dreaded." Instead, he pointed to "the little pains the constant falling of thy drops of care which wear away the heart." Calling her "my betrothed," he urged her to write him "immediately." Switching to French, which they evidently used for endearments, he closed: "Adieu Ma chere tres chere amie adieu au Recrire."[6]

Three months after writing that letter Lieutenant Davis left Fort Gibson for Mississippi. Although technically on a forty-day furlough, he had submitted his resignation in case he did not return. Obviously, he was seriously considering a permanent absence. Details of his activities in Mississippi are unknown, but they surely included discussion with brother Joseph about his future. At some point before the end of April, Jefferson Davis made the crucial decision to give up his army career in order to become a cotton planter. He would join Joseph, but not as a business partner. Joseph, owner of thousands of acres on the Mississippi River just below Vicksburg, agreed to provide Jefferson with the land essential for growing cotton.

It is impossible to know how much his impending marriage to Knox Taylor influenced Davis's decision to shed his uniform permanently. He certainly shared his thoughts and feelings with her, but none of their 1835 correspondence survives. Whether his resignation from the army inclined Zachary Taylor to look more favorably on Davis as a prospective son-in-law is also unknown, though Taylor clearly never became enthusiastic about the match.[7]

Sometime during that fateful spring Jefferson and Knox set the time and location for their marriage. At first they planned a fall wedding, but they moved the date up to June. The ceremony would take place in Louisville in the midst of Knox's relatives. Traveling by steamboat, Knox left Fort Crawford for Louisville sometime earlier. On the boat prior to its departure she met one last time with her father, but again failed to win his unqualified support for her marriage.[8]

Zachary Taylor was not adamant in his opposition, however. After Knox had reached Kentucky, he wrote to his sister in Louisville that if his daughter was still determined to marry Lieutenant Davis, he would accede to her wishes, and he wanted her to wed at her aunt's house. He also sent Knox what she described as a "kind and affectionate letter," along with what she termed a "liberal supply of money."[9]

Still, Knox was acutely aware that both her parents remained somewhat displeased with her decision to become Mrs. Jefferson Davis. Taking the most important step of her young life, she clearly wished for a blessing she did not have. She revealed her emotional trial in a wedding day letter to her mother: "But you my dearest mother I know will still return some feelings of affection for a child who has been so unfortunate as to form [su]ch a connexion without the sanction of her parents; but who will always feel the deepest affection for them whatever may be their feelings toward her."[10]

On June 17, 1835, Jefferson Davis and Knox Taylor became husband and wife. Exactly when he left Mississippi and arrived in Louisville is unknown, but on the seventeenth he obtained a marriage license, after one slight, albeit trying, delay. The clerk of court would not issue a license until Davis brought with him an uncle of Knox's to swear that she was of lawful age.[11]

Jefferson and Knox were married at Beechland, just outside Louisville, the home of her widowed aunt, Mrs. John G. Taylor, Colonel Taylor's sister. No Davises attended; Knox's cousin Richard L. Taylor acted as the groom's best man. Although neither Zachary nor Margaret Taylor made the journey to Kentucky, Taylors were there in plenitude—Hancock and Joseph Taylor, Zachary's brothers, and their families; Mrs. John Taylor with her family; Knox's older sister Ann, whose attendance especially pleased the bride, and her husband. The rector of Christ Episcopal Church in Louisville performed the service.[12]

For her afternoon wedding Knox followed her mother's advice and wore a dark traveling dress with a matching bonnet. Davis was married in a close-fitting, long-tail cutaway coat, a brocaded waistcoat, and tight-fitting pantaloons with straps that passed under his boots and buckled on the sides. In addition, he carried a fashionable stovepipe hat. After a reception with wine and cakes, held at Beechland, the newlyweds drove to the Ohio River and at 4 p.m. went on board a steamboat for Vicksburg.[13]

The historical record is silent on the bride and bridegroom's trip south. Possibly they stopped in St. Louis, for Knox mentions in a letter sent from Mississippi that Jefferson wrote to her parents from that city. Likewise, nothing specifies when they reached Joseph Davis's plantation. There, on land almost enclosed within a huge bend in the Mississippi River—known as Davis Bend after its predominant landowner—they would make their home. Twenty-seven years old, Jefferson would begin life as a planter and a husband.[14]

No documents detail their brief time at Davis Bend. Because Jefferson did not yet have his own house, the young couple lived with Joseph and his wife. While Jefferson began the task of making the acreage Joseph had provided suitable for crops, a cheerful Knox evidently enjoyed her role in a new place. Her only surviving letter from Davis

Bend has a happy tone. She was pleased to have heard from her mother, whom she missed. But the delight Knox expressed about her "beautiful colt" bespoke her satisfaction. After inquiring about her sisters and brother, she asked her mother to give "my love to Pa" and to write "as often as you can find time and tell me all concerning you." The final sentence was eerily ironic: "Do not make yourself uneasy about me; the country is quite healthy."[15]

In the antebellum years the question of health in the hot, humid summer months always occupied the minds of those who lived in the Deep South. Before anyone had any idea of the germ theory of disease, the heat and the humidity, especially in low places, were thought to threaten sickness, particularly fevers, which could be quite serious, even lethal. Without doubt Margaret Taylor expressed her concern about her daughter's spending a summer in the Mississippi lowlands. Jefferson Davis shared that concern. In August 1828 on his way home from West Point, he requested that the army extend his leave, in part because the sickly season had begun in the lower Mississippi Valley. Yet at the time of his wedding he was confident that Davis Bend was a salubrious location. He would never have brought his adored Knox there otherwise. Usually no one thought of any particular location as unhealthy until the heat and humidity really built up, and often not until people started getting sick. August, an oppressive month, was much more likely to harbor the conditions conducive to sickliness than the more moderate June.[16]

Sometime shortly after August 11 when Knox wrote her mother, Jefferson took his wife some 125 miles south to Locust Grove, the home of his sister Anna Smith in West Feliciana Parish, Louisiana. The rolling countryside of West Feliciana was considered much healthier than the flat river land at Davis Bend. In the summer months antebellum southerners often journeyed short distances to gain a little higher elevation, which meant for them slightly cooler temperatures, especially at night, and as they saw it a less fertile disease environment.[17]

Yet Jefferson and Knox were not to escape the scourge of the southern summer. Very soon after their arrival at Locust Grove, Jefferson fell ill with fever. The next day Knox was struck down. Placed in separate rooms, they both became desperately ill with malaria.[18]

Characterized by recurrent fever and chills, malaria is an ancient disease. Hippocrates, the father of medicine, described its major symptoms in the fifth century B.C. It is produced by four different parasites of the genus *Plasmodium*, with mosquitoes serving as the transmitter to humans; and the specific plasmodium infecting a person is critical in determining the severity of the disease. The most benign form, vivax malaria, had long been known in Northern Europe and during the early decades of the nineteenth century was widespread in the United States. The most dangerous species, *Plasmodium falciparum,* was restricted to the South, chiefly the Deep South, because it required an especially warm climate to survive. Endemic in Africa, *Plasmodium falciparum* first reached the South in the bodies of African slaves during the late seventeenth century. *Anopheles quadrimaculatus,* a local mosquito ranging across the region, became an effective transmitter. No place was more hospitable to this potentially lethal form of malaria than the swampy area of the lower Mississippi River Valley.[19]

Every strain of malaria spawns severe chills, which cannot be relieved even with numerous blankets, followed by high fever, frequent nausea, and intense headaches. In extreme cases major organs like the liver, the kidneys, and even the brain can be massively affected. Delirium can occur; coma may follow. Even before the nineteenth century, the curative powers of quinine had been recognized, and its use was widespread in Louisiana. Nothing is known, however, about the medical treatment, if any, given the Davises. The record does not say whether a physician was in attendance or whether one of the widely available published medical guides was used.

For days the lives of both Knox and Jefferson were in serious jeopardy. Family tradition relates that Jefferson emerged from delirium to hear Knox singing "Fairy Bells," a favorite song. Rising from his sickbed, Jefferson struggled toward his beloved and reached her side only in time to witness her death. Knox Taylor Davis died on September 15, 1835, and was buried in the family cemetery at Locust Grove. She was but twenty-one and had been Mrs. Jefferson Davis for only three months.[20]

Jefferson himself remained sick and in a weakened condition for another month. Although he came away from this attack with his life, his body was not rid of malaria. Like many other victims of the disease, he experienced repetitive episodes of fever and chills. Finally, he returned to Davis Bend to try to cope with Knox's death. Her loss had delivered him a massive emotional blow. In his "Autobiography," written in the last year of his life, he spoke of "liv[ing] in great seclusion" for "many years" after her death. Her memory and his vision of that memory obviously stayed with him for the remaining fifty-four years of his life. A number of years after the tragic event, according to a family story, Davis was rummaging through an old trunk when the sight of one of Knox's slippers so staggered him that he lost consciousness.[21]

Just months before his death he received an offer for the return of a letter from Knox. His reaction underscored the power of the emotion he retained even after almost five and a half decades. "You rightly suppose it has much value to me," he responded. He went on to inform his potential benefactor that he had kept at his home in Davis Bend all of his and Knox's correspondence in a "package" in a desk, letters which he never saw again after February 1861. The old man concluded, "it would be a great solace if I could recover the letter Miss Taylor wrote to me."[22]

Now without his cherished Knox, Jefferson Davis had to set out to create a plantation, learn to be a cotton planter and a master of slaves. Now his fortunes, personal as well as financial, were tied even more closely to his eldest brother Joseph, who made the land available for Jefferson to launch his new career.

Joseph Davis was an unusual person. He was born in Wilkes County, Georgia, in 1784, and as a young man in Kentucky he clerked in a store, then read law. Following his family to Mississippi, he read more law and in 1812 established his legal practice in Jefferson County, a near neighbor of Wilkinson. Able and ambitious, Joseph Davis made his mark in his new home. In 1817 he was chosen as a delegate from Jefferson County to the first Mississippi Constitutional Convention; the next year he won a seat in the legislature. At the same time Joseph Davis was prospering, and he put his money into the major asset of his adopted state. In 1818 he and a partner bought from the United States more than 7,000 acres of rich bottomland along the Mississippi River in Warren County, some twenty miles south of the settlement that would become the town of Vicksburg and the county seat. Soon thereafter he bought out his partner and purchased even more land, pushing his total up to 11,000 acres. At this juncture he owned the entire peninsula jutting into the Mississippi, which became known as Davis Bend. In 1820 he moved his legal practice to Natchez, the most prominent town in the state, where he fraternized with the social and economic elite.[23]

In a portrait painted in 1818, Joseph Davis has the look often associated with aristocrats: a proud, intelligent countenance and long, angular features dominate. The dark eyes are engaging. The face, with an appearance frequently deemed sensitive, could be called handsome. The Joseph Davis presented in the painting makes understandable his reputation as a ladies' man.[24]

While Joseph Davis tended to his law practice and added to his for-

Joseph Davis, c. 1818 (painting by William E. West).
*Courtesy of Percival T. Beacroft, Jr., Rosemont Plantation, Woodville, Mississippi,
Gift of Estate of Jefferson Hayes-Davis, grandson of President Jefferson Davis*

tune, he never lost sight of his huge investment in Warren County. He
sold large portions of the land to friends, including John A. Quitman,
another successful immigrant to Natchez who would appear in Jefferson Davis's future, but he still retained some 5,000 acres. He wanted to
begin transforming this virgin land into a productive plantation,
though he was not ready to leave Natchez. As a result, he made
arrangements with his brother Isaac, who agreed to move to Davis
Bend and begin the work of transformation. In 1827, shortly after Isaac
built a dwelling place, a massive storm hit, destroying the house, injur-
ing him, and killing his infant child. The storm had a substantial
impact: the plantation was thereafter known as Hurricane; Isaac left,
never to return; Joseph decided to become a resident planter.

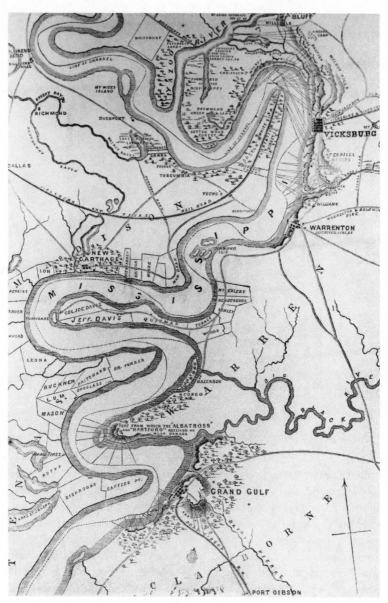

Davis Bend.

Wartime map from Harper's Weekly, May 23, 1863

When Joseph went upriver from Natchez to Davis Bend, he took with him his new wife and three daughters. In New Orleans on October 5, 1827, the forty-three-year-old Joseph Davis married sixteen-year-old Eliza Van Benthuysen, whose widowed mother had lived in Natchez before moving to the Louisiana metropolis where she ran a boardinghouse. Eliza Davis was the same age as Joseph's oldest daughter, Florida. His younger two, Mary and Caroline, were eleven and four, respectively. Although Joseph had three daughters living with him, there is absolutely no record of any marriage; nor is the name of their mother or mothers known. Joseph Davis's biographer suggests that perhaps he perceived the isolation of Davis Bend as more hospitable to his unusual family than the town of Natchez.

As a planter, Joseph Davis thrived. The bottomland of Hurricane plantation, enriched over the centuries by the periodic floods of the Mississippi, yielded cotton crops that made him immensely wealthy. By 1830, he owned 102 slaves, which placed him among the largest and richest slaveowners in the state. In the mid-1830s he built a mansion that would also be called Hurricane.

A substantial three-storied house of stucco-covered brick with two-storied galleries all around, Hurricane conveyed in authority and dignity what it may have lacked in architectural grace. Thick walls and small windows helped keep the interior cool despite the heat and humidity of the long summers. Each floor had four rooms. On the first floor, a wide entrance hall separated the public rooms on the right from the master bedroom and private office on the left. Each of the upper floors contained four large bedrooms and a bathroom, installed by plumbers from Cincinnati, with water supplied from an attic tank kept filled by a slave-operated pump. A large annex extended west of the main structure, with a brick-paved dining room on the first floor and above it a large room with many windows used for entertaining. Behind this wing a brick building of two stories housed the kitchen, laundry, a storeroom, and six bedrooms for the house servants. In the early 1840s, Joseph added to the southwest a cottage with squared Doric columns on all four sides; this became his office and library and sleeping quarters for overflow guests.

Having reached the highest level of the southern ruling class, composed of those who owned the most land and the most slaves, Joseph in 1835 welcomed his youngest brother. The possibility of settling close to home had always appealed to Jefferson, who in 1824 had confided to a sister, "I hope someday to be permanently settled near you." In the early 1830s he had discussed with Joseph and his brother-in-law William Stamps the feasibility of joining one of them in a farming venture. Stamps did propose a partnership, but Jefferson decided instead to join Joseph at Davis Bend. Joseph, who thought of Jefferson more as a son than a brother, obviously wanted him close by, and clearly made the best proposition. According to Stamps, Joseph encouraged Jefferson to resign his commission and provided him the land to begin his career in agriculture.[25]

Joseph offered Jefferson a part of Davis Bend adjacent to Hurricane that became known as Brierfield. A land appraiser who saw it at that time described the tract as "an old burn, with stumps of trees, some cane & many briers, so that I afterwards thought the place was well named when I heard it called Brierfield." The area lay to the east of Hurricane on the southern side of Davis Bend, facing the Mississippi. With its two and a half miles of river frontage, the property totaled more than 900 acres. Dense brush and bramble coated much of the ground; stands of hardwood denoted the ridges; lakes and sloughs dotted the acreage. Of course, as part of the alluvial lowlands along the Mississippi, it did not have much elevation. Both Brierfield and Hurricane ranged between 80 and 85 feet above sea level.[26]

Turning the almost primeval-looking Brierfield into a productive cotton plantation would necessitate arduous work. In the fall of 1835, an emotionally distraught and malaria-ravaged Jefferson Davis was in no condition to commence such an undertaking. Emaciated and suffering also from a persistent cough, he seemed almost like a consumptive specter. Therefore a decision was made, with Joseph undoubtedly having an important say: the weakened, sad widower would go to Havana for the upcoming cold months. That autumn Davis made the easy sea voyage from New Orleans to Cuba. With little interest in social life, he spent most of his time wandering and sketching among the hills and fortifications. The former soldier also enjoyed watching the troops drilling, but he was a bit too attentive for the authorities, who told him to refrain from his drawing and observing. Informing him that they knew he had been an army officer, the Spanish evidently feared that Davis was doing more than entertaining himself. No evidence suggests, however, that the recovering Davis had any clandestine motives.[27]

Sometime in the late winter or early spring of 1836, Davis returned to Davis Bend and plunged himself into the task of plantation building. To make Brierfield fit for cultivation and human habitation would require a vast amount of physical labor. In Jefferson Davis's world that labor was provided by black slaves. The young would-be planter could not imagine clearing Brierfield and growing cotton without them. He owned but one, James Pemberton, who would have a central role in the opening of Brierfield, but he and Pemberton alone could not make cultivated cotton rows out of the tangle of Brierfield.

It is likely that Joseph advanced him money to begin the building of a slave force. Late in her life Jefferson's widow reported that Joseph had loaned him $10,000 to buy his first group of slaves. Certainly Jefferson did not possess that kind of money, nor did he have any other likely source. Borrowing money with Brierfield as collateral would have been difficult because he had no title to the land. Although Joseph surely gave the place to him, and although both brothers always spoke of Brierfield as Jefferson's, Joseph never conveyed legal title to his youngest brother, either in 1835 or 1836 or at any other time. Though certainly genuine, Joseph's generosity did not come uncircumscribed. In the next decade he also gave a plantation to his eldest daughter and her husband, without including the title.[28]

Jefferson Davis's first purchase of slaves occurred in Natchez in Joseph's presence, either in 1835 or in 1836 just after his return from Cuba. On this buying trip Jefferson bought sixteen slaves, both men and women, of unknown ages. Except for James Pemberton, they were the first slaves he owned; by October 1836 he possessed twenty-three slaves between five and sixty years of age.[29]

These slaves went to Brierfield. Some agricultural activity most probably began there in 1835, though contemporary records are unrevealing. Writing in 1890, Davis's widow claimed that he planted a crop in 1835. Fifteen years earlier, William Stamps, who should have known, placed the beginning of real labor at Brierfield in 1836. Certainly by that year a full-scale assault on the wilderness was underway. At the outset some of Joseph's slaves assisted Jefferson's bondspeople in taming Brierfield.[30]

The initial task consisted of finding the appropriate spots for cabins that would shelter the slaves. The location chosen was on a ridge along a road about a mile east of Joseph's residence. There the slaves cut trees and put up a cabin, the first structure at Brierfield. Afterwards this site would hold the central buildings of the plantation, including the master's home and the slave quarters.

Jefferson Davis took charge at Brierfield. Although he still resided at Hurricane with Joseph and Eliza, he appeared at Brierfield every day. One of the slaves he acquired in the first lot in Natchez remembered that at times Davis would even remove his jacket and join in cutting down trees. But along with his own active involvement, Davis relied on a crucial assistant—James Pemberton, who served as Davis's overseer, the person who actively directed the work of the other slaves under the master's orders. In so utilizing Pemberton, Davis was exceptional, for the overwhelming majority of planters employed white overseers. Pemberton occupied this critical post until his death in 1850. The other slaves recognized Pemberton's special status; one even called him the "master man." Pemberton knew his position, however. When he gave his fellow slaves their daily orders, he always cited his authority for doing so: "Masr Jeff" said so. Master and slave forged a powerful personal bond. When the slaveowner was away, news from this slave invariably reached him, and the slaveowner always wanted to be remembered to his slave.[31]

Slowly the trees, the cane, the bramble disappeared. By 1837, at the latest, Davis made an excellent cotton crop. Quarters were erected for the slave force, which at first grew slowly, then more rapidly. In 1838 Davis owned twenty-five souls, only two more than in 1836. The next year saw no increase, but by 1840 he had made significant additions. At that time he possessed around forty, which meant that between 1839 and 1840 the number of his slaves increased by 60 percent. What portion came from natural increase and what portion from purchase is unknown, though at that period Davis was buying slaves in New Orleans.[32]

Not surprisingly, Davis's slave force consisted chiefly of young people. As a beginning planter, who commenced with only one inherited bondsman, he would logically want to obtain youthful slaves, who would presumably have a long work career before them. In 1840 he also had an exceptionally balanced sex ratio, twenty-one men and eighteen women. The federal census for that year broke them down into the following groups: children under ten, three boys and six girls; older children and young people between ten and twenty-four, eight males and six females; young adults between twenty-four and thirty-six, five men and four women; adults between thirty-six and fifty-five, four men and but one woman; old people over fifty-five, one of each sex. Of this total of thirty-nine, the census reported that twenty-nine were occupied in agriculture, meaning that the youngest and possibly oldest did not work in the fields. Although the record is silent on the familial relationships among these slaves, the substantial number of children coupled with an almost exact sexual division in the next two age categories suggest slave families. This possibility could also mean that natural increase provided a superb way for slavemaster Davis to expand his slave population.[33]

As Jefferson became a planter in his own right, he remained close to Joseph. After all, he still lived under Joseph's roof, where he would stay until after his second marriage. He also turned to his surrogate father for advice. At the same time no one questioned his ownership of Brierfield; very few people even knew that Joseph had never relinquished the title.

In business transactions Brierfield and Jefferson were considered independent of Hurricane and Joseph. Between 1838 and 1844, Jefferson used the factorage house of Oakey, Payne & Hawkins in New Orleans to handle his marketing and supply needs. George E. Payne, who handled Jefferson's affairs in these years, testified that he worked with Jefferson, not Joseph, and not the brothers together. According to Payne, the cotton received from Jefferson was clearly marked "Brierfield," and all proceeds from its sale went directly into Jefferson's account, which in the spring of 1842 had a positive balance of $1,000, a considerable sum at that time when cotton prices were depressed and the annual per capita income of free Mississippians totaled around $92. Payne's firm furnished and paid for whatever items Jefferson ordered, including slaves, and debited his account. Everything went upriver by steamboat to Davis Bend with invoices and bills of lading in Jefferson's name. Jefferson was succeeding as a planter, though information about his finances is scarce. A friend congratulated him on "escap[ing] the vortex of Speculation, as also its twin Sister *credit*." His land had come free of charge, and Joseph was always there as a lender of last resort, though no evidence indicates that any cash ever came from Joseph after his outlay of $10,000. Moreover, taxes were minimal. Between 1836 and 1841, Jefferson's annual payments on his slaves never exceeded $16. The total taxes on his personal property, including slaves, ranged from $28.19 in 1842 to $56.82 in 1845.[34]

Between the brothers harmony prevailed. When Jefferson took off on an extended trip to the Northeast during the winter of 1837–38, Joseph looked after affairs at Brierfield. He reported on the health of the slaves and the harvesting of the corn and cotton to Jefferson in January 1838. He also indicated that the ginning of cotton had been delayed, which meant that it would be "Some time to Come" before he could send Jefferson's crop to market. The next month he wrote that because of the severe winter at Davis Bend he had been unable to start spring planting. He continued that Jefferson's "people [slaves] are about as usual they have done as well as they Could but like mine have been hindered by the weather from effecting much." While traveling in the summer of 1838, Joseph informed Jefferson that in Louisville he had purchased "Some linsey & c for the Supply of the people Sufficient for yours & mine." By all accounts the Davis brothers had established a close, effective business relationship. Clearly, Jefferson was thought of as an independent man, but Joseph gave advice and assistance when needed.[35]

Love and respect characterized their personal interaction. Joseph's letters communicated all of his doings, not just plantation business. He surely took Jefferson into his confidence on family, financial, and political matters. When he learned in August 1838 that his young protégé planned to spend "the Season" at Davis Bend, Joseph worried "that you may Suffer from the influence of the Season & the increased exposure. . . ." He warned the younger man "against an error that I have too often committed & which you I think are Some what liable to an attempt at *too much*." Yet an obviously concerned Joseph acknowledged Jefferson's maturity: "You Can judge better being on the Spot than I can." For his part, Jefferson continued to rely on his oldest brother for guidance and support. To Joseph, he was always "affectionately your Brother."

While Joseph remained special, Jefferson also maintained other family ties that had been so important to him when he was far away from Mississippi. His mother's adoration of her youngest child had not diminished. Staying with daughters either in Wilkinson County or West Feliciana Parish, Jane Davis still hoped to see and hear from him more often, but she assured her last-born of "the Sincere love of your affectionate Mother." Reciprocating, Jefferson helped provide for his mother's needs by having his nephew draw on his New Orleans factor. His sister Lucinda reported to him "how mutch pleasure" his letters gave her. The newsy, affectionate communications that he received from his nieces made clear just how comfortable they were with their "Dear Uncle." Their correspondence leaves no doubt that Uncle Jefferson made them feel important as individuals in their own right as well as in his life. Joseph's daughter Florida articulated the sentiment all her cousins obviously shared: "I Know you love me."[36]

Joseph's wife Eliza, only three years younger than Jefferson, did not disguise her opinion of her brother-in-law, whom she addressed as "My dear brother," and penned detailed letters to him when away from Hurricane. Their affinity clearly included playfulness, for on one occasion when Jefferson had been left alone at Hurricane, she wanted to know how he was succeeding as a housekeeper.[37]

After his Cuban trip only once in the next eight years did Jefferson venture far from the homeland of Davises. In November 1837 he left for an extended trip to the Northeast. His first major stop was New York City, where he stayed with Eliza Davis's brother, Watson Van Benthuysen. After a sojourn of at least two weeks he departed for Washington, the focus of his journey. Along the way, in Baltimore, Davis became "too unwell to proceed." He related to Joseph that an army surgeon traveling with him "stopped and attended to me." Davis provides no clue about the nature of his illness, though he seemingly recovered quickly. The very next day he was "much better," so much so that he went a short distance in the country to see the finest short-horn Durham cattle he had ever seen.[38]

The following morning he once again proceeded toward Washington, reaching the national capital on December 26. His physical recovery had only been temporary, however, for he arrived "with a severe cough and considerable fever, which latter became intermittent." There flulike symptoms confined him to his room at Brown's Hotel for almost a week. By January 1, 1838, he felt "free of disease," though the inclement weather made him "fearful of exposure." Thus, he remained "a prisoner."[39]

Once improved, Davis went to the Capitol to renew his friendship with his old companion of Transylvania and Fort Crawford days, George W. Jones. Now a delegate to Congress from Wisconsin Territory, Jones lived in a boardinghouse on Capitol Hill, as did so many senators and representatives. "Overjoyed" to see his visitor, who yet "look[ed] quite ill," Jones invited Davis to share his quarters and join his mess at the boardinghouse. When Davis agreed, Jones had his luggage transferred from his hotel. Jones took it upon himself to introduce Davis to a number of political luminaries, including President Martin Van Buren, various senators and congressmen, and members of the cabinet. Davis told his brother that he had attended a public reception at the White House, but on that day, "being weak of body and luke warm of spirit," he had not been formally presented to the president. Family tradition narrates another visit to the mansion for breakfast with President Van Buren when the two men talked of the army, of politics, and of Davis's shoes made in New Orleans, which the president greatly admired.[40]

Although Jefferson Davis certainly enjoyed his reunion with

George Jones and meeting new people who made him a part of their social life, one occasion led to a serious accident. Davis went to a "large party" with Jones and Senators William Allen of Ohio and Lewis Linn of Missouri. About midnight Jones and Linn decided to go home. Searching for their comrades, they found them in "the banqueting room" still eating, drinking, and having a good time. Even so, they all decided to leave—Davis and Allen in a carriage with Senator John J. Crittenden of Kentucky. After reaching Crittenden's abode, Allen stated, he and Davis decided to go the rest of the way on foot, walking up Capitol Hill in order to "digest our supper and wine." As they started up the hill with Allen in the lead, they missed the bridge spanning Tiber Creek (which at that time flowed just beyond First Street not far up the hill) and plunged into the creek. In Allen's words, "Davis fell headforemost upon the stones and was nearly killed." Though inebriated, Allen managed to get Davis back to Jones's room. When he arrived, Davis had "blood, mud, and water trickling down [his] face." Alarmed at Davis's cuts and his bleeding, Jones roused Linn, a physician as well as a senator, who treated the "mute" Davis and dressed "the terrible wounds on his head." The next morning when Jones tried to wake the injured man, he found Davis "speechless and almost dead," and called Dr. Linn. Immediately, the doctor responded and used camphor and laudanum, "soon restoring him to consciousness and life again." According to Jones, Dr. Linn believed that without prompt treatment Davis would have died. Whether that diagnosis was correct is impossible to ascertain, but in all likelihood the fall resulted in a concussion as well as lacerations.[41]

In this instance Jefferson Davis had obviously imbibed too much alcohol, though in later years both Jones and Davis's widow insisted that he never drank to excess. Yet Senator Allen, whom Jones described as drunk, admitted that both he and Davis needed the fateful walk to help them handle their consumption of food and drink. In his thirtieth year Jefferson Davis still enjoyed a good time that included parties and spirits. He was also fond of smoking a pipe, at least since army days. One army chum reminisced about Davis "sucking the cob" at Jefferson Barracks. In the future Davis did seem to keep his drinking under control, though always taking pleasure in a glass of whiskey. Relishing his pipes and cigars throughout his life, Davis never gave up smoking despite his recurring bronchial problems.[42]

Not all of Davis's northern activities revolved around social events, however. The record does not reveal the full motives behind this extensive trip, yet one purpose is apparent. Once again, he was thinking about the army. Although the extant documents are silent on exactly what caused him to reconsider the decision he made in 1835 to resign his commission, they do make clear that he was rethinking that choice. By all accounts his career as a planter had begun auspiciously; business associates and relatives, including Joseph, talked about his success in his new work. Perhaps, then, he wanted to remove himself physically and emotionally from the scene of his great sadness.[43]

Talk abounded that in 1838 Congress might add three new regiments to the army, and unquestionably Davis wanted to position himself to receive a commission in one of them. From Washington he described to Joseph, obviously privy to his intentions, his efforts to accomplish this goal. "Tomorrow I hope I shall be able to call on such persons as I know in public life here and adding the Missi. delegation to whom I must become known, review the whole & then endeavor to estimate what influence I can bring to bear on my purpose." In April 1838 Congress did augment the size of the army, but by only one regiment, not three. Whether that smaller increase adversely affected Davis's chances is unknown, but no appointment ever came to him.[44]

With the arrival of spring, Davis bade his farewells and set out for Mississippi, returning by the western route. Leaving Washington on April 5, he first went north to Philadelphia, then west to Pittsburgh. There he boarded a steamboat for the trip down the Ohio and Mississippi Rivers and back to Davis Bend and Brierfield.[45]

At home Davis did not devote all of his time to learning about the cultivation of cotton and the management of slaves. In his words, "located in a very retired place . . . the cane break in which I lived," he undertook the ambitious reading program that as a young army officer he had outlined to his sister Lucinda. Books were available in Joseph's richly stocked library, which both brothers undoubtedly kept adding to.[46]

In this library political economy and political philosophy held a central place. From the British giants John Locke and Adam Smith to the American founders Thomas Jefferson and James Madison, Davis sought to understand the founding principles of his country. He also immersed himself in the classic legal treatises by the Englishman Sir William Blackstone and the American James Kent. Legislative and congressional debates, along with newspapers and other periodicals, both American and British, kept him abreast of contemporary political events and thought.

Jefferson Davis as a young man.

Southern Historical Collection, Wilson Library, University of North Carolina, Chapel Hill

He did not overlook literature. Renewing his acquaintance with Latin authors, he went on to consume Shakespeare and other English writers such as Lord Byron and Oliver Goldsmith. Two special favorites were the notable Scotsmen Robert Burns and Sir Walter Scott. In addition, he spent considerable time with the Bible, committing a substantial portion of it to memory. His correspondence began to contain literary quotations. Borrowing from Burns, he began one letter: "I long hae thought my honored friend A something to hae sent ye."[47]

At the same time Jefferson Davis was absorbing the printed page, he was also engaged in an ongoing colloquy with Joseph. The two brothers—surrogate father and surrogate son—spent many hours discussing numerous topics besides agriculture and slaves. Indicating his respect for Jefferson, Joseph consulted him on investment strategy. Both men were avid admirers of horses and had superb animals. While traveling, Joseph described in detail the magnificent "Natures Nobles" he saw on a horse farm in Kentucky.

Politics occupied a central place in the brothers' deliberations. Although Joseph had not been in public office for many years, he retained an active interest in Mississippi and national politics. Jefferson, of course, had never previously been involved in politics, but he came to share Joseph's fascination. The course of the Mississippi legislature and the outcome of state elections keenly interested them. In Washington in the winter of 1838, Jefferson evinced interest in congressional goings-on and enjoyed the company of politicians, both old friends, like George Jones, and new acquaintances.

Slavery as a political question also came under the brothers' scrutiny. Jefferson reported on the abolition-petition controversy that was generating so much heated debate in Congress. Events much closer to home greatly upset Joseph. On hearing speeches in Kentucky urging local planters to reduce their slave population and not tie their futures to "the Cotton planters and Sugar planters" farther south, he was so distressed that he wanted to respond personally. "You may readily Suppose the feelin[gs]," he wrote Jefferson, "of any Southern man on hearing Such principles in Such a place."[48]

At this time a strong partisan rivalry between the Democratic and Whig parties divided the country and Mississippi. The Davis brothers lined up with the Democrats, though the record does not reveal the genesis of their party loyalty. It is reasonable to assume that Joseph made his choice first, before Jefferson, and that he had an influence on his youngest sibling's decision. Without doubt, the person of Andrew Jackson was a formative force. The Davis family had been admirers of Jackson at least since the Battle of New Orleans, and for Jefferson the general who became president had been a hero since childhood. As a United States senator, Davis recalled that the first vote he ever cast was for Jackson for president.[49]

Additionally, both Davises saw Jackson's Democratic party as a bastion of the states' rights political philosophy they associated with their political saint, Thomas Jefferson. The Virginia and Kentucky Resolutions of 1798 and 1799 composed by Jefferson and his comrade James Madison became their political creed. The Resolutions emphasized states' rights, limited federal powers, and strict construction of the Constitution. The Davis brothers disliked the views of Jefferson's arch-antagonist Alexander Hamilton, whom they perceived as the great advocate of federal power and a broad or loose interpretation of the Constitution. For them the Whig party represented a continuation of Hamilton's political and constitutional views.[50]

The Davises made a logical choice. The Whig party did not in general champion states' rights, though in the late 1830s there were some states' rights Whigs in Mississippi and other southern states. Still, most states' rights stalwarts dressed in the Democratic uniform, and their number increased after the rapprochement in 1837 between the most prominent states' rights politician, Senator John C. Calhoun of South Carolina, and the Democratic party. The Calhoun-Democratic alliance had a direct impact in Mississippi, where it ensured that the Democratic party would be the majority party in the state.

In their home county, however, the Davis brothers found themselves in the minority. Dominated by wealthy planters, Warren County was a Whig stronghold, as were the other rich cotton counties along the Mississippi south to Adams County and Natchez. Unlike the Davises, most rich slaveowners in the river counties subscribed to Whig economic and financial policies and did not become excited by the doctrine of states' rights and strict construction. They kept their counties in the Whig column.[51]

The documentary record provides little information on Jefferson Davis's early attitudes on specific issues. After he became a senator, he told a friendly newspaper editor that up to 1837 he had taken no part in politics except to vote. Later in life he declared that he had made up his mind on one momentous issue. If the Nullification Crisis between South Carolina and the United States government in 1832–33 had resulted in armed conflict, he had, he maintained, decided to resign from the army rather than participate in a war against a state. The crisis, of course, was resolved without violence; so Davis never had to confront that decision.[52]

Nothing charts precisely the growth of Jefferson Davis's interest in becoming more than a political spectator. After expressing his doubts about President Van Buren's financial policy in an 1839 letter to George Jones, an obviously self-conscious Davis remarked, "You perceive that when I write of Politics I am out of my element and naturally slip back to seeding and ploughing. . . ." Yet politics did attract him. Joseph's wealth and prominence would certainly give Jefferson an immediate identity among Warren County Democrats, but anything beyond that entrée would necessitate his own effort.[53]

He began inconspicuously. In August 1840 he became more than an onlooker when he attended a Democratic meeting in Vicksburg and wound up being named as one of around 100 delegates to the party's state convention in Jackson. Two years later he once again found himself chosen to attend the gathering of Democrats in Jackson, and in 1843 he traveled all the way along the political road from observer to participant.[54]

At age thirty-five, Jefferson Davis became the Democratic candidate for the state House of Representatives from Warren County and Vicksburg. The party had not intended to sponsor him, but when its original choice ran into difficulty with certain groups, Warren County Democrats decided to make a change, even though the election was rapidly approaching. Less than a week before the balloting, the county convention on November 1, 1843, turned to the untried Davis for its standard-bearer. Even though he knew that he faced an extremely tough contest in heavily Whig Warren, Davis readily accepted the nomination. Later, he admitted that he expected to lose, but despite that conviction he leaped at the chance to make the race.[55]

He made a spirited run. It was now only a few days before the balloting, so little time remained for campaigning. The Democratic paper in Vicksburg praised Davis as "a sterling Democrat," who would make an excellent legislator. Even the Whigs recognized him as an intelligent and honorable man, and they certainly took his candidacy seriously, for they brought out their biggest name, not Davis's actual opponent, for the only speaking engagement. Seargent S. Prentiss, a Vicksburg attorney famed as an orator, spoke for his side.[56]

The speeches, delivered at the courthouse in Vicksburg on the very day of the election, November 5, presented contrasting styles. Although the arrangement was for each man to have fifteen minutes, Prentiss told Davis that he could never hold to such a limitation. Davis agreed that Prentiss could extend his time, provided that he stayed on the subject. The "great stump orator" held the podium and the crowd for three hours with a speech that even the Democrats called a "brilliant, dazzling thing." Davis himself remembered that Prentiss argued "closely and powerfully." Still, undaunted by his opponent's performance, Davis rose and, according to his partisans, "successfully replied" with a "classical and chaste" speech of thirty minutes in which he "[m]aintained his position." Obviously, he knew he could not match Prentiss's fireworks, but his exertions satisfied his supporters.[57]

The only substantive matter discussed in the debate was the repudiation question, the defining political issue in Mississippi from the late 1830s to the mid-1840s. In the economic boom of the 1830s, Mississippians of all political persuasions clamored for banks to provide desperately needed credit, and by 1837 the state had chartered twenty-seven banks. In that year the legislature created the Mississippi Union Bank, "a quasi-official state institution." To ensure its success the legislature pledged the faith of the state through the issuance of $15.5 million to provide part of the necessary start-up money. As required by the state constitution for any measure that called for financial backing by the state, the bill came back before legislators in 1838. Once more it was approved, but with a supplement that called for the governor to purchase $5 million of bank stock, the money to be raised by the sale of state bonds. This act changed the relationship between the state and the bank; the state became a stockholder, not simply a backer of the bank. Despite this significant alteration, the amended charter did not return to the legislature in 1839 for a second approval.[58]

When the economic collapse caused by the Panic of 1837 hit Mississippi, many Democrats wanted to refuse to pay the Union Bank bonds. They cried for repudiation to preclude the taxation of hardworking, struggling Mississippians to pay bondholders, most of whom resided in the Northeast or in England. Whigs countered that the faith and good name of the state were on the line. A contract entered into by the state, they argued, had the same legal force as a contract between two private partners; as a result, repudiation meant dishonor.

By the time of Jefferson Davis's initial race, the dispute had been decided by the Mississippi legislature's repudiation of the debt. Still, the topic of repudiation retained both its volatility and its partisan nature. Among the Democrats, however, a minority believed the bonds legitimate. Through this political minefield the novice Jefferson Davis navigated carefully. Although he did think payment of the bonds illegal, he did not support legislative repudiation. Instead, he insisted that the courts provided the proper forum to settle the matter. Because the Mississippi constitution permitted the state to be sued, Davis and others argued that the anti-bond forces could go to court claiming that the failure of the amended charter to go before two legislatures made it unconstitutional. At some political risk, Davis adhered to this stand. He never backed the majority Democratic position of legislative repudiation, though he was placed in that camp by enemies, especially during the Civil War. Almost to the end of his life he angrily denounced those who branded him a repudiator.[59]

In his single recorded campaign appearance Davis stated his case against Prentiss, who attacked the Democratic party as the haven of repudiation. In all probability the words of neither Prentiss nor Davis had much effect on the outcome of the election because as it traditionally did, Warren County went Whig. Davis garnered 512 votes to 685 for his victorious Whig opponent.[60]

Although a loser this first time out in electoral politics, Jefferson Davis had done himself immense political good. His party saw him as one ready to take up the Democratic banner in spite of the late hour and the long odds. Likewise, his willingness to compete directly against the Whig titan Prentiss revealed him as a man not cowed by eminence. A Democratic editor proclaimed that Davis emerged from his encounter with Prentiss "untouched . . . triumphantly, suc[ce]ssfully and honorably." Designating him "no *ordinary man*," party stalwarts in his home county "anticipat[ed] for him a proud and honorable career."[61]

Warren Democrats thought they had a possible rising political star. One month after his defeat, his county colleagues again sent him to the state Democratic conclave, scheduled in Jackson for early January 1844. With their help at that meeting, Davis moved his party activity from the county to the state level. The convention chose him as one of the party's six electors for the fall presidential election. That selection clearly signaled that Jefferson Davis had moved beyond "clearing fields in the primeval forests" of Davis Bend for the larger world of political engagement.[62]

While Davis was beginning his serious involvement in politics, his personal life was also moving in a new direction. Riding from Hurricane in December 1843 to Vicksburg for the Warren County Democratic meeting, Jefferson Davis stopped by Diamond Place, the home of his niece Florida McCaleb, only a dozen miles from her father Joseph's seat. There he delivered to Varina Howell a message from Joseph, who was eager for the young woman from Natchez to make her way to Hurricane. Soon, Davis was off to Vicksburg.

CHAPTER FIVE

"It Was What I Wished"

Varina Banks Howell was the daughter of Joseph's old friend William B. Howell of Natchez. A native of New Jersey and son of a governor of that state, Howell migrated to the Natchez area after serving as an officer in the War of 1812. There he met and in 1823 married Margaret Louisa Kempe, daughter of a well-to-do landowner. Over the next years Howell tried a number of businesses, but succeeded in none. The wealth of his in-laws and his wife's inheritance provided critical financial resources Howell needed for his wife and brood of children.[1]

Soon after his arrival in Natchez, Howell became acquainted with another immigrant to Mississippi, Joseph Davis. The two grew to be fast friends, and Joseph, already a successful attorney, took Howell "under his wing and sponsored him in Natchez society." They remained steadfast friends, though Howell never found the prosperity that Joseph was beginning to enjoy. Unlike Joseph, who gave up town life for the prospects at Davis Bend, Howell clung to Natchez. He lived with his growing family on the river bluff just south of town in the Briars, a substantial but not palatial house provided by Margaret Howell's father. That William Howell named his firstborn Joseph Davis Howell underscored just how close he felt to Joseph Davis, whom the Howell children always called Uncle Joe.

On a visit to Natchez in 1842, Joseph invited the eldest daughter of his companion to visit him at Hurricane. Both William and Margaret were happy for young Varina to go, and she would have gone but for dedication to her studies. The proposed trip was postponed until December 1843, when Varina, chaperoned by her tutor, Judge George Winchester, went aboard a steamboat at Natchez and headed upriver toward Vicksburg and Davis Bend.

Varina Banks Howell, c. 1844.
Courtesy of Varina Margaret Webb Stewart

Joseph's seventeen-year-old guest was born just across the river from Natchez on May 7, 1826, on her maternal grandparents' plantation in Concordia Parish, Louisiana. Growing up in Natchez, Varina associated with children from the first families of the thriving town, though the Howells enjoyed neither the financial means nor the security of these wealthy people. She also received for a young girl of that time a remarkably good education. In one year, 1836, she attended Madame Greland's, a fashionable boarding school in Philadelphia, but that was not her most influential educational experience. For a substantial time in Natchez, she had the immense good fortune of having a superior private tutor, Judge Winchester, like her father an immigrant from the North. Born in Massachusetts, Winchester had established a friendship with the Howells and a respectable legal practice that led to his appointment to the bench. Taking quite a fancy to young Varina Howell, Winchester took it upon himself to educate her. Over a period of a dozen years, and without a fee, Winchester guided his only student through a course including Latin, the English classics, and French. Bright and interested, Varina worked hard at her books, even putting off a holiday with her Uncle Joe to finish her study with Judge Winchester. In later years she wrote that she learned so much more from her teacher than the content of particular subjects. "The pure, high standard of right of which his course was the exemplar" stayed with her throughout her life.[2]

When Jefferson Davis first met Varina Howell, he saw a slim girl of more than average height, with striking dark hair pulled closely around her head. A broad nose and ample mouth with full lips dominated a face more handsome than beautiful. Widely set, doleful dark eyes gave her almost a haunting appearance. Yet she looked like the young maiden she surely was.[3]

Jefferson Davis certainly made an impression on this teenager. The very next day in a letter to her mother, Varina portrayed him as "a remarkable kind of man," though she had difficulty making up her mind about him. Whether he was young or old, she could not decide, but, she supposed, "he is old, from what I hear he is only two years younger than you are." Varina discerned in him "an uncertain temper, and . . . a way of taking for granted that everybody agrees with him when he expresses an opinion, which offends me." Yet at the same time she described him as "most agreeable," with "a peculiarly sweet voice and a winning manner of asserting himself." The young girl perceived an older protector. "He is the kind of person I should expect to rescue one from a mad dog at any risk, but to insist on a stoical indifference to the fright afterward." She also admired his refinement and cultivation, even though she did not believe she would ever like him so much as Uncle Joe. That this puzzling man was a Democrat perturbed her. In her world gentlemen like her father and Judge Winchester were Whigs; evidently neither of these men had ever bothered to tell her that dear Uncle Joe also identified with the Democratic party.[4]

The day after Jefferson left the message that his brother was eager to see Varina, Joseph sent a niece with horse, driver, and carriage for the young woman and her luggage. Once at Hurricane, Varina settled in for a lengthy visit, not departing for two months. Obviously enjoying Uncle Joe's hospitality and her stay in his mansion, she discovered an unexpected attraction—that same Jefferson Davis, with whom she spent much time. He captivated her. Now she described "a very gay fellow," "look[ing] about thirty; erect, well-proportioned, and active as a boy." On horseback he almost took her breath away: "He rode with more grace than any man I have ever seen, and gave one the impression of being incapable either of being unseated or fatigued."[5]

Jefferson Davis, c. 1845.
National Portrait Gallery

Equally fascinated, Davis discovered his emotions racing. Clearly he had experienced nothing remotely resembling these feelings since Fort Crawford and Knox Taylor. Only one month after meeting this girl half his age, he proposed marriage. Depicting her as lively and intelligent, Davis found her irresistible and himself enchanted. Varina responded positively to his entreaties, obviously sharing his sentiments. They spent two intense months together, except for Davis's political journey to Jackson in early January 1844. When Varina embarked on the steamboat to return to Natchez, he was desolate. "I wished myself so earnestly on the Boat that was bearing you off," he wrote shortly after her departure, "that had you called me . . . could I have found any other excuse for going back I should have substituted your feeling of desolation with either surprise, annoyance, or confusion."[6]

At this point Davis faced a situation he knew well—the problem of parental approval. A dutiful young daughter, Varina wanted to tell her parents of her new love and to obtain their blessing on her hopes for marriage. An understanding Davis accepted her decision to return alone, though he surely would have wanted to be with her when she talked with her parents. Just as certainly, and aware of their age difference, he did not want to press Varina into marriage or even be perceived as pressing her. At first the Howells were unsure; at least Margaret Howell had some reservations. After all, Jefferson Davis was her contemporary, only two and a half years younger, and old enough to be Varina's father. She also knew about the deep love he had for his first wife and the hard blow struck him by her death. Within a short while, however, she agreed to permit Varina to follow her heart. During this period Judge Winchester had also been Varina's champion, commending Davis and supporting the match between his favorite damsel and the older suitor.[7]

Love for Varina Howell enveloped Jefferson Davis. He told "My own Dearest Varina" that the house had been "particularly dull" since her departure. When the mail put off by a steamboat seemingly contained no letter for him from her, "my heart sunk within me," he confessed. A few hours later, however, when his sister-in-law Eliza handed him an envelope, he was elated. "It was more than I had hoped for," he exulted, "it was what I wished, it came to dispel my gloomy apprehensions. . . ." When Varina wrote to inform him that her mother no longer objected to their betrothal, he wanted to rush immediately to Natchez. Seeing her "every day and all day" was his goal, and he assured her that "my spirit is always with you." In the eleven months of their engagement, March 1844 to February 1845, he was at times with her in more than spirit, for he visited Natchez more than once, though no details of any visit, save the last, survive.[8]

Throughout that year Jefferson constantly pledged his love. He sent his "deepest truest purest love" with the declaration that he would renew these assurances when he saw her. On another occasion he dramatized her importance to him: "the first wish of my heart is my first though[t] my first prayer this morning need I say that wish is for your welfare." Anticipating their marriage, Jefferson completely committed himself: "your spirit is with me. I feel it's presence, my heart is yours, my dreams are of our union, they are not dreams, for I will not wake from them." As with his first love, he also expressed endearments in French. "Adieu, au revoir, ma chère, très chère, plus chère Varina Dieu te benisse." Varina was "mon ange."[9]

Her desire that he burn her letters brought forth a vigorous remonstrance: "If the house was on fire those letters with the flowers you have made sacred by wearing and the lock of your hair" would be the first things he would save. He asked that she retract her request because honoring it would inflict more pain on him than she could wish. He assured her that no one besides himself would see them, unless he died, and he did not expect to meet his end for some time. Unfortunately, however, Varina's courtship letters have not survived.[10]

Davis also devoted much attention to Varina's health, which was not always good in 1844. In his initial communications after she left Hurricane, he urged her to take care of herself. In order to prevent injury to her "angel eyes," he advised against reading at night or keeping a light on in her bedchamber. A week later, rejoicing at the news that she was well, he wrote, "again I entreat you to take care of my wife." Illnesses that she suffered in the autumn and winter elicited concern and anxiety from the absent sweetheart, and the pair considered postponement of their wedding.[11]

Davis continuously insisted to his betrothed that a bright future awaited them. If he were even half as good a person as she claimed, then "surely such little faults as you suppose you may commit could never disturb the harmony of our lives." When finally they were together, she could instill "goodness and purity" into him, which would make him even more worthy. About her he had no doubt, though he did issue a caution. He confided that "there is but one species of error which an honorable woman is capable that could distress me if committed by my wife—e.g. such love of admiration, or excess of politeness as might induce one to fear that ridicule, or even detractive remarks were secretly made, but of this as a morbid feeling in its extent I have long since informed you as one of my many weaknesses." Even so, he did not mean to suggest that his fiancée had any such traits. "You are always such as I wish you," he confirmed.[12]

Nevertheless, one matter had come up that occasioned at least some disagreement. Varina evidently raised the possibility of their living someplace besides Davis Bend and even of his changing his occupation. Jefferson replied that if it were his "will" to decide how and where they lived, her wishes would be critical in his decision. He reminded her that he had often said, "we are controlled by a master not likely to regard either your wishes or mine." Still, Jefferson had every confidence that Varina could "meet the exigencies and yeild to the necessities our fortune imposes." His life as a cotton planter at Davis Bend had been decided upon. No room for discussion remained. Then, almost as a parent, he addressed her: "It is well however to be prepared for the worst which is within the range of possibilities as blessed are they who expect nothing, for surely they shall not be disappointed."[13]

That parent-child dimension appeared more than once. Part of it was the mid-nineteenth-century social convention, especially in the South, in which husbands normally assumed the role of protector and guardian of the wife. The substantial difference in Jefferson and Varina's ages could easily have led to an exaggerated form of that custom. Early in her engagement a possibly confused Varina called her father by Jefferson's name. Disturbed, she shared the misnomer with Jefferson, who replied with a question: "Was it a mistake of langua[ge] if it so may be called to think of one thing and speak of another, or have you, my dear child, been sick again?" The adult solicitous of the child's well-being also occasionally took on the pet name of "Uncle Jeff."[14] Davis's wedding photograph graphically portrays the difference in their ages. Whereas Varina has a girlish appearance, almost demure, Jefferson no longer looks young. The long, angular features give him an aloof, or even aristocratic, countenance to accompany the resolute bearing of a mature man. The penetrating eyes dominate a face that seems to wear a sadness earned from experience. The look of constraint evinces a person who kept his emotions in check, even at this time of joy.[15]

The day before they married, he counseled: "Pray be calm and meet the contingency of this important change as becomes you, as one who has 'a hurt for every fate.' " He spelled out what she could anticipate from him: "I will try to do better than I have ever promised to fulfill brighter hopes than I have ever inculcated and failing in this, my sympathy shall pour oil upon your wounds, my heart shall beat warmly to relieve you from the chills of misfortune's winter and my form shall screen you from the lightnings of an angry destiny." Finally, the eager bridegroom broke through. "I wish you would put in that Lion pawing up the dirt, without which I fear you will find the picture incomplete."[16]

The wedding took place on February 26, 1845, at the Briars. Postponements had occurred because of Varina's recurring illnesses in the late fall and early winter, but toward the end of February, with spring budding out along the lower Mississippi River, she rallied. With Jefferson in Natchez on one of his periodic visits, the decision was made to hold the ceremony promptly with only close relatives and a few Natchez friends present. For the second time no Davises attended Jefferson's marriage. According to Varina's later testimony, the wedding was neither an elaborate nor an expensive affair. The bride wore "a

Wedding picture of Jefferson and Varina Davis.
Courtesy of Varina Margaret Webb Stewart

white embroidered Indian muslin with touches of lace, and a dark suit for her departure." One of her two bridesmaids, a cousin, picked from the garden a rose that Varina placed in her hair. Her maternal grandmother gave her some jewelry—"a bracelet, necklace, brooch, and pendant earrings of cut glass with antique gold settings." Her groom had given her an engagement ring, a large emerald with diamonds set in gold. The rector of Trinity Episcopal Church in Natchez, the Howells' religious home, officiated at the 11 a.m. ceremony. After the exchange of vows, a wedding breakfast was served upstairs at the Briars in a room scented with white flowers from the Howells' garden.[17]

Thereupon bride and groom boarded a steamboat to begin their wedding trip. Their ultimate destination was New Orleans, but first on the itinerary were stops with certain of Davis's relatives. Downriver from Natchez they disembarked in West Feliciana Parish, Louisiana, to visit Jefferson's sister Anna and her family at their home, Locust Grove, where Knox Taylor Davis had died a decade earlier. While there Jefferson and Varina walked to the family cemetery and placed flowers upon Knox's grave. Next, the couple traveled about twenty-five miles north to Woodville, Mississippi, where Jefferson's mother still lived at Poplar Grove with her daughter Lucinda, son-in-law William Stamps, their children, and other grandchildren. Now eighty-four years old, Jane Cook Davis was "so infirm" that she could not rise from her chair. Varina remembered her as "still fair to look upon," even though she was nearly blind, almost deaf, and practically mute. Jane Davis greeted the newlyweds affectionately, telling them that she had always wanted her baby to remarry. Every day she asked for them. They both responded, but Varina told her mother that Jefferson was so sensitive about his mother's mental failing that "I never stay with her while he is there." Despite the sadness of Jane Davis's decline, "the tender love [Jefferson] evinced for his sisters and family" along with "the warmest reception" given her by her in-laws impressed the new Mrs. Jefferson Davis.[18]

After a sojourn at Poplar Grove, Jefferson and Varina once more returned to the river and a steamboat, this time bound for New Orleans. Even as they awaited the boat, Varina admitted in a letter to her mother that she missed home and confessed that whenever she thought about her, she began crying like "an overgrown baby." She hurried to add that "Uncle Jeff" never saw the tears and she quickly got over her momentary unhappiness. When the couple arrived in New Orleans, where they put up at the St. Charles Hotel, the city's smartest, Varina was not grieving. On the very first night the Davises attended a soirée at the St. Charles, where Varina later recalled being introduced to "the first poet I had ever encountered." Many years later, she recollected being charmed by the man she thought was an uncle of Oscar Wilde. She also thought well of one of her husband's old commanders, General Edmund P. Gaines, and his wife. After enjoying themselves for some six weeks in the cosmopolitan center of the lower Mississippi Valley, the Davises once more embarked on a steamboat, this one to take them upriver back to Davis Bend.[19]

Even before he married, Jefferson Davis's political world had expanded far beyond the borders of Warren County. On January 8, 1844, Davis interrupted his early romance with Varina to attend his third state Democratic convention. There his party named him an elector at large for the upcoming presidential race, one of six; each congressional district had an elector, and two, including Davis, were chosen for the state at large. At that time in Mississippi, accepting the post of elector involved considerably more than having one's name placed on the presidential ballot. Electors were expected to campaign actively for the national ticket.[20]

The convention that chose Davis as an elector also endorsed a preferred slate—former chief executive Martin Van Buren for president and James K. Polk of Tennessee for vice president—and directed the delegates to the Democratic National Convention in Baltimore to support the nominations of Van Buren and Polk. In Jackson, Davis made clear that Van Buren was not his first choice, though he had been instructed by the Warren County delegation to vote for the former president. In one of the major addresses to the assembled Democrats, Davis announced that while he was aware of Van Buren's claims on the party and he certainly recognized the New Yorker as a good Democrat, he preferred John C. Calhoun of South Carolina. But the preeminent states' rights politician, who had mounted his greatest effort to gain the Democratic presidential nod, was stymied by Van Buren's forces in the South as well as the North and had decided to withdraw from the contest by the time Davis presented his name to the Mississippi convention. Davis did not know of Calhoun's decision because it did not become public knowledge until February.

Davis insisted that Calhoun merited the support of Mississippi because he was the best candidate on the critical issues: lowering the tariff, annexing Texas, reducing the size of the federal government, and redressing the niggardly treatment the South had received on coastal defense. Davis maintained that the coastal regions of both the South Atlantic and the Gulf of Mexico had been "treated ungenerously and unjustly" in comparison with the Northeast. Although Davis specified four individual issues on which he believed Calhoun strongest, a single foundation underlay his preference. He wanted a southerner, and Calhoun was the obvious choice. Davis urged his fellow delegates to consider "the necessity we have for a Southern President" to secure the goals most important to the South. "The South has borne long," he cried; "let her be true to herself, that justice may be done."

Although the convention rejected Davis's plea for Calhoun, it did not reject Davis. A Democrat in attendance remembered that the speech so impressed the assemblage it gave the speaker a standing ovation when he finished. Davis did get the convention to adopt unanimously a resolution stating that if "any contingency" should defeat the nomination of Van Buren and Polk, the Mississippi delegation should think of Calhoun as second choice. Then the convention moved on and with unanimity selected the delegates to the national convention and the presidential electors, including Jefferson Davis.[21]

Accepting his selection as a presidential elector propelled Davis into the center of Mississippi politics. A rowdy spectator sport that arose from the whirlwind of Jacksonian Democracy, this rough-and-tumble political world had thrived for more than a decade. White manhood suffrage had existed since 1832, and the sovereign voters required wooing and intermingling from their prospective officeholders.[22]

The equality of all white men was the bedrock of political Mississippi. This was emphatically not a political world in which rich planters controlled candidates and elections while sipping sherry and juleps in elegant drawing rooms. Energetic campaigning antedated Davis's entry into the arena and did not diminish during his time as a participant. From 1844 until 1860, Davis participated fully and willingly in the demanding ordeal set up by Mississippi voters for those who wanted their allegiance. Braving abominable roads, poor transportation, nasty weather, uncertain accommodations, Davis and his fellow aspirants made their treks through towns, villages, and countryside.

Although Varina's later claim that before the campaign no more than a dozen men outside Warren County knew his name was surely an exaggeration, Davis was in many ways still a political novice, and he knew it. He made his preparations accordingly. Assuming into the spring that Van Buren would carry the party's standard, Davis wrote directly to him for information that would help in Mississippi. After identifying himself as a Democratic elector and mentioning that the two of them had met, though Van Buren probably did not remember him, Davis went straight to the point. "You will oblige me and many other Democrats of this section of the country," Davis told the presumed candidate, "by giving your opinion" on three questions—the annexation of Texas, the constitutional power of Congress over slavery in the District of Columbia, and particulars about Van Buren's vote on the Tariff of 1828. Davis expected these issues "to be opened" and thought they "could not be otherwise as well closed" as with the candidate's own response. Davis also asked a companion from his Washington trip, Senator William Allen, for statements to counter charges of defalcation and extravagance during Van Buren's administration as well as material on the tariff and the Bank of the United States. Confessing his inexperience, Davis admitted, "I have mingled but little in politics and as you perceive by this letter have an arsenal poorly supplied for a campaign."[23]

Despite his doubts, Davis embraced his task: "Labor is expected of me and I am willing to render it." He did not, however, work for Van Buren, who had never excited him, but for former Tennessee congressman and governor James K. Polk. The Tennessean snared the nomination when Van Buren was blocked by southerners distressed over his opposition to annexing Texas. The requirements of the campaign forced Davis to realize that politics at this level was a demanding calling. As he explained to his fiancée, he had discovered "as many have done before me that whilst attending to the public my private affairs had got much out of joint." The party had set up a rigorous schedule that would take him to almost every part of Mississippi. From June until the election in November, he spent most of his time on the road. Davis usually traveled with other Democrats, often with Henry Stuart Foote, a fellow candidate for elector and another rising Democratic star, who would have a significant place in Davis's political life for much of the next two decades.[24]

Highlighting the campaign, or the canvass as it was called, were the public speeches given by both Democrats and Whigs at every stop. The importance of these addresses cannot be exaggerated, for they were central to the political culture and to the success of an individual politician. "One of the most remarkable characteristics of the Southern people before the war was their universal enjoyment of public speaking and their intense appreciation of good popular oratory," asserted a contemporary of Jefferson Davis's, who also successfully appealed to Mississippi voters. "In consequence," he continued, "the art of fluent speaking was largely cultivated and a man could hope for little success in public life unless he possessed this faculty in some degree."[25]

Recognizing this truth about Mississippi politics and that "public speaking was a new thing to me," Davis worked at becoming a more effective orator. He did begin with a distinct asset, what one political opponent described as "a musical and well modulated voice." Throughout the canvass observers assessed his performance. A Democratic witness commented on his first appearance at Natchez in mid-June: "he rose gracefully and with a mild impressiveness of manner that commanded universal admiration." For almost two hours Davis held the attention of his audience with a speech that "gave universal satisfaction." According to this commentator, Davis adopted a particular style: "He addresses the reason, the judgement, the intellect; but has no words for the Passions. Convincing the head, he stoops not to warm the affections, or to fire the heart with emotion." This writer wanted

Davis to "animate the perfect, but somewhat inanimate statue of his eloquence with some of the strong outlines of passion." Doing so, and in conjunction with "his inimitable style of passionless argument," would enable Davis to "rouse the will and the passions, enlist the feelings and captivate the imagination." Then he "would rank among the foremost of our Mississippi orators."[26]

Throughout the next five months of speechmaking, other critics made similar remarks about Davis's chaste style. The "beauty of his style and the cogency of his reasoning" impressed one. Another described him as "an elegant, calm, and deliberate speaker" with "argumentative powers" of "the first order." While praising these attributes, some wished for "more animation and warmth of action," which after a time Davis began to provide.[27]

The heat of a long Mississippi summer evidently began to seep into his speeches. In Noxubee County in early August he gave a "soul-stirring speech" of one hour; a week later in Aberdeen his oratory had an "elec[t]rical" impact on a large crowd. He could employ the vernacular to good effect: "the Whig party claim to be the decency party, raise their coons and roll their balls, but they remind me of a certain *insect* which rolls its ball backwards and down hill."[28]

Davis had clearly improved, whether or not he had become what a Democratic partisan judged "the most eloquent and pathetic speaker in the southern country." He also received exceptionally high marks from another aspiring Mississippi Democrat who first encountered Davis in late July at Holly Springs. Analyzing Jefferson Davis as an orator, Reuben Davis, who was not a relative, recalled that when Jefferson "made his salutation . . . there was nothing particularly imposing in his appearance or manner." But "from the moment he began to speak with all the ease and eloquence of which he was so consummately master, he seemed to expand and etherealize into the very spirit of oratory." Davis's "soft and mellow utterance, his lucid argument," delighted his listeners. "Dignified and commanding, soft and persuasive, his speech was from beginning to end a finished speech of logic and oratory," which brought forth "rapturous applause" from the crowd.[29]

During at least sixteen speeches in eleven different counties, Davis concentrated on what he defined as the basic difference between the two parties. In his view, the central question facing Mississippians was as old as the country—constitutional interpretation and the power of the central government. He presented the Democratic party as the legitimate heir of Jefferson, "the sage and apostle of democracy."

Davis emblazoned states' rights and strict construction on the Democratic banner, while the Whigs, as Davis represented them, embodied the consolidation and broad construction of Hamiltonianism and the Federalist party. The Democratic party, Davis emphasized, would always strive for lowering the tariff and would never permit the rechartering of the Bank of the United States because the Constitution did not specifically allow for either a protective tariff or a national bank. In contrast, Davis declared that the Whigs cared little about the words of the Constitution in their determination to aid manufacturers and augment the power of the federal government.[30]

During the campaign Davis did not focus on the issue that had brought down Van Buren and ignited the South, the annexation of Texas. Lying immediately west of Louisiana and just southwest of Arkansas, Texas had been on the southern political horizon for almost a decade.[31] After successfully revolting from Mexico in 1836, Texas claimed to be an independent country. Because American immigrants, chiefly southerners, led the revolt and dominated the new republic, many in both Texas and the United States wanted Texas in the Union, but the existence of slavery in Texas put off many in the North and made acquisition a delicate issue. Such political considerations held back both Andrew Jackson and Martin Van Buren from advocating annexation. When the Virginian John Tyler became president in 1841, the political calculus changed. The southern-oriented Tyler administration believed with some justification that Great Britain had designs on Texas that included the abolition of slavery. It foresaw a threat to slavery in the South, and thus, in the administration's perception, to the security of the entire country. Ambitious to remain in the White House, Tyler, who had been cast out of the Whig party for his opposition to its nationalist economic policy, also saw Texas annexation as a way to stir up political excitement in the South that might lead to a second Tyler administration. In the end Texas did create a furor in the South but did not keep Tyler president. Instead, it caused a southern Democratic revolt against the anti-Texas Van Buren, which cost him the party nomination in 1844 and led to the selection of the strongly pro-annexation James K. Polk.

Texas generated such a volcanic reaction in the South because it bore to the bedrock of southern values. Pro-Texas rhetoric linked annexation with southern honor by claiming that failure to annex would brand the South as inferior to the rest of the country: southerners must be unworthy Americans if only slavery, their fundamental social institution, barred Texas. Moreover, Texas symbolized the future. According to Texas proponents, only antisouthern and anti-slavery feeling in the North could prevent annexation, and therefore force the South to face a dismal political and economic future. Although tens of thousands of square miles in the Louisiana Purchase existed for more free states, little remained for additional slave states because the Missouri Compromise blocked slavery in most of the pur-chase. Texas provided the possibility of continued political parity for the South. If the North could exclude Texas, then the South would be confined within its boundaries and could anticipate becoming a weaker and weaker minority. The magnet of land was also wrapped up in Texas. From its beginning the American nation, including the South, had marched steadily westward—across the Appalachians, to the Mis-sissippi Valley. Texas was next. Closing the gate to Texas shut out southerners from western expansion and from equal participation in the great American future.

The contemporary accounts of the canvass depict Henry S. Foote as the major Democratic spokesman for Texas, a division of labor that did not mean Davis was cool on Texas. As early as January 9, 1844, he joined Foote and John A. Quitman in addressing a public meeting in Jackson convened to call for joining Texas to the Union. In May, he served on a Committee of Twenty appointed by the Texas Annexation Association to prepare an address to Mississippians explaining the necessity for immediate annexation. When Davis did touch on the Texas issue during the canvass, his listeners "found him not one jot behind" the most enthusiastic boosters for turning the Republic of Texas into the state of Texas.[32]

To Mississippi voters, Davis made clear his concern about the South and the southern future. Connecting the South directly to the Democ-ratic belief in strict construction, Davis argued, "We of the South are now in a minority, we must continue to be the minority, our only reliance is on the constitution as a barrier against legislative encroach-ment. . . ." In Davis's judgment, expecting the majority to respect southern rights simply because it should made as much sense "as asking mercy of the wind and waves." He hoped for a direct consideration of "whether the domestic institutions of the south shall be considered an objection to the extension of the southern states by the acquisition of adjoining territory." In this wish Davis was unsuccessful, for the larger question of the extension of slavery never became a major campaign topic. Yet it stood at the center of the Texas matter because all, North and South, recognized that if Texas came into the Union, it would do so as a slave state.[33]

The strenuous efforts of Davis and his fellow Democratic warriors during the summer and fall of 1844 were rewarded. Traditionally Democratic, Mississippi remained safely in that column. Collecting 57 percent of the popular votes, Polk won easily over his Whig opponent Henry Clay and garnered Mississippi's six electoral votes. Although all the Democratic campaigners won plaudits from the party, Davis received special notice. Even before the actual election, the major Democratic paper in the state heaped praise upon him: "He is a gallant soldier and has covered himself with honor in the present campaign." A fellow Democratic activist reported that Davis gained "new laurels" whenever he appeared during the canvass. After the electoral triumph he served as one of the managers for a victory ball held in Vicksburg in early December.[34]

The Democratic win in Mississippi was part of a national Democratic victory that made James K. Polk the eleventh president of the United States. Davis wasted no time in participating in the honored Jacksonian custom of seeking jobs for the party faithful. In early December he joined with other Democratic notables requesting President-elect Polk to appoint a fellow elector to a federal patronage post in Mississippi. That practice did not unsettle Davis, who later in the winter told one of his state's senators that more Democrats than he had thought would be applying for positions. As a result, Davis "hope[d] our friends will not allow such of our enemies as shall have the impudence to place themselves in like attitude, to profit thereby."[35]

At the same time Jefferson Davis found himself in the political limelight, he was beginning married life for the second time. When he and Varina returned to Davis Bend from their wedding trip, they took up residence at Brierfield in a cat-and-clayed house, in which straw and clay were melded for chinking, designed by Jefferson and built with the assistance of James Pemberton and other plantation slaves. As an architect, Davis did not match the man for whom he was named, Thomas Jefferson. Although located amidst a magnificent grove of oaks with slave quarters on both right and left, the house was not distinguished. Large rooms that "opened on a paved brick gallery, surrounded by lattice work," characterized the structure. The windows were unusual because a "miscalculation" placed the sills at chest height. To admit as much air as possible and encourage circulation, Davis constructed outer doors six feet wide, which did help keep the house cool. Varina recollected that opening them seemed to make that entire side of the house disappear. To her, the deep fireplaces "looked as though they had been built in Queen Elizabeth's time, to roast a sheep whole."[36]

The newlyweds appeared to be making a good beginning. Varina spoke of busy and happy days with Jefferson, reading, writing, riding, including "many races when the road was smooth." They also visited neighbors, and Hurricane, where they saw Joseph and Eliza every day. Varina spent time tending to her flowers and vines. In addition, she took up the duties of a plantation mistress, running a household and caring for sick slaves.[37]

Shortly after their arrival at Brierfield, the new husband reported satisfaction with his young wife. To his mother-in-law, whom he called "my dear mamma," he described the happiness of their humble lifestyle: "We should not probably be more happy if the walls of a castle sheltered us, than we are beneath the protection of our rugged hut." He thought that Varina grew "calmer discreeter happier & lovelier with each passing day." He was quite pleased with the attention his relatives had given his bride and delighted that "they harmonize together better than I had hoped."[38]

While Jefferson and Varina were adjusting to each other and to relatives, particularly Joseph and Eliza, Jefferson was actively engaged in running Brierfield. The planting and cultivation of cotton and grain demanded special attention, but Davis continued to clear away the trees, cane, and brambles that had once pervaded the plantation. "For several days past I have been enveloped in smoke" from preparing more land for cotton, he wrote his factor. Increasing the production of cotton troubled him, for he believed the staple had been overproduced. Still, he did not know what else to do. Worried about the low price of cotton, which had plunged to less than 5 cents per pound in the prolonged depression following the Panic of 1837, Davis opined that the United States "must drive all the other countries out of the cultivation of cotton and if the price does not improve then all of our own people except those most favorably situated must give way also." Still, he wanted "through this long vista of depression [to] look forward to brighter things."[39]

Neither domesticity nor agriculture occupied all of Davis's attention, however. The political name he had made for himself during the campaign of 1844 opened up other possibilities. His Democratic friends in Warren County considered him not only "a free-hearted, open, manly, bold *Mississippian*, and a Democrat to the core," but also a man "destined to be the pride and ornament of our state." When Warren Democrats convened in late June 1845, with Davis present, they once again chose him as a delegate to the state convention, but they also unanimously resolved to present his name to that body as a nominee for a seat in the U.S. House of Representatives.[40]

In Jackson on July 8, Mississippi Democrats did select Davis as one of their four congressional candidates, but his triumph did not occur without opposition. Even though they were chosen to represent different sections of the state—Davis, for example, the southwestern—each candidate had to make a statewide race, not simply one in his bailiwick. With their preponderant majority in the entire state, the Democrats maintained the at-large election system to preclude any Whig's getting elected in an area of special Whig strength, such as Davis's own region. Three other Democrats avidly desired the southwestern slot, chief among them Dr. William Gwin, also of Warren County. The record does not provide details for the brief, albeit vigorous skirmish that ended with Davis's victory. After leading handsomely on the first ballot, Davis easily vanquished Gwin by 51 to 34 on the second, and won the nomination. Now, in 1845 as in 1844, he would have to canvass the state, this time asking Mississippi voters to elect him.[41]

The nomination struggle in Jackson did not surprise Davis. In fact, even before the state convention he had been attacked in the Vicksburg press. Once more the old banking issue appeared, though in a different form. In 1845 the question was framed around the Briscoe Bill, a measure that the legislature had enacted back in 1843. When first put forward in 1842 by Democratic legislator Parmenas Briscoe, it proposed to expunge all debts owed to the defunct Union Bank, which would have aided a number of Briscoe's friends and relatives who were indebted to the bank. That bill failed, but Briscoe brought it back the next year, and it passed the state House of Representatives. The Senate, however, amended the bill so that the bank's debtors would be legally liable for what they owed in order to permit the bank's creditors to gain something for their investment. Thus amended, the legislation got through both houses and upon the governor's signature became law in July 1843. And in January 1845 its constitutionality had been affirmed by the Mississippi High Court of Errors and Appeals. Still, many Democratic stalwarts decided that their party's antibank identity necessitated adherence to the original Briscoe Bill, which, of course, had never become law.[42]

Although most Mississippi Democrats adopted that position, Davis did not. He believed that the bill that had been enacted was fair and had been judicially sanctioned, and he said so publicly. At the same time he made sure that no one could mistake him for a bank partisan. "To show that my opinion on the subject of bank forfeiture, is free from the bias of any personal interest, I will state that I have never owned a share of bank stock, nor borrowed a dollar from a bank," he declared in a public letter that he had printed and placed before the state convention. Despite his unequivocal declaration, accompanied by a denunciation of paper currency, Davis worried that his opposition to the initial version of the Briscoe Bill would lead to his defeat. Even though he differed on this issue with the majority of his party, he prevailed in Jackson.[43]

His victory despite the Briscoe Bill fracas delighted his home newspaper, the *Vicksburg Sentinel,* and brought forth its praise: "Doubly triumphant is the securing of such a man in public life. It is a triumph of straight forward frankness and honesty over intriguing, non committalism, and duplicity which we grieve to say has too much heretofore characterized our public men." This enthusiastic editor wanted Davis "to be known in other parts of the state as he is at home; and we know that he will become everywhere else as much beloved and esteemed as he is here."[44]

Even before he had secured the congressional nomination, Davis's neighbors demonstrated their admiration for him by inviting him to give the eulogy during the ceremonies held in Vicksburg to commemorate Andrew Jackson, who had died on June 8. After the usual self-deprecation, Davis agreed to memorialize a man whom he idolized and idealized. "From my childhood I was attached to General Jackson," he informed a friend. Later, he continued, "my confidence and respect for him increased," and "my affection and admiration followed him to the grave, and cling to his memory."[45]

On June 28 two military companies, Masonic Lodges, Mechanics' Mutual Benefits Societies, several fire companies, and "a numerous train of citizens with their beautiful badges and insignia" marched through Vicksburg. When this "imposing and beautiful spectacle" reached the Presbyterian church, the ceremonies commenced. After music and a prayer, Jefferson Davis rose. Comparing Jackson's character and patriotism favorably to George Washington's, Davis portrayed the fallen hero as a man who "never hesitated between the prompting of self interest and the demands of honor and duty." Jackson's "moral firmness, his high sense of duty," guaranteed that he would act solely to

Mississippi, c. 1845.

From Papers of Jefferson Davis, *II, with permission of the LSU Press*

benefit his country, never just himself. In Davis's scenario, Jackson as president viewed with "agony" the possibility of civil strife among Americans. The speaker concurred with Jackson's watchword: "The Union it must be preserved." "Long live that maxim, and may our Union ever be preserved by justice conciliation and brotherhood, without a spot, without a stain of blood that flowed in civil war." Accordingly, citizens must protect "the pure fire of liberty," which they can do if they "catch the Flame before it sinks." Davis's remarks touched the proper chord, for approbation and praise came his way.[46]

Davis's new prominence manifested itself in yet another way. During this period on at least two occasions, friends and associates called on him to mediate grave differences between notable Mississippi Democrats. With John A. Quitman he settled a serious dispute between two Jackson editors in which both agreed to retract personally offensive remarks. In another instance, and again in concert with Quitman, he adjusted a matter between Congressman Jacob Thompson and Dr. William Gwin that could easily have led to a duel. Such controversies were supremely important in the honor-conscious South, and for mediation disputants would rely only on men they considered of reputation and distinction.[47]

With eulogies and conventions behind him, Jefferson Davis once more set out on the campaign trail, even though he started out ill. With eyes "inflamed" and "the white of one . . . *entirely* red," his wife reported that he looked "very badly," and she also detected other undisclosed "symptoms of sickness." Worried about when she would see her husband again, Varina began to understand his commitment to politics, which made her "jealous" because politics absorbed too much of him. But despite his poor health and his wife's concern, Davis, between August and November 1845, canvassed Mississippi from counties bordering Louisiana in the south to those adjacent to Tennessee in the north, covering an untold number of miles. He was surely not outdone by a Whig opponent who traveled 800 miles on horseback and another 400 by steamboat while visiting twenty-eight counties and making thirty-eight speeches.[48]

The campaign itself mainly replayed 1844 without Texas, annexed in March. According to Davis, annexation was good for all Americans, and it had removed Texas from the political stage. At the outset, Davis had to confront a mini-rebellion in Democratic ranks when yet again enemies in Warren County tried to yoke him with the Briscoe Bill. Promptly, candidate Davis reiterated his firm anti-bank views that gave "general satisfaction" to Democrats. These professions along with the support of leading party newspapers quickly squelched the unhappy dissidents.[49]

Davis based his campaign for Congress on the traditional Democratic platform, with one notable addition. Emphasizing that Democratic and Whig ideals remained starkly different, Davis urged Mississippi voters to stand with him and his party on their principles of strict construction and states' rights. He condemned the Whigs for supporting a new national bank and high tariffs, which in his rhetoric hurt an agricultural people. A lower tariff and no national bank were his cries, and once in Congress, he told his audiences, he would help ensure the success of President Polk's program, which included reducing the tariff. Although he concentrated on these core issues, Davis also introduced a topic to appeal to Mississippians, a proposed navy yard for Ship and Cat Islands on the Gulf Coast. He pronounced such an installation essential for a proper defensive posture; besides, in his judgment, Mississippi had long been shortchanged on federal expenditures.[50]

Davis's speechmaking through the weeks of summer and autumn received high marks. A Democratic observer applauded him as "one of the first orators, and most effective speakers in the State." Others made equally positive assessments: "eloquent and convincing," "as effective . . . as we ever witnessed," "a master hand," "a masterly defense of the democratic party." The *Vicksburg Sentinel* was effusive, praising "his trumpet tones, his eagle look, and bold, free 'form and gesture.' " Even his Whig opponents spoke of him as "a handsome speaker," though they decried his attempts to mislead the voters.[51]

Davis's partisans gave his campaign performance unqualified commendation. A Democratic newspaper identified him as "one of the brightest stars in the state." Every Democratic sheet echoed the *Marion East Mississippian* in its celebration of "this eloquent champion of democracy," who presented "a clear, bold and eloquent exposition of his opinions." Lauding Davis, the *Vicksburg Sentinel* acclaimed him as "the impersonation of the true spirit of the South," informing its readers that it would watch "this brilliant and noble son" of the state "not with a cold approval, but with enthusiasm," for "we predict that he becomes the Calhoun of Mississippi."[52]

On November 3 and 4, Mississippi voters registered their absolute satisfaction with Davis and his fellow Democrats, all of whom won handily, with around 60 percent of the vote. Of the four Democrats, Davis gained the second highest vote total, 27,645, some 300 fewer than Jacob Thompson, an incumbent. Winning by such a margin would indicate that Davis ran well in all parts of the state, and he did, though he and his colleagues faltered in Whig strongholds like Adams and Warren Counties. In only one month Jefferson Davis would make another journey to Washington, D.C., this time as a United States congressman.[53]

Before heading north, Representative-elect Davis received another accolade from his community. Citizens attending a public meeting in Vicksburg on November 5 selected Davis to present the welcoming address at the anticipated visit of John C. Calhoun. En route by steamboat from New Orleans to Memphis for a conference on the federal government and western waterways, Calhoun was scheduled for a stopover in Vicksburg. But mechanical problems delayed the boat, and although it docked briefly, Calhoun did not disembark. He promised Davis that on his return trip he would pay a call on the city. Once again a public gathering was called to formulate plans for an appropriate reception for the venerable statesman, and for the second time in eight days Jefferson Davis was named to give the formal greeting.

The choice of Davis came from the respect Vicksburgers felt for him, not from any closeness between him and Calhoun. He had undoubtedly met Calhoun, then a United States senator, during his stay in Washington in the winter of 1837–38, but nothing suggests that they had seen each other since then. Although Varina Davis later claimed that an intimate friendship existed between her husband and Calhoun even in 1845, no surviving documents record a particularly close relationship between the two men, either then or later.[54]

Preparations had been made when on November 18 at about 4 p.m. word came by steamer that Calhoun would reach Vicksburg in an hour or so, but that news turned out to be more than a little optimistic. When the vessel carrying Calhoun finally arrived at ten o'clock, many of those assembled to greet him had gone home. A substantial crowd remained, however, including "the attentive cannoneers," who "gave the great Carolinian a salute that shook the hills and waked a thousand echoes from the opposite side of the river." Calhoun was escorted from the landing through the streets to a hotel where he was introduced to a crowd of between 300 and 400.[55]

After the introduction, Davis rose for his official greeting. He had worried over his speech and prepared it carefully, with Varina writing it out in her "best hand." She disclosed that before speaking, Davis's anxiety verged on dread. Although he was a veteran and effective stump speaker, he had never spoken before such an august personage. He admired Calhoun enormously and obviously wanted the great man to think well of him. In addition, this would be the first time his wife would hear him speak in public, and according to her he requested that she not look at him while he spoke. As she reported the event, all his worries had been for naught. Although he began tentatively, "his voice grew round and clearer until it filled the large hall to the echo."

Only Varina in her *Memoir* provides any details about Davis's remarks. In her summary he welcomed Calhoun and the assembly, then "passed in rapid review" through current issues like the tariff and Texas. Following "a strong appeal" for strict construction and a paean to the country, he recounted Calhoun's distinguished public career. Not surprisingly, the Vicksburg newspaper accounts, albeit terse, had a partisan tone. The Democratic sheet satisfied itself with commending Davis's "accustomed eloquence," while its Whig counterpart thought the thirty-minute speech somewhat too prejudicial for the occasion.[56]

After Calhoun tendered brief comments of gratitude, ladies were presented to him and then dancing began. Although Calhoun did not really know Jefferson Davis and had never met Varina Davis, she certainly captivated him that November evening. Her older brother, who attended the reception, wrote to their mother that Calhoun "did not leave [Varina] an instant during his stay in the room, which was about three hours." Before leaving, the sixty-three-year-old Calhoun informed young Joseph Howell that despite his sister's youth, "he had never met with a lady with whose manners he was more pleased, or of whose talents he had a higher opinion." The twenty-one-year-old Howell thought that "the old man indeed seemed quite struck with her," so much so that "he walked with no one else talked with no one else, and seemed to have no use for his eyes except to look at her and Mr. Davis." In Joseph Howell's reading of the situation, that singular attention miffed several other ladies, one especially whom he described as wearing a dress that "expos[ed] more of her person than . . . any *lady* would care about." Sometime after midnight Calhoun finally left Varina's side and "amid loud plaudits" departed for his steamboat.[57]

In less than six months Jefferson Davis had participated significantly in celebrating two of the dominant political leaders of Jacksonian America, Andrew Jackson himself and John C. Calhoun. To Davis, Jackson stood as the unblemished hero and the formative leader of his party, who embodied patriotism and the majesty of the nation. He identified Calhoun as the great contemporary expositor of the sacred states' rights creed and the paramount guardian of southern rights in the Union. Although Davis revered both, they had become bitter personal and political enemies during Jackson's presidency when Calhoun served as Jackson's first vice president and then as a U.S. senator from South Carolina. Their personal conflict resulted from two enormously able, ambitious, and proud men vying for power. Ambition and pride also marked their political strife, a discord massively amplified by the Nullification Crisis, in which Jackson boldly proclaimed national supremacy in the face of Calhoun's insistence on the absolute rights of individual states. Glossing over these sharp and deep differences, Davis saw them both as patriotic Americans and good southerners and as believers in states' rights and the Union. Balancing these potentially contradictory ideals formed Davis's political vision.

For Jefferson Davis the evening with Calhoun was yet another singular event in a notable year highlighted by his second marriage in February and his election to Congress in November. In the midst of these happy occasions Davis had to deal with one sad event. While campaigning in northern Mississippi, he received the news of his mother's death on October 3. Immediately he rode to Woodville. Eighty-four years old, Jane Davis died at the original Davis property in Mississippi, Poplar Grove, by that time the home of her daughter Lucinda and son-in-law William Stamps. The precise date of the funeral service is unknown, but with Jefferson present she was buried in the family cemetery at Poplar Grove. Although Varina's later account is mistaken about Jefferson's whereabouts at this unhappy time, there is no reason to doubt her testimony that he was "much overcome" by the loss of his mother. He had never expressed any but positive sentiments about Jane Davis, who had always cherished her youngest child and had never given him reason to doubt her affection. Following the funeral, Davis returned to the hustings, with his next recorded appearance in Natchez on October 22.

With a major political victory and the Calhoun fête behind him, Congressman-elect Jefferson Davis left Vicksburg on November 19 for Washington and the opening of Congress. He did not travel alone. Accompanying him was reelected Congressman Robert W. Roberts, as well as Varina and his niece Mary Jane Bradford. At that time most representatives and senators did not take their wives and families to the capital. The expense of a family in Washington, the paucity of suitable housing, and the relative brevity of many congressional sessions all combined to make almost a literal brotherhood among lawmakers.

That Jefferson brought along Varina signals graphically that they very much desired to be together.

Jefferson's absence from Brierfield during the long campaign had not dampened their enthusiasm for each other. While traveling around Mississippi courting voters, he wrote openly to his young wife that he missed her. During his political peregrination, Varina kept busy as a plantation mistress. As part of caring for the slaves, she oversaw the making of clothes for them, a task in which she participated, at times rising at dawn to ensure accomplishment of the work. She also spent time with "the cotton book," which meant that she was keeping track of the critical autumn activity, picking cotton.

Her social life focused on the Hurricane family and on her older brother, Joseph Davis Howell, who lived at Brierfield while his brother-in-law was away. All got along quite well. Although Varina complained to her mother about "my *usual pains*" and once suffered from swollen neck glands, for which she used leeches, her brother thought that her health had improved since her marriage. Varina's letters from these months, along with those of people close to her, describe a happy, fulfilled young woman, though she surely missed her "Jeffy."[58]

Jefferson's political triumph pleased her immensely, but she wondered whether she was "proper proud of [her] good man" because she saw the victory "as a just tribute to his merit." She contemplated her role as wife, and she clearly wanted to succeed in it. Writing to her mother, she talked about what she had to do in order to be a good wife. "I feel that Jeff's love is only to be returned by the practice of self control, and that it is the only mode of gaining his esteem and confidence." Although she characterized her husband as caring and responsive, she told Margaret Howell that even if he were not, "your approbation must always be incentive to do what I know you will say I should do for God's sake."[59]

When the Davis party departed from Vicksburg, no one anticipated what Jefferson afterwards called "a very severe trip." They took the northern route to Washington—by steamboat up the Mississippi and then the Ohio to either Wheeling, Virginia (now West Virginia), or Pittsburgh, and finally overland to the capital. An early winter blast turned the journey into an ordeal. Ice clogging the Ohio stopped boats some forty-five miles downstream from Wheeling, requiring all passengers to disembark. With the ground covered with snow and no public conveyances available, Davis by "considerable maneuvering" procured a common woodshed and nailed stanchions on the sides and planks to them. Sitting atop the baggage on this ersatz sled, the Davises and their companions took two cold days and one spill down a frozen hillside to reach Wheeling. Along the way they spent the night at "a fine looking frame house" where, Varina learned, her mother with a small son had stayed many years earlier. In Wheeling the four passengers shifted to a stage for a jolting ride in which they often found themselves pitched up to the roof. "On several occasions" when the stage threatened to leave the snow-choked road, the men piled out to chock wheels. During this journey Varina reported that Jefferson cheered the group, "always ready with some pleasant story, making light of the discomforts, and sometimes singing 'We'll tough it out till morning.' " Finally, after some three weeks of "peril, discomfort, and cold," the travelers reached Washington.[60]

No one would have mistaken the national capital in 1845 for a grand city. The great English writer Charles Dickens pictured it as "the city of Magnificent intentions" with "spacious avenues, that begin in nothing, and lead nowhere." The federal district appeared more like a half dozen country villages than a unified city. Neither the Capitol nor the Washington Monument had been completed, and the city lacked basic amenities such as gaslights on the streets and any semblance of a sewage system. An omnipresent noisome odor resulted from the nearby swamps and trash-filled vacant lots. In addition, cows, swine, and geese as well as dogs and cats roamed the streets, contributing to the stench.[61]

Upon reaching this somewhat ragged place with grand aspirations, the Davises stopped at the National Hotel on Pennsylvania Avenue. After about ten days they found rooms for themselves and their niece in a nearby boardinghouse, also on Pennsylvania Avenue. Most congressmen and senators who had come to Washington without wives and families lived in boardinghouses, or messes, as they were called. In the Davis mess were two more Mississippians, Jacob Thompson and Stephen Adams, both with wives, and several others. When Davis's old friend George W. Jones visited during that winter, he too joined the mess.[62]

By the time Jefferson Davis had completed his arduous trek to the capital, the first session of the Twenty-ninth Congress had already commenced. On December 8, one week late, he appeared at the Capitol, was sworn in, and took his seat. The chamber of the House of Representatives that Davis entered was "a beautiful and spacious hall, of semicircular shape, supported by handsome pillars," and still illuminated with candles. The height to the top of the entablature was 35 feet to accommodate a ladies' gallery at the south end and a larger public gallery. Decorative scarlet curtains hanging in the galleries also muffled sounds. Above the members rose a 57-foot dome with painted caissons to represent the dome of the Pantheon in Rome. At the center of the dome, a handsome cupola served both to please the eye and admit light. All congressmen had their own desks and chairs arranged in groups of three in a semicircle facing the speaker's rostrum. Above it stood a plaster statue of liberty atop an eagle with wings spread.[63]

Freshman representative Jefferson Davis began his congressional career as a member of the majority, with Democrats comfortably outnumbering Whigs. Most of the Democrats wanted to use their dominance to help President Polk enact his program of traditional Democratic measures, such as lowering the tariff and reestablishing the Independent Treasury, and of spurring the westward march of the United States all the way to the Pacific Ocean. Although only in his first term, Jefferson Davis began setting forth ideas and themes that would mark his public life for the next decade and a half.

Davis had been in the House for some two months when he rose on February 6, 1846, to make his first major congressional speech during the debate on the Oregon question. A fellow representative described his appearance as "prepossessing—tall, slender, with a soldierly bearing, a fine head, an intellectual face; there was a look of culture and refinement about him that made a favorable impression from the first, and the attainments he displayed, even in conversation, commanded the respect of those who met him." In his remarks Davis talked about the uniqueness of his country and the inevitability of American progress. The Oregon matter before Congress involved both ownership and boundaries. Since 1818 the United States and Great Britain had agreed to a joint occupation of the area, with the agreement providing that either party could give notice of one year for terminating joint occupation. That was precisely what President Polk, absolutely confident about his country's title, wanted to do. But while notification of termination was straightforward, establishing a border was more complex. The Democratic platform of 1844 had called for the occupation of the whole of Oregon, with its northern boundary at 54°40', far up into British Canada. Britain, recognizing that in Oregon Americans enjoyed a numerical advantage of almost seven to one over its own citizens, decided to give up its claim to the territory in return for American acceptance of a northern boundary at 49 degrees, extending the American-Canadian border from the Rocky Mountains on westward to the Pacific Ocean. That possibility angered many Democrats, especially from the old Northwest, who wanted the president to uphold the party platform, even if it meant war.

In his address to the House, Davis steadfastly backed the president in his advocacy of notice and his acceptance of 49 degrees. Speaking at length on the right of Americans to colonize Oregon for agricultural purposes, he announced: "Our people have removed the 'Far West' into Oregon." He maintained, "American hearts have gone over the mountains, and American laws should follow," and found the secret of American expansion in "the energy and restless spirit of adventure, which is characteristic of our people." In his view, these qualities explained why hardworking citizens "left the repose of civil government to plunge into the haunts of savage beast and savage men." According to Davis, settlers "have gone to the school of the wilderness" from which they would produce an agricultural country that would benefit many. Declaring that this mission sharply contrasted the Americans in Oregon with the British, who were satisfied with fur trading and had no interest in opening and cultivating the land, he maintained that the westward movement should continue "until our people shall sit down on the shores of the Pacific and weep that there are no more forests to subdue." Davis had absorbed enthusiastically the doctrine of Manifest Destiny, which proclaimed that the superior American culture and people should predominate from ocean to ocean in order to bring civilization and progress to the backward, lesser races, whether Native Americans or Mexicans.

Despite his ardent convictions about an American Oregon, the prospect of war troubled Davis. Disagreeing with the bellicose rhetoric reverberating through the chamber, Davis said simply that war did not provide "the purifier" nor blood the "aliment" for free institutions. Although he admitted that at times republics, including his own, had been "cradled in war," he cautioned that "more often they have met with a grave in that cradle." Advocating the boundary compromise as a policy of peace, he urged approval of 49 degrees. In his judgment, nothing but "national rights or national honor" could justify war, and he perceived neither in this question. Here he could find only the termination of a treaty on agreed-upon terms. In the end, the position that Davis supported prevailed. During the summer the United States and

Great Britain assented to a plan that made Oregon solely American and drew its northern boundary along the 49th parallel.[64]

The advance of American institutions toward the Pacific was not the only brand of progress that Congressman Davis championed. The first session of the Twenty-ninth Congress had to decide what to do about James Smithson's gift to the country. An Englishman, Smithson in 1829 bequeathed his fortune to a nephew with the provision that if the nephew died without an heir, the money should go to the United States. When that happened, more than $500,000 was delivered to the U.S. government in 1838. After various proposals for its use had been submitted, including the founding of a national university, the House in December 1845 created a special committee to consider the creation of the Smithsonian Institution. Placed on the seven-man committee, Jefferson Davis became an ardent proponent of using the money for establishing the Institution, which to his mind would benefit science and encourage "the diffusion of every kind of helpful knowledge." To those who argued that the government had no authority to take charge of education, Davis answered that the proposal did not put education under governmental aegis. Instead, the work accomplished under the auspices of the Institution would aid science and assist in spreading new information throughout the country. His commitment was firm and deeply felt: "Knowledge [is] the common cement that unite[s] all the heterogeneous materials of this Union into one mass, like the very pillars before us." The House did eventually pass a substitute bill, though it did not alter the purpose which Davis supported so fervently. President Polk signed the bill into law in August.[65]

During this session Davis also distinctly enunciated his vision of the Constitution and his concept of federal power. His opportunity occurred during the debate over the Rivers and Harbors Bill, an internal improvements measure that included providing federal funds to construct harbors in river ports and to improve navigation in rivers. Davis registered a strong dissent to the claim that the constitutional mandate of providing for a navy conferred a right for river and harbor improvements in order to promote commercial maritime activities as a "nursery for seamen." In his judgment, the proposal before the House sought simply "to appropriate money, not to execute a granted power . . . to substitute the discretion of the Government for the specific enumeration of objects for which, by the Constitution, appropriations are permitted." The proposition advanced by proponents that constitutional justification derived from "a sort of floating right" by which the government could determine "the means necessary and proper" to effect its chosen end appalled Davis. He denounced this formulation as "wholly irreconcilable to the very idea of specific grants, or the existence of reserved and sovereign powers within the States. When the States entered into a union, and established this Government as the agent of their league," he lectured his fellow lawmakers, "they gave to it certain carefully enumerated powers, with authority to make all *laws* which should be *necessary and proper* for carrying those powers into execution."

Davis went on to make absolutely clear his conception of the relationship between the states and the federal government, which undergirded his reading of the Constitution. "To all which has been said of the inherent powers of the Government, I answer, it is the creature of the States; as such it could have no inherent power, all it preserves was delegated by the States, and it is therefore that our Constitution is not an instrument of limitations, but of grants." As such, "whatever was then deemed necessary was specifically conveyed; beyond the power so granted, nothing can now be claimed except those incidents which are indispensable to its existence; not merely convenient or conducive, but subordinate and necessary to the exercise of the grants." After this discourse on strict construction, really an exposition of John C. Calhoun's constitutional theories, Davis called on the memory of his hero—and Calhoun's archenemy—Andrew Jackson, who in Davis's view had checked with the presidential veto the internal-improvements mania and the Constitution-stretching of his time. "Let Democrats remember," he cried, "and make the application." Not all Democrats heeded Davis's call, however, and the bill passed the House and the Senate also. But, harking back to his famous predecessor, President Polk vetoed the act.[66]

Committed to faith in the beneficence as well as the efficiency of American technological progress, Davis also championed the professionalism beginning to mark the industrializing economies. In congratulating the American army for its victories in May 1846 in several small but sharp encounters against Mexican troops in the Rio Grande Valley, Congress extolled the virtues of American fighting men. Davis participated in the chorus, but he added another verse praising the professional training undergone at West Point by most officers in the engagements. American courage and spirit could not have prevailed, Davis argued, without the "military science" resulting from a professional education. He agreed that neither George Washington, Andrew Jackson, nor Zachary Taylor, the American commander along the Rio Grande, had experienced such an education, but he insisted that all of them understood the need for a school like West Point to train men for the profession of arms. According to Davis, battlefield success depended upon fortifications properly constructed and situated and on artillery correctly handled, and only professional training could guarantee those outcomes. Davis maintained to the House that the events along the Rio Grande proved the worth of West Point.

Davis's praise of professionalism got him in trouble with some colleagues for what they perceived as a condescending attitude toward ordinary Americans. Among those offended was Andrew Johnson, Democrat of Tennessee, who not for the last time took issue with Jefferson Davis. While emphasizing the necessity of professional education so that soldiers could effectively handle complex military matters, Davis declared that not just any blacksmith or tailor could do so. Johnson, a former tailor, took exception to remarks that he deemed made "an invidious distinction," and proudly identified himself with workingmen. He thundered "that he knew we had an illegitimate, swaggering, bastard, scrub aristocracy, who assumed to know a good deal, but who, when the flimsy veil of pretension was torn off from it, was shown to possess neither talents, information, nor a foundation on which you can rear a superstructure that would be useful." Davis hastened to make clear that he intended no such slight; rather, he "merely said that scientific education was as necessary in the art of war as was the proper training in any other occupation or profession." He went on to apologize, for he had no intention "of wantonly wounding the feelings or of making insidious reflections upon the origins or occupation of any man." The reporter noted: "the debate in all its stages not being of an entirely pleasant nature."[67]

Although slavery as a political or ideological issue did not become central in Davis's initial congressional session, he did not hesitate to speak forthrightly on behalf of the South's major social institution when the occasion presented itself. He certainly did not believe that slave property should be kept out of Oregon by congressional mandate. Only ten days after Davis took his seat, a Massachusetts representative declaimed against slavery, asserting that whenever it existed, "the high moral character and perfectibility of man was not to be found." Riposting, Davis asked whether the speaker had forgotten that John Adams, John Quincy Adams, and other worthies hailed from a state that for a long time had tolerated slavery. Uneasy about the "envy, jealousy, and sectional strife" that he saw "eating like rust in the bonds our fathers expected to bind us," Davis ascribed these negative characteristics to certain northerners, not to southerners. Focusing on the monument at Bunker Hill just outside Boston as a symbol of freedom and union, he declared that the South gloried in the nation and in national triumphs. He condemned abolitionism while he distinguished the "manly and patriotic sentiments" of northerners who loved the Constitution and the Union. "Yes, sir, when ignorance, led by fanatic hate, and armed by all uncharitableness, assails a domestic institution of the South, I try to forgive, for the sake of the righteous among the wicked—our natural allies, the Democracy of the North."[68]

Jefferson Davis did not spend all of his working time on the floor of the House listening to colleagues and making speeches. From the outset he recognized the importance of directly serving his constituents, and he realized that many voters expected tangible results from those they elected. Davis had no doubt about who had sent him to Congress and who would control his tenure there. He worked on his correspondence until two or three in the morning, and with only Varina's assistance, he franked every letter and document sent back to Mississippi. She worried about the effect on his eyes, which became so red and painful that she wrote her mother they "even lose their beauty to me." She wished he would work less and go out more. Despite Varina's concern, Davis did participate in the social season, attending and enjoying parties and dinners with his wife. Illness also continued to assault him, with recurrent painful earaches and high fever, but never deterred his work for long.[69]

Myriad concerns occupied the attention of the freshman congressman. He made sure that Mississippi newspapers, even some of the Whig persuasion, received pertinent government publications. To the House he presented private petitions requesting action on military pensions and various matters involving land titles. He worked to get Mississippians appointed to West Point and other federal positions. In these endeavors he used whatever tack he thought would be effective. Attempting to get a midshipman's warrant in the United States Navy for a young Mississippian, Davis reminded the secretary of the navy that "we of Mississippi have less than our proportionate share of Navy appointments." When bureaucratic or congressional action was slow in coming, he remained active. Reporting to a constituent that he did not yet have the answer to a land problem, he went on, "not willing to delay any longer I write now to assure you that your case shall not be neglected." He told his correspondents that he would be "glad at all times" to hear from them and that he wanted to serve them "whenever and however I can."[70]

Congressman Davis stood as a stalwart administration man, though he never became a party robot. On matters it identified as crucial, the Polk administration could count on him. He was especially active in defending Secretary of the Treasury Robert J. Walker, formerly a U.S. senator from Mississippi, against charges of venality. In fact, he attached himself to Walker both politically and socially. Yet as a member of the House committee to investigate accusations that the celebrated Massachusetts Whig senator Daniel Webster had been guilty of malfeasance when serving as secretary of state under John Tyler, Davis refused to let the inquiry turn him into a zealous partisan. Convinced of Webster's innocence, Davis voted to absolve him of any wrongdoing. Davis's general performance impressed another notable Massachusetts Whig, ex-president, now congressman, and often acerbic, John Quincy Adams. Although Davis was a good Democrat, he was a skilled political trader as well as a party loyalist. In the summer of 1846, he delayed leaving Washington for service in the Mexican War until the House had decided on tariff reduction. In return for promising President Polk that he would remain in Congress until the crucial vote, Davis won the president's pledge that he would direct the secretary of war to fill promptly all of Davis's military requisitions.[71]

While Jefferson Davis learned the political ways of Washington, the capital electrified Varina Davis. To her the people looked so grand and sophisticated; the social life she found exhilarating and the talk at times almost intoxicating. She attended parties and gave her own, proudly informing her mother that she was known for "giving the most delightful little hops of the season." Whether guest or hostess, Varina carefully noted her clothes and her impressions. Picturing her new hat of black silk velvet with a long drooping plume on the shoulder and white velvet flowers inside, she reported, "it becomes me very much." At a White House dinner she contrasted herself, in a "black watered silk, and a white polka dress made of bobbinet, and trimmed with my wedding lace—a white japonica in my hair," with Mrs. Polk, who appeared, in Varina's eyes, "dressed to death." President Polk fared no better; "an insignificant looking little man," she called him. Nothing excited her more than the intelligence and cleverness of so many of the men and women she met. Participating in a conversation with her husband and former president John Tyler, whom she thought impressive, especially thrilled her. She vividly remembered one "delightful evening" when a congressman and the vice president of the United States "talked to each other and to me of Byron and Wordsworth, of Dante and Virgil." Even after four and a half decades her enthusiasm and wonder at the place and the people leap from the pages of her *Memoir*.[72]

But although Washington captured her spirit and imagination, Jefferson remained the center of her world. She confided to her mother that she did not desire "any admiration but Jeffy's," and she esteemed his speeches, copies of which she sent her parents, as "*great* of *course*." When she had to choose between going to social functions or staying at home with a sick husband, she remained by his side. On those occasions, caring and tender, she nursed a husband who in her own words always bore suffering "patiently." But she was obviously thrilled when they went out together, and especially with "Jeff's elegant manners." She did not even mind his "flirt[ing] to his heart's content" at one of her own gatherings. Even in the midst of this social whirl, Varina still thought seriously about herself. "My manners are much improved," she stated to her mother. And she noted with pride, "I have lost a great deal of that emb[ar]rassed angry looking manner which made me [appear] to so much disadvantage." Clearly, Washington was a maturing as well as a stirring experience for the young woman of nineteen.[73]

For his part, Jefferson evinced emotions equally strong and solicitous. Sometime in the spring of 1846 the Davises engaged a place in Virginia no more than a day's travel west of Washington, where they could escape the rising heat and humidity of the city. From this retreat in late June, Varina wrote her husband that she had become ill with an undisclosed malady. Responding immediately, he thanked her for the "sweet letter . . . bearing on its face that ardent love you have always manifested. . . ." Anxious about her illness, he wanted to be present "to cheer [your] heart and to relieve [your] pain." He wished her with him, but reflection convinced him that she would be better off in the cooler climate. Before joining her, he was waiting for the vote on the tariff bill, but he made clear that "if my presence is necessary to you all other things must yield." Unmentioned in his communication was any reference to a tension that in the previous two weeks had grown between them and might easily have contributed to Varina's distress. By early June, Jefferson Davis had made a unilateral decision that would be crucial for his future and his marriage. He had decided to join the forces heading for the Mexican War.[74]

CHAPTER SIX

"It May Be That I Will
Return with a Reputation"

War broke out between the United States and Mexico because of James K. Polk's expansionist policy. Not only was he determined to have an American Oregon, he also coveted California, the area below Oregon, which belonged to Mexico. At the same time President Polk was negotiating with Great Britain over Oregon, he was also attempting with intimidation and money to settle territorial matters with Mexico. When Texas entered the Union as a state in December 1845, it claimed the Rio Grande as its boundary. Mexico, never having recognized Texas's independence, broke diplomatic relations with the United States to protest the annexation; and it insisted that the southern and western boundary of Texas rested on the Nueces River, around 130 miles north of the Rio Grande. Polk moved on two fronts, in the summer ordering a military force to cross the Nueces and in the fall of 1845 sending a diplomatic mission to Mexico with instructions to secure by purchase his territorial goals: the Rio Grande boundary; New Mexico as a land bridge between Texas and California; and, the great prize, California itself. But, confronting a public opinion extremely hostile to giving up any more territory, the Mexican government unceremoniously rebuffed Polk's financial overtures.

Even before the complete failure of his attempt to buy what he wanted, Polk had ordered an army of some 4,000 men under Brigadier General Zachary Taylor from the Nueces to the Rio Grande. While Mexico considered this movement an invasion, Polk wanted to position himself to defend American interests if war occurred after his diplomatic gambit failed, as it indeed did in March 1846. With word of the Mexican rebuff, he began to prepare a war message to Congress arguing that Mexico refused to recognize legitimate American claims. In the meantime two opposing forces glared at each other across the Rio Grande, and with such proximity conflict was almost inevitable. In late April an exchange of fire between Mexican and American units on the northern side of the river left eleven Americans dead. When that news reached Washington two weeks later, President Polk, proclaiming that Mexico had killed American soldiers on American soil, sent a war message to Congress on May 11. Responding promptly, Congress in two days voted men and money along with a declaration that war was the consequence of Mexican aggression. By that time, north of the Rio Grande, two pitched battles had taken place between the contesting armies, both resulting in American victories.[1]

From the beginning, Congressman Jefferson Davis fell into step with the Mexican War. On May 11 he cast his ballot for the declaration of war and for raising men and money to fight it. Shortly thereafter the president asked for Davis's opinion on appointments of officers for a new regiment. In his response Davis commented generally on the rank given those placed in the additional unit and suggested specifically a name for its commander. From the battle zone itself he heard from a former friend in uniform, "We have war in earnest on the Rio Grande." When tidings of the American victories at Palo Alto and Resaca de la Palma reached Washington, Davis requested a suspension of House rules to propose a resolution specifying awards for all those engaged. Congress did commend all, but only General Taylor received a medal.[2]

In Mississippi, war fever reigned. "TO ARMS TO ARMS!!!—MISSISIPPI-ANS!!!," the cry of one newspaper reverberated throughout the state. In almost every county, militia units rushed to volunteer for service in the conflict. One Davis correspondent captured the ardor: "We are in great excitement, drums, beating, fifes, playing, flags flying, meetings holding, and 'To Arms, to arms,' in large Capitols stuck up at every corner of the streets, and at every fork of the roads." In the eyes of this enthusiast, patriotism had superseded partisanship. "There is no Whig & Democrat now!" he wrote. "We are all one; striving shoulder to shoulder to prepare for the coming strife." All hungered for news from Taylor's army.

Eager to join the fight, by June some 17,000 Mississippians in twenty-two separate militia organizations congregated at Vicksburg, the point designated for volunteers to be received into the United States Army. Bitter disappointment followed the information that the

War Department had authorized from the state only one regiment of infantry for twelve months' service. That directive held despite an effort by the governor to have the quota increased. In Vicksburg, the receiving officer selected ten companies to make up the First Mississippi Regiment. For this virgin unit of 936 officers and men, the initial order of business was the election of field officers, a colonel, a lieutenant colonel, and a major. The secretary of war had directed that officers be selected according to the laws of each given state.[3]

Davis took a direct part in Mississippi events. He joined with others in the state's congressional delegation to recommend to President Polk the appointment of John A. Quitman of Natchez as one of the new brigadier generals. Then, in a letter to a friend, which appeared in the *Sentinel and Expositor* and several other sheets in the state, he announced that he would very much like to command a Warren County unit. He thought his military education and experience would enable him "to be of service to Mississippians who take the field." "If they wish it," he declared, "I will join them as soon as possible, wherever they may be."[4]

The men of the First Mississippi certainly knew about Davis and his interest in leading them. The Democratic editor in Vicksburg pumped Davis as "a man of military knowledge—experience—sagacity—character, and high and soldier like bearing." Furthermore, this champion of Congressman Davis proclaimed, "He is burning to leave the luxurious Halls of Congress and join his brethren on the Soldier's field of toil and glory!" In addition, of the ten companies chosen for the regiment, three came from Davis's home counties, two from Warren and one from Wilkinson, where he enjoyed particularly strong support even among Whigs. Of course, Davis's statewide campaigns of 1844 and 1845 had given him a name and reputation throughout Mississippi. And he had clearly signaled that he would accept command of the regiment if offered to him.[5]

Although Davis surely had his partisans among the volunteers, he was not the only person desirous of the colonelcy, and he was still in Washington when the vote took place on June 18. Five names, including Davis's, were placed in nomination, including two major generals in the Mississippi militia, one of whom had been in the Second Seminole War. On the initial ballot, that veteran, Alexander B. Bradford, a fifty-six-year-old Whig from Marshall County in the northern part of the state, won a plurality with 350 votes. Davis ran a strong second with 300; the remainder were scattered. Under the laws of Mississippi, Bradford was elected because militia elections did not require a majority. Bradford, however, expressed the view that the colonel of the regiment should have a majority, not merely a plurality, and he immediately resigned. On the second ballot Davis emerged as almost the consensual choice, winning more than two-thirds of the votes. Now he was a full colonel and regimental commander, quite an advance beyond his previous highest rank of first lieutenant.[6]

While Davis made himself visible both in Washington and in Mississippi as an advocate of the Mexican War and a possible participant in it, the subject became a major issue in his private life. From the onset of hostilities he had been talking with Varina about once again donning a uniform. She left him no room to doubt her wishes. Forcefully opposing his volunteering for active service, she termed their discussion "a struggle." Although "it was carried on in love," she found it "not the less bitter." Finally, Jefferson promised Varina that he would not volunteer.

That promise he did not keep. Almost as soon as he made it, he broke it. Despite his wife's vigorous resistance, he decided unilaterally that once again he would become a soldier, but he did not forthrightly share with her that resolution. The allure of the war was simply too potent. He saw duty calling; with his nation drawing its sword, he could not envision remaining at home while his countrymen and literally his neighbors rushed to its defense. Moreover, the conflict presented an opportunity to test his education and military training on a battlefield, a powerful magnet for a former professional soldier. Combat could also mean military glory for himself, an ambition shared by so many from his time and place. Finally, though he never articulated this consideration, Davis knew what accomplishments in war could mean for his political career. Since George Washington, military heroes had captivated Americans. Davis's own personal hero, Andrew Jackson, had secured his place with American voters because of his performance at New Orleans in 1815. Antebellum Mississippians lived in a society filled with militia companies and militia officers. Military rank, even won as political patronage, carried prestige and respect. For Davis, as for most of his constituents, nothing else could match the esteem and honor of upholding the flag on the field of battle.

Davis's decision stunned his wife. Telling her mother that she "found out last night accidentally that he had committed himself about going," she confessed, "I have cried until I am stupid, but you know there is 'no use crying, better luck next time.' " Still, she grieved, "I am so miserable I feel as if I could lay down my life to be near you and Father." She supposed that he could not help deciding to go, and in so doing violating his commitment to her, but her hurt was real. "Jeff thinks there is *something* the matter with me, but I *know* there is not," she informed Margaret Howell. She did qualify her lament: "if Jeff was a cross bad husband, old, ugly, or stupid I could better bear for him to go on a year's campaign, but he is so tender, and good that I feel like he ought never to leave me." But he probably will, and "god only knows how bitter it is to me." Still, "I can bear it." Bearing it, however, would mean joining her parents. "If I must lose my only treasure, I *will* be with those *equally* dear to me."[7]

Despite his wife's obvious distress, Congressman Davis did not bend from his determination to become Colonel Davis. When the verdict from Vicksburg along with a tender of the commission as colonel of the First Mississippi Regiment reached Washington, he readily accepted. Even so, he kept his bargain with President Polk, not leaving Washington until July 4, the day after he had voted with the majority in the House for the Walker Tariff. The Davises returned home by the same northern route they had taken to Washington some eight months previously. This time, they had a most pleasant journey. Instead of snow and ice, Varina remembered, "the whole mountain sides were rosy with the blossoms of the laurel, and nothing could have been more attractive than the scenery." On this trip Jefferson focused his attention on the three matters most crucial to him: his wife, his political career, and his return to uniform.[8]

Varina's well-being deeply concerned him. Her health still worried him as it had for the past month, and he really wanted her to remain in the North for the summer, but she was determined to go back to Mississippi with him. What to do with her while he was away at war also caused him anxiety. From a steamboat on the Ohio River, he wrote his beloved sister Lucinda that if "circumstances warranted," he would send Varina to live with her. Acknowledging what he perceived as possible difficulties with his wife, he told Lucinda, "To you and your family alone of all the world could I entrust her and rest assured that no waywardness would ever lessen kindness." But he indicated that Varina would "probably" live with her mother during most of his absence. Staying at Hurricane would not work, for Varina "could not be contented" with Eliza, "nor would their residing together increase their good feeling for each other." That fact, Davis confided, "distresses me as you will readily imagine, but if you ever have an opportunity to understand Varina's character, you will see the propriety of the conclusion, and I feel that you will love her too much to take heed of the weaknesses which spring from a sensitive and generous temper."[9]

Although he found making arrangements for Varina vexing, he never forgot that he remained a sitting congressman. He left Washington with Congress still in session, though he did not resign. From the steamboat the *Star Spangled Banner*, on July 13 Davis wrote a public letter "To the People of Mississippi," explaining his early departure from the capital and reporting on his actions while there. First, his being chosen by Mississippians to lead them into Mexico accounted for his heading home early. He had accepted that post of responsibility because he believed his military education and experience meant both that his service was due his country and that he could help the Mississippi regiment. He hastened to add that he had not abandoned any critical measures that would face close votes. He had even stayed on after getting his commission to vote for the lower Walker Tariff, which did pass the House, and he was also certain it would gain approval in the Senate. Then he recounted his activities on subjects ranging from the Independent Treasury and Oregon to his support for the effort to obtain alternate sections of public land to aid in building the Mississippi & Alabama Railroad. Defending the administration's Mexican policy, he maintained that it had tried to resolve differences with that country but had been spurned. When Mexico crossed the Rio Grande and attacked our troops, Davis asserted, the president and all Americans had to defend the flag. Defining his sense of the relationship between his constituents and himself, he announced that he had "acted upon all measures as seemed to me best to accord with the principles upon which I was elected, and most likely to correspond with the wishes and interests of the people of Mississippi." He concluded by declaring that he had striven to be a good representative for Mississippi but that the voters would have the final judgment. "I will cheerfully submit to your decision."[10]

Traveling west and south, Davis also reflected upon and prepared for his return to the army. During much of the journey he "studied a little pocket edition of military tactics." Varina recalled that when she protested his absorption, her husband "explained agreeably the mysteries of enfilading, breaking column, hollow squares, and what not." To Lucinda he recounted how proud his election as colonel made him. He also unhesitatingly expressed his hope that his service might enhance his name and fame. If the opportunity arose, "it may be that I will return with a reputation over which you will rejoice as my Mother would have done."[11]

When Jefferson Davis reached home on July 13, he did not have much time to arrange his personal and business affairs. The orders he received before leaving Washington directed the First Mississippi to proceed immediately to the Rio Grande Valley and join General Taylor. In preparation for being transported to the war zone, the regiment had already gone downriver to New Orleans even before its colonel had officially taken command.[12]

At Davis Bend, Colonel Davis, in consultation with Joseph and Varina, made arrangements for the settlement of his wife and the management of his plantation during his absence. Although Jefferson and Varina had undoubtedly discussed these matters on their way south, details of the decisions made en route and in Mississippi have not survived. Varina would spend much of her time at Brierfield, with a niece of Jefferson's coming over from Hurricane to join her every night; the remainder chiefly with her parents in Natchez; but some time also with Joseph. To look after Brierfield, Davis decided to leave his slave overseer, James Pemberton, in charge. Davis and Pemberton discussed whether the slave should accompany his master to Mexico or remain on the plantation. According to Varina, her husband permitted James Pemberton to make the final decision, and he decided to stay at home. Of course, Joseph was just one mile down the road, if needed. Thus, the situation at Brierfield continued just as it had been with Davis in Washington, but for Varina's sometime presence. After the decision about Pemberton, Joseph provided his brother with one of his slaves, Jim Green, as a servant, and a fine Arabian horse named Tartar. With wife and plantation secure under the watchful eye of Joseph, Colonel Jefferson Davis set out for his regiment.[13]

Reaching New Orleans on July 17, Davis found his men encamped three miles below the city at Chalmette Plantation, the site of the Battle of New Orleans. Organized in ten companies, the regiment had an aggregate strength of 936 officers and men. Besides Davis, the other elected regimental officers were Lieutenant Colonel Alexander K. McClung, former federal marshal of the Northern District of Mississippi, and Major Alexander B. Bradford, the man who had a plurality on the first ballot for colonel. Davis found conditions atrocious; the troops were in open fields exposed to the rainy weather, with mud and water knee-deep. The awful sanitary conditions and neglected hygiene led to a lengthening sick list. Davis immediately got his unit moved to some empty cotton sheds closer to the city. This improved location did not completely satisfy volunteers eager to get to the war they had signed up to fight. Though chafing, the troops enthusiastically welcomed their commanding officer, for whom they had been waiting with "intense anxiety" and whom they believed would make a "gallant commander." Davis set promptly to work getting his regiment on board ships bound for the war. He was distressed that the percussion rifles he had been promised in Washington had not yet arrived.[14]

The avenue he took to prod delivery of the rifles revealed the army officer still operating as politician. On July 22, the date his first three companies sailed, he requested Secretary of the Treasury Walker to check on the whereabouts of the rifles. Walker evidently acted, for the rifles were eventually dispatched from New Orleans on revenue cutters controlled by the Treasury Department. In that same letter Davis also reported on Democratic political affairs in New Orleans. In Davis's view, Secretary Walker had great strength in the city, but something needed to be done with "the Custom house officers," who, Davis told Walker, "hang a dead weight upon you." In addition, he advised Walker that the Democratic newspaper could accomplish "much good if unembarrassed—more harm if rendered hostile to us." An observant, loyal, and ambitious Democrat, Jefferson Davis clearly did not want the Polk administration to forget about him.[15]

He also handled his own political position quite cautiously. Although he had accepted the commission as colonel, left Congress early, and actually assumed command of his regiment, he had not yet resigned his seat. His failure to do so did occasion some adverse comment in Mississippi, but the Democratic party in the state generally backed him on this point. The major Democratic newspaper pronounced that no obligation required him to depart officially; "on the contrary, we think he ought not resign." According to the *Mississippian,* the current session of Congress would not last much longer, and plenty of time remained for Davis to resign and a successor to be chosen for the next session, should he remain in the army. Davis had obviously discussed this matter with party officials, for on July 15 the *Mississippian* announced, "we think we are authorized to say he will not." Davis had left with Joseph a letter of resignation to be submitted at the appropriate time, if it came. Davis clearly did not want to act precipitously. If the war ended quickly and the First Mississippi disbanded, he wanted to redeem his congressman's seat, not simply return to private life. Not until mid-October did Joseph forward Jefferson's official resignation to the governor.[16]

Although politics did not disappear from Colonel Davis's field of vision, he focused on the military task at hand. Advance elements of the First Mississippi departed New Orleans on July 22 for Brazos Island, just north of the mouth of the Rio Grande, the staging area for reinforcements arriving from the United States. The next day, four more companies embarked; the remainder, with Davis amongst them, left on July 26. On the twenty-eighth the regiment came ashore, but it did not find the core of Taylor's army.

When Mexico did not give in or offer negotiations after Taylor's initial victories, Polk decided to step up the pressure. After all, his goal from the outset had been California, especially, and New Mexico. Always willing to risk war, he would not be deterred because it had begun. Now the administration directed General Taylor to invade northern Mexico, with the purpose of occupying that portion of the country in order to press Mexico to agree to American territorial demands. With the city of Monterrey his major target, Taylor had decided to establish the base for his invasion at Camargo, Mexico, around 240 river miles up the Rio Grande. When the Mississippians arrived, the bulk of his army was either already there or underway. Back at the mouth of the river and Brazos Island newly arriving units gathered and awaited steamboats to transport them to Camargo.[17]

The First Mississippi had come to a truly inhospitable spot. A treeless, sandy barrier key, Brazos Island was between three and four miles long and about two miles wide. In the middle of the summer the troops faced a merciless environment. When, after a few days, the regiment moved to the mouth of the river, conditions changed not at all. There were still no trees even along the low banks of the river. One soldier recorded, "I never experienced such heat from the sun in my life—never saw so many flies." And in what another called "a lone and desolate beach," there was no fresh water. Storms could bring welcome, though temporary, relief from the sun's rays, but they also left an unwelcome legacy: "every thing one eats and drinks has its own portion of land intermixed." Homesickness and diarrhea affected many of the young soldiers, who lived in tents pitched "on the ridge of serried hills which skirt[ed] the sea shore."[18]

The wait by the sea did not sit well with the regimental commander, who "chafed at delay." To Secretary Walker, Davis complained, "We

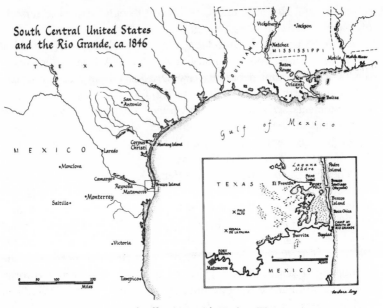

Seat of Jefferson Davis's Mexican War.
From Papers of Jefferson Davis, *III, with permission of the LSU Press*

have met delay and detention at every turn." Finally, the rifles arrived, but he asserted that the quartermaster at New Orleans had acted either "most incompetently or maliciously." Then the percussion caps, essential for firing the rifles, were held up. One of Davis's officers perceived that Davis's disgust at inefficiency and the halt at the mouth of the Rio Grande was aggravated by "the Col.'s heart being altogether set on military glory." For about a month, however, Davis had to cope with his own frustration and with an unhappy group of soldiers in a miserably hot and unhealthful place. In these weeks he concentrated on what he thought a responsible commander should enforce, the discipline and training of his troops. Unlike a number of the volunteer regiments where attention to the basics of military life was rare, the First Mississippi underwent a crash course in soldiering. Drill and then more drill occupied the men; guard was mounted and relieved in the regulation manner. At least one young soldier complained in his diary about this "strict Military Discipline." Davis even developed a manual of arms for using rifles that employed percussion caps. Because of these special weapons the First Mississippi acquired an appellation that stuck: "the Mississippi Rifles."[19]

While struggling with conditions in his pestilential camp, Davis did not forget his young wife back in Mississippi. In a tender, hasty note from New Orleans, "your Hubbie" spoke "with a heart full of love to own Winnie," a favored nickname. From southern Texas, their disagreement over his joining the army and his view of her proper conduct occupied his attention. Noting the "extraordinarily quiet voyage" across the Gulf of Mexico, he told Varina that the calmness of Gulf waters was fine, but her "agitation" concerned him much more. "May God have preserved you as calm," he preached. Acknowledging an "affectionate letter" from her, he adopted his fatherly stance, expressing pleasure that she was engaged in "useful and domestic things." He went on to lecture. "However unimportant in themselves each may be, it is the mass which constitutes the business of life, and as it is pursued so will it generally be found that a woman is happy and contented." Then he urged that "the season of our absence may be a season of reflection bearing fruits of soberness, and utility, and certainty of thought and action." He made absolutely clear his feeling that his reputation depended in no small part on her conduct. "My love for you placed my happiness in your keeping, our vows have placed my hono[r] and respectability in the same hands." Two weeks later, he sermonized: "Be pious, be calm, be useful, and charitable and temperate in all things."

Their marriage was not simply patriarchal or one-sided, however. He reported that he had not forgotten Varina's request "on the subject of profanity and have improved." The genuine affection and playfulness they shared also shone brightly: "Hubbie would kiss the paper he sends to his wife, but is in the midst of men, who though talking & whistling and wondering . . . have time enough to observe any thing the Col. does—I send a kiss upon the wires of love and feel earth, air & sea cannot break the connection."[20]

One connection which Davis reestablished was with his former father-in-law and now commanding general, Zachary Taylor. Upon his arrival on the Rio Grande, Davis received a warm welcoming letter from General Taylor. The estrangement between the two men, which went back more than a decade to Davis's army days and his courtship of Knox Taylor, had ended about two years earlier. In an apparently accidental meeting on a steamboat traveling between Vicksburg and

Natchez, they reconciled their past differences and commenced what would mature into a sincere friendship. Taylor did not hide his feelings: "I can assure you I am more than anxious to take you by the hand, & to have you & your command with or near me." But, Taylor said, the limited transportation meant that not all units could be moved inland at once, and those that disembarked on Brazos Island first were the first to leave. Hence, the script seemed to read, more waiting.[21]

Yet Taylor did give the First Mississippi priority over several other regiments that had preceded it to the coast. He also evidently informed Davis that he would ensure that the Mississippi Rifles would always be with him. When orders to start upriver arrived, the men began going on board the steamboats that would convey them up to Camargo, and by August 26 all the companies were underway. But though the regiment had departed from its hated sandspit, it had hardly set out on a pleasure cruise. The regimental quartermaster recounted a wretched journey: "Everybody dissatisfied, unhappy, the boat fetid & stinking, & many, very many, sick. I was suffering dreadfully with the universal complaint, diarrhea, so hot, such a dreadful stench from the necessities, biscuit half cooked, no place to poke one's head in where a moment's comfort could be found, night or day. The sick strewed about, some delirious & crying out for their friends. I became so weak that I could scarcely walk."[22]

At last the First Mississippi reached Camargo, a hot, dusty town with summer temperatures reaching well above 100 degrees. It rested on the San Juan River, three miles above its confluence with the Rio Grande. Though no paradise, Camargo was in Mexico, and there the Rifles joined the army poised for invasion. That force, which by September had swollen to 15,000 men, made its home in white tent cities outside the town.[23]

As Colonel Davis got his troops ready for the advance to Monterrey, some 100 miles southwest of Camargo, the First Mississippi had already suffered substantially from disease. By the end of August, 108 men had been discharged for health reasons, another 70 were listed as sick, and a number had died. In sum, the Rifles had already lost between 20 and 25 percent of their strength. In the midst of all this sickness, Davis himself, despite his medical history, escaped any debilitating illness.[24]

At Camargo, Davis was pleased with his reunion with Zachary Taylor, who had been promoted to major general because of his victories on the lower Rio Grande. Not all the troops, however, had full confidence in the plain-looking and stocky Taylor, who often, even in his mode of dress, seemed more like a farmer than a military chieftain. On one occasion a young regular officer found the commanding general attired "in a big straw sombrero, a pair of enlisted men's trousers, which were too short for him, a loose linen coat, and a pair of 'soldier shoes.'" Seeing Taylor for the first time, a company commander in the Rifles described him as "a rough looking man and I do not think he has the appearance of a great man." These depictions help explain Taylor's famous sobriquet, "Old Rough-and-Ready," which dated from the Second Seminole War and reflected both his self-identification with his soldiers and his basic disinterest in military pomp.[25]

Finally the drills and preparations ended; in mid-August, Taylor ordered his army to plunge into Mexico. Because of a shortage of animals and wagons for transportation, he decided to lead a lean strike force of around 6,500 men to Monterrey, leaving the remainder to guard the base at Camargo and the Rio Grande supply line. Commanding an army made up of both regulars and volunteers, Taylor divided his invading legions into three divisions—two of regulars, the first under Brigadier General William J. Worth and the second under Colonel David E. Twiggs; and a volunteer division under Major General William O. Butler. The division of volunteers was further separated into two brigades, with the First Mississippi and the First Tennessee making up one led by Davis's friend Brigadier General John A. Quitman from Natchez. Troops had been moving out of Camargo for three weeks when the Rifles took up the march on September 7, cutting striking figures in their uniforms of red shirts worn outside white duck pants and their black slouch hats.[26]

As Taylor's column wound its way southward, the climate and the topography changed, even though the heat and humidity of Camargo were not shaken off quickly. For the initial portion of the trek basically similar conditions obtained, but by the time the army reached the handsome town of Cerralvo, sixty miles from Camargo, the increasing elevation made for notable changes. A green countryside, cooler temperatures, and good water greeted the invaders, who could also make out the Sierra Madre Mountains. In his journal, a Mississippian recorded, "The mountains all the time in the distance, Oh beautiful! How beautiful!" From there on to Monterrey the marching conditions were ideal for infantrymen.[27]

Finally, on September 19, Taylor and his divisions arrived before Monterrey. There Governor J. Pinckney Henderson of Texas with two regiments from his state joined the American force. While the commanding general decided how to approach the city, the First Mississippi along with other units went into camp under circumstances far different from those at the mouth of the Rio Grande or at Camargo. The encampment was situated in a beautiful park, known as San Domingo, covered with pecan and walnut trees and well watered by a large, bubbling spring. The Americans named their hospitable place Walnut Springs. En route to Monterrey, General Taylor did not know whether the Mexicans would defend the city or withdraw deeper into the interior. The cannon shot that saluted his initial reconnaissance provided a quick and harsh answer. If he wanted Monterrey, he would have to take it by force.[28]

Monterrey seemingly provided a strong position for General Pedro de Ampudía and his 10,300 defenders, 7,300 regulars and 3,000 local conscripts. The city was nestled between mountains on the east and west, with the Santa Catarina River flowing at its rear and turning north at the eastern end of the town. A plain to the north made for an open front, and, of course, from that direction the Americans approached. If Taylor undertook a frontal assault, he confronted substantial defensive works anchored on the Citadel, a fortified former church just north of the center of the city. The Americans called it the Black Fort because of the massive walls darkened by weather and neglect. On the western edge of Monterrey, two peaks—Independencía north of the river and Federación on the south bank—dominated approaches from that direction. On the opposite, or eastern, end stood three strongpoints; the redoubt El Diablo and the stone fort La Tenería (so called because the basic structure had once been a tannery) on either side of a deep ravine, along with the fortified Purísima Bridge across it, blocked any enemy.

To capture Monterrey, Taylor would have to attack. Investing the city was not an option because he had left behind in Camargo the heavy artillery, which he thought too difficult to haul through the countryside. The general's plan of assault derived from information brought in by engineer officers who had reconnoitered the Mexican defenses. Their report indicated that the two western guardians, Independencía and Federación, could be turned and then seized from the rear. They were not heavily defended to stop such an attack because the Mexicans did not consider such an action possible. To accomplish this turning mission Taylor assigned Worth's division of regulars. To prevent the Mexicans from reinforcing their threatened western positions, the rest

Battle of Monterrey.

From Papers of Jefferson Davis, *III, with permission of the LSU Press*

of the army would demonstrate against the eastern defenses. On Sunday, September 20, Worth set out from the American camp, and on Monday launched his assault.

For the demonstration promised Worth, Taylor directed Twiggs's division of regulars to move against the Tenería and other installations on the Mexican right. At 8 a.m. on Monday, the twenty-first, Twiggs's division left Walnut Springs and maneuvered through cornfields and across stone walls toward the enemy works, all the while trying to stay out of range of the guns in the Citadel. As the troops approached the line from which they would commence their attack, they came under heavy shelling to their front and right. The formation broke, with some men heading toward the rear, others toward the city, but west of where they should have been. Most of these soldiers entered Monterrey, becoming trapped and even lost in the patchwork of narrow streets.

On Monday, September 21, the Mississippi Rifles and their colonel went into battle for the first time—or "saw the elephant," as the American soldiers termed combat. With his diversionary tactic failing almost as soon as it started, Taylor ordered Butler's volunteer division forward in support of the battered Second Division. Quitman's brigade was pitted against the Tenería, the First Tennessee facing the northern ramparts and the Rifles fronting the northwestern wall. Moving at double-quick, both regiments soon came in range for the cannon firing from El Diablo and the Tenería. About 300 yards from their target and receiving a torrent of lead from musket balls and solid shot, the Tennesseans and the Mississippians formed in lines and opened fire. Unhappy at the range from which his riflemen were engaging, Colonel Davis complained to one of his officers, "Damn it, why do not the men get nearer to the fort? Why waste ammunition at such distance?" The Rifles then advanced to only about 180 yards from the fort, but at that moment the Mexican guns grew silent.[29]

During this lull both regiments awaited instructions from General Quitman, with Colonel Davis fuming at the delay. What happened next cannot be precisely reconstructed because there are so many different versions of events. Although a directive never came from the brigade commander, each regiment, almost simultaneously, decided to carry the fight forward. On the brigade left, Colonel William Campbell called upon his First Tennessee to rush the fort, while on his right identical cries came from Lieutenant Colonel McClung on the extreme left of the Rifles and from Davis in their center. The red-shirted soldiers responded enthusiastically. "Away we went like so many devils hooting and yelling," exclaimed a participant, "with nothing but naked rifles no bayonets even." Surging forward, the Rifles breached the walls, with McClung the first man on the parapet, and drove into the fort. The First Tennessee did likewise. Throughout the action Davis was in the thick of the fight with his men. On Tartar, then on foot, always waving his sword, he exhorted his troops onward and entered the fort with them. The Tenería was in American hands.[30]

After the capture of the Tenería, the American attack ground to a halt. Because no one above regimental level, from Quitman to Taylor, had carefully thought through the battle, no plans existed to take advantage of the opportunity presented by the sudden fall of the Tenería. Losing cohesion and without direction, soldiers from both regiments were milling around inside the fort. At this moment, Davis organized a small group of Tennesseans and Mississippians, "cheered [it] to the charge," plunging into the ravine behind the Tenería and crossing the creek to strike at El Diablo. But from this position Davis received orders to pull back as part of a general withdrawal from the city directed by Taylor. During this movement some Mexican lancers came out from the Citadel to hit the Americans, many of whom were falling back in disarray. Quick reactions by Davis and his old West Point chum, Albert S. Johnston, an aide to General Butler, rallied enough men into line to beat off the lancers. Nightfall brought to a close a long day of hard fighting in which the First Mississippi and its colonel had been baptized in the stern ordeal of combat.

In the Rifles' sector, Tuesday the twenty-second was quiet. That morning the regiment was moved into the Tenería, where it remained inactive through the day. But at the other end of the American front, significant events were taking place. General Worth's troops, who had successfully stormed both Federación and Independencía, captured the Bishop's Palace, the strongpoint on the former. With the Stars and Stripes flying over the two prominences, the Americans had secured the western side of Monterrey. Back in the Tenería, the Rifles had to cope with the elements—a norther blew through, dropping temperatures and bringing a cold rain. Davis's men had no blankets and no food because the regimental quartermaster had been unable to get an escort to bring his supply wagons forward. The hungry and weary Mississippians spent a cold, wet night.

Wednesday, September 23, brought another day of tough fighting, but of a very different kind. Early in the morning Quitman directed Davis to take a patrol of several companies, including one Tennessean, across the ravine to reconnoiter El Diablo. To their surprise, the Americans discovered that formidable work abandoned because General Ampudía was bringing all of his troops, except those in the Citadel, back to the main plaza in the center of the city. Davis led his detachment forward until it came under heavy fire, when he stopped to await reinforcements. Shortly thereafter the rest of the Rifles came up and once more the advance began. Their attack was taking place in the far eastern part of the city, bypassing and isolating the Citadel.

Davis and his men fought in a deadly maze. Densely packed in close streets, masonry houses with large iron and wooden grates and heavy shutters that opened from inside out as well as rooftop parapets made for ideal defensive positions. Musket balls poured in from every direction upon the volunteers totally unfamiliar with street warfare. The arrival of some Texas soldiers helped immensely, for they understood the construction of the houses. With guidance from the Texans, the Mississippians and Tennesseans with axes and crowbars tunneled their way through the adobe walls of houses, raced through courtyards, and mounted stairs to fire from rooftops. They fought the Mexicans on their own terms, from house to house, and would not be denied.

Engaged in this bloody work, the men were cheered by the presence not only of their own colonel but also of their commanding general, who had ridden into the city and actually directed some troops in their assaults on individual houses. As the Rifles neared the central plaza, they found all the streets barricaded and swept by a severe fire. To continue their progress, the soldiers had to construct a defense across a street, which they could use as a shield. For this purpose they employed baggage and pack saddles found in houses, but the shooting stopped before they could put the shield to use. At nightfall the lead elements occupied a two-story stone house overlooking the cathedral that dominated the square. Once again the Rifles and their colonel had acquitted themselves well under desperate conditions.[31]

As Generals Taylor and Ampudía assessed the events of the day, they had different perspectives. With Worth, acting on his own initiative, as successful on the right as the force under his own eye had been on the left, Taylor stood poised once again to hammer the Mexicans from two directions and drive them into the Santa Catarina, though such an assault through the center of Monterrey would surely demand a high price in American blood. Ampudía faced a much more difficult situation. Despite outnumbering his enemy and holding strong defensive positions as well as interior lines, he had not been able to thwart the American advance. To continue the battle could decimate his army and result in terrible damage to the city. As a result, at 11 p.m. Ampudía sent a message to Taylor offering to abandon the city and the Citadel, which he still held, provided he could march away with his army and remaining equipment. On the morning of the twenty-fourth, Taylor responded negatively, demanding a surrender without terms and an answer by noon. Before that hour, Ampudía requested a personal meeting with his opponent. The commanders met at 1 p.m. and agreed to form a joint commission to draw up arrangements for a capitulation.

General Taylor appointed three negotiators: General Worth, his senior regular officer; Governor Henderson; and Colonel Jefferson Davis, who served as secretary for the Americans. They met with Ampudía's three appointees during the afternoon. By that evening they had drawn up articles for a formal capitulation, which each side signed. Generally they followed the form suggested by Taylor. Ampudía agreed to surrender the city and all public property except the personal belongings of his officers and men plus one artillery battery. He would also give up the Citadel and within one week retreat to an agreed-upon line running from thirty-five miles west of Monterrey to around fifty miles south of it. For his part, with the city in his hands, General Taylor agreed to honor an eight-week armistice.

From its signing, the armistice stirred considerable discussion. General Taylor believed that he was following his original orders to achieve an early peace and occupy much of northern Mexico, which the administration could then use as a lever in its attempt to pry New Mexico and especially California from the Mexican government. Taylor's timing was a bit off, however, for, as yet unbeknownst to the general, President Polk had decided that only additional campaigning would prod Mexico into serious negotiations. Three weeks later when the documents stipulating the terms reached Washington, the Polk administration repudiated the agreement and instructed General Taylor to rescind the armistice. On the battlefield itself, Taylor surely had the upper hand, but his troops had experienced three days of hard fighting. To pursue the battle within the town would undoubtedly have been costly and possibly hazardous, for supplies of food and ammunition were running low, with resupply difficult. All in all, given Taylor's comprehension of his instructions and the situation of his army, his decision to accept evacuation of Monterrey with the armistice is both understandable and defensible. Not surprisingly, Jefferson Davis, who became a great champion of Taylor, certainly thought so. From his participation as a member of the negotiating team until the end of his life, he insisted that Taylor had acted wisely and for the best.[32]

Thinking about his regiment, Colonel Davis swelled with pride. Writing Joseph just after the battle, he praised the "brilliant" conduct of his men in the "severe conflict." In his official report to his brigade commander, Davis spoke about "the duty we had to perform [being] both difficult & perilous." Even so, among his troops, "I saw no exhibition of fear, no want of confidence, but on every side the men who stood around me were prompt and willing to execute my orders." In truth, the Rifles had fought well in two tough, bitter days that had been expensive in blood—nine killed and fifty-two wounded. Davis understood one cause and effect of this performance when from Monterrey he told Secretary Walker, "If any moral effect could be produced by military achievement enough has been done at this place to produce it." The Mississippians, like the other American soldiers, never believed they could be stopped, and that conviction was central to their success, as was the performance of certain line officers. The Americans won despite Taylor's lack of planning and poor coordination because individual commanders like General Worth and Colonels Campbell and

Davis exhibited initiative and daring in leading determined, enthusiastic troops to victory.[33]

Jefferson Davis came out of this battle with an enhanced reputation. His commanding general obviously thought extremely highly of him. From Davis's arrival in the war theater, Taylor had looked favorably upon him by moving the Rifles relatively promptly to Camargo and ensuring that the regiment became part of the invading force. Then Davis's joining a senior regular officer and a governor on the commission to arrange the surrender of Monterrey clearly indicated Taylor's confidence in him and his influence with his commander. The men he commanded also approved of him and his conduct. Though surely a partisan, young Joseph Howell, as a private in the Rifles, did not venture far off the mark when telling his father about the confidence Davis's troops had in him: "I verily believe that if he should tell his men to jump into a cannon's mouth they would think it all right & would all say Col. Jeff as they call him knows best so hurra boys lets go ahead." In their battle reports, prepared almost immediately afterwards, his officers often noted Davis's effectiveness as a combat commander and his leadership qualities. They found him cool, decisive, and always in their midst taking every risk every other soldier took.[34]

In the exultation following the American triumph, the colonel informed his brother Joseph that although he had no privileged information, he believed the war might soon be over and the regiment disbanded. On the return of peace Davis was much too optimistic; the war would last almost two more years. Not long after writing that letter, however, Davis found himself on the way back to Mississippi. On October 18 he was granted a sixty-day furlough on the grounds of his wife's illness. With Jim Green, he promptly left Monterrey for Camargo and then the mouth of the Rio Grande and a ship. He reached New Orleans on November 1, and shortly thereafter arrived at Davis Bend.[35]

There he confronted the real reason he had undertaken a difficult two-week journey of around 1,000 miles, with the prospect of a prompt return trip. Although the evidence is sketchy and precision impossible, it is clear that the normal distress of a young wife sending her husband off to war had burgeoned into emotional turmoil that brought Jefferson Davis home. Without doubt Varina missed him. In a letter to him she related a dream that graphically portrayed the impact of their separation on her. She told him that the previous night she had dreamt that they were parting in front of a crowd, and every time she started away, he ran back to her and kissed her again. "I actually waked with your kisses so warm upon my lips," she confided, "that I could not believe you were not in my arms." Then she professed her love: "Dearest, best beloved, may God bring you these arms once more, and then at least for the time I clasp you I shall be happy."[36]

Yet more lay beneath Varina's distress than anxiety about Jefferson's absence. When he left for Mexico, the decision was made that Varina would spend much of her time near Joseph, and, as Jefferson had feared, difficulties arose. Varina later admitted that she had been "wounded" by talk in the family about Jefferson's remaining dependent on Joseph. Joseph's response that he had given Jefferson land, helped him, and looked upon him as a son failed to allay her uneasiness. Excessive concern about dependency most probably affected Varina because she expected to be treated as an adult and an equal, especially after her heady experience in Washington. On the other hand, Joseph, old enough to be her grandfather, still considered her basically the child who had called him Uncle Joe and had married his cherished brother. But Varina was no longer a child, and she certainly did not act like one. Even if all else had been smooth and calm, the sharply different perspectives held by these two ferociously strong-willed people had the potential in themselves to generate strife. Also, when at Hurricane, Varina was not only in Joseph's home but in Eliza's as well. Another woman dominated that household.[37]

Then the vexing issue of Jefferson's 1846 will must be considered. This question becomes especially troublesome because no copy survives, and it is not clear exactly when he prepared it. Varina later claimed that he did so during his leave, but most likely he drew it up in July before departing from Davis Bend, a common practice for a man going to war. And the document would have been left with Joseph, who helped write it and still owned the land Jefferson farmed. Varina most probably knew about its contents, and possibly her unhappiness exploded because this first will, like the later one in 1847, permitted Varina to reside at Brierfield during her lifetime, but shared the income with Jefferson's two widowed sisters and two orphaned nieces. Those provisions certainly upset her in 1847, because she did not feel that these stipulations admitted her primacy as wife, much less recognized her as an adult and an equal. From Brierfield a proud and angry Varina declared to her mother, "I have become quite a savage . . . and I tear my food in silence." Even so, she prided herself on her ability to manage on her own: "Woman was made to live alone, if man was not."[38]

Finally, being around children at Hurricane caused her disappointment to grow even keener. By October 1846 the twenty-year-old Varina Davis had been married for eighteen months but she had not yet had a child or even become pregnant. Her culture taught her to wish for and cherish motherhood as the highest calling of a woman. In her time the chief duty of a wife, especially one young and vigorous, was to provide children for the family and then to care for them. That after a year and a half Varina did not yet enjoy the confidence of knowing she could satisfy that desire was "a source of grief to her."[39]

Much about the dynamics of the situation that called Jefferson home can be discerned from letters he wrote Varina and Joseph in the first two months after his return to Mexico. To Varina he placed himself in the role of wise teacher and counselor as well as proud, though imperfect, husband. "My dear wife," he lectured, "you have taken upon yourself in many respects the decision of your own course, and remember to be responsible for ones conduct is not the happy state which those who think they have been governed too much sometimes suppose it." A homily followed: "To rise superior to petty annoyances to pity and forgive the weakness in others which galls and incommodes us is a noble exhibition of moral philosophy and the surest indication of an elevated nature." He made clear that he wanted "the power and the practice" in his wife to include "look[ing] over the conventionalisms of society yet hav[ing] the good sense which skillfully avoids a collision. . . ." "With the practice and without the power a woman may be respectable," he declaimed, but "with the power and without the practice she will often be exposed to remarks, the fear of which would render me as *husband* unhappy." That concern, he confessed, "belong[ed] to a morbid sensibility" that he had early on told her about. Recognizing her perceptiveness, he acknowledged that "had I not done so you must after our marriage have discovered it." Despite all the upheaval he wanted them both to "believe that all is ordered for the general good & tutor our minds to act as becomes contributors, to feel as becomes creaturis bound by many obligations to receive with gratitude whatever may be offered, and wait with patience and confidence the coming result."

One thing that Varina could anticipate was a new home that had been discussed during Jefferson's visit to Davis Bend. He said she could build whatever she wanted, but only after talking with Joseph and getting his advice. Jefferson obviously still thought that Joseph should occupy in Varina's life a position similar to that in his own. After telling her to consult Joseph, a not entirely perceptive husband counseled, "endeavor to make your home happy to yourself and those who share it with you." His closing expressed the depth of his feelings for her: "Farewell, ever with deepest love and fondest hope."[40]

To Joseph he expressed guarded optimism that all would be well with Varina. Joseph had obviously written positively about her, for Jefferson exclaimed, "God grant that all your hopes in relation to Varina be realized." Evidently at Hurricane the brothers had talked about the effect on Varina of Jefferson's going back to Mexico, and both had agreed that he should return. "If she shall be excited by my absence to such action and self command as to restore her health and spirits," Jefferson pronounced, "it will be a boon cheaply purchased by all the sacrifices and inconveniences it costs me."[41]

Although family matters concerned Davis most during his stay in Mississippi, his trip home produced other important results. As the first notable Mississippian to return from the war, Davis received a laudatory welcome. The public had been primed by newspaper accounts that after Monterrey extolled all the officers in the Rifles for "ascend[ing] the ladder of fame," but the commander received special notice: "Col. Davis was in the front and head of the battle from the opening to the close, cheering onward the men by his cool, pleasant, fearless and confident manner." Briefly, a squabble erupted over Davis's failure to list all casualties in a letter to Joseph that ended up in the *Vicksburg Sentinel*. But when those upset realized that Davis knew the *Vicksburg Whig* correspondent with the regiment would make a full accounting of all the killed and wounded, the tempest subsided. It did not at all dull the praise heaped upon Davis; the editor of the *Whig* even publicly apologized for his part in the wrangle. Of course, Davis was not the only prominent Mississippian in Mexico, but he appeared on home ground first, and he had done well on the battlefield.[42]

Davis gave a speech in the limelight before several hundred people at "a splendid collation" held at Southern Hall in Vicksburg on November 10. Enjoying the moment, he expressed appreciation for "the approbation extended so generously by my fellow citizens." He then praised "the gallant men it has been my pride and good fortune to lead in battle," proclaiming that at Monterrey they had added to "the honor and chivalry of our State." While he piled accolade after accolade upon his troops for their heroism and skill, he did not forget their colonel, emphasizing, for example, that his attention to drill led to the regiment's ability to execute difficult maneuvers during combat. Jefferson Davis's name became imprinted on the minds of thousands of Mississippians. As a political man, he reaped incalculable benefits from being a war hero, the man of the hour.[43]

Davis's reception and his response to it had two concrete manifestations. In his public address he fueled a controversy that had begun sputtering back in Mexico. After the Battle of Monterrey, the First Tennessee and the First Mississippi each claimed that it had been first in the Tenería on September 21. Surely the victory provided enough glory for all, and everyone admitted the signal contribution of each regiment, but that general acclaim satisfied neither. Although the preponderant evidence places the First Mississippi in the works just minutes ahead of the Tennesseans, the key element in the dispute was pride, not only of regiments, but also of colonels. The highly partisan politics of the time also got injected into the controversy—Campbell was a Whig and Davis, of course, a Democrat.[44]

By the time Davis reached New Orleans on his way to Davis Bend, the conflicting claims had appeared in the press. In his Vicksburg speech and in a letter to the editor of the *Vicksburg Sentinel,* he stressed that the Rifles had initially breached the walls of the Tenería. A letter in a New Orleans paper claiming that distinction for the First Tennessee brought forth a remonstrance from Davis. To its author, Balie Peyton, a Whig and friend of Campbell's who had served on General Worth's staff at Monterrey, Davis wrote asking how he intended to remove the erroneous impression created by his account. Then they exchanged letters in which Peyton said he was only repeating what Colonel Campbell had told him. Davis, in turn, insisted on a specific and public disclaimer. Although this torrent of pride threatening to sweep aside good sense finally slowed, the hard feelings generated did not easily abate. No matter Davis's motives—and they undoubtedly included pride and politics—he did not exhibit much generosity or tolerance even if he was right on the narrow factual point. Peyton believed that Davis took up the cudgels chiefly "to make a little Locofoco capital at home for Miss. consumption." Certainly Davis's stance as a stalwart advocate for Mississippi did not injure his reputation in his own state.[45]

Davis's early anointment as Mississippi's hero of the war also pushed him ahead of a fellow Mississippian, his senior in years and rank, who also happened to be his brigade commander in Mexico. In addition to having been the ranking major general in the state militia, the forty-seven-year-old John A. Quitman of Natchez was a longtime friend and neighboring landowner on Davis Bend. Moreover, Quitman harbored political ambitions, and he hoped his military service would have political benefits. He certainly felt that some of the plaudits being showered upon Davis should come his way, and he saw his subordinate stealing a march on him.[46]

Although Davis could not help what was happening in Mississippi public opinion, his conduct toward Quitman was not generous. In his official report of the battle addressed to General Quitman, Davis made respectful and politic comments about the brigade commander's helpful role in the contest. In the Vicksburg speech, however, Davis never mentioned Quitman's name, an omission that rankled the general when the news reached him. Quitman resented Davis's claiming "the merit of having done every thing," even though he had no authority "to make any disposition but under my orders." The general began to think of the colonel, he later wrote his wife, as "a selfish and fiercely ambitious man, without one particle of magnanimity in his character."[47]

That Davis did not call on Quitman's family when in Mississippi further irritated the general. The Quitmans at home were eager for a visit from the man Quitman's daughter called "our old friend 'Uncle Jeff.' " They wanted news from husband and father and had parcels to send him; but Davis never appeared, though he did probably stop in Natchez to pick up Varina on his way to Davis Bend. Possibly he did not have the time to see the Quitmans, and he did arrange to have sent to him the packages and letters they wanted him to carry back to Mexico. Davis as deliveryman did not, however, mollify Quitman, who thought the colonel seemed unfriendly.[48]

Although General Quitman and Colonel Davis undoubtedly saw each other as potential political rivals, probably more important to Davis was Quitman's position on the Mississippi-Tennessee quarrel. Quitman's official report did not take sides, a stance he considered appropriate because he commanded both regiments. Even after the controversy became public and Davis requested a declaration from him, Quitman would never state directly that the Rifles beat the First Tennessee into the Tenería, though he admitted privately that Lieutenant Colonel McClung was the first man on the ramparts and that a deep ditch had impeded the Tennesseans. With Davis back in Mexico, relations worsened, and when in January 1847 Quitman was reassigned to Winfield Scott's command, the two men remained estranged. Reconciliation would not come until after the war.[49]

As his turbulent family situation quieted, at least for a time, and proudly wearing the laurels of a publicly acclaimed war chief, Jefferson Davis on about November 20 set out on his return trip to Mexico. Ever mindful of the relationship between the war and politics as well as his own political career, he made sure before he left the country to renew his ties to the Polk administration. From New Orleans he reminded Secretary Walker of his friendship, both personal and political. Eager for information on governmental policy toward Mexico, he requested Walker to keep him informed. Then Colonel Davis outlined what he considered the proper American course—establish a line of posts across northern Mexico from Tampico on the Gulf of Mexico on to a favorable point on the Pacific, and then commence operations to seize "the entrepots of Commerce." According to Davis, such a policy would quickly bring Mexico to the bargaining table and end the war with "an early and cheap peace." Davis worried that if the fighting dragged on, the need for revenue might reopen the door for protective tariffs, undoing the good of the recently enacted Walker Tariff.

After discussing grand strategy, Davis moved on to the particulars of local Democratic politics. He was disturbed by rumors afloat in New Orleans that the customhouse officers, with Walker's blessing, intended to start a new paper. Davis informed the secretary that the city already had a strong Democratic and pro-Walker sheet, whose editor, Eliza Davis's brother, wanted to push Walker for the presidency. Davis did not think he could give permission to do so, but he did report that he had provided the journalist with a letter of introduction to Walker, and hoped the two men would meet.[50]

On December 1, the day after writing that letter, Davis sailed from New Orleans for Brazos Island. Two weeks later he reached Camargo and promptly headed south to rejoin his regiment. When he met up with General Taylor on Christmas Day, his commanding general was most displeased. The repudiation of the armistice by the administration had not set well with him, nor did he believe that the president or the government had properly appreciated or acknowledged his accomplishment at Monterrey. Now there was even more to irritate him. To solidify his position in northern Mexico and also to prepare for an advance deeper into the country, should Washington choose, Taylor in November had ordered the occupation of Saltillo, fifty miles southwest of Monterrey, and in December, the movement of troops to Victoria, over 100 miles southeast of Monterrey. Initially he planned to extend his lines southeastward to Tampico on the Gulf Coast, but the Mexicans evacuated that port before the Americans reached Victoria. While

Taylor was moving his troops about, the president did decide on a new campaign aimed at Mexico City. Much of Taylor's army would participate, but not the general himself, whom Polk pilloried as narrow, partisan, and unqualified for high command. To lead the offensive, Polk named Major General Winfield Scott commanding general of the United States Army.[51]

Under this plan Taylor was assigned a holding mission centered on Monterrey; but, to him even worse, his army was decimated. More than half, 9,000 men including almost all of his regulars, were transferred to Scott's invasion force. In these decisions, Taylor spied politics—an administration frightened by his success and popularity, and in collusion with General Scott, was now snubbing him. His suspicions had some substance; but Scott, about whom the president also harbored doubts, had not plotted against Taylor. Neither of these regular generals was a good Democrat, and nothing was more important to James K. Polk than partisan credentials and allegiance.

In Taylor's pared-down force, Colonel Davis became even closer to his commander and friend. When Taylor dispatched so many troops to Scott's gathering host, he kept the First Mississippi with him. Proud of their retention by Old Rough-and-Ready, the Rifles considered it a signal honor indicating their superiority over their rivals, the First Tennessee, among the units sent to Scott. Taylor's growing intimacy with Davis surely contributed to his decision to keep the First Mississippi in his command. As he tried to fathom the political currents, Taylor's antipathy toward the administration festered, and he placed the president, the secretary of war, and the commanding general all on his enemies' list. In his view, all three had schemed to deprive him of recognition and leave him out of the war. When General Scott arrived in Mexico and came to Camargo for a meeting with Taylor, Old Rough-and-Ready did not show up. In this instance he was not refusing to obey orders, for Scott had only requested his presence, but when Scott ordered him to abandon Saltillo, Taylor did disobey because he believed such a move would weaken his defensive posture. In fact, Taylor planned to establish his headquarters in Saltillo, then occupied by a force under Brigadier General John E. Wool that had set out from San Antonio, Texas, bound originally for Chihuahua. After Taylor and Wool agreed that going so far west made little sense, Taylor directed Wool to Saltillo, where he held the extreme right of Taylor's line. In numberless camp conversations with his general, Davis undoubtedly built up a lasting aversion to Scott as a man personally inimical toward

Taylor, though as a good Democrat he kept very private any sharing of his commander's antipathy toward Polk and the secretary of war. Davis never spoke publicly against the Polk administration, but he always defended Taylor's actions, including the Monterrey armistice.

Although Taylor seethed at what he termed a political assault on his rear by his superiors, he still had to attend to his military responsibility. Word came to him from General Wool at Saltillo that a sizable Mexican force led by General Antonio López de Santa Anna was moving northward from San Luis de Potosí toward his position. Although Taylor did not believe that an army could traverse the 150 miles of desert that dominated the road from San Luis up to Saltillo, he responded to Wool's news by leaving Victoria for Saltillo on January 16, 1847, with an escort of the First Mississippi and two artillery batteries.[52]

Arriving in Saltillo on February 2, Taylor surveyed the situation. To improve the morale of his troops and to ascertain Mexican whereabouts, Taylor sent the bulk of his force, including the Rifles, twenty miles southward to Agua Nueva on the tableland at the foot of the Sierra Madre. To Varina, Davis described the location as "a beautiful and healthy position." He informed her that "we came expecting a host and battle, have found solitude and externally peace." "We are waiting," he explained, "only action or such excitement as reconciles man to repose."[53]

At this point General Taylor still held to his conviction that his enemy could not cross the wasteland before him. He even disregarded his engineers' opinion that Agua Nueva could be easily bypassed by Mexican cavalry, cutting off the 4,000 Americans there, including Taylor. Although Old Rough-and-Ready did not have a clear sense of his foe's location or intention, his soldiers had no doubt about him. A company commander in the Rifles, who back at Camargo had expressed misgivings about the general, now characterized him as "a good man and a good officer—The army has great confidence in him." On the march from Monterrey to Saltillo one of his soldiers saw the commanding general ride by with a troop of horsemen and described the image that endeared Old Rough-and-Ready to his men: "Do you see, at their head, a plain-looking gentleman, mounted upon a brown horse, having upon his head a Mexican sombrero, dressed in a brown, olive-colored, loose-frock-coat, gray pants, wool socks, and shoes; beneath the frock appears the scabbard of a sword; he has the eye of an eagle, and every lineament of his countenance is expressive of honesty, and a calm determined mind." To his troops, confident that they "can not be

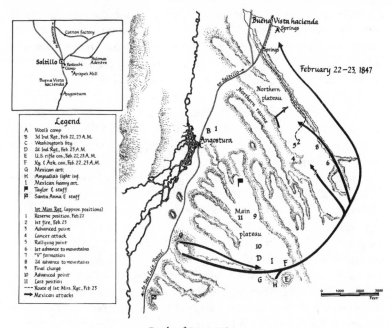

Battle of Buena Vista.

From Papers of Jefferson Davis, *III, with permission of the LSU Press*

whipped by a Mexican army," Taylor was one with them, indomitable and imperturbable.[54]

That confidence in themselves and in their commanding general was critical, for Taylor quickly found himself and his army in a spot little short of desperate. By February 20 no doubt remained. Santa Anna was just south of Agua Nueva, advancing toward Saltillo with almost 20,000 men, a force more than three times the size of Taylor's legions. And in that small force only the First Mississippi and some batteries had ever before seen combat. But though Taylor was basically isolated, far from any reinforcements, and defeat could mean the literal destruction of his entire army, he never hesitated. Old Rough-and-Ready would stand and fight. Unlike Monterrey, this contest would not take place in an urban area but in open country. Still, as always, the topography would be critical in the planning and flow of battle.

The ground that the Mexicans and Americans fought over resembled the landscape on an arid moon where the crust had been tormented and torn by violent shocks and explosions. Three miles beyond Saltillo the main road south passed by the Buena Vista hacienda, then bore right, or west, as it traversed a narrow pass, La Angostura, before settling down for a run of around fifteen miles to Agua Nueva. Immediately to the west of the road, a web of sharp, ragged gullies ripped the ground, and around a half mile farther west a wall of mountains rose up. East of the road several plateaus, including two broad ones, peppered with rocks and desert shrubs, reached out for about a mile and sloped up toward the Sierra Madre, which barricaded the eastern edge of the area. Rocky and at times wide and deep ravines hacked the earth between and among the plateaus.

Having ridden through and thought about this forbidding landscape, General Wool decided that artillery well placed in the narrow pass supported by infantry would bring the Mexican advance to a dead stop and protect Saltillo. The gullies on the American right he correctly judged impenetrable for cavalry and practically so for any sizable body of infantry. With the plateaus on his left angling in a basically east–west rather than north–south direction, and often cleft by ravines, Wool could not envision the Mexican army making a sustained move that way either. Thus, to get to Saltillo, Santa Anna would have to come straight at the Americans in La Angostura, where, Wool was confident, he would be thrown back. Zachary Taylor basically accepted Wool's defensive tactical plan.

When Santa Anna reached Agua Nueva on February 21, he was disappointed that his enemy had fallen back toward Saltillo. Still, he saw more opportunity for his side in the terrain in front of him than Wool did. The gullies were out, and he certainly did not believe he could drive straight through La Angostura and onto more level ground where his numbers might prove decisive. An advance across the ravines would be difficult to maintain, but at their extreme eastern end the plateaus left the ravines largely behind, making for a slender stretch of basically open ground almost at the base of the Sierra Madre. If Santa Anna could get a combined infantry-cavalry force far enough along that route before the Americans realized what he was about, then he could turn their position at La Angostura, fall upon the rear, and capture the supply depot at Saltillo. Simply put, he could smash Taylor's army and cut off any escape.

Santa Anna decided to strike immediately, though his men were exhausted and hungry after their long, debilitating trudge across the desert. The Mexican general did not want to give the Americans time to strengthen their defenses. Issuing a proclamation calling for the expulsion of the invaders, Santa Anna strove to spur his troops to a supreme effort. He ordered two divisions east toward the Sierra Madre to undertake the flanking operation. At the same time, to occupy the Americans and keep their attention away from his main strike, he mounted a diversion straight up the road toward La Angostura. Both assaults would have artillery support. After a cold, wet night on February 22, the twenty-third dawned with a storm-cleansed, bright sky. At 8 a.m. the Mexican attack opened the Battle of Buena Vista or, to the Mexicans, the Battle of La Angostura.

That morning Jefferson Davis and the Rifles were in Saltillo with Taylor. Late in the afternoon of the twenty-second, Taylor, convinced that a major engagement would not take place that day, had left Wool in charge and returned with the First Mississippi to Saltillo to ensure that his supplies were adequately protected. Satisfied that the garrison could fend off any Mexican cavalry attacks and secure the army's provisions, Taylor planned to head back to the scene of the impending battle at first light. After a few hours' sleep the general, along with most of the First Mississippi, started south. Colonel Davis had left behind in Saltillo one of his captains with two companies to defend the supply depot. And that afternoon they did beat off a feeble effort by a band of Mexican cavalry.

As Old Rough-and-Ready and his entourage reached the Buena Vista hacienda around 9 a.m. on the twenty-third, they met the pandemonium raging in the American army. To this point the fight had not gone well for Taylor's men. Initially, Wool reacted decisively and successfully to the Mexican thrust toward his left. When the Mexican move was discovered, Wool dispatched additional units to the threatened point, and in fierce fighting the Americans halted the advance. Then, in the fog of combat—first-time combat for the American infantry regiments locked in this struggle—confusion and seemingly contradictory orders caused the commander of the Second Indiana to order a retreat that opened the gates for the Mexicans. Taking advantage of this gap in the American line, Santa Anna pushed his troops forward. His plan seemed to be on the verge of succeeding, with the Americans fleeing and the avenue around their left flank and to their rear broad and inviting. By the time Taylor appeared on the battlefield, the Mexican infantry was pressing down the broad plateau that would take it behind La Angostura to Buena Vista hacienda.

With Americans on the run, Old Rough-and-Ready confronted a deteriorating, even desperate situation. According to some accounts,

General Wool counseled withdrawal. Taylor refused, fearing that with his mostly green troops any general retreat could turn into an uncontrollable rout. He would stand. In this instance Taylor's calmness, courage, and solidity were as important as his soldiers' confidence in him. He did not rattle, much less break.

Davis and the Rifles hesitated near the hacienda only long enough to fill their canteens, and following Taylor's instructions, deployed on the northern plateau to meet the Mexicans flooding toward the American rear. As he ordered his men to advance toward the enemy, Davis to little avail also implored straggling and retreating soldiers to join his band, but he did get Wool to promise to send help as soon as possible. Despite the odds—his eight companies, numbering fewer than 400 men against at least a full division and possibly as many as 4,000 Mexicans—Colonel Davis never wavered. "No one could have failed to perceive the hazard," Davis observed in his report. Attacking forthwith he believed absolutely essential, at "whatever sacrifice." He pushed his red-shirted troops forward at double-quick time until they came within rifle range of their foe. At that point, he called a halt and then ordered his men to "advance firing." With Davis leading on horseback, the Rifles screaming a "loud yell of defiance, which rang on the ear more like the roar of angry lions than the shout of men . . . rushed forward" under what one officer called "one of the heaviest fires I ever saw." Not to be deterred, the Mississippians successfully navigated an abrupt ravine in their path and continued to pour a torrent of lead, twenty-one rounds of cartridges, upon the "close and dense rank" of the Mexicans. The powerful shock of this charge crumpled the Mexican onslaught. The American rear had been saved, for the moment.[55]

The danger had not evaporated yet. The collision with the Mexicans had cost the Rifles dearly; most of the casualties suffered in the battle occurred during this bloody fighting. The colonel himself suffered a painful wound when a musket ball pierced his right foot near the ankle, driving shards of brass from his shattered spur and bits of his sock into his flesh. Even so, he refused to leave the field, having his wound wrapped while he remained on horseback. Aware of his exposed location, however, he pulled his regiment back to a stronger defensive position. As the Mississippians withdrew in good order, the Third Indiana came up to reinforce them. At this juncture some refugees from units previously overrun and scattered also appeared.[56]

Almost immediately all of these Americans found themselves facing still another grave crisis. Stymied, Santa Anna attempted to regain the initiative by sending an additional brigade of cavalry to his right flank to act as catalyst for yet another try to get behind his enemy. As Colonel Davis peered to his front, he saw about 400 yards distant "a body of richly caparisoned lancers," in fact, about 2,000 of them. These troops, in Davis's words, "came forward rapidly and in beautiful order—the files and ranks so closed, as to look like a solid mass of men and horses."[57]

Davis had to act quickly, for a thunderous cavalry charge could overrun his position and plunge straight to the Saltillo road, along the way crushing the American left and exposing the rear. Davis's men had never before confronted a massive cavalry charge, and he did not think he had time to form the classic infantry defense against men on horseback, the hollow square. Instead, he deployed his forces in what became the famous V, the Indiana troops making up the right arm and the Rifles the left, with an artillery piece on their left end. Davis styled his formation "a reentering angle," which would permit his riflemen to catch the Mexican cavalry in a converging fire as it bore down on the American position. With his troops stationed as he wanted, Davis repeatedly urged them not to shoot until the enemy was almost in their midst. In his battle report Davis praised the steadiness of his soldiers "as they stood at shouldered arms waiting an attack." As the Mexican horsemen approached, their speed decreased from a gallop to a trot until at 30 to 80 yards, depending upon the account, they came to a walk. Perhaps the unusual alignment in front of them gave them pause, or perhaps the slowdown was simply momentary before a racing charge. At that moment a few shots rang out from the American side, then both sides of the V hurled "a volley so destructive, that the mass yielded to the blow, and the survivors fled." Now artillery from the middle plateau rained shot and shell on the bloodied lancers. The Rifles in conjunction with the Indianans and the artillery had shattered the cavalry charge. For a second time the Saltillo road had been secured.[58]

With this turn of events the scene of heaviest action shifted to the center—but not before a respite caused by a brief rainstorm, and by a Mexican stratagem of using a white flag to help extricate troops that after the failure of the cavalry attack were trapped against the eastern mountains. Thinking the Mexicans in retreat, Taylor ordered a general American advance across the main plateau. Santa Anna was not yet through. He too directed an all-out assault on the American center.

First Mississippi Regiment at Buena Vista (watercolor by Samuel Chamberlain).
San Jacinto Museum of History Association

Once more the two sides became entangled in bloody combat, with the outcome seemingly hanging in the balance, but the superbly handled American artillery added immensely to the punishment inflicted upon the Mexicans. Then, late in the afternoon, the Mississippi and Indiana Regiments made it across the rugged ravines and joined what General Wool called "the hottest as well as the most critical part of the action," protecting the crucial artillery batteries from Mexican infantry. Davis proudly reported that even after their arduous day, the Rifles "advanced upon the enemy with the alacrity and eagerness of men fresh to the combat." When night fell, the exhausted men of both sides practically dropped in position. The Americans had recovered the ground they had lost on the main plateau, and all expected the fighting to resume on the morrow.[59]

The morning of February 24 revealed, instead, that Santa Anna had completely withdrawn, leaving the field to Taylor and his little army. The struggle had resulted in a significant American victory. Triumph at Buena Vista ensured not only the security of Taylor's force, but also the American occupation of much of northern Mexico, and in addition greatly enhanced the heroic image and political appeal of Old Rough-and-Ready. Yet Taylor's role at Buena Vista was much the same as at Monterrey. He had not really directed the battle, but presided over the battlefield and left many of the critical decisions and deployments to his subordinates. And again on the regimental and battery level, a number of American officers, including Colonel Jefferson Davis, turned in excellent performances under extraordinarily trying conditions.

After the fighting halted on the twenty-third, Colonel Davis went to a field tent for "surgical aid" and from there was transported by wagon to the hospital that had been set up in Saltillo, where he arrived at about 10 p.m. Writing to Varina two days later, he described his wounded foot as "painful but . . . by no means dangerous." Although the injury never threatened to require amputation of foot or leg, it still hobbled him. For two years he had to use crutches to get around, and for three more the afflicted foot at times caused him extreme pain. During that period the bone exfoliated, and the shattered pieces either worked themselves out or were removed surgically, each generating intense anguish. This battlefield wound would occasionally bother Davis throughout his life.[60]

Jefferson Davis was enormously proud of his regiment and himself, though he always touted his men. At Buena Vista the Rifles suffered the heaviest casualties of any unit, thirty-nine killed and fifty-six wounded, or almost one-quarter of their strength on the field, underscoring that they had been in the maelstrom most of the day. In Davis's official report he recorded, "my regiment equalled—it was impossible to exceed—my expectations." With pride he later talked about "that terrible engine of power, disciplined Mississippi courage. . . ." As for himself, he knew that General Taylor thought his performance exemplary. In his official report Taylor left no doubt: "[Davis's] Distinguished coolness and gallantry at the head of his regiment . . . entitle him to the particular notice of the government." Davis's subordinates in the First Mississippi hailed his leadership as decisive, courageous, and effective. Major Bradford summed up their collective opinion: "I am pleased to say that I observed with pleasure the devotion you manifested towards your Regiment & your country. . . ."[61]

From that time until his death more than four decades later, Davis never doubted that the Rifles had saved the army, both in their initial charge and then in the defense. He always believed that his V-formation had been both a brilliant innovation and a critically important deployment. Whether or not brilliant, it indisputably showed imagination and decisiveness in an acute emergency. Without question, those two actions on the northern plateau saved the American rear at crucial junctures, though it cannot be proven that they were mostly responsible for the American victory. The Third Indiana had an instrumental part in the second fight. Also momentous was the afternoon contest on the central plateau, in which the First Mississippi significantly participated. Serious recent students of the battle point to the artillery as making the real difference for the Americans, and, of course, those guns helped Jefferson Davis. Throughout the day the field artillery, superbly handled by regular officers like Captain Braxton Bragg, who would reappear in Davis's future, provided mobile and ferocious firepower all over the field. The Mexicans could not match it. At the same time, the Rifles and their colonel performed splendidly and contributed conspicuously to the American triumph.[62]

After Buena Vista, the war began to wind down for the First Mississippi. With Mexican and American attention centered on Winfield Scott's campaign, which got underway in early March 1847, Taylor's force became basically an army of occupation, guarding supply lines and tangling with guerrillas. During the spring the regiment prepared for its homeward journey. A volunteer organization, it had been mustered in for one year, and its twelve months would be up in June.

On May 17, near Monterrey, a parade was held to honor the Rifles, with Old Rough-and-Ready appearing in full regulation uniform, a rare display, to pay his respects to a unit that he had grown to admire greatly. As the ceremony concluded, Colonel Davis brought the Rifles to attention with each man standing as nearly as possible where he had stood the evening before the Battle of Monterrey. A witness pictured "a solemn sight," with "great gaps" marking the places that had been occupied by those who had fallen. To this observer "the Regiment looked like an old comb with most of the teeth broken out." The First Mississippi had embarked for Mexico with more than 900 officers and men, but would return home with only 376 battle-tested veterans. Following the parade, the regiment retraced its route to Camargo, on to the mouth of the Rio Grande, and finally to New Orleans, which all companies reached in early June.[63]

The First Mississippi and Colonel Jefferson Davis disembarked in New Orleans to a tumultuous welcome. Even before leaving the mouth of the Rio Grande, each man in the regiment received a new blue uniform presented by the Mississippi legislature. In the Crescent City on the afternoon of June 10, a "grand and imposing" parade marched to Lafayette Square, the site of the official celebration. After welcoming remarks, Davis rose to respond, resting his wounded leg on a chair because he could not yet walk. In his brief comments he thanked the multitude for their celebration of his brave men, who had unflinchingly faced the enemy and performed magnificently. Both those who fell and remained beneath Mexican soil and those who returned he crowned true heroes, who did their duty and "gave themselves to their country." Davis thought the reception tendered by the city glorious, for "next to approval of his own conscience," he told the gathering, "the soldier values the approbation of his country." Thereupon the throng made its way to the Place d'Armes, where tables 300 feet long groaned with "everything that the heart could wish."[64]

Two days later Davis and four companies headed upriver on steamboats for Natchez and Vicksburg. In Natchez, an excited crowd, including Varina Davis, greeted the victorious soldiers. Once more, Colonel Davis spoke for "the brave men he had the honor to command," who had fought superbly and prevailed against great odds, saying he owed to them "all that, under the circumstances, one man could owe to another." And again he thanked the people for "the very kind reception that had been extended" to him and all who served with him. Then came "the sumptuously loaded board," some twenty toasts, bands playing, and cannon thundering. After the festivities, Davis and Varina rode to the river landing "in a barouche nearly hidden with flowers. . . ." In Vicksburg a five-gun salute welcomed the party, and a procession with nineteen separate units wound to the square for speeches. Then all moved on to Camp Independence, where the regiment had been organized, for barbecue and liquid refreshment, accompanied by thirteen regular toasts with ten more in response from the Rifles.[65]

Although Mississippi hailed its entire regiment, the commander received special accolades. While the Rifles were still in Mexico, the correspondent of the *Vicksburg Whig* applauded Davis, who had "more than distinguished himself" and "attracted the attention of the whole army, and receives and merits unqualified praise." This journalist, who lived with the regiment, reported that the men under Davis's command "conceived him to be superior to any officer in the army—those of them who have no personal fondness for him, prefer him as a commander to anyone else." One of his officers added that even among those who felt Davis's manner too abrupt and even chilling, "their confidence he possesses in the highest degree." A publicly announced "spontaneous project" called for funds to present him with a sword. "Davis is one of those brilliant meteors that shoots along and illuminates the military horizon of the world, at intervals, long and far between," exclaimed an eastern Mississippi newspaper. Davis was adjudged qualified "for any station that a Republican government can bestow." This heroic image even spawned verse, with one poem closing,

The Son of our State whom so proudly we claim;
The soldier and leader—the foremost in fame.[66]

A year earlier Davis had told his sister that his service in Mexico might give him a significant reputation. He could hardly have imagined the result. And this renown would spread far beyond the borders of his state.

CHAPTER SEVEN

"At Present All Is Uncertainty"

Jefferson Davis returned from Mexico in the late spring of 1847 as an authentic war hero, with all the status a war hero commanded in his culture. Observers proclaimed that he could win any state office, and none was too good for him. The editor of the *Ripley Advertiser* declared that Davis would go through the state like " 'a streak of lightning' getting more votes and with more hearty good will than any man who has run for office in Mississippi this many a year." The state Democratic convention adopted as the party motto a command Davis had given at Buena Vista: "Forward—guide centre—march!"[1]

Davis's overwhelming popularity in Mississippi had manifestations far beyond the borders of his home state. Still running a war, President Polk had more officers to appoint, including a new brigadier general. Always favoring partisan credentials and personal loyalty, the president wanted to appoint Robert Armstrong, a longtime friend of his as well as a former associate and subordinate of Andrew Jackson's. The politician Polk found politics blocking his way, however. He informed Armstrong that "public sentiment" clamored for Jefferson Davis, and his failure to heed it "would probably have produced the most disastrous consequences." To ensure that Mississippi remained Democratic, Polk told his friend, he had "to yield" and appoint Davis. And even though the Mississippian was clearly not his preferred choice, the president described Davis as a "scientific and gallant officer," who "richly merit[ed]" his promotion. His decision made, Polk on May 19 wrote Davis praising his performance in Mexico and tendering him a commission as a brigadier general in the United States Army to command a brigade of volunteers.[2]

When Davis received the commission, he was not at all sure that he wanted to return to the army, even as a general. Without question he liked the military, and he had certainly succeeded as a regimental commander. But now he had questions about the army, and he also had to weigh his options as a civilian. A Taylor partisan, Davis knew that Winfield Scott directed the primary war theater, with John Quitman a new major general in that command. Given these circumstances, Davis had to doubt his role should his assignment place him with Scott's force. Away from the army, his luminous stature in Mississippi offered seemingly limitless possibilities. Even before his return, there was talk of his replacing United States Senator Jesse Speight, who had died on May 1. In addition, many urged that he be given the Democratic nomination for governor.

Davis did not make this critical decision without seeking advice. Although he certainly discussed his options with Joseph and most probably with Varina, whose preference he could not doubt, no records reveal their deliberations, except to indicate that Joseph expected his brother to be offered the Senate seat. Davis also consulted his former commanding general and fast friend, Zachary Taylor, who had no doubts. While he believed that Davis deserved both a general's star and any political reward, he advised against the army. He shared Davis's view, erroneous as it turned out, that the war would not last much longer. Moreover, he expressed his opinion that whatever fighting remained would take on more of "a guerilla character," in which "little of reputation c[ould] be gained." Taylor therefore urged Davis to go to the Senate, if his private affairs permitted.[3]

Davis decided on the political course. In a June 20 letter he thanked President Polk profusely, but turned down the brigadier-generalship on constitutional grounds. He maintained that because volunteers were really militia troops, they had a constitutional right to serve under the immediate command of officers appointed by state authority, even after they entered the service of the United States. Thus, Davis said he could not take command of such units in violation of his principles. No evidence indicates that he had previously held such convictions, but they gave respectability to his negative response, in no way disparaging the president or the war and also enabling him to mask his choice of political office.[4]

At the moment Davis declined the commission, he did not know absolutely that the Senate appointment was his. Yet the available evidence indicates that hope alone did not underlie his refusal of the president's offer. As early as May 1847, various newspapers had asserted that Governor Albert G. Brown would surely award the vacant post to

Davis, and in mid-July, Davis informed a political confidant that he was "really obliged to Governor Brown for feelings which by others I had been led to believe that he did not entertain towards to me." Zachary Taylor leaves no question that Davis saw the Senate as considerably more than a mere possibility. Commenting on Davis's correspondence to him, Taylor in June wrote a son-in-law that Davis was deciding between a civilian and a military position.[5]

Even though certainty is impossible, the record forcefully suggests that sometime early in the summer Governor Brown let Davis know how he intended to fill the Senate vacancy. After all, Brown was a shrewd politician who knew as much about the public mood in Mississippi as anyone else. He undoubtedly saw Davis as a potential rival, but he had no intention of turning the wounded war hero into a political martyr. Besides, other leaders pushed him to appoint Davis. When, on August 10, Brown sent Davis formal notification of the appointment, he received in return the prompt acceptance he expected. As all had anticipated, public acclaim resounded through the state. Praising the governor's action, the leading Democratic newspaper proclaimed, "No selection could have given greater satisfaction to the *whole* State than this." The Whig press exuberantly joined the chorus: "In this appointment the Governor has, without doubt, given expression to the wishes of a large majority of the people of the State."[6]

Davis would be making his second trip to Washington in as many years, but sharply different circumstances marked the occasion. In the fall of 1845 he had been an unknown freshman congressman. Two years later he would enter the Senate with a national reputation as an enormously popular military hero, who had rapidly ascended to the highest level of Mississippi politics. In 1845 he had taken his young bride with him to the capital, but this time he would leave her behind.

Jefferson Davis went to Washington alone because the family difficulties that had first brought him home from Mexico erupted again. His arrival at Davis Bend in June 1847 seemed to inflame what had been at best a simmering détente between wife and brother. That summer Varina wrote her mother decrying "this miserable business of Brother Joe's," which had given Jefferson "more pain if possible than expected." The evidence makes clear, however, that Jefferson's distress did not result chiefly from anything Joseph did, but rather from Varina's behavior. Addressing her directly, he did not mince words: "You had an opportunity when I came to you cripple, so as to be confined to the house, to quarrel with me as much as would have satisfied any ordinary person. . . ."[7]

Although it appears that Joseph and Varina's competition for Jefferson's affection and attention underlay the discord, at least two specific matters generated abundant agitation for Varina. First, the old issue of Jefferson's will arose once more. A new will drawn up in 1847 evidently replicated central portions of the 1846 version, which had surely upset her. The terms of this one also stipulated that she could live at Brierfield and would receive income from the plantation during her lifetime, but, as before, she would share these proceeds with certain of her husband's relatives. Also, as in 1846, she would not control the estate, much less inherit the property, a situation that she found intolerable.[8]

Compounding the matter of the will which so offended Varina were the plans for a new residence at Brierfield. During Jefferson's leave at Davis Bend in the fall of 1846, he had agreed to build a new and larger home, but beyond that general determination, he and Varina had settled on no specifics. As the plans matured in the autumn of 1847, Varina reacted furiously, angry at both Jefferson and Joseph. She was distressed mainly because the house was being designed to accommodate not only Jefferson and herself but also his widowed sister Amanda and her children. The house would have a central section separating two wings and two kitchens, one for each family.

Though the general cause of Varina's unhappiness is clear, the precise origins are less so. That she would have to share her home with another woman rankled her. She also identified Joseph as a source of trouble, blaming him for trying to dictate particulars of construction. She told her mother that decisions concerning the house were not always conveyed to her, even though "I always speak as if it were mine and no one else's." At the same time she admitted that all family members remained "affectionate" with her.[9]

Jefferson, in contrast, pointed to Varina herself. He claimed that she had proposed that Amanda live with them, and he planned the house design on her wishes. Then, according to Jefferson, Varina changed her mind and announced that to live with Amanda would be "a source of *misery*." He even told Varina that she had been generally disagreeable about the design, rejecting several proposals before finally agreeing to one. The question of fault or responsibility aside, the two women did like each other. Alone at Brierfield with her husband in

Mexico, Varina enjoyed visits from Amanda, who was living at Hurricane, and she liked Amanda's daughter, Malie, who often spent the night with her. Eventually, according to Varina, they "declined" to live together because, as Varina put it, neither of them would be subordinate in the household.[10]

In the fall of 1847 Jefferson Davis became quite impatient with his wife and emphasized his displeasure with her by leaving her at home when he departed for Washington. Because their months in the capital when he served in the House had been so exhilarating for Varina, he had to know how much it would hurt her not to accompany him. When she told her mother that she "had rather die than take leave of him," she may have spoken truthfully, but she had no choice in the matter. She also reported that Jefferson "went from [her] comfortable, and as happy as the circumstances would admit of." The circumstances obviously were not at all happy.[11]

Jefferson was blunt. "I will be frank with you," he wrote from Washington about why he had refused to bring her with him. Even though he headed north "with body crippled, even shattered, and mind depressed," he had felt compelled to go without her because his "dread of constant strife was so great." "I cannot expose myself to such conduct as your's when with me here," he declared. "I cannot bear constant harassment, occasional reproach, and subsequent misrepresentation." To him, his wife's misdeeds had been numerous and serious—her attitude about the house; her not caring for him when he was hurt; her grumbling about servants, then becoming angry when he found "a kind companion," Amanda, to take charge of the household when he was away; her accusing his relatives of having "a mercenary motive"; her general complaining and bitterness. It had been too much: "henceforth I will not answer your assaults or insults." He growled that unless she changed, her conduct "would render it impossible for us ever to live together."

While admonishing his wife, Jefferson Davis revealed once again his view of their relationship. He had hoped that "left in our separation to the full force of your affection for me, you would have enjoyed more equanimity than when we were together." Admitting that "I cannot bear to be suspected or complained of, or misconstrued after explanation, *by you*," he inveighed, "circumstances, habits, education, combativeness, render you prone to apply the tests which I have just said I cannot bear." He expected that she "would have grappled with substantial facts," which would have led her to "a line of conduct suited to the character of your husband, and demanded by your duties as a wife." "You should," he intoned, "as a moral duty as a social obligation exercise such prudence and self-control in all things as will conduce to your health physical and mental."[12]

In the midst of this blistering lecture, an obviously angry husband still professed his love for what he saw as an errant wife. At one point he even suggested that Varina may have acted unintentionally. "We are opt by viewing our own heart, to contrive our acts differently from others, and conscious of your love for me, you may not have understood how far your treatment of me was injurious." Despite his discouragement at most of her letters, in which he detected little beneficial change in her attitude, he mentioned the "community and affection" they shared. In April 1848 he even let her know that Mrs. Robert Walker had offered to have Varina stay with her at the Virginia springs and elsewhere after the congressional recess. His love for her had obviously not diminished, and because of that, "it would always make me happier to be with you, if kind and peaceful." Trying to convey those feelings, he closed this spring letter: "Affectionately your husband Truth & Love ever attend upon you—Good night." He also sent her tangible symbols—a cameo of him enclosed in a band of gold for her wrist, a small gold chain, and a gold pen and pencil. Despite this showing of a softer side, he did not invite her to Washington and would remain apart from her until his return to Mississippi in the late summer of 1848.[13]

No evidence remains that clearly illumines Varina's reaction to her husband's harsh preaching, though his soft words and endearing gifts tempered its severity. None of her letters to him during this nine-month separation has survived, or been discovered. Although she did cherish her presents, she probably divulged less than the entire truth when to her mother she announced, "in trying to do my whole, I am happy, and absolutely look upon Jeff's pleasure or displeasure as a minor consideration to my own duty."[14]

When Jefferson Davis was getting underway for Washington, he not only had to deal with an extraordinarily tense family situation but also had to cope with poor health. His war wound had been flaring up and he had suffered from "a severe attack of sickness" marked by fever, most likely malarial. When he made public appearances in Jackson and Vicksburg, observers commented on his "very feeble health." Even after he reached Washington, his foot remained troublesome. He stood with crutches when he took his oath of office in the Senate chamber on

December 6. During the winter his foot did improve, but not until spring did he report, "my health is almost restored."[15]

Even though emotional stress and physical problems plagued him, Brierfield was thriving. Before he got home in June 1848, Joseph let him know that all was well at Brierfield, both crops and slaves. The plantation he had built had become prosperous, with the rich alluvial soil producing bountiful harvests of cotton. During Davis's stay in Washington, the same arrangements made for his military absence took effect. James Pemberton, his overseer as well as slave, still had responsibility for the operations at Brierfield, under Joseph's watchful supervision, of course. As senator, Jefferson Davis could rest assured that capable and loyal men, one black, the other white, watched over the major source of his financial well-being.[16]

On November 11, 1847, Davis steamed up the Mississippi River from Vicksburg with his senatorial colleague and fellow Democrat Henry S. Foote as traveling companion. Davis and Foote had known each other at least since the campaign of 1844, when both, as rising Democratic stars, served as presidential electors. Although they got along at this point, strains would develop over the next two years, growing into animosity. In a week they reached Cincinnati, where former president John Tyler, who happened to be in the city, came on board their vessel for a visit. Then they continued up the Ohio River and finally headed east, arriving in Washington on November 25. Davis initially registered at Gadsby's New Hotel on the corner of Pennsylvania Avenue and Third Street, but soon moved to Mrs. Owner's boardinghouse on Capitol Hill.[17]

On December 6, Davis went to the Capitol for his swearing in as a U.S. senator. He entered a Senate chamber that had long been in use and would house the Senate until it moved to newly constructed quarters in the north wing in 1859. A compact, semicircular room, 75 feet at its longest, 45 at both its widest and tallest, this space provided a human-sized home for the sixty senators. The principal light entered from the east side above the vice president's chair, which sat on an elevated platform; apertures at the top of the dome and a chandelier added illumination. Marble columns of the Doric order formed a screen on either side of the vice president's post. The senators' mahogany desks were arranged in concentric semicircles on gradually rising platforms, one long-armed chair and a cuspidor for each. Heat came from open fires—four grates beneath the shelves in the corridor behind the vice president's place—and from two Franklin stoves near the main entrance. Davis's desk was located on the far right side of the last row to the right of the vice president, next to his old friend William Allen of Ohio.[18]

When he took his Senate seat, the thirty-nine-and-a-half-year-old Jefferson Davis was a vigorous person, though the wound he sustained at Buena Vista yet hobbled him and he was getting over his most recent malarial attack. A young reporter who saw him in the Senate in 1848 pictured him as "handsome, possessing a symmetrical figure, well up to medium size, a piercing but kindly eye, and a gamy chivalric bearing." This observer, who liked Davis because of his "genial personal kindness," thought him "a fluent and sometimes an eloquent speaker," with "a fine, sensuous voice."[19]

Politically, Davis found himself in the majority, for the Democrats had a comfortable lead of seventeen over the rival Whigs, though that party outnumbered the Democrats in the House of Representatives. Not surprisingly, Davis found himself appointed to the Committee on Military Affairs; in addition, he served on the Pension and Library committees as well as on the Board of Regents of the Smithsonian Institution. Viewing the prospects for this first session of the Thirtieth Congress, he saw the war as the major issue. Despite vigorous Whig opposition to the conflict that had developed in 1847, Davis was convinced that under the leadership of President Polk, whom he found optimistic and confident, the Democrats could "discomfit the enemy," at home as well as in Mexico. One measure that he discounted was the Wilmot Proviso, introduced in Congress back in 1846 by David Wilmot, a Democratic representative from Pennsylvania, and brought up again in the most recent congressional session. The proviso, which drew overwhelming bipartisan support from northerners in Congress, proposed to prohibit slavery in any territory taken or purchased from Mexico. Davis foresaw no real problems with the measure, a noxious proposition to southerners, predicting that it "will soon be of the things which were." In this monumental underestimation he may have followed the lead of Zachary Taylor, who had made that judgment while sharing with Davis his opinions on political matters.[20]

As a new senator who wanted to remain a senator, Jefferson Davis kept his own political situation in sharp focus. Governor Brown's naming him to the Senate did not guarantee a lengthy tenure because the legislature meeting in January 1848 would elect a man to finish the two years left in Jesse Speight's unexpired term. From the moment he accepted the appointment, Davis intended to stand for election, and he very much wanted the legislature to choose him. As he confided to a friend, "I now feel greater interest than I should have done had I remained at home, because to be beaten under present circumstances is to be recalled."[21]

Even though Davis ran as the incumbent with his war hero's image, victory was not a foregone conclusion. A tradition of Mississippi politics worked against him—dividing the Senate seats between the northern and southern sections of the state. Davis's senior colleague Foote lived in Jackson, considered in the southern part, and as Davis well knew, some Democrats in northern Mississippi thought their area deserved the position Davis held. They intended to support Roger Barton, an attorney in Holly Springs, who had been in the legislature and had twice before tried for the Senate. Long a champion of Davis, the leading party newspaper, the *Jackson Mississippian*, publicly refused to take sides and praised both men as "Democrats of the sternest school."[22]

Davis did not sit idly by. Within a week of reaching Washington, he requested that a political associate in Mississippi mail him a "list of Correspondents" because he had not been able to locate "the books and papers" he had left in the capital back in the summer of 1846. In order to keep abreast of state affairs, he also asked that the editor of the *Mississippian* be reminded to send him the paper. Davis did not focus his attention only on Democrats, however. Aware that many Whig legislators who recognized they could not elect one of their own preferred him to any other Democrat, he made known his pleasure in their support. When Mississippi's lone Whig congressman, Patrick Tompkins, wrote to inform Davis of rumors that he would refuse Whig backing, Davis answered on the same day that he would happily accept Whig votes because as a senator he represented the entire state, not just his party. Proclaiming that no one could doubt Davis's partisan credentials, his home county Democratic newspaper asserted that he would never, and should never, make a "quixotic" pledge to spurn Whig aid.[23]

When the legislature met, Jefferson Davis overpowered Roger Barton. With the Democrats dominating the body by more than a two-to-one majority, any Democratic candidate who commanded their allegiance would win easily, but if a bitter division wracked their ranks, the thirty-five Whigs could decide the outcome. Caucusing on January 10, 1848, in the Hall of Representatives, the Democratic legislators decided without contention that a majority would be required for nomination and that no one could vote in the caucus unless he pledged to support its nominee before the legislature, guaranteeing, of course, victory for the party's choice. Because all knew that only Davis and Barton were contestants, the caucus dispensed with formal nominations and proceeded directly to the voting, which it had agreed to do viva voce rather than by ballot. Davis's power was unmistakable; he won by 54 to 34, sweeping the south of the state and doing well in the north. In an unusually short time he had moved to a position of remarkable strength in the overwhelmingly dominant political organization in his state. The next day the full legislature chose Davis by acclamation; Whigs as well as Democrats voted for him. A reporter described a crowded Hall of Representatives, with many ladies present, for "Mississippi was about to reward her hero, and the people flocked together to witness the triumphal ceremony." It was an "extraordinary occurrence," cried the *Mississippian*, while proudly proclaiming Senator Davis "the pride and boast of the State at home and abroad."[24]

Secure now that he had been elected in his own right, Davis turned his attention to policy matters. From the outset he involved himself with issues arising out of the ongoing Mexican War. Just over three weeks after taking his seat, he visited the White House along with Senator Lewis Cass of Michigan, a senior Democrat, to press President Polk to relieve General Winfield Scott. Davis wanted Zachary Taylor in Scott's place, and he also relayed to the president information from army friends indicating the Mexican government would welcome a peace mission. Although Polk shared the senators' unhappiness with Scott, he was unwilling to go with Taylor, and left Scott in command. As for peace, Polk wanted it but had determined more punishment would be required before Mexico would make the territorial concessions he demanded.[25]

When Davis began his senatorial duties, deep division on the war, basically following partisan lines, divided both country and Congress. The Whigs were never happy with the conflict and by late 1847, with Mexico City in American hands and the shooting basically stopped, they took the political offensive, attacking the administration for dragging out the war for unwarranted territorial aggrandizement. The Whig-controlled House of Representatives had gone so far as to pass a resolution declaring that the war had been "unnecessarily and unconstitutionally begun by the President of the United States." Crying for a prompt cessation of hostilities, Whigs had an ally in the nominal Democrat Senator John C. Calhoun, who had never supported what he thought of as an offensive war and who had become deeply concerned by talk among some Democrats of annexing all of Mexico. Facing this combined Whig-Calhoun pressure, and with a public generally yearning for peace, President Polk and his party found themselves forced to defend both intentions and measures.[26]

This antiwar opinion underlay the Whig-led attack on the Ten Regiment Bill. With more troops needed in Mexico, the administration wanted Congress to authorize ten additional regiments for the regular army. Accordingly, Senator Cass, chairman of the Committee on Military Affairs, reported a bill doing just that. Whigs resisted a larger regular army, which they saw as evidence that Polk had no intention of quickly ending the war. Although they opposed increasing the size of the regular military establishment, the Whigs had no intention of allowing themselves to be accused of failing to provide the forces needed in Mexico. As a result, they called for additional militia units.

During the Senate debate Davis spoke for the Ten Regiment Bill, though as a proud former commander of militia troops he did not disparage their virtue. He argued that the surest way to convince the Mexican government to negotiate seriously was the rapid augmentation of U.S. forces. Our enemy, he told his fellow senators, could not miss that signal. He made clear that he did not doubt the bravery and fighting ability of citizen-soldiers, but he insisted that the critical question concerned the kind of service intended for these new units. He pointed out that because these troops would perform chiefly garrison and guard duty, regulars would be preferable; they would more readily submit to the necessary discipline than militia volunteers, who should not be "wasted in the mere duties of the sentinel." Davis maintained that the administration wanted peace, not further combat, but to ensure the commencement of negotiations as well as their satisfactory outcome the U.S. Army would have to continue occupying the territory it had conquered. A month after first giving his views, Davis summarized: "Again, I will state as my reason for wishing to increase our army so largely, the belief that its visible strength must be such as to destroy in the enemy all hope of resistance before he will seriously incline to peace."[27]

Senator Davis did not hesitate to support the president's war policy, even against the opposition of Calhoun, whom he so admired. In the eyes of many, Polk had made an offensive move by his initial order to General Taylor to advance all the way to the Rio Grande; but Davis countered that because Mexico disputed the American claim to all of Texas, not just the area below the Nueces River, Polk had not acted in a belligerent fashion. The president, Davis insisted, had shown great "forbearance" in his dealings with an intransigent foe. He also denied that either he or the administration desired to take all of Mexico, but some land would have to be given up, and he defended the proposition that if Mexico did "not give us peace willingly, we will coerce a peace." Denouncing those who branded the war as odious, Davis proclaimed that "the events of this war will live in the history of our country and our race, affording, in all ages to come, proof of the high state of civilization amongst the people who conducted it—proof of the intelligence which pervaded the rank and file who fought its battles—proof of the resources of such a Government as ours, wholly unembarrassed in the midst of war, conquering one nation and feeding another!"[28]

During the congressional struggle over the course and future of the war, a peace treaty arrived in Washington. Even though this agreement contained the cession of the territory Polk had gone to war to obtain—chiefly California and New Mexico, which placed more than 500,000 additional square miles under the American flag—the president wanted to reject it. Recognizing the general public desire for peace, however, he concluded that he simply had to submit the treaty to the Senate for ratification. When the senators voted on March 10 to endorse the Treaty of Guadalupe Hidalgo, Jefferson Davis cast his ballot for approval, but not before he had tried to alter the stipulated boundary to include much of present-day northern Mexico. Because Mexico was unlikely to accept such a substantive change, Davis was in fact proposing to continue the war so that the Mexicans would be forced to agree to new terms. Although Davis's effort had the support of several Democratic colleagues, northern as well as southern, it fell far short of obtaining a majority. Attempts by Whigs to delete all territorial acquisitions also failed. After those two futile moves, the Senate ratified the treaty by 38 to 14, with Davis voting aye. The Mexican War was over.[29]

The war was not the only question on which Davis discovered himself differing with Calhoun. As a member of the House in 1846, he had refused to follow the great Carolinian's constitutional justification for federally sponsored improvements on western rivers, finding specious the argument that defined rivers, even the Ohio and Mississippi system, as inland seas. During an April 1848 discussion of an appropriation to repair the Cumberland Island Dam because its disrepair was disrupting shipping in the Ohio River, Davis spoke in favor of spending the money, but only because the federal government had constructed the dam. Although agreeing that the government should pay to maintain what it had built, he took pains to repeat that in general he opposed all internal improvements because they rested upon "an assumption of power not conferred by the Constitution." He rejected both regulation of commerce and Calhoun's specific brief on buoys and lighthouses as the basis for this expenditure. His support derived solely from the particular circumstances of this instance.[30]

Even though issues of war and peace as well as constitutional interpretation occupied Senator Davis, he did not neglect service to his constituents. He recommended several veterans of the First Mississippi Regiment for army commissions. For others who had served with him he worked to ensure the government's attention to their applications for bounty lands. Letters soliciting appointments to West Point for young Mississippians received his attention as did the collectorship of customs at Natchez. The editor of the *Washington Union,* a semiofficial organ of the administration, got a note from Senator Davis requesting that he send the newspaper to a Mississippi voter. He also asked Secretary of the Treasury Robert Walker to help his father-in-law, William B. Howell, obtain the postmastership in Natchez. As in the House, he still plugged away at trying to get a navy yard for Ship and Cat Islands on the Mississippi Gulf Coast.[31]

As the congressional session moved into the summer, Congress and Jefferson Davis confronted directly the issue that would dominate the national legislature over the next two years and would remain at the forefront until it tore the Union apart: slavery in the territories. The question arose in the most unlikely of places, Oregon, which still had no territorial government, even though the treaty with Great Britain had been signed in 1846. Although debate focused initially on Oregon, it aroused such fervor because all recognized that Oregon would serve as a dress rehearsal for the Mexican Cession, California and New Mexico. Tabled since February 1848, the Oregon bill was brought up at the end of May and talked about intermittently for three weeks until an antislavery senator proposed to extend to the territory the Northwest Ordinance of 1787, which would bar slavery. Countering, Jefferson Davis offered an amendment to prevent prohibition of slavery in Oregon. Now the Senate riveted its full attention on this vexing and volatile matter. On July 12, Davis rose to defend his proposition; even more important, he would present for the first time in Congress his vision of slavery and the territories, the topic that would occupy so much of his thought over the next dozen years.[32]

"Deeply impressed with the gravity and importance of the subject," Davis spoke about "the grave and melancholy questions" that emerged from it. He identified as central "political strife, for sectional supremacy." That drive led directly to "an interference with domestic affairs of the people in one portion of the Union, wounding to their pride and sensibility, and unwarranted by the compact of the confederation." Such an intrusion might result in "a discrimination against one section of the Confederacy, the palpable object of which is totally to destroy political equality. . . ." On this point Davis followed Calhoun's dictum that sectional parity was fundamental to the constitutional past and must continue unchanged because no other arrangement could guarantee tranquillity for the nation.

Davis forecast that this treacherous tack menacing sectional equality would bring about "the foreboding fear" of Thomas Jefferson: sectional political parties. That in turn, Davis worried, could only "hasten" what he perceived as "the inevitable goal" of those who assaulted the honor of the South while they strove to deprive southerners of their constitutional rights, "the disunion of the States." The South, he cried, can never "consent to be a marked caste, doomed, in the progress of national growth, to be dwarfed into helplessness and political dependence."

He called for a turning away from such a destructive course by the assertion of "patriotism and enlightened statesmanship," which had marked earlier epochs of the country's history. Davis certainly saw himself performing this role, for he averred that he had no desire to impose slavery on Oregon. Instead, his chief goal was to protect the constitutional rights of southern Americans. He informed his fellow senators that he neither claimed nor wanted more than strict constructionists ever had—to keep the federal government from exercising unconstitutional powers that had never been granted to it. In his reading, the U.S. Constitution had nowhere authorized Congress to prohibit slavery in any territory.

Senator Davis took his constitutional text on what he termed the founding document's recognition of property "in persons," pointing specifically to the provisions requiring the return of fugitives from service or labor and permitting Congress to outlaw the international slave trade after twenty years. With this view almost all contemporary interpreters concurred, even supporters of the Wilmot Proviso, though a contrary opinion held by some radical antislavery writers argued that because the word "slavery" never appeared in the Constitution, the framers had refused to give it their blessing. Moreover, these proponents of an antislavery Constitution maintained that the power given Congress to ban the international slave trade meant the Founding Fathers thought slavery temporary. More crucially, they argued, the ban signaled that Congress held the authority to act on other aspects of slavery. This antislavery reading of the Constitution never triumphed in Congress before the Civil War.[33]

Davis went on to say that the federal government had recognized slavery in treaties completing the acquisition of the Louisiana Purchase and Florida as well as ending the War of 1812. He claimed that his foes had no such stronghold. Even when he admitted that the Constitution did allow the government to make rules for territories, he, like most southerners, construed that grant narrowly, to refer solely to territories as public lands. To him the constitutional phrase "territory or other property" demonstrated his conclusion "too distinctly to require elucidation." Only needful measures like the creation of territorial courts could be passed. As for the power inherent in the federal government's right to acquire territory, Davis grasped his states' rights standard: because the federal government acted as the agent of the sovereign states, "the acquisition must inure to the benefit of the States, in whose right alone it could be made." In the same sense, Congress could not turn over any decision regarding slavery to the settlers in a territory because they had no claim to sovereignty; only the states were sovereign, except where the Constitution made an explicit grant of power to the federal government.

In addition, Davis addressed a concept that would become even more fractious in the upcoming clash over organizing the Mexican Cession: the legitimacy of the laws of the previous owner. He ridiculed the proposition that the preceding legal provisions retained their legitimacy until replaced by new American legislation; in his opinion the Constitution automatically and in full force followed the flag, protecting all American citizens in all of their rights. No other view contained any logic. If he were to give any credence to this illogical and wrongheaded consideration, he said he could use it for Oregon, where the American claim came from Spain, in whose empire slavery existed at the time the title was transferred to the United States. Thus, it would still be legal. Of course, in the Mexican Cession the reverse would obtain, for Mexico had abolished slavery.

No matter whether that premise would help or hurt his cause, Davis dismissed it as preposterous. "Shall the citizen," he asked his colleagues, "who, rejoicing in the extended domain of his country, migrates to its newly acquired territory, find himself shorn of the property he held under the Constitution by the laws of Mexico? Shall the widow and orphan of him who died in his country's quarrel, be excluded from the acquisition obtained in part by his blood, unless they will submit to the laws of the power he bled and died to subdue?" His answer resounded: "Never, Never! Reason and justice, constitutional right and national pride, combine to forbid the supposition."

Finally, Davis confronted those who asserted that the South demanded nothing more than an abstraction. If that were the case, he wanted to know why the opponents of the South "so obstinately resisted" its claims. He did not minimize principle, announcing, "The men who have encountered past war for the maintenance of principle, will never consent to be branded with inferiority—pronounced, because of their domestic institutions, unworthy of further political growth." In Davis's mind the political future moved the subject from the abstract to the concrete. As he comprehended the ultimate goal of many of his opponents, they desired to forbid the extension of slavery in order "to obtain in the future such preponderance of free states as will enable them constitutionally to amend the compact of our Union, and strip the South of the guarantees it gives." "The lust of power, and an irrational hostility to your brethren of the South," he identified as prompting what he saw as an unjustified attack, which if kept up could end only by "staining the battle-fields of the Revolution with the blood of civil war."

Davis did not believe that destruction of the Union and fraternal bloodletting were inevitable, however. Praising the tradition of compromise and pledging southern loyalty to that custom, he pointed to the three-fifths provision in the Constitution and the Missouri Compromise of 1820 as examples of the forbearance that had been synonymous with American patriotism. He was willing, he told his listeners, to adhere to that honorable practice of finding a middle way because "to compromise is to waive the application, not to surrender the principles on which a right rests, and surely give no claim to further concession." While asserting he would forever cling to principle, Davis enunciated clearly that he would make a deal, but only if the other side evinced a willingness to meet him at least partway.

At the time Jefferson Davis explained at length his position on the territorial issue, the Senate was seeking a path around the formidable political barrier erected by the Oregon version of that question. With President Polk's backing, an effort was already underway to extend the Missouri Compromise line westward from the Rocky Mountains to the Pacific Ocean, thus making Oregon free because it lay north of the 36°30′ boundary that separated slavery from freedom in the Louisiana Purchase. Even as the Senate considered the Missouri extension, which was overwhelmingly opposed by northerners of both parties, it tried yet another initiative produced by a special committee chaired by Delaware Whig John M. Clayton. This measure, which took on Clayton's name, had two major provisions. First, it created a territorial government for Oregon that allowed an antislavery ban by an unofficial provisional government to stand until the new territorial legislature decided for or against slavery. Second, it established territorial governments for California and New Mexico, but specifically prohibited them from acting on slavery. Instead, in those territories it turned the decision on the legality of slavery over to the federal judiciary. Although the Senate narrowly approved Clayton's offering, the House refused to go along chiefly because of powerful northern opposition, linked with a few southern Whigs who claimed to be worried about ceding southern rights to the courts.

Congress seemingly faced adjournment with Oregon still unorganized and no mechanism in sight to handle the looming problem of the Mexican Cession. The Senate hoped that an appeal to the past might win last-minute approval for extending the Missouri Compromise line. With Davis in the majority, the Senate passed the bill on August 11 and sent it to the House. Led by Whigs, northern congressmen remained adamant and removed all reference to the Missouri Compromise in the Oregon bill that went back to the Senate. There, most southerners, including Davis, refused to ratify the measure without the Missouri Compromise provisions, but at almost the last hour three slave-state senators broke ranks, and the Senate put its seal on the House bill by the narrow margin of 28 to 25, with Davis on the losing side. Although President Polk had threatened to veto any organization of Oregon without mention of the Missouri Compromise and would have negated the Wilmot Proviso, he did sign this Oregon act with the notation that he did so only because the territory rested north of 36°30′. Through all the weeks of congressional wrangling, one circumstance was crystal clear—in both houses the overwhelming majority of northern members of both parties opposed giving the South what almost all southerners considered their rights, a fact not lost on Jefferson Davis.[34]

While speaking for what he judged the constitutional rights of the South and slaveowners in the territories, Davis did not hesitate to defend openly the South's "paternal institution." Noting the existence of slavery among the Hebrews of the Old Testament, Davis claimed biblical legitimacy and sanction. When he discussed the racial slavery practiced in his section, he praised its positive impact on the blacks, whom he described as being far better off than either the free blacks in the North or those recently emancipated in the West Indies.[35]

According to Davis, a major reason for the well-being of the slaves rested in a critical fact: "slaves are capital; and in the mind of the master, there can be no contest between capital and labor—the contest from which so much of human suffering and oppression has arisen." In Davis's definition of slavery, kindness and self-interest meshed to restrain "the sordid and vicious" practices that prevailed with hired labor. In his script the slaves themselves recognized the validity of his interpretation of their situation. Three months earlier he had pronounced them "happy and contented," living in "the kindest relation that labor can sustain to capital." As a result he had no fear at all of slave "insurrection," informing the Senate that he had "no more dread of our slaves than I have of our cattle." An added boon from southern slavery was the equality of all whites because Davis argued that real social equality could never occur where the same race performed as both "master and menial." Although he spoke sincerely about his sense of the political and social interrelationship among southern whites, his defense of slavery oversimplified and made much gentler an affiliation between master and slave that in reality was both more complex and harsher. But as advocate for his side, he felt no need to make the case for his opponent.[36]

Davis linked the alleged benignity of slavery to territorial expansion by invoking a version of the hoary diffusion theory that had been periodically touted by exponents of slavery expansion since the time of Thomas Jefferson and James Madison. In Davis's rendition, the master-slave connection took on a more kindly character when slaves were dispersed and owned by many individuals who maintained personal contact with their bondspeople. Confining slavery geographically meant, in Davis's view, large holdings, often with "agents" or overseers standing between masters and slaves, making for a harsher system. Thus, Davis avowed that the absence of limits would secure the best treatment of slaves. Moreover, affirming that slavery became the preferred form of labor only in frontierlike conditions, Davis claimed that as population density increased, free workers became more profitable. For Davis, however, the implementation of this social law in the South faced severe difficulties because the slaves composed "a distinct race" that must be kept in bondage even when unprofitable, for white and black could not live together peaceably in any other relationship.[37]

Even so, Davis foresaw a future that might lead to what he described as having happened in the Northeast—a slave population so decreased that emancipation could be contemplated and even enacted. And Davis could not resist noting that northeasterners only began condemning slavery as "the sin and opprobrium of the nation" after slavery had disappeared from their region. Continued expansion westward and southward, he speculated, might eventually lead toward the tropics, where blacks could congregate in communities separated from whites and relieved from "the condition of degradation." Holding out that possibility, he denounced abolitionists for their "indecent intrusion on the domestic affairs of others—I ask what remedy do you propose?" He answered his own question by claiming that his enemies had none, for they knew the impossibility of emancipating a distinct race. Even if the states agreed, Davis asserted that the federal government did not have sufficient funds. Besides, he posited, the end of slavery would result in the demise of cotton and that would ruin the northern economy. His conclusion was obvious: immediate, radical change simply could not occur; only the longest-term kind of solution could be taken into consideration.

Although no reason exists to doubt the sincerity of Davis's argument, he did skim over difficulties and inconsistencies. His "distant future" when slavery might vanish was so far off as to be practically unimaginable. For example, he knew that in Virginia, the state with the largest number of slaves, servitude had survived for two centuries. He never suggested a chronology. Doing so honestly would have entailed setting forth a time frame basically impossible to comprehend and one that certainly would not attract any support from antislavery battalions. Davis also thought of himself and his brother Joseph as kind masters, and he defended their stewardship of their slaves. Yet both owned large slave corps with overseers operating between them and their human property, as did many of their social friends. Whatever Davis precisely intended, he clearly did not mean exactly what he said.

Over the next two years Davis amplified his wide-ranging and vigorous defense of slavery. As he explained to a friend in 1849, "it is time for our justification before the uninformed and that we may be understood by posterity as well as by contemporaries that the long continued and gross misrepresentations of our slave institutions should be answered." Davis believed this duty especially pressing, for "in an evil hour some of the most distinguished southern stat[es]men admitted that slavery was an evil." Such an admission, Davis professed, "takes from us all gro[und] of defence save that of presen[t neces]sity, and not only warrants the attempts of others for its abolition but also demands of us constant efforts to remove the obstacles to its abatement." On the floor of the Senate he announced that "the decree of God" underlay slavery, which he found "sanctioned in the Bible, authorized, regulated, and recognized from Genesis to Revelation." To a Mississippi audience he emphasized that slavery made possible white equality. "No white man in a slave community," he preached, "was the menial servant of anyone." Yes, he acknowledged the permanence of fundamental social distinction; but in the South he insisted that it rested on color and race, whereas in the North and in Europe, wealth denoted the division.[38]

To his overall justification of slavery Davis conceded only one exception, the professional slave trader whose confinement of slaves impaired their health. In the Senate he admitted "the odium which exists against this class of traders," even observing that his own community shared it, as he did personally. Giving on that particular, he almost immediately pulled back by asserting that such men were usually northerners, "who came among us, but are not of us."[39]

Publicly and privately Jefferson Davis stood foursquare behind the institution that he had known since childhood and that provided the foundation for his and Joseph's prosperity and way of life. His constituents applauded. When the *Mississippian* announced its publication of his Oregon speech, the paper praised it as "conclusive and unanswerable; and so we think every candid and unprejudiced mind will regard it."[40]

With the adjournment of Congress on August 14, Senator Davis departed for Mississippi by the western route. After stopping in Kentucky, he reached home by mid-September and almost immediately discovered himself in the midst of a presidential contest that had a special resonance for him. Zachary Taylor was the candidate of the

Whigs, not Davis's Democratic party. Since early in the year Davis had seen presidential politics infecting congressional deliberations.[41]

Davis's relationship with Taylor placed him in an unusual situation. Their friendship had continued on an intimate level even after both had returned to the United States. Taylor, who called Baton Rouge, Louisiana, home but also owned a large cotton plantation in Jefferson County, Mississippi, not far from Davis Bend, really considered Jefferson and brother Joseph as family. When Taylor stopped by Hurricane after visiting his Mississippi plantation, he wrote Jefferson that he did not think of himself as a guest, but rather amid "near & dear relatives." He shared his political views openly and in detail with Davis, partisanship notwithstanding. Basically a nonpartisan professional soldier before the Mexican War, Taylor inclined more toward the Whigs as his heroic image made him an increasingly attractive presidential possibility. The old general was undoubtedly influenced by his feeling that the Polk administration had treated him shabbily.[42]

Widely and correctly seen as close to Taylor, Davis found himself the focal point for a number of people eager to learn the general's position on partisan and policy matters. Before Taylor made clear his intention of joining the Whigs, certain politicos explored the possibility of fitting him with a Democratic uniform. These would-be president-makers sought Davis's advice and enlisted him as a liaison to Taylor. But even though Davis was devoted to his friend and believed his "true position" was on the Democratic side, he never thought Taylor would sign up with the Democrats, and he had no detectable influence on the general's eventual decision to go with the Whigs.[43]

When Taylor did receive the Whig presidential nomination in early June 1848, Davis had to cope with an uncomfortable political decision, but he never wavered. A loyal Democrat, he declared his unequivocal support for his party's nominee, Senator Lewis Cass. He told Mississippi audiences that while he respected and even cherished Zachary Taylor, his personal creed meant his vote would go for Cass. Privately he expressed identical sentiments, telling a friend his affection for Taylor "will be opposed by my convictions, and adherence to measures." At the same time, Davis did not campaign enthusiastically for the Democratic ticket, though he did make a few speeches, all fairly close to Warren County. His less-than-vigorous support for the Democratic standard-bearers did not generate unhappiness in the state party, which expressed considerable empathy for his position. Pointing to "considerations of a private character" that would keep Davis from actively participating in the race, the *Mississippian* pronounced Davis's motives "highly commendable" and certainly approved by Mississippi Democrats.[44]

Despite his relative quiet during the campaign, Davis remained forthright about his commitment to his party. Even before the election year, he publicly asserted that Mississippi Democrats should attend the party's national convention and meet with their northern brethren. He also maintained that "the South should fraternize with the Democracy . . . the party of strict construction, of checks and balances, and constitutional restraints." According to Davis, strict construction should forever abide as "the political Shibboleth of the South." Voting patterns on the territorial issue in the recently adjourned session of Congress troubled him, however. That so many northern Democrats insisted on the Wilmot Proviso and refused to meet the South even partway, as in the extension of the Missouri Compromise line, caused him to question the general commitment of northern Democrats to southern constitutional rights. He worried about the possibility of "a *geographical* division," which he had "always deprecated, and which must be the *precursor* of *disunion*." Despite his concern, he had not yet come close to giving up on his northern associates, whom he believed could end any potentiality of a sectional party if they would "brave the abolitionists." He had no doubt that Cass as president would prove true on the critical issue and veto the Wilmot Proviso should it ever pass Congress, though he did not consider the Michigan senator a great man.[45]

Jefferson Davis genuinely liked Lewis Cass and sincerely believed he would block the Wilmot Proviso, but he did not have complete faith in the solution Cass proposed for the territorial question, popular sovereignty. Borrowing the concept, Cass at the end of 1847 presented popular sovereignty as a way around the proviso that would satisfy the South but not alienate the North. Based on the supreme Democratic principle that the people are sovereign, popular sovereignty first declared the Wilmot Proviso unconstitutional and then stipulated that the settlers in a territory, not the Congress or anyone else, should make the decision on slavery.[46]

Popular sovereignty added to its political allure by leaving the time frame for the crucial decision on slavery conveniently vague. Although the doctrine implied that settlers could accept or reject slavery during the territorial stage, its advocates did not talk about territorial legislatures. The theory also asserted that all settlers had to abide by the basic principles of the Constitution. Northerners who took the implication as the chief thrust could argue that the first territorial legislature could ban slavery if it wanted to do so, but southerners, like Davis, who stressed the constitutional-principles theme, declared that a decision on slavery had to await statehood, for territories lacked the authority to decide so fundamental a question. Only a state possessed the requisite authority. As defined by southern Democrats, popular sovereignty became an extension of their traditional doctrine of states' rights. The inherent inconsistency and vagueness that provided so much of popular sovereignty's political beauty troubled Davis, though he recognized the political utility. Professing loyalty to popular sovereignty, both northern and southern Democrats could interpret it as they wished while banishing the inflammatory Wilmot Proviso from their political vocabulary.

Although the lack of guarantees and the obvious obfuscation bothered Davis, the Democrats offered more on paper than the Whigs, whose northern and southern wings were so divided on the proviso that the Whig convention wrote no platform. That posed no problem for southern Whigs; they presented Zachary Taylor as one of their own, a slaveowning cotton planter, who would never betray the fundamental interests of the South. With his fervent friendship for Taylor, Davis never mentioned any doubts, even though some of Taylor's observations in correspondence should have cautioned him against assuming that the two men would agree on how to handle the territorial issue.[47]

In November the country elected the heroic general as its president, an outcome that did not surprise and could not have disappointed Jefferson Davis. Even in staunchly Democratic Mississippi, Taylor's popularity was evident; he lost the state by fewer than 800 votes. Talk about the prospective Taylor administration even included the Democrat Jefferson Davis, with rumors that he would accept a place in the cabinet. Denying such a possibility, the *Mississippian* editorialized: "We freely say, that the democracy of Col. Davis, in our opinion, is above suspicion." No surviving evidence suggests that either Taylor or Davis seriously considered such a maneuver, but Taylor remained concerned about Davis's political career, always counseling Davis to act as he must. He assured the younger man that not even possible political differences could alter his personal regard and friendship. As for Davis, he was eager for Taylor to succeed as president, going so far as to share thoughts with one of Taylor's closest Whig advisers.[48]

After only two months in Mississippi, Jefferson Davis headed back to Washington for the short second session of the Thirtieth Congress, from December 1848 to March 1849. Taking the southern route down-river to New Orleans and then on to Washington, Davis traveled alone, once again leaving Varina behind. He arrived in Washington on December 1, and established residence, along with several other southern Democrats, at Mrs. Duvall's boardinghouse on Missouri Avenue near 4½ Street, where he remained throughout the session.[49]

Two political forces dominated this post-election Congress. First, basking in Zachary Taylor's victory, Whigs wanted to hamper or undermine any congressional initiative that might possibly upstage Taylor's administration, which would begin with his inauguration on March 4, 1849. Second, John C. Calhoun labored mightily in his supreme attempt to overcome party loyalty and achieve his long-desired southern unity. These two currents intersected when southern Whigs, supremely confident about Taylor's prospects, set about torpedoing Calhoun's effort. Senator Davis was not central in either camp, though he had an interest in both, and he did support Calhoun.[50]

Davis was surely concerned about the circumstance prompting Calhoun to believe that he could substitute sectional for party allegiance— the territorial issue, specifically the possibility that the Wilmot Proviso would become law because northerners in both parties backed it. A move led by northern Whigs in the House against slavery in the District of Columbia heightened southern concern about the intentions of antislavery politicians and caused an uproar among southerners. Public opinion in the South knew no division on the proviso, and considerable activity in the slave states publicized that opposition. Davis had already noted with distress the northern unity behind the proviso; besides, he considered Calhoun the great sentinel of southern rights in the Union. When the congressmen and senators from the South caucused to consider Calhoun's ideas, Davis participated, and he signed the resulting address, which called for a united front against the North and insisted on equal southern rights in the territories. Although Calhoun gained the support of a substantial majority of southern Democrats, he failed to obtain his cherished solidarity, for southern Whigs overwhelmingly rejected his handiwork. Totally convinced that the slaveowning cotton planter Taylor would act for their benefit, southern Whigs wanted neither Calhoun nor anyone else undermining what they envisioned as their glorious political future.

Winter did not find Senator Davis deeply involved in legislative activity. He was worried, however, by what he saw as a potential danger to Taylor's presidency in Henry Clay's scheduled return to the

Senate in December 1849. A major Whig leader since the party's incep-
tion, the magnetic Clay commanded the loyalty of many of the faithful
in Congress, and he resented that Zachary Taylor, not Henry Clay,
would sit in the presidential chair. Davis worried that Clay's influence
coupled with his jealousy might sabotage Taylor. At the same time, he
counseled a Taylor adviser on the general's cabinet. On the vexing territorial issue, southern Whigs in the House tried to bypass the proviso
by admitting immediately all of the Mexican Cession as a single state,
but they failed. When Congress adjourned on March 3, 1849, all was
ready for the inauguration of the new president. Having served as one
of three senators on the committee arranging the ceremony, Davis was
present when his former father-in-law took the oath of office as the
twelfth president of the United States. Then, after attending a brief
special congressional session, he left in late March for home.[51]

Davis returned to a state abundantly exercised by the seemingly
inexorable growth of antislavery rhetoric and political strength. Both
Whigs and Democrats from south-central Mississippi gathered in Jackson on May 7 to consider the general situation. This group in turn
called for a statewide convention to meet in October to assess the condition of affairs and propose a proper course for the state to follow.
Convening in the summer, official bodies of both the Democratic and
Whig parties chorused support for the autumn assembly.[52]

Jefferson Davis was in the midst of this activity. After appearing at
the May meeting, he gave a major address in Jackson. He began by saying that he had not come "to articulate [his] indignation" at the North
but to get "fresh instruction at the hands of the people," though he was
"gratified" to find "vigilance and unanimity" on a question that
involved "the feelings and interests of the whole community." Defining the war waged by antislavery forces as "both wounding and insulting" to the South, he urged that the time had arrived for the South to
put aside the "long supineness" that had characterized its response to
northern attacks and assert its legitimate rights. Northerners, who
argued that the South should remain quiet because no real danger
existed, Davis castigated for giving advice akin to "the lulling of the
vampire fawning the victim which he will destroy." If the South continued to give in, he asserted, "the equality given to us by our fathers is
to be destroyed," because the North would soon have three-quarters of
the states and could then alter the Constitution at will. Even when faced
with such an enemy, Davis found no "spirit of disunion" among southerners, and he certainly opposed "hasty action." "We should make no

ultimatum we do not mean," he concluded, but "when all other things failed then was left the stern appeal—*to arms.*"[53]

During the summer and fall, Senator Davis participated energetically in Democratic party affairs. He attended the party's state convention that nominated his former Mexican War commander John A. Quitman for governor; by this time the two men had put their wartime estrangement behind them and renewed their friendship, at least publicly. Then, in October, Davis toured northern Mississippi, mounting the podium in towns like Aberdeen, Canton, Holly Springs, and Kosciusko. He spoke on behalf of Democratic candidates and spread his alarm at the surging antislavery sentiment in the North, highlighted by the formation in 1848 of the Free Soil party with adoption of the Wilmot Proviso as its chief end. He also wanted to make sure voters did not forget their junior senator. Proudly and correctly, he reported to Varina that he had been received with "most flattering demonstrations of regard."[54]

Davis took this opportunity to proclaim his loyalty to the Democratic party and to praise his political home. Pledging his fealty to party candidates, he declared that Mississippi Democrats knew no internal division; all acted as one. "Our creed," he announced, is grounded "on the immutable basis of truth, and will descend from generation to generation such as it came to us." Praising that creed's permanence, he reached for a metaphorical illustration: "Temporary excitement, faction or error, like enveloping mists, may obscure it for a while, yet it will stand, as the house which the wise man built on a rock." Davis's efforts were not in vain, for the Democrats won a smashing victory: the governorship, both houses of the legislature, and all four congressional seats.[55]

Although Senator Davis made every exertion for the electoral triumph of his party, he confided to a friend, "My heart just now is in union and action of the South against Abolitionism, which may as a generic term include all the associations making war on the slave holding states." In the late summer of 1849, he prepared a long public letter spelling out his views for fellow Mississippians. He started out by sounding his now constant alarm that antislavery agitation had moved beyond a few fanatics to become "the heart of a great political organization" that "aim[ed] at political dominion over us, and str[uck] at our prosperity, our property, and domestic security." Our assailants, he informed his readers, "have taken a variety of names, such as antislavery men, non-extensionists, emancipationists, liberty party, free soil party, etc., but considering them one family, differing somewhat in their mode of attack, but not at all in the final purpose of it, I will refer to them by their patronymic, as abolitionists." If the activities of this "systematic, calculating, sectional organization" had not yet aroused some southerners, Davis averred that only inattention could explain the resulting laxness.[56]

According to Davis, this movement posed such a grave danger to the South because of its substantial political influence in the North, often holding the balance of power in and between the Democratic and Whig parties. Southerners, Davis proclaimed, "no longer hear[d] of compromise for sectional equalization," but the outcry of "the unsatisfiable horse leech—give! give!" Facing such opponents, the South had to hold fast to its constitutional rights or "consent to be the subject, to sink in the United States Congress to the helpless condition which Ireland occupies in the British parliament." Davis believed that the time had come for the South to make its stand. Non-resistance, he predicted, would have a fatal outcome; besides, "our friends in the North" had been shackled by the inability or unwillingness of the South to present a united front behind a specific platform. Although he never specified the particular position the South should take, Davis clearly adhered to Calhoun's view that the South confronted a major crisis focused on the territories and should come together in agreement on some kind of ultimatum. Based on his actions in the Senate and his words on the stump in Mississippi, Davis could certainly support compromise proposals, such as extending the Missouri Compromise line or resurrecting the Clayton Compromise, but he was convinced that a positive impact from any proposition required a solid South. Simultaneously, Davis confidently preached to Mississippians that if the South could forge unity, it could prevail, for the South still had enough political friends in the North to obtain congressional approval for a compromise measure that carried the authority of the South speaking with a single voice.

Davis's hope for southern unity enjoyed an auspicious beginning at a bipartisan, statewide meeting held in Jackson on October 3, where notables from both parties had substantive roles. This was not simply a Mississippi assembly, for John C. Calhoun had been instrumental in getting it together, though his involvement was kept secret lest his reputation for sectional radicalism sink the entire effort. Davis participated in the deliberations and supported the published resolutions, which in large part repeated his public letter—the South faced a massive threat and the time for action was now. Furthermore, one of the resolutions called for all slave states to send delegates to a convention scheduled to take place in Nashville, Tennessee, on the first Monday of June 1850, "to devise and adopt some mode of resistance to these [northern] aggressions."[57]

Within three weeks after his speaking tour through northern Mississippi, Jefferson Davis left once again for Washington. This time Varina, along with two of his nieces, traveled with him, and they reached the capital before December 1. They established residence at Donohoo's Building on Pennsylvania Avenue next door to the United States Hotel; they took their meals via "a little bridge" that connected Donohoo's with the hotel dining room. At the outset several other southern senators and representatives shared the Davis "mess," but by the following summer when Congress finally adjourned, only one remained. In his political lodgings, the Senate chamber, Davis had a different seat; his desk remained to the right of the vice president's chair but was now in the middle of the third row beside John C. Calhoun's.[58]

As Senator Davis settled in for what he believed would be a difficult session, his own status occupied his attention. After his appointment to the Senate in 1847, the Mississippi legislature in January 1848 elected him in his own right, but only to serve out the remaining two years of that term. Thus, Davis once more had to have his name placed before the legislature that would sit in the winter of 1850. Although he had every reason for confidence, as early as the summer of 1849, he foresaw "many screws which will be tightened on me." Mostly, he feared that the traditional sectionalism of Mississippi politics—the same apprehension he had experienced his first time before the legislators—would work against him. Davis's senior colleague Henry Foote lived in southern Mississippi, and all five statewide candidates nominated by the state convention in the summer of 1849 also hailed from that area. Davis also worried that his political opponents would emphasize his friendship with Zachary Taylor and not separate it from his allegiance to the Democracy.[59]

Without question, some Democrats in northern Mississippi hoped to defeat Davis. There was talk that Roger Barton would make yet another try, but a potentially more dangerous foe emerged in Congressman Jacob Thompson from Oxford. Eager for Davis's seat, Thompson pushed his northern residence, asserting that it was his section's turn for the Senate post and that Davis could wait. He also argued that in relation to the Democratic party in the presidential election of 1848, "Davis to say the very least stood in a negative position."[60]

Davis met these criticisms head-on. Disturbed that any portion of the state might oppose him because he was from another, he insisted that as senator he represented all of Mississippi. As his political trek back in October showed, he always strove to shore up his position in the northern counties. As for the charge that he had been insufficiently stalwart in 1848, he wondered how many of those against him would have tried to defeat Taylor for the party's sake, if they had had his relationship with the general-become-president. Stressing his party loyalty, Davis told Mississippi Democrats he did not want the "organization and harmony" of the party disturbed by his name coming before the caucus of Democratic legislators. He declared that no office and no candidate was important enough for "a course which might lead to such evils." The Democratic party, strong and united, was the watchword Davis put forth.[61]

Davis worried needlessly. Faced with his strength, even in the north, Jacob Thompson's candidacy never materialized. When the legislators voted on February 12, 1850, to fill the six-year term, Davis won easily. On the first ballot he received exactly one-half of the votes, 64 of 128, with perennial candidate Roger Barton in second place, gaining 33, and the remainder scattered. On the second ballot Davis's total soared to 79 of 129, with Barton far behind at 37, and the rest again scattered. Now, after his second resounding victory in as many years, no one doubted Jefferson Davis's political authority in his state.[62]

While securing his own political position, Senator Davis confronted a vexing situation with his former father-in-law and fast friend, President Taylor. He undoubtedly wanted Taylor to succeed in the White House, even though they wore different partisan uniforms. Before the inauguration he shared political confidences with Taylor's closest advisers. After Taylor took the oath of office, they remained close, with the younger man even venturing to express candid criticism. Obviously responding to such criticism, Taylor wrote frankly in mid-September 1849 defending his administration and insisting that harmony prevailed in his cabinet. Furthermore, Taylor claimed that most citizens would be pleased with his presidency. He admitted the inevitability of "blunders," but hurried to add that he believed they would be attributed to his head, not his heart. Then, Taylor shifted to his paternal persona, telling Davis to pursue the political course directed by his "good sense, interest, and honor." Even if Davis ended up opposing the president, Taylor reassured him that political disagreement would not "interrupt our personal intercourse, or my esteem & friendship for you." That pledge would undergo a stern test in the first session of the Thirty-first Congress.[63]

At the same time Jefferson Davis coped with a complex political world, he and Varina were trying to get beyond the emotional minefield that had lacerated their relationship since his return from Mexico. When Jefferson was in Mississippi during the summer and fall of 1849, the situation between them obviously improved substantially, because he took Varina with him when he went back to Washington. Her *Memoir* leaves no doubt that she thoroughly enjoyed her return to the city. Because of Jefferson's commitment to his work, the couple did not often go out at night, but Varina delighted as before in lively conversation with notables like Representative Robert Toombs, a hearty, leonine Georgian, and Senator Daniel Webster, the majestic personage from Massachusetts. She remembered with great pleasure a "high tea" given by a leading Washington hostess for the Swedish writer Frederika Bremer, which the Davises attended along with others from the capital's political and social elite. The couple also appeared on the guest list for a dinner given by a wealthy, influential banker, W. W. Corcoran.[64]

In a photograph probably taken in 1849, the twenty-three-year-old Varina Davis looks beyond the camera with brooding eyes. Her dark hair, pulled back in matronly fashion, frames a pensive expression. Full lips and a broad nose give her face a sensual quality, with an appearance youthful but not girlish. The picture portrays a purposeful young woman, and during this time Varina was certainly trying to meet the criticism her husband had earlier poured upon her. Showering endearments upon Jefferson, she talked about his "sweet eyes," called him "sweetest" and herself "your affectionate wife." When she thanked him for giving her Charles Dickens's *The Haunted Man and the Ghost's Bargain*, she related that she most admired the character of Milly, who saved her spouse and her father-in-law through her goodness and innocence. To emphasize her efforts to improve herself, Varina reported that she had been reading Sarah Stickney Ellis's *Guide to Social Happiness*, which she told her husband would not interest him because it dealt with "woman and woman's trials," but, she hastened to add, "it will help 'Winnie' to be 'Wife.'" Published in New York, the *Guide* was one of many books on the role of women and the family written by this prolific English author. A volume of moral instruction, it advised

Varina Davis, c. 1849.

*Picture Collection, Louisiana and Lower Mississippi Valley Collections,
LSU Libraries, Louisiana State University, Baton Rouge*

women to find happiness through selflessness and acceptance of their place in the world as ordained by God. According to Sarah Ellis, a woman won the respect and affection of others by studying how to please them, not by waiting for others to please her.

Whether or not Varina fully made herself over in Jefferson's image of her cannot be known with certainty. A brief unpleasantness evidently occurred between her and the Taylor women in the White House, but during the months in Washington the rancor of the recent past between husband and wife did not surface. She remained with him through the session, though when the summer heat appeared, she spent some time with a niece of Jefferson's in Pennsylvania. No evidence suggests that Jefferson was at all unhappy or displeased with his young wife during this Washington interlude.[65]

The relative quiet on the domestic front was not matched on the political front. When Congress convened on December 3, 1849, sectional anger and emotion reverberated through both houses. A wise old veteran of more than four decades in Washington, Senator Clay of Kentucky found sectional bitterness "stronger than I hoped or supposed it could." This palpable hostility mangled attempts to get Congress underway when a closely divided House could not elect a speaker and organize itself. Certain northern Democrats would not support their party's nominee because he was a southerner; likewise, some southern Whigs would not back their party's choice because he came from Massachusetts and also because the Whig caucus formally refused to oppose the Wilmot Proviso. For three weeks raucous behavior and intimations of violence marked the barren voting. After fifty-nine frustrating ballots, the House in desperation managed to pass a resolution authorizing the election of a speaker with only a plurality, not the usual majority. On the next vote Howell Cobb, a Georgia Democrat, became speaker. Thus the Democrats would control both houses, for they had a clear majority in the Senate, which had been meeting and adjourning from day to day.[66]

With Congress finally ready for business, the reading of President Taylor's message became the order of the day. For president and Congress, attention focused on the territorial issue, with California the flashpoint, because the rush of settlers after the discovery of gold mandated some form of governmental organization. Trying to bypass the political snake pit of the Wilmot Proviso, Taylor proposed the immediate admission of California as a state, pointing out that Californians had met in convention and written a constitution, but not revealing his administration's role in facilitating that process. The president knew that everyone in the territorial debate, including Calhoun, agreed that a state could decide its own position on slavery within its jurisdiction. Accordingly, he considered his intention to skip the territorial stage a brilliant stratagem that would preclude a bitter struggle over the proviso and California. That California would join the Union as a free state because its constitution prohibited slavery did not deter the slave-owning Taylor, who did not believe slavery would ever get to California, and, more fundamentally, did not think that slavery should expand at all beyond its 1849 borders. His message also indicated that New Mexico would soon follow California, with the clear implication that he wanted it too admitted as a free state without any territorial period. Zachary Taylor was convinced that the finality of his plan would end the trauma over slavery that had afflicted the country since the close of the Mexican War.[67]

Because Taylor's plan would effectively shut the South out of the Mexican Cession, however, it generated an uproar among southerners. Southern Democrats denounced it as the executive proviso, and even southern Whigs turned anxious because Taylor left them precariously exposed to Democratic charges that their president and their party were uncaring about southern rights. As for Jefferson Davis individually, he was deeply troubled; in his mind the major issue combined fairness and sectional balance. Southern Americans, himself included, had fought and bled for the cession, and he believed profoundly that they possessed an absolute right to emigrate to it with their property, including human property. Moreover, Davis had fully adopted Calhoun's position that the maintenance of southern rights in the nation depended upon sectional parity. Without the political power stemming from that equality, he feared an increasingly strident antislavery North endangering both the rights and the safety of the South.

The southern citadel remained the U.S. Senate, where the fifteen slave states and the fifteen free states had the same number of senators. Already the mushrooming northern population had reduced the South to a distinct minority in the House. Davis saw the result: the House had passed the proviso and had blocked the extension of the Missouri Compromise line as well as the Clayton Compromise. Thus, while he believed retaining the sectional balance in the Senate utterly essential, Taylor's design would destroy it. In addition, what he saw as the unwarranted, hasty admission of California and New Mexico as states meant that southerners would never have a chance to take slaves into any part of the cession. They would not even be permitted to compete for any part of this new national domain. Even more important, the admission of California would signal the beginning of the decline of southern power in the Senate to the same level as in the House. Taylor's message advised that New Mexico would soon have a constitution and deserved statehood, and, all knew, as a free state. Oregon and the vast bulk of the unorganized Louisiana Purchase were already free soil. As a result, the South and slavery had nowhere else to expand. As Davis perceived the matter of California, it involved both the future security of the South and the preservation of the Union he cherished. Writing to a political friend, he hoped Congress could "avoid the precipice on the brink of which I believe we now stand."[68]

Reacting to Taylor's message, Davis stood forthrightly in opposition. He united with the rest of the Mississippi delegation in informing Governor Quitman that the admission of a free California seemed inevitable and asking for his, the legislature's, and "if practicable" the people's advice on what the state would see as the proper course in "this emergency." He also joined with other southern Democrats in resolutions demanding that the president send Congress all correspondence with agents it had dispatched to California and New Mexico. The southerners believed these documents would expose Taylor as the real force behind the push by westerners for immediate statehood with free constitutions.[69]

While Davis strove to throw up defensive walls, an old Senate hand moved in a different direction. Deeply concerned about what he perceived as a genuine danger to the Union, Henry Clay worked diligently for three weeks to come up with what he termed a compromise that could calm emotions, decrease tensions, and resolve issues. On January 29, 1850, he presented his proposal to the Senate, calling on the more powerful North to make "a more liberal and extensive concession" than the South. In that vein Clay described the net effect of his eight individual propositions as a comprehensive solution to the territorial problem in particular and sectional animosity in general. Moreover, according to Clay, southern rights were guaranteed. Yet, however soothing the words he aimed at the South, southern Democrats, Jefferson Davis among them, found little comfort in Clay's prescription.

A close inspection of what Clay actually put before the Senate reveals that while he may have spoken with a southern accent, his proposed actions had a decidedly northern tone. Following Taylor, he would immediately admit California as a free state; yet, unlike the president, he would move to organize the remainder of the cession with an unspecified number of territorial governments. Although Clay made no mention of the Wilmot Proviso, his suggestion would result in barring slavery. In the first place, he asserted that Mexican law prevailed unless specifically superseded, eliminating the possibility of slavery because Mexico had abolished the institution. Then he addressed an issue that had become increasingly controversial, the boundary of Texas. When admitted as a state in 1845, Texas claimed the Rio Grande as its southern and western border, which meant that much of eastern New Mexico would end up in Texas, a slave state. Clay redrew the line, giving Texas the Rio Grande in the south, but placing the border with New Mexico so far east that a substantial portion of central and western Texas would become part of New Mexico. Clay also proposed that the U.S. government assume the debt Texas had incurred as an independent republic. There were no southern victories here, for Clay not only slammed the door on slavery in all of the Mexican Cession, he also intended to lop off a sizable portion of Texas.[70]

In addition, Clay wanted adjustment on four other contentious points. In one instance he called on Congress to abolish the slave trade in the District of Columbia, a demand long urged by many northerners. Then, Clay ostensibly addressed southern anxieties and grievances. Congress should declare that it had no authority to prohibit the interstate slave trade and that it was "inexpedient" to outlaw slavery in the District, without residents consenting and the approval of Maryland, in addition to making "just compensation" to the slaveowners. Finally, Clay requested that Congress pass a stronger fugitive slave law.

Even though Clay clearly intended for the last three resolutions to reassure and pacify the South, that section would really benefit little. He only called on Congress not to act on the interstate slave trade and slavery in the District; and by claiming that it was "inexpedient" to abolish slavery in the District, he implied that Congress could do so if it wished, a power that most southerners vehemently denied. Of course, the great majority of southerners did like the idea of a more effective fugitive slave law, though the measure that eventually won congressional approval did not include Clay's provision for some procedural protection for the alleged fugitives.

Agreeing with many of his fellow southerners, especially southern Democrats, Jefferson Davis perceived no sectional equity in Clay's proposed settlement. On the very day Clay presented his resolution, Davis rose to say that he saw no compromise anywhere. Replicating the stance he had taken in 1848, he articulated what he thought was a fair way to handle the Mexican Cession, proclaiming to the Senate, "I here assert that never will I take less than the Missouri compromise line extended to the Pacific ocean, with the specific recognition of the right to hold slaves in the territory below that line."[71]

Two weeks later, on February 13 and 14, before a packed chamber and filled galleries, Senator Davis delivered his full-dress response. He began by announcing that he believed his "duty" required him to present his views on the "dangerous doctrines" Clay had offered. His reaction had not come sooner, he explained, because he could not get the floor. "I now come to lift the glove [Clay] then threw down, and trust in the justice of the cause in which I stand." He had hoped that

Clay would put forward a true compromise, but had to confess disappointment because he now had to place Clay on the side of "the preponderating aggressive majority." Davis found this situation so fraught with danger because it was not "merely the result of passion." Instead, he averred, considering "the cold, calculating purpose of those who seek sectional domination, I see nothing short of conquest on the one side, or submission on the other." Insisting to the Senate that the basic drive of his political opponents aimed for political power in order to destroy southern constitutional rights so they could harm his section, Davis informed the lawmakers that the South needed both the North and the national government to halt their hostility against "an institution so interwoven with its interests, its domestic peace, and all its social relations, that it cannot be disturbed without causing their overthrow."[72]

Davis then recounted his unchanged interpretation of slavery and the Constitution. Although slavery antedated the formation of the Union, Davis argued that it derived from that document recognition it would otherwise not enjoy. According to him, the Constitution provided for a national responsibility for slavery in obligating states to return fugitive slaves as well as in authorizing Congress to tax slaves and in giving them a role in representation. To Davis these provisions led to only one logical conclusion: "As a property recognized by the Constitution, and held in a portion of the States, the Federal Government is bound to admit it into all the Territories, and to give it such protection as other private property receives."

Defending the right of slaveowners to enter the Mexican Cession, he even reasserted the diffusion theory in his testimony that "whatever the evil of slavery," geographical expansion would not enhance it. In contrast, he contended that "the immediate connection" between master and slave "preserves the domestic character, and strictly patriarchal relations." Davis claimed that cruelty could only exist on large plantations where intermediaries intervened between owners and bondspeople. Here, of course, he was referring, willy-nilly, to his and Joseph's operations, but he avoided any suggestion that large plantations and brutality were necessarily synonymous. He maintained, rather, that the *potential* for a hostile relationship could obtain only on great estates. At the same time, he hurried on to assert that whatever cruelty did occur between master and slave, it "probably exists to a smaller extent than in any other relation of labor to capital."

Senator Davis took issue with Clay on all points involving the Mexican Cession. Regarding California, he rejected the notion that the South should be satisfied because Congress never denied the right of slavery to go there; rather, Californians themselves pursued the admission of California as a free state. He declared he could never accept "the will of the conglomerated mass of goldhunters, foreign and native" as sufficiently authoritative to keep out citizens of the United States supposedly protected by the "equal privileges" of the Constitution. "Why, sir, what choice is there between this and the Wilmot Proviso?" Davis found none, announcing that he preferred the latter because "the advocate of the Wilmot proviso attempts to rob me of my rights, whilst acknowledging them, by the admission that it requires legislation to deprive me of them. The other denies their existence."

On the rest of the cession, he contested Clay along two lines. Again repeating his case from his speech on Oregon in the Thirtieth Congress, he declared that the Constitution followed the flag. The contention that Mexican law still prevailed in American territory he dismissed as preposterous. By way of ridiculing the notion of any continuation of Mexican authority, Davis asked rhetorically whether Roman Catholicism remained the religion. Next, he denied Clay's claim that nature banned slavery throughout the cession. In contrast, he saw opportunity for slave labor in mining and in agriculture dependent on irrigation, where slaves were perfect for the construction of necessary dams and ditches. As Davis saw it, denying slaveowners to any part of the cession deprived them of real economic possibilities.

Davis stressed that he and the South did not request any political gifts, only their rights. "We want something substantial, something permanent," he affirmed. Offering to compromise principle for sectional peace, he would accept extending the Missouri Compromise line because of tradition. Congress should establish territorial governments for California and New Mexico that would protect the rights of all. He saw no need for the "irregular" admission of new states. The territorial phase that had obtained with all other territories should certainly be employed in this instance also. In his opinion the northern majority had the power to settle "this distracting question" if it would give the South "some substantial proposition, such as magnanimity can offer, and such as we can honorably accept. I being one of the minority in the Senate, and the Union have nothing to offer, except an assurance of cooperation in anything which my principles will allow me to adopt, and which promises permanent, substantial security."

On Texas, Davis likewise discovered no room for discussion. In his judgment the provisions of the act annexing the republic of Texas back in 1845 were still in force, and they set the boundary at the Rio Grande, on both south and west. He did not believe that Congress could discard the law and make new borders wherever it saw fit. Texas had legal guarantees set by Congress in a solemn pact, guarantees which Davis perceived as inviolable.

He had little more use for the rest of Clay's plan. Even entertaining the possibility that Congress could abolish slavery in the District of Columbia distressed him mightily. Such a step would mean that southerners were not equal to other Americans because they could not bring their property to the seat of the federal government. To Davis, that eventuality was simply unacceptable. Neither did he expect anything from a new fugitive slave statute, which he termed "a dead letter" in any state where public opinion opposed the returning of any escaped slave. "I would sooner trust it to day to the sense of constitutional obligation of the state," he maintained, "than to the enforcement of any law which Congress can enact against the popular opinion of those among whom it is executed."

Drawing to a close, Davis vigorously denied that either he or the South embraced disunion. Although he did acknowledge that perhaps "seeds of disunion" could be found, he said they were quite scattered and most certainly could not be equated with Mississippi's call for a convention of slave states, which arose from "patriotism, and a high resolve to preserve if possible, our constitutional Union." He diagnosed the health of the Union as most disturbed by the northern press that so incessantly harped on the South. After applauding the loyalty of his state and his section, Davis testified to his personal devotion to the Union. The son of a Revolutionary War soldier, he recalled one of his earliest childhood lessons as "attachment to this Union." He also reminded the Senate that from boyhood into adulthood he had proudly worn the uniform of the country, and he still looked on the flag "with the affection of early love. . . ."

The South, he cried, was American. Explaining that the South had shared in all the toil and danger, Davis demanded that the Congress not deny its constitutional rights. "If so," he warned, "self-respect requires that we should assert them; and, as best we may, maintain that which we could not surrender without losing your respect as well as our own."

Both sections benefited each other. The commercial and manufacturing North needed southern agriculture, which provided its "life-blood." Using Carthage, Tyre, and Venice as illustrations, he lectured that history taught the fate of states without a powerful agricultural base. Sorrowfully, he declaimed that if "this spirit of sectional aggrandizement, or, if gentlemen prefer, this love they bear the African race, shall cause the disunion of these States, the last chapter of our history will be a sad commentary upon the justice and wisdom of our people."

Even as Jefferson Davis dealt with momentous public issues creating such "a bubbling cauldron" that, as he phrased it, "at present all is uncertainty," a grave private matter intruded. In response to a Virginia congressman's praise of the First Mississippi at Buena Vista, Democratic representative William Bissell of Illinois, who had commanded the Second Illinois on that field, spoke up on February 21 for his regiment, saying that the Mississippians had not been within a mile and a half when the Second Indiana gave way. Davis, as always prideful about his and his unit's performance at Buena Vista, on the next day identified himself as "the proper person to answer any charge which a responsible man may make against the Mississippi Regiment." He penned a note asking "whether the information I have received is correct." Bissell replied promptly that, desiring only "to do justice" to those under his "own observation," he had made no attack on the First Mississippi. This statement failed to satisfy Davis, as he wrote Bissell, because it seemed to him that the Illinoisan still denied that his men stopped the Mexican assault, instead "assert[ing] that the merit of that service is due others."[73]

After this exchange each man enlisted a friend to act as an agent, or in the language of the southern code of honor, a second, to ascertain whether the apparently different positions could be reconciled— Democratic congressman Samuel Inge of Alabama for Davis and Democratic senator James Shields of Illinois, a brigade commander in Mexico, for Bissell. When Shields and Inge met, the latter suggested, at Davis's behest, that Bissell add a sentence at the beginning of the final paragraph of his February 22 letter detailing the First Mississippi's having saved the day at Buena Vista. For Bissell, Shields declined. On February 27, Davis informed Bissell that because a satisfactory answer to his initial inquiry still had not been received, he should name someone to arrange with Inge "the necessary preliminaries" to a duel. Immediately, Bissell picked Major Osborne Cross of the United States Army.

Although a duel seemed imminent, combat on the field of honor was averted. On the evening of February 27, Major Cross and Senator Shields met with Congressman Inge, and the three were joined by Whig senator William Dawson of Georgia and Democratic congressman William Richardson of Illinois, who came with a prepared settlement—the withdrawal of all correspondence after Davis's first letter, and Bissell's adding at the point Davis had earlier indicated a more succinct version of the language Davis had proposed. This time the wording would be: "But am willing to award them [the First Mississippi] the credit due to their gallant and distinguished service in the battle." Cross, Shields, and Inge agreed. Then Davis's letter of February 22 as well as Bissell's amended reply of the same day were sent to the *Washington Union* with the declaration that the dispute had been honorably adjusted. There were also reports that President Taylor had intervened. The two disputants certainly appeared to hold no grudge, for just a couple of days later a reporter spotted them in the House engaging in "friendly chat."

A second personal matter concerning Davis stemmed from the different stands he and his senatorial colleague Henry S. Foote took on Clay's plan. Whereas Davis vigorously opposed Clay's measures, Foote became an ardent advocate of a general settlement based on them. A native Virginian and an attorney, Foote had migrated to Mississippi in 1830 and practiced law in several towns, including Vicksburg and Jackson. Active politically, he served as a surveyor general of public lands, as a legislator, and in both 1840 and 1844 as a presidential elector. Then, in 1847, he won election to the United States Senate. Short, with a large bald head, "Foote was never known to deliberate." Rather, his trademark became mercurial political shifts, a fiery temper, and fierce language on the stump and in Congress. An avid supporter of Calhoun and his Southern Address in the winter of 1848–49, Foote in March 1850 angrily accused the Carolinian of disunionism, then in the very next month defended his cause and his "holy work." Having insulted a fellow senator in 1850 by calling him "a calumniator," Foote found himself physically threatened, whereupon he drew a pistol on the floor of the Senate but just as quickly handed it to an associate. Although Davis and Foote had started out as political allies and at least friendly acquaintances on the personal level, their relationship had degenerated considerably prior to the stress of 1850.[74]

On Christmas Day 1847 the two men had an altercation that resulted in violence, and certainly presaged future difficulties. Along with other messmates, they had adjourned after breakfast to the sitting room of their boardinghouse when a dispute about popular sovereignty arose. Their disagreement, heated by language Davis termed "offensive," though unrecorded, prompted him to ignore his war wound, cross the room, and assault Foote. After friends separated them, Foote started to leave but at the door turned, announcing he had "struck first." Denouncing him as a liar, Davis shook his fist in Foote's face, threatening "to beat him to death" if he "dared" to repeat that claim. At first silent, Foote then hit Davis, who in return knocked Foote down and commenced beating him until pulled back by others. Thereupon, Davis proposed that he and Foote go to his room, where he had pistols, and lock the door. Foote found the proposal unreasonable. Inferring that his antagonist thought he would not get an equal chance, Davis prepared to assault him once again, but Foote denied any such implication. Others in the room intervened, urging that the matter be dropped as a "Christmas frolic" and kept private. Later, Davis told a friend he believed that that agreement had ended the matter.[75]

It erupted again, however, approximately two years later. Davis learned that in New Orleans, Foote was boasting about having hit Davis, who had taken the blow, not "resent[ing]" it. Davis sent a note by Albert Brown asking Foote either to admit or deny that he had made such a statement. In Davis's account, Foote sent a lengthy reply, which denied the charge, but not so explicitly as Davis desired. A second request produced a similar response. At that point Davis was prepared to challenge Foote to a duel, but Brown and Robert J. Walker persuaded him that Foote's denial had been sufficient. In addition, they argued that many people would not view a challenge favorably because they considered Foote unequal to Davis "in a trial with deadly weapons."[76]

Obviously, considerable tension remained between them. In the summer of 1848 they engaged in a small-minded squabble over the presentation to Congress of a flag from the Mexican War. When they divided over Clay's scheme, more was involved than simply two senators taking opposing sides on a political issue. Each harshly accused the other; Foote indicted Davis as a disunionist while Davis damned Foote as a submissionist. Moreover, both men claimed to speak for their state, and both aspired to use the congressional struggle to become the dominant force in Mississippi politics.[77]

In the midst of the varied and tense reactions to Clay's overtures, John C. Calhoun died. A giant of American politics, who from his arrival in the House of Representatives in 1810 had been a force in national affairs, Calhoun had exercised an enormous influence on Jefferson Davis. Davis was convinced that Calhoun had enunciated the correct interpretation of both the constitutional and the political Union. He shared Calhoun's constitutional view that the sovereign states had created the Union through a written document in which they delegated only carefully stipulated powers to the federal government, with all others retained by the states. He believed this states' rights doctrine, in turn, offered constitutional protection to the South in the Union. On the political front, Calhoun fervently believed that the South must maintain an equality in the Union. Without that equality and the political strength drawn from it, Calhoun feared that the South and slavery were mortally endangered. Likewise, Davis in 1850 did not think that the slave South could survive without an equal status, now lodged in the Senate, to block what he considered a northern drive to control the country.

In his last public act Calhoun opposed Clay's plan, finding nothing in it for the South and calling for new guarantees to preserve southern parity in the Union. Terminally ill with tuberculosis and wracked with pain, an emaciated Calhoun appeared in the Senate on March 4 for what would be his final speech. He was so weak that his address had to be read for him; by the end of the month he was dead.

The Senate, the national capital, and South Carolina paid their ceremonious homage. Thousands followed the cortège to the Potomac River and a ship waiting to bear the body on the first stage of its return to South Carolina. As one of six senators appointed to accompany Calhoun's remains back to his native state, Davis left Washington on April 22 and three days later reached Charleston, where he participated in the public ritual that lasted for several days. After Calhoun's burial, he arrived back in Washington on April 30.[78]

Senator Davis returned to a political battleground where the contesting forces plotted tactics and jockeyed for advantage. President Taylor stood resolute, willing to accept only his plan—California and New Mexico statehood alone. Holding and desiring to strengthen their firm free-soil position, northern Whigs overwhelmingly lined up with the president, though the most prestigious northern Whig in the Senate did not.

Daniel Webster of Massachusetts, who along with Clay and Calhoun formed what has been designated the Great Triumvirate, rose in the Senate, even before Calhoun's death, to pronounce himself for compromise. He began his oration with the famous words: "I wish to speak to-day, not as a Massachusetts man, nor as a northern man, but as an American. . . ." With his massive head and brooding eyes, and his incomparable oratorical skills, the majestic Webster projected a formidable presence. Although his embrace of compromise, including a fugitive slave law, caused angry outcries among antislavery men, especially in Massachusetts, Webster provided compromise a lustrous ally and a potent voice. Moreover, southern Whigs, who felt betrayed by Taylor's adamant demand for a free California and New Mexico without any political offerings to the South and also abandoned by most of their northern associates, could claim in Webster a northern Whig friend who supported a general settlement that included a fugitive slave law and excluded the proviso. Webster's tacking toward compromise did not surprise Jefferson Davis, who earlier had predicted that with almost all northerners moving in the other direction or hunkering down, the Massachusetts powerhouse might do just what he did. Northern Democrats also added their troops to the pro-compromise battalions. Generally speaking, northern Democrats were more conservative on sectional and slavery issues than northern Whigs, and in adopting popular sovereignty they had repudiated the Wilmot Proviso. Thus, they had no difficulty with the general scheme of compromise.[79]

The final major bloc was composed of southern Democrats, most of whom utterly opposed both Taylor's strategy and Clay's proposal. Davis started here, never wavered, and became a leader of southerners trying to bar the admission of California and the compromise plan, while Foote broke with the majority of his southern Democratic brethren and became a major proponent of the compromise. In Davis's judgment, the South had to insist on recognition of its rights, and this must be done now because as time passed, the South would only grow weaker in comparison with the North. That all southerners did not see the situation as he did troubled him greatly, for he believed that a unified South could obtain a respectable deal, such as extending the Missouri Compromise line to the Pacific Ocean. Viewing the upcoming Nashville Convention from this perspective, he hoped it would spur the southern unity he believed essential for southern safety.[80]

During the spring, pro-compromise senators, with Henry Foote among the leaders, decided on a new course, grouping all of Clay's individual proposals into a single inclusive bill known as the Omnibus. Although Clay had initially opposed that approach, it was decided upon by a select Senate committee appointed in April to consider the slavery question as a whole, not just as it pertained to the Mexican Cession. On May 8, the committee presented its handiwork, which addressed all the points Clay had originally brought up, but with a few notable changes. Important to southern Whigs were two provisions: creating territorial governments for New Mexico and Utah specifically prohibited from passing any law on slavery, thus precluding the proviso; and pushing the Texas boundary farther west, though still not to the limits Texas claimed.

Although the creation of the Omnibus did not change the political order of battle, it did make for some unusual alliances. The two groups who most opposed the bill, northern Whigs and southern Democrats, came together to sabotage it, though their long-range goals differed sharply. Jefferson Davis was quite active in this legislative marriage of convenience, being generally cited as a manager of the partnership. Another was William Henry Seward, Whig of New York, an important supporter of free soil in general and the proviso in particular. The crafty Seward, with his bushy eyebrows and beaklike nose, had gotten close to President Taylor, although his actions in the Senate did not aim so much toward supporting Taylor's programs as toward establishing himself as the northern Whig champion of antislavery. In his major speech, he talked about a higher law than the Constitution. Observers noted the collaboration between the tall, erect Mississippian committed to defending southern equality and slavery, as well as the rights of slaveowners in the territories, and the short, stooped New Yorker dedicated to asserting northern supremacy, assaulting slavery, and blocking slaveowners from the territories. In the short term, however, they shared a common purpose—destroying the Omnibus.[81]

Into the summer the struggle over the crowded legislative vehicle continued. The unending wrangle in what would become the longest session of Congress to that time coupled with a thermometer pushing past 90 degrees caused one harried reporter to cry that the capital was hot as Egypt. This climate led to utter exhaustion, numbing enervation, increasing irritability, and breaking health. Yet almost everyone clung to their posts, though always searching for new tactical advantages.

Away from Washington, the possibility of congressional action undermined a once promising effort that Davis had backed to forge unity in the slave states. The Nashville Convention met in June, but realizing the division in southern opinion, the delegates merely passed resolutions affirming southern rights and went home, though they did resolve to reconvene after the adjournment of Congress to assess its work.

Jefferson Davis did not flinch or bend. The positions he held throughout the steamy summer matched those he had staked out back in the seemingly long-past winter. First and foremost was his opposition to immediate statehood for California, which he thought unfair and more important desperately wounding to the South. The admission of California, he informed the Senate, "obliterated" all protection for the minority South by giving one section control of both houses of Congress. Expressing a deep conviction, he went on, "I feel we have reached the point at which the decline of our Government has commenced, the point at which the great restraints which have preserved it, the bonds which have held it together, are to be broken by a ruthless majority, when the next step may lead us to the point at which aggression will assume such a form as will require the minority to decide whether they will sink below the condition to which they were born, or maintain it by forcible resistance."[82]

Even so, California did not consume all of his attention. Always insisting that American possession of the cession negated Mexican law in that area, he moved late in July to repeal explicitly the Mexican statutes abolishing slavery. He lost on a basically sectional vote, which meant that the status of slavery remained murky, but Clay's argument that it would be illegal was still a possibility. In addition, the Texas boundary continued to be central to Davis, with his efforts directed toward Senate validation of the borders Texas claimed, the Rio Grande in the west as well as the south. The one section of the Omnibus that he could support, the proposed fugitive slave law, seemed to offer the South little in the face of hostile public opinion in the free states. From that base he spoke against providing jury trials for alleged fugitives because the hostility would lead to no enforcement. At the same time, he opposed an attempt to have the federal government recompense the owners of escaped slaves. Southern safety, he explained, lay in "rigid adherence to the terms and principles of the federal compact." If the South admitted any power of the federal government over slave property, such as that government's interposing its financial strength between slaveowner and slave, he asked, "where shall we find an end to the action which anti-slavery feeling will suggest?" To him the Constitution obligated the government to return fugitives, not purchase them.[83]

Even in the midst of what Davis perceived as a fateful time for his state, his section, and his country, he never forgot the elementary but crucial tasks of the politician. During the previous Congress, a Mississippian who said that he was "in humble life . . . a common farmer, and make no pretensions to Aristocracy," thanked Davis for sending documents, telling him that no one else in the state delegation had "so far condescended from his high *pinnacle of Congressional glory*, as to favor me with anything of importance from *Headquarters*." Although, as Davis himself reported to a constituent, "the slavery question . . . renders it very difficult to transact any local business," he made every effort. Presenting petitions, forwarding government publications, making recommendations and requests for federal appointments, advocating the construction of a marine hospital in Vicksburg and land grants for a projected railroad from Brandon, Mississippi, to the Alabama state line, Davis never flagged in recognizing that Mississippi voters expected his services, an expectation in which he totally concurred. Responding to a concern about the postmastership in Jackson, Davis underscored his conception of his relationship with voters back in Mississippi; he informed his correspondent that he had "kept all the letters I have received on the subject as forming a guide to my future course." One constituent for whom he was certainly successful was himself. In March he received payment of $3,678 ($2,950.26 plus interest) as reimbursement for his personal expenses incurred in outfitting the First Mississippi Regiment.[84]

While Davis battled the Omnibus and tended to constituent service, for the second time in four months he had to face the loss of an important person in his life. On a wickedly hot Fourth of July, Zachary Taylor spent much of the day outdoors participating in Independence Day activities. Upon returning to the Executive Mansion, he gorged himself on cold liquids as well as raw fruits and vegetables. Shortly thereafter he was struck with acute gastroenteritis and grew steadily worse. After a lifetime of surviving frontier hardships and battlefield dangers, the old general died in his bed in the White House on July 9. Among family members and close associates at his bedside were Jefferson and Varina Davis, who related that the president's final words were addressed to his former son-in-law. Although details of their personal relations during the months of the congressional session have not survived, the two men clearly retained their close ties in spite of their fundamentally opposed approaches to California and the rest of the Mexican Cession, though both for different reasons wanted the

Omnibus overturned. Taylor had obviously adhered to the pledge he earlier made to Davis: the younger man should take his own political course, no matter its direction, but he would never lose the affection and friendship of his first father-in-law. In turn, Davis retained genuine fondness and deep respect for Sarah Knox's father, who had become his wartime commander and his friend.[85]

Taylor's death did alter the political alignment, for it removed an implacable foe of compromise from the White House. Through all the maneuvering in Congress, Taylor did not move at all, demanding the admission of California as a free state and the same for New Mexico upon application, with nothing else added. Ascending to the executive chair, Vice President Millard Fillmore of New York did not share Taylor's obdurate aversion to compromise. Although Fillmore did not start out as a champion of the Omnibus, he soon climbed aboard, putting behind it all the power of his administration, including Webster as the new secretary of state.

Initially, presidential backing did not seem to matter. As summer with its wilting heat dragged on, the political prospects of the Omnibus seemed more akin to the constantly shifting breezes of spring. On some days it appeared that nothing could deter the smooth-running Omnibus, on others that it would sputter and stall. Finally, at the end of July with the Senate ready to vote, the sad-faced opponents of the Omnibus feared the worst. Then, with astonishing rapidity, the finely crafted mechanism began to come apart. It all started on July 31 with a motion to delete a particular provision about the governance of the territory east of the Rio Grande prior to a final settlement of the Texas–New Mexico boundary. When that move succeeded, other parts began to clank. Within hours all had broken and failed. As an exasperated Clay walked out of the Senate chamber, opponents rejoiced, including Jefferson Davis, with a "gleaming smile" upon his countenance. "The *great omnibus* broke down," a Mississippi congressman wrote home. "A mountain has been in labor and a mouse has been born."[86]

Although Davis and fellow resisters of the Omnibus delighted in its wreck, their joyous mood was short-lived. Despondent and frustrated at the ruin of his hopes, an exhausted and sick Henry Clay departed torrid Washington for cool Newport, Rhode Island. Clay's departure opened the way for others equally committed to compromise to steer a different form of settlement through the Senate. At the forefront of this legislative initiative was Democrat Stephen A. Douglas of Illinois, who, like Seward, would have a momentous role in Jefferson Davis's political future. With short, stubby legs, Douglas stood only five feet four inches, but he had broad shoulders, a massive head topped with thick black hair, and incredibly dynamic energy. He had always believed that the best chance for a successful compromise lay in presenting separate measures to the Senate and constructing majorities for each, with the core supporters of compromise, chiefly northern Democrats and southern Whigs, voting for almost every bill, and additional votes coming from elsewhere on particular matters, such as northern Whigs for California statehood and southern Democrats for a fugitive slave law. In this new drive Douglas enjoyed the crucial backing of the Fillmore administration, which was essential to get the necessary cooperation from northern Whigs, whether in the form of aye ballots or abstentions.

Using these tactics, Douglas and the administration prevailed. Almost immediately after the demolition of the Omnibus, Douglas went to work in earnest, and by mid-September the Senate passed each part of the compromise, though the final version did not track exactly the propositions Clay had offered back in the winter. California was admitted as a free state and without qualification, but the rest of the Mexican Cession was handled differently. The Senate created two territories, New Mexico and Utah, without the proviso and with the stipulation that either could enter the Union free or slave as each state constitution prescribed, though the New Mexico bill contained some different wording that implied a territorial legislature might prohibit slavery. After much debate the Texas–New Mexico border was set where it now exists. Although Texas did not get its desired western boundary on the Rio Grande, it received considerably more territory than Clay ever wanted to give. This agreement was critical, for jingoistic politicians in Texas threatened to use force to impose the boundary of their choice, possibly resulting in an armed clash with both New Mexicans and U.S. Army troops in the territory. Also, the federal government would pay the Texas debt. A Fugitive Slave Law, which made the federal government responsible for returning escaped slaves, passed, with no provision for a jury trial for the alleged fugitives. Finally, as Clay wished, the slave trade in the District of Columbia was abolished, though slavery itself remained untouched there.

The House followed the Senate in passing each element of the compromise, and on September 20, President Fillmore signed the final bill. What was known as the Compromise of 1850 had become law. It offered the South considerably more on both the territorial issue and the particulars of the Fugitive Slave Law than had Clay's original package. Whether the Compromise of 1850 was a true compromise or not has divided historians, but it had surely become much less one-sided in its journey through Congress. Yet despite general approbation from all parts of the country on the apparent settlement of so many difficult issues, passage of the Compromise did not please Jefferson Davis at all. Detailed studies of legislative history give Davis a perfect voting record in the anti-Compromise bloc. In the end, his votes matched closely the positions he had held throughout. He voted against California as a state, against the adjusted Texas boundary, and against outlawing the slave trade in the District of Columbia. He said yes on the fugitive-slave legislation. Omitting the proviso and allowing for the possibility of a future slave state won his vote for the Utah bill, but he was recorded as not voting on New Mexico. The possible implication of language regarding slavery during the territorial phase may have deterred him, or he could possibly have been unofficially paired (meaning that a proponent and an opponent mutually agreed to miss the vote), for almost two dozen senators were absent.[87]

He always saw California statehood as the most crucial question, for it would immediately and directly affect the sectional balance of power, and he battled it with all his strength and power. On August 2, Davis, along with nine other southern senators, pledged in writing "to avail ourselves of any and every means" to prevent admission unless the Missouri Compromise line applied. Then, on the thirteenth, the day the Senate passed the California bill, he was one of ten southerners who signed a solemn protest against California statehood that they wanted printed in the *Senate Journal*. At the end, facing defeat, but still denouncing the admission of California, Davis announced that because he knew the outcome, he would no longer argue the merits of the bill and would offer no further opposition, not "for want of will, but for the want of power." His feelings about California bored so deep that he even entertained the notion of physically taking the California bill from the secretary of the Senate and "tearing it to pieces," but because only six other southern senators indicated a willingness to participate, the great ripping never occurred.[88]

Throughout the futile struggle to throttle California statehood and strangle the Compromise, Davis vehemently denied that either he personally or those he represented desired disunion. "I have not spoken of disunion to the Senate," he proclaimed. Disunion was "an alternative not to be anticipated—one to which I could only look forward as the last resort." Nor did "threats of civil war" exercise him, for he "believe[d] it to be a phantom of politicians." In his opinion, the people of the country did not want sectional conflict. As for himself, he spoke proudly. "I, sir, am an American citizen," calling the Union "my country." Yet his constitutionalism required a qualification: "I am a citizen of the United States, it is true, because I am a citizen of a State," and "allegiance, I know, is first due to the State I represent." Davis insisted that while his "affections begin" with his Mississippi, they "are not bound by the limits of the State." He ringingly declaimed, "I belong to no State and no section, when the great interests of the Union are concerned." That declaration was not without constraints, however, for he continued, "I belong to the State which is my home when the Union attempts to trample upon her rights." The tension inherent in Davis's massive labor to hold these two taut lines, which often pulled against each other, exploded in his response to those senators who dared name him a disunionist. He riposted in "monosyllables."[89]

Although Davis emphasized his loyalty to the Union, he did not accept the Compromise of 1850 as ending discussion or settling all matters, at least not right away. When Congress finally adjourned on September 30, a "weary" and "disgusted" Davis prepared to leave for Mississippi, where he intended to carry on his campaign against what Congress had wrought.[90]

CHAPTER EIGHT

"The Cloud Which Had Collected"

When Congress adjourned on September 30, Jefferson Davis left Senate debates and defeats behind, but he took his deep concern about the Compromise of 1850 home with him. He departed from Washington immediately after the session, stopped briefly in Baltimore where Varina had preceded him to shop for furniture, then headed south, and reached Mississippi in mid-October. Almost at once he plunged into a three-week speaking tour through the west-central part of the state.[1]

Davis was eager to mingle with his constituents. On the floor of the Senate, he had claimed that they shared his view of the iniquity of the Compromise. When Henry Foote asserted that the state's voters agreed with him, Davis responded that as soon as both men could confer with Mississippians, his stance would be substantiated. Additionally, Davis believed it imperative to share his sense of the peril the South faced from the antislavery North as well as to expose what he saw as the sham of the Compromise.[2]

Davis mounted the hustings with the overwhelming majority of Mississippi Democrats shouting huzzas for him. The *Jackson Mississippian* had already proclaimed that he enjoyed the "unqualified approval" of his party, while the *Vicksburg Sentinel* decreed him "faithful" and announced that "the most enthusiastic reception ever given to a public man in Mississippi awaits him at the hands of the people." Across the state cries rang forth that he "commanded the spontaneous admiration of her people," that he "st[oo]d up manfully and with judgement for our rights and honor." Later, when the legislature convened, it commended Davis and the four congressmen for their conduct while it censured Foote for his.[3]

From the stump in major towns like Vicksburg and Jackson as well as smaller places like Brandon and Lexington, Davis chorused his Senate lines. To places he could not reach in the time he had in Mississippi, he dispatched public letters carrying the same message. The admission of California he denounced as "unconstitutional," fashioned not by real citizens but by "mere trespassers upon the public domain." Using an even harsher term, he denigrated it as "a *fraud*" on the South. Equally unconstitutional was the abolition of the slave trade in the District of Columbia, in which Congress exercised a power never transmitted by the Constitution to the federal government. Davis continued with strong language, calling the Texas boundary settlement "the dismemberment of Texas." And he identified a single culprit as underlying all: "the ruling, directing power of hostility to the slave institutions of the South." In his judgment the antislavery North had inflicted "a wrong" on the South and would go so far as to "involve us in total ruin." That implacable opposition to what he understood as southern rights and constitutional principles "nerved" him to fight unceasingly against the bulk of the Compromise.[4]

Because he could discover no compromise at all in the bills passed by Congress, he urged Mississippians to continue their resistance against northern aggression and usurpation by maintaining their opposition to the Compromise in particular and to the denial of their constitutional rights in general. Davis's prescription for the stand he thought essential was simultaneously clear and quite murky. "If the doctrine of passive resistance shall prevail," he warned, "we shall receive the contempt of the enemy." Mississippi must "make a manly and determined resistance now and demand new guards for her security."

Although he mentioned several forms of possible activities such as non-intercourse and public meetings, he focused on a vintage Calhounian program. Mississippi should hold a state convention, demand that Congress recognize the constitutional rights of all citizens, including slaveowners, especially in the territories, and call on other slave states to follow suit. Despite the failure of the Nashville Convention, whose feeble second gathering in November ended in a fiasco, Davis was unquestionably convinced that united action by the South would guarantee recognition and preservation of the rights he felt so vital. If the North failed to react as Davis expected, at that moment, but not before, the South would have to contemplate leaving the Union. Such "a catastrophe we will sincerely deplore," he said, but "responsibility" for it, he hurried to insist, "will rest not on our heads, but upon those regardless of social and political obligation [who] have undermined the foundation on which the Union was erected." He viewed this dreaded eventuality as unlikely because it could only occur following a Mississippi convention, a southern convention, and a congressional refusal to accept southern demands.

Thus, Davis never believed that he advocated disunion, and he vehemently shoved aside all attempts to stigmatize him as a disunionist. In fact, he dismissed as false the very notion of framing the issue as union or disunion. He described himself and all others opposing the Compromise as the real unionists, because they were struggling to maintain the constitutional Union. He professed an abiding loyalty to that Union, the Union of equals. Allegiance to the constitutional Union, he preached, was neither impractical nor treasonable. He contended that nothing he had advocated or done aimed at destroying it.

While arguing for his state to reject the Compromise as a valid settlement and claim its legitimate constitutional rights, Senator Davis made it indisputably clear that he would follow the lead of Mississippi. The course set by the people of Mississippi would be his course. Whatever determination his fellow citizens made, he "trust[ed] the decision w[ould] be made calmly and deliberately upon principle, by reason, and equally uninfluenced by headlong passion or unmanly fear."

Davis returned to Brierfield on November 6. After only two weeks at home, he once again set off for Washington, reaching the city on the evening of December 4 and taking his seat in the Senate the next day. Having made the trip alone, he set up bachelor's quarters at Mrs. Henry Hill's boardinghouse on Capitol Hill. His leaving Varina behind did not signify any reappearance of undue distress and tension between them. For the short second session of the Thirty-first Congress, he expected to stay in Washington no more than around three months. Besides, according to her own testimony, Varina at this time was "by no means strong." Writing a friend in January 1851, she spoke of "a *misfortune*" that had befallen her back in the fall and kept her bedridden for a month. The language in which she described herself as being in "*such a situation*" prior to her "misfortune" strongly suggests pregnancy and miscarriage, though the record provides no conclusive evidence.[5]

Jefferson's correspondence contains no hint of husbandly displeasure. Although Varina boasted that he wrote twice weekly, only one of his letters is known—one written just after he arrived in the capital. Already he missed her "sweet presence" and had begun anticipating the time when again he would "clasp my own Winnie in my arms." His closing revealed his deep feelings for his young wife, but the fatherly tone crept in: "Good bye sweet wife, and as you will not allow me to kiss you for an angel, be one now in the presence of Our God, and the absence of [your husband]." As for Varina, she did not expect Jefferson to mourn unduly his single status, sharing with another homebound congressional wife her opinion that both husbands would engage in "flirting" with "no kind friend to tell us!" Although she did depict herself and her correspondent as "sisters in affliction," nothing indicates that she harbored any serious concern about her husband's behavior. Other comments that she had made on his flirtations in Washington carried no connotations of disdain or jealousy. Neither did this letter convey or even imply harsh sentiments or censure.

After the tumult that had characterized its immediate predecessor, calmness predominated in this congressional session. On the Compromise no new fighting occurred, though enforcement of the Fugitive Slave Law drew attention. Vigorous antislavery opposition had sparked unrest, especially in Boston, where a mob had forced release of an alleged fugitive. Addressing this matter, Davis repeated what he had previously said about northern public opinion—without its support, the law would be unenforceable and useless. At the same time he adamantly opposed using the U.S. Army for enforcement because he believed that any state could refuse to enforce a law. But when a state chose to deny the supremacy of public laws, only one more step would break apart the Union. Although southerners were constantly assaulted for their states' rights views, Davis pointed out that no southern states were acting in such a manner.[6]

During the debate over the execution of the Fugitive Slave Law, Davis spoke emotionally about the Union. He described "the charm which invests and binds [it] with greater force than bands of brass and steel." "This Union," he informed the Senate, "is held together by historical associations and national pride. It is held together by social links, from the fact that fathers and sons, mothers and daughters, brothers and sisters, and boyhood friends, live in extreme ends of the Union." In Davis's description, "so many unseen, close, and daily increasing points of contact" kept the Union whole. All together made for a "magic power." In his opinion the Union could "only be rent in twain by something which loosens these rivets." He identified antislavery and sectional politics as the "lever" that might do the loosening. He found especially worrisome the possibility that politicians would have "to manufacture bonds to hold the Union together." If that sad day ever came, he saw the Union as "gone—worthless as a rope of sand." Of course, in striving to maintain southern equality, Davis was clinging desperately to bonds that two previous generations of politicians had fashioned.[7]

Davis also reiterated in the strongest possible language his conception of the power of Congress and of the federal government when he opposed granting public land to construct asylums for the indigent insane. "I do not consider our Government as one founded for great eleemosynary purposes," he declaimed. "This government was established as the agent of the States in their foreign relations, and as an umpire between the States in their relations one to another, not to dispense charities to the indigent, nor to establish workhouses or houses of correction for the vicious within the States."[8]

His position in this instance was not at all unusual or isolated. Back in 1849 he had objected to the purchase of the artist George Catlin's paintings of Indians. After praising the accuracy and quality of Catlin's work, he still resisted because for Congress to buy them would denote a marked departure "from the simple republican character of the Government." Taking such a step would result in "Congress becom[ing] the patron of art, the caterer to the tastes and refined pleasures, as well as the law-makers of the republic." In similar vein, a year later he steadfastly contested a proposal to buy the corrected copy of George Washington's Farewell Address. Congress had already bought the first president's papers, he noted, and while he venerated Washington as did all patriots, he did not think that meant purchasing everything related to him from walking sticks to battlefields. Where would it stop? he asked. In his mind, emotion should not rule. He concluded that as representatives of the people, senators should not draw on public money to gratify sentiment.[9]

In addition, Davis expressed strong reservations about what he deemed seemingly uncontrollable growth of government publications. The possible publication of a report from the Patent Office, which included a substantial section devoted to the agricultural bureau within that agency, particularly distressed him. "I hold that it is no part of the duty of Congress to publish works on speculative philosophy, or compilations of agriculture, or any similar subject not connected with legislation." Congress "ha[d] become the great book-maker of the country," a situation he deplored and wanted to halt.[10]

At the same time he continued to advocate science and invention, and he also served as a regent of the Smithsonian Institution. In his declamation against the government as publisher, he made one exception: reports connected with inventions ought to be published. Davis also wanted to strengthen laws protecting rights of patent holders, those with "inventive genius." And he supported additional appropriations for the U.S. Navy to carry out astronomical observations, arguing that the work was essential for science. As a Smithsonian regent, he became chairman of the building committee considering a general plan to improve the Mall, at that time described as "a large common . . . presenting a surface of yellow or white clay, cut into by deep gullies, and without trees except one or two scraggly and dying sycamores." The ideas of New York landscape architect Andrew Jackson Downing excited Davis. Calling them "most beautiful and useful," he envisioned the Mall transformed into "an extended landscape garden, to be traversed in different directions by gravelled walks and carriage drives."[11]

In the winter of 1851, Davis also struck out at two prime perquisites of senators, a move that attracted few allies. Davis believed firmly that his and all other speeches should be reported as spoken, not after having been edited. "I often address the Senate without having prepared myself as to what I was going to say," he admitted candidly. As a result, he "always f[ou]nd in such cases that the reporter ha[d] failed to report me correctly." Still, he maintained that the remarks uttered should be the remarks printed, even granting that reporters would inevitably make mistakes. Most of his colleagues did not agree; nor did many join him in calling for abolition of the franking privilege. Even though Davis himself made liberal use of it, he could find no "justice" in a system that taxed individuals "not for their own benefit, nor for the benefit of the country at large." "I do not perceive the least propriety," he asserted, "in giving to a member of Congress the right to send to his friends at the expense of the Government such documents as he may think proper to bestow on them, and to leave others either deprived of mailable matter or charged with the expense of paying for its transportation."[12]

With the adjournment of Congress in mid-March 1851, Senator Davis left for Mississippi by the western route, stopped briefly in Louisville, and reached Davis Bend on March 26. After a short stay, he journeyed downriver to New Orleans on business. While there he also visited his in-laws; William Howell had moved to that city in his unendingly unsuccessful search for financial security. By April 16, Davis had returned to Brierfield.[13]

Within two weeks, he plunged into the greatest contest he had yet known in his political career. Not only did the lengthy crisis over the Compromise of 1850 strain national party alliances, it also broke down party lines in the South. The great majority of southern Whigs had opposed Taylor and supported the Compromise, while the bulk of southern Democrats fought both the president and the Compromise. Each side experienced defections, especially Democrats both in and out of Congress who felt their comrades had gone too far in opposing the Compromise. Defining the Compromise as safe for the South and as politically defensible, these Democrats, with Henry Foote a major figure among them, made common cause with their partisan foes. In three states—Alabama, Georgia, and Mississippi—this political storm shook traditional political alignments from their moorings. There, the overwhelming majority of Whigs along with a minority faction of Democrats moved into what they called the Union or Constitutional Union party. The mass of Democrats, joined by a sprinkling of Whigs, also dropped old labels, now calling themselves Southern Rights men or State Rights Democrats.[14]

One of the three states where parties became totally deranged, Mississippi obviously did not escape this convulsion jarring southern politics. For Whigs in the state, the Union party was politically as well as ideologically attractive. To be sure, by defending the Compromise and wrapping themselves in the folds of the Union, they staked out superb political ground, but the Union movement also provided an opportunity for recouping lost fortunes. Mississippi Whigs had been in a distinct minority since the Calhoun-Democratic rapprochement of the late 1830s. During the 1840s they had not elected a governor nor controlled a legislature, though they did hold a few state offices and had elected a congressman from a safe district centering on the southwestern river counties. From what one stalwart termed their "hopeless minority" position, the Whigs hoped to rejuvenate their party, albeit under a new banner.[15]

The path of the major Democratic bolter was also clear. When Henry Foote championed the Compromise in the Senate, he found himself an outcast among Democratic leaders in his state. Heavily Democratic, the legislature in late 1850 had censured him while praising the others in the congressional delegation for fighting the Compromise. Within the Union party, Henry Foote had a possible political future in Mississippi; without it, he had none.

The immediate political context surrounding these partisan shifts in Mississippi bore the imprint of Governor John A. Quitman, a Democrat and an extremist on sectional issues. When he learned that the Compromise of 1850 had won congressional approval, he called a special session of the legislature for November 18 to consider withdrawing from the Union. He soon began making public speeches advocating that route, and simultaneously he plotted secretly with officials in South Carolina, the most radical southern state, on the most efficacious method to bring about secession. Without question, Quitman believed the predicament of the South required leaving the Union, and he wanted his state in the vanguard. Although the legislature refused to go as far as Quitman desired, it did keep alive the question of Mississippi's future by decreeing elections in September 1851 for delegates to a November state convention that would determine the state's fate. Only by agreeing to postpone the convention for a year could Governor Quitman and his fellow radicals get legislators to authorize such a meeting.[16]

While the legislature met during the last two weeks of November 1850, a group calling itself "friends of the Union" also had gathered in Jackson, Mississippi. These friends proclaimed their platform in ringing terms: embracing the Compromise as safe for the South and championing the Union. Denouncing the governor as treasonable and the crisis as possibly catastrophic, they declared old party lines obliterated and pleaded for all lovers of the Union to come together into a newly created Union party. Doing so served political as well as ideological purposes. Potential Democratic recruits could more easily move into an organization that did not bear the name Whig, their longtime and despised antagonist. With this newly built political vehicle, Unionists planned to storm the state in 1851, control the state convention, win the gubernatorial election, and wrest dominance away from the Democrats. With the close of Congress in the spring of 1851 and the appearance back in Mississippi of Senator Foote, a strong campaigner and marvelous stump speaker, Unionists were ready.

Although their opponents attempted to besmear Unionists as "submissionists" to northern and antislavery usurpation of southern rights, they protected themselves by appropriating the famous Georgia Platform as their own. Written in December 1850 by Georgia Unionists to expound their creed, the platform was no Milquetoast document. It proclaimed that Georgia "will and ought to resist," with secession if necessary, any action by Congress directed against slavery in the District of Columbia or in other places within congressional jurisdiction that was "incompatible with the safety, and domestic tranquility, the rights and honor of the slave holding states." The same reaction would follow should Congress deny admission to a slave state, prohibit slavery in either New Mexico or Utah Territories, or pass any bill "repealing or materially modifying" the Fugitive Slave Law. The Georgia Platform, now also the Mississippi Platform, bristled with southern weaponry.[17]

The Democrats sustained difficulties matching their new political rivals. First, they assumed an altered name. To underscore their ideological benchmark and to attract sympathetic Whigs, they prefaced their traditional appellation with "State Rights." Even so, State Rights Democrats were seriously divided among themselves, all the way from outright secessionists like Governor Quitman to the much more moderate Jefferson Davis. Assessing the stance of twenty-three formerly Democratic newspapers, one observer reported them in four camps, ranging from steadfastly unionist to "avowedly" disunionist. Davis recognized the "great confusion" plaguing what had recently been the almost omnipotent Democratic party.[18]

Aware that the continued dominance of his party was at stake, Davis also knew that more was involved than a critical fight between State Rights Democrats and Unionists. He and Foote, whom he characterized as "industrious as a bee" and "reckless of truth," were in a bitter contest for influence and prestige. In the Senate he had declared that he, not Foote, spoke for Mississippi. Moreover, the powerful position he had attained with his reelection to the Senate and his popularity with most Democrats were in jeopardy. Additionally, in May the campaign began for September election of delegates to the state convention set for November, the centerpiece of State Rights hopes. Davis's published speaking tour, scheduled between May 10 and June 13, demonstrated just how serious he judged the situation—twenty speeches in as many different towns in central and northern Mississippi.[19]

Even though he had been away from his plantation and his wife since late November, but for a few days, at this moment his political work was paramount. Not sharing her husband's sense of urgency, Varina wanted him home for a longer time. His response left no doubt about his priorities: "Your claim on my time though first could my heart decide it is interrupted for a longer period than I anticipated when we parted." "Circumstances," he told her, "have pressed" me "immediately" into the service of the State Rights Democratic party. He said he would not see her again until mid-June. As if consciously stressing the critical nature of the moment, he closed: "I commenced to talk to you my own dear Winnie but the people are crowding in on me and I have now asked them to sit down and let me close my letter."[20]

Mississippi, 1851.

From Papers of Jefferson Davis, *IV, with permission of the LSU Press*

Davis understood that he carried a major responsibility as the recognized leader of the State Rights party. He knew that Quitman had pushed too far too rapidly and that following his lead would result in "disaster and disgrace," as a political correspondent put it. Ready for his task, Davis started in Jackson on the evening of May 7, when "a large procession" marched to his lodgings and escorted him to the Capitol. There in the Senate chamber waited a substantial crowd, including many women. For some two hours he held his audience "spell bound," in the words of the reporter from the *Mississippian*. Sending him off along the dusty roads of the state, the newspaper announced it would not summarize the speech because Davis intended to visit every county so that the people themselves could hear his message.[21]

The next day he began his tour with a traveling companion, former governor and new congressman Albert G. Brown, who during the previous fall had been rhetorically as well as politically with Quitman. After sharing podiums with Brown for a week, Davis was next joined by congressional candidate William McWillie, who spent several days campaigning with him. Beginning in the center of the state, Davis headed north, and then turned east. All in all, he made twenty-four appearances before returning to Jackson for the State Rights Democratic party convention on June 16.[22]

His speeches during this five-week trek fulfilled his own description of himself as unchanging or unbending. During debate on the Compromise, he admitted, "If I have one defect which stands out more prominently than the rest, I fear it is that I adhere to my own opinion when others believe that arguments enough have been offered to warrant a change." These 1851 addresses did not deviate in substance from those he had given either in the Senate or on the stump the year before—the Compromise was no compromise but a defeat for the South; the admission of California was no less than an executive proviso and most importantly ended sectional equality; slaveowners did not receive the declared right to take their property into the territories; Mississippi and the South must demand their constitutional rights. Davis maintained that several avenues were available for southerners to make their displeasure known, from a boycott of northern goods to building up southern industrial strength to a state- or sectionwide convention. Never, however, did he speak for disunion. He did defend the right of secession, but he emphatically insisted that the situation did not mandate resorting to that drastic step.[23]

All along his route, party faithful heaped accolades upon him. The *Mississippian* judged the tour a rousing success, with large numbers attending almost every speech. Identifying Davis as the "untiring friend" of southern rights, the *Vicksburg Sentinel* characterized his canvass as "little less than a triumphal march." An eyewitness reported on one address to the *Mississippian:* "Every eye was riveted on the speaker. Tears were on many a cheek. The orator touched the heart and convinced the reason."[24]

Of course, the Unionists viewed him quite differently. With a keen sense of where Davis was most vulnerable, the Unionist press depicted no faithful servant, but rather a misguided evangel who propounded ultra doctrines that would surely endanger Mississippi and destroy the Union. When Davis tried to shun the designation of disunionist, his opponents accused him of fearing "to avow" secession directly, though he acted in every way to aid forces bent on breaking up the Union.[25]

In Jackson for the state convention of his party, a weary Davis strove mightily to throw off the disunion shroud Unionists had woven for him and his comrades. He understood how effective Unionist rhetoric had been; he was aware that Quitman's radicalism left the State Rights cause in a precarious position. Although the long statement of principles adopted by the convention repeated familiar points, it also quite specifically in a final resolution written by Davis attempted to disclaim once and for all the accusation that the party favored disunion: "That the advocates of State Rights are the true friends of the South, and of the Union; and that no right can be more clear or more essential to the protection of the majority, than the right of a State peaceably to withdraw from the Union, without denial or obstruction from any quarter whatsoever; but whilst we assert the right, we consider it the last remedy, the final alternative; and also declare that the exercise of it by the State of Mississippi, under existing circumstances, would be inexpedient, and is a proposition which does not meet the approbation of the Convention."[26]

In addition to adopting a platform, the convention also had to select a gubernatorial candidate to run against Foote, who had been nominated for the governorship at the Union party gathering in May. Contemporary evidence points to Davis as the preferred choice of his party, and "a decided majority" of the committee appointed to choose a candidate supported him. Informed of the committee's wishes, Davis agreed to accept, provided that Quitman concurred. Quitman's status and ambition placed both party and Jefferson Davis in a difficult position. Quitman was the previous governor, but not the incumbent because he had resigned in early February 1851 after his indictment by a federal grand jury. The charge of violating the Neutrality Laws by assisting a Cuban-American group to invade Cuba was dropped a month later, however. Quitman saw nomination as vindication; besides, he had long labored for the Democratic party and had put up critical guideposts along the road to the State Rights party. Davis recognized the legitimacy of Quitman's claims, but also his liability.[27]

This political tug-of-war ended with Quitman as the State Rights nominee, for he absolutely refused to step aside, even when the committee spurned his plea to turn from Davis. Although Quitman failed with the committee, he succeeded with Davis, who finally informed the group in a note transported by Quitman's friends that he refused to accept its nomination. Quitman's candidacy muddied the State Rights position on disunion. Despite the platform's outright rejection of secession as policy, Quitman as the personification of extremism undermined that declaration, though even he had begun to bend to the obvious—in the summer of 1851, most Mississippians wanted no part of secession.

The convention over, Senator Davis immediately returned to the hustings, now concentrating on the southern counties, and much of the time accompanied by Congressman Brown in his home district. Davis stepped into a political conflagration, for as a veteran politico recalled, "Mississippi was in a blaze from east to west, and from north to south." With the massive effort to win delegates in the September election in full swing, Davis, Quitman, Foote, the congressmen, and numerous other politicians were all canvassing the state. Moving through political heat that matched the torrid Mississippi summer, Davis did not alter his text. He continued to lecture audiences that a hostile northern majority had denied southerners their constitutional rights in the common territories. He reiterated his conviction that his state and his section had to assert themselves against a determined antislavery enemy. He wanted Mississippi to act in conjunction with other states, even including South Carolina, despite the latter's radical reputation. He was in touch with leaders in that state, though no evidence points to his influencing their actions, or vice versa. And he remained convinced that such a show of unity and resolve would result in the South's achieving its goals.[28]

Simultaneously, Davis struggled to throw off the disunion yoke placed on him and his fellow State Righters by Unionists. He derided the proposition that the contest was in any way between union and disunion. Emphatically denying that he or his party agitated against the Union, he proudly proclaimed himself a dedicated unionist. Although he repeated his belief in the right of secession—to him a legacy from 1776—he stressed that current conditions did not necessitate such drastic action. Furthermore, he declared that he knew of no one in either his party or the state who advocated secession, except for one man who claimed to be already out of the Union.

Davis kept up a brutal pace despite the enervating weather, and associates praised him for doing "much good," but the incessant travel and constant speechmaking were taking their toll on his physical strength. His weakened condition confined him to his room during much of the State Rights convention in Jackson. Then in mid-July, following a speech in Fayette, exhaustion led to illness, which forced him to retreat to nearby Brierfield. After resting for only a week, he once again took to the stump, this time in northern Mississippi.[29]

As before, he faced a demanding job, with at least fifteen stops publicly scheduled in the month remaining before election of convention delegates. Even before he really got underway, a supporter described him as "worn and jaded." Yet he kept mounting rostrums in towns and villages in the northern counties. Crowds poured out to hear him, and his voice rang out with the same themes he had been hammering on since May. Reports, friendly to be sure, praised his effort: he "held the crowd in breathless attention until the hour of dinner"; "the gallant Davis . . . [told] a plain eloquent tale of our wrongs with dignity, truth and power."[30]

As the campaign for electing delegates wound down, Davis's body simply refused to keep going. In Oxford on August 16, "a slight chill" forced him to curtail his remarks; around two days later, in Pontotoc, he collapsed. Quite ill, he finally had to give up his speechmaking; nursed by friends, he remained there for more than two weeks, until regaining sufficient strength to travel to Memphis and a steamboat home.[31]

"A shadow of his former self," Davis reached Brierfield in mid-September practically invalided by the most serious illness to strike him since his initial battle with malaria more than a decade and a half earlier. The almost nonstop campaigning through the sultry Mississippi summer had so worn down his resistance that he succumbed to fever and chills, undoubtedly a recurrence of malaria. The massive pressure generated by the enormous political stakes for Davis and his party probably contributed to a further affliction, a severe eye attack.[32]

Although he had been bothered previously by inflamed eyes, never before had he suffered anything approaching the severity of this attack. Varina recalled that he could not "bear a ray of light upon either eye," though the left one was more severely afflicted. For some three weeks "he slept all day, arose after sundown, and walked through the house all night." After little more than a week at home, Davis wanted to consult Dr. Samuel Cartwright, a noted physician in New Orleans as well as a family friend, but he did not believe that he could yet make the trip downriver.[33]

Davis was not able to go to Dr. Cartwright, but he did relate to the doctor his symptoms and his regimen, which had led to a partial recovery. After a time of keeping himself in "mild and uniform light," Davis told Dr. Cartwright that "the inflammation has greatly [su]bsided, and the sight of that eye which was entirely blind has been partially restored." Although he still dealt with "great irritability in the nerve of the eye," "the cloud which had collected between the coatings of the cornea, and which entirely covered the pupil . . . has receded so as now to appear like a clear drop of water which swells the cornea on one side (the outside,) and encroaches very little on the pupil, though it covers about a third of the iris." He went on to report that "the eye has ceased to weep, and has rather an unnatural dryness, and heat, but without any engorgement of blood vessels."[34]

Although it is impossible to be absolutely certain, it is most probable that Davis's disorder resulted from a herpes simplex infection of the cornea of the left eye, a condition known as herpetic keratitis. Davis's description points to that diagnosis, as does the established connection between herpetic keratitis and malaria. The type I herpes simplex virus does have a positive relationship to heat, sunlight, and febrile illness like malaria, as well as emotional stress. Certainly during the summer of 1851, Davis was exposed to heat and sunlight, did come down with malaria, and most assuredly felt tremendous emotional stress.[35]

Davis's own delineation of his symptoms meshes with modern clinical reports, including redness, tearing, and decreased vision. His emphasizing the cornea indicates that he had most likely developed metaherpetic keratoiritis, with severe stromal involvement. The stroma makes up approximately 90 percent of the corneal substance. As the stroma of his left cornea began to disintegrate from the inflammatory process, it weakened, allowing a prominent membrane (Descemet's) to protrude forward because of the intraocular pressure of the aqueous humor, forming what is termed a descemetocole, which Davis refers to as appearing like "a clear drop of water."

Davis recovered slowly from this siege, but his eye problem did not disappear. The type I herpes simplex virus can recur, given the proper physical and emotional conditions. Moreover, a usual course of herpetic keratitis fits Davis's clinical history, with his ongoing and ultimately even more serious ophthalmological difficulties.[36]

While weakness and disability hobbled Davis, his party was knocked off its political feet. The Union party swept the state, capturing 57 percent of the vote, with a margin exceeding 7,000. This outcome distressed Davis, who in midsummer had still thought his party, his cause, and his prestige would prevail. Postmortems were quickly produced. Astute State Righters realized that Quitman had been an albatross in two different ways. First, his extremist reputation made it too easy for Unionists to cast the disunionist net over the State Rights party. Quitman had simply "outstripped the views of the people" when he "recommend[ed] secession as the proper cause" for the state. Second, with his "poor and flat" speaking style, Quitman could not match Foote on the stump.[37]

During the joint canvass by the two gubernatorial candidates, in June and July, Foote consistently bested his opponent. Relations between the men so deteriorated that a threat of violence came to hover over the campaign—a threat that was finally realized on July 18, when they pummeled each other with fists and feet. As a result, Quitman called off all further joint appearances, arriving thereafter in a particular place roughly two days after Foote. This tactic backfired, however, for it enabled Foote to boast that Quitman was afraid to meet him face-to-face. Quitman took the defeat of his cause as a personal repudiation, which in a significant way it was, and resigned as the Democratic State Rights nominee for governor on September 6, only two months before the election.[38]

Although Quitman's notoriety and his oratorical shortcomings certainly did not help his party, a more fundamental cause underlay the State Rights debacle. A significant number of Mississippians were not prepared for extreme measures. Though not thrilled with the Compromise of 1850, they did not consider it so awful or so dangerous as to require preparation for disunion, much less disunion itself. That fact enabled the Union party, with a former Democratic notable at its head and reciting the Georgia-become-Mississippi Platform, to present itself as the state's responsible, conservative defender.

The election for convention delegates revealed an evaporation of the normal, overwhelming Democratic majority. Winning handily, Unionists carried all but eighteen counties, mostly in the Piney Woods of southern Mississippi, and elected better than a two-to-one majority of convention delegates. Contributing heavily to the State Rights rout was a significantly lower turnout. In the election for convention delegates, 49,643 Mississippians voted, compared to 56,113 in the 1849 gubernatorial contest, and 57,717 in the November election. The overwhelming majority of those who stayed home had usually lodged in the Democratic tent, for in 1849 the victorious Quitman won 33,117 votes, but in 1851 the State Rights delegates managed to garner only 21,241. Thus, many Democrats who would not support what they perceived as extremism still refused to vote for a party made up chiefly of Whigs and led by a man most Democratic leaders branded a turncoat or traitor.[39]

Even though the convention campaign left the Democratic State Rights party "scattered to the four winds of Heaven," party stalwarts labored "to retrieve the fortunes of the day." That so many traditional Democrats stayed home on election day—party leaders estimated as many as 7,000 or more—provided hope that the decision in September could be reversed in the gubernatorial election, if the right candidate replaced Quitman. Almost as one man, party managers turned to Jefferson Davis. Only days after Quitman's withdrawal the committee designated by the State Rights state convention to fill any vacancies selected Davis, announcing in a public letter that the press and people of Mississippi had already named him. Even Quitman joined the chorus.[40]

From Brierfield on September 17 an ailing Davis responded positively to the invitation: "Under such circumstances, I have only to reply that my whole political life has been devoted to the Democratic cause, and the maintenance of those principles in which originated the party of strict construction, and faithful adherence to the Constitution. It is not in an hour when clouds have darkened our fortune that I can refuse any poor service it is still in my power to render. That cause, and those principles, seem more dear to me now than in the day of their triumph." After tying the State Rights banner to the Democratic staff, he closed by saying that as soon as his health permitted he would prepare an address to the people. Having consulted with friends, he emphasized his commitment to this newly accepted mission by resigning from the United States Senate. This also permitted Davis to contrast himself with Foote, who had not given up his Senate post, even though he had been the Union party nominee since May.[41]

The news that Davis had entered the field rejuvenated the downcast and defeated State Righters. Proclaiming that "the very mention of him sends an electric thrill through every heart," the party's major newspaper hailed Davis as the man who led the "sons and brothers" of Mississippians "to victory," and "who never quailed himself, and whose smiles and voice cheered them on in the most doubtful and trying moment of battle." With that man "now a candidate for the highest office within your gift," the *Mississippian* asked the critical question: "Can you vote against him?" A compatriot believed Davis "stronger in the State of Mississippi, not only than any man, but than any principle." "The people," he maintained, "had a confidence in his integrity and trustworthiness that surpassed anything I have known. . . ."[42]

Giving up the Senate seat he had cherished and worked so hard to keep for a difficult immediate challenge and an uncertain future demonstrated conclusively that in Davis's mind, something utterly fundamental was at stake. He obviously felt an obligation to his party, which he still considered to be the Democrats, for ideological as well as political-tactical reasons. Like other State Rights leaders, he knew that the September drubbing had left the party in shambles and that, with no effective gubernatorial standard-bearer, it would remain so and end up crushed in both the governor's race and the legislative elections. Such an outcome would mean that Foote would dominate state politics, an outcome that did not bode well for Jefferson Davis. Besides, his pride was on the line. He had told the U.S. Senate that he spoke with the voice of Mississippi; he had traversed much of the state preaching a gospel that he believed in deeply. When the committee asked him to step forward, everything was in jeopardy: career, cause, reputation. He acted to vindicate all.

Davis had agreed to make the race, but his eye difficulties still severely restricted his activities. He and his advisers recognized that they had little time left to reverse the Unionist tide. Because of his impaired vision, the committee drafted and sent him a public announcement. At first, he listened to the document being read, then objected to "turgid" phrasing, and finally "discarded the whole paper." Then, according to Varina, he dictated another statement to her. Dated September 25, this long address to "The People of Mississippi" basically repeated the message Davis had been proclaiming since spring. He made sure to underscore his longtime loyalty to the Democratic party and Democratic principles, but he also declared that he always considered himself the representative of the people. As such, his opposing the Compromise of 1850 in the Senate matched the stated position of Mississippi in the spring of that year. One stand he never took, he insisted, was for disunion. Denouncing those who tried to make union or disunion the question, he once again pledged his love for the Union and proclaimed the only legitimate issue to be preserving the constitutional rights of Mississippi by Mississippians.[43]

This public letter, which was issued in "extra-form" in Jackson and appeared widely in the state press, was not the only vehicle the Davis camp used to reach voters. In late September a hastily written biography appeared, with "A Citizen of Mississippi" listed as author. That citizen was in fact Collin S. Tarpley, a well-known Jackson attorney, a prominent Democrat, and a friend of Davis. Published in Jackson, this twenty-nine-page pamphlet recounted Davis's career, describing him as a Democrat and stressing his service to the nation as well as his unswerving loyalty to Mississippi in both peace and war. According to the biographer, selflessness, integrity, honor, and devotion to his state formed Davis's credo.[44]

Despite Davis's personal popularity, the State Rights leadership knew that in the effort to defeat the Union party they faced two notable, intertwined problems: the Unionists' momentum and the stain of disunion clinging to their party. Although Unionists with their rhetorical broadsides through the year had certainly made a hefty contribution toward plastering that designation on their opponents, perceptive State Righters acknowledged responsibility within their own camp. The editor of the *Mississippian* admitted to Davis that public talk of a confederacy of southern states damaged the party. All attempts at caution, he warned, would lead nowhere "while letters from half-crazy members of the party, are thrown before the public to influence the election." Unionists never let up, though some of them privately admitted that while Davis believed in the right of secession, he had not advocated disunion. Noting Davis's replacing Quitman, a major Unionist newspaper asserted that a change in men did not change the message. The *Vicksburg Whig* proclaimed, "The people of the State have decided that the reins of Government shall not continue in the hands of agitators, and we think that the course of Gen. Foote will be sustained in November, by a much larger majority than has been announced in the recent convention election."[45]

To prove that prediction wrong and to demonstrate his political powers, a convalescing, though far from recovered, Jefferson Davis left Brierfield in late October to present himself and his case to the voters. Against his doctor's advice, but with the left eye covered and goggles to deflect sun and dust, Davis traveled through Vicksburg on the twentieth and on to Jackson, before heading for north Mississippi on the twenty-first. Aware that if he were to have any chance, he would have to generate enthusiasm and a large turnout in this traditionally Democratic citadel, Davis planned to spend all of his time in the area. With only two weeks until the voting, he could not hope to cover all of the northern counties; yet the party announced that he would make at least a half dozen public speeches. His last appearance was at Holly Springs on November 3, election day.[46]

In this final almost desperate exertion, Davis continued to denounce the Compromise of 1850 and condemn the Union party. Still, acknowledging that Mississippians had made clear their acceptance of the Compromise, he declared himself "bound by every principle of his cherished democracy" to accept the popular verdict. He saw only one issue remaining: whether Mississippians acquiesced approvingly or disapprovingly, and in his opinion the decision of voters should turn on that question. To nudge them toward disapproval, and himself, he accentuated his Democratic heritage, declaring that he would always be found "clutching to the last the flag staff of the good old banner of Jackson and Jefferson and Madison Democracy."[47]

Davis did not prevail. In spite of his vigorous, albeit brief, campaign, he lost to Henry Foote. Even so, he narrowed considerably the Union margin of victory. In the convention election Unionists had won by more than 7,000 votes; Davis lost by only 999. He brought back to the polls many Democrats who had sat out two months earlier. Running strongly across the state, except in Whig strongholds along the Mississippi River, he polled 28,359 votes, or one-third more than the State Rights delegates had obtained in September. He carried twenty-six counties, making inroads in the north and adding in the south. Several knowledgeable politicians on both sides thought that had the election been held a couple of weeks later, Davis could have completely closed the gap and beaten Foote.[48]

Whether or not more time would have enabled Davis to win can never be known, but the defeat did not at all tarnish his standing in his party. To the contrary, he emerged with status enhanced. That at a dire moment he gave up his Senate seat and cast his political fortunes with his party in Mississippi, and then, given his physical condition, made an almost herculean attempt to turn back the Unionist tide, brought an outpouring of support. He was told that his friends now admired him as no man had been admired since Jackson. "I regard your future political sky as being without a cloud and of Italian azure," wrote one State Rights leader, who added the salve, "and that your course will be necessarily onwards and upwards, until you reach the Presidency."[49]

Yet, although losing the governor's race did not diminish Davis's personal political standing, his party suffered a notable setback. His was an individual performance, for his close run did not help many of his comrades. Of the four Democratic State Rights congressional incumbents, all of whom had opposed the Compromise, only Albert G. Brown, whose district included the only part of the state to vote State Rights in September, would return to Congress. Unionists thrashed State Righters in the contests for the state House, winning sixty-three of ninety-eight seats. Only the state Senate remained a State Rights refuge; the party won nine of sixteen contested seats and retained a considerable advantage, twenty-one to eleven.[50]

Davis attributed the State Rights defeat to what he called "a false issue," which "proved a bond to unite the minority, Whigs, with a portion of the Democrats and give the State to the so-called Union party." That issue was, of course, the question of disunion. Despite his massive effort of six months, from May to November, Davis had been unable to break its power. Now, his enemies personal and political predominated in Mississippi politics. But the Union party had emerged out of a fortuitous set of political circumstances, which also allowed it and Henry Foote to capture votes and offices. As 1851 closed, no one knew how long either the particular situation or the Union party would last.[51]

His political career stymied, Jefferson Davis settled in at Brierfield, planning more than a brief stay for the first time since entering Congress back in 1845. He and Varina now lived in the new house he had agreed to build in 1846 while on furlough from Mexico. Construction had commenced by early 1849, utilizing local builders and the labor of his slaves, with much of the lumber cut and milled on the plantation.[52]

In contrast to Joseph, Jefferson did not build an impressive mansion, though he spent around $6,000 on what one of its builders termed "a costly residence." A one-story home, sprawling as a live oak, the new Brierfield was long and low. Raised on piers about three feet from the ground, its branching wings provided spaciousness without ostentation. Inviting porches ran the entire length, front and back. The fluted Doric columns supporting these deep galleries and the massive doorway centered in the portico gave the home a gracious if not grand appearance.

Although not a typical Greek Revival southern mansion, Brierfield had many traditional features, such as the wide central hall and the front windows that reached 12 feet from the floor. These and ceilings about 16 feet high aided the ventilation in the nine rooms. Two imported Carrara marble mantels in the parlor and the library, along with two chandeliers in the dining room, added refinement to rooms with unadorned millwork and plain plaster walls. The east and west wings were accessible from both the front and back porches. Perpendicular to the west wing, which contained the dining room as well as a bedroom, and set apart from the main structure, the kitchen and pantry were in turn connected to the back porch by a covered service walkway. The home also contained a shower bath, though no particulars about it have survived. Behind the big house stood many smaller buildings, including three latticed cisterns, a commissary, an outhouse, and a bellstand.[53]

The Davises first moved into the house following their return from Washington in the fall of 1850. To a friend in January 1851, Varina called it "quite new." At that time she did not use lyrical phrases to describe her home, which "not least in my catalog of evils is large enough for two families." Of course, it was originally designed for two, hers along with that of Jefferson's widowed sister Amanda; but the absence of a second kitchen attested to the scrapping of those plans. Setting up housekeeping with Jefferson back in the Senate, she found the house "desolate, damp, and lonesome," with "even the cats shunning it." She and her eight-year-old sister Maggie occupied two rooms "in one end of this barn."[54]

By the time a weak and weary Jefferson returned in November 1851 from his exhausting, futile six-month political campaign, Varina had a more positive outlook. By all accounts they had overcome the marital difficulties that had plagued them between 1846 and 1850. When Jefferson was desperately ill at home, she cared for him and adapted her habits of reading and writing "in light that was not sufficient to show the position of the furniture." With husband and wife together, Varina recounted happy times. Books, mail twice a week, visits from neighbors, gardening, and horseback riding occupied their time. She delighted in "the daily ride on our fast racing horses, with races on the smooth road wherever we found one." "Nothing could be more pleasant," she rhapsodized, "than the dense shade through which we could ride for miles, in air redolent of the perfume of the moss, flowers, wild crab-apple and plum blossoms."[55]

Reading held an important place in their lives. After resigning,

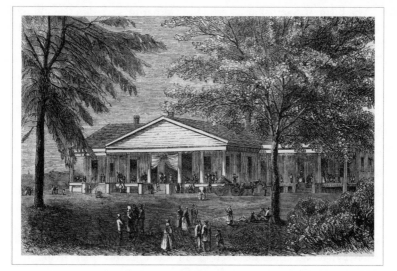

Brierfield.
From Harper's Weekly, *September 15, 1866*

Davis requested the Senate secretary to send his books as well as the *Congressional Globe* on to Mississippi. Although the historical record does not reveal what the Davises actually read at Brierfield, it does indicate what the senator checked out of the Library of Congress during the winter of 1851. Those books included writings of the first-century Jewish historian Josephus, a volume of George Sand's works, medieval French tales, an early novel by the popular English writer Edward Bulwer-Lytton, the memoirs of an English peeress, sermons by the English clergyman Reginald Heber, onetime Anglican Lord Bishop of Calcutta, an encyclopedia of natural history, and *Ure's Dictionary of the Arts* . . . , in reality an encyclopedia of engineering and technology. Their taste in reading clearly ranged widely, from current affairs to history to fiction to religion to technical items.[56]

In the summer of 1852 the Davises knew great joy, the birth of their first child. Born on July 30, Samuel Emory Davis was named for his grandfather Davis. This event was especially joyful because Varina had been married for seven years without giving birth and had experienced at least one miscarriage. She had even given up "all expectations" that she would ever become a mother. Before Samuel's arrival her own mother and several siblings had come to Brierfield to be with her.[57]

The birth of Samuel also caused his father to alter significantly his outlook on the future. Since his departure for the Mexican War in 1846, his will, influenced by Joseph, had not left his property to Varina, but divided its income between her and certain of his sisters. Varina would be permitted to live at Brierfield, if she chose, but if she did not, the plantation would be sold with the proceeds divided as the income. Now, with a son to inherit, he destroyed the will that had so distressed his wife. Making a ceremony of its destruction, he built a fire, even in July, and called in a builder working at Brierfield to witness the flames consuming the document.[58]

Although the ceremony pleased his wife, Jefferson now had to contend with a "misunderstanding" of "a very irritating character" with Joseph. In some unknown manner Joseph came to believe that Jefferson desired to sell Brierfield plantation, though no surviving evidence indicates that he had any such intention. Emphasizing the emotional distance that had arisen between the brothers, despite their living just over a mile apart, Joseph sent a letter to Jefferson asking about price so that he could buy the place. Jefferson replied that he had never thought about selling and had no wish to do so. Not only did Jefferson have to confront difficulties with his brother; at this time Joseph's wife, Eliza, complained to her brother-in-law that he, Jefferson, had not treated her kindly, causing her great pain. She claimed further that Varina had spoken irritably to her and rejected her affection. Now, Eliza determined to return " 'Measure for Measure.' " Joseph blamed the women for his and Jefferson's estrangement. To a friend he expressed deep affection for his youngest brother, but vowed to prevent Varina or any of her family from gaining control of any Davis property.

In all probability their estrangement affected Jefferson's immediate decisions about managing Brierfield. This episode also illustrates once more the onerous position Jefferson occupied between Joseph and Varina. Pleasing or appearing to grow closer to one almost invariably meant increasingly stressful relations with the other. Jefferson seemingly could not stand in the same emotional location with the two people who meant most to him, his wife and his brother–surrogate father.[59]

According to Varina, these "family troubles" contributed in spring 1852 to another breakdown in her husband's health. He was eating poorly and "thin to attenuations," in her words. Moreover, his eye problem returned, becoming serious by late summer, with Davis himself speaking once more of his "opthalmic disease." Certainly emotional stress could have led to a recurrence of herpetic keratitis. Attempting to aid recuperation, in the fall he took a month's sojourn to New Orleans and to the Mississippi Gulf Coast, where he visited relatives, consulted with Dr. Cartwright, rested by the sea, and did get better. By the first of the new year he reported his health "much improved."[60]

Simultaneously delighted and dismayed with his loved ones, Jefferson Davis turned his attention to the land that in the preceding fifteen years had been transformed from a tangled wilderness into a prosperous plantation. In 1850 Brierfield contained more than 1,200 acres, with 450 cleared. Through the next decade Davis opened up an additional 350 acres, giving him a total of 800 acres for cultivation. He raised the crops and animals normal for large agricultural enterprises in the Deep South: corn and other grains for both human and animal consumption; horses for pleasure; cattle, poultry, and swine for food; oxen and mules for work. In addition, gardens produced vegetables for the black and white inhabitants, and an orchard contained an impressive variety of fruit trees, including apple, peach, pear, and plum.[61]

Although Brierfield was home to a varied assortment of people, animals, and plants, everyone and everything on the place had a single overriding mission—growing the cotton crop that made everything else possible. The enormously rich, alluvial soil could produce two bales to the acre, an impressive yield for that day. By the 1840s Davis was harvesting several hundred bales each year. During the 1850s, his output remained in that range, reaching at least 600 bales of around 400 to 450 pounds each.[62]

Modern scholarly methodology offers proof that Davis operated an enormously productive enterprise. Productivity is judged chiefly by the output per hand or slave—in the case of cotton, the number of bales divided by the available workforce. In Warren County in 1860 the cotton crop averaged 3.77 bales per hand, based on the number of slaves between fifteen and fifty-nine years of age. Analyzing the 6.8 bale-per-hand yield on one plantation, a knowledgeable student of antebellum Mississippi cotton culture pronounced it "exceptionally large" for the county. Brierfield's production far surpassed even that total, equaling or exceeding the highest county average of 8.93 bales. At the end of the decade between 500 and 600 bales were being ginned yearly on Brierfield. In 1860, Davis owned fifty-seven slaves aged between fifteen and fifty-nine, giving him an imposing average of between 8.8 and 10.5 bales per hand. In tandem, the fabulously rich soil and Davis's slave labor enabled him to outpace most of his fellow planters.[63]

To market his cotton, Davis followed the practice of Joseph and most other planters and used a factor. Factors in the slave states offered a full array of financial and commercial services for their planter clients. In the role of broker or seller's agent, factors received and sold shipments of cotton or other major staples such as rice, cane, and tobacco where they found the best price, either in the United States or Europe, placing the proceeds in an account the planter maintained with the factor. Then, with the income on hand or forthcoming, the factor acted as banker and furnishing merchant—holding deposits, honoring drafts, loaning money, providing supplies that could vary from expensive European furniture to inexpensive slave shoes to slaves themselves. For these services, factors received a commission of around 2 percent of the income generated by the sale of the planter's crop.[64]

In his career as a cotton planter, Jefferson Davis utilized only a few factors, preferring to concentrate his business rather than spread it out. From the late 1830s to the early 1840s, he used George E. Payne, a partner in a New Orleans firm. Later in the 1840s, he dealt with William Laughlin & Company, also in New Orleans; Laughlin eventually became a nephew-in-law, marrying one of Joseph's daughters. Throughout the 1850s Davis worked chiefly with Jacob U. Payne (no relation to George), whom he had first met in the mid-1830s at either Vicksburg or Warrenton. Payne, who became a lifelong friend, moved to New Orleans in 1840 and eventually became a partner in the firm of Payne & Harrison.[65]

Surviving records detail a range of transactions between the planter and his factors, especially Jacob Payne. Davis trusted Payne completely, even permitting him to decide when, in which market, and at what price to sell Brierfield cotton. Davis was evidently satisfied, for no evidence even hints at any complaint about Payne's decisions. Aside from selling Davis's crop, Payne & Harrison regularly paid bills incurred by Davis and honored drafts drawn on his account. From New Orleans they shipped upriver to Brierfield everything from personal or decorative items like mirrors, a shower bath, and millinery to essential products for the plantation like flour, pork, molasses, and parts for the cotton gin. Payne also filled special orders such as Davis's request that the factor procure a talented slave cook for the Brierfield kitchen.[66]

In running Brierfield, Davis had to contend with the vagaries of the weather, as did every other farmer and planter, but as his plantation fronted the Mississippi River, he also at times had to cope with a particularly destructive force of nature: floods. Rising river waters often threatened the vulnerable lowlands of Davis Bend. No coordinated levee system existed, and no public agency exercised control or authority over levee construction or standards. Although the Davis brothers and other planters in the Bend did strive to build levees that would protect lives and property, their barriers could withstand only so much high water. In the late 1850s, the Mississippi smashed at Davis Bend levees with a force unseen for three decades, even bringing Jefferson home from Washington to face impending or actual disaster. In May 1858 the plantation suffered damage from floodwaters. Then, in the spring of 1859, the river cascaded across Brierfield, covering land not flooded in "the memory of man," according to Davis, with a "strong current" running across the main ridge. He reported that the appearance of flora in some of the inundated areas indicated that the land had not been underwater for a century. This deluge even exceeded what contemporaries along the river called the great flood of 1828. This time the Davis brothers evacuated some 900 animals away from the Bend to higher ground, though they were able to maintain the slaves safely at Hurricane and Brierfield. This abnormally high water had been "unexpectedly injurious" to him, Davis confided to a friend.[67]

Despite setbacks as in 1859, all signs point to Davis's prospering as a cotton planter. In 1850, the federal census reported the cash value of Brierfield at $25,000; ten years later the amount had tripled to $75,000. Illustrating the usual undervaluation by local authorities, the Warren County assessor in 1850 evaluated Brierfield as worth $16,770, the same figure that had been used in 1846; by 1857 the assessed value had increased only to $20,000. In conformity with the generally low tax rates in the South, Davis's taxes on both real and personal property remained slight through the decade. In 1853, for example, he paid Warren County $38.31 on his land and $154.74 on his personal property, including slaves, cattle, a pleasure carriage, two watches, one clock, and 400 bales of ginned cotton. In 1860 his tax bill went up, but only to $261.43. Davis's slaves added enormously to his wealth; the 113 that he owned in 1860 were worth, conservatively, $80,000. He also invested in land away from Davis Bend. In 1857 he purchased a lot on the Mississippi Gulf Coast; and in 1857 and 1859, in partnership with Joseph and a third investor, more than 10,000 acres of swamp and overflow land in Arkansas. Also in 1857 he sold for $6,000 some land in Louisiana that he had bought earlier.[68]

Clearly Jefferson Davis was a wealthy man, though precision concerning his annual income is impossible. Very late in her life Varina claimed that before the Civil War, Davis made between $35,000 and $40,000 annually at Brierfield, though she also said the sum declined toward 1860. Although it is impossible to verify those numbers, it is possible to estimate the income derived from his cotton crop. Knowing the range of his cotton production and the price of cotton in the New Orleans market permits calculating the proceeds from these cotton sales. In the 1850s the price varied from a low of 7.4 cents per pound in 1851 to a high of 12.4 cents per pound in 1856, with 11.2 cents the decennial average. Selling 500 bales of cotton weighing 450 pounds each would generate $25,200. Of course, higher prices were available in certain months during a year and at times in other markets, including European. Because Davis and Payne strove for the highest possible price and because Davis had the financial strength to wait for better prices, it is likely that Davis did somewhat better than average. Then, additional income could have come from such endeavors as selling wood to steamboats for fuel, as Joseph surely did. Thus, Varina's numbers may be close to the mark. Whatever the exact figure, Davis was an exceptionally rich man for his time and place. In 1860 the per capita income of free people in Mississippi was only $124, $20 less than the national average and $150 less than the highest regional average, the western south-central states. In addition, Davis's factor Jacob Payne testified that Davis generally paid as he went along, making every effort to avoid debt. Thus, little of his income had to be used for paying either principal or interest.[69]

During the 1850s, Davis had to manage Brierfield without the assistance of his trusted slave overseer James Pemberton, who died sometime in 1850 while his master was in Washington. After Pemberton's death, Davis turned to white overseers, as the overwhelming majority of planters had always done. Planters usually changed overseers regularly and complained about them even more often. Overseeing was an extremely difficult job, for the overseer often received a twofold and contradictory charge from his employer—keep the slave force reasonably content, but also produce the largest possible crop. Between 1850, when Davis hired his first white overseer, and 1861, at least seven different men worked the Brierfield slaves. On a visit home in 1857, Davis sounded the lament of planters across the South: "The business of the place I have still and the generous, brotherly love of that class called overseer, brings candidates 'to manage' for me." Davis paid his overseer from $800 to $1,000 annually, a salary level common on large cotton plantations. The high turnover occurred because he found his overseers falling short in different areas, from failure to prepare satisfactorily for an overflow from the Mississippi to what he called "mean & vicious . . . conduct." One overseer behaved toward a slave or slaves in some unspecified manner that caused Davis to say the man could no longer deal with slaves because of "the loss of moral power consequent upon his conduct."[70]

Davis's long absences from Brierfield made a normally difficult situation even more troublesome. He was in Washington most of 1850 and for three months in 1851. Then he went back as a cabinet officer between 1853 and 1857, when he returned to the Senate and where he remained until 1861. While serving in the cabinet, he hired a family friend, Dr. George McElrath of nearby Warrenton, to supervise Brierfield. McElrath's duties involved hiring overseers, ordering supplies, and drawing drafts. Joseph, who lived just over one mile away, could act almost as the resident planter. That had certainly been the practice from Jefferson's entrance into Congress in 1845 until his resignation from the Senate in 1851.[71]

After that time his relationship with Joseph and Joseph's with Brierfield became more complex. The difficulties obviously began in 1852 with the will and the rumor about selling Brierfield, and for a period Joseph had little to do with affairs at Brierfield. In 1853, he complained to a sister and brother-in-law about the "management" of Brierfield, but acknowledged that he "had no right to turn [the overseer] off." Later, in 1855, Jefferson had to intervene when unpleasantness arose between Joseph and Dr. McElrath over another Brierfield overseer. Jefferson's consistent laments about the state of his plantation upon his periodic visits from Washington certainly do not indicate any close, consistent attention by Joseph. Yet, in 1855, Jefferson went out of his way to explain in detail to Joseph his plans for an extensive building program at Brierfield. And Jefferson made sure that Joseph could have no doubt about his continued deep affection and respect: "Whilst I may sometimes estimate men differently from yourself I can have no relations to others which would interfere with those I bear to you, and whoever is your enemy must needs be mine." Near the end of the decade the brothers seemed close to where they had been at its beginning, with the two of them investing together in Arkansas lands and Joseph advising Jefferson's overseer.[72]

Jefferson Davis operated his plantation with slave labor from the day he and James Pemberton began hacking at the tangled growth that would become the cultivated fields of Brierfield. Black slaves were utterly central to the development, maintenance, and prosperity of the place. In 1835, Pemberton was his only slave; by 1840, he owned 39. During the 1840s that number increased to 72, and in the final antebellum decade to 113.[73]

Certain common traits characterized Davis's holdings from 1840 to 1860. First, his force consisted overwhelmingly of young slaves. In 1840 over half of his slaves were under twenty-four, while but seven were thirty-six or older, with only two over fifty-five. That spread of ages did not change fundamentally down to 1860, even though the total number of slaves almost tripled. In 1850, the ages of the Brierfield slaves broke down as follows: twenty-five under fifteen; forty between twenty and thirty-nine; three between forty and forty-nine; four over fifty. In 1860, the pattern remained quite similar: fifty-one under fifteen; fifty-three between twenty and thirty-nine; two between forty and forty-nine; seven over fifty.

The continuing imbalance toward younger slaves on Brierfield strongly indicates that only a small percentage of Davis's bondspeople lived past forty. The modern calculation of slave life expectancy puts it at only thirty-six years in 1850. Although that seems frightfully young by contemporary standards, it was only four years less than that for a white American in 1850 and exactly the same as that for the Dutch and French populations in the decade. Still, the paucity of older slaves is striking, for even with that life expectancy a substantial percentage of people would live past fifty. No evidence suggests that Davis made a habit of selling older slaves. Besides, no lucrative market existed for slaves past forty, especially in the lower Mississippi Valley, where planters clamored for fit, vigorous men and women to toil in the cotton and sugarcane fields. Moreover, just down the road at Hurricane, Joseph's much larger slave force also had a shortage of senior slaves. In 1850, 17 of his 239 exceeded the age of fifty; in 1860, only 13 of 355. Thus, neither Davis brother watched many slaves grow old in his service. This rarity of the elderly also helps explain why the master of Brierfield evinced such affection for the ancient slave known as Uncle Bob. He had practically no peers.[74]

The sex ratio at Brierfield did change between 1840 and 1860. When Davis began buying slaves in the late 1830s, he purchased a roughly equal number of each sex. By 1850, however, the balance had shifted toward females, who outnumbered males by forty-three to twenty-nine. Yet that imbalance was concentrated in the youthful population, for among the slaves under fifteen years of age, girls dominated by four to one, twenty to five. But an almost equal division, twenty men and eighteen women, characterized the age group that would have produced the most children as well as provided the prime field hands, twenty to twenty-nine. A decade later a turnabout had occurred, with the men predominating by sixty-five to forty-eight. A sharp increase among the males brought about this change. In the critical range from twenty to thirty-nine years, males had an almost two-to-one advantage at Brierfield: thirty-four to nineteen. But a balance characterized the young; twenty-eight girls and twenty-three boys were under fifteen.

Although surviving documents cast no light on the reasons underlying the diversity and shifting sexual ratios among the different age groups, the specifics of what changed over time do suggest possible explanations. The random nature of the birth of male and female babies could account for the sharp change that took place among the younger slaves, from heavily female in 1850 to almost evenly balanced in 1860. No records indicate the purchase in the 1840s of numerous young girls, nor does any logical reason explain why Davis would have done so. That the sexual disparity disappeared by 1860 suggests that perhaps Brierfield had a sufficiently large slave population to have produced a more normal male-female split in the under-fifteen age group. That in the late 1830s Davis bought basically equal numbers of young men and women could certainly account for the balance in the key twenty to thirty-nine age group in 1850. The disparity that became evident by 1860 probably resulted from his purchase of more male slaves in the 1850s. There is no substantive evidence that he sold slaves in any significant numbers.

But Davis certainly kept buying slaves, though it is impossible to be precise about when he purchased them or the details of all his purchases. Surviving documents indicate that he once bought from a niece a slave that she was unable to manage. He also bought skilled slaves, including a blacksmith purchased in New Orleans for $2,700; a "valuable servant" named Caroline for Varina; and a cook named Jacques, who drowned in a bayou.[75]

One special purchase involved finding an acceptable cook. When Davis asked Payne & Harrison in the summer of 1852 to send him a cook, the firm responded that his request was "the most difficult matter we have had for some time." After advising Davis of the general scarcity of available slaves, the company said that it had alerted a slave trader in the city to look out for a likely prospect. Payne & Harrison also thought that several candidates would have to be sent upriver for trials before Davis found just the one he wanted. But in just a week, Davis's factor reported that a trader had offered a seemingly qualified woman. The trader wanted $850, indicating that by winter she would probably bring $1,000. And he was willing to send her up to Brierfield for a two-week trial. Payne & Harrison wrote Davis that sum would cover her transportation costs, but he would be liable for any accident or illness that might befall the slave, including her running away. Unfortunately, the documentary record goes no further.[76]

In late 1857, Davis negotiated with Payne & Harrison to buy a "lot of negroes." Questioning whether all of the slaves were worth the asking price, he found one man described as "small," a woman as "common," and two boys, ages eleven and twelve, "hardly to be called hands." After discussing prices and looking carefully at the description of the slaves, Davis offered $10,000 for the group. He also informed his factor that while he would not have time personally to examine these blacks, he would have it done.[77]

Although the historical record covering Jefferson Davis as a slave-owner is disappointingly thin and does not permit extended analysis, sufficient evidence survives to make clear that the welfare of his human property occupied much of his attention. Davis was motivated by a combination of self-interest and the precepts of evangelical Protestantism that took hold in most of the South during the first third of the nineteenth century. Self-interest taught that decent care of valuable property resulted in healthier and more productive laborers, while religion preached the need for Christian stewardship by one group of God's children toward another. In a critical manifestation of that outlook, numerous slaveowners—Davis included—considered their slaves an extension of their Christian family, using terms like "my people," which Davis employed extensively, rather than the hard word "slave."[78]

Davis did strive to supply the basic physical needs of his bondspeople. He provided ample food, chiefly the pork and cornmeal that were the principal elements of the slave diet across the South. Supplements came from chickens and eggs raised in the slaves' own chicken coops, along with fruits and vegetables in season. This diet probably furnished sufficient calories, but also undoubtedly failed to supply all needed nutrients. When present at Brierfield, he and Varina often tended ill slaves. He built a hospital for them, which he enlarged in 1855, and also scheduled visits from a physician, usually Dr. McElrath. In one instance he sent a slave girl with an unusual affliction all the way to New Orleans by steamboat for Dr. Cartwright's treatment.[79]

Davis took note of matters spiritual as well. Varina remembered worship held every Sunday in the chapel at one end of Joseph's hospital. The Davises engaged an Episcopalian chaplain for the whites, but not for the blacks, who preferred either Baptist or Methodist services, the two denominations favored by slaves as well as whites almost everywhere. Accordingly, the Davises brought in ministers of these two persuasions alternately: a Baptist minister would preach for two weeks, then a Methodist for the next two. Whether or not slave preachers functioned on the Davis plantations is simply not known, though Varina spoke of Uncle Bob as being "eloquent in prayer." The existing documents neither confirm nor deny the activity of slave preachers, who had considerable influence on many farms and plantations. Marking the end of life, slaves on Brierfield received special allotments for the supper that highlighted the wakes for the deceased. Burial followed in the slave cemetery, located just to the southeast of the Davis residence or the big house.[80]

As did most slaveowners, the Davis brothers recognized families among their slaves, despite the absence of any statutory provision or protection for the slave family. Jefferson's first slave and overseer, James Pemberton, had a wife and at least one child. On Hurricane, Joseph certainly acknowledged the family of the remarkable Ben Montgomery, a literate and extraordinarily capable slave, who ran the plantation store and kept accounts.[81]

Brierfield slaves lived in cabins. The exact number of cabins is not known, though they were arranged in rows, a common placement, near the big house. Davis did want adequate housing in his slave quarters, the usual designation for the structures as well as the area in which they were placed. In 1855, from Washington, he detailed for Joseph the additional construction he had ordered for Brierfield to address what he saw as overcrowding in the quarters. An illustration of a portion of Brierfield's slave quarters appeared in *Harper's Weekly* just after the Civil War; it pictured typical clapboard cabins of both one story and a story and a half.[82]

In particular cases Davis treated his slaves with dignity. Perhaps this attitude came in part from his long close association with James Pemberton, whom he entrusted with substantial responsibility and considered a friend, always handing him a cigar when they parted.

Slave cabins at Brierfield.
From Harper's Weekly, *September 15, 1866*

Complementing his experience with Pemberton, he also maintained close relations with his brother's slave Ben Montgomery. When in Washington, he corresponded with Montgomery, who forwarded Davis mail and apprised him of affairs at the Bend during Joseph's absences. Although the circumstances are completely unknown, in 1859 Jefferson took out a life insurance policy for $3,500 on Ben Montgomery and a female slave. In addition, the assignments and leeway Joseph gave Ben Montgomery clearly attest to the eldest brother's conviction about the ability and worthiness of at least some slaves. Many years later Varina recalled other instances such as her husband's permitting slaves to choose their own names and calling them by their chosen name.[83]

Davis, of course, owned slaves chiefly for labor—and labor they did. As on all large plantations, the work seemed unending. The cotton crop consumed the greatest exertion, from preparing the soil and planting in late winter and early spring through cultivation in late spring and summer to harvest in fall and early winter. In addition, corn and other grains demanded attention, as did the hundreds of animals. In slower periods, efforts were directed toward construction and maintenance of buildings, fences, and ditches, and, in the Mississippi floodplain, levees. To ensure that all able-bodied men and women were available for physical work, the plantation had a nursery to care for young children.[84]

In a most unusual assignment for bondsmen, Jefferson and Joseph in 1851 armed and led a contingent of their slaves in an attempt to halt the construction of a cutoff at the narrow eastern end of Davis Bend where less than one mile of dry land separated coils of the great river. Successful diversion of the river would have removed the riverfront from the Davis properties and isolated them. In 1850 Joseph had gone to court and obtained an injunction against the diversionary initiative. When his legal victory did not stop the digging, he and Jefferson undertook the use of force. Unfortunately, there is no record as to whether any actual clash occurred between the Davis-led slaves and the other side. No more confrontations or threats of confrontation seem to have taken place, though it appears that the attempt to create a cutoff continued sometime later, perhaps during the war. Then, in 1867, the river itself rushed across the narrow neck, turning Davis Bend into Davis Island.[85]

The family tradition that both Jefferson and Joseph were benevolent masters for their time and place does generally fit the available evidence, but the familial story goes considerably further in holding up the Davis brothers as model masters running plantations on which the slaves barely realized they were slaves. According to this script, Joseph set the pattern of an unusually humane system, which his youngest brother and protégé followed. A key element in this version of slavery on both Hurricane and Brierfield involved the slave jury, where any slave accused of violating a plantation regulation was tried by a jury of peers, that is, by other slaves. The master intervened only to ameliorate harsh sentences, as when Jefferson supposedly reduced a penalty of 5,000 lashes to an extra hour in the field. In the same vein, the whip, the pervasive symbol of white authority in the slave South, was unseen, for Jefferson forbade corporal punishment, specifically whipping.

This view of slavery under the Davis brothers originated with Varina in her *Memoir,* published in 1890, and in her subsequent correspondence and in letters written by Joseph's granddaughter almost two decades later. Although these two women should certainly have been excellent witnesses of slavery at Brierfield and Hurricane, they were both looking back from the late nineteenth and early twentieth centuries, when southern whites were romanticizing old plantation days, including slavery. Additionally, no other contemporary documents verify this plantation Eden. That such a fascinating system of slave management run by two such prominent individuals in such an accessible location completely escaped notice is puzzling.[86]

The testimony of Jefferson Davis's slaves generally affirms the family tradition, albeit with few details and some caveats. In late 1865 a group of Davis's former slaves petitioned the governor of Mississippi, requesting the release from prison of their ex-master. Admitting that "he tried hard" to maintain slavery, the petitioners also declared, "Some of us well know of many kindness he shown his slaves on his plantation." Much later, in the 1930s, several men and women who had belonged to him were interviewed by whites during an attempt sponsored by the federal government to obtain firsthand accounts of the slave experience. In these conversations extremely elderly people were trying to recall conditions and events of their early youth. Moreover, these black former slaves were being questioned by whites in Mississippi during the heyday of white supremacy and racial segregation. Under such circumstances, legitimate doubts can be raised about both accuracy and candor, but the dominance of certain themes lends credibility. The comments by former Brierfield slaves concentrate on three topics: they recognized that they had been owned by an important man; they described him as a kind master, especially to children; they remembered being bought or sold by Davis. One did mention the slave jury, but gave no details.[87]

In one area the Davis brothers were unusual, though not unique. Each gave substantive authority to certain slaves. For a decade and a half James Pemberton served as the only overseer on Brierfield, watching the number of slaves increase from a handful to more than seventy. Varina was surely accurate in her observation that her husband was never able to replace him. After all, seven white men served in the ten years after Pemberton's death. Joseph's dealings with Ben Montgomery and his sons matched Jefferson's with Pemberton. There could have been others. Visiting the Davis plantations during the Civil War, a Union naval officer remarked that the slaves he encountered there "offer[ed] a strong contrast to many on the River," observing that they "seem[ed] more intelligent than those I have seen elsewhere." He found some "educated" and some possessing "quite a mechanical genius." Although this officer specified neither numbers nor names, it seems likely that he encountered some of the Montgomerys.[88]

When overseers stepped beyond the bounds of conduct Jefferson Davis considered acceptable, he acted, but the bounds are unknown, for no rules for overseers on Brierfield have survived. In 1855 he let an overseer go, calling him "a low man" because his unspecified "conduct disqualified him for the proper management of the people." Two years later, Davis reported that after he had fired another overseer for improperly administering medicine which had caused the death of a slave girl, he learned "so much more that is mean & vicious in his past conduct."[89]

Despite his honest wish that his slaves receive decent treatment, Davis understood that slavery did not exist without punishment. He evidently was "averse to bodily castigation," except when unavoidable. And, of course, he or his agents made that decision. In penalizing slaves Davis could be inventive. One of Davis's male slaves who "annoyed him greatly" for an unknown offense ended up in his master's version of solitary confinement. Davis had the offender placed in "a little prison-house of logs, with top door to hand his victuals through." After being incarcerated for two weeks, the slave was released, "fully subdued and never gave his master more trouble." In January 1861 Joseph discovered that slaves from both Hurricane and Brierfield had been involved in a "contraband trade in corn & whiskey," which meant buying and selling or bartering illegally with whites or other blacks. Joseph told Jefferson in Washington that the slaves judged guilty had been punished, but he did not give details.[90]

Jefferson Davis's almost continuous absence from Brierfield between 1853 and 1861 and his incessant difficulties with overseers, along with complaints about conditions, do not correlate with the traditional view of Brierfield as a plantation paradise. His hiring of overseers whom he subsequently dismissed for misconduct meant that at times his own actions resulted in the mistreatment of his slaves. Back at Brierfield in mid-1855 after an absence of almost two and a half years, Davis revealed that "the place had fallen into bad condition but under the present overseer promises better hereafter." That promise was not kept, however, because when Varina returned home in the spring of 1857, she found abject neglect: "All the locks spoilt, sheets cut up for napkins, towels and napkins swept from the land—nothing even to cook in. . . . I just sat down and cried." That a perfectly run plantation would have witnessed an almost perpetually revolving door of over-seers and occasioned such laments from the owners seems most unlikely. That thoroughly happy slaves would have participated in contraband trade and other activities requiring solitary confinement seems equally improbable.[91]

In sum, judging by both the standards of his time and the findings of modern scholarship on slavery, Jefferson Davis was a reasonably humane master, but no evidence presents Brierfield as unique or as some idyllic garden for its enslaved inhabitants. Brierfield slaves worked very hard, and they felt the arbitrary and, at times, intemperate authority of ever-changing overseers. Moreover, the reported activities and punishments clearly demonstrate that the restrictions and rigors of bondage chafed at least some of them.

Davis deemed the slaves themselves an unfortunate race that he and his fellow masters had to tutor and care for. He believed bringing Christianity to the transplanted Africans the greatest missionary work of all time. Whether he concurred in the opinion of his friend Dr. Samuel Cartwright that blacks composed a distinct species cannot be ascertained, yet it is unlikely that he shared such an extreme view. At the same time he did think that God had created blacks to become "tillers of land and drawers of water," though he was obviously just as convinced that some slaves had special capabilities, as witness his dealings with James Pemberton and Ben Montgomery. According to Varina, in 1846 he talked with Pemberton about freedom. Varina says that the slave wanted to "take care of his mistress" at his master's death; but if she died also, he would want his liberty. No existing record suggests that Davis ever contemplated emancipation for any other slave.[92]

Davis envisioned no early end to slavery. His long-term hope seems to have been that somehow westward migration would take slaves out of the United States by way of Mexico and Central America. Such a fanciful dream certainly included an open-ended time frame for slavery, for in the unlikely event such an exodus took place, it would only happen in the unforeseeable future. In his fundamental outlook on race and race relations, Davis shared much with almost every other southern white and a considerable number of northern whites as well. He believed blacks inferior to whites, and also that where blacks were present in large numbers, social peace required the superior race to possess absolute legal control and power over the inferior. Thus, slavery must remain in place.[93]

CHAPTER NINE

"I . . . Have a Field of Usefulness"

Just after his gubernatorial defeat, Jefferson Davis told a former Senate colleague that he was "separated from the exciting strife of politicians . . . ," but he exaggerated. Reestablishing himself at Brierfield did not mean retirement from politics, only from public office. In December 1851, one month after his defeat, Warren County State Rights Democrats named him as a delegate to the party's state convention, scheduled for Jackson early in the new year. Informing Davis that they wanted him to speak to the assembly and counsel with them, party leaders expected him to attend.[1]

Despite their setback in November, Davis and his fellow Democrats were not at all despondent, even though their nemesis Henry Foote was about to occupy the governor's chair. Events in Washington contributed notably to their positive outlook. Leading southern Unionists tried but failed to make local parties national by restructuring the Whig party into a national union organization that could attract conservative Democrats as well as Whigs. Sectional rivalry and ingrained partisan loyalties proved too powerful, however, for southern Unionists to effect a reorientation of parties on the national level, matching what they had accomplished in their states. At the same time State Rights Democrats worked strenuously and ultimately successfully to make sure that the national Democratic party recognized them and their organizations as the legitimate Democrats in their bailiwicks.[2]

The conjunction of these two results placed Democrats who had signed on with Union parties in a precarious political position. Their hopes as Unionists were dwindling because national occurrences signaled the permanent localization of Union parties. Moreover, as State Rights Democrats succeeded in winning acknowledgment as true Democrats, the Democrats-become-Unionists found their status with their old party in jeopardy. As one State Rights chief in Mississippi chortled to Davis, Foote was having "to chew the cud of disappointment."[3]

In this environment, Davis took as his major task the promotion of Democratic reunification in Mississippi. Addressing the state convention, he emphasized his identity as a lifetime Democrat, merging the Democratic and State Rights parties. He said that all who desired to be Democrats were welcome and should come into the party. He announced to Union Democrats that if they wanted the traditional policies of a low tariff, strict construction, and states' rights, they had to rely on the Democratic party.

Underscoring his party loyalty, he advocated selecting delegates for the national Democratic convention and denied as false charges that he would not support the national ticket. He assured the assembled party activists that he had always backed the Democratic candidate for president and surely intended doing so in 1852. He stressed his belief in certain hallowed principles that only the Democratic party upheld. In a public letter following the state gathering, he made clear his sense of the relationship between party and principle: "Party consultation and party organization are the means, not the end. Principles alone can dignify a party, and party allegiance can rightfully claim no more than the just application of its principles to measures and men."[4]

On the eve of the state convention, the leading Democratic newspaper had sounded the trumpet of reunification. "Let it be a gathering of the olden time," cried the *Mississippian*. "Political brethren, who have been for a time estranged upon settled issues, have met together in the preliminary meetings, and now let them meet in the old wigwam, with the hatchet buried as the questions are buried which caused it to be uplifted, resolved to do all for the cause of Democracy."[5]

Throughout 1852 Davis kept up his effort to rebuild the Democratic party. He wanted a "family re-union." It bothered him that some of his State Rights associates did not approve of his push for party unity. To one of them he wrote, "you remind me that in healing up our party divisions I cooperate with those who stabbed me; I remember more keenly the stab which was given to the state, but have no purpose of revenge which will prevent me from acting with those who return to the standard of Democracy, and aid us in future to uphold the principles of state sovereignty and federal limitations which it was unfurled to sustain."[6]

Davis made an exception, however. Even though he argued that Henry Foote "was too small to be treated as an obstacle round which the course of the democratic party should be bent," his antipathy toward his former gubernatorial foe led him into an ugly verbal battle in the press. When Foote accused Davis of leading a secessionist band, Davis responded with a vigorous denial while he charged Foote with forgetting the "propriety of his office." Their public quarrel brought forth pleas even from pro-Davis newspapers for both men to back away from an unseemly squabble. A political friend gave Davis blunt advice: "It is best to let Foote have rope, for the Scamp is hanging himself faster than even his enemies could desire." Assuring Davis that Foote was politically dead, this observer warned against making any new issues with Foote because doing so could lead to a "personal collision," which would not do Davis any good. Davis did finally withdraw from the public argument, though he retained a potent animosity toward Foote.[7]

The course of the legislature that met in the winter of 1851–52 highlighted Foote's political problems. It gave the remaining year of his Senate term to a Whig, and a former Union Democrat got Davis's seat. Although the Union party did well in filling the two vacancies, Democrats succeeded in getting the lawmakers to postpone electing a senator for the six-year term beginning in 1854. When Governor Foote tried to get the legislature to go on record approving the Compromise of 1850, he failed. With the drive for Democratic unity fully underway by the time he became governor on January 10, 1852, Foote could only watch helplessly as his Democratic support began disappearing.[8]

When in May the national Democratic convention nominated Franklin Pierce of New Hampshire for president and William R. King of Alabama for vice president, a largely reunified Mississippi Democratic party, with Jefferson Davis in the forefront, enthusiastically embraced the ticket. Davis had met then-Senator Pierce during his visit to Washington back in 1838. To Mississippians he praised Pierce as a foe of abolitionists and a patriot who had served in Mexico. In Davis's opinion, Mississippi, the South, and slavery could not have a stronger friend in the White House. When he contemplated the reunion of Mississippi Democrats and the satisfaction of the party's national ticket, Davis shed the anxiety that had cloaked him, quoting Shakespeare, "Now is the winter of our discontent made glorious summer."[9]

As soon as news from the convention in Baltimore reached Mississippi, Jefferson Davis stepped forward to champion the ticket. He spoke in Vicksburg on June 8 and the next day before a large public meeting in Jackson. Signaling Davis's place among Mississippi Democrats, the state party organ hailed him as "the gallant son of Mississippi—the favorite of all—[who] was welcomed with appropriate honors." The state delegation to the national convention had attempted to get the vice-presidential nomination for him. Even though that effort did not succeed, one delegate reported to a friend, "I assure you he holds a very high stand in the Union both as a man of talents and of high toned integrity and worth."[10]

After his initial appearances in Vicksburg and Jackson, Davis made some campaign speeches, chiefly in northern Mississippi, with one stop in Memphis. The recurrence of eye problems in September severely curtailed his autumn political activities, though he did write a letter for publication in a New Orleans newspaper. When he spoke, he sounded the same themes: states' rights and strict construction would remain secure with Pierce and the Democratic party. About the Whig nominee, Major General Winfield Scott, Davis had little good to say. The animus he had felt since 1847 was still quite alive. He did admit that Scott had been a good soldier, but he emphasized that the general had no experience in civil affairs, a lack that had never bothered him in Zachary Taylor's case. Moreover, he found Scott's personal characteristics especially unsuited to the presidency. He described Scott as a quarrelsome man, "petulant, vain and presumptuous."[11]

The result of the election certainly pleased Davis, and another outcome just as surely surprised him. Nationally, Pierce trounced Winfield Scott by 254 to 42 in the electoral count, though the popular vote was much closer. He won easily in Mississippi, with 61 percent of the vote, underscoring the reunification of the state's Democrats. Only a month after the election Pierce wrote a warm, friendly letter to Davis, telling him that because of "the circumstances" of their initial acquaintance and their "present positions," he should not be surprised if the president-elect "much desire[d]" to see him and obtain advice. Then Pierce became more specific; he wanted to consult with Davis on the South, and especially on the makeup of the cabinet. Although Pierce did not offer Davis a cabinet post, he mentioned the possibility, assuring Davis that he most wanted, and knew he would receive, "free and useful suggestions." After asking whether Davis planned an early trip to Washington or could even possibly come up to Boston, Pierce informed the Mississippian that his opinion on the cabinet would be "definitively formed" by late February, when he intended to go to the capital. In the meantime he requested that Davis respond through a private friend in Boston, ensuring confidentiality. Although Davis's reply has not survived, it pleased Pierce, who called it a "noble spirited letter."[12]

From the outset Pierce was clearly considering Davis for his cabinet. The president-elect wanted to overcome past Democratic division over the Compromise by including in his official family men who had both opposed and supported it. This intention angered southern Democrats who had gone into Union parties. They believed they deserved presidential accolades and favors; but they did not prevail. Writing from Washington in January 1853, Congressman Albert Brown told Davis the word among politicians placed him in the cabinet, and even Davis's critics shared that opinion. Because the appointment seemed probable, Brown declared that he would not press his own claims. It *"will be glory enough,"* Brown announced, to have our "recognized leader" sit in the cabinet.[13]

By early February, Pierce had definitely decided on Davis. Pierce had met with Virginia senator Robert M. T. Hunter, who had traveled to New Hampshire carrying the message that southern states' righters wanted Davis in the cabinet. Brown described Hunter as a "willing witness" in the states' righters behalf, who was "fully impressed with the importance of having them gratified." On February 2 a telegram from one of Pierce's advisers asked Davis to be in Washington by the fifteenth. Davis wired back that he could not make it by that date. The reply flashed south, "Please meet in Washington as soon as possible." Political confidants urged Davis to accept Pierce's offer for the benefit of the cause and the party. Still uncertain, Davis left Brierfield on February 22 by steamboat bound via New Orleans for Washington, where he arrived on March 5 and immediately conferred with Pierce. He accepted Pierce's offer of the War Department, though he later claimed that he intended to decline the cabinet so that he could run for governor again in 1853, rearguing the old issues before Mississippi voters. In Washington, however, he said he confronted the same argument put to him in Mississippi—to turn down Pierce could damage the State Rights cause. Thus, Jefferson Davis once again took on a political role in the national capital, but this time in an executive position.[14]

Having accepted Pierce's offer, Davis rented a furnished house on 13th Street just east of the White House and established himself at the War Department. The department was located just west of the executive mansion on the southeastern corner of Pennsylvania Avenue and 17th Street, in a drab two-story brick building built in the 1820s. Running along about one-third of the front, a colonnade painted white and ornamented with Corinthian pillars attempted to provide some distinction. Davis located his office in three rooms at the rear of the first floor near the stairway.[15]

In a photograph taken in 1853, the forty-five-year-old Jefferson Davis confronted the camera, clearly middle-aged, but just as obviously vigorous and confident. His large, pale eyes distinguished and softened an angular face. One who saw him noted his "clear-cut, sharp, refined face" and dignified bearing. Despite his bouts of eye disease and recurring problems with malaria and neuralgia, Davis retained what another observer called a "distinguished appearance," with a "demeanor and conversation" that "impressed" people around him. Even a staunch political opponent described him as "a gentleman and a scholar, smart as a steel trap. . . ." An English visitor to the capital city depicted him as a "polished man, more so certainly than any of the others [in the cabinet]." And a well-known Washington hostess and close friend remembered him as "exceedingly slender, but his step was springy, and he carried himself with such an air of conscious strength and ease and purpose as often to cause a stranger to turn and look at him."[16]

When Davis became secretary of war, both the War Department and the U.S. Army it managed were small and ossified. The secretary's immediate staff totaled only eleven: a chief clerk, seven clerks, and three messengers. There was no assistant secretary and really no other civilian employee of executive rank. By law, the army had an authorized strength of 13,821, but it actually numbered only 10,417, a force far too small to accomplish its major mission: protection of settlers on the advancing frontier. Organized in eleven different geographic commands, the great majority of troops were dispensed in far-flung, isolated posts on the western frontier.[17]

This army consisted of two parts so distinct that it seemed at times each wore its own uniform. One, the bureaus or staff agencies, operated under the direct supervision of the secretary of war. There were eight bureaus—adjutant general, quartermaster, pay, subsistence, medical, engineers, topographical engineers, and ordnance. Each had a chief who ruled his universe almost as a medieval fiefdom. That a number of these officers had occupied their positions for a long time, two since 1818, only added to their bureaucratic power and political influence. Movement rarely occurred within the officer corps. Officers assigned to a staff bureau remained there, as did those assigned to the combat arms.

Jefferson Davis, c. 1853.
Museum of the Confederacy

The combat or line force looked to the commanding general of the army for its orders. Throughout Davis's tenure in the War Department, the post was held by sixty-seven-year-old Major General Winfield Scott, who had been a general officer since 1814 and commanding general since 1841. A veteran of the War of 1812 and the Mexican War, Scott was a first-rate soldier with a distinguished record, capped by his impressive campaign from Vera Cruz to Mexico City in 1847. Scott's quest for military glory was matched by his ambition for political preferment, evidenced by his garnering the Whig nomination for president in 1852. Although he did run as a major party candidate for the nation's highest office, he never resigned his commission because in his time the rules did not require resignation from the military to run for office.[18]

The army's bifurcated organizational structure included a divided chain of command. While the secretary of war traditionally directed the administrative business of the department and the activities of the bureaus, he did not exercise authority over the commanding general, who considered the president his sole superior. Because the Constitution made the president the commander in chief of the armed forces, it would seem that the secretary of war as his personal choice to oversee the War Department would have authority over all of its parts. Matters had not turned out that way, however. Almost an institution in himself, the able, vain, corpulent, and highly successful General Scott zealously guarded his independence. In his mind the secretary was simply another clerk who would depart before too long.

For decades the department had been basically dormant, with one exception, in the late 1810s and early 1820s, when John C. Calhoun was secretary of war. But since then initiative, planning, and thought had become uncommon commodities in an increasingly encrusted establishment. Seniority dominated all else. With no retirement policy, generals and other officers remained on active duty until too physically or intellectually enfeebled to continue, and sometimes even longer. As a result, promotions occurred at a glacial rate. Rigid rules governed all practices. The one exception was the Mexican War, when the small regular army augmented by volunteers won a foreign war. After 1848, however, procedures in the War Department hastened back into their hidebound pattern.

Jefferson Davis brought to the war office a background vastly different from his predecessors. Like them, he was a politician, but he also had graduated from West Point, had been an officer in the regular army for seven years, had commanded a regiment in battle in Mexico, and had served as chairman of the Senate Committee on Military Affairs. Even more important, he possessed a great interest in the U.S. Army, an institution he viewed as both guardian and benefactor of the nation. Moreover, the geographic expansion of the country and the technological changes affecting so many areas of national life excited him. In his mind, the army was vital to both.

As a cabinet officer, Jefferson Davis joined six other men in President Pierce's official family. Perhaps the best known nationally was the capable secretary of state, William L. Marcy of New York, a former governor, United States senator, and secretary of war for James K. Polk. Caleb Cushing of Massachusetts, scholarly, hardworking, and a defender of southern property rights in slaves, became attorney general. James Guthrie of Kentucky, physically robust and quite wealthy, presided over the Treasury Department. A slight, quiet former congressman from North Carolina, James C. Dobbin, ran the Navy Department. The great patronage machine known as the Post Office

Department was given to the Pennsylvanian James Campbell, who had little experience but important connections. For the newest addition to the cabinet, the Department of the Interior, Pierce chose Robert McClelland of Michigan, who when in Congress had voted for the Wilmot Proviso, but later had become a proponent of the Compromise of 1850. In making his choices Pierce covered both the essential geographic bases and the party's ideological spectrum, but he certainly did not assemble a distinguished group. It was, however, a congenial cabinet; for the only time in American history no changes occurred during an administration.[19]

Franklin Pierce himself brought no special distinction to the White House. Born into an active political family in New Hampshire, he rose to a dominant position in the state party. At the same time he became a successful attorney, noted for his ability to sway juries. He had sat in both houses of Congress between 1833 and 1842, where he compiled an unremarkable record as a loyal Democrat, but he had been away from Washington for more than a decade. He had also served as a brigadier general in Mexico, though he did not emerge with a notable war record. Throughout his career he evinced an unshakable devotion to the classical Jeffersonian doctrine of strict construction and states' rights, which meant to southern Democrats that he occupied their constitutional ground. An affable man with good political instincts but without great intelligence, Pierce suffered a great personal tragedy just after the election when his only remaining child, a lad of eleven, was killed before his very eyes in a railroad accident. That terrible event turned his wife into a recluse and delivered a fearsome emotional blow just as he entered the presidency.

Perhaps that trauma helped turn him toward Jefferson Davis. For unknown reasons Davis already thought of Pierce as a friend, though the record reveals no contact between the two men after their introduction in the winter of 1838 until Pierce's letter in December 1852. Because Pierce was assigned to Winfield Scott's command, they never saw each other in Mexico. Through the next four years a real friendship did develop, with the president and his war minister becoming devoted to each other. Varina reported warm, cordial visits from Pierce, with "intimate talks," and one winter when she was ill, his plowing through massive snowdrifts to ascertain her condition. When Davis met with Pierce on the president's last day in office, the chief executive did not conceal his feelings: "I can scarcely bear the parting from you, who have been strength and solace to me for four anxious years and never failed me." Davis often evinced similar feelings, holding to them even into old age. Two decades after leaving the cabinet, he said that "equal magnanimity and generosity of heart" characterized Pierce's personality. He could be even more complimentary: "Pure grand and good man, I never knew him to falter in the maintenance of sound principle." Davis's immense personal regard for Pierce overcame his political judgment; he could never admit the disastrous reality of his friend's presidency.[20]

As an active politician, Davis knew certain of his cabinet colleagues, but he had been familiar with none. He had known Guthrie the longest. Davis remembered that they had met when he was a schoolboy in Kentucky and Guthrie a law clerk. Even though they had not maintained an active friendship over the decades, Guthrie did become Davis's closest social friend in the cabinet. He seemingly had cordial relations with all the others, particularly Cushing, but details are not plentiful.[21]

Taking over the War Department, Davis was temporarily without his wife. Because he had made such a hurried trip to Washington and because he was not absolutely sure about its outcome, he left her in Mississippi with their young son. But Davis left no doubt about his feelings. Writing from Washington in mid-April, and clearly referring to his estrangement from Joseph, he closed: "Farewell my dear and let us hope that happier days will come when our trials have passed, but there can be none in which you will be dearer and nearer to the heart of your husband." He urged her "always to speak freely and explicitly of everything which concerns you, because it must be equally my affair."

The distant husband and father was eager for his family to join him. He confessed to Varina that he missed her and was "ever full of love" for her, and as for young Sam, or "le man," an ancient endearment meaning sweetheart, the doting father wanted the little boy "to run to his daddy as fast as he can." Even though he anticipated their arrival, he cautioned Varina to wait for warmer weather in Washington so that she and the child would not have to endure a change of climate. In the meantime his niece, Mary Jane (Malie) Bradford Brodhead, and her husband, a Democratic senator from Pennsylvania, kept house for him until Varina's arrival in the summer.[22]

Davis started out and remained a hands-on secretary, seeking involvement in all aspects of his department's operations. A man as dedicated and as ambitious as Davis, who also had a vision of what he wanted to accomplish, could master the small domain of the antebellum U.S. Army. No doubt existed about his placing his imprint on the

War Department. According to a contemporary observer, Davis knew "every detail of his office from 'brass howitzers to brass buttons.'" Another made the same point, asserting that "the Government could never be cheated out of the value of a brass button or a cadet's jacket while Davis remained Secretary of War."[23]

At the outset Davis put in long hours. He left home between 9 and 10 a.m., not returning until after 6 p.m. After some two months he was confined to his room with facial neuralgia, which his niece attributed to overwork. Upon recovery, he began returning to his house at four and taking long walks in the evening. Whatever the precise reason, Malie Brodhead believed that her uncle looked "better, far better," with a healthier complexion, and "his face fuller." Formal office hours at the department were certainly not too taxing. Although Congress had instructed the war office to remain open from 8 a.m. to 6 p.m., the department did not adhere to that schedule. Winter hours were officially 8–4, but were often shorter, while the so-called summer hours in effect from April 1 to October 1 were 8–3. Of course, the secretary could remain after the front door closed, and Davis's drive and energy wore down some of his subordinates. At times his lunch was sent from home to his office. As late as 1856 Davis still complained, "My days belong to everyone more than to myself."[24]

The papers that crossed Davis's desk and received his personal attention ranged from the most essential to the extraordinarily trivial. The critical documents included departmental budgets, major reports, general policy, congressional requests for information, directives to generals and other key subordinates, and politics. While he dealt with these substantial matters, he also devoted considerable time to massive amounts of marginal material. He commented on an incredible number of topics. He placed an endorsement on seemingly every letter to the department involving military or civil appointments, whether for an officer's commission, for a place at West Point, or for a watchman. He also monitored assignments of officers made by bureau chiefs and commanders, even acting on requests by junior officers to transfer from one duty to another. The issues Davis regularly ruled on were legion: the number of horses that would be allowed on a cavalry expedition into Sioux country; whether soldiers working on a military road would receive extra pay; the hiring of counsel for a lieutenant facing a court-martial; complaints about a former military storekeeper at an arsenal. In 1855, when a group of West Point seniors requested permission to grow beards, the secretary himself gave the answer. Responding negatively,

Davis declared that beards would disrupt "the uniform appearance of the corps," reminding the future officers that the country's most distinguished soldiers—Washington, Jackson, Taylor, and Scott—had all been cleanshaven. In the War Department, Davis developed an administrative style of seeing everything, of paying attention to the smallest detail, and of personally acting on almost all matters. He saw himself as responsible for the department, and either could not or would not delegate that responsibility.[25]

Yet even as he immersed himself in all the details, Davis did have priorities. On at least two occasions after leaving the War Department, the first in 1859 and the second in the final year of his life, Davis listed what he deemed his most notable accomplishments as secretary. In both instances, the specific items can be grouped together under four general rubrics: technological innovation, intellectual environment, defense and exploration of the West, and strengthening the regular army. Davis's judgments expressed over the decades basically correlate with those he made in office. He omitted only one important area, his strenuous effort to bring about army reorganization, perhaps because he had such limited success.[26]

Secretary Davis strove mightily to reform the organization and structure of the army, aiming toward greater efficiency, enhanced professionalism, and a clear, unified chain of command. Believing the total separation between the bureaus or staff and the line units harmful because it underlay inefficiency and spawned insular views, especially among officers, Davis advocated change. He wanted to reduce the number of bureaus, placing the commanding general over all and having officers move back and forth between staff and line assignments. Although he never backed away from this goal, he failed to persuade Congress to act, unable to overcome inertia and the entrenched power of the bureau chiefs. He could not even obtain the union of two most closely allied bureaus, the Engineers and the Topographical Engineers. In fact, the bureaus remained untouched until 1903. Davis also wanted Congress to create a retired list for regular officers to break the suffocating stranglehold of seniority and make room for new men and ideas. This proposal failed, too.

While reorganization foundered, Davis did succeed on two other fronts. Noting the size of the army in his first annual report, Davis acknowledged that Congress had authorized a force of 13,821, but pointed out that the actual strength was only 10,417. In the secretary's opinion, even with full ranks the army could not possibly fulfill its mission. Though he argued that Congress should authorize an increase in the size of the regular army, he also realized salary levels had to go up in order to attract officers and men to fill the additional positions. The resignations of officers and desertions of enlisted men were already serious problems. In 1855 Congress responded, creating four new regiments and enacting a higher pay scale. Scholars of the antebellum army concur that these two measures notably affected both the capability and the morale of the army.[27]

Davis has also generally received accolades for the quality of the officers he named to the new regiments. From the outset he maintained that "military merits alone" would govern the selection and assignment of regular officers, assuring one general he would not be looked at through "a political medium." The top positions in the newly created units went mostly to professionals on active duty or to graduates of West Point and veterans of the Mexican War who had left the service. On one colonelcy Davis held out for his selection against considerable political pressure from the president himself for another candidate. Finally, he told Pierce that he would submit the name, but would not sign the recommendation. Facing such opposition, Pierce relented, and Davis got his choice as colonel of the Second Cavalry Regiment, Albert Sidney Johnston, his friend from West Point days.[28]

Despite his concern for professional qualifications in senior officers, Secretary Davis clearly realized that he operated in a political environment. As a former chairman of the Senate Committee on Military Affairs, he knew full well that maintaining good relations with Congress was critical. After all, he would have to obtain congressional approval for much of what he hoped to accomplish. And he did consult with key representatives and senators in shaping legislation and in attempting to get it passed, though he certainly did not succeed in all cases. When the four new regiments were added to the army, he also understood the political dimension involved in filling the ranks of the junior officers. His actions would have an impact on his and the administration's relations with Congress. Davis took seriously the recommendations of major congressional figures when they made plain their wishes. When criticized by Senator Stephen Douglas of Illinois for not naming individuals he preferred, Davis replied that he would have certainly paid attention to the senator's preferences, if only they had been made clear before appointments had been made.[29]

Davis made his imprint in another crucial area, though in so doing he jettisoned his political instincts and stained his imprint with an unsightly blemish. He entered the War Department concerned about command; he wanted to exert his authority over the entire army, the commanding general included. But aiming at this target guaranteed an intense struggle, for Winfield Scott would relinquish no independence or authority without a strenuous fight. And the two strong-willed men did not begin as comrades.

Davis's antipathy toward the commanding general dated back to the Mexican War, when he had seen Scott through Zachary Taylor's eyes. Taylor was convinced that Scott had conspired against him by depleting his command and leaving his army perilously exposed. Davis shared that conviction, and since 1847 nothing had occurred to shake it. When the Senate in 1851 attempted to give Major General Scott the rank of brevet lieutenant general for his services in Mexico, Senator Davis objected, averring that Zachary Taylor, who first defeated the Mexican army and Santa Anna, was just as central to the American triumph as Scott. In addition, he condemned the positive comparison made by Scott's supporters between their hero and George Washington. The promotion failed, and Scott correctly viewed Davis as working to deprive him of the rank he eagerly desired and believed he merited. Then, in the presidential campaign of 1852, Davis publicly excoriated the general as a man, though he did admit that Scott was a good soldier.[30]

Scott did not look forward to having Davis as the new secretary of war. When his former subordinate and rival Zachary Taylor had occupied the White House, Scott had transferred his headquarters to New York City. After Taylor's death he moved back to Washington, but in January 1853, President-elect Pierce was unwilling to force his defeated opponent to remain in the capital and acceded to the general's wish to return to New York City. By the time Davis was sworn in as secretary of war, army headquarters had once again been removed.

But though the general was not physically present, he clearly occupied much of the secretary's attention. Davis was determined to demonstrate that in the chain of command he, not Scott, came immediately after the president. Instead, however, of sitting down with Scott to discuss the matter of proper command arrangements, he began by forcing Scott to comply with regulations that the commanding general had customarily bypassed. Davis directed that Scott's travel vouchers be rejected unless the travel had been authorized by a superior, just as was required for every other officer. Davis also demanded that Scott explain why he had authorized a leave of absence for a regimental commander in circumstances violating army policy. In these instances, the secretary of war was insisting that as the constitutional commander in chief's personal choice to run the War Department, he had command authority over the commanding general.

The problem was that in his dealings with Scott, Davis permitted personal animus to become entangled with his more valid concerns. In 1855, when Congress did create the rank of brevet lieutenant general for Scott, to date from 1847, the general legitimately applied for his back pay. Even though making the payment was clearly the intention of Congress, Davis opposed it so vigorously that an opinion from the attorney general was required before he relented. A year earlier, in clearing up Scott's Mexican War accounts, Davis challenged the general's final claim and referred the matter to President Pierce. Even after the president found in part for Scott, Davis kept probing and recalculating until he persuaded Pierce to deprive the general of almost the entire sum.

Scott met Davis at every turn. The general refused to accept voluntarily Davis's version of the chain of command, contending that the secretary could give him orders only when acting upon an express presidential directive. The contest went to Pierce for decision. Acting upon an opinion of the attorney general which supported Davis's position, the president made clear that the secretary of war had command authority over the commanding general of the army.

Jefferson Davis had won a satisfying victory and had established an important precedent, but he could not affirm that in doing so he had always acted appropriately. Attempting to besmirch each other, the two men ranted like spoiled adolescents. Scott informed Davis that he would treat all of Davis's letters as official, "whether designed as private and scurrilous, or public missives of arrogance and superciliousness." He characterized them as "examples of chicanery and tergiversation, of prodigality in assertion and utter penury in proofs and probabilities." At one point, Scott declared: "My silence, under the new provocation, has been the result, first, of pity, and next, forgetfulness. Compassion is always due to an enraged imbecile, who lays about him in blows which hurt only himself, or who, at the worst, seeks to stifle his opponent by the dint of naughty words."[31]

Davis likewise leaped into the epistolary gutter. "Your petulance, characteristic egotism and recklessness of accusation have imposed on me the task of unveiling some of your deformities. . . ." Davis went on to tell the general that his reputation had been "clouded by grovelling vices" such as "querulousness, insubordination, greed of lucre and want of truth." Although Davis's depictions of Scott were apt, he was seemingly unaware that he had descended to his antagonist's level. To Davis, Scott matched Foote in vileness. To make matters even more embarrassing, Congress in December 1856 called for all the correspondence, publishing it in a volume of more than 250 pages for the entire country to see personal hostility and professional jealousy turned into acrimonious hatred.[32]

In his campaign to belittle Scott, Davis evidently had a willing ally. Afterwards, Varina related the story of a dinner party she gave with General Scott among the guests. Scott was an acknowledged gourmand, and according to her, if he disliked a dish, he made his displeasure plainly known, with no regard for the feelings of his hostess. On the day of her dinner, she went to the general's cook and paid him $5 to make one of Scott's favorite soups. At the table, when Scott tasted the soup, he muttered unpleasantly. When Varina questioned his remarks, he replied, "It is not good," professing that only his own cook could properly prepare the particular recipe. To Scott and the assembly, Varina responded that the soup had come from his own cook. "I am very sorry," she said, "that my efforts have been a failure." In Varina's recounting, Scott made no more complaints, but she admitted that their relations were "strained."[33]

As Davis confronted organizational challenges and dragged himself down into a nasty personal squabble, he also devoted attention to the technological status and intellectual environment of the army. Technology had always fascinated him; technological advance was a desirable dimension of the progress he embraced, equating it with his country. Commenting on machine tools he had seen in operation, he observed that "the ingenuity of man has set in motion complicated machinery which seems to be endowed with reason." He called them "wonderful." And he was surely determined to ensure that the army benefited in every possible way from new technology and innovative ideas.[34]

The advent of the rifle underlay a major change in weaponry. It had been well known that shoulder arms with rifled barrels overmatched smoothbore muskets in both accuracy and range, but primitive bullets negated their advantage. Thus, when Davis entered the War Office, the musket remained the basic infantry weapon in the U.S. Army. By the mid-1850s, however, advances in bullet design heralded the triumph of the rifle. As secretary of war, Davis ordered tests that confirmed the superiority of the rifle with new ammunition. In 1855 he ended the manufacture of smoothbores in all government armories, converting them to the production of rifles. This shift did not signify the sudden disappearance of muskets, but it did mean that only rifles would be produced in the future. Experiments by the Ordnance Bureau also led to substantial improvement in the metallic composition of cannon. In addition, Davis took great pride in having iron substituted for wood in gun carriages.[35]

Aware that rifled weapons would alter the battlefield, Davis believed the army needed a new tactics manual. The person named to prepare it was Captain William J. Hardee, a promising young officer who had studied tactics in France and had earned a fine reputation in the Mexican War. From late 1853 into the summer of 1854, Hardee worked diligently, often in close collaboration with Secretary Davis, who consulted with him almost daily. Borrowing heavily from French thinking, Hardee's treatise emphasized speed and fluidity in tactical formations enabling infantry to maneuver more rapidly and effectively. Upon the completion of *Rifle and Light Infantry Tactics*, Davis arranged for its publication and for distribution throughout the army and even to state militias.[36]

Because Davis encouraged innovation in general, whether old-fashioned ingenuity or technological advances, inventors found a ready welcome in his office. He wrote a political associate that new projects came to him weekly and often even daily. He considered them all, even though many would lead to "the more rapid and certain killing of our fellow men." Not all, however, directly involved human destruction. The development of a wagon body that could also be used as a pontoon or a boat excited him. After personally witnessing trials of this wagon-boat, he supplied them to units in the West, where they performed effectively. His positive reaction to suggestions for improvements on items ranging from stirrups to bridles and bits for cavalry to scabbards for swords evinced his receptiveness to new ideas and ways of accomplishing time-honored tasks.[37]

Aware of the stultifying intellectual atmosphere pervading the War Department, Davis wanted the American army to learn from experiences and practices of more sophisticated forces. As did most military authorities of his time, Davis believed the French army the best in the world and French military thought the most advanced. When he presented his case for organizational reform to Congress, he often drew upon French examples to buttress his arguments. For the edification of his office, he ordered for the War Department library publications by both French and German authors on various military topics.[38]

In his best-known enterprise designed to draw on European examples and expertise, in 1855 Davis dispatched three officers across the Atlantic on what one scholar terms "the most ambitious military mission of the antebellum era." Prompted by the ongoing Crimean War, Davis charged his team to tour the principal nations of Europe—he specified England, France, Prussia, Austria, and Russia—and study their military systems. The secretary's instructions called for attention to particular matters, including the organization of armies, rifled arms, ordnance with emphasis on recent changes, transport for men and horses, and permanent fortifications. Once in Europe, the Americans could not abide by Davis's wish that they start out at the seat of war in the Crimea; because Russia would not permit a visit within its lines, the Americans finally reached the battle zone only after the Russians had evacuated their major stronghold. Observing and studying, the mission remained abroad for a year, not returning to the United States until April 1856. Its report to Davis constituted an important installment in the struggle to upgrade and modernize the U.S. Army, though it by no means became a plan of action dictating immediate change.[39]

Another element in Davis's attention to the army's intellectual condition involved West Point. Always defending his alma mater as a force for national sentiment and as essential for the country's security, Davis regarded it as the critical training ground for the officer corps that would lead the army. As secretary, he participated actively in the governance of the Military Academy. In 1854 and in 1856 he visited West Point for detailed inspections. More important, in 1854 he approved and instituted a major curricular change adding a fifth year to the program, an altered design that lasted until 1861. Although the required subjects remained heavily concentrated in technical areas, the added courses emphasized the humanities and military topics. The extent of Davis's involvement even included advice on where individual courses should be placed in the curriculum. Davis believed the extra year would produce a better-educated graduate and a better-prepared officer.[40]

Jefferson Davis made his chief concern the great American West, for in it so many of his interests overlapped and intersected. Defending that vast area, especially the settlers stretched out from the prairies to the Rockies and on to the Pacific, Davis accepted as a basic responsibility. Moreover, he gloried in the West as emblematic of American strength and progress, asserting that for many peoples the great distances and imposing mountains would destroy unity, but for determined and ingenious Americans those seeming obstacles would become powerful signs of national greatness.[41]

Davis argued that the only feasible way to defend over such enormous distances mandated significant improvements in land transportation. He testified that a strong naval enemy could devastate Pacific ports before any reinforcements could arrive via the lengthy, time-consuming water route. He also maintained that the troops and posts guarding the ever longer line of settlements and the growing number of settlers heading west had to have more effective transport for communications, supply, and operations. To Davis, a transcontinental railroad provided the only sensible solution to the problems of topography and distance.

Advocating that the federal government itself construct the railroad in the national territories, Davis differed with a number of his traditional political and constitutional allies. While they found the federal government as railroad-builder a sharp departure from strict construction, Davis perceived no such interpretive difficulty. He built his case on three main points: the Constitution gave to the federal government the responsibility for national defense; the federal government owned the territories; the railroads would be constructed on federal property chiefly for military purposes and would not discriminate against any citizen or part of the nation. As a result, Davis could discern in his stance no problem for disciples of strict construction and states' rights. Just as Davis did not convince all his detractors, his railroad never got built, for Congress could never decide on a route, much less on the appropriate role of the federal government in building the projected line.[42]

The transcontinental railroad turned into a volatile political issue. Because everyone assumed that, at least for some time, only one railroad would be built, intense competition erupted among cities and states in the Mississippi Valley, all desiring to reap the expected economic rewards of becoming the iron tracks' eastern terminus. This struggle then was swept up in the larger sectional contest between North and South, with the battle becoming so fierce that Congress could not agree on where to place the railroad. Facing its inability to act, Congress directed the War Department to investigate several likely routes and report on the most feasible. Where the political will had failed, science would make action possible.[43]

Jefferson Davis relished this assignment because he thought he knew what the studies would reveal. Since the Mexican War, the Topographical Engineers had devoted considerable resources to surveying and mapping the newly acquired Southwest in order to find the best route between Texas and California. The results convinced the chief of the Topographical Engineers that his men had charted a superb path all the way to the Pacific—from San Antonio westward across Texas to El Paso, then along the 32nd parallel through southern New Mexico to California and the Pacific. He shared this conclusion with numerous pro-railroad groups and politicians. Concurring, the Pierce administration in late 1853 bought from Mexico the Gadsden Purchase, an additional tract of land extending New Mexico farther south to ensure the straightest track. Jefferson Davis eagerly accepted this determination. Not only was it based on scientific exploration, it also took the most southerly line across the continent and would surely benefit the South. He could see no reason for anyone to deprive his section of what seemed to him simply a natural advantage.

During his first year as secretary, Davis sent four separate reconnaissance parties into the field. The routes to be checked stretched from the far north down to the 35th parallel. Initially, the 32nd parallel option was omitted because of all the work already done on it, but realizing gaps existed in the desired information, Davis directed another group to fill them. The chosen four possibilities did not come solely from the secretary or the Topographical Engineers; rather, they largely represented the possibilities with the strongest political backing. Determined to preclude the appearance of sectional favoritism, Davis mostly stayed away from southern partisans in his assignments of officers to these teams. He expected science to confirm what he thought he already knew.

But when the reports came in, they did not settle the question. Basically reconnaissances rather than detailed surveys of railroad lines, they suggested, but did not definitively point to, the best and most cost-effective way west. While presenting much valuable scientific and geographic information, they showed that several routes were practicable, not just the 32nd parallel line. Thus, science had not provided the conclusive answer Davis had expectantly awaited. Still, he informed Congress that the 32nd parallel remained the best choice, emphasizing the negative features in all its competitors while downplaying them in his favorite. Just as the surveys did not change Davis's mind, they altered few other opinions. Political gridlock continued to immobilize

Congress, ensuring that no transcontinental railroad project would commence before 1861.

Although convinced that railroads provided the long-term solution to the problems of distance and topography in the West, Davis also moved to improve in the short term the army's ability to cope with each. As early as 1851 in the Senate, he advocated using camels in the Southwest, persuaded that they would prove superior to horses and mules in that region's desertlike conditions. Upon becoming secretary of war, he obtained congressional authorization to purchase and employ camels, and in 1855 sent an expedition to the Middle East to buy and bring back the beasts. This was not some fanciful scheme, for he knew that Napoleon had used camels in his Egyptian campaign, that Arabs and Turks used them, and that the contemporary French army had experimented with them. The record makes clear that Davis had two goals for his camel force: basic transportation and direct military involvement against Indians, when camels could carry light cannon and infantry as well as substitute for cavalry horses. He believed camels would give American troops, and thereby American settlers, an advantage against both the topography and the Indians in the vast arid area stretching westward from central Texas.[44]

The experience with camels proved Davis's judgment sound, even though experimentation was not completed until after he left the cabinet. The officers who handled the trial trek from Texas to California rendered enthusiastic reports. Those positive reactions pushed Davis's successor in the War Department to urge continued congressional support, but Congress did not see fit to do so. Although the camel corps never became as important as Davis envisioned and railroads would soon make the concept obsolete, this short-lived affair underscored his willingness to innovate.

The possible use of camels was an example of Davis's attempt to generate discussion on the best methods for the army to employ in fighting hostile Indians. Taking for granted that the Indians would have to give way in the face of white migration, Davis wanted to use the army as effectively as possible. He even sent troops into southern Florida to herd the hardy, resilient Seminoles across the Mississippi River to the Indian Territory, but his concentration focused on the West. He suggested altering the army's basic tactical approach because he did not think the increasing number of small posts with equally small garrisons could do much more than protect themselves. Instead, he wanted fewer but larger forts accessible by railroads or navigable rivers that would become bases for strong columns sent into Indian country during the campaigning season. Davis's plan was never fully adopted but in all likelihood would not have proved any more successful than the program he criticized. The fundamental American problem lay not in tactics but in manpower. There were never enough soldiers to protect and guard everyone and everything, as Davis recognized when he admitted to Congress that concentrating troops in certain areas would expose "portions of the frontier to Indian hostilities without any protection whatever."[45]

Far away from the frontier, Secretary Davis's involvement in public works helped persuade him that the federal government should retain tight control over certain tasks he considered critical. In 1853, President Pierce gave Davis direct responsibility for two notable public works projects: the construction of the Washington Aqueduct, designed to carry water from near the Great Falls on the Potomac River above Washington into the city, and the tremendous expansion of the Capitol. Although neither was completed during Davis's time as secretary, he pushed the work forward on both, closely overseeing the supervising officer from the Corps of Engineers. He even took approval of artistic decisions under his purview.[46]

Davis's convictions about the need for government monopoly extended beyond public structures in the federal district. He successfully resisted congressional pressure to shut federal armories and purchase all arms from private contractors, maintaining that efficiency and innovation would be best guaranteed by federal manufacture of all arms. He was unsuccessful, however, when he advocated congressional funding for a national armory. Refusing to support private contracting for clearing western rivers, Davis left no doubt about his reasons: ". . . the public interests will be best subserved by entrusting public works to specially instructed and experienced officers, who, in the execution of their duty, have no interest adverse to that of the Government—whose professional reputation, gained by long years of toil and exposure, is staked on the skillful and successful completion of the works; whose hope of honorable employment and future advancement in the public service, to which their lives are devoted, give assurance of vigilance and zeal; who have no pecuniary inducement to slight the work, who are urged by all the highest motives—that influence men to the faithful execution of the trusts confided to them."[47]

While Jefferson Davis strove to implement his policies in the War Department, he had his family with him. Varina came up in the summer of 1853 with Samuel and two of her younger siblings. Because, unlike Congress, an administration did not adjourn, the Davises searched for a full-time residence. Starting out in the house Jefferson had rented on 13th Street, in the fall they moved to 14th Street between F and G, only one block east of the White House, before finally settling in late 1854 in an imposing mansion at the corner of 18th and G Streets, just a block west of the War Department. Davis paid an annual rent of $1,500 for this three-story, twenty-room house with hot and cold running water. Although 18th and G remained the Davis home address for the duration of his stay in the cabinet, the Davises engaged summer places just outside the city to escape Washington's heat during that season.[48]

Whether in their town houses or summer country homes, husband and wife enjoyed a close, affectionate relationship. On a trip away from Washington, Jefferson wrote: "Farewell for a little while my dear Wife and be assured that in the mean time whether sleeping or waking the fondest affections are with you which can be offered by the heart of YOUR HUSBAND." Varina matched him, writing lovingly about him to her mother, and sharing her deep feelings about her Jeff with a close friend. She also remembered shared pleasures in dinner parties and stimulating conversations. She worried for a time about his recurring anxiety, which she attributed to his difficulties with Joseph, but she thought his health generally improving, though he remained quite thin.[49]

Concern about health prompted a three-week excursion Davis took in the late summer of 1853. In company with Alexander D. Bache, whom Davis had known at West Point and who had superintended the Coast Survey, Davis left Washington on August 17 for his first recorded trip to New England. Stopping in Boston, the secretary and Bache visited the Bunker Hill Monument, the Charleston Navy Yard, Faneuil Hall, and Harvard College. Then they headed north for the White Mountains of New Hampshire, where they spent several days, including one night on the summit of Mount Washington. Finally, on August 27, the party reached its ultimate destination, the Coast Survey camp at Blue Mountain, Maine, at an altitude of 3,000 feet and some eighty miles north of Portland. Davis reported to Varina that he was "far up in the mountains and 'far down east' in Maine, the wind sweeps over the tent with the chilly feeling and hollow sound of wintry weather, but every thing is so well arranged that the portable stove renders the inside of canvass very comfortable." After some time at Blue Mountain, a refreshed Davis headed back to Washington, reaching the city on September 9.[50]

The great joy of both Jefferson and Varina was young Samuel, but a year old when he and his mother joined his father. For Varina, the pride of motherhood and the pleasure of having her own baby were palpable. She described Samuel to her family as "the sweetest thing you ever saw." Gleefully, she recounted his antics, such as learning "to fight and scratch," and crowing and flapping his arms to signal he wanted the chicken he saw on the table. His early words like "Aam" for his name and "mammam" for Mama delighted her. Taking him for rides pleased her greatly. The proud father beamed about "Le man," who would run to his father when called. Once, Jefferson told Varina that he wanted "to run back and kiss the dear boy." Varina remarked that her husband was "absorbed" in the child "to a fearful extent."[51]

In the summer of 1854, great joy turned into massive sadness. Although young Sam experienced his share of childhood ailments, he appeared vigorous and healthy. Then, in June, an unknown illness struck him; possibly he had been exposed to measles. Jefferson called in the best physicians in the city, but to no avail. Varina reported that her "child suffered like a hero," always wanting his mother by his side, but not crying before he died, not yet two, on June 13. Two days later the funeral was held at the Davis house, followed by burial in Oak Hill Cemetery in Georgetown. Friends and officials, including the president and other cabinet members, attended what an eyewitness termed "a very affecting scene."[52]

Mother and father were devastated. Varina depicted herself as "tortured," while Jefferson spoke of her "irreperable grief" that caused periods of "painful depressions." An acquaintance portrayed Jefferson as "overwhelmed with affliction and look[ing] worse than I have seen him for many years." He had not faced such an emotional trauma since Sarah Knox's death almost two decades before. Varina recalled an anguished man who "walked half the night and worked fiercely all day." "A child's cry in the street well-nigh drove him mad," she wrote. To the end of his life he never forgot the brief existence of his first-born.[53]

During this time of extreme anguish, no record indicates that Jefferson Davis turned to religion for special comfort and consolation. Davis identified himself as a Christian, and he certainly knew his Bible, allusions to it often appearing in his speeches. Late in life, Varina said his knowledge of the Bible surpassed any other layman's she knew and matched most ministers'. Even so, no evidence suggests that at this point Christianity was central in his life. Raised in a Baptist home, edu-

cated initially in a Roman Catholic academy, married twice to Episcopalian women by clergymen of that denomination, Davis did not fervently embrace any of these creeds. Unlike his eldest brother, Joseph, a
stalwart of the Natchez Episcopal Church when he lived in that town,
Jefferson did not become a church leader. When at Davis Bend, he
attended services held by an Episcopalian chaplain brought by Joseph
to Hurricane. From 1845 to 1861 when in Washington, he went to the
Episcopalian Church of the Epiphany at 1317 G Street, and in 1857
bought a pew when they were offered for sale. Yet before the Civil War
he was never confirmed in that or any other congregation. Jefferson
Davis's finding of a personal God active in his life awaited an even
greater trial.[54]

Having experienced the death of a young child, as did so many parents of their time, Jefferson and Varina found their grief assuaged by
the arrival of new Davises. Although Varina had been married for
seven years prior to Samuel's birth, her second baby arrived on February 25, 1855. Margaret Howell Davis (Maggie) was named for her
maternal grandmother. Then, on January 16, 1857, less than two years
later, Varina gave birth to Jefferson Davis, Jr., but only after a difficult
pregnancy. Both parents delighted in these additions to their once
depleted household.[55]

In the midst of their domestic life, both happy and sad, the Davises
led an active social life. Friends like President Pierce and James
Guthrie visited often, and the Davises developed new friendships, as
with New York senator William Henry Seward, who entered their circle by braving a snowstorm in his sleigh to deliver a nurse during an illness of Varina's. Family members also appeared in the capital. Varina's
mother came after Samuel's death and before her namesake's birth,
staying several months. In the late summer of 1856, Joseph arrived with
his wife and daughter. His visit underscored his reconciliation with Jefferson, the brothers having gotten past the difficulties that had divided
them since 1852. Joseph was especially pleased with his new niece,
making a fuss over her and giving her $60 in gold.[56]

Beyond good friends and family, Secretary and Mrs. Davis kept a
calendar filled with receptions and dinners. Diplomatic affairs introduced them to a variety of people from the papal legate to a delegation
of Japanese princes, in Washington following the initial contact
between the United States and Japan. Varina hosted dinners for members of Congress and for bureau chiefs and other senior officers; "General's dinners," she called them. Proud of her skills as a hostess and the

success of her parties, she told her mother that she was "universally acknowledged to give the finest dinners in Washington, with the most elegant decorations."[57]

As during her previous residences in Washington, Varina especially enjoyed the company of the sophisticated people she met. This woman whom a close female friend called "funny & smart" relished the environment of the capital city, so different from the world of Davis Bend and Warren County. She played the observer with men like the self-consciously intellectual senator from Massachusetts, Charles Sumner. She reported that he liked to talk with southern ladies, in whose presence he said nothing about his strident antislavery views. Instead, he prepared setpieces on various topics like Demosthenes, Platonian theory, or lace. She recollected one occasion when he gave her "an interesting résumé of the history of dancing." She was really impressed, however, when with her husband she conversed at length with eminent scientists attending conferences in Washington. Because of Jefferson's longtime interest in the Smithsonian Institution, the Davises often saw its director, Professor Joseph Henry, whom Varina thought "a most attractive man, whose wisdom made his 'face to shine.' " Other encounters that excited her involved the eminent Louis Agassiz of Harvard and John LeConte, the noted geologist from Georgia.[58]

Books retained their place of consequence in the Davis household. From the Library of Congress, Jefferson borrowed historical and literary titles covering a broad range of topics. As always, Shakespeare was on a list that also included the Roman writer Apuleius, the seventeenth-century Spanish dramatist Pedro Calderón de la Barca, and the popular contemporary British novelist Maria Edgeworth. The first description of Ceylon in English, by Robert Knox, caught the Davises' attention, as did the diaries and correspondence of the British diplomat James Harris (1746–1820), first Earl of Malmesbury.[59]

Whether reading or participating in an active social life, Jefferson Davis never lost sight of the main business of a man who identified himself as a "politician." Early in his secretaryship he established a visible political connection between himself and the president he served. In July 1853 President Pierce traveled to New York City to attend the Exhibition of All Nations, taking with him three cabinet officers, Cushing, Guthrie, and Jefferson Davis. Making public appearances along the way, the presidential party reached New York City on the fourteenth.[60]

At each stop, from Wilmington, Delaware, through Philadelphia, Trenton, Princeton, and Newark, as well as in New York City, Davis made a brief address. In addition to praising President Pierce, he sounded the same themes in all his remarks. He gloried in his American citizenship and declared his pride in marching under the flag, "loved as the insignia of our States united." Strict construction as the foundation for the band of Union among equals was his watchword, for, as he told listeners in Trenton, "on fraternity our Union was founded." He also proudly pointed to American success with what he called "the useful sciences." Asserting that energy and science underlay national destiny, he announced, "We are on our way to American industry and inventive genius compared with that of the Old World—to see the progress of American mind in its contest with matter."

Everywhere Davis revealed a deft political touch, making sure he forged a link with each audience. In Wilmington, he praised Delaware for its role in creating and maintaining the Union. In the three New Jersey stops, he reminded his hearers of their state's heroism in the Revolution and lauded the New Jersey plan, which he said provided for the equality of states in the United States Senate. The glorious future he foresaw was central in Philadelphia and New York City; he noted that Pennsylvania coal and iron and New York trade would be critical in the certain American conquest of the West.[61]

Davis also made his presence felt in a quite different political arena. For professional politicians, access to patronage was absolutely critical—patronage meant rewarding labor and loyalty, and its dispensation also enabled a politician to demonstrate his power and influence. States' rights politicians across the South perceived Davis as their conduit to patronage for their partisans. Davis took this responsibility seriously, working on behalf of his political friends and curbing the power of southern Democrats who had been active in Union parties. Eager for a strong southern man to become minister to France in order to assist the hoped-for acquisition of Cuba, Davis strove successfully to get the appointment for John Y. Mason of Virginia. The creation in 1855 of four new army regiments placed him at the center of patronage decisions, working closely with Congress and the president. Of course, the distribution of federal jobs in Mississippi always occupied much of his attention. When in 1856 he informed a former Louisiana congressman he had but little influence in securing official posts for his friends, Davis clearly dissembled. Throughout his tenure in the cabinet, he wielded considerable authority over patronage decisions both within and without his department.[62]

As a central figure in the Pierce cabinet, Davis was directly involved in major policy matters apart from his duties as secretary of war. As a result, his hand was evident in both the leading foreign policy initiative and the most important domestic issue of the administration. Pierce and his advisers shared an ardent desire to reach a goal that had eluded administrations for decades—the acquisition of Spanish-owned Cuba, the Pearl of the Antilles. The same vision of Manifest Destiny that had propelled the United States to the Pacific Ocean led expansionist-minded Americans to covet Cuba. Some underscored its strategic location as making its annexation essential; many southerners saw it as a perfect new slave state, for slavery already existed on the island.[63]

Davis held both views, and, indeed, believed possession of Cuba imperative for the South. That belief underlay his desire to place a southern man in the Paris embassy. When Pierce named John Mason to the post, he matched his choices for the other two crucial European capitals, each with Davis's enthusiastic approval. To London he sent the strongly pro-southern James Buchanan of Pennsylvania, and to Madrid, the zealous, volatile Pierre Soulé of Louisiana.[64]

The administration tried to keep open all options for obtaining the prize. It always considered purchase, just as it continuously hoped revolt against Spanish rule would place Cuba in its hands. Even the use of armed force was not ruled out. The president also received pressure from groups wanting to mount privately sponsored attacks on the island from the United States. Never consistent in its approach, the administration sometimes followed one avenue, then another, and occasionally almost all at once.

Despite his genuine desire and considerable exertions, President Pierce failed to obtain Cuba. Perhaps his best chance came in the spring of 1854, when Spanish authorities in Cuba confiscated the cargo of an American merchant ship. Attempting to build on the national outrage caused by the seizure, Pierce requested Congress to adopt provisional measures as the emergency demanded. Congress, however, did not respond promptly. Subsequent attempts to buy the island or to intimidate Spain were poorly handled, and eventually unsuccessful. Growing sectional opposition in Congress to what many northerners perceived as a strategy to expand slavery helped immensely in dooming Pierce's hopes. And after mid-1854 no chance remained for a congressional majority on any initiative marked as a southern measure.

Although the Pierce administration would win no accolades for its particularly inept Cuban diplomacy, Davis ardently defended its actions. On the stump he argued that the administration had "done all in its power to accomplish so desirable an object." He blamed the failure to acquire the island on Congress for refusing at critical moments to back the president.[65]

While Jefferson Davis took a forthright stand on Cuba, his position was not so clear-cut on filibustering, the efforts by certain Americans to employ privately raised and financed forces and set off from the United States to take various parts of Mexico and Central America as well as Cuba. Filibustering and filibusters were not new to Davis. His fellow Mississippian John A. Quitman stood in the forefront of those striving to prepare an expedition against Cuba. Moreover, strong pro-filibustering sentiment ran through Mississippi. In public speeches Davis spoke in favor both of the basic concept and of specific filibustering expeditions.[66]

But filibusters and their most fervent advocates expressed serious doubts about Davis's fidelity to their cause. They suspected that in 1854 he had been instrumental in preparing a presidential proclamation enforcing the Neutrality Laws which really blocked Quitman's enterprise. This was the point at which Pierce decided to turn away from violence and seek instead a negotiated purchase. Although the record is incomplete on this matter, Davis was surely privy to the innermost deliberations on Cuban policy, and he certainly never denounced the proclamation that so incensed the filibusters.[67]

While it is impossible to ascertain precisely Davis's position on filibustering, no doubt exists about his role in President Pierce's most fateful decision—one of the most momentous in all of American history—to back the proposed Kansas-Nebraska bill. In its beginnings Kansas-Nebraska had nothing to do with sectional politics or slavery. Its originator, Senator Stephen A. Douglas, Democrat of Illinois, was a great proponent of development, and by the early 1850s settlement had reached the western borders of Iowa and Missouri. As Douglas viewed the situation, the logical step was to organize officially the adjacent Nebraska Territory. Otherwise, settlers could not keep on following the horizon. Moreover, the possibility of transcontinental railroads underscored the need for congressional action because a central route could run through Nebraska. A Nebraska bill made it through the House at the close of the Thirty-second Congress, but failed in the Senate. When the Thirty-third Congress convened in December 1853,

Douglas, chairman of the Senate Committee on Territories, came forward with another Nebraska measure.[68]

It was at this juncture that sectional politics consumed Douglas's plans. He recognized that to win passage he needed southern backing, which he had not gotten when the Senate had earlier rejected organizing Nebraska. Obtaining those votes meant he would have to find a way to permit the possibility of slavery in the new territory. As it stood, the Missouri Compromise prohibited slavery in Nebraska because the entire territory lay north of 36°30'. To get past that restriction, Douglas fastened on the Democratic doctrine of popular sovereignty, which had been employed in the Compromise of 1850 and promulgated in the Democratic platform of 1852. In turning to popular sovereignty, Douglas actually copied language from a Compromise bill. Even so, he did not propose the overt repeal of the Missouri Compromise.

For southerners, Douglas did not go far enough. Political rivalry between southern Whigs and southern Democrats, along with the desire of the latter to stamp their authority on their party, underlay the demand that Douglas include open repeal. Southern Democrats perceived nothing radical in their requirement; both the hailed Compromise of 1850 and their own party platform embraced popular sovereignty. To the southerners those endorsements signified the Missouri Compromise had already been superseded in law and in party doctrine. Douglas readily accepted the southern conditions. He was totally committed to popular sovereignty; and besides, expansion and development, not slavery, was paramount to him.

No evidence places Jefferson Davis in any of these discussions, though the prospect of overturning the Missouri Compromise surely pleased him, for he had long thought it unconstitutional. Finally, on Saturday, January 21, 1854, Douglas had the repeal inserted in his measure, which also created two territories, Nebraska bordering free Iowa and Kansas next to slave Missouri. But because this new version did abrogate the Missouri Compromise, Douglas wanted presidential approval before he introduced it in Congress. Timing was a problem, however. Douglas was not ready until Saturday night, and because of the congressional calendar he had to present his bill on Monday morning or face delay. The difficulty confronted by Douglas had to do with the president, who did not usually transact business on Sunday.

On Sunday morning Douglas appeared with a group of southern Democratic senators and congressmen at Jefferson Davis's door. They wanted Davis to get them an audience with President Pierce, even on

Sunday. The southerners saw Davis as their champion in the cabinet, and all knew of the closeness between him and the president. Initially Davis demurred, telling his callers they were either a day early or a day late. But after hearing Douglas's case for the necessity of immediate action, Davis went with them to the White House. There, Davis had a private meeting with Pierce, explaining to him the purpose of the visit. Then the president agreed to see the waiting solons. Their argument persuaded him to accept this draft of the bill, which voided the Missouri Compromise and called for two territories. In so doing, Pierce changed his mind, for just the day before he had indicated his unwillingness to broach directly any Missouri repeal. In that cabinet meeting only Davis and one other had spoken for the direct approach. True, Pierce did not find reconsideration difficult, for his new stance placed him squarely on his party's campaign platform, and he did have doubts about the constitutionality of the Missouri Compromise line. Douglas had a further concern: Pierce's reputation for being swayed by whoever spoke to him last. Thus, Douglas got the president to write out the statement on repeal that would go into the bill. With President Pierce's endorsement, Kansas-Nebraska became an administration measure.[69]

That Monday, Douglas introduced the Kansas-Nebraska bill, and the congressional contest commenced. In the Senate, Democratic predominance made for relatively easy passage, by 37 to 14 on March 3. In the House, the battle was hot. Strenuous opposition led by northern Whigs joined by numerous northern Democrats put the outcome in doubt. In that chamber only the president's exercise of the full force and influence of his office enabled the advocates of Kansas-Nebraska to prevail. Jefferson Davis took an active part in the administration's campaign, communicating ideas on legislative strategy to congressional leaders. At last, on May 22, the House gave its approval by the narrow margin of 113 to 100, with half the northern Democrats opposing their president. Eight days later Franklin Pierce signed the Kansas-Nebraska Act into law. He and the southerners had triumphed, but at the enormously high cost of splitting the Democratic party.[70]

President Pierce's signature on the legislation did not end the trouble over Kansas-Nebraska. In a fundamental sense it was only beginning, for during the next two years the more southerly territory, Kansas, became at the same time a microcosm of the increasingly virulent fight over slavery and a severe political test for Pierce and his administration. When settlers began moving into Kansas, most had the same motives that had prompted Americans to head west since the colonial era—cheap land and along with it opportunity. Few had any direct interest in slavery. The territory faced the usual fractious issues, such as land titles, locations of county seats, and local taxes, that marked the opening of new territories. But in Kansas the bitter struggle between northern and southern zealots overpowered normal difficulties and processes.[71]

Both northern and southern extremists were active in Kansas, each determined to control the destiny of the new territory, to make it either free or slave. Highly publicized activities of New England abolitionists aimed at ensuring that Kansas became free soil prompted a vigorous response from staunch proslavery men, especially in Missouri. At first, the Missourians could set the course in Kansas, for they were so close, and most of the earliest immigrants were from Missouri and other slave states. But in their zeal to demolish any possibility of free soil, they overplayed their hand, engaging in election fraud, legislative intimidation, and even violence.

Jefferson Davis knew firsthand about events in Kansas. The proslavery leader in Missouri, Democratic senator David R. Atchison, whom Davis had known since Transylvania and who had stood at his door on that portentous Sunday morning, kept him posted. In relating Kansas incidents to Davis, Atchison held nothing back. According to Atchison, antislavery men in Kansas had pledged to keep out slaveholders, but "our people are resolved to go in and take their '*niggers*' with them. . . ." Reporting in September 1854 that within six months his side would have "the Devil to play in Kansas," Atchison made clear just how far he was willing to go: "we will be compelled, to shoot, burn & hang, but the thing will soon be over, we intend to '*Mormanise*' the Abolitionists." But "the thing" did not end soon. Eighteen months later an embittered Atchison was still talking about keeping his "wrath warm."[72]

Davis viewed Kansas through two lenses, one political, the other official and administrative, though they surely became intermingled. Politically he wanted Kansas to end up slave country and eventually a slave state. Success in Kansas would redound to the credit of Pierce and his administration, including Jefferson Davis. Between 1854 and 1857 Kansas remained a federal territory, much of it frontier with a strong Indian presence beyond the area of white settlement in the eastern part. The U.S. Army was responsible for controlling these Indians and for maintaining order if the territorial civilian authority broke down. But there were not enough troops to do both jobs thoroughly.[73]

Secretary Davis knew about the manpower problem. He wanted a militia established in Kansas to operate under the command of the regular army. He even requested the governors of Kentucky and Illinois to make militia available for use in Kansas, if necessary. Confronting increasing pressure to operate against the Indians in order to protect emigrants traveling westward through the territory, Davis did recommend moving regular troops west, but the president decided against him. A loyal subordinate, Davis strove to have the army carry out its mission in settled Kansas.[74]

He assumed an active role in army affairs. Following Pierce's directives, Davis instructed his officers to support the civilian officials and refrain from becoming involved in the increasingly nasty political fracas. The army found itself in a most difficult situation because the unending political strife led to the election of two legislatures, one proslavery, the other free-soil. In addition, with almost all Kansans armed, violence became endemic and killings commonplace. Still, Davis ordered his commanders not to consider sectional origins of settlers or their political outlook, only to make sure that all abided by the law. On one occasion, he reprimanded an officer for disbanding the free-soil legislature, even though it was extralegal. Yet many raised complaints that the army did not act so forcefully as it should have against the armed bands, especially the so-called "border ruffians" who came over from Missouri chiefly to burn and pillage. With its small numbers and instructions to support civilian control, the military conducted itself responsibly.[75]

Even with the army's presence and even with Pierce's trying three different territorial governors, affairs in Kansas did not improve. The fury and storm in the infant territory kept it on the front pages of the nation's newspapers. Failure to manage events in Kansas plagued Pierce and helped deny him nomination for a second term in the White House. When Jefferson Davis left the War Department in March 1857, he did not leave Kansas behind. It would reappear nine months later in a critical form in the Senate, where Davis then represented his state.

Although Davis's administrative and political duties in Washington took up much of his time, he always directed a major part of his political attention toward Mississippi. Even as Davis entered Franklin Pierce's cabinet, his chief political goal was to redeem himself in Mississippi. Greatly distressed because Mississippi voters had rejected him for a man he called "an empty demagogue," Davis talked about running for governor again in 1853 on his platform of 1851 in order to obtain a ringing affirmation of his views. He also thought about the United States Senate; he and his political associates believed that because he had resigned in 1851 for his party, he deserved to be returned. In fact, even before Davis agreed to join the cabinet, he told President Pierce the Mississippi legislature might send him back to the Senate, and if it did so, he would accept.[76]

The Mississippi legislature was to elect a United States senator in January 1854, and during 1853 Davis received conflicting advice on the course to follow. While his friends wanted him in the Senate and believed their party owed him the post, they differed on whether he should make himself available. Davis was told that if he indicated a wish for the Senate seat, no other contender would challenge him and with the "utmost ease" he would prevail. But other advisers urged him not to enter the contest because he might lose. And because of his status, a defeat would injure the cause of states' rights and deliver a terrible blow to the Democratic party in Mississippi.[77]

Davis confronted a dilemma. He clearly wanted to return to the Senate, often saying, "I preferred the Senate to any other public post." The Senate also meant vindication; Davis spoke about "the pride I would certainly feel in receiving such an endorsement as would answer the industriously circulated report that I had been tried and condemned by constituents." To the inquiries asking him to declare his preferences, he provided the same equivocal answer. He always underscored his "rule of conduct which require[s] me as a democrat to serve my party where they require me, not where my taste or ambition may indicate." He also consistently asserted: "to advance the doctrine of state rights is my first wish and whatever will most promote this end will be most acceptable to me." But just as insistently he refused to commit himself: "If the use of my name would serve to strengthen the Democracy, it is, as it has been at their service; but if it would tend to divide and weaken them, I ask of my friends to consider all personal feeling for me as but dust in the balance, thus I will be assured they justly appreciate me." An astute politician, Davis recognized that in the fierce contest of 1851 he had become "especially odious" to Union Democrats, who had now rejoined their State Rights brethren. Thus, Davis realized he might have to wait for those wounds to heal completely. Such an outcome he could understand and accept. As he wrote confidentially to a close political colleague, "in my present position I am sufficiently content and have a field of usefulness wide enough to satisfy me." Davis clearly could not bear the possibility of another defeat, and would take no initiative that risked one.[78]

At the same time, he kept in close touch with partisan affairs in his home state. Regular and full reports of activities and rivalries arrived in his mail. Central in this correspondence was the success of the reunited Democrats in holding together despite Henry Foote's efforts to disrupt the state Democratic convention held in May 1853. In the summer and fall of that year, the Democrats mounted a vigorous and successful campaign, electing their candidate for governor, John J. McRae, an avowed Davis partisan, and winning control of both houses in the legislature. McRae and his fellow Democrats certainly heeded Davis's admonition "to teach all the necessity for organization and the value of party allegiance." This triumphant Democratic performance ended Foote's political career in Mississippi. Now a man without a party, he gave up hope of getting his Senate seat back, and in January 1854 left for California. A pleased Jefferson Davis watched the political destruction of the hated Foote as Mississippi once again became a Democratic bastion flying the states' rights banner. A letter from Governor McRae attributing Democratic success to Davis's position in the cabinet surely gratified the secretary of war.[79]

The newly chosen legislature would select a United States senator. The chief combatants of 1851 did not clash again; Foote was no longer in the state, and Davis's name was never brought forward. The post went to Congressman Albert G. Brown, who politicked vigorously for it. A popular and veteran Democrat, who had also been governor, Brown was a confirmed and vociferous champion of southern rights; he had been an ideological mate of Quitman and a stalwart of the State Rights campaign of 1851. At that time he and Davis had been close political associates, and Brown recognized Davis as party leader. But with his election to the Senate, the ambitious Brown became Davis's rival for dominance among Mississippi Democrats. Brown had found an ally in Quitman, who resented Davis's role in preventing his Cuban venture and who also had reservations about Davis's firmness on southern issues. Even before the senatorial election, Brown felt rebuffed by what he considered Davis's noncommittal response to his personal request to be given the consulship in Havana. Afterwards their relationship deteriorated. To friends Brown denounced Davis as arrogant and overbearing; one of them noted that Brown "hates Davis as he does the Devil." Without doubt Brown chafed at Davis's strength in Mississippi. Describing the control Davis and his associates exercised in the state Democratic convention of 1855, Brown groaned that they made it "impossible for me to do my friends or myself justice." Despite Brown's popularity and his growing animus, he could not shoulder Davis aside. As one of Brown's senatorial allies discerned, Davis was "too strong" for him.[80]

One reason Davis held such sway in Mississippi was the careful attention he paid to the political fundamentals of patronage and service. In the cabinet he exerted great influence over federal jobs in Mississippi. The positions of federal timber agents and postmasters and the like came under his scrutiny. He also reassured a Mississippi congressman that a favored newspaper would get "a fair show" in the distribution of federal printing. His former constituents continued to seek his aid on a range of topics, including the reinstatement of a midshipman expelled from the navy. When a Mississippi geologist unknown to Davis visited Washington, the secretary welcomed him at home, then took him to the White House for an introduction to the president, and on to the War Department to meet engineer officers. Grumbling about Davis's success in dispensing patronage and providing service, a political opponent recognized that those "who held office from his kindness" and those who "have felt his kindness & received his favors," including "the most influential Democratic editor in the State," would stand on Davis's side.[81]

By 1855, Davis no longer doubted the proper way to plan for his political future. He now concentrated on the Senate seat the Mississippi legislature would fill in January 1856 for a full six-year term to begin on March 4, 1857. To emphasize his claim on Mississippi Democrats, he made his only trip home during his secretaryship to coincide with the state Democratic convention of 1855. Traveling much of the way by train, he departed Washington on May 26, having a most unusual experience en route. Although the surrounding circumstances are unclear, a family accused Davis and an army officer accompanying him of theft. The two men were arrested in Augusta, Georgia, but when the accusers learned who Davis was, they dropped the charges in embarrassment.[82]

Davis arrived in Jackson on June 2; he spoke that night, addressed the conclave of Democrats two days later, then moved on to Vicksburg, where he made another speech. An observer there noted Davis's "dignified manner, and easy, confident and agreeable oratorical style." In his remarks Davis decried antislavery activities and defended the

Pierce administration, but his chief interest was the convention itself. He and his loyalists totally dominated the body. A miffed, albeit admiring, Albert Brown described the scene: "Davis was present directing affairs in person. His friends got possession of the convention and managed every thing their own way." "I need hardly add," Brown continued, "that every possible opportunity was given Davis to make an impression. He made it." Brown could only fall back on a hope, "Whether for good or evil time will tell."[83]

Aware that he could not afford another season of equivocation, Davis made his wishes widely known. A Mississippi congressman reported on Davis's attitude: the secretary would feel "personal gratification" for the world to see that "Mississippi still loves him as his devotion to her assumes." When legislators wrote asking about his intentions, Davis "replied to all of them that a Seat in the Senate is the only position he would now accept." Davis also made known his distress that other senators who had stood with him in fighting the Compromise had had their stances validated by reelection, and he had not. Davis's closest political friends informed him they would be in Jackson to protect his interests. In December he prepared for publication a letter to his longtime supporter Collin S. Tarpley announcing that he would proudly accept the Senate seat, if offered. He grounded his case on his proven loyalty to Mississippi and his desire to ensure political victory for states' rights.[84]

In the approaching contest Davis had once more to contend with sectional rivalry in Mississippi. Because Brown lived in the southern part of the state, a number of north Mississippians maintained their region should have the other seat. Proclaiming the rights of north Mississippi, Jacob Thompson made yet another try for the Senate. Thompson declared that he could hold most northern legislators and draw enough strength from other areas of the state to stop Davis. In his campaign, he had Brown's aid. Thompson did make an effort, and was evidently willing to employ almost any tactic. The Democratic editor in Vicksburg alleged that Thompson, in a futile attempt to gain his support, offered "*pecuniary* favors to any reasonable amount."[85]

The legislature convened in January 1856. Before the balloting for senator, Davis's letter to Tarpley was printed as an extra and placed on the desk of every legislator. Thompson proved no match for the Davis juggernaut. On January 14 the Democratic caucus gave Davis 59 percent of its 85 votes and the senatorial nomination. Two days later the

Democrat-controlled legislature cast 91 votes for Davis, with 33 scattered, to award him the prize he coveted. When his cabinet term ended, he could move straight to the Senate.[86]

In spite of all his exertions to gain victory, just a week before the election Davis proudly announced in a letter to a loyal political operative that he had not joined other hopefuls in politicking for the seat. Here, he surely rationalized. He was right when he said that he had not been in the state for the meeting of the legislature, but he had worked very hard and his trusted confidants were in Jackson. In fact, an opposition newspaper had sharply criticized him for his highly visible campaign. Perhaps he was preparing himself for possible defeat, or perhaps he was defining the politics of this election quite narrowly. Whatever his thinking, with his win he concluded a most impressive political performance.[87]

As Jefferson Davis anticipated returning to the Senate, fundamental changes reshaped the political landscape. By 1856 the venerable Whig party had disappeared, ravaged by the battles over slavery and pummeled by new disputes arising over immigration and religion. Two parties appeared seeking to replace the Whigs as the second major party and Democratic opponent. Generated by a sharp increase in Roman Catholic immigrants chiefly from Ireland and Germany, a growing nativism and anti–Roman Catholic sentiment gave rise to the American party, popularly called the "Know-Nothings." Originating in secret lodges, chiefly in northern cities, this party quickly became a home for many old Whigs, both North and South. Another group struggling to gain favor was an organization that embraced the concept of free soil and condemned the South—the Republican party. Directing their message only toward the free states, the Republicans had no interest in cultivating support in the South, which they branded as basically un-American.[88]

Both the Know-Nothings and the Republicans troubled Davis. He denounced the former for secrecy and animus toward immigrants and Roman Catholics, castigating their program as "both saddening and disgusting." He refused to believe that many Americans would join any political party espousing such doctrines, and was sure it would quickly depart the political scene. In this view, Davis proved correct. After meteoric success in numerous contests in 1855, the party failed in the presidential election of 1856. It rapidly disintegrated, plagued by sectional differences over slavery and smashed in the North by the surging Republican party.[89]

The Republican party was a different creature altogether. The party platform of 1856 ringingly affirmed the virtues of the Wilmot Proviso while condemning slavery as a "relic of barbarism." No major party had ever before so completely repudiated the South. From the southern perspective, the party loomed like a giant tidal wave ready to thunder over and crush the political world finely crafted by three generations of southern politicians. The mere possibility of a Republican president terrified most southerners. When the Republicans in 1856 carried eleven of the sixteen free states, no one could doubt that their message had found a responsive audience in the North. Among southerners, for the first time since the crisis of 1849–51, this realization prompted widespread talk of severing the Union.

Davis certainly heard the calls to break up the Union. He still believed in the right of secession, and he did not cut his political ties to the sectional extremists, often called "fire-eaters." In May 1856 Congressman Preston Brooks of South Carolina responded to a vitriolic attack by Senator Charles Sumner on his state and a kinsman by brutally assaulting Sumner on the floor of the Senate. Although flayed by Republicans, Brooks was praised by southern extremists and fêted in his home district. Davis sent a message to a dinner in Brooks's honor: "I have only to express to you my sympathy with the feeling that prompts the sons of Carolina to welcome the return of a brother, who has been the subject of vilification, misrepresentation, and persecution, because he resented a libellous assault upon the reputation of their mother."[90]

At the same time, as in 1851, Davis did not believe the situation of the South warranted drastic action. Writing to a major Georgia political leader, he summarized his view: "In a single sentence then my idea of our present condition is, that we should make all the preparation proper for sovereign States—should hasten slowly, and be temperate in all things."[91]

Davis still had confidence in the Democratic party and its adherents in the North. In his opinion, all who stood on the Democratic platform of 1852 honored southern rights. His association with Pierce and with fellow cabinet members like Cushing convinced him that many northern Democrats were prepared to stand by what he saw as the South's constitutional guarantees. For 1856 he argued that political necessity required a northern candidate for president because it was the North that must settle the only issue which "disturbs and endangers the harmony of our Union"—slavery. Thus, he thought it best to have a northern leader "entirely worthy of the trust." He preferred Pierce to be nominated for a second term, but that was not possible. Many Democrats blamed the Pierce administration for the massive defeats the party had suffered in state and congressional elections in 1854–55. But Davis gladly accepted his party's nominee for the presidency, James Buchanan of Pennsylvania, whom he knew well. And Buchanan's victory in 1856 confirmed his faith in his country.[92]

Profoundly loyal to the United States, Jefferson Davis did not hide his sentiments. Affirming his devotion to the Union, he told an Indianapolis editor he had never advocated disunion. He proudly pointed to what he saw as his unblemished lineage: his father had fought in the Revolution; three brothers had been with Jackson at New Orleans; he had served his country since entering West Point at age sixteen. When asked his opinion about establishing a southern military academy exclusively for southern youths, Davis answered directly, "I fear the tendency would be to create and increase sectional jealousies." In contrast, he emphasized what he considered one of West Point's greatest virtues: its alumni were "more free from purely sectional prejudices, and more national in their feelings than the same number of persons to be found elsewhere in our country."[93]

On the morning of March 4, 1857, Secretary of War Jefferson Davis tendered his resignation to his friend and chief Franklin Pierce. He went immediately up Pennsylvania Avenue to the Capitol. At noon he was sworn in as a senator from Mississippi. From his seat in the Senate chamber, he would confront a ferocious challenge to his vision of the Union.

CHAPTER TEN

"The Darkest Hour"

The spring of 1857 found Jefferson Davis and his family bound for Mississippi. After the brief special session of Congress ended on March 14, and with the prospect of a long congressional recess, Davis prepared for the first time in almost four years to return to his home state with his wife and children. Acknowledging that the family would no longer be permanent residents of the capital city, Davis gave up the mansion at 18th and G, arranged to auction the furniture, and rented rooms until all the Davises were ready to travel. Although Davis had certainly enjoyed serving as secretary of war, he did not find the assignment profitable. To his eldest brother he quoted Charles Dickens, saying he looked on his cabinet position "somewhat as Mrs. M'Cawber did on the corn trade," which she found "gentlemanly, but it is not remunerative."[1]

Neither departure from Washington nor the actual trip home ended up as a simple matter. Because Varina was still quite weak from bearing young Jeff only two months previously and by her own admission worn out "in spirits and energy" from the auction, her husband decided she could not leave immediately, and the Davises took temporary rooms with a friend. With the weather cold outside, Varina reported a suffocatingly hot house inside. In addition, severe colds afflicted father and children, with Jeff Jr. ending up with pneumonia. A debilitated Varina experienced great difficulty in nursing her baby. Finally, on April 24, the Davises boarded a train for Wheeling, Virginia, on the Ohio River, where they transferred to a steamboat for the journey on to Mississippi. Even before departing, Maggie contracted chicken pox, and along the way her little brother broke out with it. Describing herself as "weary, weary," their mother wrote about the incessant crying of both. In early May, the landing at Hurricane on Davis Bend was a welcome sight.

Even so, arrival at Brierfield did not mean rest for the tired travelers. The house had suffered from the absence of its owners. Cataloguing the disarray in her home, Varina listed such things as sheets cut to make napkins and the disappearance of pots. To her mother, she confessed, "I just sat down and cried." As for Jefferson, his plantation needed his attention, and he set out to get it in order.[2]

Even as Davis faced reordering his plantation, including the hiring of a new overseer, he did not neglect his political duties. On May 18 he went to Vicksburg for a reception given him by the town. After a procession headed by a military contingent reached the courthouse square, Davis spoke to a large, enthusiastic crowd. Later in the month he journeyed to Jackson for a much larger event. Sixteen guns heralded the honored guest's arrival in an open coach drawn by four white horses. It moved toward the statehouse through massive portals adorned with a garland banner carrying the inscription: "Welcome Jeff Davis." With 3,000 people crowding around, Davis's speech scheduled for the House chamber in the Capitol was relocated to a hastily constructed platform on the grounds.[3]

Davis's speech in Jackson expanded upon themes from his remarks in Vicksburg and laid out what he would be saying through the autumn in numerous Mississippi towns. "Profoundly grateful" to Governor John McRae for his generous introduction, Davis identified himself completely with his state. Proclaiming "he was thrice and four times happy to meet again his fellow-citizens . . . ," Davis declared he had returned from Washington "unchanged in heart. Its pulses were ever with Mississippi." He also defended the Pierce administration as "unflinchingly true" to the principles of states' rights, which he correlated directly with defense of southern interests. Additionally, he presented President Buchanan and the Democratic party as bastions of the Constitution and southern rights. In contrast, he pictured the Republican party as a danger and a threat to the South and slavery. Denying that he intended to alarm anyone, Davis predicted that 1860 would bring "the monster crisis," what he termed "the ordeal of fire" for American patriotism. He hoped for the best, but charged Mississippians to prepare for the worst. As a Mississippian he would stand fast: "If there was danger he would share it; Mississippi's peril was his own. He would aid her in averting or overcoming it, or with her he would perish." Three weeks later he appeared with Senator Brown and Governor McRae at the state Democratic convention in Jackson, justifying the policies of the Pierce administration to the largest party gathering to that time.[4]

In the summer Davis thought about his family as well as plantation and politics. Varina had never fully regained her health following Jeff Jr.'s birth, and at the end of June he took her and the children to the Mississippi Gulf Coast, where they hoped sea breezes and saltwater would foster restoration. Varina and the children remained for the rest of the summer, enjoying their beach vacation. Varina liked her stay so much that in the fall Jefferson spent some $2,000 for beachfront property near the village of Mississippi City.[5]

Back amid the heat and cotton fields of Brierfield, an obviously lonely Davis expressed openly how much he missed his loved ones. Using an unpleasant personal experience to contrast the coast with his riverfront plantation, he told his wife, "I am the victim of gnats and I am now suffering from one which met me with an evil eye, yesterday evening, and straight rendered my eye so evil that I write with pain." "Oh Winnie you cannot know how dreary the house seems," he wrote. "When busy in it some unexpected noise seems like that of the children, and when coming back from the field or elsewhere every thing there is wanting which constituted the place's charm and made it home." But the pleasure and revival of health stemming from the coastal sojourn reconciled him, making him "happy in the deprivation which is necessary to those great goods to us all." To his little ones he sent special greetings: "Kiss my dear Daughty and sweet little Boy for their old Tady who loves them 'too much.' " He closed, "Farewell my dear Wife until a happier hour, but in all hours bright or gloomy you are the unclouded object of your husband's love and he prays for your welfare and our speedy reunion."[6]

Varina stayed in touch with her husband, corresponding in a similarly endearing tone. She often emulated the language of her babies. "Jeffy!!! bit boy, smart boy, grand old boy, big as him's Fader—him was big again as when his Fader left him and not a single tooth." Varina called Jeffy especially sweet and good, but not "precocious however—and I am thankful for it." Mother thought Maggie "the smartest thing I ever saw," and she played about in the sea "like a fish." She left no doubt about her feelings for her husband: "Take care of yourself my own old Ban, and write when you can. God bless and keep you is the prayer of your devoted wife."[7]

While his family delighted in the holiday, Jefferson's mind never strayed far from politics. As so often, his attention focused on central and northern Mississippi, the part of the state essential for his party and for his own success. Preparing for a lengthy speaking tour, he altered his plans upon discovering that no notices of his schedule had been distributed from Jackson. A careful politician, Davis knew that without advance notice he would draw small crowds in rural areas, which in his mind would mean a "valueless" exercise. As soon as he could, he telegraphed notices to the northernmost counties, informing Joseph he would travel rapidly by public transportation, then get a horse and buggy for places "I must visit."[8]

He left Jackson on September 1 and spent two weeks in the northern counties speaking in towns like Hernando and Holly Springs. He basically repeated the themes of his earlier address in Jackson, though he specified preparations he thought the South should make, such as not hiring northern teachers and encouraging southerners to write schoolbooks in order to preclude "abolition poison." Democratic partisans were delighted with his appearance among them and with his platform performances.

On September 15 he left Memphis for Davis Bend and then went on to retrieve his family on the coast, where he arrived on September 27. He remained there for around three weeks before returning to Brierfield. While on the coast he made two additional speeches, at Mississippi City and Pass Christian. The addresses repeated what he had said at the other end of the state, but he also dwelled on material progress. Heretofore he had expressed pleasure at the agricultural and commercial prosperity he saw, and he had called for more factories in the state. But the disappearing wilderness along the Gulf brought forth full expression of his convictions: "The ring of the saw and the hammer, the hum of the manufacturing village . . . give life and activity to the scene, and the solemn dirge of other days is made pensive in our ears." But this was only "the first step in the line of progress which lies before us." Praising the timber industry and the anticipated railroad that would connect the coastal region to the interior as well as to the commercial worlds of Mobile and New Orleans, Davis depicted them as not only vehicles of economic growth but also harbingers of the future. That future too necessitated state pride and self-reliance for "the feeling of State independence, to sustain the rights and fulfill the destiny which we were permitted to hope Mississippi would realize in the future."[9]

At Mississippi City, Davis spoke in more detail about slavery. He told his audience that during the presidential campaign of 1856 the slavery question "had acquired a distinctness and a gravity which he had not seen equaled." And although all the speeches and editorials had not silenced the enemies of slavery, he discerned at least one powerful benefit. "They had relieved us of Southern apologists who prayed for toleration to African slavery as an admitted evil, but one for the introduction of which we were not responsible, and of which we could not get rid—an admission which not only excused abolitionists, but which, if true, demanded of every honest man among us that he should cooperate in all well directed efforts for its abatement." As for Davis, he did not deny that "this relation of labor to capital had defects" and admitted it was abused by "the vicious, the ignorant and the wayward," but he hastened to add that the same situation obtained even with parents and children and husband and wife. Yet, in any comparison, Davis maintained that slaves fared better than apprentices, day laborers, pensioners, and asylum or prison inmates. He discovered the reason in "the universal principle of self interest," which made the master "usually kind and attentive to the wants of his slave, who, in the language of Holy Writ, 'is his money.' "

Davis defined the institution of slavery as "the most humane relations of labor to capital which can permanently subsist between them, and the most beneficent form of government that has been applied to those who are morally and intellectually unable to take care of themselves." Black Africans had been transferred from barbarism to civilization, taught "useful arts," and introduced to Christianity. By any practical standard, he declared, "African slavery, as it exists in the United States, [is] a moral, social and a political blessing."[10]

In mid-October the Davises packed up for the return to Brierfield, where they prepared to go north for the opening of Congress. Before leaving Mississippi, Davis on November 4 made yet another appearance in Jackson before the state legislature, but he added nothing significant to what he had been saying across his state for the past six months. His address displayed confidence in slavery, progress, prosperity, and the Democratic party balanced by wariness toward antislavery politics and concern about preparations against potential hazards. He left no doubts in the minds of Mississippians that in him they had a loyal, watchful guardian of their rights and their social system.[11]

In late November, the Davis family left Mississippi by steamboat heading upriver, and arrived in the national capital after a trip of some ten days. The Davises rented for $400 annually a house at 238 G Street, between 17th and 18th Streets, close to their former residence, but considerably smaller. This dwelling had two good parlors and bedrooms, but Jefferson found it cramped, cold in winter and hot in summer. Even so, during congressional sessions the family lived in it until late 1859, when they made what would be their final move in Washington, two blocks north to 249 I Street.[12]

When Senator Davis took his seat for the first session of the Thirty-fifth Congress, he was a consequential man in his state, in his party, and in his country, a status he clearly recognized. A contemporary photograph captured that status. Although the deepened lines on his cheeks indicated aging since 1853, his pale eyes were still luminous. They peered ahead confidently even while the face evinced care. This face had a past and a future written on it. In a Senate dominated by Democrats, Davis was named chairman of the Committee on Military Affairs, and in President Buchanan he counted a longtime friend. They were political confidants; Buchanan had even consulted him on cabinet appointments.[13]

To underscore Davis's political stature, at the beginning of 1858 a national news publication, *Harper's Weekly*, devoted its entire front page to him, with a photographic representation, a biographical sketch, and a commentary. The reporter stated that Davis was beloved in his home state, though many northerners thought of him as a sectional extremist or fire-eater. Contradicting that perception, the writer depicted a quite different Davis. He described the Mississippian as precise, cool, even cold, full of statistics and principles, without emotional excitement, though with a "kind and gentle disposition." According to the article, Davis was the last person in Congress a visitor would pick out as a fire-eater.[14]

As the Senate began conducting business, Senator Davis seemed almost like Secretary Davis. He brought to the floor a measure increasing the size of the regular army. Advocating the addition of two companies to each regiment, Davis said the demands of the frontier required action. He argued that even with the additional regiments authorized during the Pierce administration, the army was still stretched far too thin, with too many posts to garrison and too much territory to defend. He also maintained that augmenting existing regiments with new companies was more efficient than creating more regiments. Although Davis made a logical, solid case, the Senate was in no hurry to make the army larger. There was the traditional American reluctance to a strong standing army, but many Republican senators also feared the thwarting of their free-soil goal because they envisioned the troops aimed at Kansas.[15]

Jefferson Davis, c. 1858.
(McMlees' Gallery of Photographic Prints), The Rhode Island Historical Society

Kansas, which had devoured the Pierce presidency, remained vora-cious, reaching for the new Buchanan administration. Before the initial session of the Thirty-fifth Congress, Kansas appeared in the form of the Lecompton Constitution, which had emerged from the turmoil and bitterness of Kansas politics. Territorial politics were so inflamed that the proslavery and free-soil camps refused to participate in the same political process. Attempting to cope with this volatile situation was Robert J. Walker, newly installed as territorial governor by President Buchanan. A former United States senator from Mississippi and cabi-net officer under James K. Polk, Walker had long been a political friend of Jefferson Davis. But at the outset of his governorship Walker alien-ated many southerners when he announced that climate would prevent Kansas from becoming a slave state. He also declared that the constitu-tion prepared for Kansas should be submitted to a popular vote, with the issue of slavery submitted separately.

In 1857, when proslavery forces decided to hold a constitutional convention to prepare for statehood, free-soilers boycotted it. Meeting in Lecompton, this convention drafted a proslavery constitution to accompany the application for statehood. Aware that the free-soilers significantly outnumbered them, the proslavery men, in opposition to Governor Walker's promise and wish, did not submit either the full constitution or the issue of slavery to a general vote, in which both would have undoubtedly failed. Instead, they provided for only a partial referendum. Kansans could vote on a provision governing the future admission of slaves in the territory, but they could not express their opinion on the slaves already there. Holding true to Kansas form, the free-soilers did not participate in the December referendum, in which the constitution with slavery won easily, 6,226 to 569. Meanwhile, a new free-soil legislature called for another referendum in which voters could say aye or nay to the entire constitution. The proslavery forces boycotted this January 1858 polling, which rejected their constitution by more than 10,000 votes. These facts were as well known in Washington as in Kansas.[16]

For President Buchanan and his party, the Lecompton Constitution demanded a major decision. On the face of things, it was a fruit of popular sovereignty, the gospel of their party. But popular sovereignty meant the wishes of the majority, and everyone knew full well that no majority in Kansas desired the Lecompton Constitution, that it had been engineered by a minority. Many northern Democrats therefore could not help but see Lecompton as a mockery of the popular sovereignty they espoused, and simply could not accept it—a feeling reinforced by the continuing and politically potent cries of Republicans for free soil. If the president and southern Democrats nonetheless made an all-out effort for Lecompton, the ensuing struggle could fracture party unity.

Despite the potential danger, that is precisely what President Buchanan and the southerners decided: to adopt Lecompton as their own, to battle for admission of Kansas as a slave state. From Buchanan's point of view, all the legalities had been observed. Even though the convention had disregarded his advice to submit the constitution to a popular vote, it had that right. And previous conventions in other territories had followed that model. When the free-soilers refrained from voting, that was their choice. In addition, southerners dominated the party, in the Congress and in the cabinet. Moreover,

Buchanan had long been close to many prominent southern Democrats. For the president, personal proclivity and potential political benefit seemingly coalesced.

The southern Democrats realized the Lecompton Constitution provided an opportunity to add a slave state, and promptly. Southerners
wanted to test the willingness of the nation to admit another slave state
into the Union; not since 1845, when Florida and Texas were admitted,
had it done so. Many southerners believed that if a slave Kansas were
refused admission, the great battles over constitutional rights would
have been fought in vain, especially since the United States Supreme
Court, in the *Dred Scott* decision handed down in March 1857, had
sanctioned southern positions on slavery and the territories. Despite
some confusion caused by the numerous opinions accompanying the
decision, the Court did specifically declare the Missouri Compromise
line unconstitutional, decreeing that Congress had no power to bar
slavery from any territory, the common property of all citizens. Southerners also feared that if they let Kansas go by, they might never have
another equally good chance. Kansas bordered slavery; it abutted Missouri and was just northwest of Arkansas. Many southerners felt it was
now or never.[17]

From his service in Pierce's cabinet, Jefferson Davis certainly knew
the reality of Kansas politics. In the Senate his chief concern was to
protect what he considered the South's constitutional rights in the territories, rights the *Dred Scott* decision had affirmed. Davis saw as equally
important congressional willingness to admit a slave state, for in his
mind admission offered a concrete test of the moral and constitutional
equality defining his sense of the Union.

His Mississippi speeches made his views quite clear. Calling Kansas
"the pivot of this sectional conflict," Davis termed it especially important because of geography, its proximity to Missouri and Arkansas, and
he foresaw negative consequences if it were lost to the South. Although
he had not seen the document written at Lecompton, he assumed it
would either overtly authorize slavery or keep silent about it. To him,
because of the *Dred Scott* decision, either approach was fine. Dismiss-
ing as irrelevant the dispute about submission to a popular vote, he
pointed out that constitutions can come directly to Congress. While
Davis condemned Walker's statements on slavery and his hostility to
Lecompton, he assured Mississippians that President Buchanan would
stand with the South on constitutional grounds. He also believed that

unity among southern senators and representatives would mean speedy admission of Kansas because a sufficient number of northern Democrats would side with the South to guarantee a positive outcome. Although he did not expect it, Davis did address the possibility that Kansas would be denied admission solely because of slavery. Then, as he saw it, the South would have to stand or "be degraded. Submission to such an invasion of our rights would cover us with moral leprosy." Even so, he did not prescribe any precise course, but advocated only "stern resistance."[18]

When the president decided to put his office behind Lecompton, he knew there would be a struggle, but he expected his party ultimately to follow his lead just as it had taken up the banner of Kansas-Nebraska behind Pierce. With Kansas admitted as he anticipated, the everlasting war over slavery in the territories would surely end. The struggle, however, turned out to be more intense than he had thought. The ablest and most prominent northern Democrat in Congress, the man who had managed the passage of the Kansas-Nebraska Act, Senator Stephen A. Douglas, refused to support Buchanan. Ever since 1854, Douglas had made popular sovereignty his political creed; he had stumped the North for it. He could not accept the mockery Lecompton made of his doctrine, certainly not with the Republicans mounting a major campaign for his Senate seat, which came up in 1858. In his march away from the president and the southerners, Douglas took with him a sizable number of northern Democrats and their constituency within the party.

Nonetheless, although Douglas's defection created a glaring gap along the party's northern front, President Buchanan forged ahead. A running debate on the Kansas question had existed since the opening of Congress, but the real struggle began on February 2, 1858, when Buchanan sent the Lecompton Constitution to the Capitol, along with a message urging its adoption. Senator Davis was optimistic that Lecompton would prevail, and in the Senate southern power and presidential muscle carried the day, despite Douglas's opposition. Twenty-five of thirty-seven Democratic senators were southerners, and no more than three northern Democrats would align with Douglas. After six weeks of debate and maneuver, the Senate on March 23 accepted the Lecompton Constitution, 38 to 25.[19]

All involved knew, however, that a ferocious struggle would occur in the House of Representatives. There the Democratic majority was much smaller—128 to the Republican 92 and the American 4. Moreover, among the Democrats the southerners were not so prominent, outnumbering the northerners by only 75 to 53. Buchanan and the southerners recognized that hard work lay ahead, but they were convinced that cracking the whip of party regularity, offering and threatening patronage, and other devices could deliver a majority, just as they had back in 1854 for Kansas-Nebraska. And the same man directed the administration's effort, Alexander H. Stephens of Georgia, a former Whig. The cadaverous-looking Stephens, who weighed less than 100 pounds, enjoyed a deserved reputation as a brilliant floor manager and a master of parliamentary procedure. And he set out to give Buchanan and the South what they wanted. But after herculean exertions and a legion of stratagems, Stephens and Buchanan failed. Northern opinion had turned too strongly against Lecompton. On April 1 the House passed a bill that would return the Lecompton Constitution to Kansas for a closely supervised vote.

With the two chambers deadlocked, a conference committee offered the only chance of adjustment. In the committee a compromise was fashioned to camouflage the failure of the president and the southerners to have Kansas admitted as a slave state. Known as the English Bill for its chief author, Democratic Congressman William H. English of Indiana, the settlement turned on the extraordinary request accompanying the Lecompton Constitution that Kansas be given 23 million acres of public land, about six times the normal award to a new state. English's measure reduced the grant to around 4 million acres and returned the Lecompton Constitution to Kansas for voters to decide whether they wanted it with the reduced land grant. For southerners this approach had one great advantage: they could legitimately say that Congress had not rejected a slave state. In addition, although most realized that Kansas would vote against Lecompton, they would not soon face the prospect of a free Kansas, for the English Bill stipulated that if Kansas turned down Lecompton, the territory could not reapply for statehood until it had a population of 90,000. For northerners the English Bill meant that Kansas would have a federally sanctioned opportunity to vote on the Lecompton Constitution. On April 30 this approach won approval in both houses, though Douglas remained in opposition, and President Buchanan signed it into law. In the summer Kansans made their decision, drubbing Lecompton by 11,300 to 1,788. Kansas would not become a state until 1861.

Despite congressional rejection of the Lecompton Constitution, Senator Davis did not view the outcome as a defeat. On the contrary, he considered the English Bill a notable success. During the deliberations of the conference committee, Congressman Stephens had obtained Davis's help in framing the measure. Davis also called the Mississippi delegation together to lobby for the English Bill, gaining the support of Senator Brown and all the representatives but one. Because he believed passage of the bill imperative, he left his sickbed to be present when the Senate voted.[20]

Thereafter, Davis always claimed the English Bill had been a "triumph of all for which we contended and the success of a great constitutional principle." To support his contention, Davis occupied narrow and technical ground. According to him, Congress had not rejected but in fact admitted a slave state. Yet, in so doing, Congress had pointed to a flaw in the application, the outsized land grant. He even claimed to prefer the English Bill to the original Lecompton Constitution. And if the people of Kansas decided not to accept the congressionally mandated change in the acreage granted, they had the right to do so. This assessment he pushed in Mississippi, in the press and from the podium. Praising Buchanan for his stance throughout the struggle, he applauded the president's "Roman firmness and integrity of purpose." He told Mississippians he had "the most unlimited confidence in that noble old patriot," who had fought valiantly and successfully for their rights. In his mind the English Bill "relieved" the country from a terrible danger, for had a legitimate application for the admission of a slave state been rejected, "our honor, our safety, our respect for our ancestors, and our regard for our posterity would have required the South to meet [the issue] at whatever sacrifice."[21]

In drawing his conclusion, Davis could proclaim that the Democratic party remained a shield for the South and that the Union he cherished still existed. Yes, Douglas had broken ranks on this question, and Davis condemned him for this specific act only, making no effort to discipline him or drum him out of the party. He presented Buchanan, as he had Pierce, as the representative northern Democrat, reminding Mississippians that southern Democrats had never asked their northern brethren to concur in "their abstract opinion" about slavery, but simply to recognize their constitutional rights. The passage of the English Bill affirmed the moral and constitutional equality of the South. Davis opted to underscore that interpretation rather than confront the harsh fact of the defeat of the Lecompton Constitution, caused in large part by the opposition of the leading northern Democrat in Congress.[22]

On February 13, just eleven days after President Buchanan submitted his message on the Lecompton Constitution to Congress, Senator Davis was "confined by a painful illness." His condition worsened, a severe cold led to laryngitis, and, more dangerously, his "left eye became intensely inflamed." The disease that had first downed him in 1851 struck again, and this time even more ferociously.[23]

For two months Davis was in great pain and literally prostrate. He lay speechless, barely able to take nourishment, muffling screams, and communicating only through a writing tablet. Because his sensitive eye could not bear light, Davis was confined to a darkened room. On one occasion when light streamed into his chambers to make an examination of the eye possible, Varina wrote of "the emaciated hand that wrung mine at every pang." Confronting such pain, Davis exhibited remarkable self-control, so much so that physicians expressed amazement at his stoical demeanor. But unsurprisingly, one of his doctors and a friend noted depression. Varina, who nursed him diligently and acted as his amanuensis, concentrated on her husband's will to overcome his affliction.[24]

During this protracted illness Davis had several regular visitors who showed their concern and helped him pass through his ordeal. Old army acquaintances Colonel Edwin Sumner and William Hardee, now a brevet lieutenant colonel, spent hours sitting in almost total darkness talking about army matters and reading to the invalid. The British ambassador, Lord Napier, often stopped by. From the political world two men came daily. Davis's close friend Democratic senator Clement C. Clay of Alabama spent many hours, including nights, at the bedside of his stricken comrade. Then, from the other side of the partisan aisle and the opposite end of the sectional spectrum, Republican senator William Henry Seward of New York also appeared for an hour every day, and "sometimes oftener." According to Varina, Senator Seward brought news of congressional proceedings and made every effort to build the patient's spirits. Even in the aftermath of 1865, Varina commented on Seward's "earnest, tender interest," which she believed "unmistakably genuine."[25]

Davis had the services of extremely able physicians. Dr. Robert Stone, a highly regarded ophthalmologist in Washington, called on Davis at least daily. Then, the Davis family's physician and friend Dr. Thomas Miller brought in Dr. Isaac Hayes of Philadelphia, perhaps the most eminent ophthalmologist of his day in America. Attending a conference in Washington, Dr. Hayes undertook to examine Davis. The medical men evidently agreed on treatment, at the time the accepted therapy for his illness—the patient remained quiet in a darkened room and took special medication.[26]

Davis was unquestionably suffering from another siege of metaherpetic keratoiritis. The cold and fever that had gripped him, as well as the intense stress over Kansas, could easily have contributed to the timing of the new assault on his left eye. Dr. Stone's clinical notes specifically talk about ulceration of the cornea. His description indicates a ruptured healing descemetocele filled with iris tissue and a threatened abscess of the eyeball, as well as a possible hypopyon, an accumulation of pus in the anterior chamber of the eye. After two frightful months, Davis began getting better. On April 19 he informed Joseph, "My health is now restored except the affection of the eye, and the consequent influence upon the sight."[27]

Late in April he briefly took his seat in the Senate, and after mid-May he appeared regularly. His trips to the Senate to vote on Lecompton and the English Bill had required incredible efforts. Describing Davis upon his return to the Senate, a reporter underscored how ravaging his illness had been: "a pale ghastly-looking figure, his eye bandaged with strips of white linen passing over the head, his whole aspect presenting an appearance of feebleness and debility."[28]

Even though Davis came through this trial, his eye problem was not yet over. Good vision did not return to the left eye, which periodically still caused difficulties. In the spring of 1859 he wrote his mother-in-law, "The eye of which the sight was almost lost has slowly recovered and hopes are entertained that by quiet and proper treatment during the approaching summer the sight may be restored so as to make it again useful for looking in two directions." At least part of his treatment included surgery; by early June he had had a surgical procedure performed on the eye in Washington. Although no details survive, he probably had a hypopyon, which would involve an incision of the cornea to drain pus from the anterior chamber of the eye, a not uncommon technique in Davis's time.[29]

Although Davis never again experienced eye disease that remotely resembled the seriousness of the 1858 attack and the 1859 surgery, they left their marks. He turned to eyeglasses, with evidently some temporary help. As time passed, however, the degenerative ocular process connected with his affliction continued, and in all probability phthisisvalbi set in. As a film covered the left eye, he could see only light and darkness, but could no longer distinguish objects. Contemporaries used various terms when they mentioned the eye. A close friend mentioned "clouded"; another observer called it "discolored"; even the word "blind" was used. In photographs taken in 1859 and 1860, Davis did not look directly at the camera. Instead, he presented a profile which emphasized his right side and hid his left side and his damaged eye.[30]

Although Davis did return to the Senate, he was far from fully recovered. He remained quite weak, with little appetite, was much thinner than usual, and could not see well enough to write. His attending physician wanted him to get away to a cooler climate for rest and recuperation. When Congress adjourned in mid-June, the Davis family prepared for a lengthy sojourn in New England.[31]

On July 3 in Baltimore, Jefferson, Varina, and both children—Maggie now three and a half and Jeff Jr., eighteen months—embarked on the *Joseph Whitney*. Arriving in Boston on the morning of July 6, Jefferson and Varina spent the day touring the sights until late afternoon, when they took an overnight steamer bound for Portland, Maine, disembarking there the next morning. During the subsequent three months the Davises enjoyed the refreshing summer and early fall of Maine. They saw much of the state, from Portland to Augusta, Penobscot Bay, Bangor, and just over fifty miles east of Bangor the Coast Survey camp on 1,475-foot Humpback or Lead Mountain, where Alexander Bache once again greeted his old friend. Varina remembered joyful excursions on the water, clambakes, picnics or "basket parties," fresh fish and vegetables adorning tables, quiet nights because of the absence of nocturnal insects, and the kindness of so many people.[32]

When on October 6 the Davises finally left Maine, they stopped once again in Boston. Here they stayed over a week, longer than they expected because Jeff Jr. came down with a bronchial illness. During this stopover, in company with numerous other dignitaries, Jefferson toured Boston Harbor and visited Marshfield, the estate of Daniel Webster. After Boston, the Davises made a brief stop in New York City before returning to Washington on October 22.[33]

The trip certainly aided Davis's physical condition. As early as mid-August he reported that since his arrival in Maine his health had "improved steadily." One of his hosts recalled his "pleasant face," even though he was not completely well. But he got better over the weeks;

Varina thought "hourly." According to her, the trip accomplished precisely what had been hoped: "health came back to his wasted form, and his sight improved daily."[34]

And the trip had an unexpected dimension. Hailed as a notable public figure, Davis often found himself called upon to give speeches, and give them he did. From impromptu remarks on board ship on the Fourth of July to addressing a crowd of 5,000 at a Democratic rally in New York City on October 19, Davis spoke at least eight times, including before the Maine Democratic convention, at the state militia encampment, at the Maine Agricultural Society, and at a Democratic ratification meeting at Faneuil Hall in Boston. This public recognition surprised and delighted him. He told one audience it overwhelmed him; to another, he spoke of the "constant acts of generous hospitality" shown him. Bowdoin College in Brunswick, Maine, Franklin Pierce's alma mater, even awarded him an honorary doctor of laws degree. All the while he enjoyed renewing old political friendships and making new ones.[35]

In each of his public appearances Davis emphasized the same themes, starting with the single heritage of all Americans. When called for remarks on the Fourth of July aboard the *Joseph Whitney*, he talked about the "common sense of nationality beat[ing] in every American bosom." Those in any section who wanted to divide the country, he denounced as "trifling politicians" engaged in a futile endeavor: "They are like the mosquitoes around the ox; they annoy, but they cannot wound, and never kill." He touched upon the shared Revolutionary legacy of all Americans and "the fraternity of our revolutionary fathers," when all states aided one another in a common cause. And he assured listeners that should danger arise anew, Mississippi would rush to the side of Maine, and he was sure Maine would do the same for Mississippi. Fanatics who wanted to do away with the constitutional Union, like Senator Seward, who appealed to a "higher law," he branded as "traitors." "We became a nation by the constitution," he declared, "whatever is national springs from the constitution; and national and constitutional are convertible terms."[36]

Obviously referring to slavery, Davis insisted that local matters should remain local concerns. He refused to discuss Maine issues because as an outsider he would not interfere. America had been built on the principle of "each willing to sacrifice local interest, individual prejudice or temporary good to the general welfare." The Founding Fathers had rightly turned from consolidation; he argued their respect for local or community interests—read states' rights—underlay the success of the Constitution. He believed the great majority of Americans wanted to continue in that tradition, ensuring the continued development and prosperity of the country.[37]

Davis also underscored other common interests binding the different parts of the country into a whole. Although he expressed his conviction that agriculture was "the basis of all wealth," he gloried in the economic diversity of America. He saw New England as a center of manufacturing that bought quantities of the major southern staple, cotton, and the South in turn purchased manufactured goods from New England. "This is an interweaving of interests, which makes us all the richer and all the happier."[38]

Davis evinced little patience with the Republican message proclaiming the aggressiveness of the slave states. He wanted to know how the migration of American citizens with their legal slave property into a territory could possibly be defined as aggressive. "We have nothing to aggress upon," he announced, adding that even if the South wanted to be aggressive, it no longer possessed the power to do so. As for the Republican charge that the Supreme Court would accede to southern wishes and declare slavery legal in the free states, Davis termed it a "palpable absurdity." On the contrary, he said, the Court would have to overturn any such wild law should Congress enact it. In Davis's view, the states absolutely controlled slavery within their borders, except for the right of transit for a slaveowner traveling with his property.[39]

At the same time he squarely faced the issue of slavery. In his judgment, the political agitation wracking the country rested on slavery, or, more precisely, on the northern fanatics meddling in somebody else's affairs. "With Pharisaical pretension it is sometimes said it is a moral obligation to agitate, and I suppose they are going through a sort of vicarious repentance for other men's sins." He did not hesitate to defend southern slavery. In the citadel of abolition, Faneuil Hall, he demanded to know who gave abolitionists the right to call slavery a sin. He could find no denunciation of it in the Constitution and no teaching against it in the Bible. In contrast, he claimed slavery had helped blacks more than anything else, to Christianize and to civilize them.[40]

Throughout these speeches Davis sounded a note of optimism but one tempered by reality. If "each man should attend to his own business, that no community should arrogantly assume to interfere with the affair of another," he believed, "every American hand [would] unite in the great object of National development." He employed what he hoped would be a resonating metaphor. Observing the interaction between the sea and the land along the rocky Maine coast, Davis watched the waves rush onto the cliffs, only to be thrown back. But when the tide receded, "I saw that the rock was seamed and worn by the ceaseless beating of the sea, and fragments riven from the rock were lying on the beach." "Thus the waves of sectional agitation are dashing themselves against the granite patriotism of the land," he went on. "If long continued, that too must show the seams and scars of the conflict. Sectional hostility must sooner or later produce political fragments." The danger should be stopped now, he concluded. And he provided the prescription: Americans should heed the lessons of fraternity and union from the Revolution.[41]

All these speeches received positive assessments. Davis often spoke before large audiences that gave him enthusiastic receptions. Of course, he addressed chiefly Democrats, not Republicans. Still, after the bitter battle over Lecompton and Douglas's break with the president, the warm response to Davis was remarkable. The reports in the Democratic press repeated the reactions of those who actually heard the speeches. Even Republican newspapers approvingly noted Davis's emphasis on the Union.[42]

Davis delighted as much in his political reception as he did in the climate. Repeatedly, he thanked his audiences for their hospitality and attentiveness. As a result, he saw "a brighter sky" and felt "a firmer foundation beneath [my] feet." Looking back after three months, he found no reason to abandon his hopefulness. He wrote to Franklin Pierce that his tour persuaded him "temperate true men" could make a great difference by visiting in opposite sections. He had discovered that "The difference is less than I had supposed."[43]

While Davis in New England experienced a renewed conviction about the American future, he was taken aback by a totally unanticipated assault on him by southern states' rights zealots. Certain reports of Davis's remarks aboard the *Joseph Whitney* had him proclaiming the inviolability of the Union, which violated the states' rights creed. But though Davis certainly praised the blessings of the Union, he never declared it inviolable, for he had long believed in the right of secession. In the South, fire-eating newspapers, such as the *Charleston Mercury* and the *New Orleans Delta*, vilified him for betraying his section and for turning his back on his political friends. Davis's phrase "trifling politicians" especially angered them, for they assumed he meant them. One disgusted fire-eater denounced "corruption & treachery of Southern

Politicians (Jeff Davis in particular)." An Alabama editor castigated the speech as "a pitiable spectacle of human weakness and political tergiversation."[44]

The outbursts had important ramifications in Mississippi, where Davis had long upheld the states' rights banner but also had foes eager for an opening against him. Immediately upon seeing an account of the Fourth of July address, a close political and personal friend in Vicksburg wrote telling Davis he needed to correct the report. Understanding the potential political danger, Davis responded immediately, denying that he ever said the Union could not be dissolved. He declared his record on states' rights needed no defense. He went on to say he had not spoken from a prepared text and his words had been twisted. But he proudly stood by his positive sentiments about the Union. At the same time, he condemned politicians who refused to see the benefit of the Union and for personal grievance or arrogance wanted to destroy it. He concluded that they "trifle with a grave subject, and deserve rebuke from every reflecting citizen of the United States." With Davis's permission requested and granted by telegraph, the letter appeared almost immediately in the *Jackson Mississippian*. Three weeks later the *Mississippian* carried another lengthy response from Davis defending his position to a constituent.[45]

Meanwhile Albert G. Brown moved rapidly to exploit an excellent opportunity to best Davis as a defender of the South and slavery. Speaking to his fellow Mississippians in the fall, he made his most extreme statements since 1851, telling his listeners they must give up either the Union or slavery. Like many Republicans, but unlike Davis, Brown asserted that the country could not survive part slave and part free. In his view, it was "madness" for anyone to assume the tide of abolition could be turned back. Declaring all must soon "stand in the breach as one man determined to do or die in defense of our common heritage," Brown claimed to quote Oliver Cromwell, "Pray to the Lord, but keep your powder dry."[46]

Politically knowledgeable Mississippians recognized the reality of a political contest. Long a champion of Davis, the *Jackson Mississippian*, the major Democratic newspaper in the state, made every effort to shore up his standing among states' rights loyalists. Not only did it readily publish Davis's own statements, it also joined in his defense, condemning sheets like the *Delta* and the *Mercury* for trying with "unjustified censure" to drum Davis out of the states' rights camp. Emphasizing Davis's sterling credentials, the *Mississippian* also delighted in both the correctness of his remarks in New England and the positive reception he received. "Mississippi may well experience a feeling of just pride in these attentions to her distinguished statesman. The honors showered upon him are reflected back on her." While the *Mississippian* erected defensive barricades around its hero, the *Vicksburg Whig* welcomed him to the conservative ranks. Never a Davis partisan during the Whig-Democratic rivalry, the *Whig* during that period spoke for the party whose name it carried. In the great struggle of 1850–51, it championed the Union-Democrats and ever since had branded Davis as too radical. Now, however, this hometown paper praised him for "the most eloquent" tributes to "the value and permanence" of the Union. At the same time, it delighted in what it saw as confusion among some fire-eating editors "dumbfounded" by his speeches. The *Whig* bored to the core of what was happening: "As Jeff. Davis goes North, Brown comes South." "Davis goes to Portland and Brown goes to the Equator," chortled the editor. "If Davis should penetrate further into Maine, we shall probably hear of Brown bathing in the crater of a volcano."[47]

The turmoil in Mississippi prompted Davis to make a personal journey to the state. Varina remembered his need to check on his plantation, but he made sure his visit coincided with the meeting of the legislature. Taking the western route, Davis left Washington on October 28 and reached Brierfield on November 5. Three days later he went by train from Vicksburg to Jackson. There he spoke before what was called the largest crowd ever to gather in the Hall of Representatives in the Capitol. An eyewitness described Davis as worn and having aged but with a clear mind and a voice still vigorous.[48]

He started out with his traditional opening; it was a privilege to be among those he loved, those who trusted and honored him, and those for whom he worked. But he savaged those who he said had intentionally misrepresented him: "For the wretch who is doomed to go through the world bearing a personal jealousy or a personal malignity, which renders him incapable of doing justice, and studious of misrepresentation, I can only feel pity, and were it possible to feel revengeful, could consign him to no worse punishment than that of his own tormentors, the vipers nursed in his own breast." Then he plunged straight to his main purpose, defending himself. He had been surprised and delighted by his reception in New England, and by discovering the South had friends there. He also justified his record on states' rights and "the equality of the South," claiming no one had been more vigilant than he. But he repeated that he had never advocated disunion "except as the last alternative." It is not time now, he announced to the assembly.

In his view, the passage of the English Bill along with the sentiment he found in New England proved that the South was not isolated. The Democratic party remained a bulwark for protection of southern constitutional rights. Despite this positive assessment, Davis did not advocate complacency. If in 1860 the abolitionists elected a president, Mississippi would have to decide whether to let the government "pass into the hands of your avowed and implacable enemies." He defined that eventuality as "a species of revolution by which the purposes of the Government would be destroyed and the observance of its mere forms entitled to no respect." At that point he thought Mississippi would have a "duty" to "provide safety" for itself outside the Union and prepare itself by constructing armories and railroads, for example. Still, he reaffirmed his contention that secession was "the last remedy— the final alternative." He clung to the Union, concluding, "I love the flag of my country with even more than a filial affection."[49]

Before returning to Washington, Davis also addressed citizens of Vicksburg in a shorter version of his speech before the legislature, saying he "d[id] not yet despair of the Union" because of the "many sterling and patriotic Democrats at the North," who still upheld the constitutional rights of the South. The Republicans were another matter, however. Davis did not believe that even if elected in 1860, "an Abolition President" should be allowed to occupy the presidential chair. The South would never be secure, and he would feel "disgraced by living under an Abolition government." In that case, he acknowledged, appeal might have to go to "the God of Battles"; but not yet. After three weeks of stressing his political position, reinforcing his allies, and affirming his loyalty to his state and its values, Davis once again headed northward. He left Vicksburg on November 28 and arrived in Washington by December 6. When the second session of the Thirty-fifth Congress convened, he was in his seat.[50]

Despite Davis's public letters, his newspaper support, and his flying trip home, his friends told him he needed to do more. Warning that his political foes constantly distorted his stand on critical sectional questions, they urged him to collect his New England speeches and publish them in book form. They also let him know that Albert Brown was already engaged in preparing a volume of his speeches. Initially, Davis demurred, citing "diffidence." But he hurried on to say that if public duty demanded it, he would not permit his personal feelings to control his actions. Yet he feared that the labor required in such an endeavor exceeded his physical capability, especially his inability to work at night. Early in 1859, however, he began preparation of such a collection, gathering all the newspaper reports of his addresses during the summer and fall of 1858. Because he wanted them in the precise form they had originally appeared, he made no revisions. He added to the eight speeches he gave in New England and New York City extracts from two on the Compromise of 1850 and the discourse he had just made before the Mississippi legislature in November.[51]

Published in Baltimore, the fifty-six-page book was out by April 1859. It was dedicated "To the people of Mississippi," and the preface clearly spelled out his hope and his intent: "I have been induced by the persistent misrepresentation of popular addresses made by me at the North during the year 1858, to collect them, and with extracts from speeches made by me in the Senate in 1850, to present the whole in this connected form; to the end that the case may be fairly before those whose judgment I am willing to stand or fall." Davis worked hard to distribute the book, for which there was a substantial demand outside as well as inside Mississippi. In that effort, Varina, even though in the later stages of her fourth pregnancy, was most helpful. In fact, she worked up until the day prior to her delivery, telling her husband, "it gives me pleasure to be doing something which seems to bring us nearer to each other."[52]

As the 1850s drew to a close, the Davises approached the completion of a decade and a half of marriage. At this moment in their life together, they were devoted to each other and did not hesitate to express their feelings. That in the spring of 1859 Varina worked on mailing political materials so late in her pregnancy powerfully confirmed her commitment to her husband. But there were joyous times apart from work. Varina's account of their New England trip dwells on the pleasures she and Jefferson shared during those months, and Jefferson specifically commented on how much she enjoyed their time together in that region.[53]

Their words and actions toward each other demonstrated the bond they shared. On the eve of Varina's giving birth to their third living child, Jefferson was at Davis Bend battling a flooding Mississippi River. "I do so long to see you my dear Husband," she wrote. "It saddens me to realize that there is so very much in ones being the first love of early youth." She confided to him that since he had been away, she had often "experienced that queer annihilation of responsibility, and of time, and gone back fourteen years to the anxious loving girl, so little of use, yet so devoted to you." But reality intruded: "my grey head, swollen feet, and household cares awakes me from the dream." Fearful, she verged on "becoming sentimental," saying he might "wish my romance had been indefinitely postponed"; but she closed with the assurance, "hourly my prayer is that 'the Lord bless thee, and keep thee.' " Three months later identifying him as her "only love" and her "all," she made clear her adoration for "my precious good Husband."[54]

Jefferson matched that devotion. When he learned by telegraph that Varina had become seriously ill after the delivery, he informed his father-in-law that his anxiety had become "so uncontrollable" he could not feel "joy" about the new baby boy, only "depression." Thinking of nothing else, he left Mississippi on a hurried trip back to her side, where he stayed for six weeks. While there, he took pains to make arrangements for "some cool and healthy retreat" where Varina could spend the summer. Within the month he took the family to the village of Oakland, in a hilly section of western Maryland.[55]

Father and mother certainly delighted in their children. To her mother, Varina depicted the antics of "very smart" Maggie, and Jeffy "so big, and white, and fat." The two played together, with Jeffy "stirring around like mad." When Jefferson was at Davis Bend, Varina kept him posted. Maggie knew he had a wax doll for her in his trunk, while Jeffy shouted fifty times a day, "I love my Daddy, I love Mr. Davis, I do." In one letter she reported that Jeffy, "as red as a burr," had eaten two large mutton chops for breakfast. She called him "the best child on earth," who from the minute he was born, she felt, "would be 'friend of my bosom the balm of my life.' "[56]

The proud father was enchanted. At fifty, he had little ones around his feet. In early 1859, he wrote Franklin Pierce that both the older children "have grown rapidly and the little girl is now quite a companion to me. . . ." He found Maggie bright, and said she was better at meeting people than were her parents. He thought charming her habit of waiting by her gate for someone to unlock it, and then going to a house where she was known to wait until "her hiding place" was discovered. As for Jeff Jr., Jeff Sr. portrayed him at two as "a large strong fellow and the most manly little fellow I ever saw." Admitting his partisanship, the father added, but *"public opinion* in which I retain full confidence" concurred. Davis did more than write about his feelings. On one occasion, a visitor to his home in Washington discovered him lying on the floor with the two children climbing over him, and Varina recounted his gamboling on Humpback Mountain with Maggie on his shoulders.[57]

As usual, books formed a part of the Davis household; the records of the Library of Congress reveal an eclectic lot borrowed between 1857 and 1860 under Senator Davis's name. The volumes numbered several contemporary novels, mostly by American and English women, Louisa Stuart Costello, Letitia MacLean, and Catherine Maria Sedgwick. There was also a collection of British drama and the Italian epic poem *Orlando Furioso* in English translation. Their borrowings included the memoirs of the famous French writer Alexandre Dumas (in French) and of the English playwright Richard Sheridan, as well as a two-volume literary history of Southern Europe. Accounts of travel in Spain and in the American West indicate the Davises' abiding interest in that genre. Their taste in history ranged widely: the memoir of a Russian princess in the court of Catherine the Great, two studies of Napoleon I, David Ramsay's *History of South Carolina* (1808, reissued in 1858), and *History of the National Flag* (1852) by a grandson of Alexander Hamilton.[58]

When on April 18, 1859, Jefferson and Varina welcomed a newcomer to their family, an old family wound reopened. Although Varina's physician worried that she was in "such a very unfavorable condition" before delivery and feared puerperal fever, after the birth Varina reported her most "comfortable confinement." Yet her physical improvement was paralleled by an emotional decline after a disagreement between her and Jefferson over the baby's name. Varina had planned to name him William Howell Davis for her father. Jefferson had a different intention, however, and he made a decision diametrically opposed to his wife's wishes. The child was named Joseph Evan Davis, in honor of his uncle, Jefferson's surrogate father and Varina's nemesis. Even though Varina said Jefferson had the right to make the decision, his doing so greatly upset her. Distraught, she cried to her mother that she had wept herself so sick she had to take quinine. She confided she could not participate in paying "the highest compliment in a woman's power to a man whose very name was only suggestive to me of injustice and unkindness from my youth up to middle age." She expressed unhappiness that the infant looked like a Davis. She prayed he would outgrow the resemblance, and if not, she assured herself, it would be solely an external likeness, "unless Howell & Kempe blood has run out."[59]

Joseph Davis, c. 1859.
Special Collections, Howard-Tilton Memorial Library, Tulane University

The iron emotional triangle of the Davis family endured unbroken and unbending. Varina had no use for Joseph, letting him know how she felt in word and deed. When Joseph had tried to give her money to buy "a fine dress" for Buchanan's inaugural, she refused, in spite of his saying he had only the "kindest" affections for her and loved her like a father. Passing through Washington in 1859 on his way to Europe, Joseph offered to defray all expenses for Varina, her three children, and a nurse to accompany him and his family. He told her that he believed she would be "an agreeable traveling companion to talk about all we saw there." Again, she turned him down.[60]

Two years later, in a private conversation with her, Joseph discussed their "estrangements." According to Varina, Joseph said the naming of little Joseph after him had "obliterated" all memories of ill feelings between them. Varina responded that the naming was Jefferson's choice, not hers, and she had given in. Then she informed Joseph she knew how much Jefferson loved him, and she granted she would teach her children to respect him for the assistance he had given their father at "the outset of life." But, as for herself, "I owe you nothing, & perfectly appreciate your hostility to me." Continued discussion produced no reconciliation.[61]

Since the fall of 1846 Jefferson Davis had been navigating the treacherous shoals separating the two people he cherished most. Seeming to side with one or honoring the other generated a ferocious reaction from brother or wife, each perceiving disfavor. During those years he had discovered no formula that would temper the rigid triangle.

In the late 1850s, Jefferson Davis confronted a political world as thorny and treacherous as the relationship between his wife and his sole living brother. The continued success of the Republican party deeply troubled him because of his understanding of its self-proclaimed mission, disregarding the constitutional rights of southerners as Americans and destroying the southern social system. He continuously attacked Republicans for what he judged their unthinking hostility to the South and southern institutions. The Republicans' "greatest evil" had already occurred—"the perversion of the Northern mind and . . . the alienation of the Northern people, from the fraternity due to the South."[62]

Republican leaders talking about a higher law and an irrepressible conflict greatly distressed him. In response, he emphasized that a written Constitution formed the law for Americans, which he defined as "the plighted faith of our fathers" and "the hope of our posterity." To Davis, references to a higher law were irresponsible and fraught with danger. In the Senate, he identified the first advocate of a higher law as "the tempter" in the Garden of Eden, who led mankind down the road of sin and to the loss of liberty and happiness, all the way to death. As for an irrepressible conflict, he simply could not detect one. The North and the South with their different labor systems had lived together for generations. From an economic viewpoint, he maintained that the agricultural South and the manufacturing North complemented each other, each contributing to the growth and development of the entire country. As for attitudes toward labor, he rejected Republican assertions that slavery belittled labor. His version was quite different. In the South whites outnumbered blacks; most whites worked and were not at all "degraded" by labor. On the contrary, slavery exalted all whites including those who worked: "Nowhere else will you find every white man recognized so far as an equal as never to be excluded from any man's house or any man's table."[63]

Davis also denied the South had any aggressive intentions; instead, he labeled the Republicans as aggressors. He could discern no aggression in the demand of southerners for their constitutional rights. Rather, Republicans aggressively assaulted even the Americanism of southerners. Davis saw a concrete and dangerous manifestation of Republican belligerence in a notable incident of October 1859. On the sixteenth of that month, the avenging angel of abolition, John Brown, a bloody veteran of Bleeding Kansas, hurled his fury and twenty-two followers against slavery at Harpers Ferry, Virginia. Brown's hope to spark a slave uprising failed utterly. No slaves rose; he and his men were trapped in the town. Two days later it was over; ten of Brown's men were dead or dying, and seven were captured, including Brown himself. Although major Republican leaders repudiated Brown's violent tactics, a notable group of respectable northerners had financed his venture. And John Brown became a folk hero in the antislavery North. In the Senate, Davis condemned what he called "a murderous raid" and "a conspiracy against a portion of the United States, a rebellion against the constitutional government of a State." He supported the creation of an investigating committee, and as a committee member took an active role in the Senate's inquiry.[64]

The possibility of a Republican victory in the 1860 presidential election presented a vexing personal and political dilemma to Davis. He did not want the failure of the Union, which he considered "the grandest achievement of uninspired human intellect to be found in the records of time." "Young as a nation," he proudly told his fellow senators, "our triumphs under this system have had no parallel in human history." To Mississippi Democrats he enunciated his confidence "that a sanguine temperament does not mislead me to the belief that the mists of sectional prejudice are steadily though slowly floating away and . . . promises to our country a happier day than this." Still, he worried that if victorious, the Republicans might actually destroy the constitutional Union he cherished, and if so, he wanted no part of the country, for it would no longer be his conception of the Union created by the Founding Fathers.[65]

In Mississippi extreme sectionalists or fire-eaters, with Albert Brown in the lead, clamored for prompt secession if the Republicans won, and they had a receptive audience. Commenting favorably on Brown's fire-eating speeches, the *Mississippian* prophesied that disunion would greatly benefit the South. The state Democratic convention of 1859 resolved unanimously that the state would regard the election of a Republican as "a declaration of hostility," requiring Mississippi to be prepared for any eventuality. Senator Davis could disregard these sentiments only at his personal political peril.[66]

On the stump in Mississippi, Davis could at times match the rhetoric of any fire-eater. To the state Democratic convention, he announced that a Republican victory would mean "the despotism of a majority," and Mississippians would have to decide if "you will become the subjects of a hostile government." Seven months earlier in Vicksburg he had proclaimed that should an abolitionist be chosen president, he "would rather appeal to the God of Battles at once than attempt to live longer in such a Union." To a Jackson audience late in 1859 he vowed that even if Mississippi seceded alone, "he would 'hug her to his heart.' " He also urged preparation for potential separation, and even conflict. Work should be pushed on a railroad to connect Jackson with the Gulf Coast, a project Davis had long supported and believed crucial for the state's economic development. He wanted volunteer companies raised, arms and ammunition stockpiled. But he always placed caveats alongside those declarations and pledges. He would substitute "abolitionist" for "Republican." He would specify the Republican's being elected on a particular platform, for example, endorsement of the higher-law doctrine. He held to what he had earlier said, that he was equally opposed to "slavish submission" and to "the brainless intemperance of those who desired a dissolution of the Union, and who found in every rustling leaf fresh evidence of volcanic eruption."[67]

On the floor of the Senate he was always careful. Professing his loyalty to his country, he stated in the winter of 1858, "I think I have given evidence in every form in which patriotism is ever subjected to a test." He also denied having ever announced that the election of a Republican president would mean dissolution of the Union. He insisted that only if any individual became president "not to administer [the government] according to the Constitution, but to pervert it to our destruction, to make this Government one of hostility to us, we would with the right hand redress our wrongs." Thus, according to his script, the fate of the Union rested in the hands of the Republicans, especially their platform writers and their candidate. Senator Davis balanced along an extraordinarily thin tightrope.[68]

The Republican party did not present Davis with his only political difficulties. On both the state and the national level, confusion ruled within his own Democratic party, burdening him with concerns and hazardous challenges. Pressure from the sectional left in Mississippi did not end with the question of secession. Albert Brown spoke out forcefully on filibustering; to applause he advocated governmental backing for offensive campaigns in Mexico, Central America, and the Caribbean. He also said Congress must enact a law to protect the rights of slaveowners in the territories, especially in Kansas. In the Lower South, including Mississippi, there was also agitation to reopen the international slave trade, prohibited by Congress since 1808, though Brown did not push this issue.[69]

Senator Davis met both. Although he embraced neither, he carefully tailored his responses to retain his political base in Mississippi. From the public platform, he denounced filibustering, but repeated his support for an American Cuba. He predicted that in time the United States would acquire the island through purchase. When he steadfastly opposed reopening the international slave trade, he emphasized states' rights, arguing that the states, not the federal government, knew best their own interests regarding slaves. Asserting that Mississippi had access to all the slaves it wanted, he was confident the state did not want the trade renewed, though he would not speak for other states. Davis made absolutely clear that his opposition did not rest on moral grounds. On the contrary, he said the trade had a powerful moral impact, bringing heathen Africans in touch with Christianity. To his constituents his positions rang true; the *Mississippian* praised "the correctness" of his stance.[70]

The territorial issue did not only stir up Democrats in Mississippi, it also sparked the turbulence roiling the national Democratic party. The breach between the Buchanan administration and southerners on the one hand and Senator Stephen Douglas on the other widened after the senator won reelection by narrowly turning back a vigorous Republican challenger named Abraham Lincoln. In the 1858 contest the territorial question was central. Lincoln spoke for the traditional Republican doctrine of free soil. He and his party still maintained that Congress should exercise its constitutional authority to prohibit slavery in all territories, even though the Supreme Court in its *Dred Scott* ruling denied that Congress had power to exclude slavery from any territory. Facing a powerful and popular Republican onslaught, Douglas knew he could not stand naked on *Dred Scott* and survive politically, despite his oft-repeated declaration that he would abide by the Court's ruling. Ever inventive, he found a way around *Dred Scott,* while continuing to claim that he backed the Court and its decision. In what became known as the Freeport Doctrine, Douglas argued that despite *Dred Scott,* slavery could not survive unless local law supported it; *Dred Scott* would have no impact in a territory unless the territorial legislature enacted statutes affirming it. Douglas insisted that he was here simply holding to a policy he had long espoused: popular sovereignty.[71]

The southern Democrats condemned the Freeport Doctrine, derisively terming it "squatter sovereignty." In the southern view, the Supreme Court had settled the matter, and Douglas, who for years had said he would abide by the rulings of the Court, should abide by his own promise. Their fight disrupted the party in Congress. At the opening of the first session of the Thirty-sixth Congress, party schism prevented the election of a Democratic speaker of the House. Although the House was closely divided, with Republicans having a plurality, Democrats and American party members, mostly from the South, could combine to command a majority. But the Democrats could not unite among themselves, much less with the Americans. For two months congressmen wrangled while the House remained unorganized. Not until February 3, 1860, when the Republicans put forward one of their most conservative men, one who had even supported the Fugitive Slave Law, was a speaker selected. Democratic division also appeared in the Senate, but with the party holding a safe majority and the southerners dominant, Douglas was the immediate loser. To show their displeasure at what they considered his apostasy, the southerners and the administration loyalists stripped him of his chairmanship of the Committee on Territories.

On the Senate floor Davis flayed Douglas as "full of heresy" for Freeport, and he certainly supported removal of Douglas from his chairmanship. At the same time, he said he did not attack Douglas as a Democrat, nor did he feel "personal animosity" toward the Illinois senator, for whom he had "a great many kind remembrances" of the many years they had worked together. Davis even offered to turn over his Committee on Military Affairs to Douglas—an offer other chairmen also made. Douglas refused all. Both he and his antagonists recognized the powerful symbolism of depriving him of the post he wanted, a position equated with national development and territorial policy. Hounded in the Senate, the Illinois senator looked to 1860, when, he had grounds for believing, his popularity in the free states would bring him the Democratic presidential nomination, and vindication. Although Davis and Douglas injected levity into their oral jousting, both claiming to be no more than members of their party's "rank and file," each man realized, as did their colleagues, that a menacing fissure still ran through their party.[72]

The administration and the southern Democrats, with Davis in the forefront, wanted to close that rift on their terms. Their method was to provide the party with a territorial policy that Douglas could not accept without a shameful recantation. When Davis rose in the Senate on February 2, 1860, to present a series of resolutions, he acted for himself, but also for his wing of the party, which wanted to ensure its unity on vexing territorial questions. The Democrats discussed the proposals, and on March 1, Davis substituted a modified set, though it had no substantive alterations. There were seven resolutions. Five of them concentrated on reaffirming traditional southern and Democratic views on the Constitution and slavery, the equality of all citizens, the correctness of fugitive slave legislation, and the right of territories to choose or reject slavery when they applied for statehood. The fourth and the fifth were the controversial ones. The former echoed the *Dred Scott* decision, declaring that neither Congress nor a territorial legislature could prohibit slavery in any territory. The latter, and most critical, stipulated: "That if experience at any time prove that the judiciary and executive authority do not possess means to insure adequate protection to constitutional rights in a Territory, and if the territorial government shall fail or refuse to provide the necessary remedies for that purpose it will be the duty of Congress to supply such deficiency."

These resolutions had been approved by President Buchanan and an overwhelming majority of Democratic senators. The Democratic caucus of the Senate had even gone on record favoring them, with two notable exceptions: Stephen Douglas rightly saw them as an assault on his presidential ambitions, and Albert Brown recognized they effectively undermined his own bill mandating congressional action to protect slavery in the territories. Although the resolutions commanded a clear Senate majority, no vote on them occurred before the Democratic National Convention, which opened on April 23. Finally, in late May, the Senate passed them with one change, a specification that under number five, no conditions existed calling for action. According to Davis, that stipulation had no practical value, but it gained northern votes.[73]

Although the partisan political motives underlying Davis's resolutions have been clearly understood, their actual content and their fundamental intent have usually been misunderstood. All Republicans, Douglas and his band, and most historians have said Davis called for a federal slave code for the territories, that he wanted Congress to pass legislation guaranteeing the right of slave property in all territories just as state codes guaranteed the right of slave property in the slave states. That is precisely what Albert Brown proposed; but not Jefferson Davis.[74]

In his resolutions Davis repeated his long-held premise that the territories belonged to all citizens and so all could take their legal property into the federal domain. But Davis had no interest in forcing slavery into any territory, a point he made in a Maine speech. To a Democratic rally in Portland he stated that if the inhabitants of a territory refused to adopt "police regulations" for the protection of property, "it would be rendered more or less valueless." Referring specifically to slave property, Davis continued, "the insecurity would be so great that the owner could not ordinarily retain it." Thus, the right to own slaves would remain, but "the remedy withheld, it would follow that the owner would be practically debarred by the circumstances of the case, from taking slave property into a territory where the sense of the inhabitants was opposed to its introduction." Davis gave his final assessment: "So much for the oft repeated fallacy of forcing slavery upon any community." As an editor in Mississippi noted, this position seemed closely parallel to the Freeport Doctrine. Both Davis and Douglas maintained that unless a territory actively protected slavery, slaveowners would not enter. But Davis still upheld his constitutional position, confirmed by *Dred Scott*, that slaveowners possessed a basic constitutional right.[75]

Davis's goal in the Senate was to get a statement of principle, not a specific statute. To an Alabama congressman he made clear his intent: "Our right is equality and the duty of the general government is to give adequate protection to every constitutional right which was placed under its care." If existing laws provided "adequate protection," Davis believed it "unwise" to request additional legislation "under the apprehension that they might not hereafter be effectual." Besides, he reminded his correspondent, "there is danger of over action by our friends." Analyzing the political forces involved, Davis made a shrewd observation: "As the smaller of the contending armies it behooves us carefully to reconnoiter ground before we advance to occupy it." In the Senate, Davis maintained that *Dred Scott* provided the South with the required protection. As a result, Congress would not have to act until experience demonstrated that the executive and judiciary had trampled upon the rights of slaveowners. In making his case, he rejected Brown's arguments that in Kansas these rights had already been violated.[76]

Davis did not believe the South could obtain the kind of legislation Brown proposed; more important, he did not think it necessary, or even desirable. He had been convinced that in addition to *Dred Scott*, common-law property rights would protect slaveowners in any territorial judicial proceeding. He also confided to a friend that he and many of his colleagues knew the Supreme Court of Kansas would declare unconstitutional any antislavery law passed by the territorial legislature. Davis kept saying he wanted no factual case brought forward or discussed, but only a statement of basic principles.[77]

He hoped his design could build a bridge over the chasm dividing northern and southern Democrats on the territorial question. But he had no intention of constructing a span wide enough to accommodate Douglas, unless Douglas came to him. Without question, his bringing up the resolutions in the winter of 1860 just weeks before the party's national convention was not accidental. Even so, despite his best efforts, he never succeeded in getting his position denoted as moderate by a majority of northern Democrats.

Davis, Douglas, and other senators now debated in a new chamber. On January 4, 1859, the Senate as a body had marched from its old quarters into the new northern wing of the Capitol, part of the building's expansion that Secretary of War Davis had overseen. Two years earlier the House had moved to its new home at the opposite end of the Capitol. The Senate's much-larger rectangular chamber was over 113 feet long and more than 80 feet wide, with 36 feet to a ceiling highlighted with intricately designed glass and iron skylights. Modern gas lighting illuminated the room; gold arabesques decorated its walls. The vice president's elevated chair occupied the center of the northern wall; the galleries above seated almost 700 people, one for ladies and gentlemen, another for gentlemen only, and a third for press. Facing the vice president's dais, the senators' desks, which had been brought from the old chamber, were arranged in a semicircle with an aisle dividing them. Davis sat on the vice president's right in the middle of the second row, amid several other southerners, with Douglas only three desks away.[78]

During 1859 and 1860 in the Senate, Davis did not spend his time solely on the territorial question, though it was certainly the most important item of business. Military matters also occupied his attention. Always defending appropriations for the army, he fended off senators who wanted severe retrenchment. He also chided lawmakers for their penchant for creating new posts but providing insufficient funds to garrison them adequately. Basically, Davis fought a largely successful action to retain the gains he thought the army had made during the Pierce administration. He also continued his vigorous support for a transcontinental railroad, built with federal assistance. As before, he struggled against his strict-constructionist associates, who did not think the federal government should aid railroads. Again, Davis based his contention on requirements for defense and federal ownership of the territories. To avoid the problems of selecting a route, he suggested authorizing private companies to present plans for construction; he argued that they would make decisions on the best way west on engineering and commercial bases, not politics. Then, accepting the best proposal, the government could provide alternate sections of land in the territories and advance as much as $10 million, to be repaid from the railroad's profits. He did not succeed.[79]

Davis never forgot Mississippi. He sent government documents such as Patent Office reports and volumes from the Pacific railroad survey to his constituents. He was active in filling a federal attorney's slot; the appointment of local postmasters received his careful attention. He tried to help a Woodville man obtain a reexamination of his patent application for cotton gin improvements, and he intervened with the secretary of war for a West Point cadet charged with drunkenness. A ledger he used illustrates the care he gave to his political base. Containing more than 400 pages with about 80 percent filled, the volume begins with a catalogue of Mississippi's newspapers by town and county. There is also a roll of correspondents, individual and institutional, again by town and county, with an alphabetically arranged table of contents.[80]

In the midst of Davis's normal senatorial duties and the consideration of momentous national problems, private matters intruded into the public arena. Despite serious political and ideological differences, Davis usually remained on good terms with his senatorial colleagues, at least in public. Even with their competitiveness in Mississippi and Brown's dislike for him, he and Brown did not openly reveal personal animosity. In 1857 Davis willingly agreed to let a group of mutual friends reconcile him and Senator Robert Toombs of Georgia, over differences stemming from old Unionist–State Rights charges. But on June 8, 1858, a situation arose suddenly that could have ended in disaster.[81]

During Senate consideration of the army appropriations bill, the Finance Committee proposed to strike a provision providing $100,000 for breech-loading guns. In the ensuing debate sharp words passed between Davis and Judah P. Benjamin of Louisiana. The two men disagreed over whether the secretary of war had requested the money to buy new weapons or to rework old ones. Benjamin accused Davis of making "a sneering reply"; Davis responded that if Benjamin found it "disagreeable, I hope he will keep it to himself." Benjamin riposted, "When directed to me, I will not keep it to myself; I will repel it *instanter.*" Davis snapped, "You have got it, sir." Some evidence suggests that the *Congressional Globe* purposefully omitted Davis's most offensive remark: he had "no idea that he was to be met with arguments of a paid attorney in the Senate chamber." When Benjamin asked if he had heard correctly, Davis affirmed that he had.

Thereupon a duel seemed imminent. Almost immediately Benjamin sent Davis a challenge. When Davis read it in the Senate cloakroom, he realized he had stepped across a boundary. Promptly tearing up the note, he informed a colleague, "I will make this all right at once. I have been wholly wrong." On the floor of the Senate, he publicly expressed regret: "I cannot gainsay . . . that my manner implied more than my heart meant." To his fellow senators Davis confessed, "I always feel pained, nay, more . . . when I am involved in a personal controversy with anybody." Admitting that he became angry and had "intended to be offensive," and acknowledging that when he stated a conviction he could seem "dogmatic and dictatorial," Davis apologized to the Senate and to Benjamin, toward whom he felt "kindness and respect," for his unacceptable display of emotion. Thanking Davis, Benjamin said admiration and esteem still characterized his feelings toward the Mississippian. The incident was over.[82]

Even though Davis had recovered from the serious illness that had prostrated him in the spring of 1858, physical and emotional stress maintained a tenacious grip. That the Benjamin incident took place soon after his return to the Senate following the lengthy, painful struggle for his eye is probably not accidental. Not only did his eye keep bothering him into 1859, but Davis also reported other maladies, chiefly facial neuralgia, probably deriving from his eye illness. In 1859, he even consulted with a prominent British physician who was visiting Washington.[83]

A reporter who observed him in the Senate in May 1860 penned a vivid word picture. Initially struck by "the face of a corpse, the form of a skeleton," he urged: "Look at the haggard, sunken weary eye—the thin white wrinkled lips clasped close upon the teeth in anguish. That is the mouth of a brave but impatient sufferer. See the ghostly white, hollow, bitterly puckered cheek, the high, sharp cheek bone, the pale brow full of fine wrinkles, the grizzly hair, prematurely gray."[84]

Indeed, photographs from the time depict a face showing great strain. One taken for McMlees' Gallery portrays a haggard visage that had changed dramatically in five years. Davis's hair and the fringe beard he had just started have become permeated with gray. The new beard, along with thin lips pressed tight, elongate his angular face. The pale eyes peer far off and away from the camera as he tries to mask the affected left one. Even though the famous Mathew Brady photograph from 1860 presents a well-groomed and composed man, the worn, tension-filled face reveals the scars of ravaging physical illness and enormous emotional pressure. Despite the obvious pain and strain, Davis did not turn from the unprecedented challenges facing him, his party, and his country. His determination and willpower continued to propel him. His wife understood when she wrote: "his mind dominated his body in so great a degree that he was able to endure nearly what he pleased."[85]

Jefferson Davis believed the presidential election of 1860 would be absolutely critical, a conviction shared by most southerners and many northerners. Its momentousness derived from the potential triumph of the Republican party, which sustained its unrelenting ideological and political onslaught on the South. But Davis was also aware that danger lurked in waters plied only by Democrats. The same division over the territorial issue and chiefly between the southerners and Douglas that had plagued the party since Lecompton remained deep.

The Democrats confronted two massive obstacles: a platform and a candidate. Most southerners demanded a platform containing at least Davis's resolutions on the explosive territorial issue. The Alabama Democratic convention had even instructed its delegation to the national convention to bolt unless such a platform was adopted. Calling such provisions a slave code for the territories, a substantial number of northerners rejected it. At the same time, a majority of northerners supported the candidacy of Stephen A. Douglas, who would command the allegiance of more than half the delegates. But, according to Democratic rules, nomination required a two-thirds vote of the convention. With southerners, including Davis, resolved to deny Douglas the presidential nod, he had practically no chance of amassing the necessary two-thirds. Thus, a successful convention would necessitate compromise on both platform and candidate. Northerners and southerners alike would have to step back, giving way on both Davis's resolutions and Douglas's candidacy. Unless such an outcome could be arranged, the party faced cataclysm.[86]

Although Davis did not underestimate the political obstacles endangering his side, he thought it could surmount them. He envisioned the track for victory in a reprise of Zachary Taylor's 1848 campaign. The Democrats needed a man "recognized in both sections as true exponent of their opinions." Because in the national convention the territorial question would generate "a hazardous controversy" that Davis could conceive no way to avoid, he wanted no platform adopted. He believed the nominee would have to be a northerner, for to gain sufficient northern backing any southerner would have to make too many dangerous compromises. He had already picked out his ideal choice: Franklin Pierce. Most important, according to Davis, Pierce met two essential requirements; no one else could save the party from "a controversy as to 'the platform,' " and he could win. Moreover, Davis liked Pierce, who he believed would protect southern rights as defined by the Supreme Court and interpreted in his resolutions. He could also expect to exercise considerable influence himself in a second Pierce administration. Davis counseled an obviously interested Pierce, advised him to remain above the fray, and refused to meet his friend in New York City out of fear that personal contact would tarnish Pierce with his southern identity. Davis's efforts were not secret, for the Douglas camp was aware of the pro-Pierce activity.[87]

Davis kept to this course despite considerable talk about his trying for the nomination. In 1859 the Mississippi Democratic convention by a five-to-one margin voted to recommend him for the presidency to the national convention. From New England came positive soundings about his "qualities of mind and character," including one from a notable Massachusetts Democrat who would soon become notorious in the South, Benjamin F. Butler. Davis's own choice, Franklin Pierce, reported that Davis was "rapidly gaining ground" in Pierce's home area. Among southern politicians, he stood high on the list of favored potential candidates. These notices made heady news for a man as ambitious as Davis. A fellow senator, albeit a critical one, wrote: "Jefferson Davis is burning up with ambition and . . . What Jeff will do if not nominated *God* only knows." Davis's career to 1860 gives every reason to accept Andrew Johnson's opinion on the matter of ambition, but this time Davis was absolutely convinced that everyone, himself included, had to put aside personal goals for the sake of the party, which, to Davis at this point, meant the country. As a result, he spurned all overtures and parried all attempts to push his name. He feared "a division of the Democracy must be a forerunner of a division of the States."[88]

On April 23, 1860, the Democrats gathered for their quadrennial assembly in Charleston, South Carolina, the citadel of southern fire-eating and an incredibly inopportune site for judicious deliberations and reconciliation. Before Charleston, Davis met in Washington with former cabinet associate Caleb Cushing, who supported the basic southern position and who would be named presiding officer of the convention. Davis also sent an emissary to Charleston, urging his friends, especially in the Mississippi delegation, to recognize their most important task as stopping Douglas, not writing a particular platform. A group of southern congressional leaders went to Charleston, while others, including Davis, maintained telegraphic contact.[89]

The convention paid no heed to Davis's wishes or the efforts of congressional managers on the scene. Before considering nominations, it took up the platform, making an early casualty of Davis's hope for no such document. Attempting to force its will on the party and on Douglas, the anti-Douglas combine with southerners in the vanguard demanded a platform embodying Davis's resolutions on slavery and the territories. In the atmosphere of strident southernism pervading Charleston, the southern offensive received public cheers. Yet the Douglas forces refused to break, or even to bend. When the platform committee endorsed the southern position (because in it each state had one vote, and the southern-administration alliance controlled a majority of states), the Douglasites prepared a minority report stating that all matters involving slavery in the territories and the duty of Congress should be left to the Supreme Court. On the floor, with voting by individuals rather than by states, the minority version prevailed by a narrow margin. At the announcement of the result, Alabama led delegations from the Deep South out of the hall.

The bolters did not go far. They set up nearby, adopted the rejected majority platform, but made no nominations. They acted as if they wanted to rejoin the convention, but attempts to pull all back together failed. Sensing their opportunity, the Douglas camp rushed to get the much-desired nomination for their man. Chairman Cushing foiled them, however, by ruling that two-thirds of the original number of votes were still required for nomination. When the convention upheld Cushing, Douglas's chances slipped. Although delegates cast fifty-seven ballots, Douglas never reached two-thirds of those still in their seats, much less two-thirds of the original delegates. Finally, recognizing they could not reach their goal, his supporters adjourned on the tenth day of the convention to meet once more in Baltimore on June 18. In similar manner, the bolting delegations, which had not only lost on the platform but also failed to force the choice of a compromise candidate, decided to come back together on June 11 at Richmond, Virginia. Although most bolters were southern, they called themselves National Democrats.

This crushing outcome did not kill Davis's hopes. He did not even lash out at the Mississippi delegation for not heeding his advice. Aware of popular sentiment back in his home state, on the floor of the Senate he commended the delegates for asserting their state's "equality of right." At the same time, he exerted every effort to get the convention back together. He conferred with Cushing upon the latter's return to Washington. In addition, he joined with eighteen other southern members of Congress in a public letter urging the eight bolting delegations to postpone the Richmond meeting until after Baltimore. All the delegates should appear in Baltimore, the missive said, rejoin the convention, and work to gain approval for a satisfactory platform and a strong nominee. The lawmakers argued that a reunited convention could thus hold together "our party, the sole conservative organization remaining in the country." In mid-June, still pressing his friends to make "an honest effort" to save the party, Davis unrealistically clung to Pierce but worried that southerners could not agree on any single candidate. But even more troubling were signs that the northern majority would insist on Douglas and, as he feared, destroy the party. Yet Davis did not want to give up. To Pierce he wrote, "The darkest hour precedes the dawn and it may be that light will break upon us when most needed & least expected."[90]

But for Jefferson Davis darkness descended. In Baltimore the Democratic party failed to mend itself. The Douglas forces stood fast, even turning away some of the seceding delegations in favor of hastily chosen replacements favoring the Illinoisan. The disarray within the

party turned into public dismemberment when each of the two dominant groups in the aborted convention called itself the Democratic
party. For the first time since its creation, the Democratic party could
settle upon neither a standard-bearer nor a platform. The Douglas loyalists hung on, giving their nomination to their hero, while the break-
away southerners chose John C. Breckinridge of Kentucky, vice
president of the United States. By 1860 standards Breckinridge was a
sectional moderate, but he was a staunch southerner. The Democratic
party stumbled out of Baltimore, reeling from the political wreck that
had split it asunder.

Even before the fracturing of the Democracy, the centrifugal forces
tearing American politics led to the entry of another group in the presidential field, chiefly in the South. This new entrant called itself the
Constitutional Union party, though it was more accurately an ad hoc
reaction to particular circumstances rather than a party. The almost
simultaneous occurrence of Democratic disruption, the Republican
threat, and the presidential election coalesced non-Democrats into a
unit. Almost all Constitutional Unionists had been conservative
Whigs, and many had shared the brief life of the Know-Nothing party.
Calling for patriotism and forbearance as the watchwords of all Americans, they cried for all to stand on the Constitution. Their nominations
went to old-line Whigs, John Bell of Tennessee for president and
Edward Everett of Massachusetts for vice president. At best, theirs was
a desperate exercise.

In the midst of this political splintering, Jefferson Davis had no
doubt about his path. He vigorously supported the ticket of Breckinridge and Senator Joseph Lane of Oregon. In a public letter sent to
Mississippi, he admitted his distress about the division of the party but
said Democrats should congratulate themselves that they had "enough
of vitality to bear amputation, and adhering to fundamental principles, to give us good candidates on a good platform." Addressing a
ratification meeting in Washington just after the nominations, Davis
praised them as based on the Constitution, fraternity, and states'
rights. Before another gathering in the capital, he condemned the
Douglas party as "the spurious and decayed off-shoot of democracy,"
while he praised the Breckinridge party as "the cause of our common
country." He also served on the National Executive Committee
formed in Washington. As an experienced national politician, Davis
knew a divided Democratic party faced mortal danger in the presidential contest. As a result, he became a leader in the attempt to arrange a

truce that would involve combining the forces of Bell, Breckinridge, and Douglas, with each man stepping aside for a new choice around whom all anti-Republicans could rally. According to Davis, Bell and Breckinridge agreed, but Douglas refused. As a political professional, Davis could have little doubt what the failure of combination meant. Breckinridge himself told Varina, "I trust I have the courage to lead a forlorn hope."[91]

The election that placed four candidates before the voters was not at all what Jefferson Davis wanted. His goal had been a united Democratic party facing the leading Republican, Senator William Henry Seward, who had popularized two key Republican phrases, "the higher law" and "the irrepressible conflict," even while becoming Davis's friend. Davis believed a concentrated Democracy could defeat Seward and put the Republicans to flight. But the autumn of 1860 found his beloved Democracy severely wounded, and with the advent of the Constitutional Unionists he knew the Democrats could not even count on sweeping the Upper South and the border states. Worst of all to Davis, the energetic and enthusiastic Republicans presented a solid front behind their candidate. While the Democrats had not been able to get past the controversial Douglas to a unifying man, the Republicans had spurned the highly visible Seward for someone they perceived as more electable, Abraham Lincoln of Illinois, a man Davis did not know at all.[92]

Despite his undoubted disappointment and apprehension, in September Davis headed for Mississippi to campaign, leaving Varina and the children behind. In the fall of 1860 Mississippi was one giant political carnival: barbecues, torchlight processions, fireworks, flag presentations, and speechmaking pervaded the state. A galaxy of public figures, congressmen, the governor, former governor, even Henry Foote, who returned in a futile effort for Douglas, joined Albert Brown and Davis in courting the voters. "Wielding the battle axe of Richard," as a friendly editor characterized him, one more time Jefferson Davis traveled the roads and spoke from rostrums throughout the critical central and northern counties, in so many familiar towns and villages—Jackson, Oxford, Holly Springs, Corinth, Columbus, Enterprise, Benton, and Vicksburg. His tour included a rally just across the state line in Memphis, where he spoke for two hours. For places he could not reach, he prepared public letters. For six weeks, from September 21 until election eve in early November, he knew little rest from his political labors.[93]

Davis delivered a clear message, though on one crucial point—the question of secession—he equivocated. He made clear that he considered Breckinridge the strongest spokesman for southern interests, and the best hope to maintain his vision of the constitutional Union. Besides praising the Breckinridge campaign, Davis concentrated on attacking the Republicans, paying but little attention to either Douglas or the Constitutional Unionists. In his words, a Republican victory would present southerners with "a very bad and disagreeable Union." Any southern man who would either live under or accept office from a Republican administration would immerse himself in "self-disgrace and self-degradation."[94]

Across the state Democratic speakers cried that a Republican victory would mean the secession of Mississippi. Few could doubt the claim of the editor of the *Mississippian* that 99 percent of Breckinridge's supporters favored secession if Lincoln were elected. When handed a written question asking whether secession would be justified upon Lincoln's election, Davis answered yes, but. He responded that he had really been asked whether he believed Lincoln a Black Republican, because he felt bound by resolutions of the legislature and the Democratic state convention. These declared that in the event of a Black Republican's victory, "on the avowed purposes of that organization," Mississippi would discern a hostile act and be prepared to cooperate with other southern states in whatever fashion required. Davis hastened to add that the declaration did not necessarily mean secession would be the remedy decided upon, but it did mean at least the possibility of secession. Once more, he repeated his conviction that anyone who denied the right of any state "to judge in the last resort of its wrongs and the remedies to be applied, repudiated the Democratic creed, and reject[ed] every common sense idea of State sovereignty."[95]

After a month and a half of traveling through much of the state and talking with voters, Davis certainly had a sense of his constituents' attitude. In Vicksburg just before the election, he moved ever closer to the shouts resounding through the state:

If Mississippi in her sovereign capacity decides to submit to the rule of an arrogant and sectional North, then I will sit me down as one upon whose brow the brand infamy and degradation has been written, and bear my portion of the bitter trial. But, if on the other hand, Mississippi decides to resist the hands that would tarnish her star on the National Flag, then I will come at your bidding, whether by day or by night, and pluck that star from the galaxy, and place it upon a banner of its own. I will plant it upon the crest of battle, and gathering around me Mississippi's best and bravest, will welcome the invader to the harvest of death; and future generations will point to a small hillock upon our border, which will tell the reception with which the invader met upon our soil.[96]

Finally, the fateful day arrived. In Mississippi, Breckinridge received 59 percent of the popular vote, sweeping the state except in the southwestern river counties, the old Whig stronghold, where Bell did well. Bell wound up with 36 percent and Douglas a dismal 5 percent. But the country did not go as Mississippi did. The news flashed across the land that Abraham Lincoln had been elected president. By carrying every free state but New Jersey, which he divided with Douglas, Lincoln amassed 173 electoral votes, a clear majority. Yet he garnered but a minority of the popular vote; just 40 percent of American voters cast their ballots for him, and practically none in the slave states. His name was not even on the ballot in ten of them. Suddenly, talk about what to do if a Republican were elected moved from the theoretical to the practical.

Lincoln's election prompted a flurry of activity in the southern states. Public discussion weighed various courses of action, while governors summoned legislatures and legislatures called for elections to choose delegates to state conventions to determine state action, if any. In Mississippi, Governor John J. Pettus prepared his message to a special legislative session that would convene on November 26. Jefferson Davis, who during the campaign had not insisted on immediate secession in case of a Republican victory, was at Brierfield for a brief respite before returning to Washington for the opening of Congress.[97]

From Brierfield on November 10, he made his first important statement on how the South should meet the long-feared election of a Republican president. Responding to a request for his views from Robert Barnwell Rhett, Jr., editor of the leading fire-eater journal the *Charleston Mercury,* Davis urged caution. In an obvious attempt not to fuel Rhett's eagerness to dissolve the Union, Davis said he knew nothing of the public mood in his state, even though he had just spent six weeks mingling with voters. He told Rhett that he saw no reason to rush ahead; moreover, he doubted whether the Mississippi legislature would call for a state convention or even appoint delegates to a possible southern convention. To Davis all the planting states shared a "common interest of such magnitude" that they would eventually act in unison for protection, but only after they consulted together. In his judgment South Carolina should not secede alone. Secession should not take place before the slave states had been able to cooperate in a common venture. Apologizing for his inability to "give more precise information," Davis closed by assuring Rhett he had given his confidential opinion.[98]

Davis carried this cautious approach to Jackson, where he met with the governor and other members of the congressional delegation. Governor Pettus had asked the congressmen and senators to confer with him about his recommendation to the special session of the legislature. All but one congressman attended. After considerable deliberation, a proposal was made to advocate immediate secession. The governor and a majority of the delegation favored that policy; but not Davis. He opposed secession as long as any hope remained for a peaceful settlement of the sectional dispute. During the conference, Davis received a telegram from two southern members of Buchanan's cabinet appealing for his prompt return to Washington for consultation on the president's message to Congress. He left immediately. Although he departed while deliberation continued, he announced he would abide by whatever decision was made. After his departure, his reluctance to embrace immediate secession caused comment within the group.[99]

Arriving in Washington on November 27, Davis encountered a gloomy atmosphere and one filled with uncertainty. "Men's faces wear a somber and melancholy aspect, and the place has lost its usual pleasantness," wrote one reporter. Davis and other southerners believed they could count on their old personal and political friend President Buchanan standing by them in this crisis. Yet the hurried wire to Davis signaled that Buchanan might not stand so stalwartly as the southerners expected. And an even greater unknown confronted them—the Republican party. With the prospect that their bitter political enemy would take over the executive branch, southerners wanted some glimpse of what policies Republicans intended to follow. Their congressional leader, Senator Seward, had been bypassed for the presidential nomination in favor of Abraham Lincoln, who had not been in Washington since his single term in the House a decade and a half earlier. Few southerners knew him, and none had a clear sense of what he would do or how congressional Republicans would respond to his leadership.[100]

Senator Jefferson Davis entered the second session of the Thirty-sixth Congress as an acknowledged leader, not only of the South in Congress but also in national affairs. *Harper's Weekly* termed him "emphatically 'one of those born to command.' " Northerners on both sides of the partisan aisle recognized him as the most influential southerner. Senator Seward had no doubt about Davis's stature.[101]

Although what Davis hoped for from Congress is quite clear, precisely what he anticipated is murky. He desperately wanted a settlement on terms that would salvage southern rights and honor. And he thought the Republicans had to take the initiative, because it was their continued demand that Congress ban slavery from all territories in spite of the *Dred Scott* decision and their refusal to admit the constitutional equality of the South underlay the crisis. His knowledge of Seward, the Republican he knew best, and their mutual respect gave him reason to think a deal possible between the Republicans and the South. According to Varina, Seward had admitted to her husband and her that many of his utterances were chiefly for political effect. Thus, facing a real crisis like this one, Seward might temper his extreme declarations. Just before Congress began, a knowledgeable observer reported the Republicans would concede "what the South are justly entitled to demand and that thus the Union will be saved."[102]

No record survives of any Davis-Seward conversations during these weeks. Seward did not commit himself until he learned what Lincoln would and would not accept. His most intimate political confidant traveled to Illinois to meet with Lincoln, and Seward absented himself from Washington for some time. What Seward would have done had he been in charge is unknowable, but in the immediate aftermath of the first Republican presidential triumph, he had no intention of breaking with the president-elect. In the end, Seward, like Lincoln, opposed any compromise acceptable to the Deep South.

By the time Congress convened on December 3, hope among the southerners seemed to evaporate. From their point of view, President Buchanan was at best equivocal. He did take the position that the federal government possessed no power to hold the Union together, but he simultaneously denied the constitutionality of secession. He clearly would not be a sturdy champion for the South. On the other side, the Republicans seemed utterly intransigent, giving in on nothing consequential to the South. A pessimistic Davis was quoted as saying, "no human power can save the Union." He even looked with disfavor upon a Mississippi congressman for agreeing to serve on a House committee created to search for a settlement. On December 14 he joined others in signing a statement "To Our Constituents," proclaiming that "the argument is exhausted" because Republicans would grant nothing that "will or ought to satisfy the South." "The honor, safety, and independence" of the South, these solons continued, required secession by each state.[103]

The South was in motion. With no acceptable overture forthcoming from Republicans, with no compromise in sight, legislators and voters in the Deep South put their states on the road to secession. Congressional southerners knew full well the mood in their states. In Davis's state "but one opinion existed," according to a longtime Democratic operative. On December 20, Mississippians voted for delegates to a secession convention scheduled for January 7, 1861. A former congressman still in the state informed Davis that the pressure for immediate secession was "growing every day more intense." Then, also on December 20, South Carolina seceded. As Davis saw it, the Union had cracked, but it was not yet broken.[104]

Still, the forces ripping the Union apart appeared unstoppable. In the Senate on December 10, an almost desperate Davis said that appeals to sentiment would no longer suffice and pleaded for evidence from Republicans that southerners erred when they perceived only hostility. He was eager to see signs of friendship, and ready to trumpet them to the South. Although the Republicans sent Davis no satisfactory signal, the Senate on December 20 did establish a Committee of Thirteen to find a settlement, if possible. When appointed to this committee, Davis declined, saying it was useless; but he was urged to reconsider. On the next day he agreed, "avowing my willingness to make any sacrifice to avert the impending struggle." Even at this late date, he did not concede. A reporter for the *New York Herald* characterized him as "moderate but firm." A hometown newspaper headline read: "Jefferson Davis for Moderation," and a Republican congressman reported his information did not locate Davis among the seceders.[105]

Meeting immediately, the Committee of Thirteen took up as its main order of business the Crittenden Compromise, a series of proposals named after their author, Senator John J. Crittenden of Kentucky. A veteran Whig who had never given up his loyalty to the dead party, and a protégé of Kentucky's most famous political son, Henry Clay, Crittenden attempted to emulate the great compromiser. Although Crittenden's complete package contained ten individual propositions, the critical item recommended restoring the Missouri Compromise line and extending it to the Pacific Ocean, leaving California intact. In order to get around the Supreme Court's declaration that Congress could not prohibit slavery in any territory, Crittenden presented the extension as an amendment to the Constitution. While a longer Missouri Compromise line addressed southern demands for equality, it repudiated the central plank in the Republican platform by permitting the possible extension of slavery.

The Committee of Thirteen would decide the political life or death of the Crittenden Compromise. The membership consisted of Crittenden, who became its leader, though not officially chairman; five Republicans; and seven Democrats, including prominent men like Davis, Douglas, and Seward. At the outset the committee adopted a procedural rule, moved by Davis, that it would take action and report favorably to the full Senate only with the concurrence of both a majority of Republicans and a majority of the other members. From Davis's perspective, any measure without Republican agreement had no meaning at all. From its initial meeting on December 22 until its final gathering six days later, the committee remained totally divided. The Democrats, including Davis and the other Deep South member, Robert Toombs, along with Crittenden, gave their ready assent to the program. Davis was sincere in his willingness to accept Crittenden's plan, a sincerity noted by many witnesses, Crittenden and Douglas included. But the Republicans absolutely refused. Repeatedly, they declined to move at all from their platform declaration against slavery in any territory. Taking a slightly different tack, Davis offered a resolution to amend the Constitution stating that slave property was like all other property and neither Congress nor a territorial legislature could discriminate against it. Again, all Republicans voted no. An exasperated Douglas finally asked the Republicans to spell out what settlement they would accept. Nothing was forthcoming. Recognizing its failure, the committee on December 31 reported to the Senate that it could not agree on the Crittenden Compromise or on any other measure.[106]

At this point, Davis gave up. A few years later he wrote, "My hope of an honorable peaceable settlement was not abandoned until the report of the Com." He agreed with Judah Benjamin that the Republicans "will make no Compromise, agreement or concession whatever." The new Republican chieftain, Abraham Lincoln, stood ramrod-straight on the territorial issue, telling Republicans in Congress to stand fast and make no compromise on this key point. Lincoln knew little of the South; if he had known more, he would have been aware that men like Davis, Benjamin, and numerous others were not radicals. Moreover, they were receiving ferocious pressure from their states, where the fervor for secession dominated public opinion. Whether such knowledge would have made any difference to Lincoln's posture is impossible to know, but he was fundamentally ignorant of his southern political foes.[107]

While paralysis gripped Congress, the slave states bustled with activity that commanded Davis's attention. Elections for delegates to secession conventions occurred in several states in addition to Mississippi. Even more important, on December 26, Major Robert Anderson, commander of the U.S. Army garrison in Charleston, moved his men from Fort Moultrie to Fort Sumter, at the mouth of the harbor. This transfer outraged South Carolina authorities, who, following the state's secession, believed they had an understanding with the Buchanan administration that the military situation in Charleston would not be altered. The Carolinians, along with southern congressional leaders, including Davis, pressed Buchanan to order the soldiers back to Fort Moultrie. The president was under heavy pressure from his southern friends to countermand Anderson, and from northern members of his cabinet, joined by an increasingly strident northern public opinion, to hold fast. A vacillating and wavering Buchanan ultimately decided against the southerners. A disgusted Davis called the president's treatment of South Carolina "perfidious." According to Davis, Buchanan's "weakness has done as much harm as wickedness would have achieved. Though I can no longer respect or confer with him and feel injured by his conduct," Davis explained, "yet I pity and would extenuate the offences not prompted by bad design or malignant intent."[108]

Davis and other southern leaders worried about a collision in Charleston Harbor between South Carolina and the United States. Attempting to negotiate for Fort Sumter as well as other posts, the state sent a mission to Washington. Although the president would not enter into negotiations, Davis and others extracted a promise from him not to use force. Thereupon the southern leadership set out to persuade the eager Carolinians not to initiate hostilities. The Carolinians left no doubt they considered the occupation of Fort Sumter an affront which they intended to remedy, by force if necessary. When Governor Francis W. Pickens asked for advice, Davis in frequent messages implored him not to act and maintained that a premature strike would only hurt the southern cause. He reminded Pickens, "the little garrison in its present positi[on] presses on nothing but a point of pride, & to you I need not say that war is made up of real eleme[nts]." Moreover, Davis assured him that "we shall soon have a Southern Confederacy that shall be ready to do all which interest or even pride demands."[109]

Throughout December, as chances of a settlement acceptable to them receded, southern senators and congressmen talked about their future options. Davis was certainly involved in these conversations, a number of which took place in his home on I Street. After the Committee of Thirteen failed, the southerners set their course. On January 5, 1861, with Davis present, a caucus of senators from the states moving toward secession made the decision to call for the creation of a Southern Confederacy. The formative meeting was to be held in Montgomery, Alabama, in mid-February, by which time delegates from all the Deep South states from South Carolina to Texas could be chosen and travel to Montgomery.[110]

The chief concern prompting this timing was the desire to have concrete action taken before March 4, presidential inauguration day; these southerners wanted no part of a United States with Abraham Lincoln and the Republican party controlling the executive branch of the federal government. Initially they thought they needed to maintain their presence in the Senate to block measures designed to strengthen federal powers that Lincoln might use to intimidate or even force back the seceded states. But, as Davis informed Governor Pettus, careful counting revealed that a sufficient number of Democrats, northern and southern, would remain to stop any such initiatives before March 4 and even after, should Lincoln call a special session of Congress. They failed to consider that Lincoln might do what he actually did—act unilaterally, without Congress, which he did not bring to Washington until the summer.

Davis had serious reservations about remaining in his seat after his state went out. He repeated his argument of 1850 that a sitting senator should involve himself in the constructive work of the government, not devote himself to obstruction. He asserted he would have no legitimate role after his state left the Union. If this conviction had come into conflict with the need temporarily perceived by the southerners for the necessary votes to defeat augmentation laws, it is impossible to know what Davis would have done. But he never faced that quandary. He let it be known that he would hold his seat in the Senate until he received official notification of Mississippi secession, then he would leave.[111]

From the time he left Jackson in late November until he departed from Washington two months later, Davis kept in close touch with his constituents. From as early as December 1859 he was active in advising the governor on the purchase of weapons for state forces, even corresponding directly with manufacturers. He also kept state officials apprised of his interpretation of events in Congress. In addition, he advised on the secession convention and on the ordinance of secession itself. Realizing that his state with its new status would call on him, on January 9, he telegraphed Governor Pettus: "Judge what Mississippi requires of me and place me accordingly." On January 23, the governor issued a proclamation announcing the appointment of Jefferson Davis as major general of the Army of Mississippi.[112]

The weeks after Davis's return to Washington were tense for him and for his wife, as the sectional tension and polarization also affected Washington's social life. In early December, Varina confided to a friend that she would no longer associate with Republicans, but she spurned secessionists, having little use for what she called the "blathering" of disunionists. And she also noted that the uncertainty spawned fear. "*Everybody is scared,*" especially the president, she informed her husband.[113]

Varina still relished Washington society, where she had an almost regal presence. She was quite close to Buchanan, and even when her husband lost faith in him, she confessed that she still "love[d] the dear old man." Presenting him with her Christmas gift, a pair of slippers, she told him she hoped "they may sometime remind you of the great regard with which I shall ever remain faithfully your friend." One of her closest friends began calling her "Queen Varina," which delighted her. The appellation caught on. "Warmly attached" to the capital city, she told her seamstress and a group of confidantes that she preferred to stay in Washington than to go south. On New Year's Day 1861, she described the disruption: "This town is like some kind of mausoleum, comparatively, no one visiting, no dinners or parties—just a sullen gloom impending over all things." Not wanting to give up all of the attractions in Washington, Varina unsuccessfully implored her free black seamstress to go south with her.[114]

Jefferson carried on under terrible strain. What he had dreaded for more than a decade had finally come to pass; his Union was no more. He did not exaggerate when he claimed he had been not only "conciliatory in spirit, but deeply anxious to avoid the issue if it could be consistently done with due regard to the rights the safety and the honor of the

South." Yet, as a politician, he recognized that opinion in Mississippi had rushed beyond him. He could not and would not let his state embark in this radically different direction without him. Moreover, he did believe deeply that fundamental constitutional rights of the South had been violated. In addition, Republicans did frighten him because their vision of America excluded him, his state, and his region. What he viewed as Republican unwillingness to accept the *Dred Scott* decision, to honor constitutional precepts, and to compromise, along with the sustained Republican attack on southern institutions and on southerners as Americans, persuaded him that his beloved Mississippi had no other recourse. By the turn of the year, Davis's health gave way, his body no longer able to carry the burden. On Christmas Eve, Varina's seamstress depicted him as "careworn, and his step seemed to be a little nervous." In early January he went to bed under a physician's care, afflicted chiefly with painful facial neuralgia.[115]

Just before he succumbed to physical and emotional pain, on January 10, Davis gave his last major speech in the Senate. Although he uttered still another paean to the Union he loved and held forth on what he termed the "wailing cry of patriotism" heard through the land, he knew the end had come. "To-day, therefore," he announced, "it is my purpose to deal with events." As for the dangerous situation in Charleston Harbor, he blamed President Buchanan for a "perfidious breach" of promises made to him and others that had brought South Carolina and the federal government almost to the point of conflict. To the Republicans he spoke harshly. Despite warnings by responsible southerners that continued enmity toward institutions and deprivation of rights would generate a powerful southern reaction, Republicans had refused to listen. Attributing much of the responsibility to Republican ignorance of the South and southern politics, he informed them they fatally misjudged when they deemed secession "a mere passing political mood" and "a device for some party end." Instead, something fundamental was at stake. Republicans, Davis charged, had forced upon the South a choice it did not want to make: "the destruction of our community independence or the destruction of the Union which our Fathers made."

In concluding, Davis acknowledged that he was probably making his last argument in the Senate. He maintained that the southern determination not to accept a coercive government did not mean the failure of self-government. It remained in the states. Separation had now become inevitable; two confederacies would exist. He saw one critical issue, how best to effect that separation. He hoped for a policy of peace, which would make possible the reconstruction of the Union when all had the will to do so. But he left no doubt that if peaceful separation were not permitted, "then it is an issue from which we will not shrink; for, between oppression and freedom, between the maintenance of right and submission to power, we will invoke the God of battles, and meet our fate, whatever it may be." He told his Republican antagonists, "I leave the case in your hands."[116]

Now he waited only on Mississippi, and on his health. Official notification of his state's secession reached him by telegraph on January 19, with the information that his "immediate presence" was required in Jackson. His illness had caused him to cancel a proposed trip through South Carolina to consult with Governor Pickens and his advisers. Yet, in spite of his physician's protests, on the twenty-first he left his sickbed to join four other colleagues in bidding farewell to the Senate he loved and the country he cherished. When, the next day, Jefferson Davis boarded a train with Varina and his children, he departed from Washington and from the United States.[117]

CHAPTER ELEVEN

"Our Cause Is Just and Holy"

The Davises' homeward journey took them southwestward through Virginia, Tennessee, and northern Alabama into Mississippi. Along the way Jefferson conferred with political leaders, made several speeches defending secession and warning about the prospect of a bitter war. In Jackson at the end of January 1861, he accepted his commission as major general of the Army of Mississippi, began organizing the force, and repeated his fear that war loomed. After a brief stay, the family made the final leg of their trip, reaching Vicksburg on February 1 and heading immediately for Davis Bend.[1]

At Brierfield with their children for the first time since the fall of 1857, Jefferson and Varina expressed pleasure at their return home. To a friend back in Washington, Jefferson reported, "I found much to be done and have entered upon to me the most agreable of all labors planting shrubs and trees and directing the operations of my field— . . . ploughing and cleaning up for another crop." Settling in, they sent instructions for the shipment of possessions they had not brought with them.[2]

Yet, simultaneously Davis also looked toward the state capital of Alabama, a quiet riverport of around 9,000 people, half of them black. At Montgomery on February 4, delegates from six Deep South states gathered to create a southern confederacy. Davis awaited word from that conclave, for he knew his name would be considered for a major position in the new country, either commanding general of the army or chief executive. Among leading politicians he possessed unique credentials; no one else could match his combined political and military experience. Writing to a Mississippi delegate, he discussed both the presidency and command of the army. After the ritual disclaimer that he wanted neither, he concluded, "in this hour of my country's severest trial [I] will accept any place to which my fellow citizens may assign me."[3]

The men who met in Montgomery assumed three distinct identities, performing tasks matched by no other single group in American history. Initially, they organized as a constitutional convention to draft the document that would provide the foundation for their new republic. Then, they constituted themselves as an electoral college to select a provisional president and vice president. Finally, they designated themselves a unicameral Provisional Congress to enact statutes that would give substance to the Confederate States of America.

Their organic law illustrated their commitment to the Constitution of the United States, which in their minds the Republicans had subverted. In fact, some among them wanted simply to replicate the document they had cherished. But alterations were made to clarify points most southerners claimed were at least implicit in the federal Constitution. The Confederate Constitution explicitly protected slavery and raised states' rights to a first principle. It also prohibited a protective tariff. To cleanse what they deemed the corruption of the system they had left behind, the delegates provided for a single six-year term for the president. With no possibility of reelection, politicking would not be the hallmark of a Confederate president's administration. Satisfied that they had depoliticized their chief executive, these constitution-writers then set out to rein in the rapacity of legislators. In an effort to prevent logrolling and pork-barrel projects, the president received a line-item veto on appropriations bills. Moreover, a two-thirds vote in both houses of Congress was required for any appropriation not requested by the president. In their handiwork they underscored that their president "should not be a party leader but instead should stand as a patriot rallying the people to the cause of Southern independence."[4]

With the provisional Constitution adopted on February 8, the delegates became electors. Their choices for president and vice president would be only provisional; the election of a regular president and vice president by popular vote and a constitutional electoral college was set for the fall. As in the constitutional deliberations, the delegates voted by state. Although many ambitious politicians were in Montgomery, intense politicking did not characterize the selection process; numerous participants commented on the absence of traditional pressures and lobbying. Those same participants, and observers as well, described a determined harmony pervading all activities. These self-appointed electors wanted the man they perceived as best for their Confederate States of America.[5]

In Montgomery, and even before, one name always came up: Jefferson Davis. Among southern political leaders, no one else could match his combined political, military, and administrative experience. And because armed conflict might occur, his military background carried special weight. Davis had another attribute that appealed to many, his conservatism. He had never been a fire-eater, and was not perceived as a fomenter of secession. This identity assumed particular importance because the delegates in Montgomery were acutely aware that only seven slave states had seceded while eight remained in the Union. To attract the Upper South and border states, the new government would have to exhibit moderation and judiciousness. Thus, Davis's name appeared on everyone's short list.[6]

But Davis was not the only possibility. Everyone recognized that because of its size, location, and the prominent men in its delegation, Georgia would have an influential voice in the selection. No other state sent men with the reputations of Howell Cobb, Alexander Stephens, and Robert Toombs, all of whom had had impressive political careers. And Cobb, a former congressman, governor, and secretary of the treasury, had been named president of the convention. Still, Georgians would have to settle on one of their luminaries, and in addition each had liabilities. Cobb did not relish the responsibility of the presidency and made his feeling widely known. Stephens was almost too conservative; in Georgia he had spoken against immediate secession and on the first ballot in the secession convention had voted against that course. Although the prospect of becoming president pleased Toombs, he had a different problem. In Montgomery his highly visible penchant for excessive imbibing made for serious doubts about his fitness for the post. The dean of fire-eaters, Robert Barnwell Rhett, Sr., a member of the South Carolina delegation, was clearly interested and may have believed it his due, but not even a majority of his fellow Carolinians considered him qualified. Younger than Rhett but his equal as a proponent of secession, William Lowndes Yancey of Alabama had supporters among some zealots, but not very many.[7]

Yet, in spite of these possible contenders, the balloting held little suspense. With four votes needed to win, no one seriously challenged Davis. The testimony makes clear that he was the choice of Mississippi, Louisiana, and Florida; in addition, he had a majority in South

Carolina, even though some of the Palmetto Staters worried about his conservatism. Alabama also came to him, influenced by commissioners sent by the state to Virginia, who reported that leading men in Virginia wanted Davis. In Georgia, Cobb, Stephens, and Toombs canceled one another out. If the Georgia delegates had united behind one, especially Cobb, and pushed hard, they might have sparked a contest. But without a serious challenge from Georgia, Davis triumphed easily. In all likelihood he would have won anyway. When on February 9 the delegates met to elect a chief executive, they placed in nomination only one name: Jefferson Davis. No one else received a vote. Then with the same unanimity Alexander Stephens was chosen vice president. The entire process took only half an hour. Via telegraph the result flashed to Mississippi.[8]

From Vicksburg a messenger was immediately dispatched to Davis Bend, arriving late in the afternoon of February 9. He found Davis in the garden at Brierfield assisting Varina with rose cuttings. Upon reading the telegram, Davis "looked so grieved" that, his wife later remembered, she feared some family calamity. She recorded that, "after a few minutes' painful silence," her husband shared the news "as a man might speak of a sentence of death." According to Varina, he neither wanted nor expected the presidency. Years afterward Davis repeated that he never desired the position; later he even claimed he thought he had helped arrangements in favor of Howell Cobb. Yet he knew the Montgomery gathering would in all probability name him to a major post, whether military or civilian, and unlike Cobb he never sought to remove his name from consideration for president. Still, the notification forced him to confront the enormous responsibility placed on him.[9]

He did not shirk it. He informed Varina he would have to leave immediately for Montgomery. When he departed from Hurricane Landing on February 11, slaves rowed him out to mid-river to catch a steamboat bound for Vicksburg. Going aboard the familiar boat, Jefferson Davis could not know he would not see Brierfield again for seven years and would never return as a slaveowner or as a resident planter.

Davis's trip to Montgomery took five days. When he disembarked at Vicksburg, the town put on a great celebration—bands, militia units, speeches. A similar event awaited him in Jackson, where he resigned his general's commission and in a brief address promised to do his duty as president. To reach Montgomery from Jackson by train, Davis had to go north to Grand Junction, Tennessee, then east through northern Alabama to Chattanooga, and south to Atlanta. When he reached Atlanta at 4 a.m. on the sixteenth, a waiting throng wanted a speech. Later in the morning, Davis spoke to this crowd just as he had to some two dozen others at every stop along the way from Jackson, except in Tennessee, which had not yet seceded. To enthusiastic listeners he talked about independence as the southern destiny; he said he hoped for peace, but would accept war if necessary for independence. A reporter characterized the entire trip as "one continuous ovation."[10]

After his address, Davis departed Atlanta on the final portion of his journey. At the rail junction of West Point, Georgia, a delegation from Montgomery met the president-elect. Following brief speeches, Davis and other dignitaries escorted by militia companies boarded a train for the run to Montgomery, with Davis speaking in "eloquent style" at two stops in eastern Alabama. Finally, at 10 p.m. the train puffed into Montgomery, where a large, excited crowd and salvos of artillery greeted its arrival. Stepping from his car, a tired Davis made a few remarks emphasizing his perception of transpiring events. A new time had come: "Our separation from the old Union is complete. NO COMPROMISE; NO RECONSTRUCTION CAN BE NOW ENTERTAINED."[11]

Amidst tremendous applause, Davis headed for the Exchange Hotel and bed. But another big, exuberant gathering clamored for him. At 10:45 p.m., he appeared on the hotel balcony to underscore his sense of the moment. "Fellow Citizens and Brethren of the Confederate States of America—for now we are brethren, not in name, merely, but in fact—men of one flesh, one bone, one interest, one purpose, and of identity of domestic institutions." After pointing to what he called the "homogeneity" in the Confederacy, he said the new nation would prevail. He left no doubt about his own commitment. "I will devote to the duties of the high office to which I have been called all I have of heart, of head and of hand."[12]

Because the inauguration was set for Monday, February 18, Davis could rest on Sunday from his tiring journey. He remained in bed until well after 10 a.m. The remainder of the day he spent working on his inaugural address. For this occasion Davis had no intention of extemporizing; he would speak the precise words he wrote.[13]

Inaugural day dawned with a cloudy sky; it was cold, with frost covering the ground. Promptly at 10 a.m. the chief marshal accompanied by aides representing the seven Confederate States appeared in front of the Exchange Hotel. The parade was formed with a brass band in front, followed by militia companies wearing sky blue pants and bright red coats. Then came Davis and Alexander Stephens, in a barouche lined in saffron and white, mounted with silver, and drawn by six magnificent gray horses. Next, also in open carriages, came an array of dignitaries from the Provisional Congress, the several Confederate states, and the city. Citizens in carriages and on foot completed the parade. The sun broke through the overcast as the procession moved up Market Street toward the Alabama Capitol, perched on a commanding hill. As the long line approached the Capitol, the thousands of cheering spectators filling the sidewalks and streets became more numerous. An additional 5,000-plus waited on the Capitol grounds.

At the Capitol, Davis and Stephens stepped down and, accompanied by their escort, ascended the steps of the portico and went into the building. Some women had made a beautiful wreath and placed it on Davis's arm. More bouquets were showered upon him. After brief, formal introductions to the Provisional Congress, the official party and members of Congress emerged and took their places on a wooden platform that had been constructed in front of the portico. A grand cheer accompanied by an artillery salute greeted them. At 1 p.m., just after the invocation, Howell Cobb introduced Jefferson Davis, who rose "amid a storm of applause" and faced the crowd.[14]

In his inaugural address Davis cogently and forcefully defined the Confederate cause. He began by proclaiming that the Confederacy "illustrates the American idea that governments rest upon the consent of the governed, and that it is the right of the people to alter or abolish governments whenever they become destructive of the ends for which they were established." Fusing the southern past to the southern present, he said the southern people had "merely asserted a right which the Declaration of Independence of 1776 had defined to be inalienable." Because the Union of the fathers had been "perverted from the purposes for which it was ordained, and had ceased to answer the ends for which it was established," southerners in "a peaceful appeal to the ballot-box declared that so far as they were concerned, the government created by that compact should cease to exist." Confederates would emulate their ancestors: "Doubly justified by the absence of wrong on our part, and by wanton aggression on the part of others, there can be no cause to doubt that the courage and patriotism of the people of the Confederate States will be found equal to any measures of defense which honor and security may require."

Davis sounded no call to war, however. He announced that "our true policy is peace." Identifying the Confederacy as agricultural, Davis stated that the new country wanted to engage in commerce with "the freest trade which our necessities will permit." And he spoke confidently about trade, for he shared the widespread southern assumption that the overarching requirement for cotton in the United States and especially in England "would invite good will and kind offices."

He then congratulated the new nation on its peaceful gestation and birth. There had been neither "aggression upon others" nor "domestic convulsion." He found both the industrial and agricultural sectors of the economy functioning "as heretofore." Yet, Confederates feared not. If anyone "desire[d] to inflict injury upon us," the result would be "the suffering of millions," which would "bear testimony to the folly and wickedness of our aggressors."

His closing became more personal. "You will see many errors to forgive, many deficiencies to tolerate," he told his audience, "but you shall not find in me either a want of zeal or fidelity to the cause that is to me highest in hope and of most enduring affection." He had not sought and did not merit his office, but "generosity" had bestowed it upon him. "Upon the continuance of that sentiment and upon your wisdom and patriotism I rely to direct and support me in the performance of the duty required at my hands." Davis concluded by celebrating what he described as "a people united in heart, where one purpose of high resolve animates and actuates the whole—where the sacrifices to be made are not weighed in the balance against honor and right and liberty and equality." He then called on "the God of our fathers" to continue "His favor" upon the Confederates in their effort to carry forth the principles which he had permitted their fathers to "establish and transmit. . . ."[15]

In the evening hundreds jammed Estelle Hall for a reception. For a long time President Davis stood shaking the hands of well-wishers. A substantial portion of the celebrants was female, and a number of them showed their excitement with more than handshakes. An observer noted that Davis "was abundantly kissed and rekissed." According to one reporter, many males "thought there was too much waste of that delectable commodity, at such an early period in the history of the Confederation." But neither the women nor the president seemed to mind.[16]

President Jefferson Davis understood the monumental task he confronted. To his wife he wrote: "We are without machinery without means and threatened by powerful opposition but I do not despond and will not shrink from the task imposed upon me." Literally, he had to construct a government from nothing. The seven states in the Confederacy had governments, of course, but there had never been any central governmental apparatus. Appointing the cabinet became Davis's first order of business. The Provisional Congress had stipulated six agencies—State, Treasury, War, Navy, Attorney General, and Postmaster General. They replicated the departments of the old Union, except for the newest one, Interior, for which the Confederates saw no need, in no small part because to them it was symbolic of too powerful a central government. Davis later claimed that politics played no part in his selection process, but this was only partially true. Although he had no personal political debts to pay or party factions to satisfy, he did have geographic considerations. The officers he chose represented each state in the Confederacy, except for his home state. After deciding not to include the vocal, radical, and controversial Barnwell Rhett, who did not even have unanimous support within the South Carolina delegation, Davis proceeded to name his official family.[17]

With the view that everyone shared his dedication to the new cause, Davis appointed men without even asking them. Three people turned him down—Robert Barnwell, the leader of the South Carolina delegation whom he knew and trusted, because of a desire to leave politics; his friend Clement Clay, because of ill health; and Yancey, probably because he felt the cabinet would restrict his independence. Two others, Toombs and John H. Reagan of Texas, initially refused, but for the sake of unity eventually agreed to serve. The two most notable appointees were former United States senators, Toombs for the State Department and Judah P. Benjamin of Louisiana for attorney general. One of their colleagues in that chamber, Stephen R. Mallory of Florida, took over the Navy Department. The position of postmaster general went to Reagan, who had sat in the House of Representatives. The two who had not previously held national offices were Christopher G. Memminger of South Carolina and LeRoy P. Walker of Alabama, who went to the Treasury Department and War Department respectively. Although not overall a distinguished group, Davis's cabinet compared favorably to most in the old Union. Two men would hold their posts and render stellar service throughout Davis's presidency, Mallory and Reagan. Benjamin also remained for the duration and became Davis's closest cabinet counselor, though he would head three different ministries and become controversial. Toombs, who accepted his appointment only reluctantly, departed first—for a general's commission and the battlefield, where he did not duplicate his political distinction. The two most unlikely choices, Memminger and Walker, had different experiences. Neither was really qualified, but the former stayed until 1864 and struggled valiantly, if ineffectively, with the Confederacy's increasingly catastrophic financial situation; Walker, simply incapable of handling his assignment, departed after only seven months. At the outset Davis promised his official advisers that he would be candid with them, and from them he asked for the same frankness.

From the beginning Davis established the work habits that would mark his tenure as chief executive. Upon his arrival in Montgomery he turned part of his suite at the Exchange Hotel into his office. Then in early March he moved to a nearby building designated as Government House, indicating its new function. Three rooms on the second floor became the president's office, where he transacted most official business during his stay in Montgomery. Varina described a long workday, specifying that he did not come home at night "until his cabinet peels off." Consulting with it at length on major matters, Davis often kept the cabinet in session for hours. He also spent considerable time conferring with influential members of Congress. Preparing the army bill, he and Congressman William Porcher Miles, chairman of the Military Affairs Committee, spent days closeted together.[18]

The lines waiting to see the president seemed unending. At least fifty men came every day with plans, suggestions, or pleas. To all, Varina reported, her husband responded "in softly modulated dulcet accents," if he could keep his temper. Davis described himself as "constantly engaged" and "so crowded and pressed." Even with major meetings and decisions plus endless streams of visitors, Davis's administrative style repeated the pattern he had followed as secretary of war. He looked at almost every piece of paper addressed to the president; his personal comments appeared on them all, whether important or trivial. One caller remarked that Davis seemed "overwhelmed" with paper.[19]

Passing through Montgomery, the English journalist William Russell painted a full word picture of the new president. Davis held his "slight, light figure . . . erect and straight." Russell described "a fine full forehead, square and high, covered with innumerable fine lines and wrinkles, features regular, though the cheek-bones are too high, and jaws too hollow to be handsome; the lips are thin, flexible, and curved, the chin square, well refined, the nose very regular with wide nostrils, and the eyes deep set, large and full—one seems nearly blind, and is partially covered with a film." To Russell, Davis's face seemed "anxious," and he had "a very haggard, careworn, and pain-drawn look, though no trace of anything but the utmost confidence and the greatest decision could be detected in conversation."[20]

As Davis immersed himself in his work, Varina and the children joined him, arriving in Montgomery on March 1. While alone, Jefferson made clear how much he missed his family. En route to Alabama, he asked Varina to "kiss my dear children and tell them to be good and love one another." He wrote lovingly, "I am always with you in spirit and so will be while life lasts." Reporting on his journey to Montgomery, Davis wished both wife and children could have shared the outpouring of support that greeted him along the way. "I thought it would have gratified you to have witnessed it and have been a memory to our children."[21]

When Varina and the children reached Montgomery, they found Jefferson living at the Exchange Hotel. All the Davises remained there until mid-April, when they moved two blocks to a house that had been leased by Congress for an executive mansion. The two-story "Confederate White House" had been built in the 1830s and renovated in the Italianate style in 1855. Varina supervised redecoration of the house, which she called "roomy enough for our purposes," and even returned to Brierfield for personal items before the family took up residence in their new home.[22]

As first lady, Varina made strong and generally positive impressions. William Russell described her as "a comely, sprightly woman, verging on matronhood, of good figure and manners, well-dressed, ladylike and clever." Numerous people noted her quick mind and her wit. The perceptive wife of a member of the South Carolina delegation, who would become a great friend, Mary Chesnut, recorded, "she is awfully clever—always." Varina's first levee, given on March 6 at the Exchange, was a success. Thereafter she gave regular receptions at the residence, and Jefferson attended most. But even in the midst of a busy social schedule she took great delight in her children and enjoyed her role as mother. "She is well received," commented one observer, "and admired more as a true Southern lady than as the wife of the chief executive."[23]

The only qualification to the positive assessment concerned her frequent public statements that she harbored no animosity toward northern friends. Mary Chesnut recognized that Varina found "playing Mrs.

Varina Davis, c. 1860.
Museum of the Confederacy

President of this small Confederacy slow work after leaving . . . Washington." Without doubt she missed that capital city. Privately she called Montgomery "a strange community," depicted the Confederate Congress as "the Botany Bay, no I am too polite to say that, but bear garden of the South," and complained about the sanitation. She did not totally disagree with the new attorney general, who informed a northern friend: "We will show you what a true Republican government is— no pâté, no champagne, no salmon, no nothing—people don't give dinners here: but only nice tea parties."[24]

But family and active social life did not deter President Davis from his work. He gave great attention to the creation of an army. He had long believed that secession would result in war, though he considered conflict might be avoided if all the slave states left the Union. In building the Confederate States Army, Davis concentrated his efforts on three major tasks. He strove to have Congress adopt a lengthy enlistment policy. Aware of the time required to prepare civilians for military service, and fearful war was imminent and that it would be long, he wanted soldiers signed up for the duration of any conflict, or for at least three years. He failed. Most congressmen advocated only a six-month period of service, convinced either that no fighting would occur, or if it did, the struggle would be brief and successful. Davis's pleas did get twelve-month enlistments, but no more. Also recognizing the critical importance of a trained cadre, Davis courted officers from the U.S. Army. Because of his time as secretary of war, he had considerable knowledge of the officer corps. In this area Davis experienced success. Although most officers from the South resigned upon the secession of their home states, Davis's overtures ensured that many offered their services to the Confederacy. In addition, Davis knew his country faced a perilous shortage of military equipment, especially weapons. He dispatched agents to both the United States and Europe to procure as much as possible as soon as possible. But until the spring of 1862 the Confederacy remained unable to arm all its soldiers.[25]

The army did not occupy all of the president's attention, however. In setting up departments, he followed advice to embrace the old federal bureaucracy and its rules, at least initially. Thus United States postmasters became Confederate States postmasters, and officers of the United States courts became officers of the Confederate States courts. This process of governmental creation was materially assisted by former civil servants in Washington who volunteered their services and expertise in Montgomery. Some even appeared with copies of regulations and procedures that could be promptly distributed and implemented.[26]

Although the tasks, both civilian and military, were unending, to Davis one seemed foremost: diplomacy. He identified three diplomatic fronts, though he realized their interconnection: the slave states still in the Union; Europe, especially Great Britain; and the United States. Acutely aware that eight slave states had not seceded, Davis wanted to signal that the Confederacy respected them, wanted their friendship, and eagerly awaited their joining the Confederacy. He signed a law declaring the Mississippi River would remain open for commerce from all states, and he talked about trade and good relations. He also dispatched emissaries to present the Confederate case to these states.

Like most Confederates, Davis believed Europe would react positively to the Confederacy. When they referred to Europe, they really meant Great Britain and to a lesser extent France. They thought that Great Britain would welcome the division of the United States, and more important, they were absolutely convinced that British prosperity depended upon southern cotton. As a result, Davis and his advisers could not envision Britain's permitting any serious interference with the cotton trade. To impress upon the British and others that the Confederacy had only peaceful intentions with an eagerness to trade, Davis did not delay in sending a mission abroad, though his choices for commissioners revealed both his ignorance of foreign affairs and his penchant for correlating commitment to the Confederacy with suitability for important assignments. He named the voluble Alabama fire-eater William L. Yancey, who would concentrate on Great Britain; Ambrose Dudley Mann, who had considerable diplomatic experience in the old Union and was a Confederate and Davis loyalist, but also an ineffectual lightweight; and Louisianian Pierre Rost, who knew a number of influential men in his native France. This irregular team received no special instructions and possessed no authority to conclude any particular agreements with the European powers. They were simply to convey the message of friendship and trade.

Although Davis did think about the other slave states and Europe, his most pressing problem in the late winter and early spring of 1861 centered on relations with the United States. Davis obviously wanted recognition of Confederate legitimacy, but his immediate concern focused on the military posts within Confederate borders still garrisoned by United States troops. As individual states seceded, state authorities gained control of almost all federal posts within their jurisdiction. No clashes resulted and no casualties occurred. Yet upon the formation of the Confederate States, four remained in Union hands— two far away in the Florida Keys; Fort Pickens at Pensacola, Florida; and the most visible, Fort Sumter in the harbor of Charleston, South Carolina. Davis wanted the soldiers withdrawn from Pickens and Sumter.

President Davis was prepared to offer compensation for these forts as well as for all the federal property that had already come under Confederate authority. To communicate his position and carry out negotiations, he sent a special mission to Washington. Although there had been some indication that the Buchanan administration might have received the Confederate delegation, it arrived after Lincoln had come into office. And President Lincoln had no intention of treating with the Confederates. Though formally rebuffed, the southerners did manage to establish an informal channel with Secretary of State William Seward. Although never meeting, Seward and the Confederates communicated through Justice John A. Campbell of the United States Supreme Court, an Alabamian who had not yet resigned. Initially Seward promised that Fort Sumter would be evacuated, but every time the Confederates pressed for details, he equivocated. They assumed he spoke for Lincoln, but in fact Seward was struggling to influence his president's decisions. And always all dealings were strictly unofficial.[27]

As President Davis awaited developments in Washington, South Carolina fully occupied him. The situation in Charleston was extremely volatile, for South Carolina officials talked about attacking Fort Sumter on their own. Even before he left Washington, Davis had cautioned Governor Francis Pickens against precipitate action. From Montgomery he was in almost daily telegraphic contact with Pickens, always urging the governor not to act unilaterally. Pickens kept insisting that South Carolina must have Sumter, as soon as possible. The president was delighted when the Confederate Congress on February 22 passed a resolution charging the Confederate government with responsibility for the forts still held by the United States. At that point he stated to Pickens, "I hope you will be able to prevent the issue of peace or war for the Confederate States from being decided by any other than the authorities constituted to conduct our international relations. The most ardent and sensitive should believe that we will not be unmindful or regardless of the rights and honor of South Carolina." On March 1, Davis took control when he dispatched Brigadier General Pierre G. T. Beauregard to assume command of all forces in the Charleston area. A professional soldier, veteran of the Mexican War, and former superintendent of West Point, Beauregard had orders to get all in readiness, but to prevent any attack on Fort Sumter, "unless in self defense."[28]

Davis tried to ensure that any military action in Charleston Harbor would result only from his direct orders, then hoped for positive word from Washington. There the fledgling Lincoln administration confronted a crisis of its own. On the day after his inauguration Lincoln learned that Major Robert Anderson, commanding at Fort Sumter, had informed the War Department that dwindling supplies made it impossible to hold the bastion for very long, a month or six weeks at the most.

Fort Sumter became the prize in the first great contest between the Union and Abraham Lincoln and the Confederacy and Jefferson Davis. The stakes were more political than military, for the Sumter garrison, massively outnumbered and outgunned by the Confederates, could not hope to win a fight. On the political front the rewards and dangers were much greater. Some of Lincoln's advisers recommended withdrawal from Fort Sumter. The commanding general of the U.S. Army, Davis's old nemesis Winfield Scott, informed the president that he could not mount a mission to succor Anderson before Sumter's supplies ran out. But Lincoln did not want to pull out; in his mind doing so would mean conceding the Confederacy's independence, and possibly the end of his cherished dream of keeping the Union whole. On the other hand, he realized that a straightforward military reinforcement not only would provoke a Confederate reaction but might also push both the Upper South and the border states into the Confederacy, thus doubling the Confederacy's base and courting disaster for the Union. Although over the next several weeks Lincoln received numerous suggestions and opinions for dealing with this vexing problem, it always seemed to come down to these same two basic choices: attempt to reinforce Fort Sumter or give it up. At times he appeared inclined toward one, then the other. He never wanted to begin a war, but he desperately wished to keep the flag flying.

As Lincoln groped toward a decision, Davis received reports and warnings about what might happen. Former Senate colleagues still in Washington and Confederates retaining ties in the capital revealed to Davis and other prominent men in Montgomery that division reigned in Republican circles, basically between a peace party headed by Seward and a war party led by several major Republicans in and out of the cabinet. In mid-March one of Davis's delegation wrote Vice President Stephens that Seward had indirectly begged for time. "If we force an answer," the diplomat reported Seward as saying, "he is whipped in the cabinet; if he have some time he is sure he can carry his views." Two weeks later Justice Campbell corresponded directly with President Davis. In a lengthy message he recounted his dealings with Seward, in which the secretary of state repeatedly maintained that Sumter would be evacuated. Campbell thought Lincoln knew what Seward was about, but he did make clear that Seward declared all his assurances he made on his *"own."* Campbell did not doubt that Sumter would soon be abandoned, but about Pickens he was unsure. He concluded that what he termed "the inactive policy is as favorable to you as any that this administration could adopt for you and that I would not interrupt it."[29]

Yet even before Campbell's message, Lincoln had made a decision. On March 29 he ordered that an expedition for Fort Sumter be made ready to depart by April 6. Rejecting both reinforcement *and* withdrawal, he had decided simply to resupply Fort Sumter, sending in no additional soldiers or guns, only food and medicine for the troops already there. In this way the calculus of power in Charleston Harbor would apparently be left unchanged. It was a masterful maneuver, providing the first clear sign of the political genius that would make Lincoln such a formidable president and war leader. Despite Lincoln's directive, Seward kept trying to forestall the ultimate showdown by substituting Fort Pickens for Fort Sumter as the target of Federal action. He failed. On April 6 Lincoln, never admitting the legitimacy of the Confederacy, dispatched a messenger to Charleston with a notice for the governor of South Carolina. Two days later Governor Pickens and General Beauregard read Lincoln's message: he would resupply only, and if not resisted, he would make no attempt at reinforcement "without further notice, or in case of attack upon the fort."[30]

Now it was Jefferson Davis's turn to make *his* first desperate decision. Despite the optimistic word from the Confederate mission to Washington, by early April Davis and his advisers considered "threatening" the Federal military activity known to them. From their point of view, they occupied peaceful and defensive ground because the United States had no legitimate claim to Fort Sumter or Fort Pickens. Both were equally important to Davis, though more attention in Montgomery and Washington focused on Sumter. If the question of Sumter had been resolved, the problem of Pickens would have moved immediately to the forefront. On April 6 Davis eagerly desired "peace between those who though separated have many reasons to feel towards each other more than the friendship common among other nations." At the same time, as president of the Confederate States of America, he could not dismiss the critical importance of the forts. "We have waited hopefully for the withdrawal of garrisons which irritate the people of these states and threaten the respective localities, and which can serve no purpose to the United States unless it be to injure us." He said his government had taken no action and did not want to use force. But now "the idea of evacuation had been abandoned," and he contemplated that perhaps all along the United States had followed a policy of deception. In Davis's mind, Lincoln controlled the "problem" of the forts. Any attempt to relieve or to maintain Fort Sumter, whatever the term employed, Davis saw as an assault on the Confederacy. At that point the Federal presence did more than touch upon pride; it became a powerful threat to vital interests of his government. To a visitor Davis was blunt: "they mean to compel us into a political servitude we disown and spurn."[31]

Potent arguments supported the contention that the Confederates should take Fort Sumter. The first was that the Union occupation mocked the independence of the Confederacy. According to this thinking, the Confederate States of America could not stand as an independent nation so long as another power maintained an uninvited military force within its borders. Second, the administration justifiably worried that despite the Confederate command structure in Charleston, zealots in South Carolina might strike against the fort on their own initiative. Such an action would undermine the authority of the Confederate government and commit it to a course it had not decided upon. The Confederate leadership also recognized that a move against Fort Sumter would mobilize the citizens behind their government and, perhaps more important, bring the Upper South, especially Virginia, within the Confederate fold. It was the weight of these considerations that directed Davis's course, though some thought was given to the possible adverse impact on potential northern friends of the Confederacy. Davis recognized the difficulty stemming from actually shooting first, but as he informed his commander in Pensacola, "to relieve our territory and jurisdiction of the presence of a foreign garrison that advantage is overbalanced by other considerations."[32]

He made his decision. On April 10 the War Department ordered General Beauregard to demand the surrender of Fort Sumter. If the Federals refused, Beauregard was instructed to take the fort. The next day Beauregard sent officers out to the fort. Presented with the alternatives of surrendering or facing an attack, Major Anderson said he would fight, but he added that unless he received new supplies in a few days, he would have to evacuate. Aware that war or peace now rested in the balance, Beauregard reported Anderson's response to the War Department. The new directive sent to Beauregard held firm to the government's fundamental position, though it did give the general some latitude. If Anderson would provide a specific date for evacuation, Beauregard was not to open fire. Late on the night of April 11, Beauregard's messengers returned to Fort Sumter with their new ultimatum. After considering his situation and his options, Major Anderson announced he would withdraw at noon on the fifteenth, unless before that time he received additional supplies or further instructions from his government. Because the Confederates were aware that supplies and possibly reinforcements were en route, Anderson's qualifications made his response unsatisfactory. Beauregard's deputation notified Anderson that Confederate batteries would commence firing in one hour. At 4:30 a.m. on April 12, Beauregard's guns began pouring shot and shell on Fort Sumter. Thirty-four hours later Anderson surrendered.[33]

For Jefferson Davis and his government the immediate response to Fort Sumter confirmed the rightness of their decision. The thrill of action and triumph rushed through the Confederacy. In the Upper South, where secession had been stymied, reconsideration proceeded promptly. Davis sent envoys to each state urging them to join the Confederacy. When Lincoln now called for 75,000 volunteers to put down what he defined as a rebellion, the Upper South turned toward the Confederate States of America. Over the rest of April and in May, Virginia, North Carolina, Tennessee, and Arkansas seceded and bound their futures to the Confederacy. In the border states of Maryland, Kentucky, and Missouri, secession was stalled but uncertainty prevailed. Kentucky even proclaimed neutrality between the United States and the Confederate States. The war Jefferson Davis had both long feared and anticipated was at hand. He had spoken of its costing "thousands of lives and millions of treasure." But even with his foreboding he could not foresee the destruction that lay ahead.[34]

With Abraham Lincoln's call for troops to put down what he termed a rebellion, and his announcement of a blockade of the coast of the rebellious states, it was clear to Jefferson Davis and his cabinet that the firing on Fort Sumter had signaled the end of the first phase of their revolution and the start of an even more perilous period. Judah Benjamin informed a friend that the Confederate leadership considered Lincoln's proclamation "an unmistakable declaration of war."[35]

Confronting the onset of war, Jefferson Davis acted vigorously. He led the call for additional volunteers to man the Confederate Army, whose numbers were rapidly increasing. On April 17 Davis invited applications for letters of marque, which would legalize Confederate privateers to prey on northern shipping. He also summoned the Provisional Congress back to Montgomery for a special session to begin on April 29.

In his message to the assembled lawmakers, Davis acknowledged that hostilities had begun and insisted that war had been forced upon the Confederacy. He had convened Congress so that it could "devise the measures necessary for the defense of the country." He then engaged in a lengthy recounting of the sectional conflict, focusing on his interpretation of northern aggression and the justification for secession. But secession did not mean the Confederacy wanted war. He reminded Congress that he had sent a commission to Washington in pursuit of peace. After receiving assurances that the Union also desired peace, he and the commissioners were surprised when Lincoln would not negotiate. Davis did not believe the Confederates had been treated fairly: "The crooked paths of diplomacy can scarcely furnish an example so wanting in courtesy, in candor, and directness as was the course of the United States Government toward our commission in Washington." Still, hoping to avert bloodshed, Davis reported that he had offered the commander at Fort Sumter an opportunity to avoid armed conflict, but was refused.

The president expressed confidence in his country and his countrymen. After detailing the responsibilities of the different departments of government, Davis proudly recited "that in every portion of our country there has been exhibited the most patriotic devotion to our common cause." He made absolutely clear his own sense of the moment: "We feel that our cause is just and holy; we protest solemnly in the face of mankind that we desire peace at any sacrifice save that of honor and independence; we seek no conquest, no aggrandizement, no concession of any kind from the States with which we were lately confederated; all we ask is to be let alone; that those who never held power over us shall not now attempt our subjugation by arms. This we will, this we must, resist to the direst extremity." And he predicted the Confederacy would prevail because "a people . . . united and resolved cannot shrink from any sacrifice which they may be called on to make . . . however long and severe may be the test of their determination to maintain their birthright of freedom and equality as a trust which it is their first duty to transmit undiminished to their posterity."[36]

With the advent of war, Davis wished to participate in it directly in some way. Although some advisers urged him to lead Confederate forces in the field to defeat the northern invaders, he decided against exercising his responsibilities as constitutional commander in chief in that capacity. But he did reveal his determination to appear personally at threatened points and with his soldiers. After the opening of rail connections between Montgomery and Pensacola, Davis decided to visit Pensacola himself. Accompanied by his wife and Secretary Mallory, he left on May 14 for the nine-hour train ride. In Pensacola he conferred with his commander, Brigadier General Braxton Bragg, and along with Bragg and the general's staff, he reviewed troops drawn up on a white sandy beach. As the reviewers galloped along the line, "the wildest huzzas" greeted them. After spending one night, Davis and his party departed.[37]

Back in Montgomery on May 15, the president contemplated changing his residence and his capital. To Confederates the most important state was Virginia, "mother of the South," primary force in the Revolution, home of heroes like Washington and Jefferson. Without Virginia many Confederates believed their country incomplete. In the aftermath of Fort Sumter, Davis had dispatched emissaries to the unseceded slave states urging their alignment with the Confederacy. To Richmond he had sent Alexander Stephens, and the vice president had labored there effectively. On April 17 Virginia seceded; on the twenty-seventh the Virginia convention offered Richmond as the national capital; on May 7, Virginia officially joined the Confederate States of America. As Virginia and the Confederacy became one, Jefferson Davis was elated.

The decision to accept Virginia's invitation and move the capital was a quite logical one, and not only because of the state's historic primacy. The accession of Virginia moved the border of the Confederacy all the way to the gates of Washington. The initial armed clash between the two sides would likely take place in northern Virginia. Further, Richmond was the most important industrial center in the new nation, and included the greatest iron-making facilities in the South. This industrial might demanded protection. Thus, the 100 miles between Washington and Richmond became the most priceless real estate in the Confederacy. Moreover, the limitations of Montgomery's size and resources were becoming more and more apparent. On May 20, Congress passed a resolution to move the government, which Davis readily signed. The next day Congress adjourned, and officials began the preparations for transferring a government.

On the evening of May 26, President Davis, accompanied by Secretary Toombs and three others, departed quietly by train for the new capital. Despite efforts to keep the journey low-key, at stops along the way crowds approached the train calling for the president. Davis always appeared and often made a few remarks. During the evening meal at his hotel in Goldsboro, North Carolina, Davis's table was "thronged with beautiful girls, and many were bedecking him with garlands of flowers, while others fanned him." On May 29 at 8 a.m. the presidential train reached Petersburg, Virginia, where Governor John L. Letcher and the mayor of Richmond met it. According to a reporter who had been on the train, the trip had been "one continuous ovation." Escorted by governor and mayor, Davis and his party covered the final twenty miles into Richmond, which would be Davis's home for the next four years.[38]

The hilly city at the falls of the historic James River stretched east to west along its banks for more than two miles and pushed northward. A visitor to Richmond, the great English writer Charles Dickens, described the town as "delightfully situated on eight hills, overhanging James River; a sparkling stream, studded here and there with bright islands or brawling over broken rocks." The capital of Virginia since 1780, Richmond by 1860 had become the twenty-fifth-largest city in the United States, with a population approaching 40,000. Just over a third of the inhabitants were black, four-fifths slave and one-fifth free. They were quite visible on the streets and at myriad tasks. Only New Orleans exceeded Richmond's thriving slave market, from which thousands of bondspeople began their trek to the Deep South. The city had also become a manufacturing center, with manufactured products valued at thirteenth among all cities in the old Union. Richmond boasted the largest flour mill in the world and the Tredegar Iron Works, the second-largest foundry in the world. Its tobacco market outranked all others. Steamboats plying the James, and railroads reaching north to the Potomac, down the Atlantic coast, and into the heart of the Deep South, made it a transportation hub. And above the industrial and mercantile enterprises along the river impressive homes, churches, and public buildings adorned the high ground. Crowning a high hill was the Capitol, a Roman temple designed by Thomas Jefferson.[39]

At the depot a great crowd awaited the president; cannon announced his arrival. In an open carriage drawn by four horses, Davis, with Governor Letcher and the mayor, moved through the cheering populace to the Spotswood Hotel, his temporary home. No formal parade or ceremony was held because Davis wanted none. Despite his fatigue when he reached the hotel, he spoke for ten minutes. He identified Virginia as "the mother of the South in this act"; her cradle had rocked Washington, Jefferson, Madison, Monroe, and many others. According to Davis, those sons of Virginia had provided a model government that had been perverted. Now the Confederacy would save their legacy. After some rest, the president on horseback rode at five-thirty in the afternoon to an assembly area for troops, where the men in uniform gave their commander in chief a reception "enthusiastic in the extreme." Back at the Spotswood, several thousand cheering citizens called for the president. At 9:30 p.m. he spoke briefly, emphasizing the themes of his earlier remarks; then he retired. The next day President Davis held a public reception at the Governor's Mansion, the women at 11 a.m. and the men at noon. Several thousand appeared. "No formal introductions or courtly display" marked this affair. An approving reporter noted, "The bearing of the President and manner of reception were dignified and simple, so that the humblest as well as the highest felt at ease."[40]

Davis's family followed him immediately by train. On the morning of June 1 Davis met Varina and the children, and a large crowd gathered to cheer the first family. Between the station and the hotel many floral bouquets were thrown into the Davis carriage. When one little girl's bouquet fell short, the president ordered the carriage stopped and the flowers picked up and handed to him, whereupon he gave them to Varina. According to an eyewitness, this "simple, unaffected" act "created a spontaneous burst of applause from the people."[41]

That evening citizens congregated in front of the Spotswood to serenade the chief executive and his family. Davis responded from a window. His brief words echoed what he had been saying about the Confederacy since his arrival in Montgomery. Confederates fought for their birthright for which their fathers had bled in the Revolution: "the richest inheritance that ever fell to man, and which it is our sacred duty to transmit untarnished to our children." To secure this inheritance, Davis was sure "there is not one true son of the South who is not ready to shoulder his musket to bleed, to die or to conquer in the cause of liberty here."[42]

Although Davis was surely pleased to have his family with him, he focused his attention on moving Confederate forces northward, to the Virginia side of the Potomac River. The Federals, who had already occupied Arlington and Alexandria, directly across the river from Washington, were concentrating, and talk abounded of an imminent advance. Even before he reached Richmond, Davis kept himself informed about the military situation in Virginia through communication with Robert E. Lee, who had been commanding Virginia state troops and whom Davis named Confederate commander in the state. The president ordered General Beauregard to proceed to Virginia and take charge of the army facing Washington. He also directed another new Confederate general, Joseph E. Johnston, a native Virginian and career officer, to take control at Harpers Ferry, the strategic spot at the foot of the Shenandoah Valley where the Shenandoah River flowed into the Potomac.[43]

In addition to appointing and placing generals, Davis worked energetically to get fighting men positioned on his northeastern frontier. To the Virginia front he directed units from many states, including those as far away as the Mississippi Valley. In getting troops to Virginia, Davis had to contend with two problems that would last as long as the Confederacy, the views of governors and the desire for local defense. As in the United States, raising an army in the Confederacy involved both the central government and the individual states. Congress authorized volunteers and set their term of enlistment; the president called for them; and the governors raised regiments. At the outset governors were eager to cooperate, and impressive numbers of men came forward. But at the same time governors wanted considerable influence on critical matters: the organization of volunteers, the appointment of officers, the disposition of weapons seized from Federal arsenals, and even the deployment of units. President Davis as well as Secretary Walker continuously strove to explain to governors what they already knew, that statutes passed by Congress governed both the types of units acceptable for Confederate service and the appointment of officers once organizations came under Confederate authority. Moreover, the Constitution specified the president as commander in chief. Davis also told state leaders the crisis required units to leave their native states to defend against the impending invasion of Virginia. Most governors eventually agreed and materially aided the president, though the effort to negotiate over a multitude of issues and gain that cooperation required much of Davis's time.[44]

One state chief executive proved particularly troublesome: Joseph E. Brown of Georgia. An ardent secessionist, Brown initially praised Davis. Even though he had never met the Mississippian, Brown considered Davis an excellent choice for president, "as his wisdom and statesmanship are known to all to be of the most profound and highest order." But Brown's actions quickly belied those words. Extraordinarily jealous of his gubernatorial prerogatives, and often declaring the requirements of his state more important than those of his new country, Brown demonstrated an amazing capacity for tenacious obstructionism and perverse obstinacy. He stalled the transfer of former Federal arsenals and forts to the Confederacy, and in the interval shifted the best weapons to his own armory. He tried to forbid regiments to join the Confederate army, and if they did so, he insisted that all state-owned arms must remain in Georgia. He wanted more troops for coastal defense, even though there was no immediate threat to his coast, and fought at every step sending units to Virginia. Davis and Walker both exerted themselves to work with the pettifogging Brown, often giving in for the sake of harmony. With Joseph Brown, Davis learned quickly that selfless commitment to the Confederate cause did not extend to all public officials. Although he did not upbraid or denounce Brown, he did not dispute Howell Cobb's description of Brown as "the miserable demagogue who now disgraces the executive chair of Ga."[45]

At the same time Davis treated with governors, he maintained constant communications with his two field commanders, Beauregard and Johnston. The president was an active, involved commander in chief. Whether he wrote directly or through Secretary Walker, General Lee, or General Samuel Cooper, formerly the adjutant and inspector general of the U.S. Army whom Davis had placed in that same role in the Confederate army, the president made suggestions and issued directives. Adopting the policy he would follow throughout the war, he told Johnston he wanted him to hold Harpers Ferry as long as possible, but as the commander on the scene Johnston must use his own discretion. To both generals he sent word that he was forwarding reinforcements as rapidly as possible.[46]

Davis did not have easy decisions to make. Both Beauregard and Johnston faced greater numbers, and each general pleaded for additional troops. Beauregard also urged Davis to give up the Shenandoah Valley and send Johnston to join him so that the combined Confederate armies could move against the Federals. While Davis liked the prospect of forward movement, he thought it far too premature to give up the Valley, critical politically and logistically. Responding, he told Beauregard to await the new troops he hoped would make an offensive possible.

In mid-July a restless Beauregard sent an aide to Richmond to present a more ambitious, even grandiose, plan. In it he again wanted Johnston to unite with him, and after they dispatched the enemy in his front, the combined armies would head west and defeat the Federals in the Valley. Thereupon Johnston would march into mountainous western Virginia and whip the Union forces coming eastward from the Ohio River. Then the victorious Confederates would reunite and threaten Washington. Although this design seemed logical, even flaw-less, on paper, it had little connection with reality—Johnston had barely half the 20,000 men Beauregard awarded him; Confederate suc-cess would depend upon utterly stationary Federals. Logistics did not intrude in this fanciful stratagem: the Confederacy possessed neither the transportation nor the supplies to support such complex move-ments.

Davis gave Beauregard's impossible design more attention than it merited. He permitted Beauregard's aide to present it to Lee, Cooper, and himself at a conference in Richmond. The deliberations indicated that the president and Lee had been discussing strategy and that they had agreed on the appropriate course for their armies. Lee responded, with Davis's assent clearly signaling his agreement. Gently noting the incredible complications in the proposal, Lee pointed out the enormous difficulties involved. Then he added that before any Confederate com-bination could succeed, the Federals would have to be drawn farther into Virginia. Attacked prematurely, the Federal hosts would simply fall back behind their impregnable defensive lines. The Beauregard-Johnston union would have to await the proper moment.

Even though preoccupied with the situation along the Potomac, President Davis had to be ready for the third session of the Provisional Congress, scheduled for June 20, the first meeting of Congress in Rich-mond. At the same time, during the first half of June he battled mani-festations of his old comrade, malaria, with what Varina called "congestive chills" striking him a dreadful blow. Yet he struggled to keep up with his work. When Congress convened, Davis presented a brief, upbeat message. Reporting that North Carolina and Tennessee had joined the Confederacy, he also asserted in an overstatement that the border states would have done likewise but for Lincoln's subversion of civil authority and declaration of martial law. Noting the probable invasion of Virginia, he expressed confidence that the patriotism of the Confederate army would thwart the enemy. In conclusion, he applauded the Confederate people for their "attitude of calm and sub-lime devotion to their country," praising the "courage with which they are already preparing to meet the threatened invasion in whatever pro-portions it may assume."[47]

While dealing with essential military and civil matters and in spite of illness, Davis made himself quite visible in Richmond, regularly visit-ing army units camped in and near the capital city on their way to the front. Obviously enjoying himself, and occasionally accompanied by aides and other dignitaries like Governor Letcher, he rode to the encampments, spoke to the soldiers, and mingled with them. Hurrahs and cheers greeted his appearance. A perceptive observer noted that "Jeff Davis is very good at that sort of thing"—making the president and commander in chief a real person to the men in the ranks.[48]

The War Department kept those units moving north as rapidly as possible, for conflict seemed imminent. On July 16 the Federal army under Brigadier General Irwin McDowell advanced toward Beauregard, who informed Richmond and prepared to strike the Federals. Immediately Davis ordered Johnston to travel by train from the Valley and link up with Beauregard. But on July 21 before Beauregard could mount his attack, McDowell assaulted the Confederates.[49]

President Davis wanted to do more than deploy armies; he wanted to participate with them on the battlefield. On the morning of July 21, with his nephew and aide-de-camp Joseph R. Davis, he left Richmond by special train. Although many believed the president would take the field and actively direct the fighting, Davis gave no indication of any such intention. By the time he reached Manassas Junction, the sounds of battle could be heard. At Confederate headquarters, Davis and his nephew were furnished horses and guided toward the action. As Davis rode forward, the initial and accurate reports of a Confederate defeat turned into news of Confederate victory. The timely arrival by rail of Johnston's brigades enabled the hard-pressed Confederates to turn the Federals back and put them to flight. Witnessing the signs of the Confederate triumph, Davis waved his hat to all he met, made several short, impromptu speeches as he rode along the lines, and received cheers from his troops.

After nightfall, Davis met with his two generals at Beauregard's headquarters. They exchanged congratulations; the president promoted Beauregard to full general and asked about plans for pursuit. After some discussion, the three men recognized the impossibility of pressing forward in any organized fashion. The First Battle of Manassas, or in Union terminology the First Battle of Bull Run, was over. After this battle as after so many Civil War battles to follow, the victorious army was too spent and too disorganized to follow up its tactical victory with effective pursuit. Later, looking back at what seemed a missed opportunity, each commander tried to blame the others for failing to order an advance. But on the night of July 21, the president and his two generals recognized and accepted reality. Davis did want to announce the victory, and he sent a dispatch proclaiming, "Our forces have won a glorious victory," killing many of the enemy as well as taking numerous prisoners and capturing much matériel. He declared, "Too high praise cannot be bestowed whether for the skill of the principal officers or for the Gallantry of all the Troops."[50]

Davis spent the next day touring the battlefield, conferring with generals, and visiting encampments. He particularly searched for a seventeen-year-old stepnephew reported as seriously wounded, but he did not find the young soldier before he succumbed to his wounds. After spending a second night, Davis left for Richmond at mid-morning on July 23. "A vast concourse" had gathered at the Virginia Central depot to meet the train coming from Manassas. When the crowd learned that the president had arrived, it rushed to find him. Even though tired, Davis responded with "fervid eloquence" to the "enthusiastic citizens." He passed "the highest encomiums upon our heroic soldiers, and particularly the two eminent men in command— Beauregard and Johnston. Too much praise cannot be bestowed on officers and men," he exclaimed, "for all determined to conquer or die." He "paid a glowing tribute" to the "honoured dead," which according to a reporter on the scene, "could not fail to dim with tears the eyes of the least feeling among his hearers." Brave men had preserved "the sacred soil of Virginia," and Davis predicted "a yet bloodier and far more fatal lesson awaits [our enemies] unless they speedily acknowledge that freedom to which you were born."[51]

Yet Davis had no illusions about the difficulties ahead. In a conversation with a friend, he said he believed the Confederates would do "all that can be done by pluck and muscle, endurance and dogged courage—dash and red-hot patriotism, & C." Still, Mary Chesnut reported, a "sad refrain" ran through his remarks. Davis expected a long war in which Confederates "would have many a bitter experience." In his mind, "only fools" could doubt the courage or the determination of the North. Yet he did not doubt his own courage or determination or that of his countrymen.[52]

Jefferson Davis recognized that he faced an absolutely committed foe; he also knew that the material resources on his side did not match those of his enemy. His experience in national affairs, especially in military matters, made him acutely aware of the equipment available to the Union army, as well as the war-making potential of the northern economy. In addition, he was aware that the Confederacy had far fewer men of military age.

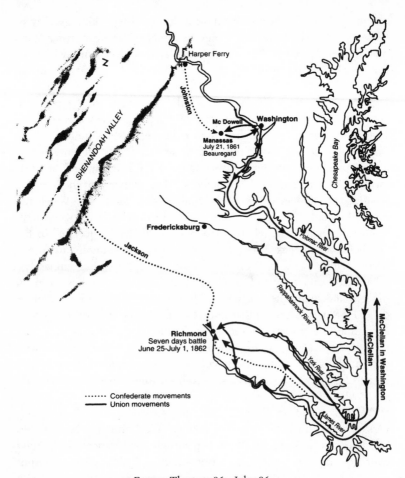

Eastern Theater, 1861–July 1862.
From W. J. Cooper and T. E. Terrill, The American South: A History *(2d ed.),*
with permission of the McGraw-Hill Companies

In fact, substantial disparities existed between the two sides. In 1860 the total population of the Confederate States was just over 9 million, while the Union total exceeded 22 million. In the most crucial category, white males aged eighteen to forty-five, the North enjoyed an advantage of around three to one. As it began its struggle for independence, the Confederacy commanded but 10 percent of the industrial capacity of the Union. In 1860 the North had produced over 90 percent of the country's firearms, pig iron, locomotives, cloth, boots, and shoes. The

Union also had twice the density of railroads per square mile, as well as considerably more mileage of canals and macadamized roads. Moreover, almost all of the rails within the Confederacy had been purchased from the North or Great Britain.[53]

Davis undoubtedly expected a long war, but his activity on the financial front gave no indication of that expectation. He had little understanding of public finance, and his treasury secretary, Christopher Memminger, no more. Neither grasped the magnitude of the financial requirements of fighting a great war. Although both believed that King Cotton would ensure British help, they did not think concretely about how that assistance would translate into defraying the cost of their war. Davis rightly deemed as impractical proposals for the government to purchase the cotton crop and transport it to Europe in order to build up Confederate monetary reserves. Most of the 1860 crop had already been sold and the 1861 crop would not be available until the autumn. A lack of ships made for an equally fundamental problem, besides the naval one of getting a large, unescorted transport fleet past Union warships. Davis would not support a government squadron of blockade-runners, for until late in the war he considered blockade-running a private affair.[54]

There are three major methods of financing a war: taxation, borrowing, and fiat money, with taxation the least inflationary. But antebellum Americans had been very lightly taxed, and on a per-capita basis southerners even less than northerners. Confederate authorities never embraced taxes. At the outset Congress was unenthusiastic, and initially Davis did not make a strong case for the necessity of taxation. Taxes would eventually be levied, but too late to have a positive impact on the financial situation.

The Confederate government preferred borrowing. Because European loans never provided sufficient funds, the government had to depend on its own citizens. In 1861 Congress authorized the issuance of $115 million in bonds. Yet, with most of its capital tied up in land and slaves, the amount of liquid capital to invest in bonds never met the demands. Recognizing the problem presented by illiquidity, Congress permitted investors to pledge the proceeds from their crops for bonds, the so-called "produce loans." Even so, most of the bonds were bought with treasury notes, or fiat money. Moreover, the sums generated were woefully inadequate. Paper money became the porous, crumbling financial foundation of the Confederacy. To pay its war bills Congress in 1861 authorized $170 million worth of treasury notes, redeemable in specie at face value within two years after the close of the war. But they never became legal tender as they did in the Union because a majority of Congress, along with the president and secretary of the treasury, envisioned constitutional and practical difficulties. The printing presses ran faster and faster, eventually pouring out a paper money avalanche of $1.5 billion. States and even localities also issued their own notes. Inflation kept pace, accelerating continuously, until by 1863 it was hurtling forward at runaway speed. In 1861 the price index went up some 60 percent; the next year, 300 percent; and by 1863 the Confederate economy had become unmanageable. In January 1864 the inflation rate exploded past 600 percent. The Confederacy literally drowned in a sea of paper money. President Davis never comprehended the dimensions of the disaster.

Preparing for war, the Confederacy confronted a unique social situation. Neither secession nor the formation of the Confederate States of America was conceivable without slavery, and the more than 3.5 million slaves within the Confederacy's borders formed a key part of the Confederate war effort. Their availability for agricultural work would enable almost all potential white soldiers to don a uniform. Moreover, slaves could perform essential labor on fortifications and other military construction, permitting most whites to serve in the combat arms. Yet a potential liability existed. Throughout the long history of slavery in the South, white men had always been omnipresent on farms and plantations. If demands of the war denuded the countryside of that group, no one could foretell the influence on order, discipline, and subordination within the slave force.

Cognizant of the dangerous war in which he found himself, Davis considered his country. Its huge size, stretching over 1,000 miles from the Atlantic Ocean westward to the vastness of Texas, and totaling some 800,000 square miles, was surely an asset, yet also a liability. To defeat the Confederacy, the Union would have to invade and occupy its territory, a formidable task. But Davis would have to defend his extensive borders.

President Davis often talked about the unity predominating among southerners. In his mind, "the magnitude and supreme importance of the present crisis" overrode and replaced all previous distinctions among those who became Confederates. Yet he recognized that a "national character" had not predated the formation of the new country, that one would have to be developed while fighting the war. In the autumn of 1861 he urged the brigading of troops by state because he saw "state pride" as "the highest incentive for gallant and faithful service." The lack of national feeling also convinced Davis that he must temper the military maxim of concentration. He believed he had to maintain a visible military presence throughout his country, or he would face "dissatisfaction, distress, desertion of soldiers, opposition of State Govts." In the midst of the war he told one of his commanders, "the general truth, that power is increased by the concentration of an army, is, under our peculiar circumstances, subject to modification. The evacuation of any portion of territory," he continued, "involves not only the loss of supplies, but in every instance . . . troops." He could envision a reaction so vigorous it could result in the "*collapse*" of the Confederacy. He struggled constantly with the difficult problem of concentration.[55]

Davis thought about more than defense. From the beginning, he emphasized that the Confederacy wanted to be left alone, but Abraham Lincoln would not grant his wish. With war upon his country, Davis was eager for his enemy to feel the pain and horrors brought by the conflict. He agreed with the many Confederates who pressed him to take the fight into the North. He informed his brother Joseph he would much rather have Confederate armies on the Susquehanna River than the Potomac. His desire to invade the North did not mean he wanted to capture territory, however. "My early declared purpose and continued hope," he wrote a supporter, "was to feed upon the enemy and teach them the blessings of peace by making them feel in its most tangible form the evils of war."[56]

Despite his undenied desire to order his generals beyond his borders, Davis could not do so. Reality constrained him. He knew quite well his War Department could not arm all the troops that had flocked to the Confederate standard. He could see no use in proclaiming that the Confederacy had shifted to the offensive when he could not back up his words with actions. Even in the face of criticism, he did not think he could explain his reasoning. "I have borne reproach in silence, because to reply by an exact statement of facts would have exposed our weakness to the enemy." Thus, he could only "pine for the day when our soil should be free from invasion and our banners float over the fields of the Enemy. . . ."[57]

Even though he could not send all Confederate armies northward, Davis was clearly an aggressive commander in chief, who wanted to strike the enemy whenever possible. As he instructed one of his generals, Confederates should grasp "the opportunity to cut some of his lines of communications, to break up his plan of campaign; and defeating some of his columns to drive him from the soil. . . ." He was forced to opt for a fundamentally defensive strategy, but he never accepted a static defense. And he always desperately desired to turn the tables and take the offensive.[58]

From the outset Davis personally directed the Confederate military machine. He believed he had real military ability, as did many other Confederates, who commented both on his opinion of himself and on his broad knowledge. He did employ advisers and assistants, but rarely did they become policy-makers. The highest-ranking Confederate officer, Adjutant and Inspector General Cooper, oversaw implementing regulations and maintaining the official record. He had occupied the same position in the pre-1861 U.S. Army, where Davis knew him well. The president trusted Cooper, an encyclopedia of military rules and procedures, and relied on his advice on interpreting regulations in areas like promotion; but Cooper did not have an influential voice in formulating policy.

From the earliest days in Montgomery, Davis basically acted as his own secretary of war. Considering no matter too trivial for his attention, he did not assign Secretary Walker primary responsibility for any activity. Much correspondence and many directives went out over Walker's signature, but all the major decisions, and many minor ones, were Davis's. That situation did not change with the move to Richmond. As the war became larger and the demands upon the War Department even greater, Davis's involvement remained so total that no room existed for Walker to act independently. The president's hand was on almost everything, including a Virginia civilian's offer of his home to care for wounded and a private's request for transfer to be near his brother.[59]

Even though Walker had little responsibility, the administrative demands of his job simply overwhelmed him. He had no pertinent experience and but limited ability. By midsummer Davis concluded that Walker could not handle his duties, a judgment in which other cabinet members concurred. Even more important, lawmakers had lost confidence in Walker, and when Congress adjourned on August 31, it left behind a committee to look into the operations of the War Department. Davis knew Walker had to go. To ease his departure the president refrained from officially communicating displeasure with his service and offered a foreign post, which Walker declined. He preferred appointment as a brigadier general and returning to Alabama.

Agreeing, Davis made him a general and sent him back to Alabama, but with an empty assignment. Even though he soon resigned his commission, Walker never wavered in his support of the president.[60]

When Walker resigned on September 16, Davis had no ready replacement in mind. He did question whether any civilian could do the job, and some wondered whether he would appoint a general. Davis decided to make an interim appointment; on September 17 he made Attorney General Judah Benjamin acting secretary of war.[61]

While President Davis had found his secretary of war not up to his task, he had no qualms about his chief adviser in uniform. Upon reaching Richmond, Davis kept Robert E. Lee by his side. Although the general did not have a formal title after Virginia forces were placed under Confederate authority, he acted as Davis's adviser. The two men had known each other since West Point, where Davis was a year ahead of Lee. They had never been close, but their paths did cross. Still on active duty in late 1849, Lee sought Senator Davis's counsel on whether he should accept command of a proposed, privately sponsored assault on Cuba. Lee turned down the offer. As secretary of war, Davis worked in harmony with Lee, who served as superintendent of West Point from 1852 until 1855. The secretary made clear his opinion of the Virginian when in 1855 he had Lee appointed to the permanent rank of lieutenant colonel and named assistant commander of the Second Cavalry, one of the new regiments created by Congress.[62]

In Richmond, the president and the general got along quite well. Davis wanted and needed Lee's advice on Virginia. More important, their discussions revealed that they shared similar views on the Potomac front. The Manassas campaign and their common reaction to Beauregard's fanciful scheme demonstrated their harmonious outlook. Even so, only a week after Manassas, on July 28, Davis felt compelled to send Lee to Trans-Allegheny Virginia to unite disputatious Confederate commanders and to thwart a Federal advance.

As Jefferson Davis contemplated the defense of his country, he was aware that Virginia and the Richmond-Washington corridor would always have critical importance, but he also recognized the centrality of the Mississippi Valley. As a resident of the Valley, Davis did not require a primer on the absolute need to defend the Mississippi River, the great highway into the heart of the Confederacy. Even so, leaders in the area apprised the president of its importance and urged him to make appropriate arrangements for its defense.[63]

To bring military order to the Mississippi Valley and assert Confederate authority, Davis wanted to appoint a commander to oversee all military operations. No obvious choice stood out. Two of his leading generals, Joseph Johnston and Beauregard, already had crucial jobs in Virginia. The president also felt he needed Robert E. Lee in Virginia. The man Davis esteemed more than any other as a military commander was in far-off California, though newspapers reported Albert Sidney Johnston riding eastward. Davis did not believe he could wait upon Johnston's arrival, even though he thought northern fear of the torrid summer in the Deep South would preclude any immediate attack down the Mississippi. No one yet knew that this war would be fought in all seasons on all fronts.[64]

Davis's selection for the West revealed a president who placed enormous trust in men he had known and respected during his formative years and who counted loyalty to the cause a primary qualification for high position. In mid-May, Leonidas Polk, Episcopal bishop of Louisiana, and a man of charm and persuasiveness, wrote the president about the necessity for a commander in the Mississippi Valley; then he offered his services in any capacity. Davis had known Polk at West Point, but since then they had not been in touch. Nor had Polk had any contact with anything military since his graduation in 1827, for he immediately resigned his commission to enter the ministry. Ordained in 1830, he was eight years later named missionary bishop of the Southwest, a vast territory extending into a half dozen states, and in 1841 he was chosen bishop of Louisiana.[65]

Responding to Polk's letter, Davis invited his former fellow cadet to visit. In June the tall, imposing cleric met with the president, several cabinet members, and General Lee. Impressed with Polk's earnestness and commitment, Davis on June 25 appointed him major general and assigned him command of the region from the mouth of the Red River to the northern border of Tennessee, to include the Tennessee River Valley. In this instance, the commander in chief gave a critical post to a military neophyte. But in his episcopal duties Polk had traveled widely in the Mississippi Valley, becoming familiar with its geography and people. Besides, Davis did not believe he had a more propitious choice. In addition, he was confident Federal dread of the tropical summer in the lower Valley would keep the enemy in place for a few months. In the meantime, Polk could assert Confederate authority and solidify defenses.[66]

When the new general departed Richmond, Kentucky was the major question in the West confronting the administration. When war broke out between the United States and the Confederate States, the border state of Kentucky proclaimed neutrality and forbade forces of either side to cross its borders. With adherents of both the Union and the Confederacy vying for the state's political allegiance, both belligerents initially honored Kentucky's wishes. But it was only a matter of time before armies bent on strategic advantage would break that artificial barrier. Eager for the state of his birth to secede formally and join his new nation, Davis did not want his soldiers to enter Kentucky first. Although aware of that policy, General Polk, rightly convinced that his enemy planned an early move, decided his mission required him to occupy Columbus, Kentucky, on the Mississippi River before the Federals did. Without giving prior notice to the War Department, Polk's forces violated Kentucky's neutrality on September 3 by occupying Columbus and immediately setting up fortifications.[67]

Polk's strike caused a crisis. The heavily pro-Union Kentucky legislature resolved by a three-to-one margin that the state had been invaded. At the same time the governor resigned, casting his lot with the Confederacy. Acutely concerned about the implications of Polk's action, Governor Isham Harris of Tennessee beseeched Davis on September 5 to order the general's immediate withdrawal because the presence of Confederate troops "injure[s] our cause in [Kentucky]." In his endorsement on Harris's telegram, Davis instructed Secretary Walker to direct Polk to retire from Kentucky and to explain his actions. Later the same day that Harris's message arrived, the War Department received Polk's wire declaring military necessity made taking Columbus essential. Polk's dispatch had been written before the president's directive reached him.[68]

Davis had to decide between a governor distraught over political fallout and a general defending his movements as militarily indispensable. After reading Polk's account, the president sent him a countermanding order: "the necessity must justify the action." Davis's response permitted Polk to make the final decision, and the general held his ground. Believing the individual on the spot best knew the immediate circumstances, Davis as commander in chief was always reluctant to overrule a field commander, and this one told the president that he absolutely had to act as he did. Davis upheld Polk because he thought he had little choice. Respecting Harris's judgment, and no political novice himself, Davis realized that in the short term his decision might be harmful to the Confederate cause in Kentucky. Yet he also knew that military might would ultimately settle the state's fate.

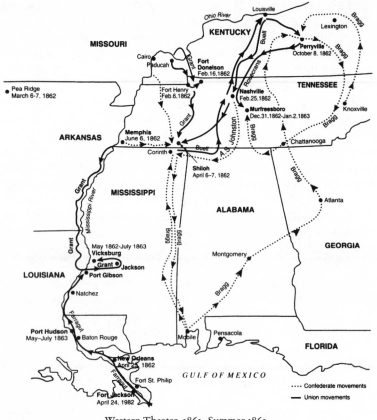

Western Theater, 1861–Summer 1863.
From W. J. Cooper and T. E. Terrill, The American South: A History (2d ed.), with permission of the McGraw-Hill Companies

On the scene he had a commander who had moved decisively to bolster his position. In standing behind Polk, Davis asserted his conviction that taking the offensive where possible was appropriate.[69]

Just as Davis affirmed Polk's intrusion into Kentucky, he once again fell prey to malarial symptoms. Wracked with intermittent fever, feeble, and weak, he went to bed. Although pressed by cabinet members to leave the capital for a nearby country seat to recuperate, the president stayed on. Then, at the end of the first week in September, from his second-floor sickroom he heard a familiar step. Immediately, he sent for Albert Sidney Johnston to come up and see him. Of that moment

Davis later said, "I felt strengthened and reassured, knowing that a great support had thereby been added to the Confederate cause."[70]

For reasons not completely clear, Davis considered Johnston a great soldier. The two men went back a long way, having been friends at Transylvania and West Point. Five years older than Davis and two years ahead of him at the Military Academy, Johnston seems to have been his friend's youthful beau ideal, a view the younger man held to tenaciously. For a time as junior officers they served together in the old Northwest. Both fought at Monterrey, and both received Zachary Taylor's praise. They also resigned from the army at almost the same time. No longer a soldier, Johnston emigrated to Texas, where he engaged in a variety of occupations. In 1855, Secretary of War Davis got Johnston appointed as colonel of the newly created Second Cavalry Regiment. By 1861, Johnston had been promoted to brevet brigadier general and was stationed in California as commanding general of the Department of the Pacific. After getting news that his adopted state of Texas had seceded, Johnston resigned his commission and set out overland for the Confederacy. Just over six feet tall, powerfully built, and with penetrating eyes, Johnston made a striking impression. No sterling combat record marked his career; but in 1861, Davis and many others—among them, Winfield Scott—shared the view that Johnston possessed great military ability, a conviction Davis never lost. Memories of shared experiences helped shape Davis's confidence that this man he had been admiring for almost four decades would perform superlatively in the great test of his chosen profession. Having already appointed Johnston to the rank of full general, the president now named him commander of Department No. 2, embracing parts of Mississippi, Tennessee, and Arkansas, as well as all military operations in Kentucky, Missouri, Kansas, and the Indian Territory. For this critical and difficult command, the president thought Johnston "the only man who seemed equal to it." In Davis's mind, the heartland of his country had found its defender.[71]

Sidney Johnston's command included Missouri, another torn and divided border slave state that demanded President Davis's attention. In March a state convention had rejected secession, but after Fort Sumter the pro-southern governor, Claiborne Jackson, called on Missouri to join her sister slave states. A civil war broke out in the state, and by midsummer the Union side had the upper hand. With the governor and the legislature decamping, the convention took over state governmental responsibilities. In June, Governor Jackson along with Davis's former U.S. Senate colleague David R. Atchison traveled to Richmond to see the president and request military assistance. Although concerned about the commitment of Missourians, especially the paucity of troops, Davis requested and obtained a $1 million congressional appropriation for Missouri.

Events in Missouri moved rapidly. On August 5, Governor Jackson issued a proclamation declaring Missouri independent. Five days later, Confederate forces defeated a Union army at Wilson's Creek in the southern part of the state. Led by Sterling Price, an immensely popular former governor, the victorious Confederates moved north and asserted authority over much of the state. But Price's advance was basically a raid because he had insufficient strength to hold territory. Reorganized and larger Federal forces drove Price back down to the southwest corner of the state. In the meantime, on November 3 a rump meeting of the pro-Confederate Missouri legislature met near the Arkansas border and passed an ordinance of secession. The Confederate Congress thereupon admitted Missouri as the twelfth Confederate state. But although Missouri senators and representatives sat in the Congress, the state's Confederate government existed in exile for the entire war.[72]

When dealing with the West, President Davis dispatched generals and orders and received visitors, but in Virginia he could go personally to his major army in order to discuss important matters. Moreover, that opportunity permitted Davis to join his troops at the front, which always pleased him. In late September, troubled by his lengthening, thinning defensive line, as well as by the increasing strength of the Federal army facing him, General Joseph Johnston requested that either the secretary of war or the president come to his headquarters at Fairfax Court House for a conference. Davis decided he would go, and on September 30, he took a 6 a.m. train out of Richmond.

He was met by Johnston with his two ranking officers, Beauregard and Gustavus W. Smith, a Kentucky native and West Pointer who was living in New York in 1861 when he decided to join the Confederate army and was commissioned a major general. Riding the four miles from the station to headquarters, Davis raised his hat to acknowledge the cheers of soldiers and civilians along the route. While at Fairfax Court House, on October 1, Davis reconnoitered toward enemy lines. He also "rode many miles visiting the encampments." Yet the most critical part of his trip was a conference with the three generals.

After some discussions of army organization, the generals raised the point that most interested them—going on the offensive. They wanted to cross the Potomac, flank the Federals, force them out of their fortifications, and then attack them. An obviously interested president listened; he had even brought with him maps of river crossings. To carry out their proposed plan, the generals insisted they needed substantial reinforcements of seasoned troops. Davis told them they were asking for the impossible. No such body of experienced men existed; only new troops were available. Besides, he confided, arms were still limited. Although he could not provide ingredients for a major offensive, Davis proposed raids across the Potomac against enemy batteries. This time General Johnston demurred, probably arguing correctly that such assaults involved too much risk for the potential gain. Thus, with the decision that Johnston's army would retain its defensive posture, Davis on October 4 returned to Richmond.[73]

President Davis did not appoint generals and establish war policy in a vacuum. He was a public figure acting on a public stage. As a veteran politician, he understood the importance of public opinion. He well knew that he had to conduct political and military campaigns as "a joint operation."[74]

Davis enjoyed great popularity in 1861, and if such had existed, certainly would have received a quite high approval rating for his performance in office. The general public, men in the army, those in civil office all testified to the widespread support for the president. The *Richmond Enquirer* spoke for many in its observation that "the Chief Magistrate of the Confederate States, not only enjoys the unqualified confidence of the Southern people, but he has deserved it." Observers often feared for the country without him. Secretary Mallory was convinced that should Davis die, "general dejection would ensue, and indeed our cause would have received a heavy blow & great discouragement."[75]

Testifying to his commanding public image, Davis had no opposition when he stood for election on November 6 as president for a full six-year term. In Montgomery, he and Alexander Stephens had been given provisional appointments, to serve for one year. That the country was fighting a war certainly contributed to the absence of opponents, as did the continuing determination of most Confederates to present a united front. Yet Davis's public standing was also consequential in his confronting no challenger. Even Joseph Brown did not think anyone should oppose Davis and Stephens. Summing up the general opinion, the *Richmond Examiner* declared Davis should be chosen, "not merely because he commands the popular confidence, but he deserves it."[76]

The election of Davis and Stephens did not mean that a team ran the executive department. Although in Montgomery the president had consulted with the vice president, after the move to Richmond those consultations took place less and less frequently. Telling a friend the president did not include him in military decisions, Stephens revealed no dissatisfaction. At this early point Davis excluded Stephens chiefly because of his concentration on military affairs, an area in which he did not see Stephens as a valuable adviser. In time, however, this tendency extended to other areas as well. Even though the president met often with his cabinet, the vice president had no special place. Of course, in basically disregarding his vice president, Davis followed the practice of all American presidents to 1860, and of most afterwards. Yet, by thus isolating a proud, sensitive man, Davis helped create a notable opponent of his administration. By paying the vice president just a little attention, he could have helped prevent the distance growing between them.[77]

Although in 1861 Stephens was not a political antagonist, elsewhere Davis confronted vigorous criticism, even enmity. The harmony so vigorously touted in Montgomery did not survive Montgomery. Robert Barnwell Rhett, Sr., Davis's first serious as well as venomous critic, emerged in Montgomery and remained in the forefront of opposition throughout the war. Robert Barnwell, who knew Rhett well, believed the origin of this personal and spiteful enmity lay in resentment because Davis occupied the position that Rhett, often called the father of secession, believed was rightfully his. Whatever the cause, Rhett's fury exploded shortly after Davis's selection as provisional president. When the Provisional Congress appropriated money to lease a home for the president, Rhett cried tyranny. From the podium of his newspaper, the *Charleston Mercury*, Rhett hurled denunciations that the president was "egotistical, arrogant, and vindictive," and decried his "terrible incompetency and perversity." He characterized his voting for Davis as one of the "greatest errors of my life." Rhett's opposition centered on Davis the man and president, not on policy. Anything Davis said or did, Rhett found poisonous and reprehensible.[78]

In the first year, Davis had the cooperation and respect of most governors, with whom he worked closely in building and deploying an army. Only Joseph Brown acted in a way that foreshadowed his joining

Rhett on the front line of Davis enemies. The shrewd Brown eventually drew Stephens and some of the vice president's friends into his orbit. In the autumn of 1861 a close Georgia associate of Stephens denounced Davis as "the prince of humbug," with no ability, only hunger for adulation. The Brown-Stephens alliance, which Toombs also joined, would become the strongest and most tenacious political opposition the president would face.[79]

An old political hand, Davis was not surprised by political opponents, though from the beginning he made clear his creed that allegiance to the Confederacy should outweigh all prior personal and political differences. Moreover, loyalty to the cause should subsume personal ambition. Offering a generalship to his old antagonist from the Mexican War, William B. Campbell, and giving a lieutenant's commission to young Henry S. Foote, Jr., illustrated his belief, as did his response to the request of an ardent foe of secession in Tennessee that the government release him from a charge of disloyalty. Davis did so, saying he did not believe past positions important. Only current loyalty to the Confederacy mattered.[80]

Discussing appointments with Tennessee governor Isham Harris, the president articulated his conception of the Confederacy and his identity with it. The governor expressed concern that Davis had paid too little attention to previous political affiliations in awarding army commissions to Tennesseans. According to Harris, "positive political necessity" required more military slots for former Whigs. In response Davis thanked the governor for advice that "shall not be disregarded," and urged him to write frequently and candidly. Explaining his previous appointments, Davis wrote that "the magnitude and supreme importance of the present crisis" caused him "to forget the past." Moreover, he "regard[ed] all good and true men *now,* as belonging to the *one party* of the South in which *all* are loyal, and *all* are equally entitled to recognition and honor."[81]

Davis certainly expected such loyalty and commitment from the professional soldiers leading his armies. But in the summer and fall of 1861 two occurrences fundamentally undermined that expectation. Davis's reaction to them would have massive consequences for him and for his country. These instances tested him as commander in chief while underscoring his understanding of the Confederate movement.

When, on August 31, Davis sent to Congress his ranking of the five full generals in the Confederate army, he ignited a firestorm of resentment. Back in March, Congress had passed a law setting full general as the highest rank in the army; the statute also stated that rank previously held in the United States Army should govern placement in the Confederate States Army. Even before First Manassas, the president had appointed four full generals—both Johnstons, Lee, and Samuel Cooper—and after the battle he rewarded Beauregard with promotion to the highest rank.

Even so, there had been no official seniority list until Davis's August message. It named Cooper as senior, followed in order by A. S. Johnston, Lee, J. E. Johnston, and Beauregard. In assigning seniority Davis did not go by rank held in the United States Army, except for making Beauregard the most junior. Cooper and Lee had been colonels, A. S. Johnston a brevet brigadier general, and J. E. Johnston a brigadier general. The younger Beauregard had been only a major.

President Davis gave various explanations for this ranking. He claimed to have followed West Point class and standing within a class—Cooper, 1815, A. S. Johnston, 1826, Lee and J. E. Johnston, 1829 (second and thirteenth respectively), Beauregard, 1838. He also said he placed A. S. Johnston and Lee ahead of J. E. Johnston because they had been line officers, while J. E. Johnston's generalship derived solely from his staff assignment as quartermaster general. In addition, he maintained that the law applied neither to Lee nor to J. E. Johnston, because both had entered the Confederate army from Virginia state forces where the former outranked the latter. But while each of these reasons may have had some validity, Davis was clearly rationalizing what he had done. The oldest, at sixty-three, Cooper would always work in Richmond, where he would sign a multitude of orders and directives. The president wanted no question about his authority. He believed A. S. Johnston to be his best soldier, and from his arrival in Richmond he had become increasingly confident in Lee. Thus, J. E. Johnston was left in fourth place.[82]

Joseph Johnston would have none of it. Always inordinately sensitive about rank, and especially careful in career activities to look out for himself, Johnston felt he had been insulted and his honor impugned. He was the only man to have held a permanent brigadier's rank, and he had no doubt that his name should have headed Davis's list. Angry and hurt, he penned a lengthy, agitated missive to the president in which he announced: "I now and here claim, that notwithstanding these nominations by the President and their confirmation by Congress, I still rightfully hold the rank of first general in the Armies of the Southern Confederacy." He maintained that by placing him fourth, Davis had broken him in rank. After writing the letter, Johnston kept it for two days, and then decided it exactly expressed his feelings and sent it. In the words of his most important biographer, the general had written "an ill-judged and foolish letter," which should never have been forwarded.

Jefferson Davis was taken aback. Johnston's language was surely inappropriate from a military subordinate to a superior; but, even more important, the letter told Davis that his general cared more about rank than the cause. He shared Johnston's protest with his cabinet, terming its tone "intemperate." He also read to his official family his brief but sharp reply: "I have just received and read your letter of the 12th instant. Its language is, as you say, unusual; its arguments and statements utterly one-sided; and its insinuations as unfounded as they are unbecoming." This was the official end. Never again during the war did the two men correspond about this matter, though its memory embittered Johnston for the rest of his life. In his reaction Johnston had revealed the human flaws of pride and ambition, which Davis could not countenance, for the Confederate purpose was far too serious to permit indulgence in such luxuries. This incident fundamentally altered the relationship between president and general; for quite different reasons, neither man ever again trusted the other.[83]

This affair with Johnston was not the only conflict Davis experienced with a general in the late summer and fall of 1861. Between August and October, Beauregard sent several fault-finding letters to the War Department, pointing to shortcomings, including food shortages. He even wrote to friendly congressmen, who read the charges to their fellows. The president resented Beauregard's involving members of Congress to publicize his opinions about supposed deficiencies in the War Department and his unhappiness about his command relationship with Joseph Johnston. After Judah Benjamin became acting secretary, the correspondence became increasingly acrimonious. In a number of lengthy, forbearing letters Davis attempted to ameliorate the situation, telling Beauregard he understood his frustration, but adding that everyone, including Benjamin, was doing all possible for the army. He also urged Beauregard to concentrate his energy on the real enemy in his front. Indicating he did not occupy his own post out of choice, Davis said he "labor[ed] assiduously in my present position," and "my best hope has been, and is, that my co-laborers, purified and elevated by the sanctity of the cause they defend, would forget themselves in their zeal for the public welfare."[84]

Discontented as Johnston's deputy and aware of his popularity—friends had even mentioned him for president in place of Davis—Beauregard now moved his self-promotion to a higher level. He filled his official report on the Battle of Manassas, dated October 14, with puffery and rhetorical excesses, strongly implying that he alone made the victory possible and would have marched on Washington if the president had not prevented his doing so. In addition, he pointedly noted that even before the battle, Davis had quashed his grand offensive plan. Poorly disguised as a mere battle report, this promotional tract was sent to congressional allies as well as to the War Department.

Davis first learned about the report from a summary printed in a Richmond newspaper. This time Beauregard had gone too far, and the president determined to set the record straight. He said he could handle the personal cuts, but worried that Beauregard's claims made the administration look bad and could undermine public confidence in its ability to manage the war. Thereupon, he rounded up documents to prove he did not stop any advance, and even obtained a corroborating statement from Joseph Johnston. When the president forwarded Beauregard's report to Congress, he attached an endorsement spelling out where he believed the general had erred.

Writing to Beauregard, Davis expressed surprise and disgust. That the report's text confirmed the newspaper account astounded him, "because if we did differ in opinion as to the measures and purposes of contemplated campaigns, such fact could have no appropriate place in the report of a battle." More than anything else, Davis found unacceptable Beauregard's descriptions of nonexistent plans and especially what "seemed to be an attempt to exalt yourself at my expense." In Davis's mind, his general had certainly not heeded his admonition to put cause above self. Davis now doubted the depth of Beauregard's commitment, a doubt that would only grow.[85]

As president, Davis served as both civilian and military leader. Those roles merged because Davis devoted himself to the military struggle to secure Confederate independence, but he conflated his own and his administration's actions and policies with patriotism. He could believe he had overcome the ambition that had been so central in his career both because of his absolute allegiance to the Confederate cause and because he was at the top. When he detected others acting for personal advantage, he suspected lack of commitment to the cause that had become all-encompassing for him. Aware that securing Confederate independence would be a herculean task, he was convinced Confederates had to put aside or suppress all personal concerns in accomplishing this sacred mission. He was also confident that he himself had done so.

Although building an army and fighting a war overwhelmingly pre-occupied President Davis, he tried to shore up his diplomatic front. When Robert Toombs resigned as secretary of state in July, Davis replaced him with Robert M. T. Hunter of Virginia. Davis had known Hunter in the United States Senate, where he had sat from 1847 to 1861. Moreover, the president wanted a Virginian in the cabinet, and Hunter seemed a logical choice. The advent of Hunter did not change the chief diplomatic goals of the Confederacy: recognition, especially by Britain and France, and assistance in lifting the blockade.[86]

Davis not only put a new man in the State Department, he also reconstructed his most important foreign mission. By autumn the orig-inal team sent to Europe had accomplished little. With high hopes for early intervention dashed, a frustrated Yancey resigned. At that time Davis decided to replace the commissioners with ministers plenipoten-tiary in the major capitals. To London, he sent James M. Mason, holder of an illustrious Virginia name and former chairman of the U.S. Senate Committee on Foreign Relations, but no Anglophile. For Paris, he chose another ex-senator, John Slidell of Louisiana, a most capable politician and a man at home with French culture and the French language.

Mason and Slidell came closest to succeeding in their mission before they ever landed in Europe. In October they left Charleston by blockade-runner. In Havana, they transferred to the British mail packet *Trent* for their trans-Atlantic voyage. But on November 8 the *Trent* was stopped by a U.S. Navy sloop, and Mason and Slidell were removed, before the *Trent* was permitted to continue. Although northern public opinion initially applauded the capture, the British voiced outrage. The British government dispatched an ultimatum to Washington demand-ing an apology and release of the two diplomats. In the tense weeks fol-lowing, talk of war reverberated on both sides of the Atlantic.

Davis denounced the seizure, charging that the United States had violated rights "held sacred even amongst barbarians." He certainly wanted the *Trent* crisis to lead to a break between Britain and the United States, even to war. His friend Ambrose Dudley Mann wrote from London that his sources predicted a joint Anglo-French move to raise the blockade.

With no ability to affect the outcome of the dispute, Davis could only wait and hope. But he waited and hoped in vain. The British gave the United States time to make a considered response. Ultimately unwilling to risk an armed clash with Britain, the Lincoln administration decided to release Mason and Slidell, with an accompanying declaration that the Union naval officer who had captured them acted without instructions. Britain accepted this explanation, and on January 1, 1862, Mason and Slidell resumed their journey. The settlement of the incident left the Confederacy unrecognized and the blockade in place. More important for the long term, having worked out a satisfactory solution to the crisis solidified relations between the two nations. The Confederates faced a daunting task in seeking to disrupt that association.

The British stance on the blockade compounded Confederate diplomatic difficulties. The Confederacy wanted the British to find the Union blockade of Confederate ports ineffective. Doing so would mean the blockade was not legally binding on neutral countries, like Britain and France. The crucial issue under international law was whether a blockade was physically effective. The Confederacy supported the stand that the United States, as a neutral power, had taken in previous European wars: for a blockade to be legal, the blockading power had to seal off absolutely access to its enemy's ports. By pointing to the numerous vessels that successfully ran the Union blockade, the Confederates attempted to prove its ineffectiveness. But Britain, the world's greatest naval power, had always argued that patrolling warships trying to stop vessels from entering or leaving enemy ports made a blockade effective and legal. In this instance, while the Confederacy advocated the customary American position, the Union stood where the British traditionally did. Not wishing to create a precedent that could rebound against its interest in a future conflict, the British government in early 1862 declared the blockade legal.[87]

As Jefferson Davis formulated military and foreign policy, he had the comfort of his family in Richmond. At first the Davises lived at the Spotswood Hotel, where he had bedrooms as well as a private table and parlor, though the press of people turned them into quasi-public spaces. The family itself almost made a crowd: Jefferson, Varina, the three children—Maggie, Jeff Jr., Joe—and Varina's younger sister Margaret (also known as Maggie). In addition, Varina was once again pregnant.[88]

The Davises did not long remain hotel residents, for on August 1 they moved to the newly acquired Executive Mansion of the Confederate States. Located in the city's Court End neighborhood at 12th and

Clay Streets, a short distance northeast of the Capitol, the mansion stood "on the brow of a steep and very high hill . . . sharply defined against the plain at its foot." Its fourth owner, Richmond merchant Lewis Crenshaw, sold the house to the city, which, in turn, leased it to the Confederate government as the presidential residence. Although it had an outer surface of gray stucco, the house became known as the White House of the Confederacy. Crenshaw had recently transformed the two-story, neoclassical house built in 1818 into a three-story Italianate mansion. He installed gas-burning chandeliers, called gasoliers. Following upper-class taste of the mid-Victorian period, he added richly ornamented interior details and furnishings of the American Rococo Revival style. Gilded, tasseled, and tufted, Crenshaw's residence proved worthy of a president.[89]

On the first floor of the White House were most of the public rooms—the state dining room, a receiving parlor, and a more formal drawing room. Visitors entered an oval entrance hall before proceeding to the central parlor, or they turned right, went through a side door, and ascended the main staircase or went beyond the stairs into a small private library. On the second floor the offices of the president and his private secretary occupied the center of the house, behind a small waiting room. The master bedroom with dressing room flanked one side of these offices, and a large nursery the other. There was also a water closet. In the new third story were rooms for aides and guests. The family dining room shared space in the basement with a warming kitchen, butler's pantry, storage room, and perhaps a sleeping area for servants. Outbuildings included quarters for slaves and a gardener, a stable and a carriage house, and a two-story brick kitchen.

As first lady, Varina maintained an active social life—lunches, teas, receptions. In the White House, she received almost every evening, with guests crowding into the first-floor public rooms. She was a gracious hostess, though she often retired early from weariness caused by her pregnancy, which occasionally required her to stay in bed. Everyone was pleased when on December 6, a new baby named William Howell Davis joined the family. Naming the new son for Varina's father produced no marital unhappiness.[90]

As presidential wife in Richmond, Varina strongly resembled the cabinet and Senate wife of Washington. Clever, strong-minded, willing to express her opinion, including even her continued "unaltered feelings" for her northern friends, she drew other women to her. In Mary Chesnut's words, she could exert "great force." At the same time,

White House of the Confederacy, looking down Clay Street, April 1865.
Library of Congress, copy print, Museum of the Confederacy

her sharp wit and biting comments could repel. She sometimes squabbled with other notable wives, like Charlotte Wigfall, whose husband, the Texas politician Louis Wigfall, had been an ardent supporter of Davis before and after secession but soon became a bitter foe. One observer noted that "quiet smiles or decided laughter convey & cover rifle balls." Varina was even called "the Empress Eugénie."[91]

She displayed two sides of a forceful personality. Secretary Mallory found her "a truthful, generous good woman," whose "perception of the ridiculous is perfectly riotous in its manifestations." Yet he commented that she "lack[ed] precisely what she plumes herself upon,—refinement & judgement; and her attempts at mimicry though they sometimes amuse, are not only usually failures, but they present her in a light at once undignified and unamiable." The acutely perceptive Mary Chesnut also caught both Varinas, describing her as kind and as "affability itself," but remarking on a lack of civility and a willingness to be unnecessarily abrasive in contretemps.[92]

A special familial pleasure for Jefferson came from a visit from brother Joseph, whom he had not seen since leaving Mississippi. In his

White House of the Confederacy in its wartime setting.
Museum of the Confederacy

new position, the youngest yearned for counsel from the oldest. Writing Joseph in mid-June, Jefferson had said he expected soon to have "a good house" and urged his brother to visit. "Your advice to me," he continued, "always desirable is now more than at any previous period coveted." Much to the president's delight, Joseph journeyed to Richmond, arriving on July 21 with an entourage including his wife Eliza, two grandchildren, and three others. Initially they put up at the Spotswood, but when Jefferson occupied the White House, he insisted that Joseph come along. At first Joseph objected, but when Jefferson indicated he would return to the hotel unless his invitation was accepted, Joseph agreed. He, Eliza, and the grandchildren moved into the White House, where they joined Jefferson and Varina at receptions.[93]

Joseph also brought news of Brierfield. Since becoming president, Jefferson had not had much time to think about his plantation, but he did get occasional reports. His friend and factor Jacob Payne wrote about supplies for Brierfield and the favorable season for picking cotton. In December, his overseer Nicholas Barnes informed his employer about "your Place & Bisness." Predicting a crop totaling 70,000 pounds of seed cotton, Barnes thought it would exceed the 1860 production. He also noted an ample corn crop. In addition, he declared the slaves were "well and doing Vary well."[94]

During the five-week visit of the Joseph Davises, Eliza Davis attentively noticed the brother-in-law she had known for three decades. Like other watchful observers, she detected the emotional and physical impact of his presidential duties. Eliza judged him "sadly changed," thinner than usual and affected by mood swings, "at times cheerful & again depressed." Although he could receive bad news stoically, "without the slightest evidence of *feeling* beyond a change of color," contemplating reversals and failures could make him "gloomy." Eliza was also bothered by the unending stream of callers that made it impossible for him "to take his meals in peace." Varina remembered that when he ate under "any excitement," dyspepsia flared, afflicting him for days.[95]

For Jefferson Davis the official business that both buoyed and dispirited him was never far away. As 1861 drew to a close, he made ready for the final session of the Provisional Congress scheduled to convene in mid-November. As with all his congressional messages, this one was carefully prepared, with the cabinet fully consulted. In a confident tone the chief executive touched upon many items from the Post Office Department to financial matters, but he concentrated on three topics—the military effort; diplomatic goals; and the enemy.

Upon Confederate armies he heaped great praise. They had defeated the Federals on battlefields from Virginia to Missouri and had halted the northern invasion. He also asserted that substantial progress had been made in arming and equipping the fighting men, who were now better able to confront their opponents. For this improvement he credited both the government and private ventures, though he hastened to add that these advances must continue. "If we husband our means and make a judicious use of our resources," he informed the solons, "it would be difficult to fix a limit to the period during which we could conduct a war against the adversary whom we now encounter."

In addition, he told the legislators that the administration was ardently pursuing diplomatic recognition by foreign countries. He believed recognition would result in assistance for raising the blockade. To that end, he said, the government was actively engaged in proving to foreign nations that because of its porousness, the blockade was ineffectual under international law. Delivering this message in the midst of the *Trent* crisis, the president expressed optimism that the Confederates would realize their diplomatic goals. Even so, he proclaimed that "the successful prosecution of the war" did not necessitate ending the blockade because the Confederacy could redirect its economy and become "more and more independent of the rest of the world."

Davis reserved harsh words for his foes. In his judgment, the war waged against the Confederacy had become "barbarous." The Union had "bombarded undefended villages" and participated in "arson and rapine, the destruction of private houses and property, and injuries of the most wanton character even upon non-combatants," especially along the Confederate border. He condemned the successful Union naval assault on Port Royal, South Carolina, as designed "to pillage," and, most frightening, "to incite a servile insurrection in our midst."

Even facing such a savage adversary, Davis betrayed no doubt about the ultimate outcome of the struggle. After noting the Confederates' "humble dependence upon Providence . . . to whose rule we confidently submit our destinies," he concluded: "Liberty is always won where there exists the unconquerable will to be free, and we have reason to know the strength that is given by a conscious sense, not only of the magnitude, but of the righteousness of our cause."[96]

CHAPTER TWELVE

"The Noblest Cause in Which Man Can Be Engaged"

Presidents of the United States had traditionally hosted public receptions on New Year's Day, and on his first New Year's Day as president of the Confederate States, Davis did likewise, opening his White House for all who wanted to come. From 11 a.m. until 3 p.m. on January 1, 1862, Jefferson Davis welcomed callers to the Executive Mansion. Standing just within the parlor fronting the main entrance hall of the house, Davis greeted each visitor, introduced by an aide at his side. Although he received without Varina, kept in her room by illness, Davis's "hearty cordiality" charmed the guests, "a continuous throng" that kept the president busy shaking hands. "A very large bowl of apple brandy toddy" and the Armory Band helped create a cheerful mood.[1]

As Davis greeted 1862, he led an infant nation striving for independence, and he commanded armies stretching from the Atlantic coast across the Appalachians to the Mississippi River and even beyond. What a month later he called "war on so gigantic a scale" was surely underway.[2]

Early in the new year Davis prepared for his inauguration as the first elected president of the Confederate States. The ceremony was set for February 22, birthday of George Washington, the father of the original American republic, whom the Confederates claimed as their own Founding Father. To make the connection as powerful as possible, Davis would give his inaugural address below the great equestrian statue of Washington on the Capitol grounds next to the Virginia statehouse, now the home of the Confederate Congress.

Cold temperatures, dark skies, and heavy rain made for a dismal day. After a morning in his office, Davis with Varina went by carriage from the White House to the Capitol, where he met Vice President Stephens, members of Congress, and the cabinet, along with other dignitaries. Because of the nasty weather, some proposed holding the ceremony inside, but Davis said no. The procession moved out to the statue of Washington, where a platform had been erected and covered with an awning. Despite the downpour and the mud almost ankle-deep, "a dense and eager crowd" jammed every approach to Capitol Square. Observers commented on the multitude of umbrellas, resembling "the appearance of a plantation of immense mushrooms." A band played "Dixie."[3]

Following the invocation, shortly after noon, Davis rose to speak. He did not seem to notice the rain falling directly on the speaker's stand, but someone quickly held an umbrella over him. Mostly reading from his prepared text, Davis spoke "in a fine manner and with a loud voice." He began by proclaiming that through the Confederate States "we hope to perpetuate the principles of our revolutionary fathers. The day, the memory, and the purpose seem fitly associated." That purpose, he explained, was simply "to maintain our ancient institutions." In order to secure the Confederate cause, Davis "pledge[d] a zealous devotion of every faculty to the service of those who have chosen me as their Chief Magistrate."[4]

In his brief remarks Davis emphasized the righteousness of the Confederate mission while he pointed to the "lights" and the "shadows" characterizing the initial year of the Confederate experience. Yet despite the "trials and difficulties," he had no doubt about the final result of what he termed "this great strife." Although assured, Davis did not say ultimate victory would come easily; it would require a "determined spirit," one even greater than already exhibited. "To show ourselves worthy of the inheritance bequeathed to us by the Patriots of the Revolution, we must emulate that heroic devotion which made reverse to them but the crucible in which their patriotism was defined." In closing he turned to God: "I trustingly commit myself, and prayerfully invoke thy blessing on my country and cause."

After Davis finished and the cheers ended, the ceremonies continued with the oath of office administered to president and vice president. At the conclusion of the official activities, the band struck up "La Marseillaise." That evening from 8 to 11 p.m. the president and first lady hosted a reception at the White House. Even though torrents of rain still pelted the city, several hundred well-wishers attended. A reporter noted that Varina performed with "rare grace and unaffected dignity." Though pale, the president "appeared cheerful and in good spirits."[5]

During the late winter and into the summer of 1862, Davis's spirit would be sorely tested by circumstances all along his far-flung battle lines. In Virginia, he kept in close touch with Joseph Johnston. Occupying the positions he had held since First Manassas, Johnston faced a greatly strengthened Federal army under a new commander, Major General George B. McClellan. Both Davis and Johnston realized he would have to withdraw to more defensible lines. Summoned by the president, Johnston arrived in Richmond on February 19 to assess his situation. Davis involved the entire cabinet in a lengthy discussion covering a wide range of military topics, from strategy to the technical difficulties in moving heavy guns.[6]

At the meeting Davis and Johnston agreed the Confederates should pull back, probably all the way to the Rappahannock River, in order to place a significant natural barrier between them and McClellan's host. At the same time, Davis wanted to salvage as great a quantity as possible of the weapons and other supplies that had been accumulated to support Johnston's army. Upon leaving the capital, Johnston believed he possessed the authority to withdraw whenever he deemed best. The president certainly concurred, telling his general, "as has been my custom I have only sought to present general purposes & views. I rely on your special knowledge & high ability to effect whatever is practicable in this our hour of need." But Davis wanted to know what his commander intended. As he had earlier written, "Please keep me fully & frequently advised of your condition, and give me some early information. . . ." But keeping his commander in chief so apprised of his intentions was not primary for Johnston. He worried about leaks of military information within the administration, and he remained guarded with the president.[7]

When, on March 13, Johnston informed Davis that he had largely completed his withdrawal behind the Rappahannock, the president was surprised. "I was as much in the dark as to your purposes, conditions, and necessities, as at the time of our conversation on the subject about a month since." Johnston's report that he had been forced to destroy a massive quantity of supplies also distressed the president, who knew the difficulty in replacing them. The destruction was not all Johnston's fault, for a clogged rail line south from Manassas Junction hindered movement. Moreover, poor planning and coordination within various bureaus and the War Department, which Johnston had complained about, contributed to the confusion and inefficiency. Yet Johnston, as senior commander on the spot, could not escape all responsibility for this logistical disaster.[8]

Despite this unexpected turn of events, Davis had to deal with the present. Once Johnston had established himself south of the Rappahannock, Davis again journeyed to see his general at Johnston's headquarters near Fredericksburg. On March 22 they talked and even reconnoitered Federal positions north of the river. President and general on horseback began to ford the river when a dog belonging to their guide's son followed along. The boy yelled, "Come back Jeff." Turning in his saddle, Jefferson Davis smiled.[9]

But more important than dogs or reconnaissances were discussions about McClellan's intentions and the appropriate Confederate response. Johnston correctly believed that McClellan would not come straight at him, but he did not know precisely how his opponent would attempt to get around him. Using Federal naval superiority, McClellan had decided to turn Johnston's right flank by taking the water route down the Potomac and on down the Chesapeake Bay all the way to the confluence of the York and James Rivers with the Bay. There he would come ashore and threaten Richmond by advancing up the Peninsula, the land between the rivers. By late March, Davis knew of McClellan's move, which placed a massive army some seventy-five miles southeast of the capital.[10]

This maneuver posed a serious problem for Davis and Johnston, who had to decide whether to concentrate all their forces to oppose McClellan or to leave contingents elsewhere to guard against other Union forces, particularly the sizable group left behind at Fredericksburg. The numerical disparity made the situation even more desperate. McClellan commanded more than 100,000 men on the Peninsula; 40,000 remained at Fredericksburg. Johnston had little more than 40,000 in his main army and around 12,000 men in McClellan's path along the James and York Rivers. In western Virginia almost 20,000 Confederate troops were in and around the Shenandoah Valley.

To make the critical decision on how to meet this crisis, President Davis on April 14 held an all-day council of war in Richmond. He hosted Johnston and two of his generals along with the secretary of war and Robert E. Lee, once again Davis's military adviser. Johnston urged concentration at Richmond of all forces in Virginia reinforced by all available units from the Carolina-Georgia coast, but he had no interest in fighting McClellan on the Peninsula, which he believed utterly futile. Instead, he wanted to strike northward with the bulk of the newly thrown-together force in a campaign beyond the Potomac, leaving a garrison to protect Richmond. Davis and Lee raised serious questions. They saw no guarantee that McClellan would follow Johnston without first marching into Richmond and then following with his vastly superior numbers. They were unwilling to risk the capital and the army. The capital was also endangered from the south, for the enemy had successfully invaded the North Carolina coast at Roanoke Island, only 100 miles below Richmond. Besides, Lee thought the Peninsula a good place to fight because the restricted land space could work to the Confederate advantage. He also worried that stripping the coast would result in the fall of Savannah and Charleston.

Davis sided with Lee: the Confederates would fight on the Peninsula. Although Johnston would not get all the reinforcements he wanted, the president did give him the troops in northern and eastern Virginia and did begin bringing up individual units from the Carolinas. By May, Johnston commanded the largest army yet assembled by his government, around 70,000 men. Still, Johnston's pessimism remained; he saw no way he could stop McClellan's juggernaut. He simply did not believe he could operate successfully on the ground assigned.[11]

Turning toward the West offered Jefferson Davis no relief. Although he had absolute confidence in Sidney Johnston, the general was deeply concerned about the means available to defend his vast front extending from the Appalachians westward across the Mississippi. Johnston centered his line in central Kentucky because of the state's political and military importance, but a determined Federal push in several locations, particularly up the rivers leading into the southern interior, could unhinge his position. To plead for more resources, he had written a letter early in 1862 and sent it by a staff officer to Davis. As Davis read the message on January 14, the officer remembered the president's features contracting as he exclaimed, "My God!" He explained that he would do what he could but could send neither sufficient arms nor sufficient men to Johnston because he did not have them. Moreover, every other commander was making identical demands. Johnston would have to raise troops in Tennessee. "We commenced this war without preparation," Davis concluded, "and we must do the best we can with what we have."[12]

The next news from the West was even worse. In early February a combined army-navy Federal force advanced up the Tennessee and Cumberland Rivers under the direction of a determined, compact general, with the cigar stuffed in his mouth seemingly a permanent part of his anatomy. Just south of the Kentucky-Tennessee border, Ulysses S. Grant assaulted and captured Forts Henry and Donelson, the respective guardians of the two rivers. The Confederates mounted a futile, and at Donelson an embarrassing, defense, with almost the entire force there surrendered. Grant's success made Sidney Johnston's position in Kentucky untenable and Nashville, on the Cumberland, indefensible. Johnston had to retreat all the way through Tennessee into northern Mississippi. His entire front caved in. This catastrophe was compounded in far-off northwestern Arkansas, where in early March at Pea Ridge the major Confederate army west of the Mississippi suffered a severe defeat. Reconquering Missouri became a distant hope.[13]

The rapid and unexpected collapse of Johnston's front occasioned a great public outcry. The concomitant fall of Nashville and the news that the garrison at Fort Donelson had surrendered without trying harder to fight its way out fueled the clamor. Letters poured in to the president about the calamity, including one from the Tennessee congressional delegation. Some writers begged Davis to take command in the field to salvage the cause. This hammer blow affected the president personally. A cabinet member reported him "distressed and almost gloomy." The capitulation at Fort Donelson especially perplexed him; he could not understand Confederates giving up without fighting. Although he had no intention of altering his role by taking active command of a field army, he understood the import of what he described to Joseph as "recent disasters in Tennessee." He realized he would have to exert every effort to "retrieve our waning fortunes in the West," lest support for the Confederacy in that region decline precipitously.[14]

In this bleak time Davis still clutched one certainty, the ability of Sidney Johnston. To his favorite soldier he penned a consoling message, yet one acutely perceptive about the war he was waging and the country he was leading. "We have suffered great anxiety because of recent events in Ky. & Tenn.," he admitted, "and I have been not a little disturbed by the repetitions of reflections upon yourself." While eagerly awaiting Johnston's full report, the president wrote, "I made for you such defense as friendship prompted, and many years of acquaintance justified." Still, he went on, "I needed facts to rebut the wholesale assertions made against you to cover others, and to condemn my administration."

The political veteran told his general the public did not understand the military situation because it believed Johnston's force much stronger than it actually was. The Confederate game of bluff had been working on the home front as well as against the Federals. But now "a full development of the truth is necessary for future success." Informing Johnston that he must not protect anyone out of generosity, Davis stressed that "the question is not personal, but public in its nature." As he would so often do, Davis maintained he could absorb adverse blows, and he was certain Johnston could as well, but he underscored that "neither of us can willingly permit detriment to the country."[15]

Davis advised Johnston that he would strive to augment his army. And he had already begun calling for reinforcements from all over the West, including the river force at New Orleans, to succor Johnston. General Beauregard waited in Corinth, Mississippi, for these disparate units. Even before Fort Donelson, Davis had ordered Beauregard to leave Joseph Johnston's army to assist Albert Sidney Johnston in his huge command. As the victorious Federals pursued the retreating Confederates, they divided their forces, one under Grant ascending the Tennessee, another initially sent to Nashville, and a third along the Mississippi. President Davis urged Johnston to strike one Federal column. He recognized that Johnston, even reinforced, would be no match for the united Union host, but he hoped his general could isolate one element of his enemy and inflict a blow of such magnitude that sagging morale would rebound. He told Johnston he anticipated victory, and as with all his commanders asked to be kept fully and regularly informed.[16]

Sidney Johnston did not disagree. In early March he sent an aide to Richmond to affirm that he remained optimistic and intended to fight, but not until he had crossed the Tennessee River. Later in the month he sent a lengthy message to the president, saying he expected the criticism leveled against him. But he had been so busy trying to cope with the disastrous situation, he had not had the opportunity thoroughly to investigate events at Fort Donelson. After sketching his current understanding of what had happened there, Johnston said he had no interest in attributing blame to subordinates for past errors. Instead, he was concentrating on future operations. He also hoped Davis would soon visit his army, and if the president decided to assume command, he would happily assist. In the meantime, Johnston planned to join with Beauregard and turn on the enemy before he could reunite. He believed the result would silence all critics. In this message, the president saw what he saw in himself, a selfless patriot eager to destroy the enemy.[17]

On April 6, Johnston flung his hurriedly assembled and incompletely organized army at the most advanced Federal column under Ulysses Grant, encamped on the western side of the Tennessee River just across the Mississippi state line from Corinth. Shiloh, the name of a little country church, became the Confederate designation for the greatest and bloodiest battle of the war to that date; together casualties on both sides reached some 24,000. On the first day the Confederates seemed on the verge of fantastic success against the surprised Federals. Intent on driving Grant back into the Tennessee River, the gray lines pressed inexorably forward in vicious fighting. But as daylight began to disappear, the Confederate attack was halted. Tidings of a great victory flashed to Richmond, but there was terrible news for the president: Sidney Johnston had died on the battlefield, mortally wounded while rallying his troops on the front lines. Command passed to Beauregard, who late in the afternoon stopped the assaults.[18]

Reinforced the next day by units arriving from Nashville, Grant drove the Confederates back across the ground they had purchased so dearly, and Beauregard withdrew to Corinth. This was not the great victory that had been initially reported and celebrated in the capital. Still, Shiloh—or Pittsburg Landing, as the Union called it—would have enormous consequences. The battle ended all thought of a quick and easy Union triumph in the West; the Confederates could and would fight.

For Jefferson Davis, the disappointment in the outcome at Shiloh could not match his distress at Sidney Johnston's death; he pronounced the loss "irreparable." Privately he wept, mourning Johnston's loss as "the greatest the country could suffer from." Later he confessed to the general's son, "My dear Boy, I cannot think calmly of your Father. I cannot speak or write of him without immotion." In his memoir he wrote that in Johnston's "fall the great pillar of the Southern Confederacy was crushed, and beneath its fragments the best hope of the Southwest lay buried." Based on reports coming to him that he surely wanted to accept, Davis also believed that in halting the Confederate attack Beauregard had given up Johnston's great victory, a belief he clung to all his life. The question of whether Beauregard's decision to halt prevented a decisive Confederate triumph has no simple answer. The weight of scholarly opinion holds that the Confederate assault had spent itself, and neither Johnston nor anyone else could have driven Grant into the Tennessee River, though not all students of the battle agree. As for leadership, riding along the front lines like a regimental commander, Johnston demonstrated a flair for inspiring volunteer troops on the battlefield but revealed little mastery of tactics or full understanding of the role of a commanding general.[19]

While coping with frustration and grief in the West, Davis also had to deal with the enemy almost at his doorstep. McClellan was slowly and methodically pushing Joseph Johnston back up the Peninsula toward Richmond. In mid-March, to help deal with this massive military responsibility, Davis brought Robert E. Lee back as his military adviser. After some difficult months in western Virginia, and following the fall of Port Royal, South Carolina, Lee had been sent to shore up the coastal defenses of South Carolina and Georgia. Although Davis worried that ordering Lee to return to Richmond could risk the safety of Charleston and Savannah, he decided he had to have Lee by his side. On March 13, Davis charged Lee with conducting "military operations in the armies of the Confederacy" under the president, though Lee was not specifically designated commanding general. Still, he had Davis's authority, and after Sidney Johnston's death, he outranked every other officer in the Confederate army but Adjutant and Inspector General Cooper.[20]

On March 14, at almost the same time Davis appointed Lee, he vetoed a bill passed by Congress creating the office of commanding general of all Confederate armies. In rejecting the bill, Davis has usually been faulted for his unwillingness or inability, or both, to relinquish any authority. Yet Davis had been involved in preparation of the initial bill; but when a provision was added permitting the commanding general on his own initiative to take the field, Davis balked and tried unsuccessfully to have that stipulation deleted. He had legitimate reasons for his objections to the proposed statute. In his veto message he assured Congress that he "fully approve[d]" the proposition to have an individual "under direction of the President" head the army. After all, he had just given Lee such a commission. His problem lay elsewhere, and he had tried unsuccessfully to get Congress to reconsider his concern. He specifically rejected the portion of the measure that permitted the commanding general at his choice to take the field and command any army he pleased, without presidential authority. In Davis's mind, this provision completely undermined the constitutional vesting of the president as commander in chief. As he bluntly put it, "The Executive could in no just sense be said to be Commander in Chief if without the power to control the discretion of the general created by this act." Davis had a sound constitutional position; besides, no president would willingly give up the power Davis zealously guarded. Davis may not have wanted anyone to carry the title commanding general of all armies, but he had Lee, to whom he had given similar powers, and before Shiloh he had his most trusted general in command in the West.[21]

Lee occupied a critical position and exercised considerable influence, particularly in the East. As the intermediary between the president and Joseph Johnston, he transmitted Davis's wishes and attempted to glean information about Johnston's intentions. Davis and Lee wanted to strike McClellan; an unhappy Johnston doubted the wisdom of defending Richmond, much less attacking the stronger enemy. He remained uncommunicative and even secretive. On May 14 Davis and Lee visited Johnston's headquarters for a full discussion, but even though the three men talked until quite late—so late that Davis and Lee spent the night—no conclusion was reached. Responding to Davis's inquiries about his plans, Johnston replied that because he had insufficient strength to take the offensive, he had to bide his time and hope his adversary would make a mistake. Two days later, with Johnston in Richmond's suburbs, a presidential message received the same vague response; the general could only wait for McClellan. Even this crisis did not allay the tension between president and field commander.[22]

With Lee, however, the president enjoyed a sharply different relationship. During their time together in the late spring and summer of 1861, and again between March and May of 1862, when they saw each other almost daily, the two men developed a rapport, even a trust. As Davis told an aide, "Genl Lee acts in accord with [me]." Lee was not so cautious or timid as Johnston, nor was he plagued with the concern that action might injure his reputation. He and Davis agreed that the Confederates could not keep waiting until Johnston perceived a blunder by McClellan. In addition, neither wanted to give up Richmond without a desperate fight. Publicly responding to concerns expressed by the Virginia legislature, the president declared on May 14 "that it would be the effort of his life to defend the soil of Virginia and to cover her capital." Determined to impede McClellan, Davis and Lee bypassed Johnston completely. Without Johnston's knowledge or input, they decided to use the small contingents in the Shenandoah Valley combined under Major General Thomas J. "Stonewall" Jackson, nominally a part of Johnston's command. The Davis-Lee stratagem was phenomenally successful. Their first goal was the disposition of the 40,000 Federal soldiers at Fredericksburg intended for McClellan's army. In a brilliant campaign Jackson turned the Shenandoah into his playpen, outmarching, outfighting, and outgeneraling several Federal commanders. Jackson's triumphs influenced the Lincoln administration to hold the Union forces at Fredericksburg to protect Washington, if that became necessary.[23]

Still, Federal cannon could be heard in Richmond, and the peals of the city's church bells reached Union lines. During the last week in May, Johnston finally saw an opportunity for an attack. He believed he could bring a superior force against the smaller portion of McClellan's army on the Richmond or northern side of the rain-swollen Chickahominy River. Holding to his pattern, he did not inform Lee or Davis of his plans. On May 31, he struck. Despite delays, poor coordination, and disjointed attacks, the Confederates drove their enemy back. The sounds of the Battle of Seven Pines, less than ten miles from Richmond, brought the commander in chief to the field. At Johnston's headquarters Davis and Lee could find no one who could tell them exactly what was happening. Johnston himself had ridden toward the fighting, and Davis and Lee followed. Reaching the battlefield, the president joined officers in attempting to rally troops who had been repulsed. At nightfall, as the Confederates regrouped to continue their assault on the following morning, a shell fragment severely wounded Johnston. Federal artillery still raked the area; a member of the president's party commented on shells falling among them and cutting up trees. Seeing Johnston carried from the field, Davis dismounted, offered the general his hand, and asked if he could do anything. Shaking his head, Johnston said he did not know how seriously he had been hurt. Obviously moved, Davis wrote his wife that "the poor fellow bore his suffering most heroically." But as the litter-bearers carried Johnston to the rear, Davis knew he had to find a new general to defend Richmond and save the army. And given the dire circumstances, he could not delay. He decided almost immediately on Lee. No one else was available; none of Johnston's generals had distinguished themselves. Besides, the president had "perfect confidence" in Lee. During their ride back to Richmond in the gathering darkness, Davis told Lee that he would be assigned to command the army. The next day the Battle of Seven Pines played out with the Federals retaking the ground they had lost.[24]

The military difficulties had profound political and social manifestations that certainly affected Jefferson Davis. In late February, in his brief message to the initial session of the First Congress, he publicly acknowledged the "serious disasters" that had befallen the country. He found their genesis in the government's attempt to defend all of its territory with a paucity of "the means for the prosecution of the war on so gigantic a scale." At the same time he called the losses of Roanoke Island and Fort Donelson "humiliating." Yet even while admitting unpleasant realities, he remained undaunted about his cause. "I cannot doubt," he told the senators and representatives, "that the bitter disappointments we have borne, by nerving the people to still greater exertions, will speedily secure results more accordant with our just expectation, and as favorable to our cause as those which marked the earlier periods of the war."[25]

The president's message, however, salved neither popular dismay nor congressional unrest. Members of Congress wanted to know why Roanoke Island and Fort Donelson had been lost, and demanded that the administration take measures to bolster the war effort. Critics lashed out, cursing the president and even wishing for his capture by Union forces. Lining up with the opposition, Robert Toombs wrote Vice President Stephens that "Davis's incapacity was lamentable." In this pessimistic environment Davis worried about a possible attempt to establish a border-state confederacy. Deeply troubled as he was by the mounting criticism, he was reported by one government official as mentioning resignation.[26]

Both in and out of Congress the cries for change began to focus on the cabinet. After his inauguration as the first elected president, Davis had to submit his cabinet choices for confirmation by the permanent Senate. One member of the group had become a lightning rod for critics of the administration: Judah Benjamin, still interim secretary of war. Initially deaf to anti-Benjamin talk, Davis was determined to retain him. But he soon realized that doing so would cost too high a political price, because Benjamin had quarreled with too many notable people, including Beauregard and Joseph Johnston. Johnston had even said at a Richmond dinner party that the Confederacy could not win with Benjamin in the War Department. These disagreements spilled over into politics as champions of the two men took up their arguments. Benjamin also became the scapegoat for the feeble and futile Confederate defense of Roanoke Island. In addition, a tinge of anti-Semitism colored the opposition of some. Cries of "we must get more talent into the Confederate Government or be ruined" were really aimed at Benjamin.

Yet Davis did not want to give up Benjamin. He recognized the secretary's considerable ability and had begun to value him as a counselor.

The president's opportunity arose when Secretary of State Hunter decided to leave the cabinet and accept his election to the Confederate Senate. Davis quickly shifted Benjamin to the State Department, a much less controversial post and in the public view not nearly so prominent.

Moving Benjamin necessitated a new man for the most important ministry. Davis believed Sidney Johnston the best possible choice for secretary of war, but he also regarded his favorite general as indispensable in the West. With Johnston's appointment an impossibility, Davis concentrated on Virginians. After Hunter's departure, no one from the Old Dominion belonged to the official family, and the president wanted his host state represented. After considering different names and hearing his cabinet advisers' opinions, he decided upon George W. Randolph, a grandson of Thomas Jefferson. Educated at Harvard and the University of Virginia, and a successful attorney in prewar Richmond, he was serving as a brigadier general in southern Virginia. Randolph was delighted with his appointment, promising Davis that "my best energies shall be devoted to the cause so dear to us all." Aside from the Virginia connection, it is not clear precisely why the president chose Randolph, but Randolph was a popular selection, and he worked to make himself a good secretary. According to a cabinet colleague, Randolph possessed solid credentials: "a man of plain, practical mind, a good deal of what is called common sense, and is not afraid to express his opinions."[27]

Davis still had one other political requirement to meet before completing his cabinet reorganization. Every member had been a Democrat in 1860, though Benjamin had originally been a Whig, and all had supported secession. Davis felt pressure to include someone who had an untainted Whig background or who had been a Unionist. Although he did not like thinking in terms of any pre-Confederate political distinctions, he accepted the necessity of broadening the political background of his official family. But after shifting Benjamin and appointing Randolph, he had no openings. At this point Attorney General Thomas Bragg volunteered to step down, creating a vacancy. Bragg told Davis he made the suggestion because he believed his position the easiest to fill. Reluctantly accepting Bragg's offer, Davis named as his successor Thomas H. Watts of Alabama, a former Whig and Constitutional Unionist. With his new cabinet set, the president on March 17 sent his nominations to the Senate: Benjamin for State, Memminger for Treasury, Randolph for War, Mallory for Navy, Watts for

Justice, and Reagan for Post Office. The Senate promptly confirmed them all.

While coping with political disgruntlement and reorganizing his cabinet, President Davis was also concerned about manpower needs in his armies. Even before 1862, he expressed disquiet to his cabinet about the impact of the expiration in the spring of the twelve-month enlistments. In his February message to Congress he repeated that concern in a public forum. Between April and June 1861 tens of thousands of southerners had rushed to the colors, but many signed up for only one year. Thus, between April and June 1862, serious depletions could affect Confederate military strength, at a time when the enemy was literally at the gates of Richmond and invading the heartland. The question Davis faced: how to maintain the force under arms? Pleas and exhortations to defend homes and soil resounded throughout the country, but Davis feared they would not keep enough soldiers under arms. For a president embarked on a holy mission and publicly extolling both the sanctity of the Confederate cause and the determination of its citizens' support, his own crusade and his rhetoric seemingly clashed with reality. In his understanding of the Confederate cause, no one would leave any post until final victory. Yet he clearly worried that thousands would do just that, jeopardizing the prize of liberty. Emotionally he had to contend with the dissonance, and politically he had to confront what he saw as a fundamental crisis.[28]

In so doing, Davis acted both boldly and timidly. He did not launch a great public campaign pointing out the sharp divergence between the country's need and the citizens' willingness to meet it. In contrast, he acted almost stealthily, albeit resolutely. On March 28, he sent a special message to Congress, decrying the patchwork system for raising armies. "Frequent changes and amendments," he wrote, had made things "so complicated as to make it often quite difficult to determine what the law really is." Then he proposed legislation declaring that all persons between the ages of eighteen and thirty-five legitimately eligible for military service "shall be held to be in the military service of the Confederate States." He requested that "some plain and simple method be adopted for their prompt enrollment and organization, repealing all the legislation heretofore enacted which would conflict with the system proposed." Jefferson Davis had quietly advanced the first national conscription law in American history.[29]

In less than three weeks Congress, by a two-to-one margin in the House and almost four to one in the Senate, passed the Conscription

Act, which basically followed Davis's sketchy outline, the initial draft of the statute having been prepared in General Lee's office. Every white man between eighteen and thirty-five would go into Confederate service unless exempted, and those already serving would have to remain for three years dating from their initial enlistment. There were some loopholes and exceptions, however. Following the time-honored practice applied to militia service in previous wars, including the Revolution, a drafted man could hire a substitute from the pool of men not drafted. Then, in a supplementary law, Congress exempted men in several occupations judged critical, including Confederate and state civil officials, railroad workers, miners, telegraph operators, teachers, and clergymen.

While conscription preserved the armies, it generated considerable public discussion, and led to the hardening opposition of the wiliest and most intransigent of Davis's political foes. Opponents in and out of Congress cried despotism. They depicted states' rights trodden underfoot by the march of consolidation and individual liberty throttled by a power-mad state. Those who sustained the president and the new departure emphasized the absolute necessity of drastic measures required by the mortal threat to the country.

Davis himself accented both the constitutionality of conscription and his continued devotion to states' rights. He never saw the Confederate government as abolishing state governments or even empowered to intrude into the particular affairs of states. Moreover, in his message requesting a draft law, he praised "the entire harmony of purpose and cordiality of feeling" between himself and the chief executives of the states. But he was convinced the Constitution made the central government responsible for national defense; specifically, it authorized Congress to organize and maintain armies. In his view, the constitutional brief for conscription permitted no dissent. If in individual instances the government abused its authority, then the courts could protect the rights of those involved.

Although many Confederates were concerned about the potential hazards of governmental power embedded in conscription, they generally muted or greatly moderated their reservations. One did not. Governor Joseph Brown denounced conscription as the most heinous kind of power grab; he denied that conditions warranted such an extreme act. Brown alternated between constitutional objections and concern about his prerogatives in Georgia, wanting no challenge to whatever authority he chose to claim or exert in his state. Even though he promised not to place obstacles in the way of implementing the law, he asserted that every draft-age male in Georgia belonged by definition to the state militia, precluding any call to service by the national government. The governor pursued his demurrals in several venues, including long, windy, demagogic letters to the president.

Davis believed he had to respond to Brown's missives. His silence could signal an unwillingness to rebut an opponent's arguments or an admission that the government had no case. Although he penned letters almost as long, his were not quite so windy and not at all demagogic. Instead of using general but succinct language to make his case, Davis went over his interpretation of the constitutional issues in painstaking detail. In the summer a fifty-two-page pamphlet appeared containing the correspondence between the two men. It did not help the reputation of either, nor did it become a catechism of Confederate constitutionalism.[30]

The same session of Congress empowered Davis to suspend the writ of habeas corpus in parts of the country endangered by enemy attack. Aware of the ingrained southern commitment to the individual liberty of whites, both Congress and president moved cautiously. When the same kinds of states' rights and constitutional objections to conscription were leveled against suspension, Congress amended the original law with a provision that the authorization would expire thirty days after the beginning of the next congressional session. This authority did lapse on September 17, but was reinstated to last until February 13, 1863. Davis, in turn, employed this power sparingly and judiciously, much more so than his counterpart in the United States. Davis never invoked it without prior congressional approval. He immediately put portions of the Peninsula under martial law and quickly extended military control to Richmond, yet Davis regularly overruled generals who tried to impose martial law without his permission. Neither did the Confederacy try civilians by military commissions, though the War Department did imprison civilians.[31]

Passing a conscription law and giving the president power to suspend habeas corpus did not stave off military disasters, however. At the end of April the largest city and the most important commercial center in the Confederacy fell, the worst defeat yet and all the more traumatic because so unexpected. Back in the autumn of 1861, Davis had assigned vigorous young Major General Mansfield Lovell, a Maryland-born West Pointer, to direct the defense of New Orleans, though the president explicitly refused to give him authority over the naval elements.

Lovell worked energetically to build up the defenses both near the city and downriver at Fort Jackson and Fort St. Philip, designed to protect against a river attack. In cooperation with Governor Thomas O. Moore, some 30,000 troops were raised to oppose any invasion.[32]

President Davis had given little thought to any danger at New Orleans. He was so much more concerned about Virginia, Tennessee, and the upper Mississippi River that he did not hesitate to transfer the bulk of Lovell's defense force to points he considered more threatened. Even the flotilla of armed steamers outfitted to help protect the water approaches to the city was ordered upriver to aid in holding the area above Memphis. To defend New Orleans, Davis confidently relied on the two forts on either side of the Mississippi some seventy river miles below the city. As late as April 17, he assured Governor Moore that those bastions could prevent any naval force from ascending the Mississippi. He did not comprehend that river forts would have an extremely difficult time turning back a powerful, determined fleet. After midnight on April 24 just such a force successfully passed the forts. Nothing stood between the victorious Union navy and a practically defenseless city. On the twenty-ninth the Stars and Stripes again flew over the Crescent City.[33]

The surprising news from New Orleans stunned the capital and tore at the president. A niece of his visiting at the White House disclosed that the shock "like to have set us all crazy here." She described Richmond as "depressed," anxious that "the cause of the Confederacy seems drooping and sinking." Varina recollected the tidings as a "terrible disaster." When Davis was informed, he reportedly "buried his face in his hands."[34]

The disappointment of Shiloh, the devastation of Sidney Johnston's death, anxiety over manpower needs, the debate over conscription, McClellan's inching inexorably closer to Richmond, the catastrophe of New Orleans—all bore down on the president. While he had to confront this cascade of troubles, he also had to keep a clear head amid the swirl of wild entreaties and suggestions generated by the desperation many felt. Two Confederate senators proposed a night attack on McClellan employing exotic tactics—"5000 [men] *stripped naked* to storm the camps of the enemy with the bayonet only & Kill everybody with clothes on."[35]

Davis struggled to cope. Portraying him as "miserable," his niece confided to her mother, "I fear he cannot live long if he does not get some rest and quiet." The constant reverses "distress him so much."

During these trying days Varina remembered an evening when he spoke about "the weight of responsibility distress[ing] him so he felt he would give all his limbs to have someone with whom he could share it." Trying to comfort her husband, she began reading the adventure novel *Guy Livingstone* by the English writer G. A. Lawrence. The story of a magnificently courageous hero so captivated Davis that "he took no notice of time." Previously he had spent little time with adventure novels, but Varina reported the book now helped "driv[e] out thoughts of more serious things."[36]

In this dark moment Davis also began to think about God and religion in more personal terms than ever before. As an adult Davis had often attended religious services, usually Episcopalian, the denomination of Varina and his brother Joseph, and in 1857 he had even purchased a pew in the Church of the Epiphany in Washington. By all indications he thought of himself as a Christian, and as Confederate president he regularly asked for divine blessing on his cause. Yet he had never become a member of any church and could not even recall whether he had ever been baptized.

In the winter of 1862, he and Varina began talking seriously about his joining the Episcopal Church. He had grown close to the Reverend Charles Minnigerode, rector of St. Paul's Episcopal Church in Richmond, who told Davis: "I look upon you as God's chosen instrument." By the beginning of May, the president had made his decision. On May 6, at 9:30 a.m., the Reverend Minnigerode came to the White House and in a private ceremony baptized the president. Later that morning Bishop John Johns presided over a special confirmation service at St. Paul's in which Davis and two others were confirmed. Just short of his fifty-fourth birthday, Jefferson Davis became a member of the Episcopal Church, publicly affirming his Christian faith. Varina later claimed that following his baptism and confirmation, "a peace which passed understanding seemed to settle in his heart."[37]

As Jefferson Davis moved toward making public confession of his Christian faith, he also prepared to send Varina and the children away from Richmond. Ever since McClellan's arrival on the Peninsula he had worried; by May the approach of the Federal multitude seemed so ominous that he decided that to ensure his family's safety, it must leave the capital. Although husband and wife wanted to share this moment of peril, rationality overcame emotion. Because Varina did not want to miss Jefferson's confirmation, the service was scheduled just days before her departure.

Several sites had been discussed as a refuge for the first family, but finally the decision was made for Raleigh, North Carolina, around 160 miles south of Richmond and a day's journey by rail. On May 10, Varina left with her four children, Jefferson's niece, servants, and blank checks to cover expenses. For the first six weeks she resided at the Yarborough Hotel, then moved to the campus of St. Mary's School. Except for one brief return to Richmond, she would remain in North Carolina until mid-August.[38]

This time apart cemented the emotional closeness that had been growing between husband and wife. They literally did not know whether the Confederacy would survive or whether they would ever see each other again. Jefferson even sent her a pistol with instructions to practice firing it. They wrote often and hid nothing. In his first letter Davis bared his emotional dependency: "I am quite desolate and at every look meet something of yours or the children to remind me that I am alone."

Throughout Varina's absence he repeatedly expressed the pain of this forced separation. The day before she left he penned a brief note expressing what every letter repeated: "My heart is with you." After three weeks he told her, "our separation seems to me very long. Our house is dreary at night and no loving sounds greet me in the morning." He called on God to "give you to my arms and bring to us peace and freedom from further sadness like that we are now doomed to bear." The sense of danger intensified his feelings: "Oh my wife how I long to be with you in this hour of our distress." His constant prayer asked for the protection of God.[39]

The four children, ranging from seven to less than a year, preoccupied their anguished father. "I go into the nursery," he confided, "as a bird may go to the robbed nest, but man's tenacious memory preserves the pain." In every letter he wanted to know about them and entreated, "Kiss my dear children tell them to love one another and to be good always." To his oldest, daughter Margaret, called affectionately "Polly," he wrote directly, thanking her for her "sweet little letter." He told her she and her brothers "must be good children so that Mother will tell me how happy the children made her when Father was away." He shared his innermost feelings: "it is very lonely to me at night your little beds make me feel desolate when I see them without the dear ones I used to kiss in their sleep."[40]

Jefferson Davis wrote about more than his loneliness. He underscored the importance of his family. As for himself, "I belong to the country," but his wife and children he did not count as public property. "My ease, my health, my property, my life I can give to the cause of my country," he disclosed to Varina, but "the heroism which could lay my Wife and children on any sacrificial altar is not mine. Spare us Good Lord." Davis described how his sense of his mission was plagued by struggles with others. "The great temporal object is to secure our independence and they who engage in strife for personal or party aggrandizement deserve contemptuous forgetfulness." He admitted that when people he had trusted were "detected in secret hostility, I feel like mustering claws were in me, and that cramping fetters had fallen from my limbs." "To me," he claimed, "who have no political wish beyond the success of our cause, no personal desire but to be relieved from further connection with office, opposition in any form can only disturb me in so much as it may endanger the public welfare."[41]

Making clear that he now considered his wife his adult partner, Jefferson shared military information with her, including thoughts about upcoming battles. He often mentioned his determination to defend Richmond. After providing details on Seven Pines, he delineated his and Lee's intentions. Applauding Lee's entrenchment before the capital, Davis said every great general since Julius Caesar had made good use of the shovel. But the ultimate purpose was not to defend. He and Lee wanted to employ maneuver to force the enemy out of his works, "compel[ling] him to meet us on the field," where the president had "much confidence in our ability to give him a complete defeat, and then it may be possible to teach him the pains of invasion and to feed our army on his territory." And by late June he indicated a growing optimism about his army in front of Richmond and about its commanding general.[42]

Varina responded with equal warmth and devotion to her husband's declarations and concerns. She told him, "We have been so much together of late years that my heart aches when I can not kiss you good night, and feel that I have you to lay my hand on when I wake." His "precious" letters she treasured. Regularly she used endearing names, spoke of how much she missed him and wanted to touch him. "A fond sweet tender good night, dearest Banny, shut your eyes and you will feel a kiss on your lids from your wife." Her recurrent prayer: "May God keep you dearest free from harm and bring you safe to the arms of your devoted wife. . . ." Her supplication continued, "may God in his mercy spread over you his shield and bring you safely to me if not in triumph, well, and unharmed."[43]

Wife did not hide her anxieties from husband. Rumors of Confederate reverses upset her; news of fighting kept her awake at night. But most of all she worried about him. His description of his own worry and loneliness distressed her: "The vision of your beloved form wandering in our nursery among the empty beds is too much for me." Her greatest consolation was their joint faith. "May God keep you in His Holy Keeping & bear you up in this your time of need." She was confident that "the peace which passeth all understanding," along with his "christian reliance," would sustain him, no matter the difficulty.[44]

On a more worldly level Varina gave wifely advice and also expressed gratitude to aides who had become partial substitutes. Aware that he often rode out to the army, she urged caution. She also reminded him not to expose himself either to too much sun or too much night air, and warned against smoking too much, his penchant when especially troubled. She had left two aides—his nephew Colonel Joseph R. Davis and Colonel William Preston Johnston, son of Sidney Johnston, along with Jefferson's private secretary Burton N. Harrison—living at the White House. Noting their closeness to her husband, Varina both asked them to watch over him and thanked them for doing so, imploring Johnston to keep the president out of the night air and to let her know if a chill affected him.[45]

Her letters were full of the children's well-being and activities. Their health was a constant concern. The father read about Maggie's hearty appetite and her getting a pony along with a sidesaddle. Then there was Maggie's kitten, "Stonewall," who rebuffed the attention of the young Davises. Varina reported on five-year-old Jeff's pride in coming out victorious in a boys' squabble, and recounted her glee at his claim to be in love and kissing the favored little girl. Young Joe desired to pack up and "do to pappa." Devoted to her young ones, Varina clearly relished her role as mother, and wished to share her joy with her husband.[46]

But joy turned into desperate concern over baby Billy, or "Witty Billy," as she called him. Through May and into June she recorded a series of problems: feeding difficulties necessitated her finding a wet nurse, horrific boils plagued the baby, intestinal trouble became increasingly serious. Varina feared cholera. A deeply concerned father dispatched a Richmond doctor. Finally, in mid-June, Davis made a hurried trip to Raleigh to visit his "angel baby," returning only when satisfied the child was getting better. Care brought continued improvement, and Varina happily related the baby's growing strength. Mother and father felt an almost tangible relief.[47]

In Raleigh, Varina did more than write letters to her husband and look after children. The household she managed required her to keep track of expenses. The deaths of soldiers she knew, and their growing number, disturbed her and occasioned letters of condolence. Even so, she enjoyed an active social life, even commenting on the hospitality and kindness of the people in Raleigh, which made it "a pleasure to be with them." Her basic personality had not changed, however. A luncheon host reported: "she is a very smart, intelligent and agreeable person, quite independent, says what she pleases and cuts at people generally." She also found time for reading what she rightfully termed "solid books," specifically the great New England historian John L. Motley's *The Rise of the Dutch Republic* and *The Lives of the Queens of Scotland* by the English historical writer Agnes Strickland.[48]

Varina's full days did not bring her satisfaction with life in a place she depicted to a friend as "this N. Carolina Sleepy Hollow." She wanted to get back to Richmond, to her husband and the capital. Although she did make a brief trip there in mid-July, another month passed before Jefferson decided conditions were safe enough for her permanent return.[49]

When Jefferson Davis named Robert E. Lee to command his most visible army, he and Lee had already forged a mutual bond; but Lee had numerous doubters. His performance in western Virginia had been uninspiring, and protecting the South Carolina–Georgia coast did not equal leading an army in battle. Moreover, his private advice to the president had been private, and not available for public judgment. Davis had no doubts, however. He saw Lee in his own image—a man totally dedicated to the Confederacy, with no interest in seeking or gaining personal advantage. Lee never complained about assignment or rank; he also never became involved with Confederate politics, except when directed by the president on issues like conscription. Davis's confidence in him was "unbounded." In addition, president and general shared a common strategic vision and approach to the war. Both preferred the offensive, and they believed that risks had to be taken, "movements which are not without great hazard," in Davis's words. And to get "at the Enemy," both were willing to take them. Convinced that military boldness was essential for Confederate victory, Davis grasped and applauded Lee's audacity. After the war Davis avowed that between him and Lee "there was such entire accord that he wrote to me as fully as he thought. . . ."[50]

In command of what he had termed the Army of Northern Virginia, Lee saw only one way to drive McClellan from the gates of Richmond and rescue the faltering Confederate standard. He would maneuver McClellan out of his fieldworks into the open. As he designed his strike, he developed the plan he and Davis had attempted to get Johnston to implement. Lee would mass his forces on McClellan's right, threaten his supply lines resting on the York River, and force him to fight in the open, where Lee and the president thought the Confederates could prevail. Agreed on the need for a powerful thrust, they also concurred on bringing Jackson from the Valley to enhance their chances. To Varina, Davis wrote, "General Lee rises to the occasion . . . and seems to be equal to the conception."[51]

Just as Davis had confidence in Lee, the general trusted the president. Realizing that Johnston's secretiveness had frustrated Davis, Lee always kept him fully informed on both his intentions and his actions. He understood the faith Davis had in him, and he respected his commander in chief as a man as well as president. As the great battle for Richmond loomed, Davis embraced Lee's daring plan, which he had undoubtedly helped formulate, yet he began to worry that denuding the city's defenses to augment Lee's attack would gravely endanger the capital. Understanding the president's anxiety, Lee reassured him, "Directions have been repeated to the Officers commanding the lines & batteries around Richmond to hold their positions at all hazards." Late in life, Davis remembered Lee's assurance that if McClellan did attack first, "before he reaches the outerworks of Richmond I will be upon his heels." Lee's skills as a subordinate equaled his ability as a commander.[52]

With Lee so close, President Davis could indulge his penchant for visiting the army, the troops as well as the commanding general. As the June days passed, he detected a palpable improvement in morale. He and Lee enjoyed a friendly as well as respectful relationship, and the president came out often, perhaps too often. During the initial major engagement of the Seven Days, the battle for Richmond that lasted from June 25 until July 2, Davis appeared with an entourage at the scene of heavy fighting, shots whizzing all about. Facing this cavalcade, a formally correct Lee saluted and asked the president to whose army the group belonged. A startled Davis answered that it was not his army. Thereupon Lee replied that neither was it part of his army and certainly it was in the wrong place. Now composed, Davis responded that if he withdrew, all would probably follow; the president then promptly retreated out of Lee's sight. Davis never revealed any hard feelings, underscoring the rapport that had developed between the two men.[53]

The Seven Days had enormous consequences. Lee did not succeed in destroying McClellan's army or even in cutting its supply lines, for McClellan shifted his base to the James River. Lee had, of course, turned back the immediate threat to Richmond, but, more important, he had seized the initiative for the Confederacy. A pleased Jefferson Davis wrote glowingly to his wife of Lee's achievement. He had found a general who not only comprehended his view of the war but had proved his mettle on the battlefield. In a fundamental sense Lee replaced the dead Sidney Johnston. Davis viewed Lee as a confidant and friend, not just as a superb general. When Lee assumed command of the Army of Northern Virginia, he no longer retained an office in the War Department. His appointment as military adviser to the president was never formally terminated, though Davis later recalled that because of Lee's repeated requests he did relieve him of the responsibility. In fact, the basic relationship between the commander in chief and his senior general in the field never changed. Davis regularly called on Lee for counsel on matters far removed from the Army of Northern Virginia, and until the end Lee remained the president's closest military adviser.[54]

While President Davis had a profoundly successful search for a general in the East, he did not have the same good fortune in the West. After Shiloh, Beauregard fell back to Corinth, the strategic rail junction in northeastern Mississippi. Calling this critically important town the key to the lower Mississippi Valley, Beauregard proclaimed to the War Department he would hold it "to the last extremity." He faced a difficult task, for a huge Federal force under Major General Henry W. Halleck, the overall Union commander in the West, was making its way toward Corinth. Much like McClellan in Virginia, Halleck approached slowly and cautiously, but he came closer and closer to Corinth. Even though he had been reinforced since Shiloh, Beauregard was outnumbered by at least two to one. He could not possibly withstand a siege or a direct assault. Like Lee before Richmond, his only hope lay in maneuver and quick strikes to disrupt and possibly defeat his enemy. Unlike Lee, Beauregard considered the risks in such a campaign far too great. As a result, he adopted the only course he left himself: retreat.[55]

He withdrew fifty miles south to Tupelo. News of his withdrawal shocked Davis. This general who bragged about how vigorously he would defend a site he deemed essential had departed without firing a shot. When pressed to explain his retrograde movement, Beauregard pleaded that the urgency of his business precluded an early explanation. His pride in the mastery of his retreat did not boost him in Davis's opinion. Davis wrote to Varina, "there are those who can only walk a log when it is near to the ground, and I fear he has been placed too high for his mental strength, as he does not exhibit the ability manifested on smaller fields." He dispatched an officer from his personal staff to inspect the army and obtain answers to a series of written questions about Beauregard's actions. The president also began thinking about whether to reassign this general who talked and wrote, but did not fight.[56]

Thus, Davis was appalled to learn in mid-June that without requesting permission from the War Department or even prior notification Beauregard had placed himself on sick leave, departed for a salubrious resort, and turned his army over to his second-in-command, Braxton Bragg. To Davis, who knew something about illness on the job, this smacked of dereliction of duty. He did not hide his feelings, sarcastically telling Varina "the sedentary life at Corinth must have been hard to bear. . . ." In the cabinet, talk was of abandonment, absence without leave, desertion. In Davis's view, Beauregard had once more placed his own personal concerns ahead of duty and cause, this time in a crucial situation. If Beauregard believed his army could do without him, Davis concurred. On June 20 he relieved Beauregard and moved Bragg from interim to permanent commander.[57]

Beauregard was furious. Believing his removal solely the result of a presidential vendetta, he castigated Davis as "that living specimen of gall and hatred." He called on his political allies to rescue him, asserting that if they did not, "I shall think but poorly of them & of human nature." Later the two senators from Louisiana did present to the president a petition with sixty congressional signatures decrying the general's removal and urging his reappointment. From that moment Beauregard was convinced that Davis would never give him a fair chance. Over time his enmity only hardened, and the gulf between general and president steadily deepened.[58]

Sacking Beauregard meant appointing another commanding general, and Davis had no doubt as to the proper man. The new chief in Tupelo had been with the army since before Shiloh. A West Pointer, the forty-five-year-old Bragg had fought in Mexico, where his artillery battery had a vital role at Buena Vista. After his marriage to a Louisiana sugar heiress, he used her resources to buy his own sugarcane plantation, which he left the army to manage. Upon secession he became commander first of Louisiana state forces and subsequently of Confederate Pensacola. A stern man, with a bad temper and little sense of humor, the bushy-browed Bragg was no hail-fellow-well-met, but he was a tough, effective trainer of troops and a superb organizer. At this point Bragg enjoyed a good reputation in the army and had even been promoted to full general after Shiloh. Not knowing Davis well, he doubted that the president had a good impression of him, though his brother Thomas had served as attorney general between November 1861 and March 1862.[59]

But Davis did look favorably upon Bragg, forming his opinion early in the war. Based on what he had learned in late 1861 about units trained by Bragg at Pensacola, he considered the general the best commander of volunteer troops in the entire Confederate army. His confidence grew so that by early 1862, he believed Bragg one of his ablest generals. Moreover, he thought Bragg was honest and direct with him. From close friends and family members he received positive reports on Bragg's performance at Shiloh and in Mississippi. But even more important, Davis perceived Bragg as the opposite of Beauregard, a general who placed the cause before self. During the initial months of the war, Bragg never complained about his station in a backwater. He diligently trained troops and sent them off to other generals who had the prospect of directing them in battle. Bragg seemed to have that most valuable combination, ability and commitment. Davis could hope his new western leader could become a second Lee.[60]

While Bragg was familiarizing himself with his responsibilities, Lee in Virginia confronted new dangers. Although he had thwarted McClellan's advance and seized the initiative, the Federal general remained on the Peninsula with his massive army. In guarding against McClellan's resurgence, Lee learned that another Union force under Major General John Pope was moving southward from Washington into central Virginia. To counter Pope's advance, Lee in mid-July dispatched 15,000 troops under Stonewall Jackson, but kept most of his army in front of Richmond. A month later Lee recognized that Pope constituted a major threat and marched with the bulk of his force toward this new menace. President Davis did not stop his general because he realized the necessity of this decision.

McClellan did get underway, but not toward the capital; instead, he withdrew down the James River and up the Chesapeake Bay from whence he came. With McClellan heading toward a possible junction with Pope, Lee knew he had to move quickly. Employing a daring maneuver to get to Pope's rear, he drew the Federal commander all the way back to Manassas. On the site of the first great Confederate victory, Lee gained another stunning triumph, the Battle of Second Manassas, on August 29 and 30. Through all of his marching and fighting, Lee kept Davis fully informed, writing almost daily. The president never doubted. With every confidence in this general, he worried only about Lee's personal safety.[61]

Fresh from his battlefield success, Lee contemplated his course. Within a few days he decided to lead the first major Confederate advance into Maryland. On September 3 he wrote the president of his plans, emphasizing "we cannot afford to be idle," even though he did not consider his army "properly equipped" for a full-scale invasion. The very next day, Lee sent another message underscoring his convictions about the benefits of crossing the Potomac River. Unless the president overruled him, he would move into Maryland, and if all went well advance into Pennsylvania. By September 6, he was across the Potomac.[62]

Although Lee never received specific authorization for his undertaking, he had no reason to doubt presidential approval. Never during the Maryland campaign or thereafter did Davis express any reservation about the propriety of Lee's decision. Moreover, just after the Seven Days he voiced his hope that the Confederate success could lead to an invasion of Maryland, a hope Lee shared. To an officer, Davis confided that Lee "is fully alive to the advantage of the present opportunity, and will, I am sure, cordially sustain and boldly execute my wishes to the full extent of his power."

Not only did Davis approve, he attempted to join Lee. Despite Lee's warning about the hazards of the journey, even the possibility of capture because of the continued Federal presence in northern Virginia, Davis left Richmond on the morning of September 7. But when he reached Warrenton, he realized that Lee was too far away, and the next day he returned to the capital.[63]

As Lee entered Maryland, Braxton Bragg had begun a massive offensive that would carry him all the way from Tupelo to Kentucky. Taking command of the Army of Tennessee, Bragg faced the same overwhelming Union numbers that had caused Beauregard to fall back from Corinth. The War Department told Bragg he could adopt the

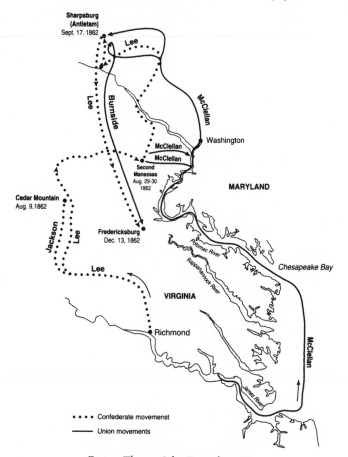

Eastern Theater, July–December 1862.
From W. J. Cooper and T. E. Terrill, The American South: A History *(2d ed.), with permission of the McGraw-Hill Companies*

strategy he thought best. Apprised about Bragg's army by the report of an aide sent out to inspect it, President Davis hoped General Halleck would divide his force, giving Bragg the opportunity to attack a portion of his enemy. Halleck did just that when he dispatched a substantial segment under Major General Don Carlos Buell eastward to Chattanooga, Tennessee, an important rail junction and the gateway to Atlanta.[64]

Bragg had worked on organization and training and now felt his army ready for action, though he had not been permitted to reshape his officer corps fully. He requested that the president waive regulations requiring promotion by seniority so that meritorious young generals could be advanced to replace some less able senior men. Among those Bragg had in mind in the latter category was his ranking major general and Davis's friend Leonidas Polk, who detested his commander. Davis would not relax the rule, however.[65]

Considering his options, Bragg decided on an imaginative and daring plan. When the Confederate commander in East Tennessee called for help, Bragg dispatched a division. The rail trip from Tupelo to Chattanooga was long and involved—some 800 miles, south to Mobile, by ferry across Mobile Bay, up to Montgomery, over to Atlanta, and finally Chattanooga. In addition, different gauges on the rail lines necessitated several changes of trains. Bragg watched this single division make a successful transit and then decided to follow with the bulk of his command. Reaching Chattanooga before Buell would not only secure the city but also open up the possibility of a Confederate advance into middle Tennessee or even into Kentucky. In an impressive operation Bragg put his infantry into motion on July 21, transferred it to Chattanooga in less than three weeks, and arrived ahead of Buell.

Like Lee, Bragg did not ask for Davis's specific permission to implement his strategy, but he too kept the president informed. Davis was delighted with the possibility that the Confederates could retake Tennessee and possibly move into Kentucky. He was also satisfied that Bragg had left a sufficient force in Mississippi to protect the state, and even to mount a concurrent advance into western Tennessee.[66]

In Chattanooga, Bragg thought about his movement northward and attempted to coordinate operations with Major General Edmund Kirby Smith, commander of the Department of East Tennessee. A full general, Bragg outranked Smith, only a major general, but the War Department issued no order extending his official authority over Smith's department. When they were together, Bragg was clearly in charge, but when apart, the relationship turned murky. The trouble stemmed in part from army organization. In structuring army commands, Davis basically used geographical boundaries, the system widely employed in the pre-1860 U.S. Army and by his opponents between 1861 and 1865. These departments could be huge or small and their limits could change. Sidney Johnston's Department No. 2 had originally extended from the Appalachians across the Mississippi; after his death and Beauregard's dismissal, it eventually became several departments, including the Department of East Tennessee. Each departmental commander reported directly to the War Department in Richmond, in reality to President Davis, who was literally as well as constitutionally commander in chief.

Although Davis has often been faulted for this departmental structure, it had nothing intrinsically wrong with it. The fundamental arrangement was logical, though arguments can be made about the appropriateness of particular borders. The arrangement did have one severe drawback, however. Departmental boundary lines could hamper coordination and cooperation if neighboring commanders disagreed on military plans or had poor personal or professional relationships. Davis usually did not extend commands geographically or formally place one general in overall command. Instead, he relied on normal authority of rank and on common commitment to the cause. He refused to consider that form could affect substance.[67]

With his experience in the army and as secretary of war, it seems that Davis would have routinely extended command boundaries. Yet he did not. He did not see the problem so many of his critics have highlighted. Most important, he believed commitment to the cause would override bureaucratic boundaries and personal feelings. As he wrote Bragg about Smith, "he has taken every position without indicating the least tendency to question its advantage to himself, without complaint when his prospects for distinction were remote, and with alacrity when dangers and hardships were to be met." The president described Smith as he perceived Bragg, as a patriot in his own image. He evinced no doubt: "Upon your cordial cooperation I can, therefore, confidently rely."[68]

At the outset Bragg and Smith initiated harmonious relations and agreed upon a common strategy. Meeting in Chattanooga on July 31, they concurred on a plan to do precisely what Davis had three days earlier pressed upon Smith. After Smith and Bragg combined, the president wanted them "to crush Buells column and advance to the recovery of Tennessee and the occupation of Kentucky." Because Bragg was still awaiting his artillery and wagon trains, Smith would move first against the Federal detachment holding Cumberland Gap. Having eliminated that potential threat to the rear of a Confederate thrust into Kentucky, he would return to Bragg, whereupon the two would march north, attempt to cut off Buell, and at the least relieve Nashville before crossing into Kentucky.[69]

But it was not to be. Almost from the moment he left Chattanooga, Smith began to think about Kentucky. Identifying Cumberland Gap as a time-consuming nuisance, he suggested to Bragg that he bypass it and strike out for Lexington in the center of Kentucky's rich Bluegrass region. Bragg was dubious, for he needed Smith's numbers to defeat Buell, and he also told his fellow commander that he could not yet support a northward advance. But he did not order Smith to return. On his own, Smith could not resist the lure of Kentucky. He had thought about it for too long, eager for the glory, though anxious about the task. On August 14 his troops turned toward Lexington. Having given up the initiative to a junior general, Bragg could only react. Two weeks later he started north, paralleling Smith's track but some 100 miles to the west. Because Buell fell back so quickly, making Nashville unattainable, Bragg kept on toward Kentucky, with his lead elements in the state before September 10.

As his armies entered Maryland and Kentucky, Jefferson Davis was acutely aware of the relationship between military events and politics. Although Maryland had never seceded and Lee had no thought of occupation, it was a slave state and thousands of Marylanders fought in Confederate gray. Davis certainly wished for a political return. In his aborted attempt to join Lee, he had as a traveling companion Enoch L. Lowe, a former governor of Maryland, now pro-Confederate and a voluntary exile in Richmond. Although Lowe had no formal position, both Davis and Lee clearly hoped that he could help the Confederate army with civilian affairs in his native state. Lowe continued on from Warrenton, and did meet with Lee in Maryland, but military events soon nullified his mission.[70]

Unlike Maryland, Kentucky had been admitted to the Confederacy and its senators and representatives sat in the Confederate Congress, even though the Union had occupied the state since Sidney Johnston's withdrawal. Eager to reverse that circumstance, Davis emphasized to Bragg and Smith the importance of popular support by Kentuckians for the Confederate army. To that end they tried to make sure Kentucky officers accompanied the Confederate troops, especially John C. Breckinridge, former vice president and presidential candidate, now a major general in the Confederate army. Breckinridge was ordered from Louisiana to join Bragg, though he did not arrive in time. While Davis and his generals desired both public backing and recruits for the army, they also realized that a serious commitment by sympathetic Kentuckians would require evidence that the Confederates intended more than a temporary stay in their state. The presence with Bragg of Richard Hawes, the Confederate governor of Kentucky, who had been

in Richmond conferring with Davis and the state's congressional delegation and who carried with him a substantial sum of Confederate
money, underscored the political aspirations of the president.[71]

President Davis sent specific instructions on politics to his commanders, directing them to issue proclamations spelling out their intentions
and the goals of the Confederate government. Because from the start
the United States had refused to negotiate and had striven to subjugate
the Confederate States and its people, he emphasized that the Confederacy waged war solely in self-defense, having "no design of conquest." It even still adhered to the policy of free navigation on all
western rivers, Davis asserted, leaving unnoted that the Union now
controlled most of them. That this "relentless" enemy had devastated
"our homes" and "our fields," Davis further noted, forced the Confederates to transfer "the seat of war" in order to demonstrate that "if
such a war is to continue its consequences shall fall on those who persist
in their refusal to make peace." He concluded that the people of Kentucky and Maryland should insist that the United States desist, and if
the response was negative, then exercise their sovereignty by agreeing
to a separate peace treaty with the Confederacy.[72]

But Davis's high hopes were dashed. At first Lee moved easily
through western Maryland, an area of little pro-Confederate sentiment
and few slaves. Neither the Confederate side nor Lee's army experienced any popular rush. Lee was, to be sure, delighted to be feeding
and provisioning his army on the northern side of the Potomac, but his
ambition to go forward into Pennsylvania was foiled. Once more
against Lee, General McClellan was slowly following the Army of
Northern Virginia, unaware of his opponent's intentions until the gods
of war favored the Federal commander: a misplaced copy of Lee's
orders containing troop dispositions and planned movements fell into
his hands. With this information McClellan pushed more aggressively,
forcing Lee to regroup his dispersed units. On September 17, along
Antietam Creek near the village of Sharpsburg, the two armies fought
viciously, the bloodiest single day of the entire war, with some 23,000
casualties. Although Lee held his own tactically despite being heavily
outnumbered, the brutal struggle had enormous strategic repercussions. Lee could no longer maintain his forces north of the Potomac,
and by September 20 had safely recrossed the river.

Confederate fortunes fared no better in Kentucky. Initially the Confederate offensive met and even exceeded expectations, thrilling President Davis. Smith marched rapidly, brushed aside all opposition, and

took Lexington on September 2. Roughly 100 miles to the west, Bragg also experienced exhilarating success. Outpacing Buell, he placed his army in central Kentucky between Buell and the great Union base at Louisville. But the Confederates failed to maintain their momentum, chiefly because the voluntary command structure broke down completely and indecision plagued the two commanders.[73]

With a numerically superior Buell in his front, Bragg rightly decided Smith should join him to fight the great battle for Kentucky. But when Bragg urged Smith to effect the combination, Smith responded that he could not leave the Bluegrass region exposed. Bragg never did issue an order; of course, if he had, Smith might have chosen not to obey, on the technical ground that Bragg was just another department commander. This was not a scenario that Jefferson Davis had envisioned—generals not cooperating, with the senior unwilling to command and the junior refusing to heed a call.

Cooperation never materialized, and Bragg even lost control of his own force. To get closer to Smith, Bragg moved eastward, permitting an unopposed Buell to secure Louisville. Still, no Confederate junction took place, for Smith's units were scattered. With their military alignment verging on disarray, the two generals turned to politics. Both men journeyed to Frankfort, the state capital, where they oversaw the formal inauguration of Hawes as governor, in hopes it would rally pro-Confederate Kentuckians.

In Frankfort, Bragg learned that a reinforced Buell was already in the Bluegrass. At that moment Bragg's authority seemed to dissolve. Trying to devise a plan to strike Buell, he could not even get the senior general in his own army, Leonidas Polk, to carry out his instructions. In addition, Polk persuaded other top commanders to follow him. Spread-out troops and fragmented information led to the confusion that dominated Bragg's decisions. Finally, on October 8, several divisions under Polk almost stumbled into what became the Battle of Perryville. The Federals were also poorly handled, and a bloody tactical stalemate resulted. Yet the strategic outcome was profound, with Bragg concluding he must return to Tennessee.

Although both offensives failed, their aftermaths were quite different. Not just the technical commander of his army, Lee overwhelmingly commanded the allegiance of his officers and men. Moreover, the commander in chief fully backed him, never faulting him for the failure of the Maryland campaign. The Army of Tennessee was a different story. Although Braxton Bragg was the authorized commander and enjoyed presidential support, he did not have the trust of all his officers, particularly those most senior.

After the retreat into Tennessee the strife so apparent in Kentucky reached literally into Jefferson Davis's office. Smith dispatched a private messenger to Richmond to convey his judgment that Bragg's ineptness lost the Kentucky campaign. Further, he requested that he never again serve under Bragg, and if any blame for the failure were placed on him, he wanted to be relieved. Finally, he requested permission to come to the capital and personally present his case to the president. Polk, who had done much to hurt and little to help his commanding general, tried to get other generals to call for Bragg's removal. He made negative and even untruthful statements about Bragg, going so far as to say Bragg had lost his mind. All the while he boasted that had he been in charge, the Kentucky operation would have been a glorious success.

Bitterly disappointed at the outcome in Kentucky, and realizing that no army could function amid this swirling backbiting and recrimination, Davis ordered the three generals to Richmond for individual conferences. Smith and Polk repeated what they had been saying, with the latter asserting that Bragg had lost the confidence of his generals. Bragg related his version, did not acknowledge any personal blame, and volunteered for reassignment, should the president think it for the best. After listening to each man, Davis made a calamitous decision. He continued Bragg in command of the Army of Tennessee; he left Polk in that army and promoted him to lieutenant general; he retained Smith as commander of his department, also promoted him to lieutenant general, and told him to cooperate with Bragg. In sum, he made no changes at all.[74]

In a letter to General Smith, Davis extolled the patriotism of all three, emphasizing that Bragg had never denigrated Smith. Moreover, Bragg "evinced the most self denying temper in relation to his future position." Once again, the president permitted his perception of commitment to influence his judgment about effectiveness. He acknowledged that Bragg was not perfect, then followed with "all [generals] have their defects." He went on to explain he did not have a ready replacement, spelling out the situations of the other four full generals. Just as before Kentucky, when the commander in chief had denied Bragg's request to reorganize his officer corps, he now, in a much more troubling time, refused to do so himself. The Kentucky campaign dramatically demonstrated the disharmony afflicting the most important field army in the heartland of the nation. For all the right reasons a ruthless, even a pragmatic, commander in chief would have instituted dramatic changes that included transfers, promotions of junior officers, and perhaps dismissals. Although fundamental overhaul was needed, for emotional and practical reasons Jefferson Davis stood fast. The cancer he did not even attempt to excise was left to grow more virulent.[75]

President Davis's frustration about the outcomes in Kentucky and Maryland was matched by his disappointment at results on the diplomatic front. Richmond was convinced that the British people supported the Confederate cause. Summertime battlefield successes buoyed hope for European intervention—either through mediation or outright recognition—which would substantively aid the Confederacy, even secure independence. Both James Mason in London and John Slidell in Paris legitimately expressed optimism that Britain and France were finally heading toward involvement, even though the Lincoln administration had made clear its adamant opposition to such action.[76]

Although Confederate diplomats pressed for recognition, claiming they had established a government and a nation, the British and French governments responded from self-interest. Napoleon III was a willing listener to entreaties from Slidell, who enjoyed direct access to the court. The cotton shortage caused by the blockade hurt French industry, but more important, Napoleon's imperial ambitions had propelled him to full-scale intervention in Mexico. That venture made him receptive to Confederate offers of cotton and alliance, for the United States vehemently opposed the new French presence in North America. Napoleon's ambition led to perhaps the greatest Confederate diplomatic success, the Erlanger loan; in Europe a French banking house sold for the Confederacy bonds secured by cotton. In all, £1.75 million were raised and used for Confederate military purchases. Napoleon also advocated some form of European intercession in the American war, but would not act unilaterally. With the British navy ruling the seas, the French required British agreement before undertaking any substantive initiative.

The British situation was more complicated. Although the British continued to proclaim neutrality and after February 1862 had denied James Mason even unofficial meetings with government ministers, influential elements in both Parliament and the cabinet did favor moving toward involvement. The disruption of cotton imports had an adverse economic effect on the textile districts. Besides, Britain could not look with disinterest upon a weakened United States; in addition, there was a powerful humanitarian concern to stop the awful bloodletting before it led to anarchy, including the horrible possibility of race war. Yet other influential voices emphasized the difficulties inherent in any operation, not the least of these being the Lincoln administration's warning that British intervention would mean war. During the summer and autumn of 1862 leaders engaged in serious discussions about the proper course, often in secret cabinet meetings, and for a time it seemed the outcome would favor the Confederacy. In early October, Chancellor of the Exchequer William Gladstone made a public speech that included the famous lines: "We may have our own opinions about slavery, we may be for or against the South; but there is no doubt that Jefferson Davis and other leaders of the South have made an army; they are making, it appears, a navy; and they have made what is more than either—they have made a nation."

Despite those ringing words, prevailing opinion in British governmental circles demanded undisputed battlefield evidence of the Confederacy's ability to win. Second Manassas signaled affirmatively, but Lee's reverse north of the Potomac along with Bragg's retreat from Kentucky dampened interventionist desires. Even Secretary of State Benjamin's claim that the Maryland campaign proved the Union could not destroy the Confederacy did not lessen the impact of Lee's failure. Then, in the aftermath of Antietam, when Abraham Lincoln made emancipation a Union war aim, it became exceedingly difficult for Britain to assume any pro-Confederate stance. Finally, in November, the cabinet decided against taking any active step aimed at ending the American conflict. This was not necessarily a permanent decision, for events on the battlefield could still spark reconsideration.

For Davis, however, the British decision meant that the Confederacy continued to stand alone. He complained that alleged European neutrality had in fact injured the Confederate States. "It is manifest that the course of action adopted by Europe, while based on an apparent refusal to determine the question, or to side with either party, was in point of fact," he asserted to Congress, "an actual decision against our rights and in favor of the groundless pretensions of the United States." In his view, Britain and France had wrongly refused "to treat us as an independent Government." In spite of these unjustifiable setbacks, Davis still exhibited public confidence, proclaiming that his country's "just place in the family of nations cannot long be withheld. . . ."[77]

From the spring on through 1862, while Jefferson Davis wrestled with affairs of state, the war also became intensely personal for him.

Not only did Varina and the children become temporary refugees, Davis Bend also felt the shock of war. Brother Joseph reported that the fall of New Orleans along with a rising Mississippi was forcing him to remove from the Bend some of his and Jefferson's stock and slaves, in his language always "people." Attempting to find an appropriate site for relocation, Joseph was staying with Owen B. Cox, a former overseer who lived near Clinton just west of Jackson and valiantly aided his old employer in this troubled time.[78]

Summer witnessed no improvement. Joseph rebuked the overseers still on the brothers' plantations as "worthless rascals," who had not prevented looting by slaves. Then an outbreak of measles among Brierfield slaves slowed and even precluded additional removal. A Yankee raiding party made a call at Brierfield and Hurricane, carrying off slaves, horses, and equipment. In addition, raiders plundered both homes and burned the Hurricane mansion to the ground, the flames visible from Vicksburg. For unknown reasons they spared Jefferson's vandalized home from the torch.

Finding a new home proved exceedingly vexing; only poor land at prohibitive prices was available. Joseph told Jefferson that the flood and the burning of cotton had seriously damaged his finances, though he did pay Confederate taxes for both of them. He also expressed uncertainty about how he could maintain their human and animal property. Joseph's wife Eliza chorused the litany of travails, writing her brother-in-law about her husband's difficulties and the general displacement caused by the war.

Joseph especially worried about the slaves. At one point he described Brierfield and Hurricane as mostly deserted, but then many of the slaves who had left on their own just as voluntarily returned. He brought more into the interior with him, and he hired out others to work in hospitals and on military projects. Confronting so many problems with limited means, he asked Jefferson to indicate exactly what he wanted done with his slaves. He informed his brother that their nephew Hugh Davis, who resided in Wilkinson County, had offered to take and care for them. He added that until he received Jefferson's response, he would carry on as before.

By the fall the seventy-eight-year-old family patriarch had decided to move to Texas because he and others he knew feared the Federals would overrun the state. Informing his brother of this decision, Joseph offered to take all the slaves. But in November an illness felled him for three weeks, and with Eliza also sick and weak, the elderly planter concluded that such a journey was simply impossible. He renewed his search for a temporary residence, finally finding a 1,300-acre plantation called Fleetwood in Hinds County, near Bolton's Station, between Jackson and Vicksburg, which he bought before ever seeing it. When he got to Fleetwood, he found it less than satisfying, "a poor place with miserable huts for a part only of the negroes." "I cannot feel that it is home," he admitted to his brother. He also wrote Jefferson of the availability of a nearby place.

Although Jefferson confided to a Mississippi friend that he barely had time "to bestow a thought" on his private affairs, he was distraught about his slaves and especially about his brother, worrying particularly about Joseph's trips back and forth to Davis Bend. He helped financially by sending $3,000 to aid in provisioning his slaves. He did not want to send them to his nephew, preferring if possible to settle them near Joseph. After Joseph made his decision to move in at Fleetwood, Jefferson acquired the property close by that Joseph had mentioned. Through Joseph's agency, he purchased 1,565 acres for $15 per acre plus the cost of hogs, all to be paid for within three years. According to Joseph's granddaughter Lise Mitchell, who was living with her grandparents, Jefferson's unnamed acreage was more desirable than Fleetwood. She termed it "much more valuable, though also in need of repairs and improvements." She also commented on the poor quality of soil: "it seems a waste of labor to cultivate it, particularly so to one who has planted on the rich delta lands of the river, as Grandpa has." No longer did the Davis brothers command plantation showplaces fronting the Mississippi. War had literally driven them to hardscrabble farms.[79]

The upheaval at Davis Bend that disrupted plantation life and turned Joseph Davis into a refugee intensified President Davis's reaction to growing civilian distress. In late 1861, he had noted the enemy's beginning to overstep his definition of civilized warfare, but by the summer of 1862 he saw horror becoming pervasive. The penetration by Federal forces into so many areas of the Confederacy brought thousands of civilians into the swath of battles, raids, and occupations. Some Federals welcomed the havoc wreaked upon persons and property while others for a time tried to control destruction. But such boundaries proved impossible to maintain. Civilians and their property could not escape the whirlwind that accompanied marching and fighting by great armies. In Davis's mind their barbarity was dramatized by the actions of Major General Benjamin F. Butler, his erstwhile political supporter, now the Federal commander of occupied New Orleans. Reacting to several incidents in which the city's women had been less than respectful to his troops, Butler in May issued his famous or infamous "woman order," which declared that any woman insulting or contemptuous of Federal military personnel would be treated as a prostitute. Even though the Lincoln administration never officially approved it and nothing untoward actually occurred to any woman, to Confederates the order became symbolic of what they conceived as uncivilized war. Then the next month Butler executed a civilian who had taken down and destroyed a United States flag.[80]

Privately and publicly Davis condemned what he considered Butler's outrages. To Varina, he deplored "the brutal tyranny" that reigned in New Orleans overseen by an ogre "properly surnamed the Beast." In his August message to Congress, he denounced Butler's "contumelious" behavior. Four months later, he issued a public proclamation excoriating Butler as "a felon deserving of capital punishment . . . an outlaw and common enemy of mankind," who would be hanged if captured.[81]

Davis matched his revulsion toward Butler with general condemnations of what he perceived as a new and horrific direction taken by his foe. In a public proclamation dated September 4, he denounced an enemy who "laid waste our fields, polluted our altars, and violated the sanctity of our homes." Earlier he wrote to General Lee that the United States had "chang[ed] the character of the war from such as becomes civilized nations into a campaign of indiscriminate robbery and murder." To Congress, the president was blunt: "Humanity shudders at the appalling atrocities which are being daily multiplied under the sanction of those who have obtained temporary possession of power in the United States. . . ."[82]

Davis had no doubt that these horrors merited retaliation. Most Confederates agreed, and a number told him so. He informed Congress that "stern and exemplary punishment" should be meted out to those who deserved it. He also brought up the subject of retaliation with the cabinet, the discussion revolving around how to carry it out, a worrisome question. The fact that his armies had not yet reached into the territory of his opponents restricted Davis's options. He could not impose the civilian suffering and destruction that came only with invading hosts. Besides, at this point he did not want to blame northern citizens for the conduct of their military and political leaders, though he did say they could not remain "wholly guiltless" if the atrocities continued without any effort to repress those responsible for them.[83]

President Davis had only one realistic option: turning on prisoners of war. Immediately, however, this possibility raised concerns. If Confederates violated accepted practices and began executing prisoners, even in the name of retaliation, they would become just as barbaric as their enemy. Even more important, the Lincoln administration would surely do likewise to its prisoners. Thus, except in very particular circumstances, such as responding to a specific act against captured Confederates, venting anger and frustration on prisoners offered no satisfaction. Despite his growing scorn for the Federals' methods of waging war, Davis never did discover an appropriate or gratifying way to repay ferocity. Only successful invasion of the free states would have offered that opportunity, and he never had it.

For Davis, the Emancipation Proclamation represented the culmination of the savage war waged upon his country. Lincoln issued his preliminary proclamation just after Antietam on September 22, with the final version promulgated on January 1, 1863, the date it took effect. Using his authority as commander in chief, Lincoln freed all slaves in states and areas of states still engaged in rebellion against the United States. Across the Confederacy the edict generated an outrage, which Davis conveyed in a message to Congress, damning the proclamation as "the most execrable measure recorded in the history of guilty man." For its backers he had only "profound contempt," and he tried to present the proclamation as "impotent rage" from a government that could not conquer the Confederacy by defeating its armies.

In assaulting the proclamation, Davis articulated both central tenets of the proslavery argument and fears of white southerners: "We may well leave it to the instincts of that common humanity which a beneficent Creator has implanted in the breasts of our fellowmen of all countries to pass judgment on a measure by which several millions of human beings of an inferior race, peaceful and contented laborers in their sphere, are doomed to extermination, while at the same time they are encouraged to a general assassination of their masters by the insidious recommendation 'to abstain from violence unless in necessary self-defense.' " In contemplating this monstrous deed, he did identify one virtue. Now all Confederates could see "the complete and crowning proof of the true nature" of their enemy. For his part, he would react directly. Davis proposed to turn over to state authorities all Union commissioned officers captured in any state covered by the proclamation. At that point, "they may be dealt with in accordance with the laws of those States providing for punishment of criminals engaged in exciting servile insurrection." But the Confederate government never adopted any such policy. Emotion stemming from anger and horror said yes, yet practical recognition of the undoubted repercussions on captured Confederate officers dictated no. Once again, President Davis found no practical way to satisfy his overwhelming desire for retaliation.[84]

Viewing his enemy as increasingly loathsome, Davis instituted important changes in his western command structure that he hoped would help his armies fight more effectively. In his major eastern army he knew he could depend upon Robert E. Lee. But in the West he had no such security, and he had not ended the disharmony rampant among the generals in the Army of Tennessee. For some time he and Secretary of War Randolph had been contemplating a new design for the heartland—a unified command for that immense area, with the creation of a department akin to Sidney Johnston's Department No. 2.[85]

The situation Bragg left behind in Mississippi upon his departure for Tennessee undoubtedly contributed to the discussions in Richmond. In the force remaining to defend the state, command relations were unclear, with two men, each a major general, vying for control. Moreover, once in Tennessee and committed to the Kentucky campaign, Bragg exercised no real authority in Mississippi. President Davis became directly involved in trying to sort out the confusion. He had relied on Major General Earl Van Dorn, a West Pointer, professional soldier, and Mississippian, but he ended up disappointed, especially by Van Dorn's defeat at Corinth in early October, believing justifiably that his commander had been outgeneraled.[86]

Davis determined to do better by Mississippi. It was his native state, and the great Confederate river bastion Vicksburg was practically his hometown. He acted even before the fiasco at Corinth, for on October 1 he appointed a new commander for the Department of Mississippi and Southeast Louisiana. For Davis this appointment not only brought new hope to Mississippi, it also solved a nagging political problem in South Carolina.

Central in Davis's decision-making was John C. Pemberton, a Philadelphia-born West Pointer who followed his Virginia wife into the Confederacy. Pemberton was one of those officers who without ever having done anything to warrant it enjoyed an excellent military reputation, an opinion shared by Davis. His Confederate service began in a Virginia cavalry regiment and took him to the South Atlantic coast, where he served under Lee. When Davis in March 1862 called Lee back to Virginia as his military adviser, Pemberton took over.

Despite his military standing, the transplanted Pennsylvanian never became acceptable to the South Carolinians, especially Governor Francis Pickens, who implored Davis to remove Pemberton. Pickens said that the general might have a fine military record, but he could not generate public support. Although the president defended Pemberton, amazingly calling him "one of the best Generals in our service," he finally realized that political reality in South Carolina required a change. Having come to this conclusion, he knew he wanted Beauregard in Charleston, and suggested his name to Pickens. In Davis's mind, the South Atlantic command was a good post for Beauregard because it entailed chiefly coastal defense requiring engineering skills which Beauregard possessed. There was no significant field army. Moreover, the Carolinians liked him; to them he was still the hero of Fort Sumter and First Manassas. In late September he superseded Pemberton.[87]

This assignment made Pemberton available for reassignment. Davis promptly promoted him to lieutenant general and dispatched him to Mississippi. The president assured his fellow Mississippians of Pemberton's loyalty and ability. Upon his arrival in the state, Pemberton made a positive impression on leading citizens, including Joseph Davis, who had not thought much of Pemberton's predecessors, remarking, "When Van Dorn was made a General it spoiled a good captain. . . ."[88]

The western boundary of Pemberton's department was the Mississippi River, the great highway flowing north to south through the heart of the Confederate States. Beyond it lay the vast reaches of what the Confederates termed the Trans-Mississippi. Officials and citizens of Arkansas, Louisiana, and Texas, as well as Confederate refugees from Missouri, often felt isolated and likened themselves to uncared-for stepchildren. Distance made communications difficult, though not impossible, for the Confederacy still controlled the Mississippi between Port Hudson, Louisiana, and Vicksburg. Additionally, many troops from those states had gone east to fight as far away as Virginia, while few had come west. Wide correspondence and conversations with members of Congress and visitors to Richmond made President Davis quite aware of circumstances and attitudes in his Far West.

In the summer and fall of 1862, he heard regularly from civilian and military officials. In late July, the governors of the four states jointly signed a letter to the president underscoring their personal loyalty and that of the people in their states. At the same time they spelled out what they saw as fundamental needs to sustain allegiance, an overall commander along with an infusion of arms and money. Similar pleas came to Davis's desk from others in the region.[89]

Acknowledging the "discontent and despondency" permeating the region, Davis wanted to respond as positively as he could, but he had to tread carefully because military and political concerns often merged, complicating choices. Many Missourians, especially, clamored for Sterling Price, enormously popular but an indifferent general, whom Davis did not trust for an important command. Davis worked with favorite sons, like Thomas C. Hindman in Arkansas and his former brother-in-law Richard Taylor, whom he ordered from Virginia back to Louisiana, under an overall commander. Davis had initially tapped Major General John B. Magruder, an energetic, enthusiastic officer who had performed well on the Peninsula and had the potential to rally civilians and soldiers and become an effective leader. But Magruder had barely departed Virginia when Davis recalled him because of allegations of intemperate behavior, including intoxication. Believing he could not wait for the final adjudication of Magruder's case, he appointed Major General Theophilus H. Holmes in Magruder's stead.[90]

Davis's choice of Holmes was both curious and unfortunate. Although a contemporary of Davis's and an 1829 graduate of West Point, Holmes, who suffered from deafness, appeared older, as indicated by his sobriquet "Granny." His Confederate service had been undistinguished through the Seven Days, when, as a division commander, he gave a lackluster performance. But even though Holmes had no obvious political gifts and had demonstrated little military talent, Davis assigned him to command the Trans-Mississippi. Holmes expressed reservations, writing the president that he doubted his ability to handle the post, a remonstration stemming not from modesty but self-awareness. Davis, who interpreted Holmes's genuine misgivings as merely "diffidence," maintained his belief in the general's patriotism and in his professional capability.

When he took command in Little Rock in early August, Holmes discovered serious problems that seemed to grow only worse. He even told Davis that had the president comprehended the gravity of the situation in Arkansas, he would surely have sent an abler general. Disaffection plagued both the civilian population and the soldiers. Holmes's forces were vastly understrength and ravaged by disease. Facing such intractable difficulties, he was unsure what course to set. He asked the president to send directions, which he would gladly carry out. But Davis instead reasserted his faith in Holmes, promoting him to lieutenant general and instructing the general to use his judgment. Once again the president held fast to his conviction that he could not give operational orders to his field commanders.[91]

With Holmes and Pemberton, Davis had placed two unproven generals in critical posts. He clearly believed in Pemberton's potential, for he assigned the Pennsylvanian to defend his home. Yet General Pemberton, whose chief mission was to protect Vicksburg, had never participated, much less commanded, in a major battle. Davis's mysterious trust in Holmes is unfathomable but for the importance the president attached to loyalty to the Confederate cause. As a student of military history, Davis understood that "a great General is so rare that their names mark the arch of history." He had no illusions that the Confederacy would prove an exception to what he considered a truth of history. He had demonstrated that he could assess military ability, but in these two instances hope and faith prevailed over perceptive appraisal.[92]

Holmes and Pemberton controlled either side of the Mississippi, yet neither could command the other. Although Davis certainly recognized the vital strategic importance of the river and the need for joint action, he only urged his generals to cooperate, despite the debacle in Kentucky. While exhorting them, he always stipulated that the two commanders retained the discretion to act as each deemed best. The motivation for making the Mississippi a military as well as a geographical boundary rested on a political judgment. Command in the Trans-Mississippi region had to remain west of the river.[93]

Appointing Holmes and Pemberton did not end Davis's revamping of his western front. He and Secretary Randolph decided to name a single commander for much of the vast area. Even though the president had stood by Bragg, vociferous dissatisfaction with the general continued, cries the politician Jefferson Davis heard. Even Bragg himself urged that a sort of super-commander be placed over him. Only four men ranked Bragg: Cooper, who would never take the field; Lee, who was indispensable in Virginia; Beauregard, whom the president judged unqualified; and the recuperating Joseph Johnston.[94]

By late autumn Johnston had recovered and on November 12 he reported to the War Department for duty. Although he and his commander in chief had certainly experienced differences, Davis still believed Johnston to be "a good Soldier." He did not classify Johnston with Beauregard on either intellectual or moral grounds. Moreover, numerous appeals for Johnston from prominent westerners arrived in Richmond. Johnston was the obvious choice for what was called the Department of the West, not quite a replication of Sidney Johnston's Department No. 2 because it stopped at the Mississippi River. In his new assignment, Joseph Johnston would oversee Smith, Bragg, and Pemberton, and he would have responsibility for defending the two major Federal targets, middle Tennessee and Vicksburg.[95]

Johnston's orders were specific and inclusive. His geographic "command" was spelled out in detail. He was also directed to establish his headquarters at Chattanooga or wherever he thought would "best secure facilities for ready communication with the troops within the limits of his command." Finally, he was given complete authority to "repair in person to any part of said command whenever his presence may for the time be necessary or desirable."[96]

Despite the straightforward language in this order, Johnston perceived ambiguity and want of clarity. With the Department of the West, Davis was attempting to construct a theater command of the type that would become so popular in World War II. But Johnston, like most Civil War generals, could not envision commanding without actually leading troops in the field. He felt Bragg had the preferable job, though he was Bragg's commanding officer. Further, Johnston could not contemplate assuming authority without relieving the commander on the spot, an act unthinkable to him. In addition, the three departmental commanders would still report directly to the War Department without having to go through Johnston's headquarters. Johnston interpreted this as bypassing him, though that was not the key. As much as anything else, this arrangement had to do with staff requirements; Richmond could handle so much more than Johnston's headquarters. Besides, the telegraph should enable all participants in any decision to remain in close communication. Still, Johnston, who craved certainty, saw himself surrounded by uncertainty.[97]

Uneasy in this new position, Johnston fretted that he had been given an assignment that could only end in failure and his blemished reputation. Upon reaching Chattanooga, he wrote to his friend Senator Louis Wigfall, "Nobody ever assumed a command under more unfavorable circumstances." Little more than a week later he chorused, "A great mistake has been made in the arrangement of my command." Johnston's recovery from his wound at Wigfall's home in Richmond had placed him in the orbit of anti-Davis politicians. Entering the Confederacy as a staunch supporter of Davis, the Texas senator for reasons not entirely clear became an inveterate opponent. Politicians like Wigfall saw Johnston as an ally, perhaps a pawn, in the campaign against Davis. They surely fed the general's inclination to distrust his commander in chief, to see him as petty and self-serving. This proclivity, plus Johnston's natural disposition to protect himself by exercising extreme professional caution, almost ensured that he would take little initiative, and certainly no risks. Davis at this point, however, retained confidence in Johnston's military ability. He certainly did not think he had given Johnston an empty assignment.[98]

Johnston had another fundamental reservation about his job, and this time in a military sense he was undoubtedly right. He believed strongly that a proper defense of the Mississippi River demanded placing Holmes and Pemberton in a unified command. In his view, the importance of that unity far outweighed bringing Bragg and Pemberton together, for he considered them too far apart ever realistically to help each other. But though Johnston was militarily correct about interconnection on the Mississippi, he never reflected on the possibilities within his command. He never ruminated about how the transfer in the summer of most of Bragg's army from Mississippi to Tennessee might affect either a mobile defense or reinforcement for a quick strike.

Even before Johnston left Richmond, he suggested to Secretary Randolph that the Department of the West combined the wrong departments. Randolph listened empathetically, for he agreed and assured the general that he had tried unsuccessfully to persuade the president. Davis remained adamant about Holmes's retaining an independent command, though he definitely wanted Holmes to cooperate with Pemberton and Johnston. The reasons for Davis's insistence that the Trans-Mississippi stay separate were fundamentally political. He believed it essential that citizens west of the Mississippi entertain no doubts about the government's determination to defend them. To Davis, that meant an army and an independent commander in place, even though he realized that Federal penetration of the river would level a terrible blow against his cause. Given the dilemma he confronted, he put his faith in an almost abstract notion of cooperation, relying on Johnston, Pemberton, and Holmes to find a solution to his conundrum.[99]

The disagreement between Davis and Randolph over the Trans-Mississippi led to the secretary's resignation. Over time Randolph had grown increasingly dissatisfied with his role. Davis wanted a war minister he could respect and with whom he could discuss policy matters, large and small. Yet he never delegated substantial authority to Randolph or any other secretary. He wanted all major and myriad minor decisions cleared with him before any directives left the War Department. He did not even always consult the secretary, whom he would on occasion bypass by sending instructions directly through General Cooper.

After numerous discussions with the president on the value of the armies in Arkansas and Mississippi acting together, Randolph in late October authorized Holmes to cross the river. He received a stinging remonstrance. Upon reading the message, Davis said he had in mind only "co-intelligent action," and he thought any departure of Holmes from Arkansas, even if temporary, "would have a disastrous effect." Without an endorsement, Randolph sent this communication on to Holmes to become part of his instructions. On November 14 Davis informed the secretary that he should always go through "the established channel." When Randolph asked for clarification, Davis stipulated matters that must come before him, including "the removal of an army, the transfer of a Genl. . . . the assignment of general officers," and finally, anything "material to the public defense." Pointing to the "usage" and "advantages" of "free conference," Davis made clear that while he welcomed discussion, he did not countenance the secretary's giving orders. The next day Randolph brusquely responded: "Conceiving that I can no longer be useful in the War Department I hereby resign my commission as Secretary of War." Davis's immediate reply was equally curt: "As you have thus without notice and in terms excluding inquiry retired from the post of a constitutional adviser of the Executive of the Confederacy, nothing remains but to give you this formal notice of the acceptance of your resignation."[100]

The president acted quickly to replace him. This time there would be no interim appointment. Davis wanted another Virginian, specifically James A. Seddon, a Richmond lawyer and a planter in nearby Goochland County, who had been influential in the Virginia Democratic party since the 1840s. Although he had no experience with anything military, Seddon readily accepted. And he was a popular choice. Even the hypercritical *Richmond Examiner* called his appointment "a fortunate event." Laboring long hours, the cadaverous-looking Seddon learned quickly and worked effectively with Davis. He would hold the post for more than two years, longer than any other man. On western matters, Seddon's arrival signaled no attempt to change policy, for he shared Davis and Randolph's view of the importance of the western theater and was an enthusiastic supporter of Joseph Johnston.[101]

As Seddon settled in at the War Department and Johnston traveled to Chattanooga, Davis decided he must make a western trip. He knew he was setting up a new organization with a new commanding general who doubted its efficacy. Additionally, he wanted to visit Bragg's army to assess firsthand esprit de corps and preparedness. Finally, he believed he needed to heed calls from his own part of the country indicating that only his presence could restore morale and reinvigorate commitment to the Confederate cause. Davis wanted to show the people in the heartland that their government and their president cared about them. Thus, despite the prospect of renewed conflict between Lee and the Federal army along the Rappahannock, only fifty miles from the capital, Davis prepared for a lengthy but, in his mind, essential journey.

On December 9, accompanied by two aides and a servant, he left Richmond by train. Rolling through southwest Virginia into Knoxville, where he made a few remarks, the presidential party reached Chattanooga on the evening of the eleventh. The next morning, with a band playing "Bonnie Blue Flag," the presidential train, colors flying, departed early and arrived that evening at Murfreesboro, Bragg's headquarters and only thirty miles south of Nashville.

The thirteenth was an active day. Accompanied by Bragg and Johnston, the president reviewed troops and briefly addressed the soldiers, expressing his complete confidence in their devotion and ability. He also visited with many officers at his quarters. One recalled the occasion: "He was quite agreeable and gentlemanly in manner, and on the whole I was rather favorably impressed by him." In this personal inspection of the Army of Tennessee, Davis found it in "fine spirits and well supplied." Davis was confident it could halt any Federal advance, though lacking the strength to take Nashville.[102]

Davis was no imperial traveler. An observer noted that "his dress was plain and unassuming and his baggage was limited to a single leather valise, with the initials 'J.D.' marked upon the side." This eyewitness described "a man rather above the middle stature; of slight but well proportioned figure," with handsome features. A sprinkling of gray in his hair along with gray whiskers and "graceful manners" added dignity. An "expression of good humor" dominated his countenance as he spoke in a "voice soft and persuasive, yet distinct and full toned. . . ."[103]

Davis's party, including General Johnston, left Murfreesboro at 6 a.m. on Sunday, the fourteenth, for Chattanooga, and ultimately Mississippi. In East Tennessee he got the welcome news of Robert E. Lee's smashing triumph at Fredericksburg. Late the following afternoon he started toward his home state, passed through Atlanta and Montgomery, where he spent a day, and on to Jackson, arriving without fanfare on December 19. Next morning he boarded a train for Vicksburg, but along the way stopped for a short visit to Fleetwood and his own property before moving on. In Vicksburg, he examined defensive works and reviewed troops. Then he turned back to Jackson and on up to North Mississippi to confer with Pemberton, who was celebrating the great Confederate success at Holly Springs on the twentieth, which destroyed Grant's supply base and caused the Union general to abandon his overland thrust toward Vicksburg. Once again Davis reviewed troops before returning to Jackson and Christmas dinner with a niece.[104]

From Tennessee to Mississippi, the main topic of discussion between the president and his commander in the Department of the West concerned proper steps for the defense of the two states. Davis told the army bearing its name that Tennessee must be held at all costs and at the same time that he considered Mississippi critical—so critical that he personally ordered a division from Bragg to reinforce Pemberton. During their journey, Johnston pressed Davis to order Holmes east of the river. The general believed 40,000 troops essential to secure Vicksburg, yet he had but half that number. Davis did not disagree, and on December 22 he penned a long letter to Holmes emphasizing the grave situation confronting the Confederates. If Vicksburg fell, the Confederacy would be sundered and the Trans-Mississippi cut off from the rest of the country. He called for help, but still permitted Holmes to decide if he could do so and yet protect his command. When Davis showed Johnston the letter, the general was upset that the president had not directed Holmes to cross the river. He was convinced that only the timely arrival of Holmes could guarantee the safety of Vicksburg. He had even been trying to get Senator Wigfall to press Secretary Seddon to see that Holmes received unequivocal orders to join Pemberton.[105]

Holmes responded by telling Davis he would obey any order, but because the president had left the final decision in his hands, he could not reinforce Pemberton. He had so few troops; they were widely scattered; and he was dealing with at least two different serious Federal threats. If he went to Pemberton's aid, he told Davis without exaggeration, Arkansas would be left unprotected and could easily fall. Moreover, in his opinion, distance and road conditions made rapid movement impossible. Replying, Davis said that if Holmes had correctly assessed his situation, which he surely had, then he had acted properly to remain in Arkansas.[106]

A major problem resulted from the small size of Holmes's force. He had only 10,000 men spread over much of the state, no more than half the number Davis and Johnston thought available. Numbers posed a problem everywhere: Bragg had around 45,000 and faced a stronger enemy; Smith could add only some 10,000; Pemberton was outnumbered by more than two to one; Holmes likewise faced a considerably stronger foe. There were simply not enough Confederate soldiers to guarantee the safety of all threatened points, and for military and political reasons Davis deemed Tennessee, Mississippi, and Arkansas all critical. Success confronting such complex problems and enormous odds would require the most resolute and daring leadership.

While on this tiring journey and dealing with such momentous matters, Davis found time to write his wife. He informed her of his safe arrival in Tennessee and apprised her of his view of the Army of Tennessee as well as reports about public opinion. He did not neglect family matters, however. "Kiss my dear Children for their loving Father," he told Varina, "they can little realize how much I miss them." Every child he encountered reminded him of his own, "but none can equal their charms. . . ." As for "my long worshipped Winnie," he drew on Robert Burns: "She is na my ain Lassie / Though fair the lassie be for well ken I my ain lassie / By the kind love in her eye."[107]

Responding, Varina tried to comfort her husband. Although she reported on Fredericksburg and other public matters, she focused on the children. Maggie often spoke of her absent father; Jeff, "full of fun," had learned to whistle "Dixie"; Joe asked about him and "talked of pappas letter." As for baby Billy, "To night I was dressing for dinner, and Billy was sitting on the floor . . . and my skirt tilted him over—He got so mad he fought me, and would not be taken up."

Varina made clear she understood the enormous pressure bearing down on him. "I am now, as heretofore oppressed with a sense of my own inability to say anything which will either distract your mind, or lighten your troubles, but be assured if I cannot participate I always remember that your heavy responsibilities and overtaxed mind prevent you in every act of life from doing that which your heart would indicate." She implored, "take care of yourself, and try to look forward to peace and rest with the children. . . ." She concluded with a pledge: "remember that there is one person who should success not be given you in unstinted measure, would only be the more devotedly your wife."[108]

While his wife offered private solace, Davis displayed public optimism. During his lengthy journey he made a number of short speeches, but just before leaving Mississippi he gave one longer address, in Jackson. Accepting an invitation from legislators, Davis on December 26 spoke for ninety minutes to a packed House chamber in the Capitol. He began, as he had on so many occasions before 1861, by identifying himself with those he had always striven to serve, the people of Mississippi. He told his listeners that even though in his current station he tried to make "no distinction between the various parts of the country," he had to acknowledge that "my heart has always beat more warmly for Mississippi." Now all Confederates, he professed, were involved in a great war with an enemy of "malignant ferocity" bent on destroying every vestige of liberty. He presented the issue as simple and fundamental: "will you be slaves . . . will you renounce the exercise of those rights with which you were born and which were transmitted to you by your fathers?" He knew the answer of Mississippians, "that their interests, even life itself, should be willingly laid down on the altar of their country." Praising sons of Mississippi already in uniform, he called on all others to "devote themselves to the noblest cause in which man can be engaged."

Davis declared the defense of the state crucial. To lead that effort he had appointed two men to defend "the land of my affections," lauding Pemberton and Johnston as accomplished generals whose "capacity and resolution" would protect Mississippi. Asserting that he wanted to carry the war to the home fields of the enemy, the president admitted he lacked the power to do so. Even so, he declared that in the past year the Confederates had vastly improved their capacity to wage war. He was confident that the support of the people would enable the Confederate cause to prevail. He had no doubt that the magnificent people of Mississippi would rise to this occasion and secure their independence.[109]

After his speech, Davis and Johnston went back to Vicksburg for two days. On the twenty-eighth, Davis returned to Jackson. He departed for Mobile the next day. On that same day, Pemberton repulsed General Sherman's river-based assault on Vicksburg. In mid-afternoon on December 30, Davis's train chugged into the Alabama port. Once again he reviewed troops, and in the evening from the balcony of his hotel spoke to a crowd composed mostly of soldiers. Celebrating the heroism of Confederate troops, "an army of heroes," he proclaimed they could never be conquered. "Independence" or "domination of the Yankees" was at stake, and he was sure about the outcome. That the Confederates had turned back both Grant and Sherman in Mississippi fueled his optimism. Closing, he said that "the welfare of the people was the sole motive which actuated him . . . ," and vowed always to give "the utmost of his energies" to securing their liberty.[110]

After inspecting Forts Gaines and Morgan guarding the entrance to Mobile Bay, Davis on the last day of the year began the final leg of the trip back to Richmond, passing through Montgomery; he spoke briefly in Atlanta on New Year's Day evening. On January 2, 1863, his train went through Augusta and Charlotte on to Raleigh, where he gave an optimistic twenty-minute speech applauding North Carolina's contribution to the Confederacy and providing an account of his western tour. He saw no reason to doubt the ultimate outcome of the struggle because everywhere he had found a determination to defeat the Yankees. He declared that his every act was aimed at victory. "The cause," he said, "is above all personal or political considerations, and the man who, at a time like this, cannot sink such considerations, is unworthy of power." In Petersburg on January 4, Davis assured the 1,000 to 1,500 well-wishers who greeted his train that "as certain as the earth now revolves upon its axis, so surely will peace and independence be established."

Finally, later that day, he reached Richmond and home. He had been on the road for twenty-seven days, covered approximately 3,000 miles, made numerous public appearances and speeches, all the while engaged in what he called "promoting the noble cause. . . ."[111]

CHAPTER THIRTEEN

"Lift Men Above All Personal Considerations"

There was no New Year's Day reception at the White House to usher in 1863. President Davis had not yet returned from his lengthy western journey. Once back in Richmond, he did make a public appearance on the night of January 5, when several hundred people congregated outside the Executive Mansion for a serenade. Davis appeared on the portico, accompanied by an aide who introduced "the president of the United States," but quickly corrected himself in front of the mirthful crowd.

Addressing "Friends and Fellow Citizens," Davis seized the inadvertent cue just given him: "Of the title as corrected, I am proud—the other I would scorn to hold." Applause greeted both alacrity and sentiment. In his remarks the president emphasized themes that he equated with his cause. As he had from the beginning, he identified the Confederacy: "the last hope, as I believe, for the perpetuation of that system of government which our forefathers founded—the asylum of the oppressed and the home of true representative liberty." The "ancestors" of his audience had declared "the great principles of human government," which Confederates embraced as their own. Davis said of his countrymen: "You have shown yourselves in no respect to be degenerate sons of your fathers. You have fought mighty battles, and your deeds of valor will live among the richest spoils of Time's ample page."

This clarion call once again underscored the powerful bond cementing white liberty and black slavery. That the Confederate cause still included protecting slavery posed no problem to Davis. Almost two years of war had not altered his conviction, shared with the overwhelming majority of his fellow citizens, that the Founding Fathers had perceived no contradiction between their devotion to liberty and the right to own slaves. Before the war, the Constitution had given form to that liberty and that right. With the war, the Confederate States offered the only hope that the Revolution and the constitutionalism of the Fathers could survive. In his mind he simply carried on their legacy when he praised the valor of a people fighting for a liberty that included the right to own slaves.

Davis also excoriated the barbarism of the enemy. He found them guilty of every crime from murdering to burning to plundering, in their blurring the line between combatant and civilian. But now their savagery had advanced to an even more horrendous level. According to Davis, the Federals plotted "to be your masters, to try to reduce you to subjection" by "disturb[ing] your social organizations on the plea that it is a military necessity." Referring to the Emancipation Proclamation, he said the Lincoln administration claimed it only wanted to preserve the Union, but he asked how it could do so "by destroying [our] social existence. . . ." To shouts of approval, he denounced Yankees as worse than "hyenas."

Though admitting that war was utterly evil, the president saw "the severe crucible" as essential, for it alone could "cement us together." He believed that the vicissitudes of war "we have been subjected to in common, and the glory which encircles our brow has made us a band of brothers, and, I trust, we will be united forever." Now soldiers of every state are "linked in the defense of a most sacred cause."

For the defenders of Confederate liberty, Davis envisioned a bright future. He announced that the enemy had been halted in Virginia, Tennessee, and Mississippi. The Confederacy was growing proportionately stronger than the Union. "Now deep resolve is seen in every eye, an unconquerable spirit nerves every arm," he proclaimed. That determination existed on the home front as well as in the ranks. "With such noble women at home, and such heroic soldiers in the field, we are invincible." He closed with an appeal to the Almighty: "May God prosper our cause and may we live to give to our children untarnished the rich inheritance which our Fathers gave to us."[1]

One week later, Davis's message to the third session of the First Congress covered much of the same ground. He praised the valor of Confederate soldiers and commended the southern people for their efforts. He proudly averred "that these Confederate States have added another to the lessons taught by history for the instruction of man; that they have afforded another example of the impossibility of subjugating a people determined to be free. . . ." Condemning what he termed "the appalling atrocities" of the Yankee invaders, Davis singled out Benjamin Butler as an outlaw deserving execution. And with the Emancipation Proclamation, this bestiality was now threatening the monstrosity of servile insurrection and race war. Even facing so blood-thirsty a foe, Davis showed no doubt. "The energies of a whole nation devoted to the single object of success in this war have accomplished marvels. . . ." "With hearts swelling with gratitude," he concluded, "let us, then, join in returning thanks to God, and in beseeching the continuance of his protecting care over our cause and the restoration of peace with its manifold blessings to our beloved country."[2]

Although in his speech and message Davis included the just-visited West in heralding Confederate military success, almost immediately he had to struggle again with the disease he had traveled so far to treat. In the Army of Tennessee, his palliatives had not effected a cure. The pestilence afflicting the army did not long remain in remission. During the turn of the year, Braxton Bragg fought the futile Battle of Murfreesboro (in the Union designation, Stone's River). On the last day of 1862, his attack drove back the Federals, causing him to commu-nicate news of a great victory. But after a desultory January 1, his renewed assault on the second was a bloody failure. Even though the two sides had battled to a tactical draw, Bragg realized he could not maintain his army at Murfreesboro and fell back about twenty-five miles.[3]

Coming so rapidly after the report of a triumph, Bragg's retreat brought disappointment to Richmond; but more important, it reener-gized the anti-Bragg feeling within and without the army. This antago-nistic outpouring so affected Bragg that he took the unusual step of asking his generals in writing whether they approved of his retreat and whether they retained confidence in him as a commander. The replies stung. While some support was voiced, a widespread judgment called for his resignation.

Jefferson Davis did not know quite what to make of his general. He retained his faith in Bragg's ability; he had fought the enemy and still held a position in middle Tennessee. Even so, the president could not fathom Bragg's requesting his subordinates' opinion of his actions. The lack of confidence among so many generals worried him, though it certainly should not have surprised him. He was legitimately con-cerned that such an attitude could eventually infect the entire army, rendering it unlikely to fight effectively for Bragg. Also, he recognized that Bragg did not belong to the select company of generals who could "overcome the distrust and alienation of their principal officers" and on their own "excite enthusiasm & . . . win affection of their troops. . . ."[4]

On January 21 the president directed General Johnston, then touring his department, to proceed to Bragg's army and report on whether Bragg should be replaced. Davis reminded the general, "as that army is a part of your command, no order will be necessary to give you authority there." Within a week Johnston arrived at Bragg's headquarters at Tullahoma, Tennessee.[5]

Although Bragg was his subordinate, Johnston acted more like a timid guest than a commanding general. He did talk with Bragg, but with few others. He made no attempt to conduct extensive interviews and actually determine the relationship between Bragg and the Army of Tennessee. As a result, in his reports to the president, dated February 3 and 12, he assessed positively the state of the army, the command relationships in it, and in addition gave Bragg a ringing endorsement.[6]

Joseph Johnston did not approach this assignment as a commanding officer. What his most astute biographer terms his "delicate sense of honor" made him impotent. The critical fact was that if Bragg went, Johnston would replace him. Everyone—Johnston, Bragg, Davis, and Secretary of War Seddon—understood that. While Johnston did want the army, a position he considered eminently preferable to his theater command, his sense of honor precluded any involvement in opening the slot, even making a professional judgment. He wanted the president to force him to take the post while he protested the decision. He believed that if he found anything askew, he could be accused of engineering Bragg's removal. He was deeply troubled about such perceptions for his reputation, telling his friend Senator Wigfall it "would not look well & would certainly expose me, injure me." The president assured Johnston that his command authority obviated any such criticism. Similar assurances from his political patron Senator Wigfall and from Secretary Seddon, known to Johnston as a friendly supporter, who even suggested that he keep Bragg as chief of staff, did not move the general. He was unwilling to act. Honor, yes, fear of public disfavor, yes; but Johnston had never been willing in any critical situation to make any decision that might reflect adversely upon him. In this instance his inaction was absolutely in character.[7]

That characteristic was evident when President Davis on March 9 finally took the issue in his own hands and ordered Johnston to take over the Army of Tennessee and send Bragg to Richmond. It had become apparent to the president that Johnston had not reported accurately. Letters from Leonidas Polk, his old acquaintance and Bragg's archenemy and senior subordinate, castigated the commanding general but urged his appointment to a post that could utilize his talent for discipline and organization. In this instance Polk was surely right. At about the same time Bragg's report on the Battle of Murfreesboro reached the War Department; in it Bragg lambasted several of his generals, including John C. Breckinridge. Further, Congress was becoming restive about Bragg.[8]

Johnston even managed to sidestep this direct order. He wired that Bragg's wife was quite ill, making it impossible for Bragg to go to Richmond. Of course, Johnston could easily have assumed command of the army and left it to Bragg and the War Department to decide on the general's travel plans. Then, on April 10, Johnston said that his own illness prevented his taking the field; Bragg had to stay.[9]

At this point Davis and Seddon stopped trying to make any change. Johnston had written that if Bragg went, the army needed a new commander promptly. If Johnston would not accept the position, no other full general was available. Given Johnston's repeated assertions of punctilio and persistent refusal to act, the president had to consider that removing Bragg might so offend Johnston that he would refuse or resign, leaving the West with no senior commander. Furthermore, given the structure of army command, Davis really had no option, barring radical action. Once more Davis proved unwilling to eradicate the plague afflicting the Army of Tennessee by firing Bragg along with the carping, backbiting corps and division commanders. The army needed radical surgery, which the senior physician would not and could not bring himself to administer.

As he entered the third year of his presidency, Jefferson Davis's work habits had not changed since the early weeks in Montgomery. In Richmond he used two different offices. His official workplace was located on the third floor of the former Customs House on Main Street just a block below Capitol Square. The building housed the Departments of State and the Treasury as well as the Office of the President. Davis usually walked the half mile from the White House past the Capitol and down the hill to the Customs House.[10]

Davis's business office was neither impressive nor large; it measured around 24 feet long by 18 feet wide, furnished with two tables, a few chairs, and maps covering the walls. The cabinet also met here. A single soldier guarded the door. His private secretary's office adjoined, and immediately opposite the presidential rooms was the office of his personal aides; they had unrestricted access to him, and at least one was always present.[11]

Davis had a second office in the White House where he also worked, especially when ill, though he never held cabinet meetings there and rarely formal conferences of any kind. The office was located centrally on the second floor between the master bedroom and the large nursery, with doors opening to each. It contained only a desk, table, chairs, a map, and bookcases. A small outer chamber, occupied by the private secretary, provided a buffer between the president and callers. In addition, Davis used a small, informally furnished library off the drawing room, also accessible from the entry hall—a "snuggery," one cabinet member termed it—for intimate discussions.[12]

President Davis devoted long hours to his extensive duties. Never an early riser, he did not usually begin his workday until 10 a.m., but regularly worked far into the night. One hour every morning he generally gave to any visitors who happened by. Then he had numerous formal appointments as well as conferences with advisers. Rarely holding to a fixed schedule, he quite often found himself running as much as an hour late for meetings. Although no one expected him to be on time, those who worked with him attested to his diligence and dedication. In the evening he returned to paperwork. He was literally "indefatigable," but at a frightful cost to his health.[13]

Davis's preoccupation with detail helped keep his days and nights full. He was consumed with minutiae that one War Department employee rightly termed "little trash which ought to be dispatched by clerks in the adjutant general's office." He unquestionably tried to keep himself aware of literally everything going on, particularly in the army. He also believed his duty required that kind of detailed attentiveness. Yet in a fundamental sense he simply continued the practices he had begun as secretary of war and reinstituted in Montgomery. The larger war he was running by 1862 did not cause any basic alterations in his administrative style.[14]

His sending as many as 200 papers to the War Department in a single day caused no surprise, and illustrated his involvement. He questioned nominations for junior artillery officers. He involved himself in deciding whether two pieces of artillery went to the navy or Charleston. He acted on a request to permit a junior officer to resign rather than face a court-martial. A letter from a captain wanting a transfer from Virginia to the Mississippi Valley received a presidential endorsement. Another captain who felt he had been overlooked for promotion also got the president's personal attention. Matters like the promotion of two lieutenant colonels in a Louisiana regiment took his time, as did the proposal from a Virginia civilian to raise a force of artillerists in Mexico for service in Texas.[15]

Technology and weaponry continued to fascinate Davis. He spent time thinking about and talking about proposals both reasonable and fanciful. He responded personally to the inventor of a device for the "artificial elevation" of cannon. He scheduled an appointment with a man who claimed to have developed a new breech-loading gun. Sabers for the cavalry and their virtues versus the pistol carbine generated discussion. He even dealt with a plan for "a flying machine to be used for war purposes."[16]

President Davis spent considerable time in conferences, both cabinet meetings and talks with one or more officials. The cabinet usually met two or three times a week, the deliberations lasting between two and five hours. In these meetings Davis brought myriad topics before his official family, such as conscription, political questions, potential cabinet members, and diplomatic issues, though only rarely military strategy. He encouraged free discussion and invited different viewpoints. The meetings were not tightly run, however, chiefly because of Davis's discursiveness. In the midst of discussions he would commence on what one cabinet officer called "episodical questions," which included his early army career, horses, and history.[17]

The president involved the cabinet fully in the preparation of his major messages to Congress. About a month before Congress convened, he would call the cabinet together for a lengthy "free conversation" in which he and the members would go over topics that required attention. Around a week later he presented a rough draft and asked for criticism. The numerous corrections on the document indicated to the ministers their leader's concern about the message. Davis did care, but there was a second reason for all the editorial activity, and only a single member knew about it. The initial version of the message was prepared by Judah Benjamin. He and Davis made the decision to relieve the president of such a time-consuming task. Then Davis went over Benjamin's work and brought it to the meeting. The secretaries made any suggestions they wished; Benjamin, with their knowledge, was responsible for incorporating the adopted ideas and preparing a fair copy. Thereupon, the cabinet considered it once more. At this meeting the entire message was read, giving the last opportunity for additions or deletions. Finally, Benjamin had the responsibility to prepare the official copy for the president to submit to Congress.[18]

Judah Benjamin came to occupy a special place among Davis's counselors. "A stout dapper little man" with a full, olive-colored face and "the brightest large black eyes," Benjamin had a "lively, agreeable manner" and "elegantly polished speech." Born in 1811 in St. Croix in the Danish West Indies, of Sephardic Jewish parents, Benjamin as a boy migrated with his family to the United States. In his adopted Louisiana, he became a notable and wealthy attorney as well as a successful politician, rising to the United States Senate. Davis had not been close to Benjamin before 1861. But he valued the Louisianian's brilliance and early on in the war began to appreciate his absolute personal loyalty, rebuffing all attempts, some accompanied by anti-Semitism, to drive Benjamin from his cabinet. Besides his great intellectual ability and undoubted fidelity, Benjamin brought an optimism, buoyance, almost insouciance, that countered Davis's heavy sense of responsibility and constant worry and anxiety. His omnipresent smile and wit never withered, no matter the news. By the end of 1861, Benjamin spent many hours with Davis discussing every aspect of Confederate policy. His becoming secretary of state in March 1862 gave him the time to spend on nondepartmental matters, such as congressional messages, for there was little diplomatic business to transact, and even that decreased after 1862.[19]

Benjamin was not the only cabinet officer to spend considerable time with the president. Davis spent hours almost daily with his war ministers, Randolph and Seddon. He liked to discuss with his secretary of war all aspects of the war, both important and unimportant; strategy, conscription policy, assignments of full generals, and resignations were all fit topics for president-secretary conferences. Employees in the War Department reported on their bosses' returning from at times marathon deliberations. Although President Davis made almost every decision, large and small, he wanted to talk them out before deciding.[20]

He was a deliberate decision-maker. Although he did not dodge making decisions, he did not act quickly. According to Secretary of the Navy Stephen Mallory, a close associate over the war years, Davis's caution and thoroughness made immediate action quite unlikely. Wanting to explore all possible dimensions of any question, Davis sought out discussion. He wanted others' opinions, and he got them—from his cabinet, from members of Congress, from friends, but most especially from his war ministers along with Benjamin and Lee. Then he decided, and once he had charted a course, he clung to it with barnacle-like tenacity.[21]

President Davis also had a private secretary and personal aides to help him carry out his duties. He employed only two private secretaries: Robert Josselyn, a contemporary and veteran of the First Mississippi Regiment, who served for the initial year; and most important, Burton N. Harrison, whom he appointed in February 1862. Born in New Orleans in 1838, Harrison spent his youth mostly with relatives in Maryland because of his father's death. He gravitated to the University of Mississippi, chiefly at the urging of a kinsman, the noted educator Franklin A. P. Barnard. But, again upon Barnard's encouragement, he quickly moved on to Yale, where he finished in 1859. Barnard, now president of the Mississippi institution, brought him back as an assistant professor of mathematics. All the while he pursued legal studies. This bright, ambitious, and handsome young man came to Davis's attention through his fellow Mississippian and ardent supporter L. Q. C. Lamar, who strongly recommended Harrison.

Burton Harrison was twenty-four years old when he came to the White House. At first, he reported his job as not very taxing, but the pace quickened and never let up—drafting letters for the president, writing letters in the president's name, delivering documents between the Capitol and the presidential offices, making appointments, greeting visitors. He sat just outside the president's door overseeing the passageway to Davis's presence. Not only an essential person in Davis's public family, Harrison also became part of the private family, living on the third floor of the White House until his marriage in 1864. The president treated him like a grown son when his oldest boy was only five. Varina found him delightful. In the postwar years Harrison became a prominent New York attorney, but he never forgot his unique status with the Davises and remained steadfastly loyal to them until his death in 1904.[22]

In addition to Harrison, Davis from the beginning also had personal aides. In April 1862, Congress authorized the president to increase his personal staff to four with the rank of colonel in the Confederate army; later, the number was raised to six. He employed different people in this position, including a nephew, Joseph R. Davis, and Robert E. Lee's son, George Washington Custis Lee, both of whom went on to become general officers and compile notable war records. There was James

Chesnut of South Carolina, former United States senator and husband of the diarist Mary Boykin Chesnut, who became a great friend of Varina; and Francis K. Lubbock, who had been governor of Texas. Others serving in this capacity included Joseph C. Ives, New Yorker, West Pointer, and engineering officer, and the Irish-born William M. Browne, a graduate of Trinity College, Dublin, and in the late 1850s a pro-southern and pro-Davis journalist in Washington. But without doubt the closest to Davis was William Preston Johnston, son of the lamented Albert Sidney, who joined the president's staff the month his father died and remained until 1865. Just past thirty, Colonel Johnston, like his fellow Yale alumnus Harrison, was treated like an adopted son by the Davises. Johnston even spoke of the president's acting "almost fatherly to me."[23]

President Davis employed his aides chiefly in two ways. First he utilized them as secretaries, designating them to draft letters for him and even directing them to respond directly to certain correspondents, always specifying they were writing for the president. In the latter case he provided instructions for the content of the letters. These assignments could keep pens scratching until midnight.[24]

The president also used these men as private inspecting officers by dispatching them to various commands to disclose conditions directly to him. Johnston went to the Army of Tennessee in both 1862 and early 1863; Ives visited that same army in December 1863 and Browne in early 1864. In 1863 Chesnut and Lee received orders to proceed to Beauregard's South Atlantic command. Lee at times also acted as a liaison between his father and the president. The aides were not sent secretly; they always reported to the commanding general and stated their mission. They simply provided Davis with a direct and unobstructed view of a command by someone he trusted. That most of these assignments went to armies and departments commanded by Beauregard or Joseph Johnston underscored the president's doubts about both generals.[25]

Although Davis's sense of duty and the burden of office consumed him, he did have a passion that relaxed him—horseback riding. His health permitting, he rode late in the afternoon, sometimes for several hours. Varina never knew how long he would be gone. At times he returned long after dark, occasionally as late as 10 or 11 p.m. The military camps dotted around Richmond regularly received unadvertised visits from the commander in chief. He often took an aide, family member, or friend with him, but on many occasions he rode alone. When with a companion, he conversed about favorite subjects such as horses, dogs, and his early army career in the West.

A superb rider, "graceful and easy in the saddle," as one observer described him, Davis also displayed surprising physical stamina for a man with his chronic health problems. Neither driving rainstorms nor the ice and slush of winter deterred him. Without hesitation the president would plunge into overflowing streams. Rides of fifteen miles were not uncommon, and he could wear out his young aides.[26]

Although Davis sometimes rode alone and varied his human companions, he was always accompanied by a cigar. Despite repeated bouts with bronchial troubles, he never gave up cigars. He smoked them constantly and routinely offered them to visitors. Upon informal occasions and in relaxing moments, they were omnipresent. But in periods of great strain he also puffed away; according to Varina, he smoked most then. Even when sick, he cherished his cigars. Once when ill with dyspepsia, he appeared late to greet two visitors, who commented on his "suffering." Still, he offered cigars—"the strongest, blackest I had ever seen," said one. After lighting up, the other remarked that with such cigars he was amazed the president "did not suffer from a worse ailment. . . ."[27]

That the president rode without a bodyguard caused some concern about the possibility of assassination. Presidential security was generally lax. A full-time military detail was not formed for the White House until February 1864, though sentinels had been posted earlier. A fire in the basement helped prompt this action, even though its origin was never determined. An interviewer who talked with Davis late in life claimed the former president said he had confronted one suspicious situation in Montgomery and had twice been shot at on rides around Richmond. But in a private letter Davis disputed the accuracy of the published account, leaving the question of real threats unanswered.[28]

While Jefferson Davis was directing a great war, his wife strove to make the Executive Mansion a home for him. She presided over a full house: not only her husband and their four children, but usually her sister Maggie and occasionally other relatives of hers and Jefferson's resided there. For two years Burton Harrison was a permanent resident, and various aides at different times added to the number.

Varina was a mother with an active brood—Maggie, age eight; Jeff Jr., six; Joe, four; and Billy, not yet two. She gloried in them and in her motherhood. The children were visible in the house, even making unannounced appearances at functions. Jeff wrestled and raced with his little dog, and also had goats that he hooked up to a wagon. He and Maggie adored ponies, and all liked to ride close by their father, or even in his lap. Jeff and Joe had their own Confederate uniforms. A close friend depicted Varina's "infant family," commenting on "wonderfully clever and precocious children—but unbroken wills." One time "the nursery contingent" rose up. "They fought, screamed, laughed. It was bedlam broke loose." Mother "scolded, laughed, cried."[29]

For assistance the first lady could call on a range of servants. In the Executive Mansion of a slaveholding republic and with the slaveowning background of its occupants, a striking diversity marked the domestic staff. There were slaves, of course, but also free blacks as well as white women. The Davises brought only two slaves from Brierfield, one of them Jim Pemberton, the son of Jefferson's first slave, longtime companion, and overseer. Over the course of the war, they hired at least six others. In addition, several free blacks and two white women worked for the Davises. These people performed a variety of tasks: manservant, maid, nurse, cook, butler, dining-room servant, coachman, groom for the horses. The impact of the war wrecked the stability of this group. Decamping became so common, especially among those hired, that Mary Chesnut called them "mere birds of passage." Even the trusted Jim Pemberton ran away to the nearby Federal lines in the summer of 1864. Attempting to cope with the instability and turnover, Varina strove to find replacements, particularly to hire slaves, her task made more difficult by deteriorating Confederate finances.[30]

She needed servants, for she was an active hostess. At the White House, she and Jefferson gave numerous receptions. In addition, the president invited cabinet officers, generals, friends, and visitors to informal dinners, and even breakfasts. Varina also entertained her own friends at teas and luncheons. She served eggnog on Christmas Eve and even gave "a matinée musicale." Her White House was a lively place. Trying to make herself and her stage as attractive as possible, she attempted to obtain clothes and even furniture from Europe, though the blockade made the arrival of such purchases problematical.[31]

Her table could be sumptuous, though at other times simple. One meal included gumbo, ducks, liver, chicken in jelly, oysters, claret soup, champagne, salad, and chocolate jelly cake. Another time brains *en papillote* adorned the table. Guests also noted the plain simple food. In this area Varina did not have a demanding husband, for he cared little about what was put before him. From at least the time of their marriage,

Jefferson ate what little he did because his body required food, not because he relished it. By the last months of the war sumptuousness had totally disappeared, with only the "plainest and scantiest of fare" on the table.[32]

Varina invariably still received plaudits as a hostess and social companion, but this approbation did not indicate the emergence of a different Varina. "A most refined, accomplished, and excellent lady, bright pleasing and intelligent in conversation and an elegant entertainer," concluded one who had enjoyed her company. A Confederate official called her "a lady of great good sense and of much more than ordinary cultivation." A Virginia lady remembered her as "very clever and brilliant in society. . . ." There were other depictions of a "gracious mistress of a salon" and "a woman of warm heart, and . . . witty. . . ." Clever and quick-witted many found her, a cleverness that still often manifested itself in a withering tongue that could "blight with sarcasm." An Irish visitor recoiled at what he called her "smart sneers." This caustic mode some observers attributed to a lack of refinement or a deficiency of cultivated manners.[33]

The first lady was never imprisoned in the White House or ostracized by Richmond society. Varina recollected "a certain offishness" in Richmond, which she put down to the "inundation" pouring into the city. At the same time she recalled her good fortune in finding friends, some women she had previously known and new ones, including members of the so-called First Families of Virginia. Moreover, she developed friendships among those who, like her, came with the tide of Confederates. Perhaps the most notable of these was the South Carolinian Mary Boykin Chesnut. Varina certainly spoke her mind, and women who would be her friends had to accept that directness.[34]

She surely had enemies, women who detested her. Most of this animus was directly related to the personalities and politics of the war and was immediately connected to her husband. Lydia Johnston and Charlotte Wigfall, wives of Joseph E. and Louis T. respectively, who had been prewar friends but turned bitterly against her, were leaders in this brigade.[35]

In 1863 Varina was thirty-seven and had borne five children in nine years. She was also caught up in the trials of a great war. Her appearance had become much more matronly. A Richmonder depicted "a tall commanding figure, with dark hair, eyes and complexion, and strongly marked expression. . . ." Her lips were "firmly set," though "beautifully softened by the unusually sad expression of her dark, earnest eyes." This observer thought her "a handsome woman" with presence, "but by no means coming under the description of the feminine adjective 'pretty.' "[36]

As a presidential wife in wartime, Varina strove to fulfill her sense of public duty. Like many other Richmond women, she and others in her house were often seen on their porch plaiting straw and making hats and bonnets. She also made every effort to provide food for the many army officers who kept coming and going from the White House. In addition, she distributed provisions collected for families in need. She covered the walls and mantel of her reception room in the White House "with chains and all kinds of knick-knacks of wood, made and presented to her" by prisoners of war. One endeavor that attracted many prominent women in Richmond, visiting and nursing at hospitals, she absented herself from. Her husband believed she should stay away in order "not to expose the men to the restraint my [Varina's] presence might have imposed. . . ."[37]

Varina found the war and her role in it difficult, even though her experience was different from the great majority of women of her class. They remained in the countryside and, with husbands and sons absent, had to cope with the increasingly arduous problem of providing for families and managing increasingly restive slaves. Varina told her friend Mary Chesnut, "I live in a kind of maze: disaster follows disaster. . . ." "Nothing," she said, "seems to do its appointed work." She fantasized that her husband was a dry goods clerk, and they could "dine in peace on a mutton scrag at three and take an airing on Sunday in a little buggy with no back, drawn by a one eyed horse at fifty cents an hour." In late 1863, she wondered, "Is [it] self government or self immolation that we are testing?" Although she prayed for Confederate success, she feared she was not "one of those whose righteousness makes their prayer available."[38]

She also worried about her parents, displaced by the fall of New Orleans. They did get to North Carolina in the summer of 1862, but the next year William Howell fell desperately ill in Montgomery. Upon receiving the news, she left promptly by train, accompanied by William P. Johnston. But her father died on March 16, a day before his oldest daughter could reach him. Johnston reported Varina "greatly overwhelmed and grieved." She had little time to bemoan her dead father, for she found her mother quite sick, "wasted to skin and bones." Even though she wanted to return quickly to Richmond, she believed her mother's illness required her to remain in Montgomery. To Jefferson she wrote emotionally of her misery being away from him and her children. "Do kiss my darlings for me especially my daughter and thre[e] little sons," she beseeched, "and dear Husband believe me your devoted Wife."[39]

A major reason for Varina's distress about being away from Richmond was her concern over Jefferson's health. It had been wretched since February and would deteriorate during the spring into summer. Davis could seem like a hospital ward all by himself. Yet again his old nemeses assaulted his fifty-five-year-old body—headaches, fever, bronchitis, laryngitis, an eye infection, dyspepsia, possibly even pneumonia. Absent from his office in the Customs House for almost a month in April and May, Davis was devastated by recurrent illnesses. Feeble and wracked with pain, he kept to his task, telling Joseph in early May, "my official duties have not been suspended at any time," though he had to defer personal interviews when he lost his voice. At a public ceremony in mid-month, the president appeared "frail in health." He would improve, then suffer a relapse. Battling so many afflictions, his body could not remain healthy for long. Still, his underlying physical strength plus his absolute determination to meet his duty to the cause kept him going.[40]

Despite Davis's ordeal, he retained his presence and could be impressive. In mid-June a visiting British army officer noted that "his face is emaciated and much wrinkled"; this eyewitness also commented on Davis's extreme thinness and observed the beginnings of a stoop. At the same time, he described his host's good features, "especially his eye which is very bright and full of life and humor." The president impressed this worldly visitor with his "agreeable, unassuming manners, and by the charm of his conversation."[41]

Whatever his physical disability and the pressure that ground down on him, Davis had a powerful tonic in his children. Those around him remarked on his adoration of his little ones and his joy with them. He enjoyed taking them for rides. When small boys in nightclothes interrupted an evening meal or social gathering, a proud father welcomed and said prayers with his little men, then sent them on to bed. According to Secretary Mallory, the president's children considered him "their pleasantest playmate."[42]

Despite repeated illness and constant overwork, President Davis never turned into a social hermit. He did not make a habit of publicly mingling with Richmonders, telling them that "constant labor in the duties of office, borne down by care, and with an anxiety which has left me scarcely a moment for repose," permitted little time for what he termed "social intercourse among you." Yet he did preside effectively at official functions.[43]

He most relished informal gatherings at the White House. He spontaneously invited to dinner or to breakfast individuals or groups of cabinet members, military officers, congressmen, friends, and visitors to Richmond. No special preparations were made, for these guests ate whatever was being served the family. Attendees portrayed a "plain and unpretending" host, who conversed about many subjects from bridles to his school days in Mississippi. The evening affairs, often closing with cigars, could go on quite late.[44]

Davis also demonstrated a genuine generosity to individuals serving the cause whom he discovered in unfortunate circumstances. One winter night he noticed the sentinel at the front door of the Executive Mansion wore no overcoat. Informed that overcoats had not been issued, the president acted, and soon the garments were distributed. When he learned that a regiment camped in the city had received no breakfast, these soldiers had food delivered to them by noon. One morning an elderly woman came to him at the White House. She identified herself as the oldest living relative of George Mason, a Revolutionary hero, and said that all her property was within Federal lines. To support herself, she needed a job. The president got her a position at the Treasury Department.[45]

He regularly took his own time to thank people for sending him presents and helping him. His personal letters expressed gratitude for items ranging from hats to Bibles, from eyeglasses to tea sets. Once when suffering from a boil, he received a Richmond woman's remedy, a flaxseed poultice. It evidently worked, for upon recovery he made a visit to her home to voice his appreciation.[46]

The president did have another side, however. As Secretary Mallory observed, "few men could be more chillingly, freezingly cold." Davis's frosty demeanor chilled those he perceived as motivated by less than total concern for the public welfare, for the cause. Just as with generals, he refused to flatter or to cultivate goodwill with members of Congress and other politicians he identified as consumed with their own private interests. Their self-esteem he discounted. If they did not attain his perception of his own devotion to the cause, they deserved at best only formal courtesy from him. In his judgment, the crisis demanded superhuman exertions and selflessness, and he could not deal effectively or humanly with those who did not measure up. He had no patience with human folly. His friends' attempts to counsel him in this matter went unheard, for, in Mallory's words, "he could not do this; it was not in his nature . . . to coax men to do their duty in the condition of their country."[47]

Considering the military situation in the two major theaters of war, Commander-in-Chief Davis faced what had become an ever-present dichotomy: in Virginia, achievement and stability; in the West, disappointment and turmoil. In early May, Robert E. Lee again demonstrated his battlefield wizardry in defeating the huge Federal army at Chancellorsville, just west of Fredericksburg. But this stunning victory came at an extraordinarily high price. Among the mortally wounded was Lee's great lieutenant Stonewall Jackson, who died on May 10. The government put on a state funeral in Richmond for the fallen hero, attended by an unwell and feeble president. The body was then transported to Jackson's Shenandoah Valley home in Lexington for burial. For Davis, the death of Jackson did not match Sidney Johnston's as a personal blow, but he recognized Stonewall's special place, stating that "a great national calamity has befallen us. . . ." To a visitor at the White House after the funeral, he remarked, "I am still staggering from a dreadful blow. I cannot think."[48]

Even though Lee had to cope with the loss of Jackson and was involved in reorganizing his army, he eagerly advocated another advance into enemy country. He knew the temper of the president who wrote his general, "I readily perceive the disadvantage of standing still. . . ." Davis only regretted that he could not provide Lee with "the means which would make it quite safe to attempt all that we desire." Neither Lee nor Davis, however, required certainty or safety before action.[49]

The two men decided they needed a face-to-face discussion. Because of his health, Davis had Lee come to Richmond. In a mid-May conference with Davis and Secretary of War Seddon, Lee placed before them an ambitious plan: he would take his army, with all the reinforcements the president would give him, and strike across the Potomac. To make the advance of the Army of Northern Virginia even more menacing to the enemy, Lee wanted the Atlantic coast virtually stripped and those troops organized under General Beauregard in central Virginia. From there Beauregard could pose a threat to Washington that would tie down Federal troops, and he could quickly take advantage of any success Lee might have in the North.[50]

Lee had several goals for his offensive. They were discussed in Richmond, and during the following six weeks were spelled out in letters between general and president. He certainly wanted to feed and supply his army on northern soil. Northern Virginia had sustained too many armies for too long. In addition, an invasion would carry the war to the enemy, an aim he and Davis shared and savored. He also believed his army almost invincible, certainly capable of inflicting a devastating defeat on his opponent. Such a thunderous victory in enemy country would surely have enormous value, perhaps even lead to peace. Most assuredly it would relieve the pressure bearing down on the lower Mississippi Valley, specifically Vicksburg.

Davis brought before his cabinet the question of whether to authorize Lee's project or to keep him on the defensive, shifting units from his army to Mississippi. All supported Lee's thrust except Postmaster General John Reagan, the only member from west of the Mississippi. The cabinet's position affirmed by the president so troubled Reagan that he requested the president to reconsider. Aware of the gravity of this decision, Davis agreed to reopen the discussion. According to Reagan, the cabinet spent an entire Saturday going over every aspect of every issue, with the outcome the same. An impromptu gathering on Sunday reaffirmed what had already been decided. Even though he did not prevail, Reagan was impressed by his chief's deliberate thoughtfulness: "his whole course of conduct showed him to be reasonable, conservative and just."[51]

Davis's decision to go with Lee was quite understandable and sensible. Lee was without question his best general, and Davis knew it. Moreover, no other general had even approached Lee's record in the field. Success by Lee on enemy territory had enormous potential. Besides, Lee's advance appealed to Davis's aggressiveness and his overwhelming desire to inflict pain on his enemy. Davis later wrote he hoped Lee could win a battlefield victory north of the Potomac that would have "ensured peace on the only basis we were willing to accept it, Independence." Further, the president could not know what use would be made of troops sent from Lee to Mississippi. Would they arrive in time, and more important, would they be employed effectively? Lee put it elliptically, speaking of "the uncertainty of [their] application." Neither Davis nor Lee ever said directly, but both knew, that Joseph Johnston had never exhibited decisiveness, much less boldness. While Davis blessed Lee's move, he did not strip the Atlantic

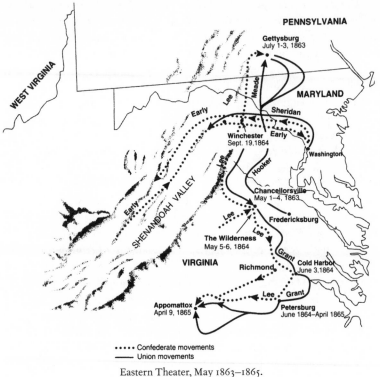

Eastern Theater, May 1863–1865.

From W. J. Cooper and T. E. Terrill, The American South: A History *(2d ed.),*
with permission of the McGraw-Hill Companies

coast, ordering those men along with Beauregard to Virginia. That was simply too much of a gamble, for it risked losing Charleston and Savannah, and perhaps the Carolinas. The political dangers were too great.[52]

When President Davis turned toward the lower Mississippi Valley and his home, he had to cope with a troublesome situation. The fundamental command problem in the Department of the West had never been solved. General Johnston still adamantly refused to take literal command. Despite repeated efforts by Davis to tell him that he was in charge, and by Seddon, who tried to placate Johnston's suspicions by emphasizing his friendship for the fussy general, Johnston demurred. To get around Johnston's insistence that distance made his assignment impossible, the president suggested that he place a division at Selma or Meridian to expedite movement, but nothing happened. Johnston satisfied himself by proclaiming that a choice between defending Mississippi and Tennessee was a political decision, one that should be made in Richmond, not by a general in the field. In a basic sense he was right. Yet he never suggested, much less tried, any stratagem that would give him the flexibility to hold both. And he certainly never issued orders forcing Davis to make that hard decision, a choice that for political reasons, including public opinion and his estimation of Confederate unity, the president really could not make.[53]

While Richmond and Johnston frustrated each other, their supposedly common enemy acted. Frustrated by his previous setbacks, General Ulysses Grant was determined to win the great prize: Vicksburg. The spring of 1863 found him charting a new course. Convinced no direct approach would work, he dedicated himself to finding a way to place his army in the rear of the great fortress. He realized he could march his soldiers down the Louisiana side of the Mississippi; the issue was getting them back to the eastern bank. He initially attempted to cut or dig a route for transports through the swamps and streams, to no avail. Finally, he decided on a daring move. In mid-April, navy transports and gunboats were sent on a run past the Vicksburg batteries. It worked. Now he had both soldiers and ships below the city. In the meantime, he ordered a huge cavalry raid from north to south through Mississippi to disrupt the Confederates. That was also a smashing success. By the end of April, his army had crossed the river. Now, to confuse his foe, he would strike eastward toward Jackson, then reverse himself, going back toward the river. For this campaign he jettisoned a supply line. His men would live off the land while they turned Fortress Vicksburg into Prison Vicksburg. Grant had formulated a brilliant plan, which could only be foiled by quick response, decisive action, and smooth cooperation.[54]

Grant's two opponents were not up to the challenge. Pemberton had courage, and would certainly hold steadfastly to what he saw as his duty, but did not understand Grant's design until it was far too late. He assumed that Grant would act as he himself would, cautiously and conservatively. Pemberton was simply outclassed in this campaign of maneuver. Besides, he spent much of his energy trying to separate himself from Johnston's authority. Although Pemberton initially thought about searching for Grant and briefly came out of his fortifications, he took Davis's order to hold Vicksburg to mean that he must physically remain within the city, where he was so much more comfortable. It became his anchor of certainty in a sea of uncertainty. He never seemed to comprehend that he could prevail only by preventing a siege. Confused, Pemberton clung to the city while Grant moved easily through the countryside. Later, a direct order from Johnston finally moved him out; outside the town he thought chiefly about interrupting Grant's nonexistent supply lines, but bewilderment and ineptness doomed him. In lopsided engagements, Grant easily pushed him back, and by May 18, Pemberton was trapped in Vicksburg.[55]

Joseph Johnston also assisted. To meet the grave threat to his home state, President Davis did not wait for the commanding general of the Department of the West to decide his presence was required. Shortly after learning that Grant had crossed the Mississippi, Davis ordered Johnston to Mississippi. Upon arriving in Jackson on May 13, Johnston telegraphed that because Federal forces had inserted themselves between Jackson and Vicksburg, he had arrived too late. Once again Johnston and Richmond became bogged down in a futile, stupefying dialogue about his command authority. Although Johnston did say only a quick strike could save Pemberton and Vicksburg, he orchestrated none. He said he must wait for reinforcements because he was outnumbered. As Davis urged action, wiring, "we cannot hope for numerical equality and time will probably increase the disparity," Johnston was quarreling with the War Department over how many men he actually had.[56]

In Mississippi, Joseph Johnston occupied himself principally with fashioning a cocoon of security. He did instruct Pemberton to attempt a junction with him, and eventually urged his subordinate to evacuate Vicksburg in an effort to save his army. But Johnston never undertook any serious measure to effect any combination, or even to thrust at Grant. He saw only defeat. Having concluded the president had placed him in a position where he could only fail, Johnston wanted the record to show that he had been given an impossible assignment and, outnumbered, he could not succeed. He rationalized that no other general had ever faced such odds. Concerned mostly with protecting his name and fame, he wanted to ensure that no one could blame him for Confederate failure. He responded to his wife's expressed concern about his reputation: "Don't be uneasy on the Subject." He continued that once everyone realized he did not have a powerful army, he would be judged as a soldier "who discharge[d] his duty manfully & responsibly [and] will always be respected. . . ." The administration could not blame him. Revealing a modicum of self-awareness, he told his wife, "I cannot be a great man, Nature & the President will it otherwise." Here

Johnston was half right. He did not possess the moral strength and self-confidence for greatness as a captain, but the president wanted nothing so much as for him to prevail.[57]

Throughout May and June, the situation in Mississippi utterly frustrated Jefferson Davis. Even though seriously ill, he was consumed with Mississippi and Vicksburg. To one correspondent he wrote of his keen "anxiety." Almost daily he sent dispatches to Johnston, Pemberton, or Governor John Pettus. From many Mississippians, including Pettus and brother Joseph, came cries for help. Davis answered that he was doing all he could, and he did scour the Confederacy for troops. Five thousand went from Beauregard, but he could spare no more and neither could Bragg help. The president called on his new commander in the Trans-Mississippi, Lieutenant General Edmund Kirby Smith, to send assistance. But, as with Holmes, he left it to Smith's discretion, and concentrating on threats perceived in Louisiana, Smith said he could not try to relieve Vicksburg. A harrowed Davis urged Pettus to call for a levy en masse. He even wired Johnston, "if my strength permitted I would go to you."[58]

Davis operated with severe handicaps, and with increasing desperation. As always, Johnston provided the scantiest information. The president informed Lee that he could get no more from Johnston than the two of them could a year previously. An official in the War Department described the general's communications as "brief unsatisfactory, almost captious letters." Additionally, by relying on figures provided by Seddon, Davis overestimated Johnston's strength; the actual number of reinforcements arriving in Mississippi never equaled the paper strength of the units sent. Davis was also unreasonably optimistic about the prospects for a massive rush of Mississippians to Johnston's side. Furthermore, he too never fathomed what Grant was about. Although he did understand that to prevail the Confederates had to strike Grant in the field, he kept pressing his generals to hit that great Confederate fiction, Grant's supply line. In conclusion, he kept hoping, and in his anguish even believing, that despite a complete absence of evidence for it, Johnston's supposed great ability would surface, enabling the general to do something dramatic. But there was no miracle. On July 4 Pemberton unconditionally surrendered his army of 31,000 to Grant. Hearing this news, the last Confederate river bastion at Port Hudson, Louisiana, followed suit four days later, also succumbing to a siege. Now the Union controlled the entire length of the Mississippi. The Confederacy had been sundered.[59]

No offsetting good news reached Richmond from Lee. The high hopes he and Davis placed on his offensive were obliterated on the hillsides around the small town of Gettysburg, Pennsylvania. In June Lee marched his army west into the Shenandoah Valley, then north into Pennsylvania. Like Grant in Mississippi, he abandoned reliance on a supply line. The Army of Northern Virginia advanced easily and rapidly, its lead elements reaching the Susquehanna River. With news that the Federal army, under its new commander, Major General George G. Meade, was fast approaching, Lee ordered his forces to concentrate on Gettysburg. During the first three days of July, Confederates and Federals engaged in a mighty struggle which cost more than 50,000 casualties. Suffering losses totaling almost one-third of his army, Lee was forced to fall back across the Potomac. But the severely battered Union army, with casualties reaching one-fourth of its strength, could not mount a vigorous pursuit. Lee's second northern thrust had ended like the first, a blood-soaked strategic failure. During the campaign Davis had been anxious. Varina recalled his saying at the time that if he could join Lee, the two of them could "wrest a victory from those people." Although the outcome surely disappointed the president, he did not perceive catastrophe. Recognition of the Battle of Gettysburg as a major turning point would have to await time and perspective.[60]

But from the moment he heard about the fall of Vicksburg, Davis understood full well its meaning. On July 14 he portrayed himself "in the depth of the gloom in which the disasters on the Missi River have shrouded our cause." He craved to know whether the calamity had resulted from "mismanagement, or it may have been that [victory] was unattainable." He was convinced that he had done all possible to give his commanders on the scene the means to defeat Grant. In one sense, he was right. He had done all he could, short of voluntarily giving up Tennessee and the central South along with the Trans-Mississippi. From his viewpoint, the latter course would mean suicide for his country. And that action he neither could nor would take.[61]

But then he had personally given Pemberton and Johnston their commands. They did not do well for him, though each performed in character. Never having previously directed an active campaign, Pemberton, inexperienced and of limited ability, contrasted strongly with his formidable opponent. Davis, impressed with the heroism of the Confederates withstanding Grant's siege, always emphasized Pemberton's bravery. Pemberton was undoubtedly brave, but bravery alone never won a battle. Exculpating Pemberton and himself left Johnston as the villain. There was certainly much responsibility for the official commanding general to absorb. He had done practically nothing with what he had, even after admitting he confronted a grave crisis. The supremely cautious and self-protective Johnston proved once again that he was no Lee. Davis wanted a court of inquiry, which he believed would indict Johnston's performance. One was called, but it never met. For the beleaguered Confederates, the press of war did not permit such luxuries.[62]

There were also problems equally as fundamental as personal traits. No one really perceived what Grant was doing. Johnston had the best sense, but would never act. Pemberton was clueless and Davis held tenaciously to the idea of Johnston as malefactor, never recognizing or admitting that Grant had no supply lines to cut. Numbers also posed a basic difficulty. Grant initially crossed the Mississippi with only 23,000 men, but his strength quickly went up to 40,000, and by July he had 70,000 investing Vicksburg. Pemberton's force numbered but 31,000, and Johnston reinforced never had more than 25,000, discounting the garrison at Port Hudson. Neither Smith nor Bragg could ever furnish sufficient troops to equalize the two sides in Mississippi. Used together under vigorous, imaginative leadership, Pemberton's and Johnston's forces might not have been able to defeat Grant, but they could have given him a contest. No such Confederate generalship was available in Mississippi in May and June of 1863.[63]

Even as he fought despair generated by Vicksburg, Davis focused on public opinion in his state. Though aware the loss of Vicksburg could sap morale, he prayed for the reverse—that the heel of the invader would engender a renewed surge of spirit and resistance. He would not waver. "In proportion as our difficulties increase," he declared, "so must we all cling together, judge charitably of each other, and strive to bear, and forbear, however great may be the sacrifice, and bitter the trial." In his bleakness, he became almost fatalistic: "it is not for man to command success, he should strive to deserve it, and leave the rest to Him who governs all things, and disposes for the best, though to our short vision the Justice may not be visible."[64]

Confederate battlefield reverses in Pennsylvania and Mississippi were matched by rebuffs on the diplomatic front, making for a barren summer. In early June when prospects seemed much brighter, Vice President Alexander Stephens, from his home in Crawfordville, Georgia, wrote the president suggesting the time might be right for peace overtures to the Lincoln government. Stephens was especially concerned about the breakdown in exchanging prisoners of war caused in part by the Confederate reaction to the Emancipation Proclamation. He worried that captives faced increasingly barbaric treatment. Stephens proposed that he undertake a mission to Washington to discuss prisoner policy, with the "hope that *indirectly* I could now turn attention to a general adjustment upon such basis as might ultimately be acceptable to both parties," and end the war. Stephens made clear that he "entertain[ed] but one idea of the basis of final settlement or adjustment; that is, the recognition of the sovereignty of the States and the right of each in its sovereign capacity to determine its own destiny." Thus, the states that had chosen to enter the Confederacy could remain there. At this point Stephens was not scheming to undo Jefferson Davis's great cause.[65]

At about the same time, Davis heard from General Lee on the peace issue. Lee hoped the Confederacy, particularly through his offensive, could encourage division in the North, emboldening those who favored peace, even if with reunion. He did not advocate reunion, however. Instead, he envisioned it as a possible negotiating ploy; specific terms, he said, could wait for an actual peace proposal.[66]

President Davis responded positively, bringing Stephens to Richmond and discussing "very fully" with him the administration's policy. Davis also brought the enterprise before the cabinet, which provided its assent. President and vice president agreed on the substance of their proposition, but not on the means of delivering it. Davis wanted Stephens to join Lee and arrive in the North with the might of a successful army at hand. Stephens envisioned a purely diplomatic approach. He got his way, for the advent of wet weather made road travel difficult.

On July 3, Stephens took a ship for the trip down the James River to the Union lines at Norfolk, and thence, he anticipated, up the Chesapeake and the Potomac to Washington. He carried formal instructions from President Davis authorizing him to negotiate prisoner exchanges and other procedures. Whether he had any informal powers to discuss a cease-fire or peace negotiations is not known. His ship made contact with a vessel of the Union navy on the fourth; Stephens communicated his mission and requested safe passage. This message reached Washington along with the news from Gettysburg and Vicksburg. Lincoln curtly refused. Stephens could only return to Richmond.[67]

Across the Atlantic, Confederate fortunes fared no better. Repeated attempts to get Britain to reconsider its policy on intervention or recognition failed. Davis finally concluded that maintaining a diplomatic mission in the country was not only futile but embarrassing. At the beginning of August, he directed James Mason to leave London, breaking off efforts to establish official relations with Britain. The rejected envoy retreated across the English Channel to Paris. Revealing his unhappiness with the British, Davis two months later agreed with Benjamin on the necessity of expelling the remaining British consular agents in the Confederacy. The stated cause was their interference with Confederate sovereignty by advising soldiers who claimed British citizenship to disregard Confederate laws. At the end of the year in his message to Congress, Davis condemned Britain's so-called neutrality, which he asserted really helped the United States and injured the Confederate States. But having done so, he admitted, "we are without adequate remedy against the injustice under which we suffer."[68]

In this season of debilitating illness and setbacks, both domestic and foreign, President Davis in mid-August sat for his only portrait painted during the war. In contrast to vivid word pictures graphically describing a worn but still vital man, the Baltimore artist John R. Robertson did not present realistically the individual before him. In Robertson's painting one sees a man composed by the artist. Davis's eyes have no flash and look more serene than saddened. Showing but flecks of gray, his hair and chin whiskers basically retain their color. His cheeks are not at all sunken nor his brow pleated with care. The broad brow and sensitive mouth are those of a noble and idealized leader.[69]

Throughout these torturous months President Davis faced political opposition. Shrill invective continued to spew from his bitterest personal enemies. Always at the forefront, Robert Barnwell Rhett ranted about a "silly and disastrous" president who had brought the country to the verge of ruin. His fellow South Carolinian James H. Hammond condemned Davis as "a Marplot always." Matching this scathing language, Robert Toombs damned the chief executive as a "stupid, malignant wretch." The vice president's brother Linton imagined action, fantasizing that "*perhaps*" only a Brutus could save the Confederacy from the "*little, conceited, dogged* knave and fool."[70]

This band of viciously hostile critics remained small. They never managed to stir up formidable personal animosity toward the president, a failure that angered them. Across the Confederacy, Davis's

Jefferson Davis, 1863 (painting by John Robertson).
Museum of the Confederacy

dominant image was that of a patriot striving to secure the great goal—independence. Legislatures, patriotic groups, and military units all adopted resolutions of support, which buoyed him. After traveling through much of the South, an English visitor concluded, "People speak of any misfortune happening to [the president] as an irreparable evil too dreadful to contemplate."[71]

While Davis escaped widespread personal hostility, however, considerable opposition was building to components of his war policy. Hostility to conscription lay at the heart of this anti-administration sentiment. From the initial law enacted in the spring of 1862, some defined enforced service as despotism, a perception that intensified with the new statute passed the following fall. This act raised the upper age limit of eligibility to forty-five but, most important, added a controversial new exemption, one white man on every plantation with twenty or more slaves. This feature, coupled with the substitution provision retained from the original bill, led to cries of a rich man's war but a poor man's fight.

Yet what became known as the Twenty Negro Law had another side. Powerful economic and social forces demanded that exemption. Slavery was about the control of a race whites considered inferior. With so many white males from farms and plantations in uniform, the issue of regulation in the countryside became acute. Compounding the problem was the sexual dimension of the southern social ethic, which dictated that white men must protect white women from supposedly predatory black men. But in many regions of the Confederacy, white women had to deal directly with black males, without the presence of white male authority. Moreover, slaves provided the labor critical for the production of foodstuffs essential for the war effort. Without white men to oversee and guarantee that work, food production could suffer. War had not changed the social and economic realities of slavery, only exacerbated them.

Although Jefferson Davis was certainly aware of the complexities arising from slavery, he had them repeatedly accented. Governor John Milton of Florida did not mince words when he asserted that without the exemption for overseers "the result will probably be insubordination and insurrection." A South Carolina merchant wrote the president that agricultural production in his area could not be maintained without the exception. Weighing both social and economic considerations, Howell Cobb informed Davis that altering the provision "will be attended with the most serious injury." "The negroes have thus far generally behaved pretty well," judged an old Mississippi associate, "but now that the men are all gone it is very doubtful how long they will continue in a state of subordination." "If all the efficient white men are taken away," this friend foreboded, "our whole system of slave labor will fail us and general want will come upon the country—and possibly general massacre of women and children."[72]

At the same time, news detailing the deleterious impact of the Twenty Negro Law reached Davis's desk. As early as December 1862, a close political ally, a Confederate senator from Mississippi, stated to the president, "never did a law meet with more universal odium." He described its effect upon the poor as "calamitous." A Georgian called the provision a "poison [that] is being infused in the minds of the poor, and is being carried to the army by the poor conscripts," where "insubordination may result." Davis was also informed that "demagogues" used this specific exemption to urge people "to believe that it is a war for the defence of the institution of slavery, an institution in which they have no personal interest. . . ."[73]

President Davis confronted a terrible dilemma, aware that both views contained fundamental truth. He knew that white authority in the countryside was an absolute necessity, but as a veteran of antebellum Mississippi politics he also understood the political cost of even seeming to favor the rich. He had always preached the Confederate gospel in which he deeply believed—the cause meant a mighty battle for liberty for all whites, never a crusade for slaveholders. Yet it was simply impossible to maintain social control and agricultural production and simultaneously satisfy cries of class favoritism. Davis could only hold course, leaving many unhappy, from those who desired more overseers exempted to those who wanted none.[74]

The practice of substitution also fomented divisiveness and class resentment among Confederates. Davis's correspondents catalogued the negative consequences of wealthier citizens hiring substitutes while poorer men could not take advantage of that alternative to service: "It is shocking and shameful to see the crowds of young men—below 40—aye, even below 30—who are lounging about the country." Joseph Davis called on his brother to have substitution as well as exemption repealed. By 1863, two sides really did not exist on this issue. The president admitted that "the measure of substitution has done much harm and has been prolific of crime." Yet he wishfully declared that new regulations issued by the War Department eliminated the worst abuses. Outcries continued until, at the beginning of its next session in December, Congress, with presidential support, abolished substitution and also made the men who had purchased proxies liable for conscription.[75]

By the second half of 1863 the course of the war had added two serious liabilities to the Confederate war effort: desertion and hunger. Both derived from the same cause. The ferocity of the war and the deepening Union penetration into Confederate territory wreaked havoc on the home front, disrupting traditional social organization as well as normal production and distribution patterns. Parents and wives left behind as sons and fathers went off to fight could no longer protect their homes and provide for their families. Confederate soldiers had gone to war to protect liberty, and to defend home and family. Yet with home and family often undefended and uncared for while facing social disorganization, privation, and advancing Federals, many soldiers rethought their primary duty. Desertion afflicted every army, including

Lee's, and the number who simply walked away kept increasing. Some returned to the colors; others did not. This redefining of patriotism presented a growing problem to Confederate authorities, who watched their armies lose men while their enemy became stronger and stronger.

The desertion question was well known to Davis. All his commanders talked about it, and he worried about filling the ranks in his armies. But he also understood the primary motive behind the soldiers' decision to leave their posts. He personally read letters detailing the need: citizens petitioned for the discharge of a native son because the county no longer had a competent miller; a father, with three sons in the army, asked for one to be discharged because illness made it impossible to run his farm; a mother needed her son to come home and manage the family farm; a woman "out of Employment . . . very nearly out of bread, out of spirits" wanted to draw her boy's pay, a private now a prisoner of war. Even Joseph wrote requesting the discharge of the son of a friend, who had already lost two in the war, and was now too sick to run his plantation. Davis was not impervious to these pleas, which were amplified when he examined files of men sentenced to death for desertion. A cabinet member related the case of a soldier who left his unit upon being told the enemy had driven his wife and children from their home. All were sick and destitute, and one child had already died. This husband and father departed without permission, though he did return, whereupon a court-martial convicted him of desertion. Upon reading this record, Davis said that under similar circumstances he would have done precisely as this soldier did. The president set aside the sentence and ordered the man restored to the ranks.[76]

Understanding and empathy did not fill battle lines, however. In August, Davis issued a proclamation promising "amnesty and pardon" to all who returned to "their proper posts of duty" within twenty days. Although he included several reasons why men might have gone absent without leave, he excluded any wish "to escape from the sacrifices required by patriotism." In contrast, he praised the "courage and fortitude" demonstrated by Confederates in more than two years of frightful combat. In his words, the terrible war had become even more monstrous because of the enemy "design to incite servile insurrection and light the fires of incendiarism wherever they can reach your homes. . . ." The Federals took that barbarous route because "of their inability to prevail by legitimate warfare. . . ." "Fellow-citizens," Davis cried, "no alternative is left you but victory or subjugation, slavery, and the utter ruin of yourselves, your families, and your country."

"The victory is within your reach," he exclaimed. All that was required to ensure Confederate success was for those "called to the field by every motive that can move the human heart" to join their comrades now facing the foe. Before closing he focused on a critical group, calling upon his "countrywomen, the wives, mothers, sisters, and daughters of the Confederacy" to employ "their all-powerful influence . . . and take care that none who owe service in the field shall be sheltered at home from the disgrace of having deserted their duty to their families, to their country, and to their God." Davis's appeal pointed directly to the core of his problem: thousands of Confederate soldiers were placing their families first.[77]

By 1863 many Confederate civilians experienced real want. The combination of runaway inflation pushing prices to astronomical levels—early in 1863, seven dollars were required to buy what one dollar had bought in 1861, for the war inflation was stratospheric—and the breakdown of the transportation system caused serious food shortages, especially in urban areas where people had to buy basic foodstuffs. This deplorable situation led to riots in several cities, notably Richmond in April 1863. In the capital city, overcrowding meant even greater demand for shrinking supplies. Led by women from poorer neighborhoods, a crowd of around 1,000 gathered, marched to Capitol Square and the Governor's Mansion, then moved into the business district, smashing windows and doors and grabbing what they could. A full-scale riot was underway. The mayor, the governor, and the president all appeared and strove to quell the mob. Although accounts differ on which official took the lead, the evidence overwhelmingly points to the governor, who ultimately threatened to have the Public Guard fire upon the rioters unless they disbanded. Davis is recorded as addressing the crowd, or more likely part of it, in a quiet, moving tone that was not threatening. Before blood was shed, the rioters dispersed. Disaster was averted, but the Richmond Bread Riot underscored the plight of many impoverished Confederates.[78]

Although President Davis acted to stop the Richmond rioters, he recognized that they and many other Confederate citizens were suffering. He asked Congress to assist those whose property had been destroyed by the government for defensive purposes. Tax policy also addressed the issue. Congress in 1863 placed a levy on exempted overseers, enacted a progressive income tax, and put a 10 percent tax in kind on agricultural products. The last stipulated that after reserving subsistence for his family, a farmer would turn over 10 percent of the surplus to the government, which, in turn, would be distributed among soldiers' families. The tax in kind was double-edged, for the tax collectors became to many farmers government oppressors. The president also hailed efforts by states and localities to assist those deprived by war. The Confederacy fell far short of fulfilling needs for assistance, but seven decades before the New Deal and under extremely difficult circumstances, it tried, however stumblingly. For the government and the president, significant relief could only come if the battlefield could relieve pressure on the home front.[79]

Jefferson Davis did not have to experience the vicissitudes and viciousness of war vicariously. His brother Joseph, Joseph's property, and his own were caught in the tornado of war twisting through Mississippi. In late 1862, Joseph, with the human and animal property of both brothers that he could bring from Davis Bend, had relocated at Fleetwood in Hinds County, west of Jackson. During the following spring Joseph undertook unfruitful farming operations while worrying about his wife Eliza's worsening health. Even here, as he wrote Jefferson, "much anxiety" and "uncertainty" about Federal military movements preyed on his mind. Moving to Fleetwood did not take Joseph to safety, for Grant's campaign placed his new homestead in harm's way.[80]

In late May 1863 Federal troops arrived at Fleetwood. The elderly Joseph, who was given just thirty minutes to get his furniture outside, could only watch helplessly as the men in blue burned buildings and carried off personal valuables, provisions, and slaves. Joseph believed that false promises along with force motivated the blacks to leave. Whatever the causes, all but a few were gone. Jefferson's nearby place received identical treatment. By mid-June, Joseph told his brother that "never since the war began has appearances been so bad." "Affairs here are depressing," he wrote. Despite his own travail, Joseph regularly expressed concern for his youngest sibling's welfare.[81]

Following the ravaging of Fleetwood, Joseph traveled a short distance to the farm of Owen Cox, a former overseer on Hurricane and now a helpful friend. From Cox's, he narrated the disaster for his brother, including the news that their sister in West Feliciana Parish, Louisiana, had also suffered grievous depredations. In spite of Eliza's illness, Joseph set about repairing wagons and carts to take him, her, and granddaughter Lise Mitchell away from the fury.

Even before the baleful tidings of destruction inflicted on Fleetwood reached him, Jefferson was distraught. "It has been to me a constant source of deep anxiety to know that you were exposed to the malignant outrages of the cruel foe with whom we are at war," he wrote. He even suggested that Joseph come to Richmond with wife and granddaughter. His words conveyed palpable distress: "It is sad to me to know that you and Sister Eliza are in your old age denied the repose required and to feel powerless to give you the personal assistance which in the order of nature is due from me. God I trust will shield you. . . ."[82]

Then yet more terrible news reached Richmond. Just after the fall of Vicksburg, Federals showed up at Cox's farm. There Joseph had hidden personal belongings of Jefferson he had managed to bring from Brierfield, thinking these would be safe at what he considered an anonymous farmstead. He might have been right but for a slave belonging to Cox who had run off to the Union army. Returning with the soldiers, this bondsman revealed the hiding places. From Saturday until Monday the bluecoats assaulted—tearing, wrecking, burning, pillaging. A box of correspondence did survive, wending its way up the chain of command all the way to the War Department in Washington and in the early twentieth century to the Library of Congress. Aside from those few papers, almost the sole surviving items were a writing desk and a marble bust of Jefferson and Varina's firstborn, Samuel. The latter escaped because the white caretaker, held under guard during the rampage, claimed it represented his own dead child. Upon getting word of this pillaging, the president pressed for particulars. The resulting accounts only added detail to the story of destruction. They were punctuated by Joseph's report in mid-August that everything hidden at Cox's had been destroyed or carried off.[83]

Joseph had become a wandering refugee. Three difficult weeks on the road with wife, granddaughter, and a few slaves brought him in August all the way to western Alabama. After a short stay for the bedridden Eliza to regain some strength, in early September he turned his small caravan back toward Mississippi, heading for Lauderdale Springs above Meridian and just inside the state. Though supposedly a healthy location, Joseph found it hot and unhealthy. But he hoped to hire out his slaves to the military hospital there; besides, Eliza, who had survived two months under extremely arduous conditions, was simply too weak to move. Within the month she was dead. From Lauderdale Springs, Joseph let Jefferson know that Cox had brought the bust of Samuel to him.

Late in the year Joseph went back to Jackson, hoping to generate an expedition to recover the slaves still at Brierfield and Hurricane. A cavalry raid did take place, but it did not please the old planter. To Jefferson, he termed it "murderous," accusing the Confederates of firing on slaves, killing several. The blacks had been armed by the Federals to protect and slaughter cattle, but according to Joseph they fired only in self-defense. Frustrated that he could not bring about another effort to reclaim the bondspeople at Davis Bend, Joseph once more started east. Reporting on his final visit to their Hinds County property, Joseph informed Jefferson that nothing remained, not even hogs. For the president Vicksburg was a personal as well as a national disaster.

Scanning his far-flung battle lines, President Davis could see little brightness. With the fall of Vicksburg and Port Hudson, the distant Trans-Mississippi became almost a separate territory. Recognizing that the closure of the Mississippi River fundamentally altered the status of the westernmost segment of his country, Davis assigned his commander more complex and varied duties. Since March that position had been occupied by Lieutenant General Edmund Kirby Smith, an energetic officer who always relished independent command. A good choice for this vast, difficult domain in place of the loyal and conscientious but nervous and incompetent Theophilus Holmes, Smith set out to stabilize and make an imprint on his command.

The commander in chief understood the difficulty of Smith's task, realizing that its political dimensions equaled, even exceeded, the military ones. Davis knew that west of the river, sentiment existed to separate the Trans-Mississippi states from the Confederacy, a feeling he attributed to "unreasonable men [who believe] they have been neglected and timid men [who] may hope that they can make better terms for themselves, if their cause is not combined with that of the Confederacy." To counter this view, Davis assured political leaders in his distant Far West that "no effort shall be spared to promote the defense of the Trans-Missi. Dept. and to develop its resources so as to meet the exigencies of the present struggle." To overcome any thought of local primacy, he asserted to the governor of Arkansas, "the states of the Confederacy can have but one fortune." He admitted that in the great struggle localities would not suffer equally; still, "the prize for which we strive—independence—must be gained by us all, or we must all share a fate which to every man fit to be a freeman would be worse than torture and death."[84]

The president shared his sense of the political complexities and dangers with his commander. Warning Smith about the separatist sentiment, he directed the general to demonstrate Confederate commitment through public assurances and industriousness. Although Davis knew Smith could not "give to each section all that local interests may suggest," he never contemplated voluntary surrender of territory. Always aware of the newborn fragility of Confederate nationalism, he worried that any such concessions also meant loss of loyalty and troops. The president counseled Smith to take political leaders into his confidence, telling him that doing so was the surest way to make for "valuable coadjutors."

Davis also laid out an ambitious program for General Smith, whom he envisioned as a director of economic development and active politician as well as military commander. He wanted Smith to develop the mineral wealth and industrial potential of the region from mining ventures to ironworks capable of casting cannon and rolling sheets for ironclads. A powder mill was essential. Davis urged tanning and textile operations along with those for building gun carriages and wagons. In sum, the Trans-Mississippi would become self-sufficient. To assist in these endeavors, he was sending skilled workers because of their paucity in the area. He also informed Smith that officials from the Treasury Department were en route to handle critical financial tasks. Arms and ammunition were coming by sea and then through Mexico. Closing, the president admitted the distance between the goals he had set and his ability to help Smith reach them: "It grieves me to have enumerated so many and such difficult objects for your attention when I can give you so little aid in their achievement."[85]

General Smith understood the nature of his command. He informed Richmond that too few troops were available to defend all significant, threatened places. He needed arms and money. The citizens and the state troops he found "luke warm" and "disheartened," with little hope of success. But he also reported good crops and detailed promising work on textiles and ordnance. In addition, the general acted to incorporate political chieftains into his leadership team by calling a meeting in Marshall, Texas, in mid-August, to which he invited notables from the four states in his department. They responded; to this gathering came governors, members of Congress, and other prominent men from Arkansas, Louisiana, Missouri, and Texas. At its conclusion the conferees in published proceedings proclaimed the fidelity of the Trans-Mississippi and their confidence in ultimate Confederate victory.[86]

Given the realities of the Trans-Mississippi, President Davis did what he could. He realized that without substantial improvement in Confederate military fortunes, the vast area lay largely beyond the regular orbit of the Confederate States. One realistic goal he pursued: to strive to maintain Confederate authority in order to sustain general allegiance to the government of the Confederate States.

Much closer to home, Davis's best general and his most successful army required his careful attention. Back in Virginia after Gettysburg, Robert E. Lee offered to resign. Although he did not believe he had totally failed in Pennsylvania, the campaign had not fulfilled his expectations. On August 8 he wrote the president: "the general remedy for the want of success in a military commander is his removal." Then he mentioned his health, "the growing failure of my bodily strength" and his not having "recovered from the attack I experienced the past spring." Although the extent of Lee's illness was then unknown, he had developed cardiovascular disease, which he would never overcome.

A surprised president rejected this suggestion. In an amiable, even intimate response, Davis tried to buoy his friend while at the same time acknowledging dependence upon him. Davis could find no substantive failure. Regretting that Lee still did not feel completely well, he entreated the general to "take all possible care of yourself, that your health and strength may be entirely restored. . . ." He was also bluntly honest and complimentary: "To ask me to substitute you by some one in my judgment more fit to command, or who would possess more of the confidence of the army, or of the reflecting men in the country is to demand an impossibility." Nor was there anyone else, he could have added, who had his confidence and on whom he could absolutely rely. This episode in no way diminished the trusting, confidential relationship between the general and the president.[87]

Twice, in late August and in early September, Davis called Lee to Richmond for consultation. The chief topic was the Army of Tennessee. As had been the case since the death of Sidney Johnston, that army generated the most vexing problem for the commander in chief. Its internal destructiveness seemed endemic, and squabbling among its general officers appeared permanent. There was also strategic peril. During the summer Braxton Bragg and his army had been maneuvered out of middle Tennessee by the Union commander Major General William S. Rosecrans. Bragg fell back into northern Georgia, losing Chattanooga along the way. Moreover, a strong Union force had advanced into East Tennessee, occupied Knoxville, and severed the most direct rail connection between Virginia and the West. During Bragg's withdrawal, Davis urged him to isolate and fall upon a portion of Rosecrans's army. Aware that Bragg needed more men, the president tried to help. Following Vicksburg, the Department of the West was abolished and the Department of East Tennessee placed under Bragg's authority. In addition, Joseph Johnston, left with a small force in Mississippi, was directed to send reinforcements. Davis also dispatched an aide to see the governors of Georgia and Alabama, urging them to forward state troops.[88]

Davis wanted Lee's advice on how he should handle the situation, both pressing and dangerous. He also wanted more; he wanted Lee to go to Georgia. The Virginian just as clearly did not want the assignment, but as a soldier he would follow orders. He articulated several reasons for not going: he knew little of the Army of Tennessee or its strategic circumstances; his health was not good; and most important, he had no obvious replacement. At that moment the Army of Northern Virginia faced a powerful Federal host little more than fifty miles north of Richmond. It became painfully clear that no one else was readily available. Lee obviously did not have sufficient confidence in any of his subordinates. The only full general in the East was Beauregard in Charleston, but Davis had already decided he was unfit to command a major field army. Thus, Lee would stay in Virginia; but the president decided to assist Bragg further by sending substantial reinforcements from Lee's army, more than two full divisions under Lee's senior corps commander, Lieutenant General James Longstreet.[89]

For Davis, dispatching Longstreet's detachment to the Army of Tennessee represented neither caving in to pressure to protect the West nor embracing defensive warfare. With good reason, he was legitimately concerned about the fate of the Army of Tennessee, now standing at the gateway to the heart of the Deep South. Moreover, a major triumph around Chattanooga could have momentous results. In this instance Davis acted in character. He undertook a considerable risk for victory.[90]

As Longstreet moved by rail through the Carolinas into Georgia, Bragg prepared to strike. After being outgeneraled in Tennessee, he regrouped. In the difficult, sub-mountainous terrain of northwestern Georgia, he managed to get powerful segments of his army between separated elements of his enemy. He planned to beat Rosecrans in detail, but it never happened. The virulent animus and hostility plaguing the army prevailed. Orders were disregarded or disobeyed; cooperation was a foreign concept. As a result, several promising battle plans self-destructed. Finally, on September 19, just as Longstreet arrived, Bragg managed to get an attack underway. Despite the poisonous relations that

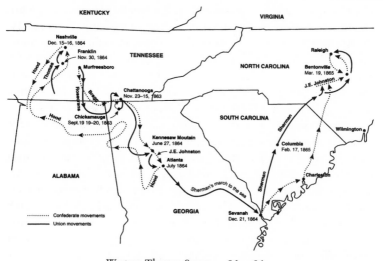

Western Theater, Summer 1863–1865.

From W. J. Cooper and T. E. Terrill, The American South: A History *(2d ed.), with permission of the McGraw-Hill Companies*

affected operations, on that day and the next the Army of Tennessee won its greatest victory of the war, the Battle of Chickamauga. Longstreet's troops had a decisive part in the struggle. But though the Confederates drove Rosecrans from the field, they did not destroy his army or prevent his retreat to Chattanooga.

This smashing triumph did nothing to change the personality of the army's high command, however. Instead of congratulating each other on a hard-fought victory, the generals blamed each other for not winning more stupendously, for not destroying the enemy. But this time the generals went beyond accusations and diatribes. Bragg relieved Leonidas Polk, his senior subordinate and bitterest critic, along with another lieutenant general, for not obeying orders. Before his dismissal Polk had met with several other generals, including Longstreet, who immediately became a stalwart in the anti-Bragg camp, to discuss ways of getting Bragg replaced. Polk and Longstreet undertook a letter-writing campaign. After Polk's dismissal anti-Bragg corps and division commanders drew up a petition to the president demanding Bragg's removal. Twelve general officers signed it.

Davis initially attempted to mollify the disputants and paper over the conflict. He told Bragg that removing Polk would only cause trouble.

But Bragg wanted the disobedient, malcontent bishop-general gone; he even preferred court-martial charges. Yet Bragg did not comprehend the breadth or depth of his generals' opposition to him. Aware that he had cured nothing, the president worried and contemplated a western trip. At that moment his aide James Chesnut was in Georgia on an assignment. After meeting with men on both sides of the acrimonious quarrel, Chesnut wired on October 5 that Davis's presence was essential. The president responded that he would depart immediately.[91]

On October 6 President Davis left Richmond by train accompanied by aides William P. Johnston and G. W. C. Lee and General Pemberton, whom he asked to join his party. For the second time in less than a year he was heading west to combat the cancer that had been assaulting the Army of Tennessee. The loss of the main rail line in East Tennessee required an itinerary that carried him south through the Carolinas to Atlanta, then northward to Bragg's army, spread along Missionary Ridge and the adjoining high ground overlooking Chattanooga and the Federal occupying force.

The four-day journey was not difficult, but neither was it quiet. Roomy cars made for comfortable travel, but at each little town people clamored for the president, who spoke and shook hands to "ovations." Reaching Atlanta on the evening of the eighth, Davis received a rousing welcome, with Governor Brown and a crowd on hand. After an introduction by Brown, the president spoke from the platform with a sure political accent. He complimented Georgia for her performance during the war, underscoring the conduct of her soldiers on so many battlefields. He also praised the cooperation he had received from the governor. With Brown aboard, Davis's train next morning steamed toward northern Georgia. In a brief stop at Marietta, Brown again introduced Davis, who basically repeated his Atlanta remarks.[92]

That night the president arrived at his destination. As he detrained, hundreds of soldiers greeted him with cries for a speech. After mounting his horse, he raised his hat and shouted: "Man never spoke as you did on the field of Chickamauga, and in your presence I dare not speak. Yours is the voice that will win independence of your country and strike terror to the heart of a ruthless foe." Amid shouts, he waved and rode to Bragg's headquarters on Missionary Ridge, where he spent the night.[93]

Saturday he toured and inspected Confederate lines. "Plaudits" and "still louder cheers" predominated during his ride through the army, although at times the welcome was more subdued because of the proximity of the Federal lines, in some instances no more than 1,000 yards away, with pickets in plain sight. William P. Johnston called the president's reception "truly gratifying." That evening Davis appeared on the porch of the farmhouse serving as Bragg's headquarters to speak briefly to around 100 soldiers who had gathered hoping to see him. Beginning by lauding their gallantry at Chickamauga, he continued, "[you] had given still higher evidence of courage, patriotism, and resolute determination to live freemen or die freemen. . . ." He closed with the conviction that "under the blessings of Providence" the Confederacy would succeed, and the Army of Tennessee would advance its banners from the Tennessee to the Ohio. According to an observer, the president's words were "rapturously and repeatedly cheered."[94]

Davis performed these public tasks admirably, but the main purpose of his visit was to root out the malignant growth strangling the army's high command. To that end he conversed with Bragg and other generals. All had the opportunity to tell their stories, and the commander in chief listened to all who wanted to talk. What he heard confirmed what he had been told. Unrestrained, even virulent dissatisfaction with Bragg permeated the general officers' ranks. One of the newest arrivals was perhaps the most denunciatory. Longstreet said to Davis that at Chickamauga, Bragg was not active on the field as Lee would have been.[95]

After three days of discussions Davis made an incredible decision. Deciding he could not make a change in commanders, he stuck with Bragg, even though he acknowledged "the painful fact" that "the harmony and subordination" essential for success were absent. He tried to ameliorate this unhappy condition by confirming Bragg's sacking of Polk and a corps commander. Rationalizing that he was helping Bragg and the army, he replaced Polk with Lieutenant General William J. Hardee, then in Mississippi, a solid, experienced officer who had previously served in the Army of Tennessee, but who had been at odds with Bragg after the Kentucky campaign. Upon assigning Hardee, Davis admitted the rancor still rampant in the army and silently confessed that he had not eliminated it. "I rely greatly upon you," he told Hardee, "for the restoration of a proper feeling, and know that you will realize the comparative insignificance of personal considerations when weighed against the duty of imparting to the Army all the efficiency of which it is capable." Emphasizing how his perception of commitment could distort reality, he even hoped to find a place in the army for Pemberton, at that moment perhaps the most discredited Confederate general. To

Bragg he reiterated the point that the circumstances "should lift men above all personal considerations and devote them wholly to their country's cause." Davis's absolute conviction that the Confederacy demanded commitment to cause over anything personal became in this instance a mantra. He clung to his creed despite a year of futility in pacifying the venomous relations menacing the Army of Tennessee.[96]

The decision to retain Bragg as commanding general of the Army of Tennessee was disastrous. Perhaps back in December 1862 Davis could have reasonably hoped that his visit to the army, along with Joseph Johnston's oversight, would alleviate hard feelings and enable Bragg to succeed as a commander. Ten months later no such rationalization had any legitimacy. When Davis said he had no one else to substitute for Bragg, he was again referring to full generals. Of course, Johnston was nearby and available, but Davis understandably would not consider him. He blamed Johnston for Vicksburg; besides, Johnston's performance with the Department of the West and at Vicksburg did not indicate he would make a strong army commander. At this moment the president needed to move beyond the prescription of reliance on rank structure in the Confederate army. With Polk already gone, he could have relieved Bragg, which would have dispensed with the two chief antagonists. Then he would have had to risk turning to a lieutenant general, perhaps Longstreet or Hardee, in hopes the appointee would restore the unity and positive outlook so desperately needed. His not doing so is extremely difficult to understand, for he knew that virulent illness still contaminated the army. He blindly or desperately rationalized the palliative of substituting Hardee for Polk as effective therapy, adding a massive dose of wishful thinking. In only six weeks his woefully inadequate treatment resulted in catastrophe.

Upon leaving this brave, mishandled army, the president addressed to it a public statement in which he forcefully restated his view of the Confederate cause. After praising the officers and men for "gallantry and patriotic devotion," he designated them as "defenders of the heart of our territory," telling them that "the hopes of our cause greatly depend upon you," and much remained to be done. Large portions of the country had been "devastated by your ruthless invader, where gentle women, feeble age, and helpless infancy have been subjected to outrages without parallel in the warfare of civilized nations." They eagerly await your arrival for their "deliverance," he cried.

Davis said the Confederacy had been "forced to take up arms to vindicate the political rights, the freedom, equality, and State sovereignty which were the heritage purchased by the blood of your revolutionary sires." He posited but a single alternative: "slavish submission to despotic usurpation, or the independence which vigorous, united, persistent effort will secure." "Nobly have you redeemed the pledges given in the name of freedom to the memory of your ancestors and the rights of your posterity," he assured the soldiers. But, the president went on to say, completion of their mission would necessitate "continuance in the patient endurance of toil and danger, and that self-denial which rejects every consideration at variance with the public service as unworthy of the holy cause in which you are engaged."

With the reference to the subduing of personal goals and desires, Davis came to the present moment on Missionary Ridge. He claimed all shared a "common destiny" that demanded from each man "obedience and cordial cooperation." "No higher duty" could he imagine "than that which requires each to render to all what is due to their station. He who sows the seeds of discontent and distrust prepares for the harvest of slaughter and defeat." Commending their bravery and determination, Davis called on the soldiers to "crown" those attributes "with harmony, due subordination, and cheerful support of lawful authority, that the measure of your duty may be full." Davis's ringing pronouncement to the army encamped along Missionary Ridge contrasted sharply with his feeble action.[97]

The president's visit to the Army of Tennessee completed the initial segment of what turned out to be a monthlong journey through the heartland of his country. From Missionary Ridge, Davis returned to Atlanta on October 14 and started west, still accompanied by aides Johnston and Lee. Reaching Montgomery on the fifteenth, he consulted with Thomas Watts, his recently resigned attorney general and newly elected governor of Alabama. In Montgomery, Davis went aboard a steamboat for an overnight run down the Alabama River to Selma. When the boat docked at daylight, the mayor welcomed the presidential party and conducted it to breakfast. In Selma, Davis gave a speech and visited the Confederate naval foundry before boarding a train for Demopolis. In that town he spoke, lunched with a member of Congress, and met with Generals Johnston and Hardee. The generals joined the president for the trip on to Meridian, Mississippi, where, after a tiring day, Davis spent the night. On the morning of October 18, he took a brief twenty-mile train ride to Lauderdale Springs to see his brother Joseph and mortally ill sister-in-law Eliza, who died six days later. There he also conferred with Governor Pettus.[98]

Back in Meridian on the nineteenth, the president changed his plans. Instead of leaving immediately for Mobile, he decided to remain in Mississippi and visit Jackson, which had suffered grievous damage when taken by Federal troops in mid-July. But before going to the state capital, he traveled a short distance south to Enterprise to review troops. On "a very hot & dusty day" he looked them over and then spoke to them from a hotel porch. During his remarks a heckler took a verbal blast when Davis declared he would "not be interrupted by blackguards—my foot is on my native hearth."

After staying the night in Enterprise, Davis set out early on October 20 for Jackson. Because of torn-up rails, he had to detrain twelve miles east of the city at Brandon and continue on horseback. The twenty-first began drizzly but cleared while the president rode around observing the destruction. To Colonel Johnston the burned-over town presented "most gloomy pictures." In a speech in the Capitol, Davis appealed to Mississippi to rise up and throw off the invader. Then he returned to Brandon, ate supper, and reboarded the train. But after only ten miles, the cars lurched as the engine ran off the tracks. "We had made blue beef of a misguided cow," wrote Johnston. Thus delayed, Davis did not get back to Meridian until the next day.[99]

From Meridian, the president headed east. He spent two days in Mobile reviewing troops in the area, and he also gave a brief speech asserting that the Confederate cause was stronger than it had been a year earlier. Leaving Mobile, Davis traveled up to Montgomery and on over to Atlanta. There, on October 29, he saw Governor Isham Harris of Tennessee and Vice President Stephens, who described a president "in excellent Health and spirits." To an apprehensive Stephens, Davis expressed confidence that Bragg would achieve positive results in Chattanooga.[100]

The following morning Davis departed for Savannah. Along the way he made brief remarks. At Macon a "hurrahing" crowd greeted him and "carried him off in triumph" to a hotel, where he addressed a large gathering. After dinner a special train transported him on to Savannah. Even though Davis tried to sleep, people at stations along the route waited to see him. At Griswoldville, only ten miles east of Macon, some forty blacks who labored in a pistol factory gathered in hopes of seeing the president. Informed of this unusual assemblage, Davis stepped from his car and circulated among the workers, took each hand, and spoke individually to each man. Thereafter at stops he would rise and shake hands. At 8 a.m. he reached Savannah, where dignitaries ushered him from the depot to a hotel and a quiet breakfast. Afterward he went by boat to examine the coastal fortifications. Artillery batteries saluted his arrival. He came ashore, inspected the soldiers, and praised the patriotism of Georgians. According to one of his uniformed audience, "his remarks fell with electric effect on the men, and at the conclusion we gave him three hearty cheers."

The presidential party returned in carriages late in the afternoon. That evening a former West Point classmate provided a magnificent feast: oyster soup, stewed terrapin, fried oysters, wild duck, mutton chops, custard, coffee, and sherry. After this meal a torchlight procession called for a speech; Davis complied from the hotel balcony. Then he was off to the Masonic Hall for another address. There, Johnston related, he shook hands with 1,000 well-wishers, "leaving him rather exhausted and miserable." After the president finally got to bed, a crowd serenaded him. Next morning after breakfasting on stewed and fried oysters, he received a committee from Charleston, attended church, and talked with the mayor, who put on a sumptuous dinner: okra soup, stewed shrimp, boiled and roasted wild duck, and vegetables.[101]

On the morning of November 2 Davis left Savannah and its lavish board. Bound by train for Charleston, he spoke twice en route and at 1 p.m. arrived in the birthplace of secession, where booming cannon announced the presidential train. Accompanied by a cavalry escort from the depot, four carriages, with Davis and General Beauregard in the lead vehicle, traversed the streets to City Hall. Thousands of citizens thronged the route: "the men cheered and the ladies waved their handkerchiefs in token of recognition." At City Hall, after the mayor's introduction, Davis addressed a large crowd. He began by recalling his previous visit when he accompanied the body of John C. Calhoun. Davis was confident that great statesman "in our trial watches over us with all a guardian angels care." Praising the patriotism and devotion of South Carolina, he emphasized the valor of the proud defenders of the city. The enemy certainly desired Charleston "as the nest of the rebellion," but he did not believe they would ever capture it. Yet if it ever did fall, he would want only "rubbish" remaining, no "prey for yankee spoils." He told his listeners he had come to confer with General Beauregard and learn the needs for defense. Though he had no doubts about the fidelity of the Palmetto State, he urged constant vigilance. "But let us not be inactive," he cried, "let then all our efforts in this our crisis be directed to the future." The politician Davis was in action. According to an eyewitness, he gave many hands a hearty shake, meeting "every one as if he had met an old friend." Then he reentered his carriage for the drive to his lodgings, the mansion of a former governor. During the subsequent two days, the president inspected troops and works in and around the city, including visits to islands guarding the harbor.[102]

From Charleston, Davis's train chugged north toward Richmond. On November 5 he was in Wilmington, North Carolina, where he spoke and toured nearby fortifications, telling defenders they were fighting for their liberty, their homes, and their sweethearts. He gave his final public remarks in Goldsboro, and November 7 arrived back in Richmond.[103]

It had been a remarkable trip. The president had been on the road for thirty-two days. He had made at least twenty speeches; he had conferred with numerous political and military leaders; he had met literally hundreds of his fellow Confederates. Davis had taken on a herculean effort to show his concern for the heartland of his country and to rally all citizens in what he constantly called "our crisis." Everywhere, from war-ravaged Mississippi to the protected Atlantic coast, he had been enthusiastically received. His reception gave credence to one editor's claim that the president enjoyed "the heart and confidence of the people." Even the severely critical *Richmond Examiner* was impressed with Davis's undertaking: "He has inspired new life, courage and hope everywhere and among all classes. The bare sight of his sad, worn, attenuated features has drowned the voice of faction, aroused the warmest patriotism and harmony among the masses." The *Examiner* called for "a tremendous and enthusiastic welcome home to our second Washington." The *Examiner* exaggerated, for Davis had not quieted all his critics, but no one doubted who was president.[104]

While President Davis strove to uphold morale and struggled with military reverses and command problems, Confederate voters were choosing a new Congress. Balloting for the Second Congress began in May 1863 and spilled over into 1864, for there was no national election day. These were strange elections for a society used to lengthy campaigns, engaged canvassing, and in-depth coverage by numerous newspapers, which together helped produce impressive turnouts. The Union controlled Kentucky and Missouri and most of Arkansas and Tennessee, as well as southern Louisiana, northern and western Virginia, and coastal areas in both Carolinas. Obviously, ordinary elections could not be held in these places. The standard format was election by general ticket rather than by district, with small numbers of soldiers and refugees making up the electorate. There were variations: a general ticket for occupied districts with ballots cast by voters in non-occupied districts plus soldiers and refugees; district voting with only soldiers and refugees generally participating. Even in the unoccupied areas of the Confederacy the situation was far from normal. So many voters were absent in uniform, and shortages of everything from skilled labor to paper greatly reduced the number and thoroughness of newspapers. Under these circumstances, electoral participation dropped to extremely low levels. Almost everywhere the soldier vote was consequential, and the army was a stronghold for the president.[105]

By the time of these contests, discontent brought on by the ravages of war affected a substantial percentage of the Confederate population. Yet the elections did not turn into a referendum on either the Davis administration or the president personally. Opponents of one or both disagreed with themselves as often as they agreed. Both Henry S. Foote, Davis's former enemy in Mississippi, now a congressman from Tennessee, and Louis Wigfall abhorred Davis, but Wigfall vigorously supported strong war measures while Foote denounced them as tyrannical. Moreover, former fire-eaters, who were Davis-haters but devoted Confederates, had no political bonds with ex-Unionists who talked about reconstruction, or peace without independence. Such wide divergences made most unlikely an organized or unified opposition.

These basic differences help explain the absence of a rival party. Additionally, the Whig collapse in most of the South in the mid-1850s left a vacuum not filled before the secession crisis, and much of the area where a Whig-based opposition had held on, like Kentucky and Tennessee, was under Federal domination. Furthermore, at the birth of their new nation, Confederates, in the language of the Founding Fathers, denounced the legitimacy of parties. Anti-partyism became an article of political faith. Almost nobody, even Davis's most fervent antagonists, advocated parties.

Davis took no active part in the elections. He did not back any slate of candidates, nor did he urge voters to return those who championed his policies and throw out those who did not. His stance illustrated his view of Confederate politics. He considered the old politics of partisan identity along with the striving for partisan advantages part of a jettisoned past. Even though before 1861 he had mastered that brand of politics, it had failed to save the Union. Davis believed partisanship had contributed massively to its destruction. Such politics would certainly not preserve the Confederacy. The cause had become his politics, and he wanted to believe that all Confederates were as committed to it as he. He was a Confederate, meaning, in his mind, that ideology and politics had merged. His office and the vigor of his administration did galvanize opposition; but because his opponents did not have a legitimate institutional home, he could blame objections on fractious, selfish individuals, who put pride and place ahead of the cause.

The results of this congressional election did not signal any radical change. Incumbents fared poorly in the unoccupied states: fewer than half were returned from those districts, in contrast to two-thirds returning from occupied districts. Turning out those in office certainly spoke to discontent, though almost 54 percent of all House incumbents were reelected. The outcome did not signify the triumph of former Unionists or Whigs, or a repudiation of Davis. Each election was almost idiosyncratic, given local concerns, the dwarfed electorate, the poverty of campaigning, and the dearth of newspapers. The new Congress, which would not convene until May 1864, generally supported the president as readily as did the old. Disaffection had not prevailed. Loyalty to the Confederacy and to the president remained powerful.

The returns, in conjunction with congressional roll calls, reveal a striking fact about Confederate politics. The most helpful suggestion for understanding the basic division in Confederate politics posits two groups: those who pursued "the politics of national unity" and those who advocated "the politics of liberty." The former supported almost any legislative measure and the growth of executive power in the name of Confederate independence, while the latter depicted acts like conscription and suspension of habeas corpus, as well as a powerful executive, as dangerous threats to fundamental rights and liberties. In Congress, politicians who stood strongly against a vigorous national government hailed overwhelmingly from states like Georgia and South Carolina, still largely untouched by Federal intrusion. Senators and representatives from Union-controlled states and areas almost invariably backed the strongest possible war legislation. No delegations offered stauncher support for Davis's forceful war policies than those from Kentucky and Missouri, who represented basically phantom states and districts.[106]

As useful as the definitions associated with national unity and liberty may be in comprehending Confederate politics, they do not fully explain Jefferson Davis, for he did not perceive them as antagonistic. As he said so often, national survival or Confederate independence meant liberty; failure would mean slavery. Thus, national unity or defense assumed primacy, and that view underlay his constitutionalism and advocacy of energetic government. For Davis, this outlook antedated the war. In the 1850s he parted with many of his strict-constructionist colleagues when he upheld a vital governmental role in the construction of a transcontinental railroad. Additionally, he believed in direct government involvement in arms manufacture. Both were required for national defense, and in accordance with the Constitution.

This perspective carried Davis in directions he could not have anticipated when he took the oath of office in Montgomery. By the end of 1863, with the energetic leadership of the president and the concurrence of Congress, the Confederate government had become powerful and active. Not only did Congress authorize conscription and suspension of habeas corpus, it also passed legislation enabling Confederate functionaries to impress war matériel, even including slaves; they did so from farms, plantations, factories, from wherever they found needed goods and persons. Payment was made according to official schedules, but the government set the prices, and no citizen could legally resist impressment. Recognizing the centrality of railroads, Congress as early as 1862 appropriated money for construction where deemed necessary for the war. In 1863 a law was passed giving the executive broad discretionary power over railroad operations, though Davis never put them under direct government control as he was often urged to do. The government also became intimately involved in war industries. As the major purchaser it fundamentally directed private businesses like iron mills, both large and small. It also became the primary manufacturer of certain items. The Confederate navy, its hopes of purchasing European-built ships dashed, became a shipbuilder, and the Ordnance Bureau of the War Department constructed at Augusta, Georgia, the largest gunpowder factory in North America.

President Davis had his way with Congress. A vigorous and potent chief executive, he obtained from Congress legislation that in 1860 or even 1861 almost all southerners would have decried as horrendously despotic. Congress never stymied him on a critical matter. Aside from personal characteristics, there were understandable reasons for Davis's success. As in most wars, and certainly the case in the United States between 1861 and 1865, executive power surged at the expense of legislative. Davis was the war leader who approached Congress speaking the language of military necessity and national survival. Most senators and representatives were ardent Confederates who believed steps taken toward national authority were better than Union victory. Additionally, for security reasons the Confederate Congress conducted most of its sessions in secret. Those private deliberations, coupled with scant reporting, meant that public pressure barely affected debates, and bills went through the legislative process with little outside scrutiny. Furthermore, the stalwart pro-Davis cohort—anchored on the men from the occupied areas plus those who voted for the administration's war policies despite opposing the president personally—represented an unbeatable combination. The frustrated minority that disliked the measures as well as the man flailed away, often with personal diatribes against the president. Henry Foote denounced Davis as "vain, selfish, overbearing, ambitious, intriguing, and a slave to his prejudices and partialities. . . ." He shouted for "the people to rise, sword in hand, to put down the domestic tyrant who thus sought to invade their rights." But vicious verbal barrages could not derail Davis's legislative success.[107]

Although enjoying substantial legislative leeway, Davis did not dictate to senators and representatives. His political background and his devotion to traditional American constitutional practices influenced his dealings with Congress. As well as sending messages setting forth what he wanted and why, Davis during congressional sessions also met constantly with legislators. He recognized that contact with members was important for them to have a venue to present their needs and wishes as well as for him to press his case. Individuals brought concerns about appointments and questions about patronage. Entire state delegations trooped in for conferences, sometimes called by Davis, to discuss affairs in their states. Davis listened and tried to explain his policy.

The president could be considerate and gracious, though he stiffened when he spotted any deviation from his definition of commitment to the cause. Following a visit to the president, one congressman depicted him as "out of temper." His upbraidings could ruffle feelings, and he did make enemies. But until the end he never lost the goodwill of a congressional majority or the upper hand in legislative matters. His success with Congress enhanced his belief that commitment to the cause, his definition of Confederate patriotism, would enable his country to prevail. In addition to these business meetings, the president often entertained the solons in the White House, both in small groups and at large receptions. The discussions and the socializing did not guarantee he would have his way with Congress, but they did not hurt.[108]

Shortly after completing his western travels, President Davis took to the road again, but this time only a short distance, some seventy-five miles northwest of Richmond, to the Army of Northern Virginia at Orange. Through his presidential-aide son, Robert E. Lee had let Davis know that he and his army would be delighted to see their commander in chief. Davis was pleased to go. He always liked being around troops, and he could discuss personally with his trusted friend and top soldier his thoughts on the western military situation. Accompanied by two members of his staff, one of them G. W. C. Lee, he took the train on Saturday, November 21, and arrived in a driving rain. He was greeted by General Lee, and the two men repaired immediately to Lee's headquarters, where they spent the day. On Sunday the president and the commanding general attended St. Thomas Episcopal Church in Orange, the pews clogged with officers wanting to see the two chieftains together. The president visited some units, though the inclement weather knocked out a scheduled review. On the twenty-fourth, Davis was back in Richmond.[109]

President Davis had barely returned to Richmond when disaster struck. On November 25, the Federal army in Chattanooga under Ulysses Grant, who had taken over after Davis's visit, assaulted Missionary Ridge. Late in the afternoon, attackers in blue broke Bragg's line and routed the men in gray. The beaten and demoralized Army of Tennessee did not halt its pell-mell retreat until it reached Dalton, Georgia, some twenty-five miles south of Chattanooga. Grant not only crushed Bragg, he also blasted Davis's fantasy.[110]

This time no question arose about Bragg's future with the army. Even the crusty general realized he had none; three days after the debacle he resigned his post. Bragg's reports to Davis combined honest self-appraisal with charges assailing subordinates for what happened. Writing of his "shameful discomfiture," he called the defeat "justly disparaging to me as a commander." He also admitted that he and the president "both erred in the conclusion for me to retain command here after the clamor raised against me." But in almost the same breath he hurried to blame the loss on the scurrilous conduct of others, especially Major General John C. Breckinridge, who Bragg claimed had been drunk during and after the battle. Bragg asserted that "warfare" against him "has been carried on successfully and the fruits are bitter."[111]

Davis knew that Bragg had to go, though the magnitude of the calamity shocked him. He had convinced himself that he had set the army in the right direction. He hoped, even expected, that Bragg would go on the offensive around Chattanooga, or at least drive the Federals from East Tennessee. Neither eventuality occurred, however. Even before Missionary Ridge, Bragg's hesitancy and Federal initiatives disappointed Davis. Disharmony also still plagued the army. Although Polk was gone, he was not the only Bragg antagonist, and Longstreet had overtly joined the opposition. With Bragg's initial blessing, Longstreet marched off to East Tennessee, where he basically disregarded his commanding officer and acted independently. But he had no more success than Bragg; by the end of November he had suffered bloody failure.[112]

Confronting such a shocking and dispiriting defeat, the president had to do more than merely replace Bragg. He also had to restore confidence in the army and the country. When Bragg departed, his senior subordinate, Lieutenant General Hardee, was named interim commander, but Hardee informed the War Department that he did not want the regular job. Bragg had advised Davis to send to the army "our greatest and best leader," and then, like a man cognizant of his plight, added, "yourself if practicable." Although the president had no intention of assuming any field command, he immediately thought about his best commander: Lee. He was not alone. Howell Cobb, the influential Georgian, a stalwart Davis backer and a Confederate major general with a key assignment in his native state, appeared in Richmond to campaign for Lee. Regarding Lee's appointment as "almost essential to the success of our cause," Cobb declared he would "spare no pains or effort in pressing the matter upon the President." And Davis did listen to him.[113]

While Cobb pressed, Davis for the second time in two months discussed with Lee the latter's taking over the Army of Tennessee. Lee stated that he had "considered with some anxiety the condition of affairs in Georgia & Tennessee." He also suggested Beauregard as Bragg's successor. To the president's query about his going, Lee answered as he had in October: he would go, but he had no one in his army who could replace him. Obviously aware of the sour-tempered officer corps in the Army of Tennessee, Lee wondered whether he would receive "cordial cooperation." Wrestling with an enormously important and difficult decision, the president on December 9 called Lee to Richmond for consultations. Upon departing for the capital, Lee believed that he would be sent west. But after several days of discussion, Davis took a different course. He decided that Lee was irreplaceable in Virginia.[114]

With Lee removed from contention, Davis had few alternatives. The time had passed to take the risk and appoint a lieutenant general in an attempt to cleanse and rejuvenate the army. Hardee had already begged out, and with his bad relations with Bragg and poor performance in East Tennessee, Longstreet was not an option. Lee had brought up Beauregard, but Davis continued to have serious reservations about Beauregard's character and ability and would not trust him with a major field army. That left only Joe Johnston.[115]

There was certainly a clamor for Johnston's appointment. Even after Vicksburg Johnston's public reputation survived, as he had predicted. Important westerners were eager for him; after a western tour, presidential aide James Chesnut told Davis that "every honest man" he saw thought highly of Johnston. Davis's old acquaintance Leonidas Polk, who had done as much as anyone to wreck the Army of Tennessee, also urged that Johnston be placed over it. Pro-Johnston politicians pushed for him; Senator Wigfall lobbied vigorously, especially with Secretary of War Seddon. Aware of Davis's antipathy to Johnston, men like Wigfall—who was enjoying what he termed the "low state" of the administration after the defeat at Missionary Ridge—saw Johnston's assignment as a way to embarrass the president; they were not so much pro-Johnston as anti-Davis. Seddon finally concluded that Johnston was the only reasonable choice. Likewise, Lee favored him.[116]

At last, making a decision he did not relish, Davis did name Johnston. Although he held Johnston responsible for Vicksburg, he still believed in the general's military ability. On December 16 Johnston was ordered to Dalton to become the commanding general of the Army of Tennessee. A popular move, the choice of Johnston also benefited the president politically. Even the ardently pro-Lee Cobb accepted it as the best "under all the circumstances." Yet Davis did what he did, not because of politics or large-mindedness, but because he could find no acceptable alternative. As Seddon wrote, "the president, after doubt and with misgiving to the end, chose [Johnston], not as due exaltation on this score, but as the best on the whole to be obtained."[117]

Even as he struggled with the aftermath of Missionary Ridge, President Davis greeted the fourth and final session of the First Congress. In a lengthy message dated December 7, he outlined his ambitious legislative program. He also offered a mostly realistic assessment of the Confederacy's position and provided a vigorous restatement of his conviction that his course could not fail. He wanted Congress to amend the conscription law to extend the ages of eligibility, to abolish substitution, and to tighten exemption provisions. In asking for new taxes, the president made no attempt to cover up the jumble and morass of Confederate finances. He told the lawmakers he would "deem it my duty to approve any law levying the taxation which you are bound to impose for the defense of the country in any other practicable mode which shall distribute the burthen uniformly and impartially on the whole property of the people." And he urged taking steps to brake the accelerating monetary disaster by passing legislation recommended by the secretary of the treasury to reduce the quantity of Confederate notes in circulation, by requiring their exchange for interest-bearing bonds. The gross excess of the notes, Davis correctly maintained, was responsible both for runaway inflation and for the "spirit of speculation," which he condemned. Open about the financial mess, Davis also conceded that Confederate diplomacy in Europe had failed, though he blamed the British government because it refused to uphold international law regarding blockades and the rights of neutrals. The president acknowledged that the enemy occupied much of the country and admitted the "grave reverses" headlined by the fall of Vicksburg and the recent disaster at Missionary Ridge.

Despite these setbacks, the president expressed no doubt about the ultimate outcome of the war. Even though "our success in driving the enemy from our soil has not equaled the expectations confidently entertained at the commencement of the campaign," Davis asserted, "his progress has been checked." In Texas, in Louisiana, and at Charleston, Confederate arms prevailed. Yet declaring the army "to be in all respects in better condition than at any previous period of the war" was surely overstatement. He celebrated gallant Confederate soldiers battling a monstrous foe, who utilized uncivilized and "inhuman practices" in a relentless, albeit vain, attempt to conquer the Confederacy. Turning to history, Davis conveyed confidence: "Whatever obstinacy may be displayed by the enemy in his desperate sacrifices of money, life, and liberty in the hope of enslaving us, the experience of mankind has too conclusively shown the superior endurance of those who fight for home, liberty, and independence to permit any doubt of the result."[118]

CHAPTER FOURTEEN

"We Are Fighting for Existence"

A new year arrived with the chief executive signaling confidence. On January 1, 1864, he and his wife hosted an afternoon reception at the White House, with aides "in full fig, swords and sashes" serving as ushers for the guests, both military and civilian, including members of Congress. The large numbers in attendance left their mark on the president and first lady. Davis's right arm became "stiff with the New Year's shaking" and Varina's "hand tender to the touch." Two and a half weeks later, the Davises announced they would receive at the Executive Mansion every Tuesday between 8 and 10 p.m. With the final session of the First Congress still sitting, well-dressed ladies and gentlemen filled the public rooms of the house to find a cordial president greeting guests and introducing Varina to those unknown to her. The political motive behind these galas became evident when Davis discontinued them a month after they began, timing that coincided with the adjournment of Congress.[1]

Even with his active social and political calendar, President Davis's thoughts never strayed far from his fighting men. On February 10 he penned a public letter to "Soldiers of the Armies of the Confederate States" that was issued as a general order and carried in newspapers. He began by congratulating them for their "many noble triumphs" achieved in the "long and bloody war" gripping the nation. Special gratitude went to those who could have left the service upon expiration of their enlistments, but who instead "heeded the call only of your suffering country." Although as president he could not share "your dangers, your sufferings, and your privations in the field," he assured them, "with pride and affection my heart has accompanied you in every march; with solicitude it has sought to minister to your every want; with exultation it has marked your every heroic achievement."

Turning to the anticipated spring campaign, the commander in chief expressed confidence in his soldiers. "Your resolution needed nothing to fortify it." In the coming arduous battles the Confederates, with ranks rebuilt and superb leadership, could defeat an enemy become less "formidable" because of exhaustion. Evincing no doubt, Davis reiterated his vision of the Confederacy: "Assured success awaits us in our holy struggle for liberty and independence, and for the preservation of all that renders life desirable to honorable men." His closing called on God to protect "the citizen-defenders of the homes, the liberties, and the altars of the Confederacy."[2]

But the Federal juggernaut aimed at Davis's stalwart troopers was not exhausted. The Union had in the field its most powerful force yet, which outnumbered Confederate defenders by more than two to one. Equally as important, momentous changes had occurred in the Union command structure. In late winter President Lincoln promoted to lieutenant general Ulysses S. Grant, the first to hold that regular rank since George Washington, and placed the victor at Vicksburg and Chattanooga in command of all Union armies. Grant went east to set up his headquarters with the Army of the Potomac and direct its operations against the most successful Confederate general, Robert E. Lee. He turned over his old command to Major General William T. Sherman, with instructions to carry the fight to the Army of Tennessee, then at Dalton, some ninety miles north of Atlanta. Although Atlanta was not the chief goal of Sherman's campaign, it became a great political and psychological prize. Defending the city was central for the Confederates because it was a railway hub and the gateway to central Georgia, Alabama, and South Carolina. General Grant intended an all-out offensive all along the far-flung battle lines.[3]

To meet this powerful enemy, the Confederate command had both an old and a new look. In Virginia, Lee began his third campaign season as the resolute guardian of his native state and the Confederacy's eastern flank. Even though the Army of Northern Virginia had been augmented by James Longstreet's return from his futile foray in East Tennessee, its 60,000 men equaled no more than 60 percent of its foe's. Lee and his men faced a severe test.

The new faces belonged to veteran soldiers in different assignments. President Davis ordered General Braxton Bragg to Richmond as his military adviser, or personal chief of staff, a position not occupied since Lee's departure in June 1862. Here Bragg's talent for organization might best be utilized. He would have little impact on the eastern theater, for Davis and Lee were so close, but he brought with him intimate knowledge of the Army of Tennessee, whose new commander had not enjoyed the best relations with the president. Davis could only hope that with the major field army he had been wanting, Joseph Johnston would display the military ability that so many believed in, including the president.

Although Johnston was glad to have an army, he did not arrive in Dalton with a different attitude toward Davis. During the fall of 1863 and on into 1864, he whined incessantly about anyone's believing he bore any responsibility for Vicksburg. He viewed his new command as vindication and a triumph over the president, but he still mistrusted Davis. With one colleague he shared his conviction that "Mr. Davis will not place me in any position where there is any chance or possibility of success." As the astute Mary Chesnut perceived, Johnston's "hatred of Jeff Davis amounts to a religion. With him it colors all things." "Being such a good hater," she observed, "it is a pity he had not elected to hate somebody else than the president of our country."[4]

A major reason for Johnston's continuing venomous view of Davis was his close relationship with Louis Wigfall. The rabidly anti-Davis senator kept telling the general that the president hated him and that he should never trust the commander in chief. Wigfall described Davis as a man who, to gratify his personal likes and dislikes, would "sacrifice everything except personal popularity & power." Wigfall even confided, "We have fears for the future unless he can be controlled." A close friend and confidant filling letters with such sentiments only exacerbated the prickly and self-appointed martyr's propensity to think the worst of Davis. This deep-seated attitude did not augur well for future relations.[5]

At the outset Johnston and Davis disagreed fundamentally over military operations. Johnston understood he had to rebuild morale and confidence in the Army of Tennessee, and he worked effectively to do so. Recognizing the terrible cost of the internal squabbling, he asserted, "if I were President, I'd distribute the generals of this army over the Confederacy." The conflict with Richmond came over what to do with the army. Davis urged Johnston to go on the offensive, or at least to plan for such a move. He even sent a personal emissary, Brigadier General William N. Pendleton, formerly Johnston's chief of artillery, to confer with Johnston and convey the presidential view. Secretary of War James Seddon and General Bragg also explained to Johnston what was desired and promised to provide all possible assistance. Responding to the president, Johnston expressed serious misgivings about undertaking any such operation. In addition, in early April he sent Colonel Benjamin Ewell from his staff to Richmond to present personally his views. Meeting with Bragg first and then the president, Colonel Ewell emphasized Johnston's shortages in men and transportation. Both Bragg and Davis acknowledged Johnston's needs and declared they would do what they could, but they said Lee too was outnumbered and made clear the severe limits of available resources. Davis pressed his desire for an offensive. His detailed knowledge of the Army of Tennessee impressed Ewell, as did his "affability and courtesy" during the discussion. Despite the harmony of this conference, it changed no minds.[6]

The president still wanted and expected his general to strike, but Johnston thought only in defensive terms. Davis overestimated the capability of the Army of Tennessee, which like its counterpart in Virginia confronted a stronger foe. Even though its ranks increased between December and May to 60,000, including the return of Leonidas Polk, along with some 14,000 troops from eastern Mississippi, as well as units from Mobile and South Carolina, Sherman counted nearly 100,000. The numbers were not so central, however, as Johnston's basic mind-set. For him in the spring of 1864, as in 1863 and 1862, no offensive movements could be undertaken unless everything was just right. Of course, that condition never obtained, and Johnston would never risk his army or his reputation. On a letter to Bragg in which Johnston stated firmly he would have to await the enemy's initiative, the president noted: "read with disappointment."[7]

The great Federal onslaught commenced in May. On the fifth, Grant slammed into Lee on almost the same ground that had witnessed Chancellorsville a year earlier. For two days the antagonists fought bitterly in what became known as the Battle of the Wilderness. Grant could not break Lee, but neither could Lee drive Grant back. For a full month following the Wilderness, the Army of the Potomac and the Army of Northern Virginia grappled in blood-soaked combat that ended literally at the gates of Richmond on the fields of the Seven Days. Whenever he could, Lee struck at Grant, but none of his thrusts succeeded. His flank attacks no longer stung with the fury of those he had mounted in 1862 and 1863. Between May 5 and June 4 the casualties reached appalling levels: about 25,000 Confederates and 50,000 Federals.

Through these sanguinary weeks Davis and Lee were in constant communication. As he had always done, Lee kept the president regularly informed, at times daily, about his operations and intentions. In response, Davis strove to provide the men and material Lee needed. He even ordered General Pierre Beauregard to come with his organized brigades from the Carolinas to Virginia and direct operations south of the James River. As Federal cavalry raids arrived practically at the outskirts of Richmond, Davis himself directed troop movements that helped thwart the enemy. He kept Lee posted on these activities.[8]

In Georgia, the situation was simultaneously the same and quite different. In the face of Sherman's advance into the rough, submountainous terrain of North Georgia, which began on May 7, Joseph Johnston fell back constantly, relinquishing defensive position after defensive position. He never seriously attempted to strike Sherman. In contrast to Virginia, little heavy fighting occurred, for Sherman, unlike Grant, did not regularly attack his opponent. He preferred flanking movements that Johnston always met with retreat. Only at the Battle of Kennesaw Mountain on June 27 did Sherman make a Grant-like assault, which Johnston bloodily repulsed. By July 9 Johnston had fallen back all the way to the southern bank of the Chattahoochee River, only ten miles from Atlanta.

During this campaign Johnston did not alter his practices. He provided little operational information to his superiors in Richmond. Numerous messages flowed from the Army of Tennessee to the War Department, but they consisted overwhelmingly of routine administrative matters. Johnston did not divulge his plans. Still, however tightlipped he remained, there did exist an informal conduit extending from his headquarters to Richmond through Lieutenant General John B. Hood, a hard-charging, combat-scarred veteran of the Army of Northern Virginia and Chickamauga, recently promoted to corps command. During the winter of 1863–64, while in Richmond convalescing from the amputation of his left leg at Chickamauga, Hood spent time with both Jefferson and Varina Davis on informal and social occasions. Always an aggressive fighter, he talked to Davis about the need for an offensive course in Georgia. With confidence in Hood's combat prowess, Davis made him a lieutenant general and assigned him to the Army of Tennessee. Hood departed from Richmond in the president's favor. Delighted to have Hood, in spite of his maimed arm from Gettysburg as well as an absent leg, Johnston welcomed his new corps commander in his tent almost every day. He was unaware that Hood regularly wrote to Bragg about Johnston's defensive outlook. Surely Hood's conduct was unprofessional, but the administration shared responsibility, for neither Bragg, Seddon, nor the president ever alerted

Johnston about Hood's backdoor dispatches. Although Johnston's secrecy frustrated the War Department and Davis, Hood's information increased concern that Johnston never intended to fight his army.[9]

While Confederate armies gave ground in Virginia and Georgia, the distant Trans-Mississippi became more and more the domain of General Edmund Kirby Smith. Promoted to full general in February, Smith also exercised increased civil authority. President Davis understood that neither he nor his administration could directly control policy in what became known as "Kirby Smithdom." In late April he wrote General Smith: "As far as the constitution permits, full authority has been given to you to administer to the wants of your Dept., civil as well as military." To procure desperately needed supplies and weapons, Smith organized an agency to collect, even to the point of impressment, and dispose of cotton, chiefly in Mexico. Despite speculation, problems with currency, and opposition by private owners of cotton, this program did furnish many necessities. On the military front, Confederate forces halted two Federal advances, one coming southward from Little Rock, the other moving up the Red River in Louisiana. This military success had limited impact, for the Trans-Mississippi remained strategically isolated and could not fundamentally affect events east of the great river.[10]

As his armies confronted Grant's spring offensives, the commander in chief was enmeshed in a complicated political world. Accounts of war weariness and even reluctance to continue the struggle reached his desk. As early as the summer of 1863, Davis was told by men he knew and trusted that "the *Cause* is in its last agonies, and will soon expire, never, never, to be revived." A close ally in the Confederate Senate disclosed that traveling across much of the country had left him with "a feeling of *despondency.*" "The day I ever dreaded *has come,*" he wrote, "the *enthusiasm* of the masses of the people *is dead!*" Davis read that citizens felt "the keen calamities of the present" and wanted relief. He saw reports that military setbacks had left many with "a chilling apprehension" about the future.

But simultaneously with these bleak missives he received word of renewed commitment by Confederate citizens. In certain instances, military reverses had even stimulated patriotism. "Success or utter annihilation is the stern resolve of the people here," wrote an old Mississippi associate. Heartened, Davis showed no signs of wavering from his course. To the initial session of the Second Congress, which convened in early May, the president repeated his conviction about his cause and its citizens. Confederate armies, he declared, "still oppose with unshaken front a formidable barrier to the progress of the invader, and our generals, armies, and people are animated by cheerful confidence."[11]

Davis knew, however, that his political opponents continued to cry out against him and his war policies. Two measures passed by the final session of the First Congress stepped up the drumbeat that despotism trampled upon liberty: the new Conscription Law, which extended eligible ages from seventeen to fifty, curtailed exemptions, and authorized the War Department to detail men to jobs it deemed critical; and the statute granting the president the power to suspend the writ of habeas corpus for six months, with governing conditions spelled out. Critics of these measures repeated their warning that principles such as personal liberty and states' rights were too precious to restrict, much less sacrifice, even for political independence. In contrast, President Davis and his supporters reiterated that the struggle for independence took precedence, for Confederate failure would mean slavery.[12]

Although individual opponents were scattered across the shrinking Confederacy, the most potent opposition to Davis and his vigorous war program arose in two states, Georgia and North Carolina. There the chorus propounding personal liberty and states' rights blended ideological purity with political self-interest. In Georgia, Governor Joseph Brown had long cloaked his anti-Davis stance in the mantle of states' rights. Claiming the sacred rights of Georgia to be under siege, he tried to remove from the reach of conscription all state civil and military officials. He also denounced the power to suspend the writ of habeas corpus as emblematic of the most heinous tyranny. In addition, he wanted the legislature to take a strong stand against this dangerous, usurping central government. Yet in his clamor against Davis and Confederate power, Brown never made any class appeal by calling on the poor to refuse to fight a rich man's war. Neither did he ever urge the creation of an anti-administration party. Brown's chief concern was Brown's power. He strove to maintain as much control as possible over affairs within Georgia borders, but he was a realist who understood the danger posed by Federal invasion.

In the spring of 1864, Governor Brown secured an articulate ally, Vice President Stephens. An ideologue totally dedicated to his own conception of personal liberty and states' rights, Stephens now broke publicly with the administration. Because of illness as well as dissatisfaction with policy, the vice president did not go to Richmond for the final session of the First Congress, but he did write a long letter to Davis detailing his views of how the Confederacy should fight the war. In this epistle he took exception to the president's position, which he termed "execrable." He wanted no conscription, no impressment, no suspension of the writ of habeas corpus. The positive action of Congress in these areas pushed Stephens into open opposition, a course that Davis never tried to block with soothing words or flattering overtures. In a lengthy address before the Georgia legislature in mid-March, Stephens denounced the Davis administration as the embodiment of tyranny; the escape from oppression in 1861 had ended up in the dungeon of despotism.[13]

The vice president and his close collaborators, his younger brother Linton and close friend Robert Toombs, lived in their own world, with room for neither war nor invasion. It was as if the entire Confederacy replicated the pastoral quiet of their central Georgia home. They acted as if the spring of 1864 simply continued the spring of 1861, without Fort Sumter and three years of bloody warfare. Consumed by their personal visions of the political holy grail and a growing hatred for Davis personally, they spoke of popular liberty, the rights of Georgia, and even a settlement with the Union that would leave slavery intact.

These raging Georgians howled, but they accomplished little. Davis and his definition of the Confederate cause had stalwart supporters in the state, such as Howell Cobb and Confederate senators Benjamin Hill and Herschel Johnson. Like Senator Johnson, a friend of Stephens's who worried about increased executive authority, many Georgians refused to follow the dissidents' lead. Maintaining trust in Davis, Johnson condoned no direct attacks on the administration and rebuffed all talk of replacing the president. Cobb, Hill, Johnson, and their backers called on all Georgians to rally to the cause and its leader. They prevailed. The Brown-Stephens team could not even persuade the legislature to adopt a strong anti-administration stance. Davis himself never became personally involved in this fracas, except to counter in direct fashion Brown's long, argumentative letters. Although Davis loyalists may have exaggerated when they claimed that Brown's machinations had "recoiled" upon the wily governor, the president's position in Georgia was not undermined.[14]

In North Carolina, the situation was potentially more dangerous for President Davis and could have become explosive, but for the consummate political skills of Governor Zebulon Vance. Although Vance is usually coupled with Brown as a gubernatorial opponent of Davis's administration, in fact, he was no such thing. Considerable antiwar and even anti-Confederate feeling existed in the state, particularly in the Appalachian region. In addition, widespread unhappiness caused by overzealous impressment and conscription officers increased hostility toward the Davis administration. The able journalist and veteran of Tarheel politics William W. Holden led a vigorous effort to direct this disaffection and distress into a peace movement, in which the state would at least consider a separate peace with the United States. Holden took on Vance in the 1864 gubernatorial contest. To stymie this activity and Holden, Vance operated on two fronts. He pressed Davis on issues such as peace overtures and impressment and conscription excesses while simultaneously appealing to the loyalty and patriotism of North Carolinians. He wanted no party organized to oppose the president. Vance's strategy worked. Winning more than 75 percent of the vote, including almost 90 percent of the soldier vote, in the summer election, Vance smashed Holden while isolating and crushing the antiwar and anti-Davis faction.

Davis took Vance seriously, and exercised considerable judgment in his dealings with the governor. Not only was Vance the chief executive of an important state, he also spoke Davis's language of patriotism. He told the president that "the true men of the state are going to work every where," and he expected to prevail. Moreover, on two occasions the governor visited the president to exchange views and explain what was happening in North Carolina. The president saw Vance as a stalwart Confederate who could keep his state loyal. When Vance reported outrages by Confederate officials, Davis strove to effect corrective action. To the governor's counsel on peace initiatives, the president detailed his efforts, most recently the aborted Stephens mission. He also said that he thought Lincoln would respond positively only to an offer of surrender.[15]

Although Davis was forthcoming and positive, he did reveal his sensitivity to criticism that implied any reasons for his decisions beyond the sole benefit of the Confederate cause. Bristling when he inferred that Vance had questioned the motives behind certain presidential actions, including appointments, Davis apprised the governor of his "regret that you have deemed proper in urging your views to make unjust reflections upon my official conduct. . . ." In order to avoid controversy, Davis said he preferred to remain silent, "but public interests are involved which preclude this course." If unchallenged, Vance's comments "would tend to create hostility to the Government and undermine its power to provide for the public defense." Davis felt he had "a duty to respond." Even so, he prepared a sober and moderate, though lengthy, letter in which he made clear that he took no personal umbrage. Replying promptly, Vance disabused the president of any such implications. "It was very far from my intention," he wrote, "to raise any issues of disagreeable & unprofitable character with you." Both men successfully endeavored to prevent disagreements from hampering their working relationship.[16]

In spite of a cacophony of tirades and screeds, the political opposition to the president accomplished little. No state, not even Georgia or North Carolina, took off on an independent course. Neither did any other political leader seriously challenge Davis's authority or prestige in the Confederacy. By the autumn of 1864 the Confederacy had become geographically diminished but the president's position remained undiminished. He continued to stand at the center.

In the president's own house, Davis and his wife stood as one. Just after the war she said they "liv[ed] in the closest friendship," and she was even "cognizant of a great deal relating to his official conduct." Davis reacted sharply to perceived slights or insults to the first lady. In the southern code such reactions underscored the husband's role as guardian and protector of the wife, but also the fact that the man's own public and private identity was based in part on treatment of the woman. A man of honor demanded that other men demonstrate respect for his wife. During the winter of 1864, a general visiting the White House neglected to speak to Varina, though she was in the room. Recognizing his oversight and having intended no rudeness, he called again to apologize for the omission. Davis refused the apology.[17]

Earlier, Davis had revealed an extraordinary sensitivity about esteem shown to Varina and to his own self-image. In the fall of 1863, just before leaving Richmond for assignment in Charleston, Brigadier General Henry Wise, a former governor of Virginia, sent a present of wooden spoons as "a memento" of a pleasant visit with Varina. From Charleston, Wise asked his son-in-law Dr. A. Y. P. Garnett, who often treated members of the Davis household, to find out whether the gift had been received. When Dr. Garnett inquired, he did not talk with Varina but with her sister, who relayed Varina's positive answer. Varina also sent word for Dr. Garnett to give her love to General Wise and tell him that she would write a personal note. When Garnett so informed Wise, at the same time he playfully noted newspaper stories about the president's kissing girls on his western trip.

Davis learned of this communication and took singular exception, inferring that Garnett had connected Varina's mention of love to his own supposed osculatory activities. He demanded an explanation from Garnett, who replied that he had simply delivered a message, with no intention of tying it to reported accounts of presidential behavior. Davis was satisfied, but Wise was disgusted. In an indignant letter to the president, Wise accused him of duplicity. He stated that when Davis was in Charleston, they had laughed at talk of the alleged kissing. Wise quoted Davis as declaring the story false, but "it is one of those sort of things *which a man cannot* deny." Wise maintained that he had nothing but respect for Varina, but he told his son-in-law the president was "a small, weak, little jaundiced bigot & vain pretender." An obviously angry Wise fumed that he was inclined "to kick his 'seat of honor,' if he has any." In this instance, Davis certainly overreacted. He needlessly made an enemy of General Wise, and only Garnett's forbearance averted a quite ugly situation. The record does not reveal what Varina thought of this epistolary huffing and puffing.[18]

As 1864 began, the first lady continued to lead an active social life. While she of course presided over numerous formal receptions in the White House, she also hosted popular ladies' luncheons on Saturdays. Sometimes she and Angela Mallory chaperoned "gay society" on steamer excursions on the James River. Then there were gatherings at friends' houses, where festivities included the tableaux and pantomimes popular in the capital.[19]

But during the spring, her upbeat mood faltered. The depreciation of Confederate currency affected even the first family. Acknowledging that "everybody is in trouble," Varina informed her friend Mary Chesnut that they were going to give up their carriages and horses. Apprehensive about the military situation, she feared a siege of Richmond was inevitable, a forecast that "utterly depressed" her. If that eventuality should come to pass, she intended to send her children away to safety.[20]

Then, on the last day of April, horror struck. During the middle of that Saturday, five-year-old Joe was playing on the piazza on the southeast side of the White House, most probably walking along the railing. For the moment out of sight of his Irish nurse and unseen by anyone else, he fell to the brick pavement twelve feet below. Both his legs were broken, and his skull fractured. The crushed child lived but a short time. His mother had just gone to take some food to her husband's office in the Customs House. A servant brought news of the accident.

Mother and father rushed home to watch and hold their boy in his last moments of life. An eyewitness recorded Varina's "flood of tears and wild lamentations." "Unutterable anguish" marked Jefferson's face, which "seemed suddenly ready to burst with unspeakable grief, and then transfixed into a stony rigidity." His wife recalled his crying out, "Not mine, oh, Lord, but thine." Turning away a courier, he moaned, "I must have this day with my little child." Exercising "terrible self control," the father with his burden of "heavy sorrow" paced the floor of his bedroom throughout the night.[21]

Friends rushed to the White House, and Burton Harrison took charge of the arrangements. The funeral was held at Hollywood Cemetery on the western edge of the city overlooking the James River, with many children sprinkled through the large crowd. Flowers covered the new grave. "Passionate in grief," Varina spoke "in the deepest affliction" of the cherished little boy who was no more.[22]

Neither Jefferson nor Varina had time to dwell on their horrendous loss. She was again pregnant, and some seven weeks after Joe's death she gave birth on June 27 to her last child and second daughter, Varina Anne, her namesake. Writing to a friend shortly afterward, she reported herself exhausted and still too unwell to think about the future. Grief and the debility of childbirth sapped her energy and strength. The president once more heard the alarm bells that signaled Federal troops close to the capital, and southward in Georgia he faced yet another crisis in command.[23]

In Virginia, Lee and Grant still battled. On June 3 at Cold Harbor, less than ten miles from Richmond, Lee bloodily smashed Grant when the Federal general tried to ram his way into the capital. After that setback, Grant moved south across the James River toward Petersburg— Lee and Richmond's railroad link to the Deep South. Lee was initially unsure about his adversary's intention, but when he comprehended Grant's objective and his and his government's peril, the Confederate commander rushed troops to the endangered town, where Beauregard employed them effectively to hold back Grant. Arriving with his main force in Petersburg, Lee strengthened the Confederate position and prepared to hold the strategic town as long as possible. With both sides manning ever stronger entrenchments and forts, Grant could not drive Lee out of his defenses and Lee could not budge Grant.[24]

Grant's successful lodgment south of the James fundamentally altered the Confederate strategic situation in Virginia. If Lee was to protect Richmond, he had to remain at Petersburg in front of Grant. In his defensive lines he no longer had the option of maneuvering his entire army, for such movement would uncover the capital and leave the way open for Federal troops literally to walk into the city. But no evidence indicates at this point that either Lee or Davis seriously considered abandoning it. As the Confederate capital, Richmond had enormous symbolic significance. It was also critically important as a source of essential war matériel, being the leading manufacturing center in the Confederacy, with the country's largest ironworks. Richmond's loss would have had a devastating impact on the Confederate war effort.

Lee dreaded this static warfare, which he considered extremely dangerous to his cause. Even before he crossed the James, he remarked that if he were forced to withstand a siege, then his ultimate defeat would be a matter of time. Still hoping that maneuver could loosen Grant's grip and enable him to strike, Lee tried to replicate the phenomenally successful strategy of 1862 when Stonewall Jackson's triumphs in the Shenandoah Valley rattled Washington and held up reinforcements intended for McClellan. In mid-June he ordered Lieutenant General Jubal A. Early to the Valley with 10,000 men—soldiers Lee could ill afford to spare. His little army up to 15,000 with the addition of 5,000 troops already defending the Shenandoah, Early threw back a Federal incursion and set off down the Valley toward the Potomac River and Maryland. Crossing the river, the Confederates on July 11 came within sight of Washington, before superior numbers forced them to turn back. Early's campaign did create a stir within the Federal capital and caused Grant to send an entire corps from the Army of the Potomac. But 1864 was not 1862. Even after dispatching reinforcements to Washington, Grant, with more than twice the strength of Lee, remained far too formidable for any offensive the Confederate general could mount. By the end of summer, Petersburg was clearly under siege.

Through the summer Davis and Lee kept in their usual close touch, and the president approved and supported the decisions his general made. When Lee requested Davis's views on his plan for Early, he received no countermanding instructions. Always hungering to have his armies on northern soil and have his enemy experience the pain of war, Davis shared his commander's aspirations for Early's advance. Davis and Lee also planned a raid on a large Union prisoner-of-war camp at Point Lookout in eastern Maryland, an operation they hoped would coincide with Early's presence in the state. But the absolute secrecy imperative for success could not be maintained, and the foray was canceled.[25]

While regular messages continued to pass between Davis and Lee, the proximity of the Army of Northern Virginia to Richmond permitted the two men to meet more often. The general came to the capital, but the president, accompanied by various companions, also rode out to army headquarters. These rides could cover more than twenty miles, and the visits could last far into the night. Sometimes Davis did not leave Lee until the moon was up. Such excursions could also place him in danger. On at least two occasions, despite the presence of guides, the presidential party rode beyond Confederate positions. But in each instance cries from men in gray brought an unharmed president back within friendly lines. Once, visiting a battery on the James, Davis came under fire from Federal units only a few hundred yards away. Seemingly unperturbed, he finally yielded to the pleas of officers, "smiled, turned," and withdrew.[26]

Although the commander in chief concurred with Lee's vigorous thrusts at Grant, he watched with increasing concern Johnston's retreat toward Atlanta. Davis certainly did not want to yield the city "before manly blows had been struck for its preservation." Hood's messages fed his fear that Johnston would not strike at Sherman. He shared his anxiety with a friend who quoted him: "I had hoped & trusted from day to day that I should get news of a general battle, and I felt sure we should succeed but day after day came and went and there was no fight, while the army was still falling back, back, back!" General Bragg and others in the administration had already reached that conclusion. In mid-July a War Department official recorded in his diary: "A very gloomy view of affairs in Georgia prevails in the cabinet."[27]

A major reason for the distress permeating the administration was that no one, including Davis, knew Johnston's intentions. The general had become no more open in his communications to the War Department. He did admit that because of the numerical disparity and the nature of the country, he had been unable to halt Sherman's progress. Yet, as he told his wife, he reported to Richmond only in "a general way," and in monumental misjudgment or self-deception he asserted that his superiors took "no interest in any partial affairs that may occur in this quarter. . . ." After two months of continuous withdrawal, Davis grew anxious to know what his commander intended. The president was also concerned about what he saw as Johnston's "want of confidence." Did Johnston plan to fight for Atlanta? Did he contemplate withstanding a siege in the city? Did he envision continued retreat toward Savannah or Mobile? Johnston gave Davis every reason to expect the third alternative when on July 11 he "strongly recommended" the immediate removal of Federal prisoners of war from Andersonville, some 100 miles south of Atlanta. Then, what chance would Johnston have against Sherman in the plains of central Georgia if he had not been able to stop him in the much more defense-friendly terrain above Atlanta?[28]

Davis aimed to ascertain Johnston's purpose, if possible. He sent Bragg to the Army of Tennessee to sound out Johnston. He also had Secretary of War Seddon request from Senator Benjamin Hill an account of a discussion he had had with Johnston. Both general and senator presented similar reports. Hill said that Johnston hoped Sherman would attack him, and if so was confident of victory. Moreover, Hill relayed Johnston's conviction that he could hold his lines in front of the Chattahoochee River for a month or more. But Hill conveyed to Seddon his opinion that Johnston would not strive to gain the initiative. Hill also journeyed to Richmond to present his account directly to the president. Likewise, Bragg sent word to Richmond that Johnston had "ever been opposed to seeking battle. . . ." Unknown to Davis, Bragg played a devious role while with the army. He posed as Johnston's friend but really listened to Hood's criticisms and sent a negative dispatch back to the War Department. Although he had been duplicitous in his personal dealings with Johnston, that conduct did not fundamentally affect his findings, for Johnston had steadily maintained that he could only react to Sherman.[29]

Despite the obvious signs of his commander in chief's anxiety, Johnston remained guarded and recalcitrant, even defensive. In fact, Johnston was a troubled general who shared potentially embarrassing doubts only with his wife, never with his superiors. At the beginning of the campaign in early May, he sounded reasonably confident; he did not believe Sherman could succeed "unless we have bad luck." But only a week later, his tone changed: "I have been very much disappointed to do so little with so fine an army—& one so devoted to me." He confided, "I have never been so little satisfied with myself. Have never been so weak." His relinquishing of so much territory distressed and humiliated him. Confessing his inability to counter what he termed Sherman's "Engineering system," he informed his wife on June 18 that he might have to cross the Chattahoochee. With that admission he implored her to burn his letter promptly. Twelve days later he expressed to Senator Hill complete confidence in his defensive position. On the last day of June, he harked back to the self-protective mantra he had employed before. He told his wife that no other general had ever faced his predicament. "Such a warfare was never before waged," he moaned.[30]

Johnston did make one positive recommendation. He regularly urged the War Department to unleash a cavalry force against Sherman's long rail supply line, which stretched back to Chattanooga and on up to Nashville. Always claiming his own mounted arm was too weak for such an assignment, he wanted the troops sent from Mississippi or elsewhere. To help obtain the War Department's agreement on this maneuver, he called on Governor Brown and Senator Hill to lobby for it. One strong Confederate cavalry force did exist in Mississippi, under Major General Nathan Bedford Forrest, the ablest Confederate cavalry commander. Whether Forrest could have done more than temporarily interrupt Sherman is most unlikely. No doubt exists, however, on two other relevant matters. Johnston never considered any assault on the railroad by a portion of his own army akin to Lee's employment of Early. And Davis never considered sending Forrest against Sherman's rear, for he believed the cavalryman essential for the defense of Mississippi. In June, Forrest was instrumental in turning back a Federal attack on the northern part of the state. Of course, the president could have jettisoned Mississippi and directed Confederate forces there toward central Tennessee, where they might or might not have forced Sherman to turn away from Johnston and head back to Tennessee. Davis was not prepared to take that drastic step and shrink his country. The emotional and political costs would have been exorbitant.

Confronting yet another troubling situation with the Army of Tennessee, Davis once more called on his best soldier and most trusted counselor. "*Gen. Johnston,*" Davis wired to Lee, "has *failed* and there are strong indications that he will *abandon Atlanta.*" Underscoring his conclusion, the president had learned that the line Johnston had told Senator Hill he could hold for more than a month had been given up in a week. Stating that "the case seems hopeless in present hands," Davis broached the possibility of Johnston's removal and asked Lee, "Who should *succeed* him?" Lee cautioned the president not to act hastily. He thought it "a grievous thing to change commander of an army situated as is that of the Tennessee," a concern Davis shared. The president told Senator Hill that removing Johnston would be dreadful, but he feared he would have to do it. Lee agreed, adding, "Still if necessary it ought to be done."[31]

While Lee was wary about changing commanding generals in Atlanta, Davis's two closest cabinet advisers had decided that drastic and immediate action was essential. Judah Benjamin, never a Johnston admirer, had long questioned the general's strategy. He saw only disaster if Johnston were retained. Secretary Seddon expressed the same opinion, though he had reached it from a different starting point. He had usually backed Johnston and in December 1863 had enthusiastically pushed for Johnston's assignment to the Army of Tennessee. Now he advised Davis that Johnston must go.[32]

Finally, the president turned to Johnston himself. On July 16 he requested from the general information about the "present situation, and your plan of operation. . . ." Replying that same day, Johnston reiterated lines that he had been speaking since the Peninsula in 1862. His opponent outnumbered him, which meant that his "plan of operations must, therefore, depend upon that of the enemy." This exchange convinced Davis that his concerns about Johnston's confidence were justified. Now he had to act. The following day he relieved Johnston for failing to stop Sherman but chiefly for "express[ing] no confidence that you can defeat or repel him. . . ."[33]

In relieving Johnston, Davis compared his campaign to Lee's. Although both generals had retreated before a superior foe, the president viewed their circumstances and performances as quite different. Lee had battled all the way and with Early had even tried a daring, albeit unsuccessful, move to regain the initiative. At Petersburg, he had Grant as much at bay as Grant had him. With a bloodied and weary army, Grant could neither overpower nor dislodge the Confederate defenders. Lee knew he could hold on for a considerable time. Moreover, throughout the weeks from the Wilderness to Petersburg he had kept Davis thoroughly informed and had promptly posted the president on his intentions and actions.[34]

In contrast, Johnston, in the same amount of time, had fallen back over twice as great a distance and through country more advantageous for defense. He never seriously tried to grasp the initiative, and he constantly cried for help from outside his army. He never slowed down or weakened Sherman, who reached Atlanta relatively more powerful than Grant at Petersburg. According to a compatriot, Davis worried that Johnston thought "his army is not for the defense of the country, but that he must at all hazards protect the army." Perhaps most important, Johnston never confided in Davis. He never gave the president any reason to have confidence in him. Of course, that would have been difficult because he had so little in himself.[35]

Removing Johnston meant replacing him. With Sherman at the gates of Atlanta, a decision could not be put off, and with Davis determined to fight for the city, no time remained to bring in someone from outside the Army of Tennessee. Given the situation, Davis had few choices. The army's two senior lieutenant generals were unavailable for different reasons. Leonidas Polk had been killed by Federal artillery just prior to the Battle of Kennesaw Mountain, and William Hardee had withdrawn his name from consideration back in December 1863, under conditions not nearly so pressing. The remaining two were Polk's successor Alexander P. Stewart, who had received his third star only in late June, and the impatient Hood, who had been advocating offensive moves.

Of course, the president wanted the opinion of Robert E. Lee. It had become habitual with him to seek Lee's counsel before making any major decision regarding the Army of Tennessee. When Davis posed Hood's name, he got an unenthusiastic response. Lee acknowledged Hood's "gallantry, earnestness & zeal," but feared for his success "when the whole responsibility rested upon him." Lee suggested the more experienced Hardee. Four days after this exchange the president sent Secretary Seddon by train to confer with Lee about Johnston's replacement. Upon Seddon's return, he and Davis closeted themselves to make a decision. From Davis's perspective, Hardee had already expressed an unwillingness to take over the army. On the other hand, Hood was eager for the command and no one doubted he would fight. Davis promoted him to the temporary rank of full general and gave him the opportunity.[36]

Hood fulfilled Davis's expectations; he fought desperately for Atlanta. In a series of bold assaults in and around the city, he tried to throw Sherman back. He failed, though he did the best he could. Military historians have often condemned Hood for destroying the fine army he had inherited from Johnston, but some have been impressed by his effort. He started out with inferior numbers. Then his headlong attacks lacked the careful planning that would have increased his chances of severely hurting Sherman. In addition, he had no luck. Hood had learned to fight in the Army of Northern Virginia in 1862 and 1863, and on the battlefield he tried to emulate the combative Lee.

But he was no Lee. And by mid-1864 even Lee could not drive his enemy back.[37]

During a difficult spring and summer, Davis did not spend all of his time on his two major armies. His workdays continued long and extended well into the night. Friends worried about the constant pressure and about the impact on his health of the late hours as well as the absorption in detail. He was urged to turn over small matters to others; but such counsel did not comprehend the sheer impossibility of his doing so. Neither his ingrained administrative style nor his concept of his duty would permit any substantive delegation of authority or tasks.[38]

Yet the president did not neglect his public obligations. When 1,000 prisoners of war were returned to Richmond, he joined a large crowd in Capitol Square to welcome them. Greeted by hearty cheers from the soldiers, Davis praised them for their bravery in captivity and promised they could soon rejoin their units. He also had the sad task of visiting Lee's celebrated cavalry chieftain, Major General J. E. B. Stuart, who lay dying in a Richmond home. He had been mortally wounded just north of the city while repelling a Federal cavalry raid. Returning to the Executive Mansion, Davis knelt in prayer and, according to his wife, asked God to spare Stuart's life "to our needy country."[39]

Davis's family concerns extended beyond the travails in the White House to include the tribulations of brother Joseph. Joseph had thought about Georgia as a sanctuary, but decided the trip would be too arduous. As a result, the spring of 1864 found the displaced old planter in Tuscaloosa, Alabama, with his granddaughter Lise Mitchell still by his side. His wandering had finally come to a halt. He informed Jefferson he was "feeble" but not sick. He reported on family trials and slaves, some of whom remained with him. He hoped to find work for them and to plant some corn in order to help feed them. Jefferson worried about his elderly sibling and wanted him in Richmond. Declining the invitation, Joseph said the expense would be too great; besides, Jefferson did not need the added bother of having him at hand. Joseph did want to send Lise for "the advantages" he saw in the capital city, but she would not leave him. With cares and sadness pressing upon him, Joseph wrote of happier times as "only the faint shadow of the past." The old man and the young woman would stay in Tuscaloosa to the end.[40]

The president's moods ranged from grim to light. After he spoke to the former prisoners, some women friends asked if the men would like going back to the army. Davis answered, "it may seem hard." Then he pointed to some twelve- to fourteen-year-old boys playing nearby and said they too "will have their trial," possibly with rats as their rations. On other occasions his spirits were buoyant and he would indulge his fondness for telling stories. One companion heard incidents involving two of his heroes, Andrew Jackson and Zachary Taylor. Visitors to the presidential office were invariably impressed by his charm and graciousness.[41]

In July an acute observer described a man yet vigorous but visibly affected by the enormous burden constantly with him. A slight stoop barely bowed his frame of just under six feet. His hair and chin whiskers were now "iron-gray," and "his face was emaciated and much wrinkled." But to this eyewitness, Davis's broad forehead along with strong mouth and chin signified "great energy and strength of will." His eyes still captivated, even though one was damaged.[42]

In mid-July a visit from two northern men who came to talk about the possibility of ending the war provided an occasion for President Davis to define once again his sense of the Confederacy. These men, Union officer James F. Jaquess and Methodist minister James R. Gilmore, had no official status, though they had been granted passage from Washington into Confederate lines. Upon their arrival in Richmond, they made clear in their request for an interview that they came as private citizens. They also specified they brought no message from President Lincoln, but they declared themselves familiar with his views. Davis readily agreed to see them and, accompanied by Judah Benjamin, met them in Benjamin's office. He agreed with his guests that he could not leave untried any approach that might result in peace. He told them he wanted peace and deplored bloodshed as much as they did, but claimed that "not one drop of the blood shed in this war is on my hands." "I can look up to my God and say this," he went on, because he had striven for a dozen years to prevent war, but he had failed.

The war came, he asserted, and "Now it must go on till the last man of this generation falls in his tracks, and his children seize his musket and fight our battle, *unless you acknowledge our right to self government*." Insisting that Confederates were not battling for slavery, Davis claimed that slavery had never been the key issue. In his words, "it was only a means of bringing other conflicting elements to an earlier culmination.

It fired the musket which was already capped and loaded." "We are fighting for Independence," he proclaimed, "and that, or extermination, we *will* have."

Davis repeatedly emphasized that peace required independence. Upon being told that the North would never relent in its determination to maintain the Union and that the northern people might eventually want to hang Confederate leaders, Davis responded, "There are some things worse than hanging or extermination. We reckon giving up the right of self-government one of those things." Throughout the discussion Davis never wavered in his complete confidence that the Confederacy could and would prevail. He pointed to Grant's inability to break Lee and the massive casualties he had incurred while trying, and he stated that Sherman's lengthening supply line rendered his situation increasingly perilous, whether or not Atlanta fell. As his visitors departed, Davis spoke directly: "Say to Mr. Lincoln from me, that I shall at any time be pleased to receive proposals for peace on the basis of our Independence. It will be useless to approach me with any other."[43]

In just six weeks, the assurance Davis expressed to his northern visitors was sorely tested. From the moment he had taken command of the Army of Tennessee, Hood had been trying to drive Sherman away from Atlanta. He did not succeed. A month and a half after he inaugurated his fight for Atlanta, he gave up all hope of saving the city. On September 2 Federal troops marched in. The news dealt "a stunning blow" to Davis and his advisers. "No hope," Mary Chesnut wrote. "We will try to have no fear."[44]

President Davis recognized the danger to his army and even more to his cause. Preserving Atlanta had been the psychological as well as military goal of the campaign. Davis had removed Johnston specifically because the general would not promise to defend the city. The president wanted it defended, and Hood had complied, though unsuccessfully. Atlanta's fall opened the way both to central Alabama and on to the Gulf of Mexico, as well as to central Georgia and South Carolina on to the South Atlantic coast. Davis believed he had to rally public opinion in the threatened region and show support for the Army of Tennessee and its aggressive general.

For the third time in less than two years, he decided that a western trip was essential. Accompanied by aides Francis Lubbock and G. W. C. Lee, he left Richmond by rail on September 20 for Georgia. His route took him via Charlotte and Augusta; there in order to bypass captured Atlanta he had to turn south and then back north through Macon, where he arrived unannounced early on the morning of the twenty-fourth. At stops along the way crowds, including many women, gathered at depots to see him. Observers commented on his worn, burdened look; one reflected, "poor man he pays for *his* honors." Yet Davis still spoke in firm and vigorous voice. His brief remarks always emphasized his continuing confidence in the Confederate cause and called for all able-bodied men to join the ranks. In Macon he stopped with General Cobb and gave a talk before traveling on to Hood's headquarters at Palmetto, twenty miles southwest of Atlanta.[45]

On a rainy Sunday, September 25, he reached the end of his journey. In visiting the army, he had two goals. Hoping to boost morale, he was eager to show his unflagging belief in the soldiers, and at the same time he wanted to stand publicly by his young commander. He spoke extemporaneously to Tennessee troops gathered at the station to meet him. "Be of good cheer, for within a short while your faces will be turned homeward and your feet pressing the soil of Tennessee." Although those words brought forth shouts of approval, his inspection of the army highlighted the problem he faced. The president with generals and their staffs rode by the drawn-up units, but this review did not replicate those of 1862 and 1863. This time Davis received salutes but heard no cheers. The silence did not necessarily mean that the troops had turned against their commander in chief. They had just been through weeks of hard, bloody fighting, which ended in defeat. According to reports, some were angry and a few even called for Joe Johnston; many others simply did not feel like hurrahing. Still, the reception given Davis provided a telling commentary on the condition of the army. And he was affected. One officer described him as "careworn," with a "scornful expression" on his face. The commentator thought the president and the senior commanders "all looked uneasy and apprehensive." The generals told Davis about morale problems and questioned the competence of the commanding general. Yet the president did not consider firing Hood, who had done precisely what had been expected of him. Besides, no ready replacement was at hand.[46]

In addition to dealing with the matter of esprit, Davis discussed strategy. Hood proposed to move his army into North Georgia, believing that this maneuver would draw Sherman away from Atlanta. If Sherman refused to oblige the Confederates and headed south from Atlanta, Hood would be close on his heels. A receptive Davis authorized Hood to proceed with those plans, with one alteration. Should

Sherman try to force Hood away from his communications, as they expected he would, Davis directed his general to fall back westward on Gadsden, Alabama. There he would have secure supply lines coming from the Southwest, and he would also be closer to Lieutenant General Richard Taylor, commander of the Department of Alabama and Mississippi. Davis knew he could not approve a retreat by Hood after he had removed Johnston for following such a policy. He also knew that retreat toward the Atlantic Ocean or the Gulf of Mexico could have but one result. Furthermore, he believed an advance would help morale. Aggressiveness he always preferred and in this instance considered essential, so he supported Hood.[47]

After settling the future course of the Army of Tennessee, Davis traveled on to Montgomery, where he stayed with Governor Thomas Watts, addressed the Alabama legislature, and on September 28 met with Richard Taylor. Taylor expressed surprise at Hood's offensive intentions because he thought Hood's forces too weak to undertake such a campaign. He also informed the president that he himself had insufficient resources to provide any assistance to Hood. Davis brought up the possibility of obtaining help from the Trans-Mississippi. Replying that none existed, Taylor pointed out the practical impossibility of moving large numbers of troops across the Mississippi. He went on to tell his former brother-in-law that many soldiers would refuse to come east. According to Taylor, loyalty to the Confederate government had waned considerably west of the river. Both soldiers and civilians felt that Richmond had neglected their homeland. Davis, of course, had no way to project directly the authority of the Confederate government in the Trans-Mississippi.

General Taylor was not alone in his reservations about Hood's plans. Braxton Bragg also warned Davis that Hood's weakness along with Sherman's overwhelming force made remote any chances of success, for Federal forces outnumbered the Confederates by more than two to one. Their combined opposition did not change Davis's mind, for neither did adopting a defensive stance guarantee victory.[48]

Command structure as well as strategy received Davis's attention. In this area, political considerations took primacy. The removal of Joseph Johnston had caused unrest that only intensified after the fall of Atlanta. Although Davis had no intention of sacking Hood, he did want to placate his critics and at the same time help his effort to boost public morale. He contemplated creating a new theater command, similar to the old Department of the West. This new one would be termed the Military Division of the West, with boundaries reaching from Georgia to the Mississippi and including Hood's and Richard Taylor's forces. The commander would have to be an experienced full general. Because Lee was required in Virginia, and Bragg and Johnston were impossibilities, there was only one choice—Beauregard. Davis's opinion of Beauregard had not improved, but if he wanted a grand command in the West in the autumn of 1864, he had no alternative. And he was prepared to make use of Beauregard's public reputation and popularity.[49]

Even before leaving Richmond for Georgia, Davis had this new structure and Beauregard in mind. He asked Lee about Beauregard's availability and willingness to accept a western post. Because neither Lee nor Beauregard was satisfied with the latter's difficult position in Virginia as Lee's deputy, both generals eagerly welcomed the president's suggestions. At Palmetto, Davis broached the possibility to Hood, and in Montgomery to Taylor. Both agreed. On his return to the capital, Davis met with Beauregard in Augusta. They discussed both Hood's strategy, which Davis had already approved, and Beauregard's job. Beauregard backed Hood's northern move and accepted his new assignment, commanding general of the Military Division of the West.[50]

Beauregard's orders dated October 2 made clear his authority and the character of his duties. He was authorized to establish his headquarters wherever he thought best, within the limits of his command. "Your personal presence is expected wherever in your judgment the interests of your command render it expedient," his instructions read. They also made clear that he was the commanding general. Davis certainly gave Beauregard authority to command, but Beauregard, like Joseph Johnston before him and like so many other Civil War generals, could not conceive of commanding without actually leading troops in the field. General responsibility over a geographical area or theater rather than a specific army made Beauregard uncomfortable. The instructions that "he would be without troops directly under him" and that "he was not superseding General Hood" left Beauregard unsure about his new post. But his desire to be on his own, and the president's promise of support, persuaded him to accept the assignment.[51]

The device of the Military Division of the West and the selection of Beauregard as its commanding general constituted a masterstroke. It provided advice and restraint for a young field commander. It muted public criticism after Atlanta. It resurrected an old hero to repel the invader from the southern heartland.

After his western tour, the president headed back to Virginia, with stops in Augusta and in Columbia. In Augusta he met to discuss military matters with Beauregard, Cobb, and also Hardee, whom he had reassigned from the Army of Tennessee to command the South Atlantic coast. On October 3 he also made a major speech. In spite of inclement weather, he had a substantial audience. Davis rode in a carriage from the railroad station to the nearby speaker's platform. When he stepped down from the carriage, women crowded around to get a glimpse of him, even to kiss his hand, according to a reporter. Davis then journeyed to Columbia, where he was the guest of his former aide General James Chesnut. At Chesnut's home a group of small boys came to serenade him. On the fourth, the mayor welcomed him, and he spoke to a large assembly. Afterwards, in Mary Chesnut's words, his hand was "nearly shaken off." That evening the Chesnuts, with the governor of South Carolina in attendance, provided a sumptuous dinner that belied reality and harkened back to the halcyon days of 1861— boned turkey stuffed with truffles along with stuffed tomatoes and stuffed peppers on elegant old china. A sixty-year-old Madeira accompanied this feast. When Davis departed, a wealthy Columbian provided some dozen bottles of fine wine for the president to take on the train.[52]

Finally, on October 6, after more than two weeks on the road, he got back to Richmond. As on his two previous western trips, he had made critical decisions on military policy, and in public appearances, impromptu talks, and major speeches he had toiled strenuously to rally his fellow citizens.[53]

Just before leaving Richmond for this trip, President Davis wrote two letters that highlighted themes he stressed on his western journey. On September 19 he penned a circular to six governors, from Virginia westward to Alabama, in which he preached the gospel of unity. Several states had issued proclamations requiring all aliens either to enter the army or leave the state. Pointing to the essential labor provided by foreigners in Confederate factories and workshops, Davis urged the state leaders to rethink their policies in this instance. In his view, all Confederates must join together in making their utmost contribution to the war effort. At the same time, he assured the governors he wanted no clash between the central government and state governments and would raise no issue that could lead to conflict. Unity must be the watchword. On the day before his circular went out, he requested Senator Herschel Johnson of Georgia to combine with him in striving to produce "the support of a public opinion which will drive to the army all who belong to it, and all who ought to belong to it. . . ."[54]

On his trip to and from Hood's army, in addition to a number of short talks, the president gave at least four major addresses, in which he tried to generate renewed enthusiasm for a cause that he insisted remained virtuous and was not lost. Carried in newspapers, his words reached far beyond his immediate audience. Before even reaching Hood's headquarters, he addressed a Macon meeting that had been called to discuss aid for Atlanta refugees. He also spoke in Montgomery, and on his return in Augusta and Columbia.[55]

Acknowledging the continuing importance of local identity, Davis praised each state for its participation in the war. In Macon, he called himself a son of Georgia because of his father's birth in the state and said he would never forget that Georgians had battled so valiantly. Before Alabama lawmakers, he applauded the exertions their state had made in behalf of the Confederacy. In Columbia, he expressed gratitude for all South Carolina's sacrifices during the conflict. In all of these speeches he also defended his removal of General Johnston and his opposition to Governor Brown's policies.

Davis concentrated on four major topics in these addresses. First, he regularly conceded Confederate setbacks, but always hastened to add that "our cause is not lost." The president declared the Army of Tennessee could and would strike back at the enemy, just as Lee had done in Virginia. Sherman would never be able to maintain his communications, Davis predicted. Moreover, he prophesied that the invading Federal host would meet the same fate that befell the French in Russia a half century earlier. According to this script, Sherman, like Napoleon before him, would suffer harassment and eventually destruction. On his return in speeches at Augusta and Columbia, Davis said he came away from visiting with Hood and Taylor more confident than ever. He was convinced the revived, rejuvenated Army of Tennessee would soon drive the invaders from Georgia. Speaking directly to those who were giving up on the Confederacy, Davis maintained they were simply unaware of what had been done in the army and what would be done. He assured doubters that he did not doubt the future.

In order for the army to accomplish its task most expeditiously, Davis exhorted absent soldiers to return to the ranks. His second major theme was the large number of men away from the army. Admitting that as much as two-thirds of the army's strength was absent, and most of that number absent without leave, he urged all to return promptly. He refused to dwell on reasons for absence; instead, he called on all men to meet their patriotic duty. "The man who repents and goes back to his commander voluntarily, at once appeals strongly to Executive clemency." In contrast, Davis asked where those who stayed away would shield themselves after the war, "when every man's history will be told . . . ?" He pressed all citizens to help push the absentees back to the colors.

His attempt to enlist everyone's help in repopulating the army led Davis to his third basic theme, addressed chiefly to the group he believed most influential in this critical endeavor: women. Praising them for being "like the Spartan mothers of old," he celebrated their "sacrifices which, if written, would be surpassed by nothing in history." In the war, they had performed their great duty. "You have given up all. You have sent your husbands, your fathers, your sons to the army. . . ." Moreover, these wives, daughters, and mothers had "buoy[ed] up the hearts of the people."

But now, Davis proclaimed, "you must do more." He said Confederate women "must use your influence to send all to the front, and form a public opinion that shall make the skulker a marked man, and leave him no house wherein he can shelter." Davis even incorporated romance. "And with all sincerity, I say to my young friends here, if you want the right man for a husband, take him whose armless sleeve and noble heart betoken the duties he has rendered to his country, rather than he who has never shared the toils, or borne the danger of the field."

From the letters that crossed his desk, the president knew that many mothers and wives wanted their men back home to provide sustenance and protection. In numerous areas of the Confederacy, invasion and conquest by Union forces had broken down the normal social and economic order. The president also knew that pleas from women affected the troops—whether or not he or his commanders granted leaves or resignations. The desertion rate gave indisputable proof that their women's entreaties moved soldiers to leave their units for home. In these speeches, he attempted to convince women that their ultimate safety depended upon the defeat of the enemy. Given this reality, he told them they must stand stalwart until their men could accomplish their crucial mission. He pleaded with them not to establish safe havens away from the battle lines.

Davis's final point underscored precisely why the return of the absent soldiers was so critical. He asserted that only battlefield victory would guarantee Confederate success. Declaring the war not a revolution but a struggle of "a free and independent people" to protect their rights by creating "a better government when they saw fit," he announced independence the only Confederate hope. He had striven for peace, he professed, but to no avail, for all his efforts had been rebuffed. He demanded the independence of the Confederate States, and Abraham Lincoln absolutely refused this condition for ending the war. Thus, military triumph was essential. To secure this imperative purpose, Davis defended his administration's legislative program. "We are fighting for existence," and that struggle, he averred, demanded war measures. Even though he could not predict "how many sacrifices it may take," he again expressed no doubt about the final outcome. In his mind, all Confederates comprehended the enormity of the stakes. Moreover, "I believe that a just God looks upon our cause as holy, and that of our enemy as iniquitous." Harking back to Old Testament prophets and centuries of Christian sermons, Davis declared that God "may chastise us for our offences, but in so doing He is preparing us, and in His good Providence will assist us, and never desert the right."

Back in Richmond, the president received word that his arduous labors had been productive, at least in part. It was far too early to know whether men were returning to the army, but the public seemed to respond. Before going, Davis had been condemned publicly and privately for "indulg[ing]" his "pitiful personal feelings" in making policy. Accusations of "unworthy motives" prompting presidential actions spouted from his opponents. In contrast, both Georgia senators hailed Davis's effort. "Your visit to Georgia has been decidedly beneficial," wrote Senator Johnson, who said the presidential presence helped "heal the heart burnings." Senator Hill concurred: "the spirit of the people has evidently improved." Echoing this assessment, the editor of a Macon newspaper especially cheered Beauregard's appointment because it would enable friends of the administration to refute charges "that you are implacable in your resentments and know not how to forgive." Even those troubled by Davis's stalwart oratorical defense of himself found continuing personal attacks even more disquieting. According to this view, public morale, the "last great element of defense," depended at least partially upon faith in the president. Davis's trip also sparked a meeting of several governors in Augusta.

These chief executives came together and passed resolutions entreating all Confederates to reunite zealously behind the war effort.[56]

Despite such heartening statements and actions, Davis's most inveterate foes held fast to their implacable opposition and different vision. Yet, as before, extremism and enduring divisiveness undercut their ability to make headway. The most potent unit, the Brown-Stephens combine, advocated a convention of states that would negotiate peace, perhaps with reunion, a tactic generally known as reconstruction. A handful of congressmen and Holden districts in North Carolina joined in. But all to no avail. A public letter from one congressman generated no enthusiasm. In North Carolina, fervor for peace went down with Holden. Governor Brown could not even persuade his own legislature to stand with him. For most Confederates, talk of giving up independence went too far. The *Richmond Examiner,* which regularly excoriated the president, spoke for them when it denounced Brown and his proposal for reconstruction. Even in the fall of 1864, the overwhelming majority of Confederates, including officeholders on both state and national levels, still stood stalwart for independence. No serious competitor had risen to challenge the president.[57]

Although Davis remained adamant against any kind of separate state action and utterly opposed any negotiating terms that did not make independence a sine qua non, he demonstrated a willingness to try different approaches to reach his goal. As the presidential election of 1864 approached in the United States, numerous Confederates hoped for a Democratic victory over Abraham Lincoln that would result in ending the war. Lincoln worried they were right. Confederates wanted to do all they could to help all opponents of Lincoln. Davis doubted that his government could have much impact except through steadfastness on the battlefield. He wrote Governor Vance that he foresaw no change in Federal policy "until the enemy is beaten out of his vain confidence in our subjugation." Yet he had been told that significant numbers of antiwar and anti-Lincoln northerners, especially in the Middle West, were eager for peace, even if it meant Confederate independence.[58]

Word of this latent fifth column came to the president from several different sources. In the late spring of 1863 Clement L. Vallandigham, a major Democratic figure in Ohio, whom Lincoln had banished from the United States for antiwar activities, showed up in Richmond touting himself as a leader of forces who wanted Lincoln defeated and the war ended. He talked with civilian and military officials, though not directly with the president. Later that year, Confederate prisoners of war who escaped from confinement in Ohio claimed the Confederacy could make positive use of restive northerners. In March 1864 a Missouri Confederate traveled to Richmond and claimed to Davis that 490,000 men in states from New York to Iowa, but mostly in the Middle West, stood ready to aid the Confederacy and were prepared to challenge the Lincoln administration, by force if necessary.[59]

Davis was persuaded to help his alleged allies in the North. He hoped for "the adoption of some action that might influence popular sentiment in the hostile section." In February 1864 the Congress appropriated $5 million to fund clandestine enterprises. It was decided to mount this campaign of subversion from Canada, where Confederate agents could more easily meet with antiwar activists and Confederate sympathizers. In April the president appointed Clement C. Clay, Jr., of Alabama and Jacob Thompson of Mississippi to oversee the operation. Davis had long known each man, and Clay had been a particular friend, though the friendship had recently been buffeted by political disagreement and misunderstanding. Equally important, because of previous public service in the 1850s—Clay in the United States Senate and Thompson in the House and in James Buchanan's cabinet—both were well known among northern Democrats. Neither was eager for the assignment, but convictions about duty and the promise of presidential support gained acceptance from both. Given oral instructions by the president, they ran the blockade from Wilmington, reached Bermuda, and journeyed on to Canada. Thompson carried $1 million in specie with him.[60]

Clay and Thompson engaged in an amazing variety of ventures. A major goal was to funnel financial aid to Lincoln opponents who would take an active role in stirring up antiwar sentiment. There was talk of a massive uprising in the summer and of disrupting the Democratic convention to be held in Chicago. The Confederates plotted to liberate captured soldiers from prison camps on Lake Erie and near Chicago and to destroy military property. Men who schemed to burn New York City also received money.

Clay and an associate even met with the influential Republican editor of the *New York Tribune*, Horace Greeley, who wanted to talk about peace. Greeley was accompanied by one of Lincoln's private secretaries. Although Clay and Thompson had no authority to negotiate any peace, they did hope for a propaganda success by placing blame on the

United States for preventing peace by demanding unacceptable terms. There was no chance for any consequential outcome, for Lincoln had told Greeley he would listen to talk of peace only when it included restoration of the Union and the destruction of slavery—the exact opposites of Davis's conditions.

Although the Confederate mission lasted into 1865, it produced few positive results. Clay and Thompson reported that something always went wrong to disrupt their plans. Yet, aside from things going wrong, they confronted two insuperable obstacles. First, the number of northerners ready to take an active part in stopping the war had been greatly exaggerated. Second, Union military triumphs, especially at Atlanta and in the Shenandoah Valley, where during September and October Jubal Early's small army was decimated, stifled opposition to the war. Then Lincoln's reelection in November made unmistakably clear that the United States would not relent in its war against the Confederate States.

The secret war waged by the Confederates had another dimension. There were schemes to kidnap Lincoln and other high Union officials. They received a boost following an unsuccessful cavalry raid on Richmond in the late winter of 1864. Confederates discovered papers on the body of a Federal colonel killed in the fighting declaring that the goals of the raiders included burning the city and killing Davis and cabinet members. When Davis turned these documents over to the press, their publication caused a great outcry among Confederates. For Davis, the purported aims of burning and killing fit his characterization of his enemy as inhuman and murderous. He later termed them "infamous instructions." When sent copies, high-ranking Union officers completely disavowed them, and they could not be tied to Lincoln. Still, Confederates clearly believed them genuine. Even today scholars disagree on the authenticity of the papers.[61]

The existence of Confederate plots to abduct Lincoln and others cannot be doubted, but connecting them directly to President Davis is much more difficult. He certainly knew about the machinations of Clay and Thompson and about other efforts, chiefly in Maryland, to free Confederate prisoners of war and recruit for the army. Yet he consistently denied authorizing any kidnapping, which he said would end in killing because he claimed he did not believe Lincoln could be captured unharmed. He also turned aside other schemes he defined as criminal, such as a proposal to send ships into northern ports loaded with infected blankets, beds, and other items to introduce yellow fever and smallpox into the population. Nor did any other responsible Confederate official ever cite Davis's involvement in any such intrigues. Even so, modern historians have built a strong circumstantial case in which Davis sanctions attempts to kidnap Lincoln. Davis's immersion in detail and his awareness of all aspects of Confederate military operations lend credence to the argument that he would have known about and authorized abduction attempts. Still, no documentary evidence has come to light which proves his involvement.[62]

Although Davis's clandestine war sputtered, the strategy he had approved for the Army of Tennessee functioned as designed. Even before Beauregard reached the army, Hood had started for northern Georgia. Receiving word that the Confederates had advanced north of the Chattahoochee River, Sherman moved out of Atlanta to find Hood. For the better part of a month, the two armies played a cat-and-mouse game in northwestern Georgia and northeastern Alabama. Neither commander enjoyed this contest. Although Hood had accomplished his purpose of drawing Sherman out of Atlanta, no battle had occurred. Sherman, who had promised to pummel Hood, chafed at the futility of the chase. To Sherman, with his army some sixty miles behind Hood, the possibilities in a march through central Georgia contrasted vividly with the fruitless pursuit of Hood.[63]

While Sherman thought of Savannah, Hood had visions of Confederate divisions in Tennessee. The strategy decided on by Hood and Davis at Palmetto and agreed to by Beauregard at Augusta permitted an offensive campaign only so long as Sherman dutifully followed. Should he turn back to Atlanta and strike for the sea, then Hood was to become the hunter. Hood's new plan dropped that contingency. The Army of Tennessee would forget about Sherman and invade Tennessee.

Hood conveyed his intentions to Beauregard at Gadsden, Alabama, on October 20. Initially Beauregard exhibited little enthusiasm, but after two days of discussion he altered his opinion, even indicating some excitement about the plan. He authorized Hood to go forward into Tennessee and urged on his subordinate the absolute necessity for speed. Hood had to get into middle Tennessee before the Federals were ready for him. His decision made, Beauregard informed the War Department and the president of the change in operations. Hood in a message to Davis also made clear that his offensive was no longer tied to Sherman's location. No directive came from either the department or the commander in chief countermanding Hood's invasion.[64]

After a series of alterations in his plan, Hood arrived in Tuscumbia, in northwestern Alabama on the Tennessee River, the place he and Beauregard had finally agreed upon as a jumping-off point for the thrust into Tennessee. But Hood failed to heed Beauregard's admonition to make haste and get into Tennessee as quickly as possible; instead, Hood stayed for three weeks in Tuscumbia. The dashing, even impetuous Hood sat down. Not until November 21 did he advance into Tennessee. The reasons for this delay have never been convincingly explained, though they surely included increasingly fractious relations between Beauregard and Hood, logistical difficulties, and changes in Hood's confidence and emotional state.

The three-week halt certainly diminished Hood's chances for success. While he trooped between Gadsden and Tuscumbia, Sherman turned back to Atlanta and began the march to the sea. He placed Major General George H. Thomas, with 30,000 men from his own army to be reinforced by additional units, in charge of defending Tennessee; but Thomas did not begin getting his troops positioned until November 4. Disarray pervaded Federal concentration efforts to such an extent that when Hood finally did get underway, he came close to cutting off and isolating from Thomas a sizable portion of his force.

Hood's Tennessee campaign was crucial for Jefferson Davis and the Confederacy—and Davis knew it. He understood that giving Hood command of the Army of Tennessee involved risk. He did so because he saw no other way to obtain what he believed necessary, a battlefield victory. In the autumn of 1864 he backed Hood all the way. He did not cancel Beauregard's authorization. Before Hood left Tuscumbia, he wrote a long, rambling letter expressing the hope that his general might beat the Federals in detail and "advance to the Ohio River." To Beauregard he spoke of Hood's "reach[ing] the country proper of the enemy" from where he could "change the plans for Sherman's or Grant's campaigns."[65]

While Hood marched in place at Tuscumbia and Davis in Richmond waited on Hood to move, the Second Confederate Congress convened for its second session on November 7. On that day the president submitted his message, which contained much of the same spirit that characterized its predecessors. To the world, Davis still expressed optimism about Confederate prospects, though he did concede that the lawmakers were gathered during "a time of such public exigency."

The military situation occupied his attention. Acknowledging the fall of Atlanta, he discounted its importance by claiming that the enemy had gained no significant advantage from its capture. He emphasized the progress he found on his side. From the Trans-Mississippi, where Confederate arms had won victories in every state, to Virginia, where districts previously occupied by Federals were now in Confederate hands, the fortunes of the Confederacy had improved. These improvements included retaking portions of Alabama, Mississippi, and Tennessee. Even the most powerful Federal army, unable to have its way, was still at bay at Petersburg.

Moving away from geographic reporting, Davis asserted that ultimate Confederate triumph did not depend upon holding any specific area or place, even Richmond. In his view, "the indomitable valor of its troops" and "the unquenchable spirit of its people" controlled the outcome of the war, in which the Confederacy would surely prevail. "There is no military success of the enemy which can accomplish its destruction," he declared. In this sense Davis reified the Confederacy; it became more idea than physical space, or even a government.

Part of the message dealt with foreign affairs and finances. Davis once again condemned European powers for not recognizing the legitimacy of the Confederate States, which in his opinion the proper reading of international law required. As for finances, he gave a bifurcated accounting. Pointing to the report of the secretary of the treasury, he pronounced the national budget sound, with the public debt capable of redemption. What Davis termed "the chief difficulty" on the financial front resulted from the depreciation of treasury notes. Yet he said that appropriate taxation strategies, which the secretary had outlined, could remedy the harmful situation. The horrors of runaway inflation were not mentioned.

Although not completely forthcoming on the deleterious financial situation, which he did not totally comprehend, Davis fully understood the manpower crisis in his armies. He focused on two areas. He wanted the exemption law tightened so that "no pursuit or position should relieve any one who is able to do active duty from enrollment in the Army, unless his functions or services are more useful to the defense of his country in another sphere." Entire classes of men, he argued, could not be exempt. He requested additional authority for the War Department to regulate exemption and to curb abuses.

The president devoted considerable space to the relationship of slaves to Confederate military performance. Regretfully, he informed Congress that its law of February 1864 providing for the impressment of 20,000 slaves to serve as teamsters, cooks, and laborers had not worked; it was too restrictive on tasks slaves were allowed to perform. He asked for twice as many slaves, with extended duties.

He went further. He underscored that the slave bore two relationships to the state, as property and as person—a condition that had obtained through the history of slavery in the South. Davis noted that because the impressed slaves required training and encountered hazard, their duties "demand[ed] loyalty and zeal." Those attributes, he said, involved person more than property. Accordingly, he thought it appropriate that the government should "acquire for the public service the entire property in the labor of the slave, and to pay therefor due compensation rather than to impress his labor for short terms." That procedure would eliminate the division between person and property caused by impressment; those two dimensions would be combined in government ownership just as in any private slaveowner. Moreover, Davis suggested that Congress might want to consider manumission for "zealous discharge of duty" and "faithful service." Should Congress reach that conclusion, Davis said he stood ready to support it.

Although willing to propose state ownership of slaves and to suggest the possibility of their eventual emancipation, Davis was unwilling at this moment to utilize slaves as soldiers. Until the white population proved insufficient to man the armies, he did not think it wise to arm slaves and make them combat soldiers. Yet, even in taking this position, he made his priorities dramatically clear. "But should the alternative ever be presented of subjugation or of the employment of the slave as a soldier, there seems to be no reason to doubt what should then be our decision." This potential choice he still called an "improbable contingency," however.

After public discussion of a topic unthinkable in 1861, Davis concluded his message with a hope and a declaration. He trusted that what he saw as a "fast-growing" desire for peace among the northern people would influence the Lincoln administration to end the war. But no matter what the United States did or did not do, the Confederate States would never submit. "In the hope that the day will soon be reached when under Divine favor these States may be allowed to enter on their former peaceful pursuits and to develop the abundant natural resources with which they are blessed, let us, then, resolutely continue to devote our united and unimpaired energies to the defense of our homes, our lives, and our liberties."[66]

Despite Davis's courageous words, the outcome of Hood's Tennessee campaign struck a mighty blow against his cherished independence. Hood never came close to the enemy homeland. Because of mismanagement, lack of planning, and horrendous judgment Hood squandered whatever chance he had had of succeeding. Eight days into the campaign, through both ineptness and plain bad luck, he missed a marvelous opportunity to isolate and defeat a major Federal column. The next day, November 30, at Franklin he flung his brave men in a furious frontal assault against a strong Federal position. It was a bloodbath; the Army of Tennessee lost one-fourth of its strength, including six generals killed. The wounded army trudged on to Nashville, where two weeks later General Thomas, by then outnumbering Hood by more than three to one, battered the once proud Army of Tennessee. The crippled remnant, fewer than 20,000 men, limped southward, reached the Tennessee River by Christmas, and retreated through northwestern Alabama into Mississippi.

After the war Jefferson Davis tried to exempt himself from complicity in Hood's project. Calling the invasion "ill-advised," he claimed in his memoirs he had no knowledge until after the fact that Hood had decided not to follow Sherman. He even denied Hood's fatherhood of the plan and insisted that Beauregard forced it on Hood. But the contemporary documents leave no doubt that Davis knew from the beginning what Hood was about. He hoped, as did his two generals, that Hood would succeed in Tennessee. He hoped that Sherman would be compelled to leave Georgia. He hoped the invasion of Tennessee would lead to victory that would rejuvenate the Confederate military effort in the West.[67]

Approving Hood's offensive, he gambled again, just as when he appointed Hood army commander. This time the stakes were even higher than before Atlanta because conditions were more desperate. The evidence from the Atlanta campaign gave no indication that the Army of Tennessee could do more than delay for brief moments Sherman's inexorable advance. But a resounding win in Tennessee might have made a substantial difference.

While Hood wrecked his army in Tennessee, Sherman marched triumphantly to the sea. Even before Hood started into Tennessee, Sherman on November 16 set out from Atlanta to make good on his promise to make Georgia howl. Unsure of his target, Confederate commanders were unwilling to concentrate the meager forces they had. Never facing substantial opposition, Sherman moved quickly through the basically undefended Georgia countryside. Five days before Hood's catastrophe at Nashville, Sherman's army arrived before Savannah. As the suffering survivors of Franklin and Nashville struggled to reach the Tennessee River and safety, Sherman occupied Savannah on December 21; now the eastern Confederacy had been halved. In the Confederate West, November and December had been disastrous for Jefferson Davis and his cause.[68]

Worry and growing concern reached into the Executive Mansion, where Varina shared with a close friend the emotional toll these desperate times were taking on her and her husband. Just after Jefferson's return from his western trip, she informed Mary Chesnut in South Carolina, "We are in a sad and anxious state here." Repeating herself with emphasis in the same letter, she confided, "Strictly between us, *things look* very anxious *here.*" Varina said she could not read and spoke of being "so constantly depressed" that she dreaded writing. She sewed constantly and never stopped her household duties. She reported her husband "extremely well—for him—but very anxious." Fully understanding the crucial nature of Hood's campaign, she wrote on November 20, "Affairs west are looking so critical now that before you receive this you and I will be in the depths or else triumphant." There was no triumph, only ever-deepening depths.[69]

The increasing vexations of daily life underscored the bleakness. The exorbitant cost of provisions affected the Davises, who had to purchase food and supplies like any other citizens. Although Varina admitted that the deprivations suffered by the first family did not match those of most people, it by no means escaped the exponentially exploding prices and the severe shortages. By the summer and fall of 1864, the cost of basic items had passed beyond exorbitant but kept spiraling upward—bacon $9 a pound, Irish potatoes $25 a bushel, chickens $30 a pair, milk $4 a quart, whole ham $7 a pound, baby shoes $20 a pair, wood $50 per cord. Varina contemplated selling some fine material to obtain money. She also sent her horses to be sold, though the next day they were returned, bought for her by anonymous friends. Still, she feared she could not provide food for them. The president had already sold all the horses he could spare. The basic diet at the White House consisted of rice, cornmeal, and what an aide called the "plainest and scantiest of fare." Meat was served only a few times a week. Varina recorded that the meager table was not her choice, but what she could find and afford.[70]

In the midst of this cheerless time, the first lady still found delight in her children. To Mary Chesnut, she lovingly recounted their looks and activities. Baby Varina Anne, nicknamed "Piecake," she treasured as "exquisite." "In pink she looks like a little rosebud." She described her oldest, Maggie, now almost ten, as "so soft, so good, and so very *lady-like*." Jeff Jr., who would be eight in January, had picked up all sorts of habits at school such as "antics and astounding tricks with strings and bows and arrows," and "seem[ed] in a fair way to graduate in down street dialect."[71]

As 1864 drew to a close, Varina Davis strove to bring enchantment into her house. Despite immense difficulties, she orchestrated with the help of friends a pageant of joy in which for a brief moment reality was suspended. Upon learning that the orphans in the Episcopal Home had been promised a Christmas tree, she included them in her plans. She was determined that no one would be disappointed. For the orphans she oversaw the collection and refurbishment of old toys. Rag dolls, for example, were cleaned and plumped out, with their faces painted and beads used for eyes. On Christmas Eve around twenty young people gathered at the White House to prepare the presents and string apples and popcorn for the tree. The completion of those tasks was the signal to bring out the eggnog, with homemade gingersnaps and lady cake. She permitted her own children to stay up and participate in the festivities. When the little ones had gone to bed, the stockings were stuffed—molasses candy, apples, an orange, a pair of woolen gloves, small whips plaited by the family with colored crackers, and balls of tightly wound rags covered with old kid gloves. During the night, the president had cake sent out to the White House guards.

The holiday spirit reigned on Christmas Day. The children rose early to see their surprises. Each servant was handed a small gift. Jefferson received from his children loving letters which their Grandmother Howell had helped them write. Presents for the president and his wife came from devoted friends and followers: for him, a pair of chamois-skin riding gauntlets embroidered on the back; for her, six cakes of "delicious soap" made from ham grease, and some fine linen thread. After breakfast the family walked to St. Paul's for services. Following church the Davises returned to a spectacular Christmas dinner, with turkey, roast beef, and mince pie, along with a delight for the little Davises, a life-sized spun sugar hen on a nest of blancmange eggs.

The evening had its own festivities. At 8 p.m., all returned to St. Paul's for the orphans' Christmas party. The appearance of presents created great excitement. The president began to help pass them out, but in his enthusiasm put too much into outstretched little hands. Thus, according to Varina, he was reassigned to rescue tots who had become entangled in strings of popcorn. After the memorable celebration, the holiday closed with a dance at a neighbor's house, but without refreshments. Guests enjoyed what Varina designated a " 'starvation party.' "72

The next day reality returned. Although no official reports of Nashville had been received, news and rumors were filtering in. The *Richmond Examiner* announced what many felt; the year ended on a blacker note than anyone had thought possible.73

CHAPTER FIFTEEN

"The Issue Is . . .
Very Painful for Me to Meet"

No glittering social events marked New Year's Day 1865 in Richmond, a cold clear Sunday with snow on the ground. Wearing a woolen cap, Jefferson Davis attended church, but the president and first lady hosted no reception at the Executive Mansion. Throughout the Confederacy, despondency and even despair greeted the turn of the year.[1]

President Davis could have no doubt about conditions in his country and their impact on his position and his leadership. Friends and supporters reaffirmed their continued loyalty to the cause and to him, but they also warned of general unrest and war weariness among the people. These were not scare tactics. As the loyal Howell Cobb wrote, "It is due you to know the state of feeling in the country." Cobb, the veteran politician, went on to inform Davis, "It is useless to disguise the fact that there is a deep despondency in the public mind—extending in too many instances to disaffection." There were even reports that stridently anti-Davis men like Senator Wigfall were scheming to take power from him.[2]

In Richmond, political actions spoke volumes. On January 17 the Virginia legislature unanimously passed a secret resolution demanding the appointment of Robert E. Lee to command all Confederate armies. Although the lawmakers tacked on generous sentiments about Davis, they made clear they wanted a new hand directing the war. The next day they called for the entire cabinet to resign. In the Congress, with the enthusiastic championship of Vice President Stephens, opponents of the president and his policy worked actively to present peace resolutions, calls for state conventions, and generally to condemn the president's policies.[3]

On the battle lines the outlook became only grimmer and grimmer. On January 15, Fort Fisher, the bastion guarding the ocean approach to Wilmington, North Carolina, fell, closing the last port open to blockade-runners. The news had a "stunning effect" in Richmond. A distraught President Davis called the loss "unexpected" and immediately wired the Confederate commander to find out whether the fortress could be retaken. Within a week Sherman began his invasion of South Carolina. Facing no more opposition than in Georgia, the blue legions moved easily through the state. By the middle of February they had forced the evacuation of Charleston and captured Columbia, much of which went up in flames. The major Confederate western front now moved toward North Carolina, where only a pitiful remnant of the Army of Tennessee stood in the path of Sherman's triumphant divisions. At Petersburg the gray lines became feebler and feebler as an overwhelmingly outmanned Lee stretched his men perilously thin to keep pace with Grant's southwestward extension around the city.[4]

President Davis fully understood the grave conditions confronting his country and his presidency. A visiting Confederate admiral judged him "deeply impressed with the critical state of the country." On January 8 Davis stated to a sister that he was facing "bitter trials," including constant anxiety caused by the proximity of the Federal hosts. Two weeks later he had a private conversation with a leading Virginia public figure in which he acknowledged the widespread "despondency and distrust." He was even reported to have said that some kind of revolution could occur. To overcome these dangerous attitudes, he expressed a willingness to take any action that would help. Varina underscored the atmosphere of crisis surrounding her husband and herself when she confided to a longtime friend that "ours have been the carking cares of poverty, and danger, always pressing upon us even in sleep."[5]

Although Davis comprehended the gravity of the crisis gripping the Confederacy, even admitting the terrible effect of the "long and severe pressure" inflicted upon the population by a relentless war, he still blamed "malcontents." They had seized upon the situation and "created a feeling hostile to the execution of the rigorous laws which were necessary to raise and feed our armies, then magnifying every reverse and prophesying ruin they have produced public depression and sown the seeds of disintegration." As always, Davis had difficulty coping with the abundant evidence that not all Confederates shared his utter commitment to the Confederate cause. He could not contemplate failure. Varina certainly spoke his mind in saying that "everything also even to extermination we expect to bear unless the liberty for which we began it is granted to us." "The foundations of our political life," she continued, "are laid deep in the blood of our nearest and dearest. I am sure it has not been shed in vain."[6]

Davis's commitment and determination never wavered in these trying times. He continued to express the belief that his side, the right, would prevail. In conversations with members of Congress and others he continued to evince confidence in the Confederate cause. In a public address before thousands in early February he spoke in ringing terms that sounded more like 1862 than 1865. Applauding a people "plucking from adversity new courage and resolution," he told the crowd that "his heart beat high with hope." Battlefield success still represented the best chance for peace and independence, and, as he had been doing for months, he called on absentees from the army to return to duty. When that took place, he had no doubt that Confederate victories would follow.

His own loyalty he made absolutely clear. "His life was bound up with the Confederacy," he announced. "With the Confederacy he would live or die." He thanked God that "he represented a people too proud to eat the leek or bow the neck to mortal man." Davis's closing combined a cry for unity with unbridled optimism: "Let us unite our hands and hearts, lock our shields together, and we may well believe that before the next summer solstice falls upon us, it will be the enemy who will be asking us for conferences and occasions in which to make our demands."[7]

During this fourth winter of the war President Davis dealt with three major policy matters, all aimed at securing independence for his country and all revealing his absolute commitment to his understanding of the Confederate cause. Even in this bleak moment no other politician had risen to challenge Davis's leadership. Yet there was another Confederate who enjoyed greater popularity and who commanded universal respect: Robert E. Lee. By 1864 he had become a national hero, the selfless and valiant patriot. Lee was without question his nation's most successful soldier, a general who had so often won stirring victories against tremendous odds. To many beleaguered southerners Lee was the only person who could overcome the seemingly insuperable difficulties pressing upon the Confederacy. As one official confided to his diary, "Nearly all desire to see Lee at the head of affairs."[8]

Mounting criticism of Davis's direction of the war accompanied the cheering of Lee. In the aftermath of Hood's defeat and Sherman's march through Georgia, Davis became an inviting target. He had erred in removing Joseph Johnston; he had mismanaged the western war; he had interfered with generals in the field. The bitterly hostile *Richmond Examiner* claimed it had discovered the source of the Confederacy's troubles way back in the Mexican War: "For the horns of this V are not like the horns of a dilemma; one of which you can always choose to be impaled upon; but he gores us with both horns like a bull."[9]

Although wild talk was heard about a military dictatorship, attention centered on giving Lee more authority over military affairs. The Virginia legislature called for his elevation to supreme command. In Congress, House and Senate secretly passed a joint resolution asking for Lee to be made general in chief. In the midst of these unmistakable strictures on his direction of the war, Davis remained calm. The possibility of promoting Lee did not distress him; he had previously offered Lee wider responsibilities in addition to the Army of Northern Virginia, which the general had declined. Even so, the president had continuously utilized Lee as a military adviser on questions far beyond Virginia. Still, Davis zealously guarded his executive authority and prerogatives.[10]

Finally, the president and Congress worked out a solution. Congress passed a bill creating the position of general in chief, which Davis signed. On February 6 he named Lee to the post. In appointing Lee, Davis wrote him, "the honor designed to be bestowed has been so fully won, that the fact of conferring it can add nothing to your fame." Accepting the appointment, Lee remained the deferential subordinate. "I know I am indebted entirely to your indulgence and kind consideration for this honorable position." He certainly still recognized Davis as commander in chief. The messages the two men exchanged on the promotion did not portend any change in their relationship, either personal or professional. And none occurred.[11]

Even before the decision to have a commanding general of all Confederate armies, Jefferson Davis had become involved in two major diplomatic efforts, one directed toward Europe that he initiated, the other with the United States which he accepted. Each signaled the perilous conditions of Confederate fortunes, but simultaneously dramatized Davis's unshakable faith in his nation.

In January, President Davis became engaged in another attempt to discuss peace with the United States. This effort originated with Francis Preston Blair, Sr., a Kentucky native and notable old Jacksonian. In late 1864 Blair came up with a scheme to end the fighting and hasten reconciliation between the South and the North—the two sections would join together and attack the French in Mexico. He took his plan to President Lincoln and desired to present it to Davis. Lincoln wanted nothing to do with any foreign military action, but agreed to permit Blair to go to Richmond and see what transpired.

On January 12, 1865, Blair arrived in the Confederate capital. His visit was kept secret, though rumors of his presence and its meaning swirled about. When they saw each other, Blair and Davis renewed their prewar friendship before turning to the real purpose of their meeting. Blair asserted that with the war over slavery practically finished, his goal was to reunify the country as quickly as possible. He worried that if the conflict continued, the huge armies employed by both sides would eventually threaten democracy. He could even envision monarchy because foreign powers might pick apart an exhausted America. To preclude these dire possibilities, Blair prescribed a foreign war to restore national harmony. He said that Davis, if he chose, could move west and lead the southern forces from Texas.

In response, according to Blair, the Confederate president was quite receptive to the idea of ending the war. Davis pointed out that more than once he had tried for peace talks. But he thought the reestablishment of sectional accord would necessitate the passage of some time. He did agree that a joint military venture to defend shared values would help the process, though he had doubts about actually mounting one. If the Lincoln administration was serious about peace, Davis said he would either send delegates to Washington or receive a Union delegation in Richmond. Still, he expressed grave reservations about Secretary of State William Henry Seward, whom he declared he would not trust in negotiations. Davis believed that back in 1861 Seward had been duplicitous in his dealings with the Confederate emissaries in Washington. Acknowledging that he did not know Lincoln, Davis requested Blair's opinion. Blair described the Union leader as a fair, honest man; Davis replied that this positive assessment satisfied him.

Blair returned to Washington carrying a letter to Lincoln in which Davis wrote that if Lincoln would promise to receive Confederate agents, he would promptly make the necessary appointments and "renew the effort to enter into a conference with a view to secure peace to the two countries." Lincoln would have nothing to do with talk of "two countries." He prepared a reply in which he instructed Blair to tell Davis that he would receive any person Davis may "informally send me, with a view of securing peace to the people of our common country." On the twenty-first Blair delivered Lincoln's response to Davis.

In this proposed conference Davis perceived an opportunity to silence critics who faulted him for not pursuing peace more vigorously. Davis had not altered his opinion that Lincoln would require terms including the end of slavery and the restoration of the Union. Perhaps he was wrong, and if so, he would welcome an end to hostilities. On the other hand, if the result turned out as he expected, it could only help Davis and his cause. If the talks made clear that Lincoln demanded the equivalent of unconditional surrender, his detractors would be quieted, for at this point most were unwilling to give up the Confederacy. Even the *Richmond Examiner* proclaimed peace on those terms "impossible." Active in Congress on the peace issue, Senator William A. Graham of North Carolina spoke for many like-minded politicians when he admitted the South was weary of war and surely wanted it over, but concluded that giving up "a great Government" run by men chosen to maintain it would be enormously difficult.

Having decided to participate in a conference, President Davis had now to select his envoys. To help make his decision he took the unusual step of talking with Vice President Stephens, who was in Richmond for the congressional session, and he also brought the matter before his cabinet. All thought Assistant Secretary of War John A. Campbell a good choice. He had been an associate justice of the United States Supreme Court and in 1861 had acted as liaison between the Confederate mission in Washington and Seward. After discussion Davis named two others: Robert M. T. Hunter, his former secretary of state and subsequently a member of the Confederate Senate, where he backed the administration and served on the Foreign Relations Committee; and Vice President Stephens. Initially Davis resisted appointing Stephens, for several months now a vocal opponent of the administration; but he was persuaded by arguments that the vice president, who was well known in the North, was an especially appropriate choice and that anti-administration forces would try to exploit the omission of Stephens, an articulate advocate of peace talks. In the end, Davis made politically astute as well as able choices for his commission.

On January 29 the three men left Richmond for Petersburg and the Federal lines. They hoped to be allowed to pass through and go on to Washington. Although the president announced their departure on a peace mission, his instructions made success almost impossible in the way they spelled out the commission's assignment: "an informal conference with [Lincoln's representatives] upon the issues involved in the existing war, and for the purpose of securing peace to the two countries." Lincoln had never countenanced any language including the concept of "two countries," as Davis well knew. Judah Benjamin, who drafted the directive, tried to gloss over the point, but Davis put in "two countries." Those words caused a delay at General Grant's headquarters, with urgent messages to and from Washington before the Confederates were allowed to proceed. They went aboard a Union vessel and on down the James River, but not to Washington. They stopped at Fortress Monroe, where Secretary Seward awaited them along with President Lincoln, who at the last minute had decided to participate personally.

On February 3 the five men actually met on Lincoln's steamer. Their discussion would become known as the Hampton Roads Conference. They decided on an informal session with no documents read and no notes taken; there were also no aides, only one steward. After brief pleasantries, the serious talk began. Leading for the Confederates and making no mention of "two countries," Stephens asked if a way existed to stop the war. Lincoln responded that he knew of only one way: end the rebellion. Stephens then pushed the possibility of a Mexican action. His colleagues also brought up the issue of an armistice during which negotiations could proceed. Lincoln quickly brought reality to the Confederates. There would be no joint Mexican venture and no armistice. Hostilities would cease only when those rebelling against lawful authority quit the struggle and returned to the Union. In addition, all executive decisions regarding slavery would remain intact. Seward then informed the commissioners about the Thirteenth Amendment prohibiting slavery, recently sent to the states for ratification. In Stephens's account, Lincoln talked about giving additional time to the southern states to ratify and about compensation for slaves. Although historians do not agree on whether Lincoln made such an offer, none disputes his fundamental requirement for peace: the dissolution of the Confederate States of America.

Their mission a complete failure, the three commissioners returned to Richmond. They gave the president a written report. Although they declined the president's request that they include an assessment of the conference, their recital of events left no doubt about the position of the United States. Making sure the newspapers had the report, Davis passed it along with all pertinent correspondence to Congress. In his covering message, he did not hesitate to make judgments. The enemy, he pointed out, declined to negotiate with the Confederate States. Furthermore, he continued, our opponent refused "to give to our people any other terms or guaranties than those which the conqueror may grant, or to permit us to have on any other basis than our unconditional submission to their rule. . . ."[12]

The public reacted as Davis both desired and anticipated. Denouncing such terms, one editor stormed, echoing Patrick Henry, "Forbid it, Almighty God! Now, let us cease all bickering, and strike for life and liberty." Another discovered "new life . . . visible everywhere." Senator Benjamin Hill informed the president that the outcome at Hampton Roads had revived the war spirit in Georgia. Calling Davis's handling of the matter "the most admirable master stroke," Hill chortled at the discomfiture of Stephens and Governor Brown and opined that many absentees would now return to the army. In Richmond on February 6 Virginia governor William Smith called a public meeting to reaffirm Confederate loyalty. Three days later an even more impressive affair took place. A band led a march from the Governor's Mansion to the African Church, a substantial structure often used by whites for large gatherings. During the afternoon and evening an estimated 10,000 people congregated in and around the building to listen to ringing speeches by Benjamin, Hunter, and others.[13]

Speaking at both assemblies, Davis hurled defiance at his foe. Thunderous applause greeted his unexpected appearance on the sixth. Excoriating Lincoln as "His Majesty Abraham the First," he proclaimed that Confederates would "teach the insolent enemy who had treated our proposition with contumely in that conference in which he had so plumed himself with arrogance, he was, indeed talking to his masters." He especially fulminated against the Thirteenth Amendment. In the African Church, Davis again slammed Lincoln and his demands while praising the nobility and ultimate triumph of the Confederate cause with which he so proudly and utterly identified himself. On these occasions Davis glimpsed his countrymen as he wanted to believe them, equally as determined as he not to let their cause fail. On the rostrum he became a man possessed; conviction and enthusiasm spurred his oratory. Applause and cheers repeatedly interrupted. Calling Davis's address on the sixth "the most remarkable speech of his life," his dedicated critic, the editor of the *Richmond Examiner,* confessed he had never been "so much moved by the power of words spoken for the same space of time." Davis even impressed Alexander Stephens, who, despite his having given up on the Confederacy after Hampton Roads, sat on the podium at the African Church with Davis and other dignitaries. Stephens termed the president's performance "brilliant," even though he considered Davis's predictions of victory "the emanation of a demented brain."[14]

Even after the failure of the Hampton Roads Conference and the flare of renewed enthusiasm, including the boisterous celebrations in Richmond, talk of peace ventures never entirely disappeared. A suggested military convention between Lee and Grant died stillborn, though Davis gave it his blessing—"two countries" again. Senator Hunter spoke about saving whatever possible from what he termed the "wreck," but then backed away. On one occasion Hunter, Graham, and a third colleague visited the president and urged negotiations based on abandoning independence. When Davis inquired if they represented the Senate in an official capacity, they demurred. When he asked about a Senate resolution, there was none. After the war Davis's former rival from prewar Mississippi, Albert G. Brown, also a Confederate senator, faulted everyone, including himself, for waiting on everyone else to take the lead on peace, which resulted in no one stepping forward. Secretary of the Navy Stephen Mallory claimed that if the Senate had passed a resolution for peace, Davis would have agreed to Lincoln's terms, but his chief could not act unilaterally.[15]

Davis gave no indication at this point that he would have entertained anything other than his public condition, independence. He made clear he was "unwilling to seek peace by the surrender of the Confederacy." Some, he admitted in a postwar letter, had come to call that attitude a sin; "that sin was mine," he attested. Although Davis unequivocally demanded the survival of the Confederate States of America, he was prepared to pay an enormous price for that endurance—the voluntary relinquishment of slavery. Despite his making political capital out of Lincoln's demands on slavery, Davis stood prepared to give up the venerable institution, if the sacrifice could secure Confederate independence.[16]

The sharply different approach to slavery introduced by the president in his congressional message of November 1864 provided the background for an unprecedented initiative designed to obtain recognition from Great Britain and France. In late December 1864 Davis, with Secretary of State Judah Benjamin's strong support, had made the momentous decision to sacrifice slavery on the altar of hope for

European intervention. Davis came to this position despite the provision in the Confederate Constitution forbidding Congress to enact any law denying property rights in slaves. He also did so without congressional authorization, though he did inform congressional leaders about his intentions. Davis saw this step as an extra-constitutional war measure essential for national survival.[17]

The Confederate president's overture offered gradual emancipation in return for European recognition and assistance. Benjamin's written instructions to his diplomats in Europe did not mention slavery directly. Instead, he told them the Confederacy was willing to act if the British and French had "*objections* not *made known* to us, which have for four years *prevented the recognition of our independence. . . .*" In language expressing Davis's sentiment, Benjamin declared that to secure independence "*no sacrifice is* too great, *save that* of honor."

To take this plan across the Atlantic and oversee its implementation, Davis selected a wealthy Louisiana sugar planter, Duncan F. Kenner, who was close to Benjamin and also chairman of the Ways and Means Committee of the Confederate House of Representatives. Having concluded soon after the fall of New Orleans that slavery threatened Confederate success, Kenner was enthusiastic about this new direction. In addition to the written directives he carried, Kenner had also received oral instructions from Davis. Moreover, the president made him a minister plenipotentiary to ensure that neither James Mason nor John Slidell could thwart the presentation of the revised Confederate position to the British and French governments. Kenner did not get started until mid-January, and by that time no Confederate Atlantic ports remained open to blockade-runners. He therefore undertook a harrowing and secret journey: he passed through enemy lines in northern Virginia, crossed an ice-filled Potomac River, and traveled incognito, chiefly by train, on to New York City, where he took passage on a German liner for Great Britain.

He arrived in Britain on February 21, 1865, and went on immediately to Paris, where he met with Mason and Slidell. Working with them, Kenner spent a month striving to achieve his goal. He failed. As before, Napoleon III said he was willing to help the Confederacy, but only in conjunction with Great Britain. As always, the British refused. Both governments stated that the issue of slavery had not controlled their previous reactions to the Confederacy. It is doubtful whether even an earlier offer of emancipation would have persuaded Great Britain to recognize the Confederate States, but 1865 was in any case far too late.

The Confederacy was tottering, and the British knew it. Duncan Kenner was still in Europe when the end came.

The Kenner Mission was not the only instance that revealed Davis's willingness to sever slavery from the Confederacy. When in his congressional message of November 1864 he urged government ownership of slaves and even broached the possibility of emancipation for faithful service, he said that he did not yet advocate making soldiers of slaves, though he did indicate that if the ultimate crisis ever came, he would consider such a role for bondsmen.[18]

Arming slaves and sending them into combat would have meant a fundamental uprooting of the traditional southern worldview. That action went far beyond government possession of slaves, or even freeing some of them. The antebellum proslavery argument placed blacks beneath whites racially and socially. To have them fight would give them characteristics of manhood previously denied them and put them on an equal basis with whites, at least in one absolutely critical area. As teamsters, cooks, and laborers, slaves surely helped the Confederate war effort, but in these capacities they served in distinctly inferior roles. The white men did the fighting. But with slaves as combat soldiers the sharp distinction between superior and inferior could no longer hold. Combat service also brought up the question of freedom. Would slaves fight to maintain slavery, or would freedom become a requisite badge for bearing arms? Would the government offer freedom as an inducement or reward? What about the aftermath of the war? If becoming a soldier led to becoming a free man, then certainly the postbellum social order would markedly differ from the world southern whites and blacks had always known.

The Confederacy had come into existence over slavery, and with slavery as its fundamental social institution. It is impossible to imagine the breakup of the Union without the presence of slavery. Seceding southerners spoke about building a slaveholding republic, and the Confederate Constitution declared slavery a bedrock of the new nation. The southern white conception of liberty had long been intimately tied to slavery for blacks. That connection was central in the initial formation of Confederate identity. The widespread mention of slave soldiers in the winter of 1865 underscored the feelings of desperation seeping through the Confederacy.[19]

As early as 1863, already concerned about the course of the war and viewing slaves as an underutilized asset, a few southerners had suggested using them as soldiers. Newspapers in Jackson and Montgomery, for example, called for slave soldiers to ensure Confederate victory. Infrequent letters, the earliest in 1861, also arrived on President Davis's desk with the same outlook. One correspondent based his case on the conventional white view of the master-slave relationship: "Cannot we, who have been raised with our negroes and know how to command them, make them more efficient than the Yankees can?" Although these writers made salient points, they gave no indication that they had thought through the potential repercussions of taking the path they proposed.[20]

Discussions about slaves as fighters became much more serious in January 1864, when the best division commander in the Army of Tennessee proposed slave soldiers. A native of Ireland who had immigrated to Arkansas, Major General Patrick Cleburne asserted he could see no other way to meet urgent manpower needs. Cleburne's proposal carried the signatures of thirteen other officers. This project created considerable excitement among various commanders in the army. To one, it was a "monstrous proposition"; another said following through on it would "involve our cause in ruin and disgrace." Visiting the army at that time, Governor Isham Harris of Tennessee was appalled. He alerted Davis, imploring the president to smother the proposal because public knowledge of it "would produce the greatest possible discontent." Davis, who also heard directly from the army, agreed: "Deeming it to be injurious to the public service that such a subject should be mooted, or even known to be entertained by persons possessed of the confidence and respect of the people," Davis directed General Joseph Johnston to quash the matter. The suppression basically succeeded; Cleburne's proposition did not become widely known.[21]

A year later the situation had changed dramatically. No one now doubted the existence of a grave manpower shortage in Confederate armies. Since his western trip in the autumn of 1864, Davis regularly pleaded for soldiers to return to the colors. In early 1865 he made a special plea to southeastern governors for men to stop Sherman. At the same time, cries for slave soldiers increased both in the press and in letters to Davis. As one Virginian wrote, he saw no other way to overcome "the perils of our country." At the great African Church conclave, Secretary Benjamin made a forceful appeal to save the Confederacy by putting slaves on the battlefield.[22]

But even in this dark hour, opposition remained powerful. Many white southerners simply could not conceive of breaking the bond between white liberty and black slavery. They could not imagine their new nation jettisoning the institution that in their minds guaranteed social harmony and social safety. This disagreement over slave soldiers revealed the fragility of Confederate nationalism. Forged in the furnace of war, it had not had sufficient time to solidify. It remained brittle, susceptible to sharp blows along visible seams.

Although at one on the sanctity of slavery in the Confederate nation, opponents of slave soldiers did not follow a single path. Senator William Graham declared slaves as soldiers "inexpedient and dangerous," but he also argued that enrolling slaves would violate the *Dred Scott* decision. Robert Barnwell Rhett raged against what he called governmental interference with slavery, which, to him, mocked strict construction and states' rights. Governor Joseph Brown saw nothing but evil in any plan for slave soldiers. In making known their opposition, two consistent allies of the president bore to the heart of the fundamental Confederate dilemma. The former United States senator from Florida, David L. Yulee, told Davis that if the Confederate government ever treated slaves "other than *as property* a social revolution is begun in the South, the end of which may not be foreseen." Howell Cobb was even more emphatic: "the day you make soldiers of them is the beginning of the end of the revolution. If slaves will make good soldiers our whole theory of slavery is wrong."[23]

This disagreement among Confederates was not chiefly a debate about emancipation. The arguments largely concentrated on the virtues of placing slaves in combat and what that step would mean for Confederate government and society. Some did consider that freedom would be at least an implied result of any positive decision on slave soldiers, but others did not draw such a conclusion. Congress certainly did not. Although the ultimate outcome cannot be known, slaves serving successfully as soldiers would surely have wrenched the traditional social order.[24]

Decisive in this matter was the opinion of Robert E. Lee, the single most prestigious and influential person in the Confederacy. Privately, Lee had decided that the Confederacy should employ slaves as soldiers, despite the risk to the social order. He saw no other way to fill the ranks. In a public letter to a congressional sponsor of slave soldiers, Lee in mid-February 1865 wrote that placing slaves in the army was essential. He also maintained that those who served honorably should be freed.[25]

In the midst of this argument Jefferson Davis's stance was clear. Although he did not make numerous public statements, he did not keep his views secret. He advocated slave soldiers. As he wrote in February to an Alabama friend, "it is now becoming daily more evident to all reflecting persons that we are reduced to choosing whether the negroes shall fight for us or against us." For the country's defense Davis wanted "all the able bodied men we have without distinction of color." He also expected that service would lead to emancipation, certainly for a number of those who served. Back in November 1864 he had signaled Congress his willingness to emancipate for less than combat. In the final spring he made his position unequivocally clear to Governor Smith, a stalwart backer of slave soldiers. The president promised the governor "to seek legislation to secure unmistakably freedom to the slave who shall enter the Army with a right to return to his old home when he shall have been honorably discharged from the Military Service." Davis committed himself to work for freedom plus the right for the ex-slave to live as a free man at his former home, the property of the individual who had previously owned the freedman. Thus, to save the Confederacy he was willing to challenge the privileges of private property and to contemplate a quite different postbellum society: whites, slaves, and a substantial, albeit unknown, number of free blacks, who had been enslaved, all living on the land of the white property owner.[26]

The legislative initiative to put uniforms on slaves took place in two venues. At Governor Smith's urging, and aware that General Lee believed the enlistment of slaves necessary, the Virginia legislature in early March adopted a resolution calling for slave soldiers, though nothing was said about emancipation. The Confederate Congress witnessed a hard, close battle. The effort to get an act through would certainly have failed without General Lee's public support. Davis had lobbied privately, but his formal appeal for congressional action did not come until March, when he chided the lawmakers for not sending him a bill to sign. The measure passed the House by a margin of only three, and on the initial try failed by one vote in the Senate. Thereupon the Virginia legislature instructed the states' two senators, who had voted no, to support the bill. They did so. Congress passed it on March 13.

This law did not, however, guarantee emancipation as a reward for service. In fact it stated that no change could take place in the relationship between slaves and owners, except with the consent of both the owners and the states in which they resided. This provided for a double veto on emancipation. Davis tried to accommodate this provision by having the War Department regulations governing the enlistment of slaves require that masters consent to freedom before slaves could be enrolled. How many slaves would have joined the army and how the numerous issues involved in slaves as soldiers would have worked out will never be known. Before the collapse of the Confederacy only two companies were organized, both in Richmond.[27]

President Davis's dispatch of Duncan Kenner to Europe and, especially, his shift on slave soldiers leave no doubt that he understood the gravity of the situation facing his country in the winter and early spring of 1865. In a March message to Congress he described the Confederacy as "environed with perils." Yet it is not possible to chart in detail his reaction to rapidly deteriorating Confederate fortunes. He kept his public statements positive, while his private anxieties and fears were not chronicled. His total commitment to the Confederate States of America made contemplation of failure intensely painful, if not impossible. But the rational Jefferson Davis knew that catastrophe was looming. Two years after the war, in a letter to his former boss, Judah Benjamin referred to "the anxious hours when we could not but perceive that our holy and sacred cause was gradually crumbling under a pressure too grievous to be borne, and when we looked every where for some sign of sympathy, some promise of help, some ray of hope."[28]

During these horrendous months Davis also struggled with his health. In December 1864, neuralgia struck another hard blow, and the manifestations plagued him for weeks. In a generally weakened state, he still tried to spend full days at his office in the Customs House. Yet at times he had to remain in the Executive Mansion. On one occasion an ill president lying on a divan met with a worried General Lee. Still, the president refused to let illness hobble him. When he appeared at the African Church rally following the Hampton Roads Conference, a War Department official noted how feeble he looked. But he also had good days when he took the horseback rides that relaxed him, at least briefly.[29]

Even with the awful public pressures and the lingering physical maladies, Davis could still impress people. His face, despite thinner and more sallow cheeks, marked a man of "extraordinary determination," an Irish visitor remarked. Even though he looked "thin and careworn," with his hair and chin whiskers "bleaching rapidly," his gray eyes remained "bright & clear." In March 1865, an eyewitness pictured "a graceful, spirited gentleman." Davis showed his spirit at a wedding where he gleefully claimed his "tribute kiss" from the blushing bride.[30]

During most of the winter and spring President Davis worked with a different lineup at the top of the War Department. On February 1

Secretary James Seddon gave up his office. Taking personally the Virginia legislature's call for wholesale changes in the cabinet, he felt that as a Virginian he should not stay in because the legislators of his state had lost faith in the official first family. Davis tried to dissuade him, but to no avail. In accepting Seddon's resignation, the president bid farewell to a trusted, loyal lieutenant. In a demanding job and under difficult circumstances, Seddon for more than two years had ably served his president. Davis recognized that service upon Seddon's departure: "you have devoted yourself with entire singleness of purpose to the public welfare . . . your labors have been incessant, your services important and your counsels very valuable. . . ."[31]

Seddon's successor was a capable man who had solid credentials. Well known to Davis, John C. Breckinridge of Kentucky had been a notable antebellum politician, including service as vice president under James Buchanan and as the southern Democratic candidate for president in 1860. Since 1861 he had served competently as brigadier and then major general in the Confederate army, in both western and eastern theaters. Davis and his new war minister seemed to get along, but Breckinridge did not hold office sufficiently long to demonstrate how the relationship would have developed.

Even before Seddon left, Davis had reassigned General Braxton Bragg from the position of military adviser to the president to take over command of Confederate forces around Wilmington. Bragg's leaving in mid-October 1864 occasioned no fundamental changes in the Confederate high command. As military adviser, Bragg had never become a confidant of the president, as Lee had been back in 1861 and 1862. Moreover, Bragg's presence in Richmond between February and October did not alter Davis's continued reliance on Lee, not only for Virginia affairs but also for matters reaching far beyond the state.

Thinking of himself as chief of staff of the Confederate army, Bragg had functioned almost as a co-secretary of war. Drawing on his organizational interests and skills, he devoted much time to such areas as officer ranks and promotions, conscription, prison, and transport. He effected some positive changes, such as reformulation of the authority for conscription. Davis also used him in conveying directives to the Army of Tennessee, and, of course, on special assignment to report on Joseph Johnston before Atlanta. But Bragg's tenure was too brief and too late to have a fundamental impact on the way Davis ran the War Department. And Bragg never replaced Seddon as a counselor to the president.[32]

During the months he had Bragg, and even after the turn of the year when he confronted the disintegration of his armies and his country, Davis continued to immerse himself in a sea of minutiae. His administrative practice did not change at all. He wanted to know why a lieutenant from Louisiana was promoted in a South Carolina artillery unit; he even entered a dispute over seniority between two captains in a Virginia regiment. A plan to promote several captains in General William Hardee's command generated a directive to the adjutant and inspector general. In early spring 1865 Davis gave directions in a controversy over a local commander's right to revoke a general order for a special assignment. Late in April he instructed Breckinridge on the promotions of lieutenants on general staffs.[33]

Although President Davis's absorption in detail remained unchanged into the spring, the Confederate military situation changed dramatically. The deterioration that had marked the end of 1864 gained momentum. By late February, Sherman was poised to enter North Carolina, where once again he faced his foe of a year earlier, Joseph E. Johnston. When Congress called for a commanding general of Confederate armies, it also requested that the president reinstate Johnston. Resisting, Davis wanted nothing more to do with a general who he believed had repeatedly failed him and the country. He went so far as to prepare a lengthy memorandum explaining to Congress why he would not recall Johnston. But, exercising restraint and avoiding unneeded confrontation, he did not submit it. Holding the document also saved considerable embarrassment, for a few days later he did reassign Johnston. Lee said Johnston was needed to try to bring order out of chaos in North Carolina. Having no real choice, Davis acquiesced. To a political supporter, he placed the best possible interpretation on his action. He complied with Lee's wish, Davis wrote, "in the hope that Genl. Johnston's soldierly qualities may be made serviceable to his country when acting under General Lee's orders, and that in his new position those defects which I found manifested by him when serving as an independent commander will be remedied by the control of the General in Chief."[34]

General Johnston's new assignment did not please him. To Mary Chesnut he confided that "he was very angry to be ordered to take command again." His wife remarked that he "went off in the devil of a bad humor." Preferring to criticize what he considered mistakes made by Lee and others, Johnston asserted that he was returned only to preside over a surrender. Johnston's command consisted of the remains of the Army of Tennessee along with troops from Bragg and Hardee, altogether around 20,000 men. This paltry force could at best do no more than briefly delay Sherman's powerful legions. Johnston did make an effort. In mid-March at Bentonville he actually attacked a portion of Sherman's army. Although the Confederates gained initial success, numbers soon prevailed. Sherman's route to Virginia lay open, though Johnston kept his small force intact.[35]

In Virginia, Lee was trying to cope with increasingly desperate difficulties. Grant's continuous extension of his lines gravely endangered Lee's control of the railroads—utterly essential for the protection of both his army and Richmond. Grant was about to surround him, and Sherman was fast approaching. Lee discerned that his only chance lay in falling back west and south toward North Carolina and uniting with Johnston. With the combined armies, even though still outnumbered, he would strike Sherman, and if he prevailed, he would turn on Grant. Any hope for success required Lee to act before Sherman reached Grant or the latter cut off his escape route.

Understanding the military reality behind Lee's design, Davis concurred. The president recalled that he and Lee were of one mind on what had to be done and how to do it. Davis claimed that both men recognized the value of Richmond as a symbol and a manufacturing center. They wanted to hold the city as long as possible, but not risk the capture of Lee's army. According to Davis, they were ready to abandon Petersburg as early as March, but the combination of mud-softened roads and weak draft animals convinced Lee that he could not move that quickly.[36]

Aware that Richmond would soon fall, Jefferson Davis planned accordingly. For the second time he prepared to send his family south, specifically to Charlotte, North Carolina, and if necessary, farther on. The spring of 1862 with the Federal host at the gates of the capital was certainly traumatic, and Davis could not know the outcome. But three years later, conditions were massively different. This time he knew the city would have to be given up. Varina sold some of the furniture in the White House, with the remainder scheduled for packing and storage. An anxious Jefferson checked on the safety of the railroad near Charlotte. He also gave his wife all his gold, save for a single five-dollar piece. In addition, he obtained a pistol for her and showed her how to use it. According to Varina, he instructed her: "You can at least, if reduced to the last extremity, force your assailants to kill you, but I charge you solemnly to leave when you hear the enemy are approaching; and if you cannot remain undisturbed in our own country, make for the Florida coast and take a ship there for a foreign country." Leave-taking was especially painful, for all realized they might never see each other again. The father found it particularly difficult to part with his children; the two oldest begged to remain and clung to him. On March 29, escorted by Burton Harrison, Varina, the four children—ranging in age from ten years to nine months—her sister Maggie, and two servants left by train.[37]

President Davis stayed on. He would not leave until the last possible moment, which came somewhat sooner than expected. Before Lee could orchestrate his withdrawal from Petersburg, Grant on April 2 broke through the Confederate lines. Immediately the news flashed to Richmond. It was a balmy Sunday morning. Postmaster General John Reagan, who had been at the War Department when the telegram arrived, headed to the White House to inform the president. On the way he met Davis en route to church. After listening to Reagan, Davis continued on.[38]

When Davis entered St. Paul's, one who saw him often noted his appearance: "the cold calm eye, the Sunken cheeks, the compressed lip, were all as impenetrable as an iron mask." During the service, the sexton brought a dispatch to the presidential pew, Lee's telegram saying that Richmond must be promptly evacuated. Upon reading it, Davis rose and quietly walked out.[39]

He went to his office in the Customs House. There he received Lee's most recent report emphasizing that this night he had to abandon his position. Although Davis had known that Lee would soon give up Petersburg, that it happened so suddenly surprised him. As he later wrote, he did not believe that eventuality "so near at hand." He called together his cabinet, the governor, and the mayor, and informed them of what had transpired at Petersburg and must happen in Richmond. Preparations were underway to pack up all archives possible and remove the government. Davis also wired Lee asking if he could give any more time before the required evacuation. In front of his staff the hard-pressed general growled that he had given plenty of notice about the extreme fragility of his position. No, read the reply, he could provide no more time.[40]

That evening President Davis walked back to the Executive Mansion for the final time. To inquiring citizens who stopped him, he confirmed that the government would leave the city. After gathering up a few belongings he "sat on a divan in his study, sad, but calm and dignified," conversing with those around him. When the carriage arrived to take him to the Richmond and Danville depot, he lit a cigar and got in. At the station he waited in the office of the railroad's president until the special train was ready. Then, with General Samuel Cooper and his cabinet, except for Breckinridge who followed later, he climbed aboard, and at 11 p.m. the locomotive chugged out of the city. Davis and his party left a quiet city, but by next morning much of it was on fire, flames spreading from the demolition of ammunition works to engulf entire blocks.[41]

Davis's destination was Danville, some 145 miles southwest of Richmond and just above the North Carolina line. From the capital the train clanked slowly through the night. As the cars passed a rural station early on the morning of the third, a crowd cheered the president, who sat by a window. Acknowledging the notice, he "smiled," but an eyewitness thought "his expression showed mental and physical exhaustion." In his diary Secretary Mallory recorded that "general gloom" pervaded the atmosphere. Reaching Danville at 4 p.m., the president was greeted by an enthusiastic assembly of citizens and escorted to the residence of Major William T. Sutherlin, a mansion on the outskirts of town. The Sutherlin house became the new center of the Confederate government.[42]

At this point Davis had no thought of surrendering the Confederacy. He did not consider his cause lost. Before leaving Richmond, he had brought up with Lee his cherished vision of troops swarming back to the colors. He told Bragg in North Carolina that his military goal remained the prevention of a junction between Sherman and Grant. He was not certain how long he would stay in Danville, however. Although he had engineers look into constructing defensive works for the town, he wrote his wife he was not ready to decide on a future seat of government. But he did emphasize that he did not want to leave Virginia. He just did not know where the necessary buildings for the executive departments and Congress could be found.[43]

His public stance exuded confidence and determination. In a proclamation to the "People of the Confederate States" dated April 4, he declared, "it is my purpose to maintain your cause with my whole heart and soul." Yet he did not deny that serious reverses had occurred. The seat of government had been temporarily moved to Danville because military exigencies required the evacuation of Richmond. But this setback did not sound the death knell for our "most sacred cause"; instead, it meant "a new phase of a struggle, the memory of which is to endure for all ages, and to shed ever increasing lustre upon our country."

Relieved from protecting fixed points, Confederate armies could defeat in detail enemy forces drawn far from their bases, Davis asserted. Even if events necessitated withdrawal from Virginia or any other state in the upper Confederacy, he promised Confederate divisions would return. "[N]othing is now needed to render our triumph certain, but the exhibition of our own unquenchable resolve. Let us but will it, and we are free." In his view, the enemy had the "impossible task of making slaves of a people resolved to be free."[44]

Circumstances quickly overtook these stirring words. Davis expected Lee to reach Danville, or at least to position himself to protect the town and especially the government. But the general, now on a desperate march for survival, could not match the speed and power of his foe. Grant's presence on his southern flank had already forced him due west rather than southwest, making Danville an impossible goal. By April 8 Lee found units of Grant's army in his front as well; they blocked the way west. Breckinridge had reported to Davis that Lee's situation was bleak. An officer from Lee slipped through the lines and reached Danville on the night of the eighth. The president was then holding a cabinet meeting in the Sutherlin dining room. Although Davis put the young man at ease upon his arrival, his words shocked: he did not believe Lee could reach safety; he thought surrender imminent. Still, the president sought to get dispatches to Lee. But the young officer was right. On Sunday, April 9, at Appomattox Court House, General Lee surrendered the Army of Northern Virginia to General Grant. On the tenth, even though no official news had reached him, Davis informed Joseph Johnston that "little doubt" existed about Lee's fate.[45]

When, later that day, President Davis received reliable information that Lee had indeed surrendered his entire army, the chief executive prepared to move his government. This time the destination was Greensboro, North Carolina, fifty miles south of Danville and close to Joseph Johnston's headquarters. The presidential train pulled out of Danville around midnight and steamed into Greensboro the following afternoon. Unlike their counterparts in Danville, the citizens of Greensboro did not provide a cheery, warm welcome for the president. Antiwar sentiment had grown, but fear of reprisals from Federal raiding parties also governed conduct.[46]

The quarters of the Confederate government and its leader dramatized their plight. Offices were set up in railroad cars; most cabinet members also slept in coaches. Davis's aide and nephew by his first marriage, the grandson of Zachary Taylor, John Taylor Wood, fitted out an empty room in his lodgings for his uncle. Even though they governed a disintegrating country, these men enjoyed a full commissary in Greensboro, which provided substantial rations. Secretary Mallory pictured the attorney general with a hoecake in one hand and bacon in the other, the secretary of state dividing his attention between a bucket of stewed apples and a haversack of hard-boiled eggs, and the postmaster general using his bowie knife to cut a ham.[47]

At Greensboro, President Davis's chief goal was to devise a plan to carry on the war. To that end, he called both General Johnston and General Beauregard to confer with him. Although he issued no proclamation as he had done at Danville, he was no less determined. An aide described him as still having "a great deal of fight." To Governor Vance he implored, "we must redouble our efforts to meet present disaster. An army holding its position with determination to fight on, and manifest ability to maintain the struggle," he insisted, "will attract all the scattered soldiers and daily and rapidly gather strength." Davis appealed to the governor to join him in exercising moral leadership "to revive the spirit and hope of the people." When Beauregard appeared, his interview with the president left no doubt that the commander in chief intended to continue the war.[48]

Davis held two critical cabinet meetings on the afternoon of the twelfth and the morning of the thirteenth. Johnston and Beauregard attended both. At the first, the president spoke earnestly about promptly gathering deserters and conscripts to create an army large enough to give the Confederacy a chance. Although the two generals demurred, Davis clung to his view and adjourned the deliberations until the next morning when Secretary of War Breckinridge would be present.

The session on April 13 Postmaster General Reagan termed "solemnly funereal." As he did so often, Davis began with small talk, but soon he became serious. He admitted the scale of recent disasters, but did not think them fatal. Then he asked Johnston and Beauregard for their views. The soldiers replied they saw no course but to sue for peace. They had no force capable of keeping up the war and did not believe one could be raised. The cabinet officers were polled. Only Benjamin advocated war. Reagan actually brought up what no one else had been willing to mention: capitulation. For the first time, the official family had broken ranks; it no longer stood as one with the president. During this discussion, Davis's expression did not change. According to Mallory, he "sat with his eyes fixed upon a scrap of paper which he was folding & unfolding alternately." Finally, he authorized General Johnston to seek terms from Sherman. At Johnston's request, the president dictated a statement for Johnston to present to Sherman, which Johnston signed. The proposal did not mention the word "surrender"; instead, it called for a cessation of hostilities so that civil authorities in the states could act to end the war. Although Davis had no confidence this initiative would succeed, he agreed to it.[49]

After this conference Jefferson Davis received the official dispatch from his first soldier reporting his Appomattox surrender. Davis's demeanor changed. He had been talking about carrying on the war west of the Mississippi. After reading the message he passed it along and turned away. According to a junior officer, Davis "silently wept bitter tears." Robert E. Lee, Jr., who happened to be in Greensboro on his way to Johnston's army, recalled that the president "seemed quite broken."[50]

But Davis could not dwell on that bitter loss. Even though "depression is universal & disorganization is setting in," as John Taylor Wood recorded in his diary, Davis had to act. He and his party had to move on, but with a different status. From Richmond to Danville and on to Greensboro, Davis had been a head of state with armies, though vastly weakened, to command and a fully supportive cabinet. Now his armies had either been surrendered or were melting away. Moreover, both his senior commanders and most of his cabinet officers believed the war lost.[51]

Davis and his advisers had become fugitives, forced to keep moving south. Davis hoped to reach Confederate forces in the Gulf states or even in the Trans-Mississippi where he could carry on the fight. To him waging a guerrilla campaign was not an acceptable option. He believed the social price far too high. His closest aide, William Johnston, reported him as saying, "Guerrillas become brigands, and any government is better than that."[52]

The first goal was Charlotte, around eighty miles to the southwest. Because Federal cavalry had cut the railroad between the towns, the presidential party had to turn to horses and wagons. In a driving rainstorm and accompanied by a cavalry escort, the president on horseback headed out with his beleaguered group. Davis impressed a cavalry captain, who noted that he rode "very erectly" and appeared neither frail nor weak. On the journey to Charlotte, evidence grew that the end had come. Fearing reprisals, some people refused to take the president into their homes. On April 16, for the first time, Davis and several cabinet secretaries camped out.[53]

During his sad retreat from Richmond, Davis had not forgotten his family. Varina and the children had reached Charlotte after four days riding slow trains. Upon their arrival Burton Harrison closed the windows on their coach because of the "most shocking language" used by some deserters to revile the first lady. Although the townspeople did not rush forward to extend hospitality, decent rooms were found for the family in a private home. She reported to her husband that discouraging rumors dominated her news. She professed her love for him and her faith in his strength and ability. She also expressed her eagerness to come to him with the baby, but did not know when she could. The activities of the children she detailed for the absent father, from Billy's being bad to Jeff's generally behaving to the baby's teething. "I am very well off," she assured him. Varina had shown her own strength. Mary Chesnut found her "as calm and smiling as ever," even under "*altered skies.*"[54]

As for the husband and father, he wrote of his love and his concern, though his outlook changed. From Danville he described his hurried departure from Richmond and the kindness of the local townspeople. He sent kisses to the little ones and letters for them. Always he prayed to God to watch over his loved ones. "Everything is dark," he lamented just before leaving Greensboro. Telling her he would come to her if at all possible, he urged her to go on to Abbeville, South Carolina, where friends had offered safe haven.[55]

When Jefferson arrived in Charlotte on April 19, Varina had traveled on to Abbeville. In Charlotte the presidential office was set up in the Bank of North Carolina. Davis also found comfortable lodgings in a private home. The presidential entourage found the town a congenial stop. Preston Johnston informed his wife they were "living splendidly at this place," with "all good things to eat and drink." Shortly after Davis's arrival, word came that Sherman and Johnston had agreed to terms based largely on the Greensboro proposal. While Sherman submitted the agreement to his government for its approval, Johnston requested instructions from his president. Davis asked for written opinions from his cabinet members, who told their chief to accept it. In his response Secretary of War Breckinridge, who had participated in the Johnston-Sherman discussion, gave blunt advice. He stated that Johnston's army had dwindled to fewer than 15,000 men and could make no headway against the huge Federal forces. Moreover, he pointed out that Confederate ports were closed and that Federal armies could move at will through much of the Confederacy. He saw no possibility of assembling, equipping, and maintaining a large army east of the Mississippi. An understatement followed, "I think we can no longer contend with reasonable hope of success." Accepting this counsel, Davis agreed to the terms, though he doubted the Federal administration would approve them.[56]

Yet Davis still hoped for some miracle. To General Bragg he reiterated his abiding conviction, "Could we be assured that the spirit of the country would rise to the level of the occasion I should feel confident of final success, and am not without hope that recent disaster may awake the dormant energy and develop the patriotism which sustained us in the first years of the war." In a brief, impromptu address to soldiers, he declared, "the cause is not yet dead." "Determination and fortitude," he claimed, could yet bring victory.[57]

Davis tried to busy himself with the duties of chief executive. He deliberated with his cabinet about Joseph Johnston's peace negotiations. He worked to obtain artillery and cavalry for the defense of Charlotte. He also sought information on Federal movements in South Carolina and Georgia. Governor Vance came to town to confer about his proper course. Davis talked of crossing the Mississippi and suggested that Vance come along with as many North Carolina troops as he could muster. After a momentary silence, Breckinridge said further fighting served no purpose. Sadly, Davis concurred. Yet, when approached by officers who had escaped capture at Lee's surrender or were not present at Johnston's, he encouraged them to head south and keep up the fight.[58]

While in Charlotte, Davis learned that his great antagonist Abraham Lincoln had been assassinated. All accounts of the occasion agree that Davis voiced regret at Lincoln's death. He also observed that Lincoln would have been more lenient on the South than his successor was likely to be. Davis expected no favors for himself or his fellow Confederates from Andrew Johnson.[59]

On the twenty-third, President Davis attended church and heard a sermon entitled "And Thus It Must Be." That afternoon he wrote his wife a long letter, which he sent by messenger. Lee's surrender "destroyed the hopes I entertained when we parted," he explained. He admitted that deserters and stragglers were not now coming back into the ranks. "Panic has seized the country." "The issue," he confessed, "is one which it is very painful for me to meet." He envisioned agonizing options: "On one hand is the long night of oppression which will follow the return of our people to the 'Union'; on the other, the suffering of the women and children, and carnage among the few brave patriots who would still oppose the invader, and who, unless the people would rise en-masse to sustain them, would struggle but to die in vain." He was convinced no bias marked his judgments. He always prayed for "wisdom and fortitude" to equal his responsibilities. "I have sacrificed so much for the cause of the Confederacy that I can measure my ability to make any further sacrifice required, and am assured there is but one to which I am not equal—My wife and my Children—How are they to be saved from degradation or want is now my care."

As for that safety, he directed her to sail for a foreign port or to go to Texas, whichever "may be more practicable." He knew she had little money, but if he could sell his land, she would have enough to secure her "from absolute want." He planned to leave Charlotte quite soon, and if "a devoted band of Cavalry will cling to me," he might get across the Mississippi. But should he be unable to accomplish anything positive in the Trans-Mississippi, then "I can go to Mexico, and have the world from which to choose a location."

Before closing, he remembered their beginnings and pointed to her strength. "Dear Wife, this is not the fate to which I invited [you] when the future was rose colored to us both; but I know you will bear it even better than myself, and that, of us two, I alone, will ever look back reproachfully on my past career." He asked that she kiss his children many times for him. And then closed: "Farewell, my dear, there may be better things in store for us than are now in view, but my love is all I have to offer, and that has the value of a thing long possessed, and sure not to be lost."[60]

He did not tarry long. On April 24 President Johnson rejected the Johnston-Sherman pact, instructing Sherman that he could only offer Grant's terms at Appomattox. With hostilities scheduled to resume in forty-eight hours, Johnston went back to Sherman. On April 26 he surrendered. That day Davis's party got underway. It was smaller because General Cooper and the attorney general, who had resigned, remained behind. Again with horses and wagons, Davis, the other five cabinet officers, aides, and a cavalry escort struck out toward Abbeville, in western South Carolina near the Georgia border.

Davis's group took a week to traverse its route of just over 180 miles to the small town. Only the presence of an escort of some 3,000 cavalrymen indicated that their horses and wagons constituted anything more than another small caravan of people displaced by the war. Crossing the state, the president was received with kindness and consideration; he slept in a private home every night. Once when he requested a drink of water, the lady of the house asked if he was Jefferson Davis. Upon his positive answer, she pointed to her baby crawling down the steps and said he was named for the president. Davis gave her a gold coin and told her to keep it for his namesake. At various points women offered him flowers and wreaths, and children scattered flowers before him. On one occasion a young woman noted tears on his cheeks. Viewing these scenes, John Wood recorded, "my heart rises to my throat whenever I see [them]."[61]

During this trek Davis was cordial and sociable. He chatted pleasantly with all, including cabinet members, aides, Carolinians he encountered, and soldiers in his escort. All reported him calm and relaxed, at least outwardly. In "very bright and agreeable conversation," often with a cigar in his mouth, he talked about men, books—especially by Sir Walter Scott and Lord Byron—dogs, how to build roads, and generally about earlier days. Not much business was transacted. When on the twenty-fifth the secretary of the treasury resigned and departed because of ill health, Davis appointed Reagan as acting secretary. On May 1 General Bragg joined the company.[62]

As he journeyed westward across South Carolina, Jefferson heard from his wife, who had sent a messenger with a response to his long letter from Charlotte. She let him know she was leaving Abbeville for Washington, Georgia, and eventually, she hoped, on to Florida, then abroad to Nassau or England; but she wanted his guidance before making final plans. She too testified to the powerful bond they had cemented since 1861. Replying to his lament about the blasting of the rose-colored future they had once envisioned, she told him, "It is surely not the fate to which you invited me in brighter days, but you must remember that you did not invite me to a great Hero's home, but to that of a plain farmer." "I have shared all your triumphs," she added, "been the *only* beneficiary of them, now I am but claiming the privilege for the first time of being all to you now these pleasures have past for me." She saw her future solely with him, and she wanted to join him as soon as possible. She envisioned a reunion in the Trans-Mississippi, where she was confident he could prevail.[63]

Davis reached Abbeville on the afternoon of May 2. He stopped at the home of Armistead Burt, an ardent supporter who had been a prewar congressman. Burt had been Varina's host until her departure two days earlier. That afternoon Breckinridge thought the president should hear directly from the officers commanding his escort. The men were talking about the future and what plans had been formulated, if any. Davis called a conference for 4 p.m. in the Burt parlor, with Breckinridge, Bragg, and the six cavalry brigadiers in attendance. On this occasion as at Greensboro and Charlotte, Davis talked about continuing the war. Admitting the bleakness of the situation, he professed it no worse than the black days of the American Revolution. Taken aback, the cavalry commanders remonstrated while Breckinridge and Bragg kept silent. The commanders voiced a unanimous opinion: they could envision no military future. Davis inquired of them why with such an outlook they stayed in the field. To protect him, they answered, to get him to safety. Though shaken by the finality of their declaration, Davis called his safety inconsequential and adjourned the meeting. He would never again meet with military commanders as their commander in chief.[64]

Throughout his long retreat Jefferson Davis retained command of himself. He spoke bravely and talked about carrying forward the fight, but at Greensboro, Charlotte, and Abbeville he consistently acknowledged and acted on the realistic assessments of his secretary of war and his military commanders. Those who discussed official matters with him, including critical and astute men like General Beauregard and Governor Vance, commented on his attentiveness, his grasp of information, his close questioning. Even on that cheerless afternoon in the Burt parlor he impressed. One brigadier recorded that he had never seen the president "show to better advantage." According to this officer, "the union of dignity, graceful affability, and decision, which made his manner usually so striking was very marked in his reception of us."[65]

Although the presidential party had initially expected to stay in Abbeville at least several days, news of approaching Federals changed those plans. Following the council of war, the bulk of the escort was paid and dismissed from service. Toward midnight on May 2 a much smaller band left for Washington, Georgia, around fifty miles to the west. Davis pushed his companions through the night, and in a gray suit rode into Washington late in the morning of May 3. During the march Benjamin had peeled off for a dash to Florida, and at Washington,

Mallory also went his own way. Breckinridge, who was in the rear over-seeing the disbanding of cavalry units, made it to Washington the next day. The townspeople greeted Davis warmly. Even his blustery politi-cal opponent Robert Toombs participated, offering his erstwhile foe use of his house as well as funds and a horse.[66]

Learning that his wife had recently departed toward the southwest, Davis decided to follow. At this point what had been a retreat turned into flight. All pretense of an organized government and official mili-tary activity was dropped. Davis would strive to move rapidly, accom-panied by aides Preston Johnston, John Taylor Wood, and Francis Lubbock, ten volunteer cavalrymen, and John Reagan. Davis and Rea-gan even adopted new identities: the president as a Texas congressman trying to get home and Reagan as a judge from that state.

Davis's intentions were clear. His advisers had been urging him to travel swiftly so that he could either reach the Mississippi River or get out of the country through Florida. Davis never planned to leave his country, unless a sea journey from Florida turned out to be the only way he could reach Texas, even if he had to go by way of Mexico. He had not yet given up his cause.[67]

Late on the morning of May 4 Davis rode out of Washington with his few companions. All carried their belongings on their horses but the president, who had a pack mule. Still working in his treasury capacity, Reagan came on that night. Arriving in Washington during the after-noon, Breckinridge decided not to ride after Davis. Instead, he hoped to mislead Federal pursuers by moving due south with some cavalry-men. Davis and his associates kept to country roads and avoided towns; they covered thirty miles before halting for the night.[68]

On the sixth the president made two important decisions. First, he directed the wagons carrying the gold designated for the Trans-Mississippi to proceed apart from his party. He wanted to move more rapidly than the loaded wagons permitted. At this point each man with Davis was given some gold coins. With $25,000 in gold left and with a guard detail under Captain Watson Van Benthuysen, a relative of Joseph Davis's wife, the treasury train turned due south for Florida. On this day scouts reported that Varina Davis's wagons were not far ahead and traveling in the same general direction. In addition, word had been received that stragglers planned to plunder their supplies. Davis decided to ride ahead in an attempt to find and protect his family. Around midnight he located Varina's encampment near the village of

Dublin. Although it had been six weeks since he sent his family away from Richmond, the same people made up Varina's weary troops—her four children, her sister Maggie, and two servants. All were still under the care of the loyal Burton Harrison, who, except for a few days between Charlotte and Abbeville, had been with them all the way. A handful of volunteer officers had also added themselves to provide security.

Davis chose to unite the two parties, even though the combination would slow him down. On Sunday, the seventh, he rode with Varina in her ambulance. The surroundings matched the desolation of the fleeing family. They journeyed through sparsely settled piney woods, with little cultivation and houses ten to fifteen miles apart. A member of the escort described one campsite as a "miserable piece of woods very confined & bad water." During the day information reached the caravan that former soldiers in Dublin planned to raid the wagons on the pretext that they hauled government property. Members of the escort rode into the village and stymied the plot by announcing they would fight any attackers. In the night came a report that the Federal military had learned Jefferson Davis was traveling with his wife in a single wagon train. Davis decided that once more he would have to separate himself from his family in order to dash ahead.

By this time no organized Confederate resistance existed east of the Mississippi, though Davis did not know it. On May 4 General Richard Taylor had surrendered all the forces in his department, and five days later General Nathan Forrest bade his men farewell. Only Edmund Kirby Smith in the Trans-Mississippi kept the Confederate flag flying. For Jefferson Davis that banner had become his rainbow in the West.

As Confederate commands disappeared, the U.S. Army increased the intensity of its search for Jefferson Davis. In the aftermath of Lincoln's death, President Johnson issued a proclamation calling for Davis's arrest and offering a reward of $100,000 in gold. The Johnson administration accused Davis of complicity in planning Lincoln's assassination. In southern Georgia the search for Davis was directed by Major General James H. Wilson from his headquarters in Macon. On May 6 Wilson discovered Davis had been in Washington, and he realized that the only possible escape route ran through southern Georgia. The next evening the Federals heard that the Davis party had passed Dublin.

Davis surely wanted to escape the Federal cavalry patrols fanning out all around him. At dawn on the eighth he and his escort departed, leaving Varina and Burton Harrison to plug along with their vehicles and encumbrances. But heavy rains and high water slowed the president and his men. By evening Varina's group caught up with Jefferson at the hamlet of Abbeville, where everyone prepared to spend the night. Around midnight Davis received information about nearby Federal mounted units. He immediately instructed Burton Harrison to get the wagons underway, and Harrison did so in the midst of a terrible rainstorm. The president said he and his people would come on as soon as their horses were rested. Before daylight on May 9 the president's party rejoined his wife's. Early that morning both husband and wife washed in a creek before renewing their migration.

The trek continued until late afternoon, when the tired journeyers halted in a clearing by a stream a mile north of the tiny village of Irwinville. According to John Wood, they had come 202 miles from Washington. After resting men and animals, Davis intended to ride on during the night. Then reports that plunderers were about to storm the camp caused him to delay. If no attack took place, he still intended to leave at dawn. In the tent he shared with Varina he went to bed fully clothed. But in the drizzly predawn light, firing broke out along the creek. A servant sounded the alarm. Some thought marauders had struck, when suddenly Federal cavalry burst into the camp. Then the musketry became brisk. Two regiments, the Fourth Michigan and the First Wisconsin, had approached the camp from different directions and were shooting at each other. At this moment John Wood went to the Davis tent, where he told Varina the enemy did not know for sure of his chief's presence and during the confusion he might be able to reach the woods and escape.

Davis agreed. When he emerged from the tent, he was wearing a water-repellent cloak with wide, loose sleeves and a black shawl that Varina had thrown around his shoulders. She then directed her maid to grab a bucket and walk with her husband to make it appear they were going to the creek for water. But a cavalryman saw them walking and ordered them to halt. In response they changed direction, yet kept heading toward the woods. Another horseman rode toward them, shouting that he would shoot. Davis turned, flung off the shawl, and advanced toward the trooper. Later he claimed he intended to use a trick he had learned from the Indians—walk up, grab the rider's heel, upend him out of the saddle, mount the horse, and attempt to escape. He believed his chances good, he said, because it was difficult for a man on horseback to fire down accurately on a target so close. But he never made the attempt, for at that instant, thinking he was about to be shot, Varina rushed to him, threw her arms around his neck, and begged the soldier not to fire. The last possible chance to get away was gone. Finally, it was all over. The journey that had begun in the garden at Brierfield ended in the piney woods of south Georgia. It had lasted exactly fifty-one months—February 10, 1861, to May 10, 1865.[69]

CHAPTER SIXTEEN

"I Have Not Sunk Under My Trials"

The shooting eventually stopped. The Federals realized that their two regiments on opposite sides of the camp were firing at each other. Two cavalrymen in blue lay dead, and several were wounded. During the melee a few fugitives managed to slip away, including John Taylor Wood. Upon restoration of order, the soldiers gathered their prisoners together and pillaged the bivouac. Davis berated the commanding officer for permitting the looting, though his remonstrations did no good. After a brief time the assemblage got underway to General Wilson's headquarters at Macon. Davis was allowed to accompany his family in one of the wagons.

Jefferson Davis was being introduced to captivity. As the prisoners approached Macon, Union troops lining the road jeered the president and his entourage. Along the way Davis had learned about Andrew Johnson's presidential proclamation accusing him of complicity in Lincoln's assassination and putting a price on his head. A heavy guard accompanied the caravan into Macon, where an immense but orderly crowd awaited the former leader. In town, General Wilson treated his star prisoner with courtesy and invited Davis, his aides, and John Reagan to dine with him. And before sending them on, the general also agreed that Davis could take his family east with him.

On the evening of May 13 the captives left Macon for their assumed destination, Washington, D.C. Their route would take them by train to Atlanta and over to Augusta, then by water down the Savannah River and on up the Atlantic. At Macon, Clement Clay, who had been arrested for alleged involvement in the plot to kill Lincoln, and his wife, Virginia, joined the group. Both were longtime friends of the Davises. Virginia Clay remembered that as she entered the railcar, Davis rose, embraced her, and said, "This is a sad meeting, Jennie." In Augusta on

May 14, the party was placed on a small steamer for the trip downriver to Savannah, where they were transferred to a similar vessel for a brief jaunt up to Hilton Head, South Carolina. There crowds of Federal soldiers and civilians mocked the captives. On the sixteenth all of the captives—including Alexander Stephens, who had been added at Augusta—were placed aboard the steamer *William P. Clyde* for their ocean voyage.

Davis had a difficult trip. Between Augusta and Savannah, recurrence of an eye inflammation caused intense suffering. But more than physical pain affected him. Virginia Clay described him as "extremely depressed" and moving restlessly about the *Clyde*. According to Stephens, Davis was also emotional. Although the former executive officers initially retained their wartime distance, they became more cordial as they traveled. By the end, an empathetic Stephens reported that Davis's "tone evinced deep feeling." Yet throughout, Davis exercised self-control. All the former Confederates respected Davis's position. At dinner all stood until Davis, at the head of the table, and his wife were seated.

The *Clyde* entered Hampton Roads on May 20 and anchored. The destination had been changed. Stephens, Reagan, and the aides were removed to continue on to their places of imprisonment. After the others had waited two days, precipitate action occurred. With practically no warning—Varina claimed five minutes—Davis and Clay were taken away. The two men were herded into a small boat bound for Fortress Monroe, which overlooked the meeting of the James River and Chesapeake Bay.[1]

The U.S. War Department had planned carefully for imprisoning Davis, whom it designated a "state prisoner." Assistant Secretary of War Charles A. Dana even came down from Washington to oversee Davis's incarceration. The post itself had a new commander, Major General Nelson A. Miles, a twenty-six-year-old war hero. According to Dana, when Davis strode into the fort on May 22, "his face was somewhat flushed, but his features were composed and his step firm"; Dana also discerned "a haughty attitude." The Federal authorities had two overriding concerns: they feared either an escape plot or a suicide attempt. These cares prompted extraordinarily tight security. Miles even had authority to place his prisoner in irons, if he deemed it appropriate.

The cells prepared for Davis and Clement Clay were not in the post stockade but in the casemate, or outer wall, of the fort. Each prisoner occupied an inner room in the casemate, with the windows heavily barred. Because the grated iron door to the outer room had not been completed, the wooden door was barred and secured from the outside. A sentry stood within the cell, and two more outside the door. Davis and Clay were under constant observation; as Clay complained to his wife, even bathing and "all the acts of nature" took place within the guard's view. The furnishings were sparse: a hospital bed with iron bedstead, a chair and table, a movable stool chest, a Bible, and within days an Episcopal prayer book. They ate food prepared in the hospital, not ordinary rations, though they were allowed neither knives nor forks. A lamp burned constantly. The omnipresent light, the changing of the guard every two hours, and the incessant tramping of the sentinels made normal sleep impossible.

On the twenty-third, General Miles ordered that manacles be placed on Davis's ankles. The ostensible reason was to secure him during the replacement of the wooden door, but in the same circumstances Clay was left unshackled. The clear intention was humiliation. When an officer appeared with the manacles, Davis, who thought the irons insulting, responded forcefully. As the blacksmith stooped to affix them, Davis flung him to the floor. Soldiers cocked muskets, but the officer in charge said no firing. He commanded that four strong men be brought in to subdue Davis. They pinned him down. Still, Davis initially managed to kick the blacksmith away. Finally the shackles were riveted around his ankles and locked together. Davis lay on his bed and covered himself with his blanket.

Within three days newspapers carried the story that Davis had been placed in irons. Many northerners, including some prominent Republicans, protested. On May 28 Secretary of War Edwin M. Stanton wired Miles inquiring about the shackles and directing their removal. Responding on the same day, Miles told the secretary they had been removed. Davis was shackled for at most five days.

Two months after Davis's imprisonment the War Department improved his circumstances. The night lamp and the guard were removed from his cell. He could also exercise outdoors, though he could never be alone and still could not communicate with anyone but official personnel. When Davis and Clay saw each other on their walks, they could not speak to each other.

In October another marked improvement occurred. With the approach of winter, Davis's attending physician, Dr. John J. Craven, recommended to General Miles that the prisoner be moved out of the dank casemate. The general concurred and received approval from the War Department to implement the recommendation. Cells were prepared for Davis as well as for Clay in Carroll Hall, where officers' quarters were located. Davis described his corner room on the second story as about 18 by 20 feet, with a fireplace, which he relished. The door leading to the gallery had a fixed iron grating; the other door, which opened into the room occupied by the officer of the guard, also had an iron grating and locked on the outside. His bed was in one corner; on the opposite side were water basin, pitcher, and a folding screen, which meant he could tend to personal matters unobserved. There was a shelf for books and a peg for clothes. Although the night lamp did not return, the tread of the guards, who could view the cell, never ceased.

Even though Davis remained in close confinement and under constant guard, his jailers did permit him to receive gifts from family and friends. Varina sent cochineal shirts, which he used every night, and an overcoat. He also received cigars and brandy, which he enjoyed. These items certainly made his captivity less spartan.

Though Davis's incarceration did not help his health, his physical condition did not deteriorate as sharply as his medical history might have predicted. He fared about as well as he did for most of his adult life. Neuralgia and boils plagued him, as did erysipelas on his face. Yet he complained more about interrupted sleep than physical maladies. He received close and careful medical attention both from Dr. Craven and from physicians sent occasionally from Washington. The U.S. government had no interest in leaving itself open to the charge that it had intentionally disregarded Davis's physical well-being. Dr. Craven and his patient developed a close tie, forming a personal as well as professional relationship. The doctor literally ministered to Davis, who spoke of Dr. Craven's kindness and solicitude. In December 1865 Craven was replaced by Dr. George E. Cooper, who equaled Craven in both the medical care given and the personal concern exhibited. Dr. Cooper improved Davis's diet and taught him to make coffee in a pot provided by Virginia Clay, who reported both Dr. and Mrs. Cooper as fast friends of her husband and Davis.[2]

The state prisoner had few visitors. In late summer Richard Taylor appeared at Fortress Monroe. Davis's former brother-in-law had spent weeks in Washington hounding President Johnson for permission to see Davis. Finally Johnson relented. Taking a steamer down Chesapeake Bay from Baltimore, Taylor remembered his full emotions as he approached Davis's casemate. Silently the two men shook hands. After a time Davis said, "this is kind, but no more than I expected of you." Taylor found him worn and with an ophthalmological inflammation. Although Davis did not complain, he indicated that the constant light and noise of the guards prevented decent sleep. He made no mention of his having been shackled. He wanted to know about his family in particular and about conditions in the South in general. Taylor wrote that he responded as positively as he could. He ended his stay by telling Davis his imprisonment had endeared him to southerners. "I think he derived consolation from this view," Taylor concluded.[3]

In the fall President Johnson dispatched Secretary of the Treasury Hugh McCulloch to check on Davis's treatment. Upon their meeting, McCulloch recorded that Davis's "gait was erect, his step elastic." The prisoner seemed "neither depressed in spirits nor soured in temper." Questioned, Davis did answer that in the beginning he had been "barbarously" treated but now had no real complaint. McCulloch gave a full assessment: "He had the bearing of a brave and high-bred gentleman, who, knowing that he would have been highly honored if the Confederate States had achieved their independence would not and could not demean himself as a criminal because they had not."[4]

Besides Taylor's single appearance, Davis saw only one other person he counted as a friend. Although by the end of 1865 Virginia Clay had won permission to visit her husband, she was not allowed to see Davis. Yet by that time the authorities permitted the Reverend Charles A. Minnigerode, Davis's former pastor at St. Paul's in Richmond, to spend time at Fortress Monroe. Davis enjoyed Minnigerode's visitations. They prayed together, and the minister celebrated communion with the prisoner. The two men could talk, and Minnigerode brought welcome news of friends and associates.[5]

As Davis tried to adjust to his captivity, preparations were underway to defend him against whatever charge or charges the United States might decide to bring against him. At the center of this effort stood Charles O'Conor, a native of Ireland who had immigrated to America as a small child and had become a luminary of the New York City bar. Soon after news of Davis's capture reached him, the sixty-four-year-old O'Conor decided to offer his considerable legal talents to the state prisoner's defense. An ardent states' rights Democrat and a classical strict-constructionist, O'Conor believed that Davis and his fellow seceders had properly interpreted the Constitution. Moreover, he was convinced that lovers of constitutional government had to thwart what he saw as the Republican rush to trample the Constitution and punish former Confederates by whatever means possible.

Volunteering to be Davis's counsel was not a simple matter. On May 31 O'Conor wrote Secretary of War Stanton saying that he intended to represent Davis and requesting permission to inform his prospective client. Stanton replied that O'Conor could do so by sending an open letter to Davis through the U.S. attorney general in Washington. On June 2 the lawyer followed Stanton's instructions. Davis accepted and was given writing materials to frame a response, which he forwarded through General Miles and the attorney general. The latter sent Davis's letter back for revisions, but Davis never got the opportunity to revise it. Despite several attempts, O'Conor never received a written agreement from Davis, nor was he permitted to visit Fortress Monroe. In the end O'Conor simply asserted that he represented Davis, a role that everyone on both sides accepted.[6]

In his determination to provide Davis the best possible legal defense, O'Conor had important northern allies. Most had been well-known figures in the prewar Democratic party, including some who had been close to Davis. Prominent among them were Caleb Cushing, Franklin Pierce, and Jeremiah Black, who had served in James Buchanan's cabinet. These men maintained contact with one another, and all concurred that O'Conor should take the legal lead. From the opposite political side came Francis Blair, Sr., who had turned to the Republicans in the 1850s but was now in the process of moving his allegiance back to the Democrats. An enthusiastic enlistee from the Republican camp, Horace Greeley, the influential editor of the *New York Tribune*, who had participated in the futile peace conversations with Clay in Canada, made every effort to aid Davis's counsel.[7]

From the outset O'Conor asserted forcefully that he took on Davis's defense to uphold principle and that he had no interest in a fee. Yet word promptly reached him that ample money existed to defray all costs, whatever they might be. From London, James M. Mason informed him that Confederate funds held primarily by Colin J. McRae, the chief Confederate financial agent in Europe, would be made available, basically in whatever amount he needed. Initially McRae placed £500 in a London bank; over the next two years that sum would increase at least sixfold. John C. Breckinridge and Jacob Thompson also guaranteed access to former Confederate resources they controlled or possessed. In addition, the Mississippi legislature appropriated $20,000 for Davis's defense, and the governor made it available to his attorneys. O'Conor continued to reject compensation for himself, though he accepted and used for expenses the money offered. Although a detailed accounting of the sources and expenditures is not possible, the Davis legal team never suffered from poor financial health.[8]

Attorney O'Conor also decided he would have only one client. If any leading Confederates were brought to trial, he believed Davis would be first, and his case would set crucial precedents for all that followed. As a result he refused to become directly connected with any other potential defendants. At the same time he viewed defending Davis as defending all his associates. One trial he shunned was that of Captain Henry Wirz, the Swiss-born commandant of the Confederate prison camp at Andersonville, Georgia. Because of the appalling mortality rate there, the government and many northerners branded Wirz an inhuman beast, even though he had had little control over the overcrowding and horrendous supply situation. Tried before a military tribunal, Wirz was convicted and condemned to death. To his regret O'Conor concluded he could not risk even paying for Wirz's counsel because he feared contaminating Davis's defense. In November, Wirz went to the gallows, the only Confederate executed as a war criminal. There were reports that Wirz had been offered his life if he would implicate Davis in what had transpired at Andersonville. Refusing, Wirz maintained he never had any dealings with his commander in chief.

While O'Conor focused on his mission to his client, he had no idea of what legal strategy his opponents intended. All information coming to him in the summer and fall pointed to a government so fractured that it could not decide how to proceed against its most notorious prisoner. O'Conor kept telling his allies they had to prepare for every conceivable eventuality. To Breckinridge, O'Conor underscored his uncertainty: "If the government has any fixed design in respect to [Davis], it is totally unknown to me. All is conjecture; but there is a prevailing impression that the government is unable to deal with the subject and is patiently awaiting some providential extrication from its doubts."[9]

O'Conor was right. The Johnson administration indeed had difficulty deciding what to do with its state prisoner. In the immediate aftermath of Lincoln's assassination and the concurrent plots against other high-ranking government officers, the War Department, with Secretary Stanton's enthusiastic endorsement, claimed that Davis was intimately involved in the conspiracy that resulted in Lincoln's murder as well as other failed intrigues. But the trials in late May of the assassin John Wilkes Booth's immediate associates brought forward no new damning evidence. In subsequent investigations this supposedly crystal-clear certainty turned murky. A few officials clung to the theory of Davis's responsibility, but most observers found the evidence flimsy, even fraudulent.[10]

Attempting to advise the president, Johnson's cabinet found itself deeply divided. Secretary of State William Seward and Stanton urged a firm policy. They wanted Davis charged with treason and tried, as Booth's compatriots had been, before a military tribunal. Led by Attorney General James Speed, others had serious reservations on both charge and venue. These men thought Davis should be brought before a civil court, if he were to be tried, because the war was over and the president's Amnesty Proclamation of May 29 granted amnesty and pardon to former Confederates, with few exceptions, including Davis. On the accusation itself, Speed argued that "any competent and independent tribunal" would acquit Davis of treason. He made three basic points: the rebellion was a general action by the southern people in which foreign powers had given belligerent rights; the United States had acknowledged those same rights in its policies on prisoners of war; the Constitution required that Davis be tried where the treasonable acts took place, and he would never be convicted in Virginia or any other southern state. Despite these divisions the cabinet finally agreed, with two dissenting votes, to recommend to Johnson that Davis be tried for treason in a civil court.

Johnson also confronted a vexing problem within the federal judiciary. If Davis were indicted and brought to trial in the most logical place, Virginia, the chief justice of the United States, Salmon P. Chase, would hear the case. In a time when justices of the Supreme Court still traveled on federal circuits and sat alongside federal district judges, Virginia was in the circuit assigned to the chief justice. Chase had a strong opinion about the role of courts in a democracy. A major Republican politician before 1861 and secretary of the treasury in Lincoln's cabinet prior to his judicial appointment in 1864, he declared he would not participate in any judicial proceeding as long as military authority remained in a state. He believed courts should not operate until "all possibility of claim that the judicial is subordinate to the military power is removed by express declaration of the President." Although Johnson was well aware of Chase's stand, he had made no such declaration.[11]

With his cabinet divided, though moving toward agreement, and with Chief Justice Chase an impediment, Andrew Johnson was unsure how to proceed. In the spring and summer of 1865 he stated unequivocally that he wanted Davis punished, and in May he helped obtain an indictment for treason against Davis and others from a federal grand jury in Norfolk. This indictment was literally lost and never became part of the record. Even so, the federal court refused warrants on the grounds that none would be issued for anyone who had surrendered to lawful authority. According to Hugh McCulloch, Johnson kept insisting that Davis deserved prosecution and conviction, and Johnson never revoked his proclamation of May 2 accusing Davis of complicity in the plot against Lincoln. But the president felt constrained by the opinion of his chief law officer.[12]

With Jefferson imprisoned and politicians and lawyers deliberating his legal fate, Varina stepped forward to take charge of her family. After her husband had been taken from the *Clyde*, she was not allowed to leave the ship. Instead, the Federal authorities sent her back down the coast to Savannah, where the U.S. Army kept her basically under town arrest. Closely watched and restricted to the town, she lived in a hotel.

Upon her arrival in Savannah, she wrote that she trudged from the docks to the hotel "quite in emigrant fashion." She had primary responsibility for her four children, with assistance only from her twenty-three-year-old sister Margaret, who had spent the war years with her, and Robert Brown, a former Davis slave who stood steadfastly by his mistress's side. Varina had very little money and practically no possessions, even clothes. According to her, Federal soldiers from Irwinville to the *Clyde* had ransacked the family belongings and taken whatever they pleased. She and her children had barely more than they wore.

Although the warm reception given her by the citizens of Savannah heartened Varina, the well-being of her little ones caused great anxiety. She feared the torrid temperatures of a Deep South summer would devastate her unacclimated brood. The baby, Varina Anne—Piecake— did come down with whooping cough, and her mother was convinced the heat made it worse. Yet potential psychological and physical harm concerned Varina even more than disease. She was greatly distressed at the taunting of her sons by other boys and soldiers. Three-and-a-half-year-old Billy even picked up the words to the popular ditty "We'll Hang Jeff Davis on a Sour Apple Tree." The social revolution accompanying the destruction of slavery engulfed her when a black soldier leveled his gun at a young Davis who had called him "uncle," a paternalistic endearment whites often used for favorite older bondsmen during slavery.[13]

Desperate to get the children away from what she considered the multiple horrors of Savannah, Varina decided to send them to Canada, under her mother's care. Margaret Howell, with her daughter Maggie and Robert Brown's aid, would oversee three grandchildren. Varina would keep the baby. The little troop of refugees left in mid-July, and by the end of the month had arrived in New York City, where friends of the Davises assisted them. Soon they went on to Montreal, where Margaret Howell settled in a boardinghouse and initially placed the two older children in Catholic schools.[14]

Maintaining her family and sending most of it to the emotional and physical safety she envisioned in Canada required financial means, a constant worry for Varina. She had very little money when she arrived in Savannah. Thereafter, a few family members and friends did contribute small amounts, but her main source of revenue came from some of the same former Confederates providing for her husband's defense, chiefly Colin McRae. From England he initially sent her £200 and then set up an account of £2,500 for her. All did not go smoothly, however, for delays occurred in the receipt and transfer of funds. Yet Judah Benjamin wrote that the bulk of the money should stay in England to ensure that the U.S. government did not learn about it and possibly confiscate it. Working with a banker in Charleston who drew drafts on the account in England, she shepherded her finances. Telling her mother not to spend too much, she made clear that her resources had definite limits.[15]

Varina kept trying to get authorization so that she could leave Savannah and join either her family in Canada or her husband. But she was bothered by intimations that if she left the country, she might not be allowed to return, thus making it uncertain she would ever see her husband again. In her first success in late July, she gained permission to depart Savannah in the care of a friend, George Schley, who lived just outside Augusta. She considered this location much more salubrious for herself and her baby. Giving them a comfortable, caring home, the Schleys treated Varina and her daughter as family. Living with the Schleys far surpassed hotel life in Savannah; but Varina remained separated from three of her children, and her prisoner-husband still faced an unknown fate.[16]

During these trying weeks of separation and difficult choices, Varina exhibited great strength and decisiveness. But in unburdening to friends she revealed painful fissures in a formidable facade. Describing herself as "broken hearted" and her eyes as "faded by tears," she spoke of "a maze of horrors" through which she had been "groping." In a September letter to Mary Chesnut she held back nothing: "As for me I have nothing—but my one little ewe lamb—my baby. I will not go through the weary form of telling you how I have suffered—But enough to content any enemy, be he ever so blood thirsty—you know I bled inwardly—and suffer more because not put in the surgeon's hands as one of the wounded—I never report unfit for duty."[17]

Despite the tribulations and hardships, Varina undertook a vigorous campaign on behalf of her husband. She had three basic goals: removing the taint of assassination from his name; obtaining better treatment for him; and winning the right to visit him. She started early and never let up. From the *Clyde* en route to Savannah, she implored Frank Blair to intercede with the president for her. During the next few months she penned petitions to powerful men like Greeley, General Ulysses Grant, and even President Johnson. She also corresponded with Charles O'Conor and his associates, who kept her fully posted on what they knew about the government's intentions and on their own.

Her crusade met with little success. By the autumn no responsible government official continued to believe that Davis had been involved with Lincoln's murder, but their attitude resulted chiefly from the absence of solid, persuasive evidence, not from Varina's disclaimers. Correspondents like Blair and Greeley promised to help, and they did bring her pleas to Johnson's attention. But they could not get her to Fortress Monroe or her husband released or tried. Caught in a tangled legal and political web, Andrew Johnson took no action.[18]

Although unable to accomplish what she wanted for her husband, Varina finally found herself freed from Georgia. In January 1866 she received permission from the War Department to join her family in Canada. Even though she continued to worry about Jefferson in prison, she seized the opportunity. But before heading north, she decided to turn west and visit Mississippi and Louisiana, where she had not been since 1861. Accompanied by Burton Harrison, who had been recently released from prison, she struck out in February. On a trip that lasted more than a month she went by train to Jackson and New Orleans, where she spent fifteen frantic days, and then upriver to Vicksburg. Along the way she visited relatives and friends, including Joseph

Davis, whom she saw in Vicksburg. She reported to Jefferson that his eighty-two-year-old brother retained his mental powers and looked much the same, except for whiter hair and increased deafness.

Visiting over, Varina started back north, with Burton Harrison still her companion. She praised him for being "all in the world" to her, as much as she could hope for in a grown son. They traveled by steamboat up to Cincinnati and then by rail to New York City. While there she conferred with Charles O'Conor and Richard Taylor before continuing on to Canada. On April 14 she reached her mother's boardinghouse in Montreal.[19]

While Varina was struggling to take care of her children and campaign on behalf of her husband, the couple could only communicate via letters, which were not confidential. For three months after their separation on May 22, 1865, no direct communication occurred between them. Finally, in late August, Davis received permission to write his wife, and on August 21 he did so for the first time. He detailed the rules governing his writing: he had to confine himself to family matters, and his letters would be examined by the attorney general of the United States before final transmission. Varina could also write to him.[20]

For the ensuing eight months this correspondence became Davis's lifeline to those he cared most about. His letters demonstrated how close he and Varina had become in the cauldron of war. His enduring solicitude for his children revealed a devoted, loving father. He also laid bare a deep and abiding Christian faith that had become central in his life and brought him invaluable comfort in his imprisonment. In addition, he talked about himself, ranging from his regimen at Fortress Monroe to his sense of his role as the incarcerated former chief executive of the defunct Confederate States of America.

Expressions of love for his wife rushed ahead like the waters in a flood. In the first letter, on August 21, he described her as "equally the center of my love and confidence." "Someday," he professed, "I hope to be able to tell you how in the long weary hours of my confinement, busy memory has brought many tributes to your tender and ardent affection." Similar professions leaped from almost every later letter. In October he told her, "you have a key to my heart and know its unuttered feelings." A month later, he wrote: "May the Lord have you in his holy keeping and send the comforter to your sorrowing heart. Shut out from the ever changing world I live in the past with a vividness only thus to be accounted all the events of all the years of our love rise before me and bear witness how very dear you are to your Husband." He left no doubt about her importance to him: "Your care protected me from many ills, your hand assuaged suffering, your voice told of happy things and breathed the music sweetest to my ears, your pious spirit recalled me from thorny paths and led me into the bosom of the Church."[21]

In addition to affirming his love, Davis also evinced great pride in his wife's vitality and her willingness to act. He marveled at how she coped with her struggle in Georgia and the difficult decisions about the children. Voicing confidence that she would make the right choices about her own and the children's future, he said he never doubted her strength and her determination. His frustration came from his inability to aid her materially. Because he knew so little of what was actually happening, he could not give sound advice. He urged her to call on his brother Joseph and their good friends for counsel, but he expressed no caveats about his wife's ultimate judgments.

As always, his children absorbed him. Varina's reports of the taunts and insults they suffered in Savannah raised his ire; he wanted to lash out at those who menaced his little ones. Aside from those unsavory incidents, word of their activities greatly pleased him. He cherished the photographs that Varina sent; in one letter she included a handprint of their baby. He was especially attentive to information about schooling. The two oldest being placed in Roman Catholic institutions in Canada pleased him because he retained fond memories of his own early education. His concern for their well-being caused him to stress to Varina that she must place her responsibility for them ahead of any she felt for him. In his opinion, they needed her desperately, while he could hold on. Anxiety came when he learned his darlings worried about their father; he wanted no such disquietude intruding into their lives.[22]

Davis also occasionally heard directly when Varina forwarded letters from ten-year-old Maggie—or Polly, the name her father preferred. Always addressing her "precious father," the little girl described her activities at school and reported on her brothers, telling him that both were good boys and well. She asked for a picture and some hair. In response a loving father said that he constantly prayed that God would watch over his "precious lambs." He counseled her to obey school rules and strive to do right. Like her, he too wanted their family together once again. His prayer was that God would see fit to reunite them, if it be God's will, "And oh! may it be his will."[23]

The Davis children in Canada.
Beauvoir, The Jefferson Davis Home and Presidential Library

Davis thought about his brother Joseph and his mother-in-law, Margaret Howell, as well. He was especially uneasy about Joseph's condition and fate, fearing that Joseph's relationship to him would bring increased hardship on his brother. He told Varina that he wanted to do much for the man who had meant so much to him throughout his life, though sadly he realized that he could do nothing. The knowledge that Margaret Howell, whom he had long termed "Ma," had taken charge of her grandchildren in Canada prompted his gratitude. He regularly asked about her and wanted his appreciation relayed to her.

Matching Davis's love for his family was his devotion to his God. During the course of the war his Christian faith had deepened, and in prison it provided enormous comfort. References to the Bible, the Book of Common Prayer, and his own prayers formed a substantial part of every letter. Discussing his Christian conviction, Davis concentrated on two topics. First, he repeatedly praised the goodness and mercy of God, who through Jesus Christ would always watch over His flock, no matter its predicament. "His goodness and my unworthiness . . . does not press one back," Davis declared, "for the atoning mediator is the way, and his hand upholds me." Second, he saw God as the architect of all events; His will controlled the world. As a Christian he accepted God's will, even when it led to unwanted results. This interpretation of an active God's power helped Davis endure having absolutely no control over his fate. He proclaimed to Varina that "all things are set in order by infinite wisdom and goodness."[24]

Davis also wrote about his activities. Aware that his wife worried about him, especially his health and the burdens of his captivity, he related in detail his physical condition and his living situation. On October 20 he described his daily routine: rose and dressed; read the morning prayer, sometimes adding a passage from both the New Testament and Psalms; breakfast; secular reading; soon after 11 a.m. appropriate portions of the Book of Common Prayer and of Scripture; afternoon, more secular reading; walk with General Miles for an hour; evening, the appointed service from the Book of Common Prayer; night, family prayer. He repeatedly told Varina not to believe the wild tales in the press about his treatment. He never failed to reassure her that his circumstances were far from awful. In the fall, when they measurably improved, he reported the improvement. In addition, he informed her that certain individuals, notably his physicians and the chaplain, treated him with care and kindness. Even the army officers on the post showed him respect and courtesy.

But his activities were few, and he confessed that the hours often dragged. Besides his religious observances and the once daily exercise, he had little to occupy his time. Outside visitors were not permitted, except for the Reverend Minnigerode, who came infrequently. He did get newspapers, though irregularly, and enjoyed them. In 1866 he tried to follow Varina's travels in their columns. Access to newspapers prompted his cautioning her not to accept at face value their accounts of his treatment.

Davis was allowed to make use of the post library, and occasionally someone sent him a book he enjoyed. Although he told Varina that the library held mostly military manuals and texts used at West Point, he did find worthy reading material. He specifically mentioned George Bancroft's *History of the United States* and Thomas Macaulay's *History of England*. He even said the technical military volumes "serve[d] the useful purpose of turning my thoughts from painful reflections, and are not without interest to me. . . ."[25]

He meditated on the meaning of his imprisonment for himself and for his vanquished country, which he now identified as the South. He did not shy away from the role of martyr. Declaring his confidence in his "ability to bear much and bear long," he let her know, "I have not sunk under my trials." "I would rather be a sacrifice for the country," he claimed, "than it should be a sacrifice for me." He hoped "the spirit of vengeance [would] be satiated by my sacrifice so that my family and countrymen would then be left in peace." With his vision of his new service to the South, Davis defined the creed he embraced as "man's dignity to bear up against trials, under which the lower animals would sink."[26]

It was not a one-way correspondence; Varina wrote as often as he did. Her letters to her jailed husband overflowed with declarations of love and praise that encouraged and sustained him. As he told her, her missives "brought the only cheering ray which ever lights up the gloom of my imprisonment." Her love knew no bounds and her admiration no limits. Naming him "my first and only love," she announced, "I bless God for every hour that I have borne your spotless name." He was "the lover of my youth and the Husband of my choice." "But I lose my sense and reason when I think of you," she confessed.[27]

Throughout these letters Varina presented an almost undaunted face and unbroken will. With God's help, she said, and secure in her husband's steadfast love, she could deal with the myriad problems she faced. She left no doubt about the importance of hearing from him: "your letters are the sweetest books to me. . . ." Yet her massive difficulties and worry about Jefferson caused intense anxiety. At the beginning of 1866 she confided to a friend that her eyes were swollen from crying. "I am so very wretched, so very hopeless," she admitted. But no matter how distraught she became, her determination to do for her children and campaign for her husband never flagged. She saw herself as head of her family and responsible for its well-being.[28]

Their "painful separation," in Jefferson's phrase, drew them closer together. Spiritually and emotionally they had become utterly intertwined. Although the end of the war brought no peace to Jefferson and Varina Davis, they confronted their new conflict as one. The visceral horror of defeat, enforced separation, and fear of an unknown future only welded more securely their close wartime bonds.[29]

Varina's pleas had not been totally in vain. In the spring of 1866

President Johnson finally permitted her to rejoin Jefferson. Just after she reached Montreal in mid-April, the War Department notified her that she could go to her husband. With her baby she immediately headed for Fortress Monroe, arriving on a cold morning in early May. She recalled an emotional reunion. First, she had to sit in an open waiting room until an officer from the fort appeared. He brought a parole she had to sign, promising not to deliver any deadly weapons to her husband. Then she was taken to a casemate and shortly thereafter joined by General Miles, who asked if she understood the terms of her parole. Following her affirmative response, another officer escorted her to Carroll Hall and up the stairs to Jefferson's cell. Upon entering the guard room, she could see the barred door. She recollected, "Through the bars of the inner room I saw Mr. Davis's shrunken form and glassy eyes; his cheek bones stood out like those of a skeleton. Merely crossing the room made his breath come in short gasps, and his voice was scarcely audible." She went in, and the door was locked behind her.

This was no temporary visit. Varina moved into quarters in the casemate, where she resided with her Piecake. Burton Harrison termed them "tolerably comfortable." Later in the month, Jefferson's privileges were broadened to allow him to walk the grounds of the fort unguarded during daylight hours. For that license he had to pledge not to attempt escape. As a result, he and his wife could spend their days together and share meals, but at night the prisoner had to remain alone in his cell.

In the autumn, their circumstances improved significantly. Varina was permitted to live with her husband in a four-room apartment with a kitchen set up for them in Carroll Hall. They still enjoyed the freedom of the post during the day, and they could socialize. The Davises became friends with Dr. Cooper and his wife, who shared food with them. Advisers and comrades came often and enlivened their home. In addition, Davis enjoyed cigars, whiskey, wine, liqueurs, and a reading chair brought or sent by well-wishers.[30]

Even though Varina and Jefferson were together and the conditions of his imprisonment had improved vastly, she never ceased her efforts to obtain better treatment for him or even release. Her husband's health genuinely concerned her. To friends as well as public figures she depicted him as desperately ill. "It is hard to see him die by inches, the victim of tortures," she wrote to President Johnson. Her fundamental position was that prison was killing him. She argued first for a less onerous regimen and then for either a prompt trial or release on parole or bail.

Varina Davis waged a vigorous campaign to secure her goals. As before, her letters went to notable men like Horace Greeley, Reverdy Johnson, a leading Maryland Democrat, and John W. Garrett, president of the Baltimore & Ohio Railroad. She also wrote directly to President Johnson, and on one occasion called on him at the White House. While in Washington, she received influential politicians, including Republicans. In the midst of her struggle, blackness and fear sometimes gripped her. To an intimate she admitted, ". . . I seem perfectly apathetic. It has taken me a long time to come to this but this *'peine fort et dur'* to which I have been subjected has crushed hope out of me." Yet her determination and drive never wavered for long.[31]

Her major weapon was her assessment of Davis's health. Not only did she fill her appeals with dire diagnoses and prognoses, she also enlisted the aid of Dr. Cooper. In May he sent a long report to the War Department detailing his patient's ills and concluding, "should he be attacked by any of the severe forms of disease to which the tidewater region of Virginia is subject, I, with reason, fear for the result." In response the department dispatched the surgeon general of the army to examine Davis. He found Davis stronger than Dr. Cooper had indicated and saw no reason why Davis would be less responsive to treatment than any other prisoner, should he contract any local malady. He did recommend removal of the night lamp and the treading sentinel. From the surgeon general's visit until Davis's release eleven months later, the War Department required weekly written medical reports on Davis.[32]

To help her campaign, Varina fired heavy barrages at General Miles. In her script he became a hateful monster who watched happily over the deterioration of his star prisoner. In a fundamental sense she orchestrated a political battle against Miles, a politically astute officer who understood his antagonist's goals and appreciated her cleverness. Rebutting her accusations of maltreatment, he countered to his superiors with a brief relating his oversight of Davis. Although Miles had started out quite hostile to Davis and never became friendly, he presided over a considerable easing of Davis's prison regime. And Miles rightly maintained that Varina Davis exaggerated her husband's physical debility. Even so, he could not best her. Against his wishes, President Johnson in September reassigned him.[33]

His replacement, Brigadier General Henry S. Burton, was more acceptable to the Davises. In fact, Varina considered the general and his wife friends and always spoke highly of them. Never exhibiting any animus toward either of the Davises, General Burton did what he could for the prisoner. He eliminated the light that so interfered with Davis's sleep, and later authorized the couple's living together in the Carroll Hall apartment.

In truth, Davis's health varied over time. In the summer of 1866 Varina and Dr. Cooper expressed grave concern. Others who visited him described him as emaciated and feeble. Yet in the fall and winter he seemed better. Even Dr. Cooper made basically positive statements in his weekly reports. Although somewhat weaker than he had been upon his incarceration, Davis in 1866 and 1867 was not measurably poorer in health than he had been for at least a decade and a half.[34]

After his wife's arrival at Fortress Monroe, Davis could enjoy family life, though truncated, and he could also have visitors. They came in numbers, including former associates like his fellow inmate Clement Clay, who had been released in April 1866, Richard Taylor, Burton Harrison, and the Reverend Minnigerode. His attorneys also appeared to consult with their client. In the spring of 1867, Franklin Pierce traveled to Fortress Monroe to see his old comrade, a visit that had special meaning for Davis.[35]

The continued absence of three of his four children sharply marked the limits on Davis's family life. The three oldest remained in Canada with Grandmother Howell. They and their father did correspond, however. Polly wrote most often, but Jeff Jr. and even little William penned notes to their father. They told him how much they loved him, missed him, and wanted him to be with them. They also gave him glimpses of their activities. Telling of his falling in a river and being pulled out by a friend, Jeff concluded, "I was only wet." Polly talked about studying hard and learning hymns and poetry. She let him know that Billy could read quite well. And she added, "I am trying very hard to be all you desire." Rejoicing in them, a proud father congratulated "My dear Daughter" on her hard work and performance in school. He sent word that their mother and baby sister had brought him great pleasure.[36]

Although thrilled to be with her husband, on several occasions Varina took trips away from Fortress Monroe. She was not restricted to the post. Most often her travels concerned her efforts to help Jefferson. Consultations with political allies and attorneys found her in

Washington, Baltimore, New York City, and even Lake George, New York, where she met with Charles O'Conor, who was on vacation. In December 1866 she went back to Montreal to see her mother, sister, and children. From there she detailed activities of their little ones for her husband, and returned with her sister Maggie, who resided with the Davises at Fortress Monroe. In March and early April 1867 she had an extended stay in Baltimore where she did talk with allies, but spent most of her time having extensive dental surgery. She reported to Jefferson that most of her teeth had been removed; in one operation under chloroform, more than a half dozen were extracted.

Keeping in touch with Jefferson on these journeys, she always declared her love. "I seem sanctified by our last long kiss as we parted," she confided, "and the memory of your love gives me confidence to do anything except risk your displeasure." From Montreal she pledged, "When I get in your 'l'arms again I shall never willingly leave you again." Yet she also realized that lack of certainty continued to plague their future. "I *have no answer* yet," she informed him in mid-March 1867. "I see no plainer." Still she hoped.[37]

Although uncertainty about what would happen troubled the Davises, the overwhelming majority of southerners had no doubt about the man who had led their failed struggle for independence. Throughout the war Davis had stood as the preeminent public man in the Confederacy. No other political leader ever mounted a credible challenge to his domination. By the last winter General Robert E. Lee had eclipsed Davis in prestige, but Lee's ascendancy did not mean that most Confederates had turned on their president. Even defeat did not signal widespread denigration of Davis. Although some southerners blamed him for the disaster, they were distinctly in the minority. A few observers made a great deal of this anti-Davis sentiment, but it had much in common with wartime opposition to the president—shrill and strident, yet localized, and largely ineffectual.[38]

When Davis entered Fortress Monroe, an angry and disenchanted South did not cheer imprisonment as the proper punishment for a castigated leader. At the same time, incarceration did serve to endear Davis to the South. Most southerners had respected him and admired his dedication to the Confederate cause, but they had not cherished him. As a prisoner Davis became a symbol for the lost Confederacy. Former Confederates did not believe they had done anything wrong. They were convinced they had acted legally and constitutionally in creating their government, and then had carried on a noble fight. Because they certainly did not think they deserved imprisonment, they viewed Davis as standing in for them. His treatment became their treatment, his bars their bars.

Thoughtful southerners made the force of this outlook unmistakable. "I cannot tell you," General Lee told a former staff officer, "how much I have suffered, & still suffer on account of Mr. Davis. . . ." A prewar congressman from North Carolina, who emphasized his constant Unionism, told a prominent Republican senator that all southerners, not just those who had been zealous Confederates, were deeply solicitous about Davis and his family. A longtime student of southern public opinion acknowledged that not everyone had agreed with Davis in the final months of the war, but everyone had believed him "true and faithful to the trust which had been reposed in him." Furthermore, Howell Cobb explained, there was no indifference in the South to Davis's fate, for southerners considered him "their representative man."[39]

Individual southerners demonstrated their feelings about Davis by their actions. To help him and his family, a group in Mississippi calling itself Ladies for the President's Family raised some $4,000. Women in Fayetteville, North Carolina, sent a check for Varina's use. A Baltimore tailor was engaged to make Davis a new coat, vest, and pair of pants. Visitors to Fortress Monroe treasured their experiences with the man they deemed their chief. Gifts of spirits and tobacco abounded. A former schoolteacher "yearned to be able to do something to testify my veneration and love for the man who has been called to suffer so much for our people." His letter included a poem. Writing from Richmond, a little girl told him that her friends called her Jeff Davis "because I love you so much." She also said that when her school class went to Hollywood Cemetery to decorate soldiers' graves, "your little Joe's will not be forgotten."[40]

This effort on Davis's behalf had two goals. One aimed to cheer and warm his time in prison; the other strove to influence what happened to him. From across the South, missives including petitions signed by hundreds of people bombarded the White House to urge President Johnson to release Davis. These southerners insisted that Davis was no criminal and certainly had taken no part in Lincoln's assassination. They maintained his actions had been honorable in leading a worthy cause. If Davis had committed a crime because he had led the Confederacy, they argued, so had every other Confederate, for Davis's fellow citizens had chosen him as their president. Thus, Davis should be freed or all other former Confederates arrested.[41]

Although Davis's imprisonment would have sparked a response from the South under any circumstances, the publicity highlighting his travails at Fortress Monroe helped build his image as a martyr and generated a surging reaction. Varina worked successfully to get her version of her husband's treatment into the press; for example, Dr. Cooper's drastic report appeared in several papers. In addition, Democratic journals often condemned Davis's jailing and treatment. But a book that came out in the summer of 1866 turned into the single most important item in this pro-Davis campaign. Entitled *Prison Life of Jefferson Davis, Embracing Details and Incidents in His Captivity, Particulars Concerning His Health and Habits, Together with Many Conversations on Topics of Great Public Interest*, and purportedly written by Dr. John Craven, Davis's first physician at Fortress Monroe, the work allegedly recounted details of harsh treatment as well as lengthy conversations between doctor and patient.[42]

Yet *Prison Life* had both more complicated origins and a more far-reaching design. Although Dr. Craven participated in creating the book, his was a distinctly secondary role. The man who conceived the idea for *Prison Life* and actually wrote it was not the doctor, but a strong Democratic partisan and an ardent supporter of President Johnson who also happened to be friendly with Dr. Craven. Searching for ways to advance Johnson's policies and hurt Republicans, Charles G. Halpine, an Irish immigrant, Union war veteran, and New York journalist, decided an account of Davis in prison that presented him as a victim of inhumane treatment stemming from Republican vindictiveness would help accomplish this mission.[43]

Prison Life did portray Davis as a heroic victim of evil men. Halpine pictured Davis as a devoted Christian and a keen student, who appreciated literature and other intellectual subjects, but had been cruelly manacled and brutalized by his wicked captors. Halpine's Davis was a kind man, who forgave those who tormented him; he even had Davis befriending and feeding crumbs to a mouse. In addition, this Davis spoke admiringly of Lincoln and numerous Union generals. According to *Prison Life*, Davis worried much more about the fate of his family and the South than about himself. Summing up this paragon of virtue, Halpine wrote: "Mr. Davis is remarkable for the kindness of his nature and fidelity to friends. Of none of God's creatures does he seem to wish or speak unkindly; and the same fault found with Mr. Lincoln—unwillingness to sanction the military severities essential to maintain discipline—is the fault I have heard most strongly urged against Mr. Davis."[44]

Halpine succeeded, but only in part. The book reached a wide audience, becoming a bestseller and making money for both Halpine and Dr. Craven. It also helped create Jefferson Davis the Martyr. As a former Confederate official noted upon reading *Prison Life*, "it shows him to be what the world will one day confess him, one of its greatest men." But Halpine made little headway on the political front. Republicans increasingly gained the upper hand over Johnson. Winning an overwhelming victory in the congressional elections of 1866, they took control of Reconstruction policy.[45]

Davis understood the purpose of *Prison Life*. He knew it had little connection with the reality of his time at Fortress Monroe. As early as July 1866 he had a copy of the book, which he discussed with visitors. One acknowledged that the book was accomplishing much good for those working to free Davis, but said that Davis deemed it "sensational in parts" and "in some things incorrect." The hero himself found it "particularly disagreeable." Davis went on to annotate his copy, pointing out the errors and falsehoods; he commented on more than 180 passages. Moreover, he felt that he had been used by Dr. Craven, whom he had considered a friend. In his mind Craven had betrayed confidences and falsified Davis's statements for financial gain. He never reconciled with Dr. Craven.[46]

Jefferson Davis remained entrapped by the vexing political and legal tangle at the heart of Reconstruction. The president, his cabinet, Congress, and the chief justice of the United States all had a stake and an influence, which often clashed. Forming the basic framework of Reconstruction was the ferocious conflict growing between the president and Congress that eventuated in the first presidential impeachment.

Andrew Johnson had assumed the presidency with unusual credentials at an unprecedented time. A strong Democratic partisan before the war, Johnson, as a United States senator from Tennessee, opposed secession and refused to follow his state out of the Union. In 1862 Lincoln appointed him military governor of his home state. Two years later, as Lincoln strove to rally Democrats who backed the war to his side, he selected Johnson as his vice-presidential running mate. Upon Lincoln's death Johnson became president of the United States.[47]

When Johnson took over as chief executive, all his political experience had been in the South. He had no northern base. At first he struck fierce oratorical blows at the vanquished Confederates, whom he condemned as traitors and rebels. As a champion of non-slaveholders before 1861, Johnson viewed secession and the resulting war as plots of slaveholding planters, who deserved the wrath of the victorious North. Jefferson Davis, with whom he had quarreled in the antebellum Congress, led the pack and merited especially stern handling.

Yet Johnson wanted to follow Lincoln's policy of reconciliation. In May he proclaimed amnesty for all ex-Confederates, excepting several categories of high-ranking officials and wealthy people who had in 1860 owned taxable property worth more than $20,000. Property, except for slaves, would also be restored. To the excluded groups he offered executive clemency upon individual applications for pardon. Johnson also moved to get the former Confederate states back into the Union as quickly as possible. Under his plan those states reconstituted themselves largely under leaders who had been prominent before 1860. They had to repudiate secession and the Confederate debt, and accept the destruction of slavery. After they had done so, Johnson expected the states to rejoin the Union, their representatives and senators once again sitting in Congress.

A reappearance of numerous southerners in Congress could of course lead to a substantial strengthening of the Democratic party. Moreover, in these new governments whites attempted to exercise close and harsh control over the freed slaves through laws known as Black Codes, which severely restricted the rights and economic opportunities of blacks. Neither of these developments troubled President Johnson. A resurgent Democratic party might very well look to him for leadership. And because he shared the general white southern view of race relations, the shackling of the freed people caused him no great difficulty. For the political and ideological goals of the Republican party, the party identified with the North and the victorious Union war effort, he had little sympathy.

Furthermore, in 1865 and 1866 Johnson made liberal use of his authority over prisoners and pardoning power. When the individuals excluded from his Proclamation of Amnesty applied to him for pardon, his response was overwhelmingly positive. Major figures like Alexander Stephens, Stephen Mallory, and John Reagan were paroled, released from prison, and permitted to return to their homes. In April

1866 the president freed Davis's fellow inmate, Clement Clay. In that same spring he also issued a pardon that had special meaning for Jefferson Davis. Joseph Davis received presidential clemency in March and in September had all his land restored to him.[48]

Republicans watched the evolution of Johnson's Reconstruction policy with horror. Former chieftains were again taking charge in the southern states, even former Confederate leaders. From the Republican perspective, it seemed that the war had caused no change. If such men returned promptly to Congress, Republican prospects would darken. A reunited and revivified Democratic party might again dominate the national government. Such a revival threatened the Republican hold on power, endangering Republican goals for the nation and grinding down the emancipated slaves. Although Republicans did not agree on the appropriate treatment of blacks, with the most radical wanting to give land and the vote, all advocated equality before the law, meaning basic civil rights. To Republicans the Black Codes seemed no more than a slightly revised version of the old slave codes. Moreover, the race riots that broke out in several cities, especially Memphis and New Orleans, in 1866 appeared to indicate that southern whites did not even intend to ensure physical safety for blacks. Republicans began to fear they had won the war only to lose the peace.

They moved forthrightly. Johnson's initiatives had taken place with Congress out of session. Upon reconvening in December 1865, Congress denied seats to the senators and representatives from the Johnson governments. The Republicans also passed measures intended to guarantee fundamental civil rights for blacks. In so doing they increased the power of the central government and challenged the power of the president. In the spring of 1866 Johnson vetoed these bills, which Congress then repassed over his veto.

Relations between the president and the Republicans that broke down in early 1866 only got worse. Although some congressional Republicans tried to reach an agreement with Johnson, accommodation proved impossible. They had sharply different visions of what the United States should become; he still clung to the traditional Democratic credo of states' rights, with a small, basically inactive federal government. Moreover, he and the Republicans had increasingly divergent political goals. The great battleground became the congressional elections of 1866. Both sides campaigned hard, but only in the North, for the southern states had not been readmitted. The Republicans routed the president, winning a veto-proof majority in both houses of Congress, an outcome that meant the Republican Congress, not the president, would direct the course of Reconstruction.

Although Jefferson Davis was never a paramount concern for either side, he became part of the political equation. Drumming the message that they had saved the Union from traitorous rebels, Republicans depicted Davis as the archfiend of the rebellion. Attempting to garner some Republican support and increasingly struggling to keep Congress at bay, Johnson needed Davis in prison to show he held the head of the Confederacy accountable. Thus, neither side could easily countenance releasing Davis.

President Johnson could not doubt that a sizable segment of the northern populace considered Davis a criminal who should be severely punished, perhaps even executed. Just as southerners sent torrents of mail to Johnson urging mercy and clemency for the state prisoner, northerners inundated him with demands for the sternest treatment. One petitioner wanted Davis to get life at hard labor with his own name branded on his forehead. Another recommended that Davis be exhibited throughout the country in female dress. Johnson also received advice to hang Davis on the Fourth of July as a national celebration.[49]

Not surprisingly, President Johnson talked to visitors and associates about the wide range of advice he received, and he also expressed different opinions to different people. Hugh McCulloch recalled Johnson's berating Davis as the "head devil among the traitors, and he ought to be hung." To Richard Taylor he indicated he wanted to let Davis out as soon as politically possible. When Varina Davis visited the White House, the president received her civilly. According to her, he said he never believed Davis had anything to do with Lincoln's assassination. Moreover, he told her he would have withdrawn the proclamation accusing Davis of complicity, but because of his insecure political position he could not do so. Only the passage of time and a softening of public opinion would permit him to act.[50]

Congressional Republicans also wavered in their conviction about enforcing the trial of Davis. In the spring of 1866, testimony before a House committee proved conclusively the spuriousness of evidence connecting Davis to Lincoln's murder. Earlier, wanting to know why the state prisoner had not been tried, the House had demanded information from the administration. After a delay of four months, a response was sent explaining the difficulties of getting Davis into court. Congress did not take issue with the brief presented in those documents. In sum, it accepted the status quo, which, of course, left Davis in Fortress Monroe. At times individual Republicans or a congressional committee expressed interest in the Davis case, but Congress never took any significant steps to control the fate of Jefferson Davis.[51]

When President Johnson, with the advice of his cabinet, decided in the summer of 1865 to try Davis before a federal court, the goal was to have the nation's highest courts define secession as treason. Directing the government's case, Attorney General James Speed, along with specially appointed private counsel, decided the trial would have to take place in Virginia, where Davis had actually commanded a war against the United States. They discarded as unworkable and probably unconstitutional the proposal that Davis go on trial in a northern state under the theory that he had been constructively present when his military forces invaded northern territory.

Yet the choice of Virginia presented two quite serious, quite different problems. First, court would be held in Richmond, and Speed and his associates had to face the question of whether any fairly and impartially impaneled jury in Davis's former capital would ever convict Jefferson Davis of treason. Failure to obtain a guilty verdict would have one fundamental result: the United States had fought a victorious war, which a Virginia jury declared unlawful.

The second difficulty involved the judges. Presiding over the Federal District Court in Virginia, Judge John Underwood did not have a reputation as a judicial heavyweight. A native New Yorker, Underwood had lived in the part of Virginia that became West Virginia during the war. Even though he had resided in a slave state, he became decidedly antislavery and a stalwart Republican, who stumped several northern states for Lincoln. In 1864 President Lincoln made him a federal judge. But Judge Underwood would not hear the Davis case by himself. Joining him on the bench would be Salmon P. Chase, chief justice of the United States. The district judge and the Supreme Court member sitting together constituted the Federal Circuit Court. Having Chase as a trial judge would add dignity and authority to the court and its decision.

But Chase also brought burdens. Long a nationally prominent Republican leader, the Ohioan had been in Lincoln's cabinet and still harbored presidential ambitions. Political considerations were a congenital part of his makeup. He even flirted with the Democrats. More important at the moment, Chase refused to hold court in any former

Confederate state. The majesty and the independence of the federal judiciary and his place in it assumed paramount importance for Chase. Until the declaration of a formal peace and the removal of all military authority, Chase asserted that a shadow of military influence hovered over the judiciary. He could reconcile himself to the district judge's holding court, but no more. As he wrote President Johnson in October 1865, "a civil Court in a district under martial law can only act by sanction and supervision of the military power; and I cannot think that it becomes Justices of the Supreme Court to exercise jurisdiction under such conditions."[52]

The year 1866 brought no changes. Despite Johnson's spring proclamation declaring peace, Chase still refused to sit because certain military processes continued. In May, Judge Underwood tried to move the matter by getting his grand jury to indict Davis for treason. An indictment carried with it the probability of a trial date. The administration was not prepared to commence the prosecution, however, and requested a continuance. Although neither the president nor the attorney general seemed averse to bail for the state prisoner, zealous congressional Republicans and a cabinet member convinced Underwood that he should not grant bail. In refusing, Underwood asserted that because Davis was in military custody, he could not intervene.

In the summer a new attorney general took office, but Henry Stanbery could effect nothing consequential. Because in August President Johnson had issued a final peace proclamation, Stanbery wanted Davis's case brought before the court session scheduled for October. But an inadvertent oversight by Congress enabled Chase to wreck this plan. When lawmakers reduced the number of justices from nine to seven, they made no new circuit assignments for them. Chase concluded that without this legislation neither he nor any other justice had the legal right to hold circuit courts. In finding ways to avoid actually bringing Davis to trial, Chase always had his hand on the political and public pulse. While a strident Republican minority wanted Davis tried and convicted, a majority was unsure what to do. Facing Chase's new barrier, Stanbery advocated removing Davis from military to civil custody. He maintained that because the war had now officially ended, military imprisonment was illegal. Within the administration Secretary of War Stanton successfully opposed Stanbery's ploy on the grounds that the absence of any federal prison in Virginia would necessitate transferring Davis to a state prison. There, Stanton argued, he could not be as securely held or as well cared for as at Fortress Monroe.

Thus, after eighteen months, Jefferson Davis was still lodged in Fortress Monroe. The perceived demands of politics, concern about legal issues, the stance of the chief justice, and legislative mishap had together kept the government from ever bringing Davis to trial, or deciding to parole or bail him. Davis's continued confinement did not result from the quiescence of his backers. His supporters from the political arena pressed President Johnson to act on his behalf. Frank Blair, Sr., Richard Taylor, Reverdy Johnson, former governor of Maryland Thomas Pratt, and others kept trooping to the White House pleading for a speedy trial or prompt release from prison. Horace Greeley presented a "Memorial" to the president with an identical plea.[53]

Horace Greeley occupied a unique niche among Davis's important northern supporters. Most of them had always been and remained staunch Democrats, but Greeley was counted among the nation's leading Republicans and edited arguably the most influential Republican newspaper in the country, the *New York Tribune*. From the time he received a letter from Varina Davis shortly after her husband's imprisonment, he climbed on Davis's bandwagon. He knew and respected Charles O'Conor, and introduced him to major political figures. He also lobbied in Washington, even writing on Davis's behalf directly to the chief justice.

But Greeley's two central contributions to Davis's case lay elsewhere. His *Tribune* published numerous pieces presenting Davis in a positive light and urging a prompt trial or bail. He also set about to raise money to support bail for Davis, should that development ever occur. In this endeavor he was astonishingly successful. Among those joining him, Gerrit Smith seemed even stranger than Greeley. An extremely wealthy New Yorker, Smith before the war had been a major underwriter for abolitionists. But even though he had opposed slavery as vigorously as Davis upheld it, Smith asserted that he would enthusiastically provide funds for Davis's bail. In the late summer of 1866 he informed President Johnson that Davis's long confinement without a trial did "deep dishonor to the Government and the country." The railroad baron and financial tycoon Cornelius Vanderbilt also signed on. Among the richest men in the country, Vanderbilt placed his name and money in Greeley's camp.

For an undertaking of this magnitude Greeley had multiple motives. He talked about his commitment to fairness, and without question he desired rapid reunion and sectional reconciliation. To that end, he saw

Davis's speedy trial or release as a significant step. Some asserted the perception of commercial advantage prompted him, but others said his pro-Davis acts sharply cut into his revenues from the *Tribune*. Whatever the mix of reasons, Greeley's work substantially aided Davis's cause.[54]

Davis's legal team was also hard at work. O'Conor led, but he received able assistance from George Shea, another New York City attorney, and William Reed of Philadelphia; in addition, he made use of others, including James Lyons, a prominent member of the bar in Richmond, and young Burton Harrison, who acted as a courier and general aide. O'Conor wrote directly to Andrew Johnson requesting better treatment and proposing a plan that would result in bail for Davis. He also visited Chief Justice Chase searching for a way to get his client out of prison. All the while, the lawyers tried to coordinate their efforts with their political allies.[55]

Two beacons guided O'Conor and his associates. First, they did not believe that in a fair trial with an impartial jury Davis could be convicted of treason. But they did have concerns about the courtroom. Talk in Congress of changing the law to make it easier to find Davis guilty troubled them. They also worried that Judge Underwood, a well-known advocate of confiscating land of former Confederates and of extending political rights to the freedpeople, would pack the jury with men, white and especially black, of his own political persuasion.[56]

O'Conor spelled out his interpretation of what he saw as the basic legal issue. His study convinced him that the Constitution had adopted the construction of English statute law on treason. As a result, he was convinced Davis "could not be convicted unless it was for having *levied* war." According to O'Conor, the case depended on whether in "any just interpretations" of the phrase, Davis had done so. O'Conor intended to argue that if Davis had, that act could not be separated from the war waged by both sides. For his construction to hold, he knew he had to prove that the United States had acknowledged the existence of "a *public war*." He foresaw no difficulty in making that case in a court of law.[57]

The possibility of being put in the dock for treason did not terrify Davis. He never in 1861 or thereafter believed he had committed any treasonable act. In his mind, when he left the Union he had acted constitutionally, and he had led a legal, national war, the Confederate States against the United States. His attorneys' conviction that they could triumph against any treason indictment in a court of law simply reinforced Davis's own conception of what he had done. In a post-prison letter to one of his lawyers, he stated that even when confined at Fortress Monroe, he remained steadfast. He rejected any suggestions of a petition for pardon, for he was "confident of the justice of our cause, and the rectitude of my own conduct." Burton Harrison, who knew his former chief well, understood that part of Jefferson Davis wanted his day in court so that he could broadcast to the country the legitimacy and virtue of his cause. As Davis saw it, any fair trial had to result in his vindication. Losing that opportunity for formal justification would be a disappointment to him.[58]

But Davis's attorneys recognized that no matter how sound their legal argument might be, it was politics, not law, that governed Davis's case. From the outset, observing the situation closely, and in contact with political allies, O'Conor and his colleagues understood that the continuing and deepening conflict between the Republicans in Congress and the president held their client hostage. They realized that neither side was willing to bend on Jefferson Davis because each feared giving political ammunition to the other. O'Conor and company also knew early on that Chief Justice Chase would not hold court in Virginia until by his definition all military authority had ended. Although Davis's attorneys fully comprehended the crucial role of politics, the vagaries frustrated them. Their hopes kept creeping upward, then plunging.[59]

Politics disrupted their plans. After the federal grand jury in Virginia indicted Davis in May 1866, his lawyers thought they could make a strong argument for bail. The case would be called in Judge Underwood's court in June. Worried about its legal position and the absence of Chief Justice Chase, the government decided to ask for a continuance. Despite both the chief justice and the attorney general letting Judge Underwood know they approved, countering political pressure caused the hard-pressed Underwood to deny bail. His ruling grievously disappointed Davis's counsel, who deputed Burton Harrison to carry the bad news to Fortress Monroe. The blow hit Davis hard, Harrison reported, "but he bore it in good part."[60]

While Davis's side was aware they had enemies in Congress and that President Johnson vacillated, they also believed that a quiet but effective foe in the president's cabinet compounded their problem. O'Conor derided him as "most venomous malignant," though without naming him. But O'Conor's friends and associates identified their hidden adversary as Seward, who, according to William Reed, had the decisive influence on Judge Underwood.[61]

Davis's defenders could only persevere and wait. Finally, in the spring of 1867, the legal and political currents seemed to flow toward them. Congress passed legislation assigning circuits to Supreme Court justices, removing a key reason for Chase's refusal to sit in Virginia. Although what the chief justice might actually do could not be predicted, Davis's counsel decided to try to bring their client to court in Virginia on a writ of habeas corpus, which they hoped would force either a trial or bail. The president, the attorney general, and the chief justice had signaled their willingness to accept a writ. In addition, Davis's side scored a major triumph when with the influential encouragement of John W. Garrett, Secretary of War Stanton decided not to oppose a writ. He agreed that if presented with a legitimate writ, the army would relinquish control of Davis.[62]

Appearing before Judge Underwood on May 1, George Shea applied for a writ of habeas corpus. On that day Underwood issued the writ, returnable on May 13, by which date he assumed Chase would join him for the circuit court. A week later the War Department ordered General Burton upon receipt of a valid writ of habeas corpus to turn Davis over to the U.S. marshal or his deputies.[63]

While the writ was forthcoming, the holding of a trial was more problematical. Without guidance from his superiors, and unprepared to manage the case, Lucius Chandler, the federal district attorney, traveled to Washington for assistance and directions. Attorney General Stanbery said he had no intention of participating; he argued cases only before the Supreme Court. President Johnson allowed this stance, though it differed totally from that taken by Speed, who had planned to take the lead in the case. Stanbery considered the government's special counsel William H. Evarts, an esteemed New York City lawyer, the attorney in charge. This position surprised Evarts, who had taken for granted that Stanbery would follow Speed's policy. Chase remained elusive as to whether or not he would attend the May term of the court in Richmond. Although Judge Underwood stood ready and eager to proceed with the trial, the three responsible federal lawyers decided that no trial could take place. They knew they were not ready.

Having made that decision, they shared it with O'Conor. In a conference held in Washington, they informed him that a trial would not occur and that bail would be granted. Thereupon Evarts went to

Richmond to tell Underwood what he did not want to hear. When court opened on May 13, the government would request a continuance and would agree to bail. O'Conor also headed for the Virginia capital.

Even before he met with Stanbery and his associates, O'Conor had put his team in motion. Although he had been schooled in exploded hopes, by mid-April he expressed optimism to Varina. Once Judge Underwood issued a writ of habeas corpus, O'Conor knew it would be obeyed. He dispatched Burton Harrison from New York to Fortress Monroe for the presentation of the writ. His legal colleagues also started for Richmond. On May 10 a U.S. marshal delivered the writ to General Burton, who accepted it. Harrison spent that Friday night in the fortress with the man he still served. He noted that the date, the tenth, marked the second anniversary of their capture.[64]

On Saturday morning, May 11, Davis walked out of Fortress Monroe for the first time since his incarceration. General Burton led Davis and his companions Varina, Burton Harrison, and Dr. Cooper to the wharf, where a crowd had assembled. No soldiers guarded the prisoner either en route to the ship or on board. On the trip up the James River, Davis had the freedom of the vessel. With news spreading about the special passenger, groups gathered at every landing to get a glimpse of him. At one the craft stopped, and a number of emotional women came on board "embracing and kissing [Davis]."[65]

Late in the afternoon the steamer reached Richmond and docked at Rockett's Landing. Throngs welcomed the former president; troops were present to guarantee order. Davis got into a carriage with General Burton, Dr. Cooper, and Burton Harrison. A unit of mounted troopers followed. Varina rode in another carriage with James Lyons. General Burton had made previous arrangements with the proprietor for the Davises to stay at the Spotswood Hotel, unless the U.S. marshal demanded custody of the prisoner; he did not. Along the almost two-mile route from the landing to the hotel, masses filled the streets. There were no shouts, no huzzas, but when Davis's carriage passed, men raised their hats and women waved handkerchiefs. At the Spotswood the owner showed the Davises to the same rooms they had occupied back in 1861. General Burton left his orderly at the door, but placed no restrictions on Davis.

That evening and the next day Davis received a multitude of visitors in his private parlor. They saw a pale man with gray hair and cheeks "thin and furrowed," but eager to greet them. He embraced former friends with warmth and enthusiasm. On Sunday, Burton Harrison noticed the large number of pretty women who charmed Davis. "I observed," he wrote his mother, "that he took delight in kissing the prettiest when they went out as well as when they went in."

Monday, May 13—according to Harrison, feelings in Richmond had reached "fever pitch." Early in the morning a host congregated in the two blocks between the hotel and the court, located in the Customs House, which had become the post office. The judicial proceedings were scheduled for eleven o'clock. Before ten, observers had packed the 40-foot-square courtroom on the third story of the Customs House. At that hour two companies of soldiers took up positions between the two buildings. General Burton led Davis from the rear door of the Spotswood and into a carriage for the short ride to court. Upon entering the Customs House, Davis was taken to the office of the United States attorney.

On the bench by himself, Judge Underwood called court into session at 11:18 a.m. The chief justice did not appear. Ten minutes later, escorted by General Burton and other officers, Davis entered and sat down alone, "flushed with excitement." The marshal invited Harrison to sit by his former chief, and he moved to join Davis. Davis's legal battery was in place: O'Conor, Shea, Reed, Lyons, and other colleagues they had invited. Evarts and Chandler represented the United States.

No surprises marked the occasion. As Harrison put it, "everything went according to our hopes" and the prearranged plan. General Burton formally delivered Davis to the court; Judge Underwood accepted him and relieved the general of further responsibility. Upon the judge's directive, the deputy marshal gave the writ on the indictment to Davis, who handed it to O'Conor. O'Conor then asked "that the court will now order such proper course as justice may require." He had received the indictment and wanted to know what came next. The judge desired to hear from the government. Evarts responded that the government intended no prosecution during the court's current term. O'Conor requested bail; Evarts raised no objection. Judge Underwood declared the charge against Davis bailable. The government proposed $100,000; O'Conor said the defense could handle that sum, and added he had ten men present ready to stand for $10,000 each. The government suggested that some of the guarantors reside within the court's jurisdiction. O'Conor replied that that requirement posed no problem.

After some discussion the judge announced that the court agreed on that amount and a partial residence requisite. He called on those prepared to act as sureties to come forward and sign the prepared

document. Three men stood for $25,000 each—Horace Greeley, Ger-
rit Smith, and Cornelius Vanderbilt; ten others stood for $2,500 each.
The condition of recognizance required Davis to appear at the Circuit Court term scheduled in Richmond for the fourth Monday in
November. After the signatures were affixed, Judge Underwood
instructed the marshal to discharge the prisoner.[66]

"The effect was electric," recorded Harrison. The courtroom
erupted with shouts, and people rushed toward Davis, who told Burton
Harrison to get him away as quickly as possible. Taking Davis's arm,
Harrison guided him out of the chamber, through a passage, by the
open door of what had been his presidential office, and down the same
iron stairs he had used as president. An excited, cheering assembly
waited outside.

Although hurrahs surrounded the return to the Spotswood, at the
hotel people held back. Davis went back to his room, where his wife
waited. After giving them moments alone, Harrison and the Reverend
Minnigerode joined them and locked the door. All knelt in prayer. "We
were all sobbing," Harrison wrote. Then the doors were opened, and a
legion of well-wishers poured in.

That night Jefferson and Varina left for Canada.

CHAPTER SEVENTEEN

"These Days of Our Hard Fortune"

Jefferson and Varina, with Burton Harrison in attendance, steamed up the coast to New York City. Pressing upon the former prisoner at his hotel, well-wishers wore him out. Harrison put him in a carriage and drove him to Charles O'Conor's residence above the city on the Hudson River, where he could have quiet and rest. Harrison described Davis as "looking very thin and haggard and having very little muscular strength." Even so, Harrison thought Davis's appearance had improved since he left Fortress Monroe. Moreover, his spirits were good. Harrison was convinced that rest would restore his old chief.[1]

News of Davis's release generated a torrent of letters expressing thankfulness for his freedom and sending him best wishes. The roster of writers included so many familiar names: Judah P. Benjamin, John C. Breckinridge, Howell Cobb, Robert E. Lee, Stephen Mallory, James M. Mason, Franklin Pierce, John H. Reagan, as well as the students of the University of Mississippi. Articulating the emotions of all, Lee wrote that Davis could conceive better than he could convey "the misery" that all of Davis's friends had felt during the imprisonment, especially their impotence in his hour of distress. "Your release," Lee declared, "has lifted a load from my heart which I have not words to tell." He prayed that "the great Ruler of the world" would protect Davis from all future harm and give him "that peace which the world can not take away."[2]

From New York City the Davises traveled north to Montreal and their family. A few days after their arrival James Mason came and took Jefferson away for a brief holiday at Mason's cottage in Niagara, where several ex-Confederates had settled. To greet the boat in Toronto, a Confederate sympathizer had organized a cheering assemblage of several thousand. After a lunch hosted by former Confederates and their

Canadian friends, Mason escorted Davis and a small party across Lake Ontario to Niagara. As they approached the Canadian town, Davis noticed the U.S. flag flying over Fort Niagara on the other side of the Niagara River. "Look there, Mason," he commented, "there is the gridiron we have been fried upon." Davis enjoyed his time with Mason, but he stayed less than a week before returning to Montreal.[3]

Although Varina informed friends of the joy in the reunited Davis clan, she also shared her anxieties, especially about her husband. She discerned a physical weakness and a general lassitude in him that particularly troubled her. She tried to no avail to spark his interest in some wartime papers they had secretly brought into Canada in Maggie Howell's trunk. In addition, Varina worried about money. Because she could not afford to maintain two houses, she intended to remain in one, on Mountain Street, until the lease expired in September. Then she would decide what to do. Her children even grumbled about their meager circumstances. Maggie complained about her unstylish hoops, and little Billy found it unfair that only he among his buddies had to borrow a crossbow. Confessing to "Great care and anxiety," Varina felt that she faced all her difficulties alone because she believed her husband "not yet sufficiently well to share my troubles." Needing respite from immediate responsibilities and the trials of recent months, she made a journey into the United States with her sister Maggie, leaving the children behind with her husband and mother. They went first to New York City, then Richmond, Charleston, and as far as Athens, Georgia, for a visit with the Howell Cobbs.[4]

While his wife traveled, Jefferson responded to an inquiry from brother Joseph, who had expressed eagerness to hear from the exile. Jefferson spoke of his emotional and mental exhaustion. Two weeks earlier, in a letter to Harrison, he had portrayed his status as "little better than a state of vegetation." He told Joseph that he knew he needed to find active employment, but the impediments were imposing. He had few funds to invest and his legal situation restricted him. "My condition does not permit me to form plans for the future," he concluded sadly. That his own children had become strangers to his family disturbed him. He hoped that he and his brother would soon meet again and the two of them would still have many days together. He wanted his sons to "have the benefit of [Joseph's] teaching and example in the formation of their character." While he worried about Joseph's well-being, he grieved that he could not do "the *much* which it is my *duty* and heart's desire to render to you." He closed: "Daily my prayers are offered individually for you and our Sisters, and my longing desire is to embrace you all once more."[5]

With Jefferson's lack of earning power, the paucity of money was a major problem. The Confederate funds that had been furnished to Varina were dwindling. Very little came from other sources, though in August students at the University of Mississippi contributed $500. The Davises did, however, pursue another Confederate source they knew about. Captain Watson Van Benthuysen, Eliza Davis's nephew, had commanded the treasure train that was separated from the president's retreat and sent to Florida, but he had not been forthcoming with the money that ended up in his hands. Upon learning of President Davis's capture, Captain Van Benthuysen, over the objection of a civilian official, had taken charge of the funds he was guarding—more than $30,000. After paying some soldiers and other expenses, Van Benthuysen proposed to divide the remaining sum, consisting of gold sovereigns, among other officers and himself, with the remainder set aside in Van Benthuysen's care for Varina Davis. The officers agreed, and the division was made. According to estimates by participants, the sovereigns designated for Varina had a value of between $6,500 and $9,000.

But none of this money ever reached Varina. In the summer of 1865 she received information about the transaction and had a nephew of her husband contact the captain, then living in New Orleans. He asserted he had no money for his aunt Varina. In January 1866 Burton Harrison got involved, and others who had been in Florida confirmed what had happened. Finally Van Benthuysen admitted he had some money, but only a presidential order would cause him to part with it. Though no longer a president, Davis signed such an order. Thereupon Van Benthuysen and Harrison met in New York City. Van Benthuysen's account differed from his former compatriots'. According to him, he owed Davis only $1,190 in gold. Even though Harrison did not believe the crafty ex-captain, he had no way of enforcing his opinion and accepted the offered amount. Davis was furious. He said Van Benthuysen had acted dishonorably, and he directed Harrison not to provide any "exonerating statement" to a man Davis considered unfaithful and deceitful. But he accepted the money.[6]

Early in the fall the Davises changed their base to Lennoxville in Quebec Province, around eighty-five miles east of Montreal. Finances dictated the move to what Varina termed "this little out of the way village." Jeff Jr. attended an Episcopalian preparatory school there. In Lennoxville the family lived in a small hotel, except for Maggie Davis, who stayed in a Catholic school in Montreal. They had no ready friends, but often visited orphaned siblings of a well-to-do English family, who resided under the care of older sisters in a grand house just outside of town. The two sets of children enjoyed each other, but there was little to do. Jefferson rarely walked about the village, though at least weekly he led his family along secluded country roads, and there were picnics at nearby Lake Massawippi. Northern sympathizers occasionally made things uncomfortable, particularly for young Jeff when some of his schoolmates serenaded him with "We're Going to Hang Jefferson Davis." Despite drawbacks, Davis was generally pleased: "This is a very quiet place and so far agreeable to me but further I have little to add."[7]

In November, Davis took his first trip back into the United States. His initial destination was Richmond because, under the terms of his bond, he had to appear in federal court on the fourth Monday in the month. Throughout the autumn O'Conor had kept him posted on the legal scene. Aware of his opponents' continuing difficulties, O'Conor still worried greatly about a trial with only Judge Underwood on the bench and a jury made up primarily of blacks. O'Conor did not believe a trial would take place, though he was not certain. "The future is absolutely impenetrable," he wrote Davis. Yet he did not want Davis to undertake the journey to Richmond unless absolutely necessary, in part because there had been talk of assassination attempts. Eventually O'Conor discounted the threats as empty rumors. He also decided he did not want to give the other side any opportunity or excuse to revoke his client's bail. Thus, he finally told Davis his presence was mandatory.[8]

Court opened on November 26 with Judge Underwood presiding, again without Chief Justice Chase, who did not appear. The government requested a continuance. The same legal and political problems continued to bedevil the administration and federal prosecutors. The defendant's lawyers readily concurred in the delay. All parties agreed to carry the case over to the spring term of the court, which would begin on the fourth Wednesday of March 1868.[9]

After the postponement, Davis planned to go on south, all the way to Mississippi. He had been told that the Canadian winter might be difficult for him; besides, he wanted to see his relatives. But he had to wait for Varina, who had not accompanied him to Richmond because her mother had become seriously ill. When the Davises moved to Lennoxville, Margaret Kempe Howell, whose postwar role in taking care of her grandchildren had been so central, had gone to see friends in Bennington, Vermont, and while there she became sick. Varina promptly went to her side and took her back to Montreal. But she never recovered. On November 24 she died, not quite sixty-two and only thirty months older than her son-in-law. After the funeral, Varina set out to join her husband, leaving the children under the care of Maggie Howell and a family friend.[10]

In Richmond, Davis consulted with his attorneys and visited with friends. For the first time since March 1865 he saw Robert E. Lee, who had come as a prospective witness from Lexington, where he was president of Washington College. Davis's appearance surprised Lee. Observing his former commander in chief, Lee relayed to a daughter-in-law, "I saw Mr. Davis who looks astonishingly well & is quite cheerful."[11]

After Varina's arrival, husband and wife departed for Mississippi. They went first to Baltimore, then took a steamer to New Orleans via Cuba, where they stopped for a week. Reaching the island just before Christmas, they stayed in a hotel run by a southern woman and reveled in the tropical weather and flora. Then it was on to New Orleans and a hero's reception for Jefferson. Varina recalled "the warmth of the welcome here no words can describe." From the city the Davises traveled north to West Feliciana Parish and Wilkinson County, where Jefferson visited two sisters and other relatives, most of whom he had not seen since before the war. Finally, he reached Vicksburg, the postwar residence of his brother Joseph.[12]

The circumstances of the two brothers had changed dramatically since their last meeting in their home county. In 1861 Jefferson had reached the political pinnacle, fulfilling an ambition both he and Joseph shared. He had risen to great power in the United States and had been chosen president of the fledgling southern republic. His benefactor and mentor Joseph, owner of 355 slaves in 1860, was one of the richest and most influential men in Mississippi. The wealth of Joseph and Jefferson placed them among the financial elite of the country, and their combined economic and political power was matched by few others in the United States.

In 1868 all was different. Jefferson's political career had crashed with the Confederacy. He had been indicted for treason by the country he had once cherished. The destruction of slavery demolished the foundation of the brothers' wealth. Moreover, the ravages of war, which had blasted the southern economy, resulted in a scarcity of money and plummeting land prices. Both Joseph's age and the labor transformation made unthinkable his return as a great planter, though he had managed to regain his land.

When President Johnson issued his amnesty proclamation in May 1865, Joseph Davis was among those excluded because of his pre-1861 wealth, but he was eligible to apply for an individual pardon. In September 1865 he did petition the president for a pardon, which was granted the following March. The pardon did not restore his land, however. A year later he applied for the return of his Davis Bend acreage and even sent an agent to Washington to lobby for him. After Joseph had evacuated Davis Bend during the war, the U.S. Army had taken over his and Jefferson's plantations. The Freedmen's Bureau eventually took charge of and operated them with former Davis slaves as laborers. Finally Joseph's effort succeeded. The president directed that all his land be restored to him, with his regaining full control set for January 1, 1867.[13]

The restoration involved both Hurricane and Brierfield. Recognizing that Jefferson's plantation would be a prime target for confiscation, Joseph claimed that he owned it in addition to Hurricane. While admitting that Jefferson had managed Brierfield, he correctly insisted that he had never actually given title to his younger brother. Thus, he was lawful owner, and he submitted documentation to support his case. Joseph's argument persuaded federal authorities, who returned ownership of both plantations to him.

Joseph had the land, but not a guaranteed income from it. He knew he could no longer farm, and suspected leasing would not work. Aside from financial considerations, he also desired the blacks on both places to retain their communities. As a result, he decided to sell both properties to his former slave Ben Montgomery and the latter's two sons, Isaiah and Thornton. Joseph expected the Montgomerys to succeed as planters, in large part because he thought they could handle the new labor situation. He also believed they could keep the Brierfield and Hurricane communities of freedpeople together.

But before Joseph finalized the sale to the Montgomerys, he communicated his intention to Jefferson, still in Fortress Monroe. His messenger was a niece who was going to see her uncle Jefferson. Joseph sent word that he would do nothing about Brierfield without Jefferson's permission. Unsure of his future, Jefferson responded that Joseph should do whatever he thought best. He also urged quick action because he feared that Joseph's close relationship to him might cause

Congress to move against his brother's ownership and interfere with any sale. Yet he had one serious reservation. He doubted whether the Montgomerys would become successful planters and make all the payments, "unless the Negroes exceed my expectations." While he agreed the Montgomerys seemed able, he told his brother, "I think they will rapidly lapse to the ignorance and vagrancy characteristic of their race."[14]

Upon receiving Jefferson's reply, Joseph moved ahead. Seller and buyers agreed on a price of $300,000 for 4,000 acres, the asserted total of Brierfield and Hurricane. This sum amounted to $75 an acre, a fair price based on the sale of similar properties at that time. The principal would be paid over nine years, with the final payment due on January 1, 1876. The interest, 6 percent annually or $18,000, would be due on January 1 of each year, beginning in 1867. No down payment was required, but Joseph took a mortgage on the property to protect himself if the Montgomerys failed. The interest payments alone would provide a comfortable living for Joseph as well as funds for Jefferson's family. Joseph added one oral caveat to the sale: should Jefferson ever return and want Brierfield, that part of the deal would be rescinded. Ben Montgomery agreed.

While in Vicksburg, Jefferson visited Brierfield and Hurricane for the first time since leaving in February 1861. Although his wife reported that his former slaves welcomed him, he saw what the war had wrought—the Hurricane mansion and other structures burned, buildings, fields, and levees in poor condition. A significant physical change had also occurred: Davis Bend had become Davis Island. In the spring of 1867, the flooding Mississippi River finally severed the narrow eastern neck of the bend. The main channel of the great river flowed between the Davis plantations and the rest of Warren County; a secondary course on the west maintained the separation from Louisiana. Both Brierfield and Hurricane could be reached only by boat.[15]

An important reason for Jefferson's journey to Mississippi was to find out whether he could count on future income from the land deal. The news was not good. When the Montgomerys made the initial interest payment, they immediately borrowed $16,000 of it for their planting operation. Thus, on January 1, 1868, they would owe $34,000, but flooding and insect infestation made for a disastrous year. They could neither pay the interest due nor repay the loan. Through these disappointments Joseph was a lenient creditor and kept faith in the purchasers, though they themselves expressed doubts that they could make the plantations profitable. The land sale clearly would not provide the steady income that Jefferson hoped for and needed.[16]

Although Jefferson enjoyed seeing his relatives, especially Joseph, whose welfare had been on his mind during his imprisonment, conditions among them and in his home state distressed him. After listing for his children the people he and Varina had seen, he added that all wanted to see the young Davises. He also observed, "The war has left our people very poor and as our relations were prominently true to our country and its cause they have suffered more from the devastation of the enemy than most others." To a friend he commented, "The desolation of our country has made my visit sad, but the heroic fortitude with which our people bear privation, injustice and persistent oppression fills my heart with pride."[17]

In Mississippi, Davis made no public statements about Reconstruction or any political developments. In his view, anything that he said, even in response to "the sympathy felt by our people," could end up harming them. Worry about possible repercussions on friends caused him to decline invitations. He kept to his family. He even decided against visiting the University of Mississippi, which had offered to save places for his sons, fearing that a visit by him could be used to harm the institution.[18]

Davis's public silence did not mean that he had no opinion about the South and Reconstruction. Congressional Reconstruction, which organized the southern states into military districts, the rise of a southern Republican party, and political rights for blacks all troubled him. He viewed the South as unjustly pummeled and punished; he saw oppression of southern whites. "My thoughts are ever turned to our oppressed countrymen and my prayers are daily offered for their restoration to freedom and prosperity," he wrote. This reaction was not unique, or even unusual. Most white southerners of his background and class shared that opinion. His hope lay in the future. "It cannot be," he stated, "that so noble a race and so fair a country can be left permanently subject, a desert." He counted on the young people, especially the students at the University of Mississippi, whom he described as "the rising hope of the state," to carry forward the work on which he and his generation had "unsuccessfully labored."[19]

Court requirements governed the chronology of Davis's sojourn in Mississippi. He came to the state from Richmond after the court session in November, and he left in late February 1868 for the term beginning March 26. The Davises went downriver to New Orleans, where they spent more time than they intended in a futile attempt to recover a $1,500 investment Varina had made in 1866 in a business that subsequently failed. They departed on a steamer for Baltimore via Cuba, where they stopped briefly, as they had done on their western voyage. In Havana the Davises socialized with ex-Confederates, one of whom described Jefferson as "wearing a look of melancholy," but "entertaining and amusing at times." He and his wife reached the Virginia capital in time for the opening of court.[20]

This time, the outcome replicated what had transpired the previous November. The government requested a continuance. Alerted beforehand of the government's plan, Davis's lawyers agreed. The case was put off until May 2. The brief, almost perfunctory hearing in the courtroom resulted from critical events taking place elsewhere in the winter and spring of 1868. On the legal front, the government's private attorneys handling the case, Evarts and Richard H. Dana, Jr., in conjunction with U.S. Attorney Chandler, prepared a new indictment charging Davis with treason. Evarts and Dana considered the earlier indictment defective. Even though they obtained a new indictment for the March session of court, they asked for a delay both because Chief Justice Chase was once more absent and because they had grave reservations about ever bringing Davis to trial. Like some of President Johnson's earlier advisers, they worried about obtaining a conviction. They pointed out that one juror could force an acquittal. And no matter the effort expended to guarantee a sound jury, a Confederate partisan could get on or intimidation might cause a dissenting vote. Dana argued that the Supreme Court in 1863 had held secession and war to be treason, a ruling that had been steadily followed. But a jury trial could end with Davis found not guilty of treason, humiliating the government.[21]

In addition to the prosecution's serious legal doubts, politics also intruded. In February 1868 the combat between President Johnson and the congressional Republicans had become even more desperate with the impeachment of the president by the House of Representatives. The Senate trial began in early March, Chief Justice Chase presiding. As long as the president and his opponents in Congress remained locked in a political death struggle, no movement on Davis would occur. Further, for the length of the Senate trial the chief justice would not sit on the circuit court. In addition, Evarts was retained as one of the president's lawyers. He could not simultaneously concentrate on defending Johnson and prosecuting Davis.

Legal and political reality dictated that Davis would remain under indictment and free on bail. Before departing Richmond, he had another visit with Lee, again in the city as a witness. In his conversations with this particular friend, Davis revealed the great anxiety caused by his precarious finances. According to Lee, Davis admitted "he did not know what he should do or what he could turn his hands to for Support." Davis said he could not concentrate on anything. He did not believe the business community could put confidence in him, for at any time he might have to appear in court, with unknowable results.[22]

Traveling through New York City, the Davises were back in Lennoxville and reunited with their children by the end of March. In the Canadian village, life continued as it had before their extensive trip, though Davis became more and more concerned about the welfare of his family. Varina remembered this as a time when she and her husband were "vexed by every anxiety that could torture us." While wrestling with apprehension, Jefferson suffered a painful accident on June 25. According to Varina, as he was carrying his baby down a long flight of stairs in the hotel, he fell all the way down. The fall knocked him out and broke two of his ribs, though Winnie Anne was not hurt. Even though his painful injuries "dreadfully enfeebled" him, Davis made up his mind about his immediate future: he would go to England.[23]

He reached that decision in part because his legal status became somewhat clearer, though not all doubt was removed. Charles O'Conor had become utterly exasperated with the government's endemic uncertainties and delays. To Horace Greeley he fumed that "something [was] very contemptible in the way this case is treated by those who direct the prosecution." O'Conor still smoldered about Seward, the person he blamed for keeping Davis's case alive within the administration. Disgusted with "playing the tail to the kite," O'Conor determined to find out what his opponents really intended. Although he understood the centrality of the impeachment crisis, he pushed for an answer, even going to Washington. But not until after the president's acquittal by the Senate in May did O'Conor get definite information. Conversation with Evarts led to the cancellation of any court appearance before the trial date, October 19. Yet within the week O'Conor informed his client that the case had been postponed until November 23. More important, for the first time he expressed confidence that no trial would ever take place. Thus, Davis certainly had time for a European trip.[24]

Jefferson and Varina thought about Europe for several reasons. One was Jefferson's health. A slow recovery from the effects of his fall and a persistent cough caused his physician to insist on a change of location and climate. When husband and wife talked about the need to find a less expensive place to live, with good schools, they thought of Europe. Money assumed a central place in that discussion and was fundamental in their decision to go abroad. Davis told a niece that he had to find a way to support his family. Varina wrote that they had no means for their children's future, save those "we have in God's promise." Understanding Jefferson's problem, Joseph suggested that he make use of his greatest asset, his name. Joseph acknowledged that his brother had never previously capitalized on his name for financial benefit, but said Jefferson's situation "produce[d] the necessity late in life of giving your mind and time to a subject uncongenial. . . ."[25]

Jefferson had tried to heed that advice. Upon his arrival in Canada in the summer of 1867, he became involved with a copper-mining venture. Investing $2,000 of his scarce funds, he hoped to make at least a little money. His associates wanted his name, which they thought might help their enterprise in financial markets such as Montreal and New York. Still searching for investors a year later, they and other owners turned to selling the property and concluded England would be an excellent site to attract buyers. Davis would go as the agent of all the mine owners with authority to execute a sale. Not only might he recoup his own investment; the commission he could earn, if all went well, could reach above $25,000.[26]

Although disposing of the mines was Davis's chief business goal, he tried to diversify. He followed Joseph's suggestion that he connect with a commission house in Liverpool, the great cotton port. The potential for a partnership with a successful British merchant did exist, but its materialization depended upon Davis's assurance that he could guarantee shipments of cotton and tobacco. Before leaving Canada he contacted friends in an attempt to gain commitments that would consign such trade to him.[27]

Davis did have reason to believe that he would find a warm reception in England. Congratulating him upon his release from imprisonment, a pro-Confederate member of Parliament who had been close to James M. Mason described to Davis what awaited him: "You would be warmly welcomed by many to whom your name has for years been a household word, who have eagerly watched the Southern struggle, and who would feel it a proud honor to be allowed to make your personal acquaintance—by none more heartily than ourselves."[28]

But with nothing certain, Davis prepared in July to cross the Atlantic for the first time, and to take his entire family. Varina certainly supported this endeavor. She had no love for Lennoxville, and she hoped the move would be therapeutic for her own and her family's wounds. Sharing with Mary Ann Cobb how she hungered for an end to the bruising uncertainty that had characterized her life since the end of the war, she said she so envied her friend surrounded by children, grandchildren, a home, and a future. Varina closed this letter blessing God that all her dear friends were not like herself, "floating uprooted." The family departed Lennoxville on July 23, and two days later sailed from Quebec on the *Adriatic*.[29]

On August 4 at 11 p.m., the *Adriatic* docked in Liverpool. Crowding the wharves, friends and English sympathizers gave the voyagers a warm, enthusiastic greeting. After a few days at a hotel, they became guests of their friends, the Norman Walkers; Walker, a Virginian, had been appointed by Davis to a Confederate post in Bermuda. After the Confederacy's defeat he moved to England, where he opened a successful shipping and cotton-buying business. Although invitations came to the Davises, they declined most. Varina said what they wanted was rest, and they went with the Walkers to their hosts' summer place in northern Wales. Jefferson stayed only a few days, but while there he explored the area, visiting slate quarries, coal mines, and Caernarvon Castle, among other interesting sites.[30]

Not until November did Davis set up a separate residence for himself and his family, at Leamington in Warwickshire. Varina remembered that it was the hunting season and her husband "attracted all who saw him." She also wrote that the local people offered many kindnesses to the refugee family. During these months Davis regained strength and added a little weight. His wife recorded that he showed more energy.

From Leamington, Davis made several short journeys. He went to London on business, and while there toured Westminster Abbey. He also traveled to Birmingham for an agricultural exposition; to Manchester, where he visited a cotton mill; and to Chester, where he attended services in the cathedral. His two sons were enrolled in school in nearby Waterloo. Earlier, in September, the Davises had quite a scare when young Billy came down with typhoid fever. Both parents rushed to Waterloo and were greatly relieved when the boy recovered.[31]

The Davises stayed in Leamington until the turn of the year, when they moved to London. At the outset they resided with Dr. O. L. Blandy and his wife, who became fast friends. In March they set up housekeeping at 18 Upper Gloucester Place, Dorset Square. The main reason for the shift to the metropolis was Davis's desire to be nearer his business contacts. He never wavered in his chief goal, to stabilize his financial footing. In addition, friends told him he should make every effort to meet and socialize with prominent people.[32]

The Davises were certainly accepted by the English social and political elite. They received many invitations from the gentry and from titled men and women, including Alexander J. Beresford Hope, a pro-Confederate member of Parliament, the Earl of Shrewsbury, Lord Abinger, Lady Lothian, Lord Henry Percy, and the Duke of Northumberland. On one occasion the Lord Chamberlain made a pew available at the Chapel Royal. At times Davis responded positively. He lunched in London clubs and spent a few days at the Earl of Shrewsbury's country house, where he reported to Varina, "Every thing is on a scale of great magnificence, but the people do not seem to feel their grandeur, so I am quite at ease."[33]

Despite Davis's profession of ease amid such wealth and luxury, lack of resources made it impossible for him and his wife to participate fully in English upper-class life. Varina told Jefferson's grandniece they "simply [could] not afford to associate on those intimate terms with such rich people." Those who knew the family observed the impact of their severely limited means. One noted that "Mrs. Davis never dines out because she can't buy a suitable dress." Varina informed a relative they saw St. Paul's, the Tower of London, and Westminster Abbey, but did not go to the Botanical Gardens or the opera because of the expense. She admitted to Mary Ann Cobb that they had to be very careful with money or fatal consequences could result.[34]

One friend brought special pleasure. Upon their landing at Liverpool, fellow expatriate Judah Benjamin expressed his delight. "I shall have the extreme gratification of pressing your hand again," he wrote his old boss. After leaving Davis's retreating caravan in 1865, Benjamin had fled to England via Florida. In his new country he had become a strikingly successful barrister, eventually, in 1870, being named Queen's Counsel. Varina recorded that after the beginning of 1869 they saw him quite often.[35]

In late December 1868 Jefferson and Varina decided to go to France. They wanted to see whether that country might provide a better home than England for their displaced family. They also desired to meet with other Confederates who had found safe haven in France. Their host was Ambrose Dudley Mann, the ex-Confederate diplomat who was utterly devoted to Davis, and who had an apartment in Paris and also a country place in Chantilly, just outside the city. They had a memorable reunion with John Slidell and his wife, who had decided to remain permanently in the country where he had represented the Confederacy. In Paris the Davises saw the sights and were expansively entertained. Emperor Napoleon III sent word that he and the empress would receive Jefferson and Varina. They refused. According to Varina, Jefferson believed that Napoleon had been insincere with the Confederacy; thus he could not meet the emperor on the civil and cordial terms expected in an audience.[36]

In mid-January 1869 Varina returned to London, but Jefferson struck off for a few days in Switzerland. On February 7 he took the night train from Paris to Geneva, then journeyed on to Lausanne and a hotel on the banks of Lake Leman. A persistent cough prompted the trip. It was thought the dry mountain air of Switzerland would help, and Davis reported that it did. He enjoyed the anonymity of his hotel, where no one knew him. In a letter to his wife, he called on his powers of description: "My window looks out on a vine clad slope . . . on this side of the lake. . . . On the other side the mountains rise grand in heights wild in their irregular forms, and covered with snow which contrasts sharply with the green swards on this side, all the more strongly for the bright sun which shines upon both." On February 10 he departed for Paris, and immediately on to London.[37]

Just before leaving for Switzerland, Davis wrote a long letter to Varina in which he talked about Paris. He had found the drive through the Bois de Boulogne enjoyable, and the Louvre impressed him greatly. A trip to Père Lachaise Cemetery moved him. Although the names on the vaults "excite[d] historic memories and sad reflections," the grave of Abelard and Héloïse especially captivated him, particularly the inscription, which announced that the two were reunited in the tomb, and the graceful columns supporting its dome. But while he described much that was positive about Paris, he had serious reservations about the city. He had come to agree with his wife's preference for London. His opinion of Paris even as a place for education had worsened, not improved. "The tone cannot be delicate," he declared, "when living objects and inanimate representations so glaringly offend against decency." He questioned whether the undoubted intellectual attractions of the city could counterbalance what he called "demoraliz-ing influences." The emphasis on nudity and "amorous passions" undermined "the cultivation and preservation of modesty." Still, if Varina wanted to send Polly to a school where she could perfect her French, he stood ready to wait for her. Of course, the Slidells and Mann would watch over her.[38]

By the time Davis returned to London, his status as a defendant in the courts of the United States had changed dramatically. When his case came before the court in Richmond on November 30, 1868, consid-erable alterations had occurred on both the legal and the political front. President Johnson had survived his impeachment trial, though animos-ity between him and the congressional Republicans still ran deep. On July 4 he issued another amnesty proclamation. Even though he had been urged, even by his attorney general, to make it all-inclusive, he excluded anyone under indictment for treason—namely, Jefferson Davis. Several reasons prompted the exclusion, particularly propo-nents in the cabinet including Seward and a general fear that pardoning Davis might provoke another congressional assault on the president.[39]

Thus, Davis still faced a charge of treason. At court in Richmond, Chief Justice Chase finally joined Judge Underwood on the bench. In the meantime, the Fourteenth Amendment to the Constitution had been ratified by the states and had gone into effect on July 28. Its third section stipulated that no person could hold office who had sworn an oath to uphold the Constitution and subsequently had participated in the rebellion. To Chase this provision offered a way around the morass of a Davis trial because there could be no double jeopardy. In conver-sation with George Shea, Chase made clear his viewpoint.

Chase's opinion dictated the strategy of Davis's defense. Davis's lawyers readily admitted that in 1845 he had taken an oath to support the Constitution. Then they submitted a motion asking that the indict-ment be quashed on the grounds that the Fourteenth Amendment had already inflicted punishment on their client. The government's attor-neys contested the point. The chief counsel, Richard Dana, countered that the Constitution was not criminal law. Instead, it created an organic political system. As a result, the section in question did not set forth a penalty; it simply stated qualifications for holding office in the system.

On December 5 the court handed down a divided ruling. Chase stated that he and Underwood could not agree. He accepted the argu-ment tendered by the defense; Underwood rejected it. Counsel for the defense requested that the fact of disagreement be certified to the Supreme Court. Chase so ordered. As the indictment remained in force, the federal attorney wanted a trial date set. Chief Justice Chase said the date could be announced after the completion of the upcoming Supreme Court term.

William Evarts, who had become U.S. attorney general in July 1868, decided the government would push no further. Given Chase's public declaration on the issue, he did not want to go before the nation's highest judicial tribunal where the chief justice might convince a majority of the court to throw out the indictment and inflict a stinging defeat on the government. According to Charles O'Conor, such fears were justified. He told Davis that Chase had urged him not to concede any "disputable point," and had confided to Davis's attorney that a judicial decision for Davis "would furnish a magnificent chapter in our history. . . ." Evarts informed O'Conor he would enter a nolle prosequi if the defense would agree to end the matter and not demand a hearing before the Supreme Court. O'Conor acceded. On Christmas Day, President Johnson issued a proclamation that guaranteed total amnesty to all participants in the rebellion, even including Jefferson Davis. Finally, on February 26, 1869, Attorney General Evarts informed Davis's counsel that directions had been given to nol-pros all indictments for treason. There were no pending charges against Davis. For the first time in almost four years, he no longer faced the threat of federal prosecution.[40]

Meanwhile, in London, Davis was no closer to making a profitable business deal than he had been when he disembarked in Liverpool seven months earlier. His hopes of becoming involved in the cotton and tobacco trade with the southern states never got off the ground. He had no success in his attempts to sell the Canadian mines. He was finally advised to concentrate on finding purchasers in Canada. Although his contacts with the English elite did lead to numerous social invitations, they generated no concrete business arrangements.

Davis did have to face the lingering English distrust of Mississippi because of the state's bond default back in the 1840s, though it is impossible to measure the influence of that feeling. During the war Union propaganda masterminded by Robert J. Walker had hammered Davis as a defaulter, a charge that still reverberated. He was eager to counter the accusation, but Judah Benjamin advised against his doing so. Benjamin declared the effort bound to fail because the English public would not countenance the detailed political and constitutional arguments Davis would make.[41]

With no breakthrough forthcoming, Davis had to cope with trying circumstances. Early on, he told Varina that only dim prospects existed for selling the Canadian property. He summarized his entire experience in a letter to his wife late in the summer of 1869. Reporting on a potential deal, he "found the matter still hanging . . . but was requested to wait until evening when I should see what I should see." All he ever saw was nothing.[42]

Davis's business disappointments added to the struggle in his family life. Both he and his wife desired to provide a superior education for their children, especially in language instruction, but they worried about being able to afford what they wanted. Though they had the two youngest at home, they kept Jeff Jr. at Waterloo, and in the spring they sent Polly to Monastère de l'Assomption in Auteuil, France. Her father missed her, yet said her "cheerful brave resolution" to take advantage of her opportunities consoled him. In April, Davis's fragile health broke under a severe onslaught of facial neuralgia. A British physician, who had known Davis in prewar Washington, saw him at this time and described "a man broken down in mind, body, and estate. . . ." He needed his wife's comfort. Away from Leamington, Davis talked about "the gloom of this dismal London day" and his sadness at being far from her. Left alone in Paris, he confessed her absence made their rooms seem desolate.[43]

Despite the setbacks and myriad difficulties, there were gratifying moments, particularly a sojourn in Scotland in the summer of 1869. On July 24 Davis, along with his friend and traveling companion Dr. Charles Mackay, departed London for Scotland. Davis had long-standing invitations from the ardently pro-Confederate James Smith of Glasgow, from John and William Blackwood, proprietors of *Blackwood's Magazine*, in St. Andrews, and from Lord Abinger, who lived near Fort William. His doctor also prescribed the Scottish climate as a bracer for a weakened Davis. He delighted in the weather and urged Varina to take herself and the children to a cooler place. The travelers stopped first in Edinburgh, where they took in the major historical points, such as the castle, the old Parliament House, Holyrood, and John Knox's home.[44]

Next, Davis headed south into the Border Country between Edinburgh and England. Captivated, he called the countryside "the best combination of the beautiful the useful and the grand that I have beheld." The historic places impressed him, especially the ruins of Melrose Abbey and Dryburgh Monastery, Sir Walter Scott's burial site, and Abbotsford, Scott's home, where Davis was permitted to see some original manuscripts. He picked several flowers, which he enclosed in letters to his wife, including a harebell from near Scott's tomb and a daisy from near the depository of Robert the Bruce's heart.

Then Davis turned north to St. Andrews, arriving on August 2 and receiving a warm greeting from the Blackwoods. John Blackwood's daughter described him as "dignified and commanding," even though his face was pale and drawn and his features attenuated. In addition to enjoying his congenial hosts, Davis toured the area and met the local people. Writing Varina, he once again enclosed a flower, another hare-bell, this one from the "ground dedicated to the 'Royal Game of Golf.' "

After St. Andrews, Davis traveled west into the Highlands, immers-ing himself in the world that Scott had described in *The Lady of the Lake*. Although the accuracy of the poet's descriptions impressed him, he wrote Varina, "the beauty and grandeur of the scenery can only be realized by visiting it." To commemorate his visit, he bought her a wonderfully illustrated copy of Scott's long poem. He continued to send flowers: little wildflowers from Rob Roy's grave and moss from a rock beneath the oak prominent in a key section of the poem. He also noted that the clear, cool climate had improved his health.

Leaving the Highlands, he went south to Glasgow, where on August 9, James Smith and his wife cordially welcomed Dr. Mackay and Davis into their home. From there the two men struck out westward to Oban and the Isle of Mull. On this jaunt he ran into Lord Abinger, who had previously asked Davis to join him at his estate near Fort William.

In Abinger's company, he and Dr. Mackay journeyed to Inverlochy Castle, Abinger's palatial mansion, which has a marvelous view of Scotland's highest peak, Ben Nevis. Here Davis had a grand time. He tried salmon fishing and grouse shooting. The scenery enthralled him: "You would find a wide field for your imagination in the midst of changing lights & shades which characterize the Scottish mountains," he told his wife.

Finally, this special holiday ended. For Davis it was a tonic; during his weeks in Scotland he seemed to escape his cares. He returned by canal and railroad to Edinburgh and took a steamer back to London. In the meantime Varina had taken the children to Yarmouth on the sea. By

August 26, when the family reunited in London, Davis had decided he must return to the United States. There was no longer any danger of prosecution, but, more important, he had to find a source of income. Because nothing had turned up in England, in September he headed back across the Atlantic. But he determined to go alone. Given the uncertainty of his future, he would not uproot his family. He would establish himself first.

Jefferson and Varina's difficult parting underscored their reliance on and love for each other. From his ship at Southampton he remembered their last moments at the train station in London. "Long after we were under way your face as last seen was before me." He stated that he wanted to run after her, "for in your failure to look back I had the evidence of the struggle you had made to suppress the manifestations of your emotions." His own feelings he did not hold back: "Before this reaches you my eyes will have turned with longing looks to the place where my treasure is, that treasure which most of all assures that the heart will be with it always." Responding to "My dearest, and best beloved," Varina spoke of the children's sadness, and as for herself, "my great object too had been suddenly taken from me."[45]

After a rough crossing, Davis's ship docked in Baltimore on the evening of October 10. He was met by brother Joseph, who was accompanied by his constant companion, granddaughter Lise Mitchell. After a few days they sailed for New Orleans, and then on upriver to Vicksburg. En route Jefferson stopped once again to visit his relatives in West Feliciana Parish and Wilkinson County.

From Vicksburg he went on to Memphis to discuss employment with the Carolina Life Insurance Company. The possibility of working for Carolina Life had come up in correspondence before he left England. Although Davis knew nothing about the firm, he had asked friends to make inquiries. The intimation was that the company intended to open a new branch office in Baltimore and considered him an excellent prospect to manage it.

But in Memphis a different decision was made. After discussions between Davis and the directors, which included an examination of the company's books, the directors asked him whether he thought his influence would be greater running a branch or the parent company. He indicated the latter. His interviewers agreed, and the sitting president acted on his earlier offer to step aside in Davis's favor. The directors then named Davis as president, with an annual salary of $12,000 plus travel expenses, a substantial income at a time when the annual earnings of an industrial worker amounted to around $350. Having sat-isfied himself about the financial stability of the business and the char-acter of the directors, Davis accepted the position.[46]

The decision to go with Carolina Life was not easy, nor was it Davis's first choice, but the job had two overriding assets: availability and a good salary. He had been approached to head educational institu-tions. Even before he went to England, Randolph-Macon College in Virginia offered him its presidency. Davis said no, in part because he was still under indictment and would not risk the future of the college by associating his name with it. Just after his arrival in Memphis the University of the South at Sewanee, Tennessee, an Episcopalian school, tendered him its top post. Declining, Davis admitted that the position "would be more congenial to my tastes than that now occu-pied," but because of the need for money to support his family, salary had to be a critical consideration. Carolina Life paid much better. Before Carolina Life there had also been talk of something with the Southern Pacific Railroad, but nothing ever materialized.[47]

Aware of the relationship between occupation and social status, Davis was anxious about how any position he took would affect his reputation and image. A proud man who had been a successful planter and politician, he wanted to make a decision about his employment that would not diminish his standing either in his own estimation or in any-one else's. He reminded Varina that even if they themselves forgot, "others will not fail to remember the difference between a man of busi-ness, and a Soldier, or a Planter, or a Senator, or a Cabinet minister, or a President, or even an exiled Representative of an oppressed people." Friends expressed an identical concern to him; they worried about a man of his stature going into the insurance business. Close associates, mostly in New Orleans, sent a circular to a select group in an attempt to raise money for Davis and his family; they also emphasized that Davis had been a planter and had no professional training for a respectable position.[48]

Although concerned about propriety, Davis faced his situation head-on. He refused to accept private donations, and as he informed his wife, "our property at Brierfield is no longer to be thought of as concerning me or you or our heirs." He had to have a paying job, and he had to go where he could find one. In a letter to Varina, who shared his interest in appropriate employment and did not prefer liv-ing in Memphis, he spelled out what he saw as economic and social reality. He bluntly stated that in Memphis—and at the moment only

Jefferson Davis in Scotland.
Museum of the Confederacy

in Memphis—he could earn a living to support all of them. He even indicated he would have sufficient income for her to live elsewhere "until all things may combine to give us a less restrained choice." He then furnished his own primer on social ranks and prejudices. The differences between the classes were greater in London than in Liverpool, just as the gap was wider in Baltimore than in Memphis. He maintained that in Baltimore the upper class would have greater prejudice against an agent of a company than the president of a company, a position he did not have there. "I have compounded with my pride for the material interest of my family, and am ready to go on to the end as may best promote their happiness," he concluded. He also had Joseph's approval.[49]

Thus did the sixty-one-year-old Davis embark on a new career as president of a life insurance company. His office at 42 Madison Street in Memphis was as unready as he was. As workmen prepared the rooms, he set about to learn the insurance business. He described his colleagues as decent fellows, and even though his lack of background in the business showed, he thought he got along pretty well. He found the work not unpleasant, though it confined him to his office more than he originally thought it would. But he hoped that as he gained experience and the company matured, he would be able to travel more. The company envisioned the entire South as its territory. Its carrying the name Carolina while situating its home base on the Mississippi River in Tennessee telegraphed that ambition. Davis and the directors envisioned expanding all the way to Baltimore, a much larger financial center, where eventually the company might be headquartered. It was even possible that Davis would end up there as president.[50]

One of Davis's first major tasks was the recruitment of agents to sell his company's product. Across the postwar South many former Confederates desperately needed gainful employment, and Davis turned to them to form the core of his sales force. Once again a president, he called on men who had worn the gray to enlist with him in this new effort. A number who had been prominent soldiers, including Braxton Bragg and Wade Hampton, signed up in almost every state, though a few turned Davis down.

As a company president, Davis faced issues common to business executives, such as the technical aspects of his industry, salary structure of employees, and marketing strategy. According to Varina, after a time he mastered the mathematics of life insurance. Although Carolina Life paid its state agents a small salary, commissions on the sales of policies constituted the bulk of an individual's income. Suggestions came from the field to alter that balance toward a higher salary level. Davis believed in a base sufficient for an agent to establish himself, but no evidence indicates that he changed the calculation of compensation. With many of the newly hired agents totally inexperienced in selling life insurance or anything else, the president received requests for advice on sales techniques. Davis's response fit with his choice of agents: "It has seemed to me a reasonable hope that southern men would prefer to insure with us rather than a northern company."

Davis was concerned about both the morale and the performance of his far-flung employees. Although he worked on building up both through correspondence, after a few months he spent considerable time traveling through the area covered by Carolina Life. He ventured all the way to the Atlantic coast and as far north as Baltimore, without neglecting the Gulf states and his own Tennessee and neighboring Kentucky. On these journeys Davis did not spend every hour on business. Stops with friends like the Clement Clays near Huntsville, Alabama, and at holiday sites such as Lookout Mountain, Tennessee, where he stayed with the poet Sidney Lanier, and the springs in the Virginia mountains provided interludes of enjoyment and relaxation.[51]

On a stopover in Richmond in early November 1870, he made his first public speech since the war, a eulogy of the man who had been his comrade and his first soldier. Robert E. Lee's death the previous month served as the occasion to gather Confederate soldiers and sailors to organize a Lee Monument Association. When Davis rose to speak in the First Presbyterian Church, everyone stood amidst what a reporter termed "a storm of applause" that seemed to shake the building's foundations. In his brief remarks Davis concentrated fiercely on the character and genius of Lee. He stayed completely away from politics, except to proclaim that Lee did nothing wrong when he resigned from the U.S. Army upon the secession of Virginia, to which he owed his fundamental allegiance. Identifying Lee as a friend since West Point and a close companion during the war, Davis emphasized his personal generosity and his military ability. Between commander in chief and commander, harmony had reigned; any differences of opinion fell aside during discussion. After concise praise of Lee's Confederate career, Davis exulted in the Christian faith that had ennobled the general in life. He gave Lee his highest accolade: "I may add that I never in my life saw in him the slightest tendency to self-seeking. It was not his to make a record, it was not his to shift blame to other shoulders; but it was his with an eye fixed upon the welfare of his country, never faltering to follow the line of duty to the end."[52]

When Davis accepted the presidency of Carolina Life, he moved into the Peabody Hotel in Memphis, where he decided to live until his life settled down. While learning about the insurance business, he joined St. Lazarus Episcopal Church. And he did have a few old acquaintances in the city. Encountering a woman he knew, he suggested a walk. Thereupon, according to his companion, "he grew very eloquent & politic, & said a number of beautiful sweet things. . . ." He could still charm.

In Memphis, Davis's health followed its traditional pattern, as his recurring problems flared up regularly. He contracted a cough in December, which he attributed to the chilly and damp weather.

Describing another siege of coughing, Davis said it made him "bark more than a watchdog." The cough stayed with him through much of the winter, though with the arrival of spring the hacking disappeared. Then he experienced chills and fever, reminders of his old foe malaria. In mid-May he blamed the alternating hot and cold temperatures for the neuralgia that plagued him.

At this time optimism and sadness coexisted in his heart and mind. He did have a positive outlook about Carolina Life and was determined to succeed in his new undertaking. Yet he simultaneously wrestled with where life had placed him. To a niece he spoke of "these days of sorrow and disappointment." Responding to a request to list his amusements, he answered: "I cannot enumerate them for they are zero." Aside from contemplating what he called "the wreck," he had two other overriding concerns.[53]

The condition of his beloved brother Joseph worried him deeply. Upon seeing Joseph in Baltimore, he commented on how feeble the eighty-five-year-old man had become. Jefferson was thankful, however, that Joseph still had his granddaughter taking care of him. To young Lise, whom he addressed affectionately as "My dear Daughter" or "My dear Niece," Jefferson declared both his love for his brother and his gratitude to her. Sometime toward the end of 1869 Joseph suffered a fall that severely dislocated his shoulder. Even though in late February 1870 Jefferson arranged a trip to New Orleans for the three of them, in part to see about the injury, Joseph's condition continued to deteriorate. Late in the spring Jefferson informed his wife that Joe could no longer take care of himself. By August both hearing and sight were almost gone.[54]

That his wife and children remained in England preyed upon him. In every letter to Varina and his little ones, he professed his abiding love for all of them. Varina tried to bring her husband into their circle. She wrote him about their activities and sent him photographs. At Christmas she described presents and mentioned sadly that she had nothing for him, not even a token. A constant was mention of sickness. Word about illness affecting her or the children greatly distressed him. She catalogued coughs and flu for all, chicken pox among the children, eye inflammation and insomnia for herself, and another ominous situation: Shortly after Davis's departure, Polly, now almost fifteen, was diagnosed with a spinal problem with potentially severe repercussions. The doctor forbade her return to school in France. Fortunately, no grim manifestations ever appeared. Even so, she continued her studies at home with governesses. Jeff Jr. and Billy were in school in Liverpool. A notable event took place in February 1870, when Varina's sister Margaret, for years a fixture in the Davis household, became engaged. Although the engagement, to a widower of German descent living in Liverpool, did not thrill Varina, both she and Jefferson gave their blessing, which greatly pleased the bride-to-be.

Upcoming wedding aside, Varina struggled with her own turmoil. Once again she had charge of her children and her home without her husband and with limited means. Although she had said he should choose where they would settle, she admitted that she "dread[ed] the return to America as a country in which we are to live and die. . . ." She described a visit to friends as "a cold plunge to go among those who are happy, and at home with a tolerably certain future." One line to her husband was particularly anguished: "This death in life is the most harrowing of all sorrows."

Jefferson was anxious about his wife's reaction to his decision to locate in Memphis. Even though she had told him the choice was his, he knew that she detested the heat of the southern summer. She had made clear that she much preferred Baltimore to any place farther south. Still, Jefferson hoped she would "realize the advantage of my position here over that I would have occupied in Baltimore, and so be thankful." Whatever his wish, he tried to allow her to make her own decision. Although he had to stay in Memphis, at least for a time, he told her his income would permit her to live elsewhere if she chose, even in Europe. Yet they both wanted to reunite their family as rapidly as possible.[55]

Worried, sad, and lonely, Davis found solace in his friendship with the Clays, especially Virginia Clay, "Ginnie" to him. He had known them since the 1850s in Washington, when Clement served as a senator from Alabama and his wife enjoyed a prominent social role. Sharing many common experiences at Fortress Monroe deepened the bond between the two men, an embrace Davis extended to Virginia. Upon his return from England, he reached out to them for his emotional lifeline. After his initial visit to the Clays' mountain retreat near Huntsville, Alabama, Davis said he would like to return, "but the vision is so sweet to me, that I fear to disturb it." He did go back, however. He wanted to know every move the Clays made. Virginia did most of the Clays' letter-writing, and Davis relished her communications. Relatives in Memphis also passed on news of his dear friends. Clement Clay's suffering from tuberculosis and his poverty generated

Joseph Davis, late 1860s.
Museum of the Confederacy

Davis's solicitation and attempt to aid his companion financially. Davis even made Clay an agent of Carolina Life, but selling insurance did not turn into a profitable enterprise for the Alabamian.

Writing often, mostly to Virginia, Davis did not hide his profound attachment to the Clays and his dependence on them. "If the evening of life has not given me mystical love," he wrote, "it has taught me the value of true love such as the sterling and sensitive nature of my precious Clays feel and inspire." Talk of their moving to Minnesota because of Clement's disease pained him. "I must see you," he implored Virginia, "there is so much I would hear and something I would say." He recounted his daydream for the three of them—a good ship, good cigars, a good library, and "sail on, on to the Port where men embark for the world unknown."

With Virginia Clay he was utterly open. He told her he thought of her as his "indulgent confessor and a sincere, cordial adviser." He poured out his desolation. "A life of disappointments has not deprived me of hope, though it so often proves the seed from which springs a new disappointment." Reacting to a gentle chiding from her about his mournful melancholy, Jefferson defended himself and underscored his need for her: "But you would not expect one whose disappointments had been greatest, whose possessions were only the true and loving hearts of those from whom he was separated, and whose future was dark where he would see, and evil where forced upon the sight, who feels decay approaching and fears he may not be able to perform the little work he hoped to achieve, to feel as he did when life was new and full of promise, and as little would you expect me, I hope, to feign any sentiment or opinion, which was entertained. Don't you feel sorry for having (given) me a chance to inflict my sorrows upon you? Forgive me, this once."

Not only a confidante, Virginia Clay also brought cheer into Davis's life. He admitted that no one else gave him the joy she did. When she could not make a scheduled reunion in New Orleans during Mardi Gras, Davis was distressed. His regret was "enhanced by the frequent thought, she would enjoy that, as either the grotesque the grand or the beautiful came into view." The scent of the flowers, "especially the orange blooms," would have delighted her. "Authors say there is nothing so difficult as a beginning," he stated, then disagreed. "In writing to you I find it hardest to stop. It is as if to leave you so near does the act of addressing you bring you to me."[56]

Despite his bouts of sadness and his frequent illnesses, Davis carried on his duties as an insurance executive. By the summer of 1870 he thought the time had come for his family to join him. After a combined business and vacation trip from Memphis to Baltimore, he went on to New York City, and there on August 10 took passage on the *Russia* for Liverpool. He traveled alone, for he had been unable to persuade either the Clays or Joseph to join him. Davis commented on the few passengers because of the Franco-Prussian War raging in Europe, and noted a correlation between American sectionalism and the conflict. He informed Joseph that northerners lined up with the Prussians while southerners stood by the French.[57]

Reaching Liverpool on August 31, he went to the home of his sister-in-law Margaret Howell Stoess. He reported to Varina in London on his safe arrival and his only partially successful effort to obtain the money they had invested in Liverpool. But before heading for London, he struck out on a brief side trip back across the Irish Sea to Dublin and up to Belfast. Then he returned to Glasgow, where he took the train to London, arriving on September 26. Although he remained in England only a couple of weeks and saw a few old acquaintances, he missed Judah Benjamin, who regretted that he had to be in France.[58]

By the beginning of October, Davis prepared to return to the United States with his family, except for Polly, who was placed under her aunt Margaret's care to continue her schooling. Plagued by lingering ailments, concerned about living in what she saw as a conquered South, and unenthusiastic about the climate of Memphis, Varina delayed their departure for some two weeks. On October 8 they went on board a steamer for the voyage west, but after a rough first night they stopped in Queenstown, Ireland. The rolling of the ship had caused a round of seasickness among the children and upset their mother. Davis said she just wanted to go ashore and "touch the sod." As a result, he sailed on by himself, and she followed with her young ones a bit later.[59]

Davis made Baltimore by October 24. Before leaving England he had received the wrenching but not unexpected news of Joseph's death. Back in the United States, he shared his feelings with young Lise Mitchell. Although in the summer he had left his brother in Vicksburg with "sad forebodings," he confessed, "my heart refused to surrender hope and I crossed the Atlantic hopeful of being able again to embrace my mentor and benefactor." He cried out: "how bitter are the waters in which I am overwhelmed."[60]

Davis expected his wife to follow him. He wanted her while in Baltimore to have her eyes thoroughly examined, and he left instructions about money. While there she oversaw the placing of both boys in a nearby Episcopalian boarding school run by a ministerial friend. She also visited with other friends; finally, with six-year-old Varina Anne she set out for her husband and her new residence.[61]

The reunion in Memphis, which Varina recalled "looked very small after London," did not bring stability to the Davises. Varina, Varina Anne (Winnie), and an Irish nurse joined Jefferson at the Peabody, but hotel life suited no one. Moreover, poor health continued to beset Varina, who was being treated by a homeopathic physician she and Jefferson had known for years. When the onset of summer heat increased her discomfort, her husband sent her with Winnie back to Baltimore, to cooler temperatures and the comfort of a number of old associations. Besides, Jeff Jr. and Billy were in school nearby.

Jefferson stayed on in Memphis to manage Carolina Life. In June the board of directors unanimously reelected him president of the company he was striving to run effectively. On occasion he complained about redoing and undoing "whatever has been done or commenced by others [that] was much worse than nothing." Even though his work kept him busy, he did not forget his family. "Kiss the dear children for me," he wrote Varina, "I miss you dreadfully and wish we had a quiet home." Laboring in the intense heat of a Deep South summer, he was pleased to accept an invitation to attend commencement at the University of the South in the Tennessee highlands. On a business trip east he also managed a detour to Lexington, Virginia, the burial place of Robert E. Lee and the home of his former aide William Preston Johnston, a faculty member at Washington College. Davis had Jeff Jr. with him, and they made a jaunt over to the Virginia springs.

Back in Memphis, Davis decided he had to move out of the Peabody, noting that the hotel had "run down very low." Friends even invited him to take meals with them. He found and rented what he termed one of "the better class" of Memphis houses, though he said it featured a "cranky" plan and not much of yard. He also worried that the small rooms and low ceilings would not please his wife, who on her journey from Baltimore had come through Richmond in a mostly unsuccessful search for any of their old furniture. Christmas 1871, at 129 Court Street, with both boys home as well as Polly from England, the entire Davis family was under one roof in the United States for the first time since the war.

While Davis strove to support his immediate family, his extended family also brought their financial troubles to him. Nieces trying to hold on to family property had difficulty dealing with the combination of low cotton prices, declining land values, and tax payments. Uncle Jeff commiserated but felt unable to help. As he wrote once to Varina, "I can wish, but can I venture in the face of our wants and uncertainties?" He did not think so.

Their situation in Memphis did not improve. At the center of Davis's disquiet was his wife's health. It concerned him that she became "nervous under suspense." She did not seem to be able to throw off nagging ailments. And he had his own usual complaints. The arrival of summer deeply distressed him, for he feared the effect of the hot, humid weather on both wife and children. Yet Varina would not leave him alone, and he said he lacked the money for a summer trip. Then, in the autumn, came cataclysm: Billy, almost eleven, and the delight of his parents, contracted diphtheria; within days he was dead. The Davises had lost their third son—first Sam, then Joe, now Billy.[62]

Mother and father were devastated. Davis called him "the bright boy . . . the hope and pride of my house." His "heart bowed down at the loss," Davis said all his disappointments and sorrows had not increased his ability to bear them. For an unwell Varina, the blow was crushing. A greatly distressed Jefferson perceived that Billy's death had substantially increased her emotional suffering. In December he confided to Virginia Clay that Varina's "grief is increasing her physical ills to a degree which has made me very anxious." To a sister he depicted a terrible situation: "Varina has for a long time suffered from a numbness in her limbs and the mental depression caused by our domestic bereavement has increased both the frequency and violence of the attacks." There seemed to be no help for anyone; "the doctors seem powerless and only advise cheerfulness."

During the spring of 1873 her health continued to give him "constant anxiety." In hopes of improving her condition, he sent her in the summer to a considerably cooler place, Drummondville, Canada, which was home to a southern seasonal colony. The village was quite near Niagara, where he had visited James Mason back in 1867. During his own business trips he wrote regularly reporting on his activities and professing his devotion. From Richmond he mailed her a sprig of grass from Joe's grave. Winnie went to Canada with her mother while Polly and Jeff Jr. spent the hot months with the Preston Johnstons in Lexington. On an eastern trip their father visited and took them on an excursion to nearby Natural Bridge, a magnificent rock formation.[63]

As Davis grappled to keep his family well and whole, his business venture came apart. The financial winds buffeting American business that resulted in the Panic of 1873 did not bypass Carolina Life. Davis reported that insurance men feared the southern death rate. The scarcity of money made very real the probability of unpaid claims as well as distraught policyholders and investors. To avert the impending collapse, Davis, at the behest of his board, traveled east to New York, Baltimore, and Richmond to find financial succor for his faltering company. He claimed to have assurance that the company could raise an additional $150,000 from new stocks dependent on chartering Carolina in Maryland and moving its headquarters to Baltimore. But while

Davis was obtaining promises of rescue, his directors back in Memphis decided they could hold on no longer. Without either asking his advice or awaiting his return to Memphis, and according to Davis "insensible of their responsibility," they transferred Carolina Life to another locally owned company. Condemning the transaction as "most loosely and unwisely conducted," Davis asserted that the new arrangement meant the abandonment of widows and orphans of deceased policyholders as well as of living policyholders and investors. Unwilling to maintain responsibility for a plan he disapproved and believed grossly unfair, on August 25, 1873, he resigned as president.

The resignation placed him in a difficult financial spot. Although he would have to pay $5,150 for his indebtedness as a stockholder, he could charge from advances and commissions only $3,500 against that sum. Moreover, during the summer the household had spent $55.36 more than it had taken in. And he no longer had a salary. He apologized to Varina for piling all this dismal news upon her, saying it was "more of money trouble than I would have you to hear in your life."[64]

"The tide of my fortune is at its lowest ebb," Davis told his wife. He was out of work; he had no income. Moreover, upon the advice of a friend he had made an investment in Alabama coal and iron mining, which soured. He recouped nothing. He even spoke of selling furniture to raise income. As he told Virginia Clay, the collapse of Carolina Life had occurred so suddenly that he had not made any arrangements for other employment. Unemployment necessitated leaving Memphis, because he considered the city too expensive for him without a good salary. Although a woman friend in Memphis offered assistance, Davis refused. He responded that "your sweet letter so delicately offers aid that it relieves me of the pain one always feels as being recognized in need." While he assured this would-be benefactor that he was not in want, he lamented to a relative, "I am too sad, too deep in anguish. . . ."

Yet he forced himself to look ahead. He knew employment was essential. Although he recognized his association with the failed Carolina Life injured his business reputation, he believed he would find another opportunity so that his family would not suffer. Wanting to look in Louisville, he informed Varina that she could either come down and join him there, or he would proceed on to Canada, and they could return together.

But these immediate plans had to be postponed, for when he reached the Galt House in Louisville, Davis fell ill with what he called an "acute attack of neuralgia." From early September to the end of October, he struggled through a series of assaults on his body. Bronchial problems and dangerous fevers led to complications that he believed placed him in mortal danger. During this protracted siege, Varina and Winnie came to him, as did Polly from Virginia.

His slow recuperation did not alter reality. Decisions had to be made. Davis's physician advised that a long sea voyage was essential for the restoration of his health, though the patient feared he would be "permanently convalescent." Finally able to travel, Davis left for the East Coast to search for employment. Varina returned to Memphis with her two daughters to begin closing down their house. There eighteen-year-old Polly began receiving young men.

From Baltimore, Davis reported that his health had improved and that he had seen an unhappy Jeff Jr., who was not prospering as a cadet and college student at Virginia Military Institute. There was no news about any job, though Davis did say that he had looked into transoceanic steamers. Most important, he brought up the subject of Brierfield.[65]

At this desperate point his attention turned to his old plantation. He had not been totally divorced from Davis Bend—or since 1867, more accurately Davis Island—for Joseph's will named him an executor, along with nephew Joseph D. Smith and a close family friend in Vicksburg, Dr. J. H. D. Bowmar. In a will dated March 1869 Joseph provided for his two living daughters and divided the proceeds from the $300,000 sale of Hurricane and Brierfield between his orphaned grandchildren Lise and Joseph D. Mitchell and the children of Jefferson Davis. He specified $150,000 for his grandchildren and $20,000 each for his nieces and nephews, leaving $70,000 unmentioned. All else was to go to the Mitchells.

Although Joseph made generous bequests to Jefferson's children, significant problems remained. Because of several floods and low cotton prices, the Montgomerys still had difficulty meeting their interest payments and had done nothing toward repaying the principal. Aware that Joseph's will directed that every generosity be shown to the Montgomerys in their efforts to make payments, the executors followed the example Joseph had set during his lifetime. They forgave, lowered, and postponed payments.

Because of his devotion to his brother and his recognition that his children stood to benefit from the land sale, Jefferson took his duties as executor quite seriously. He traveled to Vicksburg for meetings; he corresponded with Ben Montgomery about agricultural and financial matters, and on at least two occasions went to the property, both times with Dr. Bowmar. In May 1870 they made a surprise appearance, which Ben Montgomery's oldest daughter termed pleasing. The next year Ben Montgomery acted as host. He gave Davis and Dr. Bowmar a tour of the plantations and also presided at the breakfast and lunch prepared for them. In each instance he waited upon his visitors but did not sit with them. The former master was served in his old house by his brother's ex-slave, who now owned the Davis acres. But despite the Montgomerys' best efforts, Davis was convinced they could never succeed in fulfilling the purchase contract.

With his income practically nonexistent and his conviction that the Montgomerys would fail, Davis decided to press his claim to Brierfield. There were complex issues. He had never held formal title to the land, a fact Joseph had taken advantage of to reclaim Brierfield as well as Hurricane from the federal government. And in his first will drawn in 1865 Joseph specified Brierfield as his, but in the second and final document prepared four years later he made no such declaration. Posing another difficulty was the adamant opposition of Joe and Lise Mitchell, who had become Lise Hamer in 1873. They had come to believe that their grandfather never intended for their great-uncle Jeff to possess Brierfield. In their opinion, the property and all the proceeds from it belonged to them. Thus, to regain Brierfield, Davis would have to seek a legal remedy.

He did consult with attorneys, who told him he could mount a strong case. Still, pursuing his claim in court would endanger and perhaps destroy his relationship with Lise Hamer, long a cherished grandniece as well as a favorite of Varina's. Moreover, he would have to file suit in a Warren County court whose judge had been appointed by a Republican governor, a longtime bitter foe of Davis's. Davis had little choice if ever again he wanted Brierfield to be his, for the statute of limitations would bar legal action after 1875. But he wanted no suit brought unless there was every chance of success.

The possibility that a legal proceeding could tarnish his reputation also concerned him. Attorneys and friends assured him "that there could be nothing in this suit from which your bitterest enemies could deduce any thing detrimental to your character as a gentleman." Davis's chief lawyer, William B. Pittman, a native Kentuckian who had moved to Vicksburg after the war, used language that resonated with his client: "Your reputation belongs to every Confederate and I should

be untrue to myself and my late comrades if I knowingly did or suffered to be done any thing that could cast a blur upon it." The suit was
filed in the Chancery Court of Warren County on June 15, 1874.[66]

The attempt to regain Brierfield did nothing to meet Davis's need
for employment. As he lamented to Preston Johnston, he felt "a drift."
There was talk of his accepting an American agency for a large English
insurance company, which might require his going to England. The
beginning of 1874 found Davis in New Orleans, where he contemplated the journey, but given his finances did not want to go unless he
could see a strong chance for a monetary return.

Pressure for the trans-Atlantic trip also came from another direction. The physician who had treated Davis in Louisville prescribed a
sea voyage as essential to restore his strength. Equally concerned about
his health, his wife pressed him to go. From New Orleans, where Davis
was staying with his niece Mary Stamps, he went over the matter with
Varina, still in Memphis.

He also reported on his physical condition. Since his parting from
her his cough had improved, but the swelling remained in his feet.
Consulting a physician, he was assured that he had a strong heart. The
doctor attributed the swelling in the feet "to some functional derange-
ment, probably of the liver." Davis also had swelling in his head, but
was assured it had no connection with any of his other ailments. To
relieve that problem, the doctor drew out about seven ounces of fluid
and told the patient that as soon as the soreness wore off in the next few
days, he would be well.

While detailing his condition, Davis worried about his weak and
nervous wife. Both plagued by debility, each worried more about the
other's well-being, and also made absolutely clear how much they
meant to each other. Underscoring his concern, he wrote, "Oh my
beloved Winnie how dark would be the future if deprived of your
helpful, hope giving presence." He called her "the love of all my
mature life, the partner of all my great efforts, and more than equal
sharer of all my trials and sorrow." Varina matched his pledge: "How
sweet it is to an old broken-hearted woman to be addressed by the love
of her youth it is not granted to me to tell you. I do feel from the bottom of my heart that our souls are very near, and that there is no longer
any lack of that love which casteth out fear."

Davis finally decided to take passage on the *Alabama*, which
steamed from New Orleans directly to Liverpool. Varina sent his trunk
and a welcome present of cigars from a Memphis friend. Then, fearing

that her husband would back out at the last minute because of concern about money or the Brierfield suit, she went to New Orleans to make sure he sailed. She was convinced that only a sea voyage would salvage his health. On January 25, 1874, the *Alabama* departed with Jefferson Davis among the passengers. Varina gave him a parting note: "Love of my life farewell—would I could go with you but it must not be farewell my sweetest dearest & best love."[67]

The ship docked in Liverpool on February 16. Although the crossing had been rough, Davis thought he benefited, gaining both strength and appetite. On board ship, doubts about the uncertainty of what awaited plagued him, as did loneliness. Even before the *Alabama* crossed the bar at the mouth of the Mississippi, he confessed to Varina, "I won't write of what I feel in this lonely hour, for there is nothing to give you joy in the recital." Reaching England, he told her the loneliness of the ship suited him so well he was not eager to land.

In Liverpool, Davis's primary mission was to secure employment with the Royal Insurance Company, a fire and marine insurer. He stayed for the first few days with the Norman Walkers, and then moved in with Margaret Stoess and her family. Initially, Davis could feel some optimism about a job because the early inquiries generated positive responses. But hopes were dashed, and the stated reasons disturbed Davis. According to the manager of the company, the intention had been to open a southern agency in addition to the one in New York. But the agent in New York asserted that northern animosity toward Davis was so intense his appointment would adversely affect business in the North. Davis did not know whether other prospective employers shared this view, and he informed his wife he could not beg for a job. Frustrated, he stated, "I could hunt or fish or chop and hoe, but not in that way make enough to support our wants."

From Liverpool, Davis journeyed to London and put up with friends while he tried to find a position in an insurance company that wanted to open a branch or agency in the United States. Unwilling to make the first calls on his own behalf, he employed an intermediary to make inquiries. But the outcome did not change. No one wanted to enter the American market and no one wanted to hire Jefferson Davis. "I shrink from the recital of disappointments," he confided to Varina, who was rarely out of his mind. All his letters carried vows of his love, and he implored Polly to watch carefully over her mother.

Chagrined, he made a trip to Paris to see a thrilled Dudley Mann. Accompanied by a former aide, Francis Lubbock, who joined him in

London, Davis was in the French capital by March 23. There he renewed acquaintance with the Slidells and others, whose company he enjoyed. On a memorable visit to the Hôtel des Invalides, he witnessed a ceremony with bemedaled veterans, flags, and a band of drummer boys. Slidell secured him a pass to the Chamber of Deputies, where Davis observed a session so raucous that he questioned the reputation of the French as a logical people. The tantalizing possibility of association with a land company organized to aid the southern people and promote emigration to the South kept him in Paris longer than he expected, but again, nothing.

By mid-April he was back in London, where he waited for more than a week because of appointments to meet businesspeople. As before, "all the prospects thus opened have only been vague if not delusive." Disheartened, he went back to Liverpool. But before turning toward the United States, he accepted an invitation from his friend and former host, James Smith, in Glasgow. On this third trip to Scotland, Davis acquired "many pleasant memories." He took special delight in a ramble through the countryside of Robert Burns, visiting sites associated with the poet, including his birthplace and a church, tavern, and bridge that had prominent roles in Burns's poetry.

Returning to Liverpool, he embarked on the *Adriatic* on June 4 for New York. On the sixteenth he arrived there and set out immediately for Memphis. Although his efforts to become employed had failed, his time on the ocean and in Europe had improved his health. He reported that upon his return he weighed a robust, for him, 142 pounds.[68]

When Davis reached Memphis, he joined his wife and daughters in a different house, for during his absence Varina had moved across the street to 98 Court Street. She had written him that after considering more inexpensive quarters, including boardinghouses and even moving in with friends, she offered $60 a month for a house that had rented for $150. To her surprise, her proposal was accepted. She said the house was far too large, but they would live in only a small part of it. She calculated the family could make it on $110 per month, for food would cost $50. Davis responded that he knew she had done the best she could "in these days of our hard fortune."

Davis had no fixed plans. He did not know where he would ultimately settle, for that rested upon employment and he had no prospects. Travel was problematical because he needed business purposes, which meant expenses paid, and he had none. With his family unwilling to leave him alone in Memphis, he summoned Charles

Dickens to illustrate their situation: "and so we wait like McCawber for something to turn up."[69]

While continuing his quest for stability, Davis had to cope with distress caused by his only living son, Jeff Jr. In his first year as a cadet at Virginia Military Institute, a school he had chosen himself, young Davis had struggled, though he claimed to be trying. At the end of the year he had been found deficient in both academic work and conduct. Receiving the news, Davis reacted sternly: "Your instincts and pride as a gentleman will sufficiently impress you with the degree of mortification I feel at the fact of your having been found deficient not only in your studies but in your conduct." He trusted the former could have been avoided and was certain the latter could have been. The father found it "humiliating" that his son remained in school through the forbearance of the institution rather than through his accomplishment. While assuring the boy that he would do anything for him, the son had his own "fortune to make or mar, summon your just pride to sustain you. . . ." His father closed: "you to whom I leave my name and in whom I fondly hope to see it reach higher distinction, will need no words of mine to stimulate you to manly effort, or to keep you in the path of truth & honor."

No turnaround occurred, however. The superintendent ascribed the cadet's poor performance to a lack of willpower. Davis asked Preston Johnston, still in Lexington, to try to discover the problem. After a few more months with no visible improvement, Davis withdrew the unhappy young man from the school. "Jefferson's course at the Institute has given me greater pain than he could have willingly inflicted," a distraught father admitted. The boy returned to Memphis, where he enrolled in a commercial college. In this new endeavor Davis perceived a bittersweet irony. "When he learns the way to business success shall we not employ him to teach us."[70]

Despite personal turmoil and travails, Davis was not impervious to the world around him. His opinion of Reconstruction had not changed. As he saw it, the Republican-dominated federal government maintained a heavy hand of oppression over much of the South. In his mind, federal statutes to protect the freedpeople, political activity by them, the presence of soldiers, and the ostracism of leading whites mocked any idea of democracy or liberty. He especially grieved for his beloved Mississippi, groaning under what he denounced as "Yankee & Negro rule." Even so, he held firmly to principle as he envisioned it. For his generation the task continued to be "to preserve the traditions of our

Fathers." Moreover, he evinced an optimism that his definition of the right would ultimately prevail because he considered the mass of the people sound. He could foresee "republican forms and despotic practice" clashing so violently that "we may see the exceptional case of a revolution rolling backward."

Yet, in spite of these deep feelings, he did not speak out. As he told a Vicksburg group, because of his "peculiar situation" nothing he said could help the people or principles he loved. Quite to the contrary, his enemies might seize upon his words to harm those he cherished. Asserting he had made that resolution upon his release from prison, he recognized that any departure from it could result in a furor. In brief remarks at a Virginia resort in the summer of 1873, Davis contended that because the Union had turned the war into an antislavery crusade, the South had been cheated, not conquered. Confederates would have never given up if they had been able to foresee the peace that was now shackled upon them. Having made those extreme statements, he criticized northerners and especially southerners who accepted the imposed tyranny. These emotional assertions caused a minor newspaper uproar, with defenders and opponents warring over his words, their appropriateness, their meaning, and the reaction to them, as well as an alleged damaging interview given by Davis.[71]

Davis understood his special place. "A less noble people than our own would in the depths of their desolation have turned upon their leaders with reproaches instead of affectionate consolation," he wrote. "To me it has been the greatest comfort, has made me more proud of those I served faithfully, and makes me humbly wish I were more worthy of such lasting regard." Such esteem he absolutely enjoyed. The poet Sidney Lanier spoke for countless thousands of white southerners: "Believe, dear Mr. Davis, that you are always President of a very large and wholly unconquerable Republic that lies in the hearts of your grateful countrymen." Davis was also singled out in Congress: he was always excluded in any bill removing disabilities imposed by the Fourteenth Amendment. But Davis said that compliments given him for bearing his personal trials were "not fully deserved, for in the magnitude of our people's loss and oppression those of an individual are obscured even from the eye of selfishness."[72]

Race was at the heart of what Davis designated "the night of despotism" that had enveloped the South. He believed the effort to make blacks enfranchised members of the body politic both politically motivated and utterly misguided. To him as to almost all white southerners, blacks remained an inferior race displaying traits unchanged from their time as slaves. He never shared his brother Joseph's conviction that the Montgomerys, as talented as he admitted they were, possessed qualities that would enable them to succeed apart from white oversight. Calling blacks "poor creatures," Davis feared that Republicans' pushing political rights on blacks would make them "more idle and ungovernable than heretofore." He had "little faith" in "the fidelity of the free Negro." What he termed "the obtrusive insolence of the Negroes" greatly troubled him. From that perspective he justified strong actions by southern whites, including violence, to restore what he saw as the appropriate social order in the South. Although Davis recognized that slavery had been destroyed, his vision of the proper southern social order remained steadfastly Jacksonian—a democratic white polity based firmly on dominance of a controlled and excluded black caste.[73]

Although Davis mostly kept quiet on public issues, he diligently pressed his quest for Brierfield. Amassing evidence to demonstrate that it in reality had belonged to him, he called on a wide range of witnesses who had known antebellum Brierfield to attest to his ownership. Public officials, former slaves, factors, overseers, white craftsmen, and relatives all affirmed they considered the plantation Jefferson Davis's—he paid the bills and taxes; the cotton was sold in his name; proceeds were placed in his account; supplies were shipped in his name. Meeting often in Vicksburg, he participated actively with his attorneys in collecting depositions and fashioning arguments that supported his case. Davis explained the circumstances surrounding the sale to the Montgomerys and emphasized that the part of the deal involving Brierfield was to be rescinded if he wished, a condition Ben Montgomery confirmed. He also claimed that in Joseph Davis's will the unassigned $70,000 from the land sale represented the accepted value of Brierfield, which his brother understood he could not bequeath.

His opponents, Joseph's grandchildren, fought their great-uncle at every step. The once-close relationship between Jefferson Davis and Lise Mitchell Hamer deteriorated. She was now "our enemy" and her husband "a greedy knave," who misrepresented the relationship between him and Joseph and refused to acknowledge what Lise had known about her grandfather's view of Brierfield. Lise and her husband asserted that Joseph had never given Jefferson title because he wanted always to retain ownership. As for the unassigned $70,000, they argued that it simply represented the difference caused by declining land values between the sale price of $300,000 and the value at the time the will was written, and that they had residuary rights to all of it. The Hamers had three notable lawyers, all Mississippians and two of them former Confederate officers, who gave their old leader no special consideration. They hurled about the courtroom accusations of "concealment," "double dealing," and "cruel and misleading" words and actions.

In January 1876 the Chancery Court dismissed Davis's suit. Employing the doctrine of estoppel, the court ruled that Davis could not legally claim the land because his acting as an executor for four years before filing suit meant that he effectively accepted the terms of the will. To Davis, the decision smacked of political favoritism or even bribery. In his opinion the judge had misstated the evidence and omitted everything favorable to his side. He fully expected his attorneys to appeal to the Mississippi Supreme Court. Still, at this point he did not own one acre of Davis Island.[74]

While Davis energetically pursued his claim to Brierfield, he was also constantly seeking ways to generate income. His suit made that search even more imperative, for after its filing he no longer received any disbursements from Joseph's estate. And no matter how uncertain those payments, they had been most welcome. He tried a variety of enterprises. He investigated the possibility of mining in Arkansas, even going to look at the property. But those prospects seemed unpromising and stayed that way. Over the course of several years he also attempted unsuccessfully to sell the wild, still unsettled land in that state he had bought before the war. In addition, he backed an attempt to build an ice-making machine. Despite early optimism and sporadic good news, the project eventually failed, and Davis lost his entire investment.[75]

In the midst of these efforts, Davis accepted an invitation to visit Texas. Pressed to make an appearance at the state fair in Houston, he decided to attend, and in mid-May arrived to a cheering welcome. Urged on by his hospitable hosts and provided a special train, Davis went on to Austin and Dallas before returning through Little Rock to Memphis. He liked what he saw on what was his first trip to the state, except for his time in the Rio Grande Valley during the Mexican War. He commented on the beautiful countryside, especially remarking on the lovely spring flowers. He was delighted to find a number of Mississippians and their descendants. "The people have a robust, healthy look," he observed, "and are cheerful and confident of their future."[76]

Back in Memphis, Davis did not welcome the hot summer. Worried about Varina's health, chiefly what he described as "sudden attacks which for the time, say 15 to 30 minutes cause partial suffocation and is followed by intense pain in the head," and the effect of the heat on her, he wanted her and the children to move to a less torrid climate; but they would not leave him. He stated that he had no money to go anywhere. Thus, they all faced the heat together, though Winnie eventually accompanied a friend to a North Carolina spa.[77]

Finally, some opportunities appeared. When in Texas, he was informed that the presidency of the new Texas Agricultural and Mechanical College could be his. The formal offer came in a letter from Governor Richard Coke, dated June 14. The terms included a furnished residence, ground for gardens, and a salary of $4,000. Coke said that Texans wanted the man they "would never cease to love and honor" more than anyone else. An appreciative Davis seriously considered accepting. A college presidency was certainly respectable, and the post would mean financial security for his family. Besides, he liked what he knew of the state. Yet he finally said no. After expressing gratitude for the confidence shown in him and the honor tendered him, Davis simply stated that he did not believe he could satisfactorily handle the job. He turned it down in part because Varina did not want him to take it. When she first heard about the possibility of their removal to Texas, she informed her husband that she "looked forward with dread to our Texas hegira." In addition, a more inviting proposition came his way.[78]

The Mississippi Valley Society provided the potential of almost ideal employment for Davis. Based in England, the company was designed to spur European immigration and English investment in the Valley and to develop direct trade, chiefly through New Orleans, in ships it would provide. Davis had discussions about this enterprise when in England, and interested parties in New Orleans and Vicksburg wanted him to head the American operation. In August he was offered the presidency, though he declined to accept until a number of matters had been settled, including financial support from England and details of his salary. Even so, in September he set out to drum up public support for the general goals of the society.[79]

He traveled by train up to Missouri, where he also had invitations to speak from several groups. At three separate fairs or expositions he gave addresses, all emphasizing the same themes. He called on the residents of the Mississippi Valley to unite for their economic benefit, advocated what he termed a more efficient and less expensive trade between river towns and Europe, lauded the prospect of immigrants coming to the region as a boost for economic development. Davis received an enthusiastic welcome everywhere he went. Along the rail line bands serenaded and crowds cheered. His spirited audiences at Fulton, where the governor introduced him, and at Kansas City numbered in the thousands. He was pleased with his trip, and despite his hectic schedule thought his health had improved, though the constant talking had left him hoarse.

A reporter covering Davis penned a description of a man who looked generally old and unwell. White hair, a short gray beard, and bushy eyebrows marked a thin, spare figure, who could still carry himself "tolerably erect." Furrows and sunken cheeks dominated his face, but the eyes could still flash with a "quick electric gleam."[80]

On this journey Jeff Jr. accompanied his father, and after concluding the Missouri engagements, they struck out for Colorado. Davis had never before seen the Rocky Mountains. They took a drive through the snow to inspect a mine and deep in the mountains visited a noted resort. Jefferson did not forget his wife back in still summery Memphis. "You would enjoy the scenery, the wild flowers, & the *cold* air."[81]

Before returning to Memphis, Davis detoured by Fairview, Kentucky, the site of his birth. Invited to a celebration, he told Varina he experienced "an enthusiasm and cordiality—a wild burst of affection—exceeding anything I have ever had before." "Women who have lost and suffered and bearded men who have served in battle, melt in tears and vainly try to express their love," he reported. And all regretted her absence.[82]

Back from this six-week business and pleasure tour, Davis continued discussions about his place in the Mississippi Valley Society. Passing through St. Louis on the way to Kentucky, he conferred with a representative of the company. He also had conferences in New Orleans with the American directors. Even so, all matters had not been clarified to his satisfaction. He wanted more information from England before he made his final decision about accepting this presidency. He did recognize that doing so would require him to live in New Orleans.[83]

During the mid-1870s Davis began making public speeches for the first time since the war. But he was careful to steer clear of current politics, and never mentioned anything about Reconstruction. In addition to his Missouri addresses, he spoke in December before the St. Andrew's Society of Memphis, where he gave a paean to Scotland and almost everything connected with a land he had grown to cherish. Three months later, in New Orleans, at a gathering of Louisiana veterans of the Mexican War, he concentrated on the noble undertaking and lofty memories of all who had participated. He proclaimed that their service and triumph had opened the way to the great West, which had made the United States a country of vast wealth and power.[84]

In staying publicly quiet about disputatious political issues, Davis exhibited considerable judgment, for he remained quite controversial. He received two invitations to appear and speak at agricultural fairs in northern states set for the fall of 1875. The agricultural societies of Bath County, Indiana, and Winnebago County, Illinois, assured Davis that they really wanted him to come and that he would be cordially received. Agreeing to appear at both events, Davis said he wanted to advance the interests of the entire Mississippi Valley, and he also desired to see the transformation of a country he had known as a wilderness when a young soldier. But in both communities, news of Davis's scheduled appearances brought forth a storm of protests. Chagrined, representatives of the two organizations wrote Davis telling him he should not come. In each instance he gracefully bowed out.[85]

In late 1875 Davis journeyed to the Mississippi Gulf Coast, where he had not been since before 1861. He went to look at the property he had bought in the late 1850s. If he became president of the American branch of the Mississippi Valley Society, he would have to live in New Orleans, but would need someplace where the family could go to escape the steamy summer. Besides, he knew they had to get out of the Memphis house "in its dilapidated condition." Moreover, his nephew Joseph R. Davis had moved to the coast. At his own property, he found the fence gone and the grounds covered with thick bushes, but much of the surrounding area cleared by loggers. Before leaving he stopped to see an old family acquaintance who lived in a waterfront home. Although Sarah Dorsey was away, he remarked to Varina, "Beauvoir is a fine place, large and beautiful house and many orange trees yet full of fruit."[86]

As the old year ended and the new began, the Davis family endured yet another unexpected bereavement but also celebrated the wedding of their older daughter. In November 1875 news came that Varina's youngest brother, twenty-eight-year-old Jefferson Davis Howell, captain of a vessel that plied between Seattle and San Francisco, was lost at sea, the victim of a collision in dense fog. "Oh! Father let this cup pass," Davis cried, telling his wife they both suffered equally. A sharply different event took place on January 1, 1876. On that day in St. Lazarus Church, Polly, almost twenty-two, was married to J. Addison Hayes, a bank cashier six years her senior. While the father of the bride admitted to a strange feeling because another "authority" had come between him and his beloved Polly, he was quite satisfied with his new son-in-law, whom he would grow to admire and rely on. "Mr. Hayes' last words to me," he informed the new Mrs. Hayes, "were in promise to take good care of you and I do not doubt he will faithfully keep that pledge. May God bless you both."[87]

Finally, in January 1876, Davis agreed to become president of the American branch of what was called the International Chamber of Commerce and Mississippi Valley Society, with offices in London and at 33 Camp Street in New Orleans. Davis would be paid $6,000 annually plus travel expenses. Even though he enjoyed an excellent salary for the first time since the demise of Carolina Life, he still economized, yet refused to live with friends. He rented a parlor-bedroom suite on Bourbon Street, with meals available at a family restaurant across the street for $1.50 per day or $2 if sent to his lodgings. Sending this information to his wife, he said he was ready to have her join him.

Davis worked diligently. He left his quarters before breakfast and returned after nightfall. His only "lark" came when he took his niece Mary Stamps to see a young female actress, who reminded him somewhat of Fanny Kemble in her youth. Continuous discussions took place with his board on the best steps for the business and on concerns about the action or inaction of the directors in London. The board believed Davis should go to England to obtain specific information on what their English associates intended to do about financial support, though some members thought Davis should make a promotional tour through Texas before going abroad.

In May the determination was made that Davis must cross the Atlantic without delay. Worried about his wife and missing her, he wanted her to accompany him to England. She agreed, and brought Winnie and a young friend along. Jeff Jr. remained in Memphis under the care of Polly and Addison Hayes. The Davises actually sailed from New Orleans around May 24, bound for Liverpool.[88]

They docked in Liverpool in late June, and were welcomed into the home of Varina's sister, Margaret Stoess. Davis left his wife and the girls there while he went to London on business. Although well treated, he met with the same delays and indecision he had come to know so well. Nothing seemed to go right. To his surprise, he learned that the English parent of the Mississippi Valley Society lacked assured revenues. All his attempts to get hard information or concrete action led nowhere. Frustration was the result.

In August the family reunited in London for a short time. As always, Jefferson and Varina had education very much in mind, and they decided to place Winnie in a girls' school in Karlsruhe, Germany. Her traveling companion would be a fellow student. Although leaving her parents saddened her, Winnie did as told. Upon sending her off, the sixty-eight-year-old father consoled his twelve-year-old daughter: "It is true, but not pleasant that duty demands self-sacrifice. Yet it is the highest attribute of humanity to be able to give to a sense of duty, that which it costs pain to surrender." Having no doubt about her success, he wrote: "I hope the pain of separation from you will be rewarded by the fulfillment of our anxious and ambitious hopes, the one for your physical and the other for your intellectual development." He then promised he would visit as soon as possible, "for I long to have my baby in hand."

Before Winnie departed for Karlsruhe, Varina became quite ill. In considerable pain, she was regularly attended by a London physician. Searching for "drier and purer air" that would benefit his sick wife, Jefferson moved their lodgings to a different part of the city. For a month he did not leave her bedside; not until mid-October did she begin to show marked improvement.[89]

With Varina much better and no movement in his business affairs, Davis left London around October 20 to visit his daughter. En route he spent a week in Paris and Chantilly with Dudley Mann. After an enjoyable stay with his old companion, Davis traveled on to Karlsruhe alone. Seeing Winnie pleased him immensely, as did her school. He reported her happy and in good hands. He also thought it essential to keep her friend with her, considering this so important he declared he would give up smoking to produce the money, if necessary. But it never came to that. While gratified with Winnie's situation, he depicted his own disconsolation to Varina: "Thrown by adverse currents on the sands and left to be beaten but not lifted by rising tides I can if hopeless yet I trust calmly look upon the changes which are seen & foreseen."

From Karlsruhe, Davis returned directly to London, and immediately prepared to cross the Atlantic. Nothing positive had occurred or seemed likely to occur any time soon regarding the Mississippi Valley Society. Additionally, Dr. Bowmar had written that he was urgently needed in Vicksburg; the Montgomerys were foundering in their attempt to maintain their contract. But Davis would have to travel alone, for the doctors said Varina's condition necessitated her remaining in England through the winter. He agreed, and also believed her surroundings would be more cheerful than back in the South. Thus, in early November when the *Adriatic* steamed out of Liverpool, she remained behind at her sister's home.[90]

Sailing alone to New York, Davis immediately took the train to Memphis, then south to Vicksburg and finally New Orleans. From Memphis, Jeff wrote his mother that his father looked hale. But there was no other positive news. Davis feared that what he considered mismanagement by Dr. Bowmar had endangered any return for his family from Joseph's estate. In New Orleans, Davis gave his directors a negative report on his activities in London; moreover, looking ahead, he could see little certainty. His directors were disappointed that their venture seemed to be going nowhere. The Mississippi Valley Society obviously provided no future for Davis.

His business career at a dead end, Davis began to turn his attention to writing his history of the Confederacy. From New Orleans he returned to the nearby Mississippi Gulf Coast searching for a place to live. He informed his wife that he had hired a man to clear their lot, and that he had not taken any of the available houses because he feared she might not like his choice. While looking, he stayed part of the time at Beauvoir with Sarah Dorsey, who sent Varina her regards.

Back in New Orleans, he wrote his wife on Christmas Eve 1876. "This evening of the anniversary when families are wont to be united, ours are scattered far and wide," he lamented. "It is sad to me," he added, "to realize that an ocean rolls between me and my dear Winnie." He admitted that he was "weary of wandering. . . ."[91]

CHAPTER EIGHTEEN

"The Duty of Doing Justice to the Cause"

January 1877 found Jefferson Davis once again at Beauvoir, the Gulf front home of Sarah Dorsey. Idolizing Davis as the Confederate president, and believing him the great man of the age, she invited him to make her home his home. Tired of wandering, with no other attractive options, and ready to start on his memoirs, he accepted her invitation. He had already decided to make the Mississippi coast at least his temporary abode when Sarah Dorsey's offer provided him a most suitable situation. He did not have to buy anything, and he could easily move.

Forty-eight years old in 1877, Sarah Ellis Dorsey had been born in Natchez into a wealthy plantation family with holdings in Mississippi and Louisiana. Her family had known the Davises, and she was a contemporary of Varina's. An unusually gifted young woman, she received a superior education in Natchez and Philadelphia. She married in 1853, and with her Maryland-born husband Samuel Dorsey settled on a Dorsey-owned cotton plantation in northeast Louisiana. A staunch Confederate during the war, she never stopped venerating the cause and its noble leaders, particularly Jefferson Davis. Sarah became an author of some note, writing both fiction and nonfiction. In 1873 the Dorseys bought and moved to Beauvoir, where Samuel died two years later. As it had for most southern plantation magnates, the war had greatly diminished the Dorseys' wealth and property. Yet a sizable fortune remained.

Beauvoir was a raised cottage, but its considerable size, impressive flight of steps, Greek Revival details, and extensive grounds gave it the air of a "mansion . . . of vernal beauty." Built in the early 1850s to take advantage of sea breezes, the house was supported on nine-foot brick pillars above an unfinished basement. Its front broad steps rose to a verandah that extended across the front and halfway around each side. The interior, with a wide central hall and floor-length windows, was also designed to take advantage of the natural ventilation. All eight rooms of the residential story opened onto the front or rear galleries.

Architectural refinements helped make Beauvoir impressive. The exterior featured square wooden columns aligned above the basement pillars. The balustrade that flanked the steps continued along the base of these pillars, which had Doric capitals topped by a broad but simple frieze. There were also symmetrically placed chimneys as well as Doric pilasters by the doorway and three-part wooden shutters at the windows. In the interior, the frescoed walls and ceilings of the hall and parlors were notable. Their rococo themes of shells, garlands, and even mythological figures were balanced by the elaborate marble mantelpieces of the parlors. Carved door casings added more impressive detail.

The grounds magnified the distinction of Beauvoir, though it had never been a working plantation. Two cottages on either side of the mansion featured floor-length windows, smaller-scaled versions of the galleries of the main house, and pagoda-like roofs. The one on the east was prepared for Davis; it contained a bedroom and a study. The usual kitchen, stable, storerooms, and servants' quarters stood in the rear. Kitchen and flower gardens were nearby, and orange trees and vineyards covered many of the estate's acres. Running just a half-mile behind the estate, and with a flag stop, the Louisville & Nashville Railroad made both New Orleans and Mobile easily accessible.[1]

Davis's patroness wanted to give him more than room and board. She hoped that Beauvoir would become his haven, where he would be safe from the bruises inflicted by the larger world. She would become his protectress, providing sanctuary and worshipful care. Upon his arrival, she reported him in poor emotional shape. "So he is in a very troubled condition of mind . . . ," she wrote, "troubled about his affairs & anxious about his wife's health, which is not much improved." She said she had difficulty getting him involved in his memoirs.

In time he did become stronger, both physical and emotional pain subsiding. With Sarah Dorsey and various guests, Beauvoir could be a lively place. She entertained many people who came to pay their respects to her hero. She, he, and at times others engaged in what one participant called "much interesting talk" on various topics, including women's suffrage, which she supported but Davis opposed. And Sarah Dorsey could still put on a lavish dinner. Her Christmas table in 1877 included oysters, raw, fried, and in soup, turkey, mutton, beef, crabs, salmon, sweet and Irish potatoes, vegetables, cranberry sauce, and jellies. Sherry and superb claret helped it all go down. Then came the main course: a roasted peacock with feathers in full display, as if it were alive. At the close of a Christmas reception, she and Davis led off in the Virginia reel.

While Davis was getting used to Beauvoir, Varina remained in London. Even in the summer of 1877, illness still kept her from rejoining her husband. Her extended absence stirred thoughts of home: "I so often long for that old shackle-down house on Court Street where I had all my children in my own home," she confided to Jefferson. Finally, in October, she sailed from Liverpool to New York, where Burton Harrison met her and sent her on her way to Memphis and her daughter.[2]

Varina did not go to Beauvoir. While in England she learned from newspaper accounts that her husband had taken up residence there with Sarah Dorsey, whom she had known in Natchez and as a schoolgirl in Philadelphia. Varina did not welcome the regime at Beauvoir. She told Jefferson that though she was grateful for Sarah Dorsey's kindness to him, she never wanted to see the place. "Nothing on earth would pain me like living in that kind of community in her house or that of another," she asserted. Because she could say nothing positive about his benefactress, she wrote Jefferson, she would say nothing. Polly concurred, writing her mother that she did not like Sarah Dorsey. Moreover, she had given her father her opinion and said her mother should never go there. In Memphis, Varina stood her ground; she even moved into a boardinghouse when her daughter had houseguests for an extended period.

In April 1878 Jefferson urged his wife to meet him in New Orleans. Varina agreed, but made it clear she did not want Sarah Dorsey at their reunion. "I cannot see her and do not desire ever to do so again, besides I do not wish to be uncivil and embarrass you." We just have to disagree, she concluded. "I will bear my separation from you as I have the last six months—as best I can—and hope for better times the history being once over."

Varina's boycott did not end easily, but ultimately she realized her husband had nowhere else he could work on his book, and she also had no place else to go. In May she appeared at Beauvoir, where Sarah Dorsey had arranged a party in her honor, though uncertain that

Varina would appear. Harmony seemingly reigned, but Varina's performance dramatized the tension in the household. Just before the reception she ran into the nearby woods. Sarah Dorsey followed her and somehow sufficiently allayed her distress so that she returned for the gathering, where she sparkled. A truce was established between the two women that over time would lead to genuinely warm relations. Varina replaced her former nemesis as Jefferson's helpmate on his book. Then, in the fall of 1878, when Varina fell seriously ill, Sarah Dorsey nursed her with unstinting care and kindness.[3]

When Davis settled at Beauvoir, his main goal was to prepare his memoirs. Providing his own account of the Confederacy had been discussed for a decade. His brother Joseph as well as his wife had broached the idea to him just after his release from prison. At that time he responded that he was not capable of the task, either physically or emotionally. Three years later Preston Johnston urged him to undertake the work because of his special qualifications to tell the Confederate story. As early as 1869 Davis began seriously to consider taking on such a project and broached the possibility of his wartime assistant's replicating that role in a literary endeavor. Davis recognized that because his presidential papers had been scattered, a major effort would be required to collect materials. He also wondered about the best location for preparing the book.[4]

He had no doubt, however, about his purpose in writing his book or in the thrust of his account of the Confederacy. Most important to him was "the duty of doing justice to the cause. . . ." In fact, an early working title was "Our Cause." To Davis, justice entailed vindication. "My motive in writing is the Justification of the South in the act of Secession and in the prosecution of the war," he informed a friend. Davis was convinced that holding to that course would enable him "to make a valuable contribution to history before I go hence, and thus complete a long life of service to the people of the South." In addition, he hoped "to add wherever I could another leaf to her crown of glory."[5]

Not only did Davis embrace utterly the conviction that right and virtue lay with the South and the Confederate States of America, he also clung to the belief that his view of the cause would ultimately triumph. "Force," he declared, "may prevail over right, but cannot destroy truth." "Truth is not less dear to its votaries," he wrote, "because it has been borne down by physical force, and those who suffer for its sake may find consolation in its deathless character." Referring to a former Confederate who had joined the Republican party because the North had won, Davis asserted "that one who could suppose force could prove the Southern Cause to be wrong, and the sword decide the question at issue, must have fought without knowing what he was fighting for." Faithful to his gospel, Davis admitted conversion of others might not be immediate. Still, he preached, "the truth should be stated by those who alone know it, and if not in our time, it may at some time overtake swift falsehood."[6]

With absolute certainty about the righteousness of his mission, Davis found a fellow believer, William T. Walthall, to assist him. Davis had not been able to finalize arrangements with Preston Johnston. An Alabamian, Walthall had been a Confederate officer and an agent for Carolina Life in Mobile when Davis came to know him. The two men shared a common absorption in the Confederate past and a joint commitment to the holiness of the Confederate cause. Moreover, Walthall considered working for Davis, whom he believed a great man, an honor and a privilege. For his part, Davis gave Walthall high praise: "He was a faithful confederate soldier, & . . . still carries the flag at topmost."[7]

In 1875 Davis authorized Walthall, who still lived in Mobile, to find a publisher for his proposed book. Aware of Davis's plans and believing he wanted a southern publisher, Turnbull Brothers in Baltimore ardently pressed him. One of the Turnbulls even came down to Vicksburg to see him, but they stumbled over a nonnegotiable Davis demand: an advance was essential to cover Walthall's expenses during the course of the project. Davis did not like pressing for an advance, which in his mind placed obligations on him, but he realized he had no money to pay the man whose assistance he had to have. Turnbull Brothers initially protested that publishers did not give advances; then they said they needed time to decide whether to break that rule.[8]

In the meantime, Walthall had contacted D. Appleton & Company in New York City. Appleton immediately showed interest and emphasized its superior sales force. After extensive discussions chiefly between Walthall and Appleton editor Joseph C. Derby, a longtime veteran of the publishing business, a contract that included an advance was hammered out in the fall of 1876. Appleton would pay $250 per month directly to Walthall until delivery of the manuscript, specified on November 1, 1877, or "as soon thereafter as possible," with the finished product not to exceed two volumes of 800 pages each. Appleton would pay a royalty of 10 percent on the retail price of all copies sold up to 20,000, then the percentage would move up to 12.5 and jump to 15 at 30,000 copies. When Davis went over the contract in New Orleans in December, he made a few clarifying alterations to which Appleton readily agreed. Author and publisher had a firm deal.[9]

While contract deliberations were taking place, Davis initiated a massive campaign to gather documents that lasted almost to the completion of the book. He strove to bring together his own dispersed archives. In doing so he discovered that some of his papers had been irretrievably lost and that not all of the guardians of his documentary trove had been faithful either to their duty or to him. Particularly victimized was his correspondence with Lee, which Burton Harrison had placed for safekeeping with an ex-Confederate officer and avowed supporter of Davis, who then purloined what he pleased. Davis, and Walthall in his behalf, wrote Confederates of all ranks, from cabinet secretaries and generals to men considerably less prominent, who had special knowledge about critical events for recollections as well as documents. Davis also dispatched agents, including Walthall, to Washington in not always successful attempts to gain access to Confederate materials held by the U.S. War Department.[10]

Once at Beauvoir, Davis started slowly. Sarah Dorsey disclosed that his emotional and physical debility seriously hampered his labor. Throughout the four years between the beginning and completion of his book, his health adversely affected his work schedule. He and those close to him—Varina, Sarah Dorsey, and Walthall—all noted when ailments from recurring neuralgia, bronchial difficulties, eye disease, and problems with his right hip and leg regularly interrupted the process of composition.[11]

"Process" is the appropriate term, for Davis did not simply sit at his desk and write away. He dictated opinions, reminiscences, and thoughts on constitutional issues and other topics first to Sarah Dorsey, later to Varina, and at times to Walthall. And all the while he engaged continually in lengthy conversations with these three on myriad subjects designated for inclusion in the book. The dictation went to Walthall. Initially that meant the pages were sent to Mobile; but in the summer of 1877 Walthall moved to Mississippi City, just a few miles west of Beauvoir. His move made delivery easier and regular personal contact possible. Walthall took the dictated material, correlated it with the appropriate sources, and prepared the manuscript for publication. At least, that was what Davis understood Walthall to be doing. The plan was that when Walthall finished his task, he would bring the manuscript to Davis for

Jefferson Davis on the porch of his cottage at Beauvoir, probably late 1870s.
State Historical Society of Wisconsin

final review and approval. This process commenced in 1877 and lasted until 1880.[12]

While Davis and his team labored in Mississippi, his publisher became increasingly anxious about the contents of the book being prepared, as well as about what seemed like interminable delays in getting it finished. After seeing two chapters Walthall sent to New York in 1878, Appleton returned them with a caution flag. The publisher told Walthall that without fundamental changes the book would fail. Appleton did not want a long rehashing of constitutional history, but rather a book recounting Davis's actions as president of the Confederacy, which the publisher asserted was what the public wanted and would buy. Late in the year Appleton sent to Beauvoir a staff member, W. J. Tenney, a states'-rights Democrat, who excelled in getting troubled manuscripts into publishable shape. He talked with Davis, whom he grew to admire, and with Walthall. He left thinking the project was headed in the right direction.

Beauvoir, c. 1880s.
Beauvoir, The Jefferson Davis Home and Presidential Library

But no manuscript was delivered. The due date passed, then weeks more, which turned into months. Appeals streamed with regularity from New York to Mississippi. Attempting to use self-interest as a motivator, Appleton kept declaring the market was right for substantial sales. In part, sales of the book would be handled by subscription agents. When the demand from those agencies reached a certain level, Walthall and Derby responded with a printed circular stating that Appleton would handle appointments and announcements about publication. As time passed, Appleton became greatly concerned about its financial commitment. The contract was extended in December 1878, along with advances to Walthall. Still no manuscript appeared in New York.[13]

At the beginning of 1880 Appleton forcibly intervened. Derby journeyed to Mississippi in February, and was appalled at what he discovered. After a cordial reception by Davis, he asked to see the manuscript. Responding that Walthall had it, Davis confessed that he himself had seen but few finished pages, and he arranged for Derby to visit Walthall at his home. There Derby found copy that he said would not make even a 300-page book, even if it were in publishable form, which it was not. This news distressed Davis, who told Derby, "strange as it may appear, I was but little better prepared than yourself to find how little had been done in a form to be sent to the press." He had obviously not been overseeing Walthall's work with any care. The now troubled Davis said he wanted to honor the contract and return the money advanced, but he did not have the available cash. And Derby, with over $8,000 already advanced, did not want to give up on the book. He suggested that Tenney come back to Beauvoir and take over the preparation of the manuscript. Davis, who had warmed to Tenney on his earlier visit, thought this an excellent idea.

Shortly thereafter, Tenney took up residence in a cottage at Beauvoir, where he set about making a book. He looked askance at what Walthall had done, or, more accurately, not done. Although the material for the first volume had been arranged, the work had not substantively advanced in the more than two years since his first discussion with Walthall. With Tenney in charge, the pace quickened markedly. Davis relayed to a friend that the final portion was done in considerable haste.[14]

On May 1, 1880, Davis severed all connections with Walthall. Let go by the man he still looked up to as a hero, the latter expressed no bitterness toward Davis, though to a companion he did register dissatisfaction with Davis's treatment of him. He told Davis that he was unhappy with his own performance, which Davis had every right to censure. Walthall said that when he had claimed to have the manuscript ready, he meant he had looked up all the references and prepared all the material. His great error came in misjudging how long it would take him to turn what he had put together into a coherent manuscript.[15]

Finally, Tenney and Davis finished their task. In 1881 *The Rise and Fall of the Confederate Government* appeared in two fat volumes, the first almost 700 pages, the second 100 pages longer. Completion brought an emotional time. For Davis personally, publication was a momentous event; he had built his monument to his cause. On the title page of both volumes of his personal copy he penciled a quotation from the Roman dramatist and philosopher Seneca: "Prosperum et felix scelus virtus vocatur" ("A prosperous and successful crime is called virtue"). Varina described to Winnie the passion generated during the months of composition: "The weary recital of the weary war, to be compiled in a splendid but heartbreaking record of cherished hopes now blasted, brave warriors bleeding and dying, and noble men living, yet dead in that they are hopeless—this tremendous record is being given to the world, and the while as he writes the graves give up the dead, and they stalk before us all gory and downcast, but for all that a gallant, proud army, ready if they could again put on their fleshly shield to do battle for their rights." And after that painful journey, exultation: "Well, dear love, *the* book is done & coming out—'whoop La.' "[16]

Davis had clearly announced the dual purpose of *Rise and Fall:* to vindicate and to prove right and wrong. Thus these two volumes do not constitute a memoir as generally understood. Much of the first volume reads like a treatise on the compact theory of the Constitution, highlighting the constitutional legitimacy of secession, with lengthy appendices containing documents, mostly his prewar speeches, that he felt helped make his case. In addition, this argument regularly reappears throughout the book. In fact, much of the book repeats themes that Davis had long emphasized. For Davis, demonstrating that the South had acted constitutionally proved the South was right. Slavery, which in 1861 and before he had regarded as central, he now downplayed as the cause of secession. "The truth remains intact and incontrovertible," he proclaimed, "that the existence of African servitude was in no wise the cause of the conflict, but only an incident." Davis maintained that the North was wrong not only for refusing to accept the constitutional secession of the southern states, but also for prosecuting a destructive, uncivilized war and imposing an oppressive peace on honorable men who had laid down their arms.[17]

In numerous comments Davis took pride in what he considered his scrupulous fair dealing with all Confederates, even those he detested. And it is true that the overbearing and arch criticism of gray-clad opponents so often found in Confederate memoirs is basically absent from *Rise and Fall*. While Davis lauded what he saw as the principled heroism of Robert E. Lee and Stonewall Jackson and even upheld a controversial figure like Braxton Bragg, he did not directly smash men like Pierre Beauregard and Joseph Johnston, whom he held responsible for terrible disasters. A close reading leaves no doubt that he believed the former lost Shiloh and the latter Atlanta, yet personalities never assume a central place in these volumes. His attention held steadfast to his goal—vindication for his cause.

The response to the published *Rise and Fall* was predictable. Ardent Davis supporters found the two hefty volumes profound and filled with a masterly exposition of constitutional and Confederate history. Thus the *Southern Historical Society Papers* called the work one of "rare power" and "thrilling interest," and its overall assessment matched Davis's own: "this noble and triumphant defense of the Confederate cause." National periodicals, however, gave little notice to Davis's opus. Some of his friends decried the paucity of reviews even in Democratic newspapers. The *Atlantic Monthly* did publish a lengthy review, which credited Davis with a clear and forcible statement of his view of states' rights. Other substantive reviews contested Davis's interpretation of the Constitution and denounced his labeling of the North as the aggressor. All depicted him as a man of the past, out of touch with the world of 1881.[18]

Despite the lack of widespread notice, despite too its bulk and its controversial content, *Rise and Fall* sold astonishingly well. Both the publisher and Joseph Derby, so instrumental in the book's ever coming out, were quite pleased with the sales. Not everyone involved in selling it shared that pleasure, however. Agents in South Carolina and Davis's own Mississippi, which had under 1,400 subscribers and even fewer buyers, grumbled about poor sales. Yet overall, *Rise and Fall* did well. Although annual sales figures do not exist, as of November 18, 1890, 22,943 copies had been sold. And as late as 1907, Appleton stated that sales remained strong.

It is impossible to ascertain how much money the book made for Davis. Appleton had put forth a significant advance that had to be repaid. Still, Davis paid close attention to what he did receive, and in the last year of his life he sued Appleton over royalties. The contract specified that when 20,000 copies had been sold, the royalty would increase from 10 to 12.5 percent. Davis correctly argued that in 1876 his publisher had agreed when sales reached 20,000, the 12.5 percent would be paid on all copies sold, not just those over 20,000. Clearly Appleton had not been fulfilling that provision, but the case was not settled in Davis's lifetime.[19]

While Davis viewed *Rise and Fall* as his personal monument, he looked to the Southern Historical Society and its publication, the *Southern Historical Society Papers,* as the institutional guardian of truthful Confederate history. The society was organized in New Orleans in 1869, but remained basically inchoate from its birth until 1873. In that year a group of Virginians determined to shape the inter-pretation of the Confederate past took it over and transferred its head-quarters to Richmond.[20]

The two key individuals in the revitalized Southern Historical Society were the Reverend J. William Jones and Jubal A. Early. An ordained Baptist minister, Jones had been a chaplain in the Army of Northern Virginia. In that same army Early, a West Pointer and opponent of secession, served as a combat officer throughout the war, rising to the rank of lieutenant general. Like Davis, both Jones and Early extolled the Confederate experience as virtuous and patriotic. They were also committed to safeguarding their sense of the proper or positive view of its heritage. Jones became the paid secretary of the society and editor of the *Southern Historical Society Papers,* which began publication in 1876. Early was chosen president and led the executive committee.

Davis and the Southern Historical Society exalted each other. For the Virginians, having Davis as a major supporter sanctioned their claim that the Southern Historical Society represented more than the state of Virginia. The society made Davis a life member and sent him all its publications. In 1877 Jones wrote Davis: "I need not assure you again that your fame is dear to our Virginia people (whatever the few may say)—that the President of our Society, Genl. Early, and the members of the Executive committee are your warm admirers." Courting Davis, Jones added, "nothing will give us more pleasure than to do everything in our power to put right on the record the able statesman, gallant soldier, pure patriot, and accomplished gentleman who presided over the Confederacy." Providing material to Davis during the preparation of *Rise and Fall,* Jones deemed it "a high privilege" to aid in "your grand work."

In 1882 Jones also tried to get Davis to undertake a speaking tour across the South to raise money for the Southern Historical Society. In wooing Davis to accept this task, Jones employed limitless flattery. He told Davis that after canvassing opinion all over the South on the best way to generate funds, one conclusion stood out. "The universal verdict is: *If President Davis will consent to speak at prominent points in the South in the interest of the S.H.S. you can raise all of the money you need.*" Jones went on to say that he hated to ask anything more of someone who had sacrificed so much for the cause, but felt he had nowhere else to turn. Yet despite such blandishments, Davis never went on the road for the society. The aftermath of a yellow fever epidemic around Beauvoir, and his own physical limitations, kept him at home. Still, Davis was vitally interested in a secure financial future for the society, and did make one address in New Orleans in its behalf.[21]

He often heaped accolades upon the society and its leaders for their great labor in preserving the record and the memory of the Confederate past. According to Davis, the *Southern Historical Society Papers* had an especially critical place. He said the collection of "scattered records and unwritten recollections" and their publication in the *Papers* would enable "the future historian, to do justice to our cause and conduct. . . ." Finding an error in the pages of the *Papers* distressed him mightily, "especially because I have regarded them as to be the depository of authentic facts in regard to the 'Confederate States of America.' "[22]

Although Davis communicated with Jones and the society mostly through correspondence, he built up a warm personal relationship with Early. He had not before known Early personally, but a shared commitment to the glory of the Confederacy and a passion for upholding and maintaining its legitimacy brought them together. Early's position as a paid supervisor in the Louisiana State Lottery Company made possible relatively frequent personal contact because the Virginian had to appear regularly in New Orleans. On trips between Virginia and the Louisiana metropolis, Early occasionally stopped at Beauvoir. Davis also visited him in New Orleans. Early always treated Davis with the utmost respect; Davis was still president and commander in chief. Additionally, in small ways Early endeared himself to Davis. He always wore a simple gray suit, which Davis had begun doing. Davis also sincerely appreciated and thoroughly enjoyed presents that Early regularly brought or sent, especially excellent pipe tobacco. The two men discussed the characteristics of different brands. On one occasion Early gave Davis a cigar holder he himself had made from Virginia buckeye wood.

Davis came to think quite highly of Early and took pleasure in his company. He viewed the Virginian as a fellow soldier in the ongoing struggle to ensure the survival of the true faith of the Confederacy. He told Early that he had many topics he wanted them to talk over, "because there are few with whom I can agree so fully." The two men spurned other southerners, including ex-Confederates, who in their minds had become too friendly with the Yankee enemy. Davis and Early despairingly termed such people "harmonizers" because they placed reconciliation ahead of insisting on the rightness and virtue of the Confederate cause, including the constitutionality of secession.[23]

Publication of *Rise and Fall* did not fundamentally alter Davis's engagement with Confederate topics or emotions. Even though he felt a strong desire to establish his definition of an accurate Confederate record, he did not relish conflict with other Confederate veterans. "I certainly wish to say nothing but good of any who wore the gray," he wrote Early. In his book he asserted he tried "to treat with gentleness any conduct of a confederate which I could not approve and necessarily regretted." Though possessing "fixed ammunition," he did not use it; he insisted he was "very forebearing to some who have been unfair and even indignant to me." Davis's assertion that putting down others had nothing to do with his writing *Rise and Fall* was substantially correct. Of course, he did not consider his insistence on the correctness of events as an attack on anybody. He was as convinced after the war as during it that he had only the purest of motives. Thus, if anyone assaulted his interpretation, this simply showed that that person's ambition and selfishness had once more surged forward.[24]

Davis received constant advice not to participate in old battles and personal vendettas. Old friends like Judah Benjamin and new ones like Early told him that to do so would be unproductive and even injurious to him. Conscious of his position and enormously proud of widespread southern esteem for him, Davis did generally refuse to enter a public fray with any other Confederate. He did want his stance vindicated, but he was usually willing to let surrogates take on those who challenged either his sense of selfless loyalty to the cause or his interpretation of disputed decisions.[25]

His old battles were chiefly with the two generals he had been at odds with since 1861, Pierre Beauregard and Joseph Johnston. They in turn held Davis in contempt. Beauregard said, "he has no elements of greatness about him." As sensitive to criticism as Davis, but without the security of his standing in the South, both men openly condemned his leadership, going so far as to imply that his incompetence alone caused the Confederate disaster. In their memoirs—Johnston's published before *Rise and Fall* and Beauregard's after—and in articles that appeared chiefly in *Century Magazine* and were reprinted in *Battles and Leaders of the Civil War,* a popular compilation of pieces by notable people on both sides, they lambasted him and boosted themselves. A pet topic was the aftermath of First Manassas: Davis had prevented what would have been a successful Confederate attack on Washington. His shortcomings at Vicksburg and Atlanta were also highlighted. In a newspaper interview Johnston even suggested that Davis had raided the Confederate treasury during the final retreat. Beauregard's former chief of staff underscored the personal motives behind these diatribes when he urged that his former commander and Johnston should together demonstrate "that in [Davis's] constant inexorable hatred of both of you and the effort to gratify that passion of his soul, he wrecked the cause unhappily entrusted to his hands."[26]

While Davis did not publicly slam either Beauregard or Johnston, his correspondence bristled with fury at their attacks upon him. To him they were small men trying to camouflage their own shortcomings, which had contributed significantly to Confederate defeat. He said that in both the *Narrative* and wartime reports Johnston's "forte [was] the suppressio veir." Davis decried Beauregard's "egotism & malignity"; Varina encapsulated her husband's opinion of the Louisianian in equating him with another person who " 'had a firm and immutable faith in himself,' and but little in the capacity of anyone else." But at times Davis also forgot the reality of the war years, as when he strove to obtain material indicating that Beauregard and Johnston bore responsibility for restraining a Confederate advance on Washington after First Manassas. Yet he did not personally take up public cudgels against these two unhappy men. He even refused an invitation from the editors of *Century Magazine* to respond in their pages to the articles of Beauregard and Johnston, in part because he could not get a guarantee that whatever he submitted would appear unedited.[27]

There was one notable public manifestation of his displeasure. In mid-1882 he accepted an invitation to speak at the dedication of the Lee mausoleum in Lexington the following year. But when he learned a few months later that Joseph Johnston would preside over the event, he reneged, making clear that Johnston's participation rendered his own impossible. He declared he had "no desire to make any demonstration in regard to Genl. J. E. Johnston," yet he wanted all involved to understand the reason for his absence. Although Early tried to persuade him to come, the Virginian said he understood and empathized with Davis's position. The ceremony took place as scheduled, without Jefferson Davis.[28]

Davis did not spend time on war-related struggles only with old Confederates. On two occasions he took issue with northern men over his sense of personal honor and his belief in immutable principles. In a November 1884 address in St. Louis, William T. Sherman asserted that he had read letters proving Davis did not really believe in secession; instead, Davis left the Union to use the South to strike violently at the North; furthermore, he would even have used force to prevent the secession of any state from the Confederacy. Then, in January 1885, the Senate debated a similar report supposedly filed with the War Department. Davis erupted with a long letter to a St. Louis editor in which he denied Sherman's accusation, preached his gospel of principle along with Confederate purity, and challenged Sherman to produce the documents or "wear the brand of a base slanderer." Waving aside Davis's challenge, Sherman replied that he and Davis would settle the matter between themselves. Sherman never contacted Davis, who was outraged. Sherman, he wrote, "is remarkable in this; that he is not only willing to lie, but does not feel degraded by the detection."[29]

In obtaining an apology or a recantation Davis fared no better with a rising young New York politician, Theodore Roosevelt. In an 1885 article Roosevelt publicly associated Davis with Benedict Arnold, asserting that the only American traitor who could compare with Arnold was Davis. An angry and hurt Davis riposted: "You must be ignorant of American history if you do not know that the career of those characters might be aptly chosen for contrast, but not for similitude; and if so ignorant, the instinct of a gentlemen, had you possessed it, must have caused you to make inquiry before uttering an accusation so libelous and false." Although Davis wanted Roosevelt "to repel the unproved outrage," he added that he had "too low an estimate of you to expect an honorable retraction of your slander." The cocky young New Yorker did not disappoint the offended old Mississippian. "Mr. Theodore Roosevelt is in receipt of a letter purporting to come from Mr. Jefferson Davis, and denying that the character of Mr. Davis compares unfavorably with that of Benedict Arnold." Roosevelt went on to say that he did not find it surprising that his view of Davis differed markedly from Davis's own sense of himself. Then he closed: "Mr. Roosevelt begs leave to add that he does not deem it necessary that there should be any further communication between himself and Jefferson Davis."[30]

Davis would never bend on the constitutional right of secession. As he perceived it, he was always a patriotic constitutionalist, never a law-breaking rebel. He had spent much of *Rise and Fall* making and buttressing his argument, but he also regularly made it elsewhere. Clinging to that faith and considering himself an apostle of the Founding Fathers, he rejected any notion that either a rebellion or a civil war had taken place. "The States are the sovereign parties to the compact of union," he intoned, "& sovereigns *cannot* rebel." According to him, the states under the Constitution remained "sovereign communities, and war between them was not as if parts of the same body were contending with each other, it was not therefore a 'Civil War.' " That term, he maintained, could apply only "to a conflict between factions in a State such as the wars of the Roses in England, but ours was a war between sovereigns—no more a civil war than that between Germany & France." The states in the Confederacy wanted what was their constitutional right, their independence. That effort, which commenced in 1861, ended in defeat, and Davis did not anticipate it would ever be attempted again. He certainly would never advocate secession. The fact of defeat simply "showed it to be impractical, but this did not prove it to be wrong."[31]

Davis's absolute conviction that he had done nothing wrong in 1861, that he was not a rebel but a constitutional patriot, underlay his refusal ever to ask for a pardon or for the removal of the political disabilities imposed by the Fourteenth Amendment. That men he admired and even revered like Robert E. Lee and his brother Joseph did so did not budge him. He admitted that he had taken an oath to uphold the Constitution of the United States, and he insisted that he had done so even in supporting secession. When, in 1876, Davis learned that wrangling over his inclusion or exclusion was jeopardizing a general amnesty bill in Congress, he urged the chairman of the House Judiciary Committee, a Kentucky Democrat, not to allow any former Confederates to suffer because of him. He did not mind exclusion. "Further it may be proper to state," he continued, "that I have no claim to pardon not having in anywise repented or changed the conviction on which my political course was founded as well as before as during and since the war between the States." But there was more. To those who asserted that a petition for removal of the disqualifications stipulated by the Fourteenth Amendment did not necessarily mean admission of wrong, he was equally adamant. "Now sir," he lectured a friend, "if I were to ask having my disabilities removed, it would not be a confession of wrong on my part, but it would be to that extent an admission of right to impose the disability I asked them to remove. That neither you nor I can concede." He clung to those creeds as long as he breathed.[32]

While Davis labored to perpetuate his vision of Confederate history, in family matters he experienced both joy and deep sadness. In March 1877 Polly presented him with his first grandchild and namesake. Grandfather Davis was delighted. He and an unemployed Jeff Jr., who was living at Beauvoir while looking for a job, traveled to Memphis to see Jefferson Davis Hayes. This happiness was short-lived. When Davis saw the infant, he described him as "plump as a partridge." Yet in June the baby fell ill and died.

With Varina still in Europe, a distraught father wanted especially to comfort his devastated daughter. "My beloved daughter has never to me outgrown her childhood," he remarked, "and when she is suffering I feel that she should be with me." But his Christian stoicism governed his advice to his son-in-law: "My dear Son, we must all submit to the chastisement visited upon us. It is the highest stage of Christian culture which enables one, when most severely stricken, to say in true resignation, God's will be done." To help everyone through this sad time, Davis persuaded the Hayes family to come to Beauvoir for an extended visit. They stayed in the cottage just west of the main house, which had been prepared for them. For a time Davis had his older daughter, his son-in-law, and his son with him. It was a period of relaxation—reading, fishing, bathing, and driving. Davis was pleased with the restoration of his daughter's vitality and spirit.

In March 1878 joy returned when Polly gave birth to Varina Howell Davis Hayes. A thrilled grandmother was in Memphis for this event. Everything went well, and she happily informed her husband, "The baby is splendid, so good & so hearty, and she laughs what her father calls a large laugh every time she wakes."[33]

Although the Davises were quite pleased with their healthy granddaughter, another blow struck the family in the autumn of 1878. That summer, a virulent epidemic of yellow fever swept through the lower Mississippi Valley, even stretching to the Mississippi Gulf Coast. Decrying the "terrible scourge," Davis blamed the excessively hot weather for its severity and the rapidity of railroad travel for the fever's unusual geographic reach.

News that the frightful disease had arrived in Memphis caused alarm at Beauvoir. Not only did Addison, Polly, and their infant daughter live in that city, but also Jeff Jr., who had recently obtained a position in a bank. "Painfully anxious" about their children, Jefferson and Varina urged them to take every precaution. And they did move about ten miles out of the city, though Addison often went in on business. The elder Davises had an added concern when William Walthall voluntarily went to the beleaguered city to assist in caring for the sick. By late September, reports that the disease was tapering off in Memphis offered some comfort to the worried people at Beauvoir.

But on October 11 came the dreaded telegram. Jeff Jr. had been stricken with yellow fever. Walthall's daughter recorded the impact of the news: "[The Davises] looked wretchedly, Mr. Davis looked as if he had received some terrible blow that had completely crushed him. . . ."

Varina desperately wanted to go to her son's side, but travel was dangerous because of infected places and quarantines. Eventually her husband and Walthall, who had just returned to the coast, convinced her of the peril. Instead, Walthall agreed immediately to retrace his steps and take charge of the young man. But Jeff Jr. was beyond anyone's help. After a brief rally, he died on October 16 at age twenty-one.

His death staggered his parents. Davis cried out in anguish: "The last of my four sons has left me. I am crushed under such heavy and repeated blows. I presume not God to scorn, but the many and humble prayers offered before my boy was taken from me, are hushed in the despair of my bereavement." Yet even in his torment, Sarah Dorsey spoke of his "bear[ing] it manfully." He spoke of his son's letters to him, a toothpick and walking stick the boy had made for him, and a pocketknife that had been a present. "These are put away to be preserved and looked at, as long as I live," he wrote. A devastated Varina lay helpless in bed, prostrated by a dangerous fever. Sarah Dorsey said she did not leave Varina's sickbed for six days and nights, except to bathe and change clothes. Mother and father had only their two daughters remaining.[34]

The year 1878 was a bittersweet one for Jefferson Davis. While he lost his one remaining son, he regained his legal right to Brierfield. In April the Mississippi Supreme Court overturned the decision of the Warren County Chancery Court. In awarding Brierfield to Davis, the Supreme Court rejected any relevance for estoppel and said Davis had proven indisputably that he had cleared the land that became Brierfield and he had resided on and farmed the property from that time until the war years. The court asserted that under a Mississippi statute of 1844, which granted ownership to anyone who had "ten years actual adverse possession" of land, Davis clearly owned Brierfield. In Davis's legal action to recover his plantation, the court found nothing "inconsistent with the lofty integrity . . . which history attests for Jefferson [Davis]."

Although the Mississippi Supreme Court handed down a legal judgment written in legal language, politics had a controlling influence on its decision. In January 1876 a Republican judge in Warren County decided against Davis. At that point he would also have lost in the Supreme Court, for it then had three Republican justices. But by the time the court ruled on Davis's case, its makeup had fundamentally changed. Two of the Republicans had been replaced by Democrats, both former Confederate officers. The two Democrats decided for Davis; the lone Republican dissented. This realignment accompanied the end of Reconstruction in Mississippi. In 1875 the Democratic party, the agent of white Mississippians, had won control of the legislature in a bitter, violence-marred election. Five months later the Republican governor, who was facing impeachment, resigned. The new Democratic governor and legislature started to eliminate Republican power and influence on the state level. By 1878 they had largely succeeded.

The close of Reconstruction found Davis at one with almost all southern whites, just as he had been through its course. By the late 1870s he was in an even larger company, for by that time almost all white northerners agreed with white southerners that Reconstruction was wrong and should end. Davis applauded what he and most white Mississippians called the redemption of their state. Speaking in May 1878 to a group of Confederate veterans who had come to honor him, Davis declared: "Well may we rejoice in the regained possession of local government, in the power of the people to choose their representatives and to legislate uncontrolled by bayonets." The demise of the Republican-dominated regimes in the southern states, supported by the power of the United States government, signaled the triumph of his brand of constitutionalism. "The constitution of the United States, interpreted as it was by those who made it, is the prophet's rod to sweeten the bitter water from which flowed the strife, the carnage, the misery and shame of the past, as well as the foils of the present."[35]

Although the court had restored Davis's legal ownership of Brierfield, he could not take immediate possession. First, judicial proceedings were required to remove the Montgomerys. On June 1, 1880, the Warren County Chancery Court issued an order authorizing foreclosure on the Montgomery mortgage, which was in default. Appeals held up enforcement of this decree until 1881. Finally, on December 1, 1881, for the first time in his life Jefferson Davis received deed and title to Brierfield.[36]

Throughout these months of gladness and sadness, Davis's relationship with Sarah Dorsey deepened. Although he spoke of her as his "hostess," he began to feel more responsibility for the widow who had so befriended him. In time he took over management of Beauvoir as well as her other business affairs. In May 1878 she gave him power of attorney. According to her, Davis "kept a kind of oversight" over her. "Now that I am left so entirely alone & desolate in the world," she told a mutual friend, "He is kinder & more considerate than ever." Even Varina warmed to this other woman, especially after her serious illness following Jeff Jr.'s death. She said she knew of no other person except her own mother who could match Sarah Dorsey as a nurse.[37]

For Sarah Dorsey, Jefferson Davis remained the hero of the age, in her eyes "the highest & noblest in existence." When Davis first arrived at Beauvoir, a number of her relatives also made extended visits, and a half brother managed the place. But after a time he left, and the others stopped coming. Sarah Dorsey wanted to ease Davis's retirement, and realizing that he had limited means and had grown enormously fond of Beauvoir, she decided in February 1879 to sell it to him. The price was $5,500—a fair bargain, but no gift. The terms were most generous, however. She demanded no down payment and said she would accept payment over three years, with the first installment due on January 1, 1880. The sales contract also provided for her right to repurchase Beauvoir, should Davis precede her in death.

There was talk at the time, and later, that Davis and Sarah Dorsey were physically intimate at Beauvoir. No known document supports such a contention, and much circumstantial evidence contradicts it. Both he and she were quite Victorian in their attitude toward sex. In one of her novels she even downplayed its importance vis-à-vis true understanding, which she believed she and Davis had achieved. Moreover, illness plagued both of them. Davis suffered from his usual and frequently recurring range of ailments, and by late 1877 she had developed breast cancer, which would eventually kill her. Besides, for the final half of the thirty months that Jefferson Davis and Sarah Dorsey shared Beauvoir, Varina Davis also lived there.

The course of Sarah Dorsey's cancer altered the transfer of Beauvoir from her to Davis. Although she had agreed to sell him Beauvoir, she also made provision for him possibly to obtain it at no cost. Declaring that she had already done enough for her relatives, she left the place to him in her will dated January 1878. Beauvoir, along with all of her other property, was willed to Davis in fee simple, with everything to go to his daughter Varina Anne upon his death. William Walthall prepared the document at her request, and Davis was aware of its contents.[38]

In June 1879 Sarah Dorsey went to New Orleans for surgery to remove her cancer. Although she came through the operation with no problem, it provided no cure and did not lengthen her life. As death approached, Davis was summoned to the city. The end came early on the morning of July 4. At her bedside during the final moments, Davis reported that he felt "deeply grieved at her death." To Walthall, he wrote, ". . . you cannot know how deeply grateful I am to her for years of unvarying kindness & service & therefore cannot realize how sorrowfully I feel her loss." He accompanied her body upriver for interment in Natchez.[39]

Back in New Orleans, Davis on July 10 applied to the Second District Court, Parish of Orleans, for the probation of her will. Five days later, the court accepted the will as legitimate. At that point Sarah Dorsey's relatives learned that she had made Davis her sole heir. Frustrated and angry, several of them decided to challenge the will. Although Davis denounced what he termed "vile attempts by greedy, ungrateful relatives, to impugn the motives and question the validity of her will," need rather than avarice governed their conduct. Attempting to overturn the will, in December 1879 they filed suit in the United States Circuit Court, District of Louisiana in New Orleans, charging that Davis had insinuated himself into a vulnerable widow's affections. But no evidence supported their accusations, and in March 1880 the court without comment decided against the plaintiffs, upholding the validity of the will. The losers did file notice of their intent to appeal to the United States Supreme Court, but no appeal was ever made. They had no reason to think they could prevail.[40]

Davis inherited an estate worth some $50,000, but one also in debt. He promptly moved to eliminate the outstanding debt by borrowing against future revenues from the property, which he estimated at about $2,500 annually. That money came from cotton plantations in Louisiana, not Beauvoir. Davis said that Beauvoir had never produced any income for either his benefactress or himself. He maintained that he always had to struggle to keep the Dorsey property solvent; expenses consumed income. Still, although Sarah Dorsey's bequest did not make Davis wealthy, it did give him a home he came to cherish.[41]

In 1881, the year *Rise and Fall* came out and Davis actually took possession of Brierfield, he made his fifth and final trip to Europe. He and Varina both went solely to bring back their daughter Winnie, who had spent five years in the girls' preparatory school in Karlsruhe. This time he was not pursuing any business goals, either elusive or illusive. With their youngest daughter abroad, Jefferson and Varina had written often with news of home and siblings, including the sad tidings of Jeff Jr.'s death, and praise for her accomplishments. Noting her study of languages, he teased that when she returned with command of three languages, she "[would] be expected to talk three times as much as you did formerly." But the serious-minded father with high demands was also present. While he lauded Winnie's "stoical heroism" in embarking on an ambitious course in a foreign place, he did not shy away from directives: "that you should be happy and healthy are requisites to your becoming well educated, and in these are contained the measure of your power to render your parents happy when we shall be reunited."[42]

In an oppressively hot August the Davises sailed from New Orleans for Liverpool on the *Bernard Hall.* Thence they traveled almost directly to Paris for a reunion with Winnie, who had already left Germany. For around two months the reunited family enjoyed the French capital and Chantilly, where Davis stayed with his old friend Dudley Mann. The Davises also enjoyed a visit, their last, with Judah Benjamin.[43]

While Jefferson spent most of his time in Chantilly, with its "higher and drier atmosphere," Varina and Winnie usually stayed in the city. The mother desired her daughter to have "the advantage of a few months in Paris" to complete her education. She also worried about Winnie's health—overmuch, according to her husband. And the two women shopped. Jefferson urged his wife not to "allow the cares of shopping to prey upon your spirits." "Though not rich," he reminded her, "we can meet all your requirements without going to the 'poor 'ouse.'" Perhaps Varina could afford what she needed, but what really captured her attention she considered too expensive. A train ride took her to Sèvres, which she designated "the throne of ceramics," with "glowing china." The exquisite creations forged a union between her aesthetic sense and her emotions. "As I looked on the angel forms depicted there," she wrote her husband, "the longing of my life to create something that would live after me was greater than ever."

Although he did go into Paris, Jefferson enjoyed the more rural environment of Chantilly. He and Mann took long walks over the famous race course that was home to the French Derby. He saw magnificent racehorses and a massive stable that awed him; he also found impressive the forest in which hunters still stalked boar and stag. On one occasion in Paris he and Varina enjoyed the Luxembourg Gardens, especially a statue of a queen of Navarre. To the Davises the sculpture bore an uncanny likeness to his niece Mary Stamps.[44]

After more than eight weeks in and around the French capital, the three Davises headed for England and a ship home. They departed from Southampton on November 22 bound for New York. Traveling via Louisville, they were back in Mississippi before the end of the year.[45]

CHAPTER NINETEEN

"There Is Much Preparation"

After their return from Europe, Jefferson and Varina Davis settled in at Beauvoir with their daughter Winnie. The publication of *Rise and Fall* completed the task that for four years had consumed the household. No other such undertaking loomed ahead.

At Beauvoir, Davis found a satisfying home. As Sarah Dorsey had observed, the climate "renews the life of Mr. Davis." In 1882 he spoke of "loving the coast." He enjoyed the variety of fish and shellfish and even built a bathhouse on the edge of the water where, during the season, he liked to watch the flounder at night. He was delighted when oranges began ripening in late winter. The relative solitude of his seaside retreat pleased him, but he never became a hermit. He traveled, hosted visitors, and participated in some local activities. He became a member, and even a vestryman, of St. Mark's Episcopal Church in Mississippi City.[1]

Varina did not share her husband's happiness with their new home. She found the heat of the Deep South no more congenial than she ever had. Even though the sea breezes often cooled Beauvoir, it could still get quite hot. She also moaned about the seclusion in such an out-of-the-way location. "Oh, me! *I do not* like solitude," she cried, "I must be able to put my hand to a friend at least once a day in order to be 'appy." Like her distaste for hot weather, her preference for a more social environment was not new. Before 1861 she had greatly preferred Washington to Davis Bend. She called Beauvoir "a bright airy place," but she still did not care for it. "As home is here, I stay here & cultivate a few roses and take care of things." Yet, "*I do get so tired* here of the sameness," she admitted.

She confessed that her loneliness exacerbated her sadness. Writing an old friend from prewar Washington, Varina hid nothing: "So sweet so sad the days that are no more are to me that each one of you who constituted the beloved circle within which I hoped to grow old start up before me sometimes as though a living presence had been sent to crown my efforts at naturalization." She could find no joy. "*I do not* like the contemplative joys of the country and every thing that ever hurt me in my life comes up and 'will not down' there being no one else to occupy the chairs, the ghosts do."[2]

Her advancing years added to her general unhappiness. When in 1886 she turned sixty, she said she felt old. She also acknowledged that she had "grown very fleshy," a condition reporters noted and photographs confirm. In addition, she remarked that aging was more pronounced in her than in her husband. As he approached eighty, she commented, "It is in the evening of life that a discrepancy of age tells in married relations, and we are now in a condition to understand the risk." Still, she declared she certainly did not want to die, and "would see the world if I could, but only in an impersonal way—being merely a looker on."

Despite her melancholy and her self-deprecation, Varina Davis remained an impressive woman. Visiting in 1882, a Canadian who had known her during her stay in his country described her as an "exceedingly clever and accomplished lady." Charles Francis Adams, Jr., recalled a "memorable" visit with her. A Philadelphia reporter, portraying her for his readers, characterized her as a "cultured and genial woman." She could still place her social skills and bright mind on full display.[3]

Although Beauvoir was certainly rural, it was not isolated. The Louisville & Nashville Railroad tracks a few hundred yards behind the house gave easy access to Mobile and New Orleans. That access was not a secret. Even though he declaimed against the "great horror of intruders," Davis was generally a civil, and often charming, host. Numerous visitors did come, groups as well as individuals. Contingents of Confederate veterans arrived to pay their respects to their former commander in chief, who always received them graciously and stressed to them the marvelous record they had made between 1861 and 1865. Friends, new acquaintances, and even strangers found their way to Davis's door. Jubal Early was a frequent guest. Davis's Transylvania mate and longtime friend George Jones of Iowa came for a few days. Reporters from various newspapers as far away as New York, Philadelphia, Chicago, and St. Louis showed up, at times unannounced. When at home, Davis generally greeted them warmly, and most wrote positive, even admiring, articles about him. Young Charles Francis Adams stopped by in 1885, as did the newspaper baron Joseph Pulitzer and his entourage three years later. Pulitzer's wife, a distant cousin of Davis's, had met Winnie in New York and grown quite fond of her. A most unusual caller was the young Irish poet-lecturer Oscar Wilde. On a lecture tour in the United States in 1882, Wilde pronounced Davis the American he most wanted to see. When he appeared at Beauvoir, he captivated Varina and Winnie, though Davis found his demeanor and dandyish dress off-putting. Wilde left him an unrequested, signed photograph.[4]

To help them maintain Beauvoir and accommodate their various guests, the elderly Davises had considerable assistance. Even though Varina complained about trouble with black servants, as did many southern whites of her time, she managed a sizable staff that performed a number of tasks. There was a cook, a houseboy, a cleaning woman, as many as three men to tend the animals and the vineyard, and a gardener. She employed no washerwoman because she sent her laundry out.[5]

Visitors found their host a man who showed his years but remained vigorous and alert. When observers first encountered Davis, they noticed his bearing. Though a bit stooped, he walked with a "steady" step. His hair and short beard were "deeply silvered." As always his eyes captured attention, even though the useless left one revealed a "slight cast," akin to a cataract. His wide-ranging and friendly conversation impressed, and on occasion surprised, northern journalists who had come expecting to find an angry, bitter old man. Although he eschewed contemporary events, Davis talked freely about the war and about what he saw as a prosperous future for the South and the country.[6]

During these years, Davis's health did not undergo any fundamental change, except for his becoming increasingly infirm, especially toward the end of the decade. His old nemeses, malarial fever, bronchial difficulties, which resulted in prolonged deep coughs, and neuralgia, continued to bedevil him. Rheumatism also appeared as a frequent companion. At times severe attacks struck him, and an assault of fever in 1885 caused Varina to fear for his life. Yet he rallied, and as late as 1887 she described him as "unusually well." Not at all housebound, Davis traveled regularly to New Orleans and to Brierfield, and on three occasions took trips out of the state. In the final year of his life, he thought seriously about going as far away as North Carolina. He did, however, mostly give up writing, and Varina became his amanuensis. She could copy his handwriting so perfectly that, according to her, he could not tell whether he or she had written a particular letter.[7]

At Beauvoir, nothing equaled the joy that children and grandchildren brought to both Jefferson and Varina. She admitted that she lived for her daughters. Having lost all four of her sons, she could not contemplate anything happening to her girls. Winnie lived with them throughout the decade, except when traveling. Polly and her family continued to reside in Memphis until late 1884 when, because of her husband's health, they moved to Colorado. Although the Hayes family move took them far from the Mississippi Gulf Coast, Polly returned with her children for visits that exhilarated her parents.

Jefferson was a doting grandfather, constantly telling his grandchildren that their "Bampa" was eager to see them. He wrote his oldest granddaughter that he could never have "fullness of joy" while she was away. "The sheep bleat around the house, the lambs skip over the lawn, the little collie barks, but the music dearest to my heart is wanting, for the voice of my 'daughtie' is not heard." By this time Polly had three little ones, two girls and then a boy, Addison Davis Hayes, born in 1884. When his grandchildren were at Beauvoir, Davis especially liked "the loving embraces you all habitually gave me." His play with them included card games and toy soldiers. In the summer of 1889, he rejoiced at the news that Polly had given birth to a second son. Varina captured the keen sadness she and her husband felt upon the departure of their loved ones: "Our great empty rooms will answer in their old dreary way to my halting pace and to Mr. Davis's cough."[8]

Mother and father were also quite proud of their younger daughter and her achievements. To the mother, Winnie was "so faithful, so delicately modest, and so conscientious, and has such a brilliant and responsive mind." She became her father's close companion, accompanying him on trips to public gatherings and Confederate reunions. A great favorite with the veterans, in Atlanta in 1886 she was publicly christened "Daughter of the Confederacy."

Then Winnie fell in love. In 1887, while visiting family friends in Syracuse, New York, she met Alfred Wilkinson. An attorney some six years older than she, Wilkinson came from an established family, but a northern one with a notable abolitionist lineage. For a time Winnie kept her romance to herself. When she finally informed her parents, they expressed bewilderment and disappointment that their daughter could even consider marrying a Yankee. At first Davis was adamantly opposed; according to Varina, he announced: "I will never consent." But when, in the late summer of 1888, Wilkinson appeared at Beauvoir to ask for Winnie's hand, their opposition weakened, then disappeared. He charmed them both. Varina noted that her husband was particularly taken with the suitor. She satisfied herself that Wilkinson had the financial means to provide amply for her daughter. Besides, mother and father observed how devoted the two young people were to each other. They saw a radiant Winnie. Jefferson and Varina withdrew their opposition, and at age twenty-four Winnie became engaged. Yet the engagement did not lead directly to marriage. Winnie was conflicted. Although she had received her parents' blessing, she knew that many southerners strongly opposed the Daughter of the Confederacy's marrying a son of their former enemy. At the time of her father's death she had made no final decision. Ultimately she did not marry Wilkinson, or anyone else.[9]

Although Beauvoir provided Davis a comforting home, it did not produce an income. Neither did the other property he inherited from Sarah Dorsey generate any significant revenue for his use, though he did spend time managing the estate. His hopes that royalties from *Rise and Fall* would supply significant funds did not materialize. In 1877 he obtained $2,500 from the Montgomerys, but that payment would not be repeated. Despite having to struggle to get by on his available income, Davis's pride caused him to spurn monetary gifts from ardent supporters. In late 1877 and 1878 friends of Davis, spurred by William Walthall, collected $1,000 for him. Acting as their agent, Governor Alfred H. Colquitt of Georgia forwarded the money to Davis as "an insignificant token of a debt due you by a grateful people." Colquitt also said he expected to send more in the future. But Davis told Colquitt that his "sense of duty" forced him to refuse that donation and all others.[10]

Davis's hopes for financial rebuilding rested on Brierfield. After regaining the plantation, Davis hoped he could turn it into the profitable enterprise it had been before 1861. It still had the fantastically rich soil. As early as 1879, he had begun exertions toward that end. He initially concentrated on the construction of new cabins for black workers who would be essential for the success of his plans. He also renewed the business connection between Brierfield and the New Orleans factor Jacob Payne, his good friend whom he saw often when in the city.

While attempting to rejuvenate Brierfield, Davis would be an absentee planter. He did not believe his health would permit him to live permanently in what he called "the swamp." And reaching the plantation was more difficult since Davis Bend had become Davis Island. In its former configuration, the steamboat landing was directly in front of the Hurricane mansion. After the river changed course, the closest landing to Brierfield was on the southeastern part of the island, some half dozen miles through wooded lowlands from Davis's plantation. Even though Davis said that placing an agent in charge could result in difficulties, he did not believe he had any choice. He would visit regularly, especially in the late fall, after the bulk of the cotton harvest and the first frost. After all, between 1853 and 1861 he had basically run Brierfield from afar. In addition to his own well-being, he knew his wife wanted nothing to do with living at Brierfield. She had not much liked it before the war, and in 1880 it was truly isolated. Furthermore, instead of an agricultural showplace, it was downtrodden and dilapidated. Varina did not even like to visit. Contemplating a trip, she wrote, "I dread the heat, the worry and complaints of the Negro tenants, the swampy miasma and seven mile drive in the mud before we get there."

Finding the proper on-site manager for Brierfield proved elusive. Davis started off with Owen B. Cox, who in the prewar period had been an overseer for him as well as for Joseph. But Davis did not find Cox satisfactory. A key problem involved what Davis saw as Cox's conflicting responsibilities.[11]

Just like antebellum overseers, Cox had responsibility for directing the workers and making the crop, but he also ran the new plantation store. With slavery gone, free blacks had to have access to supplies ranging from food and clothing to agricultural necessities. To service his employees and tenants, Davis established a store, as did other planters across the South. They envisioned these as also potential moneymakers. Because black laborers usually had little or no cash, plantation stores extended credit, with settlement coming at the close of the crop year. Concluding that Cox had concentrated on the store and its sales rather than on the farming operations, Davis decided that two white men were necessary—one for the field, the other for the store. Cox concurred, and thereafter Davis hired two people to handle affairs at Brierfield. By the end of the decade his system not only involved an overseer and a storekeeper, but also a provision that both had to sign any order for supplies, which then had to be sent to him for final approval.[12]

To assist him in the overall direction of Brierfield, Davis called on

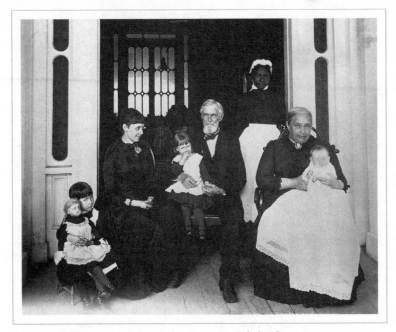

Jefferson and Varina Davis at Beauvoir with daughter Margaret,
grandchildren, and unidentified servant.
Library of Congress

his son-in-law. He even asked Addison Hayes to reside at Brierfield; his wife and children could stay at more healthful Beauvoir. Although Hayes declined to live at Brierfield, he did become central in Davis's management. He visited the plantation, bought materials, and became responsible for the annual reconciliation of accounts. At first Davis had the store accounts sent to him, and the plantation's to Hayes. Eventually all went to the latter. For as long as Hayes dwelt in Memphis, he remained intimately involved in Brierfield affairs.

Neither Davis nor his son-in-law ever discovered satisfactory overseers or storekeepers. Davis experienced trouble with his hires on myriad issues ranging from treatment of blacks to personal honesty. For Davis the 1880s replayed the 1850s. New overseers and storekeepers appeared almost annually, including, briefly in 1882, a brother of Varina's who died after a few months on the island. The inability to secure stability in those two critical positions distressed Davis. As early as 1884 he said, "the opinion grows on me that a plantation given over to agents is worse than nothing." He kept trying, to no avail. Three years later, he lamented that things had gone "from bad to worse."[13]

Frustration about agents was only one of Davis's problems, however. On an 1884 trip to Brierfield, he recounted to his wife, "since my arrival one trouble has chased another like waves, each being the herald of one to come. . . ." These included pests that attacked the cotton plants and workers who neglected the mules, essential for planting and cultivation. But Davis's most arduous and hopeless struggle was with the Mississippi River. The battle with the river was ongoing, and the flooding river usually won, adversely affecting his crop in 1882, 1883, 1884, and 1886. Only levees could protect land and crops from floodwaters. Davis strove to construct adequate levees on Brierfield, but by themselves they would not secure his acres. Other plantations on the island had to have similar protection, or Brierfield still flooded. Throughout the 1880s Davis worked with his fellow property owners to find a mutually agreeable way to share costs and devise a system that would shield all. But it never happened. There was even talk that the U.S. Army Corps of Engineers had a plan. Yet safe levees would not come for almost another half century, not until after the great flood of 1927.[14]

Farming at Brierfield brought Davis in close touch with his grand-niece Lise Hamer, who with her husband and brother operated Hurricane. As part of the foreclosure on the Montgomerys, a survey had been ordered to divide the two plantations. Davis was unenthusiastic about its outcome, and the bitterness between the old man and young woman remained. Strapped for money, Lise offered to sell Hurricane to her great-uncle, who said he could not afford it. Yet Davis did work with her on levees, helping her to obtain financing, and a warmth eventually returned to their letters. Almost twenty years after Davis's death, however, his younger relatives evinced some resentment about his lawsuit.[15]

While inadequate levees and imperfect white agents caused Davis serious difficulties, those troubles were matched by problems with black labor. At the outset of his second career as a planter, Davis assumed he would have no difficulty finding an ample number of blacks to cultivate his acres. He also thought many he called "old Negroes," or his former slaves, would again want to live and work at Brierfield. But he soon discovered that recruiting and retaining a sufficient labor force would be a major endeavor. The end of slavery meant freedom of movement for the emancipated slaves; they could no longer be compelled to remain in locations specified by white landlords. When he began actual operations at Brierfield, Davis reported that few of his former slaves were still there, and by 1884 there were none.

He finally understood that the demand for agricultural labor in the cotton counties along the Mississippi outstripped the supply. Moreover, the isolation of Davis Island made the task even more arduous. Blacks who left one plantation for another disturbed Davis; he condemned them for what was to him an absence of loyalty. As a result, he tried to prevent his workers from departing. First, he offered several types of labor arrangements. He hired day laborers who would receive wages. He also set up three classifications of tenants: those who had their own mules and farmed a piece of land at a fixed annual rate, in cotton or cash; those who worked for an agreed-upon share of the crop; and those who leased for a term of not less than five years, with allowances for improvements that benefited the proprietor.

Then he urged proper treatment of all, wage earners and tenants, to encourage their staying on. "The only way to prevent tenants from being dissatisfied & removing to other places," Davis wrote, "is to make them feel that they cannot better their condition by a change, & above all things, to prevent them from getting in debt to such an extent as to induce them to get rid of it by a change of their home." Davis wondered whether it would be better to cancel debt than carry it over for another year. But carrying over entailed two risks: the debt would never be paid; and, more critical, the debtor would abscond.

He also took other steps to keep his laborers. A key element in Davis's hiring and firing white agents had to do with their success or lack of success in dealing with the black laborers. He tried and failed to get the planters on the island to unite on certain labor concerns, such as fixing compensation and respecting the agreements between employers and employees. Davis experienced as much instability with black workers as with white managers.[16]

Still searching for workers, he turned to a new source—blacks coming west as part of an organized effort to meet the desperate need for labor on the vast cotton plantations of the lower Mississippi Valley. Agents promising better wages and conditions arranged rail transportation for travel west to huge numbers of blacks from Atlantic states like South Carolina. To secure some of them, Davis dealt with his old West Point classmate and former Confederate general Thomas F. Drayton, a South Carolinian living in Charlotte, North Carolina. Davis told Drayton he wanted healthy workers with positive traits and preferably families. When Drayton dispatched a consignment of blacks toward Mississippi, he sent a telegram informing Davis, for at the western end of the trip, especially in Memphis, competition was quite keen among prospective employers. The blacks did not always end up precisely where they were supposed to. Even participating in this interstate labor trade did not suffice. Although Davis had several rough years as a planter, even in good seasons the shortage of labor posed an insurmountable hurdle. He reported having to leave one-third of his land unplanted; but despite that kind of cutback, he found cotton left on the stalk and the ground white with cotton that would never be gathered.[17]

Although Davis periodically expressed optimism, he admitted in 1889 to a longtime Mississippi farming friend that "the result is very meager compared with what attended efforts on the same land in former times." He began thinking about leasing his plantation instead of operating it himself. That would be his "last resort," one he believed would at least check the growth of debt. But he did not lease in his lifetime. Although Davis did not make Brierfield profitable, he did not lose the land. The benefactions of his friend and factor Jacob Payne contributed significantly. Family tradition also holds that a fortuitous sale of his wild lands in Arkansas helped him handle his debt problem. In the end, he hung on. Writing in November 1889 from Brierfield, he mourned, "Nothing is as it should be, and I am not able even to look at the place."[18]

Davis's attempt to replicate his antebellum success utilizing black labor failed. Like many other former slaveowners, he found the transition to free labor fraught with difficulties. Also like many of them, he could never regain the prosperity he had enjoyed under slavery. Much of the situation was beyond their control. Seemingly intractable problems, such as overproduction of cotton and declining prices, beset the agricultural economy of the late nineteenth-century South. Nevertheless, Davis viewed his free labor force as a major reason that he was unable to make Brierfield as productive as he thought it ought to be.

Although slavery had been abolished for a decade and a half when Davis began anew as a planter, his view of the basic relationship between whites and blacks had not altered. He still believed that blacks were inferior to whites, and he did not envision any foreseeable change in the racial order. To his mind, white tutelage had always been central in any advance the subordinate race made. Thus, he had always expressed serious doubts that even the able Montgomerys could succeed on their own. His experience with free black labor at Brierfield confirmed his opinion that blacks lacked crucially important traits. He told Thomas Drayton, "The habit of drinking & gambling is so common among our negroes that for the sake of such indulgence, a large proportion of them prefer to work as day laborers instead of waiting for the larger sum they would get by making a crop & that class are always ready to drift away just at the time they are most needed."

In his general attitude about the supremacy of the white race, Davis was not at all unique. Almost every white American, as well as Western European, considered blacks an inferior race. The late decades of the nineteenth century witnessed the onrush of imperialism and the conviction that whites carried the "burden" of the lesser black, brown, and yellow peoples. Whites believed that political and economic power must reside with them and social equality was out of the question. Yet not all whites agreed on the future of blacks. Some trusted that education and the Christian religion would bring steady improvement; others were convinced that nothing could change what they viewed as the divine or natural arrangement.

By the late 1880s Davis had become more pessimistic about the progress and future of African Americans. He saw devolution. In 1889 the Virginian Philip A. Bruce published his influential book *The Plantation Negro as a Freeman*. At this time around 90 percent of all blacks still lived in the former slave states, and overwhelmingly they resided in the plantation belts, especially in the Deep South. Although Bruce based his account on personal observations in the predominantly black plantation counties of his state, he declared that the same conditions prevailed elsewhere in similar regions of the South, such as the river counties of the lower Mississippi Valley. Bruce narrated a dismal story of the degeneration of blacks in those areas where large numbers of them lived among few whites. He told of a decline in moral and productive capacity. His conclusion: the end of slavery had been disastrous for the well-being and prospects of blacks. Upon reading the book, Davis applauded Bruce: "It is gratifying to know that at last a Southern writer comprehending the true characters of the Negro, has chosen to present a real portrait for the benefit of the uninitiated."[19]

Even though Davis's general view of race was quite clear, his connections with individual blacks complicate what initially seems uncomplicated. Without question he respected individual blacks and in turn received their respect. His dealings with his slave James Pemberton and with Ben Montgomery as both a slave and a freedman illustrate such a relationship. Inviting Davis to attend the Colored State Fair in Vicksburg in 1886, Montgomery's son Isaiah said he knew Davis would have an interest "in any Enterprise tending to the welfare and development of the Colored people of Mississippi." "We would be highly pleased to have you here," Isaiah Montgomery asserted, and he closed "with best wishes for your continued preservation."

The year before Davis died, he received a letter from James H. Jones, a former Davis slave. Residing in Raleigh, North Carolina, Jones identified himself as a Republican and detailed his successful career, including a decade and a half as an alderman and a stint as a deputy sheriff. Although he had not seen Davis in fifteen years, Jones professed, "I have always been as warmly attached to you as when I was your body servant." He declared that he had never missed an opportunity to defend Davis from "any attack of malicious or envious people." He said he occasionally read about Davis and had even bought a copy of *Rise and Fall*. He also asked for a photograph. Responding, Davis wrote Jones that his letter had brought much pleasure to Varina and him. "We all here rejoiced when we heard of your honorable prosperity & have felt that it was due to your integrity [and fidelity]." Davis then assured Jones that the Davises' regard for him was undiminished. And he put his most recent photograph in the mail.[20]

At the end of his life, Jefferson Davis believed unequivocally in the superiority of his race. He also had serious reservations about black people ever achieving any kind of equality with the superior race. Yet he was no race-baiter or racial demagogue. Neither by themselves nor in conjunction with others did blacks any longer threaten what Davis considered the proper order in the South. The politics of racial demagoguery lurking just ahead in the 1890s and early twentieth century articulated a malignancy of feeling that far surpassed anything Davis ever expressed. His conviction about the innate supremacy of his race did not require hatred or viciousness.

In the late 1880s, when Davis concluded that Brierfield was not providing the income he expected and needed, he turned to writing for the first time since the publication of *Rise and Fall*. His subject remained chiefly the same: the justice and honor of secession and the Confederate cause. He declined a request to write a piece on Abraham Lincoln, though he agreed to do one on Zachary Taylor. A key figure in this new direction was James Redpath. A native Scot who immigrated with his family to Michigan around 1850, Redpath had been a Civil War journalist and had booked lecturers in the postwar years. In 1886 he became

Ruins of Brierfield (the house was destroyed by fire in 1931), looking west, 1995.
Courtesy of Patricia H. Cooper

an editor at the *North American Review,* and he invited contributions from Davis. In two successive articles published posthumously, Davis praised Robert E. Lee and once more spelled out his states'-rights constitutionalism, which legitimized secession. He also wrote a lengthy treatment of the Confederate prison camp at Andersonville, Georgia, that was not published.[21]

Prompted and aided by Redpath, he prepared a pared-down version of *Rise and Fall* for Redpath's new publishing association with Robert Belford of the Belford Company. Drastic cuts were made in the discussion of constitutional history and issues, which constituted a considerable portion of *Rise and Fall.* The coverage of the war was also reduced and the appendices jettisoned. Even so, *A Short History of the Confederate States of America,* published in the year after Davis's death, totals a hefty 505 pages.

Davis did not hesitate to emphasize his concern about money. Only with agreement on a suitable honorarium did he agree in 1888 to write the sketch of Taylor for *Appleton's Cyclopedia of American Biography.*

In the last year of his life, he reacted vigorously when a new editor at the *North American Review* sent him a check for $100 for an article rather than the $250 he and Redpath had agreed upon. Incensed, Davis returned the $100, saying he did not understand the reason for the smaller amount. A check for $250 was soon mailed to Mississippi. He also instituted a lawsuit against D. Appleton & Company over royalty payments from *Rise and Fall*.[22]

Davis contemplated writing his memoirs as well. This time he really meant memoirs or reminiscences, not a constitutional treatise or an apologia. In the summer of 1888 Redpath, who had grown to admire Davis and had become a warm friend, spent three months at Beauvoir working with Davis. He returned again in the fall of 1889 just after Davis had departed on his final trip to Brierfield. Davis often dictated to both Varina and Redpath from his sickbed, but he had not gotten much done before his death. Only two fragments survived. One known as the "Autobiography" appeared in *Belford's Magazine,* with a variant version included in J. William Jones's *The Davis Memorial Volume.* The other, "Autobiographical Sketch," was published only in Varina's own *Memoir*.[23]

Although Davis returned to writing for publication, he maintained his public silence on current political issues, with one notable exception. From the time of his return to Mississippi, he shunned any talk of public office for himself and stayed away from political disputes. He realized he could easily have been elected to either house of the Congress, but he declared his primary goal had always been to serve his state, and he recognized the liability of the controversy swirling about him. "From youth to age," he informed a Mississippi editor, "it has been my pride to represent Mississippi in military and civil service, and I would add that all her sons should realize that it is her interest which dictates my present decision." Davis professed himself satisfied and humbled with "the affection of our people. . . ."[24]

He did express his private opinion on one major national issue of the 1880s. As early as 1882 the first serious effort was underway in Congress to secure a federal appropriation for public education. Known as the Blair Bill for its chief congressional sponsor, Senator Henry W. Blair, Republican of New Hampshire, the measure got through the Senate on three separate occasions during the decade but never passed the House, and ultimately failed. In 1884 a South Carolinian asked Davis for his opinion. Replying in a private letter, Davis opposed the initiative on the grounds of strict construction and states' rights: "Unless therefore there can be found among the enumerated powers a grant to take money out of the Treasury & apply it to support of the schools, an act making such an appropriation must be unconstitutional. . . ." Money, Davis predicted, would be followed by federal control of curriculum, teacher accreditation, and textbooks—in his judgment an unmitigated disaster.[25]

While Davis's opinion on the Blair Bill did not become part of the public debate, he did stand in the spotlight on an increasingly important and divisive issue: prohibition. His involvement began when his wartime aide Francis Lubbock, who had also been governor of Texas, requested Davis's opinion on the attempt to place an amendment requiring statewide prohibition in the Texas constitution. Lubbock was a leader of the forces opposing the proposed amendment. In his response, Davis occupied the same constitutional ground he had always defended. He asserted that prohibition would mean "governmental supervision and paternity," which would violate the individual liberty at the heart of the Constitution. He contended that the world had "long suffered from the oppression of government . . . excusing the invasion into private and domestic affairs on the plea of paternal care for the morals and good order of the people."

While he agreed that "the intemperate use of intoxicating liquors is an evil" and "the root of many social disorders," he deemed the appropriate remedy to be education and Christianity, not constitutional directives. "To destroy individual liberty and moral responsibility would be to eradicate one evil by the substitution of another," Davis expounded, "which it is submitted would be more fatal than that for which it was offered as a remedy." Moreover, Davis warned that official statewide prohibition could become "the wooden horse in which a disguised enemy to State sovereignty as the guardian of individual liberty was introduced. . . ." He foresaw "the progressive march" eventually moving "from State to United States."[26]

Lubbock made Davis's letter public, drawing him into a bitter contest. For Davis, who wanted no part of public disputes, that outcome was most unwelcome but not unexpected. He had written Lubbock, "If the utterance shall avail anything for good, it will compensate me for the objurgations with which I shall doubtless be pursued by the followers of the popularism of the day." Even friendships could be strained. John H. Reagan was a major spokesman for prohibition, but the two men did not permit this difference to become personal. Davis became especially upset when prohibitionists in Texas began accusing him of opposing temperance and calling him a saloon man. Rightly believing that such charges distorted his position, he felt compelled to answer them. He sent an open letter to the *Houston Post* denying the accusations and repeating his fundamental points about strict construction and individual liberty. When the votes were counted, the antiprohibitionist side triumphed. And Lubbock gave Davis much of the credit for the victory.[27]

Davis's involvement in the prohibition wars was not restricted to Texas. In his own Mississippi, he ended up in a publicized conflict with the Reverend Charles B. Galloway, the Methodist bishop of the state. Featured in the state's newspapers, this fracas revolved around Galloway's assertion that Davis advocated intemperance and supported saloons. Davis's reaction had two components. First, he expressed his distress that "a dignitary" of the Methodist Church "should have left the pulpit and the Bible to mount the political rostrum and plead the higher law of prohibitionism." Davis proclaimed that Galloway's activity violated the separation of church and state. Second, as in his Texas statements, Davis based his position on the conviction that legalized statewide prohibition would endanger individual liberty. He claimed that "to undertake, by coercive means, the reformation of drunkards" would be a hopeless and futile task. To a friend he said he wanted no "governmental supervision of domestic habits," and he perceived another and even greater danger. "Shirk it as they may, this Prohibition means to bring the Federal Government to the supervision of our private affairs." After the Davis-Galloway exchange, the furor died down.[28]

At Beauvoir, Davis's status as the revered leader of the southern cause still brought numerous honors and requests. College fraternities and literary societies wanted his name on their rolls. Old and young wrote for autographs, photographs, and his opinion on various questions such as states' rights. A riverboat captain wanted permission to name his steamboat "Jefferson Davis." A Pennsylvanian wanted to know where he could buy a copy of *Rise and Fall.* Correspondents joyously informed him about namesakes, and one little girl in Colorado wrote, "We have a large tree in our yard named after you."

Invitations to make personal appearances and give speeches poured in. They came from a wide range of organizations and institutions. Colleges and veterans' associations clamored for visits and talks. Agricultural societies and fairs requested his presence. Groups laying cornerstones for monuments or unveiling them wanted him to join their ceremonies. In 1888 the governor of Mississippi sent a special delegation to Beauvoir to invite Davis to Jackson for the laying of the cornerstone of the Confederate monument.

Most of these invitations Davis declined, usually claiming poor health, but he did accept a few. He made the short trip to New Orleans to participate in rituals honoring the Confederacy and its heroes. Occasionally he spoke briefly, concentrating on timeworn themes—the valor and heroism of a particular individual and the glory of Confederate patriotism. In 1884 he agreed to go to his state capital and make a few remarks to the legislature. Before a joint session he proudly identified himself as a Mississippian and underscored his devotion to his state. While not forgetting the "disappointed hopes and crushed aspirations of the past," he declared that the patriotism which enabled the Confederacy to sustain for so long its mighty struggle for independence still flourished, "not measured by lines of latitude and longitude." He pictured the South in "a transition state," with all resulting changes unforeseeable. Yet he enunciated his unwavering confidence in Mississippians and spoke of "bright hopes for the future."[29]

In the fall of 1886 sentimental feelings compelled a quick journey to his birthplace in Kentucky. A group of Davis partisans in December 1885 had purchased the land on which the house stood and sent him the deed. The homestead had been torn down, and a Baptist church was set to be built on the spot. As planned, Davis in turn deeded the land to the church. He was wanted at the dedication of the new brick edifice, in which a marble tablet would specify the location as the site of Davis's birth and also indicate that he had donated the land to the Bethel Baptist Church. At Fairview he heard speeches acclaiming him and witnessed the rite of dedication. He said a few words, declaring Kentucky home country, praising his father, and speaking of the love of God. His return to Beauvoir was uneventful.[30]

His most ambitious tour had occurred earlier, in the spring of that year. Agreeing initially to go to Montgomery for the laying of the cornerstone for a monument to the Confederate dead, Davis also acceded to the urging that he continue on to Atlanta for the unveiling of the statue of his wartime ally, Senator Benjamin H. Hill, and then travel on to Savannah for ceremonies at the statue of the Revolutionary War hero General Nathanael Greene. In late April the seventy-eight-year-old Davis, accompanied by daughter Winnie, left Beauvoir in the private railroad car provided for him. In all three cities his brief public statements covered familiar ground: the legitimacy of secession, the heroism and virtue of the Confederate cause, and his pleasure in celebrating its commemoration with fellow Confederates and southerners. On every podium, dignitaries including governors and United States senators lauded the honored guest. Winnie was also introduced with great excitement at each site.

The remarkable aspect of this journey was Davis's reception. Wherever the train stopped along the route to Montgomery, crowds gathered and showered him with flowers. At the three major stops people congregated in overwhelming numbers. Newspaper accounts said 15,000 stood in a drizzle to welcome Davis to the Alabama capital; more than three times that many thronged into Atlanta; and a multitude jammed the streets and open spaces in Savannah. Davis's actual appearance at the various ceremonies generated intense emotional outbursts. When he was introduced at the Capitol in Montgomery, on almost the exact spot where he had been inaugurated in 1861, the roar was "so long drawn out that it seemed for a time he was not going to get a chance to speak." Virginia Clay, who had become Virginia Clopton, attended and remembered: "I saw women, shrouded in black fall at Mr. D's feet, to be uplifted and comforted by kind words. Old men & young men shook with emotion beyond the power of words on taking Mr. Davis's hand, & I feared the ordeal wd. Prove the death of the man."

No letdown occurred in Georgia. In Atlanta, where the approach of Davis's carriage caused the removal of hats, the eruption of a mighty cheer "was caught up by the people that lined other streets and was carried on and on until at every point in the city it could be heard." A reporter exulted: "History does not contain an account of such a grand and wonderful outburst from human throats." In Savannah the crowd surged to the platform "eager to grasp the hand of the old statesman. So great was the rush that there was some danger of Mr. Davis being crushed."

Finally, this emotionally and physically demanding trip was over. At its outset in Montgomery, Virginia Clopton reported Davis admitted feeling somewhat shaky. Back at Beauvoir after more than two weeks on the road, he collapsed. Varina worried that he was in "imminent danger." For another two weeks high fever along with acute bronchitis kept him confined and left him quite weak. His daughter joined him on the sick list; she returned with the measles. But despite the toll on his health, Davis did not want to give up such wonderful, reassuring experiences. The plaudits told him that his beloved southerners shared his view of their common cause and his dedication to it and them.[31]

The following year, 1887, he was invited to attend a combined agricultural fair and veterans' reunion scheduled for October in Macon, Georgia. Late that summer the president of the Georgia State Agricultural Society traveled to Beauvoir to prevail upon Davis to come. He succeeded. This time Davis's wife and older daughter joined Winnie and him. The scene in Macon replicated what had transpired the previous year. Varina said "the enthusiasm baffled description." A journalist observed that the first glimpse of Davis brought forth "a mighty yell" from the assembled multitude. Veterans made "a wild charge" toward Davis, "every one of them yelling." On the porch of the large house where he was staying, Davis lifted his hat and bowed; next, he leaned forward on the balustrade and grasped every outstretched hand that he could. An old Confederate flag was then brought up. After the restoration of quiet, Davis spoke: "Friends and Brethren—I am like that flag, torn and battered by storms and years. I love it for its own sake; I love it for yours. I love it as a memento of what your fathers did and hoped that you would do. God bless you." At that point he clutched the flag to his chest, burying his face and tear-filled eyes in it. Winnie took it, kissed it, and handed it back to the flag-bearer. This occasion, too, felled Davis, even before he could leave Macon. According to Varina, heart problems caused great suffering and for some days placed him in great danger. At last his attending physician permitted the return to Beauvoir.[32]

Davis's journeys occurred during a period of renewed interest in the Confederacy and the war. In mid-decade the *Century Magazine* published its enormously popular series of articles by participants that led in 1887 and 1888 to the appearance of the four-volume *Battles and Leaders of the Civil War*. In the South, public bodies and private organizations engaged in a new spurt of monument building. Additionally, more Confederate army units held reunions than ever before, and veterans' groups were organized throughout the region. The foundation was being laid for the United Confederate Veterans, founded in 1889. In the midst of this celebration, Davis became for many southerners a tangible connection with a revered past.[33]

In the spring of 1889 Davis tentatively accepted an invitation to participate in the centennial celebration of North Carolina's ratification of the Constitution. Set for late November in Fayetteville, the commemoration was predicted by its organizers to be the largest gathering in the history of the state. Asking Davis to speak on the Constitution, they used language that would encourage his assent. This opportunity, their letter read, "gives you the chance in a word to forever silence the blatant curs of high and low degree who by assailment of you have hoped to degrade the cause by you represented." The governor of the state also wrote assuring Davis that "nowhere throughout this Southern land, will your welcome be warmer or the people be more gratified. . . ." Davis held out hope that he could make the journey. He even prepared a short manuscript summarizing his constitutional views and praising North Carolina for her loyalty to principle from the Revolution forward. As the time approached, Davis realized that his health simply would not permit him to go, but he did not finally admit it until October 30.[34]

At home, far from the tumultuous excitement, Jefferson and Varina Davis thought about their lives and reflected on their mortality. Varina wrote to one friend, "Memory has summoned the past before me." "It is evident even to us," she continued, "that the night is far spent and eternal day may break upon us at any moment." Davis himself mentioned "the sad memories of the past." Time "has told heavily on me," he related to a niece, and "there is much preparation for the world of which we knew so very little. . . ." Varina said that her husband "dwells in the past." "The Shadow of the Confederacy grows heavier over him as years weigh his heart down . . . ," she noted.[35]

While Davis was committed to his immutable principles and to the memory of the Confederacy, he also looked forward. He did not believe the South or individual southerners should remain entrapped in the past or enfeebled by memories. This conviction prompted him in both his family life and public statements. Though initially unhappy and reluctant to accept Winnie's marrying Alfred Wilkinson, he did not attempt to prohibit his daughter's marriage. He even blessed her engagement. That she did not marry a man she clearly loved arose from complex reasons, but opposition by her father was not among them.

In a different sphere, Davis also embraced the future. He told audiences that their patriotism now belonged to the United States. And he took pride in what he identified as material progress in his state, especially economic diversification and greater support for public education.

Although in his time those economic and social advances never reached a level to transform Mississippi, Davis wanted and welcomed what he saw as transformation-in-the-making. To one visiting northern reporter, he sounded like the most ardent New South booster. Asserting that developing the summer resorts on the Mississippi Gulf Coast into year-round playgrounds would "afford rare chances for capitalists to make money," he saw no reason why the towns along that coast could not eventually rival winter destinations in Florida. Jefferson Davis was certainly not a man trapped in a time warp.[36]

In the last public talk Davis ever gave, he merged his devotion to the past with his hope for the future. In 1888 he went to nearby Mississippi City to speak briefly before a gathering of young men. That his listeners were young was important to him. He told them he would not otherwise have come. Beginning with words about himself, he confessed that his personal ambition along with his political dogma lay "buried in the grave of the Confederacy." But then, calling to the "Men in whose hands the destinies of our Southland lie . . . ," he announced, "the past is dead." He continued, "let it bury its dead, its hopes and aspirations; before you lies the future—a future full of golden promise; a future of expanding national glory, before which all the world shall stand amazed." His closing: "Let me beseech you to lay aside all rancor, all bitter sectional feelings, and to make your places in the ranks of those who will bring about a consummation devoutly to be wished—a reunited country."[37]

Whether Davis pondered the past or estimated the future, he always had to deal with Brierfield. Toward the end of the first week in November 1889, he left Beauvoir for the annual fall journey to his plantation. From New Orleans on November 6 he took a steamboat for the trip upriver. Aboard ship he became ill, and the captain would not put him off at Davis Island, carrying him instead on to Vicksburg. On the return, Davis disembarked on the island and drove to Brierfield. From there on the twelfth he penned his final note to his wife, telling her he planned to come back downriver right away. The omission of words signaled his feebleness: "Lest you should hear alarming write say I have suffered much but by the help of the Lord." Before leaving Brierfield the next day, Davis set down in a memory book of his overseer's little daughter the last lines he ever wrote: "May all your paths be peaceful and pleasant, charged with the best fruit, the doing good to others."[38]

He was seriously ill. An employee had sent Varina a telegram dated November 11 stating that Davis was in bed and would not see a doctor.

Jefferson Davis, c. 1888 (photograph by Washburn).
Museum of the Confederacy

Immediately she started for New Orleans and on the thirteenth embarked on a steamboat headed toward Davis Island. In the meantime Davis had followed his intentions and gotten on a southbound vessel. The two boats met on the river, and Varina joined her husband. When their boat docked at Bayou Sara, Louisiana, Davis received medical attention for the first time. According to Varina, the diagnosis was acute bronchitis complicated by serious malarial symptoms.

On November 16, a wet, miserable day, they arrived back in New Orleans. Friends waited at wharfside, as did Davis's physician and friend Dr. S. E. Chaille, and Dr. T. C. Bickham, both eminent members of their profession in the city. Varina allowed no one else to see her husband. When the rain let up, he was transported by ambulance to the home of Judge Charles E. Fenner, brother-in-law of Jacob Payne, at First and Camp Streets. Dr. Chaille told the press he saw no cause for alarm. Davis was suffering from a bad cold which might get worse, but he was resting quietly.

During the next two weeks Davis's condition remained basically stable. He sat up in bed, and his temperature was almost normal. There was even talk of his going to Beauvoir. But he did not gain much strength, and the doctors did not like their patient to speak because they said it aggravated his throat. According to Varina, his doctors gave him cordials and quinine. In constant attendance, she permitted practically no visitors. Even Jacob Payne could enter the sickroom only when Davis asked for him. She wanted to know whether her husband wished their daughters to be notified. He said no; he did not want to worry them. Alarmed by newspaper accounts, however, Polly started east, but did not reach her father in time. Winnie was in Europe.

The beginning days of December brought mixed news. On December 1 Davis was reported slightly better but still had no appetite. His daily nourishment consisted of one half-pint of milk and beef tea or broth. For the first time, the reporter covering Davis's illness indicated that prospects for recovery were dim. But a change for the better occurred on Monday, the second, and on December 3 Judge Fenner declared his guest "decidedly improved." On Wednesday, the fourth, the reporter talked with Varina, who described her husband as "frail as a lily and requir[ing] the most exquisite care," which she surely gave.

The situation worsened suddenly and dramatically. Early on the fifth he still appeared to be improving. But just before 6 p.m. a "severe congestive chill" struck him. He spurned medicine that Varina offered him. At that point he lost consciousness, which he never really regained. His doctors were summoned. Word went out that the end was near. At his bedside were his wife, his two physicians, Jacob Payne, Judge Fenner with his wife and a son, and a grandniece of Davis's. Holding his hand, Varina said she could feel occasional pressure. Then there was none. At 12:45 a.m. on Friday, December 6, Jefferson Davis died quietly.[39]

"Esto Perpetua"

During his long lifetime Jefferson Davis witnessed many changes in his country, but he held to certain verities. He saw himself as a faithful American, even though he tried to destroy the Union that to him had become subverted. He always identified himself as a constitutional patriot and true son of the American Revolution and the Founding Fathers. Professing the United States a nation created by the sovereign states that upheld it, he looked to Thomas Jefferson, James Madison, and John C. Calhoun as the great explicators of states' rights and strict construction, of the proper understanding of the nation and the Constitution. In his mind a continuum stretching over the decades connected these constitutional statesmen with their disciples of his time.

Davis cherished a vibrant United States. He shared in the sense of inevitable growth and progress that dominated the national outlook. This powerful surge pulsing through the country had two interrelated dimensions: geographic and economic. The Mexican Cession and the industrial and agricultural booms of the 1850s exemplified this combination in its inexorable march toward greater wealth and power for the country. And as a national politician Davis was willing to use the authority of the government in its own defense. As Confederate president he absolutely did so.

Certain about America, Davis also had confidence in himself and in his ability to overcome any obstacle. Moreover, his own ambition matched the ambition he had for his country. From young manhood he struggled with a wide range of serious physical maladies, but he never let their assaults on his body deter him from his course. He also knew deep sadness in his personal life, yet he never permitted that heavy veil to smother him with self-pity. His achievements underscored his convictions about himself. He wanted to succeed, and he did. He became a successful planter, a genuine war hero, and a notable politician whose career carried him into the highest councils of his country. Men spoke seriously about his becoming president.

As Davis witnessed the physical and economic development of his country, he envisioned no conflict between this progress and racial slavery. Growing up in a slave society, he accepted servitude as normal, as moral, and as American. In his public life he defended slavery on those grounds and maintained that the institution helped civilize and Christianize an inferior race. While not all Americans joined his embrace of slavery, few dissented from his belief in the superiority of the white race, an outlook shared by almost all white Americans as well as Western Europeans. On a practical level Davis conceived of slavery as adaptable and flexible. Slave labor could flourish, he believed, in many venues, such as factories and mines, not just in cotton fields. As an owner of slaves he wanted protection of slavery in his own self-interest. As a politician representing tens of thousands of other slave-owners and tens of thousands of aspiring slaveowners, he deemed guarding slavery his duty.

When geographic expansion led to conflict over slavery in the territories, he insisted on the rights of slaveowners as Americans to participate equally in the national bounty. He also feared where the energy of antislavery might lead, for he defined it chiefly as a political force—the North striving to wrest power from the South. As a result, he fought bitterly in 1849 and 1850 against the admission of California as a state because it would end the numerical equality between the free and slave states, which he believed fundamental to the Constitution and essential to secure southern rights.

But the inequality that came with California's admission did not damage his section or its interests, including slavery. His service in Franklin Pierce's administration convinced him that a substantial segment of northern opinion was prepared to honor what he considered the constitutional rights of the South. That sanguine outlook was buttressed by his satisfying, even triumphant, sojourn in Maine in 1858.

Davis rejected any notion of a contradiction between slavery and America. So many of the great national heroes who had won and preserved the independence of the nation and led its battalions against foreign foes were slaveholders—men such as George Washington, Thomas Jefferson, James Madison, Andrew Jackson, and Zachary Taylor. Furthermore, his view that the Constitution protected slavery was not at all unique. Most white Americans, northerners included, shared that interpretation, and the U.S. Supreme Court emphatically sustained it. Davis dismissed as un-American the proposition propounded in the 1850s by the Republican party that the United States could not persist, in Abraham Lincoln's words, "permanently half *slave* and half *free*." A solid majority of Davis's fellow citizens concurred with his contention that slavery and freedom could continue to coexist, as they had since the birth of the nation. In the 1860 presidential election 60 percent of the voters cast their ballots for candidates who found no fundamental problem with slavery in America. The Republican Lincoln captured only 40 percent of the popular vote, though, of course, he had an indisputable majority in the Electoral College.[1]

Lincoln's election brought on the crisis of the Union, a Union Davis did not want to break up. Although he had always preached the constitutionality of secession, he never advocated its implementation. Even in 1860 he remained convinced that significant northern support for southern rights still existed. He also had no doubts about the guarantees the Constitution gave to southern rights and slavery. But powerful political currents, to which he had contributed, gripped all southern Democrats, including Jefferson Davis. Moreover, the Republicans were caught up in their own whirlwind. Compromise proved impossible. For Davis there was no question about his course. Secession was constitutional, and his loyalty to Mississippi underlay his allegiance to the United States. He departed the Union with his state.

For Davis the Confederate States provided a way to save the America he had cherished. For him the Confederacy became the true descendant of the American Revolution and the Constitution. Preserving that sacred heritage made the Confederacy a holy cause. It must triumph, and Davis would adopt whatever measures he thought necessary to achieve victory. He contended that the Confederacy alone defended liberty. That guarding this precious liberty also involved sanctioning slavery posed him no problem. To Davis as to most white southerners, their liberty had since the American Revolution always included their right to own slaves and their right to decide about the institution without outside interference. White liberty and black slavery were inextricably intertwined.

Davis committed himself utterly to the Confederacy and directed a titanic war on its behalf. His commitment to his cause was as total as that of his great antagonist on the other side. Neither he nor Lincoln would relent. In order to save the Confederacy, Davis even led his fellow

Confederates toward an abandonment of slavery. Despite a mighty effort, the Confederacy was overwhelmed. Davis lost the war, but he clung to his cause.

Defeated, he could no longer wield a sword. Still, he interpreted Reconstruction as an extension of the Republican oppression the Confederacy had so stalwartly resisted. Even so, he said his faith in the American people reassured him that they would eventually end Reconstruction. His expectations were fulfilled, for by the mid-1870s most white northerners were rapidly withdrawing their backing for federal support of Republican regimes in the old Confederacy. The collapse of Reconstruction meant in part that northern whites came to the position southern whites had never relinquished: blacks were inferior to whites, and their fortunes should be controlled by the superior race. Because over 90 percent of black Americans still lived in the former slave states, those in control would be southern whites.

After 1865 Davis never wavered on the constitutionality of secession. Because in his mind he had acted properly under the Constitution, he had done nothing wrong in 1861. Accordingly, he never requested a pardon. But for him, secession and the Confederacy had now become part of history. Secession had failed in its attempt to create a new nation, and he did not believe it would ever be attempted again. He declared he surely would not advocate it.

Despite the dislocation and disconsolation of the postwar years, Davis in the last decade of his life became more positive about the future. He talked proudly about the grandeur of the United States, its growing wealth and power. He saw the future of his beloved South in its young people. He urged them to hold dear their Confederate heritage, but not let the past entrap them. As for himself, Davis looked back with pride on the past and on his part in what had been. At the same time, he looked ahead with the anticipation of his youth. He hoped "that crimination and recrimination should forever cease, and then, on the basis of fraternity and faithful regard for the rights of the States, there may be written on the arch of the Union, *Esto perpetua.*"[2]

Note on Sources

This book is based chiefly on the manuscript record of Jefferson Davis, his family members, and associates. Because of Davis's importance and long life, materials relating to him are voluminous and are located in numerous depositories. The Jefferson Davis Papers at Rice University has brought together almost all known Davis documents, literally tens of thousands of them. The generosity of editor Lynda L. Crist and her associates permitted me to make unrestricted use of their collection. As a result, for letters to and from Davis, for his endorsements, and also for letters of intimate family members, I mainly used photocopies from the Davis Papers. Still, I cited the location of the original document. Likewise, apart from the Davis Papers, I did not differentiate in my citations from manuscripts in archives I visited and manuscripts utilized in the form of photocopies. In addition, the work of many other scholars has been essential for me, and throughout the Notes I have tried to register my obligations to them.

I do want to mention the prominent Davis collections. The National Archives has substantial material, in several record groups, chiefly dealing with Davis's service in the United States Army, his term as secretary of war, and his presidency of the Confederate States. The Louisiana Historical Association Collection of Jefferson Davis Papers at Tulane University is composed mostly of wartime documents including presidential letterbooks, many of which have been printed in *JDC*, *O.R.*, and *PJD*, and also contains the bulk of his surviving library. Three major collections contain chiefly family letters: the Jefferson Davis Papers at both the University of Alabama and Transylvania University, and the Jefferson Davis and Family Papers at the Mississippi Department of Archives and History. Duke University possesses an important, wide-ranging collection. The significant holdings of the Museum of the Confederacy concentrate overwhelmingly on the postwar years. The sizable documentary record compiled for *Bowmar*, at the Mississippi Department of Archives and History, provides indispensable information, especially on antebellum Brierfield and on Davis family relations.

The major published materials relating to Davis merit notice. *PJD*, which in ten volumes has reached September 1864 (though the tenth became available too late for me to utilize thoroughly), constitutes an impressive achievement. Splendidly edited and superbly annotated, these volumes are absolutely indispensable for anyone working on Davis, even though from the third volume the editors have had to be increasingly selective in what they print. When my own work went beyond volume nine, I felt like a lonely traveler. In addition, *JDC* retains great value. Dunbar Rowland was a scrupulous editor, and he included many items not in *PJD*, especially speeches. Moreover, *JDC* covers the postwar period in some detail. Any serious investigator must use both sets; I have cited them regularly. For the Confederacy, *O.R.* and *M&P*, the latter containing Davis's official messages to Congress and his proclamations, remain immensely useful. *Jefferson Davis: Private Letters, 1823–1889* (New York, 1966), edited by Hudson Strode, must be used with extreme care. Strode, who published a three-volume biography of Davis between 1955 and 1964, was a lax editor, who apparently had little respect for the integrity of a document. For example, he repeatedly omitted substantive portions of letters without using ellipses, or in any other way indicating that he had done so. I have cited *Private Letters* quite sparingly, only when I could find no other source for a particular letter.

Both Jefferson and Varina Davis wrote memoirs. *R&F* is really an apologia for Davis's interpretation of the Constitution and the Confederacy, not a memoir as customarily understood. He did begin a more traditional memoir late in life, but only fragments survive, which focus on his early years. *PJD*, in the first volume, prints them. Varina's *Memoir* is invaluable, and I have used it extensively, despite its intense partisanship and its occasional confusion about dates and events. It contains much vital information, a good deal of it unavailable elsewhere.

Abbreviations Used in the Notes

AHR	*American Historical Review*
Bowmar	*Jefferson Davis v. J. H. D. Bowmar et al.*, Warren County Chancery Court, July 3, 1874–January 8, 1876, unreported, MDAH
CG	*Congressional Globe*
Chesnut	C. Vann Woodward, ed., *Mary Chesnut's Civil War* (New Haven, Conn., 1981)
CV	*Confederate Veteran*
CWH	*Civil War History*
DAB	Allen Johnson and Dumar Malone, eds., *Dictionary of American Biography* (20 vols.; New York, 1928–36)
DU	Duke University, Durham, N.C., Rare Books, Manuscript & Special Collections Library
EU	Emory University, Atlanta, Robert W. Woodruff Library, Special Collections Department
FC	Filson Club Historical Society, Louisville, Ky.
HL	Henry E. Huntington Library, San Marino, Calif.
HSP	Historical Society of Pennsylvania, Philadelphia
HU	Harvard University, Cambridge, Mass., Houghton Library

IA	Iowa Department of Archives and History, Des Moines
JAH	*Journal of American History*
JD	Jefferson Davis
JDC	Dunbar Rowland, ed., *Jefferson Davis, Constitutionalist: His Letters, Papers and Speeches* (10 vols.; Jackson, Miss., 1923)
JMH	*Journal of Mississippi History*
JSH	*Journal of Southern History*
LC	Library of Congress, Washington, D.C., Division of Manuscripts
LSU	Louisiana State University, Baton Rouge, Louisiana State University Libraries, Louisiana and Lower Mississippi Valley Collections
MaHS	Massachusetts Historical Society, Boston
MC	Museum of the Confederacy, Richmond, Va.
MDAH	Mississippi Department of Archives and History, Jackson
Memoir	Varina Howell Davis, *Jefferson Davis, Ex-President of the Confederate States of America: A Memoir by His Wife* (2 vols.; New York, 1890)
MHS	Maryland Historical Society, Baltimore
MI	University of Michigan, Ann Arbor, William L. Clements Library
M&P	James D. Richardson, comp., *A Compilation of the Messages and Papers of the Confederacy* . . . (2 vols.; Nashville, Tenn., 1906)
MU	Miami University, Miami, Ohio, Walter Havighurst Special Collections
MVHR	*Mississippi Valley Historical Review*
NA	National Archives, Washington, D.C.
m437	Letters Received by the Confederate Secretary of War
m474	Letters Received by the Confederate Adjutant and Inspector General
NYPL	New York Public Library, New York City
O.R.	*War of the Rebellion: A Compilation of the Official Records of the Union and Confederate Armies* (70 vols. in 128; Washington, D.C., 1880–1901)
PAJ	Paul H. Bergeron *et al.*, eds., *The Papers of Andrew Johnson* (15 vols.; Knoxville, Tenn., 1967–)
PJD	Lynda L. Crist *et al.*, eds., *The Papers of Jefferson Davis* (10 vols.; Baton Rouge, La., 1971–)
PMHS	*Publications of the Mississippi Historical Society*
PU	Princeton University, Princeton, N.J., Firestone Library, Department of Rare Books and Special Collections
R & F	Jefferson Davis, *The Rise and Fall of the Confederate Government* (2 vols.; New York, 1881)
RU	William Marsh Rice University, Houston
SCA	South Carolina Department of Archives and History, Columbia

SCHS	South Carolina Historical Society, Charleston
SCL	University of South Carolina, Columbia, South Caroliniana Library
SHQ	*Southwestern Historical Quarterly*
SHSP	*Southern Historical Society Papers*
TQH	*Tyler's Quarterly Historical and Genealogical Magazine*
TR	Transylvania University, Lexington, Ky.
TSLA	Tennessee State Library and Archives, Nashville
TU	Tulane University, New Orleans, Howard-Tilton Memorial Library, Special Collections
UA	University of Alabama, Tuscaloosa, W. S. Hoole Special Collections Library
UGA	University of Georgia, Athens, Hargrett Rare Book and Manuscript Library
UM	University of Memphis, Memphis, Tenn., Special Collections Department
UNC	University of North Carolina, Chapel Hill, Wilson Library, Southern Historical Collection
UT	University of Texas, Austin, Center for American History
UVA	University of Virginia, Charlottesville, Alderman Library, Special Collections Department
VD	Varina Howell Davis
VHS	Virginia Historical Society, Richmond
W&L	Washington and Lee University, Lexington, Va., Cyrus Hall McCormick Library
WM	College of William and Mary, Williamsburg, Virginia, Earl Gregg Swem Library
WPL	Clifford Dowdey and Louis H. Manarin, eds., *The Wartime Papers of R. E. Lee* (Boston and Toronto, 1961)
WRHS	Western Reserve Historical Society, Cleveland, Ohio

PREFACE

1. JD to W. L. Saunders, May 9, 1882, United Daughters of the Confederacy Texas Museum; Potter, "Jefferson Davis and the Political Factors in Confederate Defeat," in David Donald, ed., *Why the North Won the Civil War* (Baton Rouge, La., 1960), 91–114. For more general comments about JD and historians, see my "Jefferson Davis and the Sudden Disappearance of Southern Politics," in Charles W. Eagles, ed., *Is There a Southern Political Tradition?* (Jackson, Miss., 1996), 27–29, 212–13; Mark E. Neely, Jr., "Abraham Lincoln vs. Jefferson Davis: Comparing Presidential Leadership in the Civil War," in James M. McPherson and William J. Cooper, Jr., eds., *Writing the Civil War: The Quest to Understand* (Columbia, S.C., 1998), 96–111, 278–83; and Herman M. Hattaway, "Jefferson Davis and the Histori-

ans," in Roman J. Heleniak and Lawrence L. Hewitt, eds., *Confederate High Command and Related Topics* (Shippensburg, Pa., 1990), 142–71.

2. William J. Cooper, Jr., *Liberty and Slavery: Southern Politics to 1860* (New York, 1983).

PROLOGUE: *"The Saddest Day of My Life"*

1. Caroline P. Myers Manuscript Memoir, Phillips-Myers Papers, UNC; "Register of Meteorological Observations, District of Columbia, Under the Director of the Smithsonian Institution . . . (January 1861)," National Climatic Data Center, Asheville, N.C.

2. *New York Herald*, January 6, 1859.

3. *New York Times*, March 1, 1860; *Harper's Weekly*, February, 2, 1861.

4. JD to Anna Ella Carroll, March 1, 1861, *PJD*, VII, 64; *Memoir*, I, 696.

5. "When the States Seceded, from the Diary of Mrs. Eugene McLean," in *Harper's Monthly Magazine*, CXXVIII (January 1914), 284.

6. JD to Pierce, January 20, 1861, *JDC*, V, 37–38; JD to Anna Ella Carroll, March 1, 1861, *PJD*, VII, 65.

7. Elizabeth Blair Lee to Phillip, January 21, 1861, Virginia Jean Laas, ed., *Wartime Washington: The Civil War Letters of Elizabeth Blair Lee* (Urbana and Chicago, 1991), 27; William Howard Russell, *My Diary North and South* (Boston, 1863), 173–74; Joan Nunn, *Fashion in Costume, 1200–1980* (New York, 1980), 143.

8. Elizabeth Blair Lee to Phillip, January 21, 1861, Laas, ed., *Wartime Washington*, 27; *New York Herald*, January 22, 1861; *Memoir*, I, 696; JD to Anna Ella Carroll, March 1, 1861, *PJD*, VII, 65; *CG*, 36:2, 487.

9. *New York Herald*, January 22, 1861; *Memoir*, I, 698; Myrta Lockett Avary, *Dixie After the War: An Exposition of Social Conditions Existing in the South . . .* (New York, 1906), 414–15.

10. JD to Anna Ella Carroll, March 1, 1861, *PJD*, VII, 65; William M. Gwin to J. F. H. Claiborne, November 14, 1878, J. F. H. Claiborne Papers, UNC; Myers Memoir, Phillips-Myers Papers, *ibid*. Most of Davis's surviving library is in the Louisiana Historical Association Collection of JD Papers, TU (hereafter all citations to the JD Papers, TU, are from this collection unless otherwise noted).

CHAPTER ONE: *"There My Memories Begin"*

1. Uncertainty has long plagued the year of Davis's birth. For a time he believed 1807 the correct year, but then he changed to 1808. At one point he seemed cavalier about it, but later he stipulated that his mother told him 1808 was correct. I assume that she knew. JD to W. H. Sparke, February 19, 1858, *PJD*, I, lxvn., and to Crafts J. Wright, June 3, 1878, JD Papers, TR.

Some have also questioned whether Davis ever had a middle name. He used the initial at West Point, as did his mother in her will. Again, I assume that both would not have invented it. *PJD*, I, 16, 458–59; Walter L. Fleming, "The Early Life of Jefferson Davis," *Proceedings of the Mississippi Valley Historical Association*, IX, part 1 (1915–16), 157. No evidence supports Hudson Strode's claim that the actual middle name was Finis, signaling the final child. *Jefferson Davis* (3 vols.; New York, 1955–64), I, 3.

2. Many gaps remain in the Davis genealogy. For the most thorough genealogical investigation, see *PJD*, I, 488–529, IV, 402–16. My discussion in the following paragraphs is based on that material.

3. *Ibid.*, I, lxvii–lxviii, 512–13. JD to Jerome S. Ridley, February 3, 1875, *JMH*, V (July 1943), 155–56; Fleming, "Early Life," 153–56; and Janet Sharp Hermann, *Joseph E. Davis: Pioneer Patriarch* (Jackson, Miss., 1990), 3–11, all have pertinent information on Samuel Emory Davis.

4. *New Orleans Daily Picayune*, March 14, 1909; Fleming, "Early Life," 156; Hermann, *Davis*, 11.

5. Fleming, "Early Life," 157–58; Hermann, *Davis*, 16–17; Samuel Emory Davis Subject File, MDAH.

6. S. E. Davis Subject File, MDAH.

7. The house still stands, though it is now known as Rosemont. After Jane Davis's death in 1845, the family changed the name to honor her and her beloved roses. She is buried in the family cemetery on the property. Rosemont Subject File, MDAH; "Rosemont Plantation: The Childhood Home of Jefferson Davis," *Southern Accents*, X, No. 2 (March–April 1987), 137–42.

8. *PJD*, I, lxviii; JD to Jno. A. Williams, April 2, 1889, JD Collection, UVA.

9. *PJD*, I, lxviii, lxxiii; Fleming, "Early Life," 155.

10. *PJD*, I, lxxiv–lxxv; Fleming, "Early Life," 162.

11. *PJD*, I, lxxii; Fleming, "Early Life," 163.

12. *PJD*, I, lxix–lxxi.

13. *Ibid.*, 3.

14. On St. Thomas College, see Rt. Rev. John Baptist David to ?, October 26, 1818 (typescript), Diocese of Bardstown Papers, FC; V. F. O'Daniel, *A Light of the Church in Kentucky: Or the Life, Labors, and Character of the Very Rev. Samuel Thomas Wilson . . .* (Washington, D.C., 1932), 179–99 *passim;* Felix N. Pitt, "Two Early Catholic Colleges in Kentucky," *Filson Club History Quarterly*, XXXVIII (April 1964), 133–38.

15. *PJD*, I, lxxii.

16. *Ibid.;* JD to Philip Phillips, September 26, 1874, Philip Phillips Papers, LC.

17. *PJD*, I, lxxii.

18. *Ibid.*, lxxii–lxxiii.

19. Joseph Strutt, *The Sports and Pastimes of the People of England*, ed. J. Charles Cox ([1801]; London, 1903), 200 (first quotation); Ricky Jay, *Learned Pigs and Fireproof Women* (New York, 1986), 9–27 (second quotation on 15; I am grateful to Charles Royster for these references).

20. W. P. Johnston to Rosa, August 5, 1862, Mrs. Mason Barrett Collection of the Papers of Albert Sidney and William Preston Johnston, Manuscripts Collection 1, TU (hereafter all citations to the Johnston Papers, TU, are from this collection).

21. *PJD*, I, lxxii–lxxiii.

22. *Ibid.*, lxxiii.

23. *Ibid.*, lxxv; D. Clayton James, *Antebellum Natchez* (Baton Rouge, La., 1968), 223–24.

24. *PJD*, I, lxxv.

25. *Ibid.*

26. *Ibid.*, lxxiii–iv.

27. Hermann, *Davis*, 32–37; *Bowmar*, 203; S. E. Davis Subject File, MDAH; JD to Lise, February 7, 1884, October 24, 1870, Lise Mitchell Papers, TU.

CHAPTER TWO: *"Put Away the Grog"*

1. Robert V. Remini, *Henry Clay: Statesman for the Union* (New York, 1991), 17 (first quotation); Charles Caldwell, *A Discourse on the Genius and Character of the Rev. Horace Holley, LL.D., Late President of Transylvania University* (Boston, 1828), 151 (second quotation); Margaret Newman Wagers, *The Education of a Gentleman: Jefferson Davis at Transylvania, 1821–1824* (Lexington, Ky., 1943), 26–27.

2. Caldwell, *Discourse*, 70 (quotation). My general discussion of Transylvania is based on Earl Gregg Swem, ed., *Letters on the Condition of Kentucky*, in Heartman's *Historical Series Number 22* (New York, 1916; I am indebted to Charles Royster for this reference), 41–46; Wagers, *Education;* Walter Wilson Jennings, *Transylvania: Pioneer University of the West* (New York, 1955), chaps. 6–7; John D. Wright, Jr., *Transylvania: Tutor to the West* (Lexington, Ky., 1975), chaps. 5–6.

3. Wright, *Transylvania*, 58.

4. Wagers, *Education*, 5–6, 27 (quotation).

5. *PJD*, I, lxxvi. A first reading of Davis's "Memoir" seems to imply that he began in 1821, but a closer reading, along with other information, makes clear that he matriculated in the spring of 1823.

6. Wagers, *Education*, 37.

7. *Ibid.*, 17–18; *PJD*, I, lxxvi.

8. Wagers, *Education*, 32–34; *PJD*, I, 10n.

9. *PJD*, I, lxxvii–lxxviii; Wagers, *Education*, 31.

10. John Carl Parish, *George Wallace Jones* (Iowa City, 1912), 83; Wagers, *Education*, 38.

11. Wagers, *Education*, 7, 13; JD to William L. Marcy, February 10, 1851, *PJD*, IV, 159; *Memoir*, I, 29–31.

12. JD to Susannah Davis, August 2, 1824, *PJD*, I, 11; JD to [Amanda Bradford], August 2, 1824 (copy), William L. Richter, Manhattan, Kans. (1979).

13. Samuel Davis to JD, June 25, 1823, *PJD*, I, 5.

14. William Stamps to JD, ca. November 10, 1874, *PJD*, I, 12n. In 1940 Samuel Davis's remains were removed and reinterred at Beauvoir, near Biloxi, Mississippi.

15. Samuel Davis to JD, June 25, 1823, *ibid.*, 5.

16. *Ibid.*, 10, 11n.

17. JD to [Amanda Bradford], August 2, 1824 (copy), William Richter. Davis misremembered when he later stated that he had an agreement with Joseph that he could transfer to the University of Virginia after only a year at West Point. The University of Virginia did not receive students until 1826. *PJD*, I, lxxix.

18. Walter Lynwood Fleming, "Jefferson Davis at West Point," *Louisiana State University Bulletin*, I, n.s. (March 1910), 249 (quotation). My general discussion of West Point is based on Stephen E. Ambrose, *Duty, Honor, Country: A History of West Point* (Baltimore, 1966), esp. chaps. 4–5; Albert E. Church, *Personal Reminiscences of the Military Academy from 1824 to 1831* (West Point, N.Y., 1879); James L. Morrison, Jr., *"The Best School in the World": West Point in the Pre–Civil War Years, 1833–1866*

(Kent, Ohio, 1986); George S. Pappas, *To the Point: The United States Military Academy, 1802–1902* (Westport, Conn., 1993), esp. chaps. 6–10.

19. JD to Calhoun, July 7, 1824, *PJD*, I, 10; *ibid.*, lxxviii.

20. *Ibid.*, lxxviii–lxxix.

21. *Ibid.*, 28, 50, 88, 103; Morrison, *"Best School,"* appendix 2.

22. *PJD*, I, 27, 102.

23. *Ibid.*, 97–100; JD to Joseph Davis, January 12, 1825, *ibid.*, 17; Emory M. Thomas, *Robert E. Lee: A Biography* (New York, 1995), 49.

24. *PJD*, I, 39–40.

25. On Benny Havens and his tavern, see Ambrose, *Duty, Honor, Country,* 163–64 (quotations 163), and Pappas, *To the Point,* 160–61.

26. *PJD*, I, 36–41, has the court-martial proceedings.

27. On turning away and facing the wall, see Pappas, *To the Point,* 160.

28. *Memoir*, I, 52; *PJD*, I, 531; JD to Varina Davis, October 11, 1865, *ibid.*, 53n.

29. Pappas, *To the Point,* 169–73, has a full account. The riot also provided the subject for a novel, James B. Agnew, *Eggnog Riot: The Christmas Mutiny at West Point* (San Rafael, Calif., 1979). For the official proceedings, see *PJD*, I, 55–56, 60–61, 64–66, 68–69, 71, 74–75.

30. There is more than one version of Davis's exact words; I have used the one most often quoted. *PJD*, I, 61, 67, 73, 75.

31. *Ibid.*, 64, 68, 71, 75; JD to "My Dear Mollie" [Mary Stamps], May 30, 1883 (copy), Mrs. I. D. Stamps Farrar, New Orleans (1968).

32. *PJD*, I, 82.

33. *Ibid.*, 50, 53, 93–94.

34. *Ibid.*, lxxx–lxxxii; JD to "Dearest Mollie" [Mary Stamps], June 9, 1883, Mary Stamps Papers, UNC; JD to "My dear Austin" [I. J. Austin], September 3, 1882, E. Gerry Collection, MaHS; P. L. Rainwater, ed., "The Autobiography of Benjamin Grubb Humphreys, August 26, 1808–December 20, 1882," *MVHR*, XXI (1934), 237.

35. JD to Joseph Davis, January 12, 1825, *PJD*, I, 18; *Bowmar*, 209; JD to Charles J. McDonald, April 13, 1854, *JDC*, II, 350–51. Throughout this book, all italics/emphases appearing in quoted matter are in the original.

36. *PJD*, I, 30; *Memoir*, I, 51.

37. *PJD*, I, 104.

38. *Memoir*, I, 53–54; Pappas, *To the Point,* 161, has the Thayer quotation.

39. JD to Charles J. McDonald, April 13, 1854, *JDC*, II, 351.

40. *PJD*, I, 105.

CHAPTER THREE: *"Ever Ready to Render My Best Services"*

1. *PJD*, I, 106, 108.

2. JD to Susannah Davis, August 2, 1824, to Joseph Davis, January 12, 1825, to Winfield Scott, August 26, 1828, *ibid.*, 11, 17–18, 106.

3. *Ibid.*, 108.

4. Robert McElroy, *Jefferson Davis: The Unreal and the Real* (2 vols.; New York, 1937), I, 20–21.

5. On the army Davis joined, see Edward M. Coffman, *The Old Army: A Portrait of the American Army in Peacetime, 1784–1898* (New York, 1986), esp. chaps. 2–4.

The quotation comes from Henry Dodge to George Jones, April 18, 1834, *PJD*, I, 316–17.

6. *PJD*, I, 116. For a discussion of the army and army posts in the Northwest, see Francis Paul Prucha, *Broadax and Bayonet: The Role of the United States Army in the Development of the Northwest, 1815–1860* (Madison, Wis., 1953).

7. *PJD*, I, 118; JD to Lucinda Stamps, June 3, 1829, Lynda Lasswell [Crist], "Jefferson Davis Ponders His Future, 1829," *JSH*, XLI (1975), 520.

8. JD to A. J. Turner, May 5, 1880, A. J. Turner, *The Family Tree of Columbia County* (Portage, Wis., 1904), 94n.; JD to George Jones, January 5, 1872, *Milwaukee Sentinel*, February 3, 1891.

9. Mrs. John H. Kinzie, *Wau-bun: The Early Days in the Northwest* ([1856]; Chicago, 1901), 69.

10. *PJD*, I, 206; JD to George Jones, January 5, 1872, *Milwaukee Sentinel*, February 3, 1891; M. M. Quaife, "The Northwestern Career of Jefferson Davis," *Journal of the Illinois State Historical Society*, XVI (1923), 13–14.

11. *PJD*, I, 121, 125, 126, 133, 134, 287.

12. *Ibid.*, 150, 152, 163, 197–98, 211.

13. JD to James Butler, February 22, 1885, "File 1885," Wisconsin State Historical Society; W. P. Johnston to Rosa, August 28, 1862, Johnston Papers, TU; John Wentworth, *Early Chicago, Fort Dearborn, an Address Delivered at the Unveiling of the Memorial Tablet to Mark the Site of the Block-House* . . . (Chicago, 1881), 28.

14. JD to Lucinda Stamps, June 3, 1829, [Crist], "Davis Ponders," 519; JD to Thomas Jesup, February 3, 1831, *PJD*, I, 174–76.

15. JD to Colonel Willoughby Morgan, October 31, 1831, *PJD*, I, 217–18; *ibid.*, 215, 218n.; *Memoir*, I, 84–89, 150–52.

16. *Memoir*, I, 86–87.

17. JD to Lucinda Stamps, June 3, 1829, [Crist], "Davis Ponders," 519–22.

18. Florida McCaleb to JD, June 30, 1833, *PJD*, I, 271–72.

19. Florida McCaleb to JD, June 30, 1833; Lucinda Stamps to JD, July 7, 1833; Eliza Davis to JD, November 20, 1833 (quotation), and November 17, 1834; David Bradford to JD, June 18, 1834, *ibid.*, 270–72, 273–74, 303–04, 325, 341–43.

20. *Ibid.*, 233–34, 245, 249, 389–90, 396; Ellen D. Anderson to Walter Lynwood Fleming, January 13, 1908, Walter Lynwood Fleming Papers, NYPL.

21. Joseph Davis to JD, July 9, 1832, *PJD*, I, 246.

22. *Ibid.*

23. For examples of payments, see *ibid.*, 108 and n., 121, 195; *Bowmar*, 209; Coffman, *Old Army*, 50.

24. Samuel Davis to JD, June 25, 1823, *PJD*, I, 4–5, 6n.; Eliza Davis to JD, November 20, 1833, and David Bradford to JD, June 18, 1834, *ibid.*, 304, 306n., 326.

25. *Memoir*, I, 81.

26. *Ibid.*, 54, 73–74, 96; *PJD*, I, 200n.; John Carl Parish, *George Wallace Jones* (Iowa City, 1912), 294–95; Nellie Gordon to JD, September 1, 1864, JD Papers, MC.

27. Parish, *Jones*, 88–89, 294–95; JD to George Jones, December 27, 1882, *DuBuque Daily Herald*, January 14, 1883.

28. *Memoir*, I, 64; *PJD*, I, 200n.

29. *Memoir*, I, 63–64, 74.

30. *Ibid.*, 101; Memorandum by W. P. Johnston dated October 29, 1863, Johnston Papers, TU.

31. W. P. Johnston to Rosa, June 10, 1862, Johnston Papers, TU.

32. *Memoir*, I, 77; *PJD*, I, 366, 285n.; Lucius Northrop to JD, April 7, 1879, and JD to Lucius Northrop, April 25, 1879, *JDC*, VIII, 379–80, 383.

33. JD to Lucinda Stamps, June 3, 1829, [Crist], "Davis Ponders," 521–22.

34. *Memoir*, I, 63.

35. Mary Louise Dement Rugg, *Dement Dodge Patterson Williams* (n.p., 1964), 20–21; JD to Mrs. John Dement (formerly Mary Dodge), February 4, 1883, *JDC*, IX, 203.

36. *Memoir*, I, 73; JD to George Jones, December 27, 1882, *DuBuque Daily Herald*, January 14, 1883.

37. N. Matson, *Reminiscences of Bureau County in Two Parts* (Princeton, Ill., 1872), 111–14.

38. *Memoir*, I, 75–76.

39. For a solid account of the Black Hawk War, see Francis Paul Prucha, *The Sword of the Republic: The United States Army on the Frontier, 1783–1846* (Bloomington, Ind., 1969), chap. 11.

40. Charles Aldrich, "Jefferson Davis and Black Hawk," *Midland Monthly*, V (1896), 406–11; McElroy, *Davis*, I, 25–29; Hudson Strode, *Jefferson Davis* (3 vols.; New York, 1955–64), I, 71–77. One event that surely never occurred was the alleged meeting between Davis and Abraham Lincoln, who did serve in the Illinois militia. Neither man ever mentioned such an occurrence, and Davis specifically refused to substantiate it. *Memoir*, I, 131–33.

41. *PJD*, I, 240–42n., is thorough on the chronology.

42. *Ibid.*, 252–54n.

43. Memorandum by W. P. Johnston dated October 29, 1863, Johnston Papers, TU; *Black Hawk: An Autobiography*, ed. Donald Jackson (Urbana, Ill., 1955), 163.

44. John Francis McDermott, ed., *The Western Journal of Washington Irving* (Norman, Okla., 1944), 83–84; Memorandum by W. P. Johnston dated October 29, 1863 (quotations), Johnston Papers, TU.

45. *PJD*, I, 264–70, 285. On the Dragoons, see Prucha, *Sword of the Republic*, 244–46.

46. JD to Lewis Cass, July 24, 1833, *PJD*, I, 283–84; Henry Dodge to Roger Jones, September 13, 1833, *ibid.*, 289–90; *ibid.*, 314; *Army and Navy Chronicle*, II (March 24, 1836), 182–83; *American State Papers; Military Affairs*, VI, 247–48.

47. JD to George Jones, n.d., 1878, *Memoir*, I, 149; *PJD*, I, 289, 292–96.

48. *PJD*, I, 308n.

49. P. St. G. Cooke, *Scenes and Adventures in the Army: or Romance of Military Life* (Philadelphia, 1857), 219–20; [James Hildreth], *Dragoon Campaigns to the Rocky Mountains; Being a History of the Enlistment, Organization, and First Campaigns of the Regiment of United States Dragoons . . .* (New York, 1836), 37–38, 59–79 (quotations on 78).

50. Cooke, *Scenes and Adventures*, 220.

51. George H. Shirk, "Peace on the Plains," *Chronicles of Oklahoma*, XXVIII (1950), 5n.; Louis Pelzer, *Marches of the Dragoons in the Mississippi Valley: An Account of Marches and Activities of the First Regiment United States Dragoons in the Mississippi Valley Between the Years 1833 and 1850* (Iowa City, 1917), 27.

52. *PJD*, I, 374–75.

53. Dodge to George Jones, April 18, 1834, *ibid.*, 317.

54. For the expedition, consult Prucha, *Sword of the Republic*, 365–68; Pelzer, *Marches of the Dragoons*, chap. 4; Shirk, "Peace on the Plains," 2–41; [Hildreth], *Dragoon Campaign*, 140–82; Fred S. Perrine, ed., "The Journal of Hugh Evans, Covering the First and Second Campaigns of the United States Dragoon Regiment in 1834 and 1835," *Chronicles of Oklahoma*, III (1925), 174–215.

55. Perrine, ed., "Journal of Hugh Evans," 186.

56. Dodge to Roger Jones, October 1, 1834, quoted in Prucha, *Sword of the Republic*, 368. In all quoted matter I have retained the spelling and grammar of the original.

57. Perrine, ed., "Journal of Hugh Evans," *passim;* W. P. Johnston to Rosa, August 5, 1862, Johnston Papers, TU; *Memoir*, I, 155.

58. *PJD*, I, 331–40 *passim*, 374.

59. *Ibid.*, 391, 394.

60. *Memoir*, I, 95–96; Walter L. Fleming, "Jefferson Davis's First Marriage," *PMHS*, XII (1912), 25.

61. *PJD*, I, 153, 156, 164.

62. *Ibid.*, 357–81, contains the proceedings of the court-martial; all quotations come from there.

63. *Ibid.*, 389–90, 396.

64. Fleming, "Davis's First Marriage," 26; Twiggs to Thomas S. Jesup, February 7, 1835, *PJD*, I, 355.

65. Arbuckle to George A. McCall, May 12, 1835, *PJD*, I, 403.

66. *Ibid.*, 405, 410–11.

CHAPTER FOUR: *"Located in a Very Retired Place"*

1. *New Orleans Daily Picayune*, August 28, 1910; *PJD*, I, 347n.; Walter L. Fleming, "Jefferson Davis' First Marriage," *PMHS*, XII (1912), 32–33; Hudson Strode, *Jefferson Davis* (3 vols.; New York, 1955–64), I, 78.

2. Fleming, "First Marriage," 24–25; *New Orleans Daily Picayune*, August 28, 1910 (quotation); *New York Times*, October 20, 1906.

3. Fleming, "First Marriage," 25–26; *New York Times*, October 20, 1906; K. Jack Bauer, *Zachary Taylor: Soldier, Planter, Statesman of the Old Southwest* (Baton Rouge, La., 1985), 69.

4. Fleming, "First Marriage," 26–27.

5. *Ibid.*, 26.

6. JD to Knox Taylor, December 16, 1834, *PJD*, I, 345–47.

7. Knox Taylor to Margaret Taylor, June 17, 1835, *ibid.*, 407.

8. *New Orleans Daily Picayune*, August 28, 1910; Fleming, "First Marriage," 30.

9. *New Orleans Daily Picayune*, August 28, 1910; Knox Taylor to Margaret Taylor, June 17, 1835, *PJD*, I, 407; Annah Robinson Watson, *Some Notable Families of America* (New York, 1898), 9.

10. Knox Taylor to Margaret Taylor, June 17, 1835, *PJD*, I, 406–07.

11. *Ibid.*, 409; *New Orleans Daily Picayune*, August 28, 1910.

12. *New Orleans Daily Picayune*, August 28, 1910.

13. *Ibid.;* Knox Taylor to Margaret Taylor, June 17, 1835, *PJD*, I, 407; Watson, *Notable Families*, 10.

14. Knox Davis to Margaret Taylor, August 11, 1835, *PJD*, I, 475.

15. *Ibid.;* George P. Rawick, ed., *The American Slave: A Composite Autobiography Supplementary Series I* (12 vols.; Westport, Conn., 1977), VIII, 1000.

16. JD to Winfield Scott, August 26, 1828, and Knox Davis to Margaret Taylor, August 11, 1835, *PJD,* I, 106, 475. On health and high ground, see Ronald L. Numbers and Todd L. Savitt, eds., *Science and Medicine in the Old South* (Baton Rouge, La., 1989), chaps. 7–8 *passim;* John Duffy, ed., *The Rudolph Matas History of Medicine in Louisiana* (2 vols.; Baton Rouge, La., 1952–62), I, 125; Robert H. Taylor, *Antebellum South Carolina: A Social and Cultural History* (Chapel Hill, N.C., 1942), 103–05.

17. *New Orleans Daily Picayune,* August 28, 1910; *New York Times,* October 20, 1906.

18. There is a tradition that Knox Davis was already ill before heading for Louisiana; the better, though not absolutely conclusive, evidence supports my account. Cf. Rawick, ed., *American Slave,* VIII, 1000–01.

19. On malaria, see: William K. Anderson, *Malarial Psychoses and Neuroses . . .* (London, 1927), chaps. 2, 15; Herbert M. Gilles and David A. Warrell, *Bruce-Chavatt's Essential Malariology* (3d ed.; London, 1993), chap. 1; James B. Wyngaarden *et al.,* eds., *Cecil Textbook of Medicine* (19th ed., 2 vols.; Philadelphia, 1992), II, section 424; Numbers and Savitt, eds., *Science and Medicine,* 160–61; John Duffy, "The Impact of Malaria on the South," in Todd L. Savitt and James Harvey Young, eds., *Disease and Distinctiveness in the American South* (Knoxville, Tenn., 1988), 29–54; Duffy, ed., *Medicine in Louisiana,* II, 152–53.

20. *New Orleans Daily Picayune,* August 28, 1910; *New York Times,* October 20, 1906. The cemetery is now the Locust Grove State Historical Area, near St. Francisville, Louisiana.

21. *New Orleans Daily Picayune,* August 28, 1910; *PJD,* I, liv; Fleming, "First Marriage," 35.

22. JD to Miss Lee Willis, April 13, 1889, JD Association, RU.

23. On Joseph and Hurricane, see Janet Hermann, *Joseph E. Davis: Pioneer Patriarch* (Jackson, Miss., 1990); Frank Edgar Everett, Jr., *Brierfield: Plantation Home of Jefferson Davis* (Jackson, Miss., 1971); [Mahala E. Roach] to Thomas R. Roach, August 22, 1897, Roach Letters, MDAH.

24. See portrait, p. 79.

25. JD to "Dear Sister," June 3, 1829, Lynda Lasswell [Crist], "Jefferson Davis Ponders His Future, 1829," *JSH,* XLI (1975), 522; *Bowmar,* 205; Stamps to JD, November 10, 1874, JD Papers, TR.

26. *Bowmar,* 550; Everett, *Brierfield,* 6, 23–24.

27. *Memoir,* I, 165–66. No other contemporary evidence discusses the Cuban journey, but there is no reason to doubt VD's account, though she was clearly in error when she said Davis returned through the Northeast; she confused this journey with his trip of 1837–38.

28. VD to William E. Dodd, March 8, 1905, William E. Dodd Papers, LC; *Bowmar,* 553; Hermann, *Davis,* 65, 166.

29. *Bowmar,* 415, 425; *PJD,* II, 719.

30. On the opening of Brierfield, see *Memoir,* I, 163–64; *Bowmar,* 207, 211–12, 409–11, 413, 417–19, 424–26; VD to William E. Dodd, March 8, 1905, Dodd Papers, LC.

31. *Bowmar,* 417, 425 (quotations).

32. For the number of slaves in 1838 and 1839, see *PJD*, II, 719; the U.S. Census (1840) for Warren County, NA, specifies forty slaves owned by JD, but the age breakdown totals thirty-nine.

33. U.S. Census (1840) for Warren County.

34. *Bowmar*, 228–33; JD to Hugh Davis, April 17, 1842, JD Papers, MC; Lewis Sanders, Jr., to JD, November 30, 1839, *PJD*, I, 462; *ibid.*, II, 10, 34, 311, 719, and III, 455, has tax data; for per capita income, see Robert William Fogel, *Without Consent or Contract: The Rise and Fall of American Slavery* (New York, 1989), 85. For a more detailed discussion of Davis as slaveowner and planter, see below, chapter eight.

35. Joseph Davis to JD, January 19, February 19, August 27, 1838, and JD to Joseph Davis, January 2, 1838, *PJD*, I, 438 (first quotation), 442 (second quotation), 450 (third quotation), 435.

36. *Ibid.* has all of the following: Jane Davis to JD, April 8, 1836, 416 (first quotation); Lucinda Stamps to JD, May 14, 1837, 431–32 (second quotation); Florida McCaleb to JD, July 19, 1838, October 15, n.d., 448–49, 477 (final quotation); Ellen Davis to JD, December 29, 1838, September 22, 1839, 453, 460–61; Caroline Davis to JD, July 24, 1840, 470; Anna Smith to JD, August 27, 1840, 473; JD to Joseph Davis, January 2, 1838, 435. In addition, see JD to Hugh Davis, April 17, 1842, JD Papers, MC.

37. Florida McCaleb to JD, July 19, 1838, and Eliza Davis to JD, July 24, 1840, *PJD*, I, 449, 469–71.

38. JD to Joseph Davis, January 2, 1838, and Watson Van Benthuysen to JD, January 16, 1838, *ibid.*, 434, 436.

39. JD to Joseph Davis, January 2, 1838, *ibid.*, 434.

40. *Ibid.; Memoir*, I, 169–70; John Carl Parish, *George Wallace Jones* (Iowa City, 1912), 266.

41. Parish, *Jones*, 266–67; *Memoir*, I, 167–68.

42. L. B. Northrop to JD, April 17, 1879, *JDC*, VIII, 379.

43. *Bowmar*, 206–07, 228–33.

44. JD to Joseph Davis, January 2, 1838, *PJD*, I, 434–35.

45. Watson Van Benthuysen to JD, April 18, 1838, *ibid.*, 444–45.

46. JD to Ritchie, September 3, 1875, JD Papers, DU.

47. Varina Davis to William E. Dodd, March 8, 1905, Dodd Papers, LC; *Memoir*, I, 172; *New York Herald*, August 11, 1895; JD to William Allen, July 24, 1840, *PJD*, I, 467 (in the Burns quotation, JD substituted "honored" for "youthful" from Burns's "Epistle to a Young Friend").

48. VD to William E. Dodd, March 8, 1905, Dodd Papers, LC; *Memoir*, I, 172; Joseph Davis to JD, January 19, February 19, August 27, all 1838, July 23, 1840, *PJD*, I, 437–38, 442, 451, 464–65; JD to Joseph Davis, January 2, 1838, *ibid.*, 434–35.

49. JD to W. B. Tebo, August 22, 1849, *JDC*, I, 245–46.

50. VD to William E. Dodd, March 8, 1905, Dodd Papers, LC; *Memoir*, I, 172.

51. On the Whigs, Democrats, and Calhoun, consult William J. Cooper, Jr., *The South and the Politics of Slavery, 1828–1856* (Baton Rouge, La., 1978), 102–03, 113–14. Edwin A. Miles, *Jacksonian Democracy in Mississippi* (Chapel Hill, N.C., 1960), covers the Mississippi story in some detail, and Christopher Morris, *Becoming Southern: The Evolution of a Way of Life: Warren County and Vicksburg, Mississippi, 1770–1860* (New York, 1995), 151–53, addresses partisanship in Davis's county.

52. JD to W. B. Tebo, August 22, 1849, *JDC*, I, 245–46; *Memoir*, I, 89–90.

53. JD to Jones, February 9, 1839, *PJD*, I, 455.

54. *Vicksburg Daily Sentinel*, August 31, 1840; *PJD*, II, 15.

55. *PJD*, II, 35–37, 697.

56. *Vicksburg Daily Sentinel*, November 15, 1843; *Vicksburg Whig*, November 3, 1843.

57. *PJD*, II, 43–45, 698.

58. On banks and repudiation, consult Bradley G. Bond, *Political Culture in the Nineteenth Century South: Mississippi, 1830–1900* (Baton Rouge, La., 1995), 82–89 (quotation on 83), and James Roger Sharp, *The Jacksonians Versus the Banks: Politics in the States After the Panic of 1837* (New York, 1970), chaps. 3–4.

59. *PJD*, II, 698. JD to Editor, August 29, 1849, *Jackson Mississippian*, September 7, 1849; JD to Ritchie, September 3, 1875, JD Papers, DU.

60. *PJD*, II, 49.

61. *Ibid.*, 45, 47.

62. *Ibid.*, 58, 76, 697 (quotation).

CHAPTER FIVE: *"It Was What I Wished"*

1. *Memoir*, I, 187–88, 190–91. On the Howell family and Varina, see Eron Rowland, *Varina Howell: Wife of Jefferson Davis* (2 vols.; New York, 1927–31), and Ishbel Ross, *First Lady of the South: The Life of Mrs. Jefferson Davis* (New York, 1958).

2. *Memoir*, I, 189.

3. See photograph, p. 97.

4. Varina Howell to Margaret Howell, December 19, 1843, *PJD*, II, 52–53.

5. William P. Johnston to "My Dear Rosa," July 23, 1862, Johnston Family Papers, FC; *Memoir*, I, 191.

6. Ross, *First Lady*, 8–9; Rowland, *Varina Howell*, I, 75–76; JD to VD, March 8, 1844, *PJD*, II, 121.

7. Ross, *First Lady*, 11; JD to VD, March 8, 15, 1844, *PJD*, II, 120–21, 127–28.

8. JD to VD, March 8, 15, 1844, *PJD*, II, 120–21, 127–28.

9. JD to VD, March 15, September 6, 1844, and two undated letters, *ibid.*, 128, 208, 704, 705.

10. JD to VD, March 15, 1844, *ibid.*, 127–28.

11. JD to VD, March 8, 15, December 11, 1844, *ibid.*, 121, 127–28, 234, and September 27, 1844, *ibid.*, VIII, 597.

12. JD to VD, March 8, September 6, 1844, and undated, *ibid.*, II, 120, 208, 705.

13. JD to VD, November 22, 1844, *ibid.*, 224–25.

14. JD to VD, March 8, 1844, *ibid.*, 121, and February 25, 1845, Special Collections, Mississippi State University. For insightful treatments of husband-wife roles, see Bertram Wyatt-Brown, *Southern Honor: Ethics and Behavior in the Old South* (New York, 1982), chap. 8, and George C. Rable, *Civil Wars: Women and the Crisis of Southern Nationalism* (Urbana, Ill., 1989), chaps. 1–2.

15. See JD's wedding picture, p. 103.

16. JD to VD, February 25, 1845, Special Collections, Mississippi State University.

17. *Memoir*, I, 199–200; Rowland, *Varina Howell*, I, 98–99; Ross, *First Lady*, 18–19 (quotation). *PJD*, II, 235–37, has the marriage bond and marriage certificate.

18. *Memoir*, I, 200; Rowland, *Varina Howell*, I, 102–03; Ross, *First Lady*, 19–21; VD to Margaret Howell, March 9, 1845, JD and Family Papers, MDAH.

19. *Memoir*, I, 200–02.

20. For the convention, see *PJD*, II, 68–76.

21. Reuben Davis, *Recollections of Mississippi and Mississippians* (Boston and New York, 1891), 193.

22. The most perceptive study of political culture in Mississippi during Davis's time is Bradley G. Bond, *Political Culture in the Nineteenth Century South: Mississippi, 1830–1900* (Baton Rouge, La., 1995).

23. VD to William E. Dodd, March 10, 1905, William E. Dodd Papers, LC; JD to Martin Van Buren, March 25, 1844, to William Allen, March 25, 1844, *PJD*, II, 130–31, 139–40.

24. JD to William Allen, March 25, 1844, and to VD, June 22, 1844, *PJD*, II, 131, 173.

25. Davis, *Recollections*, 69.

26. JD to VD, September 6, 1844, *PJD*, II, 207; *ibid.*, 165–66, 176.

27. *Ibid.*, 179–80, 185.

28. *Ibid.*, 196–98, 202, 216. "Coon" was a derisive appellation that Democrats applied to Whigs.

29. *Ibid.*, 202; Davis, *Recollections*, 196–97.

30. *PJD*, II, xxxiv–xxxv, 165–216 *passim;* the quotation comes from a speech fragment, JD Papers, TR.

31. On the Texas issue in the South, see my *The South and the Politics of Slavery* (Baton Rouge, La., 1978), chap. 6, and William W. Freehling, *The Road to Disunion: Secessionists at Bay, 1776–1854* (New York, 1990), part VI.

32. *PJD*, II, 119, 142, 169, 165–216 *passim.*

33. Speech fragment, JD Papers, TR.

34. *Jackson Mississippian*, September 6, 1844, *PJD*, II, 220–21 (election results), 226; Davis, *Recollections*, 193.

35. H. S. Foote *et al.* to Polk, December 4, 1844, JD to Robert J. Walker, February 22, 1845, *PJD*, II, 232, 235.

36. *Memoir*, I, 202–03; JD to Margaret Howell, April 25, 1845, *PJD*, II, 244.

37. *Memoir*, I, 203–04.

38. JD to Margaret Howell, April 25, 1845, *PJD*, II, 243–44.

39. JD to G. E. Payne, February 14, 1845 (copy), Harold A. Frey, Jr., Tom's River, N.J. (1986).

40. *PJD*, II, 256–59; *Vicksburg Sentinel*, July 11, 1845.

41. *PJD*, II, 295–97. The year 1845 marked the final general-ticket election in Mississippi. Three years earlier Congress had mandated single-member districts, but it took some time for that system to be put in place. See Kenneth C. Martis, *The Historical Atlas of Parties in the United States Congress, 1789–1989* (New York, 1989), 4–7, 98–101.

42. *Vicksburg Sentinel*, June 30, 1845, and James Roger Sharp, *The Jacksonians Versus the Banks: Politics in the States After the Panic of 1837* (New York, 1970), 85.

43. *PJD*, II, 284–87, 290–91n.; *Memoir*, I, 205–06.

44. *Vicksburg Sentinel,* July 11, 1845.

45. *PJD,* II, 265–66; JD to W. B. Tebo, August 22, 1849, *JDC,* I, 246.

46. *PJD,* II, 263; *ibid.,* 266–81, has the address as printed.

47. JD and Quitman to the Public, July 10, 1845, *ibid.,* 304–05; Jacob Thompson to J. F. H. Claiborne, June 3, 1878, P. L. Rainwater, ed., "Letters to and from Jacob Thompson," *JSH,* VI (February 1940), 103. Also see JD to J. F. H. Claiborne, April 24, n.d., J. F. H. Claiborne Papers, MDAH.

48. VD to Margaret Howell, September 5, 1845, *PJD,* II, 329; W. P. Johnston to "My Dear Rosa," July 23, 1862, Johnston Family Papers, FC; *PJD,* II, xxxvi–xxxvii; *Vicksburg Whig,* October 15, 1845.

49. *Vicksburg Sentinel,* August 4, 18, 25, 1845; *Jackson Mississippian,* August 6, 1845.

50. *PJD,* II, 307–10, 312–13, 315–17, 324–25, 327–28, 336–40, 343–44, 347–53, 355–56.

51. *Ibid.,* 317, 336, 338, 344, 347, 355, 356.

52. *Ibid.,* 351–52, 356.

53. *Ibid.,* 357–59.

54. *Ibid.,* 361, 365, 370; JD to Wilson Hemingway, November 11, 1845, *ibid.,* 363–65; *Memoir* I, 208. In my research I have found no evidence for a close relationship; neither is there any in the massive archive collected for the publication of Calhoun's papers. Clyde Wilson (editor of the John C. Calhoun Papers) to WJC, September 10, 1993.

55. *Memoir,* I, 208–09, 211–12; *PJD,* II, 370; *Vicksburg Whig,* November 20, 1845.

56. *Memoir,* I, 198; *PJD,* II, xxxvii, 370–71.

57. Joseph Howell to Margaret Howell, November 21, 1845, *PJD,* II, 375–76.

58. JD to VD, August 1, 1845, *PJD,* VIII, 597; VD to Margaret Howell, September 5, 1845, *ibid.,* II, 329–30; Joseph Howell to "Dear Father," September 5, 1845, William B. Howell Papers, MDAH; Eliza Davis to Mary Davis, September 13, 1845, Lise Mitchell Papers, TU.

59. VD to "My dear Mother," November 14, 1845, Old Courthouse Museum, Vicksburg.

60. JD to Charles M. Price and George R. Fall, December 16, 1845, *PJD,* II, 384–85; VD to "My Dear Parents," December 11, 1845, JD and Family Papers, MDAH; *Memoir,* I, 215–20.

61. Charles Dickens, *American Notes* ([1842]; Gloucester, Mass., 1968), 140; Allan Nevins, *Ordeal of the Union* (2 vols.; New York, 1947), I, 39–40; Constance M. Green, *Washington* (2 vols.; Princeton, 1962), I, 155–64.

62. *Memoir,* I, 220; John Carl Parish, *George Wallace Jones* (Iowa City, 1912), 268.

63. Dickens, *American Notes,* 140; Glenn Brown, *History of the United States Capitol* (2 vols.; Washington, D.C., 1900), I, 67–68; George C. Hazelton, *The National Capitol: Its Architecture, Art and History* (New York, 1903), 218–19.

64. Henry W. Hilliard, *Politics and Pen Pictures: At Home and Abroad* (New York and London, 1892), 132; *PJD,* II, 438–63. For full discussions of the Oregon issue and Manifest Destiny, see two books by Frederick Merk, *Manifest Destiny and Mission in American History* (pb. ed.; New York, 1963), and *The Oregon Question: Essays*

in Anglo-American Diplomacy and Politics (Cambridge, Mass., 1967), along with David M. Pletcher, *The Diplomacy of Annexation: Texas, Oregon, and the Mexican War* (Columbia, Mo., 1973), and Rush Welter, *The Mind of America, 1820–1860* (New York, 1975), 66–74.

65. *PJD*, II, 395–96, 564.

66. *Ibid.*, 498–515, 519.

67. *Ibid.*, 615–18, 621–25, 627–28, 632–33, 634n.

68. *Ibid.*, 390, 463.

69. VD to Margaret Howell, January 30, April 3, 1846, *ibid.*, 419–21, 533–35; *Memoir*, I, 225, 263–64.

70. *Vicksburg Whig*, January 6, 1846; *PJD*, II, 383, 404, 409, 411, 434, 484, 549; JD to George Bancroft, December 12, 1845, to Eli Abbot, December 21, 1845, to Wilson Hemingway, November 11, 1845, *ibid.*, 384, 399, 364.

71. *PJD*, II, 424–27, 690–91; *ibid.*, 569, 649–54, 700; *Memoir*, I, 245, 252.

72. VD to "My dear parents," December 11, 1845, JD and Family Papers, MDAH; VD to Margaret Howell, January 30, April 3, 1846, *PJD*, II, 419–20, 534; *Memoir*, I, 220–27, chaps. 21–22 *passim* (quotation on 259).

73. VD to Margaret Howell, January 30, April 3, 1846, *PJD*, II, 419–21, 533–35.

74. JD to VD, June 22, 1846 (copy), Robert E. Cannon, Houston (1979, calendared *PJD*, III, 457–58); VD to JD, [June] 14, 1850, *ibid.*, IV, 119.

CHAPTER SIX: *"It May Be That I Will Return with a Reputation"*

1. For thorough accounts of Polk's goals and the coming of the war, see K. Jack Bauer, *The Mexican War, 1846–1848* (New York, 1974), chaps. 1–5; David M. Pletcher, *The Diplomacy of Annexation: Texas, Oregon, and the Mexican War* (Columbia, Mo., 1973), chaps. 9–10, 12; and Charles G. Sellers, *James K. Polk: Continentalist, 1843–1846* (Princeton, 1966), chap. 10.

2. JD to Polk, May 19, 1846, *PJD*, II, 600–01; David E. Twiggs to JD, May 4, 1846, *ibid.*, 577; *ibid.*, 583, 660, 661n.

3. *Yazoo City Whig*, May 29, 1846, quoted in Joseph E. Chance, *Jefferson Davis's Mexican War Regiment* (Jackson, Miss., 1991), 3, also 4–12; John G. Poindexter to Jacob Thompson and JD, May 1, 1846, *PJD*, II, 584.

4. Jesse Speight *et al.* to Polk, June 3, 1846, *PJD*, II, 636; JD to "A Gentleman in Vicksburg," May 12, 1846, *ibid.*, 590.

5. *Ibid.*, 589–90; *Vicksburg Whig*, May 26, 1846.

6. *PJD*, II, 670–71, 673n.; Chance, *Davis's Regiment*, 11–12. Bradford evidently acted from personal conviction and nothing else; no evidence exists to suggest any arrangement between him and Davis or any of Davis's friends.

7. VD to Margaret Howell, June 6, 1846, *PJD*, II, 641–42.

8. *Ibid.*, 675, 694n.; *Memoir*, I, 284.

9. JD to Lucinda Stamps, July 8, 1846, *PJD*, II, 695. The "circumstances" Davis referred to are not known; possibly the relatively small size of Rosemont, where the Stamps family lived, was involved.

10. *Ibid.*, III, 3–9.

11. *Memoir*, I, 284; JD to Lucinda Stamps, July 8, 1846, *PJD*, II, 695.

12. *PJD*, II, 693; Chance, *Davis's Regiment*, 20.

13. *Memoir*, I, 284–85; VD to Margaret Howell, January n.d., 1847, JD Papers, UA.

14. Chance, *Davis's Regiment*, 20; Carnot Posey to Col. George H. Gordon [1846] (typescript), Walter Lynwood Fleming Papers, NYPL; *Vicksburg Whig*, July 25, 1846 (quotation).

15. JD to Robert J. Walker, July 22, 1846, *PJD*, III, 11–12n.

16. *Jackson Mississippian*, June 24, July 15, 1846; Joseph Davis to JD, [October] 7, 1846, *PJD*, III, 55–56n.

17. JD to Robert J. Walker, July 22, 1846, *PJD*, III, 11–12. For full discussions of the government's initial policy of invasion, see K. Jack Bauer, *Zachary Taylor: Soldier, Planter, Statesman of the Old Southwest* (Baton Rouge, La., 1985), 166–74; David Lavender, *Climax at Buena Vista: The American Campaigns in Northeastern Mexico, 1846–47* (Philadelphia, 1966), 82–92; Pletcher, *Diplomacy*, chap. 14; and Sellers, *Polk*, chap. 10.

18. Eleanor Damon Pace, ed., "The Diary and Letters of William P. Rogers, 1846–1862," *SHQ*, XXXII (April 1929), 261; John A. Quitman to Eliza, August 14, 1846, Quitman Family Papers, UNC; Archibald Burns Journal, DU; Chance, *Davis's Regiment*, 24.

19. JD to Robert J. Walker, August 24, 1846, to John McNutt, August 20, 1846, *PJD*, III, 18–19, 16–17; Joseph E. Chance, ed., *The Mexican War Journal of Captain Franklin Smith* (Jackson, Miss., 1991), 9; Chance, *Davis's Regiment*, 26.

20. JD to VD, July 18, 29, August 16, 1846, *PJD*, III, 11, 13–14, 16.

21. Taylor to JD, August 3, 1846, *ibid.*, 14–15; *Memoir*, I, 199; Bauer, *Taylor*, 113–14.

22. *PJD*, III, 15n.; Chance, ed., *Smith Journal*, 13.

23. Bauer, *Taylor*, 175; Lavender, *Climax*, 93.

24. Chance, *Davis's Regiment*, 26–27.

25. Bauer, *Taylor*, 165; Pace, ed., "Rogers Diary," 262.

26. On Taylor's plans and organization, see Bauer, *Taylor*, 175–76, and Lavender, *Climax*, 92–98.

27. Pace, ed., "Rogers Diary," 263.

28. For detailed studies of the battle, see Bauer, *Taylor*, chap. 9, Chance, *Davis's Regiment*, chaps. 4–5, and Lavender, *Climax*, chap. 6. My account is drawn from them.

29. *PJD*, III, 47–48.

30. Joseph Howell to "Dear Mother," September 25, 1846, William B. Howell Papers, MDAH. The best depictions of JD in battle come from reports of regimental officers, e.g., *PJD*, III, 48, 51, 64–68.

31. For a marvelous contemporary description of the houses and streets, see William B. Campbell to His Wife, October 10, 1846, Campbell Family Papers, DU.

32. JD to Joseph, September 25, 1846, to Thomas Ritchie, January 6, 1847, *PJD*, III, 24, 110–12; *Memoir*, I, 304.

33. JD to Joseph, September 25, 1846, *PJD*, III, 24; JD to Quitman, September 26, 1846, *ibid.*, 25–29, 35–38 (quotations on 27 and 35); JD to Walker, October 12, 1846, *ibid.*, 61–62; *JDC*, I, 147–48, has casualty figures. For an insightful discussion of the attitude of Americans in Mexico, including their confidence, consult Robert Johannsen's splendid *To the Halls of the Montezumas: The Mexican War in the American Imagination* (New York, 1985).

34. Joseph Howell to "Dear Mother," October 13, [1846], JD Papers, MC; *PJD*, III, has battle reports, e.g., 48, 51, 64–76.

35. JD to Joseph, September 25, 1846, *PJD*, III, 24; John A. Quitman to "My dearest Wife," October 19, 1846, Quitman Family Papers, UNC; *PJD*, III, 74. The leave itself, dated October 18, 1846, is in the John A. Quitman Papers, MDAH.

36. VD to JD, [September 1846], *PJD*, III, 53.

37. *Bowmar,* 346–47.

38. *Ibid.,* 349–51, 357–61; *Memoir,* I, 311; VD to Margaret Howell, January n.d., 1847 (quotation), JD Papers, UA; Hudson Strode, *Jefferson Davis* (3 vols.; New York, 1955–64), I, 174.

39. "Christmas 1846" in "Christmas Days" by Mrs. M. P. H. Roach, Eggleston-Roach Papers, LSU. On the importance of motherhood, see Sally G. McMillen, *Motherhood in the Old South: Pregnancy, Childbirth, and Infant Rearing* (Baton Rouge, La., 1990), and George C. Rable, *Civil Wars: Women and the Crisis of Southern Nationalism* (Urbana, Ill., 1989), chap. 1 *passim.*

40. JD to VD, December 10, 1846, *PJD*, III, 93–95.

41. JD to Joseph, January 26, 1847, *ibid.,* 116.

42. *Vicksburg Whig,* October 29, 1846, for commendation and on October 24, November 3, 10, 12, 1846, for squabble.

43. *Ibid.,* November 12, 1846; *PJD*, III, 79–83, has the speech.

44. The preponderant evidence places the Rifles first in the fort; see *PJD*, III, 42–43n.

45. JD to Balie Peyton, November 1, 14, 1846, and Peyton to JD, November 3, 1846, *ibid.,* 77–78, 84–85; *ibid.,* 79–83, 86–88, has JD's speech and his public letter; Peyton to William B. Campbell, November 5, 1846, Campbell Family Papers, DU.

46. The best study of Quitman is Robert F. May, *John A. Quitman, Old South Crusader* (Baton Rouge, La., 1985).

47. JD to Quitman, September 26, 1846, *PJD*, III, 25–29, 35–38; Quitman to "My beloved Wife," February 20, 1847, Quitman Family Papers, UNC.

48. Louisa Quitman to "My dearest Father," November 9, 17, 1846, Eliza Quitman to Quitman, November 18, 1846, January 2, 1847, Quitman to Louisa Quitman, January 6, 1847, Quitman Family Papers, UNC; Quitman to "My dear Son," January 11, 1847, Quitman Papers, MDAH.

49. *PJD*, III, 42, 43n.; May, *Quitman,* 220. On JD's unhappiness with Quitman, see JD to Joseph Davis, January 26, 1847, *PJD*, III, 115.

50. JD to Walker, November 30, 1846, *PJD*, III, 89–91.

51. On Taylor's plans and views, consult Bauer, *Taylor,* 186–93, and Lavender, *Climax,* chap. 7.

52. The Buena Vista campaign is thoroughly covered in Bauer, *Taylor,* 194–214, Chance, *Davis's Regiment,* chaps. 7–8, and Lavender, *Climax,* chaps. 8–12. My account is drawn chiefly from them. *PJD*, III, 139–47, has JD's official report. On the pride of the Rifles, see Carnot Posey to Col. George H. Gordon, February 19, 1847 (typescript), Fleming Papers, NYPL.

53. JD to VD, [February 8, 1847], *PJD*, III, 118.

54. Pace, ed., "Rogers Diary," 272, 274; Capt. W. S. Henry, *Campaign Sketches of the War with Mexico* (New York, 1847), 276.

55. JD to W. W. S. Bliss, March 2, 1847, and Alexander Bradford to JD, March 2, 1847, *PJD*, III, 141, 144, 152; James Henry Carleton, *The Battle of Buena Vista, with*

the Operations of the *"Army of Occupation"* for One Month (New York, 1848), 77; Capt. T. W. Gibson, *Letter Descriptive of the Battle of Buena Vista, Written upon the Ground* . . . (Lawrenceburgh, Ind., 1847), 4.

56. On the wound, see *PJD*, III, 123n., 149n., and *Memoir*, I, 332.

57. JD to W. W. S. Bliss, March 2, 1847, *PJD*, III, 142.

58. *Ibid.;* JD to William A. Buck, June 21, 1859, *JDC*, IV, 56–58.

59. Wool quotation in Lavender, *Climax*, 211; JD to W. W. S. Bliss, March 2, 1847, *PJD*, III, 143.

60. JD to VD, February 25, 1847, *PJD*, III, 122; *ibid.*, 122, 143, 149n.; *Memoir*, I, 332, 359; JD to James L. Power, October 6, [1887], James L. Power Papers, MDAH.

61. *PJD*, III, 143, 184; for reports of regimental officers, see *ibid.*, 123–27, 128–39, 151–63 (quotations on 153–54); *JDC*, I, 176–77, has casualty figures; Taylor's report is in *Senate Executive Document 139*, 30:1 (serial 503).

62. JD to William A. Buck, June 21, 1859, *JDC*, IV, 56–58. For comments on the effectiveness of artillery, consult Bauer, *Taylor*, 205; Lavender, *Climax*, 225–29; Grady McWhiney and Perry D. Jamieson, *Attack and Die: Civil War Military Tactics and the Southern Heritage* (University, Ala., 1982), 37–38.

63. Chance, *Davis's Regiment*, 126–27.

64. *PJD*, III, 181–82; *New Orleans Daily Delta*, June 11, 1847.

65. *PJD*, III, 183–85; *Memoir*, I, 358; *Natchez Semi-Weekly Courier*, June 15, 1847; *Vicksburg Whig*, June 15, 1847; Chance, *Davis's Regiment*, 128–29.

66. *Vicksburg Whig*, April 2, 1847; Carnot Posey to Col. George H. Gordon, February 19, 1847 (typescript), Fleming Papers, NYPL; *Vicksburg Weekly Sentinel*, April 7, 21, July 28 (quoting *Aberdeen Advertiser*), 1847; JD to Citizens of Jackson, May 7, 1847, *PJD*, III, 171.

CHAPTER SEVEN: *"At Present All Is Uncertainty"*

1. *Jackson Mississippian*, March 26, April 23 (quoting *Ripley Advertiser*), June 11, 1847; Joseph Davis to JD, May 13, 1847, *PJD*, III, 172.

2. Milo Milton Quaife, ed., *The Diary of James K. Polk During His Presidency, 1845–1849* (4 vols.; Chicago, 1910), III, 28–29; Polk to Robert Armstrong, June 13, 1847, James K. Polk Papers, LC; Polk to JD, May 19, 1847, *PJD*, III, 175–76.

3. Joseph Davis to JD, May 21, 1847, *PJD*, III, 176; Taylor to Dr. R. C. Wood, June 23, July 20, 1847, William H. Samson, ed., *Letters of Zachary Taylor from the Battle-Fields of the Mexican War* (Rochester, N.Y., 1908), 109, 119, and Taylor to JD, July 27, 1847, *PJD*, III, 203.

4. JD to Polk, June 20, 1847, *PJD*, III, 185–86; also see JD to Robert J. Walker, June 20, 1847, *ibid.*, 186–87.

5. *Vicksburg Whig*, May 25, 1847; *Vicksburg Weekly Sentinel*, June 2, 1847; JD to Stephen Cocke, July 15, 1847, *PJD*, III, 192; see n. 3.

6. Henry S. Foote, *Casket of Reminiscences* ([1874]; New York, 1968), 349–50; Brown to JD, August 10, 1847, *JDC*, I, 92–93; JD to Brown, August 15, 1847, *PJD*, III, 207–08; *Jackson Mississippian*, August 13, 1847; *Vicksburg Whig*, August 19, 1847.

7. VD to Margaret Howell, [July] 24, 1847, JD Papers, UA; JD to VD, January 3, 1848, *The Am. Scene: A Panorama of Autographs, 1504–1980*.

8. *Bowmar,* 350, 358.

9. *Ibid.,* 354–56; VD to Margaret Howell, April n.d., 1848, JD Papers, UA.

10. JD to VD, January 3, and addendum on January 4, 1848, *Am. Scene; Bowmar,* 356.

11. VD to Margaret Howell, November 12, 1847, JD Papers, UA.

12. JD to VD, January 3, and addendum on January 4, 1848, *Am. Scene,* and on April 18, 1848, *PJD,* III, 302–03.

13. JD to VD, April 18, 1848, *PJD,* III, 302–03; VD to Margaret Howell, April n.d., 1848, JD Papers, UA.

14. VD to Margaret Howell, April n.d., 1848, JD Papers, UA. Whatever the details of her response, she has the wrong date, whether by design or because of a confused memory, for her account of the spring of 1848—*Memoir,* I, 409ff.

15. *Vicksburg Weekly Sentinel,* September 27, November 3, 1847; Zachary Taylor to Dr. R. C. Wood, October 27, 1847 (first quotation), Samson, ed., *Letters of Taylor,* 145; JD to N. D. Coleman and Others, November 2, 1847, *JDC,* I, 179; *Jackson Mississippian,* November 12, 1847 (second quotation); *Memoir,* I, 361; Zachary Taylor to JD, February 16, 1848, and JD to VD, April 18, 1848 (third quotation), *PJD,* III, 270, 302.

16. Joseph Davis to JD, May 13, 1847, *PJD,* III, 172–73; *Bowmar,* 496–97.

17. *PJD,* III, 246n., 250n.

18. *Ibid.,* seating chart facing 225; *The Senate Chamber, 1810–1859* (Washington, D.C., 1976), 5; Christian F. Eckloff, *Memoirs of a Senate Page (1855–1859),* ed. Percival G. Melbourne (New York, 1909), 5.

19. Oliver Dyer, *Great Senators of the United States Forty Years Ago (1848 and 1849): with Personal Recollections and Delineations . . .* (New York, 1889), 123–34.

20. *PJD,* III, xxxv; JD to Stephen Cocke, November 30, 1847, *ibid.,* 249; Taylor to JD, September 18, 1847, *ibid.,* 219.

21. JD to Stephen Cocke, November 30, 1847, *ibid.,* 248.

22. *Ibid.,* 249n.; *Jackson Mississippian,* December 31, 1847.

23. JD to Stephen Cocke, November 30, 1847, *PJD,* III, 249; Tompkins to JD and JD to Tompkins, both December 25, 1847, *ibid.,* 252–54; *Vicksburg Weekly Sentinel,* December 15, 1847.

24. *Vicksburg Daily Whig,* February 25, 1848; *Jackson Mississippian,* January 14, 1848.

25. Quaife, ed., *Polk Diary,* III, 269–70.

26. For general background, see David M. Potter, *The Impending Crisis, 1848–1861,* comp. and ed. Don E. Fehrenbacher (New York, 1976), chaps. 1–6. The most thorough treatment of Calhoun is Charles M. Wiltse, *John C. Calhoun* (3 vols.; Indianapolis, 1944–51).

27. *PJD,* III, 254–61, 264–65 (quotations on 258 and 265).

28. *Ibid.,* 277–88 (quotations on 278, 285, 287).

29. Potter, *Impending Crisis,* 3–5; *Senate Executive Document, 52,* 30:1, 18, 36 (serial 509).

30. *PJD,* III, 295–301 (quotation on 295).

31. *Ibid.,* 420, 421, 422, 424–35, 429–30, 431, 432, 436–37; *JDC,* I, 191.

32. *PJD,* III, 332–69, has JD's Oregon speech; all quotations come from there unless otherwise specified.

33. On slavery and the Constitution, see especially Don E. Fehrenbacher, *The Dred Scott Case: Its Significance in American Law and Politics* (New York, 1978), notably part one.

34. On the congressional struggle and its outcome, see Potter, *Impending Crisis,* 73–76, and *PJD,* III, 373n.

35. Davis defended slavery in the Oregon speech cited above; for the quotation, see *PJD,* III, 315.

36. *Ibid.*

37. On diffusion, consult Drew R. McCoy, *The Last of the Fathers: James Madison and the Republican Legacy* (New York, 1989), 265, 267–74; *JDC,* I, 313, has more on JD and diffusion in 1850.

38. JD to Dr. Samuel A. Cartwright, June 10, 1849, *PJD,* IV, 22–23; *JDC,* I, 316–17, II, 73–75.

39. *JDC,* I, 536–37.

40. *Jackson Mississippian,* September 1, 1848.

41. *PJD,* III, xxxvi; JD to VD, April 18, 1848, to Hugh R. Davis, June 4, 1848, *ibid.,* 302, 325–26.

42. Taylor to JD, April 20, 1848, *ibid.,* 307–08.

43. Robert Barnwell Rhett to John C. Calhoun, May 20, 1847, Chauncey S. Brooks and Robert P. Brooks, eds., *Correspondence Addressed to John C. Calhoun, 1837–1849* (Washington, D.C., 1930), 377; Frank Blair to Martin Van Buren, February 29, 1848, Martin Van Buren Papers, LC; JD to D. H. Lewis, March 17, 1847, D. H. Lewis Material, Sam Houston Memorial Museum, Huntsville, Texas; JD to Robert Walker, June 29, 1847, to [Simon Cameron], July 26, 1847, *PJD,* III, 190–91, 196–97; JD to Beverly Tucker, April 12, 1848, *ibid.,* 292–93.

44. *PJD,* III, xxxvi, 374–76, 388; JD to Beverly Tucker, April 12, 1848, *ibid.,* 292–93; *Jackson Mississippian,* September 1, 1848.

45. JD to Charles J. Searles, September 19, 1847, to Hugh R. Davis, June 4, 1848, to Woodville Citizens, October 23, 1848, *PJD,* III, 225–26, 325–26, 389; JD to H. R. Davis and Others, October 6, 1848, *JDC,* I, 214.

46. On popular sovereignty, see Potter, *Impending Crisis,* 56–62, and my *The South and the Politics of Slavery, 1828–1856* (Baton Rouge, La., 1978), 255–56, 263–64.

47. Taylor, for example, on April 20, 1848, informed JD that the United States should take no land from Mexico below the Missouri Compromise line—*PJD,* III, 309.

48. *Jackson Mississippian,* November 24, 1848; *Vicksburg Weekly Sentinel,* December 6, 1848; Taylor to JD, April 20, 1848, *PJD,* III, 309, and on July 10, 1848, *JDC,* I, 210; JD to John J. Crittenden, January 30, 1849, *PJD,* IV, 8–9.

49. *PJD,* III, 392n.

50. For the congressional session, Calhoun, and southern opinion, see Potter, *Impending Crisis,* 83–87, and my *Politics of Slavery,* 269–76.

51. JD to John J. Crittenden, January 30, 1849, *PJD,* IV, 8–9; *ibid.* 18n.; Cooper, *Politics of Slavery,* 272–73, 377–78, discusses the failed Whig effort.

52. The most thorough treatment of Mississippi politics between 1849 and 1851 remains, amazingly, Cleo Hearon, "Mississippi and the Compromise of 1850," *PMHS,* XIV (1914), 7–229.

53. *PJD,* IV, 19–20.

54. *Ibid.*, xxxii–xxxiii, 46–47 ed.n.; JD to VD, October 14, 1849, *ibid.*, 47.

55. *JDC*, I, 236–38; Michael F. Holt, *The Rise and Fall of the American Whig Party: Jacksonian Politics and the Onset of the Civil War* (New York, 1999), 449.

56. JD to Stephen Cocke, August 2, 1849, *PJD*, IV, 26; JD to Malcolm D. Haynes (public letter), August 18, 1849, *ibid.*, 26–44.

57. Hearon, "Compromise," 61–68, for the October 3 convention and D. W. Wallace to Whitemarsh Seabrook, October 20, 1849, Whitemarsh Seabrook Papers, LC, for JD's support.

58. *PJD*, IV, 52 ed.n., 120–21n.; JD to James W. Kingsbury, December 15, 1849, *ibid.*, 52; *Memoir*, I, 409 (although VD dates this in the spring of 1848, the evidence makes clear it is in the fall of 1849); "Plan of Senate Chamber, First Session, Thirty-first Congress," JD Papers, MC.

59. JD to Stephen Cocke, August 2, 1849, *PJD*, IV, 25; *Jackson Southron*, December 12, 1849.

60. Lewis L. Taylor to [John Duncan], September 7, 1849 (copy), William Henry McRaven Papers, MDAH; Jacob Thompson to Wm. R. Cannon, December 31, 1849, William R. Cannon Papers, LC.

61. JD to Stephen Cocke, August 2, 1849, to William R. Cannon, January 8, 1850, *PJD*, IV, 25, 55–56.

62. *Vicksburg Weekly Whig*, February 20, 1850.

63. JD to John J. Crittenden, January 30, 1849, *PJD*, IV, 8–9; Taylor to JD, September 11, 1849, quoted in Holman Hamilton, *Zachary Taylor* (2 vols.; Indianapolis, 1941–51), II, 237–38 (from this letter one can easily infer that JD had been critical).

64. *Memoir*, I, 409–18; Dinner List, January 26, 1850, W. W. Corcoran Papers, LC. Again VD places these in the spring of 1848, but she clearly describes events that occurred in 1849 and 1850.

65. VD to JD, January 25, [1850], and [June] 14, 1850, *PJD*, IV, 62, 119–20; [Sarah Stickney] Ellis, *Guide to Social Happiness* (New York: several editions were published in New York, n.d., 1847, 1848, 1850); Anna Butler to Sarah Butler, January 13, 1850 (typescript), Butler Family Papers, LSU (I am grateful to John Sacher for this reference); see photograph, p. 199.

66. By far the most thorough and most perceptive accounts of the Compromise of 1850 are especially Holt, *Whig Party*, chaps. 14–15, and Mark J. Stegmaier, *Texas, New Mexico, and the Compromise of 1850: Boundary Dispute and Sectional Crisis* (Kent, Ohio, 1996). My analysis follows them. Also see Holman Hamilton, *Prologue to Conflict: The Crisis and Compromise of 1850* ([1964]; New York, 1966), Potter, *Impending Crisis,* chap. 5, Cooper, *Politics of Slavery*, 282–310 (quotation on 284).

67. James D. Richardson, comp., *A Compilation of the Messages and Papers of the Presidents, 1789–1897* (10 vols.; Washington, D.C., 1896–99), V, 9–24.

68. JD to William R. Cannon, January 8, 1850, *PJD*, IV, 56.

69. Mississippi Delegation to John A. Quitman, January 21, 1850, *JDC*, I, 261; Albert G. Brown to J. F. H. Claiborne, March 15, 1860, J. F. H. Claiborne Papers, MDAH; JD to William R. Cannon, January 8, February 25, 1850, *PJD*, IV, 56, 82–83.

70. Holt, *Whig Party*, chap. 14, is penetrating on Clay.

71. *PJD*, IV, 63–70.

72. *JDC*, I, 263–308, has the speech; all quotations come from there.

73. JD to Francis J. Lynch, February 25, 1850, *PJD*, IV, 84. For correspondence and other relevant material, see *ibid.*, 79–82, 85–86n.; *Vicksburg Tri-Weekly Sentinel*,

March 26, 1850; Anna Butler to Robert O. Butler, February 28, 1850, Butler Family Papers, LSU (I am grateful to John Sacher for this reference).

74. Reuben Davis, *Recollections of Mississippi and Mississippians* (Boston and New York, 1891), 101, 322; Wiltse, *Calhoun*, III, 401–02, 465–66; Hamilton, *Prologue*, 93. There is no good biography of Foote, but see the biographical sketches in James Daniel Lynch, *The Bench and Bar of Mississippi* (New York, 1881), 286–88, and *DAB*, VI, 500–01.

75. JD to Howell Hinds, September 30, 1856, *PJD*, VI, 50–52; memorandum by Abraham Venable dated August 8, 1874, in Venable to JD, August 8, 1874, JD Papers, MC. A fanciful tale, with no corroborating evidence, that begins the dispute with Foote's introducing a young female friend of the Davises to an unsavory character is related in Mary A. A. Fry to Walter Lynwood Fleming, n.d., Walter Lynwood Fleming Papers, NYPL.

76. JD to Howell Hinds, September 30, 1856, *PJD*, VI, 52.

77. *Ibid.*, III, 329–31, details the flag incident.

78. For Calhoun and the compromise, see Potter, *Impending Crisis*, 100–02; *PJD*, IV, xxxiv, 344, and *Memoir*, I, 462–63, give details about JD and Calhoun's obsequies.

79. JD discusses Webster in a letter to William R. Cannon, February 25, 1850, *PJD*, IV, 82.

80. *JDC*, I, 507–08. Also see JD to James Buchanan, March 15, 1850, to Franklin H. Elmore, April 13, 1850, and Buchanan to JD, March 16, 1850, *ibid.*, 318–21, 323.

81. Robert Barnwell to JD, October 20, 1851, *PJD*, IV, 227; Stegmaier, *Texas*, 188.

82. *JDC*, I, 482–501, 504–11 (quotation, 485).

83. Texas: *ibid.*, 418, 474–80, *PJD*, IV, 109–16; Mexican law: *ibid.*, 109–16; *CG*, 31: 1, App., pt. 2, 1416–20; fugitive slaves: *JDC*, I, 512–23 (quotation 518).

84. James B. Smith to JD, February 2, 1849, *PJD*, IV, 10 (first quotation); *ibid.*, 84 (second, third quotations), 336, 338–39, 341, 360, 361, 363, 370.

85. *Ibid.*, 124n.

86. Stegmaier, *Texas*, 199; William McWillie to My Dearest Wife, August 11, 1850, McWillie-Compton Papers, MDAH.

87. Stegmaier, *Texas*, 326–28; Hamilton, *Prologue*, 191–92. While most historians view the Compromise as a compromise, Potter in *Impending Crisis* interprets it as an armistice.

88. *JDC*, I, 486, 502–06; *PJD*, IV, 124; William Walthall Diary, March 4, 1877, William Walthall Papers, MDAH.

89. *JDC*, I, 378, 381, 432–33, 509.

90. JD to Margaret K. Howell, September 15, 1850, *PJD*, IV, 132.

CHAPTER EIGHT: *"The Cloud Which Had Collected"*

1. *PJD*, IV, 134–35 ed.n.; VD to Mary Ann Cobb, January 13, 1851, Howell Cobb Papers, UGA.

2. *JDC*, I, 543–45.

3. *Jackson Mississippian*, May 31, 1850; *Vicksburg Weekly Sentinel*, October 23, November 13 (quoting *Paulding Clarion*), 1850; *JDC*, I, 589–92, 602–03.

4. *PJD*, IV, xxxv, 135–45, 373; *JDC*, I, 579–89, 592–600.

5. *PJD*, IV, xxxv, 121n., 135 ed.n.; VD to Mary Ann Cobb, January 13, 1851, Cobb Papers, UGA.

6. JD to VD, [December] 5, 1850, JD Family Papers, MDAH; VD to Mary Ann Cobb, January 13, 1851, Cobb Papers, UGA; *JDC*, II, 28–34; on enforcement of the Fugitive Slave Law, see David M. Potter, *The Impending Crisis, 1848–1861*, comp. and ed. Don E. Fehrenbacher (New York, 1976), 130–39.

7. *JDC*, II, 41–42.

8. *Ibid.*, 17–18; see also *ibid.*, I, 557–60.

9. *PJD*, IV, 16–18, 59–61.

10. *Ibid.*, 94–100.

11. *Ibid.*, 3–5, 95, 175, 176n.; *JDC*, II, 1–9 (quotation on 1).

12. *PJD*, IV, 161, 163–64.

13. *Ibid.*, 176n.

14. William J. Cooper, Jr., *The South and the Politics of Slavery, 1828–1856* (Baton Rouge, La., 1978), 304–10.

15. P. L. Rainwater, ed., "The Autobiography of Benjamin Grubb Humphreys, August 26, 1808–December 20, 1882," *MVHR*, XXI (1934), 242; on Mississippi politics in 1851, Cleo Hearon, "Mississippi and the Compromise of 1850," *PMHS*, XIV (1914), 7–229, still has the most detailed account.

16. On Quitman, see Robert F. May, *John A. Quitman, Old South Crusader* (Baton Rouge, La., 1985), chaps. 17–19 *passim*.

17. For the Georgia Platform, consult my *Politics of Slavery*, 307–08.

18. Hearon, "Mississippi and Compromise," 166n.

19. JD to David Yulee, July 18, 1851, *PJD*, IV, 218–19; *Jackson Mississippian*, May 9, 1851.

20. JD to VD, May 8, 1851, *PJD*, IV, 181; JD to David Yulee, July 18, 1851, *ibid.*, 218–19.

21. Horatio J. Harris to JD, April 17, 1851, *ibid.*, 179; *Jackson Mississippian*, May 9, 1851.

22. *PJD*, IV, 181 ed.n.

23. *Ibid.*, 389–92; *JDC*, I, 415 (quotation), II, 71–82.

24. *Vicksburg Tri-Weekly Sentinel*, June 12, 1851 (first quotation); *Jackson Mississippian*, May 23 (second quotation), 30, 1851.

25. *Vicksburg Weekly Whig*, November 6, 1850.

26. *Jackson Mississippian*, June 20, 1851; JD to James A. Pearce, August 22, 1852, *PJD*, IV, 300; Reuben Davis, *Recollections of Mississippi and Mississippians* (Boston and New York, 1891), 316.

27. For the gubernatorial struggle, see Davis, *Recollections*, 315–17; *Memoir*, I, 466–67; JD to David Yulee, July 18, 1851, *PJD*, IV, 218; May, *Quitman*, 258–59.

28. *Jackson Mississippian*, July 4, 1851; Davis, *Recollections*, 317; *PJD*, IV, xxxvi, 183 ed.n., 183–220, 392; JD to David Yulee, July 18, 1851, *ibid.*, 218; Andrew P. Butler to JD, June 16, 1851, Robert Barnwell to JD, October 20, 1851, *ibid.*, 391, 227.

29. [?] Sanders to John A. Quitman, July 13, 1851, J. F. H. Claiborne Papers, MDAH; *PJD*, IV, xxxvii, 183 ed.n.

30. *PJD*, IV, xxxvii; *Vicksburg Tri-Weekly Sentinel*, August 21, 1851 (first and second quotations); *Jackson Mississippian*, July 4, August 29 (third quotation), 1851.

31. *Jackson Mississippian*, August 29, 1851; *PJD*, IV, xxxvii, 222n.; *Memoir*, I, 467, 469.

32. *Memoir,* I, 469.

33. *Ibid.;* JD to Cartwright, September 23, 1851, *PJD,* IV, 224–25.

34. JD to Cartwright, September 23, 1851, *PJD,* IV, 224–25.

35. For my discussion of JD's eye problem, I have relied on Dr. Charles S. Bryan to WJC, January 13, March 24, 1997, and Dr. Roderick Macdonald to WJC, January 30, 1997. Pertinent medical literature includes: Gerald L. Mandell *et al.,* eds., *Principles and Practice of Infectious Diseases* (4th ed.; New York, 1995), 1336–39; Howard M. Leibowitz, *Corneal Disorders: Clinical Diagnosis and Management* (Philadelphia, 1984), chap. 16; Thomas H. Mader and R. Doyle Stulting, "Viral Keratitis," *Infectious Disease Clinics of North America,* VI (December 1992), 831–35; D. Yorston and A. Foster, "Herpetic Keratitis in Tanzania: Association with Malaria," *British Journal of Ophthalmology,* LXXVI (October 1992), 582–85. Also see *PJD,* VI, 170–71n., and Harris D. Riley, Jr., "Jefferson Davis and His Health, Part I: June, 1808–December, 1860," *JMH,* XLIX (August 1987), 195–201.

36. See chapter ten below.

37. Hearon, "Mississippi and Compromise," 209n.; JD to David Yulee, July 18, 1851, *PJD,* IV, 218–19; Powhatan Ellis to Margaret Ellis, October 8, 1851, Mumford-Ellis Papers, DU; Davis, *Recollections,* 317–18.

38. May, *Quitman,* 260–63.

39. Hearon, "Mississippi and Compromise," 209n.

40. Powhatan Ellis to Margaret Ellis, October 8, 1851, Mumford-Ellis Papers, DU; Ethelbert Barksdale to JD, September 19, 1851, *PJD,* IV, 222–23; E. C. Wilkinson to the People of Mississippi, September 16, 1851, *JDC,* II, 85–86; *Memoir,* I, 470.

41. JD to E. C. Wilkinson, September 17, 1851, *JDC,* II, 86; JD to John I. Guion, September 23, 1851, *ibid.,* 84–85; Collin S. Tarpley to JD, May 6, 1853, *ibid.,* 213.

42. *Jackson Mississippian,* September 19, October 3, 1851; Davis, *Recollections,* 320.

43. *Memoir,* I, 469; *JDC,* II, 88–107.

44. Ethelbert Barksdale to JD, September 19, 1851, *PJD,* IV, 223; [Collin S. Tarpley], *A Sketch of the Life of Jeff. Davis, the Democratic Candidate* (Jackson, Miss., 1851). The title page lists "a Citizen of Mississippi" as author, but the sketch of Tarpley in James Daniel Lynch, *The Bench and Bar of Mississippi* (New York, 1881), 366–69, identifies him as the author.

45. Ethelbert Barksdale to JD, September 19, 1851, *PJD,* IV, 223; Rainwater, ed., "Humphreys Diary," 242; *Vicksburg Weekly Whig,* September 17, 1851.

46. *Memoir,* I, 470; *Jackson Mississippian,* October 24, 1851; *PJD,* IV, xxxviii.

47. *PJD,* IV, 231–32.

48. Hearon, "Mississippi and Compromise," 215; *Journal of the House of the State of Mississippi (1852),* 256; Davis, *Recollections,* 320; Reuben Davis to JD [November n.d., 1851], *PJD,* IV, 233; *Jackson Mississippian,* November 14, 1851; Rainwater, ed., "Humphreys Diary," 242.

49. Reuben Davis to JD [November n.d., 1851], *PJD,* IV, 233; also see *Jackson Mississippian,* November 14, 1851.

50. Hearon, "Mississippi and Compromise," 215.

51. JD to John M. Clayton, November 22, 1851, *JDC,* II, 108.

52. *Bowmar,* 259, 493–94; William Ziegler to JD, February 25, 1849, *PJD,* IV, 12–13.

53. *Bowmar*, 259–60; *PJD*, IV, 237. For more detail on the house, consult Frank Edgar Everett, Jr., *Brierfield: Plantation Home of Jefferson Davis* (Jackson, Miss., 1971), chap. 5.

54. VD to Mary Ann Cobb, January 13, 1851, Cobb Papers, UGA.

55. *Memoir*, I, 469, 475–76.

56. Asbury Dickins to JD, October 27, 1851, *PJD*, IV, 229–30; "Library of Congress Loan Record," *ibid.*, 173–74.

57. *Bowmar*, 363; *Memoir*, I, 476; *PJD*, IV, 293n.

58. *Bowmar*, 350, 363.

59. *Ibid.*, 348–49, 469; Eliza Davis to JD, [1852], William B. Howell Papers, MDAH.

60. VD to Margaret K. Howell, May 25, 1852, *PJD*, IV, 301n.; JD to James A. Pearce, August 22, 1852, *ibid.*, 300; Cartwright to JD, October 16, 1852, *ibid.*, 302–04; *ibid.*, 302 ed.n.; JD to Dr. Cartwright, January 20, 1853, *ibid.*, 301n.; *Jackson Mississippian*, October 29, 1852.

61. U.S. Manuscript Census, 1850 and 1860, Warren County, Mississippi: Agriculture Schedules, NA; Joseph M. Stephenson to JD, January 5, 1852, *PJD*, V, 481.

62. Joseph Davis to JD, [October] 7, 1846, *PJD*, III, 56; JD to Payne & Harrison, November 16, 1857, *ibid.*, VI, 550; Nicholas E. Barnes to JD, December 16, 1861, *ibid.*, VII, 440; *Bowmar*, 168, 289; VD to William E. Dodd, June 16, 1905, William E. Dodd Papers, LC.

63. Manuscript Census, 1860, Warren County, Mississippi: Slave Schedules, NA; John Hebron Moore, *The Emergence of the Cotton Kingdom in the Old Southwest: Mississippi, 1770–1860* (Baton Rouge, La., 1988), 108–09, 124.

64. The best study of factors is Harold D. Woodman, *King Cotton and His Retainers: Financing and Marketing of the Crop of the South, 1800–1925* (Lexington, Ky., 1968).

65. *Bowmar*, 155–56, 167–68, 228–29.

66. *PJD*, IV, 237–40, 275; Payne & Harrison to JD, August 3, 9, 1852, *ibid.*, 299, 399; JD to Payne & Harrison, November 23, 1857, *ibid.*, VI, 163.

67. William Ziegler to JD, February 25, 1849, *PJD*, IV, 13; James Roach Diary, May 29, 1858, April 9, 21, 1859, Roach-Eggleston Papers, UNC; JD to Margaret K. Howell, March 28, 1859, to William B. Howell, April 18, 24, 1859, and to Clement C. Clay, May 17, 1859, *PJD*, VI, 241–42, 242n., 246, 247, 251; *Bowmar*, 308–12.

68. Manuscript Census, 1850: Agriculture Schedules, NA; *PJD*, III, 414; IV, 378; V, 286; VI, 130n., 546, 549; JD to Payne & Harrison, March 10, 1860, *ibid.*, VI, 548. For the value of slaves, see Michael Tadman, *Speculators and Slaves: Masters, Traders, and Slaves in the Old South* (Madison, Wis., 1989), 283–91.

69. VD to William E. Dodd, June 16, 1905, Dodd Papers, LC; Lewis C. Gray, *History of Agriculture in the Southern United States* ([1933]; 2 vols.; Gloucester, Mass., 1958), II, 1027 (cotton prices); Robert William Fogel, *Without Consent or Contract: The Rise and Fall of American Slavery* (New York, 1984), 85 (per capita income); *Bowmar*, 163; *PJD*, V, 123n.

70. The basic study of the overseer remains William K. Scarborough, *The Overseer: Plantation Management in the Old South* (Baton Rouge, La., 1966); JD to VD, July 20, 1857, *PJD*, VI, 129; JD to VD, July 27, 1857, JD Papers, TR; Joseph Davis to Payne & Harrison, July 12, 1858 (copy), *Bowmar*, 185.

71. *Bowmar*, 325–27, 329, 333–34, 345–46; *PJD*, II, 59–60n.

72. *Bowmar,* 189–90, 208; JD to Joseph Davis, September 22, 1855, *PJD,* V, 122; JD to William B. Howell, June 14, 1855, *ibid.,* 113; JD to VD, July 20, 1857, *ibid.,* VI, 129; Nicholas Barnes to JD, December 16, 1861, *ibid.,* VII, 440; *ibid.,* VI, 549 (investments).

73. Manuscript Census, 1850 and 1860: Slave Schedules, NA, has details on JD's slaveholdings.

74. Robert W. Fogel and Stanley L. Engerman, *Time on the Cross* (2 vols.; Boston, 1974), I, 125 (life expectancy); Manuscript Census, 1860: Slave Schedules (Joseph's slaves); Old Bob (sometimes Old Rob) is often mentioned, e.g., *Memoir,* I, 179–80, and JD to Joseph Davis, September 22, 1855, *PJD,* V, 123.

75. JD to Hugh R. Davis, June 4, 1848, *PJD,* III, 326; *Bowmar,* 215.

76. Payne & Harrison to JD, August 3, 9, 1852, *PJD,* IV, 299 (first quotation), and *JDC,* II, 176–77 (second quotation).

77. JD to Payne & Harrison, November 23, 1857, *PJD,* VI, 163; Joseph Davis to Payne & Harrison, December 22, 1857, and JD to Payne & Harrison, November 16, 1857 (copies), *Bowmar,* 185–86, 191–92.

78. On slavery and the master-slave relationship, see Eugene Genovese's important and influential *Roll, Jordan, Roll: The World the Slaves Made* (New York, 1974), and Peter Kolchin's excellent synthesis, *American Slavery, 1619–1877* (New York, 1993).

79. VD to William B. Howell, April 11, 1845, JD Papers, Alabama; *Memoir,* I, 179; JD to Joseph Davis, August 25, 1855, August 30, 1857, *PJD,* V, 117, VI, 136–37; JD to William B. Howell, April 18, 24, 1859, *ibid.,* VI, 246–47; JD to Cartwright, April 25, 1859, *ibid.,* 249.

80. *Memoir,* I, 179–80; VD to William E. Dodd, March 8, 1905, Dodd Papers, LC; Everett, *Brierfield,* 49.

81. *Bowmar,* 215; *Memoir,* I, 180; JD to William B. Howell, April 24, 1859, *PJD,* VI, 247; *Semi-Centennial Celebration, Mound Bayou, Mississippi* (n.p., n.d.), 19, booklet, Benjamin Montgomery Family Papers, LC; Janet Sharp Hermann, *Joseph Davis: Plantation Patriarch* (Jackson, Miss., 1990), 57–60.

82. JD to Joseph, August 25, 1855, *PJD,* V, 117; *Harper's Weekly,* September 15, 1866.

83. *Memoir,* I, 176–78; Ben Montgomery to JD, August 1, 1859, *JDC,* IV, 92–93; *PJD,* VIII, 599.

84. *Memoir,* I, 178.

85. JD to Campbell Brown, June 14, 1886, Civil War Collection (CW 82), HL; *PJD,* V, 123n.

86. *Memoir,* I, 175–76; VD to William E. Dodd, March 8, June 16, 1905, Dodd Papers, LC; Lise M. Hamer to Walter Lynwood Fleming, n.d. [1907?], January 30, 1908, Walter Lynwood Fleming Papers, NYPL. Also see Walter Lynwood Fleming, "Jefferson Davis, the Negroes and the Negro Problem," *Louisiana State University Bulletin,* Series VI (October 1908, no. 4), especially 6–7, and [Mahala Roach] to Thomas R. Roach, August 22, 1897, Roach Letters, MDAH.

87. Petition quoted in Mary Seaton Dix, "Jefferson Davis and Slavery: A Personal and Political Conflict" (unpublished paper presented to the Southern Historical Association, November 3, 1990), 3; George P. Rawick, ed., *The American Slave: A Composite Autobiography, Series I* (19 vols.; Westport, Conn., 1972), VII, 91–94,

and *Supplementary Series I* (12 vols.; Westport, Conn., 1977), VIII, 993–95, 1157–60, 1328–39 *passim*. Also see Thornton Montgomery to Lise Hamer, December 11, 1907, Lise Mitchell Papers, TU; "Talking with a Colored Fellow about Jefferson Davis," Mound Bayou, Mississippi, 1942, Folklore Division, LC, and "Speech of Isaiah Montgomery," newspaper clipping (typescript) dated February 16, 1902, Fleming Papers, NYPL.

88. *Memoir*, I, 177; David D. Porter to Lorenzo Thomas, October 21, 1863, Ira Berlin *et al.*, eds., *The Wartime Genesis of Free Labor: The Lower South* (New York, 1990), 746–48.

89. JD to Joseph Davis, September 22, 1855, *PJD*, V, 122; JD to VD, July 20, 1857, *ibid.*, VI, 129.

90. L. M. Blackford to Wm. M. Blackford, November 27, 1863, Blackford Family Papers, UVA (in this letter Blackford writes that he has just spent time with W. F. Howell, VD's brother, who was undoubtedly the source of the slave material; I am grateful to Joseph T. Glatthaar for this reference); Joseph Davis to JD, January 2, 1861, *PJD*, VII, 3. Also see the suggestive entry on manacled runaway slaves in the William Holcombe Diary, June 2, 1855, William H. Holcombe Papers, UNC.

91. JD to William B. Howell, June 14, 1855, *PJD*, V, 113; VD to Margaret K. Howell, May n.d., 1857, JD Papers, UA.

92. VD to William E. Dodd, March 8, 1905, Dodd Papers, LC; *Memoir*, I, 311–12. For an introduction to Cartwright, see Eric L. McKitrick, ed., *Slavery Defended: The Views of the Old South* (Englewood Cliffs, N.J., 1963), 139–47.

93. VD to William E. Dodd, March 8, 1905, Dodd Papers, LC.

CHAPTER NINE: *"I . . . Have a Field of Usefulness"*

1. JD to John M. Clayton, November 22, 1851, *JDC*, II, 108; *Vicksburg Tri-Weekly Whig*, December 2, 1851; Ethelbert Barksdale to JD, December 28, 1851, *PJD*, IV, 236.

2. Michael F. Holt, *The Rise and Fall of the American Whig Party: Jacksonian Politics and the Onset of the Civil War* (New York, 1999), chap. 17; Ethelbert Barksdale to JD, December 28, 1851, *PJD*, IV, 234–35.

3. Ethelbert Barksdale to JD, December 28, 1851, *PJD*, IV, 235.

4. *JDC*, II, 117–25; JD to Barksdale and Jones, February 2, 1852, *PJD*, IV, 248.

5. *Jackson Mississippian*, January 9, 1852.

6. *JDC*, II, 117; JD to ? [August–October 1852], *PJD*, IV, 297.

7. JD to ? [August–October 1852], *PJD*, IV, 293 (first quotation); JD to Barksdale and Jones, February 2, 1852, *ibid.*, 241–49 (second quotation on 241); Barksdale and Jones to JD, February 7, 1852, *ibid.*, 250–51; C. J. Searles to JD, April 8, 1852, *ibid.*, 253–54 (third and final quotations); *ibid.*, 253n.

8. *Ibid.*, 237n.; F. C. Jones to JD, March 19, [1852], *ibid.*, 252.

9. *Ibid.*, 259.

10. *Ibid.*, 258–71; *Jackson Mississippian*, June 11, 1852; Geo. H. Gordon to Carnot Posey, June 9, 1852 (copy), Walter Lynwood Fleming Papers, NYPL. Also see James A. Seddon to Robert M. T. Hunter, February 7, 1852, Charles Henry Ambler, ed., *Correspondence of Robert M. T. Hunter, 1826–1876* (Washington, D.C., 1918), 137–39.

11. *Jackson Mississippian*, July 30, 1852; *JDC*, II, 174–76 (Scott quotation on 175); *Vicksburg Weekly Whig*, September 16, 1852; JD to J. F. H. Claiborne, October 24, 1852, *PJD*, IV, 304–07.

12. Pierce to JD, December 7, 1852, January 12, 1853, *PJD*, IV, 307–08, 308n. W. Dean Burnham, *Presidential Ballots, 1836–1892* (Baltimore, 1955), 245, 352, 887, has the election results.

13. Larry Gara, *The Presidency of Franklin Pierce* (Lawrence, Kans., 1991), 44–47; Roy Franklin Nichols, *Franklin Pierce: Young Hickory of the Granite Hills* (rev. ed.; Philadelphia, 1958), 218–23, 227–30, 237–38; Brown to JD, January 1, 1853, *PJD*, V, 3–4.

14. Albert Brown to JD, January 1, 1853, *PJD*, V, 3; C. G. Greene to JD, February 2, 18 (quotation), 1853, and JD to C. G. Greene, February 13, 1853 (all telegrams), *ibid.*, 151, 5; *Vicksburg Tri-Weekly Whig*, February 19, 1853; *PJD*, V, xxxvii, 5n.; *ibid.*, VI, 141; JD to Stephen Cocke, December 19, 1853, *JDC*, II, 335–37.

15. *PJD*, V, 11n.; Lurtan D. Ingersoll, *A History of the War Department of the United States* (Washington, D.C., 1879), 110–11.

16. Photograph, p. 263; Edward K. Eckert and Nicholas J. Amato, eds., *Ten Years in the Saddle: The Memories of William Woods Averell* (San Rafael, Calif., 1978), 42; Sir Henry Holland, *Recollections of Past Life* (New York, 1872), 191; Donald B. Cole and John J. McDonough, eds., *Benjamin Brown French: Witness to the Young Republic, A Yankee's Journal, 1828–1870* (Hanover, N.H., and London, 1989), 254; George Wallis Journal, June 24, 1853, LC; Virginia Clay-Clopton, *A Belle of the Fifties: Memories of Mrs. Clay of Alabama, Covering Social and Political Life in Washington and the South, 1853–1866* . . . (New York, 1905), 68.

17. On the War Department and army, see Edward M. Coffman, *The Old Army: A Portrait of the American Army in Peacetime, 1784–1860* (New York, 1986); William B. Skelton, *An American Profession of Arms: The Army Officer Corps, 1784–1861* (Lawrence, Kans., 1992); and Leonard P. White, *The Jacksonians: A Study in Administrative History, 1829–1861* (New York, 1954), chap. 10. Those scholars are generally positive about Davis's performance as secretary of war. Cf. John Muldowny, "The Administration of Jefferson Davis as Secretary of War" (unpublished Ph.D. dissertation, Yale University, 1959), which remains the most detailed account of Davis's secretaryship.

18. On Scott, Charles Winslow Elliott, *Winfield Scott: The Soldier and the Man* (New York, 1937), is the most detailed.

19. Nichols's *Pierce* is still the most thorough on Pierce's administration, but the more recent and briefer Gara, *Pierce*, also has value.

20. VD to Margaret Howell, March 3, 6, 1854, JD Papers, UA; *Memoir*, I, 530 (Pierce statement), 559 (first quotation), 571; "Notes of Oral Discourse of Ex-President Davis: 20 October 1877," William Walthall Papers, MDAH; JD to W. P. Northend, August 28, 1883, Montague Collection, NYPL.

21. *Memoir*, I, 533–34; "Notes of Oral Discourse of Ex-President Davis," Walthall Papers, MDAH.

22. JD to VD, April 17, May 27, 1853, *PJD*, V, 10–11, 17.

23. Clay-Clopton, *Belle of the Fifties*, 69; Virginia Clay-Clopton, "A Leaf from my *Diary*," C. C. Clay Papers, DU.

24. Malie B. Brodhead to VD, May 7, 1853, Howell Family Papers, MDAH; *PJD*, V, 17n.; *Memoir*, I, 563–64; JD to Rose Greenhow, January 26, 1856, *PJD*, VI, 406.

25. For a sense of the papers, consult *PJD*, V, 154–474 *passim*, and *ibid*., VI, 379–540 *passim*. For specific examples, see V, 104–05, 406, 407, 465, 466, 467, 471, and VI, 497, 514, 517–18 (West Point incident).

26. JD to [Robert Carter], February 9, 1859, *ibid*., VI, 240, and "Autobiography," *ibid*., I, lx. My discussion of JD as secretary relies heavily on his four annual reports, all published in *JDC*, II, 292–333 (1853), 389–419 (1854), 552–71 (1855), III, 68–98 (1856). The final one is also in *PJD*, VI, 62–91. Other citations are given only for quotations or special documents.

27. In general, see Coffman, *Old Army*, and Skelton, *Profession of Arms*.

28. Coffman, *Old Army*, 60; Skelton, *Profession of Arms*, 146; JD to Ethan A. Hitchcock, June 3, 1853, *PJD*, V, 18; William Walthall Diary, April 11, 1877, Walthall Papers, MDAH.

29. JD to Charles J. Faulkner, January 25, 1855, to Robert M. T. Hunter, March 19, 1856, *PJD*, V, 97–98, VI, 17–18; Douglas to JD, March 30, 1855, Robert W. Johannsen, ed., *The Letters of Stephen A. Douglas* (Urbana, Ill., 1961), 336; David L. Yulee to JD, March 27, 1855, and JD to Douglas, April 5, 1855, *JDC*, II, 445–46, 448–50.

30. *JDC*, II, 22–28; *Memoirs of Lieut.-General Scott, LL. D. Written by Himself* (2 vols.; New York, 1864), II, 589–90, 593. On JD and Scott generally, see Elliott, *Scott*, 648–59, and especially *Senate Executive Document 34*, 34:3 (serial 880), which contains the complete correspondence between the two men.

31. Scott to JD, August 6, 1855, March 20, May 21, 1856, *JDC*, II, 488, and III, 11, 36.

32. JD to Scott, February 29, 1856, *ibid*., III, 10.

33. George T. Denison, *Soldiering in Canada: Recollections and Experiences by Lt. Col. George T. Denison* (Toronto, 1890), 73–74.

34. *JDC*, II, 262.

35. On this matter, Grady McWhiney and Perry D. Jamieson, *Attack and Die: Civil War Military Tactics and the Southern Heritage* (University, Ala., 1982), 48–49, is helpful.

36. Nathaniel Cheairs Hughes, Jr., *General William J. Hardee: Old Reliable* (Baton Rouge, La., 1965), chap. 4, provides details; on publication, see *PJD*, V, 341.

37. JD to Edouard Stoeckl, May 15, 1855, to James Buchanan, July 23, 1855 (quotation), *PJD*, V, 106–07, 115; *ibid*., VI, 55–56; Richard Delafield to George B. McClellan, October 21, 1856, George B. McClellan Papers, LC.

38. JD to John Wiley, March 11, 1854, to Alexandre Vattemare, May 15, 1855, *PJD*, V, 62, 103.

39. Skelton, *Profession of Arms*, 241 (quotation); JD to R. Delafield, A. Mordecai, and George B. McClellan, April 2, 1855, to James Buchanan, April 9, 1855, *JDC*, II, 446–48, 450–52. For a detailed discussion, consult Matthew Moten, "Mission to the Crimea: The American Military Commission to Europe and the Crimean War, 1855–1856" (unpublished Ph.D. dissertation, Rice University, 1991).

40. JD to Charles J. McDonald, April 13, 1854, *JDC*, II, 350–51; JD to Joseph G. Totten, August 19, 1854, *PJD*, V, 82–83n.; Richard Delafield to George McClellan, October 21, 1856, McClellan Papers, LC.

41. *PJD*, V, 30–31; *JDC*, II, 249–51.

42. *PJD*, V, 30–31.

43. William H. Goetzmann, *Army Exploration in the American West, 1803–1863* (New Haven, Conn., 1959), chaps. 6–7, is superb on the railroad surveys; *Report of Explorations and Surveys to Ascertain the Most Practicable and Economical Route for a Railroad from the Mississippi River to the Pacific Ocean,* published by the War Department (13 vols.; 1855–60), contains a wealth of material. JD's assessment dated February 2, 1855, is in I, 3–30.

44. *PJD,* IV, 167–70; *Senate Executive Document 62,* 34:3 (serial 881), has a detailed record of the camel effort. Also see Lewis Burt Lesley, ed., *Uncle's Sam's Camels: The Journal of Mary Humphreys Stacey Supplemented by the Report of Edward Fitzgerald Beale, 1857–1858* (Cambridge, Mass., 1929).

45. Robert M. Utley, *Frontiersmen in Blue: The United States Army and the Indian, 1848–1865* ([1967]; Lincoln, Nebr., 1981), 53–55; *JDC,* II, 391 (quotation).

46. *PJD,* V, 18, 19n., 48–49n., VI, 6–7, 7–8n.

47. JD to Luther M. Kennett, August 12, 1856, *ibid.,* VI, 36; *JDC,* II, 326–29.

48. Archibald Campbell to JD, August 20, 1853, *PJD,* V, 39–40; *ibid.,* 42n., 119n., 386, and VI, 49n.; *Memoir,* I, 558–59. For the rent, see Anthony Hyde to JD, April 13, 1855, W. W. Corcoran Papers, LC. The mansion was owned by Edward Everett, the Massachusetts educator and orator.

49. JD to VD, August 28, 1853, *PJD,* V, 543–44; VD to Mother, July 26, 1853, January n.d., March 3, 26, April 29, 1854, JD Papers, UA; Elizabeth Blair Lee to S. P. Lee, October 18, 1855, Blair-Lee Papers, PU; *Memoir,* I, chaps. 39–40 *passim.*

50. *PJD,* V, xxxix, 38 ed.n.; JD to VD, August 28, 1853, *ibid.,* 43–44. During the trip JD said that he had been in New England previously, back in the 1830s. He was undoubtedly referring to his northern trip in the winter of 1837–38, but there is no surviving record of his having visited New England at that time. *JDC,* II, 262.

51. VD letters to Mother cited in note 49 above; JD to VD, July 12, 1853, *PJD,* V, 28.

52. *PJD,* V, 69n., 73n.; VD to Her Parents, July n.d., 1854, JD Papers, UA; John H. Wheeler Diary, June 15, 1854 (second quotation), LC; statement re: Oak Hill Cemetery, June 28, 1854, JD Papers, MC. The remains were subsequently moved to the Davis plot in Hollywood Cemetery in Richmond, Virginia.

53. VD to Her Parents, July n.d., 1854, JD Papers, UA; JD to William B. Howell, October 22, 1854, *PJD,* V, 92; Henry Turner to "My Dear Sister," June 29, 1854, Quitman Family Papers, UNC; *Memoir,* I, 535.

54. Janet Sharp Hermann, *Joseph E. Davis: Pioneer Patriarch* (Jackson, Miss., 1990), 38; VD to William E. Dodd, March 8, 1905, William E. Dodd Papers, LC; *PJD,* VI, 59–60n.

55. *PJD,* V, xli, 93n., and VI, xlvi.

56. *Memoir,* I, 571; *PJD,* V, 73n., 92n., VI, 49n.; VD to Her Parents, September 15, 1856, JD Papers, UA.

57. *Memoir,* I, 546, 551–55 (quotation 553), 567–68; VD to Mother, March 26, 1854, JD Papers, UA.

58. Elizabeth Blair Lee to S. P. Lee, October 18, 1855, Blair-Lee Papers, PU; *Memoir,* I, 557–58 (first quotation), 548–51 (second quotation 549).

59. *PJD,* V, 125–27.

60. JD to VD, July 12, 1853, *ibid.,* 28 and 28 ed.n.

61. *Ibid.,* 29–32 (Philadelphia, third quotation 30); *JDC,* II, 236–39 (Wilming-

ton), 239–42 (Trenton, second quotation 241), 242 (Princeton), 246–51 (New York City, first quotation 247), 252–56 (Newark, fourth quotation 253).

62. R. M. T. Hunter to JD, May 6, 1853, David L. Yulee to JD, March 27, 1855, Miles Taylor to JD, April 28, 1856, *JDC*, II, 214–15, 445–46, III, 35; JD to Howell Cobb, October 9, November 5, 1853, Randy Reid, "Howell Cobb: A Biography" (unpublished Ph.D. dissertation, Louisiana State University, 1995), 797; JD to Mason, September 28, 1853, *PJD*, V, 45, and Mason to JD, October 2, 1853, *JDC*, II, 269–70; JD to John Perkins, Jr., January 14, 1856, *PJD*, VI, 5.

63. On Pierce and Cuba, see Nichols, *Pierce*, 266–67, 327–30, 341–43, 352–59, 366–71, 393–96, and David M. Potter, *The Impending Crisis, 1848–1861*, comp. and ed. Don E. Fehrenbacher (New York, 1976), 183–93. My account follows them.

64. JD to Gen. T. S. Jesup, March 19, 1856, JD Papers, FC, to Thomas J. Hudson, November 25, [1855], *PJD*, V, 138; *ibid.*, VI, 118.

65. *PJD*, VI, 118.

66. *Ibid.*, 119.

67. Nichols, *Pierce*, 342; John Slidell to J. F. H. Claiborne, August 25, 1855, J. F. H. Claiborne Papers, MDAH.

68. On the Kansas-Nebraska Act, see my *The South and the Politics of Slavery, 1828–1856* (Baton Rouge, La., 1978), 346–54; Holt, *Whig Party*, chap. 22; Robert W. Johannsen, *Stephen A. Douglas* (New York, 1973), 395–400, chap. 17; Potter, *Impending Crisis*, 154–67. My account follows them.

69. JD to Mrs. Archibald Dixon, September 27, 1879, Mrs. Archibald Dixon, *The True History of the Missouri Compromise and Its Repeal* (Cincinnati, 1899), 457–59; Potter, *Impending Crisis*, 161.

70. JD to John C. Breckinridge, May 15, 1854, *PJD*, V, 67.

71. On the struggle in Kansas, see Potter, *Impending Crisis*, chap. 9.

72. Atchison to JD, September 24, 1854, February 26, 1856, *PJD*, V, 83–84, VI, 13.

73. Utley, *Frontiersmen in Blue*, chap. 7, discusses the army and the Indians in Kansas.

74. JD to Brigadier General Persifor Smith, September 3, 1856, *JDC*, III, 58–59, to Governors Joel A. Matteson and Charles S. Morehead, both on September 3, 1856, *PJD*, VI, 419; Nichols, *Pierce*, 474.

75. *PJD*, VI, 418–20, calendars communications that underscore his attentiveness. See also specifically JD's endorsements on August 27, September 23, 1856, *ibid.*, 41–42, 46–47, and JD to Colonel E. V. Sumner, May 23, 1856, to Brigadier General Persifor Smith, June 27, September 3, 1856, *JDC*, III, 40–41, 48–49, 58–59.

76. Collin Tarpley to JD, May 6, 1853, and JD to William R. Cannon, December 13, 1853 (quotation), *PJD*, V, 12–15, 52–53; JD to Stephen Cocke, December 19, 1853, *JDC*, II, 335–37.

77. Douglas Cooper to JD, May 11, 1853, JD Papers, TR; Collin Tarpley to JD, May 6, 1853 (quotation), James Phelan to JD, July 19, 1853, *PJD*, V, 12–15, 35–37.

78. JD to William R. Cannon, December 13, 1853 (first, second, sixth, seventh quotations), to Eli Abbott, April 17, 1853 (fourth and fifth quotations), *PJD*, V, 53, 9; JD to Stephen Cocke, December 19, 1853 (third quotation), *JDC*, II, 335.

79. Collin Tarpley to JD, May 6, 1853, James Phelan to JD, July 19, 1853, *PJD*, V, 12–15, 35–37; F. L. Claiborne to JD, June 8, 1853, J. Mitchell to JD, July 10, 1853,

Charles D. Fontaine to JD, July 13, 1853, JD to J. J. McRae, September 17, 1853 (quotation), J. J. McRae to JD, January 13, 1855, *JDC*, II, 231–32, 233–34, 234–36, 264–65, 439; J. J. McRae to JD, January 26, 1854, JD Papers, TR.

80. J. F. H. Claiborne to JD, March 25, 1881 (enclosing two MS pages from a projected Brown memoir), JD Papers, MC; O. R. Harris to John A. Quitman, September 18, 1855 (first quotation), and Quitman to B. F. Dill, February 9, 1854, John A. Quitman Papers, MDAH; Brown to J. F. H. Claiborne, May 17, 1854, June 7, 1855 (second quotation), January 4, 1857, and John Slidell to J. F. H. Claiborne, August 26, 1855 (final quotation), Claiborne Papers, *ibid.;* John J. Pettus to JD, June 5, 1857, *PJD*, VI, 128. On Brown, James Byrne Ranck, *Albert G. Brown: Radical Southern Nationalist* (New York, 1937), remains the best study.

81. JD to J. F. H. Claiborne, April 21, 1853, to Caleb Cushing, June 18, 1853, *PJD*, V, 11–12, 22–23; Madison McAfee to JD, April 20, 1853, and JD to Stephen Cocke, May 13, 1853, *JDC*, II, 208–09, 223; D. S. Pattison to JD, November 18, 1855, JD Papers, MC; W. Barry to Wm. R. Cannon, December 12, 1853 (first quotation), William R. Cannon Papers, LC; Giles Hillyer to John A. Quitman, January 4, 1857 (second quotation), Quitman Family Papers, UNC; B. L. C. Wailes Diary, October 2, 1854, MDAH.

82. *PJD*, V, xli, xlii, 107–08 ed.n., 108–09.

83. *Ibid.*, xlii; *Vicksburg Weekly Whig*, June 13, 1855; Brown to J. F. H. Claiborne, June 7, 1855, Claiborne Papers, MDAH.

84. W. Barry to William R. Cannon, June 5, 1854 (first quotation), and William Barksdale to [William R. Cannon], December 28, 1855 (second quotation), Cannon Papers, LC; JD to Thomas J. Hudson, November 25, [1855], to Collin Tarpley, December 19, 1855, to Stephen Cocke, January 6, 1856, *PJD*, V, 137–39, 147–49, and VI, 3; William R. Cannon to JD, December 12, 1855, *ibid.*, V, 144–45, and [December 18, 1855], JD and Family Papers, MDAH.

85. John J. McRae to JD, January 13, 1855, *JDC*, II, 439–41; Wm. A. Stone to John A. Quitman, December 27, 1855, Quitman Papers, MDAH; Brown to J. F. H. Claiborne, May 19, 1855, and Thompson to J. F. H. Claiborne, November 17, 1855, Claiborne Papers, *ibid.;* [John W. Jewell] to JD, August 16, 1856, JD Papers, DU.

86. [John W. Jewell] to JD, August 16, 1856, JD Papers, DU; *PJD*, VI, 4n.; Edward Pickett to John A. Quitman, February 7, 1856, Quitman Papers, MDAH.

87. JD to Stephen Cocke, January 6, 1856, *PJD*, VI, 3; *Vicksburg Daily Whig*, January 15, 1856.

88. On the demise of the Whigs, the story of the Know-Nothings, and the rise of the Republicans, Holt, *Whig Party*, chaps. 23–26, and William E. Gienapp, *The Origins of the Republican Party, 1852–1856* (New York, 1987), are definitive.

89. *PJD*, V, 109; JD to James Buchanan, July 23, 1855, *ibid.*, 115.

90. James M. Mason to JD, September 30, 1856, Virginia Mason, *The Public Life and Diplomatic Correspondence of James M. Mason* (New York and Washington, D.C., 1906), 117–18 (calendared in *PJD*, VI, 504); JD to South Carolina Citizens, September 22, 1856, *ibid.*, 44.

91. JD to Herschel V. Johnson, October n.d., 1856, *PJD*, VI, 54–55.

92. JD to B. Tucker, October 8, 1853, *JDC*, II, 271–72; JD to Thomas J. Hudson, November 25, [1855], to William L. Ellsworth, June 5, 1856 (quotation), *PJD*, V, 139, and VI, 25–26.

93. JD to William J. Brown, May 7, 1853, to Charles J. McDonald, April 13, 1854 (quotation), *JDC*, II, 217–18, 350–51.

CHAPTER TEN: *"The Darkest Hour"*

1. JD to Joseph Davis, September 22, 1855, *PJD*, V, 123, 124n.; *ibid.*, VI, 114–15, 115n.

2. VD to her mother, May n.d., 1857, JD Papers, UA (final quotation); VD to Mrs. Franklin Pierce, May 25, 1857 (typescript, first two quotations), VD Subject File, MDAH.

3. *PJD*, VI, 117 ed.n., 118–19, 120 ed.n.; *New York Times*, June 18, 1857.

4. *PJD*, VI, 120–25, 129n.

5. *Ibid.*, xlvii–xlviii, 130n., 547–48; JD to Franklin Pierce, July 23, 1857, *ibid.*, 131–32; VD to her father, August 9, 1857, to JD, August 31, 1857, JD Papers, UA.

6. JD to VD, July 20, 1857, *PJD*, VI, 130, to VD, August 23, 1857, JD Papers, UA.

7. VD to JD, August 31, 1857, JD Papers, UA.

8. JD to Joseph Davis, August 30, 1857, *PJD*, VI, 136–37.

9. *Ibid.*, xlviii, 147–48 (Mississippi City), 548, 549; *New York Times*, October 12, 1857.

10. *PJD*, VI, 147–48.

11. *Ibid.*, xlviii, 157–62.

12. *Ibid.*, xlviii, 115n.; JD to Clement Clay, May 17, 1859, *ibid.*, 252.

13. *Ibid.*, 110n., 166n.; JD to [E. G. W. Butler], December 28, 1886, JD Papers, DU; see photograph, p. 303.

14. *Harper's Weekly*, January 9, 1858.

15. *JDC*, III, 134–69, 175–214; *PJD*, VI, 559–60.

16. The best general account of Kansas and Lecompton is David M. Potter, *The Impending Crisis, 1848–1861*, comp. and ed. Don E. Fehrenbacher (New York, 1976), chaps. 9, 12. Robert W. Johannsen, *Stephen A. Douglas* (New York, 1973), chap. 23, and Roy Franklin Nichols, *The Disruption of American Democracy* (New York, 1948), chaps. 7–10, are indispensable for Democratic and congressional details.

17. On *Dred Scott*, see Don E. Fehrenbacher's magisterial *The Dred Scott Case: Its Significance in American Law and Politics* (New York, 1978), especially parts 2–3.

18. *PJD*, VI, 149–52, 159–60 (second and third quotations), 550 (first quotation).

19. JD to William H. Sparks, February 19, 1858, *PJD*, VI, 170.

20. *JDC*, III, 228–31, 353–54.

21. *Ibid.*, 228–31 (quotation 230); *PJD*, VI, 228–29 (Buchanan quotation on 229); *Vicksburg Daily Whig*, May 26, June 1, 1858.

22. JD to Franklin Pierce, July 23, 1857, *PJD*, VI, 132.

23. JD to William H. Sparks, February 19, 1858, *ibid.*, 169–70; *Memoir*, I, 575.

24. *Memoir*, I, 575–76; Office Record Book, Dr. Robert Stone Papers, LC; JD to Franklin Pierce, April 4, 1858, *PJD*, VI, 172.

25. *Memoir*, I, 577–83; Virginia Clay-Clopton, *A Belle of the Fifties: Memories of Mrs. Clay of Alabama, Covering Social and Political Life in the South, 1853–1866* . . . (New York, 1905), 69. Unfortunately, I have uncovered no details about the

JD-Seward friendship, but during the war Seward alluded to it: see Memorandum on Dinner in 1863 by Henry Bellows in Henry Bellows Papers, MaHS (I am grateful to Charles Royster for this reference).

26. *Memoir*, I, 575–76.

27. JD to Franklin Pierce, April 4, 1858, to Joseph Davis, April 19, 1858, *PJD*, VI, 172, 176. For the illness, I have relied on Dr. Roderick Macdonald to WJC, January 29, 1997; Office Record Book, Stone Papers, LC; Harris D. Riley, Jr., "Jefferson Davis and His Health, Part I: June, 1808–December, 1860," *JMH*, XLIX (August 1987), 197–99, and other sources cited in my chapter eight, note 35.

28. JD to Joseph Davis, April 19, 1858, *PJD*, VI, 176; *ibid.*, 171n.

29. JD to Margaret K. Howell, March 28, 1859, to J. L. M. Curry, June 4, 1859, *ibid.*, 242, 254; Riley, "Jefferson Davis," 201.

30. JD to Theodore Woolfson, January 6, 1860, *PJD*, VI, 625; Dr. Macdonald to WJC, January 29, 1997; William Howard Russell, *My Diary North and South* (Boston, 1863), 173; Walter Lord, ed., *The Fremantle Diary: Being the Journal of Lieutenant Colonel James Arthur Lyon Fremantle, Coldstream Guards, on His Three Months in the Southern States* (Boston, 1954), 168; J. B. Jones, *A Rebel War Clerk's Diary* (2 vols.; Philadelphia, 1866), I, 172; James Roach Diary, March 22, 1859 (clouded quotation), Roach-Eggleston Papers, UNC; *Richmond Daily Whig*, June 3, 1861 (discolored quotation); see photographs, pp. 6, 303.

31. *Memoir*, I, 584; JD to Caleb Cushing, August 14, 1858, Caleb Cushing Papers, LC; VD to her mother, September 15, 1858, JD Papers, UA.

32. *Memoir*, I, chap. 42 *passim* (quotation 586); VD to her mother, September 15, 1858, JD Papers, UA; JD to Sidney Webster, August 14, 1858, *PJD*, VI, 203; *ibid.*, xlix–l; *A. M. C. Maine Mountain Guide: A Guide to Trails in the Mountains of Maine* (4th ed.; Boston, 1976), 104–05.

33. *Memoir*, I, 593–94, 641; *New York Times*, October 13, 1858; *PJD*, VI, 1.

34. JD to Sidney Webster, August 14, 1858, *PJD*, VI, 203; S. G. Dennis to JD, April 3, 1882, JD Papers, MC; *Memoir*, I, 588, 592.

35. *PJD*, VI, xlix–l; *JDC*, III, 279–81, 295 (quotation); John H. Pilsbury to Caleb Cushing, September 20, 1858, JD to Cushing, September 5, 1858, Sidney Webster to Cushing, October 7, 1858, F. W. Lincoln to Cushing, October 8, 1858, Cushing Papers, LC; JD to Sidney Webster, August 14, 1858, *PJD*, VI, 203.

36. The speeches: on the *Joseph Whitney*, July 4, *JDC*, III, 271–73; crowd at Portland, July 9, *ibid.*, 274–81; Maine Democratic convention at Portland, August 24, *ibid.*, 284–88; militia encampment and banquet at Belfast, September 2, *ibid.*, 288–95; Democratic rally at Portland, September 11, *PJD*, VI, 214–23; state fair at Augusta, September 23, *JDC*, III, 305–15; Faneuil Hall in Boston, October 11, 1858, *ibid.*, 315–32; New York City, October 19, 1858, *ibid.*, 332–39. I only cite the page numbers for quotations, which are in order from *ibid.*, 273, 294, 338, 327. These addresses are also printed in *Speeches of the Hon. Jefferson Davis of Mississippi, Delivered During the Summer of 1858* . . . (Baltimore, 1859).

37. *JDC*, III, 276.

38. *Ibid.*, 306, 326.

39. *Ibid.*, 332; *PJD*, VI, 220.

40. *JDC*, III, 320.

41. *JDC*, III, 287, 285, 329.

42. *PJD*, VI, 224n.; *New York Times*, October 6, 15, 20, 1858; Caroline E. Vose,

"Jefferson Davis in New England," *Virginia Quarterly Review*, II (October 1926), 557–68, cites many newspapers.

43. *PJD*, VI, 223; JD to Pierce, January 17, 1859, *JDC*, III, 498.

44. *Jackson Mississippian*, August 11, 1858; William H. Branch to R. B. Rhett, August 26, 1858, Robert Barnwell Rhett Papers, DU (first quotation); *PJD*, VI, 207 (second quotation).

45. James Roach Diary, July 26, 29, 30, August 12, 15, 17, Roach-Eggleston Papers, UNC; JD to James Roach, August 3, 1858, *Jackson Mississippian*, August 18, 1858 (calendared *PJD*, VI, 582); JD to Arthur C. Halbert, August 22, 1858, *ibid.*, 204.

46. On Brown's activities, see James Byrne Ranck, *Albert Gallatin Brown: Radical Southern Nationalist* (New York, 1937), 160–64 (quotation 163).

47. *Jackson Mississippian*, July 28 (second quotation), August 11 (first quotation), September 8, October 13, 1858; *Vicksburg Daily Whig*, July 30 (third and fourth quotations), August 7 (fifth quotation), September 14 (sixth quotation), October 12, 1858.

48. *PJD*, VI, 1, 227 ed.n.

49. *JDC*, III, 339–60 (quotations 343, 347, 349, 356, 358).

50. *PJD*, VI, 1, 228.

51. Mississippi Citizens (thirty-two signatures) to JD, October 1, 1858, Collin Tarpley to JD, December 1, 1858, *PJD*, VI, 586–87; JD to Mississippi Citizens, December 18, 1858, JD to J. L. M. Curry, June 4, 1859, *ibid.*, 229–30, 253. The Brown volume was published in New York in 1859: M. W. Cluskey, ed., *The Speeches, Messages, and Other Writings of the Hon. Albert G. Brown, A Senator from the State of Mississippi.*

52. *Speeches of Jefferson Davis;* VD to JD, April 10, 17, 1859, *PJD*, VI, 244, 609; JD to J. L. M. Curry, June 4, 1859, *ibid.*, 253.

53. VD to JD, April 10, 17, 1859, *PJD*, VI, 244, 609; *Memoir*, I, chap. 42 *passim;* JD to Franklin Pierce, January 17, 1859, *JDC*, III, 498.

54. VD to JD, April 17, 1859 (first quotation), *PJD*, VI, 244, July 2, 1859, JD Papers, UA.

55. JD to William B. Howell, April 24, 1859, to Clement Clay, May 17, 1859, to William Emory, June 15, 1859, *PJD*, VI, 247, 251, 256.

56. VD to her mother, November 21, 1858, March 1, 1859 (first quotation), JD Papers, UA; VD to JD, April 10, July 2, 1859, *ibid.*, 105–06 (quotation on loving Daddy); VD to JD, April 17, 1859, *PJD*, VI, 243–44 (other quotations).

57. JD to Pierce, January 17 (quotation), September 2, 1859, *JDC*, III, 498, and IV, 93; JD to Margaret Howell, March 28, 1859, *PJD*, VI, 241; Mrs. D. Giraud Wright, *A Southern Girl in '61: The War-Time Memories of a Confederate Senator's Daughter* (New York, 1905), 29; *Memoir*, I, 592.

58. *PJD*, VII, 30–34.

59. VD to her mother, April 25 (first and second quotations), May n.d. (third quotation), 1859, JD Papers, UA.

60. *Bowmar*, 366–67.

61. *Ibid.*, 359–61.

62. *JDC*, IV, 85–86 (quotation), 250–82 *passim; PJD*, VI, 278–84.

63. *JDC*, IV, 253–54; *PJD*, VI, 280–81.

64. On John Brown, see Potter, *Impending Crisis*, chap. 14; *JDC*, IV, 99, 107 (quotations), 157–66; *PJD*, VI, 619–21.

65. *PJD*, VI, 228 (first quotation); *JDC*, IV, 88 (final quotation), 279–80 (next-to-last quotation).

66. *Jackson Mississippian*, June 10, 14, July 8, 1859; Ranck, *Brown*, 168–90, details Brown's activities.

67. *JDC*, IV, 86–87 (first quotation); *PJD*, VI, 154 (final quotation), 228 (second quotation), 618 (third quotation); JD to Commissioners of Gulf and Ship Island Railroad, August 28, 1858, *ibid.*, 209–12. JD's caveats appear in all his speeches.

68. *JDC*, III, 173 (first quotation), IV, 158 (second quotation).

69. Ranck, *Brown*, 168–73; Joseph R. Davis to JD, June 6, 1859, *JDC*, IV, 54–55; JD to Clement Clay, May 17, 1859, *PJD*, VI, 251.

70. *PJD*, VI, 228; *JDC*, III, 130–33, 313, IV, 48, 69–71, 521–29; *Jackson Mississippian*, August 24, 1859.

71. On the internecine struggle within the Democratic party, the Johannsen, Nichols, and Potter books cited above are essential. My account largely follows them.

72. *JDC*, III, 569–88 (first quotation 583); IV, 121–39 (second and third quotations 136, final one 139); JD to William Walthall, February 21, 1880, William Walthall Papers, MDAH.

73. JD to William Lamb, September 14, 1860, *PJD*, VI, 363; *ibid.*, 275–76n.; *JDC*, IV, 348–61. The initial resolutions are in *PJD*, VI, 273–75, and the revised version in *JDC*, IV, 203–04.

74. Robert Toombs to Alexander H. Stephens, February 10, 1860, Ulrich Bonnell Phillips, ed., *The Correspondence of Robert Toombs, Alexander H. Stephens, and Howell Cobb* (Washington, D.C., 1913), 461; Andrew Johnson to George W. Jones, March 13, 1860, *PAJ*, III, 466. Potter, *Impending Crisis*, 403–04, and, much more recently, Michael A. Morrison, *Slavery and the American West: The Eclipse of Manifest Destiny and the Coming of the Civil War* (Chapel Hill, N.C., 1997), 211–12, present the consensual interpretation, but cf. the insightful article by Paul D. Escott, "Jefferson Davis and Slavery in the Territories," *JMH*, XXXIX (May 1977), 97–116.

75. *PJD*, VI, 218; *Vicksburg Daily Whig*, October 19, 1858; *JDC*, III, 569–88, IV, 110–15.

76. JD to J. L. M. Curry, June 4, 1859, *PJD*, VI, 253–54, and citations in note 75 above.

77. *JDC*, IV, 74–78; *Vicksburg Weekly Whig*, March 7, 1860; JD to William Lamb, September 14, 1860, *PJD*, VI, 363.

78. George C. Hazelton, *The National Capitol: Its Architecture, Art and History* (New York, 1903), 59, 176–77; *PJD*, VI, has a seating chart following 72.

79. *PJD*, VI, 235–36, 598; *JDC*, III, 363–76, IV, 1–30, 382–443.

80. *Vicksburg Daily Whig*, January 20, 1858; M. D. Haynes to JD, March 31, 1860, *JDC*, IV, 229; *PJD*, VI, 589–665 *passim* (specific examples 577 and 628); JD Papers, TU, has the ledger.

81. Brown Manuscript Memoirs, J. F. H. Claiborne Papers, UNC; Andrew Butler *et al.* to JD and Toombs, March 12, 1857, JD to Butler *et al.*, March 12, 1857, along with William Winder to JD, March 30, 1857, *PJD*, VI, 542.

82. *PJD*, VI, 188–95 (initial four quotations 191), 196n. (fifth quotation), 197–99n. (final five quotations); Clement C. Clay to "My Dear Wife," June 9, 1858, C. C. Clay Papers, DU; Eli N. Evans, *Judah P. Benjamin: The Jewish Confederate* (New York, 1988), 99 (sixth quotation).

83. JD to Thomas Lawson, February 1, 1859, *PJD*, VI, 600; JD to Franklin Pierce, September 2, 1859, *JDC*, IV, 93; JD to Messrs. Robinson *et al.*, September 12, 1859, *Jackson Mississippian*, October 5, 1859; Sir Henry Holland, *Recollection of a Past Life* (New York, 1872), 191; Riley, "Jefferson Davis," 261–64.

84. William B. Hesseltine, ed., *Three Against Lincoln: Murat Halstead Reports the Caucuses of 1860* (Baton Rouge, La., 1960), 121.

85. Brady photograph, p. 6; McMlees photograph, p. 303; *Memoir*, I, 198.

86. For a splendid general treatment of the election of 1860, see Potter, *Impending Crisis*, chap. 16; Nichols, *Disruption*, chaps. 15–16, remains essential for the Democrats.

87. JD to Edwin DeLeon, January 21, 1860, *PJD*, VI, 271 (first, second quotations); JD to Sidney Webster, January 9, 1860, Sidney Webster Papers, LC (third quotation, calendared *PJD*, VI, 626); JD to Pierce, September 2, 1859, January 30, 1860, *JDC*, IV, 93, 185; J. L. Foster to Stephen A. Douglas, October 17, 1859, Stephen A. Douglas Papers, Department of Special Collections, Henry Regenstein Library, University of Chicago.

88. Joseph R. Davis to JD, December 13, 1859, *PJD*, VI, 264, 265n.; *Boston Courier*, n.d., from *Jackson Mississippian*, April 18, 1860 (first quotation); Pierce to JD, January 6, 1860, *JDC*, IV, 118 (second quotation); Benjamin F. Butler to Orville Jones, n.d. [most likely 1868], Benjamin F. Butler Papers, LC; Charles Mason to Robert M. T. Hunter, April 30, 1860, Charles Henry Ambler, ed., *Correspondence of Robert M. T. Hunter, 1826–1876* (Washington, D.C., 1918), 322; W. L. Yancey to C. C. Clay, May 4, [1860], JD to C. C. Clay, November 12, 1875, Clay Papers, DU; Andrew Johnson to George W. Jones, March 13, 1860, *PAJ*, III, 466–67 (third quotation); JD to Sidney Webster, January 9, 1860, Webster Papers, LC (fourth quotation, calendared *PJD*, VI, 626); C. C. Clay to JD, October 30, 1875, JD Papers, MC.

89. JD to Cushing, April 15, 1860, J. D. Andrews to Cushing, April 29, 1860, Cushing Papers, LC; L. Q. C. Lamar to C. H. Mott, May 9, 1860, Edward Mayes, *Lucius Q. C. Lamar: His Life, Times, and Speeches, 1823–1893* (2d ed.; Nashville, Tenn., 1896), 83.

90. JD to Cushing, [May 10, 1860], Cushing Papers, LC; JD *et al.* to the National Democracy, May [7], 1860, *PJD*, VI, 289–93 (first quotation 293); JD to Pierce, June 13, 1860, *JDC*, IV, 296 (second and third quotations).

91. *PJD*, VI, 356–57 (first quotation 356), 358–60 (second and third quotations 358), 664; *R&F*, I, 52–53; *Memoir*, I, 685 (fourth quotation); JD to C. C. Clay, November 12, 1875, Clay Papers, DU; William C. Davis, *Breckinridge: Statesman, Soldier, Symbol* (Baton Rouge, La., 1974), 224–27.

92. JD to J. L. M. Curry, June 4, 1859, *PJD*, VI, 254.

93. *Ibid.*, liv, lv, 667–68; *JDC*, IV, 540–41; *Jackson Mississippian*, October 17, 1860. Percy Lee Rainwater, *Mississippi: Storm Center of Secession, 1856–61* (Baton Rouge, La., 1938), chap. 7, remains the most detailed study (quotation 136).

94. *PJD*, VI, 366 (quotations); *JDC*, IV, 540–41.

95. *PJD*, VI, 364–65; *Jackson Mississippian*, October 31, 1860.

96. *Vicksburg Weekly Whig*, November 14, 1860.

97. Potter, *Impending Crisis*, chap. 18, has the best general discussion of secession. On Mississippi, see Rainwater, *Storm Center*, chaps. 8–11, which still has enormous value, and William L. Barney, *The Secessionist Impulse: Alabama and Mississippi in 1860* (Princeton, 1974), chaps. 5–7.

98. JD to Rhett, November 10, 1860, *PJD*, VI, 368–70.

99. William Walthall Diary, March 3, 1877, Walthall Papers, MDAH; O. R. Singleton to JD, July 14, 1877, *JDC*, VII, 560–62; JD to C. C. Clay, November 12, 1875, Clay Papers, DU; Reuben Davis, *Recollections of Mississippi and Mississippians* (Boston and New York, 1891), 390–91.

100. *New York Herald*, December 11, 1860. On congressional matters, see Potter, *Impending Crisis*, chap. 19, and Potter, *Lincoln and His Party in the Secession Crisis* ([1942]; Baton Rouge, La., 1995), which is best on the Republicans, and Nichols, *Disruption*, which is superior on the Democrats. On the most important Republican, consult David Herbert Donald's superb *Lincoln* (New York, 1995).

101. *Harper's Weekly*, February 2, 1861; Samuel S. Cox, *Union–Disunion–Reunion: Three Decades of Federal Legislation . . .* (Providence, R.I., 1888), 68–69; Bellows Memorandum, Bellows Papers, MaHS; Samuel F. Butterworth to S. L. M. Barlow, December 26, 1860, S. L. M. Barlow Papers, HL; "When the States Seceded, from the Diary of Mrs. Eugene McLean," *Harper's Monthly Magazine*, CXXVIII (January 1914), 283.

102. Samuel F. Butterworth to S. L. M. Barlow, November 29, 1860, Barlow Papers, HL (quotation); *Memoir*, I, 580–83.

103. Samuel F. Butterworth to S. L. M. Barlow, December 2, 1860, Barlow Papers, HL; Davis, *Recollections*, 396; *PJD*, VI, 377.

104. Powhatan Ellis to Charles Ellis, Jr., November 29, 1860, Munford-Ellis Papers, DU; L. Q. C. Lamar to JD, December 24, 1860, *PJD*, VI, 673.

105. *JDC*, IV, 543–52; "Autobiography," *PJD*, I, lxi (quotation); *New York Herald*, December 4, 1860; *Vicksburg Weekly Whig*, December 19, 1860; Israel Washburne, Jr., to William H. Seward, December 18, 1860, William H. Seward Papers, Rhees Library, University of Rochester.

106. JD to F. H. Alfriend, August 17, 1867 (copy), Anne and Peter Holland (1995); JD to C. C. Clay, November 12, 1875, Clay Papers, DU, to William Walthall, November 21, 1875, Walthall Papers, MDAH; *New York Herald*, December 23, 1860; JD to John J. Pettus, December 26, 1860, *JDC*, IV, 560; JD interview in *Baltimore Sunday Herald*, July 10, 1887; William M. Browne to S. L. M. Barlow, December 30, 1860, Barlow Papers, HL; Cox, *Three Decades*, 77; Seward to Lincoln, December 26, 1860, Frederick W. Seward, *William H. Seward: An Autobiography from 1801 to 1834; Memoir of His Life, and Selections from His Letters* (3 vols.; New York, 1891), II, 485. The record of the committee is in *Senate Report 288*, 36:2 (serial 1090), though there are no speeches.

107. JD to F. H. Alfriend, August 17, 1867 (copy), Hollands; Benjamin to S. L. M. Barlow, December 23, 1860, Barlow Papers, HL.

108. *JDC*, V, 6 (first quotation); JD to Edwin DeLeon, January 8, 1861, *PJD*, VII, 6–7 (remaining quotations).

109. W. H. Trescot and L. M. Keitt to JD, January 9, 1861, James Buchanan Papers, HSP (calendared in *PJD*, VII, 8); F. W. Pickens to JD, January 9, 1861 (copy), Executive Council Journal Letterbook, 1861, SCA (calendared, *PJD*, VII, 8); JD *et al.* to Isaac W. Hayne, January 15, 1861 (quotation), *ibid.*, 10–12; JD to Francis W. Pickens, January 20, 1861, *JDC*, V, 39–40.

110. Elizabeth Keckley, *Behind the Scenes: Thirty Years a Slave and Four Years in the White House* ([1868]; New York, 1968), 66–67; the letters from JD to Clay and Walthall cited in note 106 above; *O.R.*, ser. 1, I, 442–44, ser. 4, I, 28–29.

111. JD to Pettus, January 4, 1861, to F. W. Pickens, January 13, 1861, *JDC*, IV, 564–65, V, 36–37; JD to F. H. Alfriend, August 17, 1867 (copy), Hollands.

112. *PJD*, VI, 622–23; JD to Eli Whitney, November 30, 1860, to John Pettus, December 26, 31, 1860, *ibid.*, 374, 559–61; W. A. Thornton to JD, January 2, 1861, *ibid.*, VII, 5; JD to John Pettus, January 4, 9, 1861, *JDC*, IV, 564–65, 570 (quotation); *PJD*, VII, 27, for the commission.

113. Elizabeth Blair Lee to S. P. Lee, December [5], 1860, Virginia Jeans Laas, ed., *Wartime Washington: The Civil War Letters of Elizabeth Blair Lee* (Urbana, Ill., 1991), 14; VD to JD, November 15, 1860, *PJD*, VI, 371–72.

114. Elizabeth Blair Lee to S. P. Lee, December [5], 1860, January 10, 1861, Laas, ed., *Wartime*, 14, 20; Keckley, *Behind the Scenes*, 69–71 (first quotation 69); VD to Buchanan, December 25, 1860, Buchanan to VD, January 20, 1861, Buchanan Papers, HSP; VD to unknown, January 1, 1861 (second quotation), in Mrs. Jefferson Davis Letters, IA.

115. JD to F. H. Alfriend, August 17, 1867 (copy), Hollands; Keckley, *Behind the Scenes*, 68 (second quotation); *Memoir*, I, 696; JD to F. W. Pickens, January 13, 1861, *JDC*, V, 36–37.

116. *JDC*, V, 1–35.

117. JD to C. C. Clay, January 19, 1861, to Anna Ella Carroll, March 1, 1861, *PJD*, VII, 16, 64–65; *ibid.*, xxxix, 27; JD to Francis Pickens, January 13, 1861, *JDC*, V, 36–37; see Prologue above.

CHAPTER ELEVEN: *"Our Cause Is Just and Holy"*

1. *PJD*, VII, xxxix, 27 ed.n.; "A Journey with Jefferson Davis," *CV*, XI (March 1903), 115–16.

2. JD to John F. Callan, February 7, 1861, *PJD*, VII, 34–35.

3. JD to Alexander M. Clayton, January 30, 1861, *ibid.*, 27–28. The states represented in Montgomery were South Carolina, Georgia, Florida, Alabama, Mississippi, and Louisiana. Delegates from Texas, which seceded on February 1, did not reach Montgomery until later in the month.

4. For Montgomery, I have relied heavily on the excellent, detailed account by William C. Davis, *"A Government of Our Own": The Making of the Confederacy* (New York, 1994). Also on the Confederate Constitution, consult George C. Rable, *The Confederate Republic: A Revolution Against Politics* (Chapel Hill, N.C., 1994), chap. 3 (quotation 59).

5. Thomas R. R. Cobb to Marion, February 11, 1861, Thomas R. R. Cobb Papers, UGA (all Thomas Cobb citations are from this collection); Howell Cobb to His Wife, February 6, 1861, Ulrich Bonnell Phillips, ed., *The Correspondence of Robert Toombs, Alexander H. Stephens, and Howell Cobb* (Washington, D.C., 1913), 537.

6. *New York Times*, January 22, 1861; *New York Tribune*, January 28, 1861; *New York Herald*, January 30, February 4, 1861; Thomas R. R. Cobb to Marion, February 3, 1861; J. D. B. DeBow to William P. Miles, February 5, 1861, William Henry Trescot to Miles, February 6, 1861, William P. Miles Papers, UNC; Robert Barnwell to James L. Orr, February 9, 1861, Orr-Patterson Papers, *ibid.*; Chesnut, 6.

7. Thomas R. R. Cobb to Marion, February 6, 1861; Howell Cobb to His Wife, February 6, 1861, Phillips, ed., *Correspondence*, 537; Davis, *"Government,"* 92–93, chap. 5.

8. J. H. Campbell to William Walthall, July 16, 1879, W. P. Harris to Walthall, July 17, 1879, J. L. M. Curry to Walthall, July 28, 1879, Duncan Kenner to Walthall, July 28, 1879, James Chesnut to Walthall, January 24, 1880, W. P. Miles to Walthall, January 27, 1880, William Walthall Papers, MDAH; Alexander M. Clayton to Editor, June 17, 1870, *Memphis Daily Appeal,* June 21, 1870; "Robert Barnwell Rhett Autobiography," 25–27, Robert Barnwell Rhett Papers, SCHS; John H. Reagan, *Memoirs with Special Reference to Secession and the Civil War* (New York and Washington, D.C., 1906), 122–23; Thomas R. R. Cobb to Marion, February 11, 1861; *JDC,* VIII, 461–63. In *"Government,"* chap. 5, William Davis strives to make the election suspenseful, but I do not find his speculations persuasive.

9. *Memoir,* II, 18–19 (quotations); VD to James Buchanan, March 18, 1861, James Buchanan Papers, HSP; "Autobiography," *PJD,* I, lxii; George T. Denison, *Soldiering in Canada: Recollections and Experiences by Lt. Col. George T. Denison* (Toronto, 1890), 70–71.

10. *Vicksburg Weekly Whig,* February 13, 1861; *New York Herald,* February 18, 1861 (quotation); *PJD,* VII, 43 ed.n.; *JDC,* V, 47.

11. *New York Herald,* February 18, 23 (first quotation), 1861; *JDC,* V, 47–48 (second quotation).

12. *JDC,* V, 48–49.

13. Davis, *"Government,"* 152; *R&F,* I, 231.

14. *PJD,* VII, 45–46 ed.n.; *New York Herald,* February 19, 1861; Howell Cobb to His Wife, February 20, 1861, Phillips, ed., *Correspondence,* 544; Thomas R. R. Cobb to Marion, February 18, 1861; Davis *"Government,"* 160; Rod Gragg, ed., *The Illustrated Confederate Reader* (New York, 1989), 59–60 (quotation).

15. *PJD,* VII, 46–50.

16. *New York Herald,* February 19, 1861; *New Orleans Daily Picayune,* February 23, 1861 (quotations).

17. JD to VD, February 20, 1861, *PJD,* VII, 54; "Autobiography," *ibid.,* I, lxii; Virginia Clay-Clopton, *A Belle of the Fifties: Memories of Mrs. Clay of Alabama, Covering Social and Political Life in Washington and the South, 1853–1866 . . .* (New York, 1905), 157; Reagan, *Memoirs,* 109–10; S. R. Mallory to Master S. R. Mallory, September 27, 1865, Stephen R. Mallory Papers, UNC (all Mallory citations are from this collection); Robert Barnwell Rhett Journal, *Index Rerum,* Aiken-Rhett Papers, Charleston Museum. Davis, *"Government,"* chap. 8, has details.

18. T. C. DeLeon, *Four Years in Rebel Capitals: An Inside View of Life in the Southern Confederacy, from Birth to Death . . .* (Mobile, Ala., 1892), 39–40; William Howard Russell, *My Diary North and South* (Boston, 1863), 172; VD to C. C. Clay, May 10, 1861 (quotation), C. C. Clay Papers, DU; "Rhett Autobiography," 56, Rhett Papers, SCHS; Davis *"Government,"* 196.

19. *Chesnut,* 62 (first quotation); JD to Francis Pickens, February 22, 1861 (second quotation), to VD, February 20, 1861 (third quotation), *PJD,* VII, 58, 53; J. B. Jones, *A Rebel War Clerk's Diary* (2 vols.; Philadelphia, 1866), I, 36; for examples of correspondence, see Albert Lea to JD, February 28, 1861, Andrew J. Lindsay to JD, March 11, 1861, Mrs. E. J. Cromwell to JD, April 29, 1861, *PJD,* VII, 64, 67, 142.

20. Russell, *Diary,* 173–74.

21. *PJD,* VII, xl; JD to VD, February 14 (first quotation), 20 (second and third quotations), 1861, *ibid.,* 40–41, 53–54.

22. *Ibid.,* xl, 54n.; *Memoir,* II, 37.

23. Russell, *Diary*, 177; Chesnut, 62 (second quotation); *Charleston Mercury*, March 11, 1861 (third quotation); "A Northern Woman in the Confederacy, from the Diary of Mrs. Euguene McLean," *Harper's Monthly Magazine*, CXXVIII (February 1914), 442; VD to C. C. Clay, May 10, 1861, Clay Papers, DU.

24. *Chesnut*, 60–61; VD to James Buchanan, March 18, 1861, Buchanan Papers, HSP; VD to C. C. Clay, May 10, 1861, Clay Papers, DU; Judah P. Benjamin to S. L. M. Barlow, April 3, 1861, S. L. M. Barlow Papers, HL.

25. "Autobiography of Wiley P. Harris," Dunbar Rowland, *Courts, Judges, and Lawyers of Mississippi, 1798–1835* (Jackson, Miss., 1935), 327; JD to Alexander M. Clayton, January 30, 1861, *PJD*, VII, 28; Reagan, *Memoirs*, 116–17; Louis T. Wigfall to JD, February 25, 1861, *PJD*, VII, 60–61; Raphael Semmes to Alexander Stephens, February 27, 1861, Alexander H. Stephens Papers, LC; Davis, *"Government,"* chap. 9 *passim*.

26. Benjamin to JD, March 14, 1861, *PJD*, VII, 68; Davis, *"Government,"* chap. 8 *passim*.

27. Louis T. Wigfall to JD, February 18, 1861, *PJD*, VII, 51. For more detail, see David M. Potter, *The Impending Crisis, 1848–1861*, comp. and ed. Don E. Fehrenbacher (New York, 1976), chap. 20, and Ludwell Johnson, "Fort Sumter and Confederate Diplomacy," *JSH*, XXVI (1960), 441–77. On Lincoln and the Republicans, Potter, *Lincoln and His Party in the Secession Crisis* ([1942]; Baton Rouge, La., 1995), remains indispensable.

28. JD to Pickens, January 20, March 1, 18, 1861, *JDC*, V, 40, 58–59, 60–61, and on February 20, 22 (first quotation), *PJD*, VII, 55, 57–58; W. P. Miles to Pickens, February 9, 1861, Executive Council Journal, Letterbook 1861, SCA; I. W. Hayne to W. P. Miles, February 19, 1861, Miles Papers, UNC; Pickens to JD, February 27, 1861, *JDC*, V, 58; Beauregard to Major J. G. Bernard, March 18, 1861 (second quotation), Letterbook, P. G. T. Beauregard Papers, LC.

29. William M. Browne to S. L. M. Barlow, March 18, 1861, Judah P. Benjamin to Barlow, April 3, 1861, Barlow Papers, HL; James M. Mason to JD, February 12, March 25, 1861, Louis T. Wigfall to JD, February 16, 1861, *PJD*, VII, 39, 81, 43; William Henry Trescot to W. P. Miles, February 17, 1861, Miles Papers, UNC; M. J. Crawford to Stephens, March 16, 1861, Stephens Papers, LC; Campbell to JD, April 3, 1861, *PJD*, VII, 88–89.

30. Lincoln quotation in Potter, *Impending Crisis*, 579.

31. Robert Toombs to Alexander Stephens, April 6, 1861 (first quotation), Alexander H. Stephens Papers, EU; JD to John A. Campbell, April 6, 1861 (intervening quotations), *PJD*, VII, 92–93; *New York Citizen*, May 4, 1867 (final quotation). On Fort Pickens, see Grady McWhiney, "The Confederacy's First Shot," *CWH*, XIV (1968), 5–14.

32. JD to Braxton Bragg, April 3, 1861, *PJD*, VII, 85.

33. *O.R.*, ser. 1, I, 297, 300–01 (all citations in chapters eleven through fifteen are to ser. 1, unless otherwise noted).

34. JD to John A. Campbell, April 6, 1861, *PJD*, VII, 92.

35. Benjamin to S. L. M. Barlow, April 16, 1861, Barlow Papers, HL. Davis, *"Govern-ment,"* chaps. 13–14, has details on JD's activities in Montgomery.

36. *M&P*, I, 63–82 (quotations on 63, 73, 81, 82).

37. *PJD*, VII, xl; Davis, *"Government,"* 323, 327, 373–74; DeLeon, *Four Years*, 69–70 (the review).

38. *PJD*, VII, xl, xli, 183 ed.n.; *Richmond Enquirer*, May 31, 1861 (quotations).

39. Ernest B. Furgurson, *Ashes of Glory: Richmond at War* (New York, 1996); Michael B. Chesson, "Richmond," in Richard N. Current *et al.*, eds., *Encyclopedia of the Confederacy* (4 vols.; New York, 1993), III, 1329–33; Charles Dickens, *American Notes* ([1842]; Gloucester, Mass., 1968), 159 (quotation).

40. *Richmond Examiner*, May 30 (first two quotations), 31 (last two quotations), 1861; *Richmond Enquirer*, May 31, 1861.

41. *Richmond Examiner*, June 3, 1861.

42. *PJD*, VII, 184–85.

43. Lee to JD, May 7, 1861, JD to Lee, May 11, 28, 1861, *ibid.*, 155, 163, 179; T. Harry Williams, *P. G. T. Beauregard: Napoleon in Gray* (Baton Rouge, La., 1955), 65–67; Craig L. Symonds, *Joseph E. Johnston: A Civil War Biography* (New York, 1992), 98.

44. On the governors, see Davis, "*Government*," chap. 14 *passim; PJD*, VII, 162–242 *passim* has numerous letters from mid-May to mid-July.

45. Brown to Alexander Stephens, February 16, 1861, Stephens Papers, EU; Howell Cobb to His Wife, May 18, 1861, quoted in Davis, "*Government*," 357. For Brown, see Joseph H. Parks, *Joseph E. Brown of Georgia* (Baton Rouge, La., 1977).

46. On the early war in Virginia, consult Symonds, *Johnston*, chaps. 8–9, and Joseph L. Harsh, *Confederate Tide Rising: Robert E. Lee and the Making of Southern Strategy, 1861–1862* (Kent, Ohio, 1998), chap. 1; Lee to Johnston, June 7, 1861 (JO200), Joseph E. Johnston Papers, HL.

47. *Chesnut*, 102; VD to Her Mother, June n.d., 1861, JD Papers, UA; *M&P*, I, 117–24.

48. *Richmond Examiner*, June 3, 11, 1861; *Richmond Enquirer*, June 19, 1861; *Chesnut*, 123 (quotation).

49. On First Manassas, consult Symonds, *Johnston*, chap. 12, and William C. Davis, *Battle at Bull Run: A History of the First Major Campaign of the Civil War* (Garden City, N.Y., 1977). On JD, see *PJD*, VII, 258 ed.n., and JD to Beauregard, July 18, 21, 1861, *ibid.*, 251, 258.

50. *PJD*, VII, 259.

51. *Richmond Examiner*, July 24, 1861 (first three quotations); *PJD*, VII, 261–63 (remaining quotations).

52. *Chesnut*, 83.

53. A good discussion is in James M. McPherson, *Battle Cry of Freedom: The Civil War Era* (New York, 1988), 318–19, 321–22.

54. *Ibid.*, 437–42, has an excellent brief synopsis of the financial situation; Reagan, *Memoirs*, 115–16. Thorough and at times provocative, albeit polemical, is Douglas B. Ball, *Financial Failure and Confederate Defeat* (Urbana, Ill., 1991).

55. JD to Isham G. Harris, July 17, 1861 (first quotation), to J. E. Johnston, [May 29, 1862], *PJD*, VII, 246, and VIII, 201, to P. G. T. Beauregard, October 20, 1861, to Edmund Kirby Smith, November 19, 1863 (sixth quotation), *JDC*, V, 147, VI, 85–87; JD to Jubal Early, April 7, 1878 (second, third, and fourth quotations), JD Papers, DU; JD to William P. Johnston, November 18, 1877 (fifth and final quotations), Arthur Marvin Shaw, ed., "Some Post-War Observations of Jefferson Davis Concerning Early Aspects of the Civil War," *JSH*, X (1944), 211. For insightful discussions of Confederate nationalism, see Drew Gilpin Faust, *The Creation of Confederate Nationalism* (Baton Rouge, La., 1988), and Gary W. Gallagher, *The Con-*

federate War: How Popular Will, Nationalism, and Military Strategy Could Not Stave Off Defeat (Cambridge, Mass., 1997), chap. 2, which emphasizes the critical role of the army.

56. JD to Joseph Davis, June 18, 1861, to John Forsyth, July 18, 1862, *PJD*, VII, 203, VIII, 293. Rable, *Confederate Republic*, 81, discusses the pressure to attack the North.

57. JD to L. Polk, September 2, 1861, to William M. Brooks, March 15, 1862 (first quotation), to John Forsyth, July 18, 1862 (second quotation), *PJD*, VII, 318, and VIII, 100, 294.

58. JD to A. S. Johnston, March 12, 1862, *ibid.*, VIII, 93. In assessing JD's basic strategic outlook, most historians have utilized some form of the "offensive-defensive" characterization vigorously presented by Frank Vandiver's "Jefferson Davis and Confederate Strategy," in Avery O. Craven and Frank E. Vandiver, *The American Tragedy: The Civil War in Retrospect* (Hampden-Sydney, Va., 1959), 19–32. In these discussions, defensive usually outweighs offensive, but cf. Harsh, *Confederate Tide.*

59. S. R. Mallory to Master S. R. Mallory, December 8, 1865; Pvt. E. C. Harvey to JD, June 20, 1861, RG109, m437, r4, f219, and J. Robert Briggs to JD, *ibid.*, r6, f236, NA.

60. S. R. Mallory Diary, September 4, 16, 1861; JD to Walker, September 9, 1861, Walker to JD, September 10, 1861 (two letters), August 13, 1864, *PJD*, VII, 333–34, 336, X, 610; *ibid.*, VII, 72n.

61. *PJD*, VII, 344.

62. On the Cuban matter, see *ibid.*, IV, 59n., and Emory M. Thomas, *Robert E. Lee: A Biography* (New York, 1995), 148.

63. Jacob Thompson to JD, September 6, 1861, Neill Brown to JD, September 22, 1861, *PJD*, VII, 329–30, 347.

64. JD to L. Polk, May 22, 1861, *ibid.*, 174.

65. Polk to JD, May 14, 1861, *ibid.*, 167. The standard biography of Polk is Joseph H. Parks, *General Leonidas Polk, C.S.A.: The Fighting Bishop* (Baton Rouge, La., 1962).

66. JD to Polk, May 22, 1861, *PJD*, VII, 174; Steven E. Woodworth, *Jefferson Davis and His Generals: The Failure of Confederate Command in the West* (Lawrence, Kans., 1990), 32.

67. Woodworth, *Davis*, 36–39, has details.

68. Harris to JD, September 5, 1861, Polk to JD, September 4, 1861, *PJD*, VII, 325–26.

69. JD to Polk, September 6, 1861, *ibid.*, 327. Cf. Woodworth, *Davis*, 39–41.

70. Mallory Diary, September 1, 4, 1861; JD to Polk, September 2, 1861, *PJD*, VII, 318; *JDC*, VIII, 232 (quotation).

71. *JDC*, IX, 206–07; Woodworth, *Davis*, 46–51; W. P. Johnston to Rosa, August 24, 1862 (quotation), Johnston Papers, TU. On Johnston, see Charles P. Roland, *Albert Sidney Johnston: Soldier of Three Republics* (Austin, Tex., 1964).

72. Thomas Reynolds to JD, August 19, 1861, *PJD*, VII, 289–93; *ibid.*, 293–94n.

73. JD to VD, October 2, 1861 (quotation), *ibid.*, 352; *ibid.*, ed.n. and 353n.; Harsh, *Confederate Tide*, 28.

74. JD to William Preston Johnston, November 18, 1877, Shaw, ed., "Observations," 211.

75. *Richmond Enquirer,* June 13, 1861; Mallory Diary, September 1, 1861; see also Jones, *Diary,* I, 64; John L. Letcher to James D. Davidson, September 14, 1861, F. N. Boney, "Governor Letcher's Candid Correspondence," *CWH,* X (1964), 173; Herschel Johnson to Alexander Stephens, May 8, 1861, Herschel Johnson Papers, DU.

76. Brown to Stephens, August 22, 1861, Stephens Papers, EU; *Richmond Examiner,* September 16, 1861; Rable, *Confederate Republic,* 90.

77. Stephens to Herschel Johnson, August 15, 1861, Johnson Papers, DU. Superb and perceptive on Stephens is Thomas Schott, *Alexander H. Stephens of Georgia: A Biography* (Baton Rouge, La., 1988).

78. *Chesnut,* 142; Davis, *"Government,"* 273, 367 (quotations); "Rhett Autobiography" *passim,* Rhett Papers, SCHS; *Charleston Mercury,* March–December 1861 *passim.*

79. Thomas W. Thomas to Stephens, October 10, 1861, Phillips, ed., *Correspondence,* 580–81.

80. Davis, *"Government,"* 352; correspondence between Foote and JD on April 24, 27, 29, 1861, *PJD,* VII, 121, 133, 142; JD to Thomas A. R. Nelson, August 13, 1861, *ibid.,* 282.

81. Harris to JD, July 13, 1861, Isham Harris Papers, TSLA (calendared *PJD,* VII, 241), and JD to Harris, July 17, 1861, *ibid.,* 245–48.

82. *O.R.,* ser. 4, I, 127–31; *PJD,* VII, 314; *Memoir,* II, 156–58.

83. Johnston to JD, September 12, 1861, *O.R.,* ser. 4, I, 605–08 (calendared *PJD,* VII, 336); Symonds, *Johnston,* 128; JD to Johnston, September 14, 1861, *PJD,* VII, 340 and 340n.; Mallory Diary, September 13, 16, 1861.

84. Williams, *Beauregard,* 96–107. For examples, see JD to Beauregard, August 4, October 20 (quotation), 25, 1861, *JDC,* V, 120–21, 146–48, 150–51, October 16, 1861, *PJD,* VII, 358–60.

85. *O.R.,* II, 484–504, has the report; Williams, *Beauregard,* 98, 105–06; *PJD,* VII, 383–84 ed.n., 384–85, 387–94, 407; JD to Beauregard, October 30, 1861, *JDC,* V, 156–57 (quotations); J. J. Seibels to His Wife, December 8, 1861, Seibels Family Papers, SCL.

86. *PJD,* VII, 266.

87. *Ibid.,* 417 (quotation), 454, and Mann to JD, January 18, 1862, *ibid.,* VIII, 20–22. Howard Jones, *Union in Peril: The Crisis over British Intervention in the Civil War* (Chapel Hill, N.C., 1992), is excellent, and chap. 4 has a good discussion of the *Trent* affair; also see Charles M. Hubbard, *The Burden of Confederate Diplomacy* (Knoxville, Tenn., 1998), chap. 5.

88. VD to Her Mother, June n.d. (received on 15th), 1861, JD Papers, UA.

89. *PJD,* VII, xlii; *Memoir,* II, 198 (quotation); for detail, see *White House of the Confederacy: An Illustrated History* (Richmond, Va., [1993]).

90. [Eliza Davis] to Mattie, August 10, 1861, Lise Mitchell Papers, TU; VD to Her Mother, June n.d. (received on 15th), 1861, JD Papers, UA; *Chesnut,* 83, 109, 159; Lise Mitchell Journal, July 1862, Mary E. Mitchell Papers, UNC; *PJD,* VII, xliii.

91. Elizabeth Blair Lee to Phil, June 14, 1861, Virginia Jeans Laas, ed., *Wartime Washington: The Civil War Letters of Elizabeth Blair Lee* (Urbana, Ill., 1991), 47 (first quotation); *Chesnut,* 80, 83, 85 (final quotation), 102, 109 (second quotation), 113, 159; Mallory Diary, June 12 (third quotation), 18, 1861.

92. Mallory Diary, June 23, 1861; *Chesnut,* 83, 102, 159 (quotation).

93. JD to Joseph Davis, June 18, 1861, *PJD*, VII, 203; *ibid.*, 205n.; Lise Mitchell Journal, July 1862, Mitchell Papers, UNC.

94. Payne to JD, October 24, 1861, Barnes to JD, December 16, 1861, *PJD*, VII, 379, 440.

95. [Eliza Davis] to Mattie, August 19, 1861 (first and fourth quotations), Mitchell Papers, TU; S. R. Mallory to Master S. R. Mallory, September 27, 1865 (second quotation); Thomas Bragg Diary, December 6, 1861 (third quotation), Thomas Bragg Papers, UNC; *Memoir*, II, 161 (fifth quotation).

96. *PJD*, VII, 412–19. On preparation of the messages, see chapter thirteen below.

CHAPTER TWELVE: *"The Noblest Cause in Which Man Can Be Engaged"*

1. *Richmond Examiner*, January 2, 1862 (all quotations but final one); Thomas Bragg Diary, January 1, 1862, Thomas Bragg Papers, UNC (all subsequent citations to Bragg Diary refer to this collection); B. Morrison to Dear Mary, January n.d., 1862 (final quotation), Miscellaneous Manuscripts, MC (I am grateful to Robert Krick for this reference).

2. *M&P*, I, 189.

3. *PJD*, VIII, 58 ed.n.; *Memoir*, II, 180–83; *Richmond Examiner*, February 24, 1862 (quotations); Mrs. Burton Harrison, *Recollections Grave and Gray* (New York, 1911), 69; Bragg Diary, February 22, 1862.

4. Reuben Davis, *Recollections of Mississippi and Mississippians* (Boston and New York, 1891), 430; Bragg Diary, February 22, 1862 (quotation about voice); *JDC*, V, 198–203.

5. *PJD*, VIII, 58 ed.n.; *Richmond Examiner*, February 24, 1862 (quotations); Harrison, *Recollections*, 69; J. B. Jones, *A Rebel War Clerk's Diary at the Confederate States Capital* (2 vols.; Philadelphia, 1866), I, 111.

6. Craig L. Symonds, *Joseph E. Johnston: A Civil War Biography* (New York, 1992), 145.

7. JD to Johnston, February 6, 1862 (copy), Joseph E. Johnston Papers, WM; Bragg Diary, February 19, 1862; *PJD*, VIII, 98n.; Symonds, *Johnston*, 145–46.

8. Johnston to JD, March 13, 1862, *PJD*, VIII, 96–97; JD to Johnston, March 15, 1862 (two messages), *JDC*, V, 222–23.

9. *Memoir*, II, 192–93; J. T. Doswell to W. S. Barton, August 10, 1885, J. L. Mayre to W. S. Barton, August 11, 1885, Statement of F. T. Forbes, August 15, 1885, R. W. Adams to W. S. Barton, August 12, 1885, W. S. Barton to JD, August 17, 1885, *JDC*, IX, 377–78, 381–82, 383–84; Jubal A. Early to JD, August 10, 1885 (quotation), JD Papers, UA.

10. On McClellan, consult Stephen W. Sears, *To the Gates of Richmond: The Peninsula Campaign* (New York, 1992).

11. Symonds, *Johnston*, 149; Joseph L. Harsh, *Confederate Tide Rising: Robert E. Lee and the Making of Southern Strategy, 1861–1862* (Kent, Ohio, 1998), 36, 192–93.

12. St. John Richardson Liddell, *Liddell's Record*, ed. Nathaniel C. Hughes (Dayton, Ohio, 1985), 39–44; for Johnston's dispositions, see Steven E. Woodworth, *Jefferson Davis and His Generals: The Failure of Confederate Command in the West* (Lawrence, Kans., 1990), chaps. 5–6, and Thomas L. Connelly, *Army of the Heartland: The Army of Tennessee, 1861–1862* (Baton Rouge, La., 1967), chaps. 3–5.

13. Woodworth, *Davis*, chap. 6, and Connelly, *Army*, chap. 6, cover the campaign for the forts, as does James M. McPherson, *Battle Cry of Freedom: The Civil War Era* (New York, 1988), 404–05, for Pea Ridge.

14. JD to Joseph Davis, February 21, 1862, *PJD*, VIII, 53; ibid., 57, 58, 64, 87–89; Bragg Diary, March 19, 1862; Connelly, *Army*, 138.

15. JD to Johnston, March 12, 1862, *PJD*, VIII, 92–94.

16. *Ibid.*, and JD to Johnston, March 26, April 5, 1862, ibid., 117, and *JDC*, V, 227; Robert E. Lee to Johnston, March 26, 1862, Johnston Papers, TU; *O.R.*, VI, 432, X, pt. 2, 407; Woodworth, *Davis*, 90; T. Harry Williams, *P. G. T. Beauregard: Napoleon in Gray* (Baton Rouge, La., 1955), 115.

17. Liddell, *Record*, 57–58; Johnston to JD, March 7, 25, 1862, *PJD*, VIII, 86, 116.

18. On Shiloh, see Woodworth, *Davis*, chap. 7, and Connelly, *Army*, chaps. 8–9.

19. JD to Earl Van Dorn, April 7, 1862, *PJD*, VIII, 135; *M&P*, I, 209–10 (first quotation); W. P. Johnston to Rosa, May 4, 1862 (second quotation), Johnston Papers, TU; JD to W. P. Johnston, April 14, 1877 (third quotation), *ibid.; R & F*, II, 67 (final quotation); Jefferson Davis Bradford to VD, April 22, 1862, JD Papers, MC; W. P. Johnston to [William Preston], May 22, 1862, Johnston Papers, TU; L. Q. C. Lamar to [presidential friend], April or May 1862, RG109, JD Letters, NA. For the debate over Shiloh, see Woodworth, *Davis*, 334n.

20. Bragg Diary, February 19, 1862; *O.R.*, V, 1099.

21. *M&P*, I, 215–16; Bragg Diary, March 14, 1862; J. L. Pugh (a Confederate senator) to Braxton Bragg, March [16], 1862, Braxton Bragg Papers, William P. Palmer Collection, WRHS.

22. Johnston to (?), April 26, 1862 (copy), Johnston Papers, WM; Symonds, *Johnston*, 158.

23. W. P. Johnston to Rosa, June 9, 1862 (first quotation), Johnston Papers, TU; *PJD*, VIII, 177 (second quotation). On Davis, Lee, and Jackson and the Valley Campaign, consult Harsh, *Confederate Tide*, 188–89. The key is not so much the originator but that all three men shared a similar view.

24. JD to VD, June 2, 1862 (first quotation), *PJD*, VIII, 209; JD to Johnston, May 23, 1862, ibid., 198; ibid., 208 ed.n., 211n.; J. W. Hinsdale Diary, July 31, 1862, Hinsdale Family Papers, UNC; John H. Reagan, *Memoirs with Special Reference to Secession and the Civil War* (New York and Washington, D.C., 1906), 141–42; W. P. Johnston to Rosa, June 9, 1862 (second quotation), Johnston Papers, TU.

25. *PJD*, VIII, 58–62.

26. *Richmond Examiner*, February 24, March 11, 1862; Louis Wigfall to C. C. Clay, May 16, 1862, C. C. Clay Papers, DU; Bragg Diary, February 5, 1862; Toombs to Stephens, March 24, May 19 (quotation), 1862, Alexander Stephens Papers, EU; *Chesnut*, 289, 292; George William Bagby Commonplace Book, March 24, 1862, George William Bagby Papers, VHS; Edward Younger, ed., *Inside the Confederate Government: The Diary of Robert Garlick Hill Kean* (New York, 1957), 88–89; William Gilmore Simms to George W. Bagby, March 24, 1862, Mary C. Simms Oliphant et al., eds., *The Letters of William Gilmore Simms* (6 vols.; Columbia, S.C., 1952–82), VI, 228–29.

27. Bragg Diary, February 6, 20, 27, March 24 (Randolph description); *PJD*, VIII, 102–03n., 105; W. P. Johnston to Rosa, August 24, 1862, Johnston Papers, TU; Randolph to JD, March 20, 1862, Autograph File, Dearborn Collection, HU (calendared *PJD*, VIII, 108); *Richmond Examiner*, February 24, 1862 (quotation). George

Green Shackelford, *George Wythe Randolph and the Confederate Elite* (Athens, Ga., 1988), is the most recent biography.

28. Bragg Diary, November 30, 1861; *PJD*, VIII, 60.

29. *PJD*, VIII, 184; *M&P*, I, 205–06. On conscription, see McPherson, *Battle Cry*, 430–33, and George C. Rable, *The Confederate Republic: A Revolt Against Politics* (Chapel Hill, N.C., 1994), 138–43.

30. *M & P*, I, 205 (quotation); *Correspondence Between Governor Brown and President Davis on the Constitutionality of the Conscription Act* (Atlanta, 1862).

31. McPherson, *Battle Cry*, 433–36; Rable, *Confederate Republic*, 145–46; *PJD*, VIII, 120; cf. Mark E. Neely, Jr., *Confederate Bastille: Jefferson Davis and Civil Liberties* (Milwaukee, Wis., 1993) and *Southern Rights: Political Prisoners and the Myth of Confederate Constitutionalism* (Charlottesville, Va., 1999), especially chap. 9.

32. On New Orleans, consult Woodworth, *Davis*, 104, 110–12; Chester G. Hearn, *The Capture of New Orleans, 1862* (Baton Rouge, La., 1995); JD to Joseph Davis, February 21, 1862, *PJD*, VIII, 53.

33. JD to Moore, April 17, 1862, *JDC*, V, 232–33; P. G. T. Beauregard to Charles Villeré, January 30, 1863, Letterbook, P. G. T. Beauregard Papers, LC; *PJD*, VIII, 576.

34. Helen Keary to Mother, May 7, 1862, *New York Daily Tribune*, August 8, 1862; *Memoir*, II, 250; *Chesnut*, 360.

35. W. P. Johnston to [William Preston], May 20, 1862, Johnston Papers, TU.

36. Helen Keary to Mother, May 7, 1862, *New York Daily Tribune*, August 8, 1862; *Memoir*, II, 301–02.

37. Minnigerode to JD, February 18, 1862, JD Papers, MC (calendared *PJD*, VIII, 52); *ibid.*, 168 ed.n.; Helen Keary to Mother, May 9, 1862, *New York Daily Tribune*, August 8, 1862; *Memoir*, II, 269.

38. Helen Keary to Mother, May 7, 1862, *New York Daily Tribune*, August 8, 1862; *PJD*, VIII, xlv, xlvii, 168 ed.n., 173n.; JD to VD, May 9, June 19, 1862, *ibid.*, 168–69, 253.

39. JD to VD, May 9, June 3, 13, 1862, *PJD*, VIII, 168, 218, 243.

40. JD to VD, June 3 (first quotation), 12, 19, 1862, *PJD*, VIII, 218, 238, 253; JD to Margaret Davis, May 20, 1862, *ibid.*, 192; JD to VD, May 19 (second quotation), 1862, JD Papers, MC (calendared *PJD*, VIII, 187); *Richmond Examiner*, June 19, 1862.

41. JD to VD, May 9 (first quotation), 16 (final quotation), June 13 (second quotation), 1862, *PJD*, VIII, 168, 178–79, 243.

42. JD to VD, May 13, June 2, 3, 11 (quotation), 19, 23, July 6, 1862, *ibid.*, 174, 209–10, 217, 236, 254, 264, 280–81.

43. VD to JD, May 19, 1862 (second quotation), *ibid.*, 188; VD to JD, May 26 (first quotation), June 12 (third and fifth quotations), 26 (fourth quotation), 1862, JD and Family Papers, MDAH (calendared *PJD*, VIII, 199, 239, 271).

44. VD to JD, May 19 (second and third quotations), June 3 (first and fourth quotations), 1862, *PJD*, VIII, 189, 219–21; VD to JD, June 5, 1862, JD and Family Papers, MDAH (calendared *PJD*, VIII, 224–25).

45. VD to JD, May 26, June 5, 26, 1862, JD and Family Papers, MDAH (calendared *PJD*, VIII, 199, 224–25, 271); VD to W. P. Johnston, June 5, 1862, Johnston Papers, TU; Johnston to Wife, June 2, 1862, Johnston Family Papers, FC.

46. Citations above in notes 43–45 plus VD to JD, July 6, August 13 (quotation), 1862, JD and Family Papers, MDAH (calendared *PJD*, VIII, 282, 338).

47. To the previous citations add JD to VD, June 12, 13, 25, 1862, *PJD*, VIII, 238, 243, 268; JD to VD, June 21, 1862 (quotation), JD Papers, MC (calendared *PJD*, VIII, 262); *ibid.*, xlvi, 254n.; *Richmond Examiner*, June 19, 1862.

48. VD to JD, May 19, 1862, *PJD*, VIII, 187–89, July 6, 1862, JD and Family Papers, MDAH (calendared *PJD*, VIII, 282); VD to [William Preston Johnston], May 22, 1862 (first quotation), to Mrs. W. P. Johnston, August 13, 1862 (final quotation), Johnston Papers, TU; Francis H. Smith to Anna Maria Smith, June 24, 1862 (second quotation), Smith Family Papers, VHS.

49. VD to Mrs. W. P. Johnston, August 13, 1862, Johnston Papers, TU; *PJD*, VIII, xlvii, 282n.

50. S. R. Mallory to Master S. R. Mallory, December 8, 1865 (first quotation), Stephen R. Mallory Papers, UNC; JD to VD, June 11 (second quotation), June 23 (third quotation), 1862, *PJD*, VIII, 236, 264; JD to [J. William Jones], August 30, 1878 (final quotation), JD Papers, MC; Gary W. Gallagher, ed., *Fighting for the Confederacy: The Personal Recollections of General Edward Porter Alexander* (Chapel Hill, N.C., 1989), 91, 93; JD's marginalia on review of John Esten Cooke's *Life of R. E. Lee* in *Edinburgh Review*, CCLXXX (April 1873), 193, 195, 197, JD Papers, TU. Recent studies by Emory Thomas, *Robert E. Lee: A Biography* (New York, 1995), and Steven E. Woodworth, *Davis and Lee at War* (Lawrence, Kans., 1995), present Lee as the more aggressive, but Joseph Harsh offers a useful corrective in *Confederate Tide.*

51. W. P. Johnston to [William Preston], July 20, 1862, Johnston Papers, TU; JD to VD, [May 30] (quotation), June 19, 1862, *PJD*, VIII, 203, 254; *ibid.*, 203n.; Harsh, *Confederate Tide*, chap. 3, 188–89.

52. Lee to JD, June 26, 1862, JD Papers, George H. and Katherine M. Davis Collection, TU (calendared *PJD*, VIII, 272); JD to W. P. Johnston, October 20, 1888, Johnston Papers, TU; Harsh, *Confederate Tide*, chap. 3 *passim*, notes Lee's twin skills.

53. Lee to JD, June 24, 1862, *PJD*, VIII, 268; JD to VD, June 13, 19, 1862, *ibid.*, 243, 254; Ezekiel Armstrong Diary, June 27, 1862, LSU; Mallory Diary, June 28, 1862, and Stephen R. Mallory to Wife, July 2, 1862, Mallory Papers, UNC; Harrison, *Recollections*, 72–74.

54. JD to VD, July 6, 1862, *PJD*, VIII, 280–81; JD interview in *Baltimore Sunday Herald*, July 16, 1887; JD to Rev. J. W. Jones, November 22, 1883, *SHSP*, XI (December 1883), 563.

55. *O.R.*, X, pt. 2, 403; on Corinth, see Woodworth, *Davis*, 102–06.

56. *PJD*, VIII, 245n.; JD to VD, June 13, 1862, and from W. P. Johnston, June 24, 1862, *ibid.*, 243–44, 267–68; JD to W. P. Johnston, June 14, 1862, *JDC*, V, 279–80; JD to F. W. Pickens, June 12, 1862, *ibid.*, 274.

57. JD to VD, June 19, 1862, *PJD*, VIII, 254; Mallory Diary, June 21, 1862, Mallory Papers, UNC; JD to Bragg, June 20, 1862, *JDC*, V, 283.

58. Beauregard to Thomas Jordan, July 12, 1862 (first quotation), to Charles Villeré, September 3, 1862 (second quotation), Letterbook, Beauregard Papers, LC; Beauregard to John L. Manning, August 2, 1886, HL (HM23371); petition, JD Papers, DU (calendared *PJD*, VIII, 390).

59. On Bragg, Grady McWhiney and Judith Lee Hallock, *Braxton Bragg and Confederate Defeat* (2 vols.; Tuscaloosa, Ala., 1991), is careful and analytical; Bragg Diary, December 3, 1861.

60. Bragg Diary, December 3, 1861, January 8, 1862; Jefferson Davis Bradford to VD, April 22, 1862, JD Papers, MC; Jas. R. Chalmers to JD, December 27, 1886, *ibid.;* L. Q. C. Lamar to [presidential friend], April or May 1862, RG109, JD Letters, NA; JD to Joseph Davis, June 18, 1861, *PJD*, VII, 204, to [John Bragg], September 1, 1862, *ibid.*, VIII, 370–71; Bragg to JD, August 23, October 22, 1861, *ibid.*, VII, 302–04, 370–72.

61. My account of Lee's campaign is drawn from Harsh, *Confederate Tide*, chaps. 4–6, Woodworth, *Davis and Lee*, chap. 5, and Stephen W. Sears, *Landscape Turned Red: The Battle of Antietam* (New Haven, Conn., 1983). For Lee to JD, see *PJD*, VIII, 339–70 *passim;* JD to Lee, July 5, 1862, *ibid.*, 277.

62. Lee to JD, September 3 (quotation), 6, 1862, *PJD*, VIII, 373, 378.

63. JD to Col. J. F. Marshall, July 11, 1862 (quotation), *JDC*, V, 293, to John Forsyth, July 18, 1862, *PJD*, VIII, 293–95. On JD and Maryland, see *ibid.*, xlvii, 383, 385, 387, 389n.

64. W. P. Johnston to JD, July 15, 1862, *O.R.*, X, pt. 1, 780–86 (calendared *PJD*, VIII, 289–90). For Bragg's offensive, I have relied chiefly on Thomas Lawrence Connelly, *Army of the Heartland: The Army of Tennessee, 1861–1862* (Baton Rouge, La., 1967), part V; Woodworth, *Davis*, chap. 9; and McWhiney and Hallock, *Bragg*, I, chaps. 12–14. I employ the designation the Army of Tennessee for the major Confederate field army in the West, though it did not formally receive that name until November 1862.

65. Bragg to Samuel Cooper, June 29, August 6, 1862, Cooper to Bragg, July 22, 1862, *O.R.*, XVII, pt. 2, 627–28, 667–68, 654–55; JD to Bragg, July 26, 1862, *JDC*, V, 298.

66. JD to VD, June 25, 1862, to Bragg, August 5, 1862, *PJD*, VIII, 269, 322.

67. Major critics of departmental organization include Thomas Lawrence Connelly, *The Politics of Command: Factions and Ideas in Confederate Strategy* (Baton Rouge, La., 1973), and Archer Jones, *Confederate Strategy from Shiloh to Vicksburg* (Baton Rouge, La., 1961).

68. JD to Bragg, August 5, 1862, to [John Bragg], September 1, 1862, *PJD*, 322, 370.

69. JD to Smith, July 28, 1862, *ibid.*, 305.

70. *Ibid.*, 379, 381n., 389n.

71. *PJD* has the following letters: Kentucky delegation to JD, August 18, 1862 (347); Hawes to JD, September 2, 1862 (372); Breckinridge to JD, July 26, 1862 (302); Smith to JD, August 11, 26, 1862 (331, 359); JD to T. H. Holmes, October 21, 1862 (455).

72. *JDC*, V, 338–39 (the correct date is September 12, calendared *PJD*, VIII, 386).

73. JD to Bragg, September 4, October 17, 1862, *PJD*, VIII, 376–77, 448.

74. Smith to JD, October 20, 1862, JD to Smith, October 29, 1862, *ibid.*, 453, 468; McWhiney and Hallock, *Bragg*, I, 323–34, 328–29; Joseph H. Parks, *General Leonidas Polk, C.S.A.: The Fighting Bishop* (Baton Rouge, La., 1962), 279–81.

75. JD to Smith, October 29, 1862, *PJD*, VIII, 469.

76. My account of Confederate diplomacy is based primarily on Frank Lawrence Owsley, *King Cotton Diplomacy: Foreign Relations of the Confederate States of America*, 2d ed. rev. Harriet Chappel Owsley (Chicago, 1959), chaps. 6–11; Howard Jones, *Union in Peril: The Crisis over British Intervention in the Civil War*

(Chapel Hill, N.C., 1992), chaps. 6–10 (Gladstone quotation on 182); Charles M. Hubbard, *The Burden of Confederate Diplomacy* (Knoxville, Tenn., 1998), chaps. 6–10; and Judith F. Gentry, "A Confederate Success in Europe: The Erlanger Loan," *JSH*, XXXVI (May 1970), 157–88.

77. *M&P*, I, 278–89 (quotations 280, 289).

78. My discussion of the Davis brothers' problems in Mississippi is based chiefly on letters from Joseph to JD between April and December 1862, printed or calendared in *PJD*, VIII: 144, 147–48, 159–60, 196–97 (first quotation), 246–47, 252, 264, 285–86, 370, 371, 398–400, 432–33, 472, 478, 507, 517–18 (second quotation), 530, and Eliza Davis to JD, August 24, 1862, 356. Also see M. L. Smith to JD, June 26, 1862, and G. W. McElrath to JD, November 13, 1862, *ibid.*, 272, 489; memorandum (copy) of details of Fleetwood purchase, Davis and Family Papers, MDAH; Frank E. Everett, Jr., *Brierfield: Plantation Home of Jefferson Davis* (Jackson, Miss., 1971), 18–19.

79. JD to VD, [May 30], June 11, 1862, to John Handy, January 25, 1863 (quotation), *PJD*, VIII, 203, 236, and IX, 39–40; VD to JD, June 12, 1862, *ibid.*, VIII, 239; *ibid.*, 519n., 556 on purchase contract; Lise Mitchell Journal, March 1863, Mary E. Mitchell Papers, UNC.

80. On 1861, *M&P*, I, 141–42; on occupied New Orleans, Chester G. Hearn, *When the Devil Came Down to Dixie: Ben Butler in New Orleans* (Baton Rouge, La., 1997). On the violence unleashed by the war, see Charles Royster's brilliant *The Destructive War: William Tecumseh Sherman, Stonewall Jackson, and the Americans* (New York, 1991).

81. JD to VD, May 28, June 25, 1862, *PJD*, VIII, 200, 269; *M&P*, I, 233–34, 269–74 (quotation 271).

82. *M&P*, I, 268, 290 (quotation); JD to Lee, July 31, 1862, *PJD*, VIII, 309.

83. *M&P*, I, 234, 290 (quotations); on retaliation, *PJD*, VIII, 292, 312n., 318–19, 346, 496, 536; Mallory Diary, August 1, 15, 1862, Mallory Papers, UNC.

84. *M&P*, I, 290–91; McPherson, *Battle Cry*, 565–67.

85. Jones, *Strategy*, Woodworth, *Davis*, and Thomas Lawrence Connelly, *Autumn of Glory: The Army of Tennessee, 1862–1865* (Baton Rouge, La., 1971), cover the Confederate West at this time.

86. *PJD*, VIII, 434n.; Josiah Gorgas Journal, October 17, 1862, William C. Gorgas Papers, LC.

87. Pickens to JD, June 12, 21, July 29, 1862, *PJD*, VIII, 238, 263, 308; Samuel Cooper to JD, June 21, 1862, *ibid.*, 263; JD to Pickens, June 12, 19, August 1 (quotation), 5, 1862, *ibid.*, 238, 255, 318, 324–25.

88. JD to Governor John Pettus, September 30, 1862, *ibid.*, 414; Ethelbert Barksdale to JD, November 11, 1862, *ibid.*, 486–87; Joseph Davis to JD, October 7 (quotation), 29, November 1, 1862, *ibid.*, 433, 472, 478.

89. Governor F. R. Lubbock to JD, June 27, 1862, and Lubbock *et al.* to JD, July 28, 1862, *JDC*, V, 287–89, 301–03; Claiborne Jackson to JD, July 28, 1862, T. H. Holmes to JD, August 28, 1862, *PJD*, VIII, 306–07, 360–63; E. C. Cabell to JD, July 28, 1862, JD Papers, DU (calendared *PJD*, VIII, 306); JD to Governor Thomas Moore, May 5, 1862, JD AES, August 26, 1862, *ibid.*, 163, 359.

90. JD to F. R. Lubbock, August 15, 1862, *JDC*, V, 318 (quotation); Bragg Diary, January 8, 1862; Thomas C. Reynolds, "Gen. Sterling Price and the Confederacy," (unfinished typescript, Missouri Historical Society), 59; W. P. Johnston to Wife,

August 15, 1862, Johnston Papers, TU; E. C. Cabell to JD, July 28, 1862, JD Papers, DU (calendared *PJD*, VIII, 306); Robert H. Chilton to JD, July 20, 1862, Magruder to JD, August 13, 1862, *ibid.*, 296–97, 297–98n., 338.

91. Holmes to JD, August 28, December 29, 1862, *PJD*, VIII, 360–63, 584–86, on November 9, 1862, T. H. Holmes Papers, DU (calendared *PJD*, VIII, 484); JD to Holmes, October 21, December 21, 1862, *ibid.*, 454–56, 561–62; W. P. Johnston to Wife, August 15, 1862 (quotation), Johnston Papers, TU.

92. JD to Francis Pickens, August 1, 1862, *PJD*, VIII, 318.

93. JD to Holmes, October 21, 1862, to George Randolph, November 12, 1862, *ibid.*, 454–55, 488.

94. *Ibid.*, 470n., 483; McWhiney and Hallock, *Bragg*, I, 325–26, 338.

95. JD to VD, June 23, 1862, *PJD*, VIII, 265; *ibid.*, 439, 446, 470n., 483.

96. *O.R.*, XVII, pt. 2, 757–58.

97. Frank E. Vandiver, *Rebel Brass: The Confederate Command System* (Baton Rouge, La., 1956), 34–35, 57–59; T. Harry Williams, *Lincoln and His Generals* (New York, 1952), 245; Symonds, *Johnston*, chap. 14; Jones, *Confederate Strategy*, chaps. 6–7.

98. Johnston to Wigfall, December 4, 1862, Mrs. D. Giraud Wright, *A Southern Girl in '61: The War-Time Memories of a Confederate Senator's Daughter* (New York, 1905), 99–100, on December 15, 1862, Wigfall Family Papers, LC; Symonds, *Johnston*, 179–81. Many scholars view the appointment as placing Johnston on the shelf; see, e.g., Connelly, *Autumn*.

99. On JD and the Trans-Mississippi, consult notes 89, 90, 105, and 106 here, along with Robert W. Johnson (Confederate senator from Arkansas) to JD, December 21, 1862, *PJD*, VIII, 558.

100. JD to Randolph, November 15, 1862, *JDC*, V, 374 (final quotation), November 12 (first two quotations), 14 (two messages), 1862, *PJD*, VIII, 488, 490–92, and Randolph to JD, November 15, 1862, *ibid.*, 495; Younger, ed., *Inside the Confederacy*, 30–31; Jones, *Rebel*, I, 188; Mallory Diary, November 19, 1862, Mallory Papers, UNC; Edward Anderson Journal, November [1862], Edward C. Anderson Papers, ibid.; W. P. Johnston to Wife, November 18, 1862, Johnston Papers, TU.

101. *Richmond Examiner*, November 17, 1862; G. W. C. Lee to JD, November 17, 1862, *PJD*, VIII, 496.

102. *PJD*, VIII, xlviii, 549–50n.; John J. Pettus and Wiley P. Harris to JD, December 1, 1862, James Phelan to JD, December 9, 1862, *ibid.*, 525, 539–44; JD to VD, December 15, 1862 (second quotation), to James A. Seddon, December 15, 1862, *ibid.*, 548–49, 551; John E. Magee Diary, December 12, 13, 1862, John E. Magee Papers, DU; R. Lockwood Tower, ed., *A Carolinian Goes to War: The Civil War Narrative of Arthur Middleton Manigault, Brigadier General, C.S.A.* (Columbia, S.C., 1983), 53 (first quotation); *New York Herald*, December 17, 27, 1862.

103. *New York Tribune*, December 25, 1862.

104. Stoddard Johnson Journal, Bragg Papers, Palmer Collection, WRHS; *WPL*, 359; James Seddon to JD, December 13, 1862, *PJD*, VIII, 548; *ibid.*, xlviii–xlix, 549–50n., 560 ed.n.; Lise Mitchell Journal, March 1863, in Mitchell Papers, UNC.

105. Johnston to JD, December 22, 1862, JD to Holmes, December 22, 1862, *PJD*, VIII, 559, 561–62; Johnston to Louis Wigfall, December 4, 1862, Wright, *Southern Girl*, 99–100; *New York Herald*, December 17, 1862; Joseph E. Johnston, "Jefferson Davis and the Mississippi Campaign," in Robert U. Johnston and

Clarence C. Buel, eds., *Battles and Leaders of the Civil War* (4 vols.; New York, 1887–88), III, 474.

106. Holmes to JD, December 29, 1862, JD to Holmes, January 28, 1863, *PJD,* VIII, 584–86, IX, 42–44.

107. JD to VD, December 15, 1862, *ibid.,* VIII, 548–49.

108. VD to JD, December 18, 21, 1862, *ibid.,* 552–53, 557–58.

109. *Ibid.,* 565 ed.n., 565–79 (quotations in order 566, 574, 571, 577, 578).

110. *Ibid.,* xlix, 587 ed.n., 587–89, 589–90n.

111. *Ibid.,* 566 (final quotation), 589–90n., IX, xli, 3, 7 ed.n., 7–8 (first quotation on 8), 9 (second quotation), 10 ed.n.; W. C. Cameron to Thomas Ruffin, January 1, 1863, Thomas Ruffin Papers, UNC.

CHAPTER THIRTEEN: *"Lift Men Above All Personal Considerations"*

1. *PJD,* IX, xli, 10–11 ed.n., 11–15; *Richmond Enquirer,* January 7, 1863.

2. *M&P,* I, 276–97 (quotations, 277, 290, 297).

3. On background and context regarding the Army of Tennessee, see Thomas Lawrence Connelly, *Autumn of Glory: The Army of Tennessee, 1862–1865* (Baton Rouge, La., 1971), chap. 4; Grady McWhiney and Judith Lee Hallock, *Braxton Bragg and Confederate Defeat* (2 vols.; Tuscaloosa, Ala., 1991), I, chap. 16; Steven E. Woodworth, *Jefferson Davis and His Generals: The Failure of Confederate Command in the West* (Lawrence, Kans., 1990), chap. 11; and Craig L. Symonds, *Joseph E. Johnston: A Civil War Biography* (New York, 1992), chap. 14. I will cite specifically only pertinent correspondence.

4. JD to Johnston, January 22, February 19 (quotation), 1863, *JDC,* V, 420–21, *PJD,* IX, 67.

5. JD to Johnston, January 21, 22, 1863, *PJD,* IX, 35, *JDC,* V, 420–21.

6. Johnston to JD, February 3, 12, 1863, *PJD,* IX, 48–49, 59–60; Lydia Johnston to Charlotte Wigfall, March 16, 1863, Wigfall Family Papers, LC.

7. Symonds, *Johnston,* 197; Johnston to Wigfall, March 4, 1863, Wigfall Family Papers, LC; JD to Johnston, February 19, 1863, *PJD,* IX, 66–68; Wigfall to Johnston, February 27, 1863 (JO 290), Joseph E. Johnston Papers, HL; Seddon to Johnston, February 5, March 3, 1863, *O.R.,* XXIII, pt. 2, 626–27, 659.

8. Seddon to Johnston, March 9, 1863, *O.R.,* XXIII, pt. 2, 674; Polk to JD, February 4, March 30, 1863, *PJD,* IX, 50–51, 118–19.

9. Johnston to Seddon, March 9, 12, 19, 1863, *O.R.,* XXIII, pt. 2, 674, 684, 708; Johnston to JD, April 10, 1863, *PJD,* IX, 137–38.

10. Mrs. Burton Harrison, *Recollections Grave and Gay* (New York, 1911), 71; *The Stranger's Guide and Official Directory for the City of Richmond* (Richmond, Va., 1863), 3–5.

11. Mallory to Master S. R. Mallory, September 27, 1865, Stephen R. Mallory Papers, UNC (all Mallory citations refer to this collection unless otherwise noted); John Louis Peyton, *The American Crisis; or, Pages from the Note-Book of a State Agent During the Civil War* (2 vols.; London, 1867), I, 120.

12. *White House of the Confederacy: An Illustrated History* (Richmond, Va., [1993]), 16, 83, 88–91; Thomas Bragg Diary, November 30, 1861, Thomas Bragg Papers, UNC (all Thomas Bragg citations refer to this collection).

13. Mallory to Master S. R. Mallory, September 27, 1865, Mallory Papers; B. N. Harrison to Prof. Quinche, March 21, 1862 (copy), Burton Harrison Papers, LC; William P. Johnston to Rosa, May 17, 1862, Johnston Papers, TU; J. B. Jones, *A Rebel War Clerk's Diary* (2 vols.; Philadelphia, 1866), II, 272 (quotation).

14. Edward Younger, ed., *Inside the Confederate Government: The Diary of Robert Garlick Hill Kean* (New York, 1957), 100.

15. Jones, *Clerk*, I, 204; John A. Campbell to Nathan Clifford, August 1, 1865, Andrew Johnson Papers, LC; AES on Seddon to JD, March 2, 1863, *PJD*, IX, 88; AES on W. P. Miles to James A. Seddon, July 15, 1863, RG109, m437, r104, f172, NA (also next three citations); AES on A. R. Wright to Braxton Bragg, August 10, 1863, *ibid.*, m474, r88, f370; AES on Capt. G. V. Moody to JD, September 3, 1863, RG109, *ibid.*, r74, f604; AES on Robert Tansill to JD, January 16, 1863, RG109, Officers; AES on G. W. Randolph to JD, August 13, 1862, *PJD*, VIII, 338–39; AES on William H. Houston to JD, August 15, 1863, *ibid.*, IX, 346.

16. JD to Thomas Randall, July 26, 1862, *JDC*, V, 299 (first quotation); Burton N. Harrison to D. R. Williams, October 24, 1862, JD Papers, DU; Josiah Gorgas Journal, August 14, 1864, William Gorgas Papers, LC; R. Finley Hunt to JD, January 26, 1864, RG109, M437, r128, f755–57, NA (second quotation).

17. Mallory to Master S. R. Mallory, September 27, 1865 (quotation), Mallory Diary, September 16, 1861, July 24, August 1, 15, 1862, Mallory Papers; Bragg Diary, November 30, 1861, January 8, 17, February 5, 19, 1862, Thomas Bragg Papers; John H. Reagan, *Memoirs with Special Reference to Secession and the Civil War* (Washington, D.C., and New York, 1906), 162.

18. Mallory to Master S. R. Mallory, December 8, 1865, Mallory Papers (quotation); Benjamin to James M. Mason, February 8, 1871, quoted in Eli N. Evans, *Judah P. Benjamin: The Jewish Confederate* (New York, 1988), 153; Littleton Washington Diary, January 1863 (transcript in possession of Douglas Gibboney, Carlisle, Pa; I am grateful to William C. Davis for this reference).

19. Walter Lord, ed., *The Fremantle Diary: Being the Journal of Lieutenant Colonel James Arthur Lyon Fremantle, Coldstream Guards, on His Three Months in the Southern States* (Boston, 1954), 165 (first quotation), 167; William Howard Russell, *My Diary North and South* (Boston, 1863), 175 (second and third quotations); John S. Wise, *End of an Era* (Boston and New York, 1899), 402 (fourth quotation); VD to Francis Lawley, June 8, 1898, Pierce Butler Papers, TU; S. R. Mallory to Master S. R. Mallory, December 8, 1865, Mallory Papers; [James R. Gilmore], *Down in Tennessee and Back by Way of Richmond* (New York, 1864), 262–65. Evans, *Benjamin*, is the best biography, though it exaggerates the relationship by pushing far beyond the evidence.

20. Younger, ed., *Kean Diary*, 30–31, 33, 100–01.

21. Stephen Mallory to Master S. R. Mallory, September 27, 1865, Mallory Papers.

22. *PJD*, II, 108–09n.; Harrison to Mother, February 26, 1862, Fairfax Harrison, ed., *Avis Sonis Facisque, Being a Memoir of an American Family: The Harrisons of Skimino* (Privately printed, 1910), 150; *ibid.*, chap. 6; Harrison to C. C. Buel, March 24, 1887, to Robert Stiles, February 23, 1898, Harrison Papers, LC; Harrison to [Constance Cary], September 12, 1864, *ibid.; PJD*, VIII, 555n.; Ishbel Ross, *First Lady of the South: The Life of Mrs. Jefferson Davis* (New York, 1958), 163. Also see the letters from VD cited in chapter twelve, note 45.

23. Abstract, Report from the Secretary of the Senate, RG109, m437, r54, f153, NA; Jones, *Clerk*, I, 184; Johnston to A. S. Johnston, February 14, 1862 (quotation), to Rosa, May 3, 24, 1862, and 1862–65 *passim*, Johnston Papers, TU.

24. *Six Decades in Texas or Memories of Francis Richard Lubbock Governor of Texas in War-Time, 1861–63[.] A Personal Experience in Business, War, and Politics,* ed. C. W. Raines (Austin, Tex., 1900), 556; W. P. Johnston to Rosa, November 29, 1862, Johnston Papers, TU; AES on J. B. Magruder to JD, January 6, 1863, *PJD,* IX, 16–17.

25. JD to W. P. Johnston, June 14, 1862, to James Chesnut, March 6, 1863, to G. W. C. Lee, April 8, 1863, *PJD,* VIII, 249, IX, 90, 130; G. W. C. Lee to JD, November 18, 1863, J. C. Ives to JD, December 8, 1863, W. M. Browne to JD, February 14, 1864, *ibid.,* X, 78, 105, 233–34; W. P. Johnston to Rosa, April 3, 7, 1863, Johnston Papers, TU.

26. W. P. Johnston to Rosa, May 8, 12, June 7, 10, July 27, 1862, February 24, 1863, Johnston Papers, TU; *Chesnut,* 84 (quotation), 503; Jones, *Clerk,* II, 15–16, 125; T. C. DeLeon, *Four Years in Rebel Capitals: An Inside View of Life in the Southern Confederacy, from Birth to Death . . .* (Mobile, Ala., 1892), 102; *Lubbock Memoirs,* 555; [Thomas Rowland] to Kate Mason Rowland, May 29, 1864, Kate Mason Rowland Diary, III, MC; JD to C. C. Clay, March 14, April 3, 1862, *PJD,* VIII, 99, 128.

27. Emma L. Bryan Reminiscences, Early Family Papers, VHS; Bragg Diary, November 30, 1861, Thomas Bragg Papers; Rev. William Wyndham Malet, *An Errand to the South in the Summer of 1862* (London, 1863), 173; S. R. Mallory to Master S. R. Mallory, September 27, 1865, Mallory Papers; J. W. Ratchford, *Some Reminiscences of Persons and Incidents of the Civil War* ([1909]; Austin, Tex., 1971), 31 (quotation); VD to JD, June 5, 1862, *PJD,* VIII, 225.

28. Jones, *Clerk,* II, 16, 218; *Chesnut,* 503; Robert B. Craddock to JD, August 5, 1864, *PJD,* X, 587; JD interview in *Baltimore Sunday Herald,* July 10, 1887; JD to J. Thomas Scharf, July 10, 1887, Scharf to JD, July 18, 1887, *JDC,* IX, 574, 576–77; J. B. Watson to JD, December 7, 1884, *ibid.,* 313–14; W. M. Gardner to Samuel Cooper, September 8, 1864, *O.R.,* XLII, pt. 2, 1238–39; *Richmond Daily Dispatch,* December 7, 1889.

29. W. P. Johnston to "My Dear Little Daughter," August 3, 1862, Johnston Papers, TU; Joseph R. Davis to JD, February 25, 1863, *PJD,* IX, 74; *Chesnut,* 529–30, 566, 595 (quotations); [Sallie Putnam], *Richmond During the War; Four Years of Personal Observations* (New York, 1867), 92; the uniforms are in MC.

30. *Chesnut,* 535 (quotation); "Slaves and Servants in the White House: Abstract," Staff Research Report, MC; VD to Kenneth Rayner, n.d., Harrison Papers, LC; VD to Mrs. Clopton, two letters, n.d., JD Papers, MC; Walter L. Fleming, "Jefferson Davis, the Negroes and the Negro Problem," *Louisiana State University Bulletin,* Series VI (October 1908, no. 4), 12–13.

31. *Chesnut,* 433 (quotation), 551; *Lubbock Memoirs,* 556; Bragg Diary, April 9, 1862, Thomas Bragg Papers; W. P. Johnston to Rosa, August 26, 1862, May 15, 1863, Johnston Papers, TU; Washington Diary, July 30, 1863; *Richmond Examiner,* December 31, 1863; Jones, *Clerk,* II, 136; "The Diary of Lt. Edward Owen, 1863–1864," *Civil War Regiments: A Journal of the American Civil War,* V (no. 1, 1996), 136. On imports, see Matilda Slidell to VD, December 12, 1862, RG109, Confederate Papers Relating to Citizens or Business Firms, NA, and Gabriel J. Rains to JD, November 24, 1862, *PJD,* VIII, 515.

32. *Chesnut,* 551; VD to Francis Lawley, June 8, 1898, Butler Papers, TU; *Memoir,* I, 155–56; *Lubbock Memoirs,* 557 (quotation).

33. *Lubbock Memoirs,* 556 (first quotation); Gorgas Journal, October 17, 1862 (second quotation), Gorgas Papers, LC; Anna Clayton Logan, "Recollections of My Life (Part II)," *Goochland County Historical Society Magazine,* XXI (1989), 21 (third quotation); Harrison, *Recollections,* 70 (fourth quotation); James Morris Morgan, *Recollections of a Rebel Reefer* (Boston and New York, 1917), 221 (fifth quotation); Nelson D. Lankford, ed., *An Irishman in Dixie: Thomas Conolly's Diary of the Fall of the Confederacy* (Columbia, S.C., 1988), 48 (final quotation).

34. *Memoir,* II, 202–03. An exchange of letters between VD and Angella Mallory, wife of Secretary of the Navy Mallory, is instructive: Mallory to VD, September n.d., October n.d., 1862, VD to Mallory, October 2, 1862, Stephen R. Mallory Papers, Lelia Abercrombie Historical Library, Pensacola Historical Museum, Pensacola, Fla.

35. Lydia Johnston to Charlotte Wigfall, January 19, August 2, 1863, Wigfall Family Papers, LC; *Chesnut,* 571.

36. [Putnam], *Richmond,* 38–39.

37. Jones, *Clerk,* II, 16 (first quotation); *Chesnut,* 478; Bryan Reminiscences, Early Family Papers, VHS (second quotation); *Memoir,* II, 204 (third quotation).

38. VD to Chesnut, April 27, 1862, n.d., 1863 (typescripts), Williams-Chesnut-Manning Papers, SCL. On the situation faced by many of Varina's social peers, see Drew Gilpin Faust's perceptive *Mothers of Invention: Women of the Slaveholding South in the Civil War* (Chapel Hill, N.C., 1996).

39. *PJD,* VIII, 222n.; *ibid.,* IX, 127 ed.n.; VD to JD, March 28, [April 5], 1863, *ibid.,* 115–16, 127–28; W. P. Johnston to Rosa, March 18, 1863, Johnston Papers, TU.

40. W. P. Johnston to Rosa, February 8, 17, July 4, 1863, to [W. Preston], January 12, 1863, Johnston Papers, TU; Jones, *Clerk,* II, 294, 297, 298, 312, 318, 321 (second quotation), 328; A. H. Stephens to Linton, July 1, 1863, Alexander H. Stephens Papers, Manhattanville College of the Sacred Heart; Gorgas Journal, April 21, July 2, 1863, Gorgas Papers, LC; JD to Joseph Davis, May 7, 1863, *PJD,* IX, 167; Harris D. Riley, Jr., "Jefferson Davis and His Health, Part II: January, 1861–December, 1889," *JMH,* XLIX (November 1987), 275–76.

41. Lord, ed., *Fremantle Diary,* 167–69.

42. *Chesnut,* 504, 530, 566; [Putnam], *Richmond,* 92; Mrs. G. H. Pattillo to JD, February 14, 1887, JD Papers, MC; S. R. Mallory to Master S. R. Mallory, September 27, 1865, Mallory Papers (quotation).

43. *PJD,* IX, 13.

44. Bragg Diary, November 30, 1861, April 9, 1862, Thomas Bragg Papers; St. John Richardson Liddell, *Liddell's Record,* ed. Nathaniel C. Hughes (Dayton, Ohio, 1985), 45–46; JD to Camille de Polignac, April 5, 1862, *PJD,* VIII, 131; Malet, *Errand,* 170–73; W. P. Johnston to Rosa, May 27, August 26, 1862, Johnston Papers, TU; Morgan, *Rebel Reefer,* 220–21.

45. J. B. Watson to JD, December 7, 1884, *JDC,* IX, 313–14; Malet, *Errand,* 163; Reagan, *Memoirs,* 163.

46. JD to Colonel S. Bassett French, January 1, 1862, to Anna R. Sanders, June 11, 1863, to Eliza C. Cannon, July 18, 1863, JD to Hannah Gaston, October 4, 1863, JD to Minnie McComas, May 4, 1864, *PJD,* VIII, 3, IX, 214, 286–87, X, 9, 389; Bryan Reminiscences, Early Family Papers, VHS.

47. S. R. Mallory to Master S. R. Mallory, September 27, 1865, Mallory Papers (quotations); W. P. Johnston to Rosa, August 1, 1862, Johnston Papers, TU.

48. *PJD*, IX, 164n.; JD to Lee, May 11, 1863, *ibid.*, 179 (first quotation); *Memoir*, II, 382–83 (second quotation). On Chancellorsville, see Ernest B. Furgurson, *Chancellorsville 1863: The Souls of the Brave* (New York, 1992), and Stephen N. Sears, *Chancellorsville* (Boston and New York, 1996).

49. JD to Lee, May 31, 1863, *PJD*, IX, 202.

50. Jones, *Clerk*, I, 325–26. On Lee, consult Emory M. Thomas, *Robert E. Lee: A Biography* (New York, 1995), 287–90, and Steven E. Woodworth, *Davis and Lee at War* (Lawrence, Kans., 1995), 229–44; yet both scholars exaggerate the differences between the general and the president.

51. Reagan, *Memoirs*, 120–23.

52. Davis to Dabney Maury, December 17, 1877, JD Papers, MC; Lee to James A. Seddon, May 10, 1863, *WPL*, 482.

53. Woodworth, *Davis*, chaps. 14–15, Symonds, *Johnston*, chaps. 11–12, and Archer Jones, *Confederate Strategy from Shiloh to Vicksburg* (Baton Rouge, La., 1961), chaps. 8–12, provide background and context.

54. Woodworth, *Davis*, chap. 15; James M. McPherson, *Battle Cry of Freedom: The Civil War Era* (New York, 1988), 626–36.

55. The best study of Pemberton is Michael B. Ballard, *Pemberton: A Biography* (Jackson, Miss., 1991), esp. chap. 8; JD to Pemberton, May 7, 1863, *JDC*, V, 482.

56. *Correspondence Between the President and General Joseph E. Johnston, Together with That of the Secretary of War and the Adjutant and Inspector General, During the Months of May, June, and July 1863* (Richmond, Va., 1864) has all the pertinent documents. The quotation is from JD to Johnston, May 28, p. 10.

57. Johnston to Lydia Johnston, June 25, 1863 (first and second quotations), John W. Johnston Papers, DU; [Johnston] to [Lydia Johnston], June 12, 29 (third quotation), 1863, McLane-Fisher Papers, MHS (I am grateful to Charles Royster for these references). On Johnston's outlook, also see Lydia Johnston to Charlotte Wigfall, August 2, 1863, Wigfall Family Papers, LC, and Louis Wigfall to Johnston, June 8, 15, 1863 (JO293 and JO294), Johnston Papers, HL.

58. Gorgas Journal, March 20, 1863, Gorgas Papers, LC; JD to [Benjamin G. Humphreys], May 1, 1863 (first quotation); JD to Governor John Pettus, May 18, June 4, 1863; JD to Bragg, June 25, 1863; JD to Beauregard, June 25, 1863; JD to Smith, May 8, July 2, 1863; JD to Johnston, May 24, 1863 (second quotation), *PJD*, IX, 162, 183, 206, 239, 240, 171–72, 254, 189; F. T. Cooper and A. N. Kimball to JD, May 8, 1863; Pettus to JD, June 3, 1863; Pettus *et al.* to JD, June 18, 1863; Joseph Davis to JD, June 3, 22, 1863; Beauregard to JD, June 25, 1863; Bragg to JD, June 26, 1863, *ibid.*, 176, 205, 230, 205, 235, 240, 246. For the daily contact, see *ibid.*, 122–264 *passim*.

59. JD to Johnston, July 8, 1863, to Lee, July 21, 1863, *PJD*, IX, 264, 295; JD to Joseph Davis, May 31, 1863, *ibid.*, 200; Younger, ed., *Kean Diary*, 46.

60. *PJD*, IX, 259 ed.n.; for Gettysburg, consult McPherson, *Battle Cry*, 653–63, and Thomas, *Lee*, 292–303; *Memoir*, II, 392.

61. JD to Robert W. Johnson, July 14, 1863 (first quotation), to Reuben Davis, July 20, 1863, to James M. Howry, August 27, 1863 (second quotation), *PJD*, IX, 276, 290–91, 357–58.

62. Jones, *Clerk*, I, 374; Gorgas Journal, July 17, 1863, Gorgas Papers, LC; JD to John Pettus, July 11, 1863, to John Pemberton, August 9, 1863, *PJD*, IX, 270, 333–34; *ibid.*, 335n. on inquiry; JD to Braxton Bragg, June 29, 1872, *JDC*, VII, 321–22; *R&F*, II, 404–16.

63. *R&F*, II, 411.

64. JD to Robert W. Johnson, July 14, 1863 (quotations), to Reuben Davis, July 20, 1863, *PJD*, IX, 276, 290–91.

65. Stephens to JD, June 12, 1863, *JDC*, V, 513–15. Thomas E. Schott, *Alexander H. Stephens of Georgia: A Biography* (Baton Rouge, La., 1988), 375–80, has an excellent discussion of this subject.

66. Lee to JD, June 10, 1863, *WPL*, 507–09 (calendared *PJD*, IX, 213).

67. JD to Stephens, June 18, 1863, Stephens to JD, July 8, 1863, *PJD*, IX, 229, 268; *ibid.*, 244–45n.; Stephens to Linton, July 1, 1863 (quotation), Stephens Papers, Manhattanville; JD to Stephens, July 2, 1863, to Lincoln, July 2, 1863, *JDC*, V, 515–19.

68. *M&P*, I, 348–59 (quotation 358), II, 539–40, 576–83; Benjamin to JD, October 8, 1863, *PJD*, X, 15–16. Charles M. Hubbard, *The Burden of Confederate Diplomacy* (Knoxville, Tenn., 1998), chap. 12, details the break with England.

69. Portrait, p. 478; "Portrait of President Jefferson Davis . . . ," flyer, JD Papers, MC; George C. Groce and David H. Wallace, *The New-York Historical Society's Dictionary of Artists in America, 1564–1860* (New Haven, Conn., 1957), 541.

70. *Charleston Mercury*, September 5, 23, 1863; James H. Hammond to James L. Orr, January 10, 1863, James H. Hammond Papers, LC; Toombs to Alexander Stephens, July 19, 1863, Alexander Stephens Papers, EU; Stephens to Stephens, April 6, 1863, Stephens Papers, Manhattanville.

71. JD to J. W. Harmon, September 17, 1863, to M. L. Bonham, December 16, 1863, to Charles Clark, December 28, 1863, *JDC*, VI, 40–41, 131, 139–40; *Richmond Enquirer*, May 1, 1863; Lord, ed., *Fremantle Diary*, 170 (quotation); George C. Rable, *The Confederate Republic: A Revolution Against Politics* (Chapel Hill, N.C., 1994), 209.

72. John Milton to JD, February 17 (first quotation), August 3, 1863, Howell Cobb to JD, May 11, 1863, James R. Magill to JD, May 16, 1863, William McWillie to JD, October 18, 1863, *PJD*, IX, 64–65, 320, 180, 182, X, 29; Albert Burton Moore, *Conscription and Conflict in the Confederacy* (New York, 1924), remains the only book on this important topic; while it still has value, a new study is sorely needed.

73. James Phelan to JD, December 9, 1862, Joseph J. Bradford to JD, February 18, 1863, Reuben Davis to JD, August 2, 1863, *PJD*, VIII, 542, and IX, 65, 319.

74. JD to John Milton, September 1, 1863, *ibid.*, 363–64.

75. James Phelan to JD, July 29, 1863, JD Papers, James S. Schoff Civil War Collection, MI (calendared *PJD*, IX, 315); Joseph Davis to JD, September 9, 1863, and JD to Reuben Davis, July 20, 1863, *ibid.*, 378, 290.

76. Citizens of Warren County, Georgia, to JD, February 25, 1863, RG109, m437, r115, f361, NA (also next two citations); Caleb Moore to JD, December 14, 1863, *ibid.*, r101, f728; Emily Nunn to JD, September 14, 1863, *ibid.*, r105, f904; Mrs. C. V. Baxley to JD, January 18, 1864 (quotation), *PJD*, X, 184; Joseph Davis to JD, March 20, 1863, JD Family Papers, MDAH; Reagan, *Memoirs*, 164. Desertion surely merits a new study to replace Ella Lonn's *Desertion During the Civil War* (New York,

1928). A recent study of the Confederate home front is William Blair, *Virginia's Private War: Feeding Body and Soul in the Confederacy, 1861–1865* (New York, 1998).

77. *M&P*, I, 329–31.

78. Michael B. Chesson, "Harlots or Heroines? A New Look at the Richmond Bread Riot," *Virginia Magazine of History and Biography*, XCII (April 1984), 131–75, is excellent; Ernest B. Furgurson, *Ashes of Glory: Richmond at War* (New York, 1996), 193–95; McPherson, *Battle Cry*, 447; *Memoir*, II, 373–76, greatly exaggerates JD's role.

79. *M&P*, I, 296; McPherson, *Battle Cry*, 615–17; Richard Franklin Bensel, *Yankee Leviathan: The Origins of Central State Authority in America, 1859–1877* (New York, 1990), 183–84; Paul D. Escott, *After Secession: Jefferson Davis and the Failure of Confederate Nationalism* (Baton Rouge, La., 1978), 140–44, 151–54, 157–59.

80. The story in this and the following paragraphs is based chiefly on letters from Joseph Davis to JD in 1863. Individual citations are not given, but quotations are specified. Where appropriate, I cite other sources. In *PJD*, IX, February 17 (64), April 9 (134–35), May 11 (180), June 3 (205), June 14 (216–18), June 17 (227–28, third quotation), June 21 (233–34, fourth quotation), June 25 (240–41), August 15 (344–45), September 9 (377–78), September 16 (393); *ibid.*, X, November 1 (45–46), [5–10] (47), 11 (61–62), December 1 (96–97); JD Papers, TR, May 7 (first, second quotations, also calendared *PJD*, IX, 169).

81. J. D. Bradford to JD, June 5, 1863, JD Papers, MC (calendared *PJD*, IX, 206–07).

82. JD to Joseph Davis, May 7, 31, 1863, *PJD*, IX, 167 (second quotation), 200 (first quotation).

83. *Ibid.*, 298–99 ed.n.; Robert E. Melvin to JD, July 22, 1863, John C. Pemberton to JD, July 29, 1863, J. D. Bradford to JD, August 17, September 16, 1863, W. H. Jackson to JD, September 11, 1863, *ibid.*, 299–301, 314, 346–47, 393, 381–82; Lise Mitchell to [Ann M. B. Miles], August 20, 1863, Lise Mitchell Papers, TU.

84. JD to Smith, July 14, 1863 (first quotation), to Holmes, July 15, 1863, to H. Flanigan, July 15, 1863 (remaining quotations), *JDC*, V, 552–54, 555–56, 563–66; JD to Robert Johnson, July 14, 1863, *PJD*, IX, 276–77.

85. JD to Smith, July 14 (quotations), November 19, 1863, *JDC*, V, 552–54, VI, 85–87.

86. Smith to JD, June 16 (first quotation), September 5 (second quotation), 11, 28, 1863, *PJD*, IX, 220–23, 371–72, 382, 412–13. Robert Lee Kerby, *Kirby Smith's Confederacy: The Trans-Mississippi South, 1863–1865* (New York, 1972), has the most detail; for the Marshall Conference, see 139–42.

87. Lee to JD, August 8, 1863, JD to Lee, August 11, 1863, *PJD*, IX, 326–27, 337–38. On Lee's health, consult Thomas, *Lee*, 277–79.

88. JD to Bragg, August 22, 1863, to Lee, September 16, 1863, to James Chesnut, August 11, to Chesnut and Alexander Stephens, August 31, 1863, *PJD*, IX, 350, 390–92, 336, 362. On events within the Army of Tennessee, I follow Connelly, *Autumn*, chaps. 6–10, and Woodworth, *Davis*, chap. 13.

89. *PJD*, IX, xliii; JD to Lee, August 24, September 8, 1863, *ibid.*, 353, 375; Lee to James Longstreet, August 31, 1863, to Mary Lee, September 4, 1863, to JD, September 6, 1863, *WPL*, 594, 595, 596 (to JD calendered *PJD*, IX, 373); Thomas, *Lee*, 309–10.

90. Cf. Woodworth, *Davis and Lee*, 255–56, and *Davis*, 228.

91. Bragg to JD, September 25, 1863, Leonidas Polk to JD, [September 27], 1863, *PJD*, IX, 404–06, 410; JD to Bragg, September 30, October 3, 1863, to Lee, October 5, 1863, *JDC*, VI, 53–56, 56–57; James Chesnut to JD, October 5, 1863, with AES endorsement, *O.R.*, LII, pt. 2, 538.

92. *PJD*, X, xlvii–xlix; *JDC*, VI, 57–58; W. P. Johnston to Rosa, October n.d., 1863 (quotation), Johnston Family Papers, FC; *Atlanta Confederacy*, n.d., in *Richmond Enquirer*, October 13, 1863.

93. *Annals of the Army of Tennessee*, I (August 1878), 237.

94. *Marietta Confederate*, n.d., in *Savannah Daily Morning News*, October 29, 1863 (first, second, sixth quotations); *Memphis Appeal*, n.d., in *Richmond Examiner*, October 24, 1863; *PJD*, X, 21–22 (fourth, fifth quotations); John Bratton to Dear Wife, October 10, 1863, John Bratton Papers, UNC; John E. Magee Diary, October 10, 1863, John E. Magee Papers, DU; W. P. Johnston to Rosa, October n.d., 1863 (third quotation), Johnston Family Papers, FC.

95. William W. Mackall to Joseph E. Johnston, October 13, 1863 (JO238), Johnston Papers, HL; *Liddell's Record*, 152–53; R. Lockwood Tower, ed., *A Carolinian Goes to War: The Civil War Narrative of Arthur Middleton Manigault, Brigadier General, C.S.A.* (Columbia, S.C., 1983), 152–53; JD to Bragg, June 29, 1872, *JDC*, VII, 321.

96. JD to Bragg, October 29, 1863 (last quotation), June 29, 1872 (first quotation), to Hardee, October 30, 1863, *JDC*, VI, 71, 72, VII, 321.

97. *Ibid.*, VI, 61–62.

98. W. P. Johnston to Rosa, October 18, 1863, Johnston Papers, TU; *PJD*, X, 29.

99. W. P. Johnston to Rosa, October 23, 1863, TU.

100. *Richmond Enquirer*, November 3, 1863; *PJD*, X, 33; Stephens to Herschel Johnson, November 14, 1863, Herschel Johnson Papers, DU.

101. *Macon Daily Telegraph*, November 11, 1863; *PJD*, X, 43, 44–45; W. P. Johnston to Rosa, October 31, 1863 (first and second quotations), Johnston Papers, TU; Eugene Verdery to Dear Sister, November 7, 1863 (third quotation), Eugene Verdery, Jr., Papers, UNC.

102. *JDC*, VI, 73–78; William Ravenel to Dear Rose, November 3, 1863 (final quotation), Frederick W. Chesson Collection, CWTI, U.S. Army Military History Institute, Carlisle Barracks, Pennsylvania (I am indebted to William C. Davis for this reference).

103. D.C. to "Miss Millie," November 17, 1863, Mary Margaret McNeill Papers, DU; *PJD*, X, 49–51.

104. *Lynchburg Republican*, n.d., in *Richmond Enquirer*, November 13, 1863; *Richmond Examiner*, November 6, 1863.

105. My treatment of Confederate politics is informed by two pathbreaking books: Rable, *Confederate Republic*, and Kenneth C. Martis, *The Historical Atlas of the Congresses of the Confederate States of America: 1861–1865* (New York, 1994). For my discussion of Confederate state activity, add Bensel, *Yankee Leviathan*, chap. 3, and Emory M. Thomas, *The Confederate Nation, 1861–1865* (New York, 1979), esp. chap. 9.

106. Rable employs these terms.

107. Henry S. Foote, *Casket of Reminiscences* ([1874]; New York, 1968), 292 (first quotation); Shelby Foote, *The Civil War: A Narrative* (3 vols.; New York, 1958–74), II, 950 (second quotation).

108. S. R. Mallory to Master S. R. Mallory, September 27, 1865, Mallory Papers; Mary B. Estill, ed., "Diary of a Confederate Congressman, 1862–1863," *SHQ*, XXXVIII, XXXIX (April, July 1935), 286, 37–38 (quotation); A. H. Garland to JD, January 30, 1863, *PJD*, IX, 46; JD to A. H. Garland, March 28, 1863, *JDC*, V, 457–60; W. L. Yancey to C. C. Clay, May 13, 1863, C. C. Clay Papers, DU; Thomas S. Bocock to JD, January 1, 1864 (copy), Harrison Papers, LC; Edwin G. Reade to William A. Graham, February 4, 1864, J. G. de Roulhac Hamilton and Max R. Williams, eds., *The Papers of William Alexander Graham* (7 vols.; Raleigh, N.C., 1957–), VI, 24; Warren Aiken to My Dear Darling, January 1, 1865, Bell Irvin Wiley, ed., *Letters of Warren Akin: Confederate Congressman* (Athens, Ga., 1959), 66.

109. *PJD*, X, xlix; G. W. C. Lee to JD, November 18, 1863, *ibid.*, 78; Walter Taylor to [Bettie], November 23, 1863, R. Lockwood Tower, ed., *Lee's Adjutant: The Wartime Letters of Colonel Walter Herron Taylor, 1862–1865* (Columbia, S.C., 1995), 90–91; B. W. Justice to My Sweet Darling Wife, November 22, 1863 (copy), St. Thomas Episcopal Church, Orange, Va.; Your Fond Husband [Andrew B. Wardlaw] to My Dearest, November 24, 1863 (typescript), Fredericksburg-Spotsylvania National Military Park (I am indebted to Robert C. Krick for the previous two references); C. E. Denoon to Brother, November 22, 1863, Denoon Family Papers, Folder No. 2, Library of Virginia, Richmond, Va.

110. Connelly, *Autumn of Glory*, chap. 10, details military events in October and November; *M&P*, I, 347.

111. Bragg to JD, November 30, December 1 (quotation), 2, 1863, *PJD*, X, 92, 94–95, 97.

112. JD to Bragg, October 29, 1863, *JDC*, VI, 69–71.

113. Bragg to JD, December 2, 1863, *PJD*, X, 97; Cobb to My Dear Wife, December 10, 1863, Howell Cobb Papers, UGA.

114. Cobb to My Dear Wife, December 10, 1863, Cobb Papers, UGA; JD to Lee, December 6, 1863, *JDC*, VI, 93; Lee to JD, December 3, 7, 1863, *WPL*, 641–42; Lee to J. E. B. Stuart, December 9, 1863, *ibid.*, 642–43; Walter Taylor to [Bettie], December 20, 1863, Tower, ed., *Lee's Adjutant*, 101.

115. Lee to JD, December 3, 1863, *WPL*, 641.

116. *Chesnut*, 482, 507; Polk to JD, December 8, 1863, *PJD*, X, 105–06; Wigfall to Johnston, December 18, 1863 (JO298), Johnston Papers, HL; Symonds, *Johnston*, 248.

117. JD to Johnston, December 16, 1863, *JDC*, VI, 132; Cobb to My Dear Wife, December 17, 1863, Cobb Papers, UGA; Gary W. Gallagher, ed., *Fighting for the Confederacy: The Personal Recollections of General Edward Porter Alexander* (Chapel Hill, N.C., 1989), 468; Benjamin Hill to [W. T. Walthall], October 12, 1878 (copy), William Walthall Papers, MDAH; Seddon to W. T. Walthall, February 10, 1879, *JDC*, VIII, 349–51 (quotation 351).

118. *M&P*, I, 345–82 (quotations in order 367, 365, 347, 369, 381, 348).

CHAPTER FOURTEEN: *"We Are Fighting for Existence"*

1. *Chesnut*, 525–26 (quotations); *Richmond Examiner*, December 31, 1863, January 2, 18, 1864; *Richmond Enquirer*, January 1, 19, 1864; J. B. Jones, *A Rebel War Clerk's Diary* (2 vols.; Philadelphia, 1866), II, 136, 152; Littleton Washington Diary,

January 1, 1864 (transcript in possession of Douglas Gibboney, Carlisle, Pa; I am grateful to William C. Davis for this reference).

2. *M&P,* I, 414–16; *Richmond Enquirer,* February 12, 16, 1864.

3. James M. McPherson, *Battle Cry of Freedom: The Civil War Era* (New York, 1988), chap. 24.

4. Johnston to Louis Wigfall, November 12, 26, December 3, 14, 1863, February 19, April 1, 5, 30, 1864, Wigfall Family Papers, LC; Richard I. Manning (aide to Johnston) to Mother, December, 22, 1863, Williams-Chesnut-Manning Papers, SCL; St. John Richardson Liddell, *Liddell's Record,* ed. Nathaniel C. Hughes (Dayton, Ohio, 1985), 169 (first quotation); *Chesnut,* 483.

5. Wigfall to Johnston, December 18, 1863, March 17, 18, 19 (quotation), 1864 (JO 298, 299, 300, 301), Joseph E. Johnston Papers, HL.

6. Benjamin Ewell Diary (Richmond 1864, quotation), Joseph E. Johnston Papers, WM; Ewell to Johnston, April 29, 1864 (JO 96), Johnston Papers, HL; Johnston to Wigfall, January 9, 1864, Wigfall Family Papers, LC; JD to Johnston, December 23, 1863, Johnston to JD, January 2, 1864, *PJD,* X, 119–21, 144–46; Seddon to Johnston, December 18, 1863, Bragg to Johnston, March 4, 7, 1864, *O.R.,* XXXI, pt. 3, 842–43, 873–74, XXXII, pt. 2, 510–11, *ibid.,* pt. 3, 584–85, 592; Memorandum by Pendleton, April 16, 1864, William N. Pendleton Papers, DU; Thomas Lawrence Connelly, *Autumn of Glory: The Army of Tennessee, 1862–1865* (Baton Rouge, La., 1971), chap. 11; Craig L. Symonds, *Joseph E. Johnston: A Civil War Biography* (New York, 1992), chap. 17; and Albert Castel, *Decision in the West: The Atlanta Campaign of 1864* (Lawrence, Kans., 1992), chaps. 1–4, present the military background.

7. JD AES on Johnston to Bragg, March [20], 1864, JD Papers, DU.

8. For an absorbing account of Lee's fight against Grant, consult Clifford Dowdey, *Lee's Last Campaign: The Story of Lee and His Men Against Grant—1864* (Boston, 1960). For the constant contact between the two men, see *WPL,* 718–68 *passim, JDC,* VI, 246–69 *passim, O.R.,* XXXVI, pts. 2 and 3 *passim.* Some messages from Lee went to Seddon, but JD saw them. Also note JD to VD, May 9, 1864, *PJD,* X, 401.

9. The best study of the Atlanta Campaign is Castel, *Decision;* also see Symonds, *Johnston,* chaps. 18–21. *O.R.,* XXXII, pts. 1–3, and XXXVIII, pts. 1–5, document communications among Johnston, JD, and Seddon; cf. the citations to primary sources in note 8 above to contrast Lee. For Hood in Richmond, consult *Chesnut,* 551, 559, 565, and with Johnston, Diary of Major Campbell Brown, January 14, 1866, George W. Campbell Papers, LC.

10. JD to Smith, April 28, 1864, *JDC,* VI, 236–37. This phase of the Trans-Mississippi is covered thoroughly in Ludwell Johnson, *Red River Campaign: Politics and Cotton in the Civil War* (Baltimore, 1958), and in Robert L. Kerby, *Kirby Smith's Confederacy: The Trans-Mississippi South, 1863–1865* (New York, 1972), chaps. 6–8.

11. Reuben Davis to JD, August 2, 1863 (first quotation), Civil War Collection, American Antiquarian Society (calendared *PJD,* IX, 319), March 21, 1864 (fifth quotation), X, 284–85; James Phelan to JD, July 29, 1863 (second and third quotations), JD Papers, James S. Schoff Civil War Collection, MI (calendared *PJD,* IX, 315); Alex Fitzpatrick to JD, January 1, 1864, Pritchard von David Collection, UT; A. G. Magrath to JD, December 25, 1864 (fourth quotation), Andrew G. Magrath Papers, SCL; F. F. Freeman to JD, March 28, 1864, *PJD,* X, 303; *M&P,* I, 448 (sixth quotation).

12. Best on Confederate politics in 1864 is again George C. Rable, *The Confederate Republic: A Revolution Against Politics* (Chapel Hill, N.C., 1994), chaps. 12–13, which informs my discussion. For more coverage of Georgia and North Carolina respectively, see Thomas E. Schott, *Alexander H. Stephens of Georgia: A Biography* (Baton Rouge, La., 1988), chaps. 19–20, and Marc W. Kruman, *Parties and Politics in North Carolina, 1836–1865* (Baton Rouge, La., 1983), chaps. 9–10. I will cite specifically only pertinent correspondence and speeches.

13. Stephens to JD, January 22, 1864, *PJD*, X, 197; Myrta Lockett Avary, *Recollections of Alexander H. Stephens . . .* (New York, 1910), 168–69 (quotation); Henry Cleveland, *Alexander H. Stephens, in Public and Private, with Letters and Speeches, Before, During, and Since the War* (Philadelphia, 1866), 761–86.

14. JD to Brown, September 12, 1863 (two letters), May 24, 1864, *JDC*, VI, 32–34, 260–61; Brown to JD, December 23, 1863, *O.R.*, ser. 4, II, 1062; Brown to James A. Seddon, January 29, 1864, to Cobb, May 20, 1864, to Colonel Wm. Browne, May 21, 1864, and Seddon to Brown, February 23, 1864, Allen D. Candler, ed., *The Confederate Records of the State of Georgia* (4 vols.; Atlanta, 1909–11), III, 458–63, 541–58, 559–62, 484–88; L. Q. C. Lamar to JD, April 27, 1864 (quotation), *PJD*, X, 369. Joseph H. Parks, *Joseph E. Brown of Georgia* (Baton Rouge, La., 1977), chaps. 13–14, has a detailed account of Brown's activities.

15. Vance to JD, February 4 (quotation), April 18, 1864, with JD AED, *PJD*, X, 220, 355; Vance to JD, December 30, 1863, JD to Vance, January 8, 1864, *JDC*, VI, 141–42, 143–46.

16. JD to Vance, February 29, 1864, *JDC*, VI, 193–97, Vance to JD, March 9, 1864, *PJD*, X, 277.

17. VD to George Shea, July 14, 1865, JD Papers, MC; *Chesnut*, 630. For an insightful study of southern honor, see Bertram Wyatt-Brown, *Southern Honor: Ethics and Behavior in the Old South* (New York, 1982).

18. JD to Garnett, November 9 (two letters), 10, 1863, Garnett to JD, November 9, 10, 11, 1863, JD to Wise, November 9, 1863, Wise to JD, November 14 (first and second quotations), 26, 1863, *PJD*, X, 58–60, 65, 68–69, 89–90; Wise to Garnett November 7, 26 (third quotation), 1863, Garnett-Wise Papers, UNC.

19. *Chesnut*, 551; Mrs. Burton Harrison, *Recollections Grave and Gay* (New York, 1911), 126; "The Diary of Lt. Edward Owen, 1863–1864," *Civil War Regiments: A Journal of the American Civil War*, V (no. 1, 1996), 136; Washington Diary, February 4, 1864.

20. *Chesnut*, 587, 594.

21. *Memphis [Atlanta] Daily Appeal*, May 21, 1864 (first three quotations); *Memoir*, II, 496–97 (fourth and fifth quotations); Harrison, *Recollections*, 182 (sixth quotation); Josiah Gorgas Journal, May 1, 1864 (seventh quotation), William Gorgas Papers, LC; *Chesnut*, 601–02.

22. *Chesnut*, 602; Harrison, *Recollections*, 182 (first quotation); VD to Mrs. Richard Griffith, May 8, 1864 (second quotation), Old Courthouse Museum, Vicksburg; Angela Mallory to Virginia Clay, May 6, 1864, C. C. Clay Papers, DU.

23. VD to Burton Harrison, July 13, 1864, Burton Harrison Papers, LC, to Mrs. Clopton [July, 1864], JD Papers, MC.

24. In addition to the Dowdey work cited in note 8 above, both McPherson, *Battle Cry*, chap. 24, and Emory M. Thomas, *Robert E. Lee: A Biography* (New York, 1995), chaps. 26–27, have value.

25. A glance at *WPL*, 646–879 *passim*, and Douglas Southall Freeman, ed., *Lee's Dispatches: Unpublished Letters of General Robert E. Lee, C.S.A. to Jefferson Davis and the War Department of the Confederate States of America, 1862–65* ([1915]; New York, 1957), 131–311, and *JDC*, VI, 142–433 *passim*, demonstrates their frequent contact.

26. Burton Harrison to William P. Johnston, September 14, 1864, Johnston Papers, TU; Burton Harrison to mother, September 17, October n.d., 1864, Fairfax Harrison, ed., *Avis Sonis Facisque: Being a Memoir of an American Family: The Harrisons of Skimino* (Privately printed, 1910), 152–55; John H. Reagan, *Memoirs with Special Reference to Secession and Civil War* (Washington, D.C., and New York, 1906), 195; Walter Taylor to Bettie, October 17, 1864, R. Lockwood Tower, ed., *Lee's Adjutant: The Wartime Letters of Colonel Walter Herron Taylor, 1862–1865* (Columbia, S.C., 1995), 197; H. T. Stanton to VD, March 24, 1890, JD Papers, DU; *Memoir*, II, 493.

27. JD to Herschel Johnson, September 18, 1864, *JDC*, VI, 338; W. D. Gale to Kate [Gale], July 30, 1864 (second quotation), Leonidas Polk Papers, UNC; Edward Younger, ed., *Inside the Confederate Government: The Diary of Robert Garlick Hill Kean* (New York, 1957), 165 (final quotation). For the context, see the Castel and Symonds works cited in note 9.

28. Johnston to His Wife, May 31, 1864 (first two quotations), McLane-Fisher Papers, MHS (I am grateful to Charles Royster for this and other references from this collection); Johnston to Braxton Bragg, July 11, 1864, *O.R.*, XXXVIII, pt. 5, 876 (final quotation); Benjamin Hill to [William Walthall], October 12, 1878 (copy, third quotation), William Walthall Papers, MDAH. Note 9 refers to the nature of the correspondence.

29. JD to Bragg, July 9, 1864, Bragg to JD, July 13, 15 (quotation), 1864, *PJD*, X, 509, 519, 523–25; Seddon to Hill, July 13, 1864, Hill to Seddon, July 14, 1864, *O.R.*, LII, pt. 2, 693–95, 704–07; on Brown's requesting reinforcements: Brown to JD, June 28, 1864, Candler, *Confederate*, III, 582, JD to Brown, June 29, 1864, *JDC*, VI, 278–79.

30. Johnston to His Wife, all in McLane-Fisher Papers, MHS: May 12 (first quotation), May 20, May 21 (second quotation), May 23 (third quotation), May 28, May 31, June 18 (fourth quotation), June 25, June 26, June 29, June 30 (final quotation), 1864. These letters, plus those he sent to the War Department, totally undermine Johnston's postwar claim in his *Narrative of Military Operations* (New York, 1874), chap. 11, that he had a definite plan to defeat Sherman.

31. JD to Lee, July 12, 13, 1864, *JDC*, VI, 291–92; Lee to JD, July 12, 1864 (two messages), *WPL*, 821–22; JD to James Lyons, August 13, [1878], James Lyons Papers, UNC; Benjamin Hill to [William Walthall], October 12, 1878 (copy), Walthall Papers, MDAH.

32. Benjamin to JD, February 15, 1879, *JDC*, VIII, 355–57; Seddon to W. T. Walthall, February 10, 1879, *ibid.*, 349–54; Younger, ed., *Kean Diary*, 151; Benjamin Hill to [William Walthall], October 12, 1878 (copy), Walthall Papers, MDAH.

33. JD to Johnston, July 16, 17, 1864, Johnston to JD, July 16, 1864, *O.R.*, XXXVIII, pt. 5, 882–83, 885.

34. On Grant, consult McPherson, *Battle Cry*, 756.

35. W. D. Gale to Kate [Gale], July 30, 1864, Polk Papers, UNC.

36. JD to Lee, July 12, 1864, *JDC*, VI, 291–92; Lee to JD, July 12, 1864, *WPL*, 822; Younger, ed., *Kean Diary*, 167.

37. Connelly, *Autumn*, chap. 15, is highly critical; Alfred H. Burne, *Lee, Grant and Sherman: A Study in Leadership in the 1864–65 Campaign* (New York, 1939), is quite positive; Castel, *Decision*, is measured, especially at 561–65.

38. John Perkins, Jr., to Joseph Davis, June 6, 1864, Mary E. Mitchell Papers, UNC; W. N. Pendleton to JD, April 23, 1864, *PJD*, X, 365.

39. *Chesnut*, 591; Jones, *Clerk*, II, 174–75; *Memoir*, II, 500 (quotation).

40. Joseph Davis to JD, April 8 (quotation), April 23, May 10, 1864, *PJD*, X, 319–20, 360–61, 407.

41. Jones, *Clerk*, II, 175 (quotations); Gorgas Journal, May 20, July 26, 1864, Gorgas Papers, LC; [James R. Gilmore], *Down in Tennessee and Back by Way of Richmond* (New York, 1864), 269, 281; W. D. Gale to Kate [Gale], July 30, 1864, Polk Papers, UNC.

42. [Gilmore], *Down in Tennessee*, 269.

43. *Ibid.*, 266–82 (quotations 271–72, 276, 280).

44. Jones, *Clerk*, II, 277; *Chesnut*, 642.

45. *Six Decades in Texas or Memoirs of Francis Richard Lubbock Governor of Texas in War-Time, 1861–63 [.] A Personal Experience in Business, War, and Politics*, ed. C. W. Raines (Austin, Tex., 1900), 553; Gorgas Journal, September 9, 1864, Gorgas Papers, LC; Jones, *Clerk*, II, 289, 293; *Richmond Examiner*, September 5, 1864; *Richmond Enquirer*, September 27, 1864; Margaret Burwell to Edmund Burwell, September 21, 1864 (quotation), Edmund S. Burwell Papers, UNC; *JDC*, VI, 341.

46. Shelby Foote, *The Civil War: A Narrative* (3 vols.; New York, 1958–74), III, 604–05 (first quotation); R. Lockwood Tower, ed., *A Carolinian Goes to War: The Civil War Narrative of Arthur Middleton Manigault, Brigadier General, C.S.A.* (Columbia, S.C., 1983), 254–55 (remaining quotations); *Richmond Examiner*, October 15, 1864; James Montgomery Lanning Diary, September 26, 27, 1864, MC; Connelly, *Autumn*, 471–72.

47. JD to L. B. Northrop, September 25, 1879, *JDC*, VIII, 415–16; William J. Cooper, Jr., "A Reassessment of Jefferson Davis as War Leader: The Case from Atlanta to Nashville," *JSH*, XXXVI (May 1970), 198.

48. Cooper, "Reassessment," 198 and n.; Richard Taylor to Governor Charles Clark, September 27, 28, 1864, Clark Administration Papers, MDAH; Richard Taylor, *Destruction and Reconstruction: Personal Experiences of the Late War* ([1879]; Waltham, Mass., 1968), 203–05; *Lubbock Memoirs*, 553.

49. JD to Hood, September 28, 1864, *JDC*, VI, 344–45; Gorgas Journal, September 9, 1864, Gorgas Papers, LC.

50. Lee to JD, September 19, 1864, Letterbook June 7, 1863–October 12, 1864, Robert E. Lee Papers, VHS; Alfred Roman, *The Military Operations of General Beauregard in the War Between the States, 1861 to 1865* (2 vols.; New York, 1883), II, 273–79; Undated manuscript on military operations, Pierre G. T. Beauregard Papers, LC; Taylor, *Destruction*, 205.

51. JD to Beauregard, October 2, 1864, to L. B. Northrop, September 25, 1879, *JDC*, VI, 348–49, VIII, 416; Roman, *Beauregard*, II, 279.

52. *Richmond Enquirer*, October 11, 1864; *JDC*, VI, 349, 356; *Chesnut*, 650–52 (quotation on 651); Invitation [Boys of Columbia] to Mr. President [October 1864], JD Papers, MC.

53. *Lubbock Memoirs*, 553; Jones, *Clerk*, II, 300.

54. JD to Johnson, September 18, 1864, to Governors, September 19, 1864, *JDC,* VI, 338, 338–40.

55. *Ibid.* has the speeches: Macon, 341–44, Montgomery, 345–47, Augusta, 356–61, Columbia, 349–56. The quotations in order come from 341, 343, 342, 354, 342, 359, 355, 357, 358, 359.

56. *Richmond Examiner,* September 5, 1864 (first quotation); Johnson to Alexander Stephens, September 28, 1864 (second quotation), Herschel Johnson Papers, DU, to JD, October 8, 1864 (third quotation), JD Papers, Schoff Collection, MI; Hill to JD, October 4, 1864 (fourth quotation), Keith Read Collection, UGA; H. L. Flash to JD, October 7, 1864 (fifth quotation), JD Papers, DU; *Richmond Enquirer,* October 4, 1864 (final quotation); Robert F. Durden, *The Gray and Black: The Confederate Debate on Emancipation* (Baton Rouge, La., 1972), 99–100.

57. Rable, *Confederate,* 272–73, 278–80; *Richmond Examiner,* November 16, 1864.

58. JD to Alexander Stephens, November 21, 1864, Alexander Stephens Papers, EU, to Vance, January 8, 1864, *JDC,* VI, 146. For general information, I have relied on and followed McPherson, *Battle Cry,* 762–67; Paul D. Escott, *After Secession: Jefferson Davis and the Failure of Confederate Nationalism* (Baton Rouge, La., 1978), 198–99; and esp. Larry E. Nelson, *Bullets, Ballots, and Rhetoric: Confederate Policy for the United States Presidential Contest of 1864* (University, Ala., 1980).

59. McPherson, *Battle Cry,* 596–98, 762–63; J. W. Tucker to JD, March 14, 1864, *JDC,* VI, 204–06.

60. *R&F,* II, 611 (quotation); Thompson to My Dear Wife, April 26, 1864, Jacob Thompson Papers, MC; JD to Clay and Thompson, April 27, 1864, *PJD,* X, 368–69; Clay to Louis Wigfall, April 24, 1864, Wigfall Family Papers, LC.

61. *R&F,* II, 507. The most detailed account of the raid is Duane Schultz, *The Dahlgren Affair: Terror and Conspiracy in the Civil War* (New York, 1998); also pertinent are Ernest B. Furgurson, *Ashes of Glory: Richmond at War* (New York, 1996), 249–58, and David Herbert Donald, *Lincoln* (New York, 1996), 489–90.

62. JD to Clay and Thompson and Thompson to my Dear Wife cited in note 60; Thompson to JD, September 12, 1864, Autograph File, Dearborn Collection, HU; JD AES dated October 13, 19, 1864, on W. Jefferson Buchanan to JD, October 13, 1864, RG109, m437, r121, f660, NA; D. H. Maury to William Walthall, June 15, 1876, Walthall Papers, MDAH; A. G. Brown Memoirs, 55–57, J. F. H. Claiborne Papers, UNC; JD to Walker Taylor, August 31, 1889, and W. P. Johnston to Henry T. Louthan, March 9, 14, 1898, Henry T. Louthan Papers, VHS; "A Proposed Abduction of Abraham Lincoln," *CV,* XI (April 1903), 157–58. The circumstantial case is made in William H. Tidwell *et al., Come Retribution: The Confederate Secret Service and the Assassination of Lincoln* (Jackson, Miss., 1988), and William H. Tidwell, *April '65: Confederate Covert Action in the American Civil War* (Kent, Ohio, 1995).

63. For the military background and Hood's campaign, I have relied on Burne, *Lee,* chap. 14; Cooper "Reassessment"; Connelly, *Autumn,* chaps. 16–17; Steven E. Woodworth, *Jefferson Davis and His Generals: The Failure of Confederate Command in the West* (Lawrence, Kans., 1990), chap. 14; and Richard M. McMurry, *John Bell Hood and the War for Southern Independence* (Lexington, Ky., 1982), chaps. 10–11.

64. Beauregard to Samuel Cooper, October 22, 24, 31 (with copy to JD), 1864, *O.R.,* XXXIX, pt. 1, 796–98, pt. 3, 841, 870; Hood to JD, November 6, 1864, J. B.

Hood, *Advance and Retreat: Personal Experiences in the United States and Confederate States Armies* (New Orleans, 1880), 272–73.

65. JD to Hood, November 7, 1864, to Beauregard, November 30, 1864, *JDC*, VI, 398–99, 413; B. H. Hill to Herschel Johnson, October 13, 1864, Johnson Papers, DU.

66. *M&P*, II, 482–98 (quotations in order, 482, 484–85, 489, 491, 494, 495, 497).

67. *R&F*, II, 569–70 (quotation); JD to L. B. Northrop, April 9, September 25, 1879, *JDC*, VIII, 376, 417–19.

68. On Sherman, consult McPherson, *Battle Cry*, 808–11.

69. VD to Chesnut, October 8 (first and second quotations), November 20 (final two quotations), 1864, *Chesnut*, 662–64, 674–75. VD actually used "X" rather than her husband's name, but the context leaves no doubt about X's identity.

70. *Memoir*, II, 529–33; VD to Mary Chesnut, October 8, 1864, *Chesnut*, 663; *Lubbock Memoir*, 557 (quotation); E. Merton Coulter, *The Confederate States of America, 1861–1865* (Baton Rouge, La., 1950), 219–22.

71. VD to Chesnut, October 8 (third quotation), November 6 (first, second, fourth quotations), 20, 1864, *Chesnut*, 662–64, 666–67, 674–75.

72. *New York Sunday World Magazine*, December 13, 1896 (quotations); Jo Higginbotham to Dear Sisters, December 25, 1864, in Joseph Higginbotham Diary, December 25, 1864, Private Collection Transcripts, MC.

73. *Richmond Examiner*, December 19, 1864, January 2, 1865.

CHAPTER FIFTEEN: *"The Issue Is . . . Very Painful for Me to Meet"*

1. J. B. Jones, *A Rebel War Clerk's Diary at the Confederate States Capital* (2 vols.; Philadelphia, 1866), II, 371–72.

2. Richard Hawes to JD, January 11, 1865, J. S. Preston to JD, December 28, 1864, Autograph File, Dearborn Collection, HU; M. W. Philips to JD, January 28, 1865, JD Papers, MC; David W. Lewis to JD, December 30, 1864, Keith Read Collection, UGA; A. G. Magrath to JD, December 25, 1864, Andrew G. Magrath Papers, SCL; Cobb to JD, January 6, 1865, Howell Cobb Papers, DU.

3. Thomas E. Schott, *Alexander H. Stephens of Georgia: A Biography* (Baton Rouge, La., 1988), 436–39; George C. Rable, *The Confederate Republic: A Revolution Against Politics* (Chapel Hill, N.C., 1994), 278–83; Steven E. Woodworth, *Davis and Lee at War* (Lawrence, Kans., 1995), 309–10.

4. Jones, *Clerk*, II, 389; JD to Braxton Bragg, January 16, 1865, *JDC*, VI, 450. On Sherman, see John G. Barrett's solid *Sherman's March Through the Carolinas* (Chapel Hill, N.C., 1956), and for Lee at Petersburg, consult Douglas Southall Freeman's magnificent *Lee's Lieutenants: A Study in Command* (3 vols.; New York, 1942–44), III, chaps. 32–34. Charles Royster, in chap. 1 of *The Destructive War: William Tecumseh Sherman, Stonewall Jackson, and the Americans* (New York, 1991), has a powerful account of the occupation and burning of Columbia.

5. Raphael Semmes, *Memoirs of Services Afloat During the War Between the States* ([1869]; Baton Rouge, La., 1996), 801; JD to Lucinda Stamps, January 8, 1865, Rosemont, Woodville, Miss.; Edward Younger, ed., *Inside the Confederate Government: The Diary of Robert Garlick Hill Kean* (New York, 1957), 192; VD to Liz [January 1865], Blair Family Papers, LC.

6. JD to Hugh, January 8, 1865, Mary Stamps Papers, UNC; VD to Liz, [January 1865], Blair Family Papers, LC.

7. Warren Akin to My Dear Wife, January 10, 1865, Bell Irvin Wiley, ed., *Letters of Warren Akin: Confederate Congressman* (Athens, Ga., 1959), 75; William A. Graham to My Dear Wife, February 26, 1865, J. G. de Roulhac Hamilton and Max R. Williams, eds., *The Papers of William Alexander Graham* (7 vols.; Raleigh, N.C., 1957–), VI, 256; Semmes, *Services*, 801; *Richmond Enquirer*, February 10, 1865.

8. Jones, *Clerk*, II, 372 (quotation), 380. Gary W. Gallagher has an excellent discussion of Lee's position in *The Confederate War: How Popular Will, Nationalism, and Military Strategy Could Not Stave Off Defeat* (Cambridge, Mass., 1997), 86–89.

9. *Richmond Examiner*, January 2, 9 (quotation), 1865; Andrew G. Magrath to JD, December 25, 1864, Magrath Papers, SCL; D. B. Fry to JD, January 8, 1865, Autograph File, Dearborn Collection, HU; Toombs to Alexander Stephens, March 23, 1865, Alexander Stephens Papers, EU.

10. Jones, *Clerk*, II, 385, 392; JD to James F. Johnson and Hugh W. Sheffey, January 18, 1865, to James A. Seddon, February 1, 1865, *JDC*, VI, 453–54, 458–61.

11. *WPL*, 891; JD to Lee, February 10, 1865, *JDC*, VI, 479; Lee to JD, February 9, 1865, *O.R.*, LI, pt. 2, 1082–83.

12. My primary sources for JD and the Blair Mission include Alexander H. Stephens, *A Constitutional View of the Late War Between the States* (2 vols.; Philadelphia, 1870), II, 584–619; Blair memorandum on conversation with JD, dated January 18, 1865, Blair Family Papers, LC; and a memorandum by W. J. Bromwell, dated January 28, 1865 (copy), Causten-Pickett Papers, *ibid. JDC*, VI, 465–78, contains the official documents (466 second quotation, 476 first quotation); *Richmond Examiner*, January 13, 1865; W. A. Graham to My Dear Wife, January 14, 1865, to David L. Swain, January 28, 1865 (quotation), Hamilton and Williams, eds., *Graham Papers*, VI, 216, 224–25; Stephens to JD, January 28, 1865, C. C. Jones, Jr., Georgia Portfolio, II, DU; JD to Mrs. D. M. Barringer, February 7, 1865, D. M. Barringer Papers, UNC; JD to James M. Mason, June 11, 1870, JD Papers, DU; John A. Campbell memorandum on Hampton Roads Conference, dated February 1865 (typescript), John A. Campbell Papers, UNC; S. R. Mallory to Master S. R. Mallory, December 8, 1865, Stephen R. Mallory Papers, *ibid.* (all future Mallory citations are from this collection). On Lincoln and slavery, cf. David Herbert Donald, *Lincoln* (New York, 1995), 559–60, and James M. McPherson, *Battle Cry of Freedom: The Civil War Era* (New York, 1988), 823–24n. For more detailed accounts, see Donald, *Lincoln*, 556–59, and Schott, *Stephens*, 439–47, which inform my discussion.

13. Schott, *Stephens*, 448 (first quotation); *Richmond Examiner*, February 7 (second quotation), 10, 1865; Hill to JD, February 17, 1865, Keith Read Papers, UGA; *Richmond Enquirer*, February 10, 1865.

14. Jones, *Clerk*, II, 411 (first quotation); *Richmond Examiner*, February 7 (second quotation), 10, 1865; *Richmond Enquirer*, February 10, 1865; Edward A. Pollard, *Life of Jefferson Davis with a Secret History of the Southern Confederacy...* (Philadelphia, 1869), 470–71; Myrta Lockett Avary, *Recollections of Alexander H. Stephens: His Diary Kept When a Prisoner at Fort Warren, Boston Harbour, 1865...* (New York, 1910), 183, 241.

15. JD to Lee, February 28, 1865, *JDC*, VI, 489; Lee to JD, March 2, 1865, Douglas Southall Freeman, ed., *Lee's Dispatches: Unpublished Letters of General Robert E. Lee, C.S.A. to Jefferson Davis and the War Department of the Confederate States of*

America ([1915]; New York, 1957), 371–72; Hunter to James M. Mason, September 19, 1870, Virginia Mason, *The Public Life and Diplomatic Correspondence of James M. Mason* (New York and Washington, D.C., 1906), 596–97; William Walthall Diary, March 4, 1877, William Walthall Papers, MDAH; JD to W. P. Johnston, March 5, 1874, Johnston Papers, TU, to J. W. Jones, March 27, 1878, JD Papers, MC; Brown Memoirs, 64–65, J. F. H. Claiborne Papers, UNC; Mallory to Master S. R. Mallory, December 8, 1865; Woodworth, *Davis and Lee*, 314–15.

16. JD to J. W. Jones, December 11, 1877, JD Papers, MC.

17. *M&P*, II, 694–97 (quotations 696–97), 709–18; Eli N. Evans, *Judah P. Benjamin: The Jewish Confederate* (New York, 1988), 274–75, 278–79; Robert F. Durden, *The Gray and the Black: The Confederate Debate on Emancipation* (Baton Rouge, La., 1972), 147–49. Craig A. Bauer gives a thorough account in "The Last Effort: The Secret Mission of the Confederate Diplomat, Duncan F. Kenner," *Louisiana History,* XXII (Winter 1981), 67–95.

18. *M&P*, I, 494.

19. For the fundamental bond between white independence and black slavery, see my *Liberty and Slavery: Southern Politics to 1860* (New York, 1983).

20. Durden, *The Gray*, 29–34; W. H. Lee to JD, May 4, 1861, Stephen Blocker to JD, July 17, 1861, O. G. Eiland to JD, July 20, 1863, Leonidas Walthall to JD, August 11, 1863 (quotation), *PJD*, VII, 148, 250, IX, 293, 339–40.

21. Durden, *The Gray*, 53–63, 64 (first quotation), 66–67; Harris to JD, January 16, 1864 (second quotation), Gen. W. H. T. Walker to JD, January 12, 1864, JD to Gen. Walker, January 23, 1864 (final quotation), JD AES [February 10, 1864], *PJD*, X, 177–78, 170, 197–98, 228–29; *ibid.*, 178–79n. On Cleburne, see Craig L. Symonds, *Stonewall of the West: Patrick Cleburne and the Civil War* (Lawrence, Kans., 1997), chap. 10.

22. JD to Andrew Magrath, January 17, 1865, to Joseph Brown, January 18, 1865, *JDC*, VI, 451–52; Durden, *The Gray*, 151–53, 159–64, 183–85; I. H. Stringfellow to JD, February 8, 1865 (quotation), Samuel Clayton to JD, January 10, 1865 (typescript), RG109, U.S. Colored Troops, NA.

23. Graham to David L. Swain, February 22, 1865, Hamilton and Williams, eds., *Graham Papers*, VI, 253; Durden, *The Gray*, 113–17, 233–35, 250–52; Yulee to JD, October 27, 1864, Pritchard von David Collection, UT; Cobb to James A. Seddon, January 8, 1865, *O.R.*, ser. 4, III, 1009–10 (quotation on 1009).

24. On the point about emancipation, see Rable, *Confederate Republic*, 364 n. 61.

25. Lee to Andrew Hunter, January 11, 1865, to Congressman Ethelbert Barksdale, February 18, 1865, Durden, *The Gray*, 206–09.

26. JD to John Forsyth, February 21, 1865, *JDC*, VI, 482 (first two quotations); *M&P*, I, 494; JD to Smith, March 30, 1865, *David Battan Catalog 14*, item 57.

27. Durden, *The Gray*, 202–03, 249–50; *R&F*, I, 518–19; *M&P*, I, 547; Rable, *Confederate Republic*, 287–96.

28. *M&P*, I, 544; Benjamin to JD, May 28, 1867, JD Papers, MC.

29. Jones, *Clerk*, II, 355, 357, 411, 426; *Memoir*, II, 206, 573–74; Josiah Gorgas Journal, February 16, 1865, William C. Gorgas Papers, LC; Harris D. Riley, Jr., "Jefferson Davis and His Health: Part II, January, 1861–December, 1889," *JMH*, IL (1987), 279.

30. Nelson D. Lankford, ed., *An Irishman in Dixie: Thomas Conolly's Diary of the Fall of the Confederacy* (Columbia, S.C., 1988), 42 (fourth quotation), 47 (first,

fifth quotations); John S. Wise, *The End of an Era* (Boston and New York, 1899), 400–01 (second, third, sixth quotations).

31. JD to Seddon, February 1, 1865, *JDC*, VI, 458–61 (quotation 461).

32. Grady McWhiney and Judith Lee Hallock, *Braxton Bragg and Confederate Defeat* (2 vols.; Tuscaloosa, Ala., 1991), II, chap. 9, details Bragg's work.

33. JD AES on James Seddon to JD, May 26, 1864, Nomination List; JD AES on S. F. Harwood to JD, September 12, 1864, mf474, r115, f628; JD AES on Hardee to JD, December 29, 1864, *ibid.*, r120, f591; JD AES on George Hodge to [?], February 6, 1865, *ibid.*, r158, f253; JD AES on John C. Breckinridge to JD, April 24, 1865, *ibid.*, r164, f606, all RG109, NA.

34. JD to James Phelan, March 1, 1865, *JDC*, VI, 491; *ibid.*, 491–503, has the memorandum dated February 18, 1865; Rable, *Confederate Republic*, 286.

35. *Chesnut*, 725 (first quotation), 729 (second quotation).

36. JD to VD, April 23, 1865, *JDC*, VI, 559; JD to Jubal Early, August 13, 1881, JD Papers, DU, and to Thomas T. Munford May 28, 1889 (copy), Munford-Ellis Papers, Thomas T. Munford Division, *ibid.*; handwritten notes 146ff. in JD's copy of Walter H. Taylor, *Four Years with General Lee* (New York, 1878), JD Papers, TU.

37. *Memoir*, II, 575–77 (quotation on 577); JD to Mary Omelia, April 2, 1865, JD Papers, MC; JD to Genl [late March 1865], with AES by John C. Breckinridge, JD Papers, DU; JD to Josiah Gorgas, March 29, 1865, Josiah Gorgas Papers, UA; Jones, *Clerk*, II, 461, 465; Ishbel Ross, *First Lady of the South: The Life of Mrs. Jefferson Davis* (New York, 1958), 214.

38. *O.R.*, XLVI, pt. 3, 1378; Reagan to Mrs. Isabel Maury, February 27, 1901, CSA Government Collection Series, MC; "Autobiography," *PJD*, I, lxiii. Ernest B. Furgurson has a fine general description of events in his *Ashes of Glory: Richmond at War* (New York, 1996), 319–25.

39. Mallory Diary, II, April 2, 1865.

40. *R&F*, II, 667 (quotation); Lee to JD, April 2, 1865, *ibid.*, 660–61; JD to Lee, April 2, 1865, *O.R.*, XLVI, pt. 3, 1378; Lee to JD, April 2, 1865, Freeman, ed., *Dispatches*, 375; Douglas Southall Freeman, *R. E. Lee: A Biography* (4 vols.; New York, 1934–35), IV, 55.

41. *R&F*, II, 667–68; JD to VD, April 5, 1865, *JDC*, VI, 532–33; *Life and Reminiscences of Jefferson Davis* (Baltimore, 1890), 42–43 (quotation); John Taylor Wood Diary, April 2, 1865, John Taylor Wood Papers, UNC (all future citations from this collection).

42. Wellford Diary, April 2, 1865, White, Wellford Papers, UNC; Mallory Diary, II, April 2, 1865; Wise, *End*, 415; Wood Diary, April 3, 1865; Myrta Lockett Avary, *Dixie After the War: An Exposition of Social Conditions Existing in the South . . .* (New York, 1906), 47. Burke Davis, *The Long Surrender* (New York, 1985), and Michael B. Ballard, *A Long Shadow: Jefferson Davis and the Final Days of the Confederacy* (Jackson, Miss., 1986), provide detailed accounts of the retreat.

43. JD to Lee, March 22, 1865, to VD, April 6, 1865, *JDC*, VI, 519–21, 533–34; JD to Bragg, April 1, 1865, *Sotheby's Fine Manuscripts and Printed Americana, Sale 6488* (1993); A. L. Rives to JD, April 10, 1865, JD Papers, DU.

44. *JDC*, VI, 529–31.

45. Breckinridge to JD, [April 1865] (copy), Burton Harrison Papers, LC; Wise, *End*, 435–37; JD to Capt. Early, April 9, 1865, Early Family Papers, VHS; JD to Joseph Johnston, April 10, 1865, *JDC*, VI, 542–43.

46. W. P. Johnston to VD, April 12, 1865 (copy), Edwin M. Stanton Papers, LC; Wood Diary, April 11, 1865.

47. Wood Diary, April 11, 1865; W. P. Johnston to Rosa, April 22, 1865, Johnston Papers, TU; Mallory Diary, II.

48. W. P. Johnston to VD, April 12, 1865 (copy), Stanton Papers, LC; JD to Vance, April 11, 1865, *O.R.*, XLVI, pt. 3, 1393; Alfred Roman, *The Military Operations of General Beauregard* (2 vols.; New York, 1884), II, 390–92.

49. Mallory Diary, II, "The Johnston-Sherman Negotiations"; John H. Reagan, *Memoirs with Special References to Secession and the Civil War* (Washington, D.C., 1906), 199–200 (first quotation); Reagan to JD, December 12, 1880, *JDC*, VIII, 535–39; Johnston to Beauregard, December 26, 1867 (JO 187), March 30, 1868, with Beauregard AES (JO 188), Joseph E. Johnston Papers, HL; Diary of Major Campbell Brown, January 14, 1866, George W. Campbell Papers, LC.

50. Lee to JD, April 12, 1865, *WPL*, 935–38; Robert E. Lee, Jr., *Recollections and Letters of General Robert E. Lee* (New York, 1904), 157.

51. Wood Diary, April 13, 1865.

52. JD to VD, April 23, 1865, *JDC*, VI, 561; Address of Col. William Preston Johnston, dated June 2, 1875, in Scrapbook *re* Thomas Jonathan (Stonewall) Jackson, Montrose Jonas Moses Collection, DU.

53. Wood Diary, April 15–19, 1865; Capt. Given Campbell Journal (typescript), Given Campbell Papers, LC (all future citations are to this collection).

54. James Morris Morgan, *Recollections of a Rebel Reefer* (Boston and New York, 1917), 231–32; VD to JD, April 1, 1865, JD Papers, DU, and April 7, 13, 1865, *JDC*, VI, 537–39, 544; *Chesnut*, 785.

55. JD to VD, April 6, 14 (quotation), 1865, *JDC*, VI, 533–34, 545; Helen Trenholm to VD, April 9, 1865, and Armistead Burt to VD, April 10, 1865, JD Papers, MC.

56. Wood Diary, April 19, 1865; W. P. Johnston to Rosa, April 22, 1865, and W. P. Johnston Diary, April 20, 1865, Johnston Papers, TU; Mallory Diary, II, "Route South"; *JDC*, VI, 568–85, has the opinions, with Breckinridge's on 572–73.

57. JD to Bragg, April 20, 1865, Philip H. and A. S. W. Rosenbach Foundation, Philadelphia; *CV*, XXII (July 1914), 304, the speech; Alexander Stephens to Linton, April 20, 1865, Alexander H. Stephens Papers, Manhattanville College of the Sacred Heart.

58. Clement Dowd, *Life of Zebulon B. Vance* (Charlotte, N.C., 1897), 485–86; *JDC*, VI, 556–57; M. W. Gary to JD, April 18, 1865, and JD AES (copy), Pegram-Johnston, McIntosh Family Papers, VHS; Mallory Diary, II, "Route South."

59. JD to C. J. Wright, May 11, 1876, *JDC*, VII, 513; Mrs. Burton Harrison, *Recollections Grave and Gay* (New York, 1911), 224; A. W. Thomson, "How Jefferson Davis Received the News of Lincoln's Death," *The Independent*, LII (February 15, 1900), 436; Mallory Diary, II, "Route South."

60. George Everhart to JD, March 30, 1886, JD Papers, MC; JD to VD, April 23, 1865, *JDC*, VI, 559–62.

61. Wood Diary, April 24–May 2, 1865; Campbell Journal; *Columbia State Sunday Magazine*, January 31, 1954; Tench Tilghman Diary, April 26–May 2, 1865, Tench Tilghman Papers, UNC (all future citations are from this collection); map entitled "Flight of the Confederate Cabinet," Monroe Cockrell Papers, DU (all future citations are from this collection).

62. Harrison, *Recollections,* 223 (quotation); Mallory Diary, II, "Route South."

63. VD to JD, April 28, 1865, *JDC,* VI, 566–67.

64. *Memoir,* II, 612; Basil W. Duke, "Last Days of the Confederacy," in Robert U. Johnson and Clarence C. Buel, eds., *Battles and Leaders of the Civil War* (4 vols.; New York, 1887–88), IV, 764; W. C. P. Breckinridge and Basil Duke to William Walthall, April 3, 6, 1878, G. G. Dibrell to W. P. Johnston, April 9, 1878, *JDC,* VIII, 151–54, 156–60, 160–64.

65. Roman, *Beauregard,* II, 390; Dowd, *Vance,* 485–86; Duke, "Last Days," 764 (quotation).

66. Wood Diary, May 3, 1865; Campbell Journal; Avary, *Dixie,* 59; Reagan, *Memoirs,* 215; *R&F,* II, 694–95.

67. Reagan to JD, August 16, 1877, von David Collection, UT; JD to Reagan, August 21, 1877, JD-John H. Reagan Collection, Dallas Historical Society, Dallas; Reagan, *Memoirs,* 212; Mallory Diary, II, "Route South"; Campbell Journal; "Autobiography," *PJD,* I, lxiii.

68. The basic sources for the final flight are: Wood Diary, May 4–10, 1865 (second quotation, May 9); Campbell Journal; Tilghman Diary, May 3–6, 1865 (first quotation, May 5); W. P. Johnston Diary, May 4–10, 1865, Johnston Papers, TU; map, "Flight."

69. Pertinent on the capture are the Wood and Johnston diaries; Burton Harrison narrative, *JDC,* VII, 6–19, IX, 226–60; VD to F. P. Blair, June 6, 1865, Blair Family Papers, LC; *Raleigh Daily News,* August 21, 1877; JD, W. P. Johnston, F. R. Lubbock to William Walthall, May 20, 1876, July 14, August 2, 1877, Walthall Papers, MDAH. JD did not attempt to escape in women's clothes; in his haste he did grab Varina's cloak, but that item was widely used in basically the same version by both men and women. After his capture, the claim that he had been disguised as a woman spread across the North. Chester D. Bradley, "Was Jefferson Davis Disguised as a Woman When Captured?" *JMH,* XXXVI (August 1974), 243–68, is authoritative on its subject. In her *The Romance of Reunion: Northerners and the South, 1865–1900* (Chapel Hill, N.C., 1993), chap. 1, Nina Silber has a provocative discussion of the northern embrace of the disguise tale.

CHAPTER SIXTEEN: *"I Have Not Sunk Under My Trials"*

1. John Taylor Wood Diary, May 10, 1865, John Taylor Wood Papers, UNC; Burton Harrison Statement, *JDC,* VII, 15–19; VD to F. P. Blair, June 6, 1865, Blair Family Papers, LC; James Nourse Diary, 287–88, James Nourse Papers, DU; Virginia Clopton-Clay, *A Belle of the Fifties: Memories of Mrs. Clay of Alabama . . .* (New York, 1905), 257 (quotation), 259–62; Myrta Lockett Avary, *Recollections of Alexander H. Stephens: His Diary Kept When a Prisoner at Fort Warren, Boston Harbor, 1865 . . .* (New York, 1910), 113–14, 118–20, 123–24 (quotation 124); John H. Reagan, *Memoirs with Special Reference to Secession and the Civil War* (Washington, D.C., and New York, 1906), 221; *Memoir,* II, 641–48.

2. For JD's imprisonment through 1865, see *O.R.,* ser. 2, VIII, 563–66, 570–71, 577, 720, 740 (all citations in this chapter are to ser. 2, unless otherwise noted); Captain Titlow's account reprinted in Chester D. Bradley, "Dr. Craven and the Prison Life of Jefferson Davis," *Virginia Magazine of History and Biography,* LXII (Janu-

ary 1954), 72–74; Clay to Virginia Clay, August 11, 1865, C. C. Clay Papers, DU; Virginia Clopton-Clay, "Prison & Prisoners," *ibid.;* JD to VD, September 15, 20, 26, November 3, December 7, 1865, JD Papers, TR, October 11, 1865, *Memoir,* II, 726–27; Edward K. Eckert, *"Fiction Distorting Fact"*: *The Prison Life Annotated by Jefferson Davis* (Macon, Ga., 1987), xxii–xxxiii.

3. Richard Taylor, *Destruction and Reconstruction: Personal Experiences of the Late War* ([1879]; Waltham, Mass., 1968), 243–47; T. Michael Parrish, *Richard Taylor: Soldier Prince of Dixie* (Chapel Hill, N.C., 1992), 454.

4. Hugh McCulloch, *Men and Measures of Half a Century: Sketches and Comments* (New York, 1889), 410–12.

5. VD to JD, December 25, 1865, JD Papers, UA, JD to VD, February 17, 1866, JD Papers, TR; *O.R.*, VIII, 975.

6. *DAB*, XIII, 620–21, on O'Conor; O'Conor to Franklin Pierce, July 5, 1865, Franklin Pierce Papers, LC; O'Conor to Stanton, May 31, June 15, 1865, Stanton to O'Conor, June 1, 1865 (copy), O'Conor to James Speed, July 3, 1865 (copy), Speed to O'Conor, July 6, 1865, O'Conor to VD, July 1, September 13, 1865, JD Papers, MC; O'Conor to Jeremiah Black, July 1, 1865, Jeremiah Black Papers, LC; O'Conor to John C. Breckinridge, July 6, 1865, John C. Breckinridge Papers, VHS.

7. O'Conor to Black, June 7, July 1, 18, August 10, 1865, J. W. Pierce to Black, June 26, 1865, Black Papers, LC; O'Conor to Pierce, July 18, 1865, Pierce Papers, *ibid.;* George Shea to Greeley, August 22, 1865, Horace Greeley Papers, NYPL; Greeley to Blair, August 29, 1865, JD Papers, MC; Cushing to Pierce, July 3, 1865, Caleb Cushing Papers, LC.

8. McRae to JD, May 18, 1867, JD Papers, MC; Thompson to Jeremiah Black, July 6, September 2, 1865, Black Papers, LC, October 9, 1865, *Dealer's Catalog*, Jacob Thompson Papers, MC; Thompson to Breckinridge, September 14, 1865, William C. Davis, "The Conduct of 'Mr. Thompson,' " *Civil War Times Illustrated*, IX (May 1970), 65; Mason to O'Conor, June 9, July 20, 1865 (copies), McRae to Mason, June 20, 1865, O'Conor to Mason, July 9, August 16, 1865, James M. Mason Papers, LC; Breckinridge to O'Conor, June 26, 1865, Breckinridge Papers, VHS; Robert Lowry to Burton Harrison, February 26, 1867, B. G. Humphreys to Harrison, March 27, 1867, Burton Harrison Papers, LC.

9. O'Conor to James M. Mason, July 9, August 16, September 6, October 19, 1865, Mason Papers, LC; O'Conor to Virginia Clay, June 29, 1865 (typescript), Clay Papers, DU; O'Conor to Breckinridge, July 6, 1865, Breckinridge Papers, VHS; F. E. Boyle to JD, October 10, 1880, JD to Louis Schade, October 5, 1888, Schade to JD, November 18, 1888, R. B. Winder to JD, December 10, 1888, *JDC*, VIII, 501–02, X, 82, 87–89, 93–95.

10. On conspiracy theories, William Hanchett, *The Lincoln Murder Conspiracies . . .* (Urbana, Ill., 1983), esp. chap. 3, is thorough.

11. McCulloch, *Men,* 408–09 (quotation on 408); Chase to Jacob Shuckers, May 15, 1866, Samuel P. Chase Papers, LC; Howard K. Beale, ed., *Diary of Gideon Welles* (3 vols.; New York, 1960), II, 335–39, 365–68.

12. McCulloch, *Men,* 409; *JDC*, VII, 141–42.

13. VD to Dr. John Craven, October 10, 1865, *Memoir*, II, 708–17 (quotation 710); VD to F. P. Blair, June 6, 1865, Blair Family Papers, LC; VD to Freda Lorenz, [1865], Phillips-Myers Papers, UNC.

14. VD to Julia Tyler, July 24, 1865, Dr. Robert McElroy, ed., "A New Davis Letter," *TQH*, XVII (July 1935), 24; Margaret Howell to VD, August [1865], JD Papers, UA, to George Shea, September 13, 1865, JD Papers, MC.

15. McRae to VD, August 11, September 25, 1865, JD Papers, UA, December 29, 1865, JD Papers MC; William Preston to VD, November 1, 1865, JD Papers, UA; VD to Octavus Cohen, August 3, 1865, to Secretary and Agent of Ladies Southern Association, December 4, 1865, from undated, untitled clipping, JD Papers, MC; Benjamin to VD, November 16, December 6, 1865, January 25, 1866, JD Papers, TR; VD to Major Edward Willis, two letters [1865], January 2, February 2, 1866, receipt dated November 20, 1865, Major Edward Willis Papers, SCHS; VD to Lise Mitchell, December 7 [1865], Lise Mitchell Papers, TU; VD to Margaret Howell [autumn 1865], JD Papers, TR; VD to Mary Chesnut, September 20, 1865, Williams-Chesnut-Manning Papers, SCL.

16. VD to General James Steelman, August 4, 1865 (copy), Andrew Johnson Papers, LC; Joseph D. Smith to "My Dear Son," September 22, 1865, Joseph D. Smith Papers, LSU; JD to VD, October 11, 1865, JD Papers, TR; Ishbel Ross, *First Lady of the South: The Life of Mrs. Jefferson Davis* (New York, 1958), 265–66.

17. VD to F. P. Blair, July 10, 1865 (first quotation), A. Johnson Papers, LC, June 23, 1865 (second quotation), Blair-Lee Papers, PU; VD to Julia Tyler, July 24, 1865, *TQH*, 24; VD to Mary Chesnut, September 20, 1865, Williams-Chesnut-Manning Papers, SCL.

18. VD to Blair, June 6, 1865, Blair Family Papers, LC, June 23, 1865, Blair-Lee Papers, PU, September 26, 1865, A. Johnson Papers, LC; VD to Grant, December 18, 1865, Autograph File, Dearborn Collection, HU; VD to Johnson, August 30, September 25, 1865, *PAJ*, VIII, 672, IX, 131–32; VD to Greeley, June 22, 1865 (copy), Greeley to VD, June 27, 1865, JD Papers, MC: Blair to VD, June 12, 1865, *ibid.*, Blair to Johnson, August 18, 1865 (draft), Blair-Lee Papers, PU; numerous letters among O'Conor, George Shea, and VD are in JD Papers, MC.

19. *O.R.*, VIII, 870, 874–75; *Memoir*, II, 756; VD to JD, April 12 (quotation), 14, 1865, JD Papers, UA.

20. The following discussion is based on the extensive correspondence between them. The notes at the ends of paragraphs will refer only to the dates for quotations. All the JD letters are in JD Papers, TR, and all from VD are in JD Papers, UA, except where otherwise specified. JD to VD, August 21, September 15, 26, October 11, 20, November 3, 21, 26, December 2, 7, 30, undated [1865], 1865, and January 16, 24, 28, February 3, 17, March 13, April 8, 21, 1866. VD to JD, August 31 (in A. Johnson Papers, LC), September 14, 22, October 1, 2, 23, n.d., November 7, 13, 27, n.d., December 7 (typescript copy in David Rankin Barbee Papers, LC), 1865, January 22, February 8, 23, March 8, April 12, 14, 16, 1866.

21. August 21, October 20, November 21, 26, 1865.

22. Handprint on September 22, 1865.

23. Margaret Davis to JD, November 30, 1865, March 2, 14, 1866, JD Papers, UA; JD to Margaret Davis, March 23 (quotation), April 9, 1866, JD Papers, TR.

24. October 20, December 30, 1865.

25. March 13, 1866.

26. September 26, October 20, 1865, February 3, 17, April 21, 1866.

27. November 3, October 23, October n.d., December 25, 1865.

28. October 23, 1865; VD to Martha Levy, January 2, 1866, Philip Phillips Family Papers, LC.

29. November 21, 1865.

30. *O.R.*, VIII, 901, 902; *Memoir*, II, 757–59 (quotation on 759), 773, 775; Geo. W. Brown to Franklin Pierce, July 14, 1866, Pierce Papers, LC; Harrison to W. P. Johnston, August 4, 1866, Johnston Papers, TU; G. Wilkins to JD, August 15, 1866, JD Papers, DU; Margaret Howell to W. T. Sutherlin, April 1, 1867, William T. Sutherlin Papers, UNC; Eckert, "*Fiction*," xxxix.

31. VD to Johnson, May 5, 19, 1866, *PAJ*, X, 476–77, 521–22 (first quotation); *Memoir*, II, 768–69; VD to Maj. Willis, June 6, 1866, Willis Papers, SCHS; VD to Greeley, September 2, October 6, November 21, n.d. [1867], 1867, Greeley Papers, NYPL; VD to R. Johnson, July 19, October 16, 1866, Reverdy Johnson Papers, LC; VD to Garrett, April 10, May 1, 1867, Robert Garrett Family Papers, *ibid.;* VD to "My Dear Old Girl," September 27, 1866 (second quotation), Blair Family Papers, *ibid.;* Burton Harrison to Mother, June 13, 1866, James Elliott Walmsley, ed., "Some Unpublished Letters of Burton N. Harrison," *PMHS*, VIII (1904), 82.

32. *O.R.*, VIII, 908 (Dr. Cooper's report), 924 (surgeon general's report), 950–83 *passim* (the weekly reports).

33. *Memoir*, II, chap. 73 *passim;* Miles to General E. D. Townsend, May 28, November 16, 1866, and to Stanton, August 24, 1866, *O.R.*, VIII, 919, 975, 955; Nelson A. Miles, "My Treatment of Jefferson Davis," *The Independent*, LVIII (February 23, 1905), 413–17; *A Statement of the Facts Concerning the Imprisonment and Treatment of Jefferson Davis* . . . (Washington, D.C., 1902), reprinted in Eckert, "*Fiction*," 142–49, and *ibid.*, xxxviii.

34. Geo. W. Brown to Franklin Pierce, July 14, 1866, Pierce Papers, LC; Burton Harrison to Armistead Burt, January 11, 1867, Armistead Burt Papers, DU, to W. P. Johnston, August 4, 1866, Johnston Papers, TU; Giles Hillyer to Burton Harrison, December 1, [1866], Harrison Papers, LC; the weekly reports cited in note 32 above.

35. Clay to Virginia Clay, November 1, December 30, 1866, Clay Papers, DU; *Memoir*, II, 774–75; JD to Pierce, May 8, 1867, Pierce Papers, LC; Charles O'Conor to George Shea, August 6, 1866, JD Papers, MC; Burton Harrison to [Mother], June 20, 1866, Fairfax Harrison, ed., *Avis Sonis Facisque, Being a Memoir of an American Family: The Harrisons of Skimino* (Privately printed, 1910), 196–97; Andrew Johnson to Edwin Stanton, June 6, 1866, *PAJ*, X, 567–68.

36. Polly to JD, September 11, November 17, 1866, March 25, 1867; JD, Jr. to JD, May n.d., 1866; William H. Davis to JD [May 17, 1867], JD Papers, UA; JD to "My Dear Daughter," May 23, 1866, JD Papers, TR.

37. VD to JD, August 14, 17, 18, December 8 (first quotation), 16 (second quotation), 1866, March 15, 18, 19 (third quotation), 20, 23, 25, [27], 28, [31], April 2, 3, 1867, JD Papers, UA.

38. Brooks D. Simpson *et al.*, eds., *Advice After Appomattox: Letters to Andrew Johnson, 1865–1866* (Knoxville, Tenn., 1987), 45–46, 48 n. 10; William Wilkins Glenn, *Between North and South: A Maryland Journalist Views the Civil War*, ed. Bagly Ellen Marks and Mark Norton Schatz (Rutherford, N.J., 1976), 153.

39. Lee to Walter Taylor, May 25, 1866, Robert E. Lee Papers, MC; Kenneth Rayner to William P. Fessenden, April 23, 1867, Kenneth Rayner Miscellaneous Manuscripts, New York Historical Society; Cobb to William Henry Seward, July 18, 1865 (second quotation), to Daniel Sickles, September 12, 1866 (third quotation),

Ulrich Bonnell Phillips, ed., *The Correspondence of Robert Toombs, Alexander H. Stephens, and Howell Cobb* (Washington, D.C., 1913), 663–65, 682–84.

40. Robert Lowry to Burton Harrison, February 26, May 10, 1867, Harrison Papers, LC; JD to Mrs. J. K. Kyle, April 22, 1866, David Rankin Barbee, "A Sheaf of Old Letters," *TQH*, XXXII (October 1950), 100–01; W. W. Stover to N. Walker & Co., May 1, 1866, JD Papers, Woodson Research Center, RU; Emily Mason, "Visit to President Davis, 4 July [1866]," Lee Family Papers, VHS; Wm. Mumford to VD, February 3, 1867, JD Papers, DU; Emily Norton to JD, January 29, [1867], JD Papers, MC. For tobacco and spirits, see also sources cited in note 30 above.

41. Consult the excellent discussion in Jonathan Truman Dorris, *Pardon and Amnesty Under Lincoln and Johnson: The Restoration of Confederates to Their Rights and Privileges, 1861–1898* (Chapel Hill, N.C., 1953), 284–89.

42. Eckert, "*Fiction,*" xxxv–xxxvi; *Prison Life* . . . (New York, 1866).

43. Eckert, "*Fiction,*" xl–xlvii, and William Hanchett, "Reconstruction and the Rehabilitation of Jefferson Davis: Charles G. Halpine's *Prison Life,*" *JAH*, LVI (September 1969), 280–89, have good accounts, which inform my treatment.

44. *Prison Life passim* (quotation 373).

45. Josiah Gorgas Journal, July 1, 1866, William C. Gorgas Papers, LC.

46. Geo. W. Brown to Franklin Pierce, July 14, 1866 (quotation), Pierce Papers, *ibid.;* Glenn, *Between North,* 273; Eckert, "*Fiction,*" 1; Mrs. John T. Broadnax to JD, March 13, 1887, *JDC,* IX, 534–36. JD's copy of *Prison Life* is in JD Papers, TU; in his "*Fiction,*" Eckert reprints the entire book with JD's annotations, though the pagination differs from the original.

47. The standard study of Reconstruction is Eric Foner, *Reconstruction: America's Unfinished Revolution, 1863–1877* (New York, 1988); the most recent biography of Johnson is Hans L. Trefousse, *Andrew Johnson: A Biography* (New York, 1989). Both inform my discussion.

48. On the releases, see Dorris, *Pardon,* chaps. 9, 11, 12.

49. *Ibid.,* 281–84.

50. McCulloch, *Men,* 410; Charles O'Conor to VD, August 29, 1866, JD Papers, MC; *Memoir,* II, 769–70.

51. Re Davis's case: Roy F. Nichols, "United States Versus Jefferson Davis," *AHR,* XXXI (April 1926), 266–84, still has enormous value; also consult Charles M. Blackford, *The Trials and Trial of Jefferson Davis* (Richmond, Va., 1900), and George Shea, *Jefferson Davis: A Statement* . . . (London, 1877; originally printed in the *New York Tribune,* January 24, 1876). An extraordinarily valuable collection of documents is Bradley T. Johnson, *Reports of the Cases Decided by Chief Justice Chase in the Circuit Court of the United States Fourth Circuit, 1865–1869* ([1876]; New York, 1972), which includes filings, writs, rulings, arguments, agreements. The entire Davis record is reprinted in *JDC,* VII, 138–227, which I cite for convenience. In addition, letters from two attorneys general to the president are illuminating: James Speed on January 4, 1866, and Henry Stanbery on December 12, 1866, *PAJ,* IX, 570–72, XI, 345–47. All of these provide the foundation of my account; individual citations occur only where appropriate.

52. On Underwood, see *DAB,* XIX, 113–14; John Niven has the best study of Chase, *Salmon P. Chase: A Biography* (New York, 1995), esp. chap. 30 and 408–10; Chase to Johnson, October 12, 1865, *PAJ,* IX, 231–32. Chase also confided in Horace

Greeley concerning his requirements for holding the trial, Chase to Greeley, June 5, 1866, Greeley Papers, NYPL.

53. Taylor to VD, November 10, 1866, Mrs. Jefferson Davis Letters, IA; George Shea to VD, October 20, 1865, JD Papers, MC; Greeley Memorial (draft and finished copy), *ibid.*, *Memoir*, II, 768; Burton Harrison to Mother, June 13, 1866, Walmsley, ed., "Harrison Letters," 81–82.

54. VD to Greeley, June 22, 1865 (copy), Greeley to VD, June 27, 1865, Greeley to Frank Blair, August 29, 1865, JD Papers, MC; George Shea to Greeley, August 22, 1865, Greeley Papers, NYPL; Greeley to Chase, May 31, 1866, Chase Papers, LC; J. Glancy Jones to James Buchanan, May 15, 1867, James Buchanan Papers, HSP; John Russell Young, *Men and Memories: Personal Reminiscences* (2 vols.; New York and London, 1901), I, 117–19 (I am grateful to Charles Royster for this reference); Smith to Johnson, August 24, 1866, *PAJ*, XI, 135; *New York Times*, June 12, November 21, 1866; *New York Tribune*, summer 1865–spring 1867 *passim*, examples September 12, 21, November 9, 1866; Shea, *Jefferson Davis*.

55. O'Conor to Johnson, November 1, 1865, O'Conor and Thomas G. Pratt to Johnson, June 13, 1866, *PAJ*, IX, 322–24, X, 583–84; Memorandum "Thursday, June 7, 1866," Bradley T. Johnson Papers, Duke. Re coordination: Stephen Mallory to Wife, June n.d., 1866, Stephen Mallory Papers, UNC, George Shea to Horace Greeley, August 22, 1865, Greeley Papers, NYPL, to VD, October 20, 1865, JD Papers, MC.

56. O'Conor to James M. Mason, December 26, 1865, Mason Papers, LC, to W. P. Johnston, December 30, 1865, to JD, October 2, 1866, to VD, October 21, 1866, JD Papers, MC.

57. O'Conor to JD, February 8, 1878, JD Papers, MC.

58. JD to James Lyons, January 27, 1876, *JDC*, VII, 483; Harrison to Mother, June 13, 1866, Walmsley, ed., "Harrison Letters," 82.

59. Geo. W. Brown to Franklin Pierce, July 14, 1866, Pierce Papers, LC; O'Conor to John C. Breckinridge, July 6, 1865, Breckinridge Papers, VHS; O'Conor to VD, October 18, November 19, 1866, January 25, 1867, JD Papers, MC; F. A. Aiken to George Shea, September 16, 1865, *ibid.*

60. Harrison to [Mother], June 20, 1866, Harrison, ed., *Avis Sonis*, 197.

61. *Ibid.*, 196–97; O'Conor to Burton Harrison, July 13, 1866 (quotation), Harrison Papers, LC; Blackford, *Trial*, 24; Reed to Mary Brodhead (JD's niece), [1866], JD Papers, MC.

62. VD to JD, March 28, [31], 1867, JD Papers, UA; VD to Garrett, April 10, May 1, 1867, Garrett Papers, LC.

63. *JDC*, VII, 166–68 (writ), 168–69 (order).

64. O'Conor to VD, April 17, 27, May 2, 1867, JD Papers, MC; Harrison to Mother, May 18, 1867, Walmsley, ed., "Harrison Letters," 83–85; William Reed to Harrison, May 5, 1867, Harrison Papers, LC.

65. On JD en route to and in Richmond, see Harrison to Mother, May 18, 1867, Walmsley, ed., "Harrison Letters," 83–85; W. Asbury Christian, *Richmond: Her Past and Present* (Richmond, Va., 1912), 284–89 (second quotation 285); Virginia King, "Three Days," in her "Reminiscences," Virginia King Papers, UNC; James Millward to JD, July 11, 1887, *JDC*, IX, 575–76; *ibid.*, VII, 169–76 (O'Conor quotation 169). All quotations come from the Harrison letter unless otherwise noted.

66. Of the three major sureties, only Greeley was present in the courtroom; agents represented Smith and Vanderbilt.

CHAPTER SEVENTEEN: *"These Days of Our Hard Fortune"*

1. Harrison to [mother], May 18, 1867, James Elliott Walmsley, ed., "Some Unpublished Letters of Burton N. Harrison," *PMHS*, VIII (1904), 85.

2. Benjamin to Mason, May 29, 1867 (copy), Accession No. 7733-A, UVA; Mason to JD, May 14, 1867, Mallory to JD, May 14, 1867, Reagan to JD, May 21, 1867, Breckinridge to JD, June 15, 1867, Cobb to JD, July 31, 1867, JD Papers, MC; Lee to JD, June 1, 1867, R. E. Lee Letterbook No. 4, DeButts-Ely Collection of Lee Family Papers, VHS; Pierce to JD, May 14, 1867, Samuel W. Richey Collection of the Southern Confederacy, MU; Students to JD, June 3, 1867, JD Papers, Alabama Department of Archives and History.

3. A. J. Clark, "When Jefferson Davis Visited Niagara," *Ontario Historical Society Papers and Records*, XIX (1922), 87–89; Virginia Mason, *The Public Life and Diplomatic Correspondence of James M. Mason* (New York and Washington, D.C., 1906), 589; George T. Denison, *Soldiering in Canada: Recollections and Experiences by Lt. Col. George T. Denison* (Toronto, 1890), 68–70 (quotation 69).

4. VD to Burton Harrison, n.d. (received June 15, all quotations), August 24, 1867, Burton Harrison Papers, LC; VD to Robert Garrett, May 3[o], 1867, Robert Garrett Family Papers, *ibid.;* VD to JD, July 10, 1867, and Howell Cobb to JD, July 31, 1867, JD Papers, MC; VD to Col. Taylor, June 3, 1867 (typescript copy), VD Subject File, 1866–1899, MDAH; *Memoir*, II, 797–99.

5. JD to Joseph, July 22, 1867, Lise Mitchell Papers, TU, to Harrison, July 7, 1867, Harrison Papers, LC.

6. M. H. Clark to VD, August 30, October 30, November 13 (copy), 1865, January 15, 27, 29, 1866; M. H. Clark to Harrison, February 20, March 20, 1866, August 26, 1867; Van Benthuysen to VD, March 13, 1866, to A. Y. Stokes, May 9, 1867; W. E. Dickinson to VD, February 8, 1866; Tench Tilghman to VD, February 24, 1866, W. Winder to VD, March 2, 1866, J. D. Smith to VD, November 21, 1865; JD to Harrison, July 7, September 4, 1867 (quotation), to Van Benthuysen, July 5, 1867 (copy); Harrison to Van Benthuysen, August 20, 1867 (copy), and Memorandum, August 21, 1867, all Harrison Papers, LC; [M. H. Clark] to Van Benthuysen, August 27, 1865, Van Benthuysen Papers, *ibid.;* Van Benthuysen to Joseph Davis, March 12, 1867, Davis Family Papers, MDAH.

7. VD to Mary Ann Cobb, July 6, 1868 (first quotation), Howell Cobb Papers, UGA; *Memoir*, II, 799–800; Virginia Frazer Boyle, "Jefferson Davis in Canada," *CV*, XXXVII (March 1929), 89–93; George E. Carter, "A Note on Jefferson Davis in Canada—His Stay in Lennoxville, Quebec," *JMH*, XXXIII (May 1971), 133–36; JD to "My dear Daughter," October 28, 1867, JD Papers, UA, to Col. Helm, October 30, 1867 (copy, second quotation), JD-Charles J. Helm Papers, UM; JD Pocket Diary, June 1, 1868, JD Papers, MC.

8. O'Conor to JD, October 2 (quotation), 18, 29, November 5, 12, 13, 1867, to VD, October 21, 1867, JD Papers, MC; JD to "Dear William [Howell]," November 6, 1867, JD Papers, Beauvoir.

9. Roy F. Nichols, "United States Versus Jefferson Davis," *AHR*, XXXI (April 1926), 276–77; *JDC*, VII, 176–79.

10. *Memoir*, II, 799–800, 803; [Margaret Howell] to "My Dear Daughter," October n.d., 1867, JD Papers, UA; *PJD*, II, 56n.; JD to Children, February 15, 1868, JD and Family Papers, MDAH.

11. Lee to Mary C. Lee, November 26, 1867, Lee Family Papers, VHS.

12. *Memoir*, II, 803–04; JD to Children, February 15, 1868, JD and Family Papers, MDAH.

13. On Joseph's pardon and the land, both Janet Sharp Hermann, *The Pursuit of a Dream* (New York, 1981), chap. 4, and Frank Edgar Everett, Jr., *Brierfield: Plantation Home of Jefferson Davis* (Jackson, Miss., 1971), chap. 9, provide details on which I have based my account. Also see Jonathan Truman Dorris, *Pardon and Amnesty Under Lincoln and Johnson: The Restoration of the Confederates to Their Rights and Privileges, 1861–1898* (Chapel Hill, N.C., 1953), 237–38.

14. JD to Joseph, December 17, 1866, *Bowmar*, 586–87.

15. *Memoir*, II, 804; Everett, *Brierfield*, 91.

16. VD to Mary Ann Cobb, July 6, 1868, Cobb Papers, UGA.

17. JD to Children, February 15, 1868, JD and Family Papers, MDAH; JD to Col. George Young, February 25, 1868 (second quotation), Evans Memorial Library, Aberdeen, Miss.

18. JD to [J. M. Howry], February 8, 1868, Howry Family Papers, LC.

19. JD to Gen. W. N. Pendleton, August 1, 1867 (first quotation), University Papers, W&L; JD to Col. George H. Young, February 25, 1868 (second quotation), Evans Library; JD to [J. M. Howry], February 8, 1868 (third quotation), Howry Family Papers, LC; JD to Joseph, July 22, 1867, Mitchell Papers, TU.

20. JD to Col. George Young, February 25, 1868, Evans Library; JD to Joseph D. Smith, March 7, 1868, JD Papers, TU; *Greenville [S.C.] Southern Enterprise*, April 22, 1868; Chronology (Box 36), JD Papers, MC.

21. To the basic sources cited in chapter sixteen at note 51, add Richard Henry Dana's informative "The Reasons for Not Prosecuting Jefferson Davis," *Proceedings of the Massachusetts Historical Society*, LXIV (April 1931), 201–09, which concentrates on the government attorneys in the post-bail period; *JDC*, VII, 179–95; O'Conor to Gentlemen, March 30, 1868, I. H. Carrington Papers, DU.

22. Lee to W. H. F. Lee, March 30, 1868, George Bolling Lee Papers, VHS.

23. *Memoir*, II, 805 (first quotation); VD to Col. Walter Taylor, July 6, 1868 (typescript, second quotation), VD Subject File, 1866–1899, MDAH; JD to Howell Cobb, July 6, 1868, *JDC*, VII, 243; JD Pocket Diary, April 2–June 25, 1868, and Chronology, JD Papers, MC.

24. O'Conor to Greeley, April 24, 1868, Horace Greeley Papers, NYPL; O'Conor to JD, April 9, 10, 18, 19, 26, May 13, 19, 27, 1868, Robert Ould to JD, April 8, 1868, JD Papers, MC; *JDC*, VII, 195–96; JD to I. H. Carrington, n.d., 1868 (typescript), JD Papers, UA.

25. *Memoir*, II, 805; JD to [Lucinda Boyle], June 4, 1868, JD Family Papers, LSU; VD to Mary Ann Cobb, July 6, 1868, Cobb Papers, UGA; Joseph to JD, n.d., 1868 (typescript), JD Papers, UA.

26. JD to Joseph Davis, July 22, 1867, Mitchell Papers, TU; Memorandum of Agreement re: Investment, July 11, 1867, Frederick Terrill to JD, August 24, 1867, January 15, July 3, 22, 1868, E. Clark to JD, July 20, 1868, JD Papers, MC.

27. Joseph Davis to JD, n.d., 1868 (typescript), JD Papers, UA; VD to Col. Walter Taylor, July 6, 1868 (typescript), VD Subject File, 1866–1899, MDAH; JD to Howell Cobb, July 6, 1868, with VD postscript, *JDC*, VII, 242–43. Because of JD's injuries, VD wrote both letters.

28. A. J. Beresford Hope to JD, June 7, 1867, JD Papers, MC.

29. VD to Mary Ann Cobb, July 6, 1868, Cobb Papers, UGA; JD Pocket Diary, JD Papers, MC.

30. *Memoir*, II, 807. Three sources are critical for places and dates in Europe: Chronology compiled by Patricia Cooper (in my possession, cited hereafter as PHC), the Chronology, and JD Pocket Diary, JD Papers, MC. I will not cite them constantly.

31. *Memoir*, II, 808; Pocket Diary, September 11, 1868.

32. Wirt Adams to JD, August 16, September 1, 1868, JD Papers, MC.

33. A. J. Beresford Hope to JD, April 25, June 2, 1869, Earl of Shrewsbury to JD, August 28, 1868, Lord Abinger to JD, April 7, 1869, Lady Lothian to JD, May 4, 1869, Calling Card of Lady Eardley, n.d., *ibid.;* Lord Henry Percy to VD, July 10, [1869], JD to VD, September 4 (quotation), November 22, 1868, JD Papers, UA; JD to Beresford Hope, August 8, 20, 1868, *JDC*, VII, 244–45.

34. VD to Lise Mitchell, April 20, 1869 (first quotation), Mitchell Papers, TU; VD to Mary Ann Cobb, January 31, 1869, Cobb Papers, UGA; Louis de Rosset to Mother, August 5, 1869, de Rosset Family Papers, UNC.

35. Benjamin to JD, August 6, 1868, JD Papers, UA; *Memoir*, II, 810; Eli N. Evans, *Judah P. Benjamin: The Jewish Confederate* (New York, 1988), chaps. 18, 20.

36. *Memoir*, II, 809–10; JD to Charles J. Leigh, December 28, 1868, Lewis Leigh Collection, Archives Branch, U.S. Army Military History Institute, Carlisle Barracks, Pa., to VD, February 7, 1869, JD Papers, TR.

37. JD to VD, February 9, 1869 (quotations), JD Papers, UA, February 7, 1869, JD Papers, TR.

38. JD to VD, February 7, 1869, JD Papers, TR.

39. For this discussion, see the sources cited in note 21 above, and add Hans L. Trefousse, *Andrew Johnson: A Biography* (New York, 1989), 337, 347. *JDC*, VII, 196–227, has the court proceedings.

40. O'Conor to JD, December 7, 1868 (quotation), January 6, 1869, JD Papers, MC.

41. Wirt Adams to JD, August 16, September 1, 1868, Alfred Bland to JD, January 2, [1869], *ibid.;* Benjamin to JD, December 20, 1868, and JD to Editor, December n.d., 1868, *JDC* VII, 246–51; James P. Shenton, *Robert John Walker: A Politician from Jackson to Lincoln* (New York, 1961), 195–98.

42. JD to VD, November 22, 1868, August 26, 1869 (quotation), JD Papers, UA.

43. VD to Mary Ann Cobb, January 31, 1869, Cobb Papers, UGA, to Lise Mitchell, April 20, 1869, Mitchell Papers, TU; JD to VD, November 22, 1868 (second quotation), January 27, 1869, to Polly May 10, 1869 (first quotation), to Dudley Mann, April 19, 1869, Polly to JD, April 30, 1869, JD Papers, UA; JD to Cora Ives, April 25, 1869, JD Papers, DU; Sir Henry Holland, *Recollections of Past Life* (New York, 1872), 191n. (third quotation).

44. On JD and Scotland, see: Smith to JD, August 7, 1868, *JDC*, VII, 244; Lord Abinger to JD, July 26, [1869], William Blackwood to JD, July 2, 1869, Mackay to JD, July 19, 1869, JD Papers, MC; JD to VD, July 26, 30 (first quotation), August 2 (third

quotation), 9, 11, 17 (final quotation), 22, 26, 1869, to [Polly], August 6, 1869, JD Papers, UA; *Memoir*, II, 810–11; Mrs. Gerald Porter, *Annals of a Publishing House. John Blackwood* (Edinburgh and London, 1898), 200–03 (second quotation 201).

45. JD to VD, September 25, 1869, and VD to JD, September 27, 1869, JD Papers, UA.

46. JD to VD, October 11, 15, November 9, 1869, *ibid.;* JD to Dr. M. Clayton, September 16, 1869 (typescript), JD-Clayton Letters, UM; JD to [Isham Harris], June 23, 1869, Forbes Magazine Collection, New York City; Isham Harris to Joseph Davis, May 27, 1869, Mitchell Papers, TU. On workers' earnings, consult Harry N. Scheiber *et al.*, *American Economic History* (9th ed.; New York, 1976), 247 (I am grateful to Paul F. Paskoff for this reference).

47. J. C. Blackwell *et al.* to JD, June 9, 1868, JD Papers, MC; R. E. Blackwell to W. L. Fleming, August 17, 1910, Walter L. Fleming Papers, NYPL; JD to Bishop Green, January 5, 1870, Small Collection, Research Center, Houston Public Library; JD to Josiah Gorgas, January 6, 1870 (quotation), Josiah Gorgas Papers, UA; JD to VD, October 11, November 9, December 25, 1869, JD Papers, *ibid.*

48. JD to VD, October 11, November 9, n.d. (quotation), 1869, JD Papers, UA; Circular dated November 17, 1869, Avery Family Papers, UNC.

49. JD to A. M. Clayton, September 16, 1869 (typescript), JD-Clayton Letters, UM; JD to VD, October 15 (first quotation), November 23 (second quotation), [n.d.] (third quotation), 1869, JD Papers, UA.

50. JD to VD, November 9, 23, December 4, 25, 1869, JD Papers, UA; JD to James M. Mason, June 11, 1870, JD Papers, DU.

51. JD to Lafayette McLaws, November 19, 1870 (quotation), Lafayette McLaws Papers, UNC; Bragg to JD, December 1, 1869, Braxton Bragg Papers, Rosenberg Library, Galveston, Texas; JD to "My dear Genl.," January 26, 1870, Charles H. Collins Collection of Historical Manuscripts, Colorado College; JD to Early, April 16, 1870, John S. Preston to JD, August 4, 1871, JD Papers, DU; William Preston to JD, January 22, 1871, John S. Preston to JD, August 4, 1870, Joseph Wheeler to JD, January 22, 1871, JD Papers, MC; JD to VD, August 1, September 18, October 3, 1872, July 14, 1873, JD Papers, UA; JD to Mary Stamps, August n.d., 1870, Mary Stamps Papers, UNC; Sidney Lanier to P. H. Hayne, August 9, 1870, Paul H. Hayne Papers, DU; John S. Preston to JD, January 24, 1871, *JDC*, VII, 288–89; *Memoir*, II, 812; Chronology, JD Papers, MC. For the Clays, see note 56 below.

52. *JDC*, VII, 281–85 (quotations 281, 282).

53. JD to VD, November 23, December 4, 1869, March 13, May 17, [summer], 1870, July 27, 1873, JD Papers, UA; JD to Mary Stamps, January 7 (fourth quotation), August n.d., 1870 (second quotation), Stamps Papers, UNC; Corinne [Goodman] to [Virginia Clay], January 23, 1870 (first quotation), and JD to Virginia Clay, November 1, 1871 (third quotation), C. C. Clay Papers, Duke; VD to Robert Garrett, December 2, 1874, Garrett Family Papers, LC.

54. JD to Lise Mitchell, November 30, December, 1869, January 14, February 14, 19, 1870, Mitchell Papers, TU; Lise Mitchell to JD, February n.d., 1870, Howell Family Papers, MDAH; JD to VD, May 31, 1870, JD Papers, UA; JD to Virginia Clay, March 22, 1870, Clay Papers, DU; Janet Sharp Hermann, *Joseph E. Davis: Pioneer Patriarch* (Jackson, Miss., 1990), 163.

55. VD to JD, October 2, December n.d. (her first quotation), 3 (second and third quotations), 28, 1869, February 28, March 4, April 1, June n.d., August 1, 1870,

and JD to VD, November 23, [November n.d.], December 25, 1869, January 17, February 26, March 13, May 17, 31, 1870, to [Winnie], June 1, 1870, to Children, June 22, 1870, JD Papers, UA; JD to Lise Mitchell, November 30, 1869 (his quotation), Mitchell Papers, TU.

56. There are numerous letters from JD to Virginia Clay, mostly from 1870 and 1871, in the Clay Papers, DU. The quotations: January 23, 1870 (first), May 31, 1870 (second and third), May 18, 1870 (fourth, seventh, ninth), February 21, 1870 (fifth), August 15, 1872 (sixth), March 22, 1870 (eighth).

57. JD to VD, August 1, 1870, JD Papers, UA; JD to Joseph, July 17, August 9, 20, 1870, Mitchell Papers, TU; PHC Chronology.

58. PHC Chronology; JD to VD, September 18, 23, 1870, JD Papers, UA; T. E. B. Braed to JD, September 6, 1870, JD Papers, MC; Benjamin to JD, September 6, 1870, and JD to A. J. Beresford Hope, October 6, 1870, *JDC*, VII, 279–81.

59. *Memoir*, II, 811; VD to JD, June n.d., 1870, JD Papers, UA; JD to Charles Stoess, October 9, 1870, JD and Family Papers, MDAH.

60. JD to [Lise Mitchell], October 24, 1870, Mitchell Papers, TU.

61. JD to VD, October 27, November 1, 1870, JD Papers, UA; *Memoir*, II, 811.

62. *Memoir*, II, 811 (first quotation); JD to VD, June 7 (seventh quotation), 30 (third and fourth quotations), September 2, 29 (second quotation), 1871, to Polly, February 11, June 29, 1871, September 7, 1872 (eighth quotation), to "My Baby of All the World," October 22, 1871 (sixth quotation), JD Papers, UA; JD to Polly, October 26, 1871 (fifth quotation), JD Papers, TR; JD to Mary Stamps, May 8, December 7, 1872, April 2, 1873, Stamps Papers, UNC; JD to Lise Mitchell, February 7, 1871, Mitchell Papers, TU; JD to James Phelan, August 6, 1872, *JDC*, VII, 326–27.

63. JD to Louise Helm, October 29, 1872 (copy, first quotation), JD-Charles J. Helm Correspondence, UM; JD to William Walthall, October 25, 1872 (second quotation), *JDC*, VII, 332; JD to Virginia Clay, December 14, 1872 (third quotation), Clay Papers, DU; JD to Lucinda Stamps, January 4, 1873 (fourth quotation), Hudson Strode, ed., *Jefferson Davis: Private Letters, 1823–1889* (New York, 1966), 361; JD to Lise Mitchell, March 21, 1873 (fifth quotation), Mitchell Papers, TU; JD to VD, July 12, August 12, 24, 1873, to Polly, August 1, 1873, JD Papers, UA.

64. JD to VD, July 12, 14, 17, 21, 27 (first quotation), August 24 (second quotation), fragment [August 25], August 26, 1873, JD Papers, UA; JD to Wade Hampton, September 6, 1873, Hampton Family Papers, SCL; JD to A. M. Clayton, August 28, 1873 (typescript), JD-Clayton Letters, UM; JD to Virginia Clay, September 8, 1874, Clay Papers, DU.

65. JD to VD, September 7 (first quotation), October 16, November 5, 6, 10, 1873, JD Papers, UA; JD to Mary Stamps, November 23, 1873 (second quotation), Stamps Papers, UNC; JD to Maj. L. Meriwether, September 6, 1873 (fourth quotation), to Mrs. Meriwether, September 6, 1873 (third quotation), Minor T. Meriwether Collection, West Tennessee Historical Society, Memphis; JD to Virginia Clay, September 9, 1873, Clay Papers, DU; JD to Jubal Early, October 21, 1873 (fifth quotation), JD Papers, *ibid.;* JD to Wade Hampton, September 20, 1873, Hampton Family Papers, SCL; JD to Louise Helm, October 20, 1873 (copy), JD-Helm Correspondence, UM; JD to Preston Johnston, October 27, 1873, Johnston Papers, TU; JD to VD, January 8, 1874, Strode, ed., *JD: Private Letters*, 377.

66. JD to VD, January 8, 1874, Strode, ed., *JD: Private Letters*, 377; W. B. Pittman to JD, June 25, 1874 (quotation), JD Papers, MC; Mary Virginia Mont-

gomery Diary, May 1, 1872, Benjamin Montgomery Family Papers, LC. On the estate and JD as executor, see Everett, *Brierfield*, chap. 10, and Hermann, *Pursuit*, 147–50, 172–73, 201–04, 206–07.

67. JD to Johnston, November 16 (first quotation), December 7, 1873, Johnston Papers, TU; JD to VD, January 5 (third quotation), 16 (second quotation), 18, 26, 1874, and VD to JD, January 1, 17, n.d. (final quotation), 1874, JD Papers, UA; JD to VD, January 8, 1874 (fourth quotation), and VD to JD, January 12, 1874 (fifth quotation), Strode, ed., *JD: Private Letters*, 377–78, 378–80.

68. JD to VD, January 26 (first quotation), February 15, 17, 26 (second quotation), March 15 (third quotation), 29, April 1, 13, 26 (fourth quotation), 1874, JD Papers, UA; JD to Polly, February 24, 1874, JD Papers, TR; JD to Mrs. S. A. Ayres, August 19, 1874, Alfred P. James, ed., "Two Unpublished Letters of Jefferson Davis," *MVHR*, XXV (March 1939), 540–42 (fifth quotation); Mann to JD, March 17, 1874, *JDC*, VII, 383; J. H. Van Evrie to JD, June 16, 1874, JD Papers, MC; JD to [Virginia Clay], August 30, 1874, Clay Papers, DU.

69. VD to JD, March 8, 1874, and JD to VD, April 1, 1874 (first quotation), JD Papers, UA; JD to Louise Helm, July 31, 1874 (copy, second quotation), JD-Helm Correspondence, UM; JD to W. P. Johnston, August 22, 1874, Johnston Papers, TU.

70. JD to VD, November 6, 1873, JD Papers, UA; JD, Jr., to JD, April 19, 1874, JD and Family Papers, MDAH; JD to JD, Jr., July 21, 1874 (first four quotations), JD to Johnston, August 22, 1874, March 22, April 3 (fifth quotation), 1875, Johnston Papers, TU; Francis H. Smith to JD, August 26, 1874, *JDC*, VII, 397; JD to Mary Stamps, April 16, 1875 (final quotation), Stamps Papers, UNC.

71. JD to A. M. Clayton, August 28, 1873 (typescript, first quotation), JD-Clayton Letters, UM; JD to Armistead Burt, November 28, 1871 (second, third, fourth quotations), JD Papers, DU; *New York Times*, January 3, 1874 (fifth quotation); *JDC*, VII, 363–78; JD to A. D. Mann, November 7, 1871, Montague Collection, NYPL.

72. JD to M. J. Dean, February 23, 1871 (copy, first quotation), Mrs. T. Walker Moore, Rosenberg, Tex. (1970); Felix Robertson to JD, November 14, 1869, John Reagan to JD, June 9, 1875, Lanier to JD, January 16, 1875, JD Papers, MC; JD to Armistead Burt, November 28, 1871 (third quotation), JD Papers, DU; James G. Blaine, *Twenty Years of Congress: From Lincoln to Garfield* . . . (2 vols.; Norwich, Conn., 1884), II, 554–55; Dorris, *Pardon*, 380–83.

73. JD to Armistead Burt, November 28, 1871 (first quotation), JD Papers, DU; JD to Lise Mitchell, November 30 (second quotation), December 30 (fourth, fifth quotations), 1869, Mitchell Papers, TU; JD to [Lucinda Boyle], June 4, 1868 (third quotation), JD Family Papers, LSU; JD to Virginia Clay, March 29, 1871 (typescript, sixth quotation), Clay Papers, DU.

74. Re: Brierfield suit: *Bowmar* and 55 Mississippi Reports, 671–814 (1878) (lawyer quotations 734, 738); re: JD's activities: JD to VD, October 23, 1874 (second quotation), March 10, May 31, June 1, 5, 9 (first quotation), 12, 14, October 22, 28, 1875, January 11, 1876, JD Papers, UA; JD to VD, October 30, 1874, JD and Family Papers, MDAH; JD to Mrs. Meriwether, January 28, 1876, Meriwether Collection, West Tennessee Historical Society; JD to Mary Stamps, July 29, [1874?], Stamps Papers, UNC; Ben Montgomery to Lise Mitchell, July 12, 1874, Mitchell Papers, TU.

75. JD to VD, February 22, 23, June 24, 1875, March 22, 25, 1876, to Margaret Davis, June 20, 1875, and T. G. Dabney to Dr. J. H. D. Bowmar, May 27, 1871, JD

Papers, UA; JD to James Robb, October 25, 1867, Gilder-Lehrman Collection, J. Pierpont Morgan Library, New York, to Dr. J. H. D. Bowmar, October 18, 1883, Old Courthouse Museum, Vicksburg; J. R. Hamilton to JD, August 2, 1874, and Albert Janin to JD, September 9, 1879, JD Papers, MC; Wm. M. Gwin to JD, December 1, 2, 11, 1875, *JDC*, VII, 466–69.

76. JD to VD, May 6, 15 (quotation), 1875, JD Papers, UA.

77. JD to A. D. Mann, August 6, 1875 (quotation), *JDC*, VII, 427; JD to Mary Stamps, June 13, August 8, 1875, Stamps Papers, UNC.

78. Coke to JD, June 14, 1875, and JD to Coke, July 8, 1875, Charles F. Arrowood, "The Election of Jefferson Davis to the Presidency of the Agricultural and Mechanical College of Texas," *SHQ*, IL (October 1945), 294–95; VD to JD, March 3, 1875, JD Papers, UA.

79. JD to A. D. Mann, August 6, 1875, *JDC*, VII, 427; JD to William Walthall, November 14, 1875, William Walthall Papers, MDAH; JD to W. P. Johnston, August 22, November 27, 1874, Johnston Papers, TU; JD to W. T. Cordner, December 7, 1876, *JDC*, VII, 520–23, and December 27, 1876, Boston Public Library.

80. JD to VD, September 9, 12, 16, 1875, JD Papers, UA; *New York Times*, September 11, 1875; William E. Parrish, "Jefferson Davis Comes to Missouri," *Missouri Historical Review*, LVII (July 1963), 344–56 (description on 354).

81. JD to VD, September 21, 23 (quotation), 1875, JD Papers, UA.

82. JD to VD, October 9, 10 (quotation), 1875, *ibid.*

83. JD to VD, September 23, November 11, December 3, 1875, *ibid.;* JD to A. D. Mann, December 11, 1875, JD Association Collection, RU; JD to William Walthall, November 14, 1875, Walthall Papers, MDAH.

84. N.80; *Memphis Daily Appeal*, December 5, 1875; *JDC*, VII, 499–507.

85. *JDC*, VII, 422–26, 434–40.

86. JD to VD, November 18, 1875, JD Papers, UA.

87. JD to VD, November 11, 1875 (first quotation), *ibid.;* JD to Polly, January 19, 1876 (remaining quotations), JD and Family Papers, MDAH; *PJD*, I, 522, V, 119n.

88. JD to VD, January 15, 22, 28, 31, March 15, 22, 25, 31, April 22, 1876, to Polly, May 27, 1876, JD Papers, UA; JD to William Walthall, May 3, 1876, *JDC*, VII, 512.

89. JD to VD, June 20, 24, 1876, to Winnie, September 21, 1876 (quotations), JD Papers, UA; *Memoir*, II, 824; JD to A. D. Mann, August 12, 1876, William P. Palmer Collection of Civil War Manuscripts, WRHS.

90. JD to VD, October 22, 25, 31, November 25, 1876, JD Papers, UA; JD to VD, October 29, 1876 (quotation), JD Papers, UA; JD to A. D. Mann, November 10, 1876, Palmer Collection, WRHS.

91. JD to VD, November 25, December 9, 24 (quotations), 1876, and JD, Jr., to VD, December 1, 1875, JD Papers, UA; JD to W. T. Cordner, December 7, 1876, *JDC*, VII, 520–23.

CHAPTER EIGHTEEN: *"The Duty of Doing Justice to the Cause"*

1. JD to VD, January [1], 1877, JD Papers, UA; J. R. Davis to W. T. Walthall, January 26, 1877, William T. Walthall Papers, MDAH (all other citations are from this collection). Bertram Wyatt-Brown has a perceptive discussion of Sarah Dorsey in his *The House of Percy: Honor, Melancholy, and Imagination in a South-*

ern Family (New York, 1994), chaps. 6–8. On Beauvoir, see Beauvoir Subject File, MDAH, *St. Louis Globe Democrat,* April 12, 1883 (quotation), *Chicago Times,* November 11, 1880.

2. JD to Polly, February 1, 1877, JD Papers, UA; Dorsey to W. T. Walthall, April 3, 5, May 1 (quotation), 1877, *JDC,* VII, 528, 529, 536; JD to A. D. Mann, April 25, 1878, A. Dudley Mann Papers, LSU; William Walthall Diary, March 4 (second quotation), April 18, December 25, 1877, Walthall Papers (all other citations to this diary are from this collection); Wyatt-Brown, *House of Percy,* 164; VD to JD, August 2, 1877 (quotation), and JD to Addison Hayes, October 22, 1877, JD Papers, UA.

3. VD to JD, September 9, 1877 (first quotation), Polly to VD, June 9, 1877, JD to Polly, November 8, 1878, JD Papers, UA; VD to JD, [April 18, 1878] (second quotation), JD Papers, Rosemonde E. and Emile Kuntz Collection, TU; Ishbel Ross, *First Lady of the South: The Life of Mrs. Jefferson Davis* (New York, 1958), 328–29.

4. See chapter seventeen, note 4 above, for VD; Joseph to JD, June 30, 1867, JD and Family Papers, MDAH; JD to A. M. Clayton, September 16, 1869, JD-Clayton Letters, UM; Johnston to JD, December 11, 1870, JD Papers, MC; JD to Johnston, December 7, 1873, January 7, 14, 1874, Johnston Papers, TU.

5. JD to A. M. Clayton, September 10, 1869 (first quotation), Davis-Clayton Letters, UM; JD to Jubal Early, September 29, 1878 (third, fourth quotations), JD Papers, DU; JD to F. Stringfellow, August 21, 1878 (fifth quotation), Frank Stringfellow Papers, UVA; VD to JD, August 2, 1877 (second quotation), JD Papers, TR.

6. JD to R. C. Holland, July 25, 1881 (first quotation), *JDC,* VIII, 6; JD to M. N. Peters, December 9, 1871 (second quotation), Simon J. Gratz Autograph Collection, HSP; JD to R. M. Orme, November 24, 1887 (copy, third quotation), Laurie C. Eason, Violet, La. (1980); JD to Judah Benjamin, May 4, 1874 (copy, fourth quotation), Pierce Butler Collection, TU.

7. JD to Walthall, November 28, 1874, Walthall Papers; JD to Jubal Early, September 29, 1878, JD Papers, DU.

8. Turnbull Bros. to Walthall, October 16, 1875, and H. C. Turnbull to Walthall, November 5, 17, 1875, H. C. Turnbull to JD, January 14, 1876, JD to Walthall, October 29, 1875, January 24, February 19, August 3, 1876, Walthall Papers.

9. The Walthall Papers contain numerous letters from the Appleton Company and from Derby to Walthall in 1876, as well as copies of the contract and amendments.

10. For gathering, see *JDC,* VII, VIII *passim,* and JD to Walthall, 1876–78 *passim,* Walthall Papers; re: Washington: Walthall to JD, November 30, December 3, 1878, *ibid.,* and W. P. Johnston to JD, January 29, 1879, JD Papers, MC; William Harris Bragg, "Charles C. Jones, Jr. and the Mystery of Lee's Lost Dispatches," *Georgia Historical Quarterly,* LXXII (Fall 1988), 429–62.

11. Dorsey to Walthall, February 23, May 1, 1877, *JDC,* VII, 523, 536–37; JD to L. B. Northrop, November 1, 1879, *ibid.,* VIII, 423; JD to A. D. Mann, April 25, 1878, and VD to Mann, November 26, 1879, William P. Palmer Collection of Civil War Miscellany, WRHS; VD to Walthall, [July 25, 1879], Walthall Papers; JD to Addison Hayes, January 19, 1879, JD-Joel Addison Hayes, Jr., Papers, UM; Walthall to S. D. Lee, November 17, 1879, Stephen D. Lee Papers, UNC (I am grateful to Bradley G. Bond for this reference).

12. Dorsey to Miss Bettie Hooks, February 10, 1877 (copy), Edward F. McCrossin, Jr., Pittsburgh (1972); JD to W. P. Johnston, April 14, 1877, Johnston Papers, TU; JD to Walthall, February 6, 1877, *JDC*, VII, 523; Dorsey to Walthall, February 23, March 10, 14, 1877, *ibid.*, 523, 525, 526, 527; Walthall Diary, June–December 1877 *passim; Memoir*, II, 829.

13. The Walthall Papers contain numerous letters from Appleton to Walthall, e.g., March 9, 1878, July 15, 31, 1879; re: Tenney, Appleton to Walthall, December 7, 1877, and Tenney to Walthall, December 18, 1877; circular dated August 1877, and Derby to Walthall, August 22, 1877, *ibid.*

14. J. C. Derby, *Fifty Years Among Authors, Books and Publishers* (New York, 1884), 493–97; JD to Derby, February 14, 1880, *ibid.*, 496; Walthall to JD, February 10, 1881, *JDC*, VIII, 592–94, and May 8, 1888, JD Papers, MC; VD to "My Dear Joe & Maggie," March 28, [1880] (copy), Mrs. J. D. Marret, Stonington, Conn. (1970), to Derby, April 28, 1880, Gratz Collection, HSP; JD to Benjamin Hill, July 30, 1880, University of Notre Dame; JD to Virginia Clay, July 30, 1882, C. C. Clay Papers, DU; JD to A. D. Mann, May 16, 1881, Breckinridge Long Papers (Autograph Collection), LC.

15. Walthall to JD, February 10, 1881, *JDC*, VIII, 592–94, to Wirt Adams, January 27, 1881 (copy), Walthall Papers.

16. VD to Winnie, April 25, 1880 (first quotation), May n.d., 1881 (second quotation), JD Papers, UA; JD's copy of *R&F* is in MC (I am grateful to the late Gary A. Crump for this translation).

17. *R&F*, I, 80.

18. L. B. Northrop to JD, July 25, 1881, *JDC*, IX, 4–6; W. N. Pendleton to JD, September 6, 1881, JD Papers, MC; *SHSP*, IX (June 1881), 285–88; *Atlantic Monthly*, XLVIII (July 1881), 405–11; *The Dial*, II (July 1881), 55–57; *The Nation*, XXXIII (July 7, 14, 1881), 10–12, 35–37.

19. Derby, *Fifty Years*, 497; D. Appleton & Company to W. L. Fleming, March 13, 1907, Walter L. Fleming Papers, NYPL; T. K. Oglesby to JD, July 29, 1881, JD Papers, MC; Wirt Adams to Walthall, September 1, 1881, and D. Appleton & Co. to Walthall, January 10, 1877, Walthall Papers; JD to D. Appleton & Co., January 31, 1889, to James Redpath, April 24, 1889, *JDC*, X, 97–98, 108; Thomas A. Bryson, "A Lawsuit Concerning the Publication of Jefferson Davis's *The Rise and Fall of the Confederate Government*," *Georgia Historical Quarterly*, LIV (Winter 1970), 540–52, and "A Note on Jefferson Davis's Lawsuit Against Appleton Publishing Company," *JMH*, XXXIII (May 1971), 149–65. Appleton's records were destroyed by fire.

20. On the Southern Historical Society and its context, see esp. Gaines M. Foster's superb *Ghosts of the Confederacy: Defeat, the Lost Cause, and the Emergence of the New South* (New York, 1987), chap. 4, and Charles C. Osborne, *Jubal: The Life and Times of General Jubal A. Early, CSA, Defender of the Lost Cause* (Chapel Hill, N.C., 1992), chap. 27.

21. Jones to Walthall, April 5, 1877, Walthall Papers; Jones to JD, December 5, 1877 (first and second quotations), December 23, 1882, *JDC*, VIII, 56, IX, 197; Jones to JD, May 19, 1880 (third and fourth quotations), JD Papers, MC, and January 6, 1882 (sixth quotation), *JDC*, IX, 141–42; *ibid.*, 162–70 (address); JD to Early, April 11, 1882, JD Papers, DU.

22. JD to Jones, May 15, 1877 (first two quotations), *JDC*, VII, 539–40, November 22, 1883 (third quotation), JD Papers, MC.

23. JD to Early, June 1, 1877, February 2, 1878 (harmonizers), January 21, 1879, March 4, 18, 1882, June 17, 1883, July 8 (quotation), September 14, 1888, JD Papers, DU, December 17, 1877, December 23, 1878, Early Family Papers, VHS; Early to JD, November 29, 1879, JD Papers, MC, August 8, 1888, JD Papers, UA; JD to W. O. Gregory, September 24, 1884, JD Papers, DU; VD to Col. Marchant, June 8, 1889 (no collection), VHS. On Early and the Louisiana State Lottery, see Osborne, *Jubal*, chap. 25.

24. JD to J. W. Jones, December 11, 1877, JD Papers, MC; JD to Jubal Early [n.d., but late 1870s] (first quotation), JD Papers, DU; JD to W. N. Pendleton, June 21, 1881 (remaining quotations), University Papers, W&L.

25. Benjamin to JD, December 20, 1868, and Thomas Reynolds to JD, January 4, 1883, JD Papers, MC; Early to JD, September 29, [1878], JD Papers, DU; JD to Walthall, February 5, 1882, Walthall Papers; JD to Lucius Northrop, November 6, 1884, A. Conger Goodyear Collection, Beinecke Library, Yale University; JD to E. G. W. Butler, August 31, 1883, E. G. W. Butler Papers, DU.

26. Beauregard to Gen. Marcus Wright, June 20, 1881 (first quotation), Letterbook, Pierre G. T. Beauregard Papers, LC; Thomas Jordan to Beauregard, October 22, 1868 (second quotation), Gratz Collection, HSP; Johnston, *Narrative of Military Operations Directed During the Late War Between the States* (New York, 1874), and Alfred Roman, *The Military Operations of General Beauregard* (2 vols.; New York, 1883), which is really Beauregard's book, though he is not listed as the author; Robert U. Johnson and Clarence C. Buel, eds., *Battles and Leaders of the Civil War* (4 vols., New York, 1887–88), I, 196–227, 240–59, 569–93, II, 202–18, III, 472–82, IV, 260–77; *JDC*, VIII, IX *passim* has many letters concerning Beauregard and Johnston; on the money matter, see IX, 31–38.

27. JD to L. B. Northrop, April 9, 1879 (first quotation), to Early, November 20, 1884 (second quotation), JD Papers, DU; VD to W. E. Dodd, June 16, 1905 (third quotation), William E. Dodd Papers, LC; Robert Underwood Johnson, *Remembered Yesterdays* (Boston, 1923), 200; for JD and First Manassas, see JD to Milledge L. Bonham, July 5, 1877, Milledge L. Bonham Papers, SCL, to Early, February 27, 1878, April 20, 1884, JD Papers, DU.

28. William N. Pendleton to JD, July 15, 1882, Early to JD, April 1, May 2, 1883, *JDC*, IX, 177–78, 205–06, 212; JD to J. W. Jones, June 24, 1883 (quotation), JD Papers, DU; JD to G. W. C. Lee, June 18, 1883 (typescript), JD Papers, UA.

29. *JDC*, IX, 472–90 (first quotation 475); JD to "My Dear Friend," August 13, 1886 (second quotation), JD Letters, UT.

30. JD to Roosevelt, September 29, 1885, Theodore Roosevelt Papers, LC; Roosevelt to JD, October 8, 1885, Elting E. Morison and John Blum, eds., *The Letters of Theodore Roosevelt* (8 vols., Cambridge, Mass., 1951–54), I, 93; Roosevelt, "The President's Policy," *North American Review*, CXLI (October 1885), 388–96, esp. 393.

31. JD to A. R. Bradley, August 12, 1883 (copy, first quotation), Beauvoir; JD to Mrs. Flora Darling, January 19, 1884 (second quotation), Joseph E. Johnston Papers, WM; JD to R. T. Daniel, June 3, 1889 (third quotation), *JDC*, X, 119; JD to A. D. Mann, November 7, 1883, Lloyd W. Smith Collection, Morristown National Historical Park, N.J.; JD to Paul Hayne, January 24, 1885, Fred A. Rosenstock-JD Papers, MDAH; *R&F*, II, 764 (final quotation); JD to J. Crafts Wright, July 17, 1878, JD Papers, UA.

32. JD to J. L. Power, June 20, 1885, *JDC*, IX, 373; JD to [J. P.] Knott, January 22, 1876 (first quotation), Correspondence by Author, TSLA; JD to James Lyons, May 15, 1879 (second quotation), James Lyons Papers, UNC.

33. JD to Winnie, April 24, 1877, JD to VD, May 1, June 11 (first quotation), July 15, 1877, to Addison Hayes, February 12, 1877 (typescript), Polly to VD, June 9, 1877, VD to JD, [April or May 1878] (final quotation), JD Papers, UA; JD to Addison Hayes, June 29, 1877 (second, third quotations), JD and Family Papers, MDAH; JD to Polly, March 26, 1877, JD Papers, TR; Sarah Dorsey to W. T. Walthall, June 29, 1877, *JDC*, VII, 558.

34. JD to C. J. Wright, September 4, 1878 (first, second quotations), to Addison Hayes, September 14, October 12, 18, 1878 (fourth quotation), to Polly, September 25, 1878, to VD, February 9, 1879 (sixth quotation), JD Papers, UA; JD to Virginia Clay, October 11, 1878, Clay Papers, DU; VD to Walthall, September 8, 1878, *JDC*, VIII, 275–76, [October 1878] (two letters), Walthall Papers; Rosa Walthall to "Dear Papa," October 14, 1878 (third quotation), and Walthall Diary, October 10–12, 1878 (typescript extracts), *ibid.;* Dorsey to A. D. Mann, October 30, 1878 (fifth quotation), JD Papers, DU.

35. *Jefferson Davis v. J. H. D. Bowmar . . . ,* 55 Mississippi Reports, 671–814 (1878) (quotations, 671, 776); Frank Edgar Everett, Jr., *Brierfield: Plantation Home of Jefferson Davis* (Jackson, Miss., 1971), chap. 10; *JDC*, VIII, 235 (JD quotations); for events in Mississippi, consult William C. Harris, *The Day of the Carpetbagger: Republican Reconstruction in Mississippi* (Baton Rouge, La., 1979), chaps. 20–21.

36. Everett, *Brierfield*, chap. 10.

37. JD to Winnie, March 30, 1878 (first quotation), to Polly, November 8, 1878, to Addison Hayes, September 14, 1878, JD Papers, UA; Dorsey to A. D. Mann, April 25, 1878 (other quotations), Mann Papers, LSU; John K. Reynaud & Co. to JD, May 6, 1879, JD Papers, MC; Exhibit A, *Stephen Percy Ellis, et al. v. Jefferson Davis,* Equity Case No. 8934, RG21, U.S. District Courts, Entry #121—general case files— Eastern District of New Orleans—Circuit Court, 21, NA, Fort Worth, Texas (hereafter cited as *Ellis v. Davis;* I am grateful to Bertram Wyatt-Brown for this reference).

38. Exhibit B, *Ellis v. Davis,* has a copy of the Dorsey will (quotation) and Exhibit C has a copy of the sales contract; Wyatt-Brown, *House of Percy,* 165–66, 168 (Wyatt-Brown and I agree on the relationship); Maud L. Walthall, "Some Facts Concerning Jefferson Davis . . ." (typescript), JD Subject File, MDAH; Walthall to Jubal Early, February 6, 1878, Jubal Early Papers, LC.

39. JD to VD, July 2, 4 (first quotation), 1879, JD Papers, TR; JD to Walthall, July 4, 1879, *JDC*, VIII, 403.

40. *Ellis v. Davis;* JD to VD, March 10, 1880, JD Papers, UA, to A. D. Mann, September 3, 1879 (quotation), JD Association Collection, RU; Wyatt-Brown, *House of Percy,* 167–68.

41. JD to Mrs. George Negus, August 4, 1879, JD Papers, UA, to J. C. Derby, February 22, 1880, JD Papers, DU, to J. D. S. Newell, January 11, 1883, J. D. S. Newell Papers, TSLA; Wyatt-Brown, *House of Percy,* 169.

42. JD to Winnie, March 19, April 24 (first, final quotations), 1877, March 30, November 27 (second quotation), 1878, VD to Winnie, April 25, 1880, May n.d., 1881, JD Papers, UA.

43. PHC Chronology; JD to Jubal Early, August 13, 1881, JD Papers, DU; J. Walker Fearn to JD, August 10, 1881, *JDC*, IX, 11; JD to Polly, July 18, 1881, JD and Family Papers, MDAH; JD to Mary Stamps, October 11, 1881 (first quotation), Mary Stamps Papers, TU; *Memoir*, II, 831 (second quotation); JD to VD, September 13 (third, fourth quotations), [September or October], 1881, VD to JD, September n.d., 1881 (fifth, sixth, seventh quotations), JD Papers, UA.

44. JD to Mary Stamps, October 11, 1881 (first quotation), Stamps Papers, TU; *Memoir*, II, 831 (second quotation); JD to VD, September 13 (third, fourth quotations), [September or October], 1881, VD to JD, September n.d., 1881 (fifth, sixth, seventh quotations), JD Papers, UA.

45. PHC Chronology; JD to Judge Tenney, November 15, 1881, University of Notre Dame; JD to Addison Hayes, December 11, 1881, JD-Hayes Papers, UM.

CHAPTER NINETEEN: *"There Is Much Preparation"*

1. Dorsey to A. D. Mann, August 4, 1878, A. Dudley Mann Papers, LSU; JD to Addison Hayes, January 28, 1882 (JD quotation), JD-Joel Addison Hayes, Jr., Papers, UM; JD to VD, July 15, 1877, to Polly, October 12, 1882, JD Papers, UA; VD to Major W. H. Morgan [September, 1888], JD Papers, LC; Maud L. Walthall, "Some Facts Concerning Jefferson Davis . . ." (typescript), JD Subject File, MDAH; William Walthall Diary, November 21, 1877, William Walthall Papers, *ibid*. For visitors and travel, see below.

2. Sarah Dorsey to A. D. Mann, August 4, 1878, Mann Papers, LSU; VD to Mrs. Gilmer, November 22, 1883 (first quotation), Jeremy F. Gilmer Papers, UNC; VD to Connie [Harrison], April 5, 1880 (second quotation), Harrison Family Papers, UVA; VD to J. C. Derby, April 15, 1880 (third quotation), Simon J. Gratz Autograph Collection, HSP; VD to Lizzie [Blair], July 24, 1883 (final quotation), Blair Family Papers, LC.

3. VD to Connie [Harrison], April 15, 1880, Harrison Family Papers, UVA; VD to Mrs. Gilmer, November 22, 1883 (first quotation), Gilmer Papers, UNC; A. K. McClure, *The South: Its Industrial, Financial, and Political Condition* (Philadelphia, 1886), 232 (second, sixth quotations); VD to Mrs. Jacob Thompson, March 26, 1885 (third quotation), Jacob Thompson Papers, MC; George T. Denison, *Soldiering in Canada: Recollections and Experiences by Lt. Col. George T. Denison* (Toronto, 1890), 72 (fourth quotation); Adams to VD, June 27, 1889 (fifth quotation), JD Papers, MC.

4. Walthall Diary, April 18, 1877, Walthall Papers, MDAH; James I. Crabbe to JD, May 10, 1888, and Adams to VD, June 27, 1889, JD Papers, MC; JD to Varina Hayes, May 17, 1888, JD Papers, UA; JD to E. G. W. Butler, August 31, 1883 (quotation), E. G. W. Butler Papers, DU; John Carl Parish, *George Wallace Jones* (Iowa City, 1912), 293–94; W. A. Swanberg, *Pulitzer* (New York, 1967), 147; Ishbel Ross, *First Lady of the South: The Life of Mrs. Jefferson Davis* (New York, 1958), 340–41, 355; Hudson Strode, *Jefferson Davis* (3 vols.; New York, 1955–64), III, 459–61.

5. VD to Winnie, February 16, 1880, JD Papers, UA.

6. McClure, *The South*, 231–38 (first, second quotations 233); *Chicago Times*, November 11, 1880 (third quotation); *St. Louis Globe-Democrat*, April 12, 1883.

7. VD to Mr. Reed, June 7, 1883, Noxubee County Mississippi Historical Society; VD to Polly, June 12, 1883, JD and Family Papers, to Mrs. James Smith, January 21, 1888, Colin Humphreys Collection, both MDAH; VD to [J. T.] Scharf,

September 7, 1885, J. T. Scharf Papers, MHS; VD to Mrs. Gilmer, December 24, 1884, Gilmer Papers, UNC; VD to Mr. Secor, May 15, 1886, JD Papers, DU; JD to Lise Hamer, December 4, 1886, Lise Mitchell Papers, TU; VD to [David] Secor, February 23, 1887 (quotation), Davis Family Letters, Historic New Orleans Collection; VD to H. T. Louthan, April 25, November 20, 1898, Henry T. Louthan Papers, VHS.

8. VD to Winnie, February 16, 1880, JD to Varina Hayes, December 19, 1882, July 19, 1884 (first, second quotations), JD to Polly, October 12, 1882 ("Bampa"), August 10, 1885, January 17, 1888, JD to [Grandson], April 26, 1889, JD Papers, UA; JD to Polly, July 12, 1882, June 11, 1889, JD to Varina Hayes, March 20, 1888, JD and Family Papers, MDAH; VD to Gaston Robbins, December 31, 1887 (final quotation), William M. Robbins Papers, UNC.

9. VD to Constance Harrison, December 20, 1886 (first quotation), Harrison Family Papers, UVA, to [W. H. Morgan], [September 1888] (second quotation), JD Papers, LC; Ross, *First Lady,* 355–58; Strode, *Davis,* III, 498–99.

10. JD to Addison Hayes, March 9, 1882, JD and Family Papers, MDAH; JD to VD, July 15, 1877, JD Papers, UA; VD to Connie [Harrison], April 5, 1880, Harrison Family Papers, UVA; Lucian Bland to J. D. S. Newell, May 19, 1881, and JD to Newell, June 12, 15, 30, 1881, February 28, 1889, J. D. S. Newell Collection, TSLA; Walthall and R. M. Sands to John B. Gordon, August 23, 1877 (copy), Walthall to Francis Nicholls, October 16, 1877 (copy), Gordon to Walthall, n.d. (received September 19, 1877), Walthall Papers, MDAH; Gordon to Jubal Early, September 15, 1877, Early Family Papers, VHS; Colquitt to JD, November 27, 1877, Gov. A. H. Colquitt Personal Letterbook, 1877–1879, Georgia Department Archives and History, January 1, 1878, JD Papers, MC.

11. JD to Addison Hayes, December 27, 1879, January 5, 1880, December 11, 1881, JD-Hayes Papers, Memphis; JD to Martin Philips, January 28, 1887 (his quotation), JD Association Collection, RU; VD to Mrs. L. W. Norwood, May 6, 1887 (copy), Ned B. Shapker, Palo Alto, Calif. (1972); contract between JD and Cox, dated December 23, 1879, Owen B. Cox Papers, LSU; *Memoir,* II, 927; JD to Polly, July 18, 1881, JD and Family Papers, MDAH. When in New Orleans, JD usually saw Payne; many letters he wrote from the city in the late 1870s and 1880s are on the stationery of Payne's company.

12. JD to Addison Hayes, September 11, 1879, December 11, 17, 27, 1881, JD-Hayes Papers, UM, February 2, 1882, JD Papers, TR; statement on Brierfield organization signed by JD on September 25, 1888, JD and Family Papers, MDAH.

13. JD to Hayes, February 2, March 9, September 23, October 13, 19, November 7, 1882, January 10, 1883, July 5, 18 (quotation), 1884, JD and Family Papers, MDAH, September 11, 16, 1879, December 11, 1881, January 28, 1882, JD-Hayes Papers, UM; JD to Hayes, February 27, March 4, 1882, to VD, December 22, 1885, January 1, 1886, B. R. Howell to JD, May 25, 1882, JD Papers, UA; Hayes to JD, March 12, 1882, JD Papers, MC; JD to J. A. S. Newell, December 17, 1883, Newell Papers, TSLA; JD to Martin Philips, November 24, 1887 (second quotation), JD Papers, Woodson Research Center, RU; Strode, *Davis,* III, 459. On postwar changes in the agricultural economy, I have benefited from two excellent books: Roger L. Ransom and Richard Sutch, *One Kind of Freedom: The Economic Consequences of Emancipation* (New York, 1977), and Gavin Wright, *Old South, New South: Revolutions in the Southern Economy Since the Civil War* (New York, 1986), chaps. 1–4.

14. JD to VD, December 9, 1884 (quotation), JD Papers, UA; JD to T. F. Drayton, January 20, 1886, JD Papers, EU; JD to A. D. Mann, May 16, 1881, Breckinridge Long Papers (Autograph Collection), LC, and December 31, 1882, Rare Books and Special Collections Department, Bancroft Library, University of California, Berkeley; JD to Addison Hayes, September 23, 1882, July 5, 1884, JD and Family Papers, MDAH; JD to Lise Hamer, March 21, June 11, December 10, 1884, Mitchell Papers, TU; JD to J. Weis[s], May 19, 1884, McCarthy Collection, Louisiana State Museum, New Orleans; Frank Edgar Everett, Jr., *Brierfield: Plantation Home of Jefferson Davis* (Jackson, Miss., 1971), 107. Re: levees, the JD Papers, MC, contain numerous letters.

15. JD to Hamer, March 21, June 11, 1884, October 20, November 4, 1885, Mitchell Papers, TU; JD to Hayes, July 27, August 3, 26, 1880, January 9, 17, 31, August 14, December 27, 1881, JD-Hayes Papers, UM; agreement dated January 18, 1881, between JD and Hamer and Mitchell, JD Papers, UA; M. E. Hamer to Prof. Fleming, January 30, 1908, Walter L. Fleming Papers, NYPL.

16. JD to Hayes, December 27, 1879 (first quotation), January 28, 1882 (copies), JD-Hayes Papers, UM; JD to Hayes, January 28, 1883 (second quotation), to VD, March 15, 1879, and statement on Brierfield organization dated September 25, 1888, JD and Family Papers, MDAH; JD to VD, December 9, 1884, December 24, 1885, January 1, 1886, and VD to JD [March n.d.], 1879, JD Papers, UA; JD to Lise Hamer, February 7, 1884, Mitchell Papers, TU.

17. JD to Hayes, January 28, 1882, JD-Hayes Papers, UM; JD to Drayton, January 20, 1886, JD Papers, EU, January 27, 1886 (copy), John G. Thomas III, Pleasant Garden, N.C. (1991); Drayton to JD, March 5, 1886, JD Papers, MC; JD to VD, December 24, 1885, JD Papers, UA. On the migration of blacks, consult William Cohen, *At Freedom's Edge: Black Mobility and the Southern White Quest for Racial Control, 1861–1915* (Baton Rouge, La., 1991), chap. 9.

18. JD to Martin Philips, February 2, 1889 (copy, first quotation), Charles Cole, Dallas (1976), November 24, 1887 (second quotation), JD Papers, Woodson Research Center, RU; JD to VD, May 17, 1887, JD Papers, TR, November 12, 1889 (final quotation), First White House of the Confederacy, Montgomery; VD to Connie [Harrison], December 23, 1886, Harrison Family Papers, UVA; *Memoir*, II, 927; M. E. Hamer to Prof. Fleming, January 30, 1908, Fleming Papers, NYPL.

19. JD to T. F. Drayton, January 20, 1886 (first quotation), JD Papers, EU; JD to Bruce, March 29, 1889 (copy, second quotation), and Bruce to JD, April 9, 1889, JD Papers, MC; on JD's earlier attitude toward the Montgomerys in particular and on race in general, see above, chapter seventeen; Bruce, *The Plantation Negro as a Freeman* (New York, 1889). For insightful treatments of postwar attitudes toward race relations, see two books which have informed my discussion: George M. Fredrickson, *The Black Image in the White Mind: The Debate on Afro-American Character and Destiny, 1817–1914* (New York, 1971), chaps. 6–9, and esp. Joel Williamson, *The Crucible of Race: Black-White Relations in the American South Since Emancipation* (New York, 1984), parts 1–3.

20. Montgomery to JD, September 27, 1886, JD Papers, MC; Jones to JD, December 1, 1888, Mrs. Jefferson Davis Letters, IA and JD to Jones, December 26, 1888, JD Papers, North Carolina Division of Archives and History.

21. Re: Redpath, *DAB*, XV, 443–44; JD to Jubal Early, September 14, 1888, JD Papers, DU; A. T. Rice to JD, March 29 (notation on envelope), September 26, 1888,

JD Papers, MC; "Robert E. Lee" and "The Doctrine of States Rights," *North American Review*, CL (January 1890), 55–66, and (February 1890), 205–19.

22. James G. Wilson to JD, May 9, 19, 1888, JD Papers, MC; Lloyd Bryce to JD, September n.d., October 3, 1889, JD to Bryce, September 26, October 8, 1889, Redpath to JD, October 31, 1889, *JDC*, X, 138–39, 141–42, 159; Redpath to Franz, November 21, 1889, JD Collection, University of Arizona; *Appleton's Cyclopedia . . .* (6 vols.; New York, 1888–89), VI, 51–55; JD, *Short History . . .* (New York, 1890); for the lawsuit, see chapter eighteen above.

23. Redpath to JD, October 31, 1889, *JDC*, X, 158–60; Redpath to Franz, November 21, 1889, JD Collection, University of Arizona; *Memoir*, I, 41–42; *Belford's Magazine*, IV (1889–90), 255–66, and J. William Jones, *The Davis Memorial Volume; or Our Dead President, Jefferson Davis . . .* (Richmond, Va., 1890), 27–42; *Memoir*, I, 3–27, 32–41; *PJD*, I, includes both: "Autobiography," liii–lxv, and "Autobiographical Sketch," lxvii–lxxxii.

24. *PJD*, I, lxv; JD to [Crafts Wright], March 15, 1879, JD Papers, TR; JD to R. H. Henry, August 29, 1879 (first quotation), *Nashville Daily American*, September 18, 1879; JD to Mrs. A. I. McCardle, November 18, 1885 (second quotation), Old Courthouse Museum, Vicksburg.

25. JD to G. C. Hodges, June 19, 1884, John Ezell, "Jefferson Davis and the Blair Bill," *JMH*, XXXI (May 1969), 121–26 (letter printed at 124–25).

26. JD to Lubbock, July 20, 1887, *JDC*, IX, 580–82.

27. *Ibid.* (quotation); Lubbock to JD [fall 1887, date in text incorrect], *ibid.*, 589–91; *Houston Post*, September 24, 1887; JD to Reagan, September 20, 1887, JD–John H. Reagan Collection, Dallas Historical Society, Dallas.

28. JD to J. L. Power, September 9, 1887, J. L. Power and Family Papers, MDAH; JD to Galloway, September 7, 1887 (first three quotations), *Louisville Courier Journal*, July 12, 1931; JD to Martin Philips, November 24, 1887 (final two quotations), JD Papers, Woodson Research Center, RU.

29. Kappa Sigma Fraternity to JD, April 23, 1883, Andrew Bates to JD, August 1, 1883, Dr. B. H. Catching to JD, August 31, 1885, Lawrence Carson to JD, May 27, 1886, Master G. H. M. McCarthy to JD, January 18, 1887, Fitzhugh Lee to JD, September 8, 1887, G. W. Acklin to JD, September 10, 1887, B. S. Leathers to JD, April 18, 1889, JD Papers, MC; Daisy Davis (no relation) to JD, April 13, 1887 (first quotation), JD Papers, Alabama Department of Archives and History; JD to J. D. Ramsey, October 30, 1888, JD Papers, UA; JD to David Boyd, June 14, 1879, David Boyd Papers, LSU; JD to J. W. Jones, October 5, 1882, JD Papers, DU; Gov. Robert Lowery to JD, May 7, 1888, Senator McAlwain Collection, MDAH; *JDC*, IX, 162–70, 206–07, 279–81 (remaining quotations). In his *Ghosts of the Confederacy: Defeat, the Lost Cause, and the Emergence of the New South* (New York, 1987), 72–73, Gaines M. Foster also noted that JD was not submerged in the past.

30. M. H. Clark to JD, December 19, 1885, July 11, 1886, JD Papers, UA; *Life and Reminiscences of Jefferson Davis by Distinguished Men of His Time* (Baltimore, 1890), 61–64.

31. R. G. Spalding to JD, March 19, 1886, Henry McDaniel to JD, April 25, 1886, JD Papers, MC; *JDC*, IX, 412–13, 419–23, 424–31 (first quotation 429), 433–39, 440–43 (third and fourth quotations 441), 445–49 (fifth quotation 446); Clopton to "My dear Annie," November 3, 1904 (typescript, second quotation), Fleming

Papers, NYPL; VD to Mrs. Gilmer, May 22, 1886 (final quotation), [Jeremy] Gilmer Memorial Album, MC.

32. W. J. Northern to Jubal Early, September 2, 1887, Jubal Early Papers, LC; *Memoir*, II, 832; undated and untitled newspaper clipping (all quotations but VD's), Mrs. Frances Sprague Scrapbook, MDAH.

33. Foster, *Ghosts*, 69–70, 104–05, 128–29.

34. W. J. Green to JD, April 18, 1889, D. G. Fowle to JD, September 27, 1889, JD to Committee, October 30, 1889, *JDC*, X, 105–07 (first quotation 105), 139–40 (second quotation 140), 153–58; JD to Green, May 31, 1889, JD Papers, MC.

35. VD to Mrs. Jacob Thompson, March 26, 1885 (first quotation), Thompson Papers, MC; VD to Connie [Harrison], December 20, 1886 (final quotation), Harrison Family Papers, UVA; JD to Virginia Clay, March 13, 1883 (second quotation), C. C. Clay Papers, DU; JD to "Dearest Mattie," October 21, 1887 (third quotation), JD Letters, Missouri Historical Society.

36. *JDC*, IX, 280–81; *St. Louis Globe-Democrat*, April 12, 1883 (quotations).

37. *JDC*, X, 47–48.

38. *New Orleans Daily Picayune*, November 15, 1889; JD to VD, November 12, 1889, First White House of the Confederacy; JD Statement, JD Subject File, MDAH.

39. *New Orleans Daily Picayune*, November 17, 18, 23, 27, December 1, 4 (first quotation), 6 (second, third quotations), 1889; VD to [W. H. Morgan], November 30, 1889 (typescript), JD Papers, LC; *Memoir*, II, 928–30; Nanny Miles to Lise Hamer, December 3, 1889, Mitchell Family Papers, TU. The death certificate (copy in the JD Subject File, MDAH), dated December 8, 1889, specified acute bronchitis as the cause of death; JD most likely developed pneumonia.

EPILOGUE: "Esto Perpetua"

1. Roy P. Basler, ed., *The Collected Works of Abraham Lincoln* (9 vols.; New Brunswick, N.J., 1953–1955), II, 461.

2. *R&F*, II, 764. Translation: "It shall be perpetual." (I am grateful to Maribel Dietz and Steven K. Ross for this translation.)

During the years I worked on this book, the assistance of many people made possible my journey with Jefferson Davis. My gratitude goes to the many librarians who helped me in discovering the riches they preside over; their number is so large that I must thank them collectively. But I do want to specify two institutions that provided me incredible service over the years. Though not technically a library, the Jefferson Davis Papers housed at Rice University has been absolutely central. Editor Lynda L. Crist and her associates, Mary S. Dix, now retired, and Kenneth H. Williams, gave me free range in their trove of Davis documents. And they willingly responded to unending inquiries. I began and ended this project there. Quite frankly, without their active help I do not think this book would ever have been completed. In addition, past and present staff members of the Museum of the Confederacy in Richmond, particularly its Eleanor S. Brockenbrough Library, were exceedingly generous during my several visits and continuous queries. I am especially grateful to Charity Coman, John Coski, Ruth Ann Coski, Cori Hudgins, and Guy Swanson.

A number of individuals provided indispensable aid in particular instances. Keith Hardison, then superintendent at Beauvoir, hosted a memorable stay at Davis's last home. Michael G. Miller and John Dale IV organized a splendid trip to Davis Island and the sites of Brierfield and Hurricane. Tracking over Davis's Mexican War battlefields would have been much less enjoyable, and in the case of Buena Vista impossible, without the companionship of W. Shelby McKenzie and J. Buford Anderson. In a visit arranged by Guy Swanson, Mrs. Frank G. Strachan welcomed me into her home, the house where Davis died. Writing about a man who suffered from serious illnesses through much of his life, I needed counsel from knowledgeable physicians. And I found them—Dr. Nicolas G. Bazan, LSU School of Medicine, New Orleans; Dr. Charles S. Bryan, University of South Carolina School of Medicine, Columbia; Dr. Roderick Macdonald, Columbia, South Carolina; Dr. Harris D. Riley, Jr., Children's Hospital, Vanderbilt University Medical Center, Nashville. All shared their expertise and their insights with me.

Others contributed significantly. A fellowship from the National Endowment for the Humanities enabled me to take a year off to begin my research. My own university generously supported my research and writing. At the outset, R.

Jackson Wilson provided invaluable assistance. Ron and Carroll Pohl became innkeepers extraordinaire during an extended stay at the Library of Congress. I found conversations with Joan Cashin, biographer of Varina H. Davis, very beneficial. Throughout the years spent on this book, Catherine Fry both prodded and encouraged me. Her interest in what she always referred to as "Mr. Davis" never flagged, and she made sure my eye remained fixed on that mark. During the actual writing, my departmental chair, Paul F. Paskoff, was incredibly accommodating to my constant calls on him. Also, in my department, Peggy Seale provided unstinting aid, while Keuren Pinkney, with good spirit, prepared many versions of my manuscript. Over the long course of my work, research assistance came from several graduate students: Bradley Bond, Richard Follett, Christopher Leahy, Robert Outland, John Sacher, and Kevin Yeager. An undergraduate, Justin Poche, helped put the notes in their final form. Mel Rosenthal, amazingly thorough and sensible, expertly guided my book through the production process.

My wife and my editor always stood by me. Patricia Cooper understood how important this book was to me, and she provided support both when things were going well and when they were not. Jane Garrett was patience and encouragement personified. Even when this book began taking much longer than either of us anticipated and completion dates had to be pushed back, she never gave up on me. I greatly value my association with her.

A marvelous attribute of historians is the time they are willing to give to the work of another. Four colleagues—Lynda L. Crist, Drew Gilpin Faust, Michael F. Holt, and Charles Royster—read the entire manuscript, and a fifth, Gaines M. Foster, read the postwar chapters. Their critical skills, thoroughness, and candor have made this a much better book than it would have been without their serious attention.

All of the people named in these acknowledgments had a hand in the making of this book. For the help each of them gave, I am enormously grateful. Yet, the book is mine, and I accept full responsibility for it.

W.J.C.

INDEX

Page numbers in *italics* refer to illustrations.